THE OXFORD HANDBOOK OF
FRIEDRICH SCHLEIERMACHER

THE OXFORD HANDBOOK OF

FRIEDRICH SCHLEIERMACHER

Edited by
ANDREW C. DOLE, SHELLI M. POE,
and
KEVIN M. VANDER SCHEL

Great Clarendon Street, Oxford, OX2 6DP,
United Kingdom

Oxford University Press is a department of the University of Oxford.
It furthers the University's objective of excellence in research, scholarship,
and education by publishing worldwide. Oxford is a registered trade mark of
Oxford University Press in the UK and in certain other countries

© Oxford University Press 2024

The moral rights of the authors have been asserted

First Edition published in 2024

All rights reserved. No part of this publication may be reproduced, stored in
a retrieval system, or transmitted, in any form or by any means, without the
prior permission in writing of Oxford University Press, or as expressly permitted
by law, by licence or under terms agreed with the appropriate reprographics
rights organization. Enquiries concerning reproduction outside the scope of the
above should be sent to the Rights Department, Oxford University Press, at the
address above

You must not circulate this work in any other form
and you must impose this same condition on any acquirer

Published in the United States of America by Oxford University Press
198 Madison Avenue, New York, NY 10016, United States of America

British Library Cataloguing in Publication Data

Data available

Library of Congress Control Number: 2023940063

ISBN 978–0–19–884609–3

DOI: 10.1093/oxfordhb/9780198846093.001.0001

Printed and bound by
CPI Group (UK) Ltd, Croydon, CR0 4YY

Links to third party websites are provided by Oxford in good faith and
for information only. Oxford disclaims any responsibility for the materials
contained in any third party website referenced in this work.

In Memoriam
Wilhelm Gräb (1948–2023)

Contents

List of Abbreviations for Schleiermacher's Works	xi
List of Contributors	xv
General Introduction	xxiii
Andrew C. Dole, Shelli M. Poe, and Kevin M. Vander Schel	

PART I SCHLEIERMACHER IN CONTEXT

A. INFLUENCES ON SCHLEIERMACHER

1. Plato   5
   Julia A. Lamm

2. Kant   21
   Peter Grove

3. Spinoza   37
   Christof Ellsiepen

4. The Reformed Tradition   53
   Jan Rohls

B. SCHLEIERMACHER AMONG HIS CONTEMPORARIES

5. Schelling and Steffens   69
   Zachary Purvis

6. "Domestic Disputes" in the Kantian Heritage: Schleiermacher and Hegel on Religion and Christianity   85
   Jörg Dierken
   Translated by Matthew Ryan Robinson

7. Schleiermacher and the University of Berlin   101
   Johannes Zachhuber

8. Schleiermacher and Friedrich Schlegel   118
   ANDREAS ARNDT

PART II SCHLEIERMACHER'S THOUGHT

A. SCHLEIERMACHER AND THE *WISSENSCHAFTEN*

9. Dialectic   137
   SARAH SCHMIDT
   TRANSLATED BY MARIELLE SUTHERLAND

10. Philosophical Ethics   155
    MICHAEL MOXTER

11. Theory of Education   171
    MICHAEL WINKLER

12. Hermeneutics   188
    CHRISTIAN BERNER

13. Philosophy of Art: With Special Regard to the Lectures on Aesthetics   203
    HOLDEN KELM

14. Psychology and Anthropology   219
    DOROTHEA MEIER

15. Theory of the State   236
    MIRIAM ROSE

B. SCHLEIERMACHER THE THEOLOGIAN

16. The *Brief Outline*   257
    PAUL T. NIMMO

17. Introduction to the *Glaubenslehre* and *On the Glaubenslehre*   272
    DANIEL PEDERSEN

18. *The Christian Faith* as Liberal Theology   288
    WALTER E. WYMAN JR.

19. Sin and Redemption   304
    KEVIN M. VANDER SCHEL

20. Person and Work of Christ 319
    MAUREEN JUNKER-KENNY

21. Trinitarian Thought 335
    SHELLI M. POE

22. Christian Ethics 351
    JAMES M. BRANDT

23. The Life of Jesus 366
    CHRISTIAN DANZ

24. Schleiermacher as a Scriptural Exegete 382
    HERMANN PATSCH

25. Practical Theology 397
    BIRGIT WEYEL

C. SCHLEIERMACHER'S PASTORAL AND OCCASIONAL WRITINGS

26. Early Writings on Ethics: *Monologen*, *Vertraute Briefe*, and *Grundlinien* 417
    OMAR BRINO

27. *On Religion* 434
    DIETRICH KORSCH

28. Sermons 450
    CATHERINE L. KELSEY

29. The *Christmas Eve Dialogue* 466
    ANDREW PACKMAN AND ANDREW C. DOLE

PART III THINKING AFTER SCHLEIERMACHER

A. RECEPTION HISTORY

30. Schleiermacher's Work and Influence on Classical Studies 487
    LUTZ KÄPPEL

31. Schleiermacher and Mediating Theology 505
    ANNETTE G. AUBERT

32. Schleiermacher and Protestant Liberalism 522
    ARNULF VON SCHELIHA

33. Schleiermacher, Neo-Orthodoxy, and Dialectical Theology 540
    PAUL DAFYDD JONES

34. Schleiermacher's Influence on Roman Catholic Theology 557
    GRANT KAPLAN

B. CONSTRUCTIVE USES

35. Constructive Theology 577
    SHELLI M. POE

36. Thinking about Race 593
    THEODORE VIAL

37. Gender 611
    RUTH JACKSON RAVENSCROFT

38. Schleiermacher and the Politics of Anglophone Religious Studies 629
    ANDREW C. DOLE

39. Friedrich Schleiermacher and the Postsecular: "Pacemaker for the Consciousness of a Postsecular Society"? 645
    MATTHEW RYAN ROBINSON

40. Schleiermacher and the Philosophy of Culture 660
    WILHELM GRÄB

Index 677

Abbreviations for Schleiermacher's works

In German

Ästhetik (Kelm)	*Vorlesungen über die Ästhetik.* In *KGA* 2.14, ed. Holden Kelm, using preparatory materials from Wolfgang Virmond (Berlin: De Gruyter, 2021)
Ästhetik (Lommatzsch)	*Vorlesungen über die Aesthetik. Aus Schleiermachers handschriftlichem Nachlasse und aus nachgeschriebenen Heften.* In *SW* 3.7, ed. Carl Lommatzsch (Berlin: Reimer, 1842)
AV	*Akademievorträge.* In *KGA* 1.11, ed. Martin Rössler with Lars Emersleben (Berlin: De Gruyter, 2002)
Bibliothek	*Schleiermachers Bibliothek nach den Angaben des Rauchschen Auktionskatalogs und der Hauptbücher des Verlags G. Reimer.* In *KGA* 1.15, ed. Günter Meckenstock (Berlin: De Gruyter, 2015)
Br. I–IV	*Aus Schleiermacher's Leben. In Briefen,* 4 vols., ed. Ludwig Jonas and Wilhelm Dilthey (Berlin: De Gruyter, 1860–63)
BzE	*Brouillon zur Ethik (1805/06),* ed. Hans-Joachim Birkner (Hamburg: Felix Meiner, 1981)
CG (Redeker)	*Der christliche Glaube nach den Grundsäzen der evangelischen Kirche im Zusammenhange dargestellt,* 2 vols., ed. Martin Redeker (Berlin: De Gruyter, 1960)
CG^1	*Der Christliche Glaube (1821–22).* In *KGA* 1.7.1–2, ed. Hermann Peiter (Berlin: De Gruyter, 1980); *Marginalien und Anhang, KGA* 1.7.3, ed. Ulrich Barth (Berlin: De Gruyter, 1984)
CG^2	*Der Christliche Glaube (1830–31).* In *KGA* 1.13 1–2, ed. Rolf Schäfer (Berlin: De Gruyter, 2003)
CS (Peiter)	*Christliche Sittenlehre (Vorlesungen im Wintersemester 1826/27) Nach grössenteils unveröffentlichten Hörernachschriften und nach teilweisse unveröffentlichten Manuskripten Schleiermachers,* ed. Hermann Peiter (Berlin: LIT Verlag, 2010)
Dial.	*Vorlesungen über die Dialektik.* In *KGA* 2.10.1–2, ed. Andreas Arndt (Berlin: De Gruyter, 2002)
Ethik (Birkner)	*Ethik [1812/13], mit späteren Fassungen der Einleitung, Güterlehre und Pflichtenlehre,* ed. Hans-Joachim Birkner, following the edition of Otto Braun (Hamburg: Meiner, 1990)
Gedanken	*Gelegentliche Gedanken über Universitäten im deutschen Sinn. Nebst einem Anhang über eine neu zu errichtende (1808).* In *KGA* 1.6, ed. Dirk Schmid (Berlin: De Gruyter, 1998)

GKS	*Grundlinien einer Kritik der bisherigen Sittenlehre*. In *KGA* 1.4, ed. Eilert Herms, Günter Meckenstock, and Michael Pietsch (Berlin: De Gruyter, 2002)
HK	*Vorlesungen zur Hermeneutik und Kritik*. In *KGA* 2.4, ed. Wolfgang Virmond (Berlin: De Gruyter, 2012)
KD^1	*Kurze Darstellung des Theologischen Studiums (1811)*. In *KGA* 1.6, ed. Dirk Schmid (Berlin: De Gruyter, 1998)
KD^2	*Kurze Darstellung des Theologischen Studiums (1830)*. In *KGA* 1.6, ed. Dirk Schmid (Berlin: De Gruyter, 1998)
KGA	*Friedrich Schleiermacher Kritische Gesamtausgabe*, ed. Lutz Käppel, Andreas Arndt, Jörg Dierken, André Munzinger and Notger Slenczka (Berlin: De Gruyter, 1980–)
KS	*Kleine Schriften 1786–1833*. In *KGA* 1.14, ed. Matthias Wolfes and Michael Pietsch (Berlin: De Gruyter, 2003)
Lucinde	*Vertraute Briefe über Friedrich Schlegels Lucinde (1800)*. In *KGA* 1.3, ed. Günter Meckenstock (Berlin: De Gruyter, 1988)
LvS	*Die Lehre vom Staat 1829–1833*. In *KGA* 2.8, ed. Walter Jäschke (Berlin: De Gruyter, 1998)
$Monologen^1$	*Monologen (1.Auflage)*. In *KGA* 1.3, ed. Günter Meckenstock (Berlin: De Gruyter, 1988)
$Monologen^2$	*Monologen, (2–)4. Auflage*. In *KGA* 1.12, ed. Günter Meckenstock (Berlin: De Gruyter, 1995)
Pädagogik	*Vorlesungen über die Pädagogik und amtliche Voten zum öffentlichen Unterricht*. In *KGA* 2.12, ed. Jens Beljan et al. (Berlin: De Gruyter, 2017)
PrTh	*Die praktische Theologie nach den Grundsätzen der evangelischen Kirche*. In *SW* 1.13, ed. Jacob Frerichs (Berlin: De Gruyter, 1850)
Psychologie	*Vorlesungen über die Psychologie*. In *KGA* 2.13, ed. Dorothea Meier with Jens Beljan (Berlin: De Gruyter, 2018)
PW	*Platons Werke*, 6 vols. (Berlin: Reimer, 1804–1828; 2nd ed. of vols. 1–5, 1817–1826)
PW (Käppel)	*Platons Werke*. In *KGA* 4.3, ed. Lutz Käppel and Joanna Loehr (Berlin: De Gruyter, 2016)
PW (Steiner)	*Die Einleitungen zur Übersetzung des Platon (1804–1828)*. In *Über die Philosophie Platons*, ed. Peter M. Steiner (Hamburg: Felix Meiner, 1996)
$Reden^1$	*Über die Religion (1.Auflage)*. In *KGA* 1.2, ed. Günter Meckenstock (Berlin: De Gruyter, 1984)
$Reden^2$	*Über die Religion, (2–)4. Auflage*. In *KGA* 1.12, ed. Günter Meckenstock (Berlin: De Gruyter, 1995)
Reden (Meckenstock)	*Über die Religion. Reden an die Gebildeten unter ihren Verächtern (1799)*, ed. Günter Meckenstock (Berlin: De Gruyter, 1999)
Reden (Peter)	*Über die Religion. Reden an die Gebildeten unter ihren Verächtern 1799/1806/1821*, ed. Niklaus Peter, Frank Bestebreurtje, and Anna Büsching (Zürich: Theologischer Verlag, 2012)
Sitte	*Die Christliche Sitte*. In *SW* 1.12, ed. Ludwig Jonas (2nd ed.; Berlin: Reimer, 1884)

Spin.	*Spinozismus.* In *KGA* 1.1, ed. Günter Meckenstock (Berlin: De Gruyter, 1984)
Spin.Sys.	*Kurze Darstellung des Spinozistischen Systems.* In *KGA* 1.1, ed. Günter Meckenstock (Berlin: De Gruyter, 1984)
SW	*Sämmtliche Werke* (Berlin: Reimer, 1835–64)
TK	*Schleiermachers Tageskalender 1808–1834*, Schleiermacher digital, ed. Elisabeth Blumrich, Christiane Hackel, and Wolfgang Virmond (Berlin: Berlin-Brandenburgische Akademie der Wissenschaften 2016), https://schleiermacher-digital.de/tageskalender/index.xql
UF	*Über die Freiheit.* In *KGA* 1.1, ed. Günter Meckenstock (Berlin: De Gruyter, 1984)
UGSA	"Über den Gegensatz zwischen der Sabellianischen und der Athanasianischen Vortstellung von der Trinität." In *KGA* 1.10 (Berlin: De Gruyter)
UHG	*Über das höchste Gut.* In *KGA* 1.1, ed. Günter Meckenstock (Berlin: De Gruyter, 1984)
UWL	*Über den Wert des Lebens.* In *KGA* 1.1, ed. Günter Meckenstock (Berlin: De Gruyter, 1984)
VHK	*Vorlesungen zur Hermeneutik und Kritik.* In *KGA* 2.4, ed. Wolfgang Virmond with Hermann Patsch (Berlin: De Gruyter, 2012)
VLJ	*Vorlesungen über das Leben Jesu.* In *KGA* 2.15, ed. Walter Jaeschke (Berlin: De Gruyter, 2018)
VTB	*Versuch einer Theorie des geselligen Betragens.* In *KGA* 1.2, ed. Günter Meckenstock (Berlin: De Gruyter, 1984)
WA	*Werke. Auswahl in vier Bände*, ed. O. Braun and Johannes Baur (Leipzig: F. Eckdart, 1910–1913)
WFG	*Die Weihnachtsfeier. Ein Gespräch.* In *KGA* 1.5, ed. Hermann Patsch (Berlin: De Gruyter, 1995)

In English Translation

BO	*Brief Outline of the Study of Theology*, trans. Terrence Tice (Louisville: Westminster/John Knox Press, 2011)
CEC	*Christmas Eve Celebration: A Dialogue*, edited and trans. Terrence Tice (Eugene, OR: Cascade, 2010)
CE (Shelley)	*Introduction to Christian Ethics*, trans. John C. Shelley (Nashville: Abingdon Press, 1989)
CE (Brandt)	*Selections from Schleiermacher's Christian Ethics*, ed. and trans. James Brandt (Louisville: Westminster/John Knox Press, 2011)
CF (1928)	*The Christian Faith*, trans. H. R. Mackintosh et al. (Edinburgh: T&T Clark, 1989)
CF (2016)	*Christian Faith*, trans. Terrence Tice, Catherine Kelsey, and Edwina Lawler, 2 vols. (Louisville: John Knox Press, 2016)
CWS	*Schleiermacher: Christmas Dialogue, Second Speech, and Other Selections*, ed. and trans. Julia Lamm (New York: Paulist Press, 2014)
Dial. (Tice)	*Dialectic or, the Art of Doing Philosophy*, trans. Terrence Tice (Oxford: Oxford University Press, 1996)

IDP	*Schleiermacher's Introduction to the Dialogues of Plato*, trans. William Dobson (Cambridge: Pit Press, 1836; reprint, New York: Arno Press, 1973)
HC	*Hermeneutics and Criticism and Other Writings*, trans. and ed. Andrew Bowie (Cambridge: Cambridge University Press, 1998)
LJ	*The Life of Jesus*, ed. Jack Verheyden, trans. S. Maclean Gilmour (Mifflintown, PA: Sigler Press, 1997)
NK	"Note on the Knowledge of Freedom (1790–1792)," "Notes on Kant's Critique of Practical Reason (probably from 1789)," and "Review of Immanuel Kant's Anthropology from a Pragmatic Point of View (1799)," trans. Jacqueline Mariña, *New Athenaeum/Neues Athenaeum* 5 (1998), pp. 11–31
NOE	*Brouillon zur Ethik/Notes on Ethics*, trans. J. Wallhauser (Lewiston: Edwin Mellen Press, 2003)
ODE	*On the Doctrine of Election*, trans. Iain G. Nicol and Terrence Tice (Louisville: Westminster John Knox Press, 2012)
ODSA	"On the Discrepancy between the Sabellian and Athanasian Method of Representing the Doctrine of the Trinity," trans. Moses Stuart. In *The Biblical Repository and Quarterly Observer* in two parts: vol. 5, no. 18 (April 1835), pp. 266–353; and vol. 6, no. 19 (July 1835), pp. 1–116
OF	*On Freedom*, trans. Albert Blackwell (Lewiston: Edwin Mellen Press, 1992)
OG	*On the Glaubenslehre: Two Letters to Dr. Lücke*, trans. James Duke and Francis Fiorenza (Atlanta: Scholars Press, 1981)
OHG	*On the Highest Good*, trans. H. Victor Froese (Lewiston: Edwin Mellen Press, 1992)
PE	*Lectures on Philosophical Ethics*, ed. Robert B. Louden, trans. Louise Adey Huish (Cambridge: Cambridge University Press, 2002)
Serm. (De Vries)	*Servant of the Word: Selected Sermons of Friedrich Schleiermacher*, trans. Dawn De Vries (Minneapolis: Fortress Press, 1987)
Serm. (Lawler)	*Fifteen Sermons of Friedrich Schleiermacher Delivered to Celebrate the Beginning of a New Year*, ed. and trans. Edwina Lawler (Lewiston: Mellen, 2003)
Serm. (Nicoll)	*Selected Sermons*, ed. W. Robertson Nicoll, trans. Mary F. Wilson (Eugene, OR: Wipf & Stock, 2004; previously published 1880)
Solil.	*Schleiermacher's Soliloquies*, trans. Horace Leland Friess (Chicago: Open Court, 1957)
Speeches[1]	*On Religion: Speeches to its Cultured Despisers (1799)*, trans. and ed. Richard Crouter (Cambridge: Cambridge University Press, 1996)
Speeches[2]	*On Religion: Speeches to Its Cultured Despisers (1821)*, trans. and ed. John Oman (Louisville: Westminster/John Knox Press, 1994)
TSC	*Toward a Theory of Sociable Conduct*, trans. R. D. Richardson (Lewiston: Edwin Mellen Press, 1995)
WGVL	*On What Gives Value to Life*, trans. Edwina Lawler and Terence Tice (Lewiston: Edwin Mellen Press, 1995)

Contributors

Andreas Arndt is Senior Professor of Philosophy in the theological faculty of the Humboldt University of Berlin. His areas of research interest include history of modern philosophy and modern theology, as well as the thought of G. W. F. Hegel, and the life and writings of Friedrich Schleiermacher. His publications include *Friedrich Schleiermacher als Philosoph* (De Gruyter, 2013), *Friedrich Schleiermachers Hermeneutik*, co-edited with Jörg Dierken (De Gruyter, 2016), and *Die Reformation der Revolution. Friedrich Schleiermacher in seiner Zeit* (Matthes & Seitz, 2019). He also serves as a general editor of the *Kritische Gesamtausgabe* of Schleiermacher's writings (De Gruyter).

Annette G. Aubert is a lecturer at Westminster Theological Seminary and a fellow of the Royal Historical Society. Her articles and books focus on the reception and analyses of nineteenth-century European religious ideas in America. She is the author of *The German Roots of Nineteenth-Century American Theology* (Oxford University Press, 2013) and co-editor of *Transatlantic Religion: Europe, America, and the Making of Modern Christianity* (Brill, 2021). Her most recent publications include *Christocentric Reformed Theology in Nineteenth-Century America*, part of the Mercersburg Theology Study Series. Her current research focuses on nineteenth-century transatlantic academic networks and the intersection of theology and science.

Christian Berner is Full Professor of German Philosophy at the University of Paris Nanterre and member of the Institut de Recherches Philosophiques. Specialist in German philosophy and hermeneutics, translator, among others, of Schleiermacher, Feuerbach, Cassirer, he has among others published *La Philosophie de Schleiermacher. Herméneutique, dialectique, éthique* (Cerf, 1995), *Au détour du sens. Perspectives d'une philosophie herméneutique* (Cerf, 2007), *L'Interprétation. Un dictionnaire philosophique* (co-edited with Denis Thouard) (Vrin, 2015).

James M. Brandt is Professor Emeritus of Historical Theology at Saint Paul School of Theology in Leawood, Kansas, USA. He has published *All Things New: Reform of Church and Society in Schleiermacher's Christian Ethics* (Westminster John Knox, 2001) and a translation, *Selections from Friedrich Schleiermacher's Christian Ethics* (Westminster John Knox, 2011) as well as numerous articles related to Schleiermacher, practical theology, and theological education. He is an ordained minister in the Evangelical Lutheran Church in America.

Omar Brino was educated at the Scuola Normale Superiore of Pisa, at the Ruhr-Universität-Bochum and at the Freie Universität Berlin, and he has taught philosophy at the University of Chieti-Pescara and the University of Trento. His primary research interests concern Schleiermacher, German classical philosophy, and the relationship between ethics, philosophy of religion, and historical hermeneutics. Among his publications are *L'architettonica della morale. Teoria e storia dell'etica nelle* Grundlinien *di Schleiermacher* (The Architectonic of Morals: Theory and History of Ethics in Schleiermacher's *Grundlinien*) (University of Trento Press, 2007), *Introduzione a Schleiermacher* (Introduction to Schleiermacher) (Laterza, 2010), and *Finitudine senza dogmi* (Finitude without Dogmas), edited with M. Forlivesi (Morcelliana, 2022).

Christian Danz is Professor of Systematic Theology at the Institut für Systematische Theologie und Religionswissenschaft, in the Faculty of Protestant Theology at the University of Vienna. His research focuses on fundamental and systematic theology, Reformed theology, historical theology in the nineteenth and twentieth centuries, ethics, and the philosophy of religion. His recent publications include *Grundprobleme der Christologie* (Tübingen, 2013), *Einführung in die Theologie Martin Luthers* (Darmstadt, 2013), *Systematische Theologie* (Tübingen, 2016), *Gottes Geist. Eine Pneumatologie* (Tübingen 2019), and *Jesus von Nazareth zwischen Judentum und Christentum. Eine christologische und religionstheologische Skizze* (Tübingen, 2020).

Jörg Dierken is Professor of Systematic Theology and Ethics at the Institut für Systematische Theologie und Praktische Theologie und Religionswissenschaft at the Martin Luther University of Halle-Wittenberg. His research lies in the areas of Protestantism and modern culture, the history of modern theology, modern theological ethics, and philosophy of religion. His recent publications include *Ganzheit und Kontrafaktizität: Religion in der Sphäre des Sozialen* (Mohr Siebeck, 2014) and *Gott und Geld: Ähnlichkeit im Widerstreit* (Mohr Siebeck, 2017). He also serves as a general editor of the *Kritische Gesamtausgabe* of Schleiermacher's writings (De Gruyter).

Andrew C. Dole received a joint PhD in religious studies and philosophy from Yale. Since 2004 he has been teaching in the religion department at Amherst College in the area of modern Western religious thought. He teaches courses in the history of Christian thought, in the philosophy of religion, the cognitive science of religion, religion and conspiratorial thinking, and theories of religion. He is the author of *Schleiermacher on Religion and the Natural Order* (Oxford University Press, 2010) and *Reframing the Masters of Suspicion: Marx, Nietzsche, and Freud* (Bloomsbury Academic, 2019).

Christof Ellsiepen serves as Dean of the Evangelischen Kirche in Heidelberg. His research centers on Schleiermacher's theory of religion and understanding of piety and on Spinoza's philosophy. His publications include *Anschauung des Universums und Scientia Intuitiva. Die spinozistischen Grundlagen von Schleiermachers früher Religionstheorie* (De Gruyter, 2006), "Frömmigkeit als Handlungsimpuls: Zum Verhältnis von Religion und Ethik nach Schleiermachers *Christlicher Sittenlehre*," in *Protestantismus–Aufklärung–Frömmigkeit: Historische, systematische und praktisch-theologische Zugänge*, ed. Andreas Kubik (Vandenhoeck & Ruprecht, 2011), and "The Types Of Knowledge (2P38–47)," in *Spinoza's Ethics: A Collective Commentary* (Brill, 2011).

Wilhelm Gräb was Professor of Practical Theology at the Humboldt University Berlin and also Professor Extraordinarius in the Theological Faculty of Stellenbosch University. His research interests included modern systematic theology, practical theology, theological ethics, and religion in modernity. His publications include *Sinnfragen. Transformationen des Religiösen in der modernen Kultur* (Gütersloher Verlagshaus, 2006), *Predigtlehre. Über religiöse Rede* (Vandenhoeck & Ruprecht, 2013), *Aufgeklärte Religion und ihre Probleme. Schleiermacher–Troeltsch–Tillich*, edited with Ulrich Barth, Christian Danz, Friedrich

Wilhelm Graf (De Gruyter, 2013), *Schleiermacher, the Study of Religion, and the Future of Theology: A Transatlantic Dialogue*, edited with Brent W. Sockness (De Gruyter, 2010), and *Vom Menschsein und der Religion. Eine praktische Kulturtheologie* (Mohr Siebeck, 2018).

Peter Grove, PhD, Dr. theol., is a pastor in the Evangelical-Lutheran Church in Denmark, having previously taught systematic theology at the universities in Aarhus in Denmark and in Kiel, Lüneburg, and Flensburg in Germany. He is the author of many publications on modern theology and philosophy of religion, of which the most important is *Deutungen des Subjekts: Schleiermachers Philosophie der Religion* (De Gruyter, 2004). His research interests especially concern German Enlightenment, Idealism, and Romanticism—not least Schleiermacher—and liberal theology around 1900.

Ruth Jackson Ravenscroft is a Bye-Fellow and Undergraduate Tutor at Sidney Sussex College, and an Affiliated Lecturer at the Faculty of Divinity, University of Cambridge. She is the author of *The Veiled God: Friedrich Schleiermacher's Theology of Finitude* (Brill, 2019), and co-editor with Simon Goldhill of *Victorian Engagements with the Bible and Antiquity: The Shock of the Old* (Cambridge University Press, 2023). Her writing sits at the intersection between theology, philosophy, literature, and intellectual history, and has focused on late eighteenth- and early nineteenth-century religious thought in particular. Her research interests include hermeneutics, religious language, gender, and epistemology.

Paul Dafydd Jones is a professor of religious studies at the University of Virginia. He is a British theologian whose scholarship focuses on Protestant theology, political and liberationist theology, constructive theology, and religion and public life. In addition to numerous articles, chapters, and reviews, he is the author of *The Humanity of Christ: Christology in Karl Barth's Church Dogmatics* (T&T Clark, 2008) and *Patience—A Theological Exploration: Part One, From Creation to Christ* (T&T Clark, 2022). He is also the co-editor of the *Oxford Handbook of Karl Barth* (Oxford University Press, 2019) and *Karl Barth and Liberation Theology* (T&T Clark, 2023).

Maureen Junker-Kenny is Professor in Theology and Fellow emerita of Trinity College Dublin, Ireland. Her research explores questions of theology and religion in modernity and modern theological and philosophical ethics, including the writings of Friedrich Schleiermacher, Jürgen Habermas, and Paul Ricoeur. Her recent publications include *Self, Christ and God in Schleiermacher's Dogmatics: A Theology Reconceived for Modernity* (De Gruyter, 2020), and *The Bold Arcs of Salvation History: Faith and Reason in Jürgen Habermas's Reconstruction of the Roots of European Thinking* (De Gruyter, 2022).

Grant Kaplan works in the areas of systematic, fundamental, and historical theology. He is the author of *Answering the Enlightenment: The Catholic Recovery of Historical Revelation* (Crossroad, 2006), *René Girard, Unlikely Apologist: Mimetic Theory and Fundamental Theology* (University of Notre Dame Press, 2016), and *Faith and Reason through Christian History: A Theological Essay* (Catholic University of America Press, 2022), and co-editor, with Kevin M. Vander Schel, of *The Oxford History of Modern Germany Theology, Vol. I: 1781–1848* (Oxford University Press, 2023). He received his PhD from Boston College in 2002 and has worked at Saint Louis University since 2007.

Lutz Käppel studied classical philology and German literature in Tübingen and Oxford. He earned his Dr. phil. 1990 and Habilitation 1998, both in Tübingen. In 1992/3, he spent a year at the Center for Hellenic Studies in Washington, DC. Since 1999, he is Professor of Classical Literature, especially Ancient Greek Literature, at the Christian-Albrechts-Universität zu Kiel. His main research fields are: ancient Greek lyric, Greek tragedy, ancient mathematics, and reception of the classical tradition. A special research area is Schleiermacher, especially Schleiermacher's work on ancient literature. In this context he is the "Geschäftsführender Herausgeber" of the "KGA" since 2019 and member of the editorial board of the "Schleiermacherarchiv." Besides a number of articles on Schleiermacher's work on Plato and Herclitus, he recently published—in cooperation with Johanna Loehr—two volumes of Schleiermacher's translation of Plato: *Platons Werke*: KGA 4.3 (2016) and KGA 4.5 (2020).

Holden Kelm is a postdoctoral research fellow at the Berlin-Brandenburgische Akademie der Wissenschaften. His publications include "Zu den Hörern von Friedrich Schleiermachers Vorlesungen und ihren Nachschriften," *Journal for the History of Modern Theology/Zeitschrift für Neuere Theologiegeschichte* (2019), *Friedrich Schleiermacher KGA 2.14. Vorlesungen über die Ästhetik*, and *Der Mensch und die Kunst bei Friedrich Schleiermacher: Beiträge zur Anthropologie und Ästhetik*, edited with Dorothea Meier (De Gruyter, 2023).

Catherine L. Kelsey is Interim Senior VP for Academic Affairs at the Iliff School of Theology in Denver, Colorado. Her ongoing research has focused on Schleiermacher's preaching (2007), Christology (2003), and influence on North American Methodism (2014). She led the editorial team that produced the fresh translation of Schleiermacher's dogmatic theology, *Christian Faith: A New Translation and Critical Edition* (Westminster John Knox Press, 2016).

Dietrich Korsch is Professor of Systematic Theology in the Protestant Theological Faculty at Philipps University Marburg. His research focuses on the history of modern Protestant theology, dogmatics, theological hermeneutics, and theological aesthetics. His publications include *Religionsbegriff und Gottesglaube. Dialektische Theologie als Hermeneutik der Religion* (Mohr Siebeck, 2005), *Martin Luther. Eine Einführung*, 2. Auflage (Mohr Siebeck, 2007), *Antwort auf Grundfragen christlichen Glaubens. Dogmatik als integrative Disziplin* (Mohr Siebeck, 2016), and *Interpreting Religion: The Significance of Friedrich Schleiermacher's Reden über die Religion for Religious Studies and Theology*, edited with Amber L. Griffioen (Mohr Siebeck, 2011).

Julia A. Lamm is Professor of Theology at Georgetown University in Washington, DC. She is author of *The Living God: Schleiermacher's Theological Appropriation of Spinoza* (Penn State University Press, 1996), *God's "Kinde" Love: Julian of Norwich's Vernacular Theology of Grace* (Crossroad, 2019), *Schleiermacher's Plato* (De Gruyter, 2021), and numerous scholarly articles. She is also translator and editor of *Schleiermacher: Christmas Dialogue, the Second Speech, and Other Selections* for the Classics of Western Spirituality (Paulist Press, 2014), and editor of *The Wiley-Blackwell Companion to Christian Mysticism* (2012). She is a recipient of an Alexander von Humboldt Fellowship (Germany).

Dorothea Meier is a research fellow in general pedagogy and theory of science at the University of Rostock. Her research interests include aesthetics, Schleiermacher's psychology and anthropology, early modern political thought, and the thought of Wolfgang Ratke. Her publications include *Friedrich Schleiermacher KGA 2.13: Vorlesungen über die Psychologie* (De Gruyter, 2019), *Schleiermachers Psychologie. Eine Phänomenologie der Seele*

(Ergon, 2019), and *Der Mensch und die Kunst bei Friedrich Schleiermacher. Beiträge zur Anthropologie und Ästhetik*, edited with Michael Winkler (De Gruyter, 2023).

Michael Moxter is Emeritus Professor of Systematic Theology at the University of Hamburg. He research centers on systematic theology, nineteenth- and twentieth-century philosophy of religion, phenomenology, and theology and jurisprudence. His publications include *Das Letzte—der Erste. Gott denken*, edited with H.-P. Großhans and P. Stoellger (Mohr Siebeck, 2018), *Konstellationen und Transformationen reformatorischer Theologie* (edited) (Evangelische Verlagsanstalt, 2018), and *Die Zeit der Bilder. Ikonische Repräsentation und Temporalität*, edited with M. Firchow (Mohr Siebeck, 2018).

Paul T. Nimmo is King's (1620) Chair of Systematic Theology at the University of Aberdeen. His publications include *Being in Action: The Theological Shape of Barth's Ethical Vision* (T&T Clark, 2007), *The Cambridge Companion to Reformed Theology* (Cambridge University Press, 2016), *Kenosis: The Self-Emptying of Christ in Scripture and Theology* (Eerdmans, 2022), and several articles on the theology of Friedrich Schleiermacher. He is the Senior Editor of *International Journal of Systematic Theology*, a co-founder of the Aberdeen Centre for Protestant Theology, and a former Steering Committee Member of the AAR Friedrich Schleiermacher Unit.

Andrew Packman is Assistant Professor of Theological Ethics and Formation at United Theological Seminary of the Twin Cities, Minnesota, USA, where he previously served as a Louisville Institute Postdoctoral Fellow. His research explores the place of affectivity in moral and religious life with a particular focus on questions of moral motivation and failure. His current project draws from social psychology, critical race theory, and the works of Friedrich Schleiermacher to construct a theological diagnosis of racism's tenacity in American life.

Hermann Patsch, Dr. theol., taught for many years as a secondary school teacher in München. His research has explored a number of areas of Schleiermacher's philosophical and theological writings, including his writings on hermeneutics and textual criticism, biblical exegesis, and lectures on the life of Jesus. His publications include *Alle Menschen sind Künstler. Friedrich Schleiermachers poetische Versuche* (De Gruyter, 1986), *Friedrich Schleiermacher KGA 1.5: Schriften aus der Hallenser Zeit 1804–1807* (De Gruyter, 1995), and numerous articles on Schleiermacher's hermeneutics, academic lectures, and exegetical works.

Daniel Pedersen is Research Fellow in Systematic Theology at the University of Aberdeen. His publications include *The Eternal Covenant: Schleiermacher on God and Natural Science* (De Gruyter, 2017), *Schleiermacher's Theology of Sin and Nature: Agency, Value, and Modern Theology* (Routledge, 2020), and numerous articles on Schleiermacher, focusing especially on Schleiermacher's theological and philosophical sources as well as the application of his though to issues at the intersection of theology and natural science.

Shelli M. Poe is Visiting Professor at Iliff School of Theology (Denver, Colorado). She is the author of *The Constructive Promise of Schleiermacher's Theology* (T&T Clark, 2021) and *Essential Trinitarianism: Schleiermacher as Trinitarian Theologian* (T&T Clark, 2017), and editor of *Schleiermacher and Sustainability: A Theology for Ecological Living* (Westminster John Knox, 2018). Her research interests include modern Protestant theology, Reformed theology, systematic theology, and constructive theologies.

Zachary Purvis is Lecturer in Church History at Edinburgh Theological Seminary, having previously held positions at the University of Göttingen, University of Wisconsin-Madison, and University of Edinburgh. He studied at Westminster Seminary California and at the University of Oxford, where he earned his DPhil. He is the author of *Theology and the University in Nineteenth-Century Germany* (Oxford University Press, 2014), awarded Best First Book from the Ecclesiastical History Society, as well as numerous articles in the theology and history of Reformation and modern Christianity.

Matthew Ryan Robinson serves in the Protestant Theological Faculty of the Rhenish Friedrich Wilhelm University Bonn. He is the author of *Redeeming Relationship, Relationships That Redeem: Free Sociability and the Completion of Humanity in the Thought of Friedrich Schleiermacher* (Mohr Siebeck, 2018) and, with Evan F. Kuehn, of *Theology Compromised: Schleiermacher, Troeltsch, and the Possibility of a Sociological Theology* (Lexington Books/Fortress Academic, 2019).

Jan Rohls is Professor Emeritus of Systematic Theology in the theological faculty of the Ludwig Maximilian University of Munich. His research interests include the history of theology, history of philosophy, Reformed theology, systematic theology, and ethics. His publications include *Geschichte der Ethik*, 2nd ed. (Mohr Siebeck, 1999), *Philosophie und Theologie in Geschichte und Gegenwart* (Mohr Siebeck, 2002), as well as numerous articles and essays treating Schleiermacher's thought.

Miriam Rose is Professor of Systematic Theology at the Friedrich Schiller University of Jena. Her areas of research interest include process theology, individuality and creativity, theological anthropology, ethics of individuality, and ecumenics. Her publications include *Schleiermachers Staatslehre* (Mohr Siebeck, 2012), *Religiöse Reden in postsäkularen Gesellschaften*, edited with Michael Wermke (Evangelische Verlagsanstalt, 2016), and *Theologie der Diaspora. Studiendokument zur Standortbestimmung der evangelischen Kirchen im pluralen Europa* (Theology of Diaspora: CPCE Study Document to Define the Situation of Protestant Churches in a Pluralist Europe), edited with Mario Fischer (Evangelischer Presseverband in Österreich, 2019).

Sarah Schmidt is director of the Schleiermacher Research Center at the Berlin-Brandenburg Academy of Sciences and Humanities. Her areas of research interest include Romantic literature and philosophy, hermeneutics, philosophy of culture, and the life and thought of Schleiermacher. Her publications include *Die Konstruktion des Endlichen. Schleiermachers Philosophie der Wechselwirkung* (De Gruyter, 2005), *Wissenschaft, Kirche, Staat und Politik. Schleiermacher im Preußischen Reformprozess*, edited with Andreas Arndt and Simon Gerber (De Gruyter, 2019), *Friedrich Schleiermacher KGA 5.12, Briefwechsel 1811–1813*, edited with Simon Gerber (De Gruyter, 2019), and *Friedrich Schleiermacher KGA 5.13. Briefwechsel 1813–1816*, edited with Simon Gerber (De Gruyter, 2020).

Kevin M. Vander Schel is Associate Professor of Religious Studies at Gonzaga University. His research centers on nineteenth- and twentieth-century Christian thought, political theology, philosophy of religion, and theological hermeneutics. He is the author of *Embedded Grace: Christ, History, and the Reign of God in Schleiermacher's Dogmatics* (Fortress Press, 2013), co-editor of *The Fragility of Consciousness: Faith, Reason, and the Human Good* (University of Toronto Press, 2017), *Theology, History, and the Modern German University*

(Mohr Siebeck, 2021), and, with Grant Kaplan, *The Oxford History of Modern Germany Theology, Vol. I: 1781–1848* (Oxford University Press, 2023).

Theodore Vial is Potthoff Professor of Theology and Modern Western Religious Thought and Vice President of Innovation, Learning, and Institutional Research at the Iliff School of Theology. He has published *Modern Religion, Modern Race* (Oxford University Press, 2016) and *Schleiermacher: A Guide for the Perplexed* (T&T Clark, 2013). His current research is in two areas: artificial intelligence and theories of human nature, and the construction of Judaism and gender in the modern world. His BA is from Brown University and both MA and PhD from the University of Chicago.

Arnulf von Scheliha is Professor of Theological Ethics in the Protestant Theological Faculty at the University of Muenster and also Director of the Institute of Ethics and Associated Social Sciences. His research lies in the areas of theological ethics, political ethics, environmental ethics, interreligious hermeneutics, and the history of nineteenth- and twentieth-century theology. His recent publications include *Eyn sonderlicher Gottesdienst. Evangelische Theologinnen und Theologen als Parlamentarier*, co-edited with Uta E. Hohmann and Catharina Jacob (Campus Verlag, 2022) and *Christentum von rechts. Theologische Erkundungen und Kritik*, co-edited with Johann Hinrich Claussen, Martin Fritz, Andreas Kubik, and Rochus Leonhardt (Mohr Siebeck, 2021).

Birgit Weyel has held the Chair for Practical Theology at the Faculty of Practical Theology in Tübingen since 2007. Born in 1964, she studied Protestant Theology in Bonn and Berlin and was ordained in 1992. She was research assistant to Wilhelm Gräb in Berlin. She received her doctorate in 1997 and her habilitation in 2004. In 2006–2007, she was a substitute professor in Munich, was appointed to professorship in 2006 in Munich, and 2013 in Berlin. Her research interests are the history of practical theology, philosophy of religion, empirical religious studies, ritual studies and practical-theological ecclesiology. She was on the scientific advisory board of the 5th Church Membership Survey of the Protestant Church in Germany, is founding chair member of the Arbeitskreis Empirische Religionsforschung e.V. and a member of the Executive Committee of the International Academy of Practical Theology.

Michael Winkler is Professor of Pedagogy and Theory of Social Pedagogy at the Friedrich Schiller University of Jena. His research centers on modern educational theory, history and theory of pedagogy, social pedagogy, and education in the family. His publications include (with Ulf Sauerbrey) *Friedrich Fröbel und seine Spielpädagogik. Eine Einführung* (Schöningh, 2018), (with Ralf Koerrenz) *Pädagogik. Eine Einführung in Stichworten* (Schöningh, 2013), and *Erziehung in der Familie. Innenansichten des pädagogischen Alltags* (Kohlhammer, 2012).

Walter E. Wyman Jr. is Professor of Religion and Weyerhaeuser Professor of Biblical Literatures, Emeritus at Whitman College. He is author of *The Concept of Glaubenslehre: Ernst Troeltsch and the Theological Heritage of Schleiermacher* (Oxford University Press, 1983), "Sin and Redemption," in Jacqueline Mariña, ed., *The Cambridge Companion to Friedrich Schleiermacher* (Cambridge University Press, 2005), "Schleiermacher's Theology," *Encyclopedia of Christianity Online* (Brill), "How Critical Is Schleiermacher's Revisionist Dogmatics? Eschatology as Test Case," in Jörg Dierken, Arnulf von Scheliha, Sarah Schmidt, eds., *Reformation und Moderne: Pluralität-Subjektivität-Kritik* (De Gruyter, 2018), and numerous other essays and reviews. His research interests include Schleiermacher, Troeltsch, and German Protestant theology.

Johannes Zachhuber is Professor of Historical and Systematic Theology at the University of Oxford. A Senior Research Fellow of the British Academy in 2017–2018 and a Visiting Fellow at the Einstein Center Chronoi in 2018–2019, Zachhuber has two distinct research foci. The first is late antique philosophy and theology, along with its reception. The second is modern and postmodern theology, focusing on the nineteenth century and continental philosophy of religion. His most recent monograph is *The Rise of Christian Theology and the End of Ancient Metaphysics* (Oxford, 2020) and he is a co-editor on the forthcoming volume from Brill, *The Philosophical and Theological Sources of the Byzantine Cosmologies*.

GENERAL INTRODUCTION

ANDREW C. DOLE, SHELLI M. POE, AND
KEVIN M. VANDER SCHEL

I.1 Historical Context and Overview of Schleiermacher's Career

Friedrich Schleiermacher's lifetime (1768–1834) coincides with dramatic developments in many areas of European society. These include, but are not limited to, the political (the French Revolution of 1789, which both unleashed democratizing energies and triggered the intensification of governmental repression and surveillance in many countries); the religious (the disestablishment and re-establishment of Roman Catholicism in France, the unification of the Reformed and Lutheran churches in Prussia, and the rise in Europe of a form of politically charged antiliberal Protestantism strikingly anticipatory of later developments in the United States); and the educational (Prussia's ambitious program to establish a world-class research university of a new type, which culminated in the founding of the University of Berlin). His career would see him engaging all of these developments.

Born into a clerical family in lower Silesia (now part of Poland), Schleiermacher followed an educational path that prepared him for both Reformed ministry and academic theology. He spent several formative years in Moravian communities, and was deeply impressed by the Pietist movement. His education was completed at Halle, where both rationalist and Pietist influences were strong. After about a decade of clerical service in Berlin and its environs (during which he published one of his best-known works, the youthful *On Religion: Speeches to its Cultured Despisers*) he returned to Halle in 1804 as Professor *Extraordinarius* and University Preacher.

Schleiermacher's tenure at Halle would prove short-lived, ending when Napoleon shut down the university following his occupation of the city in 1806. Four years later, following a period during which he was active in plans for a liberalized restructuring of the Prussian state, Schleiermacher became one of the founders of the University of Berlin, serving as the dean of its Theology faculty. He would serve the university for his remaining twenty-four years. During his tenure, in addition to his administrative responsibilities, he lectured on a broad range of topics, authored the century's most important work of Protestant dogmatics, played an important role in the unification of the Lutheran and Reformed churches, and preached nearly weekly at the university's Trinity Church. By the time of his death in 1834 he was a beloved public figure; the historian Leopold von Ranke estimated that between twenty and thirty thousand persons lined the streets to witness his funeral procession.

I.2 Schleiermacher Reception and Scholarship

From his own context and up to today, Schleiermacher's writings have generated continuous discussion and debate.[1] In his own time, Schleiermacher's works faced sharp criticism from a number of directions, including rationalist Enlightenment theologians as well as those rejecting theological rationalism in favor of a supernaturally revealed biblical faith, speculative theologians influenced by Hegel, and civic and ecclesiastical leaders suspicious of his role as a political reformer. The subsequent reception of Schleiermacher's work falls into three readily identifiable periods. For the remainder of the "long nineteenth century" following his death, he was commonly regarded as both the inaugurator of a new era in Protestant theology, one characterized by deep and intentional engagement between church and academy, and also as an important early contributor to such fields as biblical scholarship, hermeneutical theory, ethics, and what is now known as cultural theory. Some theologians, including a number of mediating theologians and members of the Erlangen school, embraced the trajectories touched off by his work and sought to carry his legacy forward, while others, such as the two distinct "schools" associated with the Protestant and Catholic theological faculties at the University of Tübingen, regarded his theological vision as flawed and in need of correction. The turn of the twentieth century saw a "Schleiermacher renaissance," particularly in the works of Ernst Troeltsch, Adolf von Harnack, and the students of Albrecht Ritschl, Rudolf Otto, and Wilhelm Herrman, who returned to Schleiermacher in taking up questions of historical consciousness and the historical understanding of religion. This period also saw the publication of substantial elements of Schleiermacher's *Nachlass*, although not yet in fully critical editions.[2]

A second period opened when the parameters of the reception of Schleiermacher's work shifted dramatically after the Great War, in ways that make some degree of historical sense. For neither the first nor the last time in history, blaming societal calamity on failure to keep to the "old ways" found a ready audience. In this case, responsibility for the trajectory of European (and particularly German) culture that culminated in the War was pinned—by Emil Brunner, Karl Barth, and other participants in the movement that eventually became known as Protestant "neo-orthodoxy"—on the liberalization of German theology of which Schleiermacher had been the principal architect. According to this narrative,

---

[1] It is no small testament to the continuing influence of Schleiermacher's thought that a number of secondary works are devoted simply to the task of chronicling research into his writings. See, for example, Terrence N. Tice, *Schleiermacher Bibliography*, Princeton Pamphlets 12 (Princeton, NJ: Princeton Theological Seminary, 1966); T.N. Tice, "Schleiermacher Bibliography: Update 1994," in *New Athenaeum/Neues Athenaeum* 4 (1995), pp. 139–94; and Martin Ohst, ed., *Schleiermacher Handbuch* (Tübingen: Mohr Siebeck, 2017), pp. 427–488.

[2] See *Schleiermacher Handbuch*, pp. 455–465.

Schleiermacher's theological program turned on a generalized account of religious subjectivity, which effectively reduced central doctrinal and historical developments to moments of religious feeling and religious experience and opened the floodgates to a progressive relaxation of the salutary restrictions on human sinfulness that characterized a more traditional and severe Protestantism. Ironically, it was this polemical perspective that largely fueled sustained interest in Schleiermacher's theological works in English-speaking scholarship. While several of his writings, such as his *Brief Outline* and commentary on Luke, received English translations by the mid-nineteenth-century and his speeches *On Religion* was translated in 1893, a full translation of his magisterial *Glaubenslehre*, or *Christian Faith*, first appeared only in 1928.[3] For several generations, it was difficult for scholarship on Schleiermacher not to engage the questions of whether his program had been correctly understood by the neo-orthodox and whether his reputation could be salvaged after their criticisms (although some solid work did largely ignore these questions).

The situation began to change after the Second World War, with the publication of several new comprehensive studies of Schleiermacher's theological and philosophical works and a new critical edition of Schleiermacher's *Glaubenslehre*.[4] The establishment of two *Forschungsstellen* (research centers) dedicated to Schleiermacher—in 1967 (Kiel) and 1979 (Berlin)— mark a transition to the third and most recent period of reception history. The early decades of this period saw the fading of the polemical energies of the neo-orthodox paradigm and the organization of a new series of critical editions of Schleiermacher's corpus, the *Kritische Gesamtausgabe (KGA)*. From the 1980s on successive volumes of the *KGA* have appeared, and the full range of Schleiermacher's corpus has been engaged by researchers interested in both historical contextualization and possibilities for contemporary application, with a greater independence from theological polemics than seems to have been possible at any earlier time. These studies have opened up a variety of new and productive avenues of research into Schleiermacher's thought and influence. These include deeper examinations of his original and expansive philosophical writings in the fields of dialectic, ethics, and hermeneutics, as well as his lesser-known contributions in areas such as aesthetics, psychology, pedagogy, and theory of the state. These newer waves of research have also enabled careful and constructive retrievals of central components of Schleiermacher's theological program, as in his Christology, trinitarian thought, his conception of sin and redemption, and his Christian ethics. And they have further allowed constructive reconsiderations of the role Schleiermacher's work might play in addressing the pressing tasks and challenges facing the contemporary academic study of theology and religion. Of the many contributors to this volume, some are founding members of this current period of

---

[3] See Friedrich Schleiermacher, *The Christian Faith*, trans. H. R. MacKintosh and J. S. Stewart (Edinburgh: T&T Clark, reprint 1999). This 1928 translation remained the standard English translation until the recent 2016 critical edition. See Friedrich Schleiermacher, *Christian Faith: A New Translation and Critical Edition*, 2 vols., trans. Terrence N. Tice, Catherine L. Kelsey, and Edwina Lawler (Louisville, KY: Westminster John Knox Press, 2016).

[4] See Emanuel Hirsch, *Geschichte der neuern evangelischen Theologie. Im Zusammenhang mit den allgemeinen Bewegungen des europäischen Denkens*, vols. 4 and 5 (Gütersloh: C. Bertelsmann, 1952; 1954); F. D. E. Schleiermacher, *Der christliche Glaube nach den Grundsätzen der evangelischen Kirche im Zusammenhange dargestellt (1830/31)*, 2 vols., ed. Martin Redeker (Berlin: De Gruyter, 1960); and Hans-Joachim Birkner, *Schleiermachers Christliche Sittenlehre im Zusammenhang seines philosophisch-theologischen Systems* (Berlin: Töpelmann, 1964).

research, whose studies have not previously appeared in English. Others are internationally respected researchers who have advanced important aspects of Schleiermacher scholarship in their respective fields.

I.3 Project of the Handbook

The current moment into which this Handbook enters is one characterized by an energetic and committed strand of Schleiermacher scholarship on the one hand, and a growing interest in a reinterpretation of Schleiermacher's work by nonspecialists on the other. Historians of Christianity and theologians in particular are paying attention anew to the view, now standard among specialists, of Schleiermacher as a theologian who attended to Scripture, church history and creedal statements, Christian ethics, the doctrine of the Trinity, and Christology (with an emphasis on the divine indwelling of Christ). It remains that there is a range of interpretations regarding the specifics of Schleiermacher's judgments on each of these topics, but the previously dominant criticisms of his work are now on the back foot.

This volume brings the authoritative interpretations of contemporary Schleiermacher scholars to the desks of specialists and nonspecialists alike. While the chapters to follow retain the complexity and detail required of a thorough introduction to the primary and secondary literature on the topics at hand, they also provide points through which those seeking entry into various aspects of Schleiermacher's thought may go in their own research and teaching. Aimed at both English and German audiences, this volume is expansive in scope, offering readers a nearly comprehensive view of the rise, work, and influence of Schleiermacher from a wide range of interpretive perspectives. Moreover, it sets the stage for continued conversations that will press Schleiermacher scholarship into new avenues of research, including constructive work.

I.4 Volume Overview

I.4.1 Schleiermacher in Context

The first part of the volume, "Schleiermacher in Context," provides a concise examination of Schleiermacher's historical context and intellectual formation. It analyzes the principal movements and thinkers he engaged in his work. This part is subdivided into two sections, the first of which examines four significant sources of influence on Schleiermacher's thought. Julia A. Lamm details Schleiermacher's extensive engagement with Plato, which included both translations of virtually the entire Platonic corpus (which work itself had significant ramifications for later Plato scholarship) and the incorporation of important aspects of Plato's philosophy into Schleiermacher's own. Peter Grove documents the importance of Kant for Schleiermacher, taking issue with the view sometimes expressed in the secondary literature that his Kantianism is most pronounced in Schleiermacher's earliest writings and seeing deep-seated Kantian notes even in his mature conception of God. Christof Ellsiepen explores the influence of Spinoza, expanding on Schleiermacher's prominent paean to this controversial figure in his youthful *Speeches* in connection with both his early pronouncement that the heart of religion lies in "intuitions of the universe" and the manner in which he correlates God and the world in his mature philosophy. And Jan Rohls engages the charged topic of Schleiermacher's relationship to his Reformed heritage, exploring the theologically and politically delicate work Schleiermacher did in promoting the union of the Reformed and Lutheran churches in Prussia as well as the ways in which Schleiermacher's positions reflected his own Reformed identity, even where he exercised the right to criticize received doctrinal formulations.

The second section considers four sources of contemporaneous influence on Schleiermacher's work. Zachary Purvis describes Schleiermacher's fraught relationships with the philosopher Friedrich Wilhelm Joseph von Schelling and his disciple Henrich Steffens, who became a colleague of Schleiermacher's early on at Halle and then much later at Berlin; affecting Schleiermacher most profoundly during the period of early Romanticism, both nevertheless shaped his later thinking, particularly on the nature and division of the *Wissenschaften*, in lasting ways. Jörg Dierken explores the relationship between Schleiermacher and G. W. F. Hegel, which developed into a significant rivalry during the period when they both taught at Berlin, with a particular focus on the different ways in which the two applied the heritage of Kantianism to the project of theorizing religion. Johannes Zachhuber argues that Schleiermacher's mature thinking was profoundly affected by his connection to the University of Berlin, through both his multifarious professional responsibilities and his ongoing reflections on the nature of the university and the place of theology within it; in giving shape to this modern university, Schleiermacher himself was shaped by it. And Andreas Arndt narrates Schleiermacher's connection to Friedrich Schlegel, who was an intimate conversation partner and a powerful "symphilosophical" stimulus during Schleiermacher's early Berlin years; their relationship deteriorated after 1800, evidenced most notably in the failure of their joint Plato translation project (which Schleiermacher would eventually complete himself), but as Arndt demonstrates, reworked versions of the ideas he and Schlegel had explored together—particularly those connected with Plato, hermeneutics, and dialectics—became prominent components of Schleiermacher's later thinking.

I.4.2 Schleiermacher's Thought

The second and largest part, "Schleiermacher's Thought," provides a detailed investigation of Schleiermacher's writings and principal areas of contribution to theological and philosophical study. This part is further divided into three sections, which reflect both the breadth of his engagement with the academic disciplines and his contribution to Protestant theology.

The first section, "Schleiermacher and the *Wissenschaften*," ranges over the various academic disciplines within which Schleiermacher taught and wrote while at the University of Berlin. Sarah Schmidt explores Schleiermacher's theory of knowledge, presented in his lectures on dialectic, with particular attention to both the development of his lectures over time and the interpenetration of dialectic and other areas of Schleiermacher's thinking. Michael Moxter engages Schleiermacher's philosophical ethical theory (as distinct from his Christian ethics) as a descriptive account of human action and cultural life that aims to reconcile virtue- and duty-based approaches to ethics. Michael Winkler documents Schleiermacher's importance for the field of pedagogical theory, with a focus on his call for the establishment of a "science of education" in his lectures on that topic; Schleiermacher understood education to be a matter of the formation of the younger generation in the direction of freedom and autonomy, always within the constraints of actually existing society and always open to revision as societies change and science progresses. Christian Berner surveys Schleiermacher's groundbreaking contributions to hermeneutics, which he defined as the "art of understanding"; focused on the task of understanding the discourse of authors operating in contexts remote from one's own, Schleiermacher's hermeneutical theory inaugurates investigations of the relationships among language, thought, and interpersonal communication that have hardly concluded today. Holden Kelm examines Schleiermacher's theory of aesthetics, which, set within the overall framework of his philosophical ethics and well integrated with his descriptions of the other philosophical *Wissenschaften*, presents artistic activity as a form of individual symbolic communication, or as an expression of the "mood" or "immediate self-consciousness" of the artist, with poetry figuring as the form of artistic production that captured Schleiermacher's greatest interest. Dorothea Meier presents Schleiermacher's lectures on psychology, which developed relatively late in his life, as an account of the "hermeneutic explication of the soul." Identifying psychology as a metaphysical approach to the investigation of the human spirit (in contrast to anthropology's empirical approach), Schleiermacher classifies human mental activity by means of a quadrilateral defined by the twin oppositions of receptivity and spontaneity on the one hand and subjective and objective consciousness on the other, with the understanding that work of this kind provides a necessary foundation for other human *Wissenschaften* (although the lectures do not develop this theme to completion). And Miriam Rose surveys Schleiermacher's lectures on the theory of the state, which anticipates later liberal political theory in certain respects, such as advocating for the importance of public opinion and favoring the independence of some social spheres—particularly religion—from state control, while remaining underdeveloped relative to contemporaneous discussions of statehood in others, as evidenced for example by his neglect of the law's function of protecting individuals and his lack of attention to the possibility of conflict internal to the state.

The chapters in the second section, "Schleiermacher the Theologian," cover a wide range of topics, some focusing on particular theological works and others on specific theological loci. Paul T. Nimmo explores Schleiermacher's work of theological encyclopedia, the *Brief Outline on the Study of Theology*, presenting it as Schleiermacher's entry into the heated debates of his time about the standing of theology among the academic disciplines. In this slender but enormously influential work Schleiermacher redefined theology as a practical science aimed at facilitating the task of church governance, and under this conception gathered together and arranged both traditional and novel theological tasks, with a particular emphasis on the importance of historical knowledge of the Christian traditions. Two chapters by Daniel Pedersen and Walter E. Wyman, Jr. survey Schleiermacher's epoch-defining work of dogmatic theology, *The Christian Faith*. Pedersen surveys the methodological and programmatic aspects of the work, focusing in particular on the technical vocabulary Schleiermacher develops in his Introduction—piety, feeling, absolute dependence, God-consciousness—recommending that this work be understood through the lens of the later, more explicitly theological parts of the dogmatics rather than the other way around. He also argues that

Schleiermacher's famous call for an "eternal covenant" between faith and science, for which he advocated in open letters that marked the publication of the second edition of his dogmatics, is simply entailed by Schleiermacher's understanding of the relationship between God and the world. Wyman focuses on the work's doctrinal sections to critically revisit the historically popular categorization of the work as "liberal" or revisionist, finding that while the work certainly deserves these characterizations in general, nevertheless its overall theological vision retains strongly conservative elements, including the centrality of the dynamic of sin and redemption and the conviction that all other forms of religion are "destined to pass over" into Christianity.

The essays included in this section evaluate core aspects of Schleiermacher's thought while also presenting a critical survey of the broader shape and interconnections between his philosophical and theological writings. Several of these chapters take up prominent themes and tensions introduced in Schleiermacher's refashioned understanding of redemption, Christology, and the Trinity, while also exploring implications for his further theological work. Kevin M. Vander Schel examines the opposition of sin and grace in Schleiermacher's treatment of redemption, arguing that these doctrines are inseparably connected in his theological vision and that his analysis of each is distinguished by its emphasis on historical and social mediation. Maureen Junker-Kenny inquires into the person and work of Christ considered as the archetype of God-consciousness, examining Schleiermacher's treatment of Christ in both the first and second editions of his *Christian Faith*, the criticism that his view departs from the historical narrative to present an "ideal Christ," and ongoing questions concerning the historical appearance of Christ as the completion of creation. Shelli M. Poe discusses Schleiermacher's reformulated doctrine of the Trinity, arguing against the misconception that Schleiermacher de-emphasized the doctrine's importance by relegating it to the status of an appendix and proposing a fuller conception of trinitarian thought that develops Schleiermacher's treatments of love, wisdom, and causality.

Chapters by James M. Brandt, Christian Danz, Hermann Patsch, and Birgit Weyel consider further theological writings of Schleiermacher, which both complement his *Christian Faith* and help to establish new subdisciplines within the academic study of theology. Brandt highlights the original achievement of Schleiermacher's Christian ethics, which moves beyond the predominant moral theories of his time to describe the forms of distinctively Christian action as a continuation of the redemptive work of Christ in history. This field, as Brandt notes, is distinct from practical theology and did not concern the practical application of Schleiermacher's theology; rather it formed the second portion of his theology that completes his theological system. Danz documents the development of Schleiermacher's lectures on "'The 'Life of Jesus,'" which were published thirty years after David Friedrich Strauss's landmark volume *Das Leben Jesu* and have long remained under its shadow. Danz maintains that these studies occupy an unusual place among treatments of the historical Jesus, as they did not seek to establish a historical foundation for Christianity but to recreate an image of the inner unity of the life of Jesus of Nazareth as it was communicated to his disciples. Patsch turns to Schleiermacher's often unheralded historical and critical studies of the New Testament, reflected in his publications on 1 Timothy, the Gospel of Luke, and Colossians, which anticipated later significant developments in form criticism. And Birgit Weyel considers Schleiermacher's contributions to the study of practical theology, a discipline he founded as a theory of church leadership and of the practice of ministry, and which he believed had a place not just in seminaries but in the university. Schleiermacher's writing in each of these fields, most of which was published posthumously, offers a fuller perspective of the detail and complexity of his unfinished theological work.

A third section examines a series of influential occasional and pastoral writings that combine features of his philosophical and theological thought. These include early writings as well as public pieces designed for a wider readership, such as his sermons, his speeches *On Religion* (1799), his *Soliloquies* (1800), and his *Christmas Eve Dialogue*. Among these works, Schleiermacher's notorious *On Religion* has exerted the widest influence. As Dietrich Korsch notes, this text served as a turning point in the modern study of religion and theology, making the broader category of religion central both to theological reflection and to the empirical study of religion. This work was soon followed, as Omar Brino indicates, by a series of writings charting the emergence of Schleiermacher's innovative ethical thought, in his *Soliloquies*, letters on Schlegel's *Lucinde*, and his 1803 critical study of existing theories, a didactic text which marked a turn away from his earlier rhapsodic writings. Andrew Packman and Andrew C. Dole engage Schleiermacher's "Christmas Eve Dialogue" of 1806, a work Schleiermacher composed as a "gift" for his friends and which has held significant interest, and posed unique problems of interpretation, for his readers down to the present day. Accompanying these occasional writings are Schleiermacher's voluminous sermons, which he composed alongside his academic duties on a weekly basis for over twenty years, and which Catherine L. Kelsey argues provide an important and underused resource for exploring both his understandings of central theological themes, such as Christology and God-consciousness, and his use of historical-critical methods of biblical exegesis.

I.4.3 Thinking after Schleiermacher

The third part, "Thinking after Schleiermacher," brings Schleiermacher's thought into critical and constructive dialogue with important contemporary movements and issues. The eleven essays presented in this part provide an analysis of the modern reception of Schleiermacher's work and also explore the contemporary influence of his thought in relation to topics such as constructive theology, race and gender studies, and the relation of the disciplines of theology and religious studies. In this manner, this part considers how Schleiermacher's writings might continue to inspire critical reflection on religion and modern Christian thought.

The first section focuses on the history of the reception of Schleiermacher's thought. In some cases, these lines of influence have been well established. Chapters by Arnulf von Scheliha and Paul Dafydd Jones respectively consider the continuation of Schleiermacher's theological legacy within Protestant liberalism and its critique in the dialectical theology of Karl Barth and Rudolph Bultmann, while also noting that in each case the reception of Schleiermacher's thought proved nuanced and complex. Both liberal and dialectical theologians retained key aspects of Schleiermacher's theology while resisting other elements of his system. Annette Aubert explores a further dimension of Schleiermacher's influence within the mediating school of the mid-nineteenth century, which sought to build upon yet also to reconfigure Schleiermacher's original theological program.

Schleiermacher's thought also found subtler avenues of influence. Lutz Käppel argues that Schleiermacher's status as a foundational figure is not limited to his impact within theology but extends to his work in modern classical studies, where his application of hermeneutics and textual criticism set the standard for generations. And Grant Kaplan traces Schleiermacher's influence within the Catholic Tübingen school, particularly in the theologians J. S. Drey and J. A. Möhler, whose work served as a precursor to the twentieth-century *ressourcement* movement that helped to shape the Second Vatican Council.

The second section of this part brings to the fore the constructive uses to which Schleiermacher's thought has been put in recent years. The first three chapters turn to liberal and liberation theologies, race theory, and gender constructions. Shelli M. Poe examines the history and publications of the Workgroup on Constructive Theology to show how Schleiermacher's work funded liberal theology and prefigures many of the theological moves currently being made in liberation theology. Theodore Vial argues that Schleiermacher is a beneficial interlocutor when thinking about race, since he contributed to establishing contemporary understandings of culture. He argues that in thinking about race with Schleiermacher, we have the occasion to interrogate the social implications of our own values. Ruth Jackson Ravenscroft takes up the theme of gender constructions in Schleiermacher's work. She argues that while his approach to gender in his ethics and politics is grounded in heterosexist and sexist assumptions, his theology is not. And she examines Schleiermacher's notion of divine transcendence and the God–world relationship to suggest that his work could be beneficial in contemporary discussions of human difference and relationality.

In the last three chapters, Schleiermacher's relationship to current academic politics, postsecular responses to religious pluralism, and modern culture are highlighted. Andrew C. Dole surveys the history of interpretation of Schleiermacher as a theorist of religion in English-speaking literature. He argues that the interpretation of Schleiermacher as an "antireductionist" and "protectivist" theorist of "religious experience," which was influentially put forward by Wayne Proudfoot, has been used to mark a clear distinction between the disciplines of "religious studies" and "theology." Though now largely abandoned, this interpretation of Schleiermacher displays the incongruity of "mediating" positions like Schleiermacher's with polarized thinking. Matthew Ryan Robinson addresses the potential of Schleiermacher's thought for postsecular theorists who attend to the challenges that arise for political entities due to religious pluralism. He argues that Schleiermacher offers innovative empirical study of these challenges in the context of the secularization of ecclesial institutions following Napoleon's invasions. Nonetheless, Robinson argues that Schleiermacher's theory of the state does not offer clear solutions for governing a religiously diverse population. In the final chapter, Wilhelm Gräb argues that Schleiermacher's philosophical ethics could contribute to a diagnosis and treatment of the crisis of modern culture. By offering a cultural philosophy that is complemented by a theology of culture, Schleiermacher is set apart from other thinkers like Rousseau, Kant, Herder, and Hegel.

I.5 Conclusion

Given the breadth and significance of the chapters that comprise this volume, perhaps it goes without saying that Schleiermacher is an influential figure in the history of Christian thought, theories and methods in religious studies, and hermeneutics. The German-language critical edition of his work, *Friedrich Schleiermacher Kritische Gesamtausgabe*, which began in 1980, and English translations of key portions of his corpus beginning in the late nineteenth century, have allowed scholars to investigate the richness of his thought. German scholars have often focused on Schleiermacher's ties to early modern philosophy, his aesthetics, hermeneutics, and theory of religion, while English-speaking scholars have often focused on the theological influences and implications of his work. Over the last thirty years, both German and Anglophone scholars have been at work translating and analyzing key texts.

As a result, a number of rich conversations are ongoing among contemporary scholars. Scholars examine Schleiermacher's place among a constellation of post-Kantian thinkers; investigate the intellectual ties between Schleiermacher and other Reformed thinkers such as John Calvin and Karl Barth; explore Schleiermacher's ethics and its relation to dogmatics; study Schleiermacher's theory of religion and its place in the modern university; and consider how Schleiermacher's work could speak to contemporary issues of race, sex, religious pluralism, language, politics, and religious studies. The appearance in 2016 of the first English-language critical edition of Schleiermacher's magnum opus, *Christian Faith* (translated and edited by Terrence Tice, Catherine L. Kelsey, and Edwina Lawler) indicates both the burgeoning Schleiermacher scholarship that has arisen over the past academic generation and the likelihood of its continuation.

As the field of Schleiermacher studies broadens into a new appreciation of Schleiermacher, especially among theologians and historians of Christianity, this Handbook serves to gather authoritative interpretations of Schleiermacher's work from both German- and English-speaking scholars, bringing together the best that Schleiermacher scholarship has to offer. We hope it is beneficial for those seeking an entry into Schleiermacher's thought, as the relatively short chapters within this volume span the range of his work and influences and point the reader to further primary and secondary literature. We also hope that the Handbook presses the conversation further, showing readers how Schleiermacher's work remains a rich resource to be mined for the benefit of constructive work.

This volume is affectionately dedicated to the memory of the author of its final chapter, Wilhelm Gräb, who passed away on January 23, 2023. Active in both German- and English-speaking circles, Gräb was known to scholars of many nations. He is remembered as a deeply learned and dedicated Schleiermacher scholar, an accomplished practical theologian and devotee of lived religion, and a reliable source of both good humor and good fellowship. Schleiermacher himself was described by his contemoraries as a "virtuoso of friendship"; Wilhelm Gräb has done much to keep alive among Schleiermacher scholars the tradition of striving after the exemplification of that signature virtue.

PART I

SCHLEIERMACHER IN CONTEXT

A

INFLUENCES ON SCHLEIERMACHER

CHAPTER 1

PLATO

JULIA A. LAMM

> There is no author who has so affected me and initiated me into the sanctum, not just of philosophy but also of humanity in general, as has this divine man.[1]
> —Schleiermacher

1.1 INTRODUCTION

Plato had a profound influence on Schleiermacher's thought in a myriad of ways. Slow recognition of this fact contributed to one of the greatest lacunae in Schleiermacher scholarship. This is all the more surprising given the fact that Schleiermacher changed the course of Plato studies by challenging our fundamental assumptions about Plato and his works. In his day, he was hailed as the "restorer of Plato."[2] Although in the past quarter century Schleiermacher scholars have increasingly acknowledged his debt to Plato, theologians and other scholars of religion (especially in the Anglophone world) remain relatively unaware of the degree to which Schleiermacher absorbed his own interpretation of Plato into the formation of his own thought and methodology. Hopefully, that will change with a new full-scale study of the topic, *Schleiermacher's Plato*.[3]

To begin to understand Schleiermacher's debt to Plato, we need to keep in mind two basic distinctions. First, we need to distinguish five periods in Schleiermacher's life where Plato inspired different responses from him: his school-boy days (1783–1785); his university years (1787–1789); his early, Romantic period in Berlin (1796–1802); his years of intensive scholarship on Plato while in Stolp and Halle, where he began his academic career (1802–1808); and his mature years as a founding member of the University of Berlin, renowned theologian, impactful church leader, member of the Royal Prussian Academy of Sciences, and political activist (1808–1834). This essay focuses on that fourth period, when Schleiermacher,

---

[1] Schleiermacher to Carl Gustav von Brinckmann, 9 June 1800, *KGA* 5.4, p. 82.
[2] Immanuel Bekker, ed., *Platonis Dialogi graece et latine, ex recensione Immanuelis Bekkeri*, 3 Vols. (Berlin: Reimer, 1816–1818), dedication: "Friderico Schleiermachero Platonis Restitutori."
[3] See Julia A. Lamm, *Schleiermacher's Plato* (Berlin and Boston: De Gruyter, 2021).

immersed in translating and interpreting the Platonic *corpus*, was also establishing the basic principles of his own constructive thought.

Second, we need to distinguish between familiar forms of Platon*ism* and Schleiermacher's particular understanding of Plato, which was distinctly modern and which focused as much on form and method as on philosophical content. The question here is whether Schleiermacher's absorption of Platonic themes can be called a form of Platon*ism*. To address that question, we need to hold together Plato's influence on Schleiermacher (which, while momentous, was never single or unidirectional) with the interpretive matrix that Schleiermacher brought to his Plato-interpretation. It is not so much that we will find a recognizable and transmittable form of Platonism as is it that we will begin to recognize *Schleiermacher's* Plato when he appears—and we will realize just how often he does appear.

Plato was always in the background—along with a host of other great thinkers, both ancient and modern. Schleiermacher had studied Greek language and literature since his early school days; he later studied Aristotle as a university student and had even planned a translation of *Nicomachean Ethics*. It was Plato, however, who played a special role for the German Romantics. There are hints of Plato, for instance, in the first edition of Schleiermacher's *Speeches* (1799).[4] In that sense, the influence of Plato on Schleiermacher was always there, although in a generalized sense. Plato's presence in Schleiermacher's thought took a new and definite form when, in 1800, he began working in earnest on what would become his monumental *Platons Werke* (hereafter *PW*).[5] Schleiermacher's *PW* would alter the course of Plato scholarship. His monumental translation of Plato's dialogues would remain *the* German translation for two hundred years and even now continues to be recognized as the "classic" one.[6] When *PW* was first published, August Boeckh, a respected classicist, praised Schleiermacher's accomplishment: "we see here exceptional insight into Hellenic language and tradition and completely new results of the most astute philological critique . . . No one has so fully understood Plato and has taught others to understand Plato as this man."[7] Nonetheless, however brilliant his translation, it was his General Introduction that rocked philological, philosophical, and literary worlds. Schleiermacher there set forth a new methodological approach to understanding the dialogues and, concomitantly, a new portrayal of Plato himself. Any answer to the question of how Schleiermacher's thought may have been influenced by Plato must therefore attend to his distinctive interpretation of Plato, as developed in his *Introductions*.

I shall proceed by describing Schleiermacher's Plato-interpretation as presented in his General Introduction to *PW*, with special attention to what was novel and what proved controversial (section 1.2); pointing out the cross-fertilization between Schleiermacher's study of Plato and the emergence of his own hermeneutics, ethics, and dialectics (section 1.3);

---

[4] See Frederick C. Beiser, *The Romantic Imperative: The Concept of Early German Romanticism* (Cambridge, MA and London: Harvard University Press, 2003), pp. 70–71.

[5] *PW*; *PW(Käppel)*, in *KGA* 4.3–8 (to date, volumes 4.3 and 4.5 have been published). Schleiermacher's Introductions to the dialogues, apart from his translations of the dialogues themselves, are available in *PW (Steiner)*. An English translation by William Dobson is available (hereafter *IDP*).

[6] Adam Schnitzer, "A History in Translation: Schleiermacher, Plato, and the University of Berlin," *The Germanic Review* 75/1 (2000), p. 53. See also Theo Hermans, "Schleiermacher and Plato, Hermeneutics and Translation," in *Friedrich Schleiermacher and the Question of Translation*, ed. Larisa Cercel and Adriana Serban (Berlin & Boston: Walter de Gruyter, 2015), pp. 77–106.

[7] August Boeckh, *Heidelbergische Jahrbücher der Literatur* 1/5 (1808), p. 83.

indicating some ways in which Plato-interpretation shaped his religio-theological writings from that same period (section 1.4); and concluding with some reflections on whether Plato's influence on Schleiermacher amounts to a form of Platonism (section 1.5).

1.2 SCHLEIERMACHER'S GENERAL INTRODUCTION TO *PLATONS WERKE*

1.2.1 Conception of the Plato Project

Like the earlier Italian Renaissance, the German renaissance of the late eighteenth century translated the "classics," although it included modern classics such as Shakespeare along with ancient Greco-Roman texts and the Bible. The goal always was to discover the spirit of the author and his (they were all male authors) time; the impetus was the conviction that only a German, and only the German language, coupled with the new historical consciousness, could translate that spirit. By the turn of the nineteenth century, several scholars were engaged in translating individual Platonic dialogues. As one scholar notes, "Outside the German sphere of influence there was no 'Platonic Question.'"[8] Friedrich Schlegel—the famous Romantic literary critic and Schleiermacher's close friend and flatmate—came up with the idea of translating the entirety of Plato's works, and he invited Schleiermacher to be his collaborator.[9] Just after having finished writing his *Speeches*, Schleiermacher wrote to Henriette Herz of the new project: "Schlegel wrote to me . . . about a great *coup* which he wishes to propose with me, and that is nothing less than to translate Plato. Oh! It is a divine idea, and I fully believe that few are as well suited to the task."[10] The grand idea was to translate, for the first time, the entire Platonic *corpus* into German; to order the dialogues chronologically using modern tools of analysis; and to offer a portrait of Plato, freed from centuries of neo-Platonic accretions.

Initially Schlegel was the leader of the project, as his name lent it weight and fame. Schleiermacher was not yet widely known, his groundbreaking *Speeches on Religion* having only been published anonymously in 1799. The original plan was that each would choose which dialogues he wanted to translate; Schlegel would write an introduction, "A Study of Plato," using the newest critical methods; they would order the dialogues chronologically for the first time; and Schleiermacher would close the work with a "Characterization of Plato." That plan fell through for a variety of reasons, foremost among them Schlegel's failure to meet deadlines, and the friendship became frayed. By 1803, Schleiermacher had become a confident Plato scholar and the Plato project became his alone. The first volume of *PW* appeared in 1804 and included the General Introduction (in addition to separate Introductions to the

---

[8] Holder Thesleff, *Studies in Platonic Chronology*, Commentationes Humanarum Litterarum no. 70 (Helsinki: Societas Scientiarum Fennica, 1982), p. 3.
[9] For a detailed account of their collaboration in the Plato project, see Lamm, *Schleiermacher's Plato*, pp. 21–31.
[10] Schleiermacher to Herz, 29 April 1799, *KGA* 5.3, p. 101.

first four dialogues) in which Schleiermacher laid out his basic interpretive principles and rationale for his ordering of the dialogues.

1.2.2 Schleiermacher's Novel Approach

In his General Introduction, Schleiermacher reviewed the full history of Plato interpretation and acknowledged his debt to the new scholarship of the eighteenth century. He concluded that, although modern scholars had removed the worst, they had not yet pushed their principles through to the point of "perfect understanding."[11] Schleiermacher's Plato-interpretation, in many ways the culmination of a century of scholarship, ushered in fresh approaches and a novel understanding of Plato that would preoccupy classicists and philosophers for the next century and which, even now, continue to engage and provoke. It was distinguished by five main interpretive principles: the internal method; the view of Plato as artist; the necessary relation between (dialogical) form and (philosophical) content; determination of the authentic dialogues; and the pedagogical progression of ideas.[12] Together, Schleiermacher maintained, these principles yielded the order of the dialogues and insight into their content.

Internal method. Schleiermacher opened his General Introduction with a deep bow to the historical work done a decade earlier by Wilhelm Gottlieb Tennemann in *System der platonischen Philosophie* (1792). Tennemann had claimed to set all dogmatic interests aside in order to discover "the system and the history of the philosophy of Plato."[13] Schleiermacher saw nothing to add to Tennemann's biography of Plato and for the most part accepted the historical dates that Tennemann had fixed in relation to the dialogues. The problem was, however, that this strictly external method of relying almost exclusively on historical markers could not by itself provide enough information to order the dialogues chronologically. Schleiermacher noted, "so little that is definite can be with certainty made out, that no particular use can be made of them for the chronology and arrangement of his writings."[14] Moreover, any information the external method could produce solely by itself would be disjointed and thus could only lead to *misunderstanding*. Schleiermacher therefore proposed his own *internal method* as a "complement" to the external method, claiming that the two mutually reinforced each other.[15] An internal method, he proposed, seeks the natural and necessary connections within and among the dialogues, and its starting point is a philological one—namely, "to adduce something relative to the scientific condition of the Hellenes at the time when Plato entered upon his career, to the advances of language in reference to the expression of philosophical thoughts, to the works of this class at that time in existence, and the probable extent of their circulation."[16] In other words, for Schleiermacher (following

---

[11] *IDP*, p. 5; *PW(Käppel)*, p. 19.
[12] For further elaboration on all these points, see Lamm, *Schleiermacher's Plato*, ch. 2: "Schleiermacher's *Platons Werke* and Its Legacy," and ch. 3: "Practicing on Plato: Interpretation, Socratic Clues, and the Emergence of Schleiermacher's Hermeneutics," pp. 21–57 and 58–85, respectively.
[13] Wilhelm Gottlieb Tennemann, *System der platonischen Philosophie*, 2 vols. (Leipzig, 1792), 1: p. x.
[14] *IDP*, p. 2; *PW(Käppel)*, p. 17.
[15] *IDP*, p. 5; *PW(Käppel)*, p. 20.
[16] *IDP*, p. 2; *PW(Käppel)*, p. 17.

Hamann and Herder) interpretation begins in language and in sifting out what is common and what unique. Language indicates thought, and thought indicates the person. Who then, according to Schleiermacher, was Plato the person?

Plato as artist. Schleiermacher argued that the key to understanding the Platonic dialogues was to understand Plato himself as an artist and his works as a single work of art. Modern scholars of Plato, having overthrown the neo-Platonic interpretation, struggled with the question of the unity of Plato's thought. Schleiermacher criticized his predecessors for making one of two mistakes: they either assumed Plato's works were fragmentary (as mere "masses capriciously and unnaturally separated from the whole body") or, at the other extreme, presented Plato's philosophy as an elaborate compartmentalized system (as a structure with "weak . . . foundations . . . and their compartments taken at random").[17] In contrast, Schleiermacher identified the unity of Plato's thought as resting in Plato himself—in his artistic genius. Plato, he declared, was a "philosophical artist,"[18] which meant that his aim was "comprehensive" and his works enjoyed an "essential unity."[19] Since there was purpose to each and everything Plato wrote, each part must be viewed in relation to every other part and to the whole. Schleiermacher described these artistic principles of interrelatedness, wholeness, and unity in terms of an organic body. This somatic metaphor was a typically Romantic one, but he found confirmation for it in Plato—specifically, in the *Phaedrus* (264c), where Socrates explains that a speech must be organized (in Schleiermacher's paraphrase) "like a living creature, having a body proportioned to the mind, with parts also in due proportion."[20] Schleiermacher applied this Socratic clue to the Platonic *corpus*. The task of the interpreter is not one of dissection; rather, it is

> to restore to their natural connection those limbs, which without dissection, usually appear so very deplorably involved one with another, I mean, not the particular opinions but the particular works–to restore them to the connection in which, as expositions continuously more complete as they advance, they gradually developed the ideas of the writer, so that while every dialogue is taken not only as a whole in itself, but also in its connection with the rest, he may himself at last be understood as *a Philosopher and a perfect Artist*.[21]

As Constanze Günthenke explains, "Schleiermacher's Platonic *corpus* is, similarly, an organic whole, a literal body of text: it is Plato the thinker himself who, as an individual, is inseparable from the coherence of the dialogues that form a continuous entity and reflect Plato's thought."[22] It follows that, in order to understand Plato as an artist, we need to understand the artistic form he employed.

Dialogue form. Perhaps Schleiermacher's strongest criticism of his predecessors, ancient and modern, was that they dismissed Plato's art form (*Kunstform*)—the dialogical form—as merely a "loose garment" (*eine lose Einkleidung*), thus as inconsequential.[23] Even Tennemann had complained that the dialogue form "becomes somewhat wide-running and

---

[17] *IDP*, p. 6; *PW(Käppel)*, pp. 20–21.
[18] *IDP*, p. 4; *PW(Käppel)*, p. 19.
[19] *IDP*, p. 7; *PW(Käppel)*, pp. 21–22.
[20] *IDP*, p. 49; *PW(Käppel)*, p. 64.
[21] *IDP*, p. 14, emphasis added; *PW(Käppel)*, pp. 28–29.
[22] Constanze Güthenke, *Feeling and Classical Philology: Knowing Antiquity in German Scholarship, 1770–1920* (Cambridge: Cambridge University Press, 2020), p. 79.
[23] *PW(Käppel)*, p. 21, my translation; cf. *IDP*, pp. 6–7.

boring; ... Why, exactly, did Plato choose this form?"[24] His answer had basically been that Plato left it to Aristotle to clean it up! Repeatedly, Schleiermacher intoned that those who held such a "depreciating view" of the dialogue form was as just "useless" and "confusing" had a fundamental *misunderstanding (Mißverständnis)* of Plato—or worse, complete lack of any understanding at all (*Nichtverstehen*).[25] His own answer to the question was that, in Plato, "form and [content] are inseparable, and no [sentence] is to be rightly understood, except in its own place, and with the combinations and limitations which Plato has assigned to it."[26] Form is essential to the living body, to the whole, and can no more be surgically separated from it than can any limb or organ. The content of Plato's philosophy, therefore, cannot be grasped apart from the form of dialogue. This, in fact, became for Schleiermacher a criterion for determining which dialogues were authentic. Understanding that essential connection between *form and content*—not only as a general principle but also as operative in any particular dialogue and in any sentence—required exquisite philological skill.

Determination of authenticity. Before Plato could be understood, even before his dialogues could be properly ordered, Schleiermacher believed it was necessary to secure "the surest canon" of his works.[27] That meant determining which works were authentic and which not. Schleiermacher therefore brought the emerging historical-critical methods to bear on Plato's *corpus*. He insisted that the authentic Platonic texts alone were

> critical ground upon which every further investigation must build, and in fact no better is needed. For the Dialogues thus authenticated form a stock from which all the rest seem to be only offsets, so that a connection with them affords the best test whereby to judge of their origin. And for the next task likewise, that of arrangement, it follows from the nature of the case, that when we have that stock we are at once in possession of all the essential grounds of general connection.[28]

This proved controversial since it entailed a rejection of the esoteric Platonic tradition, which maintained that Plato's true teachings had been reserved for his inner circle of students and passed down orally through the centuries. Proponents of the esoteric tradition, whether ancient or modern, generally view the written (exoteric) Platonic tradition as inferior—at best as merely propaedeutic, and at worst a deliberate veiling. Schleiermacher was unequivocal in his assessment of esotericism, insisting that all we have is the exoteric tradition: "as Plato's principles upon these points may be read distinctly enough in his writings, so that one can scarcely believe that his [students] needed still further instructions about them, from the publication of which he shrank, or to a puerile contrivance which indulged itself in delivering in a loud voice with closed doors, what might indeed have been as well said with open ones in a lower."[29] Schleiermacher thereby shifted his new understanding of Plato clearly away from any speculative strains of Platonism. Philology and grammar served as curbs to what he called "imaginary knowledge."[30] Once the authentic dialogues of the first

---

[24] Tennemann, *System der platonischen Philosophie*, vol. 1: p. 126.
[25] *IDP*, p. 8; *PW(Käppel)*, pp. 22–23. Cf. *IDP*, pp. 10, 13; *PW(Käppel)*, pp. 24, 28.
[26] *IDP*, p. 14; *PW(Käppel)*, p. 28.
[27] *IDP*, p. 36; *PW(Käppel)*, p. 49.
[28] *IDP*, p. 31; *PW(Käppel)*, p. 45.
[29] *IDP*, pp. 11–12; *PW(Käppel)*, p. 26.
[30] *IDP*, p. 13; *PW(Käppel)*, p. 28.

rank are determined and placed in relation to established historical markers, he said, we arrive at "a preliminary [schema] of the whole in general."[31]

Pedagogical progression of ideas. That preliminary schema, however, needed shape. How are those dialogues of the first rank to be ordered? Schleiermacher's answer: according to the pedagogical progression of ideas. This principle stands in contrast to a developmental view, common among later nineteenth- and twentieth-century interpreters, which assumed that Plato's thinking changed and matured over the years. In contrast to the developmental view, which focuses on growth in the author, Schleiermacher focused on growth in the student-reader. There is, he argued, a "progressive connection" among the dialogues, a "natural progression of the development of ideas."[32] Here again, Schleiermacher stressed the unity of Plato's thought. Plato's whole purpose was "to bring the not-yet-knowing reader to knowledge."[33] Plato, he explained, "cannot [progress] further in another dialogue unless he supposes the effect proposed in an earlier one to have been produced, so that the same subject which is completed in the termination of the one, must be supposed as the beginning and foundation of another."[34] David Schur summarizes Schleiermacher's principle of pedagogical progression nicely: "According to Schleiermacher's model of indirect communication, Plato the writer withholds what he knows, and the notion of content (what we want to get *from* the text) is therefore shifted from an immediate content to a postponed telos—the goal is not to retrieve a doctrine contained in the text, but to follow the text toward an end result."[35]

1.2.3 Schleiermacher's Ordering of the Dialogues

According to Schleiermacher, the three dialogues that initially command our attention in the preliminary overview are the *Republic*, *Timaeus*, and *Critias* due to their "objective scientific exposition."[36] The *Republic* and *Timaeus* offer the fullest scientific presentation of the two most basic disciplines, ethics and physics, respectively. That trilogy, therefore, comes last pedagogically. With that in place, our gaze moves and settles on another trilogy—the *Phaedrus*, *Protagoras*, and *Parmenides*—which is differentiated from the scientific dialogues by its *character* (having a distinctive "character of youthfulness"), *circumstance* (the constructive dialogues both presuppose and mention them), and *content* ("in them are developed the first [presentiments/*Ahndungen*] of what is the basis of all that follows").[37] All of this leads necessarily to the conclusion that this group or "whole" of three (along with some dialogues of the second order) form "the first, and, as it were, elementary part of the Platonic works."[38] That trilogy, therefore, must be the first. With these two

---

[31] *IDP*, p. 40; *PW(Käppel)*, p. 52.
[32] *IDP*, pp. 45f.; *PW(Käppel)*, p. 57.
[33] *PW(Käppel)*, p. 31, my translation; cf. *IDP*, p. 17.
[34] *IDP*, p. 19; *PW(Käppel)*, p. 32.
[35] David Schur, *Plato's Wayward Path: Literary Form and the Republic*, Hellenic Studies Series 66 (Washington, DC: Center for Hellenic Studies, 2015), http://nrs.harvard.edu/urn-3:hul.ebook:CHS_SchurD.Platos_Wayward_Path.2015, section 1, "The Problem of Literary Form," subsection 1, "Schleiermacher's Model of Unified Form and Content."
[36] *IDP*, p. 41; *PW(Käppel)*, p. 53.
[37] *IDP*, pp. 44f.; *PW(Käppel)*, pp. 55f.
[38] *IDP*, p. 45; *PW(Käppel)*, p. 56.

Table 1.1 A Trilogy of Trilogies: Schleiermacher's Ordering of Platonic Dialogues of the First Rank

First trilogy:	*Phaedrus*	*Protagoras*	*Parmenides*
Middle trilogy:	*Theaetetus*	*(Sub-trilogy:)* *Sophist* *+Statesman* *+Symposium*	*Phaedo* *+ Philebus*
Third trilogy:*	*Republic*	(*Timaeus*)	(*Critias*)

*Incomplete; *PW* ended with the *Republic*.

book-ends in place, Schleiermacher could turn his attention to the remaining first-ranked dialogues, which posed many more interpretive problems, not the least of which is the fact that there were more than three. He freely conceded that there was less certainty about the inner-ordering of this middle group than about the first and third trilogies. Nevertheless, Schleiermacher still settled on a third, middle trilogy. Applying the principles of discerning the "natural progression of the development of ideas" and attending to "a variety of particular allusions and references,"[39] he bound some dialogues closely together and identified a sub-trilogy at the center of this middle trilogy, so that the *Sophist*, *Statesman*, and *Symposium* form the heart of the heart of Plato's works. Here, ethics and physics come together for the first time. The result is what I refer to as a trilogy of trilogies (see Table 1.1).

1.2.4 Points of Contention in Schleiermacher's Plato-Interpretation

Phaedrus as first. Schleiermacher's identification of the *Phaedrus* as the first of Plato's dialogues became controversial almost immediately with the publication of *PW I,1*. Schlegel accused Schleiermacher of having stolen his idea about the placement. Schleiermacher retorted that he had his own reasons, specific to his own principles of interpretation. Their quarrel proved to be over nothing, since the idea of the *Phaedrus* as the first dialogue was pretty quickly laid to rest. That notwithstanding, some scholars continue to acknowledge Schleiermacher's insights in interpreting the dialogue—for instance, his notion that it contained the "seeds" of Plato's philosophy and his treatment of the relation between the two parts. Schleiermacher cleverly addressed the conundrum of how the two parts of the dialogue are related and, therefore, of the true subject matter of the dialogue: part 1, with the speeches on *eros*, has to do with the *impulse* (*Trieb*) toward doing philosophy; part 2, with its discussion of *dialectic* and *rhetoric*, has to do with the *method* of doing philosophy.

Rejection of esoteric tradition. Schleiermacher's rejection of the esoteric was left virtually unchallenged for well over a century, until Hans Joachim Krämer inaugurated a new

---

[39] *IDP*, p. 46; *PW(Käppel)*, p. 57.

esotericism in 1959. In this new battle over the *agrapha*, Krämer highlighted Schleiermacher's importance, albeit negatively: "It was the authority of Schleiermacher alone that brought this well-founded view [of an esoteric special teaching of Plato] almost completely to a standstill."[40] Adherents to this view constitute a relatively small but vocal circle of scholars, referred to as the "Tübingen School" of Plato interpretation, who remain highly critical of Schleiermacher, especially his alleged circumvention of Socrates' stated suspicion of writing in the *Phaedrus*.[41]

Schleiermacher's ordering. Schleiermacher's ordering of the dialogues, as a chronological ordering, was rather quickly undone. It should be restated, however, that Schleiermacher never claimed that his internal method, even when combined with the external method, resulted in a strict *chronological* order. On the contrary, he was skeptical that such was even possible. Yet, so keen was interest in the historical Plato that subsequent generations of scholars pursued the possibility doggedly. The storyline played out not unlike the first quest for the historical Jesus. The pendulum eventually swung back against those positivistic strains, such that Paul Shorey, a founding faculty member of the University of Chicago, wrote an influential essay reclaiming the Schleiermacherian idea of "The Unity of Plato's Thought" exactly a century after the publication of the first volume of *PW*.[42]

1.3 Platonic Themes in Schleiermacher's Works

During the first decade of the nineteenth century, when Schleiermacher was most intensely working on his Plato project (astoundingly, the first five of six volumes of *PW* appeared between 1804 and 1809), he was also busy working out the basic principles of his own constructive thought, in terms of both content and method. His more scholarly approach began during his "exile" in Stolp, Pomerania (1802–1804) and then took off in conjunction with his first academic appointment, at the University of Halle (1804–1806).[43] At Halle Schleiermacher lectured on hermeneutics, New Testament exegesis, ethics, church history, dogmatics, theological encyclopedia and methodology, and systematic theology. It was a creative time of incredible intellectual cross-fertilization as Schleiermacher pushed himself to think through some of the thorniest philosophical and theological questions in a new era of historical consciousness and of discovery in the natural sciences. In later iterations of those lectures, he would revise some of the content rather significantly. Nevertheless, his early drafts from Halle proved foundational for his thought in just about every area, and his work on Plato shaped virtually every aspect of his method and thinking.

---

[40] Hans Joachim Krämer, *Arete bei Platon und Aristoteles: Zum Wesen und zur Geschichte der Platonischen Ontologie* (Heidelberg: Carl Winter Universitätsverlag, 1959), p. 18.

[41] See Vittorio Hösle, "The Tübingen School," and Thomas Alexander Szlezák, "Friedrich Schleiermacher's Theory of the Platonic Dialogue and Its Legacy," in *Brill's Companion to German Platonism*, ed. Alan Kim in *Brill's Companion to German Platonism*, ed. Alan Kim (Leiden: Brill, 2019), pp. 328–348 and pp. 165–191, respectively.

[42] See Paul Shorey, *The Unity of Plato's Thought* (Chicago: University of Chicago Press, 1904).

[43] Napoleon entered the city of Halle on October 17, 1806 and closed the university.

1.3.1 Schleiermacher's Philosophy (1803–1806)

The influence of Plato on Schleiermacher is clearest in his philosophy—his *Hermeneutics*, *Ethics*, and *Dialectic*. I focus here not on those texts themselves but on the emergence of his theory regarding these topics in conjunction with his work on Plato while at Stolp and Halle.

Hermeneutics. Outside of the fields of theology and the study of religion, Schleiermacher is probably best known for his *Hermeneutics*. He was the first to set forth a general theory of interpretation (not just *hermeneutica sacra*) that applied to all texts and, indeed, to all linguistic communication. Schleiermacher first lectured on hermeneutics in 1805, while he was working on the third volume of *PW*. Without question, his hermeneutics stemmed directly out of his work translating Plato's dialogues, a task that presented him with fundamental questions of interpretation. In his struggle to understand Plato, he employed several Socratic clues—for instance, the view of a text as a living creature, as an organic whole—which he applied to Plato's *corpus* and some of which he then carried over into his general hermeneutics. In his Introductions to the dialogues, we can glean incipient expressions of principles he would articulate in lectures on hermeneutics, such as the needed skill to differentiate between the way in which language was commonly used at a particular time (the grammatical) and the unique way in which an author shaped the language anew (the technical). In short, Schleiermacher practiced his theory of interpretation on Plato.

Ethics. Plato's influence on Schleiermacher's ethics is found in the primacy he gave to the notion of the highest good and the concomitant emphasis on perfectibility and formation (*Bildung*). From his earliest scholarly pursuits, going back to his university days, Schleiermacher had been preoccupied with ethics.[44] That interest grew more concentrated through his scholarly engagement with Plato. During his lonely existence in Stolp (1802–1804), Schleiermacher sketched out his own constructive position on ethics in his sprawling *Baselines of a Critique of Previous Ethical Theories* (*Grundlinien einer Kritik der bisherigen Sittenlehre*, 1803). It was his first scholarly (*wissenschaftlich*) publication. In it, only Plato and Spinoza were deemed worthy of high praise, since both were masters of "the higher science" and sought "knowledge of the infinite and highest being."[45] Still, of those two heroes, his favorite was Plato. Both grounded the finite in the infinite, yet in Plato the infinite manifests itself in a "poeticizing" (*dichtend*) and artistically "forming" (*bildend*) manner.[46] Schleiermacher preferred Plato's artistic presentation and his formative-educative view of ethics over Spinoza's more logical presentation; most certainly, he preferred it over Kant's restrictive view of ethics. Since Schleiermacher wrote his *Grundlinien* while he was also working on the first volume of *PW*, there is considerable mutual reinforcement between them.[47]

That is also true also of his first lectures on ethics, to which he assigned the title *Notes on Ethics* (*Brouillon zur Ethik*, 1805) and which he delivered during his first semester at Halle and repeated the following year, all while translating Plato. We find in the *Brouillon* many themes

---

[44] See Brent W. Sockness, "Was Schleiermacher a Virtue Ethicist? *Tugend* and *Bildung* in the Early Ethical Writings," *Journal for the History of Modern Theology / Zeitschrift für Neuere Theologiegeschichte* 8/1 (2001), pp. 1–33.
[45] *GKS*, p. 63.
[46] *GKS*, p. 65.
[47] See André Laks, "Schleiermacher on Plato: From Form (*Introduction to Plato's Works*) to Content (*Outlines of a Critique of Previous Ethical Theory*)," in *Brill's Companion to German Platonism*, ed. Alan Kim (Leiden: Brill, 2019), pp. 146–164.

carried over from the *Grundlinien*, albeit further developed, but we also find a widening in the aperture of Schleiermacher's philosophical views that reflects his ongoing study of Plato in *PW*. For instance, he begins his *Brouillon* with this distinction: "Ethics is thus one entire side of philosophy. Everything in it appears as a producing, just as in natural science everything appears as a product. Each of these two must accept something else from the other as positive, for even knowing and acting are natural faculties and must be authenticated as such. Accordingly, all real knowing divides into these two sides."[48] Schleiermacher's understanding of these two sciences, *ethics* (philosophy of human action) and *physics* (philosophy of nature), were central to his understanding of Plato's philosophy and the pedagogical progression of ideas. According to Schleiermacher, the Platonic *corpus* culminates in the most scientific presentation of ethics in the *Republic* and of physics in the *Timaeus*—hence, in knowledge of the good and the true, and their interconnection. Thus, for Schleiermacher's Plato, the highest being is not so much the highest good as it is the identity of thinking and being.

Dialectic. Schleiermacher gave grounds for his confidence in our ability to know the good and the true—or, at least, to ever approximate such knowledge—in his Dialectic [*Dialektik*], which he defined as the "art of philosophizing" and, later, as "the art of discourse, or dialogue." He first lectured on dialectics at the University of Berlin in 1811, but the groundwork had been laid in the preceding decade in the *Grundlinien* and in *PW*, specifically through his interpretation of Plato's "dialectical method," understood as both an "art" and a "science" (*Sophist*, 265a, 253e,d). In his Introductions to Plato's dialogues, Schleiermacher distinguished between Platonic and non-Platonic forms of dialectics: the latter processes are divorced from the empirical, from love for the real, from the process and rules of knowing, and from philosophical communication; in contrast, the former involved "the dialectic play with ideas, under which, however, the relation to the whole and to the original ideas is continually progressing."[49] Platonic dialectics seeks, by means of scientific method, to bring "the [novice] of philosophy to self-consciousness, and compelling him to independent thought."[50] As he methodically moved through the dialogues, Schleiermacher consistently elided any strains of speculative forms of dialectics in Plato, hence his rejection of the esoteric tradition.[51] He embraced instead a *dialogical form of dialectics*, which he took to be genuinely Platonic, holding tenaciously to the controlling idea that "necessarily and naturally Plato's was a Socratic method."[52] Plato's influence on Schleiermacher's dialectics is found (1) in his choice of the very title *Dialectic*, (2) in his emphasis on dialectics as an (anti-speculative) *method* for knowing, and (3) in the further development of his post-Kantian ontological commitments. As Jan Rohls explains, the Platonic character of Schleiermacher's thought can be seen in his "acceptance of a transcendent or—as Schleiermacher says—a transcendental ground, of the highest being [*Sein*] as the identity of thought [*Denke*] and being [*Sein*], which is the condition for the possibility of knowledge [*Wissen*]."[53] Schleiermacher had already

---

[48] *NOE*, pp. 33–34.
[49] *IDP*, p. 37; *PW(Käppel)*, p. 50.
[50] *IDP*, p. 94; *PW(Käppel)*, p. 583.
[51] See Lamm, *Schleiermacher's Plato*, ch. 4: "Reading Plato's Dialectics: Schleiermacher's Insistence on Dialectics as Dialogical," pp. 86–106.
[52] *IDP*, p. 16; *PW(Käppel)*, p. 30.
[53] Jan Rohls, "'Der Winckelmann der griechischen Philosophie': Schleiermachers Platonismus im Kontext," in *200 Jahre "Reden Über die Religion"*, Schleiermacher-Archiv 19, ed. Ulrich Barth et al. (Berlin: Walter de Gruyter, 2000), p. 485.

been moving toward this view in the first edition of the *Speeches* (1799) and the *Soliloquies* (1800), but his immersion in Plato—and, I would add, especially in the *Sophist*—aided him in crystallizing and articulating the philosophical grounds for these commitments.

1.3.2 Schleiermacher's Religious Thought (1806)

Plato's influence on Schleiermacher's religio-theological texts from this same period of his life, although perhaps less palpable than that on his philosophy, was nevertheless significant. After all, Schleiermacher criticized those who separated philosophy from life, and theory from practice. I maintain that in two of Schleiermacher's texts on religion from this same period, both published in 1806, we find Platonic influences in terms of form, structure, and content.

Christmas Dialogue. In early December 1805, Schleiermacher, despondent over a recent romantic break-up, cancelled his ethics lecture and attended a concert by the virtuoso Friedrich Ludwig Dülon, a blind flutist. So elated and transformed was Schleiermacher by the experience that he decided, walking home that winter night, to write something on the joy of Christmas. Three weeks later, on Christmas Eve, he submitted the manuscript of *The Christmas Celebration: A Dialogue*, which was published in January 1806.[54] The form of this occasional piece—a *dialogue*—alone speaks to an influence of Plato. Yet scholars have debated whether the influence goes beyond form to include content. Some have answered in the affirmative by comparing the *Christmas Dialogue* with specific Platonic dialogues—for example, the *Symposium*, *Phaedo*, or *Phaedrus*. For the first 150 years of interpretation, focus was almost exclusively on the speeches given by men toward the end of the *Dialogue*, while the narrative section at the beginning and the stories given by women in the middle were neglected. Such myopic readings of the text began to change in the latter half of the twentieth century, especially with the rise of feminist scholarship in the 1980s.

When we take this more recent, holistic approach the *Christmas Dialogue* and read the text in light of Schleiermacher's Introductions to Plato's dialogues, it becomes clear that the Platonic influence is not restricted to a single part of the *Christmas Dialogue*, nor can it be attributed to a single Platonic dialogue. On the contrary, the entire *Christmas Dialogue* reflects Schleiermacher's interpretation of the entire Platonic *corpus*. The opening scene—which describes the festive atmosphere, the exchange of gifts, and convivial conversation among all present, including children—plays a similar role to that of the first trilogy (in particular the *Phaedrus*): it supplies both the *impulse* (joy) and *method* (loving communication). The middle section—in which three women recount stories about three women and their infants during Christmases past—plays an analogous role to that of the second trilogy (in particular the *Symposium*, *Sophist*, and *Phaedo*): it presents the *object* of Christmas (the Christ child) and the *vehicle* (mother-love). The last main section—in which three men give speeches on the meaning of Christmas in light of challenges posed by the new historical consciousness to the infancy narrative—plays an analogous role to that of the third trilogy (especially the *Republic*): it offers "scientific" (theological) presentations of basic themes from the earlier sections of the *Dialogue*. In the *Christmas Dialogue*, therefore, we have an

---

[54] Schleiermacher, *Die Weihnachtsfeier: Ein Gespräch*; translation in *CWS*, pp. 101–151.

example of a specifically Christian text by Schleiermacher that reflected, at least at a formal level, his particular reading of Plato.[55]

Second Speech on Religion, Revised. While writing his *Christmas Dialogue* and continuing to work on *PW*, Schleiermacher was also revising his *On Religion: Speeches to Its Cultured Despisers*, the second edition of which appeared later in 1806.[56] Albert Blackwell stands alone in having recognized the potential that lies in a comparison of the two editions of the *Speeches* for understanding Plato's influence on Schleiermacher: "This immersion in Plato separates the first edition of the *Speeches* from the second edition of 1806, and because of this, alterations in the latter provide a particularly sensitive index of Plato's influence on Schleiermacher's thinking."[57] Most attempts to compare the various editions of the *Speeches* have tended to focus on narrower issues—for example, shifts in terminology, such as *feeling* and *intuition*. A close examination of the revised blocks of text, only recently made possible by a new synoptic edition that lays out the three editions side by side on each page,[58] reveals substantive additions that have direct parallels to *PW*.[59]

The influences of Schleiermacher's Plato-interpretation on his revisions to the *Speeches* in 1806 (the vast majority of which were made to the second Speech) can be broken down into three basic types: First, Schleiermacher added several scattered allusions to Socrates and Plato; in the event that the cultured despisers might fail to pick up on them, he even instructed them to "go and learn it from your Socrates."[60] Second, there are several new extended discussions, including new terminology, which echo discussions in *PW*; these revised blocks suggest a much more substantive Platonic influence than the scattered allusions alone would. For instance, he absorbs into his second Speech his particular interpretation of the association of kinds from the *Sophist*. Sometimes these additions serve to crystallize a point he had tried to make in the first edition, but sometimes they introduce entirely new points. Third, the most significant revision that can be traced to Schleiermacher's *PW* is his reconceptualization of what I call "The Three," which he set forth at the beginning of the second Speech and which largely governs his theory of religion. Whereas in 1799 Schleiermacher had presented them somewhat statically in terms of the spheres of *metaphysics, morality, and religion*, in 1806 he switched to the broader, gerundive categories of *thinking, acting, and religion/piety*; he added yet further complexity to his typology by subdividing *acting* into *life* and *art*, and *thinking* into theory about *physics/metaphysics* and theory about *human behavior*. Consequently, whereas in 1799 he had set both *metaphysics* and *morals* in a negative light and placed them in an oppositional relation to *religion*, in 1806 he set both *thinking* and *acting* in a distinctly positive light and carefully distinguished them from, without opposing them to, religion. In a related

---

[55] See Lamm, *Schleiermacher's Plato*, ch. 5: "Schleiermacher's *Christmas Dialogue* as Platonic Dialogue," pp. 107–142.

[56] See my translation of the 2nd ed. of the second Speech, "On the Essence of Religion," in *CWS*, pp. 152–223. Crouter's translation is of the 1st ed. (1799), and Oman's is of the 3rd ed. (1821).

[57] Albert L. Blackwell, *Schleiermacher's Early Philosophy of Life: Determinism, Freedom, and Phantasy* (Chico, CA: Scholars Press, 1982), p. 128.

[58] *Reden* (Peter).

[59] See Lamm, *Schleiermacher's Plato*, ch. 6: "The Presence of Plato in the *Speeches* (1806), Part 1: Revising, Reconceiving, and Recasting," and ch. 7: "The Presence of Plato in the *Speeches* (1806), Part 2: Being, Non-Being, and Intuition," pp. 143–186 and 187–226, respectively.

[60] *CWS*, p. 165.

move, Schleiermacher erected the two sciences corresponding to thinking and acting—*physics* and *ethics*—as two strands that ever approximate each other, much as he saw them functioning throughout Plato's dialogues. This marks a significant, substantive revision insofar as it fundamentally alters his theory of religion. In short, Schleiermacher's Plato is pervasive in the second edition of the *Speeches*.

1.4 Concluding Remarks

Plato's influence on Schleiermacher was pervasive and profound, and in ways that are only now beginning to be appreciated. It was pervasive in that, once we know what to look for, it can be detected in his philosophical and religio-theological thinking alike. It was profound in that, as he himself confessed, "Plato is indisputably the author whom I know best and with whom I have almost coalesced."[61] Yet the influence was not unidirectional. Schleiermacher brought to his reading of Plato certain prior commitments and inclinations; moreover, his continued intensive engagement with Plato during the first decade of the nineteenth century occurred during an especially creative period of his life, with a multitude of inspirations and demands. What emerged was Schleiermacher's Plato. Once seen, Schleiermacher's Plato can be recognized in countless places. But whether it is a Platonism with a stable, transmittable form is questionable. Likewise, whether it reflects a form of Christian Platonism detectable in his theological *magnum opus*, *The Christian Faith*, is yet to be determined. Beyond debate is the fact that Schleiermacher absorbed Plato. Much as he translated Plato's ancient Greek into German, he translated Plato's method and ontology into a modern mindset, and in that sense Schleiermacher's Plato might be termed a modern form of Platonism, however unique.

Suggested Reading

Lamm, Julia A. *Schleiermacher's Plato* (Berlin and Boston: De Gruyter, 2021).
Lamm, Julia A., ed. and trans. *Schleiermacher: Christmas Dialogue, The Second Speech and Other Selections*, Classics of Western Spirituality (New York: Paulist Press, 2014).
Schleiermacher, Friedrich D. E. *Friedrich D. E. Schleiermacher: Über die Philosophie Platons*. Ed. Peter M. Steiner (Hamburg: Felix Meiner, 1996).
Schleiermacher, Friedrich D. E. *Introductions to the Dialogues of Plato*. Translated by William Dobson (Cambridge & London, 1836; reprint, New York: Arno Press, 1973).
Schleiermacher, Friedrich D. E. *Platons Werke I,1: Einleitung–Phaidros–Lysis–Protagoras–Laches* (Berlin, 1804, 1817), in *KGA* 4.3, ed. Lutz Käppel, Johanna Loehr, and Male Günther (Berlin: De Gruyter, 2016); *Platons Werke II,1: Gorgias–Theaitetos–Menon–Euthydemos* (Berlin, 1805, 1818), in *KGA* 4.5, ed Lutz Käppel and Johanna Loehr (Berlin: De Gruyter, 2020).

---

[61] Schleiermacher to Eleanore Grunow, Sept. 3, 1803, *KGA* 5.6, p. 113.

Bibliography

Beiser, Frederick C. *The Romantic Imperative: The Concept of Early German Romanticism* (Cambridge, MA and London: Harvard University Press, 2003).

Bekker, Immanuel, ed. *Platonis Dialogi graece et latine, ex recensione Immanuelis Bekkeri*, 3 vols. (Berlin: Reimer, 1816–1818).

Blackwell, Albert L. *Schleiermacher's Early Philosophy of Life: Determinism, Freedom, and Phantasy* (Chico, CA: Scholars Press, 1982).

Cantana, Leo. "Afterword: Schleiermacher and Modern Plato Scholarship." In *Late Ancient Platonism in Eighteenth-Century German Thought*, International Archives of the History of Ideas Archives/internationales d'histoire des idées 227, chapter 6 (Cham, Switzerland: Springer, 2019), pp. 165–169.

Güthenke, Constanze. *Feeling and Classical Philology: Knowing Antiquity in German Scholarship, 1770–1920* (Cambridge: Cambridge University Press, 2020).

Hermans, Theo. "Schleiermacher and Plato, Hermeneutics and Translation." In *Friedrich Schleiermacher and the Question of Translation*, ed. Larisa Cercel and Adriana Serban (Berlin & Boston: Walter de Gruyter, 2015), pp. 77–106.

Hösle, Vittorio. "The Tübingen School." In *Brill's Companion to German Platonism*, ed. Alan Kim (Leiden: Brill, 2019), pp. 328–348.

Krämer, Hans Joachim. *Arete bei Platon und Aristoteles: Zum Wesen und zur Geschichte der Platonischen Ontologie* (Heidelberg: Carl Winter Universitätsverlag, 1959).

Laks, André. "Schleiermacher on Plato: From Form *(Introduction to Plato's Works)* to Content *(Outlines of a Critique of Previous Ethical Theory)*." In *Brill's Companion to German Platonism*, ed. Alan Kim (Leiden: Brill, 2019), pp. 146–164.

Lamm, Julia A. "The Art of Interpreting Plato." In *The Cambridge Companion to Schleiermacher*, ed. Jacqueline Mariña (Cambridge & N.Y.: Cambridge University Press, 2005), pp. 91–108.

Lamm, Julia A. "Plato's Dialogues as a Single Work of Art: Friedrich Schleiermacher's *Platons Werke*." In *Lire Les Dialogues, mais lesquels et dans quel ordre? Définitions du corpus et interprétations de Platon*, ed. Anne Balansard and Isabelle Koch (Sankt Augustin: Academia Verlag, 2013), pp. 173–188.

Lamm, Julia A. "Reading Plato's Dialectics: Schleiermacher's Insistence on Dialectics as Dialogical." *Zeitschrift für Neuere Theologiegeschichte/Journal for the History of Modern Theology* 10/1 (April 2003), pp. 1–25.

Lamm, Julia A. "Schleiermacher as Plato Scholar." *Journal of Religion* 80/2 (April 2000), pp. 206–239.

Lamm, Julia A. "Schleiermacher's Christmas Dialogue as Platonic Dialogue." *The Journal of Religion* 92/3 (July 2012), pp. 392–420.

Lamm, Julia A. "Schleiermacher's Modern Platonism." In *Reformation und Moderne. Pluralität–Subjektivität–Kritik*, ed. Jörg Dierken (Berlin: Walter de Gruyter, 2018), pp. 675–697.

Lamm, Julia A. *Schleiermacher's Plato* (Berlin and Boston: Walter de Gruyter, 2021).

Lamm, Julia A. "Schleiermacher's Re-Writing as Spiritual Exercise, 1799–1806." In *Der Mensch und seine Seele. Bildung–Frömmigkeit–Ästhetik. Akten des Schleiermacher-Kongresses 2015*, ed. Arnulf von Scheliha (Berlin and Boston: Walter de Gruyter, 2017), pp. 293–302.

Rohls, Jan. "'Der Winckelmann der griechischen Philosophie': Schleiermachers Platonismus im Kontext." In *200 Jahre "Reden Über die Religion"*, Schleiermacher-Archiv 19, ed. Ulrich Barth et al. (Berlin: Walter de Gruyter, 2000), pp. 467–496.

Schleiermacher, Friedrich. *Briefwechsel 1799-1800, KGA* 5.3, ed. Andreas Arndt and Wolfgang Virmond *(Berlin: De Gruyter, 1992).*

Schleiermacher, Friedrich. *Briefwechsel 1800, KGA* 5.4, ed. Andreas Arndt and Wolfgang Virmond *(Berlin: De Gruyter, 1994).*

Schleiermacher, Friedrich. *Briefwechsel 1802-03, KGA* 5.6, ed. Andreas Arndt and Wolfgang Virmond *(Berlin: De Gruyter, 2005).*

Schnitzer, Adam. "A History in Translation: Schleiermacher, Plato, and the University of Berlin." *The Germanic Review* 75/1 (2000), pp. 53–71.

Scholtz, Gunter. "Schleiermacher und die Platonische Ideenlehre." In *Internationaler Schleiermacher-Kongreß 1984*, ed. Kurt-Victor Selge (Berlin: Walter de Gruyter, 1985), pp. 849–874.

Schur, David. *Plato's Wayward Path: Literary Form and the Republic*. Hellenic Studies Series 66 (Washington, DC: Center for Hellenic Studies, 2015). http://nrs.harvard.edu/urn-3:hul.ebook:CHS_SchurD.Platos_Wayward_Path.2015.

Shorey, Paul. *The Unity of Plato's Thought* (Chicago: University of Chicago Press, 1904).

Sockness, Brent W. "Was Schleiermacher a Virtue Ethicist? *Tugend* and *Bildung* in the Early Ethical Writings." *Journal for the History of Modern Theology / Zeitschrift für Neuere Theologiegeschichte* 8/1 (2001), pp. 1–33.

Szlezák, Thomas Alexander. "Friedrich Schleiermacher's Theory of the Platonic Dialogue and Its Legacy." In *Brill's Companion to German Platonism*, ed. Alan Kim (Leiden: Brill, 2019), pp. 165–191.

Tennemann, Wilhelm Gottlieb. *System der platonischen Philosophie*. 2 vols. (Leipzig, 1792).

Thesleff, Holder. *Studies in Platonic Chronology*. Commentationes Humanarum Litterarum no. 70 (Helsinki: Societas Scientiarum Fennica, 1982).

CHAPTER 2

KANT

PETER GROVE

IMMANUEL Kant's mature work, beginning with *Critique of Pure Reason* published in 1781, marks a new epoch in philosophy. Especially from the middle of that decade, Kant exerted an increasing influence on the philosophical discussion in Germany. Schleiermacher—from 1785 to 1787 studying at the Moravian theological seminar in Barby and from 1787 to 1789 at the University of Halle (Saale)—also became strongly influenced by him. Never becoming an orthodox Kantian, he always remained a critical reader of Kant's writings. Nevertheless Kantian philosophy is one of the most important presuppositions of Schleiermacher's thought, and it is not too much to claim that his work would have been unthinkable without Kant's.

This claim is controversial in Schleiermacher scholarship. While some scholars have indeed defended it,[1] other have attempted to refute the claim, referring to previous or subsequent influences on Schleiermacher that are allegedly of more importance.[2] Against such attempts, this chapter will attempt to substantiate the claim of Kant's importance for Schleiermacher. To do this it will concentrate on Schleiermacher's first formative period of 1789–1797, which displays a critical but constructive reception of Kant that is fundamental for the early stages of Schleiermacher's thinking. The examination will focus on his first extensive treatise and the earliest comprehensive documentation of his reception of Kant, *On*

---

[1] An early example is Wilhelm Dilthey, *Leben Schleiermacher*, vol. 1.1, ed. Martin Redeker (Berlin: Walter de Gruyter & Co., 1970). Dilthey's view of Schleiermacher's relationship with Kant is generally in agreement with this chapter's view, but he neither shows in detail how Schleiermacher stands in the philosophical debate of his time nor offers a systematic interpretation of his argumentation. An example from more recent scholarship is Günter Meckenstock, *Deterministische Ethik und kritische Theologie: Die Auseinandersetzung des frühen Schleiermacher mit Kant und Spinoza 1789–1794* (Berlin: Walter de Gruyter, 1988), a monograph on Schleiermacher's early work that interprets it as mostly the attempt at a more consistent development of Kant's beginnings and thus tends to overlook important differences between the two thinkers. An example from American scholarship is Jacqueline Mariña, *Transformation of the Self in the Thought of Friedrich Schleiermacher* (Oxford: Oxford University Press, 2008).

[2] One of the most influential contributions of this type is Eilert Herms, *Herkunft, Entfaltung und erste Gestalt des Systems der Wissenschaften bei Schleiermacher* (Gütersloh: Gütersloher Verlagshaus Gerd Mohn, 1974). Herms minimizes the importance of Schleiermacher's reception of Kant by emphasizing Schleiermacher's dependence on pre-Kantian Enlightenment philosophy on the one hand and on Friedrich Heinrich Jacobi on the other.

the Highest Good,³ which was probably written in the first months of 1789.⁴ The treatise will be supplemented by his other systematic-philosophical manuscripts from the period and by biographical sources. Schleiermacher's writings around 1800 express a much sharper criticism of Kant. The question is whether this criticism reduces or eliminates Kant's significance for Schleiermacher's thinking. Drawing lines onwards from his early writings, the article will try to show that it does not and that his early reception of Kant remains fundamental for his mature work.

2.1 General View of Schleiermacher's Early Relationship with Kant

A letter Schleiermacher wrote to his father in August 1787 gives a glimpse of the first stages of his reading of Kant and shows his early interest in Kantian philosophy. Some months previously his father had reluctantly allowed him to leave the seminar in Barby and to matriculate at the university in Halle, a stronghold of Enlightenment thought. Now Schleiermacher was attending lectures on metaphysics held by Johann August Eberhard, a philosopher in the school of Christian Wolff, and for this reason, his father advised him to bring along Kant's critical writings as "a safe guide" into "the never ending desert of transcendent notions."⁵ Schleiermacher replied:

> You recommend that I study the Kantian philosophy. From the beginning, I have had a very favorable opinion of it, just because it directs reason back from the metaphysical deserts to the fields that properly belong to it. That is why I read the *Prolegomena* back in Barby with some good friends, indeed only understanding as much as one can when one has not read the *Critique of Pure Reason*. Because I was unable to get the *Critique*, I was not able to compare the Wolffian philosophy with the Kantian during Eberhard's lectures. But I am going to do it during this fall holiday, all the more successfully because Uncle [S. E. T. Stubenrauch] is also going to read the Kantian writings then, in order to become acquainted with this *phaenomenon*, remarkable in every respect, from the source itself. But, so far as I understand Kant at present, he allows one a completely free hand in thinking about religious matters…⁶

The information this quotation gives about Schleiermacher's reading of Kant can be supplemented by other evidence. We know that he read the Kantian journal *Allgemeine Literatur-Zeitung* beginning in 1785,⁷ the year it started, and that it became part of his regular reading.⁸ The journal was important for all those who wanted to be kept informed about the philosophy of Kant and his pupils. Schleiermacher certainly did. There is evidence that he studied reviews published in the journal thoroughly, among them the review from 1786 of Kant's *Groundwork of the Metaphysic of Morals*.⁹ Schleiermacher's reading of writings of Kant

---

³ *OHG*.
⁴ Cf. Günter Meckenstock, "Einleitung des Bandherausgebers," in *KGA 1.1*, p. xli.
⁵ *KGA* 5.1, p. 88. All translations of German texts are by the author.
⁶ *KGA* 5.1, p. 92.
⁷ *KGA* 5.1, p. 31.
⁸ Cf., for example, *KGA* 5.1, pp. 146, 177.
⁹ Cf. *KGA* 5.1, p. 49.

himself, especially his *Prolegomena to Any Future Metaphysics That Will Be Able to Present Itself as Science*, dates back to 1786.[10] His reservations concerning how much he understood Kant at this time—reservations echoed in statements from the following years—seem realistic. Schleiermacher read *Critique of Pure Reason* in the fall 1787 at the earliest, probably in the second edition from that year. His *On the Highest Good* documents his familiarity with this text, as well as with the *Critique of Practical Reason* of 1788. Schleiermacher also seems to have studied Kant's *Critique of Judgement* of 1790,[11] but it is not as important for his reception of Kant as are the two first *Critiques*. Schleiermacher did not have any personal contact with Kant, apart from a short visit he paid him in 1791.[12]

However, Schleiermacher's reception of Kant's thinking is accompanied by criticism. He distinguishes between appropriation and criticism in his reception of Kant by means of a distinction between the principles of Kantian philosophy on the one hand and its consequences, conclusions, or results on the other. Early on he approves of "some of the first principles" of Kantian moral philosophy but not of "all the conclusions" that are drawn from them.[13] Later, he states things the other way around. Having declared his acceptance of Kant's "first theses" in theoretical philosophy,[14] "the principles of critical idealism," he finds in Kant's thinking "an inconsistent remnant of the old dogmatism."[15] In this connection, Schleiermacher calls the Kantianism he accepts—that is, one without dogmatist remnants—a Kantianism that "understands itself."[16] The results or conclusions that Schleiermacher criticizes are above all Kant's concept of moral feeling as the feeling of respect for moral law, his theory of freedom,[17] and his reconstruction of traditional metaphysics from the perspective of practical reason. However, as the following will show, Schleiermacher also only accepts the Kantian first principles with—partly unintentional—modifications.

Until now, I have referred to "Kant" as if Schleiermacher was here only dealing with Immanuel Kant and his philosophy. This would be an oversimplification. Kant was certainly Schleiermacher's primary focus, but his early reception of Kant shows influence from the pre-Kantian Enlightenment and from positions in early Kantianism that in some respects differ from Kant himself. In this connection the most important representative of the former is Schleiermacher's teacher in Halle, Eberhard, who represents not only Wolffian philosophy but also the later German Enlightenment in some respects.[18] From this position, he contested with Kant, editing and writing most of the content of

---

[10] Cf. Samuel Okely, "Das Tagebuch von Schleiermachers Schul- und Studienfreund Samuel Okely (1785/86)," ed. Wolfgang Virmond, *New Athenaeum* 3 (1992), pp. 200, 203–204.

[11] Cf. Peter Grove, *Deutungen des Subjekts: Schleiermachers Philosophie der Religion* (Berlin: Walter de Gruyter, 2004), pp. 29, 91, 126–127.

[12] Cf. *KGA* 5.1, pp. 218, 225.

[13] Friedrich Daniel Ernst Schleiermacher, "Freiheitsgespräch," in *KGA* 1.1, p. 160.

[14] *KGA* 5.1, p. 426.

[15] *Spin.*, p. 541; *Spin.Sys.*, p. 570.

[16] *Spin.Sys.*, p. 570.

[17] Cf. Schleiermacher, "Freiheitsgespräch"; *OF*. The compatibilism Schleiermacher argues for here is incompatible with Kant's theory of freedom. Cf. Katharina Gutekunst, *Die Freiheit des Subjekts bei Schleiermacher: Eine Analyse im Horizont der Debatte um die Willensfreiheit in der analytischen Philosophie* (Berlin: Walter de Gruyter, 2019), pp. 33–86.

[18] Cf. Peter Grove, "Johann August Eberhards Theorie des Gefühls," in *Ein Antipode Kants? Johann August Eberhard im Spannungsfeld von spätaufklärerischer Philosophie und Theologie*, ed. Hans-Joachim Kertscher and Ernst Stöckmann (Berlin: Walter de Gruyter, 2012), pp. 119–131.

two journals with the sole aim of criticizing Kantian philosophy. Eberhard's criticism focused on Kant's theoretical philosophy and has very little affinity with Schleiermacher's criticism, which has its center of gravity in Kant's practical philosophy. In recent Schleiermacher scholarship, there has been a tendency to overestimate Eberhard's influence on Schleiermacher at the expense of Kant and of the early Kantians, who mostly have been overlooked.[19] The most distinguished early Kantians influencing Schleiermacher are August Wilhelm Rehberg and Karl Leonhard Reinhold.[20] In some respects they were closer to pre-Kantian Enlightenment philosophy than Kant was and, for this reason, their presentation of his thought seems to have been easier for Schleiermacher to understand and adopt. The 1788–1789 publication of the first volumes of Eberhard's first journal, *Philosophical Magazine*, caused a vehement dispute between him and leading Kantians, including Rehberg and Reinhold. From the start, Schleiermacher followed the dispute very attentively, hoping that it would contribute to an agreement between old and new philosophy; but its course eventually disappointed him.[21]

The comparison between Kantian and Leibniz-Wolffian philosophy that Schleiermacher described in his letter of 1787 turned out in favor of the former. In February 1790, after his final expression of disappointment with the dispute between Eberhard and the Kantians, Schleiermacher declared that "my faith in this philosophy increases day by day, especially when I compare it with the Leibnizian philosophy."[22] Correspondingly, his own writings from 1789 until at least 1794 show a growing approximation to Kantian philosophy.

2.2 Schleiermacher's Kantianism

To pin down Schleiermacher's early reception of Kant and the Kantianism it produces, I will focus on his treatise *On the Highest Good*. This treatise is marked by a deep respect for "Mr Kant"[23] and is permeated with Kantian theories, although it represents a very early stage of Schleiermacher's writing on Kant. *On the Highest Good* already shows the combination of appropriation and criticism that characterizes Schleiermacher's relationship with Kant, and it touches most of the subjects connecting and separating the two thinkers.

---

[19] Cf. especially Herms, *Herkunft*; Bernd Oberdorfer, *Geselligkeit und Realisierung von Sittlichkeit: Die Theorieentwicklung Friedrich Schleiermachers bis 1799* (Berlin: Walter de Gruyter, 1995). For a balanced sketch of Eberhard's influence, see Ulrich Barth, "Die Religionstheorie der 'Reden': Schleiermachers theologisches Modernisierungsprogramm," in *Aufgeklärter Protestantismus* (Tübingen: Mohr Siebeck, 2004), pp. 265–266.

[20] For a short sketch of Rehberg's early philosophy, see Peter Grove, "Schleiermacher und Rehberg," *Journal for the History of Modern Theology* 5 (1998), pp. 10–14. For a sketch of the parts of Reinhold's philosophy that are relevant here, see Grove, *Deutungen*, pp. 143–150.

[21] Cf. *KGA* 5.1, pp. 145–146, 176–177, 190–191.

[22] *KGA* 5.1, p. 191.

[23] *UHG*, for example pp. 89, 92. Cf. footnote 46 below.

2.2.1 Autonomy

Schleiermacher's early position in moral philosophy, compared with Kant's position, can be summarized by means of a traditional distinction: He approves of Kant's principle of autonomy, the categorical imperative, as the principle of moral cognition but—in disagreement with Kant—not as the principle of execution, that is, as an actual motivator of moral action.[24]

The treatise on the highest good expresses Schleiermacher's approval of Kant's explanation of the cognitive dimension of autonomy in connection with considerations about how to determine the concept of the highest good. With reference to Kant's idea of autonomy, Schleiermacher declares that the determination has to "proceed in a completely rational manner," leaving out "foreign additions."[25] For him this excludes the idea of happiness from not only moral theory but also the concept of the highest good. Furthermore, for his own determination of the highest good, Schleiermacher adopts Kant's procedural-ethical method from *Critique of Practical Reason*: that the concept of the good must be determined only after and through the moral law.[26] Schleiermacher uses a mathematical picture to make the relationship between the law and the highest good comprehensible: The pure practical moral law relates to the highest good as a given formula relates to the curved line drawn by it.[27] Thus, he defines the highest good as the totality of what is possible through the moral law.[28]

Schleiermacher consents to Kant's explanation of the cognitive dimension of autonomy without reservations[29] and, contrary to what Schleiermacher scholars have often claimed,[30] never expresses any doubts in his early work about Kant's formalism and apriorism in ethics. With respect to the principle of moral cognition, he uses the Kantian phrase about reason as "practical of itself"[31] and gives practical reason priority over theoretical reason.[32]

Nevertheless, Schleiermacher's understanding of this dimension of autonomy does not reflect an adequate grasp of Kant's position. This is clear from his introduction of the moral law with reference to Kant's categorical imperative: "Thus, as soon as it occurs to us to subject our actions to certain principles, and, indeed, to principles of pure reason, the first thing given us is the limiting condition to which every step must be subjected: the *principle*

---

[24] For this section, cf. Grove, *Deutungen*, pp. 37–44. Cf. also Meckenstock, *Deterministische Ethik*, pp. 29–34; Michael Moxter, *Güterbegriff und Handlungstheorie: Eine Studie zur Ethik F. Schleiermachers* (Kampen: Kok Pharos Publishing House, 1992), pp. 18–30.

[25] *OHG*, p. 10 (translation modified; cf. *UHG*, p. 89).

[26] *OHG*, pp. 10–11, 13–14; Immanuel Kant, *Critique of Practical Reason*, translated by Mary Gregor (Cambridge: Cambridge University Press, 1997), pp. 54–55. Cf. Moxter, *Güterbegriff*, pp. 19–20, 24.

[27] *OHG*, p. 12.

[28] *OHG*, pp. 14, 23.

[29] Cf. also Friedrich Daniel Ernst Schleiermacher, "Notes on Kant's *Critique of Practical Reason*," translated by Jacqueline Mariña, in Jacqueline Mariña, "A Critical-Interpretative Analysis of Some Early Writings by Schleiermacher on Kant's Views of Human Nature and Freedom (1789–1799): With Translated Texts," in *Schleiermacher on Workings of the Knowing Mind: New Translations, Resources, and Understandings*, ed. Ruth Drucilla Richardson (Lewiston: The Edwin Mellen Press, 1998), p. 26; Schleiermacher, "Freiheitsgespräch," p. 161.

[30] For example, Herms, *Herkunft*, pp. 102–104; Albert L. Blackwell, *Schleiermacher's Early Philosophy of Life: Determinism, Freedom, and Phantasy* (Chico, CA: Scholars Press, 1982), pp. 24–25, 47–53.

[31] *OHG*, p. 37.

[32] *OHG*, pp. 37, 47.

of consistency [*Konsequenz*]. This is the most elementary rule, from which reason never departs in any of its actions: namely, that none of its propositions ought to contradict itself or propositions that are allied to it."[33]

"The principle of consistency" is probably identical with the principle of noncontradiction.[34] This is in line with Schleiermacher's statement of the content of the principle: that the propositions of reason—that is, in this connection, maxims—may not contradict themselves or each other. With Kant's restriction of the validity of the principle of contradiction probably in mind, Schleiermacher states that the principle he is talking about is necessary but not sufficient, or only a negative condition of moral cognition.[35] However, "with a small extension" it also contains the sufficient, positive condition.[36] This extension is the "generality" (*Allgemeinheit*) of every law of reason, which according to Schleiermacher implies the exclusion of everything that is trivial, subjective, and individual.[37] He also argues that the law must be valid for all rational persons, "and so it must stand the test of consistency."[38]

Both elements that Schleiermacher emphasizes, consistency and generality, allude to Kant's formulation of the categorical imperative,[39] but they do not express its point: the crucial issue is whether my maxim will contradict itself if it is thought as a universal law.[40] Schleiermacher reduces the categorical imperative to the demand that maxims not contradict themselves or each other, and thus to a theoretical principle applied to these which itself is unable to produce moral maxims.[41] His emphasis on consistency gives his formulation of the highest moral principle a resemblance with Wolffian ethics of perfection.[42] But the closest parallel to Schleiermacher at this point is Rehberg. Noncontradiction and the generality of maxims are main concepts in Rehberg's appropriation of Kant's ethics, an appropriation that also shows an affinity with Wolffian ethics.[43] Schleiermacher here most likely depends on Rehberg.

I have now described the unintentional modification that figures in Schleiermacher's adoption, mentioned above, of Kant's categorical imperative as the principle of moral cognition but not also as the principle of execution. This point is contained in Schleiermacher's claim that our will is not one "that can be determined by the moral law directly; rather, this

---

[33] *OHG*, p. 13 (translation modified; cf. *UHG*, p. 91).

[34] Cf. Grove, *Deutungen*, pp. 40–41.

[35] *OHG*, p. 13; cf. Immanuel Kant, *Critique of Pure Reason*, translated by Paul Guyer and Allen W. Wood (Cambridge: Cambridge University Press, 1998), pp. 279–280.

[36] *OHG*, p. 13.

[37] *OHG*, p. 13 (translation modified; cf. *UHG*, p. 91). Froese's translation of "*Allgemeinheit*" as "universal character" misses Schleiermacher's unintentional deviation from Kant at this point.

[38] *OHG*, p. 13.

[39] Cf. Kant, *Critique of Practical Reason*, pp. 24–29.

[40] Cf. Immanuel Kant, *Groundwork of the Metaphysic of Morals*, translated by H. J. Paton (New York: Harper & Row, 1964), pp. 88–107.

[41] Cf. Dieter Henrich, "Ethics of Autonomy," in *The Unity of Reason: Essays on Kant's Philosophy*, ed. Richard Velkley (Cambridge, MA: Harvard University Press, 1994), pp. 97–98.

[42] Cf. *OHG*, pp. 48–51.

[43] Cf. August Wilhelm Rehberg, Review of *Critik der practischen Vernunft*, by Immanuel Kant, *Allgemeine Literatur-Zeitung* 188a–b (Aug. 6, 1788), pp. 357–358. All the points in this review that are referred to here and in the following are developed further in August Wilhelm Rehberg, *Ueber das Verhältniß der Metaphysik zu der Religion* (Berlin: August Mylius, 1787).

can only happen indirectly, by means of subjective motivating grounds derived from that moral law."[44] The motivating ground that is needed is not a Kantian feeling of respect for moral law but a feeling that, at the same time that it is oriented towards the pure moral law, is a sensible, empirical feeling of desire, competing with other subjective motivating grounds.

In spite of this criticism, the problem Schleiermacher tries to solve is one that only becomes pressing against the background of his reception of Kant's principle of moral cognition. This principle presupposes a sharp distinction between sensibility and reason and breaks with the Wolffian idea that there is only a gradual difference between them as effects of the sole power of the soul. Besides, Rehberg also takes a position on this issue that is equivalent to Schleiermacher's.[45]

2.2.2 Cognition

When *On the Highest Good* calls Kant "the most careful philosopher to have come before us,"[46] Schleiermacher did not only have the second *Critique* in mind, for his treatise often refers or alludes affirmatively to the *Critique of Pure Reason*.[47] What does this tell about his position on Kant's theory of cognition?

The references concern various sections of the "Dialectic" of the first *Critique*, which they compare to that of the second *Critique*. The direction of thought is always from the former to the latter, such that the latter is measured by the former. Thus, Schleiermacher's argumentation is based on the "Dialectic" of the first *Critique*, which for its part is based on and incomprehensible without the theory of cognition that Kant developed in the previous parts of the book. This indicates that Schleiermacher had already adopted this theory at this time.

The most informative example is an argument against Kant's practical-philosophical reconstruction of metaphysics, an argument claiming that "also here," that is, in the practical as well as the cognitive context, we "must see ourselves as dependent on the limiting conditions of sensibility"; alluding to Kant's distinction between the concepts of understanding and the ideas of reason, Schleiermacher also discussed "the conflict of the effusive ideas of our reason" with those limiting conditions.[48] This shows that he did not agree with the Wolffian conception of sensible representations as obscure and confused and, thus, in the need of being clarified by understanding and reason. In other words, he endorsed Kant's groundbreaking thesis that human cognition is necessarily conditioned by sensible receptivity as well as by the spontaneity of understanding.[49]

A few years later Schleiermacher explicitly argued from "the principles of critical idealism."[50] "Critical" or "transcendental idealism" is Kant's own name for his theoretical philosophy. Transcendental idealism implies that "everything intuited in space and time, hence all objects of an experience possible for us, are nothing but appearances," not

---

[44] *OHG*, p. 23.
[45] Cf. Rehberg, review, p. 354.
[46] *OHG*, p. 27.
[47] Cf. *OHG*, pp. 19–25, and section 2.2.3 below.
[48] *OHG*, p. 23 (translation modified; cf. *UHG*, p. 99).
[49] This paragraph corrects Grove, *Deutungen*, p. 57.
[50] *Spin.*, p. 541; cf., for example, *Spin.*, p. 542; *Spin.Sys.*, p. 574.

"things in themselves."⁵¹ The theories that are connected with this thesis also form part of Schleiermacher's thinking, especially Kant's theory of space and time as the pure, subjective forms of sensibility. Kant's other main theory of non-empirical conditions of cognition, his theory of the pure concepts of understanding, should be mentioned as well. For example Schleiermacher wrote that understanding "demands of nature the realization of its idea and comprehends every combination of appearances only according to such rules as it has conceived for this purpose."⁵² His adoption of this theory included the argument that connects self-consciousness and synthesis of representations, from Kant's "Transcendental Deduction" of the categories.⁵³ In this connection, one can reconstruct an early step in the development of Schleiermacher's concept of self-consciousness.⁵⁴ Kant's distinction between the phenomenal and the noumenal was also important for Schleiermacher. He utilized the Kantian critical idealism for a reformulation of Spinoza that also criticizes what Schleiermacher saw as dogmatist remnants in Kant.⁵⁵

However, "Kantian" in this connection does not refer only to Kant. It refers to Reinhold as well. An example is a passage from a section in which Schleiermacher takes up Spinoza's doctrine of the properties of the infinite, absolute extension and absolute thinking, and reconstructs it by means of critical idealism.⁵⁶ The reconstruction replaces these properties with space and time as subjective forms of intuition: "If one instead of properties of the deity posits characteristics of the intuiting, then it means: The absolute material [*Stoff*] is capable of assuming the form of every capacity of representation; despite its complete, immediate non-representability it possesses an infinite (mediate) representability."⁵⁷

Reinhold's fingerprints on this can especially be seen in Schleiermacher's use of the distinction between material and form, not only in connection with the elements of cognition, as in Kant, but also at the more elementary level of representation. According to Reinhold's *Essay on a New Theory of the Human Capacity for Representation*, the material and the form of a representation are that by which it relates to the object and the subject respectively, and every representation must have a form as well as a material.⁵⁸ When Schleiermacher describes the infinite as "the absolute material" or "the unrepresentable material,"⁵⁹ he also leans on Reinhold's doctrine of the thing in itself. Absolute material or, as Reinhold says, "material per se," is the material that corresponds with the thing in itself and is without any form of representation. Therefore, the thing in itself is unrepresentable.⁶⁰ For Kant, however, the thing in itself is thinkable but not cognizable. Reinhold certainly wants to give a more precise formulation of Kant, and this is also the way Schleiermacher understood Reinhold.

---

⁵¹ Kant, *Critique of Pure Reason*, p. 511.
⁵² *OF*, p. 134 (translation modified; cf. *UF*, p. 350).
⁵³ Cf. especially Kant, *Critique of Pure Reason*, pp. 246–248, with *Spin.*, pp. 538–545.
⁵⁴ Cf. Grove, *Deutungen*, pp. 101–111.
⁵⁵ Cf. Christof Ellsiepen, *Anschauung des Universums und Scientia Intuitiva: Die spinozistischen Grundlagen von Schleiermachers früher Religionstheorie* (Berlin: Walter de Gruyter, 2006), pp. 228–271.
⁵⁶ *Spin.Sys.*, pp. 574–575, cf. Grove, *Deutungen*, pp. 150–156. For Reinhold's earlier influence on Schleiermacher, see Grove, *Deutungen*, pp. 59–79.
⁵⁷ *Spin.Sys.*, p. 575.
⁵⁸ Karl Leonhard Reinhold, *Essay on a New Theory of the Human Capacity for Representation*, translated by Tim Mehigan and Barry Empson (Berlin: Walter de Gruyter, 2011), pp. 106–114.
⁵⁹ *Spin.Sys.*, p. 567.
⁶⁰ Reinhold, *Essay*, pp. 114–119.

But the result of Reinhold's doctrine is that he makes the concept of the thing in itself inconsistent. Thus, Schleiermacher inherited from him a tendency to eliminate the assumption of such things, and so to eliminate the original Kantian transcendental idealism as well.

2.2.3 Metaphysics and Religion

One part of *On the Highest Good*, "not unlike a digression,"[61] is devoted to criticism of Kant's reconstruction of metaphysics, his doctrine of so-called postulates from the second part of *Critique of Practical Reason*, that is, the postulates of God's existence and the immortality of the soul.

The postulates correspond to Kant's third element of cognition, the ideas of reason. The ideas are indispensable for the systematization of experience but, as concepts not corresponding to any sensations, they do not constitute cognition. Thus, the idea of God does not lead to any cognition of God; in fact, it cannot even be determined by speculative reason.[62] The postulates are assumptions of conditions necessary for the realization of the highest good. To indicate their epistemic status Kant uses concepts like that of a pure practical belief of reason and various expressions for assumption (*Voraussetzung, Annahme*).[63] The postulates remedy both deficiencies of the ideas: they show that the ideas are related to objects, and the postulate of God leads to a determined concept of God.

Against this doctrine, Schleiermacher formulated arguments that draw on his conception of autonomy and on Kant's criticism of metaphysics in *Critique of Pure Reason*.

The first argument concerns Kant's idea of happiness as an element of the highest good.[64] This element forms the basis of the postulate of God's existence: a rational being in nature depends on nature and cannot warrant a happiness that is proportional to its own morality. Therefore, one has to assume the existence of a being that is different from nature and that, by its understanding and will, is the cause of nature and of the connection between virtue and happiness, that is, God.[65] Playing off Kant's moral theory against his theory of the highest good, Schleiermacher—who excluded happiness from the highest good—objects that this argumentation from the idea of happiness is inconsistent with the idea of autonomy of reason.

The second argument refers to Kant's criticism of metaphysics in the "Dialectic" of his first *Critique*.[66] It is here that Schleiermacher claims that "also here" we have to "see ourselves as dependent on the limiting conditions of sensibility." In making this claim he alludes to Kant's idea, from his exposition of the postulate of the immortality of the soul, that we are beings of the sensible world;[67] and at the same time, Schleiermacher conceives moral consciousness in

---

[61] *OHG*, p. 25, referring to *OHG*, pp. 18–25. For the following, cf. Meckenstock, *Deterministische Ethik*, pp. 148–154; Grove, *Deutungen*, pp. 119–125.
[62] Cf. Kant, *Critique of Practical Reason*, p. 111.
[63] For example, Kant, *Critique of Practical Reason*, pp. 119–121.
[64] *OHG*, pp. 18–21.
[65] Kant, *Critique of Practical Reason*, pp. 104–105.
[66] *OHG*, pp. 22–23.
[67] Kant, *Critique of Practical Reason*, p. 102.

analogy with cognitive consciousness. On this basis he doubts that the postulates rest on a "firmer basis than the natural illusion of speculative reason."[68]

Finally, arguing from the executive dimension of moral consciousness, Schleiermacher questions the demand that we realize the highest good:[69] this realization is neither necessary nor possible for the human will, which only can be determined by the moral law through subjective motivating grounds whose efficacy does not depend on the human will alone. At this point Schleiermacher also refers to the "Dialectic" of Kant's first *Critique* against Kant himself: for us the highest good can only be a regulative principle for the cultivation of our will, but Kant has made it into a constitutive principle.

Schleiermacher concludes that

> we would rather see the concepts of God and immortality remain as they were before this recent attempt [in the *Critique of Practical Reason*], in accordance with everything said about them in the "Dialectic" of pure speculative reason [in the *Critique of Pure Reason*]. And why should we not be content with this? These ideas may have real or hypothetical certainty, yes, they may even be truth or delusion. Yet, for us human beings in our present condition they will always be *inevitable*, in any of the innumerable forms which they have already assumed at various times and, God willing, will yet assume. Moreover, as such *data* they will forever retain their place in the doctrine of Happiness, for the sake of which all people are actually so deeply interested in them.[70]

What is meant by "everything said about" the ideas in the "Dialectic" of the first *Critique*?[71] If we leave the idea of immortality aside and keep to the idea of God, the relevant text in the first *Critique* is the chapter on "The Ideal of Pure Reason." Within that chapter, Schleiermacher does not refer only to the criticism of the proofs of the existence of God, which he certainly presupposes.[72] He probably also refers to the section on "The Transcendental Ideal," which has a key function in Kant's theories about philosophical theology.[73] That Schleiermacher's conclusion also draws on this section is indicated by the fact that he refers to it later in *On the Highest Good*.[74] Kant's section on the transcendental ideal is a criticism of the metaphysical concept of God, to which criticism Schleiermacher subscribes. But Kant has a reconstruction of metaphysics from the perspective of practical reason in reserve. Since Schleiermacher refutes this reconstruction, his conclusion is a radical criticism of philosophical theology. This part of his reception of Kant also has a counterpart in Rehberg's review of the second *Critique*.[75]

However, this conclusion was not Schleiermacher's last word in this matter, not even in his early work. Just a few years after *On the Highest Good*, through his Kantian reformulation of

---

[68] *OHG*, pp. 22–23.

[69] *OHG*, pp. 23–25.

[70] *OHG*, p. 25.

[71] In relation to this question, the secondary literature is not much help. Cf., for example, Herms, *Herkunft*, pp. 90–91; Meckenstock, *Deterministische Ethik*, pp. 154–155.

[72] Cf. *OHG*, p. 21.

[73] Kant, *Critique of Pure Reason*, pp. 553–559, cf. Ulrich Barth, "Gott als Grenzbegriff der Vernunft: Kants Destruktion des vorkritisch-ontologischen Theismus," in *Gott als Projekt der Vernunft* (Tübingen: Mohr Siebeck, 2005), pp. 235–262.

[74] *OHG*, pp. 30–31; cf. Kant, *Critique of Pure Reason*, p. 556.

[75] Cf. Rehberg, Review, p. 359.

Spinoza, he tried to fill the metaphysical vacuum left by his affirmation of Kant's criticism of metaphysics and his own criticism of Kant's doctrine of postulates. But Schleiermacher did not simply drop this doctrine along with traditional metaphysics. He transformed it.

Schleiermacher's doctrine of postulates is formulated in a small treatise probably from 1793.[76] It uses the same terminology, and its argumentation has mostly the same structure, as Kant's doctrine regarding God's existence and the immortality of the soul, operating with the idea of assumptions from subjective needs. To determine his own doctrine's difference from Kant's, Schleiermacher uses a distinction between two sorts of self-consciousness: the subject's self-consciousness of its human nature as such on the one hand, and its self-consciousness of certain modifications and of the state of its human nature on the other.[77] Whereas Kant had conceived religion from the former, from the subject's general self-consciousness as autonomy and striving towards happiness, Schleiermacher—leaving out happiness—conceives it from the latter, from the subject's individual self-consciousness of its concrete state[78] and, thus, he declares, "For me, all reason to believe in the religion seems to lie in the need to find an external support for the moral law, which is so contested by us from within."[79] The point Schleiermacher wants to make against Kant is that the assumption of God and immortality is not valid generally and necessarily but only individually and contingently. Thus, his doctrine of postulates does not claim a metaphysical status as Kant's does. It introduces a distinction between metaphysics and religion and lets religion take over the function of founding theology—which, until Kant, had been assigned to metaphysics.

2.3 Kant in Schleiermacher's Later Work

2.3.1 Schleiermacher's Anti-Kantianism around 1800

Until the middle of the 1790s Schleiermacher's relationship with Kant had the character of a critical but still constructive reception. The last example of this approach is Schleiermacher's notes on "*Vertragslehre*" from 1796–1797, where he invoked the doctrine of right in the first part of Kant's *Metaphysics of Morals*, published separately in January 1797.[80] In the Fall of 1797 Schleiermacher for the first time wrote not only critically but condescendingly of Kant.

---

[76] *KGA* 5.1, pp. 424–428; cf. Meckenstock, *Deterministische Ethik*, pp. 156–160; Peter Grove, "Schleiermachers Postulatenlehre: Reflexionen zu 'Wissen, Glauben und Meinen,'" *Neue Zeitschrift für Systematische Theologie und Religionsphilosophie* 42 (2000), pp. 43–65; Grove, *Deutungen*, pp. 92–100, 126–132. Herms, *Herkunft*, pp. 136–138 neglects the Kantian elements of the treatise, seeing it as documentation of Schleiermacher's reception of the philosophy of Jacobi. For the dating, see Grove, "Schleiermachers Postulatenlehre," pp. 48–50.

[77] *KGA* 5.1, p. 424.

[78] *KGA* 5.1, pp. 426–427.

[79] *KGA* 5.1, pp. 426.

[80] Friedrich Schleiermacher, "Notizen und Exzerpte zur Vertragslehre," in *KGA* 1.2, p. 56. For the appearance dates of the two parts of Kant's *Metaphysics of Morals*, see Paul Natorp, "Einleitung," in *Kants gesammelte Schriften*, ed. the Königlich Preußische Akademie der Wissenschaften, vol. 6, Die Religion innerhalb der Grenzen der bloßen Vernunft: Die Metaphysik der Sitten (Berlin: Georg Reimer, 1914), pp. 517–518.

One reason for this change is Schleiermacher's disappointment with the doctrine of virtue in the second part of Kant's *Metaphysics of Morals*, published in August 1797. In a note, Schleiermacher wrote, "So often they have kept to the dictum that the *Critique of Pure Reason* should not be a system, forgetting that the *Metaphysics of Nature* was the system. If only one could also forget that the *Metaphysics of Morals* is the system of the *Critique of Practical Reason*."[81]

The first text to document the change, a note Schleiermacher wrote on the doctrine of virtue in September 1797,[82] is more informative in its articulation of his new view of Kant. Classifying the virtues, Schleiermacher distinguishes two ways of thinking. The first of them he calls "the one of genius," the second "the correct." Referring to two instances of each way, he declares, "The former are standing on the transcendental practical standpoint; they want to make their I . . . . The latter are standing on the empirical standpoint; they only want to present their I, according to the empirical circumstances." Schleiermacher uses this distinction to position Kant: "Kant almost seems to fall under the last genus or at least he sometimes sinks so low; at least he has only given a law for the correctness," a "negative law."[83] This is in continuity with Schleiermacher's early—inadequate—interpretation of Kant's categorical imperative as the principle of consistency and generality of maxims. What is new here is that Schleiermacher criticizes this imperative for being unable to produce moral maxims. The same criticism would be expressed in his later ethics.[84]

In public, Schleiermacher expressed this new sort of criticism of Kant full blast in his anonymously published 1799 review of the aging Kant's *Anthropology from a Pragmatic Point of View*. The very ironical review considers various viewpoints from which the book appears as, for example, "almost nothing but a collection of trivia" or "a clear portrayal of the most peculiar confusion," but reaches the judgement about the real worth of the book that it is "excellent, not as anthropology but rather as the negation of all anthropology."[85] Schleiermacher's discussion of (in his estimation) Kant's unclear distinction between physiological and pragmatic anthropology culminates in the statement that "that which appears to be but a pure deification of free choice is at bottom quite closely related to a hidden realism, to which Kant still pays secret and idolatrous homage after he himself had overturned and demolished it."[86] On the way to this statement Schleiermacher indirectly characterizes its author through allusions to phrases in the book: "The one who knows nothing more or more thoroughly about what man as freely acting being makes, or can or should make, of himself, than what he finds sketched here, cannot even be a mediocre knower of himself."[87] Thus Schleiermacher himself contributes to the "Kantology" he otherwise recommends to "the blind admirers of this great man."[88]

[81] Friedrich Daniel Ernst Schleiermacher, "Vermischte Gedanken und Einfälle," in *KGA* 1.2, p. 20. "*Metaphysics of Nature*" may be short for Kant's *Metaphysical Foundations of Natural Science*.

[82] Schleiermacher, "Vermischte Gedanken," pp. 9–10. For the dating, cf. pp. 8, 11.

[83] Schleiermacher, "Vermischte Gedanken," p. 9.

[84] *GKS*, p. 87.

[85] Friedrich Daniel Ernst Schleiermacher, Review of *Anthropology from a Pragmatic Point of View*, by Immanuel Kant, translated by Jacqueline Mariña, in Mariña, "Critical-Interpretative Analysis," pp. 15–16.

[86] Schleiermacher, review of *Anthropology*, p. 17.

[87] Schleiermacher, review of *Anthropology*, p. 15 (translation modified; cf. Friedrich Daniel Ernst Schleiermacher, Review of *Anthropologie in pragmatischer Hinsicht*, by Immanuel Kant, in *KGA* 1.2, p. 365).

[88] Schleiermacher, review of *Anthropology*, p. 19.

All these quotations express a feeling of superiority to Kant that is new in Schleiermacher's writings. What is the explanation of this feeling? As the note from September 1797 indicates, it has to do with the fact that Johann Gottlieb Fichte had now replaced Kant as Schleiermacher's primary philosophical interlocutor.[89] But while Fichte never wrote in such a tone about Kant himself—only about the Kantians—Schleiermacher's new friend Friedrich Schlegel did in notes from this time, and Schleiermacher may have picked it up from him.[90] But what is more important is the question of how the change in Schleiermacher's relationship with Kant around 1800 should be interpreted. Does it mark his final farewell to Kant?

Schleiermacher's thinking saw significant development in all three areas that figure in my discussion of his earlier Kantianism. Giving up the Kantian idea of a procedural ethics, he eventually moved far beyond Kant's ethics.[91] And around 1800, in his theory of cognition, he invoked an idealism with more affinity with Fichte's, but a few years later abandoned that idealism in favor of a theory—developed in his philosophical ethics from 1804-1832 and his dialectic from 1811 to 1833—that approaches Kant's theory again.[92] In this chapter I will not have space to describe these developments in detail. Instead I will focus on Schleiermacher's development in the third area, his final theory of the idea of God, in order to reach a judgment of the lasting importance of his reception of Kant.

2.3.2 Metaphysics and Religion

It is certainly possible to draw lines from Schleiermacher's early writings to the theory of the idea of God, posited between the theory of cognition and that of religion, in Schleiermacher's dialectic and in his *Glaubenslehre* from 1821-1822 and 1830-1831.[93]

The theory has two parts, a structure that reflects Schleiermacher's distinction between metaphysics and religion. One part, which belongs to the metaphysics of the dialectic, starts from objective consciousness and thinks of God as the necessary condition of this consciousness. The other part, set out in the introduction to the *Glaubenslehre*, reconstructs the genesis of the religious concept of God from the feeling of absolute dependence as a modification of human self-consciousness. In this way, God is conceived as the transcendent ground of all cognition and being on the one hand, and as the "Whence"[94] of human subjectivity and of the world on the other.

Corresponding with this duality, an important result of the theory is a dual thesis about the validity and the content of the idea of God: as metaphysical, the idea claims general validity, but is undetermined; as religious, it is of course determined but only subjective. These metaphysical and religious ideas of God are complementary. Just to mention the function of the metaphysical idea of God for the religious idea: the metaphysical idea indirectly vouches for the personal and anthropomorphic religious idea of God against atheist criticism.[95]

[89] Cf. Grove, *Deutungen*, pp. 196-205.
[90] Grove, *Deutungen*, p. 200.
[91] See Moxter, *Güterbegriff*.
[92] See, for example, *WA*, vol. 2, pp. 150-199; *Dial.*, vol. 1, pp. 90-98, cf. Grove, *Deutungen*, pp. 218-223, 382-396, 464-480, where also agreements with Reinhold are pointed out.
[93] For the following, cf. Grove, *Deutungen*, pp. 585-612.
[94] *CF (1928)*, p. 16.
[95] Cf. *Dial.*, vol. 1, pp. 271-272; vol. 2, pp. 584-586.

This theory—in some ways the climax of Schleiermacher's metaphysics and philosophy of religion—certainly reflects new influences and developments in his thinking after the period examined above. But it also depends in many ways on Kant's contribution to philosophical theology, which Schleiermacher adopted early on. Both parts of his later theory presuppose Kant's destruction of traditional philosophical theology. That metaphysics is unable to determine the idea of God, as Schleiermacher's dialectic claims, is also Kant's conclusion in the *Critique of Pure Reason*, which is concerned with speculative reason. But Kant's influence is not limited to the destructive side of his contribution. It also extends to his doctrine of the postulate of God, the postulate that, according to Kant, brings the determination of the idea of God. The continuing influence of this doctrine on Schleiermacher as regards his argument about the religious idea of God is a natural one, in view of the fact that he had already formulated his own doctrine of postulates a few years after *On the Highest Good*. The religious part of his later theory is a successor of this doctrine, and it likewise does not make any metaphysical claims, although it does not argue from individual self-consciousness but, similarly to Kant, from general religious self-consciousness. But the metaphysical part of Schleiermacher's later theory also retains concepts from the Kantian doctrine of postulates: for example, the concept of a postulate itself,[96] and that of *Voraussetzung*.[97] And for the relationship between the religious and the philosophical idea of God it uses the concept of supplementing (*Ergänzung*), which Kant applies in a similar way in the version of his doctrine of postulates presented in the *Critique of Judgement*.[98]

To conclude: Schleiermacher's final theory of the idea of God represents one clear example of how his later work would have been unthinkable without Kant.

Suggested Reading

Dilthey, Wilhelm. *Leben Schleiermachers*. Vol. 1.1. Ed. Martin Redeker (Berlin: Walter de Gruyter & Co., 1970).

Grove, Peter. *Deutungen des Subjekts: Schleiermachers Philosophie der Religion* (Berlin: Walter de Gruyter, 2004).

Grove, Peter. "Werke: Jugendmanuskripte, erste Predigten." In *Schleiermacher Handbuch*, ed. Martin Ohst (Tübingen: Mohr Siebeck, 2017), pp. 67–76.

Herms, Eilert. *Herkunft, Entfaltung und erste Gestalt des Systems der Wissenschaften bei Schleiermacher* (Gütersloh: Gütersloher Verlagshaus Gerd Mohn, 1974).

Meckenstock, Günter. *Deterministische Ethik und kritische Theologie: Die Auseinandersetzung des frühen Schleiermacher mit Kant und Spinoza 1789-1794* (Berlin: Walter de Gruyter, 1988).

---

[96] *Dial.*, vol. 2, pp. 562–563.
[97] For example, *Dial.*, vol. 2, pp. 164, 239.
[98] *Dial.*, vol. 1, pp. 262, 267; cf. Immanuel Kant, *The Critique of Judgement, Part 2, Critique of the Teleological Judgement*, translated by James Creed Meredith (Oxford: Oxford University Press, 1986), pp. 111, 114.

Bibliography

Barth, Ulrich. "Gott als Grenzbegriff der Vernunft: Kants Destruktion des vorkritisch-ontologischen Theismus." In *Gott als Projekt der Vernunft* (Tübingen: Mohr Siebeck, 2005), pp. 235–262.

Barth, Ulrich. "Die Religionstheorie der 'Reden': Schleiermachers theologisches Modernisierungsprogramm." In *Aufgeklärter Protestantismus* (Tübingen: Mohr Siebeck, 2004), pp. 259–289.

Blackwell, Albert L. *Schleiermacher's Early Philosophy of Life: Determinism, Freedom, and Phantasy* (Chico, CA: Scholars Press, 1982).

Dilthey, Wilhelm. *Leben Schleiermachers*. Vol. 1.1. Ed. Martin Redeker (Berlin: Walter de Gruyter & Co., 1970).

Ellsiepen, Christof. *Anschauung des Universums und Scientia Intuitiva: Die spinozistischen Grundlagen von Schleiermachers früher Religionstheorie* (Berlin: Walter de Gruyter, 2006).

Grove, Peter. *Deutungen des Subjekts: Schleiermachers Philosophie der Religion* (Berlin: Walter de Gruyter, 2004).

Grove, Peter. "Johann August Eberhards Theorie des Gefühls." In *Ein Antipode Kants? Johann August Eberhard im Spannungsfeld von spätaufklärerischer Philosophie und Theologie*, ed. Hans-Joachim Kertscher and Ernst Stöckmann (Berlin: Walter de Gruyter, 2012), pp. 119–131.

Grove, Peter. "Schleiermachers Postulatenlehre: Reflexionen zu 'Wissen, Glauben und Meinen.'" *Neue Zeitschrift für Systematische Theologie und Religionsphilosophie* 42 (2000), pp. 43–65.

Grove, Peter. "Schleiermacher und Rehberg." *Journal for the History of Modern Theology* 5 (1998), pp. 1–28.

Gutekunst, Katharina. *Die Freiheit des Subjekts bei Schleiermacher: Eine Analyse im Horizont der Debatte um die Willensfreiheit in der analytischen Philosophie* (Berlin: Walter de Gruyter, 2019).

Henrich, Dieter. "Ethics of Autonomy." In *The Unity of Reason: Essays on Kant's Philosophy*, ed. Richard Velkley (Cambridge, MA: Harvard University Press, 1994), pp. 89–121.

Herms, Eilert. *Herkunft, Entfaltung und erste Gestalt des Systems der Wissenschaften bei Schleiermacher* (Gütersloh: Gütersloher Verlagshaus Gerd Mohn, 1974).

Kant, Immanuel. *The Critique of Judgement, Part 2, Critique of the Teleological Judgement*, translated by James Creed Meredith (Oxford: Oxford University Press, 1986).

Kant, Immanuel. *Critique of Practical Reason*, translated by Mary Gregor (Cambridge: Cambridge University Press, 1997).

Kant, Immanuel. *Critique of Pure Reason*, translated by Paul Guyer and Allen W. Wood (Cambridge: Cambridge University Press, 1998).

Kant, Immanuel. *Groundwork of the Metaphysic of Morals*, translated by H. J. Paton (New York: Harper & Row, 1964).

Mariña, Jacqueline. "A Critical-Interpretative Analysis of Some Early Writings by Schleiermacher on Kant's Views of Human Nature and Freedom (1789–1799): With Translated Texts." In *Schleiermacher on Workings of the Knowing Mind: New Translations, Resources, and Understandings*, ed. Ruth Drucilla Richardson (Lewiston: The Edwin Mellen Press, 1998), pp. 11–31.

Mariña, Jacqueline. *Transformation of the Self in the Thought of Friedrich Schleiermacher* (Oxford: Oxford University Press, 2008).

Meckenstock, Günter. *Deterministische Ethik und kritische Theologie: Die Auseinandersetzung des frühen Schleiermacher mit Kant und Spinoza 1789-1794* (Berlin: Walter de Gruyter, 1988).

Meckenstock, Günter. "Einleitung des Bandherausgebers." In *KGA* 1.1, ed. Günter Meckenstock (Berlin: De Gruyter, 1984), pp. xvii–lxxxix.

Moxter, Michael. *Güterbegriff und Handlungstheorie: Eine Studie zur Ethik F. Schleiermachers* (Kampen: Kok Pharos Publishing House, 1992).

Natorp, Paul. "Einleitung." In *Kants gesammelte Schriften*, ed. the Königlich Preußische Akademie der Wissenschaften, vol. 6, Die Religion innerhalb der Grenzen der bloßen Vernunft: Die Metaphysik der Sitten (Berlin: Georg Reimer, 1914), pp. 517–520.

Oberdorfer, Bernd. *Geselligkeit und Realisierung von Sittlichkeit: Die Theorieentwicklung Friedrich Schleiermachers bis 1799* (Berlin: Walter de Gruyter, 1995).

Okely, Samuel. "Das Tagebuch von Schleiermachers Schul- und Studienfreund Samuel Okely (1785/86)," ed. Wolfgang Virmond. *New Athenaeum* 3 (1992), pp. 153–210.

Rehberg, August Wilhelm. Review of *Critik der practischen Vernunft*, by Immanuel Kant. *Allgemeine Literatur-Zeitung* no. 188a–b (6 Aug. 1788).

Rehberg, August Wilhelm. *Ueber das Verhältniß der Metaphysik zu der Religion* (Berlin: August Mylius, 1787).

Reinhold, Karl Leonhard. *Essay on a New Theory of the Human Capacity for Representation*, translated by Tim Mehigan and Barry Empson (Berlin: Walter de Gruyter, 2011).

Schleiermacher, Friedrich Daniel Ernst. "Freiheitsgespräch." In *KGA* 1.1, pp. 135–164.

Schleiermacher, Friedrich Daniel Ernst. "Notes on Kant's *Critique of Practical Reason*," translated by Jacqueline Mariña. In Mariña, "Critical-Interpretative Analysis," pp. 24–29.

Schleiermacher, Friedrich Daniel Ernst. "Notizen und Exzerpte zur Vertragslehre." In *KGA* 1.2, pp. 51–67.

Schleiermacher, Friedrich Daniel Ernst. Review of *Anthropologie in pragmatischer Hinsicht*, by Immanuel Kant. In *KGA* 1.2, pp. 363–369.

Schleiermacher, Friedrich Daniel Ernst. Review of *Anthropology from a Pragmatic Point of View*, by Immanuel Kant, translated by Jacqueline Mariña. In Mariña, "Critical-Interpretative Analysis," pp. 15–19.

Schleiermacher, Friedrich Daniel Ernst. "Vermischte Gedanken und Einfälle." In *KGA* 1.2, pp. 1–49.

CHAPTER 3

SPINOZA

CHRISTOF ELLSIEPEN

> Offer with me reverently a tribute to the manes of the holy, rejected Spinoza. The high World-Spirit pervaded him; the Infinite was his beginning and his end; the Universe was his only and his everlasting love. In holy innocence and in deep humility he beheld himself mirrored in the eternal world, and perceived how he also was its most worthy mirror. He was full of religion, full of the Holy Spirit. Wherefore, he stands there alone and unequalled; master in his art, yet without disciples and without citizenship, sublime above the profane tribe.
>
> —Schleiermacher, *Speeches*[1]

THIS chapter offers an introduction into Schleiermacher's encounter with Spinoza's thought (1), and it depicts the systematic decisions influenced by this study of Spinoza, as documented in Schleiermacher's early Spinoza manuscripts focusing on the problem of individuation (2). It then turns to an outline of Spinozistic traits in Schleiermacher's further thought (3), beginning with his Spinozistic approach to the individuation problem in the early theory of religion in *Speeches* (3.1) and drawing a systematic line from the claim of the correlation of God and World in the Dialectic [*Dialektik*] to Spinoza's system (3.2).

3.1 THE *SPINOZARENAISSANCE* IN GERMANY AND LITERARY EVIDENCE OF SCHLEIERMACHER'S CONTACT WITH SPINOZA'S THOUGHT

Baruch de Spinoza was one of the most hated and most adored thinkers in the later part of the eighteenth century in Europe. His work had been largely forbidden and banned; nevertheless, his influence cannot be overestimated. Thinkers and literati like Gotthold Ephraim Lessing, Johann Wolfgang von Goethe, Gottfried Herder, Christian Wolff, and Immanuel

---

[1] See *Speeches*[1]/*Reden*[1], pp. 54f. The page numbering here follows the original 1799.

Kant had all read Spinoza's *Ethics* and worked out their own thinking in struggling against or in following Spinoza. However, the engagement with and reception of Spinoza's theses in their works remained without explicit reference or response. A proper *Spinozarenaissance* was not triggered until 1785, when Friedrich Heinrich Jacobi published the volume *On the Doctrine of Spinoza, in Letters to Mr. Moses Mendelssohn*.[2] Jacobi's aim was to show Spinoza's shortcomings not simply by disparaging him as an atheist or pantheist, but through rational and critical argument. A generation of young philosophers like Schelling, Schlegel, Fichte, Hegel, and Schleiermacher were thus exposed to a fascinating "heretic" and a novel systematic philosophy.

Schleiermacher first came upon Jacobi's book in 1787 but told his father he had to study it over again because of the "confusion" of Jacobi's philosophical language.[3] It was only six years later, during his time as a teacher's candidate in Berlin (1793-1794), that he managed to do so. At that point he studied the second edition of the *Letters*, to which Jacobi had added several important attachments in which he quoted large sequences of Spinoza's works.[4] This had been necessary because Spinoza's *Opera posthuma* were *rarissima* in Europe. Consequently, these citations were Schleiermacher's first encounter with Spinoza's text in the Latin original. The 25-year-old copied whole paragraphs and took notes, which have been preserved until today. Transcripts of this very complex material have been completely edited in the *Kritische Gesamtausgabe* (*KGA*). The titles of Schleiermacher's manuscripts show that he was not primarily interested in Jacobi at that time; instead, Jacobi's books[5] provided the vehicle to understand Spinoza.[6] In the first manuscript Schleiermacher copied the 44 paragraphs in which Jacobi had tried to give a concise account of Spinoza's philosophy and even copied some of the quotations in the footnotes as the only authentic Spinoza text in his possession at the time.[7] The second manuscript marks the literary documentation of Schleiermacher's attempt to illustrate for himself Spinoza's philosophical principles and system based on Jacobi's text, including a comparison of Spinoza with Leibniz and Kant. Schleiermacher then tried to prove his conclusions against Jacobi by copying and commenting significant parts of Jacobi's *Letters* and *David Hume*. These notes he put down in the manuscript *Spinozismus*, following the Spinoza passages copied from Jacobi's works.[8] Finally, in a third booklet he wrote down his thoughts concerning Jacobi's own philosophy, without referencing Spinoza.[9]

---

[2] See Friedrich Heinrich Jacobi, *Werke. Gesamtausgabe*, vol. 1.1: *Schriften zum Spinozastreit*, ed. Klaus Hammacher and Irmgard-Maria Piske (Hamburg: Meiner, 1998; hereafter *JWA* 1.1).

[3] See Letter No. 80, from 14 August, 1787 to J. G. A., in *KGA* 5.1, pp. 91f.

[4] *JWA* 1.1, pp. 149-267.

[5] He read also Jacobi's 1787 book, *David Hume über den Glauben, oder Idealismus und Realismus. Ein Gespräch*. See Friedrich Heinrich Jacobi, "David Hume über den Glauben, oder Idealismus und Realismus. Ein Gespräch (1787)," in *Werke. Gesamtausgabe*, vol. 2.1: *Schriften zum transzendentalen Idealismus*, ed. Walter Jaeschke (Hamburg: Meiner, 2004), pp. 5-113.

[6] See *Spinozismus. Spinoza betreffend aus Jakobi* (hereafter *Spin.*) and *Kurze Darstellung des Spinozistischen Systems* (hereafter *Spin.Sys.*), in *KGA* 1.1, 511-582.

[7] See, for example, *Spin.*, p. 514, where he copied the *Demonstration* and *Scholium* of the 28. *Proposition of Part I* of the *Ethica* quoted in Jacobi, *JWA* 1.1, pp. 94f.

[8] *Spin.*, pp. 524-558.

[9] *KGA* 1.1, pp. 583-597.

3.2 THE FUNDAMENTAL SYSTEMATIC INFLUENCE OF SPINOZA

3.2.1 The Underlying Question: The Metaphysical Problem of Individuation

Jacobi criticized Spinoza on two major points, pointing towards the accusation of fatalism. His first argument was that Spinoza claimed only physical entities to be real, while mental representations were nothing but a "copy" of the physical.[10] Schleiermacher soon realized that Jacobi had misunderstood the complex parallelism of Spinoza's concept of attributes. But Jacobi's second argument ran deeper. Jacobi viewed Spinoza as the most coherent and therefore paradigmatic rationalist and tried to show that coherent rationalism inherently leads to determinism and fatalism. The basis of the argument was Jacobi's theory of consciousness: We are by the same action(s) aware of things (*res*) and of ourselves where the former appear for us within their connection according to the laws of nature.[11] This structure of consciousness is the fundamental condition of our knowledge, which recognizes things within their causal connection and thus is based on the principle of sufficient reason. To know things means to know them through their proximate causes, which is to know their "mechanism."[12] Thus, rational knowledge is restricted to the set of finite things. According to Jacobi, Spinoza's attempt to find the "mechanism of the principle of mechanism"[13] was bound to fail. All he could get was an empty conception of the absolute with no relation to real finite and mutable things. However, Spinoza's actual claim was that the infinite and the finite are "one and the same."[14] Consequently, his task was to show how real finite things follow out of the infinite. Jacobi here refers to the philosophical question of the principle of individuation: What are the criteria by which finite things are distinguished as determined individuals? Jacobi's final judgement is that Spinoza cannot show such criteria: "Spinozism can only be successfully attacked in terms of its Individuations."[15] It is on this conclusion that Schleiermacher disagreed with Jacobi. Additionally, he was convinced that Spinoza can contribute more to the metaphysical problem of the *principium individuationis* than Jacobi believed. Thus, Jacobi had indirectly given the young Schleiermacher not only the text of Spinoza but also a focus for his philosophical endeavor: to solve the problem of individuation within a theory of consciousness.[16] In discussing this question Schleiermacher combines transcendental thought with metaphysical insights he gets from his *relecture* of Spinoza.

---

[10] Jacobi, *David Hume*, quoted in *Spin.Sys.*, pp. 578f.
[11] *JWA* 1.1, p. 263.
[12] *JWA* 1.1, p. 260.
[13] *JWA* 1.1, p. 260.
[14] *JWA* 1.1, p. 18.
[15] *JWA* 1.1, p. 234; Quoted in *Spin.*, p. 547.
[16] See Schleiermacher's note in *Spin.*, p. 546: "I remember that already in my first philosophical meditations to me, too, the principium individuationis seemed to be the main [*erste*] critical point of theoretical philosophy, but I couldn't drop my anchor anywhere."

3.2.2 In Search of a Theory of Individuation

At first sight, and according to Jacobi's conviction, a theory of individual substances like Leibniz's monadology should be superior to concepts in which an individuation is yet to be shown. Yet Schleiermacher rejects Jacobi's judgement that Leibniz is superior to Spinoza concerning the problem of individuation, arguing that Leibniz presupposes what he ought to show.[17] Moreover, in Leibniz's theory of perception an infinite connection of each individual monad to everything else is implied and he cannot show the reason for their substantial independence. Rather the individual trait of each monad, its determinate perspective (*perceptio*), indicates its "conjunction ... with the whole Universo."[18] Thus Schleiermacher determines that "Spinoza would have easily wrought out of Leibniz the transition to his view of the unity of the infinite by showing what he has so clearly demonstrated, that what seems to be individual belongs to the modification [of substance]."[19] It is in this context that "*Universum*," which will later be part of the leading term *Anschauung des Universums* in Schleiermacher's *Reden*, appears for the first time.

In Schleiermacher's reconstruction, Spinoza contributes several points to address the problem of individuation. Schleiermacher claims as Spinoza's main proposition that "there must be an infinite, within which everything finite exists."[20] This proposition is based on two assumptions: the principle of sufficient reason and the doctrine of flux of things. The latter is most interesting for the problem of individuation. The flux of things, a principle borrowed from Heraclitus,[21] stands for the non-substantial and non-stable state of finite things. One can neither speak of an individual absolute—one cannot differentiate within one absolute and no absolute can exist beside others[22]—nor of absolute individuals. Rather individuality is only a characterization of fluent finite things that do not exist from themselves. Given the totality of fluent finite things existing in the infinite, the question remains how this *in*-relation actualizes a principle of individuation of finite things. Following Jacobi's study, Schleiermacher holds that finite variable things inhere indirectly (*mittelbare Inhärenz*) in the existing infinite.[23] Schleiermacher here refers to Spinoza's theory of modes (*modi*): finite *modes* are part and modification of the infinite *modes*, which are in turn modifications of certain attributes of substance itself. Thus, the principle of individuation must be found in the realm of the infinite modes that constitute the metaphysical hinges between infinite substance and singular finite things.[24]

At first Schleiermacher considers the attribute of extension (*extensio*). Here the infinite mode is the totality of movement and rest. Schleiermacher seeks to find an illustration of what constitutes an individual within this attribute. In a very complex argument

---

[17] *Spin.*, p. 547.
[18] *Spin.Sys.*, p. 572.
[19] *Spin.Sys.*, p. 572.
[20] *Spin.Sys.*, p. 564.
[21] In 1808 Schleiermacher offered a portrait of Heraclitus (*Herakleitos der dunkle, von Ephesos*), in which he claims the flux of things as Heraclitus' main principle. See *KGA* 1.6, pp. 134–142.
[22] *Spin.Sys.*, pp. 568f.
[23] *Spin.Sys.*, p. 573; cf. also p. 567.
[24] Christof Ellsiepen, *Anschauung des Universums und Scientia Intuitiva. Die spinozistischen Grundlagen von Schleiermachers früher Religionstheorie* (Berlin: De Gruyter, 2006), p. 222; cf. also pp. 44–48.

Schleiermacher identifies a temporarily unifying coincidence of opposing modes of movement to be individual. It is Cusano's *coincidentia oppositorum*, which Schleiermacher had found in Jacobi's summary of Giordano Bruno's *De la causa, principio et uno* that provides the conceptual basis to understand what in Spinoza's thought could be classified as individual.[25] Temporarily congruent points of opposing movements, where movements occur in a determinate combination, balance, or "mixture" (*Mischung*) are designated as individuals.[26] These individuals are thus in a permanent state of flux and variability. Taking into account that their lack of substantial independence, Schleiermacher reduces their status to "pseudo-individuals" (*Scheinindividuum*).[27]

In a second step Schleiermacher searches for a principle of individuation in the attribute of *cogitatio*. Because of the parallelism or structural isomorphy of physical (*extensio*) and mental (*cogitatio*) spheres, the same argument holding for the physical domain should be applicable to mental "things" as well. Schleiermacher rejects Jacobi's view that in Spinoza only physical entities were real and mental entities only representations or "copies" of the physical.[28] Moreover, Schleiermacher maintains that Spinoza would argue that there can exist mental activity independent of physical causes. In contrast, then, causality should be found in both physical and mental modes where both spheres are isomorphic and independent of one another.[29] Accordingly, the model of individuation should apply for the mental sphere of *cogitatio* as well. The infinite modes of *cogitatio* are "reason and will" (*Verstand und Wille*).[30] Individual finite modes of these are mental realities: decisions (*Entschluß*) of the mind in which intellectual and affectual activity temporarily come together.[31]

For both spheres the indirect inherence is both a dynamic and a part-whole relation. Spinoza characterizes this relation with the term *exprimere*: to express. Jacobi literally translates with *ausdrücken*. Schleiermacher uses the term *darstellen*: "Substance must constantly . . . represent [*darstellen*] all possible modes of movement and rest, of imagination and desire."[32] This term will later recur in the *Speeches* as the correlate of *Anschauung des Universums*: Religious activity is contemplating singular things as *Darstellungen des Universums*. As this term originates here in the early manuscripts within the context of a Spinoza interpretation, it is used in a metaphysical not in an ethical sense.[33] The finite individual activity is a part of the totality of the modes of the substance from which everything is "produced." Individual determination of the finite is found in a temporary balance of opposing modes. Individuality as such is gradual and fluent, and furthermore ever-changing

---

[25] *JWA* 1.1, pp. 185–205.

[26] *Spin.*, p. 573, cf. also *Spin.Sys.*, p. 578.

[27] *Spin.Sys.*, pp. 575f.

[28] *Spin.Sys.*, pp. 579. Cf. *JWA* 1.1, pp. 20f; cf. Jacobi, *David Hume*, in *Werke. Gesamtausgabe* 2.1 (hereafter *JWA* 2.1)

[29] *Spin.Sys.*, p. 578.

[30] Here Schleiermacher follows Jacobi; cf. *Spin.*, p. 535, and §17 in *JWA* 1.1, p. 101. Spinoza's own term is *intellectus infinitus*. See Baruch de Spinoza, *Ethica ordine geometrica demonstrata* (*Opera pusthuma 1677*), ed. Konrad Blumenstock, 4th ed. (Darmstadt: Wissenschaftliche Buchgesellschaft, 1989), I, prop. 322, corol. 2.

[31] *Spin.*, p. 529.

[32] *Spin.*, p. 551.

[33] In his philosophical ethics and *Christian Ethics* Schleiermacher will later use "darstellendes Handeln" as a form of symbolizing and interacting human action. This meaning is entirely separate from the metaphysical use of *darstellen* in our context.

through interaction, but its causal force is part of the totality of modes and thus indirect expression of the one infinite absolute.

3.2.3 Schleiermacher's View of Individuation—Forming a Transcendental Spinozism

Thus far Schleiermacher's argument is only a metaphysical one. Things (*res*) show the same structural connection both in their physical and in their mental expression. The distinctiveness of his interpretation takes shape when he further considers what can be the representational object of ideas. These ideas can and do represent physical content, but as ideas they can also represent other ideas. The human mind can mentally represent not only the physical content of its bodily affections; it can also represent its mental state itself. This, again, Schleiermacher claims to be a Spinozan thought, thereby contradicting Jacobi's presentation, and it is worth noting that Schleiermacher here offers a stronger interpretation of Spinoza than Jacobi.[34]

By considering the intentional content of ideas, Schleiermacher changes the perspective on the problem of individuation. The main question is no longer what individualizes "things," but what individualizes the content of our mental representations.[35] And for this approach Schleiermacher maintains that Spinoza's philosophy can contribute significantly. Previously Schleiermacher's aim was to show how individuation can be explained by starting with a concept of the absolute: substance as the "one and only" expresses itself through principles of individuation in a totality of singular finite modes. Yet now the direction of view is reversed by starting with the finite mental representations and making a statement about the infinite: If individual things are given as a representational object of our ideas, substance must be therein represented indirectly. Spinoza's metaphysical term of *exprimere*, which Schleiermacher has translated with *darstellen*, is here given an epistemological turn: "No thing presents itself for us (*sich uns darstellen*) as a singular extended thing that is not also thought and no thing as thought that is not also extended."[36] "Every finite thing must reveal all properties of the Deity."[37]

It is at this point in Schleiermacher's Spinoza manuscripts where he makes an effort to merge his view of transcendental philosophy following Kant with the new insights he derived from his study of Spinoza. It is clear that in this attempt he is not interested in an unbiased analysis of each author in their philosophical context,[38] but rather in attaining a systematic understanding of a problem he presumes solvable only through a combination of both. On the one hand, for Schleiermacher there is no way back beyond the epistemological barrier created by Kant. On the other, Spinoza stands for a holistic, integrative view

---

[34] *Spin.Sys.*, p. 579. Cf. also Ellsiepen, *Anschauung des Universums und Scientia Intuitiva*, p. 197 and, concerning the relation of *idea* and *ideatum* in Spinoza, pp. 55–60.
[35] Ellsiepen, *Anschauung des Universums und Scientia Intuitiva*, p. 200.
[36] *Spin.Sys.*, p. 577.
[37] *Spin.Sys.*, p. 575. The term *properties* (*Eigenschaften*) refers to Spinoza's term *attributes*.
[38] Cf. Ulrich Barth, "Was heißt 'Anschauung des Universums'? Beobachtungen zum Verhältnis von Schleiermacher und Spinoza," in *Affektenlehre und amor Dei intellectualis*, ed. Violetta L. Waibel (Hamburg: Meiner, 2012), pp. 249–253, for a critical reflection on this topic.

that can bring together what had been opposed for some time. As Paul Tillich has put it, Schleiermacher ventures a "great synthesis" of Spinoza and Kant, which constitutes a crucial element for his theological and philosophical endeavors.[39]

His synthesis starts with an analogy between the Kantian forms of intuition and Spinoza's attributes. If for Spinoza every finite thing must reveal *all* properties of the Deity, why did he then treat only two of them, *extensio* and *cogitatio*, in his system? Schleiermacher answers this with following argument:

> Simply because we cannot have ideas of other properties [than these]. This can be broken down to saying: everything that cannot be viewed in space and sensed in time is lost for us. If he [Spinoza] would have pursued the cognitive transition to the insight that space and time constitute the characteristic forms of our [human] manner of representation, he would not have said *extensio* and *cogitatio* would be attributes, let alone the only attributes of the Infinite. Upon this is based the only difference between him and Kant.[40]

This difference is yet to be addressed for the coherent Spinozism that Schleiermacher aimed to create. He resolves this issue by considering the epistemological role of the two attributes of *extensio* and *cogitatio*. Their purpose is a restriction of the possible content of human mental representation. And this exactly is also the purpose of Kant's "forms of Intuition Space and Time." Consequently, Schleiermacher argues, Spinoza should have located the attributes in the realm of human thought rather than in the constitution of the absolute, because the very place of the "revelation" of the attributes is in fact the human mind itself. Only for us there are no more than two attributes of substance because we do not have mental objects other than sensations of our body and ideas of our mind.[41] Thus, coherent Spinozism leads to critical idealism.[42]

Schleiermacher furthermore sought to improve Kant's system through Spinoza's contributions. To this end he combines his theory of Spinozist individuation with the transcendental approach in order to arrive at a transcendental theory of individuation. As noted above, the *in*-relation of finite individuals in the absolute forms a tripartite structure, with the absolute substance as the underlying cause of all thing in a first level and the infinite *modi* of the attributes of substance in the second level, which in turn serve as principles of individuation of finite things in the third level. Yet on Schleiermacher's account this "second level" now is to be located in the human mind. Thus, the three-level structure is transformed into a transcendental setting of phenomena individualized through the forms of our representation. The noumenal correlate of the phenomena consequently is not representable

---

[39] Paul Tillich, *Religion des konkreten Geistes. Friedrich Schleiermacher* (Stuttgart: Evangelisches Verlagswerk 1968), p. 9.

[40] *Spin.Sys.*, pp. 574f.

[41] This is not altogether against Spinoza's own system. Spinoza claims the twofold expression of substance in those attributes as a consequence of two axioms, i.e., of two suppositions of experience that cannot be deduced. Cf. Wolfgang Bartuschat, *Spinozas Theorie des Menschen* (Hamburg: Felix Meiner, 1992), p. 38. Cf. Barth, "Was heißt 'Anschauung des Universums'?," pp. 252f.

[42] This also sheds another light on the methodological status of Spinoza's philosophical approach. Both Kant and Spinoza, according to Schleiermacher, come together in the method of a reductive approach in "finding the [way from] unconditional to the [given] conditional." See *Spin.Sys.*, p. 570: "Spinoza geht ebenfalls von dem allgemeinen Problem aus das Unbedingte zu dem Bedingten zu finden"; cf. also Barth, "Was heißt 'Anschauung des Universums'?," p. 253.

as such and we cannot determine any differentiation in it. In this manner, Schleiermacher "corrects" Kant's concept of *noumena* by drawing upon Spinoza to determine a theory of *noumenon*,[43] which adopts the purpose of the Spinozan substance as being the one in which all things inhere and which expresses itself in all things. Just as finite things inhere indirectly in the absolute, the absolute is representable only indirectly. The property of the *noumenon* is thus a "complete direct inconceivability combined with an infinite (indirect) conceivability."[44] The "revelation of the Deity" is an indirect revelation mediated through the forms of our mind in which phenomena are given to us. In actuality, there is no way to look "behind the curtain" of our consciousness and have a glimpse of the Deity or substance as it is for itself for we only have the phenomena in our mind. But with the phenomena we have the possibility of conceiving the inconceivable indirectly, through its manifold finite individuations. Hence, the *noumenon* proves to be conceivable indirectly in infinite ways. Terminologically these thoughts are bound to a concept of *Anschauung*. It is in the realm of *Anschauung* that—according to Kant—phenomena are given to us through the forms of space and time.

Therefore, the transcendental theory of individuation leads to the double conclusion of (a) a verdict of the complete direct inconceivability (*Unanschaubarkeit*) of the absolute, and (b) its infinite indirect conceivability and thus manifestation through the individual finite phenomena given to us in our mental representation (*Anschauung*). From here it is only one step further to the concept of religious *Anschauung des Universums* that emerges five years later as the central notion in *On Religion: Speeches to Its Cultured Despisers*.

3.3 Spinozistic Traits in Schleiermacher's Further Thought

Though a number of works have examined particular aspects of Schleiermacher's study of Spinoza, a comprehensive study of the influence of Spinoza on Schleiermacher's mature thought has yet to be conducted.[45] The following sections will give a short outline of Spinozistic traits in two main fields of Schleiermacher's work.

First, the Spinozistic basis of Schleiermacher's early philosophy of religion in *Speeches* is outlined. In a second approach the systematic output of his Spinoza studies in epistemological and metaphysical decisions is shown following the lectures on Dialectic.

---

[43] *Spin.Sys.*, p. 574. Cf. Ellsiepen, *Anschauung des Universums und Scientia Intuitiva*, pp. 238–245.

[44] *Spin.Sys.*, p. 575: "der absolute Stoff ist fähig die Form eines jeden Vorstellungsvermögens anzunehmen, er besitz bei der vollkomnen unmittelbaren Nichtvorstellbarkeit eine unendliche (mittelbare) Vorstellbarkeit."

[45] See Julia A. Lamm, *The Living God: Schleiermacher's Theological Appropriation of Spinoza* (University Park, PA: Pennsylvania State University Press, 1996); Katharina Gutekunst, *Die Freiheit des Subjekts bei Schleiermacher. Eine Analyse im Horizont der Debatte um die Willensfreiheit in der analytischen Philosophie* (Berlin: De Gruyter, 2019); Peter Grove, *Deutungen des Subjekts. Schleiermachers Philosophie der Religion* (Berlin: De Gruyter, 2004); Ellsiepen, *Anschauung des Universums und Scientia Intuitiva*; and Ellsiepen, "Gott und Welt. Der Spinozismus von Schleiermachers 'Dialektik,'" in *Christentum–Staat–Kultur*, ed. Andreas Arndt, Ulrich Barth, and Wilhelm Gräb (Berlin: De Gruyter, 2008), pp. 91–108. With regard to Spinoza's influence on Schleiermacher's philosophical ethics and the *Glaubenslehre* there remains a need for further research.

3.3.1 The Concept of *Anschauung des Universums*: Spinozistic Roots of Schleiermacher's Early Philosophy of Religion

Schleiermacher explicitly indicates his adoration for Spinoza in his *Speeches*. It is the first and the second name to be mentioned in his little booklet that inaugurated a new era in theology.[46] This indication is not simply a gesture demonstrating the avant-garde character of his thinking but is rooted in a deeper philosophical understanding. The new concept of religion as the heart of the *Speeches* can only be fully understood in relation to its Spinozistic foundation.[47] In fact, his explicit reference to Spinoza corresponds to a systematic influence.

Schleiermacher's concept of religion in the *Speeches* is focused on the term *Anschauung des Universums*. The Spinozistic features of this concept become especially conspicuous when one considers Schleiermacher's understanding of the term *Universum*. The complement of religious *Anschauung* is not *Universum* itself but more precisely its expression— *Darstellung des Universums*.[48] We can see this by examining which fields of religious contemplation (*religiöse Anschauung*) Schleiermacher provides for his readers in the second speech: nature and humanity.[49] Furthermore, in the disposition of exterior nature and inner life of humanity we can see another influence of Spinoza. The twofold expression of the world in extension and thought in the way Schleiermacher understands Spinoza corresponds to this disposition of exterior nature and the inner life of humanity in the *Speeches*.[50]

First, Schleiermacher discusses the manner in which religion contemplates "exterior nature."[51] Religion is not the human impression of how pleasantly or exaltedly nature is experienced, because this would only be a subjective emotive reflection that does not sufficiently take the dimension of "the whole"[52] into account. To view nature through the perspective of its laws, and in particular the laws of dynamic interdependence that Schleiermacher sees in the contemporary chemical modelling of nature, could take us further. Here, everything appears to be interconnected with everything else; nothing is separated, and nothing is the same. Individuality is relative to the dynamic process in which it is interwoven. To see a concrete individual occurrence in these laws means to see it as a relative merging of forces in the infinite dynamic sphere of nature. This is the same

---

[46] Cf. footnote 1; see *Reden*¹, pp. 54f, 128. The page numbering again follows the original 1799 edition.

[47] Ellsiepen, *Anschauung des Universums und Scientia Intuitiva*.

[48] Ellsiepen, *Anschauung des Universums und Scientia Intuitiva*, p. 350. Barth, "Was heißt 'Anschauung des Universums'?," p. 257.

[49] Ellsiepen, *Anschauung des Universums und Scientia Intuitiva*, pp. 311–349.

[50] This will be even fundamental for Schleiermacher's system of knowledge as presented in his lectures on Dialectic. Cf. *Dial.*, p. 196; and his philosophical ethics, in Friedrich Schleiermacher, *Schleiermachers Werke*, 4 vols., ed. Otto Braun (Leipzig: Felix Meiner, 1927/1928), vol. 2: *Entwürfe zu Einem System der Sittenlehre; Nach den Handschriften Schleiermachers*, ed. by Otto Braun (Leipzig: Felix Meiner, 1927/1928), pp. 248f, 532.

[51] *Reden*¹, p. 78.

[52] *Reden*¹, pp. 80f.

concept of individuality that was present in the early Spinoza studies. Such a religious consideration of nature sees "not only in every change but in all existence itself nothing other than a work of this spirit and an expression [*Darstellung*] and execution of these laws, only for him everything visible will be the actual world, formed [*gebildet*], permeated by the divinity, and one."[53] We notice here again a threefold structure. Interdependent individuals are seen as a manifestation of the laws of nature, which are penetrated and formed by the "Deity," which in turn stands for the principle of unity in this manifold world. Schleiermacher in this instance unfolds his theory of indirect inherence with respect to and including the indirect manifestation (*Darstellung*) that he has come upon through his Spinoza studies.

As a second sphere of religious contemplation, Schleiermacher presents the inner life of humanity.[54] Humanity for Schleiermacher cannot be reduced to merely intellectual or utilitarian features. He understands humanity as a qualitative term that combines general with specific connotations. Its realm is the mental sphere in the broader sense of the word, embracing both intellectual and sensual life. The inner mental life of humanity is thus contrasted with the exterior life of nature. In the context of the anthropological debate of his time, Schleiermacher associates humanity with a pedagogic aspect.[55] Humanity does not merely describe what humankind is but rather how it should develop. Thus, Schleiermacher points out that humanity is in the process of *Bildung* (education or formation), which comprises individual human development in its social relations and in its dynamic character as history.

Human individuality in this sense reflects a distinct, individual unfolding of general human gifts. In contrast to Wilhelm von Humboldt, Schleiermacher does not conceive of *Bildung* as a promotion of individual gifts, but rather individuality is found in the specific development of common human dispositions.[56] This concept of human individuality is not a subtraction-model but rather a constellation-model. That is, it is not the characteristics that are exclusive to one human being alone that are individual. Rather, what all have in common, but one has in a specific way or in a specific "mixture,"[57] are more properly said to be individual.[58] Here Schleiermacher transposes his model of individuation into the study and analysis of human mind and human development. His rejection of a substantial individuality in the sphere of human development reflects his Spinozistic insight that all individual determination is nothing but the modification of the one substance. But what is the "inner life of humanity" in a human individual? Life means polarity,[59] and human inner life unfolds in the

---

[53] *Reden*[1], p. 87.

[54] See *Reden*[1], pp. 87–104 (page numbering following the 1799 edition). For Schleiermacher's view of humanity see also his *Soliloquies* (*Monologen*), published in 1800.

[55] Cf. Johann Gottfried Herder, *Auch eine Philosophie der Geschichte zur Bildung der Menschheit* (1774) and *Ideen zur Philosophie der Geschichte der Menschheit* (1784); and Wilhelm von Humboldt, *Theoriefragment zur Bildung des Menschen* (1793).

[56] Cf. Ursula Frost, *Das Bildungsverständnis Schleiermachers und Humboldts im Kontext der Frühromantik*, in *200 Jahre Reden über die Religion*, ed. Ulrich Barth and Claus-Dieter Osthövener (Berlin: De Gruyter, 2000), pp. 859–77; at pp. 861–64.

[57] See *Reden*[1], pp. 92f, 98; and *Monologen*[1], pp. 40, 57.

[58] Cf. CG1, §17.2: "Denn jeder Mensch hat alles das, was der andere, aber alles anders."

[59] Cf. Christof Ellsiepen, "Der Begriff des Lebens bei Friedrich Schleiermacher," in *Das Leben. Historisch-systematische Studien zur Geschichte eines Begriffs*, vol. 1, ed. Petra Bahr and Stephan Schaede (Tübingen: Mohr Siebeck, 2009), pp. 487–507.

polarity of attracting and absorbing on the one hand and repulsing and exuding on the other hand.[60] The coalescing point (*Vereinigungspunkt*) of these polar forces determines a human individual soul.[61]

As a relative coalescing point, however, each individual also stands in relation with (all) others, because the polarity of absorbing and exuding lives within the reciprocal interaction with others. Hence, for Schleiermacher the formation (*Bildung*) of human individuality is essentially social.[62] Humanity is not only a promotion of human gifts—which appear in every individual in a specific modification—but humanity gains a social and collective sense. Humanity is the entirety of human mental interaction in which every human individual takes part.[63]

In this regard, humanity is not at all static but it is a dynamically corresponding and developing world of vivid interactive forces. Consequently, Schleiermacher links humanity with history. Humanity manifests itself in a historic process that results in a progression of an "individual, composite, in many ways intertwined, and elevated life."[64] Religious contemplation perceives all individual mental interaction as the work of an inner force of *Bildung* inherent to the whole of humanity in its history: The individual souls as well as their social and historical development are thus contemplated as the work of the *Weltgeist*,[65] or the spirit that enacts all.

Here once again the underlying idea is that of a tripartite structure. Human individuals participate in humanity through the total dynamic sphere of mental interaction. As such, for religious contemplation each individual appears as a distinctive qualitative expression of humanity on the one hand and as a part of the whole of humanity on the other hand. Both aspects are reflected and coalesce in Schleiermacher's concept of *Darstellung* of humanity in the individual development of a human being. Furthermore, humanity as a whole is a modification of the *Weltgeist*. Religious contemplation sees in humanity the complexion of individuality, totality and oneness. Within humanity one can consider the *Bildung* of the human individual as a *Darstellung* of humanity both in its dynamic and participative aspect.

As noted above, Schleiermacher sees both nature and humanity as objects for religious contemplation because in both one finds a complexion and correlation of individuality and totality. They are bound together in the Spinozistic view of finite individuals whose actions participate in an infinite dynamic world and are together seen as the expression of the one "spirit." This threefold structure of indirect inherence, indirect manifestation, and a

---

[60] The polarity of attraction and repulsion that Schleiermacher found as a general law in exterior nature is here transformed into the mental sphere. Cf. *Reden*[1], p. 6: "Jede menschliche Seele ... ist nur ein Produkt zweier entgegengesetzter Triebe. Der eine ist das Bestreben alles was sie umgiebt an sich zu ziehen ... Der andere ist die Sehnsucht ihr eigenes inneres Selbst von innen heraus immer weiter auszudehnen."

[61] See *Reden*[1], p. 5: "Jedes Leben ist nur das Resultat eines beständigen Aneignens und Abstoßens, jedes Ding hat nur dadurch sein bestimmtes Dasein, daß es die beiden Urkräfte der Natur, das durstige an sich ziehen und das rege Selbst verbreiten, auf eine eigenthümliche Art vereinigt und festhält."

[62] Cf. *Reden*[1], p. 237; and *Monologen*[1], pp. 17, 21, 47, 78, 126.

[63] *Reden*[1], pp. 71, 94; and *Monologen*[1], pp. 49f.

[64] *Reden*[1], p. 103.

[65] *Reden*[1], pp. 103, 107, 237; and *Monologen*[1], p. 87.

correlation of individuality and totality is implied in Schleiermacher's concept of *Darstellung des Universums*.

Thus, if the *Darstellung des Universums* is the content of religious contemplation, it is clear in consequence that religious contemplation must always begin with sensory experience of finite things. Religious contemplation is never able to "see" or "feel" the Unconditioned One itself apart from experiencing finite things. With this argumentation Schleiermacher adheres to the transcendental criticism that religion does not superpose sensory experience.

Nevertheless, religious contemplation adds something to "normal" "sensory contemplation" (*sinnliche Anschauung*). In religious contemplation finite things—material or mental occurrences—are contemplated *as* individuals existing as part of an infinite dynamic whole. Its purpose thus is hermeneutic. Religious contemplation construes[66] something *as* some thing and thus gives sense to the experienced reality. But on the other hand, it is here a specific religious sense, distinguished from regular intellectual sense-making, which is added to sensory experience: What makes the contemplation religious is seeing things in the relation of individual part and infinite whole. Thus, religious contemplation is both more than sensory feeling and other than intellectual determination.

Following Schleiermacher's argument in his *Speeches*, one can say individuality is a religious idea.[67] It cannot be seen or experienced sensorily; instead, it is religion that adds to the finite the sense of being itself a dynamic part of a dynamic infinite whole. And accordingly, totality, as the correlate of individuality in the expression of the one in the whole, is inferred from religion.

Religious contemplation is a construal of our sensory experience. It is a profound hermeneutics of the finite individual.[68] It construes the finite as a manifestation of the infinite and as such as a part of an infinite complex sphere. The finite is thus construed at the same time as an individual and as part of a totality. It was Schleiermacher's Spinozistic insight that both aspects belong together, namely that finite individuality and infinite totality correlate with and one cannot separate one from the other. Perhaps that is why Schleiermacher has chosen *Universum* to explain his theory of religion, since there both aspects are considered without separation. This moreover gave Schleiermacher's early theory of religion an ambiguity, which he most likely perceived himself. In his further work in Dialectic he therefore distinguishes the concepts of *God* and *World*.

---

[66] In German the term *deuten* has largely been approved to determine the status of religious mental action. Cf. Ulrich Barth, "Was ist Religion? Sinndeutung zwischen Erfahrung und Letztbegründung," in *Religion in der Moderne* (Tübingen: Mohr Siebeck, 2003); Barth, *Aufgeklärter Protestantismus*; Grove, *Deutungen des Subjekts*; and Jörg Lauster, *Religion als Lebensdeutung. Theologische Hermeneutik heute* (Darmstadt: Wissenschaftliche Buchgesellschaft, 2005).

[67] Ellsiepen, *Anschauung des Universums und Scientia Intuitiva*, p. 380.

[68] Ellsiepen, *Anschauung des Universums und Scientia Intuitiva*, pp. 376–381.

3.3.2 The Correlation of God and World: Spinozistic Thought in Schleiermacher's Dialectic

From 1811 onward Schleiermacher lectured seven times on Dialectic as a member of the Royal Academy of Sciences in Berlin. Although none of these manuscripts was published in his own lifetime, several of these works, along with some listener transcripts, have been preserved.[69] Schleiermacher understood dialectic as the foundational epistemological-metaphysical discipline that underlies other fields of scholarly inquiry, and it is here that the main shift to his mature thought can be found. In contrast to *Speeches* where he joined the concepts of "God" and "World" into the concept of *Universum*, his lectures on Dialectic clearly distinguish between them. Here, as Wilhelm Dilthey has put it, Schleiermacher "reiterates Spinoza's intention on the level of transcendental philosophy."[70]

In the manuscript of the 1822 lecture a definition of both terms is given: "God = unity excluding all oppositions; world = unity including all oppositions."[71] In order to understand this dense formula it is necessary to first determine which "oppositions" (*Gegensätze*) are hereby indicated and what their unity in the idea of God implies for Schleiermacher's theory of knowledge. A comparison with Spinoza's system will then help to gauge the influence of Spinoza in this field.

There are three top-level oppositions ("höchste Gegensätze") that in Schleiermacher's Dialectic mark the distinction of God and World. The first is the opposition of thinking and being. The unity of thinking and being in the idea of God is the necessary basis of the correspondence of thought and its content. In terms of a larger philosophy of knowledge, this implies the correlation of epistemology and ontology. Schleiermacher here anchors the axiomatic setting of the correlation of idea and *ideatum* in Spinoza's system.[72]

The second opposition is that of real and ideal being. The unity of both in the idea of God is the necessary basis of the polar interaction of sensory and intellectual function in thought. In terms of the philosophy of knowledge, this implies the coordination and coequality of physics (natural sciences) and ethics (humanities), which is significant for Schleiermacher's view. Schleiermacher here pursues the understanding of the so-called parallelism as a diversity of perspectives founded in Spinoza's concept of attributes (*extensio* and *cogitatio*).

The third opposition is that of universality and individuality. Their unity in the idea of God is the necessary basis of the correlation of conceptual thinking and judgment (*begriffliches und urteilendes Denken*). Judgment combines concepts, and conceptual thinking classifies ideas that result from judgments. Thus, speculative and

---

[69] See *Dial.* The only existing English translation is not based on the KGA edition *Dial.* See *Dial. (Tice).* See also Ulrich Barth, "Der Letztbegründungsgang der Dialektik," in *Aufgeklärter Protestantismus* (Tübingen: Mohr Siebeck, 2004), pp. 353–85; and Barth, "Was heißt 'Anschauung des Universums'?," p. 246.

[70] Wilhelm Dilthey, *Leben Schleiermachers*, vol. 2, in *Gesammelte Schriften*, vol. 14 (Berlin: De Gruyter, 1966), p. 247.

[71] *Dial.* p. 269.

[72] See Spinoza, *Ethics* part I, ax. 6: "Idea cum suo ideatum debet convenire."

empirical aspects of thinking are bound together. In terms of a philosophy of knowledge this indicates Schleiermacher's rejection of rational theology and its transcendental confirmation. God should not be identified with the boundary concept of the highest power, because this would still imply an opposition to its appearances. Here he again follows Spinoza, holding that "God is both [*natura naturans* and *natura naturata*] and neither of them."[73]

According to Schleiermacher, "Spinoza considers God in his causality but never isolated, and considers World in its dependence, but never isolated."[74] Thus, the strongest influence of Spinozan thought on Schleiermacher is the resulting insight, that God and World are both, distinguished and correlative. One cannot think of God without thinking World and vice versa. Because without the idea of God there would be no unity, without the idea of World there would be no multiplicity in thinking and being. Unity without its relation to multiplicity is senseless, and multiplicity without unity is chaotic. "We cannot presuppose one without the other."[75] This implies the co-extensionality of both ideas. God does not go beyond the world, because then God would enter the realm of being, in opposition to some other thing. Every single part of the infinite world is to be thought as dependent on God. To be in the world is to be in God and from God.

This insight moved Schleiermacher to transform his theory of religion. The second edition of the *Speeches* of 1806 shows a revision and especially his annotations to the third edition of 1822 try to remedy the complaint of pantheism (for Spinoza and for himself) by distinguishing God and World in this particular way. A further study of Spinoza's influence in the subsequent editions of the *Speeches* that reflect the insights of Schleiermacher's Dialectic would be well worth pursuing.[76]

Schleiermacher furthermore developed his systematic theology on the basis of this insight. Thus, his dogmatic handbook *Christian Faith*, in both editions of 1821/22 and 1830, begins with the foundational paragraphs providing the definition of religion as feeling, that is as self-consciousness of absolute dependance relating to God and distinguished from sensory feeling as a consciousness of the relative dependence and relative freedom in existing as part of the world. Both aspects of consciousness are equally constitutive and cannot be separated from one another.[77] The correlation of God and World emerges as the fundamental element

---

[73] See Lecture on history of philosophy, in *Schleiermacher Werke* III, 4.1, p. 277: "diese [unendlichen] modi sind die natura naturata als Inbegriff der Dinge, jene Attribute sind die natura naturans als das sich in diese modos zerspaltende und die Dinge aus sich erzeugende. Gott ist beides und keins von beiden." Ellsiepen, "Gott und Welt," pp. 103–104.

[74] Lecture on history of philosophy 1820, transcript by Saunier, in *Kontexte—Spinoza und die Geschichte der Philosophie*, ed. Henryk Pisarke and Manfred Walther (Wroclaw: Uniwersytetu Wrocławskiego, 2001), pp. 218–220, at p. 219.

[75] *Dial.* p. 249 (transcript 1818/19): "wir können nur fragen: wie denken oder construiren wir uns ihr [der Idee der Welt und der Gottheit] Verhältnis zueinander? Sie sind beide Correlata mit einander, d.h. wir können die eine nicht setzen ohne die andere."

[76] See Barth, "Was heißt 'Anschauung des Universums'?," pp. 245–247; and Friedrich Wilhelm Graf, "Ursprüngliches Gefühl unmittelbarer Koinzidenz des Differenten. Zur Modifikation des Religionsbegriffs in den verschiedenen Auflagen von Schleiermachers 'Reden über die Religion," *Zeitschrift für Theologie und Kirche* 75 (1978), pp. 147–186.

[77] *CG1*, §9; *CG2*, §4.

of Schleiermacher's theory of religion and theological principle even in his mature thought. Thus, a Spinozistic insight remains vital in Schleiermacher's later philosophical and theological approach.[78] A comprehensive study of the influence of Spinoza on Schleiermacher's *Christian Faith* and his philosophical ethics has yet to be conducted.[79]

In summary, one can hardly overestimate the influence of Spinoza for Schleiermacher's approach. It is, nevertheless, a post-Kantian Spinoza that Schleiermacher promotes for his own scientific system, combining transcendental critical thought with Spinoza's ideas of oneness, unity, individuality, and infinity. In this way, Schleiermacher creates a new basis for philosophy and theology that is both modern in its critical and classic in its systematic claim.

Suggested Reading

Ellsiepen, Christof. *Anschauung des Universums und Scientia Intuitiva. Die spinozistischen Grundlagen von Schleiermachers früher Religionstheorie* (Berlin: De Gruyter, 2006).
Ellsiepen, Christof. "Gott und Welt. Der Spinozismus von Schleiermachers 'Dialektik.'" In *Christentum–Staat–Kultur*, ed. Andreas Arndt, Ulrich Barth, and Wilhelm Gräb (Berlin: De Gruyter, 2008), pp. 91–108.
Grove, Peter. *Deutungen des Subjekts. Schleiermachers Philosophie der Religion* (Berlin: De Gruyter, 2004).
Gutekunst, Katharina. *Die Freiheit des Subjekts bei Schleiermacher. Eine Analyse im Horizont der Debatte um die Willensfreiheit in der analytischen Philosophie* (Berlin: De Gruyter, 2019).
Lamm, Julia A. *The Living God: Schleiermacher's Theological Appropriation of Spinoza* (University Park, PA: Pennsylvania State University Press, 1996).

Bibliography

Barth, Ulrich. *Aufgeklärter Protestantismus* (Tübingen: Mohr Siebeck, 2004).
Barth, Ulrich. "Was heißt 'Anschauung des Universums'? Beobachtungen zum Verhältnis von Schleiermacher und Spinoza." In *Affektenlehre und amor Dei intellectualis*, ed. Violetta L. Waibel (Hamburg: Meiner, 2012), pp. 243–266.
Barth, Ulrich. "Was ist Religion? Sinndeutung zwischen Erfahrung und Letztbegründung." In Ulrich Barth, *Religion in der Moderne* (Tübingen: Mohr Siebeck, 2003), pp. 3-28.
Bartuschat, Wolfgang. *Spinozas Theorie des Menschen* (Hamburg: Felix Meiner, 1992).
Dilthey, Wilhelm. *Leben Schleiermachers*, vol. 2. In *Gesammelte Schriften*, vol. 14 (Berlin: De Gruyter, 1966).
Ellsiepen, Christof. *Anschauung des Universums und Scientia Intuitiva. Die spinozistischen Grundlagen von Schleiermachers früher Religionstheorie* (Berlin: De Gruyter, 2006).

---

[78] Ellsiepen, "Gott und Welt"; Barth, "Was heißt 'Anschauung des Universums'?"
[79] Several notable treatments have laid a foundation for these future studies. In her 1996 volume *The Living God*, Lamm traces Spinoza's influence on Schleiermacher in his *Christian Faith*. Grove's 2004 *Deutungen des Subjekts* presents a study with a focus on Schleiermacher's philosophy of religion and mentions evidence of a reception of Spinozan thought. For treatments of the *Speeches* and the Dialectic, see Ellsiepen, *Anschauung des Universums und Scientia Intuitiva*; and Ellsiepen, "Gott und Welt."

Ellsiepen, Christof. "Der Begriff des Lebens bei Friedrich Schleiermacher." In *Das Leben. Historisch-systematische Studien zur Geschichte eines Begriffs*, vol. 1, ed. Petra Bahr and Stephan Schaede (Tübingen: Mohr Siebeck, 2009), pp. 487–507.

Ellsiepen, Christof. "Gott und Welt. Der Spinozismus von Schleiermachers 'Dialektik.'" In *Christentum–Staat–Kultur*, ed. Andreas Arndt, Ulrich Barth, and Wilhelm Gräb (Berlin: De Gruyter, 2008), pp. 91–108.

Graf, Friedrich Wilhelm. "'Ursprüngliches Gefühl unmittelbarer Koinzidenz des Differenten.' Zur Modifikation des Religionsbegriffs in den verschiedenen Auflagen von Schleiermachers 'Reden über die Religion.'" *Zeitschrift für Theologie und Kirche* 75 (1978), pp. 147–186.

Grove, Peter. *Deutungen des Subjekts. Schleiermachers Philosophie der Religion* (Berlin: De Gruyter, 2004).

Jacobi, Friedrich Heinrich. "David Hume über den Glauben, oder Idealismus und Realismus. Ein Gespräch (1787)." In *Werke. Gesamtausgabe*, vol. 2.1: *Schriften zum transzendentalen Idealismus*, ed. Walter Jaeschke (Hamburg: Meiner, 2004), pp. 5–113.

Jacobi, Friedrich Heinrich. *Werke. Gesamtausgabe*, vol. 1.1: *Schriften zum Spinozastreit*, ed. Klaus Hammacher and Irmgard-Maria Piske (Hamburg: Meiner, 1998).

Lauster, Jörg. *Religion als Lebensdeutung. Theologische Hermeneutik heute* (Darmstadt: Wissenschaftliche Buchgesellschaft, 2005).

Pisarke, Henryk, and Manfred Walther, eds. *Kontexte—Spinoza und die Geschichte der Philosophie* (Wroclaw: Uniwersytetu Wrocławskiego, 2001).

Schleiermacher, Friedrich. *Schleiermachers Werke*, 4 vols. Ed. Otto Braun (Leipzig: Felix Meiner, 1927/1928).

Schleiermacher, Friedrich. *Briefwechsel 1774-1796, KGA 5.1*, ed. Andreas Arndt and Wolfgang Virmond *(Berlin: De Gruyter, 1985).*

Spinoza, Baruch de. *Ethica ordine geometrica demonstrata (Opera pusthuma 1677)*. Ed. Konrad Blumenstock, 4th ed. (Darmstadt: Wissenschaftliche Buchgesellschaft, 1989).

Tillich, Paul. *Religion des konkreten Geistes. Friedrich Schleiermacher* (Stuttgart: Evangelisches Verlagswerk, 1968).

CHAPTER 4

THE REFORMED TRADITION

JAN ROHLS

SCHLEIERMACHER's relationship to the Reformed tradition has been judged in various ways. His Swiss pupil in Zurich, Alexander Schweizer, was convinced that in the main his teacher adhered to the Reformed tradition and developed it in a healthy way.[1] Wilhelm Niesel, the later General Secretary of the World Alliance of Reformed Churches, held the opposite view and spoke of an opposition between Schleiermacher's doctrine and the Reformed tradition.[2] Niesel's judgement reflects the broader criticism of Schleiermacher as the primary representative of liberal Protestantism, a claim advanced by his own teacher Karl Barth, who stridently opposed Schweizer's position that Schleiermacher continued the Reformed tradition.[3] More recently, Brian Gerrish has again renewed the claim of Schleiermacher's faithfulness to the Reformed tradition.[4] It is thus clear that the way one judges Schleiermacher's relationship to the Reformed tradition hinges on one's understanding of the Reformed tradition itself. Barth and Niesel refer to the Reformed theology of the Reformation and Protestant Orthodoxy, not accounting for its later development during the Enlightenment. Yet Schleiermacher's understanding of the Reformed tradition was deeply influenced by the Enlightenment. Thus even where he takes up certain aspects of Calvin's theology the treatment is shaped by the later development of Reformed thought. This chapter examines Schleiermacher's complex relationship to the Reformed heritage by considering his treatment of five aspects of the Reformed tradition: the development of Reformed theology; the status and authority of the Reformed confessions; the union between the Reformed and Lutheran church; the constitution and governance of the church; and Reformed teachings on the eucharist, Christ, and predestination.

---

[1] Alexander Schweizer, *Die Glaubenslehre der Evangelisch-reformirten Kirche dargestellt und aus den Quellen belegt*, vol. 1 (Zürich: Orell, Füssli und Comp., 1844), p. 92.
[2] Wilhelm Niesel, "Schleiermachers Verhältnis zur reformierten Tradition," *Zwischen der Zeiten* 8 (1930), pp. 524f.
[3] Heinrich Heppe, *Die Dogmatik der evangelisch-reformierten Kirche*, ed. Ernst Bizer (Neukirchen: Neukirchen Kreis Moers, 1958), pp. ixf.
[4] Brian A. Gerrish, "From Calvin to Schleiermacher: The Theme and the Shape of Christian Dogmatics," in *Internationaler Schleiermacher-Kongreß Berlin 1984*, vol. 2, ed. Kurt-Viktor Selge (Berlin: De Gruyter, 1985), pp. 1038–1049.

4.1 The Historical Development of the Reformed Tradition

Friedrich Schleiermacher was a member of the Reformed Church of Prussia. His father was a Reformed army chaplain in Silesia, responsible for the few Reformed parishes in this newly acquired part of the kingdom of Prussia. The elder Schleiermacher and his family lived in Breslau, the capital of Silesia, where his son was born. Schleiermacher noted that twice a year his father also had to visit the Reformed church members scattered in the province in order to distribute the sacraments.[5] His mother also came from a Reformed background. Her father, Timotheus Christian Stubenrauch, was court chaplain first in Stolpe in Pomerania and afterwards in Berlin, the capital of Prussia. Her brother Ernst Stubenrauch was extraordinary professor of Reformed theology at the university of Halle, then the main university of Prussia, and later became minister in Drossen and Landsberg an der Warthe. Beyond his family circle, Schleiermacher also had close connections to other prominent members of the Reformed church. He was acquainted with Friedrich Samuel Gottfried Sack, the head of the Reformed Church in Prussia and first court chaplain in Berlin. It was Sack who secured for him a position as tutor on the estate of the Reformed count Dohna at Schlobitten in East Prussia, following his first theological examination. Together with Sack he edited a translation of collected sermons by the British preacher Hugh Blair. Moreover, Schleiermacher remained involved in matters concerning the Prussian Reformed church throughout his life. After working as a Reformed preacher at the *Charité* hospital, the main hospital at Berlin, he became a Reformed court chaplain in Stolpe, then extraordinary Professor for Reformed theology at the Lutheran faculty in Halle and, finally, Reformed minister at the *Dreifaltigkeitskirche* (Trinity church) and Reformed professor at the newly founded university of Berlin.

It is beyond doubt, then, that Schleiermacher regarded himself as belonging to the Reformed confession. In an 1817 speech at the university of Berlin on the commemoration of the Reformation he described himself as someone who is more attached to Zwingli's doctrine than to Luther's.[6] And in his second letter to Lücke, written a few years before his death in 1829, he described himself as a theologian belonging to the Reformed school.[7] He not only took his theological examinations in the Reformed church government but was also ordained as a Reformed minister and he signed the Sigismund Confession. The Sigismund Confession was a private confession drafted in 1614 by the Reformed superintendent Füssel, in which the elector Sigismund of Brandenburg declared his reasons for converting from Lutheranism to Calvinism, following the model of the Palatinate. His private confession received official relevance when it became part of the *Corpus Constitutionum Marchicarum*, the book of confessions applicable to the Reformed subjects in Brandenburg-Prussia.[8]

Schleiermacher offered a clear account of his understanding of the Reformed tradition in a chapter concerning the Reformation in his lectures on the history of the Christian church.

---

[5] *KGA* 1.4, p. 385.
[6] *KGA* 1.10, p. 3.
[7] Ibid., p. 337.
[8] *KGA* 3.2, p. 264, n. 2.

He gave these lectures once in Halle 1806 and twice in Berlin 1821–1822 and 1825–1826. He located the background of the Reformation in the Renaissance, and specifically in the appropriation of Greek and Roman antiquity by the humanists, who profited from the emigration of Byzantine scholars to Italy. According to Schleiermacher the most famous representative among these Renaissance humanists was Giovanni Pico della Mirandola, whose work exerted a subtle but important influence upon the Reformation. Schleiermacher thus did not attribute the Reformation exclusively to certain individuals like Luther or Zwingli. Instead he was convinced that broader historical forces were concentrated in these persons.[9] Beyond the cultural transfer from East to West, he noted that the Reformation was made possible by several other factors, such as the ecclesiastical and political conditions in the Holy Roman Empire, the spread of the antischolastic humanism at various newly founded universities, the conflict between humanists like Johann Reuchlin and the theologians of the orders and, finally, Johannes Gutenberg's invention of the printing press. Schleiermacher praised Pico as well as Erasmus of Rotterdam for refusing to identify the Christian faith with any dogmatic belief. Erasmus could accept differences in doctrine so long as their consequences were not practically harmful. At the same time he was interested in the continual reform and purification of doctrine. In this regard Schleiermacher attributed to him the evangelical spirit of the Reformation, arguing that in emphasizing moral practice over doctrinal uniformity Erasmus should be regarded as superior to Luther and the adherents of the Wittenberg Reformation, whose insistence on the unity of the dogma still reflects the Roman Catholic mentality.

According to Schleiermacher the Reformation movement did not start with Luther alone, then, but had three starting points: in Saxony, in Switzerland, and in France. The latter French movement of reform, represented by Faber Stapulensis, played a mediating role between the Saxon and the Swiss reformations. Whereas in Saxon Wittenberg the critique had focused on the abuse of a singular practice, that of indulgences, the Swiss reform in Zurich centered on a consequent purification of all papal elements in the church, going back to its biblical origin. The reform of the doctrine unfolded in similar fashion. While Luther and his followers concentrated on the teaching of justification, Zwingli revised the whole Catholic doctrinal system in his book *De Vera et Falsa Religione* (1525). Zwingli furthermore proceeded in much more critical fashion than the mediating Melanchthon in his *Loci Communes* (1521), though his proposed reforms were still less radical than those of the Italian reformers Petrus Martyr, Girolamo Zanchi, Bernardino Ochino, and Lelio Sozzini, who fled to Switzerland because of the papal inquisition. These Italian reformers, inspired by the rational spirit of humanism, strove for a revision of the entirety of church doctrine by comparing it with the Bible, which finally led them to a critique of the dogma established by the councils of the early church.[10] And despite the strong attacks of the Reformed and the Lutherans their critique was based on the same principle of scriptural interpretation defended by Luther and Zwingli. In including these more radical aspects of the Reformation, Schleiermacher thus rehabilitated and incorporated into the Reformed heritage the more fundamental critique of dogma carried out by the Antitrinitarians and Socinians, whose

---

[9] *KGA* 2.6, p. 629.
[10] Ibid., p. 632.

interpretations bear special significance since they kept to the main point of Christianity in the necessity of Christ's appearance for the salvation of humanity.[11]

4.2 The Status of Reformed Confessions

The broader disagreement between the Lutherans and the Reformed concerned the understanding of the Lord's Supper. In Marburg Zwingli and his Swiss followers represented the more progressive party, opting for a symbolic understanding of the eucharist, which was in turn condemned by Luther and the Augsburg Confession (1530). And despite Calvin's critique of a pure symbolic interpretation and his closer proximity to Luther's view of real presence, the agreement between Geneva and Zurich in the Consensus Tigurinus (1548) led to a second struggle concerning different drafts of the article on the eucharist in the Augsburg Confession.[12] The Lutherans of Jena accused the Lutherans of Wittenberg around Melanchthon of tending towards the Swiss interpretation and supporting "cryptocalvinism," an accusation directed against both their interpretation of the Lord's Supper and, closely connected with it, their Christology. For the radical Lutherans, the so-called Gnesio-Lutherans, the doctrine of the real presence of Christ's flesh and blood in the eucharist rested on the presupposition of the ubiquity of Christ's body, and in the Formula of Concord (1577) the real presence was confessed simply as the affirmation of this ubiquity. According to Schleiermacher the third point of difference between Lutherans and Reformed concerned the doctrine of predestination. While Calvin accepted Augustine's teaching of a double predestination, Zwingli had at least tried to avoid the harsh consequences of this doctrine, with the result that there has never been a uniformity of teaching on this point within the Reformed churches.[13]

Schleiermacher was convinced that the Lutheran doctrine of the ubiquity of Christ's body was the first factor that encouraged the expansion of the Reformed confession in Germany, for the refusal of this position led to the acceptance of the Calvinist interpretation of the Lord's Supper, first in Heidelberg and after that in Bremen. However, the number of Reformed in the territories of the empire also increased due to the migration of Calvinist refugees from the Netherlands during their war with Spain. And Schleiermacher argued that the most relevant factor regarding the increasing acceptance of the Reformed confession in Germany was the conversion of the elector of Brandenburg to Calvinism. In this case it is also significant that his Sigismund Confession supported the Calvinist doctrine of double predestination just as little as the Heidelberg Catechism (1619).[14] As a result of these developments, there existed in the empire two Protestant confessions, the Lutherans and the Reformed. And they differed significantly in their understanding of the confessional documents, which were not as obligatory for the Reformed as for the Lutherans.

Yet even within Lutheranism there existed differences. The Wittenberg orthodoxy insisted on the literal meaning of the Formula of Concord and developed a dogmatic and polemical

---

[11] Ibid., p. 643.
[12] Ibid., p. 645.
[13] Ibid., p. 645.
[14] Ibid., p. 653.

scholasticism against both Catholics and Calvinists. In Helmstedt, by contrast, Lutheran theologians were looking for a common Protestant and Christian principle. This unifying tendency was also present in the more practical, spiritual, and mystical movements within Lutheranism that were represented by Johann Arndt, Valentin Weigel, Jakob Böhme, and the newly emerging movements of Pietism. The Reformed churches also began to splinter in contrary directions. In the Netherlands the Arminians opposed the Calvinist doctrine of the absolute divine decree and individual salvation. They did not deny the necessity of grace but insisted on the human ability to resist grace and the possibility of losing it. Schleiermacher identified this Arminian position with that of the Lutherans in the Formula of Concord. The Synod of Dort (1618–1619) called for a solution to this conflict and invited all Reformed churches; but some did not accept the invitation, among them the churches of Brandenburg and Anhalt, which did not hold to the Calvinistic doctrine of double predestination.[15] In the end, the canons of the synod only had a real effect in the Republic of the Netherlands. Within this dispute Schleiermacher favored the Arminian position, not for dogmatic reasons but because the Arminians did not simply adhere to the confessional books but supported the freedom of exegesis and interpretation regarding dogmatic statements.[16] In this respect he praised Arminians like Simon Episcopius and Hugo Grotius. English Deism and the French Enlightenment also contributed to the victory of this Arminian position in the confessions and also in Germany.[17]

Indeed, judging from his description of the period from the Renaissance to the Enlightenment within his lectures on church history, one might gain the impression that Schleiermacher shared the Arminian position regarding the confessions overall. He welcomed the Arminian freedom from any compulsion with regard to the confessions and from a literal understanding of them. At the same time, however, he opposed a repeal of the old confessions and the introduction of new ones. His reflections on the value and reputation of the confessions in his 1819 article "Ueber den eigenthümlichen Werth und das bindende Ansehen symbolischer Bücher" (On the Distinctive Value and Binding Authority of Symbolic Books) are connected with his engagement with the question of the union between Lutherans and Reformed. As many others of his day, it astonished him that some put the objections of the Enlightenment against the confessions totally aside.[18] He saw this debate in his own time as determined by two different positions. Some regarded the confessions as normative for the public teaching in the church while others viewed them as pure historical documents of the past with no relevance for the present. According to Schleiermacher, however, the bond with the confessions of the past does not entail a corresponding bond with their particular manner of expression. What is decisive is the content, not the letter, of the confessions. It contradicts the Protestant spirit, for example, if the older notions of the last judgement or of the magic work of the devil are taken literally.

Schleiermacher did not, however, support an abrogation and replacement of the old confessions. Although the confessions do not have the same relevance as the Bible,[19] both the confessions and Holy Scripture retain an important connection, as the Bible is the

---

[15] Ibid., p. 659.
[16] Ibid., p. 659f.
[17] Ibid., p. 660.
[18] *KGA* I.10, p. 119.
[19] Ibid., p. 137.

first public and lasting manifestation of the Christian spirit whereas the confessions are the first public and lasting manifestation of the Protestant spirit.[20] Where they differ is that the Bible is directed towards Christians overall, while the confessions by contrast are directed against the Roman Catholic church. Thus whereas the Bible presents the Christian faith itself, the main interest in the confessions lies in the contrast between Protestantism and Catholicism.[21] However, according to Schleiermacher, this is true only for certain confessions like the Augsburg Confession, the "Apologia," and most of the Reformed confessions. It does not hold true for the Formula of Concord or the Canons of Dort, as the aim of these confessions is the resolution of doctrinal quarrels within the Lutheran or Reformed church. Since Schleiermacher was convinced that doctrinal quarrels within the church could never be resolved by a decision of the church government, he welcomed the outcome that not all Lutheran churches accepted the Formula of Concord and not all Reformed churches took up the Canons of Dort. If Protestant confessions in a strict sense are only those that are directed against Roman Catholicism, then these confessions contain all the articles that are fundamental for Protestantism in general. The early confessions of the Reformation era gave the first public expression of the common Protestant spirit in its contrast to the Catholic Church. Thus, in the old Lutheran and Reformed confessions only those articles that formulate the contrast between Protestantism and Catholicism have continued relevance,[22] and Schleiermacher regarded a commitment of Protestant ministers to the old confessions as necessary, as it is a commitment to those articles considered in accordance with the Bible. This approach to accepting the confessions, which is not restricted by a *quatenus*—"insofar as" it is in accordance with the Bible—leaves the doctrinal opinions contained in the confessions quite open to reform.[23] Accepting the confessions thus does not entail acceptance of these doctrinal opinions but rather reflects the recognition that there is a common Protestant spirit articulated in the Lutheran and Reformed confessions despite the doctrinal differences between Lutherans and Reformed. According to Schleiermacher the unity of the church does not depend on confessional uniformity, since even in the Reformed church different doctrinal opinions, such as Zwinglian and Calvinist positions, exist side by side without destroying the unity of the church.

4.3 The Union between Lutheran and Reformed

Schleiermacher thus did not advocate for a new confession to unite the Lutherans and Reformed, as he did not regard the differing rituals and doctrinal opinions of the Lutheran and Reformed as dividing the Protestant church. This somewhat relativizing approach to the significance of confessions in the Reformed tradition is reflected in his support for the official union between Lutherans and Reformed. Already in his 1804 text "Über die Trennung

---

[20] Ibid., pp. 138f.
[21] Ibid., p. 139.
[22] Ibid., p. 141.
[23] Ibid., p. 142.

der beiden protestantischen Kirchen" (On the Separation of the Two Protestant Churches) he recommended the union because of the disadvantages of the previous separation of the Lutheran and the Reformed church in Prussia. The majority of its inhabitants were Lutherans and only a minority were Reformed, and the Reformed themselves were again split into a majority of German-Reformed and a minority of French-Reformed. Further, in this early treatise Schleiermacher maintained that a union of Lutherans and Reformed did not require uniformity in doctrine, liturgical rites, or constitution.[24] For him the ideal of a church union was found in the Moravians, the *Herrnhuter Brüdergemeine*, where Lutherans and Reformed were accepted without giving up their specific confessions. He therefore welcomed the appeal for the union by the Prussian king Friedrich Wilhelm III on the occasion of the anniversary of the Reformation in 1817. The king argued that the existing differences between Lutherans and Reformed were merely of minor importance, and that the union would be in accordance with the intention of the Reformers and the spirit of Protestantism. The Reformed courts in the empire, especially the electors of Palatine following their conversion to Calvinism, had always been interested in such a union, mainly for political reasons. The electors of Brandenburg, who were Calvinists themselves, had the same interest because the majority of their subjects were Lutherans.

In Schleiermacher's time the court chaplain August Friedrich Wilhelm Sack, one of the heads of the so-called *Neologie*, the Protestant theology of the Enlightenment, strongly supported the union, as did his son Friedrich Samuel Gottfried Sack in his 1812 treatise "Über die Vereinigung der beiden protestantischen Kirchen" (On the Union of the Two Protestant Churches). Thus Schleiermacher's defense of the union was in line with the Reformed tradition. It contrasted, however, with the position of Lutheran confessionalism represented by Claus Harms, who received support from Christoph Friedrich von Ammon, the main court chaplain at Dresden, in his 1818 pamphlet "Bittere Arznei wider die Glaubensschwäche in unserer Zeit" (Bitter Medicine for the Sickness of Faith in Our Time). Harms was an enemy of the union and declared that the only correct interpretation of the Bible was that framed by the Lutheran confessions. In his view the difference between Lutherans and Reformed was fundamental: a union was impossible.[25] In that same year Schleiermacher published his reply, "An Herrn Oberhofprediger D. Ammon über seine Prüfung der Harmsischen Sätze" (To Court Chaplain D. Ammon on His Examination of Harms' Theses). He opposed Harms' thesis that the Lutheran confessions constitute the fixed norm for the interpretation of the Bible and all dogmatic questions, a view he regarded no longer Protestant but Roman Catholic.[26] He also defended the Reformed tradition against its devaluation by Harms and Ammon. Both viewed the Reformed as far too interested in clear concepts and convincing proofs, thus as too rational. They also criticized Reformed worship as lacking all that appeals to the senses such as music and images. Schleiermacher, however, praised the rationality of Reformed theology, and he quotes Zwingli who accepted images in the church if there was no longer any danger of worshipping them.[27] He furthermore rejects the reproach that the Reformed are intolerant, pointing to the conflict between Remonstrants and Counter-Remonstrants in the Netherlands. In the end the Remonstrants were tolerated in

---

[24] *KGA* 1.4, pp. 369f.
[25] *KGA* 1.10, p. 437.
[26] Ibid., p. 27.
[27] Ibid., pp. 35f.

the Republic as a separate church alongside the main church of the Counter-Remonstrants, which was composed of Calvinist hardliners. Indeed, he argues, Lutherans had been far more intolerant if one looks at the cryptocalvinist quarrels.[28] And while Ammon had insisted that full church communion demands agreement and total consensus in all articles of faith, Schleiermacher denied this by referring to the differing understandings of the Lord's Supper in the case of Zwingli and Calvin, which did not prevent communion between Zurich and Geneva.[29] In addition, he regarded the difference between Lutherans and Reformed on several points of doctrine as a legitimate form of pluralism within Protestantism.[30]

4.4 The Constitution and Governance of the Church

Schleiermacher thus supported the union between Lutherans and Reformed. Yet he criticized the manner in which it was carried out in Prussia, which he regarded as contradicting fundamental principles of Reformed church government. The background to his protest was the king's introduction of a new order of worship in 1821 concerning the use of Berlin cathedral by both the Reformed and the Lutherans—"Kirchenagende für die Königlich Preußische Armee" (Ecclesiastical Order of Worship for the Royal Prussian Army). In his subsequent 1824 treatise "Über das liturgische Recht evangelischer Landesfürsten" (On the Liturgical Law of Evangelical Rulers), Schleiermacher argued that the sovereign does not have the right to interfere in the inner matters of the church. The right to arrange worship, the *ius liturgicum*, belongs to the congregation alone.[31] Schleiermacher quoted not only the Augsburg Confession and the "Apology" but also specific Reformed confessions like the Gallican Confession (1559), the Belgic Confession (1559), and the second Helvetic Confession (1562). These confessions attribute to the sovereign the right to punish violations of the first tablet of the Law, that is the defense of religion and the protection of the church, but not the right to participate in the church government. Schleiermacher did not deny that the *ius liturgicum* was exercised by the sovereigns since the beginning of the Reformation in Protestant territories. He argued, however, that this could not be justified by the territorial system (*Territorialsystem*) which regards this privilege to be part of the majesty's right. According to Schleiermacher it could only be justified by the so-called collegial system (*Kollegialsystem*) of ecclesiastical law, according to which the church is defined as an independent association with the power to transmit a treaty to the sovereign, who in turn names persons who exercise church government in his name. Already in his 1808 text "Vorschlag zu einer neuen Verfassung der protestantischen Kirche im preußischen Staat" (Suggestion for a New Constitution of the Protestant Church in the State of Prussia), written for the Prussian minister Heinrich Friedrich Karl vom und zum Stein, Schleiermacher complained of the church's total dependence on the state.[32] He wanted to restrict the state's governance over the

---

[28] Ibid., p. 36.
[29] Ibid., p. 59.
[30] Ibid., pp. 71f.
[31] *KGA* 1.9, p. 217.
[32] Ibid., p. 3.

church to the supervisory role indicated by the expression *ius maiestaticum circa sacra*: the rights of the sovereign, as regards the church and any other association, includes forbidding all subversive activities. However, the administration of the inner matters of the church—*ius sacrorum*—belongs in the hands of independent church institutions.

Schleiermacher's "Suggestion" still supported a mixture of episcopal and Presbyterian elements in the church constitution. In his subsequent 1817 treatise "Über die für die protestantische Kirche des preußischen Staats einzurichtende Synodalverfassung" (On the Synod Constitution to be Established for the Protestant Church in the Prussian State) he proposed local presbyteries and assemblies of ministers and elders in synods as a supplement to the consistory.[33] Yet Schleiermacher regarded the consistorial constitution as a merely provisional arrangement because of the unhealthy mixture between church and state.[34] In his view there remained two alternative forms of constitution within the Protestant church: the episcopal and the Presbyterian constitutions. The first is typical for those territories where bishops played a part in carrying out the Reformation, such as England and Sweden. The Presbyterian constitution, by contrast, prevailed in those countries in which the Protestant church was established without the help of the sovereign.[35] Schleiermacher argued that the difference between higher and lower clergy, which characterizes the episcopal constitution, has no basis in Scripture. Furthermore, such a distinction opposes the equality of all clergy, which is a point taught by many Reformed confessions. In the end therefore Schleiermacher regarded the Presbyterian constitution as the only form adequate for the Protestant church because this was the constitution Protestantism gave itself when it was not supported by the sovereign, as was the case with the Reformed church in France.[36]

This support for a Presbyterian constitution places Schleiermacher within a Reformed tradition going back to Calvin and his French followers. Whereas Zwingli in Zurich established a state church, the form of church discipline exercised by Calvin and municipal authorities in Geneva depended on a separation of ecclesiastical and political jurisdiction. Church discipline rested in the hands of elders (*anciens*), who together with the ministers (*pasteurs*), formed the consistory (*consistoire*). In the Reformed church of France this local model was transformed into a hierarchical model leading from the local consistory to the national synod. This French model was then taken over by Dutch Calvinists who settled as refugees in the territory of Jülich-Kleve-Berg, that is in those parts of the Rhineland that became part of Brandenburg early in the seventeenth century. In the Western territories of Prussia this Presbyterian constitution survived and was taken as a model by Schleiermacher. Still, the question of church governance and church constitution never played a decisive role regarding the separation of the Lutheran and the Reformed churches. The relevant points of disagreement were the understanding of the Lord's Supper and, closely connected with this, Christology and the doctrine of predestination. According to the Lutherans, disagreement concerning these points prevented the unity of the church. Yet for Schleiermacher, as a supporter of the union between Lutherans and Reformed, these doctrinal disputes lost their power to divide. His principal dogmatic work, *Der christliche Glaube*, is not a Reformed dogmatics but a description of the Christian faith according to the principles of the evangelical

---

[33] Ibid., p. 120.
[34] Ibid., p. 258.
[35] Ibid., p. 263.
[36] Ibid., p. 267.

church on the whole. Even so, and despite his support of the union, Schleiermacher always stressed that within this unified church he remained a Reformed theologian.[37] Thus one may ask whether and in what sense this Reformed background influenced his treatment of those doctrinal disputes separating the Lutherans and Reformed.

4.5 THE DOCTRINES OF THE EUCHARIST, CHRISTOLOGY, AND PREDESTINATION

Schleiermacher's treatment of the Lord's Supper begins with the conviction that Christians who take part in the eucharist experience a specific strengthening of their spiritual life as they are offered Christ's body and blood. As regards the connection between bread and wine on one hand and body and blood on the other, the evangelical church opposes first of all the Roman Catholic position that Christ's body and blood are really present independent from activities of eating and drinking. But it also opposes those views that would entirely dissolve any connection between the physical consumption of the elements and the spiritual consumption of Christ.[38] For Schleiermacher such a position is not that of Zwingli but of the Socinians and those who regard the Lord's Supper simply as a sign of confession. Zwingli, by contrast, insisted upon the connection between spiritual consumption and the Lord's Supper as a sign of confession and grateful memory. Since its beginning, two contrary positions concerning the Lord's Supper existed in the evangelical church: that of Luther and that of Zwingli. Whereas Luther's position approached the Roman Catholic view, Zwingli's tended to the Socinian position. Calvin's understanding of the Lord's Supper marked an attempt to find a middle course between the two.

Schleiermacher regarded Luther's literal understanding of the words of institution as unacceptable because the tradition of interpreting the words varies. For this reason he accepted the symbolic understanding of these words, supported by the Reformed in contrast to the Lutherans. He regarded Zwingli's interpretation, according to which Christ connects spiritual consumption with the consumption of the elements, as the clearest position, but also as a very poor one.[39] With Luther, Calvin recognized the real presence of Christ, which does not involve a spiritual consumption of Christ that takes place independently of the Lord's Supper, but rather the reality of his Christ's body and blood made present in a unique way. This presence, however, is tied to the spiritual acceptance of Christ in faith. Schleiermacher criticized Luther not only because his position approached the Roman Catholic understanding of the eucharist but also because he was unable to explain the relationship between sacramental consumption, on one hand, and the physical consumption of the elements and the spiritual consumption of Christ on the other. Yet Schleiermacher also regarded Calvin as having the same problem, and for this reason he did not expect the Calvinist understanding to prevail in the Protestant church. Instead he was convinced that further exegesis of the biblical texts would lead to an entirely new understanding of the Lord's Supper.

---

[37] *KGA* 1.10, p. 337.
[38] *CG(Redeker)*, vol. 2, pp. 347–349.
[39] Ibid., pp. 353f.

For his own part, Schleiermacher did not distinguish sacramental consumption from the physical and spiritual consumption of the body and blood. For him the spiritual nourishment that occurs outside the Lord's Supper also takes place within it,[40] strengthening the spiritual life of the believers and their community with Christ. The unworthy consumption of the Lord's Supper, on the contrary, excludes this strengthening and community. Thus Schleiermacher, in accordance with the Reformed tradition, did not speak of an unworthy consumption of Christ's body and blood, but only of the Lord's Supper. According to Schleiermacher the confessional difference between Lutherans and Reformed regarding this *manducatio impiorum* will eventually disappear in the ongoing development of the church. In its perfect form, the church will no longer know an unworthy consumption of the Lord's Supper.[41]

Closely connected with the doctrine of the eucharist is Christology, which marks the second doctrinal point separating the Lutherans and Reformed. The Lutherans developed the theory of the ubiquity of Christ's body as a presupposition to their doctrine of the real presence of Christ's body and blood in the Lord's Supper. Within the framework of the christological dogma of Christ's two natures they declared that Christ's human nature takes part in the properties, or *idiomata*, of his divine nature. Thus it participates in the ubiquity that belongs by essence to his divine nature. The Reformed opposed this doctrine because they thought that it abolished the integrity of Christ's human nature, which is finite and therefore spatially limited.

Schleiermacher's own theology, however, does not adhere to the Christology of Reformed orthodoxy. Instead, he explicitly criticized the doctrine of the two natures of Christ, arguing that Jesus of Nazareth, as a historical individual and at the same time the ideal of human piety, is like us through the identity of human nature, yet differs from us due to the strength of his consciousness of God. Schleiermacher referred to this complete consciousness of God as the peculiar being of God in Jesus, thus replacing the traditional assumption of a divine nature in Christ. He furthermore insisted upon a subsequent critical treatment of the traditional christological formulas on the basis of this new view of the person of Christ, a treatment that might retain some elements while eliminating others. Thus the preexistence of the Son of God, and with it the whole doctrine of the immanent Trinity, is to be set aside along with the christological theory of the union of the second divine person with human nature. This entails a fundamental revision of the dogmas of Nicea and Chalcedon, which were accepted and presupposed by the Reformed orthodoxy.[42] The critique of the doctrine of the two natures in Christ implies a rejection of the theory of the communication of properties between Christ's divine nature and the human nature.[43] Yet Schleiermacher shared the Reformed criticism of the Lutheran doctrine of the ubiquity of Christ's body because it undermined the integrity of the human nature of Christ.[44] This does not, however, mean that Schleiermacher shared the Reformed position on the whole.[45] Instead he rejected the christological positions of both the Reformed and the Lutherans because they

---

[40] Ibid., pp. 343f.
[41] Ibid., pp. 362f.
[42] Ibid., p. 51.
[43] Ibid., p. 74.
[44] Ibid., p. 75.
[45] Ibid., p. 76.

divide Christ by ascribing opposing divine and human attributes to him. In this respect, he preferred the Reformed position only under the presupposition of the orthodox Christology.

The third point of contention between the two confessions concerned the doctrine of predestination. The fact that Schleiermacher wrote a special treatise on this doctrine, his 1819 "Über die Lehre von der Erwählung" (On the Doctrine of the Election), reveals his interest in this question. The treatise was a reply to the "Aphorismen über die Union der beiden evangelischen Kirchen in Deutschland" (Aphorisms on the Union of both Protestant Churches in Germany), written by Karl Gottlieb Bretschneider, the Lutheran superintendent of Gotha. In his treatise Bretschneider declared that the article of the Formula of Concord that concerns the resistance of human nature to divine grace and the total inability of human persons to improve themselves contradicts the doctrine of election affirmed in the same confession.[46] According to Bretschneider the consequence of this position leads to the Calvinist doctrine of predestination, and to avoid this conclusion Lutherans should drop it and instead defend the freedom of will. In contrast to Bretschneider, Schleiermacher asked the Lutherans to stick to the Augustinian doctrine that the human person is unable to will the good, and as a natural consequence to accept the Calvinist doctrine of predestination. He regarded the Lutheran theory in the Formula of Concord as contradictory.[47] He furthermore sought to refute all of the objections brought forward by Bretschneider against the Calvinist doctrine. However, he did not revive the orthodox Reformed doctrine of predestination and he opposed the synod of Dort.[48] In particular, he rejected the Reformed orthodox dogma of an unconditioned absolute divine decree, as such a *decretum horribile* is not implied in the Confession of Sigismund.[49] Schleiermacher did not conceive of election and reprobation as directed toward particular individuals but as one divine decree concerning the entire created order, in which humanity will be reborn successively through the work of the Spirit. Thus, there is only one decree, a decree of divine love, which does not allow for the eternal damnation of particular individuals or their exclusion from the condition of the blessed.[50] The older Calvinist doctrine of double predestination, according to which only some will be saved while the rest will be eternally condemned to hell, is thus replaced by the doctrine of universal salvation. Accordingly, instead of a distinction between the elect and the damned, Schleiermacher distinguishes between those incorporated earlier and later into the reign of God.[51]

Schleiermacher's revision of the Calvinist doctrine of predestination reveals the significant manner in which the Reformed heritage continued to play a role in his dogmatics, despite his support for the union of Lutherans and Reformed. Indeed, even the starting point of his dogmatics is influenced by this heritage. For the idea of an unconditioned divine predestination corresponds to the concept of piety as the feeling of absolute dependence. Like Zwingli Schleiermacher conceives God as absolute causality, and like Calvin he begins with the *sensus divinitatis* as the consciousness of absolute dependence. This concept of absolute dependence is also reminiscent of Johann Friedrich Stapfer's "Grundlegung zur

---

[46] *KGA* 1.10, p. 151.
[47] Ibid., pp. 221f.
[48] Ibid., p. 220.
[49] Ibid., p. 197.
[50] Ibid., p. 216.
[51] Ibid., p. 218.

wahren Religion" (Foundation of True Religion) (1746), in which Stapfer, a Swiss pupil of Christian Wolff, defines religion as the total dependence on God by using the neologism *Abhänglichkeit*.[52] Here, then, as with all other articles of faith, Schleiermacher had no interest in a simple restoration of Reformed orthodoxy. Generally he accepted the objections brought forward by the theologians of the Enlightenment against the traditional dogmatic positions of Protestant orthodoxy, and his own concept of God as well as his concept of piety are, in spite of his denial of a fundamental connection between his dogmatics and philosophy, strongly influenced by modern philosophical developments, and especially by the work of Spinoza. Whoever wishes to take up the question of whether and how far Schleiermacher's thought is determined by the Reformed tradition thus must not narrowly restrict this tradition to Reformed orthodoxy alone. Rather, one also has to take into account the critiques of Reformed orthodoxy that emerge from Socinianism, Arminianism, and the Enlightenment. In this sense, contrary to Barth and Niesel, one can well say that Schleiermacher continued the Reformed tradition.

Suggested Reading

Gerrish, Brian A. "From Calvin to Schleiermacher: The Theme and the Shape of Christian Dogmatics." In *Internationaler Schleiermacher-Kongreß Berlin 1984*, vol. 2, ed. Kurt-Viktor Selge (Berlin: De Gruyter, 1985), pp. 1038–1049.

Gerrish, Brian A. "Schleiermacher and the Reformation: A Question of Doctrinal Development." In Gerrish, *The Old Protestantism and the New: Essays in the Reformation Heritage* (Edinburgh: T&T Clark, 1982), pp. 179–195.

Käfer, Anne, Constantin Plaul, and Florian Priesemuth, eds. *Der reformierte Schleiermacher. Prägungen und Potentiale seiner Theologie* (Berlin: De Grutyer, 2019).

Bibliography

DeVries, Dawn. *Jesus Christ in the Preaching of Calvin and Schleiermacher* (Louisville: Westminster John Knox, 1996).

Gerrish, Brian A. "Schleiermacher and the Reformation: A Question of Doctrinal Development." In Gerrish, *The Old Protestantism and the New: Essays in the Reformation Heritage* (Edinburgh: T&T Clark, 1982), pp. 179–195.

Gerrish, Brian A. "From Calvin to Schleiermacher: The Theme and the Shape of Christian Dogmatics." In *Internationaler Schleiermacher-Kongreß Berlin 1984*, vol. 2, ed. Kurt-Viktor Selge (Berlin: De Gruyter, 1985), pp. 1038–1049.

Heppe, Heinrich. *Die Dogmatik der evangelisch-reformierten Kirche*. Ed. Ernst Bizer (Neukirchen: Neukirchen Kreis Moers, 1958).

Käfer, Anne, Constantin Plaul, and Florian Priesemuth, eds. *Der reformierte Schleiermacher. Prägungen und Potentiale seiner Theologie* (Berlin: De Grutyer, 2019).

---

[52] Jan Rohls, *Offenbarung, Vernunft und Religion. Ideengeschichte des Christentums*, vol. 1 (Tübingen: Mohr Siebeck, 2012), p. 421.

Niesel, Wilhelm. "Schleiermachers Verhältnis zur reformierten Tradition." *Zwischen der Zeiten* 8 (1930), pp. 511–525.

Ohst, Martin. *Schleiermacher und die Bekenntnisschriften. Eine Untersuchung zu seiner Reformations- und Protestantismusdeutung* (Tübingen: Mohr Siebeck, 1989).

Rohls, Jan. *Offenbarung, Vernunft und Religion*. Ideengeschichte des Christentums, vol. 1 (Tübingen: Mohr Siebeck, 2012).

Schleiermacher, Friedrich. *Kirchenpolitische Schriften, KGA* 1.9, ed. Günter Meckenstock and Hans-Friedrich Traulsen (Berlin: De Gruyter, 2001).

Schleiermacher, Friedrich. *Vorlesungen über die Kirchengeschichte, KGA* 2.6, ed. Simon Gerber (Berlin: De Gruyter, 2006).

Schleiermacher, Friedrich. *Predigten. Fünfte bis Siebente Sammlung (1826-1833), KGA* 3.2, ed. Günter Meckenstock (Berlin: De Gruyter, 2013).

Schweizer, Alexander. *Die Glaubenslehre der Evangelisch-reformirten Kirche dargestellt und aus den Quellen belegt*, vol. 1 (Zürich: Orell, Füssli und Comp., 1844).

B

SCHLEIERMACHER AMONG HIS CONTEMPORARIES

CHAPTER 5

SCHELLING AND STEFFENS

ZACHARY PURVIS

5.1 INTRODUCTION

WILHELM Dilthey once wrote that Friedrich Schleiermacher's significance can be grasped only through biography; one must get to know the person, and the people around him, to make sense of his ideas.[1] But it is not always easy to meet the scholars of early nineteenth-century Germany on intimate terms. True, the cultural world they inhabited for some of their days, commonly characterized at least after Napoleon's downfall as the age of Biedermeier, is welcoming. But their palpable erudition, expressed in dense German or technical Latin, is punishing; their theories, potent; and the myriad webs they spun, in professional and private lives, no less perilous. Even some of their nicknames (there are others) can pose puzzles. Schleiermacher was, for instance, both the dignified "Socrates reborn" and "'the little one' [*der Kleine*] . . . with unforgettable facial expressions . . . as if the lines on his forehead and underneath his grey curls were threads pulled back and forth by a weaver at a flying shuttle."[2] The philosopher Friedrich Wilhelm Joseph von Schelling (1775–1854) was known first as indissoluble "Granite," then as shape-shifting "Proteus."[3] The natural philosopher, mineralogist, and theologian Henrik (or Henrich) Steffens (1773–1845), Norwegian-Danish but attached to Prussia, was the buttoned-up "Emperor" at evening parties in Copenhagen and "amiable," indeed "electrifying," among the German academic set.[4]

---

[1] Wilhelm Dilthey, *Leben Schleiermachers*, vol. 1. 2nd ed., ed. Hermann Mulert (Berlin: de Gruyter, 1922), p. xv.

[2] Ludwig Börne, *Sämtliche Schriften*, vol. 1, ed. Inge and Peter Rippmann (Düsseldorf: Mezler, 1964), vol. 1, p. 598; Karl Rudolf Hagenbach, "Autobiographie," Staatsarchiv Basel-Stadt PA 838a B1, fol. 191r.

[3] Caroline Schlegel to Friedrich Schlegel, October 14–15, 1798, in Friedrich Schlegel, *Kritische Friedrich Schlegel Ausgabe*, vol. 24, ed. Raymond Immerwahr (Paderborn: Ferdinand Schöningh, 1985), pp. 176–81; G. W. F. Hegel, *Vorlesungen über die Geschichte der Philosophie III*, ed. Hermann Glockner (Stuttgart-Bad Cannstatt: Frommann-Holzboog, 1965), pp. 646–83.

[4] Henrik Steffens, *Was ich erlebte. Aus der Erinnerung niedergeschrieben*, 10 vols. (Breslau: Max, 1840–1844), vol. 5, pp. 30–31; Dan Ch. Christensen, *Hans Christian Ørsted: Reading Nature's Mind* (Oxford: Oxford University Press, 2013), p. 169.

Like Schleiermacher, Schelling and Steffens were major intellectuals of their generation.[5] Schelling is, along with J. G. Fichte and G. W. F. Hegel, still remembered as one of the three great representatives of the philosophical movement of German Idealism after Immanuel Kant. Steffens is now largely forgotten, but he was Schelling's most significant disciple. He was also Schleiermacher's colleague in Halle in 1804–1807 and Berlin in 1832–1834. Both men had markedly different relationships with Schleiermacher, one mostly negative (Schelling), the other mostly positive (Steffens), with caveats, and it is these with which this chapter is concerned.

There is some consensus that Schleiermacher owed few intellectual debts to Schelling. In 1909, Hermann Süskind offered the most general outline that is still consulted.[6] What interested him most, though, was Schleiermacher the philosopher, so he trained his gaze on a small subset of Schleiermacher's expansive corpus—primarily early ethical and romantic writings, up to the second edition of *Über Religion. Reden an die Gebildeten unter ihrem Verächtern* (*On Religion: Speeches to Its Cultured Despisers*) in 1806. Perhaps counterintuitively, he concluded that Schelling's influence on Schleiermacher manifested itself more in Schleiermacher's work on religion than on philosophy. Schleiermacher developed his philosophical system independently of Schelling, through his own combination of Kant and Baruch Spinoza, in competition with Fichte and Hegel. True, Schleiermacher's system of knowledge—in his lectures on dialectic, for example—resembled Schelling's "identity philosophy," which linked subjectivity and objectivity or nature, the "ideal" and the "real," in what he called the "absolute." But Schelling prompted Schleiermacher more to revise his concept of religion as intuition in the different editions of *On Religion* and in lectures on ethics in 1804–1805 and 1805–1806. New availability of sources—not least ongoing critical editions of the writings of both scholars—will add more color and shading to Süskind's stark outline.

There is also some consensus that Schleiermacher owed more intellectual debts to Steffens. According to Dilthey, Schleiermacher "never met a spirit more closely related to him than Steffens was."[7] But the nature of those debts is rarely explored. This is due to multiple reasons. One of them is the ecclesiastical and political distance that increasingly separated Schleiermacher and Steffens from the late 1810s onward. Another is that engagement with Steffens's work requires specific technical knowledge of the history of natural science. But recent scholarship has begun to redress the balance.[8]

This chapter will sketch Schleiermacher's major entanglements with Schelling and Steffens, with emphasis on both intellectual influences and biographical matters together, for Schleiermacher's worldview and his many achievements must be understood in the context of his times and in concrete relation to his contemporaries. First, the chapter will review background features in early Romanticism. Second, it will consider Schleiermacher and

---

[5] For biographical information see Xavier Tilliete, *Schelling: biographie* (Paris: Calmann-Lévy, 1999); Otto Lorenz and Bernd Henningsen, eds., *Henrik Steffens—Vermittler zwischen Natur und Geist* (Berlin: Berlin Verlag, 1992); Fritz Paul, *Henrich Steffens. Naturphilosophie und Universalromantik* (Munich: Fink, 1973).

[6] Hermann Süskind, *Der Einfluss Schellings auf die Entwicklung von Schleiermachers System* (Tübingen: Mohr, 1909).

[7] Dilthey, *Leben*, p. 747.

[8] See Sarah Schmidt and Leon Miodoński, eds., *System und Subversion. Friedrich Schleiermacher und Henrik Steffens* (Berlin: de Gruyter: 2018).

Schelling with special reference to what Schleiermacher called his "quiet war" with Schelling, a clash of personality as much anything. This clash ran from around 1799 to 1807 but arguably culminated in 1804, when Schleiermacher reviewed Schelling's famous *Vorlesungen über die Methode des akademischen Studiums* (*Lectures on the Method of Academic Study*, 1803). Third, it will examine Schleiermacher and Steffens' rich collaboration during their time in Halle and the role Steffens seemingly played as a conduit for Schelling's ideas. Finally, it will trace the paths each followed in later years—Schleiermacher in Berlin, Schelling in Munich, and Steffens in Breslau and Berlin.

5.2 Early German Romanticism

Schleiermacher, Schelling, and Steffens all participated in early German Romanticism, the period known as *Frühromantik*, which flourished from the late 1790s to the early 1800s—Schelling in Jena, Schleiermacher in Berlin, and Steffens on the move from Jena to Freiberg to Copenhagen. This association provided an initial opportunity for them to become familiar with each other.

Romanticism was shaped by the experience of the political revolution that began in France in 1789, reaching Germany after 1792, and by the post-Kantian philosophical revolution, which disrupted previous forms of empiricism by stressing the role of the subject in producing knowledge of the world. The cradle of the movement was Jena. Near the end of the eighteenth century, the brothers Friedrich and Arthur Wilhelm Schlegel gathered there with Ludwig Tieck, Clemens Brentano, Friedrich von Hardenberg (Novalis), Friedrich Hölderlin, and others. J. W. von Goethe was nearby in Weimar. They applied the notion of revolutionary transformation to diverse fields—poetry and philosophy, biology and religion.[9] In 1797, Schelling arrived. He had attended the Protestant seminary in Tübingen, where he roomed with Hölderlin and Hegel. His early works marked him as an enthusiastic proponent of Fichte's thought and a philosophical prodigy in his own right. In 1798, he was called to the University of Jena.[10]

The early Romantics and Idealists attempted to find a first principle, an "absolute," that could reconcile polarities—God and nature, freedom and necessity, the individual and the state—which Kant's philosophy had seemingly reproduced. Fichte had argued in his pivotal *Wissenschaftslehre* (*The Science of Knowledge*, 1794) that philosophy's first principle was the self-positing ego.[11] Though Schelling initially agreed with this, he began to critique what he saw as extreme subjectivism in Fichte's idealism and to work out an alternative account that drew in part on Spinoza.[12] In publications such as *Ideen zu einer Philosophie der Natur*

---

[9] Robert J. Richards, *The Romantic Conception of Life: Science and Philosophy in the Age of Goethe* (Chicago: University of Chicago Press, 2002); Andrew Cunnigham and Nicholas Jardine, eds., *Romanticism and the Sciences* (Cambridge: Cambridge University Press, 2000).

[10] Theodore Ziolkowski, *German Romanticism and Its Institutions* (Princeton: Princeton University Press, 2000), pp. 237–268.

[11] Anthony J. La Vopa, *Fichte: The Self and the Calling of Philosophy, 1762–1799* (Cambridge: Cambridge University Press, 2001), pp. 183–230.

[12] Frederick C. Beiser, *German Idealism: The Struggle against Subjectivism, 1781–1801* (Cambridge, MA: Harvard University Press, 2002).

(*Ideas for a Philosophy of Nature*, 1797), *Von der Weltseele* (*On the World Soul*, 1798), and *Erster Entwurf eines Systemes der Naturphilosophie* (*First Outline of a System of Philosophy of Nature*, 1799), Schelling argued that nature is an organic, self-organizing whole, not opposed to but co-equal with the ego.

Schelling's approach fascinated Steffens more than anyone. In fact, Steffens postponed his course at the prestigious Freiberg Mining Academy, sponsored by the Danish government, to visit Jena, where he heard Schelling deliver his inaugural lecture. Some Europeans traveled to "Italy or Greece or the East," Steffens admitted, but they longed for a "dead past." He sought a "glorious future."[13] In Jena he became a regular in Wilhelm Schlegel's parlor, where the Jena circle met. The Schlegel brothers prodded him to contribute to their journal, *Athenaeum*, and it was through them that Steffens first made Schleiermacher's acquaintance in 1799.[14]

Schelling did not intend his philosophy of nature to replace but to complement empirical science, by reevaluating established findings. He edited the journal, *Zeitschrift für spekulative Physik*, and conducted some experiments. But the greater portion fell to Steffens. Schelling esteemed Steffens for his profound scientific knowledge; Steffens found speculative guidance for his work in Schelling's philosophy. At the Mining Academy, Steffens applied the insights in his *Beyträge zur inneren Naturgeschichte der Erde* (*Contributions to the Inner Natural History of the Earth*, 1801). In Copenhagen in 1802–1804, he applied them in wildly successful lectures. Danish onlookers quipped that Steffens had imbibed so much philosophical German from Schelling that he forgot how to think clearly in his mother tongue.[15] Throughout his life he straddled lines—theoretical and empirical, romantic and scientific. He won recognition as much in mineralogy as in literature, as the writer of many novels and fairy tales.

Schleiermacher was an honorary member of the Jena circle. He too tried to bring together Kant's critical philosophy with Spinoza in manuscripts from 1793–1794. He developed special interest in the notion of individuality, which aligned him with Friedrich Schlegel. In Berlin, he entered the world of Jewish literary salons, where he met Schlegel, with whom he shared a flat in 1797–1799. The connection helped Schleiermacher to write *On Religion*, which he published anonymously in 1799. The book was part of early Romanticism's turn to religion, which tended to be defined not in terms of ethics or belief in dogma, but rather as intuition of the infinite with the particular. Schleiermacher's speeches represented one approach. Novalis's *Christenheit oder Europa* (*Christendom or Europe*, 1799), a paean to medieval Catholicism, represented another.

---

[13] Steffens, *Was ich erlebte*, vol. 3, pp. 1–3.
[14] Henrik Steffens to Arthur Wilhelm Schlegel, July 26, 1799, in Josef Körner, ed., *Briefe von und an August Wilhelm Schlegel*, vol. 1 (Zurich: Amalthea, 1930), p. 95.
[15] Steffens, *Was ich erlebte*, vol. 5, p. 46.

5.3 Schleiermacher's Deviation from Schelling

Romanticism's halcyon days did not last. The Jena circle fractured. One split was personal. Schelling's break with Fichte occurred simultaneously with Schelling's scandalous love affair with Caroline (née Michaelis, widowed Böhmer), then married to Wilhelm Schlegel, and the anguish of all over the death of fifteen-year-old Auguste Böhmer, Caroline's daughter from her first husband. It was a double crisis: of philosophy in 1799–1802; of love and death in 1801. Wilhelm and Caroline divorced in 1803, and Caroline immediately married Schelling. Friedrich Schlegel's relations with Schelling had always been cool, due in part to their different social backgrounds, but the scandal enraged him. Schleiermacher kept abreast of everything.

Another split involved religion. Schelling reacted violently to the texts by Schleiermacher and Novalis. He responded with the satirical poem, "Epikurisch Glaubensbekenntnis Heinz Widerporstens" ("Heinz Widerporst's Epicurean Confession of Faith," 1799). The character Heinz Widerporst was created by the sixteenth-century poet Hans Sachs, whose legacy Goethe had revived. Widerporst ridicules Romanticism's interest in "other-worldliness" as a delirium. He criticizes religion for the denial of sensual pleasure. He taunts Schleiermacher as the "maker of veils," an obvious allusion to the etymology of Schleiermacher's surname. And he mocks the idea of the "intuition of the universe," which was central to *On Religion*. Friedrich Schlegel planned to print the poem in *Athenaeum*, but Goethe stopped him on the grounds that its appearance would endanger Schelling's career. Schelling thought enough of the poem, however, to published excerpts of it on his own.[16]

Yet it is difficult to assess Schelling's full response to *On Religion*. Schleiermacher and Wilhelm Schlegel gave a copy of the speeches to Schelling. Schelling had the gift "bound like a truly holy book," according to Schlegel, in "elegant black moroccan leather." Schelling himself reported that the book gave him "great joy."[17] In 1801, he tried—unsuccessfully—to win Schleiermacher as a contributor to *Kritisches Journal der Philosophie*, a new periodical he was launching with Hegel.[18]

The lines that connected Schleiermacher and Schelling knotted. Schleiermacher's notebook from 1800–1803 shows that he read Schelling closely.[19] They formulated some of their ideas with and against each other. Schelling modified Schleiermacher's concept of intuition, for example. Whereas Schleiermacher understood the intuition of the universe as the essence of religion in the speeches, Schelling described intuition in intellectual terms—as rational cognition. When Schleiermacher revised *On Religion* in 1806, he no longer defined the essence of religion as intuition. To distinguish himself from Schelling, he used the concept of feeling (*Gefühl*), which previously played only a marginal role. The two thinkers regularly criticized each other obliquely, through hints and allusions.

---

[16] G. L. Plitt, ed., *Aus Schellings Leben. In Briefen*, vol. 1 (Leipzig: Hirzel, 1869), pp. 282–293.

[17] Zachary Purvis, *Theology and the University in Nineteenth-Century Germany* (Oxford: Oxford University Press, 2016), p. 102.

[18] *KGA* 5.5, p. xxvi.

[19] Schleiermacher, *Gedanken V (1800–1803)*, *KGA* 1.3, pp. 296–297.

In 1802, Schelling delivered his *Lectures on the Method of Academic Study*.[20] They belonged to an important debate on university reform, which Kant's *Streit der Fakultäten* (*Conflict of the Faculties*, 1798) and the revolutionary-Napoleon turmoil exacerbated. In Jena alone, Friedrich Schiller had addressed the topic in 1789; Fichte in 1794. When Schelling took his turn, he was on the verge of leaving Jena to accept a chair at the University of Würzburg in northern Bavaria. The lectures developed inchoate thoughts from Schelling's *System des transzendentalen Idealismus* (*System of Transcendental Idealism*, 1800). They arguably constitute the most accessible summary of Schelling's identity philosophy. Moreover, they exercised an outsized role in the advance of modern historicism.[21]

Schelling grounded his idea of the university in the organic unity of knowledge. Each individual "science" (*Wissenschaft*) is in harmony with the other sciences. Together, they comprise an organic whole, or "absolute *Wissenschaft*." The external structure of the university should mirror the internal unity of the sciences. Philosophy was at the heart of the university. But the university did not need a separate philosophy faculty, because philosophy embodied absolute *Wissenschaft*; "that which is all things," he argued, "cannot for that very reason be anything in particular." The university should retain the three traditional higher faculties—theology, law, and medicine. These faculties taught what Schelling called the "positive sciences," devoted not to the search for truth per se but to the practical ends of people, administered by the state. The state had a legitimate interest in the positive sciences, because the common good depended on clergy, lawyers, and doctors.

In 1804, Schleiermacher reviewed Schelling's lectures for the *Allgemeine-Literatur Zeitung*, Jena's outlet "devoted," in Steffens' words, "to the connection of Schelling's philosophy with the literature of the day."[22] Schleiermacher criticized Schelling on every point. He said that the review marked his final "deviation" (*Abweichung*) from Schelling.[23] But the truth is more complex. Schleiermacher's own proposal for university reform, *Gelegentliche Gedanken über Universitäten in deutschem Sinn* (*Occasional Thoughts on Universities in the German Sense*, 1808), and his programmatic treatise on academic theology, *Kurze Darstellung des theologischen Studiums* (*Brief Outline of the Study of Theology*, 1811; 2nd ed., 1830), contained traces of Schelling's arguments. Like Schelling, Schleiermacher preserved more or less the institutional structure of the university inherited from the Middle Ages—far more, at least, than Fichte did in his own contribution to the debate. Schleiermacher also considered philosophy to be the center of the university and retained Schelling's conception of the positive sciences. Unlike Schelling, however, he argued that the positive sciences belonged in the university, not on the basis of their proximity to philosophy, but because the higher faculties had emerged naturally, the public had a legitimate interest in them, and philosophical reflection was incomplete without reference to the concrete realities they considered—even though professors in the higher faculties still needed to contribute to philosophy.[24]

---

[20] F. W. J. Schelling, "Über die Methode des akademischen Studiums," in *Schellings Werke*, vol. 3, ed. Manfred Schröter (Munich: Beck, 1927), pp. 329–374.

[21] Paul Ziche and Gian Franco Frigo, eds., *"Die bessere Richtung der Wissenschaften." Schellings "Vorlesungen über die Methode des akademischen Studiums" als Wissenschafts- und Universitätsprogramm* (Stuttgart: Frommann-Holzboog, 2011); Arnaldo Momigliano, "Friedrich Creuzer and Greek Historiography," *Journal of the Warburg and Courtauld Institutes* 9 (1946), p. 161.

[22] Steffens, *Was ich erlebte*, vol. 5, p. 12.

[23] Schleiermacher to J. C. Gaß, September 6, 1805, *KGA* 5.7, p. 307.

[24] Purvis, *Theology and the University*, pp. 86–165.

Schelling and Schleiermacher nearly became colleagues in the thick of the exchange. Schleiermacher at the time was "exiled" in Stolp near the Danish border. The Prussian Upper Consistory had harbored suspicions that his friends in the Romantic movement were dangerous influences on him, so it sent him away from Berlin. In early 1804, Würzburg offered Schleiermacher a professorship in practical theology. Schleiermacher was reluctant to settle in Catholic Bavaria, but the greater obstacle was Schelling. The possibility of working alongside each other caused them both to vent their spleens. Before his review went to print, Schleiermacher admitted being "anxious about what will become of the quiet war [*dem stillen Kriege*] in which Schelling and I are engaged."[25] In truth, their differences remained more personal than substantive.

Schleiermacher nevertheless accepted Würzburg's offer. But Prussian administrators, unwilling to lose Schleiermacher to Bavaria, intervened. Successive decrees refused his release from Stolp and promoted him to *ausserordentlicher Professor* of Theology and Preacher to the University of Halle. It happened that Schelling did not stay long in Würzburg either. He settled in Munich, where he lived and worked in 1806–1820 and 1827–1841. He established connections with the Bavarian Academy of Sciences and the Wittelsbach royal family. Schelling impressed Bavaria's Crown Prince, later King Ludwig I (r.1825–1848), who lent him support. In 1808, Schelling helped found the Academy of Fine Arts and served as its first general secretary. After the University of Landshut relocated to Munich in 1826, the king appointed Schelling as professor of philosophy. In the late 1830s, he tutored Ludwig's eldest son, the future King Maximilian II (r.1848–1864).

5.4 An Apprenticeship in Halle: Schleiermacher and Steffens

Schleiermacher's stint in Halle, 1804–1807, became one of the more fruitful periods of his career. Steffens was there amid it all. In 1804, at almost the exact time of Schleiermacher's appointment, the University of Halle called Steffens as *ordentlicher Professor* of Natural Philosophy, Physiology, and Mineralogy. His in-laws resided nearby in Giebichenstein and he accepted happily. For Schleiermacher, Halle also represented a homecoming: it was the site of his undergraduate studies under J. A. Eberhard and F. A. Wolf.

The Halle years began with trouble. Schleiermacher's radical reputation preceded him. New colleagues had misgivings: They suspected him of being a follower of Schelling, a mystic, probably a pantheist. Old teachers upped the ante. "It has now come to the point," declared Eberhard, "that an open atheist has been called to Halle as a theologian and preacher."[26] Steffens too encountered gossip: that he was an atheist, that he was Catholic, that he was in the daily use of opium and lived in a state of constant intoxication. Everyone, he said, seemed of one mind "to resist young advocates of Schelling's philosophy."[27] To Schelling, Steffens complained that Halle stunk of "old half-rotten Kantians."[28]

---

[25] Schleiermacher to Georg Reimer, November 11, 1803, *KGA* 5.7, pp. 93–94.
[26] G. L. Spalding to Schleiermacher, July 27, 1804, *Br. III*, p. 408.
[27] Steffens, *Was ich erlebte*, vol. 5, pp. 122–123, 129.
[28] Steffens to Schelling, January 1808, in F. W. J. Schelling, *Briefe und Dokumente (1775–1809)*, vol. 1, ed. Horst Fuhrmans (Bonn: Bouvier, 1962), p. 401.

Together, the young professors found their way. The greatest step for the Steffens–Schleiermacher friendship occurred one spring day somewhere along a three-hour walk north from Halle to the Petersberg, a small mountain. Schleiermacher poured out his heart to Steffens concerning his problematic love for the married Eleanore Grünow, who decided not to leave her husband. They spent the night deep in conversation in the nearby village of Ostrow. Looking back, Steffens described it in terms of religious experience. Schleiermacher was slated to preach the next morning at a commemorative service for Prussia's late Queen Mother. In the early hours, university officials called on but did not find him at his apartment. When Steffens arrived at the church, exhausted from lack of sleep, attendees exchanged knowing looks: "Since you appear here," they said, "we hope finally to see Schleiermacher." Word had already spread that he and Schleiermacher spent the night at a tavern. Schleiermacher appeared at the last minute. He had gone ahead of Steffens on the way back and composed his sermon in his head. According to Steffens, the unscripted speech "delighted everyone."[29]

Science followed the alliance. The friends understood themselves as two halves of a system: Steffens as natural philosopher and empirical investigator, Schleiermacher as ethicist and theologian. When together, they constituted a totality, a scientific whole, based on common philosophical commitments. Steffens gave greater attention to the theoretical foundation of their work. Steffens also represented the "real" sciences—to use Schelling and Schleiermacher's term—which dealt with nature and which Schleiermacher described repeatedly as necessary for a universal account of knowledge.[30] Botany and chemistry fascinated Schleiermacher, but he did not pursue them professionally. He began to consider physics and ethics in their "mutual dependence": physics had to do with products, ethics with the process that produces products. Physics and ethics perfected each other, just like Steffens and Schleiermacher did.

The duo formed their own circle of admirers, to which the philologist Wolf and the physician J. C. Reil contributed. At informal meetings over tea, they defied faculty conventions concerning professor–student hierarchy.[31] Varnhagen von Ense recalled their joint artistry and brilliance, so strong that "the theologians all listened to Steffens, and the natural scientists, to Schleiermacher."[32] In Steffens' words, "We exchanged what we knew with each other: Schleiermacher heard me lecture on physics, and he opened Greek philosophy to me, teaching me to appreciate Plato."[33] In Schleiermacher's words, "There is wonderful harmony between Steffens and me, which gives me great pleasure.... When he comes up with moral ideas in conversation, they are always mine. What I understand about nature comes from his system. Our students notice how we start from rather different angles, so that there can be nothing other than pure inner harmony between us."[34]

---

[29] Steffens, *Was ich erlebte*, vol. 5, p. 148.

[30] Jörg Dierken, "Das Absolute und die Wissenschaften. Zur Architektonik des Wissens bei Schelling und Schleiermacher," *Philosophisches Jahrbuch* 99 (1992), pp. 307–328.

[31] Steffens, *Was ich erlebte*, vol. 5, p. 152.

[32] Karl August Varnhagen von Ense, *Denkwürdigkeiten und Vermischte Schriften*, 2nd ed., vol. 1 (Leipzig: Brockhaus, 1843), p. 368.

[33] Steffens, *Was ich erlebte*, vol. 5, p. 144; Schleiermacher to Reimer, September 1806, KGA 5.9, p. 123.

[34] Schleiermacher to Henriette Herz, March 27, 1805, KGA 5.8, pp. 171–173.

Was Schelling far from their thoughts? He was present in Halle in some form. Ludwig Börne, for example, remembered a drinking party during his Halle days as a student under Steffens and Schleiermacher: some classmates got into an argument over subtleties of Schelling's idealism, exchanged insults, and "two days later blood flowed" in the streets.[35] Schelling appeared in Steffens' manuscripts too. Steffens' greatest work from Halle was the *Grundzüge der philosophischen Naturwissenschaften* (*Fundamentals of the Philosophical Natural Sciences*, 1806). Through complex formulae, the book integrated contemporary knowledge of chemistry, geology, and mineralogy on large and small scales and attempted to explain everything through Schelling's philosophy.[36]

Later, when Schleiermacher expounded his mature theory of knowledge in his lectures on dialectic, given six times, and philosophical ethics, given once in Halle and seven times in Berlin, he confirmed that Steffens' *Fundamentals* represented the "philosophical foundation with which [I am] in most agreement."[37] Competition with Fichte prompted Schleiermacher's approach. But so too did collaboration with Steffens—and there lurked Schelling.[38] For Schleiermacher developed his ideas about the systematic structure of knowledge as an organic whole with explicit reference to Steffens' book, which in turn was saturated with Schelling's thought.[39]

War caused the Halle ensemble to disband. Napoleon's troops arrived in mid-October 1806. Schleiermacher and his half-sister Anne (Nanny) crowded into Steffens' central flat with Henrik, his wife Johanna (Hanne), and their nine-month-old daughter Clara to watch the carnage that opened the Battle of Halle. They retreated to Schleiermacher's flat when Prussia's cannoneers fell to the French. Steffens, clutching Clara to his chest, barely escaped the confused throng of soldiers. But Schleiermacher's flat offered little refuge, and they were soon robbed. Into the spring of 1807, they lived and worked together in cramped quarters: women and baby in one room, men in another. The university closed its doors. The state stopped paying faculty wages. The times looked bleak. Yet Steffens later described these months as among the happiest and most productive of his life.[40]

5.5 Politics, Science, and the Church

Circumstances changed again with the Peace of Tilsit (July 1807). Upon learning that Napoleon had placed Halle under the rule of his brother Jérôme Bonaparte in the Kingdom

---

[35] Börne, *Sämtliche Schriften*, pp. 600–601.
[36] Henrik Steffens, *Grundzüge der philosophischen Naturwissenschaften* (Berlin: Realschulbuchhandlung, 1806), pp. ix–xii, 9–11.
[37] August Twesten, "Vorrede," in *Friedrich Schleiermachers Grundriss der philosophische Ethik*, ed. August Twesten (Berlin: Reimer, 1841), p. xcvii; Steffens, *Was ich erlebte*, vol. 5, p. 143.
[38] Christine Helmer, Christiane Kranich, and Birgit Rehme-Iffert, eds., *Schleiermachers Dialektik* (Tübingen: Mohr Siebeck, 2003); Gustav Mann, *Das Verhältnis der Schleiermacher'schen Dialektik zur Schelling'schen Philosophie* (Stuttgart: Vereins-Buchdruckerei, 1914).
[39] Purvis, *Theology and the University*, p. 156.
[40] Schleiermacher to Reimer, November 4, 1806, *KGA* 5.9, pp. 180–183; Steffens, *Was ich erlebte*, vol. 5, pp. 191–198.

of Westphalia, Schleiermacher departed for Berlin. He began to participate in the Prussian campaign to establish a new university as a replacement for Halle's loss.

Steffens stayed behind initially to await further political developments. Then he travelled to Copenhagen with hopes of obtaining a professorship. When his enquiries met with no success, he sought Schelling's help: "Is there no place for me near you? No southern university that wants to accept the displaced?"[41] It is curious to note that Schelling was busy at the time complaining of "plagiarizers and plunderers of *Naturphilosophie*," among whom he apparently included Steffens.[42] Disturbed, Steffens told Schleiermacher that Schelling, "through arrogance and the madness of self-worship, has sunk so low."[43] But in his memoirs, Steffens recalled, "Only one of my friends was eager and active for me.... Schelling went out of his way to get me a job as an academic in Munich. He thought he could give me hope, which was disappearing so frequently, but in the end all efforts were unsuccessful."[44] When the University of Halle reopened under Westphalian rule, Steffens, in severe financial straits, was forced to accept reinstatement.

In 1808–1810, Steffens and Schleiermacher swapped nearly fifty letters. The most tragic came when Steffens, then father of three, wrote his friend that his two youngest children had died: "There is no part of my existence that is not wounded. What is life? ... I have nothing left but silent brooding, paralysis, the grave of my children, the grief of my wife."[45] Schleiermacher replied immediately, but amid his schedule in Berlin as Reformed pastor of Trinity Church and interim director of the scientific committee tasked with overhauling Prussia's educational system, he seems to have found little time for sustained sympathy. There do not appear to be any extant letters from 1829, when Schleiermacher's nine-year-old son, Nathanael, died tragically.

The defining intellectual event of the period occurred in 1810 with the University of Berlin's establishment, the result of a remarkable political initiative under Prussia's King Friedrich Wilhelm III (r.1797–1840). In 1807, Karl Friedrich Beyme, chief of the civil cabinet, solicited proposals on the idea of a new academy in the capitol. Neither Schleiermacher nor Schelling nor Steffens appeared on the original list of academics invited to participate. But each—especially Schleiermacher—influenced the result. Schelling's contribution came from his *Lectures on the Methods of Academy Study*. Schleiermacher's came from his *Occasional Thoughts*. In Halle, Steffens gave concurrent lectures on the idea of the university, which he published in 1809.[46]

Steffens had high hopes that Schleiermacher would be able to arrange a post for him in Berlin. Schleiermacher had less sway outside of the theological faculty, but he did champion Steffens' candidacy—he even offered to take a pay cut if it would help.[47] But no professorship

---

[41] Steffens to Schelling, August 4, 1807, Schelling, *Briefe und Dokumente*, p. 386.

[42] F. W. J. Schelling, "Kritische Fragmente," *Jahrbücher der Medizin als Wissenschaft* 2 (1807), pp. 283–304.

[43] Steffens to Schleiermacher, July 9, 1807, KGA 5.9, pp. 483–484; Steffens to Schelling, July 9, 1807, Schelling, *Briefe und Dokumente*, p. 382.

[44] Steffens, *Was ich erlebte*, vol. 5, p. 282.

[45] Steffens to Schleiermacher, August 5, 1810, KGA 5.11, p. 458.

[46] Ernst Anrich, *Die Idee der deutschen Universitäten. Die fünf Grundschriften aus der Zeit ihrer Neubegründung durch klassischen Idealismus und romantischen Realismus* (Darmstadt: Wissenschaftliche Buchgesellschaft, 1956).

[47] Schleiermacher to Ludwig Nicolovius, August 1810, KGA 5.11, p. 474.

was forthcoming. The reasons are complex and disputed. Steffens' father-in-law had cooperated significantly with the upstart Westphalian government, which perhaps placed him in bad stead with Prussia.[48] Steffens' commitment to Schelling's nature philosophy set him at odds with some of Berlin's other philosophers and scientists, especially Fichte, who not only held the first chair in philosophy but also was the university's first elected rector. Ever mindful of Schelling's "betrayal" at the start of the decade, Fichte seems to have stirred up opposition.[49] In the event, Steffens did receive an appointment in 1811, but to another Prussian university—Breslau—where he taught until 1831, serving twice as rector (1821–1822; 1829–1830). He wrote a four-volume *Handbuch* to his discipline and became a celebrated mineralogist. When he traveled, his hosts regularly dragged him to see rock collections they had assembled according to his manual.[50]

Divergent views of church and state began to drive apart Schleiermacher and Steffens. United for Prussia in the "Wars of Liberation" (*Befreiungskriegen*)—Schleiermacher as a national preacher, Steffens as a mobilizer of troops and enlisted military volunteer—afterward they found themselves on opposite sides.[51] Their families kept in contact. Hanne informed Schleiermacher, for instance, of Steffens' soldierly experiences in 1813–1814, and of their former student in Halle, Alexander von der Marwitz, who died in battle in 1814. (She didn't know that Marwitz had had an affair with Schleiermacher's young wife, Henriette, from 1812, which Schleiermacher had interpreted as divine retribution for his earlier relationship with Eleonore Grünow.[52]) Other reunions occurred. (Schleiermacher eventually met Schelling in Munich, too, seemingly without acrimony.) In 1817, Schleiermacher asked Steffens to be the baptismal sponsor for his daughter Hildegard. The Steffens couple were also closely involved in Nanny Schleiermacher's engagement and wedding to Ernst Moritz Arndt.[53] But the political mood in Prussia shifted from liberal reform to reaction. Their relationship shifted too.

In Prussia, as elsewhere in Europe, conservative Restoration—putting back what had been overturned in the revolutionary-Napoleonic years—set in after the Congress of Vienna. One front on which the state campaigned was university life. Radical student fraternities (*Burschenschaften*) had acquired greater political roles. Many members had fought against Napoleon and desired to revive nationalist and liberal pan-German sentiments they had experienced on the battlefield. Unlike traditional fraternities, the *Burschenschaften* dedicated themselves to moral and spiritual reform. Many members also participated in Friedrich Ludwig Jahn's political gymnastics associations (*Turnvereine*), where they pursued such ideals as physical strength and self-sacrifice for the fatherland. At the Wartburg Festival (1817), which commingled anniversaries of the Battle of Nations at Leipzig (1813) and Martin Luther's 95 Theses (1517), demonstrations against restrictions on their civil liberties reached a climax. When the fraternity member Karl Sand assassinated the playwright August von

---

[48] Max Lenz, *Geschichte der Königlichen Friedrich-Wilhelms-Universität zu Berlin*, vol. 1 (Halle: Waisenhaus, 1910), p. 202.

[49] Steffens to Schelling, November 14, 1807, Schelling, *Briefe und Dokumente*, p. 393.

[50] Henrik Steffens, *Vollständiges Handbuch der Oryktognosie*, 4 vols. (Halle: Curt, 1811–1824).

[51] Marit Bergner, *Henrich Steffens. Ein politischer Professor in Umbruchszeiten 1806–1819* (Frankfurt am Main: Lang, 2016), pp. 105–116.

[52] See the correspondence of Marwitz and Henriette's confidante, Rahel Varnhagen, in Friedhelm Kemp, ed., *Auf frischen kleinein abstrakten Wegen: Unbekanntes und Unveröffentliches aus Rahels Freundeskreis* (Munich: Kösel, 1967), pp. 6–15.

[53] Steffens to Schleiermacher, May 18, 1817, Schleiermacher, *Br. IV*, p. 215.

Kotzebue in 1819, the German Confederation, led by the Austrian Chancellor Klemens von Metternich, passed the Karlsbad Decrees, which led to censorship of the press, state surveillance of civil servants, a ban on the gymnastic associations, and the dissolution of the fraternities.

Schleiermacher, committed to reform, supported the gymnastic and fraternity movements, though he disliked Jahn. He was even suspected of demagogic intrigue and briefly placed under surveillance. Steffens unequivocally denounced the political aspirations of both movements. He played a high-profile role in the so-called "Breslau Gymnastics Feud" (*Breslauer Turnfehde*) of 1818–1819, and published a number of widely read political statements seemingly at odds with his earlier interests in reform. Schleiermacher thought initially that Steffens' position must be based on misunderstanding and attempted to defend him.[54] But the situation became increasingly awkward for Schleiermacher. He stopped publicly supporting Steffens, and Steffens' reputation sank. In response Steffens wrote, "I do not ask that you should jump into the water every time I swim, but when I am about to drown, I expect it from your friendship."[55]

If civil politics became a wedge, theology and ecclesiastical politics widened the gap. This happened in the context of the Prussian Union of 1817, in which the king merged the Lutheran and Reformed churches of the kingdom into one single, united evangelical church. Schleiermacher remained supportive of the Union, if not the state's stubborn imposition of the liturgy, known as the "Agenda." Steffens' beliefs led him on a different path.

After 1815, Steffens yearned for a stronger religious community. Previously, Steffens wrote, "I had never felt the need to belong to a congregation, and the concept of a church was completely foreign to me. . . . Whoever was lucky enough to live in close connection with Schleiermacher . . . will find it understandable how the concept of a church was completely devoured by friendship. Unfortunately, I saw later how this rising of the church in subjective affection became an increasingly general sign of the times."[56] He found it among the Silesian circle gathered around the Lutheran pastor-professor, Johann Gottfried Scheibel, an outspoken critic of both Union and "Agenda." Scheibel emerged as a leader of the "Old Lutherans" who dissented from the Union—and faced considerable state persecution for doing so. Against Scheibel's critics, Steffens wrote *Von der falschen Theologie und dem wahren Glauben* (*On False Theology and True Faith*, 1823). His publisher advertised the book as an assault on Schleiermacher's *Der Christliche Glaube* (*Christian Faith*, 1821–1822), which Schleiermacher had written for the Union. Steffens sent Schleiermacher a copy, explaining that he had nothing to do with the promotional material. Schleiermacher later quoted Steffens' paraphrase of his own concept of religion and feeling in the second edition of *Christian Faith* (1830).

Steffens defended Scheibel again when Scheibel was suspended from office in 1830. By 1831, though, Steffens decided that his own position was precarious, and he submitted an application for transfer. He gained the support of Prussia's Crown Prince, the future Friedrich Wilhelm IV (r.1840–1861), which enabled him to move to the University of Berlin. Just as Steffens prepared to leave Breslau, Schleiermacher received a request from

---

[54] Gaß to Schleiermacher, January 1, 1819, in W. Gaß, ed., *Fr. Schleiermacher's Briefwechsel mit J. Chr. Gaß* (Berlin: Reimer, 1852), p. 167; Bergner, *Henrich Steffens*, p. 327.
[55] Steffens to Schleiermacher, June 27–28, 1819, *Br. IV*, p. 256.
[56] Steffens, *Was ich erlebte*, vol. 10, pp. 50, 60–62.

the Crown Prince to replace Silesia's recently deceased general superintendent, a high-ranking ecclesiastical administrator, and "put an end to the mischief of the 'Scheibelians' and 'Steffensians' in Breslau."[57] Schleiermacher declined the post, but he did attempt to mediate. In May 1831, Schleiermacher was supposed to be in Breslau on behalf of the government; he submitted a written recommendation instead. The same year, Steffens published *Wie ich wieder Lutheraner wurde* (*How I Became a Lutheran Again*), an account of his return to his childhood faith and his relation to the Union.

Where was Schelling in these developments? In 1809, he had published his so-called *Freiheitsschrift*, but his literary output soon came to a standstill. It was the last book he finished in his lifetime. In 1816, Schelling was among the finalists for a chair in philosophy at the University of Berlin. Fichte had died in 1814 and his position was still vacant. Hegel received the post in the end. Schleiermacher, then rector and thus chairman of the senate, cast his vote for a third party.[58] In 1817, Steffens visited Schelling in Munich. He continued to correspond regularly with Schelling, exchanging scientific data, publication details, and more personal notes. Afterward, he rushed to tell Schleiermacher: "How happy I was to see Schelling again after fifteen long years. Oh, dear Schleiermacher! I owe so much to both of you. How I wish you both would recognize each other completely!"[59] Détente may have arrived after the "quiet war," but not quite mutual exaltation.

In 1832–1834, Steffens taught alongside Schleiermacher in Berlin. They remained cordial despite falling out. From Schleiermacher's daily calendar of his last years, it appears that he regularly saw Steffens in Berlin, that they celebrated birthdays together from time to time, and that they visited each other in the evenings. In 1833, Schleiermacher traveled to Scandinavia, where among other things he pursued old interests in mineralogy. Schleiermacher's travel diary shows that he crossed paths with one "Steffens"—perhaps a relative, maybe a brother, of Henrik Steffens, who had himself remained in Berlin but had helped Schleiermacher plan and organize the trip.[60] The calendar records a last meeting with Steffens on January 22, 1834. Schleiermacher died three weeks later. As rector of the University of Berlin in 1834–1835, Steffens delivered Schleiermacher's eulogy for the academic community. He could not mask their disagreements: "I must not hide the fact," Steffens said, that the "doctrine of Christianity . . . true to me, is not his. But he was a Christian."[61]

In 1841, Schelling was called by Friedrich Wilhelm IV to fill Hegel's vacant chair in philosophy, with the purpose "to crush the dragon-seed of Hegelian pantheism."[62] His opening lectures on the philosophy of revelation attracted some of Europe's brightest intellectual stars—Steffens included—but they soon fell flat, attendance dwindled, and Schelling

---

[57] Rulemann Eylert to Schleiermacher, January 29, 1831, *Br. IV*, p. 488.
[58] Lenz, *Geschichte*, pp. 570–80.
[59] Steffens to Schleiermacher, October 15, 1817, *Br. IV*, pp. 225–226.
[60] *TK*.
[61] Henrik Steffens, "Rede in der Aula der Friedrich-Wilhelms-Universität," in *Drei Reden am Tage der Bestattung des weiland Professors der Theologie und Predigers Herrn Dr. Schleiermacher am 15ten Februar 1834* (Berlin: Reimer, 1834), p. 33.
[62] F. W. J. Schelling, *Philosophie der Offenbarung, 1841/42*, ed. Manfred Frank (Frankfurt am Main: Suhrkamp, 1977), p. 486.

gave up on public life after four years. When Steffens died in 1845, he was buried near Schleiermacher's grave in Berlin's Trinity Church Cemetery. Schelling delivered the eulogy.[63]

5.6 Conclusion

The story of Schleiermacher among his contemporaries Schelling and Steffens is complicated. This chapter has charted only some of their intersections, fraught with ironies and agonies. In Halle, Steffens helped teach Schleiermacher how to function as an academic and influenced him through the *Fundamentals*. When they separated, Steffens lamented to Schleiermacher, "It is indeed very fatal that we are so far apart!"[64] The political and theological differences that ultimately divided them should not obscure the significance of their initial close partnership. Schelling's personality ruffled the feathers of even the most sympathetic of associates. When Schleiermacher confessed that the mere thought of being near Schelling was "fatal," it is surely this factor, more than opposition to Schelling's ideas, that provoked him.[65] But Schelling's thought also left its mark on Schleiermacher, positively and negatively, as *On Religion, Occasional Thoughts*, and other texts show. In private correspondence, lectures, and publications, Schleiermacher referred often to Schelling, implicitly and explicitly. Sometimes he engaged with Schelling through a third party, as he did with Steffens. No account of Schleiermacher's work is complete without a careful examination of this background. Biographical circumstances, and sheer strength of character, remain central for any attempt to understand the influences of Schleiermacher, Schelling, and Steffens on each other in the great period of Romanticism and Idealism, reform and reaction, institution-building and system-defining.

Suggested Reading

Purvis, Zachary. *Theology and the University in Nineteenth-Century Germany* (Oxford: Oxford University Press, 2016).
Schmidt, Sarah, and Leon Miodoński, eds. *System und Subversion. Friedrich Schleiermacher und Henrik Steffens* (Berlin: de Gruyter, 2018).
Süskind, Hermann. *Der Einfluss Schellings auf die Entwicklung von Schleiermachers System*. (Tübingen: Mohr, 1909).

---

[63] F. W. J. Schelling, "Aus einem öffentlichen Vortrag zu H. Steffens Andenken," in *Nachgelassene Schriften von H. Steffens* (Berlin: Schroeder, 1846), pp. iii–lxiii.
[64] See Schmidt and Miodoński, eds., *System und Subversion*, 49.
[65] Schleiermacher to Friedrich Dohna, February 1804, *KGA* 5.7, p. 229.

Bibliography

Anrich, Ernst. *Die Idee der deutschen Universitäten. Die fünf Grundschriften aus der Zeit ihrer Neubegründung durch klassischen Idealismus und romantischen Realismus* (Darmstadt: Wissenschaftliche Buchgesellschaft, 1956).

Beiser, Frederick C. *German Idealism: The Struggle against Subjectivism, 1781–1801* (Cambridge, MA: Harvard University Press, 2002).

Bergner, Marit. *Henrich Steffens. Ein politischer Professor in Umbruchszeiten 1806–1819* (Frankfurt am Main: Lang, 2016).

Börne, Ludwig. *Sämtliche Schriften*, vol. 1. Ed. Inge and Peter Rippmann (Düsseldorf: Mezler, 1964).

Christensen, Dan Ch. *Hans Christian Ørsted: Reading Nature's Mind* (Oxford: Oxford University Press, 2013).

Cunnigham, Andrew, and Nicholas Jardine, eds. *Romanticism and the Sciences* (Cambridge: Cambridge University Press, 2000).

Dierken, Jörg. "Das Absolute und die Wissenschaften. Zur Architektonik des Wissens bei Schelling und Schleiermacher." *Philosophisches Jahrbuch* 99 (1992), pp. 307–328.

Dilthey, Wilhelm. *Leben Schleiermachers*, vol. 1. 2nd ed. Ed. Hermann Mulert (Berlin: de Gruyter, 1922).

Gaß, W., ed. *Fr. Schleiermacher's Briefwechsel mit J. Chr. Gaß* (Berlin: Reimer, 1852).

Hagenbach, Karl Rudolf. "Autobiographie." Staatsarchiv Basel-Stadt PA 838a B1.

Hegel, G. W. F. *Vorlesungen über die Geschichte der Philosophie III*. Ed. Hermann Glockner (Stuttgart-Bad Cannstatt: Frommann-Holzboog, 1965).

Helmer, Christine, Christiane Kranich, and Birgit Rehme-Iffert, eds. *Schleiermachers Dialektik* (Tübingen: Mohr Siebeck, 2003).

Kemp, Friedhelm, ed. *Auf frischen kleinein abstrakten Wegen: Unbekanntes und Unveröffentliches aus Rahels Freundeskreis* (Munich: Kösel, 1967).

Körner, Josef, ed. *Briefe von und an August Wilhelm Schlegel*, vol. 1 (Zurich: Amalthea, 1930).

La Vopa, Anthony J. *Fichte: The Self and the Calling of Philosophy, 1762–1799* (Cambridge: Cambridge University Press, 2001).

Lenz, Max. *Geschichte der Königlichen Friedrich-Wilhelms-Universität zu Berlin*, vol. 1 (Halle: Waisenhaus, 1910).

Lorenz, Otto, and Bernd Henningsen, eds. *Henrik Steffens—Vermittler zwischen Natur und Geist* (Berlin: Berlin Verlag, 1992).

Mann, Gustav. *Das Verhältnis der Schleiermacher'schen Dialektik zur Schelling'schen Philosophie* (Stuttgart: Vereins-Buchdruckerei, 1914).

Momigliano, Arnaldo. "Friedrich Creuzer and Greek Historiography." *Journal of the Warburg and Courtauld Institutes* 9 (1946), pp. 152–163.

Paul, Fritz. *Henrich Steffens. Naturphilosophie und Universalromantik* (Munich: Fink, 1973).

Plitt, G. L., ed. *Aus Schellings Leben. In Briefen*, vol. 1 (Leipzig: Hirzel, 1869).

Purvis, Zachary. *Theology and the University in Nineteenth-Century Germany* (Oxford: Oxford University Press, 2016).

Richards, Robert J. *The Romantic Conception of Life: Science and Philosophy in the Age of Goethe* (Chicago: University of Chicago Press, 2002).

Schelling, F. W. J. *Briefe und Dokumente (1775–1809)*, vol. 1. Ed. Horst Fuhrmans (Bonn: Bouvier, 1962).

Schelling, F. W. J. "Aus einem öffentlichen Vortrag zu H. Steffens Andenken." In *Nachgelassene Schriften von H. Steffens* (Berlin: Schroeder, 1846), pp. iii–lxiii.
Schelling, F. W. J. "Kritische Fragmente." *Jahrbücher der Medizin als Wissenschaft* 2 (1807), pp. 283–304.
Schelling, F. W. J. *Philosophie der Offenbarung, 1841/42*. Ed. Manfred Frank (Frankfurt am Main: Suhrkamp, 1977).
Schelling, F. W. J. *Schellings Werke*, vol. 3. Ed. Manfred Schröter (Munich: Beck, 1927).
Schlegel, Friedrich. *Kritische Friedrich Schlegel Ausgabe*, vol. 24. Ed. Raymond Immerwahr (Paderborn: Ferdinand Schöningh, 1985).
Schleiermacher, Friedrich. *Briefwechsel 1801-02, KGA* 5.5, ed. Andreas Arndt and Wolfgang Virmond (Berlin: De Gruyter, 1999).
Schleiermacher, Friedrich. *Briefwechsel 1803-04, KGA* 5.7, ed. Andreas Arndt and Wolfgang Virmond (Berlin: De Gruyter, 2005).
Schleiermacher, Friedrich. *Briefwechsel 1804-1806, KGA* 5.8, ed. Andreas Arndt and Simon Gerber (Berlin: De Gruyter, 2008).
Schleiermacher, Friedrich. *Briefwechsel 1806-1807, KGA* 5.9, ed. Andreas Arndt and Simon Gerber (Berlin: De Gruyter, 2011).
Schleiermacher, Friedrich. *Briefwechsel 1809-1810, KGA* 5.11, ed. Simon Gerber and Sarah Schmidt (Berlin: De Gruyter, 2015).
Schmidt, Sarah, and Leon Miodoński, eds. *System und Subversion. Friedrich Schleiermacher und Henrik Steffens* (Berlin: de Gruyter, 2018).
Steffens, Henrik. *Beyträge zur inner Naturgeschichte der Erde* (Freiberg: Craz, 1801).
Steffens, Henrik. *Grundzüge der philosophischen Naturwissenschaften* (Berlin: Realschulbuchhandlung, 1806).
Steffens, Henrik. "Rede in der Aula der Friedrich-Wilhelms-Universität." In *Drei Reden am Tage der Bestattung des weiland Professors der Theologie und Predigers Herrn Dr. Schleiermacher am 15ten Februar 1834* Ed. Friedrich Strauss, F. A. Pischon, and Henrik Steffens (Berlin: Reimer, 1834), pp. 25–36.
Steffens, Henrik. *Vollständiges Handbuch der Oryktognosie*, 4 vols. (Halle: Curt, 1811–1824).
Steffens, Henrik. *Was ich erlebte. Aus der Erinnerung niedergeschrieben*, 10 vols. (Breslau: Max, 1840–1844).
Süskind, Hermann. *Der Einfluss Schellings auf die Entwicklung von Schleiermachers System* (Tübingen: Mohr, 1909).
Tilliete, Xavier. *Schelling: biographie* (Paris: Calmann-Lévy, 1999).
Twesten, August. "Vorrede." In *Friedrich Schleiermachers Grundriss der philosophische Ethik.* Ed. August Twesten (Berlin: Reimer, 1841), pp. iii–cii.
Varnhagen von Ense, Karl August. *Denkwürdigkeiten und Vermischte Schriften*. 2nd ed., vol. 1 (Leipzig: Brockhaus, 1843).
Ziche, Paul, and Gian Franco Frigo, eds. *"Die bessere Richtung der Wissenschaften." Schellings "Vorlesungen über die Methode des akademischen Studiums" als Wissenschafts- und Universitätsprogramm* (Stuttgart: Frommann-Holzboog, 2011).
Ziolkowski, Theodore. *German Romanticism and Its Institutions* (Princeton: Princeton University Press, 2000).

CHAPTER 6

"DOMESTIC DISPUTES" IN THE KANTIAN HERITAGE
Schleiermacher and Hegel on Religion and Christianity

JÖRG DIERKEN

6.1 INTRODUCTION

IT is not possible to understand the work of Friedrich Schleiermacher without understanding his context, and that requires discussion of his contemporary and colleague Georg W. F. Hegel.[1] The intellectual weight of these two thinkers can hardly be overestimated. Both developed systems of thought that have left traces in nearly every area of the humanities. This makes them "classics" or points of orientation, by acceptance or rejection. Furthermore, both are inheritors, each in his own way, of the critical philosophy of Kant. As such, they extend the tradition of the Enlightenment, albeit with certain Romantic entanglements. Their significance to the institution of the university is as great as their intellectual weight. Schleiermacher stands alongside Wilhelm von Humboldt as one of the principal architects of the University of Berlin at its founding in 1810, and like Hegel, Schleiermacher was deeply involved in a practical way in systems of schooling and education. Both were moreover magnets for students and contributed to the strong reputation of the university in Berlin after its founding. And with them, religion and Christianity came to hold a central position. Only Schleiermacher was an active member of the clergy, but both had studied theology and both were philosophically minded; as such, religion was for them, broadly speaking, a rational matter. Religion is one of the sources of the formation of humanity, situated as it is in reciprocally functioning connections to nearly all social and cultural spheres of life. To the extent that religion helps to bring about the realization of freedom, religion becomes a

---

[1] An earlier German version of this chapter was previously published as "Hauskrieg bei Kants Erben, Schleiermacher und Hegel über Religion und Christentum," in *Schleiermacher/Hegel. 250. Geburtstag Schleiermachers/200 Jahre Hegel in Berlin*, ed. Andreas Arndt and Tobias Rosefeldt (Berlin: Duncker & Humblot, 2020), pp. 19–36.

location for a sense of the whole. In Schleiermacher's words, religion is a "sense and taste for the infinite," and renders the infinite intuitable in the finite. Or, to cite Hegel, religion is "self-consciousness of absolute spirit," that is, a life in which the entanglement of self and other is fully realized by the human's being raised to "God" as the "place where he feels, beholds, enjoys his freedom, infinity, and universality."[2]

Such soaring formulations are, however, clouded by polemics, and indeed precisely surrounding the topic of religion. Schleiermacher and Hegel worked very closely with one another while also competing with one another. As a result of critical observation of their different ways of thinking, the two colleagues famously were driven to a harsh mutual confrontation in 1818. Already in 1802, Hegel had publicly criticized Schleiermacher's 1799 *Speeches* on religion for its emphasis on intuition, based in feeling.[3] Contrary to thinking, such a form would be open to arbitrary contents, just like its corollary form in Schleiermacher's mature work, *The Christian Faith* (*Glaubenslehre*). In the programmatic formulation of this later work, religion is a "feeling of absolute dependence,"[4] which in Hegel's view has to do with the "animal form of rational self-consciousness."[5] This led Hegel to make the vicious comparison that a "dog would be the best Christian," since it lives principally with such a feeling in regard to its master and would experience "feelings of redemption" if given a bone to eat.[6] A quarrel between the two, which the theologian Emanuel Hirsch described as a "household war" (*häuslicher Krieg*),[7] followed in due course. This led to mutual exclusions—namely, the exclusion of Hegel from membership in the Academy of Sciences (which had been promised to him upon his hiring in Berlin) and the exclusion of Schleiermacher from the *Jahrbuch für wissenschaftliche Kritik*. This domestic dispute was only superficially papered-over at university events or in sharing insider tips on where to buy the best wine. All the while, political striving and church-political disagreements were ever-present in the background. Nevertheless, the conflict was quite productive, too: Hegel developed his philosophy of religion in reaction to the *Glaubenslehre*, while Schleiermacher critically engaged with Hegel's ideas in his lectures on aesthetics and elsewhere.[8] Moreover, both founded partially overlapping schools of thought during the years of their activity in Berlin. And in the debates that these schools carried out—over the critique and foundations of religion, or concerning history and politics—the ongoing importance and potential of

---

[2] *KGA* 1.2, p. 212; G. W. F. Hegel, *Vorlesungen über Philosophie der Religion*, vols. 1–3, ed. Walter Jaeschke (Hamburg: Meiner, 1983–1985), vol. I, p. 222; G. W. F. Hegel, "Vorrede zu Hinrich's Religionsphilosophie" (1822), in *Gesammelte Werke* [*GW*] (Hamburg: Meiner, 1968–),vol. 15, p. 137; cf. Walter Jaeschke, *Hegel-Handbuch: Leben–Werk–Schule*, 2nd ed. (Stuttgart: Metzler, 2010), pp. 279ff. All translations from the German are original to the author unless otherwise indicated.

[3] Cf. Hegel's treatment of "Glaube und Wissen," in *GW* vol. 4, pp. 385ff.

[4] CG^2, §4.

[5] Hegel, "Berliner Antrittsrede," in *GW* vol. 18, p. 24.

[6] Hegel, *GW* vol. 15, p. 137.

[7] Emanuel Hirsch, *Geschichte der neuern evangelischen Theologie, im Zusammenhange mit den allgemeinen Bewegungen des europäischen Denkens*, vols. IV–V (Gütersloh: Bertelsmann, 1952), vol. IV, p. 541.

[8] Hegel's philosophy of religion consists of a series of lectures in which religion is succinctly treated and plotted according to the ways Hegel interprets it in his systematic works. Cf. Hegel, *Philosophie der Religion*.

their teachers' categories over and beyond epochal transitions consistently proved themselves, even while undergoing constructive and destructive reversals.[9]

The following chapter analyzes similarities and differences between Schleiermacher and Hegel. It begins with their remarks on philosophy and religion after Kant, then describes the foundational concepts of Schleiermacher's theory of subjectivity in comparison to that of Hegel, and finally turns to an outline of their respective theories of the social sphere. A short conclusion will sum up the main insights.

6.2 Thinking in the Kantian Heritage

A domestic dispute presupposes something held in common. In the first place, there is the Kantian heritage: The thought of both figures takes as its point of departure the philosophy of the subject and of consciousness, in and through which the thematics of religion and God unfold. In this they are joined also by Fichte. As with Fichte, the realization of subjectivity is a central theme for both Hegel and Schleiermacher, though not as in the framing of the artificial antitheses Fichte used in his earlier philosophy, but rather as embedded in forms of life. Yet another part of the Kantian heritage as found in Schleiermacher and Hegel is the delimitation of theoretical and practical reason and the prioritization of practical reason. For each, the primacy that Kant gives to practical reason in his deontological moral philosophy is connected with a sharp critique of his bare deontological "ought," which in view of the difference between "ought" (duty) and "is" (being), loses any real moral quality the moment it is realized in being. In the ethical thought of Schleiermacher and Hegel, the performative and dynamic characterization of reason becomes more nuanced through communicative instantiations of spirit. Both thinkers' rather similar approaches to an ethics of the good display this orientation toward the ethical social environment.[10] Religion is embedded in its institutions, and in the same way those institutions reflect religion. This point leads to yet another aspect of commonality: the mutual interaction of theology and social theory. The basic idea that sets the stage for this point is that there is no principled difference between human this-worldliness and the divine beyond; rather, both are interwoven into one another. Perhaps this is to be taken with a grain of salt, as both Schleiermacher and Hegel took up Spinozistic influences in their philosophies of religion, albeit with criticism and reformulation. The philosophy of religion of both thinkers is (at)tuned to the tones of wholeness (*Ganzheit*) and totality (*Totalität*). This led to repeated accusations of pantheism, behind

---

[9] Concerning Schleiermacher's time as a professor and churchman in Berlin, see the articles from Simon Gerber, Andreas Reich, Albrecht Geck, Dirk Schmid, and Martin Rössler in Martin Ohst, ed., *Schleiermacher-Handbuch* (Tübingen: Mohr Siebeck, 2017), pp. 189ff.; Kurt Nowak, *Schleiermacher: Leben, Werk und Wirkung* (Göttingen: Vandenhoeck & Ruprecht, 2002), pp. 457ff.; Hirsch, *Geschichte*, vol. V, chs. 50–52; on Hegel, cf. Jaeschke, *Hegel-Handbuch*, pp. 505ff.; and Walter Jaeschke, *Die Vernunft in der Religion. Studien zur Grundlegung der Religionsphilosophie Hegels* (Stuttgart: Frommann-Holzboog, 1986), pp. 361ff.

[10] Schleiermacher's principal work in this regard is his philosophical ethics. See *Ethik (Birkner)*. For Hegel, see the third part of his "philosophy of right" (on "Sittlichkeit" or "ethical life") in *Grundlinien der Philosophie des Rechts*, GW vol. 14, p. 1; see also the more precise presentation of this in Hegel, *Enzyklopädie der philosophischen Wissenschaften im Grundrisse (1830)*, GW vol. 20, pp. 478–541.

which, as it was of course assumed, stood atheism. Certainly neither of them were theists—in the sense of a thinker who sees God standing apart from the natural world and intervening in its operations, nor were they pantheists in any simple sense. The former would imply a theory of two-worlds, while the latter would rule out freedom and leave everything individual to become a link in a predetermined order.[11] And atheism would cut off the possibility of an inner realization of the transcendent, to which a communicating subject leading a life of freedom in pursuit of the whole is oriented, by severely restricting its ability to be thought or symbolized. That is the limitation of Fichte's earlier position (which had triggered the *Atheismusstreit*) according to which God merges completely into the moral order and as such cannot even be thought.[12] Fichte is, however, in agreement with other classical thinkers in his understanding of freedom, according to which the life of freedom itself possesses a divine quality and must be grasped in that way in order to count as free. Since freedom is something unconditioned, as a "whole" it carries no reference to any external and is thus an idea of something self-sustaining.

As much as these and other similarities show both Schleiermacher and Hegel to be philosophers of religion in the classical (Enlightenment-Idealist-Romantic) German tradition, they also paint a picture of independent figures with marked differences. Two important ones might be mentioned at the outset. The first is illustrated by the conflict over "feeling" (*Gefühl*). What is not in question is that in contrast to dogmatic theology, with the Enlightenment era's distinction between theology and religion, the subjective dimension of religious praxis is brought into focus. However, in view of the contrast made between feeling and thinking, the extent to which access to religion proceeds primarily via the condition of the subject or primarily via objective content becomes a matter of debate. Both thinkers carefully interwove the dimensions of subjective positionality and objective content, but they did so in different ways. Schleiermacher always looked for new antitheses in his mode of reflection via contrasts, which he then sought to limit and balance out by placing two such dialectics perpendicular to one another. Thereby he creates a form of a fourfold matrix (the so-called *Viererschema*), which combines the rational operations of "organizing" (shaping nature through reason) and "symbolizing" (displaying reason by nature) with the relation of the individual (which we only can find in nature) and the universal (which is always an idea of reason), using the technique of crossing both relations in order to show the four spheres of thought and action that result from their intersection.[13] Hegel, on the other hand, is interested in a concrete negation of the difference between the subjective form of consciousness and the contents of consciousness, by means of which negation the difference subsequently reappears in a different form.

This first difference between the two thinkers in turn leads to a second, namely to different understandings of God. For Schleiermacher, God can be thought of as the final unity of all oppositions—including those of world-bound, finite consciousness—but God can only be thought of as a negation in the sense of being incomprehensible. For Hegel's God, by contrast, differences arising by means of negation are themselves incorporated substantially

---

[11] This is Jacobi's main objection against pantheistic figures.

[12] See Johann Gottlieb Fichte, *Fichtes Werke*, vol. V, ed. Immanuel Hermann Fichte (Berlin: De Gruyter, reprint 1971), pp. 175–189.

[13] For a fuller treatment of this *Viererschema* in Schleiermacher's thought, see Chapter 10 in this volume, on Schleiermacher's philosophical ethics.

into the understanding of God in Godself.[14] In looking at the philosophy of religion of both thinkers, one could say that both accept an understanding of consciousness as something finite and discursively rendered. Together with this, however, the question arises whether the resources required for discursive thought themselves remain within the ambit of discursive thought, or if instead they are raised up beyond the finitude of discursive thought into an infinite Other that is its antithesis, which through this encounter is changed and made finite. Such conceptual models obviously hold a deep connection with basic Christian paradigms. While Schleiermacher thematizes God precisely in God's persisting difference from finitude, Hegel theorizes ethics as a kind of deification in which divine incarnation and subsequent negation on the cross are appropriated into the spirit of the church community.

6.3 A Sense for All Things in the Particular

In his early years, Schleiermacher pursued a program similar to Hegel's formula of moving "from substance to subject."[15] In his romantic debut work, his speeches *On Religion*, he paid great homage to Spinoza and his notion of the unity of all things.[16] Schleiermacher's interest in Spinoza had not so much to do with how to ground a self-causing substance as a form of causality immanent in things, nor a fortiori with a concern about a self-sufficient God: one religion without any concept of God at all might be better than another with one.[17] Religion understood as a "sense and taste for the infinite" means "intuiting" and seeing the infinite through everything finite and individual, which itself becomes transparent for the infinite. Behind this multifaceted and suggestive formulation stands the idea of the "universe"— Schleiermacher's term for a world-encompassing idea of God—as the culminated reality of a reciprocal interconnectedness of all things with all things. This reality is presented, however, only in an infinite fullness in the particular, which in its difference from whatever it is not, nevertheless virtually contains all other particulars. Religion, for Schleiermacher, means perceiving this form of comprehensive-reality-in-particularity, and he explicates religion in terms of a theory of subjectivity. As its "own province in the mind" (*eigne Provinz im Gemüte*), religion is set apart, on the one hand, from the mind's faculty of theoretical reason, which stands between science and metaphysics and is responsible for objective contents; and, on the other hand, from the faculty of practical reason, which governs subjective action using moral principles.[18] That province of the mind particular to religion, however, does not refer to a separation. Religion interacts with the faculties of theoretical and practical reason in many multifaceted ways. The way that religion renders present the interconnection of the

---

[14] Schleiermacher's conceptual-philosophical perspective thus represents an epistemologically grounded negative theology, while Hegel locates the negative within the idea of God and its inner structure. Yet a further position is represented in the late thought of Fichte. For him, God is the embodiment of the fulfillment of life itself, and as such not strictly speaking conceivable. In the thinking of finite consciousness God can be reflexively present in the form of a contrast or mirror image, as long as thinking and the images used in thinking make explicit God's ineffability.

[15] Hegel, *Phänomenologie des Geistes*, *GW* vol. 9, p. 18.

[16] Cf. *Reden¹*, pp. 211f.

[17] Cf. *Reden¹*, p. 244.

[18] *Reden¹*, p. 204.

universal and the particular is in keeping with the way that religion integrates the diversity of the subject into a unity.[19] Such interaction conducts the delicate interplay of the forms of intuition and feeling that are characteristic of religion. Intuition is gripped by something "particular and finite" and sees in this the "infinite" (and, in this way, drifts in parallel to Spinoza's third, extra-discursive form of knowing, to a certain extent).[20]

Feeling corresponds with this movement as a kind of spontaneous, dynamic change within the subject, which circumvents any differences between the feeling subject and that which the subject is feeling, thereby rendering present for the subject the interconnection of the particular and the whole in an immediate way. Feeling and intuition form a relationship of complementarity that evens out the imbalance of the inner and outer, the passive and active. In the background, however, they are "one and undivided."[21] This is the point in the erotically charged closing passage of the *Speeches* where the "moment" of non-difference between intuition and feeling is compared with a sort of sexual union of the "I" with the universe, or rather with its appearance in image or form: The "I" becomes the "soul" of the "infinite world," it feels its "powers" and the universe's "infinite life just as its own. [I]t is, in this moment, my body."[22] In a kind of reverse mysticism, the universe enters into the finite, subjective "I," and in turn reveals itself to—or, better, un-limits itself in—the "I." Yet this moment is itself "secret" and incomprehensible, and it is dissolved "by the most minor disturbance" into—or better, by—other moments in which the universe and the "I," like intuition and feeling, diverge.[23] The union of the universe with the "I" becomes describable as something close to real life only, as it were, through the color-negatives of those subsequent moments. The conceptual means for dealing with this situation is a form of "necessary reflection," which "divides" moments that have been joined into a unity.[24] Neither of these is in any way downgraded: Just as that "disturbance" of unity becomes "the natal hour of all that is living in religion,"[25] so also this form of reflection that now afterward splits the unity apart and begins drawing analytic distinctions in it proves to be the methodological mode of access for giving an account of what has happened. Schleiermacher goes on to describe how nature and world and history and humanity become occasions for religious intuitions and corresponding feelings. This leads, in turn, to the cultivation of religion, realized in and by the subject in communication-based community with others. Religion itself takes on a history in the "positive" (i.e., world-historical) religions. In the religions, religion is referred back reflexively to itself as their basic "material" (*Stoff*) and impresses upon them their "higher"—and, for Schleiermacher, Christian—"potential."[26] This is the culmination point of the *Speeches*.

Hegel certainly appreciated Schleiermacher's *Speeches*, and he attributed to them a fundamentally speculative quality due to the way they join opposites into a whole. In the *Speeches*, Hegel observes, "the dividing wall between the subject and the absolutely unreachable

---

[19] In this way, Schleiermacher's account bears a formal similarity to Kant's account of the accomplishment of the act of thinking.
[20] *Reden¹*, pp. 211f.
[21] *Reden¹*, p. 221.
[22] *Reden¹*, p. 221.
[23] *Reden¹*, p. 221.
[24] *Reden¹*, p. 220.
[25] *Reden¹*, p. 222.
[26] *Reden¹*, p. 317.

object is torn down, pain is reconciled in pleasure, endless striving is satisfied in beholding [*Schauen*]."[27] Nevertheless, he continues, "this subject-objectivity of the universe" remains "again another instance of something special and subjective,"[28] and one that, in the end, dominates a multiplicity of contingent, subjective acts lacking any internal connection among them that would produce a new form of the universe. Rather than "eliminating . . . the subjective peculiarity of intuition" and producing something shared, it results in an "atomism" of virtuosos, who are always gathering "little communities" around themselves and who "resemble figures in a sea of sand ever exposed to the play of the winds"—or so the critique goes, translated into socio-philosophical terms.[29] Thus the universe can hope finally only for a kind of "searching for a longing" for "reconciliation in the here and now"— in accordance with the basic Protestant principle.[30] All of this touches on the point that Schleiermacher remains within the horizons of a philosophy of reflection on subjectivity. It is conditioned by an insurmountable difference of the finite in relation to that which grasps all things, the one and the whole—which philosophical discourse names the Absolute. This is the basic thesis of Hegel's *Glauben und Wissen*, on the philosophies of reflection on subjectivity of Kant, Jacobi (with whom Hegel categorizes Schleiermacher), and Fichte.

Evident in Hegel's critique of Schleiermacher is a sense of the superiority of his position on the problem of reflection. The problem is one that troubles any philosophical program aimed at comprehensive synthesis, including Hegel's own, yet he claims to have solved it. Hegel's approach began as a philosophy of unification, under the headings of love and life, according to which the links in the chain of love may be found in processual unfolding of life and vice versa, and thereby the differences of the finite and the infinite might be overcome. In this model, the early Hegel himself also made recourse to the subjective forms of feeling and intuition, and "God" becomes the embodiment of their realized unification. "To love God is to feel oneself in the all-things of life boundlessly in the infinite," and love is the "feeling of life that finds itself once again."[31] A similar inner recursive arc also forms the "intuited life."[32] Yet intuition reifies the intuited, while feeling can present itself in a negative form as "a loss of life."[33] The shadows of refracting reflection lie on these subjective forms that block once again the intended all-encompassing dynamic. Hegel's interests are thus aimed at solving the problem of reflection—and, indeed, to do so by means of reflective thought. Around 1800 he starts to construct increasingly complicated figures of reflection that "show the finitude in everything finite" by applying to finite difference the principle of being placed in relationship through the drawing of distinctions.[34] In place of the infinite, however, this negative dialectic knows only an incomprehensible emptiness. Hegel tackles this problem after his move to Jena in 1801 and his discovery of a speculative way of thinking through two subtly interconnected figures of thought that could enable "construction of

---

[27] Note the mutual echo here of *Schauen* and *Anschauen* in German; see Hegel, *GW* vol. 4, p. 385.
[28] Hegel, *GW* vol. 4, p. 385.
[29] Hegel, *GW* vol. 4, p. 386.
[30] Hegel, *GW* vol. 4, pp.385–6.
[31] G. W. F. Hegel, *Frühe Schriften*, in *Werke in Zwanzig Bänden. Theorie-Werkausgabe* [*TWA*], ed. Eva Moldenhauer and Karl Markus Michel (Frankfurt: Suhrkamp, 1969–1971), vol. 1, pp. 363, 346.
[32] Hegel, *TWA* vol. 1, pp. 345f.
[33] Hegel, *TWA* vol. 1, p. 345.
[34] Hegel, *TWA* vol. 1, p. 345.

the Absolute in consciousness."[35] On the one hand, the principle of reflection—that is, the separating or dividing movement—is applied reflexively to the principle itself and, as a result of this separating of the separating act, is negated. Should this process of negating reflection in reflection be taken to its fullest extent, it would form a speculative unity through opposites or antitheses. This leads to the second figure of thought: difference, distinction, or decoupling have to be set into this wholeness, which stands for the divine or the absolute. Put more pointedly, God cannot be a simple unity if God is supposed to be the unity of all things. And this difference in God, for which Hegel at first takes recourse to intellectual intuition, cannot be merely immanent to God. It must also be placed at the location contrasting God over against all others, if the true differential character is to be taken seriously. In this way of thinking, the nucleus of a kind of independence or freedom is linked into the divine and at the same time is enacted by human beings as that divine's corresponding other. This is the speculative anchor-point for Hegel, the reason why he understands religion not only in terms of truth—as a harmonizing of the self in the whole—but also in terms of freedom, as an ever-changing spontaneity that finds itself located in otherness.

Viewed in this light, Hegel's polemic against Schleiermacher's later formula of religion as a feeling of dependence may be understandable. Nevertheless, it distracts from certain rather central points in Schleiermacher's account. For the mature Schleiermacher of the *Glaubenslehre* was also convinced that religion is a matter of the self inhabiting itself as a part of a whole—and indeed each self in its own finite, relative, and individual freedom. This is what is meant by feeling. Intuition retreats behind feeling, and the realization of feeling is the culmination of the subjective condition, in which the interwovenness of the subject with the totality of the world is experienced. Still, Schleiermacher does make use of a subtle form of conceptual reflection to describe feeling, and feeling works in a highly constructed manner. Feeling in the *Glaubenslehre* is understood as a transition between the cognitive and volitional faculties. In its indifference with respect to these faculties, the connection—sometimes more passive, sometimes more active, but always partial—of the subject with an other that is also bound in the world expresses itself in an internal consciousness of their interconnectedness within a whole totality of reciprocity, for which this consciousness becomes a subjective synthesis.[36] In such a unity, feeling corresponds to a series of attempted syntheses of the absolute, which culminates in a final unity of thinking and being, subject and object, but precisely for this reason is nevertheless situated in reflective thought. In this way of bringing thinking into alignment with feeling and willing, which Schleiermacher works out in his *Dialektik*, the theory of the subject, metaphysics, and logic go together.[37] The main points of the subtle arguments in the *Glaubenslehre*, as in the *Dialektik*, together indicate that all knowing and all doing imply partial connections of the mental and the real—or, that is, of thinking and being. In this way a certain claim is always being made about their unity (the combination of which forms the absolute), in all theoretical and practical forms of life, albeit in ever finite and fragmented ways. Since feeling is situated in the transition between knowing and doing and summarily brings together the partial entanglements of thinking and being in a consciousness of reciprocity, this super-reflexive absolute is paralleled by feeling on the one hand and by its ambivalence over against reflection on the

---

[35] Hegel, "Differenzschrift," *GW* vol. 4, p. 11.
[36] Cf. *CG*², §3f.
[37] *Dial.*; cf. Andreas Arndt, *Friedrich Schleiermacher als Philosoph* (Berlin: De Gruyter, 2013), pp. 179ff.

other. By guaranteeing the unity of the subject, it renders present at the same time the whole reciprocal relationship of subject and world in the temporal course of internal states. The relational interwovenness of the subject and the world is experienced, and in this way the subject becomes an element of their totality through its relationship to itself. And as much as the subject becomes its own guarantee, it takes the "whole world up into the unity of the self-consciousness."[38] This presupposes, however, a momentary difference. It cannot be, on the one hand, the consciousness of the unity of the world and, on the other hand, a mere fleeting moment of unity. To this extent, the grounding of the feeling of dependence is joined together with a guarantee of subjective independence and freedom. The subject stands in the world, in the structure of relationality of which it is completely interwoven, always also in a position of independence. Yet at the same time it experiences itself as always already embedded in its subjective state. It is simply *there* in its self-activity and cannot, from itself, bring forth the intended unity and connectedness of the world, be that within itself or for the absolute. And exactly this is the substance of absolute dependence, which admittedly would not be perceptible without freedom.

Schleiermacher's construction has an open flank in that it does not explain religious feeling from religious states themselves, but rather opens them up indirectly, by means of what they do, via reflection. This is evident in the way that feeling is always interpreted in relation to two ideas of totality: the idea of God as a unity without multiplicity, and the idea of the world as a unity ramified by multiplicity. This permits the combination of a form of Spinozism that is reformulated in the logic of subjectivity and freedom with a strict monotheism. But the unity in question is never thought of as unity per se, but rather is always and only identified in various relations of shifting differences. God, world, and self precisely do not collapse into one. And to this extent Schleiermacher remains at a critical distance from Hegel's sort of concept-ontological "construction of the absolute in consciousness." The modes of reflection used in Schleiermacher's approach are not themselves obtained by means of reflection and stand in contradistinction to the absolute.

This is the case not only for the idea of God, which idea is interpreted consistently in correlative relationships to the idea of the world, but also for religious feeling. The indifference of religious feeling—as a result of its ambivalence—appears as "higher self consciousness" always in correlation to a "lower self consciousness" that is braided into the world, stretched out between pain and pleasure, and ever-changing.[39] This is the anchoring point for all that is historically contingent, the forms of which, in relation to the "higher," become the primary location of freedom. A criterion for measuring the degree of freedom is how easily the "higher self-consciousness" can emerge—a process that accompanies the fundamentally ethical forms of entanglement in the world as well as formation of the world. The horizon of world-formation is the kingdom of God as a potentially universal ordering of the world in freely functioning polarities. The relationship of both levels of consciousness, then, forms the measure of Schleiermacher's history-of-religions typology of pessimistically and optimistically tuned religions, and also characterizes his account of Christian life as an oscillation between sin and grace. Redemption in this account does not lead beyond the world,

---

[38] CG^2, §8.2.
[39] CG^2, §5; pp. 66ff.

but rather opens an ethically ordered way of coming home in the world. Characteristic in connection with this point is the openness for personhood. Following Schleiermacher's understanding of independence as built on the logic of subjectivity, the person is rooted in the world but in distinction from the world. The person is not merely an element of the dynamics of the world; rather, personhood means self-reliance. The ideal of the personality forms a kind of counterbalance to the pantheism motif. Personality appears in the diversity of individuality. It is thus no wonder that Schleiermacher is also regarded as being among the classical German thinkers on individuality. To the extent that the individual is distinguished from the other through its differences from the other, these differences already appear on the horizon along with individuality. In this way the social emerges in the sidelines of the individual.

Hegel's mature thinking on religion also culminates in a social philosophy. Religion realizes itself in the end as ethics and accompanies an ethical practice of life. The understanding of religion as a representation of self, world, and God is overcome in and by means of a mode of philosophy that is animated by a theoretical-contemplative structure. Both elements, one more practical and the other more theoretical, are rooted in the concept of religion found in Hegel's philosophy of Spirit. Spirit is the highest definition of the Absolute. That means that the Absolute does not remain in itself but rather realizes itself in a mode of being-in-the-other, which operates by thinking and doing. It is not a substance existing for itself apart from the world. This has consequences for the religious concept of God. God is not a given reality, but rather a thought—if perhaps an unavoidable one. And God's reality is the perceived, believed, or practical realization of God in the logic of Spirit that God incarnates. Religiously speaking this comes to expression in seeing God's becoming human as God's highest purpose. Religion is in a non-dogmatic sense God's becoming human—and indeed in such a way that, on the one hand, incarnation is understood as and rooted in the self-constitution of God but, on the other hand, is also understood as the negation of a divine being standing in opposition to the human. With regard to the former, Hegel looks to the doctrine of the Trinity. Regarding the latter, he looks to the cross as the death of an august God of the beyond and the achievement of the reception of God in faith and in the Spirit. This happens likewise on an internal-individual as well as a social-communicative level. In the process, God becomes Spirit. The being of God is its open relationship to the being of any other. Put more classically: "Spirit" is "God" only "to the extent that he is in his community."[40] Religion, the "self-consciousness of Spirit," becomes concrete in the twofold Spirit-relationship of the thinking and consciousness of God, for which the "speculative" to an extent becomes a dynamically changing "state" of the subject located in empirical contexts.[41] The socio-philosophical key concept for this structure of Spirit is "recognition."

---

[40] Hegel, *Philosophie der Religion*, vol. 1, p. 74; cf. vol. 1, p. 33; vol. 3, p. 254; and vol. 1, p. 222.
[41] Hegel, *Philosophie der Religion*, vol. 1, pp. 222, 115.

6.4 Freedom in the Communicative Formation of Community

Strong socio-philosophical influences are evident in the theories of religion of both Schleiermacher and Hegel. Theology is translated into sociology, while the relationship to God appears likewise in and through social relationships. This is valid for both thinkers, but it appears in different modes in each. For Hegel, this takes the form of a cultural-sociological approach to religion in which what a particular group "holds to be true" comes to expression in a symbolically encoded way in religion.[42] Beyond this descriptive level, religion contains further potential for the normative ongoing development of such representations. Thus, for example, what is "individual" can be first recognized as being social once individuality is known as it is "in the divine being"; that is, in the Trinity.[43] Or again, what it means to be human is approached christologically, where the one stands for all: "in one—all," to paraphrase Hegel.[44] And the pneumatological structure of Spirit is oriented toward ethical forms of life in the here and now that are similar to the becoming of God and for which forms of recognition chart the vectors.[45] The ideal of symmetry that accompanies these forms of recognition constitutes an implicit responsibility, and this responsibility flows as an undercurrent beneath the asymmetries that are bound up in all empirical social relationships.

While Hegel, in the end, transforms religious piety into practical morality, Schleiermacher is interested in making the implicit social-communicative dimension of piety explicit. Communication is a basic concept of his sociological thinking, and religion is transferred in it. For example, his Christology has the effect that the redeemer founds a new common life; the redeemer enters into this common life with his work, and indeed with his whole person.[46] And Schleiermacher's sections on pneumatology and ecclesiology parallel this, indicating the way that the pious in a communicative "order of free persons" come into communal life with Christ through enacting that community in interaction with one another in infinitely individual variation.[47] Schleiermacher also describes such communication of redemptive piety in terms of a paradigm of ethical action.[48] His uncompleted *Christian Ethics*, which seeks to describe the form of piety that had been dogmatically presented in the *Glaubenslehre* now in terms of social life, outlines in addition to liturgical-aesthetic "presentational" action also the critical mode of "purifying" and the constructive pattern of "broadening" action.[49] The proximity of religion to education becomes a significant theme in these lectures in particular.

---

[42] Hegel, *Vorlesungen über die Philosophie der Geschichte*, TWA vol. 12, p. 70.
[43] Hegel, *Vorlesungen über die Philosophie der Geschichte*, TWA vol. 12, p. 70.
[44] Hegel, *Philosophie der Religion*, vol. 3, p. 49.
[45] The social-philosophical use of the concept of recognition goes back to Fichte. While Fichte relates the term primarily to the legal relationships of the subject whose freedom can only be realized via its demarcation from others, Hegel expands the concept to comprehensive social relationships unfolding through historical-cultural evolution.
[46] Cf. CG^2, §§87ff.
[47] CG^2, §§106ff.; 113ff.
[48] Cf. *Sitte*, p. 510; *PrTh*, p. 65.
[49] *Sitte*, pp. 97ff.; 291ff.; 502ff.

That Schleiermacher's and Hegel's understandings of religion have a socio-ethical foundation and significance corresponds with the fundamentally socio-theoretical orientation of their thought in general. For all their differences, Hegel's concept of ethics (*Sittlichkeit*) and Schleiermacher's first draft of a philosophical ethics (*Philosophische Ethik*) are similar in that they describe an institutionally organized social world from the perspective of reason. In that world, empirical performances of life express themselves in intersubjective exchange, while the forms of normativity resulting therefrom (re)produce yet more life. Although their approaches converge in their subtle critiques of the Kantian logic of duty, their philosophies of the social differ significantly at other points. While Schleiermacher follows system-theoretical instincts to an extent, Hegel makes explicit the subjectivity of the will and its intersubjective, interconnecting activity using images of recognition drawn from the philosophy of Spirit.

In the formations of Hegel's objective spirit, new asymmetries are generated whose inner contradictions drive those very asymmetries beyond themselves. In this process, religion can, with likewise careening formations, remain focused on itself and its own certain form of morality without comparison or connection to the rest of the world around it. But it can also become an entity bearing up the state, for example—whether through symbolic representation of the ethical foundations of the political-legal order or in transforming the state into God on earth.[50] Hegel's understanding of the state as a constitutional monarchy with final decision-making power—an understanding that combines elements of a constitutional state and separation of powers with elements of the landed nobility—is not completely free of this deifying tendency. Religion as institutionalized in the church has its special place in the sphere of civic society, characterized as it is by economic interests, reciprocal exchange, and ever-increasing competition, as well as the fluctuations in market share and physical presence that permeate the civic arena. In this sphere of striving and division, the corporately formed church stands as a column of support for the interests of the state, one that bears up all particular interests of individuals but contributes to the ethical formation of individuals via religious communication.[51] Without question, for Hegel, religion stands in close proximity to the state. But it does not follow the lines of (subsequent) conceptions of a Christian state.[52] The institutions of state and church should in no way be collapsed into one another, and the state's duty to guarantee freedom demands freedom of religion for all citizens, regardless of confession. Religion can even function, on the basis of the structure of the freedom of spirit, to exert a kind of potential resistance over against deficient state policies. This too, then, is built into Hegel's model, even if a certain element of civil religion, so to speak, cannot be overlooked.

Schleiermacher supports the separation of religion and politics, of church and state, more strongly than Hegel.[53] He regards the state's instrumentalization of religion and

---

[50] On this point, see Ludwig Siep, *Der Staat als irdischer Gott. Genese und Relevanz einer Hegelschen Idee* (Tübingen: Mohr Siebeck, 2015).

[51] Cf. Hegel, *Rechtsphilosophie*, GW vol. 14.1, §270, Anm.; concerning the concept of a "corporation," cf. pp. 250ff.; GW vol. 20, §534.

[52] Cf. Walter Jaeschke, "Staat aus christlichem Prinzip und christlicher Staat. Zur Ambivalenz der Berufung auf das Christentum in der Rechtsphilosophie Hegels und der Restauration," *Der Staat* 18 (1979), pp. 349–374.

[53] This position, already found in the *Speeches*, remains Schleiermacher's view throughout his work.

its official organization as responsible for religion's loss of credibility. In his later thought, Schleiermacher updates the early differentiations of knowing, doing, and feeling as well as of metaphysics, morals, and religion into a concept of functional differentiation and interdependence of social spheres. Decisive for his social philosophy built on an ethics of the good is the perpendicular combination of two polarities: the "individual" and the "general," and "organizing" (the appropriation of nature through reason) and "symbolizing" (the representation of reason in nature). The key point in this well-known quadratic graphing of ethical life is that the extremes of these antitheses can be neither completely separated from one another nor wholly collapse into one another.[54] Combining the limits of the antitheses as minima and maxima yields the differentiation of the spheres: organizing activity that is overbalanced toward generality is represented by the state and bureaucracy, while organizing activity that is overbalanced toward the individual is expressed in trade, commerce, and exchange. Over against these two spheres are the two further spheres of symbolizing activity, with their accents on the general and on the individual, which are expressed respectively in the form of reproducible knowledge, as in science (*Wissenschaft*), and in the social forms of symbolic communication, as in religion and art. Corresponding institutional forms and social structures are attributed to each of these spheres, which, however, also intersect with and thus address the work of other spheres. Thus, for example, there are no institutions of science or education without the state, no religious or aesthetic communication without education, nor again any economic or political activity or corresponding responsibility without the relevant mental attitudes.[55] In this way also religion can be grasped in its own functioning from a basically socio-philosophical point of view. It serves to cultivate a kind of self-understanding that is significant for all people—namely, of human beings as free—but also of finite individuals embedded in the whole of social life. In so doing, it uses its symbolizing form to care for the potential implicit in reflective thought so that the formation of the social does not occur without proper order. And like Hegel's account, Schleiermacher's also contains certain problematic points, particularly in the way that distinctions in theoretical analysis become externalized in social oppositions like that of clergy and lay persons in the church or of rulers and subjects in the state. This is the flipside of a highly innovative theory of religion that is, however, constructed with overlapping theoretical layers.

6.5 Conclusion

Schleiermacher's and Hegel's theories of religion cannot rightfully be portrayed as variations on one another. The methodological differences are too significant, and these differences are reflected not only in tone but throughout the entire system of each. But that does not change the fact that they share basic affinities due to their Kantian heritage. This was often not seen in the former debates between the different school-traditions. Among that heritage, each takes

---

[54] This is the same structure, aimed at the absolute, as outlined in the *Dialectic*. Only, the ethics lack a detailed account of the procedures of thinking, which constitutes the focus of the *Dialectic*.

[55] On Schleiermacher's own personal involvement in the educational and religious systems of his day, see the contributions of Andreas Reich, Albrecht Geck, Dirk Schmid, Martin Rössler, and Matthias Wolfes in Ohst, ed., *Schleiermacher-Handbuch*, pp. 193–241.

as its point of departure in interpreting religion a theory of the subject according to which religion is rooted in the free act of conscious life. The religious life finds itself in its uniqueness and further develops itself in a dialectic of limits, which nevertheless immediately lead the subject to stretch beyond mere finitude. Thus, in religion, a consciousness of wholeness and of totality is entangled with an elementary understanding of freedom. In the spontaneity that comes with this freedom, religion stands for deviation, change, and becoming other, and it cannot be thought of as self-determining except insofar as it is at the same time being determined by another. The tensions in the connection of freedom and wholeness bestow an open character upon the programmatic systems of both Schleiermacher and Hegel, which is reflected also in a constructive understanding of the particular in the individual and mediated by a theory of communication or of spirit in relation to the whole: The otherness of the other—of virtually all others—reaches into the identity of individual understanding with itself right from the beginning. The Enlightenment notions of equality and freedom are part of each model, even if in substantially modified and romantically inspired ways: The theory of the subject and of the social are entangled with one another, the structure of God is translated into a kind of spiritual intersubjectivity, and piety is explained in terms of ethics. These ideas can function as anchor points for current concepts of religion and Christianity, which take into account the challenges of modernity and beyond.

Yet the most marked differences also result from the divergent ways in which each thinker takes up the Kantian heritage. Schleiermacher follows the insight of Kant's critical philosophy regarding the finitude of all thought marked by the insurmountable duality of nature and intelligence in theoretical and practical perspectives. Hegel pursues the formation of unity or synthesis that follows the sightlines of an enactment of speculative reason permeating all relational dualities. Schleiermacher's basic methodological move is to posit that final unity in the Absolute remains transcendent, and his thinking moves in a fullness of artistically balanced polarities. This is the case for feeling, as the representative of absolute unity in the here and now. Feeling, in its immediacy, is highly construed at a remove from reflection, but it first becomes interpretable only by means of reflection. Hegel, on the other hand, brings the discursive nature of finite thinking that is ever-moving through antitheses of self-application and resolution into the Absolute itself, which the finite in turn takes into itself, and the Absolute, entering into the finite, lifts it up beyond its mere finitude in the structure of spirit. In this way the images used in thinking speculatively stand in contrast to those used in thinking (self-)reflexively.

Corresponding to this is a further methodological contrast between the two thinkers, between Hegel's method of a negative dialectic and Schleiermacher's procedure of reciprocal limitations in layered, mutually balancing polarities of reflection. All of this colors many differences in tone and style of the two thinkers. Schleiermacher's artistic arrangement of antitheses gives the impression of a final balance in motion. In Hegel, the significance of the negative creates a high sensibility for that which is contradictory. Both of these—stabilization through the balancing diverse forms of exchange as well as tense internal contradictoriness—are characteristics of modernity and emerge already at its beginnings. Schleiermacher and Hegel work on these challenges in constructive ways, ways that contemporary efforts can draw upon still.

Schleiermacher's and Hegel's philosophies of religion were produced in a moment of key transition in modernity, and there is much to learn from analyzing points of overlap and divergence between the two. Part of their abiding legacy is that both thinkers understand religion as a matter of reason in the broadest sense. This is clear both for Hegel, who presents religion as reason in the mode of imagination, and also for Schleiermacher, for whom religion is not the mere opposition to rationality but the underlined contrast between religion and metaphysics that refers to the doctrinal contents of the objective consciousness. Yet as each seeks to describe the contours of rationality, their efforts cannot be simply mapped onto one another. This itself shows a tendency toward plurality that is intrinsic to reason, a tendency that is also characteristic of contemporary conceptions of reason. This plurality, a "domestic dispute," occasions further intellectual striving and discovery. The tendency toward plurality within reason is not, however, arbitrary. Both approaches lead into different orders of thinking with religious symbols about finality, and thereby indicate different ways of exploring those orders. They aim in particular at an understanding of the plurality of reason in religious matters also, rather than toward the separation of religion from reason, and they are connected with strict but likewise open forms of systematic thinking. Even today the lengths of these paths have not yet been fully traveled.

Translated by Matthew Ryan Robinson

Suggested Reading

Arndt, Andreas. *Friedrich Schleiermacher als Philosoph* (Berlin: De Gruyter, 2013).

Arndt, Andreas, and Tobias Rosefeldt, eds. *Schleiermacher/Hegel: 250. Geburtstag Schleiermachers/200 Jahre Hegel in Berlin*. Hegel Jahrbuch, Sonderband 13 (Berlin: Duncker & Humblot, 2020).

Hegel, G. W. F. *Vorlesungen über Philosophie der Religion*, vols. I–III. Ed. Walter Jaeschke (Hamburg: Meiner, 1983–1985).

Jaeschke, Walter. *Hegel-Handbuch: Leben–Werk–Schule*, 2nd ed. (Stuttgart: Metzler, 2010).

Schleiermacher, Friedrich. *Ethik [1812/13], mit späteren Fassungen der Einleitung, Güterlehre und Pflichtenlehre*. Ed. Hans-Joachim Birkner (Hamburg: Meiner, 1981).

Bibliography

Arndt, Andreas. *Friedrich Schleiermacher als Philosoph* (Berlin: De Gruyter, 2013).

Arndt, Andreas, and Tobias Rosefeldt, eds. *Schleiermacher/Hegel: 250. Geburtstag Schleiermachers/200 Jahre Hegel in Berlin*. Hegel Jahrbuch, Sonderband 13 (Berlin: Duncker & Humblot, 2020).

Fichte, Johann Gottlieb. *Fichtes Werke*, vol. V. Ed. Immanuel Hermann Fichte (Berlin: De Gruyter, reprint 1971).

Hegel, G. W. F. *Gesammelte Werke* [*GW*] (Hamburg: Meiner, 1968–).

Hegel, G. W. F. *Vorlesungen über Philosophie der Religion*, vols. I–III. Ed. Walter Jaeschke (Hamburg: Meiner, 1983–1985).

Hegel, G. W. F. *Werke in Zwanzig Bänden. Theorie-Werkausgabe* [*TWA*]. Ed. Eva Moldenhauer and Karl Markus Michel (Frankfurt: Suhrkamp, 1969–1971).

Hirsch, Emanuel. *Geschichte der neuern evangelischen Theologie, im Zusammenhange mit den allgemeinen Bewegungen des europäischen Denkens*, vols. IV–V (Gütersloh: Bertelsmann, 1952).

Jaeschke, Walter. *Hegel-Handbuch: Leben–Werk–Schule*, 2nd ed. (Stuttgart: Metzler, 2010).

Jaeschke, Walter. "Staat aus christlichem Prinzip und christlicher Staat. Zur Ambivalenz der Berufung auf das Christentum in der Rechtsphilosophie Hegels und der Restauration." *Der Staat* 18 (1979), pp. 349–374.

Jaeschke, Walter. *Die Vernunft in der Religion. Studien zur Grundlegung der Religionsphilosophie Hegels* (Stuttgart: Frommann-Holzboog, 1986).

Nowak, Kurt. *Schleiermacher: Leben, Werk und Wirkung* (Göttingen: Vandenhoeck & Ruprecht, 2002).

Ohst, Martin, ed. *Schleiermacher-Handbuch* (Tübingen: Mohr Siebeck, 2017).

Siep, Ludwig. *Der Staat als irdischer Gott. Genese und Relevanz einer Hegelschen Idee* (Tübingen: Mohr Siebeck, 2015).

CHAPTER 7

SCHLEIERMACHER AND THE UNIVERSITY OF BERLIN

JOHANNES ZACHHUBER

FRIEDRICH Schleiermacher became professor at the University of Berlin when this institution was founded in 1810 and retained the post until his death in 1834. His earliest association with the new university dates back, however, to the previous decade when he published influential reflections on the idea of the university as part of a public debate about the future of higher education. Schleiermacher notably, and successfully, defended the continuing existence of a faculty of theology as part of a modern university, although this was by no means the only purpose of his intervention. He was thus the rare case of a professor appointed in a university whose character he had decisively helped to shape.

As a professor, Schleiermacher regularly lectured on a wide range of theological and philosophical subjects. Like his colleague and rival, G. W. F. Hegel, Schleiermacher used these courses to develop his own original and creative insights in a variety of directions. His major publications during those years, notably the *Christian Faith* and the *Brief Outline*, grew out of his lecturing activity, but the bulk of his lecture notes was only published posthumously, taking up thirteen volumes in the *Sämmtliche Werke* (1834–1864) and seventeen volumes in the as yet unfinished *Kritische Gesamtausgabe* (*KGA*). Thus, a large corpus of Schleiermacher's texts owes its existence to his institutional responsibilities at the University of Berlin.

Any account of Schleiermacher's entanglement with the University of Berlin must reckon with the unusual fact that he both shaped this institution and was, in turn, shaped by it. This chapter shall do justice to this challenge by relating Schleiermacher's ideas about the university to his own work as an academic. In many ways, it will turn out, he modeled his own professional life on the ideal demanded by his own theory. It is therefore legitimate to interpret his views on higher education and his intellectual production at the University of Berlin in close conjunction.

The chapter will begin in the years running up to the foundation of the new institution and sketch Schleiermacher's part in this momentous development. Against this backdrop, the remainder of the chapter will consider Schleiermacher's work as a lecturer and administrator in the university. The chapters findings will be summarized in a brief conclusion.

7.1 Political Background

The University of Berlin was founded in 1810, but the history of Schleiermacher's relationship with this institution began truly and properly in 1806. In that year, the French emperor, Napoleon Bonaparte, waged a devastating military campaign against Schleiermacher's native Prussia.[1] On October 14, the French army claimed an easy victory in the twin battles of Jena and Auerstedt. For Prussia, this was more than a military defeat; a country that had aspired to be among the great European powers was profoundly humiliated and faced with seemingly incontrovertible evidence for the utter superiority of its military and political enemy.[2]

Schleiermacher, who had been Professor of Theology at the University of Halle since 1804, was a keen political observer of these events;[3] it was not long until they affected him personally.[4] Only three days after the decisive battles, the victorious French army marched into Halle. The local university, considered a hotbed of political opposition to the French cause, was closed on October 20 by order of the occupying force.[5] Attempts to have it reopened failed, and Schleiermacher not only faced the downfall of his home nation but also professional uncertainty and personal hardship.

In this situation, the theologian decided to relocate to Berlin.[6] This proved an inspired move. Prussia's deep fall, which was completed by the enforced Treaty of Tilsit in July 1807, finally triggered a reform movement that had been overdue. Only days after signing the treaty, the hesitant king, Friedrich William III, appointed the ardent reformer Baron vom Stein (1757–1831) as head of his cabinet. Soon, changes were afoot that laid the groundwork for Prussia's extraordinary rise throughout the nineteenth century.[7]

7.2 Debates about University Reform

Founding a new university in Berlin had been a favorite idea of vom Stein's predecessor, Carl-Friedrich von Beyme (1765–1838), who had consulted about such a plan from the beginning of the century and initiated the first, serious steps after Prussia's military defeat and

---

[1] On the historical background, cf. Paul W. Schroeder, *The Transformation of European Politics: 1763–1848* (Oxford: Oxford University Press, 1994), chs. 5 and 6; Karen Hagemann, *Revisiting Prussia's Wars against Napoleon: History, Culture, and Memory* (Cambridge: Cambridge University Press, 2015); Alexander Mikerabidze, *The Napoleonic Wars: A Global History* (Oxford: Oxford University Press, 2020), ch. 10.

[2] Kurt Nowak, *Schleiermacher: Leben, Werk und Wirkung* (Göttingen: Vandenhoeck & Ruprecht, 2001), p. 175.

[3] Ibid., p. 177.
[4] Ibid., pp. 175–177.
[5] Ibid., pp. 176–177.
[6] Ibid., pp. 177, 180.
[7] Ibid., pp. 179–180.

the loss of the University of Halle.[8] When Schleiermacher finally decided to settle in Berlin, in the latter half of 1807, he had already been earmarked as the core appointment in theology.[9] He thus immediately found himself surrounded by a crop of eager and ambitious individuals keen to use the political crisis of these years to combine the advancement of their country with the pursuit of their own visions for a modern university.

The protagonists of this movement could draw on a debate that had been conducted by leading German intellectuals, including I. Kant, J. G. Fichte, F. W. J. Schelling, H. Steffens, and Schleiermacher himself, for over a decade.[10] At the center of this debate stood the question of the purpose of universities and what future, if any, they should have. Perhaps surprisingly from today's perspective, the idea of entrusting the modernization of a country's higher education to this institution at the time appeared rather counterintuitive to many.[11] In the late eighteenth century, universities were distinctly part of the old order. They were, after all, medieval foundations and, as such, appeared to progressives as outdated as the Holy Roman Empire or the papacy. And, in fact, all these institutions were shaken to their foundations in the French Revolution and its immediate aftermath.

The university's critics could easily point to the fact that the majority of eighteenth-century innovations, whether scientific or philosophical, originated outside the university, whose professorial postholders were largely given over to the production of long-winded, scholastic treatises. England, arguably the most innovative nation during these decades, had not founded a university since the thirteenth century, but led the way by its establishment of the Royal Society in 1660. When France eventually attempted a radical reform of its education system, it put in place its famed system of *grands écoles* rather than relying on reformed universities. Closer to home, the foundation and active development of a number of professional academies in Berlin around the year 1800 indicated that Prussian leaders too could be inclined to follow the French model.[12] Some of the most celebrated intellectual giants of the period, from G. W. Leibniz to G. E. Lessing, and J. W. Goethe, developed their ideas outside the university and were often scathing about the ossified character of that institution and its uninspiring, pedantic postholders.

One reason why reformers were skeptical about the university's capacity for reform was its traditionally close association with the church, expressed through the special status accorded to the faculty of theology. There is but little doubt that the search for alternative institutions facilitating higher education and research was at least partly driven by the attempt to reduce clerical influence over this aspect of society.[13] It is therefore all the more significant that

---

[8] Max Lenz, *Geschichte der königlichen Friedrich-Wilhelms-Universität zu Berlin*, vol. 1 (Halle/S.: Buchhandlung des Waisenhauses, 1910), pp. 24–36, 71–130; Thomas Albert Howard, *Protestant Theology and the Making of the German University* (Oxford: Oxford University Press, 2006), pp. 143–148.

[9] Nowak, *Schleiermacher*, p. 181: "halb und halb berufen."

[10] On this debate, see Howard, *Protestant Theology*, pp. 156–177; Zachary Purvis, *Theology and the University in Nineteenth-Century Germany* (Oxford: Oxford University Press, 2016), pp. 89–102. Key texts are collected in Ernst Anrich, ed., *Die Idee der deutschen Universität: Die fünf Grundschriften aus der Zeit ihrer Neubegründung durch klassischen Idealismus und romantischen Realismus* (Darmstadt: WBG, 1956).

[11] Howard, *Protestant Theology*, pp. 1–2. For the eighteenth-century critique of universities, cf. pp. 80–87.

[12] Lenz, *Geschichte*, pp. 39–46.

[13] Ibid., p. 85.

Prussian reformers not only went against the grain of their time by opting for the foundation of a modern university, but that in doing so they created an institution that, although secular in its statutes, contained a faculty of theology.[14]

This outcome was no foregone conclusion. Kant's *Conflict of the Faculties*, the text that initiated German discussions about university reform, clearly targeted the existing prominence of the so-called higher faculties, not least theology.[15] While Kant stopped short of calling for the abolition of the theological faculty, one could easily conceive of such an argument as an extension of Kant's critique. The latter position was influentially advanced by J. G. Fichte. It says something about the changing political fortunes of the time that, while Kant had to battle political censorship to get his treatise published, Fichte was picked by Beyme on behalf of the Prussian government as part of a small task force spearheading the foundation of the novel university.[16]

It was in response to the solicitation of his advice that the philosopher wrote *Deducirter Plan einer in Berlin zu errichtenden höheren Lehranstalt* (*A Plan, Deduced [from first principles] for an Institution of Higher Learning to Be Established in Berlin*, 1807), a remarkable treatise setting out a radical vision for the future of higher education as it was to be realized in Berlin.[17] The omission of the word "university" from the title of this work was hardly accidental, but indicates the author's fundamental objections to the model that had persevered in the West since the Middle Ages.[18] Of the four traditional faculties, Fichte proposed abolishing three, retaining only philosophy. Law, medicine, and theology, he argued, had all arisen from the state's practical need to train lawyers, medics, and priests, not from systematic reflections. Insofar as the university was to be a place dedicated to the cultivation of pure knowledge (*Wissenschaft*), it had to be philosophical in its entirety.[19]

It is well known that Fichte saw no place for theology in his university. As a discipline drawing on insights and principles that were not generally shared knowledge, theology could not, he argued, be part of a public institution of universal learning.[20] At one level, therefore, Fichte, in keeping with the spirit of the *Conflict of Faculties*, demanded that theology should open itself up to critical enquiry if it wished to retain a place within academic debate. Even in a radically modernized form, however, theology could not retain its status as a faculty in Fichte's ideal "university" quite simply because it did not constitute its own field of enquiry. Theology does not constitute a discipline in the way Fichte understood this term, as a body of interconnected ideas deduced from the principle of universal knowledge. Rather, the legitimate topics theologians study would fall under a number of different sciences such as metaphysics, ethics, or the history of languages.[21]

---

[14] Ibid., pp. 130–131.
[15] Cf. Werner L. Euler, "Der Streit zwischen der theologischen und der philosophischen Fakultät in Kants Schrift 'Der Streit der Fakultäten,'" *Ruch Filozoficzny* 72 (2016), pp. 7–25.
[16] On Kant's own context, cf. Howard, *Protestant Theology*, p. 124; on Fichte's involvement, see p. 150.
[17] Anrich, *Die Idee*, pp. 125–218. Cf. Howard, *Protestant Theology*, pp. 160–166.
[18] Ibid., p. 161.
[19] Anrich, *Die Idee*, p. 155.
[20] Ibid., pp. 154–155.
[21] Ibid., pp. 161–162.

7.3 Schleiermacher on University Reform

Unlike Fichte, Schleiermacher was not originally invited to contribute to the early discussions about the envisaged university.[22] In fact, there is evidence suggesting that his own contribution to the debate was partly motivated by a sense of being slighted by this oversight.[23] It appears, moreover, that Schleiermacher did not know of Fichte's *Deducirter Plan* until its publication in 1817, if he knew it at all.[24] This is remarkable because to readers of the two opinions it has always seemed "as if each [of the two authors] has been looking into the other's eyes trying to refute him" on account of the "different even contradictory principles, ideas, and results" of their two texts.[25]

If Schleiermacher's manifesto can be said to have been written with an opponent in mind, this would instead have been F. W. J. Schelling, whose influential *Lectures on University Studies* he critically reviewed when they were first published.[26] Schelling's lectures were originally delivered in Jena and thus not immediately connected with developments in Berlin. Yet their eager and enthusiastic reception ensured that, like Kant's *Conflict of the Faculties*, they formed part of the wider intellectual context in which the Prussian debate took place. As Zachary Purvis has shown, Schleiermacher thought of his critical engagement with Schelling's proposals as a "quiet war," presumably in distinction from the overt military conflicts happening contemporaneously in the real world.[27]

Like Fichte, Schelling too took his theoretical starting point from the *Conflict of the Faculties*, but he drew from it nearly opposite conclusions for the practical arrangement of the university. Only philosophy was true *Wissenschaft*, but *because of that* it did not need its own faculty. Instead, Schelling's university consisted of the three higher faculties: law, medicine, and theology, each fully informed by philosophical reasoning while dedicated to what Schelling called a "positive science":

> Clearly, theology, as the science in which the innermost nature of philosophy is objectified, must have the first and highest place. Since the ideal is a higher potency or level of the real, it follows that the law faculty has precedence over the medical. As for philosophy, I maintain that there is no such faculty, nor can there be, for that which is all things cannot for that very reason be anything in particular.[28]

While Schelling's proposal, compared to Fichte's, could thus appear more conservative, it was nevertheless inspired by the same desire to reform and renew in the spirit of the age, emphasizing the centrality of philosophy. Theology may very well retain its place as the first

---

[22] Nowak, *Schleiermacher*, p. 181.
[23] Ibid., p. 182.
[24] Lenz, *Geschichte*, p. 124.
[25] Ibid.
[26] Friedrich Wilhelm Joseph Schelling, *Vorlesungen über die Methode des akademischen Studiums* (1803), in *Sämmtliche Werke*, ed. K. F. A. Schelling, vol. I/5 (Stuttgart: Cotta, 1859), pp. 207–311; Friedrich Schleiermacher, "Rezension von Friedrich Wilhelm Joseph Schelling. Vorlesungen über die Methode des akademischen Studiums," in *KGA* 1.4, pp. 461–484. Cf. Purvis, *Theology and the University*, pp. 103–105.
[27] Ibid., p. 107.
[28] Schelling, *Vorlesungen*, pp. 283f.; English translation: *On University Studies*, translated by Ella S. Morgan, ed. Norbert Guterman (Athens, OH: Ohio University Press, 1966), p. 79.

faculty, but the reason for its preeminence has nothing to do with a confessional commitment to Christianity or the church. Rather, it is derived from theology's proximity to philosophy as Schelling understood it. Schelling's program, while not banishing theology from the university, prescribed to it a root-and-branch reform in line with idealist philosophy and early historicism.

There are clear traces of Schelling's argument in Schleiermacher's proposal, published in 1808 as *Gelegentliche Gedanken über Universitäten im deutschen Sinne* (*Occasional Thoughts on Universities in the German Sense*).[29] Especially notable is the reference to "positive sciences" as the term of choice for the disciplines taught in the traditional higher faculties, and the combination of intellectual innovation and institutional conservatism. Yet the overall thrust of Schleiermacher's argument differs from Schelling's as much as from Fichte's. In fact, Schleiermacher effectively conceded to Fichte the argument that theology could not lay claim to its own systematic niche within the totality of human knowledge. While agreeing with Schelling, therefore, that theology must have its place in the modern university, Schleiermacher's justification of this thesis had to proceed in a fundamentally different manner.

Schleiermacher's essay opens with the observation, reminiscent of Aristotle, that *Wissenschaft* (science) is something human beings desire.[30] This goal, however, cannot be achieved by even the most gifted individual, but requires the collaboration of many. Science is not, therefore, an individual but a social pursuit, more specifically it is the pursuit of the group united by a common language, the nation.[31] This makes it similar to the state, but while the latter in order to act must be able to subjugate individual wills, science can thrive only under the condition of freedom. There is therefore reason for the state to support science, but equally, for both sides to mind their respective differences.[32]

Since *Wissenschaft* needs to be both taught and practiced, it is cultivated in several different institutions: schools have the primary purpose of educating and forming young people; academies on the other hand exist as the republic of letters, seeking to unite those who are masters of their fields.[33] The university for Schleiermacher forms a third in between these two. It must exist due to the dynamic nature of the system: science, in order to be advanced by the leading minds of each discipline, needs to be initiated, and this has to happen in a place dedicated to its principles. The purpose of the university, then, is to impart to young people the very idea of *Wissenschaft*, the notion of the unity of knowledge in all its diversity.[34]

Schleiermacher, then, does not diverge from Kant, Schelling, and Fichte on the centrality of the idea of *Wissenschaft* for the university. Moreover, he follows them in identifying science *stricte dictu* with philosophy. His ideal university thus is, once again, at heart a philosophical institution.[35] Yet philosophy, as Schleiermacher understood it, is necessarily

---

[29] On this text in general, cf. Nowak, *Schleiermacher*, pp. 181–186; Howard, *Protestant Theology*, pp. 166–172.
[30] Anrich, *Die Idee*, p. 223; cf. Aristotle, *Metaphysica*, ed. Werner Jaeger (Oxford: Oxford University Press, 1957), A1.
[31] Anrich, *Die Idee.*, pp. 225–226.
[32] Ibid., pp. 228–232.
[33] Ibid., p. 233.
[34] Ibid., pp. 237–241.
[35] Ibid., pp. 258–259.

embedded in the cultural contexts from which its reflection emerges and in which it takes place. The center of Schleiermacher's philosophy is ethics, but his ethics culminates in a system of goods or—to use a modern expression—a theory of culture.[36]

This rather original concept of philosophy, which Schleiermacher developed more fully in his later lectures on ethics and dialectic, underlay the defense of the traditional structure of the university he advanced in *Gelegentliche Gedanken*. Theology, law, and medicine, according to Schleiermacher, all benefit from their regular exchange with philosophy, but philosophy itself would be incomplete without those extensions. Philosophical reflection, consequently, could never be conducted in abstraction from the concrete realities of nature and culture. Schleiermacher was deeply skeptical about the ability of the human mind to construct a system of thought capable of explaining reality in its fullness. Knowledge (*Wissen*) and hence science (*Wissenschaft*) (in German the two terms are cognates) are fundamentally dependent on communication and exchange; they are always perfectible and never complete.

It was this open-ended system of science, for Schleiermacher, that facilitated theology's inclusion in the university. He did not claim that theology was an indispensable part of a system of knowledge nor accept for theology any narrow definition of science as normative. Instead, his argument for the retention of the traditional higher faculties was remarkably pragmatic: this structure had emerged "naturally"[37] and for this reason continued for such a long period of time.

The faculty of theology, in particular, was founded by the church "in order to preserve the wisdom of the Fathers; not to lose for the future what in the past had been achieved in discerning truth from error; to give a historical basis, a sure and certain direction and a common spirit to the further development of doctrine and Church."[38] In other words, theology exists because the church needs clarity about its doctrines and practices, and such clarity is achieved by permitting these issues to be openly debated in permanent exchange with all other areas of human knowledge. Theology is taught in the university because the public has an interest that this is done well, and that church ministers are appropriately trained in the same way that doctors receive a good medical education and judges a proper understanding of the law.

This is how Schleiermacher understood Schelling's term "positive science" (*positive Wissenschaft*): as a discipline constituted not by systematic deduction from the idea of knowledge but by a practical requirement. It is different from a trade because for its proper exercise a solid and permanent exchange with *Wissenschaft* proper, that is philosophy, is vital. A professor of law or of theology therefore, according to Schleiermacher, who does not actively contribute to philosophy—in the wide sense in which it includes not only metaphysics and ethics but also philology and history—deserved to be ridiculed, even excluded from the university.[39]

Schleiermacher's institutional conservatism went well beyond his preference for the retention of the traditional faculties. Many of the organizational and even ceremonial conventions inherited from its long history should, in his view, be preserved in the modern

---

[36] Cf. *OHG*.
[37] Anrich, *Die Idee*, p. 257.
[38] Ibid., p. 258, my translation.
[39] Ibid., p. 261.

university.[40] And yet, just as one would be mistaken in interpreting Schelling's affirmation of certain elements of the old university as an opposition to reform, it would be incorrect to overlook the thoroughly modern elements in Schleiermacher's proposal. The latter has, rightly, been described as an "anti-modern modernization" of the German university;[41] its far-reaching impact on the subsequent development of these institutions and, particularly, on the shape and the role of theology in these institutions were not, thus far, accidental.[42]

7.4 Schleiermacher among the Reformers

Had the foundation of the university happened as smoothly and quickly as hoped by its early proponents, the views Schleiermacher expressed in his *Denkschrift* might well not have exerted much influence. Yet the flurry of wide-ranging political reforms for which Stein's government is noted[43] pushed the plans for a new university to secondary importance. It was only in 1809, after Stein's time in office had abruptly ended, that work on the foundation of the university resumed, under the auspices of the newly appointed Wilhelm von Humboldt.[44] It quickly became clear that Humboldt had little sympathy for Fichte's radical ideas. By contrast, Schleiermacher's reasoning chimed well with the philosophy of the new minister, and while there is not much direct evidence to prove that Humboldt drew on Schleiermacher's *Gelegentliche Gedanken* when writing his own memoranda for the King,[45] there is little doubt that among all the luminaries who wrote publicly in connection with the foundation of the new university, it was Schleiermacher whose thoughts were closest to the eventual political decisions initiated by the minister and endorsed by king.[46] Ultimately, his emphatic endorsement of the traditional structures of the university, his preference for reform over revolution, and his combination of the modernizing principles of *Wissenschaft* with the inherited institutional frame not only proved attractive to Humboldt but provided the formula for the university's subsequent success.[47] As Max Lenz summarised over a hundred years ago, "Schleiermacher's thoughts, as much as he sought to coat them in the venerable glimmer of a dreamed-up past, were in their core the truly vivid and modern ones."[48]

[40] Lenz, *Geschichte*, pp. 126–127.
[41] Gert Schubring, "Spezialschulmodell versus Universitätsmodell—Die Institutionalisierung von Forschung," in *"Einsamkeit und Freiheit" neu besichtigt: Universitätsreformen und Disziplinenbildung in Preußen als Modell für Wissenschaftspolitik im Europa des 19. Jahrhunderts*, ed. Gert Schubring (Stuttgart: Steiner, 1991), p. 303.
[42] Cf. Lenz, *Geschichte*, p. 130; Howard, *Protestant Theology*, p. 156.
[43] Cf. Marion Gray, *Prussia in Transition: Society and Politics under the Stein Reform Ministry of 1808*, Transactions of the American Philosophical Society, 76/1 (Philadelphia: American Philosophical Society, 1986).
[44] Lenz, *Geschichte*, pp. 156–157; Howard, *Protestant Theology*, pp. 152–155; Nowak, *Schleiermacher*, pp. 215–216.
[45] Lenz, *Geschichte*, p. 160.
[46] Cf. Thomas Becker, "Diversifizierung eines Modells? Friedrich-Wilhelms-Universitäten 1810, 1811, 1818," in *Die Berliner Universität im Kontext der deutschen Universitätslandschaft nach 1800, um 1860 und um 1910*, ed. Rüdiger vom Bruch and Elisabeth Müller-Luckner, Schriften des Historisches Kollegs: Kolloquien 46 (München: Oldenbourg, 2010), p. 45; Howard, *Protestant Theology*, p. 155.
[47] Lenz, *Geschichte*, pp. 129–130.
[48] Lenz, *Geschichte*, pp. 129–130.

In this connection it is worth noting one "vivid and modern" view Schleiermacher held that was not, however, shared by the mainstream of his day and that, consequently, exerted little influence on the original shape of the new university. Unlike most of the Prussian reformers, Schleiermacher was remarkably skeptical toward state intervention in both science and religion. Regarding the latter, his opposition to religious establishment, nearly unique among early nineteenth-century German theologians, was expressed with aplomb in his *Speeches*.[49] *Gelegentliche Gedanken*, noted above, took an analogously categorical position in its attempt to demarcate the place of higher education in the modern state, and this too was at variance with the much more openly statist positions of Fichte and others. It is perhaps unsurprising then that on this particular point Schleiermacher remained a lone voice in the wilderness.[50] The foundation of the University of Berlin, despite following many of the insights Schleiermacher had laid out in his programmatic treatise, established a much closer connection between university and the state than Schleiermacher would have advocated. This decision was to have major consequences, not least for the theologian himself who from 1817 found himself the object of constant harassment by his government, some of it overt and some clandestine.[51]

7.5 Schleiermacher and the Faculty of Theology

In the end, the University of Berlin came into being in October 1810, and it included a faculty of theology. In the run-up to its foundation, Schleiermacher was one of the most influential players as vice president of a founding committee (*Einrichtungskomission*), though in practice often in sole charge of its operation.[52] Accordingly, his influence on the shape of his own faculty was particularly momentous. In May, he submitted two pertinent memoranda, one "On the Constitution of the Faculty of Theology," the other "On the Introduction of University Worship."[53]

The former of those is evidently based on the *Gelegentliche Gedanken* as well as his *Brief Outline to the Study of Theology*. Here, Schleiermacher wastes no time in justifying the existence of a faculty of theology whose existence, he claims, was queried by some merely "in jest" (*scherzweise*).[54] As long as the state recognizes a legitimate concern for religious matters, theology has a right to its own faculty. Such a faculty must represent the four major areas of the subject: exegetical, historical, doctrinal, and practical. Since the contest of ideas is vital

---

[49] *Speeches¹*, pp. 85–86.
[50] Lenz, *Geschichte*, pp. 187–188; Howard, *Protestant Theology*, p. 172.
[51] Nowak, *Schleiermacher*, pp. 378–385.
[52] Ibid., p. 220.
[53] Friedrich Schleiermacher, "Über die Einrichtung der theologischen Fakultät" (25 May 1810), in *Idee und Wirklichkeit einer Universität: Dokumente zur Geschichte der Friedrich-Wilhelm-Universität zu Berlin*, ed. Wilhelm Weischedel et al. (Berlin: De Gruyter, 1960), pp. 211–214; "Entwurf zur Errichtung eines Universitätsgottesdienstes in Berlin," in Weischedel et al., pp. 214–216. Cf. Howard, *Protestant Theology*, pp. 183–188.
[54] Schleiermacher, "Über die Einrichtung," p. 211.

for academic life, each of those subjects should be represented by more than one professor. Yet Schleiermacher did not think this required eight chairs; in fact, he believed that three was a sufficient number as any qualified scholar would be competent and indeed eager to contribute to at least two of these areas. As long, therefore, as appointments aim for complementarity, there will be enough diversity even with a relatively small number of professors.[55]

These reflections might be considered idealistic even for the time, but it is arguable that, with the appointment of Wilhelm Martin Leberecht de Wette (1780–1849), Philipp Marheineke (1780–1846), and August Neander (1789–1850)—"the nineteenth century's greatest department of theology," as it has been called[56]—the Berlin faculty in its early years came close to realizing Schleiermacher's ideal.[57] As for practical theology, he advised against a separate chair in "a city as rich in preachers [Kanzelrednern] as Berlin,"[58] many of whom would be willing to contribute to the faculty's teaching provision.

Throughout his memorandum, Schleiermacher's commitment to *scientific* theology is evident. He scoffs at the idea that professors should be appointed on a confessional basis as, within Protestantism at least, differences between individual scholars were often more significant than those between their churches.[59] As long as students were taught about the different confessional texts, it should be left to the ecclesiastical examination boards to ensure that their candidates conform to their respective orthodoxies. Equally notable is his distaste for the award of higher degrees to ecclesiastical dignitaries. The theological doctorate can only be awarded on the basis of "a learned theological work . . . of recognized merit," which, Schleiermacher pointedly added, "ought to be mentioned on the certificate."[60] To compensate for this rigidity, Schleiermacher proposed a second, lower degree, the licentiate obtained through "a *specimen eruditionis* and a public examination."[61]

Schleiermacher's memorandum became in practice, if not in law, the basis for the faculty's work. When proper statutes were adopted in the 1830s, they closely followed his ideas.[62] By contrast, his attempt to introduce a university-wide academic service bore fruit only years after his death, in 1847, and even then not necessarily in the way Schleiermacher had hoped.[63]

7.6 Schleiermacher as a Professor

The foundation of the University of Berlin undoubtedly marked a cesura in Schleiermacher's life and career. He was one of its most distinguished members and immediately appointed Dean of the Faculty of Theology, an office he held for the first year of the institution's

---

[55] Ibid., p. 212.
[56] Terrence N. Tice, "Schleiermacher and the Scientific Study of Religion," in *Friedrich Schleiermacher and the Founding of the University of Berlin: The Study of Religion as a Scientific Discipline*, ed. Herbert Richardson (Lewiston, NY: Edwin Mellen Press, 1991), p. 46. Cited in Howard, *Protestant Theology*, p. 178.
[57] Howard, *Protestant Theology*, pp. 194–197.
[58] Schleiermacher, "Über die Einrichtung," p. 212.
[59] Ibid.
[60] Ibid., p. 214.
[61] Ibid.
[62] Howard, *Protestant Theology*, p. 183.
[63] Nowak, *Schleiermacher*, p. 221.

existence (1810/1811) and subsequently again on three further occasions.[64] He was also, in 1810, one of four professors in charge of the new university's statutes. In fact, the latter document—adopted only in 1817—follows in its central parts the ideas first developed in Schleiermacher's *Gelegentliche Gedanken*.[65] In 1815/1816 Schleiermacher also served as the university's rector.[66]

His day-to-day activity was largely taken up by his lecturing, which was extraordinarily broad even by the standards of the time. Schleiermacher usually offered between three and five lecture courses per semester, which would be presented in three to five-hour-long lectures each week.[67] There were some exceptions to this; notably, in 1827/1828, Schleiermacher presented "The Christian Doctrine of Faith" in ten lectures per week but offered no other courses.[68] In most semesters, however, his total weekly lecturing added up to around fifteen hours. This burden did not abate until his final semester in the winter of 1833/1834, during which he offered three courses, each given in five units per week. His last lectures for all three courses are recorded for February 3. Schleiermacher died nine days later.[69]

Schleiermacher lectured from early in the morning. In the summer, his first lectures would be scheduled at 6.00 a.m., and even in the winter he would regularly start at 8.00 a.m. His lectures were well attended, roughly on a par with those of his famous rival, G. W. F. Hegel. In the winter of 1829/1830, Schleiermacher's lectures on "The Life of Jesus" attracted 251 students;[70] in the summer of 1830, his lectures on "The Doctrine of the Soul" (delivered in the Faculty of Philosophy) were attended by 229 students.[71] These numbers are all the more remarkable considering that the total number of students in the university at the time was below 2,000.[72]

Schleiermacher was famous for his unique lecturing style. He spoke from few notes. This was for him more than a matter of presentation. He believed in the virtue of sharing ideas with his hearers as he developed them. According to David Friedrich Strauss, his "method was exclusively dialectical ... [presenting to his hearers] nothing in the form of a dead note, but everything as a problem whose solution they now jointly try to find."[73] While testifying to the "deep and lasting inspiration" of Schleiermacher's talks, however, Strauss also expressed

---

[64] Nowak, *Schleiermacher*, pp. 220–221. Exact dates in Rudolf Köpke, *Die Gründung der königlichen Friedrich-Wilhelms-Universität zu Berlin* (Berlin: Schade, 1860), p. 293.

[65] Lenz, *Geschichte*, p. 436.

[66] Nowak, *Schleiermacher*, p. 223.

[67] For what follows, cf. the full list of Schleiermacher's lecture announcements printed in Andreas Arndt and Wolfgang Viermond, eds., *Schleiermachers Briefwechsel (Verzeichnis) nebst einer Liste seiner Vorlesungen* (Berlin/New York: De Gruyter, 1992), pp. 305–330.

[68] Ibid., p. 324.

[69] Ibid., p. 330.

[70] Ibid., p. 326.

[71] Werner Tress, "Professoren—Der Lehrkörper und seine Praxis zwischen Wissenschaft, Politik und Gesellschaft," in *Geschichte der Universität Unter den Linden, vol. 1: Gründung und Blütezeit der Universität zu Berlin 1810–1918*, ed. Heinz-Elmar Tenorth and Charles McClelland (Berlin/New York: De Gruyter, 2014), p. 192.

[72] Köpke, *Die Gründung*, p. 298.

[73] David Friedrich Strauss, *Der Christus des Glaubens und der Jesus der Geschichte: Eine Kritik des Schleiermacher'schen Lebens Jesu*, in Strauss, *Gesammelte Schriften*, ed. Eduard Zeller, vol. 5 (Bonn: Emil Strauß, 1877), p. 8.

his frustration with a method that made it difficult to follow the lecturer's train of thought.[74] As for the task of writing down the lectures thus delivered, this was, Strauss opined, as impossible as "photographing a dancer in full movement."[75]

In what follows, an overview will be given of Schleiermacher's lecture courses. Its main purpose is to convey a sense of the intimate bond between Schleiermacher's intellectual work and his duties as a university teacher. Schleiermacher strove to be the paradigmatic professor of his own, ideal university whose teaching and scholarly production was constantly informed by his broader intellectual concerns as much as his professorial duties gave rise to and shaped his scholarly production. For more detailed information on specific lectures, the reader may want to consult relevant chapters elsewhere in this *Handbook*.

7.7 THE THEOLOGICAL LECTURE COURSES

Pride of place must belong to Schleiermacher's famed lectures on "Theological Encyclopedia."[76] This course of lectures, which he first delivered in Halle and which almost immediately led to the publication of the *Brief Outline of the Study of Theology* (1811; 2nd ed. 1830), can be seen as flowing directly from the broader institutional reflections developed in *Gelegentliche Gedanken*.

Central, once again, is the notion of theology as a positive science whose disciplinary unity is constituted by its relationship to the Christian church, without which, consequently, the subject would disintegrate.[77] The teaching of theology, then, is inseparable from the training of church ministers. From this definition, Schleiermacher deduces a threefold division of the subject into philosophical, historical, and practical theology. Of these, he writes, "historical theology is the actual corpus of theological study, which corpus is interconnected with science, as such, by means of philosophical theology and is interconnected with the active Christian life by means of practical theology."[78]

Despite his considerable philosophical interest, Schleiermacher never lectured on philosophical theology directly, although he discussed aspects of it in his lectures on dogmatics.[79] "Lectures on historical theology," which included not only church history, but also biblical studies and dogmatics, formed the backbone of Schleiermacher's lecturing activity. Apart from the Old Testament, he covered all its fields of study: New Testament, church history, dogmatics (*Glaubenslehre*), Christian ethics (*Christliche Sittenlehre*), and ecclesiastical statistics. He also lectured on practical theology.

Perhaps counterintuitively, the largest number of his lecture courses fell into New Testament studies. Matthew and John were the subject of full courses, as were the major Pauline epistles. Shorter parts of the canon were more summarily treated. Schleiermacher also lectured on "The Life of Jesus," a highly original endeavor at the time.[80] Only a few years

---

[74] Ibid., p. 7.
[75] Ibid., p. 9.
[76] On "Theological Encyclopedia" in general cf. Purvis, *Theology and the University*.
[77] BO, p. 3 (§§5–6).
[78] BO, p. 13 (§28).
[79] Cf. *CF (1928)*, pp. 52–76. Nowak, *Schleiermacher*, pp. 251–252.
[80] Nowak, *Schleiermacher*, pp. 243–246.

after his death, however, his views seemed so thoroughly discredited by the more recent debate initiated by David Friedrich Strauss' *Das Leben Jesu* (1835/1836) that his students held back these lectures from publication in his *Sämmtliche Werke* until 1864 when, as Albert Schweitzer dryly noted, they were "brought forth to view like an embalmed corpse [, and] Strauss accorded to the dead work of the great theologian a dignified and striking funeral oration."[81]

Schleiermacher's most significant courses, naturally, were those on dogmatics, as from those lectures emerged his *Der christliche Glaube* (1821/1822, 2nd ed. 1830/1831), one of the most important treatments of the Christian doctrine of faith in the Protestant tradition. Like the medieval *Summae* and the early modern *Loci*, this book grew from the practice of teaching theology in the university. Schleiermacher conceived it as a textbook for his lectures and, once published, he regularly used it for precisely this purpose.[82]

It would be wrong to see Schleiermacher's extensive lecturing activity as a (failed) attempt at a comprehensive theological system. His understanding of theology as developed in *Brief Outline* would not have allowed for such a project. Yet Schleiermacher's ambition would be equally misunderstood if taken as a mere expression of polymathy. Rather, in line with the *Encyclopedia*, the "distinct formation of God-consciousness" in Christianity provided a center from which his theological thought flew and an organic unity towards which it was constantly aimed.[83]

7.8 The Philosophical Lectures

Schleiermacher's lecturing was, moreover, not limited to the Faculty of Theology. Among modern theologians, the author of the *Christian Faith* was arguably unique in the seriousness with which he applied himself to philosophy. Schleiermacher could claim to be a professional philosopher, although he never attained the kind of recognition in this capacity that has always been accorded to him as a theologian.

Formally, Schleiermacher's entitlement to lecture in the Faculty of Philosophy was due to his membership in Prussia's Royal Academy of Sciences, into which he was elected in 1810.[84] His eagerness to contribute to philosophy, however, ultimately derives from the principles presented in *Gelegentliche Gedanken*, according to which positive sciences, such as theology, must be included in the university because they cannot be conducted without permanent exchange with science proper, that is, philosophy. By the same token, Schleiermacher had stipulated that every professor of theology had a duty to contribute to the teaching of philosophy,[85] and he clearly strove to model himself on his own ideal.

Yet the connection between *Gelegentliche Gedanken* and his philosophical project runs deeper still. As noted above, Schleiermacher's argument in his *Denkschrift* relied on a

---

[81] Albert Schweitzer, *The Quest of the Historical Jesus*, translated by W. Montgomery, 2nd ed. (London: Black, 1911), p. 62.
[82] Ibid., pp. 251 and 253.
[83] *BO*, p. 1 (§1).
[84] Ibid., p. 283.
[85] Anrich, *Die Idee*, p. 261; Nowak, *Schleiermacher*, p. 184.

particular conception of philosophy as embedded in its cultural contexts. The contours of his philosophical system, as they become apparent from his various lecture courses, clearly correspond to precisely this kind of philosophy.

Three courses were central to this endeavor: dialectic, ethics, and hermeneutics. In his lectures on dialectics, Schleiermacher sought to develop his own systematic foundation of knowledge in evident competition with both Fichte's *Wissenschaftslehre* and Hegel's *Science of Logic*. His own estimation of the importance of these lectures is indicated by the fact that their publication was the last major project on which Schleiermacher worked, though at the time of his death only the "Introduction" existed in fully revised form.[86]

Like dialectic, Schleiermacher conceived of ethics as a "pure" (*reine*) science: whereas the former dealt with human thought, the latter treated human practice. Hermeneutics by contrast was a technical discipline, yet for Schleiermacher it held fundamental importance for all communication, philosophical as well as theological. While these three lecture courses developed the principles of what one might call a philosophy of human sociality and culture, its concrete details were explored in a number of applied courses that, in today's university, would no longer be included in philosophy. They were political theory (*Staatslehre*), educational theory, aesthetics, and theoretical psychology. Finally, Schleiermacher also lectured on the history of philosophy.

In its execution, Schleiermacher's philosophy remained fragmentary at the time of his death. Apart from his Academy lectures, he did not publish philosophical works after his appointment at Halle. It was thus in and through his lectures that he continued to pursue his ambitious philosophical project, a project whose principles corresponded closely with the philosophical vision that underlay his proposals in *Gelegentliche Gedanken*. Such facts again underline the intimate connection between the development of Schleiermacher's ideas in his mature period and the institutional structure of the university.

7.9 Conclusion

This chapter has examined Schleiermacher's relationship with the University of Berlin. Given his reputation as a leading albeit controversial theologian, it is conventional to focus in this connection on his role in, and his significance for, the Faculty of Theology. His contribution is usually summarized in the statement that Schleiermacher secured for the modern (German) university the continued presence of a faculty of theology. To this the claim is sometimes added—approvingly or disapprovingly—that he required theology to modernize in order to adapt to the modern research university emerging at the time. It should by now be clear that, while not altogether wrong, such an assessment represents a considerable simplification of a more complex reality.

Schleiermacher's contribution to the foundation of the University of Berlin proved so influential precisely because it was inspired by a comprehensive vision of the university and, ultimately, the generation and transmission of human knowledge in general. This vision in its turn was built on a phil\osophical conception of human knowledge and agency, which Schleiermacher concurrently developed and to which he was firmly committed.

---

[86] *Dial.*, pp. xlii–xlv.

Moreover, Schleiermacher's view of theology as a positive science, which grew out of and was justified by his overall conception of university education, was in fact rather elastic insofar as it resisted the notion that the discipline had to conform to a set of systematic principles. The inherently practical foundation of theology as constituted by its relationship with the Christian church permitted a wide range of approaches to its study as long as its practitioners retained an organic connection with the overall principles of *Wissenschaft*.

There was, admittedly, a tension between these two relationships that Schleiermacher stipulated for theology. As posterity has shown, theology could be challenged by science more than he had anticipated, and its scientific character could bring it into serious conflict with the church. While clearly aware of these dangers in principle, Schleiermacher arguably underestimated the extent to which developments in historical criticism in particular would radically call into question central elements of traditional Christianity only years after his death.

Whatever the final verdict on Schleiermacher's legacy, however, any investigation of his role in the University of Berlin cannot but note the exemplary way in which the theologian modeled his own existence as a professor on the ideal of his own theory. His teaching was constantly informed not only by his specialist scholarship but by his vision of the coherence of his own discipline, theology, and its place within the broader context of *Wissenschaft*. His philosophical lectures followed the same principles. At the same time, his scholarly productions flew from, and were shaped by, his professorial lecturing duties he fulfilled punctiliously. From this vantage point, the personal admiration in which he was almost universally held is easily understandable.

SUGGESTED READINGS

Anrich, Ernst, ed. *Die Idee der deutschen Universität: Die fünf Grundschriften aus der Zeit ihrer Neubegründung durch klassischen Idealismus und romantischen Realismus* (Darmstadt: WBG, 1956).

Howard, Thomas Albert. *Protestant Theology and the Making of the German University* (Oxford: Oxford University Press, 2006).

Nowak, Kurt. *Schleiermacher: Leben, Werk und Wirkung* (Göttingen: Vandenhoeck & Ruprecht, 2001).

Purvis, Zachary. *Theology and the University in Nineteenth-Century Germany* (Oxford: Oxford University Press, 2016).

Tice, Terrence N. "Schleiermacher and the Scientific Study of Religion." In *Friedrich Schleiermacher and the Founding of the University of Berlin: The Study of Religion as a Scientific Discipline*, ed. Herbert Richardson (Lewiston, NY: Edwin Mellen Press, 1991), pp. 45–82.

Zachhuber, Johannes. *Theology as Science in Nineteenth-Century Germany: From F. C. Baur to Ernst Troeltsch* (Oxford: Oxford University Press, 2013).

BIBLIOGRAPHY

Anrich, Ernst, ed. *Die Idee der deutschen Universität: Die fünf Grundschriften aus der Zeit ihrer Neubegründung durch klassischen Idealismus und romantischen Realismus* (Darmstadt: WBG, 1956).

Arndt, Andreas, and Wolfgang Viermond, eds. *Schleiermachers Briefwechsel (Verzeichnis) nebst einer Liste seiner Vorlesungen* (Berlin/New York: De Gruyter, 1992).

Aristotle, *Metaphysica*. Ed. Werner Jaeger (Oxford: Oxford University Press, 1957).

Becker, Thomas. "Diversifizierung eines Modells? Friedrich-Wilhelms-Universitäten 1810, 1811, 1818." In *Die Berliner Universität im Kontext der deutschen Universitätslandschaft nach 1800, um 1860 und um 1910*, ed. Rüdiger vom Bruch and Elisabeth Müller-Luckner; Schriften des Historisches Kollegs: Kolloquien 46 (München: Oldenbourg, 2010), pp. 43–69.

Euler, Werner L. "Der Streit zwischen der theologischen und der philosophischen Fakultät in Kants Schrift 'Der Streit der Fakultäten'." *Ruch Filozoficzny* 72 (2016), pp. 7–25.

Gray, Marion. *Prussia in Transition: Society and Politics under the Stein Reform Ministry of 1808*, Transactions of the American Philosophical Society, 76/1 (Philadelphia: American Philosophical Society, 1986).

Hagemann. Karen, *Revisiting Prussia's Wars against Napoleon: History, Culture, and Memory* (Cambridge: Cambridge University Press, 2015).

Howard, Thomas Albert. *Protestant Theology and the Making of the German University* (Oxford: Oxford University Press, 2006).

Humboldt, Wilhelm von. *The Spheres and Duties of Government*, trans. Joseph Coulthard (London: Chapman, 1854; reprint: Bristol: Thoemmes Press, 1994).

Köpke, Rudolf. *Die Gründung der königlichen Friedrich-Wilhelms-Universität zu Berlin* (Berlin: Schade, 1860).

Lenz, Max. *Geschichte der königlichen Friedrich-Wilhelms-Universität zu Berlin*, vol. 1 (Halle/S.: Buchhandlung des Waisenhauses, 1910).

Mikerabidze, Alexander. *The Napoleonic Wars: A Global History* (Oxford: Oxford University Press, 2020).

Nowak, Kurt. *Schleiermacher: Leben, Werk und Wirkung* (Göttingen: Vandenhoeck & Ruprecht, 2001).

Purvis, Zachary. *Theology and the University in Nineteenth-Century Germany* (Oxford: Oxford University Press, 2016).

Schelling, Friedrich Wilhelm Joseph. *Vorlesungen über die Methode des akademischen Studiums* (1803). In *Sämmtliche Werke*, ed. K. F. A. Schelling, vol. I/5 (Stuttgart: Cotta, 1859). English text: *On University Studies*, translated by Ella S. Morgan, ed. Norbert Guterman (Athens, OH: Ohio University Press, 1966).

Schleiermacher, Friedrich. "Entwurf zur Errichtung eines Universitätsgottesdienstes in Berlin." In *Idee und Wirklichkeit einer Universität: Dokumente zur Geschichte der Friedrich-Wilhelm-Universität zu Berlin*, ed. Wilhelm Weischedel et al. (Berlin: De Gruyter, 1960), pp. 214–216.

Schleiermacher, Friedrich. "Rezension von Friedrich Wilhelm Joseph Schelling. Vorlesungen über die Methode des akademischen Studiums," in *KGA* 1.4, pp. 461–484.

Schleiermacher, Friedrich. "Über die Einrichtung der theologischen Fakultät" (25 May 1810). In *Idee und Wirklichkeit einer Universität: Dokumente zur Geschichte der Friedrich-Wilhelm-Universität zu Berlin*, ed. Wilhelm Weischedel et al. (Berlin: De Gruyter, 1960), pp. 211–214.

Schroeder, Paul W. *The Transformation of European Politics: 1763–1848* (Oxford: Oxford University Press, 1994).

Schubring, Gert. "Spezialschulmodell versus Universitätsmodell—Die Institutionalisierung von Forschung." In *"Einsamkeit und Freiheit" neu besichtigt: Universitätsreformen und Disziplinenbildung in Preußen als Modell für Wissenschaftspolitik im Europa des 19. Jahrhunderts*, ed. Gert Schubring (Stuttgart: Steiner, 1991), pp. 276–326.

Schweitzer, Albert. *The Quest of the Historical Jesus*, translated by W. Montgomery, 2nd ed. (London: Black, 1911).

Strauss, David Friedrich. *Der Christus des Glaubens und der Jesus der Geschichte: Eine Kritik des Schleiermacher'schen Lebens Jesu*. In Strauss, *Gesammelte Schriften*, ed. Eduard Zeller, vol. 5 (Bonn: Emil Strauß, 1877), pp. 1–136.

Tice, Terrence N. "Schleiermacher and the Scientific Study of Religion." In *Friedrich Schleiermacher and the Founding of the University of Berlin: The Study of Religion as a Scientific Discipline*, ed. Herbert Richardson (Lewiston, NY: Edwin Mellen Press, 1991), 45–82.

Tress, Werner. "Professoren—Der Lehrkörper und seine Praxis zwischen Wissenschaft, Politik und Gesellschaft." In *Geschichte der Universität Unter den Linden, vol. 1: Gründung und Blütezeit der Universität zu Berlin 1810–1918*, ed. Heinz-Elmar Tenorth and Charles McClelland (Berlin/New York: De Gruyter, 2014), pp. 131–207.

CHAPTER 8

SCHLEIERMACHER AND FRIEDRICH SCHLEGEL

ANDREAS ARNDT

8.1 Remembering the Young Schlegel

In his treatise *On the Concept of Hermeneutics*, which he presented to the plenary meeting of the Berlin Academy on August 13, 1829, Schleiermacher recalled "an outstanding mind, who has just been wrested from us."[1] The reference was to Friedrich Schlegel, who had died on January 12 of the same year. It is, as I shall explain in more detail below, probably no accident that Schleiermacher chose to remember his late friend in connection with the latter's hermeneutics. And it is certainly no accident that in doing so he looked back on the turbulent time of early Romanticism by quoting "the otherwise rather paradoxical word" from the *Athenauem* Fragment 82 (1798): "that claiming is much more than proving."[2] This Schlegelian fragment is a small treatise on demonstrations in philosophy and composed of numerous notes in a variety of Schlegel's papers. Schleiermacher may have remembered that at the end of 1797 and the beginning of 1798 he had read Schlegel's philosophical notebooks in order to look for fragments for the *Athenaeum*. Thus, on January 15, 1798 he had reported to August Wilhelm Schlegel that "as he had allowed me a stroll through his papers," Friedrich had "placed the onus on my going through them like a truffle hound in order to sniff out fragments or seeds of fragments."[3] At this time Schleiermacher was living with Friedrich Schlegel in a (provisional) preacher's home in shared lodgings by the Oranienburg Gate,[4] and the reminiscence of 1829 is not the only trace that this happy and, in literary terms, productive time of cohabitation left behind in his work.

---

[1] *KGA* 1.11, p. 611. The first three parts of the following contribution are based in large part on Arndt, "Eine literarische Ehe"; the translation (by Martin Rodden) is used with permission of De Gruyter Publishing House.

[2] *KGA* 1.11, p. 611; see Friedrich Schlegel, *Werke. Kritische Ausgabe*, ed. Ernst Behler et al. (Paderborn: Schöningh, 1958–; hereafter *KFSA*), vol. 2, p. 177.

[3] *KGA* 5.2, p. 250.

[4] Due to rebuilding work, the official lodgings in the Charité hospital were not available from the beginning of May 1797 to 1800. See *KGA* 5.2, p. xvii.

The "symliving" and "symphilosophizing" in that shared home also left traces on Friedrich Schlegel, although on the theoretical level at least he seems to have been the giver rather than the receiver. Schleiermacher impressed Schlegel from the very beginning with his moral attitude, an attitude that, admittedly, casually flaunted all moral conventions, as was expressed clearly by the title of a lecture: "Immorality of All Moral" (*Immoralität aller Moral*)—now unfortunately lost. "Schleyermacher," as Schlegel wrote on November 28, 1797, "is a man in whom the person is cultivated.... He is only three years older than me, but in moral understanding he surpasses me infinitely. I hope to learn even more from him.—His whole essence is moral, and in fact of all the outstanding people I know his morality outweighs that of all others."[5] Schlegel valued Schleiermacher not only as a moral person, but also as a speculative philosophical mind, although he continued to have difficulties with Schleiermacher the theologian. Thus in 1804 he was still expressing his regret that Schleiermacher had gone to the University of Halle rather than to the University of Würzburg, where Schelling was also teaching. There he would have been drawn into the area of speculative philosophy.[6] Their different understandings of Christianity divided Schleiermacher and Schlegel for their whole lives. The young Schlegel, even when he spoke of religion, was very distanced from Christianity. When he later professed to be Christian, he meant that he was Roman Catholic, which was abhorrent to the arch-Protestant Schleiermacher.

In 1797, at the beginning of their relationship, Schleiermacher and Schlegel were not yet conscious of these and other differences. Their encounter was somewhat erotic, in the sense of the platonic Eros that leads affectively to the dialectical path toward the Idea of the Beautiful, in which the True, the Beautiful, and the Good converge.[7] It was, as all the evidence indicates, something akin to an intellectual love at first sight. In the following, I begin by describing briefly the encounter between Schleiermacher and Schlegel as well as the development of this relationship, after which I will inquire as to what traces it left on Schleiermacher.

8.2 "Symphilosophy" (1796–1802)

Following a successful trial sermon, Schleiermacher went to Berlin at the end of August 1796 from Landsberg/Warthe in order to take up a position as the reformed chaplain at the Charité hospital. As a curate in Landsberg, he had made connections within the apparently extensive social scene of the provincial town and sought the same thing in Berlin. From October 1793 to April 1794 Schleiermacher had been a candidate for the local educational authority but had lived a rather withdrawn life.[8] Now, however, he took part in the "Mittwochgesellschaft" ("Wednesday Society") of the *Aufklärer* Ignatius Aurelius Feßler, and gained entry into the

---

[5] *KFSA* vol. 24, pp. 45f.

[6] Dorothea and Friedrich Schlegel, *Briefe von Dorothea und Friedrich Schlegel an die Familie Paulus*, ed. R. Unger (Berlin: Behr, 1913), p. 17.

[7] For the Romantic interpretation of the *Symposium* see Stefan Matuschek, ed., *Wo das philosophische Gespräch ganz in Dichtung übergeht. Platons Symposion und seine Wirkung in der Renaissance, Romantik und Moderne* (Heidelberg: Winter, 2002).

[8] See *KGA* 5.2, pp. 24ff.

salon of Henriette Herz, among other things. In July 1797 Friedrich Schlegel also moved to Berlin. He met Schleiermacher at the "Mittwochsgesellschaft" and saw him again at Henriette Herz's home and at the home of a friend from his student days, the Swedish diplomat Carl Gustav von Brinckmann, who brought them closer together.[9] Their first point of contact was philosophy, particularly the study of Fichte's *Wissenschaftslehre*. On August 26, 1797, Schlegel reported to Friedrich Niethammer, the editor with Fichte of the influential *Philosophisches Journal*: "I adhere more to congenial than to scholarly circles. But I have found a preacher Schleyermacher, who is studying Fichte's writings and reads the Journal with an interest beyond curiosity and personality."[10] From September at the latest, they had been meeting in order, as Schlegel writes, "to do some Fichte."[11]

Schleiermacher reported extensively to his sister Charlotte in October on the new acquaintance: "It is nothing female, but rather a young man . . . named Schlegel . . . He is a young man of 25 years, who is of such broad knowledge, that one cannot comprehend how it should be possible to know so much with such youth, of an original mind . . ., and in his manners of a naturalness, openness and childish youthfulness whose unification with all of that is perhaps the most wonderful thing of all."[12] Above all, Schleiermacher emphasized in a letter to his sister Charlotte (October 22, 1797) that he had found a spiritual companion to whom he could "communicate my philosophical ideas so well," and

> who went into the deepest abstractions with me . . . I can not only pour out to him that which is already in me but also, through the inexhaustible stream of opinions and ideas that incessantly flows from him, bring to life much that had been slumbering. In short, since my closer acquaintance with him a new period has begun for my existence in the philosophical and literary world.[13]

Mainly, however, Schleiermacher was being pressured by Schlegel to emerge as a literary force: "He is constantly picking at me that I should also be writing, that there are a thousand things that need to be said that I of all people could say."[14] Already at this time they were planning that Schlegel should move in with Schleiermacher "in the New Year."[15] Schleiermacher reported further that for eight days he had "spent a large part of my afternoons, which I normally keep very sacred, at his place, in order to read something with him that he could not readily part with."[16] This could be a reference to Schlegel's own notebook for a *Philosophy of Philology*, that is, a theory of hermeneutics and critique on which he had been working at that time.[17]

Schleiermacher and Schlegel's companionship in the area of philosophy was the result of a convergence of independent philosophical developments.[18] In his manuscripts

---

[9] See Schleiermacher's letter to his sister Charlotte, October 22, 1797; *KGA* 5.2, pp. 177f.
[10] *KFSA* vol. 24, p. 12.
[11] "zu Fichtisieren"; *KFSA* vol. 24, p. 23.
[12] *KGA* 5.2, p. 177.
[13] *KGA* 5.2, p. 177.
[14] Ibid., p. 178.
[15] Ibid.
[16] Ibid.
[17] See Schlegel's letter to Niethammer, August 26, 1797; *KFSA* vol. 24, p. 12.
[18] See Peter Grove, *Deutungen des Subjekts. Schleiermachers Philosophie der Religion* (Berlin and New York: De Gruyter, 2004), pp. 161–170; Sarah Schmidt, *Die Konstruktion des Endlichen. Schleiermachers Philosophie der Wechselwirkung* (Berlin and New York: De Gruyter, 2005), pp. 39–56.

written in 1793/94, *Spinozism* (*Spinozismus*) and *Short Description of Spinoza's System* (*Kurze Darstellung des Spinozistischen Systems*),[19] Schleiermacher tried, independently of parallel attempts at the same time in Jena and elsewhere, to bring together Kant's critical philosophy and Spinoza, based on the 1789 second edition of Friedrich Heinrich Jacobi's *Concerning the Doctrine of Spinoza in Letters to Herr Moses Mendelsohn*. In Schleiermacher's combination of Kant and Spinoza, Kant's transcendentalism was completed by the presupposition of *objective* knowledge of things, but—according to Kant and against Spinozism—only finite things and not being as such. Finite things are "illusionary," but they are nonetheless the appearance or manifestation of the infinite. While finite things do not have any existence independent of the infinite and must be thought of as existing in the infinite (just as the infinite does not have another existence except vis-à-vis the finite), they are not simply identical. With a view to Kant, this implies that actually appearing things are regarded as the appearance of the infinite, but without knowledge of this infinite "in itself."[20]

With this combination of Kant and Spinoza, Schleiermacher's thought corresponded with the interests of the early Romantic philosophy being developed at the same time by Friedrich Schlegel and others. Thus, Schleiermacher's encounter with Friedrich Schlegel in Berlin was a meeting of equals that led to an abundance of common "symphilosophical" projects that were only realized in part. They pursued a plan for an *Anti-Leibniz* journal, as recorded in Schleiermacher's and Schlegel's notebooks,[21] they considered a joint philosophical journal, and they planned further projects.[22] The core of their symphilosophy, however, was above all the *Athenaeum* of the Schlegel brothers. Schleiermacher had been included in the planning of the journal from the beginning and he exerted influence on its conception. He not only contributed proposals for the title,[23] but also the concept of the *Literarischen Reichsanzeiger* in *Athenaeum* (1799), considered particularly offensive by the *Aufklärer* of the day, can be traced back to Schleiermacher.[24] Following the departure of Friedrich Schlegel to Jena in September 1799, Schleiermacher functioned as *Athenaeum*'s editor, overseeing the text and the printing, and mediating between the publishers and the Jena friends. Schleiermacher assisted Schlegel in piecing together his fragments for the second part of the *Athenaeum* and contributed fragments himself, as well as subsequent reviews for the journal. The translation of Plato was a further common project that should be mentioned, which contributed not inconsiderably to the rift between the friends.[25] The translation was originally Schlegel's idea, but was ultimately carried out by Schleiermacher alone and has earned him renown to this day.

Schleiermacher and Schlegel agreed not only in their basic philosophical points of view but also in their judgments on political affairs, notably on the French Revolution.[26] In

---

[19] *Spin.*; *Spin.Sys.*
[20] See Andreas Arndt, "Schleiermacher," in *Dictionary of Eighteenth-Century German Philosophers*, ed. Heiner F. Klemme and Manfred Kühn, vol. 3 (Bristol: Continuum, 2010), pp. 1019–1023.
[21] *KGA* 1.2, pp. 75–103.
[22] See the index in *KGA* 5.2, 5.3, and 5.4.
[23] *KGA* 5.2, p. xviii.
[24] *KGA* 5.3, pp. xxv–xxvi.
[25] Andreas Arndt, "Schleiermacher und Platon," in *Schleiermacher: Über die Philosophie Platons*, ed. Peter M. Steiner (Hamburg: Mainer, 1996), pp. vii–xxii.
[26] See Andreas Arndt, *Die Reformation der Revolution. Friedrich Schleiermacher in seiner Zeit* (Berlin: Matthes und Seitz, 2019), pp. 89ff.

Schleiermacher's *Speeches* he writes that the French Revolution was the "most sublime act of the universe"[27] and was therefore of religious importance. Analogous to Kant's statement, which interprets the French Revolution as a historical sign (*Geschichtszeichen*) of the progress of humankind in morality, Schleiermacher had enthusiasm about the Revolution because he thought it was a sign of the awakening of religiousness and an upcoming religious age. Schlegel took a comparable position; for him the French Revolution was the "incitement of the slumbering religion."[28] Closely related to the religious dimension of the Revolution is the aesthetic dimension, which was celebrated in the French Revolution itself (the revolutionary festivals in the French Republic) and in the enthusiasm of its German observers. In the *Speeches* Schleiermacher was the first who spoke about a "religion of art,"[29] and this connection between art and religion became predominant in Schlegel's positions.

The intensive cooperation between Schlegel and Schleiermacher was strengthened by sharing their accommodations. On December 31, 1797, Schleiermacher wrote at length to his sister Charlotte on his daily routine in their shared abode by the Oranienburg Gate. Schleiermacher typically would go to bed at 2 a.m. and would sleep till 8.30, while Schlegel would already be awake an hour earlier: "I am usually awoken by the rattle of his coffee cup. From his bed he can then open the doors which separate his room from my sleeping chamber, and we thus begin our morning discussion."[30] After breakfast each of them would work as he pleased until they spoke about their studies during a break and then had a joint lunch at 12.30. The afternoon proceeded according to a less strict timetable. Schleiermacher would listen to private collegia (e.g. at Klaproth)[31] and read some himself. Later he would devote himself to social life. When he then would return around 10 or 11 p.m., Schlegel would still be awake to greet him but would go to bed while Schleiermacher continued to work. "Our friends," Schleiermacher stated in conclusion, "have found amusement [in calling] our cohabitation a marriage, and all of them agree that I must be the wife, and have no end of fun with it."

This "marriage" did not, however, imply perfect harmony. Smaller and larger resentments soon began to emerge, resentments which had to be dealt with. At the end of 1797, Schleiermacher was already aware that their characters were very different:

> What I miss though is the delicate feeling and the fine sense for the lovely little things in life and for the fine expression of beautiful attitudes that often involuntarily reveal the whole feeling in small things. As in the way he prefers books with large print, he also likes great and strong traits in people; the merely gentle and beautiful has no hold on him, because, too analogously to his own temper, he considers everything that does not appear fiery and strong to be weak.[32]

---

[27] "die erhabenste Tat des Universums"; *KGA* 1.2, p. 196.
[28] *KFSA* vol. 2, p. 265.
[29] "Kunstreligion"; *KGA* 1.2, p. 262.
[30] *KGA* 5.2, p. 217; see on the following pp. 217–219.
[31] Martin Heinrich Klaproth was one of the founders of experimental chemistry in the eighteenth century; see also for Schleiermacher's relations to Klaproth, Ursula Klein, "Der Chemiekult der Frühromantik," in *Wissenschaft und Geselligkeit. Friedrich Schleiermacher in Berlin 1796–1802*, ed. Andreas Arndt (Berlin and New York: De Gruyter, 2009), pp. 67–92.
[32] *KGA* 5.2, p. 220.

Clearly Schlegel wanted to mold Schleiermacher according to his own ideal, though he saw his main obstacle to this in the influence of Henriette Herz. In a letter to Caroline Schlegel in January 1798, he was already complaining:

> Schleiermacher is being ruined by his association with Herz; as such and also for me and the friendship . . . they are making each other vain . . . . They give themselves credit for every lousy little exercise of virtue: Schl[eiermacher's] spirit is shrinking, he is losing his sense for the great. In short, these blasted and petty obsessions with feeling [Gemüthereien] may drive me mad! . . . The worst thing is that I see no way for Schleyermacher to rescue himself from the nooses of antiquity [i.e. Henriette Herz].[33]

Schleiermacher did complain later that Schlegel did not understand his innermost essence,[34] but would not let himself be affected by the criticism of his friend. The first major publication that he produced according to Schlegel's repeated demands was, of all things, a theory of the sociability brought about in Schleiermacher's view by women like Henriette Herz, namely, the essay *Toward a Theory of Sociable Conduct*, which appeared anonymously and remains a fragment.[35] It is perhaps telling that no response from Schlegel to this piece has been discovered, because the essay reflected the praxis of conversation in the salons like that of Henriette Herz.

Regardless of this ill-feeling and in mutual respect for the difference of their characters and views, the relationship between Schleiermacher and Schlegel initially remained untroubled beyond their domestic companionship. Schlegel's departure to Jena gave rise to an intense exchange of letters, which enabled a continuation of a "symphilosophizing" across spatial distance, which could not, however, replace the "sympersons" so important to Schleiermacher in particular. The friends supported each other's literary output. Schlegel served as a propagandist for *On Religion: Speeches to Its Cultured Despisers*,[36] and Schleiermacher as a defender of the novel *Lucinde* which—as usually is the case—was felt to be scandalous overwhelmingly by those who had not read it.[37] Concerning the *Speeches*, Schleiermacher's famous recourse to Spinoza in the second speech parallels Schlegel's interpretation of Spinoza as the mystic of the infinite or the absolute.[38] The mystic is "the master of the original science of the Absolute,"[39] and the highest masters in this discipline are Spinoza and Fichte.[40] But while for Schlegel mysticism is a *variety of philosophy*, for Schleiermacher mysticism is *beyond philosophy* or the *other to philosophy*—like religion in the *Speeches*. In consequence, mysticism stands to philosophy as religion to philosophy, and for this reason

---

[33] *KFSA* vol. 24, p. 211; on varying dates see *KGA* 5.2, p. xxxi. The origin of the salon of Schleiermacher's close companion Henriette Herz was an "alliance for virtue" (*Tugendbund*) and in Schlegel's eyes the discourse there was dominated by sentimentality and not by rationality.
[34] See the letter to Henriette Herz, July 1, 1799; *KGA* 5.3, pp. 133–137.
[35] *VTB*; see Andreas Arndt, "Geselligkeit und Gesellschaft. Die Geburt der Dialektik aus dem Geist der Konversation in Schleiermachers 'Versuch einer Theorie des geselligen Betragens,'" in *Salons der Romantik*, ed. Hartwig Schultz (Berlin and New York: De Gruyter, 1997), pp. 45–61.
[36] See his Review in *Athenaeum*; *KFSA* vol. 2, pp. 275–281.
[37] See *Lucinde*.
[38] *KGA* 1.2, p. 213.
[39] *KFSA* vol. 18, p. 7.
[40] Ibid., p. 5.

it is impossible to find a third alternative to them.[41] This separation of religion or mysticism on the one side and philosophy on the other is the main point of difference between Schlegel and Schleiermacher at that time. In his above-mentioned review of the *Speeches*, Schlegel emphasizes the *philosophical* foundation of Schleiermacher's concept of religion—and this was not a pure misunderstanding.[42] Concerning the *Lucinde*, Schleiermacher defends the novel of his friend against the accusation of immorality, emphasizing the right of poetry to depict love artistically in all variations. Both Schlegel and Schleiermacher understand love and poetry within and from a broad ethical horizon that is not morally tinctured by prudishness. Schlegel's and Schleiermacher's ethical horizon corresponds to that of morality as a historical process of the education of humanity.

In human terms, Schleiermacher and Schlegel became more and more estranged until their lives drifted apart and they independently worked out the stock of ideas they had in part "symphilosophically" developed. The temporal coincidence of Schlegel's departure from Jena in 1802, Schleiermacher's move to Stolp in the same year, and the failure of the joint Plato translation made it clear that the early Romantic epoch of the great "sym" had also come to an end in the relationship between Schlegel and Schleiermacher. The "dream of cooperation," as Georg Lukács wrote in his Novalis essay of 1907, "evaporated like a mist and after a few years the one already no longer understood the language of the other."[43] Lukács' view that the protagonists of early Romanticism could "no longer attempt an ascent on lonely paths" must be rejected, however.[44] Schleiermacher especially was to absorb and rework views he shared with early Romanticism and with Schlegel in particular, and adapt them successfully for his continuing path of thought. It is to the latter that I now turn.

8.3 Schleiermacher's Transformation of Early Romanticism

Rudolf Haym's monumental work *The Romantic School*, which was published in 1870 in Berlin almost at the same time as Wilhelm Dilthey's *The Life of Schleiermacher*, ends with a look at Schleiermacher. Schleiermacher, Haym says, had "rescued," "though in rough form," Schlegel's basic idea that "the philosophy and writing of Plato are rooted in a living, unified spirit and have to be explained in terms of this spirit."[45] Haym writes that Schleiermacher had done much more, however, in his 1803 book, *Outlines of a Critique of Previous Ethical*

---

[41] See Andreas Arndt, "Mystizismus, Spinozismus und Grenzen der Philosophie. Jacobi im Spannungsfeld von F. Schlegel und Schleiermacher," in *Ein Wendepunkt der geistigen Bildung der Zeit. Friedrich Heinrich Jacobi und die klassische deutsche Philosophie*, ed. Walter Jaeschke and Birgit Sandkaulen (Hamburg: Meiner, 2004), pp. 126–141.

[42] Andreas Arndt, "On the Amphiboly of Religious Speech: Religion and Philosophy in Schleiermacher's 'On Religion,'" in *Interpreting Religion: The Significance of Friedrich Schleiermacher's "Reden über die Religion" for Religious Studies and Theology*, ed. Dietrich Korsch and Amber L. Griffioen (Tübingen: Mohr, 2011), pp. 99–111.

[43] Georg Lukács, *Die Seele und die Formen* (Neuwied and Berlin: Luchterhand, 1971), p. 96.

[44] Ibid., p. 77.

[45] Rudolf Haym, *Die romantische Schule* (Berlin: Gaertner, 1870), p. 863.

Theory:⁴⁶ "because, for the ethical, he was not indebted to Romanticism, rather, Romanticism was indebted to him."⁴⁷ In this work, Schleiermacher had salvaged the ethical idea of early Romanticism from its fluid form and tied the "revolutionary spirit" of early Romanticism to "the law of steadfast order" and had attempted to "subject subjectivism and individualism, with their needs for feeling and imagination, to the discipline of logic and the system." This, according to Haym, corresponded to what Hegel had attempted to do in relation to the early Schelling in the *Phenomenology of Spirit* in 1807.⁴⁸ In fact, however, the systematic basic idea that Schleiermacher formulated in his book of 1803 and then further developed in his *Lectures on Dialectic* is itself also indebted to Schlegel.

The first point is the overcoming of the contradiction between idealism and realism, which is rightly considered to be a key feature of Schleiermacher's thought. Schleiermacher shared this program with Schlegel and was conscious of doing so. Thus, a letter from March 1801 reads, "The unification of idealism and realism is what all my endeavors are geared towards, and I have hinted at the ability in the *Discourses* as well as in the *Soliloquies*. The basis of this does lie very deep, though, and it will not be easy to open a feeling for this to both parties. Schlegel, who said so much that was aimed at this, is not understood, and my works have probably not yet been looked at in this way elsewhere."⁴⁹ The unification of Idealism and Realism implied not only a strong orientation toward the empirical sciences—and here too Schleiermacher is one with Schlegel—it also had consequences for systematics and above all for the founding of philosophy. This was first recognized clearly by Schlegel, who, proceeding from the historicity of human action and knowledge, determined the philosophical method as "totalization from the bottom up."⁵⁰ If the real is an irreducible constitutive moment of philosophy, then philosophy is incapable of generating any principle out of which it could develop the real deductively. Thus, writing in his review, written and published in 1796, of Jacobi's novel *Woldemar*, Schlegel opposed the notion of an "alternating proof" to Carl Leonhard Reinhold and Johann Gottlieb Fichte, who attempted to found philosophy on the basis of an unconditioned highest principle, namely, the theorem of consciousness⁵¹ or the highest principle of the doctrine of science ("oberster Grundsatz der Wissenschaftslehre"; Fichte). That is to say, as Schlegel puts it disguised in a rhetorical question, "the basis of philosophy" is an "externally unconditioned, but reciprocally conditioned and self-conditioning alternating proof."⁵² However this may be interpreted in detail, Schlegel does not think of the unconditioned, that is, the basis of philosophy, as a principle and goal (*telos*) outside of whatever is conditioned by it, but rather as a totality of self-conditioning.⁵³ In his notes for the

---

⁴⁶ *GKS*.
⁴⁷ Haym, *Die romantische Schule*, p. 863.
⁴⁸ Ibid., p. 864.
⁴⁹ To F. H. C. Schwarz, March 28, 1801; *KGA* 5.5, p. 73.
⁵⁰ "Totalisazion von unten herauf"; *KFSA* vol. 16, p. 68.
⁵¹ A first version of the "Satz des Bewusstseins" as the principle of philosophy can be found in §7 of the second book of Karl Leonhard Reinhold, *Versuch einer neuen Theorie des menschlichen Vorstellungsvermögens*, Kommentierte Ausgabe, ed. Martin Bondeli and Silvan Imhof (Basel: Schwabe Verlag, 2013), (1789) p. 128.
⁵² *KFSA* vol. 2, p. 74.
⁵³ On the theory of the alternating proof see Manfred Frank, "*Unendliche Annäherung.*" *Die Anfänge der philosophischen Frühromantik* (Frankfurt am Main: Suhrkamp, 1997) and "'Wechselgrundsatz.' Friedrich Schlegels philosophischer Ausgangspunkt," *Zeitschrift für philosophische Forschung* 50 (1996), pp. 26–50; Guido Naschert, "Friedrich Schlegel über Wechselerweis und Ironie," *Athenaeum*.

Philosophy of Philology he expresses his opposition to Fichte clearly: "the cyclization is like a totalization from the bottom up. In Fichte, however, it is a descent."[54] The "cyclization" is evidently nothing other than the alternating proof of the elements of an historical determined totality. Schlegel appealed to this method independently of Fichte: "I also myself recognized the method of the material doctrine of antiquity to be cyclical long before I knew of Fichte."[55]

Schleiermacher adopted this conception, which Schlegel had first formulated before his move to Berlin and which was doubtless the subject matter of their discussions of Fichte's philosophy at the beginning of their friendship. In a clear allusion to Schlegel's concept of alternating proof, in the *Outlines of a Critique of Previous Ethical Theory* Schleiermacher states that the highest science, that is, the "science of the grounds and the connection of all sciences," must "not for its part be based, like every individual science, on a highest principle. Rather, it can only be thought of as a Whole in which each element can be the beginning, and in which all individual things, reciprocally conditioning each other, are only based on the whole; and can thus only be thought of in such a way that it can only be accepted or rejected, but not founded or proven."[56] This has two aspects. First, the highest science can only be thought of as a whole of reciprocally conditioning and mutually supporting principles. Second, the idea of such a highest science remains problematic, because the whole (in Schlegel's terminology: the allness of the alternating proof) is inexhaustible and knowing is always only becoming and can never be completed. It is precisely for this reason that the highest science cannot be proven in the strict sense, but rather only appealed to and in this way made plausible.

At the time of his encounter with Schleiermacher, Schlegel was working on his *Philosophy of Philology*, that is, on his theory of hermeneutics and critique. As mentioned above, it is highly probable that Schleiermacher knew these first drafts and had spoken to his friend about them. Schlegel's notes were first edited in 1928 by the scholar of Romanticism from Prague, Josef Körner, who also pointed out the conspicuous parallels to Schleiermacher's hermeneutics.[57] In a groundbreaking essay in 1966, Hermann Patsch subsequently demonstrated that Schlegel, and not Schleiermacher, ought to be regarded as the initiator of the Romantic turn in hermeneutics around 1800, notwithstanding the independent significance of the Schleiermacherian theory of hermeneutics.[58] This thesis has been generally accepted in the research since then, and the reminiscence of Schlegel in Schleiermacher's Academy lecture quoted at the beginning makes it clear that Schleiermacher himself was conscious of the fact that in this area he had received essential impetus from Schlegel. From 1805 on, Schleiermacher lectured on hermeneutics in Halle und Berlin. While the *Hermeneutics* in Halle were oriented toward theology, one of the private lectures held in 1809/1810 before the opening of the University of Berlin should be regarded as philosophical.

Jahrbuch für Romantik 6 (1996), pp. 47–91, and 7 (1997), pp. 11–37; and Birgit Rehme-Iffert, *Skepsis und Enthusiasmus. Friedrich Schlegels philosophischer Grundgedanke zwischen 1796 und 1805* (Würzburg: Königshausen und Neumann, 2001), pp. 31ff.

[54] KFSA vol. 16, p. 68.

[55] KFSA vol. 16, p. 66.

[56] KGA 1.4, p. 48.

[57] Friedrich Schlegel, "Philosophie der Philologie," edited and introduced by J. Körner, *Logos* 17 (1928), pp. 1–72.

[58] Hermann Patsch, "Friedrich Schlegels 'Philosophie der Philologie' und Schleiermachers frühe Entwürfe zur Hermeneutik," *Zeitschrift für Theologie und Kirche* 63 (1966), pp. 434–472.

The 1814 lectures were divided into a philosophical and a theological part and were accordingly offered at both faculties, while the other courses were assigned to the Faculty of Theology. The essential difference between Schleiermacher's and Schlegel's concepts of hermeneutics, whose causes I cannot further go into here,[59] consisted in the fact that Schlegel, in accordance with his method of "totalization from the bottom up," conceived of a unified hermeneutical-critical approach that lead to a transcendental-philosophical dialectic. For Schleiermacher, by contrast, hermeneutics was still merely a technical discipline among the critical disciplines. Later on, in his lectures at the Berlin University, hermeneutics was also not immediately connected to the *Dialectic*, his version of the highest science, developed since 1811.[60]

From 1811, Schleiermacher, in conscious opposition to Fichte, developed an alternative to the Fichtean *Wissenschaftslehre* (*Science of Knowledge*) in the *Lectures on Dialectics*.[61] Even as Schleiermacher was lecturing at the University of Berlin in 1811 on the highest science as an independent discipline under the heading *Dialectic*, he may have remembered the conception of his former companion Schlegel, who since 1796 had wanted to deal with the problems of Kant's transcendental dialectic with a notion of "dialectic" linked to classical antiquity and to Plato, in particular: "The Greek name dialectic is of great significance. The genuine art (not the appearance thereof, as in Kant), to impart, to speak the truth, to search for, *refute*, and to *achieve* the truth collaboratively (as in Plato's *Gorgias*—cf. Aristotle), is a part of philosophy or logic and necessarily an instrument of the philosophers."[62] We can compare this with what Schleiermacher stated (according to the Twesten transcript) in the first lecture of 1811 on the explanation of the term "dialectic":

> By "dialectic" we understand . . . the principles of the art of philosophizing . . . That is, the highest and most general principles of knowledge, and the principles of philosophizing are the same. . . . We thus cannot separate constitutive and regulative principles as Kant does. . . . The name of dialectic, which had precisely this meaning in antiquity, is completely appropriate to these concepts. . . . The name relates to the art of simultaneously completing a philosophical construction with another. The dialectic . . . can be rightly called the instrument of all knowledge.[63]

---

[59] See Andreas Arndt, "Hermeneutik und Kritik im Denken der Aufklärung," in *Die Hermeneutik im Zeitalter der Aufklärung*, ed. M. Beetz and G. Cacciatore (Köln: Böhlau, 2000), pp. 211–236, and Manuel Bauer, *Schlegel und Schleiermacher. Frühromantische Kunstkritik und Hermeneutik* (Paderborn: Schöningh, 2011).

[60] Andreas Arndt, "Dialektik und Hermeneutik. Zur kritischen Vermittlung der Disziplinen bei Schleiermacher," *Synthesis philosphica* 12 (1997), pp. 39–63.

[61] *Dial.*

[62] *KFSA* vol. 18, p. 509; see Andreas Arndt, "Zur Vorgeschichte des Schleiermacherschen Begriffs von Dialektik," in *Schleiermacher und die wissenschaftliche Kultur des Christentums*. Festschrift für Hans-Joachim Birkner zum 60. Geburtstag, ed. Günter Meckenstock with J. Ringleben (Berlin and New York: De Gruyter, 1991), pp. 313–333; "Zum Begriff der Dialektik bei Friedrich Schlegel 1796–1801," *Archiv für Begriffsgeschichte* 35 (1992), pp. 257–273; "Perspektiven frühromantischer Dialektik," in *Das neue Licht der Frühromantik. Innovationen und Aktualität frühromantischer Philosophie*, ed. Bärbel Frischmann and Elizabeth Millán-Zaibert (Paderborn: Schöningh, 2009), pp. 53–64; and Marcus Böhm, *Dialektik bei Friedrich Schlegel. Zwischen transzendentaler Erkenntnis und absolutem Wissen* (Paderborn: Schöningh, 2020).

[63] *KGA* 1.10.2, pp. 5–7.

Up to this point Schleiermacher, in the wake of the rhetorical tradition, had equated dialectics with virtuosity in argumentation and nothing, not even his interpretation of the Platonic dialectic, had suggested that he wanted to award it the rank of one of the highest sciences. The only model that can come into consideration here is Friedrich Schlegel's conception of transcendental-philosophical dialectics. In 1934, also in relation to Schleiermacher's lectures on *Dialectic*, Josef Körner argued that it "exhibits certain thoughts of the Jena Transcendental Philosophy [of Schlegel]."[64] This view is being increasingly accepted in the research only today, because in order to demonstrate it, it was first necessary to rediscover and reconstruct the Schlegelian concept of dialectics.[65]

8.4 Divergent Paths (1804–1829)

The failure of the project of a common translation of Plato's complete dialogues, initially suggested and pushed along by Schlegel and then carried out by Schleiermacher alone, was doubtless the breaking point for the "symphilosophizing" of the former friends. It was Schlegel who promised nearly every month to deliver his translations, but in fact he had done almost nothing except speculate about the authenticity and historical sequence of Plato's dialogues, as a result of which he declared famous and unquestionably authentic dialogues like the *Nomoi* (*Laws*) as inauthentic.[66] Notwithstanding the fact that Schlegel had no part in the translation published by Schleiermacher from 1804 onward, Schlegel complained that Schleiermacher had used his ideas without mentioning him. Schleiermacher rejected this accusation in a letter to Schlegel from October 10, 1804.[67]

Their quarrel about the translation of Plato's dialogues marks in fact the end of the immediate "symphilosophizing" of Schlegel and Schleiermacher, but, as shown above, this was not the end of an indirect cooperation of spirit, an inner dialogue Schleiermacher held with his friend, remembering the "symphilosophy" of the former years in Berlin and Schlegel's positions and concepts. This inner dialogue with the Schlegel of the early Romanticism never came to an end. An outward sign of this ongoing inner dialogue is the fact that Schleiermacher had always a portrait of the young Schlegel, probably in his workspace, which made his wife (since 1809) Henriette jealous. On September 16, 1811, she wrote to her husband, who was in Silesia at this time, "When I went back and forth in the room quite melancholic last night, my eyes fell on Schlegel and I was very grim that the stranger was hanging there and not your portrait." Henriette removed Schlegel's portrait and replaced it with a portrait of Schleiermacher.[68] Nevertheless, this anecdote illustrates that Schlegel was

---

[64] Friedrich Schlegel, *Neue Philosophische Schriften*, ed. Josef Körner (Frankfurt am Main: Schulte-Bulmke, 1935), p. 51.

[65] Cf. Grove, *Deutungen*, pp. 438ff.; Schmidt, *Die Konstruktion*, p. 112.

[66] See Arndt, "Schleiermacher und Platon," and *KGA* 4.3, pp. xv–xxvii.

[67] *KGA* 5.7, pp. 467f.

[68] *KGA* 5.12, pp. 149f. The portrait was a work of Maria Alberti and was first mentioned in 1802; it is now lost (see Johannes Endres, ed., *Friedrich Schlegel Handbuch. Leben–Werk–Wirkung* [Stuttgart: Metzler, 2017], p. 29).

present in Schleiermacher's mind even after the break in the relationship to his former intimate friend.

The intensive correspondence between Schlegel and Schleiermacher did not come to an immediate standstill after the quarrel about the translation of Plato in October 1804, even though Schlegel changed his whereabouts often during these years (Würzburg, Paris, Cologne, Vienna) as did Schleiermacher (Stolp, Halle, Berlin), which was a serious obstacle to uninterrupted correspondence. However, it becomes clear from their letters that the differences in content increased. This was not the result of a personal alienation between the former friends, but the result of Schlegel's step-by-step inclination to Catholicism[69] and the accompanying changes in his theoretical positions. For the Protestant theologian Schleiermacher, Catholicism was diametrically opposed to his convictions—not only his understanding of Christianity, but also his philosophical and political understanding of freedom, because he, like Hegel, identified Catholicism with hierarchy and servitude.[70]

In a first letter from July 25, 1806 (the previous letter from Schleiermacher, who apparently restarted the correspondence after an interruption of nearly nine months, is not preserved), Schlegel asked for a "report on the current state of speculative philosophy" in Germany, maybe hoping that Schleiermacher would pay more attention to this philosophy, which was his old demand that he had repeated over and over again in the last years.[71] But Schleiermacher's report (in a lost letter) did not satisfy him, because Schlegel's understanding of "speculative" had changed in the meantime. It was no longer "mysticism" in the sense of a philosophy of the absolute, but, on the contrary, the limitation of philosophy as such by a theology of creation. He describes Schleiermacher's statement ironically as "heresy," because "You Spinocists" are focused on a philosophy of nature, which in truth is "hidden" or "pasted" (*verkleisterter*) materialism, but neither philosophy nor physics could say anything about the origin of nature itself.[72] The polemic against Spinozism and pantheism anticipate his later statements, as in his Fichte essay of 1808, where Schlegel criticizes Schleiermacher (without mentioning his name) for his Spinozism and his aesthetical view of religion[73]—a complete change of his positions in comparison with the "symphilosophizing" in the Berlin years. Schlegel's objections were primarily based on theological reflections, not on philosophical arguments. Those objections were not disputed in the following correspondence, but in his above-cited letter Schlegel tried to push Schleiermacher toward a "speculative" view of theological objects.[74]

Schleiermacher and Schlegel also took different paths in politics, not only in their judgment on the French Revolution—for the late Schlegel a work of unbelief and apostasy from God, whereas Schleiermacher held to his view that the revolution was legitimated—but also concerning the situation in Germany after the collapse of Prussia in 1806 and, in consequence, the "Holy Roman Empire of German Nation." Already in his letter from September 17, 1806,

---

[69] On Catholicism, see for example Schlegel's letter from June 23, 1807, *KGA* 5.9, p. 475; the final conversion took place in April 1808.

[70] Cf. Hans-Joachim Birkner, "Deutung und Kritik des Katholizismus bei Schleiermacher und Hegel," in Birkner, *Schleiermacher-Studien* (Berlin and New York: De Gruyter, 1996), pp. 125–136.

[71] See *KGA* 5.9, p. 80.

[72] *KGA* 5.9, p. 142.

[73] See *KFSA* vol. 8, pp. 69ff.

[74] See *KGA* 5.9, pp. 142f.

Schlegel wrote that this empire also includes the Netherlands and Alsace, even though they were "damaged limbs" of it, but the "center of all damage" seems to him to be Prussia.[75] Whereas Schleiermacher more and more was oriented toward Prussia and the Protestant north of Germany because he feared that Napoleon would persecute Protestantism and restore Catholicism, Schlegel thought in terms of the borders of the old empire and feared that especially its Catholic parts could be separated by Prussian politics.[76] Schlegel looked toward a greater Germany, Schleiermacher toward a smaller. Schlegel hoped for an alliance between Prussia and Austria in a letter of August 26, 1807, and he affirmed his position again in 1813.[77] In his answer, Schleiermacher suspected that Austria would be liberal enough as required to build up a united Germany.[78] A last letter from Schlegel to Schleiermacher is from 1817 and asked for the constitution of the Protestant church in Prussia.[79] Schleiermacher did not answer before Schlegel's death in January 1829. The thread of conversation was finally broken.

***

As the result of their independent developments, Schlegel and Schleiermacher met at the same theoretical and, in particular, philosophical level in Berlin and started their "symphilosophizing." Going back to the Berlin period of early Romanticism, Schleiermacher introduced early Romantic philosophy into the epoch dominated by Hegel as well as the post-Hegelian philosophical epoch. He did this by appropriating the store of ideas created in the "symphilosophical" laboratory of ideas in a systematically directed way and in doing so transformed it into a discursive form beyond the paradoxes of early Romanticism. How deeply rooted this project is in Schleiermacher's domestic and philosophical companionship with Schlegel can be gauged by the fact that all three decisive notions deriving from Schlegel—Plato, hermeneutics, and dialectics—had been worked out by Schlegel in the immediate ambit of the encounter. This does not, however, imply, as is often suspected, Schleiermacher's dependence on the ideas of his friend. It was Schleiermacher who transformed some central ideas of the early Schlegel into a systematic form in which they could live as part of the heritage of classical German philosophy.

Suggested Reading

Arndt, Andreas. *Friedrich Schleiermacher als Philosoph* (Berlin and Boston: De Gruyter, 2013).
Arndt, Andreas. "Schleiermacher." In *The Oxford Handbook of German Philosophy in the Nineteenth Century*, ed. Michael N. Forster and Kristin Gjesdal (Oxford: University Press, 2015), pp. 26–45.
Nowak, Kurt. *Schleiermacher und die Frühromantik. Eine literaturgeschichtliche Studie zum romantischen Religionsverständnis und Menschenbild am Ende des 18. Jahrhunderts in Deutschland* (Weimar: Böhlau Nachfolger, 1986).
Ohst, Martin, ed. *Schleiermacher Handbuch* (Tübingen: Mohr, 2017), pp. 32–48 and 76–137.

---

[75] KGA 5.9, p. 142.
[76] See also Dorothea Schlegel to Schleiermacher from 1806/1807; KGA 5.9, p. 334.
[77] KGA 5.9, pp. 521f.; KGA 5.12, p. 360.
[78] KGA 5.12, pp. 439f.
[79] Br. I–IV vol. 4, pp. 436f.

Bibliography

Arndt, Andreas. "On the Amphiboly of Religious Speech: Religion and Philosophy in Schleiermacher's 'On Religion.'" In *Interpreting Religion: The Significance of Friedrich Schleiermacher's "Reden über die Religion" for Religious Studies and Theology*, ed. Dietrich Korsch and Amber L. Griffioen (Tübingen: Mohr, 2011), pp. 99–111.

Arndt, Andreas. "Zum Begriff der Dialektik bei Friedrich Schlegel 1796–1801." *Archiv für Begriffsgeschichte* 35 (1992), pp. 257–273.

Arndt, Andreas. "Dialektik und Hermeneutik. Zur kritischen Vermittlung der Disziplinen bei Schleiermacher." *Synthesis philosphica* 12 (1997), pp. 39–63.

Arndt, Andreas. "Geselligkeit und Gesellschaft. Die Geburt der Dialektik aus dem Geist der Konversation in Schleiermachers 'Versuch einer Theorie des geselligen Betragens.'" In *Salons der Romantik*, ed. Hartwig Schultz (Berlin and New York: De Gruyter, 1997), pp. 45–61.

Arndt, Andreas. "Hermeneutik und Kritik im Denken der Aufklärung." In *Die Hermeneutik im Zeitalter der Aufklärung*, ed. M. Beetz and G. Cacciatore (Köln: Böhlau, 2000), pp. 211–236.

Arndt, Andreas. "Eine literarische Ehe. Schleiermachers Wohngemeinschaft mit Friedrich Schlegel." In *Wissenschaft und Geselligkeit. Friedrich Schleiermacher in Berlin 1796–1802*, ed. Andreas Arndt (Berlin and New York: De Gruyter, 2009), pp. 3–14.

Arndt, Andreas. "Mystizismus, Spinozismus und Grenzen der Philosophie. Jacobi im Spannungsfeld von F. Schlegel und Schleiermacher." In *Ein Wendepunkt der geistigen Bildung der Zeit. Friedrich Heinrich Jacobi und die klassische deutsche Philosophie*, ed. Walter Jaeschke and Birgit Sandkaulen (Hamburg: Meiner, 2004), pp. 126–141.

Arndt, Andreas. "Perspektiven frühromantischer Dialektik." In *Das neue Licht der Frühromantik. Innovationen und Aktualität frühromantischer Philosophie*, ed. Bärbel Frischmann and Elizabeth Millán-Zaibert (Paderborn: Schöningh, 2009), pp. 53–64.

Arndt, Andreas. *Die Reformation der Revolution. Friedrich Schleiermacher in seiner Zeit* (Berlin: Matthes und Seitz, 2019).

Arndt, Andreas. "'Remember That All Poetry Is to Be Regarded as a Work of Love': Ethics and Aesthetics in Schleiermacher." In *The Marriage of Aesthetics and Ethics*, ed. Stéphane Symons (Leiden and Boston: Brill, 2015), pp. 81–94.

Arndt, Andreas. "Schleiermacher." In *Dictionary of Eighteenth-Century German Philosophers*, ed. Heiner F. Klemme and Manfred Kühn, vol. 3 (Bristol: Continuum, 2010), pp. 1019–1023.

Arndt, Andreas. "Schleiermacher und Platon." In *Schleiermacher: Über die Philosophie Platons*, ed. Peter M. Steiner (Hamburg: Meiner, 1996), pp. vii–xxii.

Arndt, Andreas. "Zur Vorgeschichte des Schleiermacherschen Begriffs von Dialektik." In *Schleiermacher und die wissenschaftliche Kultur des Christentums*. Festschrift für Hans-Joachim Birkner zum 60. Geburtstag, ed. Günter Meckenstock with J. Ringleben (Berlin and New York: De Gruyter, 1991), pp. 313–333.

Bauer, Manuel. *Schlegel und Schleiermacher. Frühromantische Kunstkritik und Hermeneutik* (Paderborn: Schöningh, 2011).

Birkner, Hans-Joachim. "Deutung und Kritik des Katholizismus bei Schleiermacher und Hegel." In *Schleiermacher-Studien* (Berlin and New York: De Gruyter, 1996), pp. 125–136.

Böhm, Marcus. *Dialektik bei Friedrich Schlegel. Zwischen transzendentaler Erkenntnis und absolutem Wissen* (Paderborn: Schöningh, 2020).

Endres, Johannes, ed. *Friedrich Schlegel Handbuch. Leben–Werk–Wirkung* (Stuttgart: Metzler, 2017).

Frank, Manfred. *"Unendliche Annäherung." Die Anfänge der philosophischen Frühromantik* (Frankfurt am Main: Suhrkamp, 1997).

Frank, Manfred. "'Wechselgrundsatz.' Friedrich Schlegels philosophischer Ausgangspunkt." *Zeitschrift für philosophische Forschung* 50 (1996), pp. 26–50.

Grove, Peter. *Deutungen des Subjekts. Schleiermachers Philosophie der Religion* (Berlin and New York: De Gruyter, 2004).

Haym, Rudolf. *Die romantische Schule* (Berlin: Gaertner, 1870).

Klein, Ursula. "Der Chemiekult der Frühromantik." In *Wissenschaft und Geselligkeit. Friedrich Schleiermacher in Berlin 1796–1802*, ed. Andreas Arndt (Berlin and New York: De Gruyter, 2009), pp. 67–92.

Lukács, Georg. *Die Seele und die Formen* (Neuwied and Berlin: Luchterhand, 1971).

Matuschek, Stefan, ed. *Wo das philosophische Gespräch ganz in Dichtung übergeht. Platons Symposion und seine Wirkung in der Renaissance, Romantik und Moderne* (Heidelberg: Winter, 2002).

Naschert, Guido. "Friedrich Schlegel über Wechselerweis und Ironie." *Athenaeum. Jahrbuch für Romantik* 6 (1996), pp. 47–91, and 7 (1997), pp. 11–37.

Patsch, Hermann. "Friedrich Schlegels 'Philosophie der Philologie' und Schleiermachers frühe Entwürfe zur Hermeneutik." *Zeitschrift für Theologie und Kirche* 63 (1966), pp. 434–472.

Rehme-Iffert, Birgit. *Skepsis und Enthusiasmus. Friedrich Schlegels philosophischer Grundgedanke zwischen 1796 und 1805* (Würzburg: Königshausen und Neumann, 2001).

Reinhold, Karl Leonhard. *Versuch einer neuen Theorie des menschlichen Vorstellungsvermögens*. Kommentierte Ausgabe. Ed. Martin Bondeli and Silvan Imhof (Basel: Schwabe Verlag, 2013).

Schlegel, Dorothea, and Friedrich Schlegel. *Briefe von Dorothea und Friedrich Schlegel an die Familie Paulus*. Ed. R. Unger (Berlin: Behr, 1913).

Schlegel, Friedrich. *Neue Philosophische Schriften*. Ed. Josef Körner (Frankfurt am Main: Schulte-Bulmke, 1935).

Schlegel, Friedrich. "Philosophie der Philologie," edited and introduced by J. Körner. *Logos* 17 (1928), pp. 1–72.

Schlegel, Friedrich. *Werke. Kritische Ausgabe*. Ed. Ernst Behler et al. (Paderborn: Schöningh, 1958–).

Schleiermacher, Friedrich. *Briefwechsel 1796-1789*, KGA 5.2, ed. Andreas Arndt and Wolfgang Virmond (Berlin: De Gruyter, 1988).

Schleiermacher, Friedrich. *Briefwechsel 1799-1800*, KGA 5.3, ed. Andreas Arndt and Wolfgang Virmond (Berlin: De Gruyter, 1992).

Schleiermacher, Friedrich. *Briefwechsel 1800*, KGA 5.4, ed. Andreas Arndt and Wolfgang Virmond (Berlin: De Gruyter, 1994).

Schleiermacher, Friedrich. *Briefwechsel 1801-02*, KGA 5.5, ed. Andreas Arndt and Wolfgang Virmond (Berlin: De Gruyter, 1999).

Schleiermacher, Friedrich. *Briefwechsel 1803-04*, KGA 5.7, ed. Andreas Arndt and Wolfgang Virmond (Berlin: De Gruyter, 2005).

Schleiermacher, Friedrich. *Briefwechsel 1806-1807*, KGA 5.9, ed. Andreas Arndt and Simon Gerber (Berlin: De Gruyter, 2011).

Schleiermacher, Friedrich. *Briefwechsel 1811-1813*, KGA 5.12, ed. Simon Gerber and Sarah Schmidt (Berlin: De Gruyter, 2019).

Schmidt, Sarah. *Die Konstruktion des Endlichen. Schleiermachers Philosophie der Wechselwirkung* (Berlin and New York: De Gruyter, 2005).

PART II
SCHLEIERMACHER'S THOUGHT

A

SCHLEIERMACHER AND THE *WISSENSCHAFTEN*

CHAPTER 9

DIALECTIC

SARAH SCHMIDT

9.1 THE HISTORY AND GENESIS OF SCHLEIERMACHER'S LECTURES ON DIALECTIC

THE occasion of Schleiermacher's appointment as Professor of Theology at the University of Berlin also marks the beginning of his lectures on dialectic.[1] From 1811 to 1831—six times in total—he lectured on his epistemology, to which he had given the title "Dialectic" (*Dialektik*). The enrollment figures suggest an enthusiastic response among the students; the 63 attendees at the first lecture had increased to 148 attendees by his final course of lectures.[2] In comparison with his lectures on philosophical ethics, Schleiermacher's lectures on dialectic—in which he shaped and refined his systematic concept—took root relatively late. This does not mean, however, that no one had established a foundation for epistemology within the sciences prior to this. In Halle, Schleiermacher had been closely associated with the Norwegian Henrich Steffens, a natural philosopher and student of Schelling.[3] In his lectures, he pointed his students toward the philosophical foundation of knowledge established by Steffens, just as, conversely, Steffens advised his students to turn to Schleiermacher in ethical and theological matters. In Berlin, Schleiermacher had no recourse to colleagues, for there was no question of the philosopher Fichte—who had been appointed in Berlin and whose epistemological approach of *Wissenschaftslehre* (doctrine of scientific knowledge) Schleiermacher rejected—ever "replacing" Steffens.

Fundamental to the intuitive consonance between Steffens and Schleiermacher was Spinoza's early Romantic idea of a progressive universality of mind and nature.[4] As much as they agree in their basic philosophical structure, Steffens and Schleiermacher differ

---

[1] On Schleiermacher's role in the founding and organizing of the University of Berlin, see Chapter 7 of this volume.

[2] Cf. Andreas Arndt and Wolfgang Virmond, eds., *Schleiermachers Briefwechsel (Verzeichnis) nebst einer Liste seiner Vorlesungen* (Berlin: De Gruyter, 1992), pp. 293–330.

[3] On Schleiermacher's relation to the work of Schelling and Steffens, see Chapter 5 in this volume.

[4] Cf. Henrich Steffens, *Was ich erlebte. Aus der Erinnerung niedergeschrieben*, vol. 5 (Breslau: Josef Max, 1842), p. 143. On the influence of Spinoza on Schleiermacher's thought, see Chapter 3 in this volume.

greatly in their methodological approach and therefore also in their representation of the philosophical problem.⁵ Whereas Steffens, like Spinoza, chooses a "deductive" method, developing a compact explanation of the relationship between the finite and the infinite based on the infinite, Schleiermacher's focus in his lectures on dialectic is on a genuinely human approach to knowledge, which means a finite one. Based on one's actual knowledge, which is an eternal debate between opposing opinions, what can the human being say about knowledge as knowledge?

It becomes very clear from his paper *Grundlinien einer Kritik der bisherigen Sittenlehre* (1803) (Outlines of a Critique of the Doctrines of Morality to Date) in particular, but also in his early ethics lectures, that his Berlin Dialectic was not the first time Schleiermacher had contemplated this methodological approach.⁶ In this respect, the ethics lectures represent important milestones in the development of his ideas on dialectic. As a "formal" critique of the ethical concepts of great philosophers, his 1803 *Grundlinien* on the one hand serves as a way of reassuring himself of his ethical position, and thereby as direct preparation for his ethics lectures, but on the other hand it also reflects on the methodological foundation of knowledge and science per se. Here, Schleiermacher calls for a "science of the foundations of, and the relation between, all sciences" (*Wissenschaft von den Gründen und dem Zusammenhang aller Wissenschaften*) as a basis for all individual sciences;⁷ this should not, however, "itself be based, in turn, like those individual sciences, on a supreme principle."⁸ The lectures on ethics, too, begin with the question of the legitimation of their scientific basis and make clear the value Schleiermacher ascribed, right from the beginning of the development of his system, to the question of the methodological approach in all sciences.

Schleiermacher developed his conception of dialectic for the 1811 lecture in a relatively short time, which again emphasizes the fact he had been preoccupied with the concept for quite a while already, or, as Schleiermacher writes to Joachim Gaß on May 11, 1811, the concept had "been nagging at me for a long time."⁹ He was satisfied with the first draft—at least, that is what a few passages from letters from the years 1811 and 1812 suggest, for instance where he asserts that he has "established the basis, at least, for a relatively clear representation."¹⁰ There is evidence that there were plans for a published version from as early as 1814 during his first lecture cycles.¹¹ After that, this plan was lost in a flood of other projects; it was taken up again at the end of the 1820s. All we have today in clean copy is the introduction to Dialectic, which Schleiermacher wrote shortly before his death in 1833. Because, however, the aim of the introduction is to introduce the epistemological approach, establish dialectic as a point of intersection within the scientific system, and offer fundamental reflections on the relationship between thinking and language, it is, in terms of a final version, one document—if not the central document—of the lecture on dialectic.

---

⁵ Cf. Sarah Schmidt, "Analogie versus Wechselwirkung—Zur 'Symphilosophie' zwischen Schleiermacher und Steffens," in *Schleiermacher in Halle (1804–1808)*, ed. Andreas Arndt (Berlin: De Gruyter, 2013), pp. 91–114.
⁶ On Schleiermacher's early writings, see Chapter 25 in this volume.
⁷ *GKS*, p. 20.
⁸ *GKS*, p. 20.
⁹ *KGA* 5.12, p. 91, no. 3630.
¹⁰ *KGA* 5.12, p. 278, no. 3785.
¹¹ Cf. *KGA* 5.13, p. 219, no. 4083.

Schleiermacher's lectures on dialectic were edited for the first time as part of the collected works in 1839, a few years after Schleiermacher's death, by Ludwig Jonas.[12] This collection contains almost all Schleiermacher's manuscripts in a reliable transcription. All the lecture manuscripts by Schleiermacher that have been preserved, as well as postscripts to the lecture courses from 1811, 1818/1819, and 1822, have been available since 2002 in a historical-critical edition provided by Andreas Arndt. It contains, as an appendix, a manuscript by August Twesten on the 1811 lecture, as well as excerpts from postscripts to the 1828 and 1831 lectures that had already been published—the lecture notebooks for these have been lost.[13]

Schleiermacher's notes from 1811, supplemented with excerpts from notes by A. Twesten, is thus far the only body of texts from the lectures on dialectic that has been translated into, and introduced in, English.[14] Another short excerpt from Schleiermacher's lecture on dialectic, focused on schematism, can be found in Andrew Bowie's 1998 English translation of Schleiermacher's hermeneutics.[15]

9.2 The Idea and Conception of the Lectures on Dialectic

9.2.1 Dialectic as the Art of Dialogue

Schleiermacher defines dialectic as a "art of dialogue" (*Kunst der Gesprächsführung*), the aim of which is to create rules of mediation for the eternal debate (*Streitgespräch*)—as the manifestation of human epistemological practice—in order to approximate contingent or purely historical thinking to knowing. Such a concept of a doctrine of art requires a clarification of what knowledge is, and yet it is never possible to undertake this clarification outside the historicity of knowledge. This gives rise to the fundamental interdependency between the two parts of the Dialectic, neither of which should have priority over the other: a "transcendental" part, which reflects on the conditions for the potential generation of knowledge, and a "technical" or "formal" part, the aim of which is to orient disputatious thinking toward knowledge. Although rules can be established for guiding the emerging knowledge to a certain extent, Schleiermacher also points out that successful genesis of knowledge does not merely consist in following rules. Dialectic is therefore an art in two senses of the word: it is craftsmanship in the sense of technique or doctrine, but also an art in the sense of creative competence. The two parts of the Dialectic together with the programmatic introductory remarks—which introduce the epistemological approach and locate dialectic within the scientific system—give dialectic a tripartite structure.

The Fichtean term "*Wissenschaftslehre*" (*doctrine* of science) would suit this project, since it is concerned with a doctrine or a technique. However, Schleiermacher argues that

---

[12] *SW* III 3: 4.2.
[13] On the history and publication history of the dialectic, cf. Andreas Arndt, "Einleitung des Bandherausgebers," in *F. D. E. Schleiermacher Vorlesungen über die Dialektik*, KGA 2.10.1, ed. Andreas Arndt (Berlin: De Gruyter, 2002), pp. vii–lvii.
[14] See *Dial. (Tice)*.
[15] *HC*, pp. 269–280.

Fichte—repeating his criticism from the *Grundlinien* in the lectures on dialectic—ignores precisely this question of guiding the emerging knowledge.[16] By using the concept of dialectic in the sense of dialogue and the art, "of accomplishing a philosophical construction together with another person,"[17] Schleiermacher sees himself as in the antique tradition and refers explicitly to Plato.

Even though Schleiermacher repeatedly emphasizes the Platonic concept of the dialectic, there is no deeper philosophical reflection on Plato's concept of dialectic either in the lecture on dialectic, nor in the lectures on the history of philosophy, nor in the introduction to his translation of Plato. Even though Schleiermacher was a great admirer of Plato and remains to this day one of his most important translators,[18] the history of Schleiermacher's concept of dialectic does not point primarily to Plato. Initially, the (negative) use of dialectic in Kant's *Critique of Pure Reason* as a "logic of illusion" (*Logik des Scheins*), indicating the self-contradictory nature of reason, had an influence on, and provided a point of orientation for, the post-Kantian generation of philosophers. A positive use of the term "dialectic"— that is, where it is understood neither as rhetorical virtuosity nor as an irresolvable "logic of illusion"—can be found in *Brouillon zur Ethik* (1805/1806). Here, Schleiermacher interprets the term "dialectic" as identical with philosophizing as an activity in itself. He argues that it is the "organon of philosophy," a "continuous comparison of individual acts of cognition through language, until an identical knowledge is produced."[19] Schelling had already used the term "dialectic" in this way in *Vorlesungen über die Methode des akademischen Studiums* (Lectures on the Methodology of Academic Study) (1803), but there are good reasons for looking to Schlegel for the starting point for a positively formulated concept of dialectic, such as is found in his notebooks "Philosophische Lehrjahre" (Philosophical Apprenticeship), which deeply influenced not only Schelling and Hegel but also his roommate and ally Friedrich Schleiermacher.[20] In the first few years of their acquaintance (having first met in 1796), Friedrich Schlegel had been a pivotal source of inspiration for Schleiermacher, primarily in questions of epistemology and the philosophy of language.[21]

In this context, it is worth taking a look at the dialogic practice that Schleiermacher conceived in an early text, and which has received very little attention: the philosophical dialogue "Über das Anständige" (On Decency) (probably from the year 1800).[22] In terms of its rhetorical form, this dialogue initially sounds like a Socratic dialogue. Instead of the one-sided didactic dialogue employed by Socrates in Plato's work, Schleiermacher conceived— by employing a definition of decency that is honed within a process of dialogue—a reciprocal process of adjustment, on equal terms, between on the one hand a more conceptually abstract definition and on the other hand a more empirically and practically oriented definition of the term, each definition represented by one of the interlocutors. The concept the

---

[16] *GKS*, pp. 47ff.; cf. *Dial*.1, p. 81, §47; *Dial. (Tice)*, p. 3. Quotations from Schleiermacher's lectures on dialectic that are not taken from T. Tice's translation (*Dial. (Tice)*) have been translated by the translator of this chapter.

[17] *Dial*.2, p. 7, Std. 3; *Dial. (Tice)*, p. 3.

[18] On Schleiermacher's study of Plato, see Chapter 1 in this volume.

[19] *WA* 2, p. 164.

[20] Cf. Andreas Arndt, ed., *Friedrich Schleiermacher als Philosoph* (Berlin: De Gruyter, 2013), pp. 181–197.

[21] On Schleiermacher's relationship to F. Schlegel, see Chapter 8 of this volume.

[22] *KGA* 1.3, pp. 73–99.

interlocutors are trying to define ultimately takes shape within this dialogic "setting" of the conversation, without it being possible to ever consider the conversation ended or the definition of the concept complete.

9.2.2 The Transcendental Part: The Analysis of the Idea of Knowledge

The investigation into the foundation and form of knowledge is faced with the problem that its object "by no means lies outside of the investigation."[23] If dialectic is to orient the debate between opinions toward knowledge without itself being called into question as finite knowledge or opinion, it must find a non-disputatious point of departure. This cannot consist in actual or positive knowledge but must focus on the form of an "unconscious agency" (*unbewußte Agens*) inherent in all opinion and thought. As early as the 1811 lecture on dialectic, Schleiermacher describes this reflection on the "unconscious agency" underlying all thought as the "analysis of the idea of knowledge." Its argumentational structure barely changes throughout the individual lecture courses, but it is presented in the greatest detail in the 1822 lecture on dialectic. We comprehend the moving principle behind all statements not by interrogating opinions in terms of what they *are* but in terms of what they *wish* to be; that is, knowledge. The analysis of the idea of knowledge should ideally be structured into four steps, to which four questions can be assigned: (1) What is knowledge? (2) What is thinking? (3) In what way and why do knowledge and thinking differ? And (4) how is knowledge possible?[24]

The first step in this analysis proceeds from the situation of the dispute itself, identifying the assumptions underlying the dispute—and without which the debate would make no sense at all—as the two "characters of knowledge" (*Charaktere des Wissens*). Firstly, knowledge is characterized by the fact that it is constructed by everyone collectively, or, as Schleiermacher puts it, by the fact that the production of thought is identical. Secondly, the fact that we are disagreeing indicates a fundamental relation between the thinking and an object, for we are always disagreeing about *something*, and we postulate this *something* as the point of reference for our different lines of thought. The second character of knowledge therefore consists in the correspondence between being and thought.

The second step in this analysis of knowledge is concerned with the question of what it is that characterizes thought as thought. Similar to Kantian spontaneity and receptivity in cognition, Schleiermacher distinguishes two functions of thinking: the intellectual and the organic or sensory function. Every individual act of thinking consists in the interaction between these. For Schleiermacher, however, these two functions of thinking cannot be formally defined any further in terms of what they are capable of doing; they can merely be described in terms of their function: providing subject matter and giving form.[25] What is definable, however, is the result of their interaction: the different forms of thinking.

---

[23] *Dial*.1, p. 75, §2.
[24] Cf. Sarah Schmidt, *Die Konstruktion des Endlichen. Schleiermachers Philosophie der Wechselwirkung* (Berlin: De Gruyter, 2005), pp. 123–169.
[25] Cf. *Dial*.1, p. 97, §119.

In a third step, Schleiermacher seeks out the reason for the ineluctable individuality of thought. Perception (*Wahrnehmung*) and "thinking proper" (*eigentliches Denken*) are two sides or two directions that give us a basis upon which we try to recognize the world. Neither of the two contributes more to cognition than the other; neither is higher or lower in terms of its perfection or truth, and neither begins sooner than the other. The same is true of the forms of proper thinking: concept and judgement. In Schleiermacher's view, just like perception and proper thinking (*eigentliches Denken*), judgement and concept can be understood as differently weighted combinations of the interaction between the two functions of thinking: the organic function predominates within the judgement, and the intellectual function within the concept. When comparing Schleiermacher's consideration of judgement and concept with the concept of logic that was prevalent in that period—and Schleiermacher primarily saw Alexander Baumgarten as the representative of this[26]—two things are noticeable. On the one hand, within the Dialectic, only concept and judgement are regarded as forms of thinking; the conclusion, and with it the syllogism, are not regarded as originary forms of thinking but merely as combinations of judgement and concept. On the other hand, Schleiermacher tries to show that it is not only the case that judgements go back to concepts—concepts are also formed on the basis of judgements.[27]

In order to clarify other conditions for the potential generation of knowledge, Schleiermacher undertakes a kind of thought experiment in which he tries, through thinking, to arrive at the broadest and narrowest concept respectively, as well as the simplest and most comprehensive judgement. In so doing, he encounters the idea of an "absolute unity of being" (*absoluten Einheit des Seins*) and an "inexhaustible multiplicity" (*unerschöpflichen Mannigfaltigkeit*),[28] which both mark the limits of the imaginable or conceivable and are in absolute opposition to one another.[29]

If every act of thinking must be understood as its own, individual combination of the functions of thinking, and therefore as its own, individual combination of absolute opposition, then knowledge as knowledge of the world, or "Weltweisheit"—an internally differentiated unity "in which all oppositions [*Gegensätze*] are included"—marks the *terminus ad quem* of all emerging knowledge.[30] However, the definition of what is knowledge and what is thought does not answer the question of whether we can ever hope to approximate the differentiated, disputatious forms of thinking to knowledge. The final condition, here the fourth step, for the potential generation of knowledge is the original unity

---

[26] Cf. *Dial.*1, p. 50; *Dial. (Tice)*, p. 46.

[27] As plausible as this reciprocity is (and, we may add, as groundbreaking for modernity), Rothert asks at this point in the analysis of the idea of knowledge whether we may ascribe a supra-historical status to the forms of thinking defined by Schleiermacher (Hans-Joachim Rothert, "Die Dialektik Friedrich Schleiermachers. Überlegungen zu einem immer noch wartenden Buch," *Zeitschrift für Theologie und Kirche* 67 [1970], pp. 211f.).

[28] *Dial.*1, pp. 104f., §§147ff.

[29] Cf. Peter Weiss, "Einige Gesichtspunkte zur Problematik der Denkgrenze in verschiedenen Entwürfen der Dialektik Schleiermachers," in *Schleiermacher in Context: Papers from the 1988 International Symposium on Schleiermacher at Herrnhut, the German Democratic Republic*, ed. Ruth D. Richardson (Lewiston, Queenston, and Lampeter: Edwin Mellen Press, 1991), pp. 203–227.

[30] *Dial.*2, pp. 586f.

of the absolute as *terminus a quo*: the "Absolute," "God" or the "transcendental ground" (*transzendentale Grund*).[31]

Even though we may be permanently striving to find the transcendental ground in thinking, all attempts to grasp this through thinking will, according to Schleiermacher, ultimately fail. One form of presence of the transcendental ground is available to us, says Schleiermacher, in the "feeling" (*Gefühl*) of "immediate self-consciousness" (*unmittelbaren Selbstbewusstseins*). However, this is neither a particular feeling in the sense of an affection, nor a self-conscious self or subject engaging in reflection. Schleiermacher describes the latter as "reflected self-consciousness" (*reflektiertes Selbstbewusstsein*) in contrast to "immediate self-consciousness." It is that place where the subject can experience itself as being and thinking at the same time, without being able to substantiate this unity. In addition, because within this immediate self-consciousness we do not experience ourselves as the creators of this unity, rather, in our lack, we glimpse a hint of something beyond ourselves, Schleiermacher therefore also speaks of a "feeling of dependence" (*Abhängigkeitsgefühl*).[32]

If immediate self-consciousness is a feeling that accompanies all functions, it always has its *own* particular function, too, thus it is difficult to isolate it as pure, immediate self-consciousness.[33] Nonetheless, Schleiermacher applies the term "religious consciousness" (*religiösen Bewusstseins*) to this pure relation, which is, so to speak, a timeless self-consciousness, detached from all particular states of consciousness and purely related to the transcendental ground.[34] We cannot, however, separate the aspect of religious consciousness from immediate self-consciousness. It should be understood as a *searching* for this pure aspect rather than as a state of *having*; it is "the expression of the human striving to grasp the transcendental."[35]

Pointing to the transcendental ground, becoming cognizant of it in the feeling of dependence, and indicating that this latter condition of knowledge cannot be obtained through reflection—these all mark the interface between philosophy and religion, or rather, theology. The clearest distinction Schleiermacher makes between both perspectives on the transcendental ground is in the 1822 lecture on dialectic. This boundary is less clearly delineated, however, in the earlier lecture courses. In the secondary literature that deals with the lectures on dialectic, there has been a lot of debate around self-consciousness precisely because it represents a key interface between philosophy and religion.[36]

---

[31] Schleiermacher uses a range of different terms for this absolute opposition, as well as for *terminus ad quem* and *a quo*, within the individual lecture course and over the years.

[32] Dial.1, p. 267.

[33] Cf. Dial.2, p. 569.

[34] Dial.2, p. 569.

[35] Dial.2, pp. 569f.

[36] On the discussion of the transcendental philosophy approach, cf., inter alia, Falk Wagner, *Schleiermachers Dialektik. Eine kritische Interpretation* (Gütersloh: Gütersloher Verlagshaus Mohn, 1974), pp. 57–227; John E. Thiel, *God and World in Schleiermacher's "Dialektik" and "Glaubenslehre": Criticism and the Methodology of Dogmatics* (Bern: Lang, 1981); Hans-Walter Schütte, "Das getröstete Denken. Zu Schleiermachers Dialektik," in *Friedrich Schleiermacher 1768–1834. Theologe–Philosoph–Pädagoge*, ed. Dietz Lange (Göttingen: Vandenhoeck & Ruprecht, 1985), pp. 72–84; Sergio Sorrentino, "Schleiermachers Philosophie und der Ansatz der transzendentalen Philosophie," in *Schleiermacher in Context: Papers from the 1988 International Symposium on Schleiermacher at Herrnhut, the German Democratic Republic*, ed. Ruth D. Richardson (Lewiston, Queenston, and Lampeter: Edwin Mellen Press, 1991), pp. 227–242; Christian Albrecht, *Schleiermachers Theorie der Frömmigkeit. Ihr wissenschaftlicher Ort und ihr systematischer Gehalt in den Reden, in der Glaubenslehre und in der*

From the perspective of philosophy, what we have gained in the analysis of the idea of knowledge is the *idea* of an original unity of absolute opposition as *terminus a quo* (world) and *terminus ad quem* (God), which take on a regulative function within the process of knowledge. Insofar as it is always the case that any kind of real thinking (*reales Denken*) already points to another existing kind of thinking, the interdependency of real forms of thinking marks our epistemological position as an eternal "beginning in the middle" (*Aus-der-Mitte-Anfangen*), a position from which we cannot disembark. "If knowledge were perfected in every respect," Schleiermacher reflects, "thinking would cease."[37]

9.2.3 The Technical Part: The Reciprocity between the Forms of Knowledge

If the transcendental part is concerned with providing a foundation for real knowledge on the basis of its movement with recourse to an "unconscious agency," the aim of the technical or formal part is to orient the emerging, perpetually disputatious thinking toward knowledge. To this end, the technical part takes up the results of the transcendental part, extends this part by bringing in the level of theory development, and then concentrates on the regulative character, that is on the question of which rules for dispute resolution we can devise for the emerging knowledge.

Whereas perception, judgement, and concept were established as forms of thinking proper in the transcendental part, the technical part of the Dialectic does not only explore the elementary level of "knowledge construction" (*Wissenskonstruktion*)—the development of schemata, judgements, and concepts—or the realm of common experience. On the level of theory development, it also contrasts this level with the complex interlinking that is "knowledge combination" (*Wissenskombination*). Similar to individual perception, which can only ever take place in the context of a process of thinking that has already begun and can therefore never be a pure, entirely receptive form of thinking, Schleiermacher proves that all forms of empiricism are imbued with theory. If, for Schleiermacher, the genesis of a particular kind of thinking covers the scope of neither the narrowest nor the broadest concept or judgement, the development of the theory must also be regarded as an increasingly inductive and decreasingly deductive process in a state of always having already begun.[38]

Dialektik (Berlin: De Gruyter, 1994), in particular ch. 4; Jörg Dierken, "Das zwiefältige Absolute. Die irreduzible Differenz zwischen Frömmigkeit und Reflexion im Denken Friedrich Schleiermachers," *Zeitschrift für neuere Theologiegeschichte* 1 (1994), pp. 17–46; Ingolf Hübner, *Wissenschaftsbegriff und Theologieverständnis. Eine Untersuchung zu Schleiermachers Dialektik* (Berlin: De Gruyter, 1997); Eilert Herms, "Philosophie und Theologie im Horizont des reflektierten Selbstbewußtseins," in *Schleiermachers Dialektik*, ed. Christine Helmer, Christiane Kranich, and Birgit Rehme-Iffert (Tübingen: Mohr Siebeck, 2003), pp. 23–54; Peter Grove, *Deutungen des Subjekts. Schleiermachers Philosophie der Religion* (Berlin: De Gruyter, 2004), pp. 464–530; and Arndt, *Friedrich Schleiermacher als Philosoph*, pp. 248–259.

[37] *Dial*.1, pp. 117f., §179.2.

[38] Schleiermacher follows this architecture of the forms of knowledge in all lecture courses. However, the explanations related to the combining of knowledge and to the doctrine of judgement in the earlier lectures (1811, 1814/1815, and 1818) are fragmentary and therefore provide only a rough outline. This is

In all the lectures, the technical part of dialectic is introduced with a reflection on error. In fact, in the notes to the lecture of 1818, Schleiermacher even describes this as a "theory of error" (*Theorie des Irrthums*), a theory that, as the "supremely general" (*Allgemeinste*), should precede knowledge combination and construction and should be developed out of the rules for dispute resolution.[39] The theory of error, however, does not contain any formal definition, and certainly not any definition in terms of content, rather it emerges as a question of attitude or of the right way of dealing with our own thinking, a thinking that always claims to be knowledge. All real knowledge is thinking that contains both truth and falsity, and error exists "always only together with truth" (*immer nur an der Wahrheit*), and is "never absolute."[40] And insofar as all knowledge only arises out of the genesis of thought that is, to a greater or lesser extent, false, Schleiermacher argues it is even possible to assert that "knowledge arises from error" (*das Wissen entstehe aus dem Irrthum*).[41] In order to approximate disputatious thinking to absolute knowledge, we must replace that feeling of being convinced—a feeling that repeatedly arises—with a consciously adopted skeptical position; this is "the only means by which to arrive at conscious knowledge."[42] The first step toward dispute mediation—and we might also call this a first rule of dispute resolution—is to comprehend the fundamental historicity or contingency of thought. Only those who know that they do not yet know, and that they need an interlocutor in order to know more, are in any way capable of seriously engaging in a debate.

Further rules established by Schleiermacher in connection with his discussion of error could all be described as "maxims of reciprocity" (*Maximen der Wechselwirkung*). If the reciprocal conditionality of forms of thinking and theory development is the source of a process of thinking that never stops, it also guarantees the opportunity for infinite approximation to knowledge. This is because the one-sidedness arising from the dominance of either one of the two functions of thinking can be removed by a conscious process of relating and adjusting perception and proper thinking to one another. Although the "maxims of reciprocity" require *that* knowledge be formed not in a one-sided way but within a reciprocal process of adjustment and mediation, they have nothing yet to say about *how* this might happen. This is the point, since the first course lectures on dialectic, at which Schleiermacher introduces "critical knowlege" (*kritisches Wissen*), the "critical process" (*kritische Verfahren*) or critique, that—considering its central systematic relevance—is unfortunately developed only very briefly within *Dialectic*.

Schleiermacher describes two possible ways of developing real, individual, disputatious thinking into an identical thinking common to all: either we turn away from all differentiation into abstraction, or we turn toward these very differences.[43] The first possibility ultimately leads to a disregarding of all content and therefore to the cognitive limit of absolute unity, which is only conceivable in the abstract.[44] Much more promising is the very

---

reflected in the secondary literature, which mainly deals with the transcendental part of Schleiermacher's Dialectic.

[39] *Dial. (Tice)*, p. 4; *Dial*.1, p. 24, No. 131.
[40] *Dial*.2, p. 597; *Dial*.1, p. 60.
[41] *Dial*.1, p. 53.
[42] *Dial*.2, p. 595.
[43] *Dial*.1, p. 59.
[44] *Dial*.1, p. 179, §46.

opposite possibility. This appropriates the "individual factors" (*individuellen Factors*) and tries to comprehend the "principle of distinctiveness" (*Eigenthümlichkeit*), make "relativity [*Relativität*] itself into an object" and thereby effect "an indirect community of thought [*eine indirecte Gemeinschaft des Denkens*]."[45] In what sense thinking is relative must therefore also be clarified. However, it is only possible to judge the individual scope of validity of ostensible knowledge if the critique focuses on the context within which relative thinking claims it is knowledge.[46] Disputatious positions can then be mediated through one another, not by removing their claim to validity but by limiting it to a particular context, with the result that (in the optimal case) they are rendered no longer in conflict with one another. However, this contextualization is subject to an infinite regress. This is because the specific contexts of the disputatious thinking only become comprehensible again from the point of view of broader contexts, and these, in turn, from the point of view of even broader contexts, until it becomes necessary to establish the "total context" (*Totalzusammenhang*) in order to achieve critical mediation.[47] That which ought to proceed from dispute resolution therefore becomes, in actual fact, the prerequisite for it, and the critique can never be regarded as complete.

Within the critical reconstruction, particular weight is attached to the fact that thought, in the broadest sense, is always articulated linguistically. The critique is closely connected with philology in two ways: on the one hand, the epistemological critique must always include philological critique (and vice versa); on the other, this epistemological critique may be guided by hermeneutics in the question of how it should proceed in its task.

9.3 Dialectic in the System of Sciences: Reciprocities

As a transcendental foundation and, at the same time, a guide on the critical production of knowledge, *the Dialectic* is the methodology of all the sciences, and in this sense it can be regarded as the "organ of all the sciences" (*Organon aller Wissenschaften*) as well as the supreme science.[48] However, all sciences ultimately go back to the same object: the world; and this object emerges only in the process of knowing. In addition, it is not possible to isolate, out of the overall structure of this object, a subdomain that would thereby presuppose and, at the same time, determine all other knowledge. Comprehending the fundamental reciprocity of all sciences now gives rise to a certain reversibility of the scientific system.

The Dialectic does not give a clear answer to the question of in what way *the Dialectic* is itself determined by this growing, perpetually self-modifying total context of knowledge. One of Schleiermacher's arguments in his epistemological approach is of course precisely that form and content cannot be separated from one another. Yet this stands in contrast to Schleiermacher's concern to find a point of departure from which to make the movement itself into the object and concentrate on an "supra-historical agency" (*überhistorisches Agens*)

---

[45] *Dial.*2, p. 634; *Dial. (Tice)*, p. 58.
[46] Cf. *Dial.*2, p. 406, Std. 3.
[47] *Dial.*2, p. 411.
[48] *Dial. (Tice)*, p. 1; *Dial.*2, p. 8, Std. 4.

within thought. Both tendencies—the process of reflection on what is only ever the provisional status of *the Dialectic* and the attempt to establish "supra-historical" rules for dispute resolution—are present throughout the lecture on dialectic, right through to its conclusion. This tension or incoherence is not resolved, with the result that there is evidence for both readings.

In addition to the fundamental question of a supra-historical perspective, what is also of great interest for the system of sciences are those particular instances where two sciences encounter one another, such as the analysis of the theory of self-consciousness within dialectic and theology. The psychology lectures, which Schleiermacher began in the summer of 1818 and gave three times, also outline an interconnected theory of self-consciousness. As a pneumatology or a doctrine of the soul, psychology is as broadly defined as ethics, for the activities of the soul include acting, thinking, and feeling. In the definition of the relationship between the Dialectic and psychology, the question—connected, in particular, with the interpretation of self-consciousness—is whether Schleiermacher, by presenting psychology as a doctrine of the soul (although read in parallel), is venturing a new conception of his system of thought.[49]

Below, I consider how dialectic relates to two other philosophical sciences with which it can be explicitly and closely combined, and which, in their execution, are of direct relevance to the concept of knowledge: hermeneutics and ethics; the former with respect to the relation between thinking and speaking, and the latter with respect to the relation between thinking and acting.

9.3.1 Dialectic and Hermeneutics—The Development of Thinking within Dialogue, and the Relation between Thinking and Speaking

Hermeneutics has a special place among the relationships between dialectic and other sciences, for thinking develops within the debate, within conversation or dialogue; it is always (in the broadest sense) thought articulated in language. The relation between thinking and speaking is not addressed for the first time in the lectures on dialectic—it already features prominently in the hermeneutics lecture begun in 1805 but also in the ethics lectures begun in 1805/1806.[50] The early reflections make clear that Schleiermacher's epistemological foundation was connected, right from the start, with a consciousness of the philosophy of language. This places Schleiermacher on an axis with Hamann, Herder, and Humboldt, links primarily with Friedrich Schlegel's project of a "philosophy of philology" (*Philosophie der Philologie*),[51] and rightly marks Schleiermacher out as an important representative of the "linguistic turn *avant la lettre*" at the turn of the nineteenth century.[52] Whereas in the

---

[49] Cf. Chapter 14 in this volume, on Schleiermacher's psychology and anthropology.
[50] On Schleiermacher's hermeneutics, see Chapter 12 of this volume.
[51] Cf. Denis Thouard, "Friedrich Schlegel: de la Philologie à la Philosophie (1795–1800)," in *Symphilosophie. F. Schlegel à Jena*, ed. Denis Thouard (Paris: Vrin, 2002), pp. 25–39.
[52] Manfred Frank, "Einleitung des Herausgebers," in Friedrich Schleiermacher, *Dialektik*, ed. Manfred Frank, vol. 1 (Frankfurt am Main: Suhrkamp, 2001), p. 22.

Brouillon Schleiermacher speaks initially of an "identity" (*Identität*) between thinking and speaking,[53] the lectures on hermeneutics and dialectic differentiate this relationship as one between an inside and an outside, where "inner thought" (*inneres Denken*) has no reality whatsoever without language: "Language, however, is just the manner in which thought becomes real; for there is no thought without language."[54]

So, if we consider that languages—which are the means by which thought expresses itself—are never perfectly congruent, what role does this play in thought? In the transcendental part of the Dialectic, Schleiermacher says the reason we can never have perfectly identical, proper thinking is that both functions of thinking interact in our thinking in ways that are perpetually new and peculiar to ourselves. In so doing, their interaction knows no "first time" (*erstes Mal*) and no original form; it has always already begun, and our rational action begins "in the middle" (*aus der Mitte*).[55]

From the 1822 lecture course onward, this line of argument does not change,[56] but the focus shifts to a consideration of the extent to which thought is bound up with language. A reflection on the "material" (*materielle*) aspect of thought, the individual character of linguistic utterances, is primarily what gives rise to doubts about the general and supra-historical character of dialectic, as formulated by Schleiermacher in the 1822 lecture. The introduction to dialectic that Schleiermacher wrote in 1833 shortly before his death, which was intended for publication, likewise places a particular emphasis on linguistic difference and the implications of this for thought. He also develops a "theory of linguistic spheres" (*Theorie der Sprachkreise*) and it is not difficult here to see the close relation to Schleiermacher's theory and practice of translation: any thought expressed in language is bound up with the language of a particular linguistic sphere and is only intelligible within this.[57] The various languages are, however, only translatable into one another to a limited extent, and in every language there are "such elements (*Elemente*)" "that are irrational in relation to other languages, which also means it is not possible to produce an exact reproduction of them by connecting several elements of these languages."[58] Schleiermacher, however, is referring to the linguistic sphere in both its narrowest and broadest scope, which means that we can—indeed must—understand not only linguistic groups and national languages as a linguistic sphere, but ultimately also every person's own, individually inflected language.[59] For Schleiermacher, the

---

[53] *WA* II, p. 97, St. 15.

[54] *VHK*, p. 732: "Das Sprache ist aber nur die Art und Weise des Gedankens, wirklich zu sein; denn es gibt keinen Gedanken ohne Rede." Cf. *Dial*.2, p. 448.

[55] *Dial*.1, pp. 56–59.

[56] Reinhold Rieger (*Interpretation und Wissen. Zur philosophischen Begründung der Hermeneutik bei Friedrich Schleiermacher und ihrem geschichtlichen Hintergrund* [Berlin: De Gruyter, 1988], pp. 274, 283f.) and Karl Pohl (*Studien zur Dialektik F. Schleiermachers* [PhD dissertation, Mainz, 1954], p. 327) argue that the reason for the irreducible difference in thought in Schleiermacher's work is the spatial and temporal isolation of the human being. They refer here to the 1822 lecture course in which Schleiermacher speaks, in a somewhat condensed way, of an "original difference between the organic impressions" (*ursprüngliche Differenz der organischen Eindrücke*) (*Dial*. 2, p. 630). This is certainly not false, but a deeper reason lies in the relation between the two functions of thinking, the interaction between which is not governed by any strict norm (cf. Andrew Bowie, "Schleiermacher, Habermas, and Rorty," in *Schleiermachers Dialektik*, ed. Christine Helmer, Christiane Kranich, and Birgit Rehme-Iffert [Tübingen: Mohr Siebeck, 2003], pp. 216–234).

[57] On Schleiermacher's influence on classical studies, see Chapter 30 of this volume.

[58] *Dial*.1, p. 403.

[59] Cf. *Dial*.1, p. 404, §2.2.

difference between the languages of the various linguistic spheres gives rise to differences in the thinking that is expressed in the languages: "No knowledge in two languages can be regarded as completely the same."[60]

Because dialectic also formulates its basic rules within language, this "ineffaceable difference" (*unaustilgbaren Differenz*) between languages and thought raises the question of whether dialectic's claim that it itself lies outside the dispute—from where it establishes the principles of the dispute, "which are the same for all and appropriate to all dispute"—can be upheld. This fundamental question of the trans-temporal status of dialectic, which became prominent in the Dialectic primarily in the reciprocal relationship between the technical and the transcendental part, is resolutely answered here: "Dialectic cannot prevail everywhere in one and the same form, rather it must be established initially only for one particular linguistic sphere; and, as must be conceded in advance, it will be necessary to establish it, to a varying extent, differently for every other one."[61]

Nonetheless, no linguistic sphere should be regarded as radically separate from another. Each smaller linguistic sphere is sublated, with other linguistic spheres, into a common, larger one, and so on. The result is that although different languages cannot be perfectly translated into one another, neither are they completely untranslatable.[62] Just like thinking, language, too, is on a kind of home straight, for a modification takes place in dialogue, in translation and in comprehension, whereby the languages progressively combine into *one* language.[63] This should not be confused, however, with a lingua franca in which all idiosyncrasies are ironed out, rather it should be understood as a medium of expression that encompasses *all* linguistic performativity. How far we are from this apparently utopian goal of a total context of knowledge, which finds expression in a total language, becomes very clear if we look at the linguistic side of the process.

9.3.2 Dialectic and Ethics: Pure, Artistic, and Practical Thinking

The introductions to the ethics begin with the question of the status of the scientific nature of ethics, directly picking up on the question, from the *Grundlinien*, of two different forms of a supreme science. A supreme science in the manner of "worldly wisdom" (*Weltweisheit*) cannot exist.[64] However, dialectic can also be applied to ethics as a scientific doctrine that guides and provides a foundation for the debate, or as the "contentless reflection of supreme knowledge" (*gehaltlose Abbild des höchsten Wissens*).[65] From 1812/1813 onwards, the ethics lecture explicitly refers to the Dialectic as the site of its foundation, even speaking of a "deduction [*Deduction*] of ethics from the Dialectic."[66]

---

[60] *Dial*.1, p. 98, §125.2.
[61] *Dial*.1, p. 401, §2.
[62] Cf. *Dial*.2, p. 480.
[63] Cf. *Dial*.1, pp. 404f., §2.2.
[64] WA II, p. 245, §1.
[65] WA II, p. 537.
[66] WA II, p. 247.

In terms of its scope, however, ethics is not significantly broader than dialectic. It is one of the two empirical sciences (the other is physics). It encompasses the entire "life of reason" (*Leben der Vernunft*) and therefore—like Spinoza's ethics—practical and theoretical philosophy.[67] In this respect, dialectic can also be understood as part of ethics. The introductions to the ethics lectures explain not only the reciprocity of the sciences but also the reciprocity of rational activities: no individual rational activity—whether this is thinking, acting, or feeling—can be wholly isolated from the others in its real forms of expression. Every act of thinking is, at the same time, an action, and every action is an act of thinking. Cognition is inherent in every artistic or religious act, and an artistic act is inherent in every action, and so on. Of what significance is it to knowledge, then, that dialectic also be understood as part of ethics, and what consequences do the irreducible reciprocity and combination of rational activities have for knowledge and thought?

To answer this question, we turn once again to the lectures on dialectic. In order to consider the actual object of dialectic, Schleiermacher differentiates, as early as the 1811 lecture on the Dialectic, between a "pure [*reines*] thinking," an "artistic" (*künstlerischen*) thinking, and a "practical [*geschäftliches*] thinking." The 1822 lecture and the 1832 introduction offer a detailed reflection on these "hybrid activities" (*Mischtätigkeiten*).[68] Whereas pure thinking is exclusively directed toward knowledge, the aim of practical thinking is not to define an existence or an object adequately, but to effect a change. In order to effect a change, practical thinking also has an interest in cognition, and in this respect it is also oriented toward knowledge; its intention, however, is pragmatic. In contrast to pure thought, practical or conditional thinking is satisfied as soon as it achieves its goal, whereas pure thinking never rests in its striving for knowledge. Artistic thinking, like pure thinking, is not governed by a goal external to the thinking. In this self-referentiality, however, in contrast to pure thinking, it is only concerned with the fulfilment of the moment, with pleasure and stimulation; it is the free play of thoughts, in free association.

In reality, all three tendencies in thinking occur in combination and are initially incapable of being distinguished from one another.[69] Wherever this combination is not reflected upon, this always represents a danger to pure thinking, for both artistic and practical thinking have an important role to play in pure thinking. According to Schleiermacher, all thinking is, in terms of its development, primarily conditional, practical thinking, and without this orientation of thinking, no debate would be able to reach a conclusion. In fact, we would not even be able to survive.[70] In terms of the development of pure knowledge, however, it is precisely this tendency of practical thinking—that of declaring itself complete—that is dangerous. Free artistic thinking or fantasizing, too, has a central role to play in the *art* of dialogue within pure knowledge, in that it provides hypotheses and heuristic support. However, it only fulfils this function if it is a "known non-knowing" (*gewusstes Nichtwissen*), that is to say if the person who is fantasizing is aware she is fantasizing. Schleiermacher recommends approaching both—the danger of a pragmatic sluggishness of thought and that of an overactive imagination—with a healthy skepticism.[71]

---

[67] On Schleiermacher's philosophical ethics, see Chapter 10 in this volume.
[68] Cf. *Dial*.1, pp. 393–401, §1.
[69] Cf. *Dial*.1, p. 418, §4.3.
[70] Cf. *Dial*.2, p. 597.
[71] *Dial*.2, pp. 593f.

The intention behind this reflection on such "intermediate states" (*Mittelzustände*) within dialectic is to consider pure thinking in isolation.[72] However, the explanations Schleiermacher placed in a prominent position in the introduction (such as the theory of linguistic spheres), and was planning to publish, confirm how central this comprehension of "intermediate states" of activity is within the theory of knowledge. Only once we engage with this idea of the reciprocity of activities do such questions as the power or force of interest-oriented thinking, or the pleasure and beauty of scientific discourse, come into focus in the first place. In this respect, however, we must use Schleiermacher to go beyond Schleiermacher, which in Schleiermacher scholarship is only occasionally the case.[73]

This is because dispute resolution in the context of a "hybrid" thinking exceeds the competence of a genuinely epistemological critique, requiring a hermeneutics and a critique of culture that would be found in connection with Schleiermacher's philosophical ethics.[74] The task of outlining a critique and hermeneutics of culture—which would interpret dialectic from the point of view of ethics—would also include an examination of the "goods" or institutions of knowledge and the sciences in their significance for the process of knowledge. Here, for example, questions about the connection to the early sociology of scientific knowledge, to the archaeology and poetics of knowledge, or to research on the materiality of knowledge, mark interesting areas of investigation that have yet to be explored.

On the whole, the Dialectic can no longer be understood as a book "waiting" to be interpreted, even if many topic areas have yet to be interpreted and some treasures of thought have yet to be unearthed. The transcendental part, the relationship between knowledge and faith as well as between theology and dialectic as disciplines, has received widespread attention within secondary literature, especially within theological research. Less attention has yet been paid to the technical part, which considers knowledge "in motion," examines concrete relations of interaction, and establishes rules for resolving disputes under the banner of critical thinking.

Scholars have also attended to the question of the theoretical and scientific status of the Dialectic within the formation of Schleiermacher's system and to the associated question of the supra-historical status of dialectic. A central question within philosophical literature on the dialectic concerns the relationship between thinking and speaking, knowledge and language, and the interaction between the disciplines of dialectic and hermeneutics that follows from this relationship.

A desideratum of further research in the analysis of the transcendental part of the dialectic is wider consideration of the seldom thematized figurative (*bildlich*) thinking,[75] not least because it itself marks an open site of development within the lectures on dialectic.

---

[72] *Dial.*2, p. 595.

[73] Cf. Sarah Schmidt, "Kritik als Projekt der Moderne. Zur Reichweite und Aktualität der Schleiermacherschen Kritikkonzeption," in *Reformation und Moderne: Pluralität–Subjektivität–Kritik*, ed. Jörg Dierken, Arnulf von Scheliha, and Sarah Schmidt (Berlin: De Gruyter, 2018), pp. 551–574.

[74] On Schleiermacher's understanding of the philosophy of culture, see Chapter 41 of this volume.

[75] Cf. Sarah Schmidt, "Wahrnehmung und Schema: Zur zentralen Bedeutung des bildlichen Denkens in Schleiermachers Dialektik," in *Schleiermacher und Kierkegaard. Subjektivität und Wahrheit. Akten des Schleiermacher-Kierkegaard-Kongresses in Kopenhagen Oktober 2003*, ed. Niels Jørg Cappelørn, Richard Crouter, Theodor Jørgensen, and Claus Osterhövener (Berlin: De Gruyter, 2006), pp. 73–91; and Markus Firchow, "Zur Funktion der Oszillation in Schleiermachers 'Dialektik'," *Kodikas/Code Ars Semeiotica: An International Journal of Semiotics* 37/1-2 (June 2014): pp. 21-37.

From a critical determination of the function and meaning of figurative thinking (perception and schematism) in relation to proper thinking (judgment and concept), the relationship between dialectics and aesthetics in the framework of Schleiermacher's system might also be fruitfully examined once again.

In addition to the dialogical structure of Schleiermacher's dialectics,[76] an arrangement also reflecting a philosophy of language,[77] the relationship between figurative and discursive thinking holds significant potential for its ability to connect to the philosophical discussions of the present, a potential that has not yet been exhausted.

Translated by Marielle Sutherland

SUGGESTED READING

Arndt, Andreas. *Friedrich Schleiermacher als Philosoph* (Berlin: De Gruyter, 2013), pp. 179–259.
Berner, Christian. "La Dialectique ou 'l'art de philosopher.'" In F. D. E Schleiermacher, *Dialectique* (Paris: Cerf, 1997), pp. 7–30.
Frank, Manfred. "Einleitung des Herausgebers." In Friedrich Schleiermacher, *Dialektik*, ed. Manfred Frank, vol. 1 (Frankfurt am Main: Suhrkamp, 2001), pp. 10–136.
Helmer, Christine, Christiane Kranich, and Birgit Rehme-Iffert, eds. *Schleiermachers Dialektik* (Tübingen: Mohr Siebeck, 2003).
Schmidt, Sarah. *Die Konstruktion des Endlichen. Schleiermachers Philosophie der Wechselwirkung* (Berlin: De Gruyter, 2005).
Tice, Terrence N. "Introduction." In *Friedrich Schleiermacher, Dialectic or, The Art of Doing Philosophy. A Study Edition of the 1811 Notes*. Translated, with introduction and notes by Terrence N. Tice (Atlanta, GA: Scholars Press, 1996), pp. xi–xxv.
Wagner, Falk. *Schleiermachers Dialektik. Eine kritische Interpretation* (Gütersloh: Gütersloher Verlagshaus Mohn, 1974).

BIBLIOGRAPHY

Albrecht, Christian. *Schleiermachers Theorie der Frömmigkeit. Ihr wissenschaftlicher Ort und ihr systematischer Gehalt in den Reden, in der Glaubenslehre und in der Dialektik* (Berlin: De Gruyter, 1994).

---

[76] Cf. Udo Kliebisch, *Transzendentalphilosophie als Kommunikationstheorie. Eine Interpretation der Dialektik Friedrich Schleiermachers vor dem Hintergrund Karl-Otto Apels* (Bochum: Brockmeyer, 1981); Andreas Arndt, "Geselligkeit und Gesellschaft. Die Geburt der Dialektik aus dem Geist der Konversation in Schleiermachers Versuchen einer 'Theorie des geselligen Betragens,'" in *Salons der Romantik. Beiträge eines Wiepersdorfer Kolloquiums zu Theorie und Geschichte des Salons*, ed. H. Schultz (Berlin: De Gruyter, 1997), pp. 45–61; Dieter Burdorf and Reinhold Schmücker, eds. *Dialogische Wissenschaft. Perspektiven der Philosophie Schleiermachers* (München: Schöningh, 1998); and Bowie, "Schleiermacher, Habermas, and Rorty."

[77] Cf. Heinz Kimmerle, *Die Hermeneutik Schleiermachers im Zusammenhang seines spekulativen Denkens* (PhD dissertation, Heidelberg, 1957); Arndt, *Friedrich Schleiermacher als Philosoph*, pp. 299–325; and Manfred Frank, *Das individuelle Allgemeine. Textstrukturierung und -interpretation nach Schleiermacher* (Frankfurt am Main: Suhrkamp, 1985).

Arndt, Andreas. "Einleitung des Bandherausgebers." In *F. D. E. Schleiermacher Vorlesungen über die Dialektik, KGA* 2.10.1, ed. Andreas Arndt (Berlin: De Gruyter, 2002), pp. vii–lvii.
Arndt, Andreas. "Geselligkeit und Gesellschaft. Die Geburt der Dialektik aus dem Geist der Konversation in Schleiermachers Versuchen einer 'Theorie des geselligen Betragens.'" In *Salons der Romantik. Beiträge eines Wiepersdorfer Kolloquiums zu Theorie und Geschichte des Salons*, ed. H. Schultz (Berlin: De Gruyter, 1997), pp. 45–61.
Arndt, Andreas, ed. *Friedrich Schleiermacher als Philosoph* (Berlin: De Gruyter, 2013).
Arndt, Andreas, and Wolfgang Virmond, eds. *Schleiermachers Briefwechsel (Verzeichnis) nebst einer Liste seiner Vorlesungen* (Berlin: De Gruyter, 1992), pp. 293–330.
Bowie, Andrew. "Schleiermacher, Habermas, and Rorty." In *Schleiermachers Dialektik*, ed. Christine Helmer, Christiane Kranich, and Birgit Rehme-Iffert (Tübingen: Mohr Siebeck, 2003), pp. 216–234.
Burdorf, Dieter, and Reinhold Schmücker, eds. *Dialogische Wissenschaft. Perspektiven der Philosophie Schleiermachers* (München: Schöningh, 1998).
Dierken, Jörg. "Das zwiefältige Absolute. Die irreduzible Differenz zwischen Frömmigkeit und Reflexion im Denken Friedrich Schleiermachers." *Zeitschrift für neuere Theologiegeschichte* 1 (1994), pp. 17–46.
Firchow, Markus. "Zur Funktion der Oszillation in Schleiermachers 'Dialektik.'" *Kodikas/Code Ars Semeiotica: An International Journal of Semiotics* 37/1-2 (June 2014), pp. 21–37.
Frank, Manfred. "Einleitung des Herausgebers." In Friedrich Schleiermacher, *Dialektik*, ed. Manfred Frank, vol. 1 (Frankfurt am Main: Suhrkamp, 2001), pp. 10–136.
Frank, Manfred. *Das individuelle Allgemeine. Textstrukturierung und -interpretation nach Schleiermacher* (Frankfurt am Main: Suhrkamp, 1985).
Grove, Peter. *Deutungen des Subjekts. Schleiermachers Philosophie der Religion* (Berlin: De Gruyter, 2004).
Herms, Eilert. "Philosophie und Theologie im Horizont des reflektierten Selbstbewußtseins." In *Schleiermachers Dialektik*, ed. Christine Helmer, Christiane Kranich, and Birgit Rehme-Iffert (Tübingen: Mohr Siebeck, 2003), pp. 23–54.
Hübner, Ingolf. *Wissenschaftsbegriff und Theologieverständnis. Eine Untersuchung zu Schleiermachers Dialektik* (Berlin: De Gruyter, 1997).
Kimmerle, Heinz. *Die Hermeneutik Schleiermachers im Zusammenhang seines spekulativen Denkens* (PhD dissertation. Heidelberg, 1957).
Kliebisch, Udo. *Transzendentalphilosophie als Kommunikationstheorie. Eine Interpretation der Dialektik Friedrich Schleiermachers vor dem Hintergrund Karl-Otto Apels* (Bochum: Brockmeyer, 1981).
Pohl, Karl. *Studien zur Dialektik F. Schleiermachers* (PhD dissertation. Mainz, 1954).
Rieger, Reinhold. *Interpretation und Wissen. Zur philosophischen Begründung der Hermeneutik bei Friedrich Schleiermacher und ihrem geschichtlichen Hintergrund* (Berlin: De Gruyter, 1988).
Rothert, Hans-Joachim. "Die Dialektik Friedrich Schleiermachers. Überlegungen zu einem immer noch wartenden Buch." *Zeitschrift für Theologie und Kirche* 67 (1970), pp. 183–214.
Schleiermacher, Friedrich. *Briefwechsel 1811-1813, KGA* 5.12, ed. Simon Gerber and Sarah Schmidt (Berlin: De Gruyter, 2019).
Schleiermacher, Friedrich. *Briefwechsel 1813-1816, KGA* 5.13, ed. Simon Gerber and Sarah Schmidt (Berlin: De Gruyter, 2020).

Schmidt, Sarah. "Analogie versus Wechselwirkung—Zur 'Symphilosophie' zwischen Schleiermacher und Steffens." In *Schleiermacher in Halle (1804–1808)*, ed. Andreas Arndt (Berlin: De Gruyter, 2013), pp. 91–114.

Schmidt, Sarah. *Die Konstruktion des Endlichen. Schleiermachers Philosophie der Wechselwirkung* (Berlin: De Gruyter, 2005).

Schmidt, Sarah. "Kritik als Projekt der Moderne. Zur Reichweite und Aktualität der Schleiermacherschen Kritikkonzeption." In *Reformation und Moderne: Pluralität–Subjektivität–Kritik*, ed. Jörg Dierken, Arnulf von Scheliha, and Sarah Schmidt (Berlin: De Gruyter, 2018), pp. 551–574.

Schmidt, Sarah. "Wahrnehmung und Schema: Zur zentralen Bedeutung des bildlichen Denkens in Schleiermachers Dialektik." In *Schleiermacher und Kierkegaard. Subjektivität und Wahrheit. Akten des Schleiermacher-Kierkegaard-Kongresses in Kopenhagen Oktober 2003*, ed. Niels Jørg Cappelørn, Richard Crouter, Theodor Jørgensen, and Claus Osterhövener (Berlin: De Gruyter, 2006), pp. 73–91.

Schütte, Hans-Walter. "Das getröstete Denken. Zu Schleiermachers Dialektik." In *Friedrich Schleiermacher 1768–1834. Theologe–Philosoph–Pädagoge*, ed. Dietz Lange (Göttingen: Vandenhoeck & Ruprecht, 1985), pp. 72–84.

Sorrentino, Sergio. "Schleiermachers Philosophie und der Ansatz der transzendentalen Philosophie." In *Schleiermacher in Context: Papers from the 1988 International Symposium on Schleiermacher at Herrnhut, the German Democratic Republic*, ed. Ruth D. Richardson (Lewiston, Queenston, and Lampeter: Edwin Mellen Press, 1991), pp. 227–242.

Steffens, Henrich. *Grundzüge der philosophischen Naturwissenschaft* (Berlin: Verlag der Realschulbuchhandlung, 1806).

Steffens, Henrich. *Was ich erlebte. Aus der Erinnerung niedergeschrieben*, vol. 5 (Breslau: Josef Max, 1842).

Thiel, John E. *God and World in Schleiermacher's "Dialektik" and "Glaubenslehre": Criticism and the Methodology of Dogmatics* (Bern: Lang, 1981).

Thouard, Denis. "Friedrich Schlegel: de la Philologie à la Philosophie (1795–1800)." In *Symphilosophie. F. Schlegel à Jena*, ed. Denis Thouard (Paris: Vrin, 2002), pp. 17–66.

Tice, Terrence N. "Introduction." In *Friedrich Schleiermacher, Dialectic or, The Art of Doing Philosophy. A Study Edition of the 1811 Notes*. Translated, with introduction and notes by Terrence N. Tice (Atlanta, GA: Scholars Press, 1996), pp. xi–xxv.

Twesten, August. "Vorrede." In *Friedrich Schleiermacher: Grundzüge der philosophischen Ethik* (Berlin: Reimer, 1841), pp. iii–cii.

Wagner, Falk. *Schleiermachers Dialektik. Eine kritische Interpretation* (Gütersloh: Gütersloher Verlagshaus Mohn, 1974).

Weiss, Peter. "Einige Gesichtspunkte zur Problematik der Denkgrenze in verschiedenen Entwürfen der Dialektik Schleiermachers." In *Schleiermacher in Context: Papers from the 1988 International Symposium on Schleiermacher at Herrnhut, the German Democratic Republic*, ed. Ruth D. Richardson (Lewiston, Queenston, and Lampeter: Edwin Mellen Press, 1991), pp. 203–227.

CHAPTER 10

PHILOSOPHICAL ETHICS

MICHAEL MOXTER

SCHLEIERMACHER wrote on issues of philosophical ethics throughout his intellectual life, alongside and in addition to his contributions to Christian ethics (*Christliche Sittenlehre*), which were closely linked to the theological standpoint of his *Glaubenslehre*.[1] In contrast to his treatment of Christian ethics, Schleiermacher's writings on philosophical ethics developed a point of view, independent of Christian faith but not in contradiction to it, that offered a general account of human action and cultural life.

After a long period of reading, translating, and commenting on Plato and Aristotle (especially on the concept of friendship), and studying Kant's critical philosophy, he published an *Essay on the Theory of Social Behavior* (1799). This unfinished and soon forgotten text hinted at the free play of thoughts and sentiments, shared and communicated in private meetings of friends who are relieved from business obligations and social convention. As a counterpart to his famous *Speeches on Religion* (1799) Schleiermacher introduced his ethics of individuality in the *Soliloquies* (1800), presented as a gift for the new year and new century and as an alternative to Kant's moral claims for universality. These writings were deeply shaped by the intellectual currents of early Romanticism and the author's friendship with Friedrich Schlegel.

The *Soliloquies* were followed by a more academic, all-encompassing, and mainly critical review of existing ethical systems, the 1803 volume *Outlines of a Critique of Previous Ethical Theories*, which claimed that neither the ancient types of ethical reflection nor the modern turn to morality satisfied the requirements of true philosophical understanding. In this work, Schleiermacher sharply criticized in particular the Kantian and Fichtean concepts of duty and their pretense of universal principles. In the aftermath of this critical study, Schleiermacher began his lectures on philosophical ethics. In 1805/1806 at Halle University, Schleiermacher presented a first sketch of a more constructive understanding of the topic, *Brouillon zur Ethik*, which he developed further in 1812/1813 and continued through 1816/1817.

As a member (and later on, secretary) of the Royal Berlin Academy of Sciences, Schleiermacher furthermore addressed a variety of ethical issues, in both historical studies on Plato and Aristotle and in systematic reflections on the difference between natural and

---

[1] For a treatment of Schleiermacher's Christian ethics, see Chapter 22 in this volume.

moral law, the concept of duty, virtue, the idea of a highest good, and political philosophy. However, philosophical ethics remained an unfinished task, and his collection of remarks, outlines, and manuscripts were only posthumously published and partly framed by lecture notes of his students. Despite these challenges, his impact as an ethical thinker was nonetheless significant over the last two centuries, as it did not conform to more mainstream conceptions of moral philosophy but rather presented many insights into alternative ethical conceptions often marginalized by master thinkers like Kant or Hegel.

10.1 THE *SOLILOQUIES*: ETHICS OF INDIVIDUALITY

As the title of the text suggests, the human search for self-understanding, self-awareness, and self-reflection—enacted as an internal dialogue of the soul with itself—comes to the fore in Schleiermacher's *Soliloquies*. Only within itself does the human soul discover the holy ground of freedom, an internal and perhaps eternal word, while everything finite remains determined and transitory as the signature of the outer world. All natural things must pass; only the inward perspective confronts us with the question of who we are. However, this perspective does not isolate the individual from others and enclose human beings in an inner world without windows. It rather involves us into an eternal community of humankind, into what Leibniz and Kant had called a "realm of Spirits."

With this idea in mind Schleiermacher comments upon the rational structure of Kant's categorical imperative, which promotes universal norms by reminding us of the presence of humanity in every person. Treating each other not merely as a means to our ends, but as an end-in-itself is the most prominent version of a Kantian understanding of morality. Schleiermacher takes up this thread but argues that the implications reach beyond Kant's own formulation. At issue is not the universal subsumption of the other as simply another member of humanity or another example of a reasonable subject. What makes us human is not the abstract membership within a class of rational beings but rather an individual realization of humanity. It is not the general characteristic we have in common with others but precisely what distinguishes us from everyone else that constitutes each of us as a human person. Understanding individuality lies at the base of an idea that was concealed by Kant's abstractive approach, which leads to a purely formal and formalistic rule, a dead formula that has nothing to do with moral life. As Schleiermacher notes,

> For a long time it was sufficient for me only to have found reason in general, and . . . to believe that there is only one right action for all agents in every case, and that it is only when one knows his own situation and is given his own place that he distinguishes himself from others. . . . Now it is my highest intuition that each human person represents the human species in one's own manner and by the unique mixture of its elements, so that humankind is revealed in each of its members.[2]

As a consequence, the individual has to find her way and even personal style and learn to become what she in fact already is. The tabular form of Kantian thinking and its tendency

---

[2] *Monologen¹*, pp. 17-18.

to subsume maxims under general rules is thus replaced by a plea for personal education (*Bildung*), and the weight of reason is balanced by subjective imagination and creative insight into individuality.

10.2 ETHICS AS DESCRIPTION

Schleiermacher's attempt to develop a post-Kantian ethics that does not undercut the modern benchmarks of reason and freedom entails a methodological shift from a prescriptive to a descriptive approach. He rejects the formula of "ought-statements," and with it the is/ought dichotomy in general, since they both split up reason and reality, human intelligence and human corporeality, being and appearance. The form of ethical propositions can neither be imperative nor consultative. Or, with regard to Kant's language: Neither categorial nor hypothetical imperatives constitute the basic elements of ethics. Where an imperative is needed or "oughts" dominate the scene, ethics is bound to nothingness and negativity, and reason therefore is still left without reality and is not yet understood as a force.[3] This can only be avoided by a practical philosophy that rests on an understanding of human nature, an intuition of what "we the actors" are, a vision of what human life means. In this respect Schleiermacher continues the literature on "Human destiny" from Spalding to Fichte.[4] However, Schleiermacher does not replace the concept of ought (and duty) by simply turning back to *eudaimonism* or to the pursuit of happiness, against which Kant strongly polemicizes. Instead he argues that the presupposed difference between *is* and *ought* downplays any appropriate understanding of human action and that the dichotomy between physical and moral laws renders the reconstruction of what is presupposed in the acting itself impossible: a picture of human life as a framework of practical self-understanding. Calling for social relationships, for reliance upon unspoken habits and routines on that which goes without saying as well as upon mutual recognition and practice, does not mean running into the so-called naturalistic fallacy. This fallacy (forbidden also by Hume's famous law) is logically dependent on the fact/value dichotomy. But "facts" are one thing, and "practical reality" is something else. Whoever holds onto the gap between facts and value misses the point of practical self-understanding and reasoning. "John is the captain, he ought to be the last who leaves the ship, is true—without logical deficiencies," as A. MacIntyre argued.[5]

Searching for a scientific exhibition of human actions, Schleiermacher conceives ethics as a general theory of reason embedded in nature, and thus as the flip side of theoretical knowledge of nature including the nature of rational beings. Physics and ethics are the two counterparts in Schleiermacher's conception of the world of sciences, the former concerned with nature as such and the latter with reason insofar as it is acting in and on nature. What makes us human is precisely the impossibility of separating mind and matter, reason and brain, and soul and body. Within the harmony of both sides, nature must entail the possibility

---

[3] See *Ethik (Birkner)*, Einleitung. Letzte Bearbeitung, p. 213.
[4] See Johann J. Spalding, *Betrachtung über die Bestimmung des Menschen* (Berlin: Johann Jacob Weitbrecht, 1749); and Johann Gottlieb Fichte, *Die Bestimmung des Menschen* (Berlin: Vossische Buchhandlung, 1800).
[5] A. MacIntyre, *After Virtue. A Study in Moral Theory*, 2nd ed. (London: Duckworth, 1982), pp. 53ff.

of reason, the dynamic force of which is elucidated and clarified in ethics. Everything realized and produced by reason, everything brought about by human freedom, becomes part of ethical description under Schleiermacher's hand. Alternatives like "deontology *versus* teleology" or "modern morality *versus* premodern ethos" lead into misconstruction.

As a consequence, ethics is no longer focused on "moral law(s)" or prescriptive rules, but integrates duties, virtues, and the objectifications of human acting (namely results, structures, institutes, and organizations). Schleiermacher called the latter "goods" and thought of them as affirmative *Gestalten* of social life. According to him, philosophical ethics is thus tripartite, containing virtues, duties, and—especially—goods.

10.3 THREE FORMS OF ETHICAL THEORY

Schleiermacher distinguishes one primary and two additional forms of ethics. In antiquity, Aristotelian virtue ethics was the gold standard of ethical perspectives, oriented around competence and abilities and the idea that both are accomplished by practice alone (think of a musician who has to play guitar in order to become a guitar player). Where training is necessary to establish a habit, activity is the medium to foster human conduct and bring it to perfection. Good practice depends on knowing *how*, not necessarily on knowing *that*. It especially does not depend on abstract knowledge about norms or general rules. According to Aristotle, it is the educated and experienced person, who acts and reacts with *phronesis* (prudence), whom others should trust in practical, and especially in political affairs. One does not turn to the generalist who may possess a vast knowledge of facts and norms yet is unable to manage difficulties with success and responsibility.

In Aristotle's view, this virtue ethics is further integrated into a teleological scheme: Its leading question of how to realize a way of acting that deserves the title "good life" merges with the assertion that the essence of things is established when reaching their internal ends. In contrast, later Christian ethical thinkers and the modern paradigm influenced by them prioritized obligation, depicting God as a law-giver who oversees human action by promising gratification to those who obey his will while threatening perpetrators with punishment. This constellation is closely linked to the legal sphere and it could work even without the idea of a personal God, since obligation can be internalized as conscience and control can become self-control. Both ethical types—virtue-focused and duty-focused approaches—stand in tension to each other.[6] Where virtues are still a vivid reality, people need no advice or moral instruction by external rules. And conversely, where duties have to be inculcated, virtues as dynamic forces have faded away.

Schleiermacher's own ethics is integrative, aiming to reconcile both traditions. It interprets the approach of virtue ethics as concentrating on powers and dynamics within the individual that enable and animate a certain behavior and inspire a person to act. It orients the ethical emphasis on duty, on the other side, toward reflection on maxims and the correction of mistakes in the application of general rules to particular situations. As one's

---

[6] See MacIntyre, *After Virtue, passim.*

course of action is realized in a longer process and step by step, duties are concerned with concrete practical judgements so that nothing of importance is neglected.

Both ethical forms shed light on practical concerns, but they are not the essential form for ethics as such. Though diverging in form, that is, in the manner they constitute ethical issues, they do not substantially differ from each other. The primary and basic form of ethical theory, according to Schleiermacher, is what he called "an ethics of goods": a descriptive yet still affirmative view that refers to the results of human action and the communities by which they are achieved. The German word Gut/Güter only partly echoes the normative sense of the attribute "good"; it entails in a more substantial dimension "something given by and for practical purposes" and is intertwined with words like Landgut (estate) or Weingut (vineyard). An ethics of goods in this sense aims at a historically minded and yet critical reconstruction of the social world. Goods are established forms that prefigure a certain behavior: as results of a practice, they mediate further acting. Such goods result from human activity, but at the same time they "include and reproduce" this activity.[7] In this respect Schleiermacher's ethics displays affinities toward a normative ontology of social forms, as it is to be found in Hegel's philosophy of right and his social philosophy. What distinguishes Schleiermacher's teaching on goods from Hegel's understanding of institutions is the temporal structure of Schleiermacher's goods (they "resulted" in the past, "include" chances for the present moment, and "reproduce" new activities in the future; as a consequence they are never completed or beyond improvement). And Schleiermacher is concerned with the individual and the individual's performance while a institutionalist point of view tends to focus on reasonable circumstances and so-called objective spirit. Within Schleiermacher's concept, goods are qualified by the actions they allow and thus change continuously according to new requirements and creative answers to new situations. Goods are hubs that interlink what people have done and what they do now, making fruitful for others what someone else already has realized. In fact, goods would not be needed and realized if everyone acted only for her or his own sake and thus continuously started anew. It is essential for goods that they disclose possibilities that a solipsistic agent cannot afford alone. Goods mediate intersubjectivity and even inter-personality (as Hannah Arendt might have said), since they communicate social relations among agents.

Examples of such goods are manifold: the communication between teachers and students, the market as a medium of trade between sellers and buyers, or a religious community in which personal piety is excited by religious communication. These relationships are, on the one hand, contexts of recognition between people entering into a certain practice; on the other hand, their acts of communication are protected by institutions like universities or schools, government agencies that legally control financial contracts between money lenders and debtors, or the church as an ecclesiastical ministry. To focus on this objective approach to given forms of mutual relationship is the key issue to overcome the pure but empty account of ethical formalism Kant has introduced. Moreover, following the classical tradition, Schleiermacher also speaks of a "highest good." He defines it, however, not primarily in theological or hierarchical terms but conceives it as the totality of interaction

---

[7] See Schleiermacher, "Über das Höchste Gut. Erste Abhandlung," in KGA 1.11, pp. 535–553 (545): "daß alle alten Schulen, welche diesen Begriff verarbeitet haben ... dadurch das durch die sittliche Thätigkeit hervorgebrachte, in so fern es dieselbe auch noch in sich schloß und fort entwickelte, bezeichnen wollten."

between human persons on the one hand and reason and nature on the other. The highest good is the "organic system of all goods."[8]

10.4 A Normatively Structured Social World

Accordingly, Schleiermacher's project leads to a description of social order, one that enables persons to better orientate their further actions. The description reflects a historical process of differentiation on the one hand and a normative point of view on the other. He describes the latter as a "formula-book," the former a "picture-book."[9] But how does Schleiermacher derive his categories?

His undertaking begins on the level of an action theory that is combined with a peculiar theorem concerning life-processes as they are found in nature (and in social life as well). Human activity (like the rhythm of life in general) oscillates between bringing forth and coming back (*Aussichheraus- und Insichzurückgehen*), that is, between a more productive and a receptive or more passive dimension. Nature proceeds that way in all its life-forms and the process continues where reason comes in. Therefore, the human as rational animal is a unity of reason and body that *realizes* (in the sense of producing or establishing) reason in nature: Human beings organize their world according to insights into reason. But in order to do so, they have to *realize* (in the sense of recognize) that reason has already infiltrated and changed nature.

In this twofold perspective we can identify a quasi-evolutionary point of view. What humans share with animals is the double movement of life. On the one hand organisms establish something in the world. Think of a spider spinning a web or of bees producing honey. On the other hand, the spider web is a sensorium to refer to the particular, spider-relevant world, signaling for example captured flies or indicating an opportunity to feed. In the case of animals, the productive behavior is nothing but organic reaction of instinct. But when reason comes into the play, the products are rational products and thus can be understood as organized. Organized products convey not only signals but bear a symbolic dimension that can be recognized and acknowledged by other reasonable creatures.

For both humans and animals more generally, these two dimensions belong together. Organization is a medium for perception and perception a mode of organization. What characterizes human life is the fact that reason is embodied, and thus human beings organize with reason and for reason. What they have produced imposes a reminder for others to understand and to acknowledge the presence of reason within the product. Therefore, the human being is *homo faber* only insofar as it is an *animal symbolicum* and vice versa. In this sense, ethics refers to an anthropological description given by natural sciences (*physics* according to Schleiermacher's architecture of sciences, though in actual practice closer to biology), which is set into new light when the question is raised how to rationally continue what already has been done. This question marks the shift from physics to ethics, from

---

[8] *Ethik (Birkner)*, Einleitung. Letzte Bearbeitung, p. 220.
[9] See *Ethik (Birkner)*, Einleitung. Letzte Bearbeitung, p. 217: "Sittenlehre und Geschichtskunde bleiben immer für sich selbst gesondert; für einander sind sie die Geschichtskunde das Bilderbuch der Sittenlehre, und die Sittenlehre das Formelbuch der Geschichtskunde."

natural life to human action. Schleiermacher conceives this double structure of organization and symbolization as basic categories for human action.

He does not, however, divide them into two independent dimensions. Instead, Schleiermacher takes account of this twofoldness by introducing the concept of an oscillating movement that we can refer to as a "minimum-maximum" speculation. Since organization by humans can never take place without a minimum of symbolization, the two sides are not in opposition to each other but are gradually aligned: even when one side drifts into its largest possible expansion or in its most excellent form, the other side still remains present no matter how little or unnoticed its operations.

In a similar manner, a second difference is integrated into the architecture of Schleiermacher's ethics. In continuity with his earlier *Soliloquies* and of major importance for his understanding of reason, Schleiermacher inserts the distinction between generality and individuality. Reason is inherently "common reason," but at the same time reason is only given in human beings, whose individuality need not be denied nor abrogated in order to be and become "rational." Schleiermacher approves nothing but "individual generality,"[10] which is neither universal nor mere exemplary, neither necessary nor contingent. Here language is the decisive paradigm, since in language there are general rules and a common treasury of meanings. Nonetheless speaking a language is a highly individual activity performed in various ways and coined by a personal style.

Since there are two twofold dimensions in human action (organizing/symbolizing on the one hand, common/individual on the other) Schleiermacher generates a quadruple scheme as the basic framework of his ethics. Hence, we get four fields: (1) organizing activity dominated by generality, (2) organizing activity dominated by individuality, (3) symbolizing activity oriented toward what is held in common, and (4) symbolizing activity as mainly mediating individuality.

In order to clarify what Schleiermacher has in mind, it is helpful to identify the associated goods and institutions that are built up by activities in these four fields. Where reason shapes nature, or where things are organized under the concern of generality, we find products that can circulate between every member of society. A clock, in fact an intensively organized product of human handcraft, is made as an instrument for most general concerns. It aids in checking time and thus organizing and coordinating a wide range of activities. A clock indicates something general, local time, which is less than universal time or time as such, but is more than a personal time feeling that rests insufficient to enable a common life. As a product for general purposes, the clock can be used by everyone. It thus can be sold and be transferred to others (commerce). Thus, a market originates, money becomes important, and with it multiple forms of exchange. Commerce would not work without contracts and thus presupposes a legal order, and in the end, the existence of lawmakers, judges, and the police who execute and enforce laws. The simple act of producing a watch as an organizing activity under the prevalence of generality hints at the need of a public sphere and governmental responsibilities.

In contrast to this, an organizing activity might as well mainly bear the character of individuality. Think of a house built up for personal use, not as something one wants to sell, but a

---

[10] See Manfred Frank, *Das individuelle Allgemeine. Textstrukturierung und -interpretation nach Schleiermacher* (Frankfurt am Main: Suhrkamp, 1985).

private refuge that is arranged according to individual wants, with a library for all the books someone intends to read or a professional cooking area to fulfill dreams of haute cuisine. Even though such a house is not to be compared with any public building, this individual place can open its doors to others, and that is the case when the owner invites his friends to have a party or private gathering. Organizing activity for the sake of individual use does not principally exclude others or the community. On the contrary, even the individual as such can establish community. But in this case, it is not a matter of a market or a political society, it is just sociality (*Geselligkeit*), a way of life that flourishes amidst company.

Turning to the symbolizing dimensions of action, activities that mainly aim at generality presuppose a medium of communication (language) by means of which general insights into reality can be achieved and intersubjective knowledge about the facts can be assured. Such practice tends toward perfection when a community of investigators is established, when universities or academies are founded, to make judgments concerning claims about right and wrong. But again, action has another side: a way to symbolize and to acknowledge symbol-use that does not establish common knowledge, but is oriented toward subjective feeling and personal worldviews and beliefs. Once again, individuals are not isolated in their deepest beliefs or captured in a private language that nobody else understands. It is possible also to communicate individuality and, according to Schleiermacher, we do so in religion and its language, the various media of arts. And this communication in turn leads to the cultivation of institutions in the church or, with regard to music, in concert halls, or many others forms of cultural agencies (Table 10.1).

In all these cases, normativity lies in the background of the construction of Schleiermacher's theory. That is, if one sphere of this activity were missing or downgraded and reduced to a mere byproduct of the other spheres, human nature and especially the indispensable dimensions of human reason would be seriously impaired. A reductionist concept of human culture (be it a religious fundamentalism that does not accept the standards of sciences or, on the other side of the scale, scientists who cannot make any sense at all of religious language) will run into fallacies and end up in corruption. Yet there is another, more concrete, aspect of normativity that is linked to the minimum-maximum speculation: A society that does not understand that a private property owner owes something to

Table 10.1 Schleiermacher's Ethical Framework Ethical Goods

Types of Acting	Identity	Individuality
Symbolizing	Language/Knowledge	Feeling
Organizing	Commerce	Property
Implied Institutions		
Types of Acting	Identity	Individuality
Symbolizing	Science/University	Religious communities/Arts
Organizing	Rights/State	Free sociality

the community, or which is structurally incapable of developing a common life, will permanently risk revolt and be quickly washed away by unrest and upheaval.

Interestingly enough, then, the immanent tensions of human life that shape our behavior at the same time indicate normative limits that persons are bound to accept in order to share freedom and live in peace and harmony. There is here some proximity to an Aristotelian understanding of *mesotes* (mean, middle state between extremes), since reaction toward isolated opposite poles does not end up in compromise and in something in between. "Every opposition ... is given in twofold preponderance, sometimes a predominance of the one, sometimes of the other."[11] It is the best of both sides that comes into sight when they, in spite of their contrasts, are combined. But no point of tranquility is available within an oscillating movement, and thus sooner or later the reversal of the process sets new forces free. We come across examples of this play of oscillating and never fully balanced counterforces in Schleiermacher's ethics of duties, in rules such as, "Acquire things in such a way, that appropriation *ipso facto* brings about community"; or "Handle all forms of community-building under the *caveat* of individuality."[12] Whether a general tendency to include the respective opposite will help to decide in particular conflicts is debatable, however, a plea for fair and reasonable compensation is recognizable.

With regard to the relationship between commerce, the legal sphere, and political institutions the consideration of generality seems to imply a tendency toward a universal state, since rights, especially rights that guarantee personal freedom, indicate a global context, such that harm done to anyone is felt throughout the world as a violation of rights (as in Kant's treatment).[13] Schleiermacher admits that there is such a global tendency, and that nobody should exist without basic rights. However, he denies that this tendency leads to sameness and universal equality and hints at the individual characters of nation-states that exist in a variety of legal traditions.[14] And he argues against an understanding of political communities as resulting from a social contract, whether from a Hobbesian view or that of Rousseau, since in both versions we come across a *hysteron-proteron* fallacy (the natural order of ideas is reversed). Contracts depend on the legal sphere, they cannot constitute it.

One might here ask whether the relationship between law and commerce is so closely tied that a whole list of (modern) rights would not fit into the picture. Schleiermacher, for instance, notes, "Law and commerce essentially belong together. The legal sphere only extends so far as there are objects of exchange."[15] And furthermore his efforts to describe law as a sphere of mutual recognition are blended into etatism, when he presupposes that the difference between authority and submission is essential in politics.

The historical dimension also deserves a short comment. Since normativity results from a structured diversity of aspects that have shaped human practice, considerations of history are necessarily involved. It is clearly Schleiermacher's suggestion, that culture was developing in favor of diversification and social differentiation. Yet this surely is a

---

[11] *Ethik (Birkner)*, Einleitung. Letzte Bearbeitung, p. 197.

[12] *Ethik (Birkner)*, Tugend- und Pflichtenlehre, p. 177.

[13] See Immanuel Kant, *Toward Perpetual Peace* (1795), in Kant, *Practical Philosophy* (Cambridge: Cambridge University Press, 1996), pp. 311–352.

[14] See *Ethik (Birkner)*, Güterlehre. Letzte Bearbeitung, p. 262: "Das Recht ist über die ganze Erde verbreitet; aber es ist nicht nothwendig ein gleiches Verhältnis jedes gegen alle."

[15] *Ethik (Birkner)*, Güterlehre, Letzte Bearbeitung, p. 262.

historical statement that does not necessarily signal an irreversible trend. And should this quadruple scheme be viewed as complete? Could not new goods emerge (for example, entertainment industries, or sports or political parties)? Or is it the case that the cultural situation that emerged in Berlin at the beginning of the nineteenth century has worked out the necessary conditions for every reasonable society? In connection with the historical narrative included in the picture, one should mention the role given to family in Schleiermacher's architecture of goods. His construction leaves no place where family can immediately fit into the totality of goods. However, Schleiermacher does not intend to downplay this elementary social bond; rather, he conceives family as the historical base of cultural spheres and looks upon culture as an offspring of what family once has been. In such respects, it should be clear that Schleiermacher is not our contemporary and his description of society is not compatible with our present time. Nevertheless we can learn from it how to respond to our own situation.

10.5 TOTALITY AND ORGANISM

In his famous *Speeches on Religion*, Schleiermacher introduced the term "universe" as a placeholder for final totality, leaving open whether he was thinking of a Spinozian (or Goethean) *Hen kai Pan*, a Cartesian concept of the infinite, or a more general foundation for Christian talk of God. He shared this concept with his close friend Friedrich Schlegel, who once wrote to Dorothea Veit, "The thought of the universe and its harmony is one and all to me. In this seed I see an infinity of good thoughts, which I feel it is my real destiny to bring to light and to cultivate."[16] In later times, however, Schleiermacher avoided the term "universe" since he feared to be accused of pantheism. He used other concepts such as totality, wholeness, and, most notably, "organism" (*Organismus*). Kant introduced this latter term in his *Critique of Judgement* to differentiate the true state from a mechanistic and rationalistic version of it, an arrangement in which the king appears as the reasonable constructor of a political order that functions like a hand mill. In such a system, everyone else would play the role of a small cog in the wheel, moving under coercion, while only the king is able to express his will freely. In contrast to this, the French Revolution in its early days had, according to Kant, established a new understanding that treats the state as a lively organism, in which every part acts as a member of the common body and thus is as much indispensable as any other person, each as much an "end in itself" as the head of the body.

In that sense, talking about "organism" bears moral implications, which Schleiermacher's ethics took advantage of. With regard to its above-mentioned general perspective, that "organizing" indicates modes of action by which reason unifies nature with itself, it becomes clear that the result of this action accomplishes the structure of an "organism." "Insofar as

---

[16] See "Über die Philosophie," in August Wilhelm von Schlegel and Friedrich Schlegel, eds., *Athenäum*, vol. 2, *Erstes Stück* (Berlin: Heinrich Frolich, 1799), https://www.deutschestextarchiv.de/book/view/schlegel_athenaeum_1799/?hl=Licht&p=7, p. 15: "Der Gedanke des Universums und seiner Harmonie ist mir Eins und Alles; in diesen Keime sehe ich eine Unendlichkeit guter Gedanken, welche ans Licht zu bringen und auszubilden ich als die eigentliche Bestimmung meines Lebens fuehle."

reason has acted only when united with nature, and nature has become one with acting reason, nature must be also acting and producing with it, so the action of reason on nature is the formation of the organism out of a mass."[17] This molding of an organic whole still continues because reason cannot be satisfied by its former products. In the scope of human history, there is still a long way to go in the process, and therefore nothing in the world of goods is so perfectly organized that it does not need improvement. Otherwise ethics was superfluous.

The normative implications of this position suggest a process of shaping society (or culture in general) in such a way, that even where striving for individuality concerns us most, behavior is "rational." The proper formation of each person cannot be a moral act, unless the proper formation of others is put beside it. Every person thus necessarily excludes all others from his or her processes and its results, and for this reason is excluded from theirs in the same way. However, insofar as "one and the same activity," be it as exclusive as it may, bears a mark of commonness and being together with others, it refers to the acting of others. "Excluding and excluded activities in their respective interdependency can only together complete the organism of reason." In this organism, each exists as an "organ of reason" and, together with the things they build, each remains a part of a community, in which all rational beings conceive themselves and others as a genuine whole.[18] Once again, in this example from the lectures, Schleiermacher reminds his students of the togetherness of humankind, while he at the same time acknowledges that each community depends on local groups, shaped by language and their contingent history. A universal connection (*Totalzusammenhang*) remains out of reach. Acting as a human means acting for the sake of the human species, knowing full well that all forms of communities, peoples, and social groups are particular, contingent, and kept within bounds. Hence, the individual forms of human life remain prior to abstract pleas for universality.

This tension is insurmountable, and this is the reason why the concept of a human person stands at the core of Schleiermacher's ethics. Reason is present as identical in all human beings. However, humans essentially are individuals and as such are amidst others and lead their lives under peculiar historical circumstances. To be human means to be the center of a sphere of individual activities, and thus associated with community. Whereas examples of an animal species differ from each other by external reasons like time and location, members of the human species differ from each other for inner reasons: they differentiate themselves as individuals. In this respect, the normative idea of Schleiermacher's ethics of goods still rests on his early concept of individuality.

---

[17] *Ethik (Birkner)*, Einleitung. Letzte Bearbeitung, p. 214.

[18] See *Ethik (Birkner)*, Güterlehre. Letzte Bearbeitung, p. 265: "Jedem ist sein eigenthümliches Bilden kein sittlicher Act, als insofern das eigenthümliche Bilden anderer daneben gesetzt ist . . . Jeder so Bildende schließt von seinem Verfahren und dessen Resultaten nothwendig alle anderen aus, und sezt sich selbst eben deshalb eben so von dem ihrigen ausgeschlossen. Aber dieses Sich-ausschließen-Lassen kann nur mit der Einheit der Vernunft bestehen, sofern zugleich in einer und derselben Thätigkeit gesetzt wird, daß ausschließende und Ausgeschlossene mit ihrem Bilden nur zusammen den Organismus der Vernunft vollenden. Jeder als Organ der Vernunft sezt sich mit seiner angeeigneten Natur als ein abgeschlossenes Ganze. Jeder als selbst Vernunft sezt sich als Theil mit allen anderen in Einem Ganzen."

10.6 THE SIGNIFICANCE OF SCHLEIERMACHER'S ETHICS FOR LATER DEBATES: SIX EXAMPLES

In the second half of the nineteenth century, Schleiermacher's philosophical ethics and especially his ethics of goods built the scaffolding for a prominent and particularly influential speculative theory of culture, developed by the pioneer of German cultural Protestantism Richard Rothe (1799–1867). As a former student of Schleiermacher *and* Hegel, he designed a theology of culture to bridge the gap between Christianity and modernity by liberating the former from its ecclesiastical captivity and transforming religion into the secular. The study of ethics shows that culture needs *Sittlichkeit* as much as *Sittlichkeit* needs religion. Nevertheless, only the *Aufhebung* of the church into *a Christian state* can fit the modern situation. Rothe's ethics is based on Schleiermacher's categories insofar as individual and general ways of "perceiving" and "building" activities establish a cultural order of differentiated spheres. Intersubjectivity always is implied in these spheres, since individual products are made available for others by recognition.[19]

It was Ernst Troeltsch (1865–1923) who in early twentieth century renewed the plea for an *objective ethics of cultural goods* in contrast to that of the neo-Kantianism of his days, especially as it was adopted in systematic theology by Wilhelm Herrmann (1846–1922).[20] Troeltsch explicitly referred to Schleiermacher as the great founder of a scientific program that resists materialism as the prevailing trend of modernity and gains ground for a new form of Idealism. Culture always is in need of values that natural sciences can never generate, whereas an alliance of philosophy of history, historical knowledge, and practical orientation could provide a bulwark against the value-crisis of European culture. According to Troeltsch Schleiermacher's philosophical ethics states reasons for a broadened understanding of the sciences, including the moral or "human sciences" (*Geisteswissenschaften*). But despite its reference to history in general, it still was not confronted with historicism and its effects, at least not in the way Troeltsch himself has been. A life-long interest in Schleiermacher's insights hence shaped Troeltsch's worldview.

In more recent years Eilert Herms (b. 1940) has occupied the role of a successor and custodian of Schleiermacher's philosophical ethics.[21] Herms interprets Schleiermacher's resistance against foundationalism (i.e. the deduction of ethical norms from a unique basic principle) and as a consequence the ethical dependence on intuition (concerning human nature on the one hand and individual self-intuition on the other hand) as the possibility-condition for ethics in general. In Herms' formulation, psychology (which here does not mean empirical psychology but psychology as an ontology of the human person) serves as base of Schleiermacher's entire system.[22] An analysis of the human condition spelled

---

[19] See R. Rothe, *Theologische Ethik*, 1st ed. (Wittenberg: Zimmermann'sche Buchhandlung, 1845).

[20] See E. Troeltsch, *Grundprobleme der Ethik. In Gesammelte Schriften*, vol. 2 (Aalen: Scientia Verlag, 1962).

[21] See E. Herms, *Herkunft, Entfaltung und erste Gestalt des Systems der Wissenschaften bei Schleiermacher* (Gütersloh: Mohn, 1974); and Herms, *Menschsein im Werden. Studien zu Schleiermacher* (Tübingen: Mohr Siebeck, 2003).

[22] For a concise analysis and overview of Schleiermacher's treatment of psychology and anthropology, see Chapter 14 of this volume.

out in ontological terms counts as *pre*condition for social relations and social interaction. Both individuals and social order develop within a historical process, the categorial understanding of which is given in the ethics of goods. For Herms this ontological constitution of personhood within its world takes the place of what a more cautious and piecemeal phenomenology would call "self-understanding" or "images of ourselves." His shift to ontology culminates in a perspective according to which the unity of reason and nature is such that reason is conceived as a metaphysical entity and as an agent prior to nature that has started a unifying process somehow independent of human activities. The latter of course belong to this process and are established by it, yet human activities seem to remain sheer vessels of the stream of reasonable life. Along with this shift Herms introduces the idea that the moral status of culture will be lost when Christian belief declines. Schleiermacher's ethics becomes cultural philosophy on the basis of Christianity. In contrast, the author of the present chapter has tried to reconstruct Schleiermacher's ethics of goods by introducing only presuppositions that rest upon an intersubjective understanding of how to coordinate human activities.[23]

Among interpreters from English-speaking scholarship, William Schweiker comments on the relevance of Schleiermacher for contemporary ethics, hinting at the role that self-consciousness plays in his philosophy and theology, holding together in terms of content what is mirrored in the formal correlation of philosophical and theological ethics.[24] The actuality of Schleiermacher's ethics lies in its insight, that a rational agent shares certain commitments about the worth of life, or what it means to act as a human person. While Schweiker critizises a drive toward totalization intrinsic to the ethics of goods, he argues that this tendency is counterbalanced by theological ethics. It is only under the reign of the Holy Spirit that moral dispositions are renewed and *Bildung* and commonsense flourish. Without it secularized modernity runs into functionalism.

Brent Sockness reconstructs Schleiermacher's early writings on ethical issues and shows how young Schleiermacher found his way from a student of Johann Eberhard at Halle to Aristotle and Kant, blending these philosophers together in a *rational* understanding of the highest good that consequently does not succumb under Kant's rejection of eudaimonism.[25] Following Kant in this respect, Schleiermacher otherwise shared with the Aristotelian tradition the conviction that pure reason alone cannot move anything, especially not the human will. Referring to individuality Schleiermacher highlighted the importance of self-cultivation (*Selbst-Bildung*). For him the human self ("the soul" in traditional terminology) is neither substance (as in classical metaphysics) nor function (as in Kant's *Critique of Pure Reason*), but a bundle of accumulations given by experiences (past) and shaped by expectations (future), both influencing the present state. Thus, the self is in the making, it always remains in becoming. Sockness underlines the role of phantasy in this process and

---

[23] See M. Moxter, *Güterbegriff und Handlungstheorie. Eine Studie zur Ethik Friedrich Schleiermachers* (Kampen: Kok Pharos, 1992).

[24] See W. Schweiker, "Consciousness and the Good: Schleiermacher and Contemporary Theological Ethics," *Theology Today* 56, no. 2 (1999), pp. 180–196.

[25] See B. W. Sockness, "The Forgotten Moralist: Friedrich Schleiermacher and the Science of Spirit," *The Harvard Theological Review* 96, no. 3 (July 2003), pp. 317–348; and B.W. Sockness, "Was Schleiermacher a Virtue Ethicist? Tugend and Bildung in the Early Ethical Writings," *Journal for the History of Modern Theology / Zeitschrift für Neuere Theologiegeschichte* 8, no. 1 (2010), pp. 1–33.

acknowledges the progress made, when such becoming does not depend on human nature in general, but is generated by individual *Selbstanschauung*. Schleiermacher thus marks a step toward an expressivistic conception of selfhood (as described in the work of Charles Taylor) as the dawn of an ethics of authenticity.[26]

Interests in interreligious dialogue lead John P. Crossley to triangulate Schleiermacher's ethics in a new way. Together with the threefold philosophical ethics (goods, virtues, duties) and Christian ethics (*christliche Sittenlehre*), Crossley introduces a third branch, what he calls "religious ethics."[27] The last is not what Schleiermacher himself has developed, but something implicit in his doctrine of creation and common to all monotheistic religions insofar as they are concerned with the relationship of God and World. Here, Crossley suggests, the doctrine of creation can serve as common ground between various religions since, within Schleiermacher's dogmatics, the topic is not specific for Christian consciousness. It is only presupposed in it, and this quasi-transcendental status encloses elements that can be relevant for other belief systems as well. Even though Schleiermacher clarified the difference between philosophical ethics and his Christian ethics in many passages, he never intended to separate them by an unsurpassable divide. Instead he distinguished both for pragmatic reasons alone.[28] They made best progress in independent academic traditions and faculties. Similar to this advancement, Crossley argues, in our time there is a need for a religious ethics that unites divergent traditions for the sake of our planet. Duties such as honoring God, engaging in scientific curiosity, keeping humility toward all creatures or virtues like sustainability are elements of it.

In the end, we are left with the paradox that the ways in which Schleiermacher's *philosophical* ethics found reception and influence are colored by theological interests. In philosophy itself, Schleiermacher as an ethicist remained the great unknown, overshadowed by his merits for hermeneutics, theology, and his translation of Plato's works.

Suggested Reading

Crossley, J. P. "Schleiermacher's Christian Ethics in Relation to his Philosophical Ethics." *The Annual of the Society of Christian Ethics* 18 (1998), pp. 93–117.
Heesch, M. Art. "Philosophische Ethik." In *Schleiermacher Handbuch*, ed. Martin Ohst (Tübingen: Mohr Siebeck, 2017), pp. 267–280.

---

[26] B. W. Sockness, "Schleiermacher and the Ethics of Authenticity," *Journal of Religious Ethics* 32, no. 3 (2004), pp. 477–517.

[27] John Crossley, "The Religious Ethics implicit in Schleiermacher's Doctrine of Creation," pp. 585–608.

[28] On the distinction and connections of Schleiermacher's philosophical and Christian ethics, as well as the distinctive shape of his Christian ethics, see Kevin M. Vander Schel, *Embedded Grace: Christ, History, and the Reign of God in Schleiermacher's Dogmatics* (Minneapolis: Fortress Press, 2012), pp. 149-222; and the essays in H. Peiter, *Christliche Ethik bei Schleiermacher / Christian Ethics according to Schleiermacher*, Gesammelte Aufsätze und Besprechungen / Collected Essays and Reviews, ed. T. N. Tice, translated by Edwina Lawler (Princeton: Wipf and Stock, 2010); cf. also J. P. Crossley, "Schleiermacher's Christian Ethics in Relation to his Philosophical Ethics," *The Annual of the Society of Christian Ethics* 18 (1998), pp. 93–117.

Herms E. "'Beseelung der Natur durch die Vernunft.' Eine Untersuchung zu Schleiermachers Ethik-Vorlesung von 1805/06." In *Menschsein im Werden, Studien zu Schleiermacher* (Tübingen: Mohr Siebeck, 2003), pp. 49–100.
Schweiker, W. "Schleiermacher's Ethics: Humanistic Premise and Ecological Promise." In *Schleiermacher, the Study of Religion, and the Future of Theology: A Transatlantic Dialogue*, ed. B. W. Sockness and W. Gräb (Berlin: De Gruyter, 2010), pp. 323–334.
Sockness, B. W. "Schleiermacher and the Ethics of Authenticity." *Journal of Religious Ethics* 32, no. 3 (2004), pp. 477–517.

Bibliography

Crossley, J. P. "The Religious Ethics Implicit in Schleiermacher's Doctrine of Creation." *Journal of Religious Ethics* 34, no. 4 (2006), pp. 585–608.
Crossley, J. P. "Schleiermacher's Christian Ethics in Relation to his Philosophical Ethics." *The Annual of the Society of Christian Ethics* 18 (1998), pp. 93–117.
Dilthey W. *Leben Schleiermachers, vol. 2: Schleiermachers System als Philosophie und Theologie*. Ed. M. Redeker (Berlin: Vandenhoeck & Ruprecht, 2011).
Feil, M. *Die Grundlegung der Ethik bei Friedrich Schleiermacher und Thomas von Aquin* (Berlin: De Gruyter, 2005).
Fichte, Johann Gottlieb. *Die Bestimmung des Menschen* (Berlin: Vossische Buchhandlung, 1800).
Frank, Manfred. *Das individuelle Allgemeine. Textstrukturierung und -interpretation nach Schleiermacher* (Frankfurt am Main: Suhrkamp, 1985).
Gräb, W. "Die anfängliche Ausbildung des Kulturbegriffs in Schleiermachers Hallenser Ethik." In *Schleiermacher in Halle 1804–1807*, ed. W. Gräb and A. Arndt (Berlin: De Gruyter, 2013), pp. 77–89.
Gräb, W. "Individualität als Manifestation eines Selbstgefühls. Schleiermachers Konzept der religiösen Fundierung und kommunikativen Realisierung humaner Individualitätskultur." In *Individualität: Genese und Konzeption einer Leitkategorie humaner Selbstdeutung*, ed. W. Gräb and Lars Charbonnier (Berlin: Berlin University Pres, 2012), pp. 267–291.
Grove, Peter. *Deutungen des Subjekts: Schleiermachers Philosophie der Religion* (Berlin: De Gruyter, 2013).
Herms, E. *Herkunft, Entfaltung und erste Gestalt des Systems der Wissenschaften bei Schleiermacher* (Gütersloh: Mohn, 1974).
Herms, E. *Menschsein im Werden. Studien zu Schleiermacher* (Tübingen: Mohr Siebeck, 2003).
Kant, Immanuel. *Toward Perpetual Peace* (1795). In Kant, *Practical Philosophy* (Cambridge: Cambridge University Press, 1996), pp. 311–352.
Louden, B., ed. *Schleiermacher: Lectures on Philosophical Ethics* (Cambridge: Cambridge University Press, 2002).
MacIntyre, A. *After Virtue. A Study in Moral Theory*. 2nd ed. (London: Duckworth, 1982).
Moxter, M. *Güterbegriff und Handlungstheorie. Eine Studie zur Ethik Friedrich Schleiermachers* (Kampen: Kok Pharos, 1992).
Ohst, M., ed. *Schleiermacher-Handbuch* (Tübingen: Mohr Siebeck. 2017).
Peiter, H. *Christliche Ethik bei Schleiermacher / Christian Ethics according to Schleiermacher*. Gesammelte Aufsätze und Besprechungen / Collected Essays and Reviews. Ed. T. N. Tice. Translated by Edwina Lawler (Princeton: Wipf and Stock, 2010).

Rohls, J. "Philosophie und Religion in Schleiermachers Entwicklung." In *Einheit der Romantik? Zur Transformation frühromantischer Konzepte im 19. Jahrhundert*, ed. Bernd Auerochs and Dirk von Petersdorff (Leiden: Brill, 2009), pp. 189–215.

Rothe, R., *Theologische Ethik*. 1st ed. (Wittenberg: Zimmermann'sche Buchhandlung, 1845).

Schleiermacher, Friedrich. *Brouillon zur Ethik (1805/06)*. Ed. Hans-Joachim Birkner (Hamburg: F. Meiner, 1981).

Schmidt, S. *Die Konstruktion des Endlichen. Schleiermachers Philosophie der Wechselwirkung* (Berlin: De Gruyter, 2012).

Schweiker, W. "Consciousness and the Good: Schleiermacher and Contemporary Theological Ethics." *Theology Today* 56, no. 2 (1999), pp. 180–196.

Sockness, B. W. "The Forgotten Moralist: Friedrich Schleiermacher and the Science of Spirit." *The Harvard Theological Review* 96, no. 3 (July 2003), pp. 317–348.

Sockness, B. W. "Schleiermacher and the Ethics of Authenticity." *Journal of Religious Ethics* 32, no. 3 (2004), pp. 477–517.

Sockness, B. W. "Was Schleiermacher a Virtue Ethicist? Tugend and Bildung in the Early Ethical Writings." *Journal for the History of Modern Theology / Zeitschrift für Neuere Theologiegeschichte* 8, no. 1 (2010), pp. 1–33.

Spalding, Johann J. *Betrachtung über die Bestimmung des Menschen* (Berlin: Johann Jacob Weitbrecht, 1749).

Troeltsch, E. *Grundprobleme der Ethik*. In *Gesammelte Schriften*, vol. 2 (Aalen: Scientia Verlag, 1962).

Vander Schel, Kevin M. *Embedded Grace: Christ, History, and the Reign of God in Schleiermacher's Dogmatics* (Minneapolis: Fortress Press, 2012).

von Schlegel, August Wilhelm, and Friedrich Schlegel, eds. *Athenäum*, vol. 2. Erstes Stück (Berlin: Heinrich Frolich, 1799). https://www.deutschestextarchiv.de/book/view/schlegel_athenaeum_1799/?hl=Licht&p=7

CHAPTER 11

THEORY OF EDUCATION

MICHAEL WINKLER

11.1 SCHLEIERMACHER AND "SCIENTIFIC PEDAGOGY"

AROUND 1890, Schleiermacher was (re)discovered as one of the most important scholars in the field of educational theory. Although he was acknowledged and highly regarded in theology, he had been nearly forgotten in philosophy and pedagogy. Now at the turn of the twentieth century, he was, one might say, reinvented as a, if not *the*, founder of a modern pedagogy. From that time on, Schleiermacher was known as an influential theoretical thinker for the academic school called *Geisteswissenschaftliche Pädagogik*, which became the most successful paradigm in the first half of the twentieth century in Germany, replacing Herbartianism, the leading academic school of pedagogy and stronghold of a science of education founded by Johann Friedrich Herbart and his followers. As one of its founders, Herman Nohl, demonstrated in a famous study, *Geisteswissenschaftliche Pädagogik* started with a revolutionary attitude, calling itself part of the German Movement.[1] Even in the 1960s, many academic chairs in pedagogy in German universities were occupied by scholars educated in that paradigm, which was connected with a philosophical, cultural, and value-oriented approach to the field of education.

The role of the *Geisteswissenschaftliche Pädagogik* was contested from its very beginning. The protagonists tried to legitimate their way of understanding education by appealing to works written by great thinkers of pedagogy. They claimed to follow Wilhelm Dilthey, the founder of the concept of *Geisteswissenschaften*, but they did not realize that his concept of education was based on a mixture of phenomenological psychology and social sciences.[2] The relation between *Geisteswissenschaftliche Pädagogik*, Dilthey, and Schleiermacher's pedagogy seems somewhat puzzling, too. In fact, Schleiermacher's pedagogy was rather colonized by them because they did not realize how he had developed an approach in its

---

[1] See Herman Nohl, *Die pädagogische Bewegung in Deutschland und ihre Theorie* (Frankfurt am Main: Schulte-Bulmke, 1970), pp. 212–216.

[2] See Winkler, "Wilhelm Dilthey und die geisteswissenschaftliche Pädagogik," in *Diltheys Werk und die Wissenschaften. Neue Aspekte*, ed. Gunter Scholz (Göttingen: V & R unipress 2013), pp. 209–230.

own right, generating a theory referring to both a societal, if not socio-pedagogical, model of education and also a very open and more or less empirical approach. This approach was influenced by his strategy of analyzing a given reality through hermeneutics and dialectics.[3]

Beside such an instrumentalization of Schleiermacher's pedagogy, for many thinkers from the end of the nineteenth century on, Schleiermacher's pedagogy stood for a paradigm change. Paul Natorp, a member of the Marburg School of neo-Kantianism, first realized the relevance of Schleiermacher's pedagogy as a social pedagogy.[4] He revealed that Schleiermacher's educational theory was state of the art, even up to his own time. Natorp's insight was that Schleiermacher did not abandon the philosophical approach, seen as fundamental for educational thinking for the previous century, but demanded empirical experience and data as well. Further, he saw the center point had to be found in the complex relations between society with its historical change and the individual with its personal development, which could not be separated from historical and societal conditions.

11.2 Schleiermacher's Writings on Education: Background and Overview

Schleiermacher dealt with questions of pedagogy from his early days. He was trained in the seminar of Gedike and was later known as a sensible reviewer of books on education. He was involved in the political administration of the educational system, where he had important influence on the Prussian Reform Movement. The government, especially the Department of Education at the Minister of Internal Affairs, relied on his expertise and opinion. He was even asked to sketch curricula for school instruction. He was also a sharp observer of contemporary developments in education, and was in dialogue with important pedagogical thinkers of his time. He was familiar with relevant publications, sometimes even with books from abroad. He took part in widespread discussions, which culminated in the establishment of the modern university,[5] usually referred to as the New University formed by Wilhelm von Humboldt. In 1808, he published *Occasional Thoughts on Universities in a German Sense*.[6] From 1810 unto 1815, he worked in the sector for public instruction and in the scientific deputation, organizations attached to the Prussian Minister for Education. In addition, Schleiermacher acted as advisor and counsellor for the government in different functions to promote necessary changes and reform projects in the educational system,

---

[3] See Manfred Frank, *Das individuelle Allgemeine. Textstrukturierung und Textinterpretation nach Schleiermacher* (Frankfurt am Main: Suhrkamp, 1985).

[4] See Paul Natorp, "Schleiermacher und die Volkserziehung," in E. Troeltsch et al., *Schleiermacher der Philosoph des Glaubens* (Berlin: Buchverlag der Hilfe, 1910), pp. 57–84; cf. Natorp, *Gesammelte Abhandlungen zur Sozialpädagogik*, vol. 1 (Stuttgart: Frommanns, 1907), pp. 208f.

[5] See Ernst Müller, ed., *Gelegentliche Gedanken über Universitäten. Von J.-J. Engel, J. B. Erhard, F. A. Wolf, J. G. Fichte, F. D. E. Schleiermacher, K. F. Savigny, W. v. Humboldt, G. F. W. Hegel* (Leipzig: Reclam, 1990).

[6] See Friedrich Schleiermacher, *Gelegentliche Gedanken über Universitäten in deutschem Sinn*, in Schleiermacher, *Texte zur Pädagogik. Kommentierte Studienausgabe*, 2 vols., ed. Michael Winkler and Jens Brachmann (Frankfurt am Main: Suhrkamp, 2000). Hereafter *TP*.

driving it toward more equality and justice.⁷ Some value his work as taking the first steps toward democracy in the educational system.

Schleiermacher wrote a number of informal papers that were intended for internal use by the administration but were noticed widely in the public and by stately officials. Especially of interest were those papers concerning the role the state has to play in education.⁸ There, Schleiermacher declared for the first time that it is important to understand education as a whole, not reducing it to instruction given in schools alone. Education deals with a person's complete life, thinking, and even feeling, in a way that might be understood as competence for living, acting as a free person but aware of the necessity of social feelings and connections. Schleiermacher focused on a person's biographical identity as well as on society in a way that could be understood as a kind of religious feeling and caring for others. In doing so he realized the necessity of separating societal living and political ambitions—a differentiation that sounds familiar to liberal politics and works against a strong state influence, and which is quite similar to ideas advocated by Wilhelm von Humboldt.⁹ But Schleiermacher was also aware that states could fail, falling victim to a chaotic mass of contingencies and arbitrariness, if not despotism.¹⁰ These were critical motives remembered later in his lectures on education.

Schleiermacher's most important impact on the educational debates of his time as well as in the generations that followed emerged from the three lecture courses on education he delivered at Berlin University in 1813/1814, 1820, and in 1826. The 1813/1814 course has been preserved in short handwritten notes that Schleiermacher used as a basis for his lectures, which he delivered as free and extemporaneous speech. The lectures of 1820 and 1826 are preserved in student transcripts (*Nachschriften*), written while attending Schleiermacher's lectures and later elaborated at points. For some time, only fragments of lecture transcripts from 1820/1821 were extant, written by Friedrich Adolph Diesterweg, who himself became a famous educator. The 1820 lectures seemed to be focused on educational responses to misbehavior or to missteps in natural development and punishment. However, more recent transcripts have shown that this was a misunderstanding, as Schleiermacher treated the whole, complex subject of education here as well.¹¹ For over a century, the 1826 lectures became most popular in discussions of educational theory in the German-speaking world, as they were readily accessible in Schleiermacher's *Sämmtliche Werke* as volume nine of the third section.

This volume of the *Sämmtliche Werke* was prepared and published by C. Platz, a Protestant pastor acquainted with Schleiermacher. However, it was not a critical edition based on Schleiermacher's handwritten notes, nor could it be attributed to one of the academic students who attended the lessons personally. Following editorial principles current in the nineteenth century, Platz compiled different notes written by students without

---

⁷ Cf. the introduction to *Pädagogik*.

⁸ *TP* I, pp. 272–389.

⁹ See Wilhelm von Humboldt, *Ideen zu einem Versuch, die Gränzen des Staates der Wirksamkeit des Staates zu bestimmen* [1792], in Wilhelm von Humboldt, *Werke in fünf Bänden*, ed. Andreas Flitner and Klaus Gile, vol 1: *Schriften zur Anthropologie und Geschichte* (Darmstadt: Wissenschaftliche Buchgesellschaft, 1960), pp. 56–233.

¹⁰ *TP* I, p. 288.

¹¹ See Friedrich Schleiermacher, *Pädagogik (1820/21). Die Theorie der Erziehung in einer Nachschrift*, ed. Christiane Ehrhardt and Wolfgang Virmond (Berlin: De Gruyter, 2008).

establishing their authorship. He produced a usable edition, but one inconsonant with modern philological standards. Therefore, one cannot responsibly make use of this edition without acknowledging its limitations, particularly since Platz clearly sanitized some of Schleiermacher's remarks on the political situation.[12] Nevertheless, Platz's edition became the standard version for more than a century and a half and served as the basis for nearly all subsequent editions, including the most famous edition by Wilhelm Flitner and Theodor Schulze,[13] which in paperback form was widely used. In 2000 Schleiermacher's pedagogical writings returned to a two-volume form. These were also based on the Platz edition, but included a critical commentary showing that edition's limitations and even the passages later added to the more original writings.[14] These volumes set the stage for the critical edition of Schleiermacher's pedagogical lectures in the *KGA* (2.12), produced on the basis of entirely new manuscripts and textual evidence. The volume contains the public votes and recommendations that Schleiermacher wrote for the government and the school administration as well as all his lectures on pedagogy. The 1826 lecture in particular was produced using a completely new manuscript of student notes by Jacob Sprüngli, who studied with Schleiermacher in Berlin. His notes have been found in an archive of the University of Zürich following hints a research group at Jena University had detected. They offer a handwritten record of the 1826 lecture and represent the only authentic document representing nearly all lectures Schleiermacher delivered in the academic year 1826. They had been deciphered through a long-standing research project and can be judged as the best edition ever made of these lectures.

Despite these developments, Platz's edition remains in use, probably due to his didactically arranged presentation. It continues to provide the basic text for all the analyses and interpretations of the theoretical construction of Schleiermacher's theory, and has even been used to prepare an English translation of the 1826 lecture.[15]

Quite a few scholars turned academic attention to Schleiermacher in the decades after 1900, and especially between 1950 and 2000, indeed more so than to any other so-called classic pedagogical figure.[16] Schleiermacher's pedagogy was read in many academic seminars for teacher training and is frequently discussed in lectures on pedagogy in German universities. Though nearly forgotten in the nineteenth century, and overshadowed by the impact of Herbart's studies and writings on education throughout Europe, Schleiermacher's pedagogy began to receive significantly more attention in the 1960s. One particular study from 1935 by Albert Reble put a good amount of work into understanding the lectures and to identifying their basic concepts and constructive principles.[17] Reble referred to the complete philosophical works of Schleiermacher and suggested reading him as a philosopher of culture. Reble showed, for the first time, how Schleiermacher's pedagogy followed the path

---

[12] Cf. the edition of the lectures in *Pädagogik*.

[13] See Friedrich Schleiermacher, *Pädagogische Schriften*, 2 vols., ed. W. Flitner and T. Schulze (Düsseldorf and München: Küpper Bondi, 1957).

[14] See *TP*.

[15] See Norm Friesen and Karsten Kenklies, eds., *F. D. E. Schleiermacher's Outlines of the Art of Education: A Translation & Discussion*, Paedagogica 2 (New York: Peter Lang International Academic Publishers, 2022).

[16] An extended bibliography can be found in *TP* 2, pp. 439–454.

[17] See Albert Reble, *Schleiermachers Kulturphilosophie. Eine entwicklungsgeschichtliche-systematische Würdigung* (Erfurt: Kurt Stenger, 1935).

of the idealistic philosophy of *Geist* (Spirit), but viewed rather—in the sense of Aristotle—as a social *praxis*, in which persons are involved in creating a common culture in historical and ethical development. Reble took "culture" as a synonym for society, opening the horizon for an understanding lasting until today.

In 1964 Wolfgang Sünkel wrote a dissertation on Schleiermacher's theory of pedagogy, inspired by Ernst Lichtenstein.[18] Sünkel argued that Schleiermacher should be understood as the originator of a modern scientific approach to education, and that his works should be regarded with at least as much esteem as Herbart's had enjoyed up to that time. Sünkel opened the door for an understanding of Schleiermacher's pedagogy as a theory dealing with society as the real basis for education, and he pointed out that Schleiermacher presented a modern scientific theory. In 1975 Johannes Schurr presented his voluminous study *Schleiermachers Theorie der Erziehung*, a study more extensive than Schleiermacher's lecture itself, covering about 560 pages.[19] In some respects, Schurr's study can be read as a kind of scientific crime story, as he detected and identified within different layers of arguments many hints pointing to classical authors like Plato and Aristotle and outlining a sophisticated sketch that lays out Schleiermacher's understanding of education in a scientific way. Other studies followed, by Michael Winkler, Johanna Hopfner, and Jens Brachmann.[20] And further analyses and interpretations have since been published, at times pursuing specialized questions, such as the impact of Schleiermacher's pedagogical theory on aesthetics, on social-pedagogy, or political education.[21] Beside these studies other research has focused on narrower topics or on the relationship of Schleiermacher's pedagogy to other disciplines. Indeed it is fascinating how Schleiermacher's theory continues to inspire studies directed to an extended and comprehensive understanding of his educational ideas. In 2008 Steffen Kleint offered a new interpretation presenting an inner tension between a critical approach and affirmation in Schleiermacher's theory,[22] which seems not only a philological essay but a theory of the reality of education in general. And in 2012 Franziska Bartel reconstructed the relations between Schleiermacher's theology and his pedagogy.[23] Schleiermacher's pedagogy remains one of the most frequently and broadly discussed works in German philosophy of education,

---

[18] See Wolfgang Sünkel, *Friedrich Schleiermachers Begründung der Pädagogik als Wissenschaft* (Ratingen: Henn Verlag, 1964).

[19] See Johannes Schurr, *Schleiermachers Theorie der Erziehung. Interpretationen zur Pädagogikvorlesung von 1826* (Düsseldorf: Pädagogischer Verlag Schwann, 1975).

[20] See Michael Winkler, *Geschichte und Identität* (Bad Heilbrunn: Klinkhardt, 1979); Johanna Hopfner, *Das Subjekt im neuzeitlichen Erziehungsdenken. Ansätze zur Überwindung grundlegender Dichotomien bei Herbart und Schleiermacher* (München: Juventa, 1999); and Jens Brachmann, *Friedrich Schleiermacher. Ein pädagogisches Porträt* (Basel: Beltz—UTB, 2002).

[21] See Mari Mielityinen, *Das Ästhetische in Schleiermachers Bildungstheorie. Theorie eines individuellen Weltbezugs unter Einbeziehung der Theorie des Ästhetischen bei Schiller* (Würzburg: Ergon, 2009); Moritz Czarny, *Friedrich Schleiermacher und die Sozialpädagogik. Eine Rekonstruktion unter besonderer Berücksichtigung der strukturtheoretischen Professionstheorie* (Würzburg: Ergon, 2014); and Annika Münzel, *Zum Verhältnis von Pädagogik und Politik bei Schleiermacher* (Baden-Baden: Ergon, 2020).

[22] See Steffen Kleint, *Über die Pädagogik D. F. E. Schleiermachers. Theoriebildung im Spannungsfeld von Kritik und Affirmation* (Frankfurt: Peter Lang, 2008).

[23] See Franziska Bartel, *Die Entstehung des Erziehungsdenkens bei Schleiermacher* (Würzburg: Ergon, 2012).

and its impact on current debates can hardly overestimated, even in a diagnosis of contemporary society.[24]

11.3 Conceptual Background of Schleiermacher's Lectures on Education

Schleiermacher's lectures on pedagogy contain an ongoing plea for establishing the theory of education as a distinct academic subject offered in the faculty of philosophy. In the 1813/1814 and 1820/1821 lectures, he tried to establish an academic discipline of pedagogy in its own right, referring to the related disciplines of ethics (in philosophical and theological dimensions) and psychology. In 1826 he was more ambitious, demanding a science of pedagogy and arguing for the proper *dignity* of that subject and a distinctive academic approach to it.[25]

Schleiermacher sought to articulate his approach through a series of compromises. The first of these falls between an idealistic approach and the emerging trend toward a realistic and empirical science, analyzing the distinctive field of institutions and actions found in a given society.[26] In this case, the analysis concerned a society that was in turmoil not only through the transition from ancient institutions to modern ones, but also torn between progressive forces in Prussia and those that belonged to the *reaction* gathering at the Vienna Congress.

A second compromise appears with the insight that a theory should help to understand, to judge, and to organize institutions and practices in such a way that conditions would improve towards a modern society. Yet even there a problem emerged, as the *Reden* declare: modern society was far removed from such a humane situation, due to suffering caused by the rise of capitalism, and to the disintegration of bonds between individuals. Schleiermacher recognized that simply giving advice or outlining techniques was not sufficient to establish an ethically responsible form of education. This could only be realized by educators, teachers, and advisors on educational politics working consciously through freely made decisions. It was thus necessary to cultivate an ethical disposition (*Gesinnung*) throughout all persons of society.

Schleiermacher's manner of theorizing also reflects a third compromise. His reflections regularly drew from historical terms and concepts, reaching out to the classical Greek philosophers he knew well. But he also referred to authors from the eighteenth century and his own time, for example the philosophers of Scottish Enlightenment. As a result, his lectures on pedagogy present a model of highly educated and scholarly discourse, opening the minds of his students in every direction important for the understanding of education.

---

[24] See for example Claudia Wirsing, "Schleiermacher heute? Zur Bedeutung seiner ästhetischen Erziehung im Zeitalter pluraler Lebensformen", in *Die Aktualität der Romantik*, ed. Michael N. Forster and Klaus Vieweg (Münster: LIT, 2012), pp. 269–283; and Michael Winkler, "Friedrich Schleiermacher (1768–1834)," in B. Dollinger, ed., *Klassiker der Pädagogik. Die Bildung der modernen Gesellschaft* (Wiesbaden: VS Verlag, 2006), pp. 75–100.

[25] *TP* 2, p. 31.

[26] See *Ethik (Birkner)*, p. 94.

The lectures also became a long and difficult text, quite open to interpretation, operating more or less as both a discourse on education and a project to educate educators by teaching them to reflect on education. Accordingly, the lectures have to be read as a whole to find out what the importance and the meaning of education could be. They show Schleiermacher's attempt to construct a framework of the theory, broad enough to fill in anthropological, historical, and empirical insights, and flexible enough to enable open and creative thinking and free decisions.

The epistemological problem Schleiermacher faced was how to create a robust understanding of education that was appropriate to the evolutionary and anthropological knowledge of his time while still open to new insights gained by empirical research. His approach to this problem presents what appears as a double paradox. On one hand, he defined the theory of education with the general proposition that a pedagogy could never be valid for all times. Yet he also stated that the theory of the art of education can be determined by referring to basic structures, speaking to challenges taken on in any case of education apart from differences in content or individual persons. The second paradox lies in his insight that a theory of education cannot rely on assumptions about human anthropology. To the question of whether personal characteristics are given by birth or conditioned by one's context, Schleiermacher's theory responds that neither answer is relevant for the process of education, because we do not know which has the biggest effect on one's life. Education has to be considered as a praxis on its own; we have to organize it in a way that might be correct, regardless of whether characteristics are given by nature or by social experiences. In other words, the practice is in itself important.

While it may be surprising that a famous translator of Plato's works refers to Aristotle, it is clear that with regard to *praxis* Schleiermacher followed ideas outlined in the *Nicomachean Ethics*.[27] He denied that education might be executed as a *poesis*, as a work realizing an aim. He instead tried to identify the inner logic and rationality of education in a new mode, understanding how human beings act in their given world. To use a modern expression, he tried to understand how we are doing education. For that task, he formulated a central question leading to an educational practice worth acknowledging as a *techné*. Those who consider education as their professional work have to ask themselves questions that may sound strange: What does the older generation want to do with the younger one? What are the important aims, and what are the necessary media or instruments for this? These questions and their possible answers should be considered as a framework for a hermeneutic and dialectical discussion of the possibilities and limits of education given in a real historical and social situation on one hand and the particularity of the subject on the other.[28]

---

[27] See Hackel, Christiane, *Schleiermacher und Aristoteles. Schleiermacher als Initiator der von der Königlich-Preußischen Akademie der Wissenschaften zu Berlin herausgegebenen Aristoteles-Edition (1831–1870)*, in *Wissenschaft, Kirche, Staat und Politik: Schleiermacher im Preußischen Reformprozess*, ed. Andreas Arndt, Simon Gerber and Sarah Schmidt (Berlin, Boston: De Gruyter, 2019), pp. 145–174.

[28] Cf. *Ethik (Birkner)*, p. 5.

11.4 Primary Components of Schleiermacher's Lectures on Education

Up until to the present time, the lectures of 1826 deserve credit for being the most complex and sophisticated systematic approach to educational theory ever produced. Recent work shows that all of Schleiermacher's different lecture courses on education covered the same topics. But the lectures of 1826 display the highest degree of systematicity, and in addition offer a kind of methodology of educational thinking, describing a mindset necessary for those involved in practical education. Schleiermacher intended an ethical approach, and tried to avoid any kind of technical thinking that regarded children and youngsters as mere objects of treatment rather than confident and competent personal subjects capable of free and moral decisions. Education has to be realized as an open process undertaken by responsible actors conscious of both sides of the educational project—including both educators and children or youngsters. Schleiermacher positioned education as an ethical praxis within the ethical process in which human nature and human activities develop along tangential lines; he saw education as both a real historical process and as an open, never-ending ethical progress. Some have argued that Schleiermacher's fundamental ideal was of an eschatological end of humankind,[29] which served therefore as the ultimate aim of education. On this view the two tangents, of historical and ethical progress, could come together and connect in a future utopia. But Schleiermacher did not bring this idea into his theory of education. Education will be a part of the historical and ethical processes, and must be understood as embedded in changes in the conditions of the world, including changes for the worse. And education can act against such deterioration only by improving human understanding of it—through theory, not through direct influence.

Although one could express some reservations regarding the structure Platz gave his edition, it may be helpful to review the way Schleiermacher organized his lectures of 1826. The lectures, which should be read as a whole, have three parts: an Introduction, a General Part, and a Special Part (*Einleitung, Allgemeiner Teil, Besonderer Teil*). The Introduction presents fundamental arguments regarding the necessity of a science of education and lays the groundwork for understand education as a subject for research and understanding. It also discusses problems including that of the effectiveness of education, of the beginning and end of education, of equality and individual difference (even in view of the social status of persons), and the difference between education for girls and boys. The General Part explains the different types of action in education within the framework of education as a social activity, characterized by a tension between the effects of society and societal institutions and the intentional activities of educators on one hand, and the self-development of the subject on the other. Schleiermacher saw ways in which education shelters children against the effects of society and allows for their inner development. But education's primary and most important role is one of support. Any education worthy of the name must focus on supporting the self-development of young people, which is how autonomy is to be realized. The Special Part considers, in great detail, a great many situations in the overall educational

---

[29] Cf. Alfred Langewand, "Das Ende der Erziehung und ihrer Theorie," *Zeitschrift für Pädagogik* 3 (1987), pp. 513–522.

process, starting within the family and moving through the important social institutions of Schleiermacher's time, with results that are still worth considering today. This Part can be understood as a phenomenological analysis of the reality of education in modernity, in both its development and its internal differences and contradictions.

The opening of Schleiermacher's 1826 lectures is highly unusual for an academic work. Rather than defining education, he advised his students to recall how education is understood in daily life, arguing that this general understanding must be presumed. But he added at once: usually parents are the educators, but they work without a proper theory; and school teachers provide instruction, but do not educate in the sense Schleiermacher wanted to describe. Where instruction is concerned with particular kinds of knowledge and abilities, education refers to the living of whole active life in a general context of daily living, understood as a social and cultural living environment led by an ethical disposition. His lectures of 1813/1814 had posed the fundamental question, Where can we find a secure and stable point to begin our theory of education? After taking different approaches to this question in several lectures, in 1826 he realized that one has to combine two perspectives.

The first, and more common, perspective assumed education as an activity that occurs between two generations, an older and a younger one. But Schleiermacher did not share the optimistic progressivism of the Enlightenment. Instead, in his view history is characterized by instability, by upwards and downwards movements (he judged the reaction of his time, especially the decisions of the Vienna Congress in 1814/1815 and the following developments, as a downward movement). Such instability demands ethically founded action. The passing of generations can be judged as either historical improvement or historical decline; as Schleiermacher pointed out at the midpoint of his 1820 lectures, the historical process cannot be seen as a continuous development for the better.[30] Both improvement and decline are caused by human action, but what makes the difference is not so much a lack of sound techniques but rather a lack of sufficient consciousness of action, particularly concerning education. One needs, on the one hand, a type (*Typus*) of education that enables engaged persons to act in well-informed ways, and on the other hand, the demands and particular conditions determined by personalities and situations.

Schleiermacher added that in fact, a triangular relationship serves as the basis for identifying and collecting all the phenomena with which education needs to grapple. Because of this multidimensional structure we cannot rely on simple causal relations. This represents a systematic change, as Schleiermacher wrote in the notes for his lecture of 1813/1814: "The formation of education has two focus-points: in general, it is interested in the youth and wants to help young people to avoid errors; and in particular, education follows the feeling for that which is deficient for the common life."[31] Now, in 1826 he started with three moments in the analysis and understanding of education: the two generations and the focus on an open historical process.

We can use this as a starting point and a parameter for the hermeneutics of education, leading to what Schleiermacher termed "divination." A divination is an estimation of the situation and future a child will face, which cannot be known with certainty. Schleiermacher's position imposes limits on the hope that education will produce political

---

[30] Cf. Schleiermacher, *Pädagogik (1820/21)*, p. 169.
[31] *TP* 1, p. 224.

changes; he did not share the old and the still working dream that better education will produce better people and a better society. Education has to be understood according to its own structure and organized as an open-ended action—because for Schleiermacher the course of societal development is, at least at the present time, uncertain. No single system of education that will be viable in any historical condition can be anticipated or constructed. It is even nearly impossible to say what the effects of education will be, although Schleiermacher did speak in these terms. But, of course, without education as a praxis executed with consciousness, the ongoing development of a culture will fail. Education works to guarantee that cultural evolution will not suffer from a rollback—an insight affirmed by modern biological evolutionists.[32]

This leads to the second perspective on the starting point for the theory of education. Schleiermacher noted that regarding education as a *techné* is the real and sufficient reason to engage in it; it is obvious that he used this term to describe professional activity, based on scientific insights but also respectful of personal autonomy. Schleiermacher took on the concept of subject and subjectivity, the Enlightenment concept of the person in its identity and autonomy, in a dialectical use of the old Latin word. In Latin *subject* refers to a person without power, while in the eighteenth century a new sense emerged: the *subject* as a free, independent, and self-guided individual, with the right to speak for itself. Such a subject is mature and responsible, *mündig*, as when Immanuel Kant had commanded, "Use your own reason." But Schleiermacher realized from the beginning of his philosophical thinking that the *Subjekt* cannot be reduced to its individuality, but rather must be seen as embedded in the social conditions that make it alive in a strong sense of the word. Any education has its focus point and basic goal in the development of the person as a subject. Any human being has its sufficient reason for development in itself. The individual subject as a living being has its cause in itself. Schleiermacher used the philosophical insights of his time, but he also refers back to his psychology, which can be read as a theory of *Bildung*. It is clear that Schleiermacher used the ideas he had explained in his psychology,[33] but to these ideas must be added the point that any individual in self-development depends on other persons and on their social conditions and surroundings, which affect individual development at all times. The theory of education describes the outer conditions necessary for individual *Bildung*, framed for epistemological reasons by the relation between generations, and therefore within the ethical process. The inner side of education is explained by his psychology, and the comparison between the lectures proves a striking conformity between the ideas found in both.

The individual and subject thus cannot be thought as developing itself outside of historically given conditions of life. To use a popular formula, any child is a child of its time, and education has to acknowledge this. One has to discover and to develop one's own identity as living subject in a given society; this challenge must be mastered if subjects are to form their own identities as social and historical persons. However, Schleiermacher was firmly convinced that no one can become a person outside a living community; we cannot envision persons in isolation, since examples show us that outside of society the ability to reason, and

---

[32] See Michael Tomasello, *Becoming Human: A Theory of Ontogeny* (Cambridge, MA: Harvard University Press, 2019).

[33] See Dorothea Meier, *Schleiermachers Psychologie. Eine Phänomenologie der Seele* (Baden-Baden: Ergon, 2019).

reason itself, are reduced to a minimum. And the chance for the better development of any persons depends on the better development of social practices.

11.5 Summary and Consequences of Schleiermacher's Positions

What consequences follow from these fundamental insights? These consequences are made evident in the General and Special Parts of the lectures. To sum up, Schleiermacher's educational idea is based on the concept of becoming a free person with one's own identity, capable of acting in ways that extend beyond self-consciousness and egoism. Inspired by the early Romantics, he saw individuality as the individualization of a general given—not of reason as such, but rather a kind of social mindset, even one grounded in deep religious feeling. This mindset is developed within the spheres of society, but persons eventually realize that acting in responsible ways is something that must be learned. Yet this can be learned only in societal contexts: in ethical formed social groups and institutions to be sure, but sometimes also in the context of personal encounters. Schleiermacher is quite near to an understanding of human development commonly used by sociologists and some psychologists, one that employs Émile Durkheim's concept of socialization.

The first consequence might seem a bit odd. Schleiermacher did not think that education understood as an immediate personal relation is effective; and this marks an interesting point of difference between his concept and most other approaches. Beginning before Schleiermacher and extending to the present day, theories of education commonly focus on the personal relationship between educator (or teacher) and child (or student). They speak of interaction between these persons, who will differ both in age and in experiences and abilities. Educational theory advises the older person how to work with the child, sometimes following aims that are culturally or socially given. The educator is defined as a moral instructor, leading the student to independence and freedom. More than a few have argued that such a personal relationship will be always a strong one, seldom free of authoritarian structures—and this in addition to the fact, discovered by psychologists, that such relationships will produce in students attachments and bonding for a lifelong feeling of security and stability.

Second, the motive power behind all education and, for this reason, the central focus of education will be found in the young person itself. Schleiermacher's theory is not child-centered, as are progressive twentieth-century theories of education. The difference is a systematic one. The logical and empirical center of any education is the process of *Bildung* through which individuals mature. Of course, this seems an individualistic view, quite similar to perspectives developed by the early Romantics,[34] but much more popular two hundred years later, driven by neoliberal tendencies. Schleiermacher followed the path that early Romantic thinkers had envisioned. They focused on the integrity of persons,

---

[34] See Frederick C. Beiser, *German Idealism: The Struggle against Subjectivism, 1781–1801* (Cambridge, MA: Harvard University Press, 2002); Frank, *Das individuelle Allgemeine*; and M. Forster and K. Vieweg, eds., *Die Aktualität der Romantik* (Berlin: LIT Verlag, 2012).

emphasizing the importance of sentiments and feelings. But they never forgot the importance of social relations, even in emphasizing human freedom and dignity; there is evidence that Schleiermacher had read the theories of Scottish moralists, and even the theory of moral sentiment as a basis for market behaviors, as Adam Smith had discovered. Two of Schleiermacher's early essays, the *Monologen* and "In Search of a Theory of Sociable Conduct," dealt with these dual aspects of human life. What he discussed there remained as a basic idea throughout his philosophy, and returned as well in his pedagogical thinking.

In Schleiermacher's thinking one has to consider these two dimensions in human life, the individual and the universal. But these dimensions need to be understood as reflecting the question of equality and inequality: education can only be understood as a matter of the individual person who is developing by acting in the world as a free person. The individual person acts in two ways: receptively, in appropriating the world as given; and spontaneously, in expressing oneself in that world. Both ways create the self and the identity in a unique way, but also as formed by the historically given society and culture. Receptivity helps us to appropriate the given cultural and social world. Spontaneity is directed towards the cultural world, on which an educated person would focus in his or her own personal way.[35]

The person in their subjectivity emerges from itself, driven by nature, but never independently of a world; their action represents not only their personal identity, but also patterns formed by institutions and by practices external to these, internalized as experiences. Experiences are shaped by learning, and this again in two ways. Schleiermacher differentiated between abilities, which can be taught by teachers, and an ethical disposition and attitude, which includes the consciousness of one's personality and of one's relations to all the goods of value to life.

Third, pedagogy has to be considered as a collective affair. The members of the older generation have to think about education in a collective way, and also as individuals responsible for the organization of the conditions of the lives of the younger generation. Recall the position Schleiermacher had expressed at the beginning of his lectures: that education is a task the older generation is obligated to think about and to realize in an ethically responsible way, with the aim of enabling the younger generation to make free decisions for their own lives. But education cannot be realized beyond a given society or outside of it, say in a special "pedagogical province," as Goethe had put it. Educators need to think about possible effects of institutions and practices, and to estimate, judge, and decide what effects institutional structures and forms will have on the younger generation, and how these effects affect the whole of social life. They need to be realistic in their considerations, but also need to consider how these effects should be evaluated ethically, and always within a political horizon. Looking critically at Schleiermacher's arguments, one can hardly miss his advocacy for democratic perspectives, even if this was sometimes subtle or tacit.

Thus the questions are: How do institutions given in a society have effects on children, and what kind of effects do they have? In some respects, Schleiermacher can be seen as one of the first sociologists in education, favoring a kind of functional approach.[36] But he did not introduce the concept of socialization into his account, as Durkheim would eighty years later; and this might be the reason sociologists have not cared much about Schleiermacher, apart from

---

[35] *TP* 1, p. 191.
[36] See Otto Willmann, "Über Schleiermachers Erziehungslehre," in O. Willmann, *Aus Hörsaal und Schulstube* (Freiburg im Breisgau: Herdersche verlagsbuchhandlung, 1904), pp. 18–29.

Niklas Luhmann and from the inclusion of Schleiermacher's pedagogy in a recent volume of key works in the social sciences.[37] No one is isolated from the society in which they live, which must be taken into account, not for the individual subject alone but for the whole society. Educators must consider the relations between society and individual. Considered as a *techné*, education facilitates the rational deliberation and discussion of the ways social institutions, considered as ethical practices, work. And knowledge of the effects of social institutions may make interventions necessary. These negative effects can be derived either from within, from the natural development of the child, or from external influences.

Fourth, the results of education will be affected by the effects of social institutions that make up the world of the younger generation. These institutions have to be understood and organized so that they can be sources of ethical goods. They have to work in an ethical way, as a praxis of life, embedding the maturing person in these goods. But in contrast to the hopes of Enlightenment thinkers and the demands of national education plans (for example by Resewitz or Zöllner),[38] with their orientation towards comprehensive results—the idea that education would lead to the improvement of society and of humanity overall—Schleiermacher imposed limits on the effects of education. *Bildung*, the development of a person, should be effected by individuals themselves, in their interaction with given social institutions and practices. Schleiermacher did not accept the view that "education is an initiation and a continuation of the process of individual development by an influence from outside. In this way the state would educate, as would any good friend, and everybody would be educated lifelong."[39] Instead, he called for education to have a proper terminus. The process of education comes to and end when a person acts freely and autonomously in their given social contexts, deciding for herself or himself whether those contexts should be preserved or changed.

Fifth, how should education work and have effects? Generally speaking, education should be guided by a collective consciousness following the ethical demand to produce everything that the human process can utilize, in a way that might work as an ethical *good*. But this depends on freedom and the autonomy of subjects in their relations to given conditions. Education will be a function of these, but realized in a responsibility focused on these relations, and on the subject's acting and developing, on its *Bildung*, within these relations. Schleiermacher identifies four types of action through which subjects deal with their circumstances as they engage in the process of *Bildung*. The first is tolerance (*das Gewährenlassen*), as it were a prototype of later progressive education's principle that children are to be allowed to do what they want, not as a simple capitulation to capriciousness but as a sign of trust in the reasoning capacities of the subject. The second is protecting or sheltering action (*Behütung*). If the subject is endangered by the conditions of the social and cultural world, any educator must provide protection to ensure that the process of *Bildung* will not stop. The third is described as reaction (if not counterreaction) against evils that could affect the subject. There are two possible forms of such evil: on the one hand, evil

---

[37] See Niklas Luhmann and K. E. Schorr, eds., *Zwischen Anfang und Ende, Fragen an die Pädagogik* (Frankfurt am Main: Suhrkamp, 1990); and Samuel Salzborn, ed., *Klassiker der Sozialwissenschaften. 100 Schlüsselwerke im Portrait* (Wiesbaden: Springer VS, 2013).

[38] Cf. *TP* 1, pp. 79–99; and Helmut König, *Zur Geschichte der Nationalerziehung in Deutschland im letzten Drittel des 18. Jahrhunderts*, Monumenta Paedagogica 1 (Berlin: Akademie Verlag, 1960).

[39] Schleiermacher, *Pädagogik*, p. 260.

from the inner nature of the subject, such as tendencies for bad temper; and on the other dangers coming from outside, internalized as bad habits. The subject must respond to these. And the fourth and most important type is support or aid for the acting subject. In fact Schleiermacher states, according to the basic idea that education takes place within given conditions, that any intentional educational effort should in the end produce supportive action.

11.6 The End of Education

Space prohibits consideration of all the topics Schleiermacher discussed in the Introduction and the General Part of his lectures, although these deal with fundamental questions of education that remain important today. And it is much more difficult to give more than hints about the Special Part of the lectures, which comprise more than 250 pages in the edition of 2000. Schleiermacher looked carefully, if not scrupulously, over existing institutions and pragmatics, weighing the pros and cons in the public discussions of the time, and disputing the results of natural scientific research. In the background one finds his ethical maxims of liberty, equality, and sociability, even pertaining to gender relations.

Using the biographical narrative of a young person, Schleiermacher discussed the process of *Bildung* in the great social communities or communities of goods (*Gütergemeinschaften*), as he had termed them in his ethics. The young generation is first formed by the atmosphere of the family, and as they mature they are further influenced by religion, the state, and finally the sciences. Schleiermacher saw these communities representing clusters and patterns of meaning, if not of ethical values, that must be understood. The importance of the art of education derives from its obligation to contribute to social cohesion, especially in historical situations when societies are fragmented or subject to disturbances. Schleiermacher used these communities of goods like a superstructure of ideas to discuss actual experiences, particularly in the family and in the different types of schools. He presented his considerations as dialectics and hermeneutics for those who live or work in the concrete institutions in interaction with young people. He investigated their possible effects on individual identity and on the social process in general. He used a kind of dialectical reasoning, declaring and testing possible effects, weighing and balancing the potential benefits of different positions without giving specific advice. Sometimes he took strong positions, for example when he declared the necessity of abolishing corporal punishment in schools.[40] And he declared the importance of the ability to use language properly: without competence in language, intellectual education could not be attained.[41] Following his psychology, he held that what could be demanded of a person differs according to their age. Therefore, he differentiated three periods of *Bildung*, the first of which was formation within the family. However fully respected as a subject, a child not yet able to use language cannot yet be educated. Schleiermacher noted how personal authority will have an influence during childhood, because the child itself tends to a natural obedience that should not lead to a condition of mere

---

[40] *TP* 2, p. 267.
[41] *TP* 2, p. 331.

oppression. The second period of education is strongly connected with learning in schools, in two respects: a formal respect connected with subjects Schleiermacher addresses directly; and an informal respect, as education by the institutional structure, so to speak. The latter is important because Schleiermacher argued that the social character of a person, its *habitus*, will be formed by the institution. In the third period, the young generation undergoes training and apprenticeship, or academic studies.

Yet in every case, education ends when a person has reached the position of a consciousness of independence, beyond legitimation by any authority. It ends with the acknowledgement of a person in a transition to a public world, with open communication, which should be a free one, beyond any despotism. Education should enable a resistance against any kind of servitude in every person. *Bildung* should follow a path that frees the human spirit from all chains that have constrained it: "So that the Spirit, freed from all bonds in which it had been held, shall obtain victory."[42]

Suggested Reading

Brachmann, Jens. *Fridrich Schleiermacher. Ein pädagogisches Porträt* (Weinheim: Beltz—UTB, 2002).

Friesen, N., and K. Kenklies, eds. *F. D. E. Schleiermacher's Outlines of the Art of Education: A Translation & Discussion*. Paedagogica 2 (New York: Peter Lang International Academic Publishers, 2022).

Schleiermacher, Friedrich. *Texte zur Pädagogik*. 2 vols. Ed. Michael Winkler and Jens Brachmann (Frankfurt am Main: Suhrkamp, 2000).

Bibliography

Arndt, Andreas, Simon Gerber, and Sarah Schmidt, eds. *Wissenschaft, Kirche, Staat und Politik. Schleiermacher im preußischen Reformprozess* (Berlin: De Gruyter, 2019).

Bartel, Franziska. *Die Entstehung des Erziehungsdenkens bei Schleiermacher* (Würzburg: Ergon, 2012).

Beiser, Frederick C. *German Idealism: The Struggle against Subjectivism, 1781–1801* (Cambridge, MA: Harvard University Press, 2002).

Brachmann, Jens. *Friedrich Schleiermacher. Ein pädagogisches Porträt* (Basel: Beltz—UTB, 2002).

Czarny, Moritz. *Friedrich Schleiermacher und die Sozialpädagogik. Eine Rekonstruktion unter besonderer Berücksichtigung der strukturtheoretischen Professionstheorie* (Würzburg: Ergon, 2014).

Dollinger, B., ed. *Klassiker der Pädagogik. Die Bildung der modernen Gesellschaft* (Wiesbaden: VS Verlag, 2006).

Forster, M, and K. Vieweg, eds. *Die Aktualität der Romantik* (Berlin: LIT Verlag, 2012).

---

[42] *TP* 2, p. 404: "Damit der Geist von allen Banden, in denen er gefesselt gehalten wird, befreit den Sieg erringt."

Frank, Manfred. *Das individuelle Allgemeine. Textstrukturierung und Textinterpretation nach Schleiermacher* (Frankfurt am Main: Suhrkamp, 1985).

Friesen, Norm, and Karsten Kenklies, eds. *F. D. E. Schleiermacher's Outlines of the Art of Education: A Translation & Discussion*. Paedagogica 2 (New York: Peter Lang International Academic Publishers, 2022).

Hopfner, Johanna. *Das Subjekt im neuzeitlichen Erziehungsdenken. Ansätze zur Überwindung grundlegender Dichotomien bei Herbart und Schleiermacher* (München: Juventa, 1999).

Kleint, Steffen. *Über die Pädagogik D. F. E. Schleiermachers. Theoriebildung im Spannungsfeld von Kritik und Affirmation* (Frankfurt: Peter Lang, 2008).

König, Helmut. *Zur Geschichte der Nationalerziehung in Deutschland im letzten Drittel des 18. Jahrhunderts*. Monumenta Paedagogica 1 (Berlin: Akademie Verlag, 1960).

Langewand, Alfred. "Das Ende der Erziehung und ihrer Theorie." *Zeitschrift für Pädagogik* 3 (1987), pp. 513–522.

Luhmann, Niklas, and K. E. Schorr, eds. *Zwischen Anfang und Ende, Fragen an die Pädagogik* (Frankfurt am Main: Suhrkamp, 1990).

Meier, Dorothea. *Schleiermachers Psychologie. Eine Phänomenologie der Seele* (Baden-Baden: Ergon, 2019).

Mielityinen, Mari. *Das Ästhetische in Schleiermachers Bildungstheorie. Theorie eines individuellen Weltbezugs unter Einbeziehung der Theorie des Ästhetischen bei Schiller* (Würzburg: Ergon, 2009).

Müller, Ernst, ed. *Gelegentliche Gedanken über Universitäten. Von J.-J. Engel, J. B. Erhard, F. A. Wolf, J. G. Fichte, F. D. E. Schleiermacher, K. F. Savigny, W. v. Humboldt, G. F. W. Hegel* (Leipzig: Reclam, 1990).

Münzel, Annika. *Zum Verhältnis von Pädagogik und Politik bei Schleiermacher* (Baden-Baden: Ergon, 2020).

Natorp, Paul. *Gesammelte Abhandlungen zur Sozialpädagogik*, vol. 1 (Stuttgart: Frommanns, 1907).

Natorp, Paul. "Schleiermacher und die Volkserziehung." In *Schleiermacher der Philosoph des Glaubens*. Ed. E. Troeltsch et al. (Berlin: Buchverlag der Hilfe, 1910) pp. 57–84.

Nohl, Herman. *Die deutsche Bewegung. Vorlesungen und Aufsätze zur Geistesgeschichte von 1770–1830*. Ed. O. F. Bollnow and F. Rodi (Göttingen: Vandenhoeck & Ruprecht, 1970).

Nohl, Herman. *Die pädagogische Bewegung in Deutschland und ihre Theorie* (Frankfurt am Main: Schulte-Bulmke, 1970).

Reble, Albert. *Schleiermachers Kulturphilosophie. Eine entwicklungsgeschichtliche-systematische Würdigung* (Erfurt: Kurt Stenger, 1935).

Salzborn, Samuel, ed. *Klassiker der Sozialwissenschaften. 100 Schlüsselwerke im Portrait* (Wiesbaden: Springer VS, 2013).

Schleiermacher, Friedrich. *Pädagogik (1820/21). Die Theorie der Erziehung in einer Nachschrift*. Ed. Christiane Ehrhardt and Wolfgang Virmond (Berlin: De Gruyter, 2008).

Schleiermacher, Friedrich. *Pädagogische Schriften*. 2 vols. Ed. W. Flitner and T. Schulze (Düsseldorf and München: Küpper Bondi, 1957).

Schleiermacher, Friedrich. *Texte zur Pädagogik. Kommentierte Studienausgabe*. 2 vols. Ed. Michael Winkler and Jens Brachmann (Frankfurt am Main: Suhrkamp, 2000).

Scholz, G., ed. *Diltheys Werk und die Wissenschaften. Neue Aspekte* (Göttingen: V & R unipress, 2013).

Schurr, Johannes. *Schleiermachers Theorie der Erziehung. Interpretationen zur Pädagogikvorlesung von 1826* (Düsseldorf: Pädagogischer Verlag Schwann, 1975).

Sünkel, Wolfgang. *Friedrich Schleiermachers Begründung der Pädagogik als Wissenschaft* (Ratingen: Henn Verlag, 1964).

Tomasello, Michael. *Becoming Human: A Theory of Ontogeny* (Cambridge, MA: Harvard University Press, 2019).

von Humboldt, Wilhelm. *Werke in fünf Bänden*, vol. 1. Ed. A. Flitner and K. Giel (Darmstadt: Wissenschaftliche Buchgesellschaft, 1960).

Willmann, Otto. *Aus Hörsaal und Schulstube* (Freiburg im Breisgau: Herdersche verlagsbuchhandlung, 1904).

Winkler, Michael. *Geschichte und Identität* (Bad Heilbrunn: Klinkhardt, 1979).

Chapter 12

Hermeneutics

Christian Berner

Friedrich Schleiermacher first developed his "hermeneutics" as an exegete of the New Testament and then as a philologist and Plato translator, rather than as a Romantic theologian or Idealist philosopher competing with Fichte and Hegel. Schleiermacher gave nine lectures on hermeneutics between 1805 and 1833, first in Halle and then in Berlin, primarily for theological apprentices. In 1829, he gave two famous lectures on hermeneutics at the Berlin Academy of Sciences. It was not until 1826/1827 that the hermeneutics course was regularly supplemented by a course on philological criticism. The critical edition of Schleiermacher's hermeneutics (2012) and bourgeoning historical work in Germany and Italy have only recently made it possible to construct a much more balanced image of his hermeneutics than that which prevailed until the end of the twentieth century. Recent scholarship has now discredited the idea that Schleiermacher should be placed at the heart of a "hermeneutics" that he does not claim and that aims to be, for example, a foundation of the sciences of the mind (in Dilthey) or a hermeneutic philosophy (in Heidegger or Gadamer). Even so, interpretations that borrow from and criticize Schleiermacher undoubtedly manifest the productivity of Schleiermacher's hermeneutics, far beyond what he seems to have expected.

In what follows, we will present the structure of Schleiermacher's hermeneutics in light of this current research, and indicate the major interpretative orientations to which his hermeneutics gave rise. We will start from the general definition of "the art of understanding" to expose its main methods and then show how it fits into the aim of a philosophy of culture.

12.1 The Art of Understanding as General Hermeneutics

The proper object of hermeneutics is to determine the meaning of a text. Hermeneutics can therefore be called the "art of understanding."[1] This definition is more surprising than it may seem at first glance, because hermeneutics is traditionally defined as the art of interpretation

---

[1] *HK*, p. 119.

that aims for understanding. When we understand, we no longer interpret. Schleiermacher thus affirms that interpretation finds the principles of its method in the very analysis of understanding, which will make it possible to link hermeneutics to philosophy.[2] Thus, the epistemological aspect of comprehension completes the existential consideration of the human being as an "interpreting animal."[3] By starting from the act of understanding as such, Schleiermacher is able to posit a "general form" of hermeneutics in contrast to "special hermeneutics," where the latter collects "observations" about specific difficulties encountered by accident due to our incompetence.[4] In this respect, Schleiermacher's hermeneutics is not universal, at least not, for example, in the sense of the hermeneutics of the Enlightenment or of Nietzsche's universalization of interpretation wherein "there are no facts, but only interpretations."[5] Schleiermacher reduces the art of interpretation to the understanding of texts that are entirely and exclusively moved in the field of language. Contrary to his own claim, Schleiermacher is not the first to project the lineaments of such an art.[6] As early as the seventeenth century, most systematic logics had recognized that the correct conduct of the mind does not consist only in the correct formation of thoughts but also in explaining them correctly to others and in understanding the discourses of others. Thus, long before Schleiermacher's day, hermeneutics appeared as a complement to logic and rhetoric.

Schleiermacher aimed at a general hermeneutic of discourse mainly in order to establish principles for a special hermeneutic, the *hermeneutica sacra*. For him, holy books must be interpreted in no other way than secular books.[7] Because the Holy Spirit used human authors who were addressing a human audience, Holy Scriptures must be interpreted by using reason.[8] In other words, special hermeneutics is based on general hermeneutics, and there is no autonomous *hermeneutica sacra* but only specifications of general rules according to language, literary genre, and so forth. Therefore, we are dealing with general hermeneutics, which can be treated independently from special hermeneutics. As such, the reception of Schleiermacher's hermeneutics retained almost exclusively his attempt to elaborate general hermeneutics.

Defining hermeneutics as the "art of understanding" and thus assimilating "understanding" and "interpretation" is significant because of the assumption, first of all, that it is impossible to understand without interpretation. To dismiss this possibility seems to contradict both daily experience and logic. As for the former, it seems that we do not always have to use hermeneutics to understand. As for the latter, the process of understanding would be condemned to an infinite regression if there were not first elements that could be immediately understood. Schleiermacher recognizes that there is an ordinary understanding that is satisfied without theory because it is sufficient from a practical or aesthetic point of view. Ordinary understanding makes it possible to act, to experience pleasure, and so forth. Such

---

[2] *AV*, p. 621.
[3] See Hans-Georg Gadamer, *Wahrheit und Methode*, in *Gesammelte Werke*, vol. 1 (Tübingen: Mohr Siebeck, 1999), pp. 45f.
[4] *HK*, p. 119.
[5] Friedrich Nietzsche, "*Nachgelassene Fragmente* Ende 1886—Frühjahr 1887," 7 [60], in Nietzsche, *Kritische Studienausgabe*, ed. G. Colli and M. Montinari (Berlin/New York: DTV/De Gruyter, 1988), vol. 12, p. 315; see "*Jenseits von Gut und Böse*," §108, in *Kritische Studienausgabe*, vol. 5, p. 92.
[6] *HK*, p. 119.
[7] *HK*, p. 37.
[8] *HK*, pp. 125–126.

an understanding in ordinary life is not aware of the rules it applies and cannot reconstruct the rigorous order of its thoughts. There is, indeed, a fluidity of conversation that often leads us to understand the other immediately through empathy, or at least we have the impression that we understand.[9]

This ordinary understanding, which is often enough for us, is not what hermeneutics is all about. This is why Schleiermacher speaks of an "*authentic* understanding," one that is not blind, like immediate understanding. What hermeneutics seeks to understand is the meaning inscribed in the discourse of others, discourse that is "foreign" to me insofar as I am not its origin. The difficulty of such an understanding generally lies in the nature of language's intimate union with thought and in its non-coincidence with reality. For if Schleiermacher retains from Kant that thought does not reach the being of things as they are in themselves—not even the subject to itself, since the individual being is a phenomenon—he also agrees with Herder's *Metacritic* that reason and language are intimately united such that the "human soul thinks with *words*."[10] As a result, the communication of thoughts, which is the subject of every discourse,[11] is put to the test of identifying whether we think the same thing by using the same words and whether we build our representations identically.[12]

This thesis, which some authors such as Locke or Kant had seen on occasion, is of decisive philosophical significance with regard to the status of language as the place where truth or meaning is to be found. The question is not that of the relationship of word to reality, because according to Schleiermacher the smallest unit of understanding is the proposition, from which discourses are composed.[13] To say something about something makes the object of hermeneutics thinking, understood as judgment. Schleiermacher notes that discursive representation and perceived reality are incommensurable. That's why there are many ways of rendering what is perceived, and why every speech is a perspective.[14] This makes the concept of truth problematic in its ordinary sense, as an adequacy between discourse and being, and justifies the fact that there is a multiplicity of stories that account for things. However, the task of hermeneutics is to understand the discourse independently of the being to which it refers, that is, to establish its meaning and not its truth. This is why interpretation and hermeneutics, as that which scientifically regulates it, are the first conditions of any science. Science comes only second and is linked to the establishment of facts. The place of understanding is in the discourse: When we understand, we do not compare representations so much with things as we compare representations with discourse to see if others construct those representations in the same way. The identity of meaning in communication remains a "hypothesis" and is never given; in practice, we only have individual uses. It is in this linguistic perspective that Paul Ricœur saw in Schleiermacher a "forebearer of an important development in contemporary semantics, namely, that ordinary language functions in the interplay between identity of sense and mobility of signification."[15] By being constantly put

---

[9] *HK*, p. 198.

[10] Johann Gottfried Herder, "*Verstand und Erfahrung*". *Eine Metakritik zur Kritik der reinen Vernunft*, in *Sprachphilosophie. Ausgewählte Schriften* (Hamburg: Meiner, 2005), p. 184.

[11] *HK*, p. 120.

[12] *Dial.* 2, pp. 628f.

[13] *HK*, p. 47.

[14] *HK*, p. 1010.

[15] Paul Ricœur, "Schleiermacher's Hermeneutics," *The Monist* 60, no. 2 (1977), p. 186.

to the test, meaning is never frozen in ultimate certainty and the search for truth is carried out in dialogue, the possibility of which is, for Schleiermacher, ultimately guaranteed by the postulate of "the unity of reason."[16] That's why "dialectics," which for Schleiermacher is the discipline that presents the principles of the art of doing philosophy (the thinking that aims at knowing), is, in accordance with the common requirements of reason, the complement of the hermeneutic method. It is necessary to know what the discourse or its author wants to say before examining the reasons that the author advances to affirm that what the author says is true. It is not surprising, therefore, to articulate knowledge based on meaning and dialectic based on hermeneutics. In terms of understanding, this means that meaning does not exist in itself and that nothing allows us to say that we understand other people's words exactly as they were intended. This makes the task of understanding and interpreting "infinite" and "non-understanding will never be fully solved."[17] This is a fundamental feature of all communication and of the recognition of the other as other, which means that the discourse of others is always in some way a foreign one. In every discourse, in every thought, there is an individual element where "each is other than the other."[18] This is why translation is a particular mode of hermeneutics.[19] Schleiermacher is one of the first to have attached this paradigmatic role to translation. Starting with Dilthey, these elements will be essential for the extension of Schleiermacher's epistemology in the sciences of the mind. Dilthey makes the psychological understanding of the individual one of the individual's characteristics, as opposed to the explanation at work in the natural sciences.[20] For Dilthey, Schleiermacher elaborated the conditions of possibility and the technical methods of understanding others, which are at the foundation of the human sciences.[21]

Despite the possibilities of misunderstanding, human beings speak, write, and communicate. Faced with this undeniable fact, interpretation would be meaningless if we did not assume, despite the difficulties mentioned, the will to communicate. This is why a fundamental principle of hermeneutics states that it is always necessary to assume that the author wants to be understood.[22] Even if the author rarely takes enough care of the audience, the author is always more or less in dialogue with it.[23] This is a version of the principle of charity, rediscovered by Donald Davidson and the analytical philosophy of language in the context of the analysis of the conditions of translation and interpretation, which postulates the meaningful nature of the text as communication, a fundamental principle without which no interpretation would be possible.[24] This presupposes that the author of the speech indicates what they want to say, that is, that they give the indications of their interpretation in their speech. In other words, there can be no discourse without a willingness to communicate and therefore willingness to be understood, since the discourse will have been constructed in

---

[16] *Dial*.1, p. 190.
[17] *AV*, p. 621.
[18] *Dial*.1, p. 231.
[19] *AV*, p. 76 f.
[20] See Wilhelm Dilthey, in particular the continuation of *Der Aufbau der historischen Welt in den Geisteswissenschaften,* in Dilthey, *Gesammelte Schriften*, vol. III (Göttingen: Vandenhoeck & Ruprecht, 1924), which reproduces the principles of Schleiermacher's hermeneutics, notably pp. 224f.
[21] Dilthey, "Die Entstehung der Hermeneutik," in *Gesammelte Schriften,* vol. V, pp. 317–338.
[22] *HK*, p. 27.
[23] *HK*, p. 112.
[24] Donald Davidson, *Truth and Interpretation* (New York: Oxford University Press, 1984).

order to be reconstructed by others. This is why the discourse must be approached both with confidence, as a vector of meaning, and with mistrust, as it is likely to be misunderstood. It is this dimension that Jürgen Habermas retained by according Schleiermacher a fundamental role in the linguistic turn, alongside Johann Gottfried Herder and Wilhelm von Humboldt. In Schleiermacher, Habermas discovered a communicative theory in which subjects "are able, because of the structural relationship of their particular language to reason, to implement discourses and mobilize general convincing reasons when they encounter foreign languages or cultures and can only transcend the limits of their pre-comprehension through translation."[25] Habermas not only emphasizes the importance of the relationship between hermeneutics and philosophy because of the relationship between thought and language that Schleiermacher often makes explicit, but also finds in him the telos of dialogue as a rationally established understanding that manifests itself as early as hermeneutics in the will to understand the other, which is at the basis of the theory of communicative action.

The purpose of interpretation is to grasp the meaning of meaningful discourse. According to Schleiermacher, not everything is equally the object of hermeneutics, but only "elaborated thought,"[26] an authentic thinking, the autonomous thinking which is the motto of an enlightened reason as an affirmation of individuals who think by themselves, that is, who exercise the force of judgment and in this way create meaning.[27] Thinking is only effective in language, so we must interpret discourse directly from the language, that is, proposals or judgments that say something about something, that mean something. Hermeneutics, therefore, seeks the meaning that a subject attaches to their discourse. It wants to find what an individual wants to say in the language, that is, how the individual participates in the language,[28] by going back to their initial conception of meaning, what Schleiermacher calls in his later lectures the "seminal decision."[29] This is what happens when we let ourselves be affected by signs from others and identify what the other says, to see it as a true speech act—and therefore an act of thought—before projecting our norms of thought.[30] Schleiermacher is undoubtedly one of the first to speak of speech acts related to acts of life, as found later in Austin or Wittgenstein.[31] In short, the art of understanding is necessary as soon as we make the assumption that the discourse says something else because it means something new. Indeed, "the productive spirit always brings something that could not be expected."[32] The meaning thus goes beyond what is transmitted by the inherited language alone. The wise interpreter perceives the effort of the manifestation of innovation.[33] Hence the double relationship of the authentic author to the language: subject to the language of tradition and constrained by it, the human being who thinks freely at the same time contributes to forming the language.[34] This gives two poles to any interpretation, namely, the mind that manifests

---

[25] Jürgen Habermas, *Auch eine Geschichte der Philosophie*, vol. 2 (Berlin: Suhrkamp, 2019), pp. 439–440.
[26] *HK*, p. 120.
[27] *AV*, p. 71.
[28] *HK*, pp. 466–467.
[29] *HK*, p. 949.
[30] *HK*, pp. 740f.
[31] John Langshaw Austin, *How to Do Things with Words* (Cambridge, MA: Harvard University Press, 1962); Ludwig Wittgenstein, *Philosophische Untersuchungen* (Oxford: Basil Blackwell, 1958).
[32] *HK*, p. 26.
[33] *HK*, p. 52.
[34] *AV*, p. 71.

itself and the language of which it is a part. In this way, we can attempt to understand the message of Jesus, who spoke a transmitted language without which he could not have been understood, while at the same time saying something new.[35] This is why religion is "a spirit that forms language."[36] Schleiermacher affirms that "Christianity has made language."[37] It is in this sense that language is productive and the presence of the individual makes this difference everywhere, since the discourse participates in the life of the language that it does not just repeat. This is regularly reported by Schleiermacher as he interprets the New Testament, where Greek was grafted onto Hebrew. For Schleiermacher, the New Testament must be interpreted to grasp the originality of its message in relation to that of the Old. Thus religion, like "every new intellectual principle," is understood as "a formative linguistic spirit."[38] In other words, in order to understand the new concepts of the Christian language, psychological interpretation must complement grammatical interpretation in order to grasp the "particular emotion" that animated Christian authors.[39]

12.2 HERMENEUTICAL METHOD

In order to understand precisely, the art of interpretation develops a method that takes the discourse in its entirety and leaves no part of the interpretation undetermined. This is why an efficient method should not only look for solutions once confronted with difficulties that result from mistakes already made: "Rules must rather be a method to prevent difficulties than observations to solve them."[40] In order to prevent errors, "the hermeneutic operation must not only begin where understanding becomes uncertain," but as soon as one wants to understand. Becoming aware that one does not understand does not always coincide with the error that may be anterior. If we have not completely reconstructed the discourse and the process of thinking,[41] we will not know where the cause of the error lies. That is why authentic understanding is progressive and methodical interpretation must accompany its entire process, step by step. Compared to tradition, this methodological remark gives a new status to non-understanding: it becomes first and fundamental. Certainly, hermeneutics has always had its origin in the fact that we do not understand. But Schleiermacher goes further by declaring, "Hermeneutics is based on the fact [*factum*] of the non-understanding of the discourse."[42] This means that non-understanding is no longer *datum*, an empirical fact that it is also by virtue of our finiteness, but a methodological requirement. When we do not understand, we become aware of our intimate will to understand, which is a condition of non-understanding. On the one hand, such a willingness remains always undetermined. On the other hand, this willingness gives itself the resources to understand when it acts from

---

[35] *HK*, p. 27; pp. 509–511.
[36] *HK*, p. 38.
[37] *HK*, p. 17.
[38] *HK*, p. 38; cf. pp. 383–384, 752–753, 790f.
[39] *HK*, pp. 124–126.
[40] *HK*, p. 164.
[41] *HK*, p. 6.
[42] *HK*, p. 73.

the very beginning as if we do not understand. In other words, there is no immediate understanding in hermeneutics and that is precisely why "understanding" and "interpretation" coincide.

The art of interpretation is then that of "getting in possession of all the conditions required for understanding."[43] These conditions are not transcendental, but simply preliminary knowledge. All of the data that allow a correct interpretation must be gathered, namely knowledge of language and humanity, context, history, culture, and so forth. All these conditions can only be met once the act of understanding itself has been understood in order to know what precisely needs to be known. It is sufficient to start from the nature of the discourse, because "to understand is the reconstruction backwards to the act of the one who thinks,"[44] and to identify what "is at the very basis of the discourse."[45] Depending on its nature, discourse is entirely language. In this sense, Schleiermacher writes that the art of understanding and interpreting "only exists if the prescriptions form a system based on clear principles, drawn directly from the nature of thought and language,"[46] and that thought finds in language the very place where it is manifested. Therefore, "language is the only thing to be presupposed in hermeneutics, and everything to be found, including other objective and subjective presuppositions, must be found from language."[47] This will be the motto of the third part of Gadamer's *Truth and Method* devoted to the ontological shift in hermeneutics.[48]

Schleiermacher founded hermeneutics as a method—that's the real meaning of the term *Kunstlehre*—that provides rules for the direction of interpretation that must lead the mind to understand. Hermeneutics is a tool, the instrument of understanding, and that is why Schleiermacher most often ranks it among the technical disciplines. It was in this sense that in the 1970s Peter Szondi, in his lectures introducing literary hermeneutics, was able to rely on Schleiermacher in his methodological pretention to an objectivity of interpretation, thus reviving the claim of the scientific nature of critical literary studies.[49]

But for Schleiermacher, if hermeneutics is a *Kunstlehre*, it can also be said that "interpreting is an art."[50] Art is indeed first of all to be taken here as a "know-how," therefore as a technique. But since there are no rules for the application of the rules, which is therefore not "infallible,"[51] the interpretation can never be mechanized.[52] In this respect, hermeneutics is part of the faculty of judgment, of that talent that Kant said cannot be learned but only practiced. Interpreting therefore requires talents: a linguistic talent that makes us feel analogies and differences, and a talent to know individuality, which is the psychological talent of "knowing people." These talents are "gifts of nature" and cannot be learned.[53]

---

[43] *HK*, p. 73.
[44] *HK*, p. 456.
[45] *HK*, p. 120.
[46] *KD²*, p. 375.
[47] *HK*, p. 17.
[48] Gadamer, *Wahrheit und Methode*, p. 387.
[49] Peter Szondi, *Einführung in die literarische Hermeneutik* (Frankfurt am Main: Suhrkamp, 1975).
[50] *HK*, p. 122.
[51] *HK*, p. 122.
[52] *HK*, pp. 201, 470.
[53] *HK*, p. 123.

12.2.1 Grammatical and Technical Interpretation

We have seen that the art of interpretation must start from the linguistic nature of its object, the discourse. However, discourse is not understood from language alone, but from the relationship between the author of the discourse and the language. And language has a double relationship with the individual: on the one hand, the individual is subject to its power, and on the other hand, when the individual does not simply repeat the language, the individual contributes to its formation: "he is his organ and it is his."[54] This defines two perspectives, namely, grammatical and technical interpretation. Grammatical interpretation focuses on the reality of discourse, aiming to capture both the words and the connections that make it up. Technical interpretation seeks the power of thought, the ultimate impulse that is rooted in the individual who gives meaning to his discourse. Sometimes referred to as "psychological," this interpretation is most often referred to as "technical" because it understands how an individual has used the language, worked on it, and transformed it to express the individual's mind. The two aspects of interpretation are therefore a reflection of the constitution of any discourse as an encounter between a system, even if it is already particularized in a language, and a creative individual. This is why the two types of interpretation are complementary in seeking understanding. In the ethical formation of the community, grammatical interpretation is more assertive, and technical interpretation includes more of the constitution of the self.

Let us begin, as Schleiermacher did, by retracing the lineaments of grammatical interpretation. It is "the art of finding the determined meaning of a discourse defined from and using language."[55] Because it is based on a defined object, this interpretation is called "objective." It is also said to be "negative" because it delimits the field in which a proposal can be meaningful and excludes what does not comply with grammatical rules, which "can absolutely not be understood."[56] As a necessary but not sufficient condition of possibility, grammar makes it possible to establish the field of communication, the one where author and reader or listener can agree. The many rules and practical instructions given by Schleiermacher for this aspect of interpretation aim to establish in their univocity the signification and meanings of words in propositions or discourses as a combination of propositions.

For Schleiermacher it is necessary to reconstruct the language in its historical moment, to take into account its evolution, to avoid misunderstanding the meaning of a term, to avoid misjudging the "accent and tone" that makes us understand too much or not enough, and so on. In short, grammatical interpretation seeks the conventional meaning of words and proposals and outlines the field of communicability. Grammar is therefore the specific structure of a language in a given historical context in which individuals will be able to find ways to communicate and thus to agree.

From this perspective, the individual is first exposed to the power of language, which constitutes a world in which they are thrown. The individual finds themselves "a slave of time"[57] and of the linguistic area in which their thought is developed. However, the dual nature of language requires everyone to form their own language in a specific way, "so that the

---

[54] *HK*, p. 75.
[55] *HK*, p. 39.
[56] *HK*, p. 55.
[57] *Monologen^2*, p. 369.

deduction and sequencing, the coherence and the consequence correspond perfectly to the way of doing of his mind and that the harmony of the speech reproduces the fundamental tone of the thinking, the accent of the heart."[58] Discourse is therefore really discourse only if individuals expresses themselves, that is to say make their chords heard there. Not only do individuals need to understand on the basis of language, but they also need to understand on the basis of individuals who appropriate the language, that is, the way in which humanity transforms the inherited language by using it. This is the task of the technical interpretation, which seems to be the opposite of the grammatical part. If the latter, as we have seen, was "objective" and "negative," the technical interpretation is "subjective" insofar as it seeks access to something that does not present itself as an object, namely the individual interiority that leaves its trace without appearing as such. Technical interpretation is also "positive" according to the measure whereby it "posits" something, that is, creates or is productive in its reconstruction efforts. The discovery of individuality in the particular way a thought is exhibited is style.[59] Style emerges from the initial act that led the author to think in the particular way they say it, that is, by finding the "principle that moves the writer."[60] Style, as the singularity of composition and linguistic use, linked to the author's particularity, remains relatively stable and allows the recognition of an identity in different writings.[61] In this field, too, Schleiermacher formulates rules and gives instructions. For him, the essential thing is not only to see how the individual implements their meaning in the language, to see how they innovate by comparing it with the language of tradition, but also to grasp from the individuality of the subject how thoughts are linked and combined and what subjective dynamics govern their succession. The interpretation will therefore seek to reproduce the sequence, the combination of thoughts, in order to reconstruct identically the construction of another individual, since this is the criterion of understanding. This will require an understanding of authors' psychology, or mind, which requires knowledge of their personality, the situation that determines them, and so forth. It is obviously not easy to achieve the individuality that presides over thought insofar as the inexpressible individual, the *individuum ineffabile*, is classically defined by Schleiermacher as inaccessible.

We can therefore summarize: Just as grammatical interpretation aims at a perfect knowledge of the language, the purpose of technical interpretation "must be defined as a perfect understanding of the style."[62] Here as well as there, it is a question of rigorously rebuilding the discourse. The (re)constructive characteristic makes it possible to overcome the psychological reduction of Schleiermacher's hermeneutics, which is usual in traditional presentations of the history of hermeneutics, and thus to put it in a more direct relationship with dialectics as an art of thinking. This direct relationship is possible because understanding through reconstitution is the condition for the possibility of inscribing discourse in a practice of dialogue that aims at knowledge, that is, in the transition from meaning to truth. The two types of interpretation are complementary and neither should be preferred over the other, although they may be used in different measures, depending on the writings and the individual qualities and dispositions of the interpreters. But in accordance with the

---

[58] *Monologen²*, p. 369.
[59] *HK*, p. 156.
[60] *HK*, p. 155.
[61] *HK*, p. 103.
[62] *HK*, p. 156.

nature of the discourse, the two sides interact. There is no privilege of understanding by empathy. As Schleiermacher says, the interpreter "who would like to rush the linguistic aspect" would not only be "very wrong," but "a nebulist" who would lose in the mists of intuition the clarity required by understanding.[63] To interpret correctly, it is necessary to take both the individual and the universal into account, and the practice of hermeneutics is included both in the process of individuation and in the formation of the community, since the individual asserts themselves as well as they communicate. As we will see, it is therefore an important cultural lever.

12.2.2 Comparison and Divination

Whether taken in its grammatical or technical form, interpretation knows two methods: the comparative and the divinatory, that of "immediate intuition and that of comparison with something else." Divination is more intuitive and focuses on what seems to escape any discursive approach. Comparison tries to relate the individual to the general, the detail to the whole. Both methods are at work in each of the aspects of interpretation, even if it seems that grammatical interpretation is more comparative, whereas technical interpretation would be more like using the divinatory method of putting oneself, as much as possible, in the author's place. But each is a condition of possibility for the other. Any comparison must have primary elements that serve as comparison terms. However, these stable elements must have been initially fixed immediately, otherwise an infinite regression would prevent us from conceiving any comparison.[64] Conversely, the comparative method must confirm what has been obtained by divination, which in its immediacy may only be an uncertain discovery or even be "fantastic."[65] For if divination as a method is immediate and provides what escapes comparison, it does not claim to immediately reach the truth: it is only a moment in a research process and "is only ensured by the comparison that confirms it."[66] Its immediacy does not therefore exclude it from the reconstructive process. Once again, contrary to the interpretations proposed by Gadamer, for example, nothing in this method is reduced to mere empathy. It is always the complementarity of the methods that makes Schleiermacher's theory strong.

12.2.3 The Positive Formula of Hermeneutics

This reciprocity is often called the "hermeneutic circle." It does not simply indicate the interdependence of methods (referring to the reciprocal action between the universal and the singular), but in a general way indicates that we understand the whole from the part and vice versa. This is a version of the hypothetical-deductive method applied to the interpretation of texts and grasping their meaning. When we interpret, we make a hypothesis about how to understand the whole and the part, the totality being put to the test in a movement

---

[63] *AV*, p. 633.
[64] *HK*, p. 157.
[65] *HK*, p. 158.
[66] *HK*, p. 158.

of reciprocal determination in confrontation with the text. Understanding is always subject to correction. Most of Schleiermacher's rules of interpretation are based on this double movement and on the principle that any understanding consists in setting a part in a whole, which requires the knowledge of the part, the whole, and the connection between the two. It is the latter that we really understand. The first task of interpretation is to develop a hypothesis about the total meaning, using for example a cursory reading, even if it means "going back" later, that is, revising the provisional preunderstanding. Reduced to this movement, the "hermeneutical circle" governs all levels of interpretation. In grammatical interpretation, we understand the word from the proposition, the proposition from the discourse, the discourse from the work, the work from the "field of literature to which it belongs" and vice versa.[67] In technical interpretation, the work as an act of an author is understood from the totality of its life, the latter from the total context of the time and vice versa. When all these levels of understanding coincide, the interpretation of the discourse is "correct."[68]

Schleiermacher summarizes this as follows: "Art can only develop its rules from a positive formula which is: To rebuild the given discourse in a historical and divinatory, objective and subjective way."[69] This formula is a positive way of producing understanding, rather than a negative version that reduces itself to avoiding mistakes. Indeed, we really understand only what we can produce and therefore, in the case of received speeches, reproduce. This is an echo of the Romantic poetics of the creative subject, which can be understood in reference to Kant, who stated that since truth cannot be established by an adequacy between knowledge and its object, since we always remain in representation, it must be produced, like in the mathematics. This will be repeated in the foundation of the human sciences, which posits that the mind only understands what it has created. From there, the epistemological paradigm of hermeneutics can be exported and extended to the sciences of mind, starting with the historical sciences as it was done from Dilthey. But let us go back to Schleiermacher's formula. "Objective" and "historical" understanding is the one that captures the discourse as the effect of a grammar, by discovering the traces of its historical constitution. To do this, it compares the singular discourse with the general structure of the language. "Objective" and "divinatory" understanding captures in the discourse the transformations or alterations that the language undergoes because of the subjects involved. "Subjective" and "historical" understanding interprets the discourse from the life of the discourse maker. As for the "subjective" and "divinatory" understanding, it takes into account the current and future effects that the "seminal decision" of the speaker produces and will produce. All these levels of understanding, from the most general structure to the most singular force, must coincide in the perfect interpretation that allows for a better understanding. Here too, Schleiermacher's theory was productive. Manfred Frank has used it to reconcile structuralism and hermeneutics, taking into account the structurality of texts, on the one hand, the "innovations of meaning of a conscious subjectivity," on the other. The complementary nature of the grammatical and psychological modes of interpretation allowed him to unite "the (neo-structuralistic) argument against the centrality of the subject" and a strong "theory of

---

[67] *HK*, p. 76.
[68] *AV*, p. 641.
[69] *HK*, p. 128.

the subject" in the contemporary context of the problem of understanding and meaning.[70] In particular, it makes it possible to put into perspective the theories that think they cannot take into account the author's intention, such as Gadamer in Germany or Jacques Derrida, Roland Barthes, or Michel Foucault in France, all of whom are opposed to the idea of a rational reconstruction of the intention or even announce the death of the author.

12.3 Understanding the Author Better than He Understands Himself

For Schleiermacher, the perfect task is to "understand an author better than he understood himself."[71] By orienting the effort to understand, this aim is part of the methodological process. It "regulates" the art of interpretation, for which it draws the ultimate goal. To understand the author better means to understand better the author's discourse, since the author is only an author in their discourse. It also consists not only in making conscious a personal unconsciousness, but also in clarifying more general historical and geographical determinations concerning language, society, culture, and so on. "Understanding better," then, calls for a reflective approach to meaning, which is the privilege of superior historical knowledge, of knowing an individual and a context that escapes the author because the author is entirely immersed in it. In this respect, "understanding better" is a philological precept, a goal on which the interpretation requiring reconstruction is based. The art of interpretation does not "restore" the author's thought but understands better because it reflexively surpasses it. In other words, it is because we actually understand less well that we need to understand better. An authentic hermeneutic cannot therefore be satisfied with Gadamer's well-known statement, "It is enough to say that we understand *differently, if we understand at all*."[72] For Gadamer, we always understand differently because there is no method that can guarantee understanding. Understanding is for the human being an existential dimension that receives truth through the language of tradition and applies it to the present situation without being able to pretend to overcome historical distance by a method or by empathy. While Schleiermacher certainly recognizes that understanding is in fact not knowledge, which is why the process of understanding is always described as an infinite approximation, he is not satisfied with simply noting that "we understand otherwise." Knowing that "to understand otherwise" is contrary to the very meaning of the verb "to understand," the "perfect understanding" remains the regulative aim of any effort to understand.

Beyond the technical meaning of reconstruction, the concept of "better understanding" also has a specific meaning in the context of the aesthetic criticism of early German Romanticism. There, to understand the discourse better than its author did means to complete the work by pursuing it in interpretation and critique according to the poietic dimension mentioned above and which joins reception and creation. In the interpretation,

---

[70] Manfred Frank, *Das individuelle Allgemeine. Textstrukturierung und Textinterpretation nach Schleiermacher* (Frankfurt am Main: Suhrkamp, 1985), pp. 247f.

[71] *HK*, pp. 39, 114.

[72] Gadamer, *Wahrheit und Methode*, p. 302.

which is productive and creative, potentially infinite, the work is enriched and approaches its achievement, the interpretation contributing to the determination of its meaning, which transcends the author. Then the work of understanding, which involves interpretations, again becomes infinite. In this second sense, the maxim inviting us to "understand a discourse better than its author himself understood it" is no longer a simple hermeneutical rule. It becomes an ethical imperative inviting readers to develop the mind, this time in the form of a passage from technical hermeneutics to philosophy.

12.4 Hermeneutics and Culture

The art of understanding and interpreting, which establishes a regular meaning, that is, builds the identity of representations, therefore plays a fundamental role in culture. We have seen that as an art, that is, a rigorous practice that starts from a non-understanding, interpretation makes it possible to identify the cognitive dimensions of the act of understanding according to its philological model. However, careful observation shows that since the rebirth of science and the occupation with interpretation, the more attached interpretation has been to its principles and the more it has contributed to intellectual development in every sense. This finds in Schleiermacher a striking example in the activity of translation, a particular case of interpretation that shows what is generally worthy of hermeneutics, namely that the mind "can only blossom and fully develop its own strength through contacts with what is foreign."[73] This is obviously, in the contemporary era of the globalization of exchanges and of multicultural and pluralistic societies, of great relevance. Dilthey, in following Schleiermacher, made it a central question: "How do we understand ... what is foreign?," he asked in his reflections on historical life.[74] More recently, Charles Taylor writes that answering this question is "the great challenge of this [the twenty-first] century, both for politics and for the social sciences."[75]

For Schleiermacher, the work of interpretation as art contributes to intellectual development and makes it possible to link the speculative and empirical. In other words, it is part of the history of the development of the mind in nature and promotes its deployment, which defines, according to Schleiermacher, ethics. For him, ethics is in fact the speculative discipline that explains how the mind is embedded in nature, which is empirically realized in history. Hermeneutics, which directs interpretation and achieves understanding, participates in such an ethical process by promoting the development of the mind, allowing the thinking mind to discover and understand itself.[76] For this to happen, we must focus on discourses, and hermeneutics depends on the interest we take in texts. This is an interest that only the search for a rigorous method of interpretation can bring. Schleiermacher names three interests that have led to the art of interpretation, to hermeneutics as a method, and

---

[73] *AV*, p. 92.
[74] Dilthey, *Gesammelte Schriften*, vol. VII, p. 225.
[75] Charles Taylor, "Understanding the Other: A Gadamerian View on Conceptual Schemes," in *Gadamer's Century: Essays in Honour of Hans-Georg Gadamer*, ed. Jeff Malpas et al. (Cambridge, MA: MIT Press, 2002), p. 279.
[76] *AV*, p. 621.

contributed to the development of the spirit: the historical interest, the aesthetic interest, and the speculative interest.[77] The interest is historical when the interpretation of texts allows us access to data, for example, to old knowledge about nature. This is, for humanity, the most general field of the art of interpretation. It is aesthetic when it is the taste or pleasure that invites us to develop interpretation, as is the case, for example, in the presence of works of antiquity. Finally, and this is undoubtedly the main thing, the interest can be speculative, that is, purely scientific or religious. Since thinking and speaking are coextensive, hermeneutics, by allowing us to understand foreign discourses, puts us in the presence of the mind, and both art and science are grounded in the highest levels of the human spirit.[78]

12.5 Conclusion

Schleiermacher said in his lectures, "Every moment in life has more or less strength to determine the future; and I don't completely understand a discourse when I don't understand its determining force for the future."[79] To be sure, Schleiermacher did not take the measure of the fecundity of his hermeneutic considerations only in the field of philology, but also in relation to the epistemology of the human sciences, in critical literary theory, and in philosophy. The history of the reception of Schleiermacher's hermeneutics thus illustrates in its own way the formula inviting readers to understand this author better than he understood himself.

Suggested Reading

Arndt, Andreas, and Jörg Dierken, eds. *Friedrich Schleiermachers Hermeneutik. Interpretationen und Perspektiven* (Berlin/Boston: De Gruyter, 2016).
Berner, Christian. *La Philosophie de Schleiermacher. Herméneutique–Dialectique–Ethique* (Paris: Cerf, 1995).
Scholtz, Gunter. *Ethik und Hermeneutik. Schleiermachers Grundlegung der Geisteswissenschaften* (Frankfurt am Main: Suhrkamp, 1995).

Bibliography

Austin, John Langshaw. *How to Do Things with Words* (Cambridge, MA: Harvard University Press, 1962).
Davidson, Donald. *Truth and Interpretation* (New York: Oxford University Press, 1984).
Dilthey, Wilhelm. *Gesammelte Schriften*, vols. V and VII (Göttingen: Vandenhoeck & Ruprecht, 1924).

---

[77] *HK*, p. 621.
[78] *HK*, p. 622.
[79] *HK*, p. 383.

Frank, Manfred. *Das individuelle Allgemeine. Textstrukturierung und Textinterpretation nach Schleiermacher* (Frankfurt am Main: Suhrkamp, 1985).

Gadamer, Hans-Georg. *Wahrheit und Methode*. In *Gesammelte Werke*, vol. 1 (Tübingen: Mohr Siebeck, 1999).

Habermas, Jürgen. *Auch eine Geschichte der Philosophie*, vol. 2 (Berlin: Suhrkamp, 2019).

Herder, Johann Gottfried. "*Verstand und Erfahrung*". *Eine Metakritik zur Kritik der reinen Vernunft*, in *Sprachphilosophie. Ausgewählte Schriften* (Hamburg: Meiner, 2005).

Nietzsche, Friedrich. *Kritische Studienausgabe*. Ed. G. Colli and M. Montinari (Berlin/New York: DTV/De Gruyter, 1988).

Ricœur, Paul. "Schleiermacher's Hermeneutics." *The Monist* 60, no. 2 (1977), pp. 181–197.

Szondi, Peter. *Einführung in die literarische Hermeneutik* (Frankfurt am Main: Suhrkamp, 1975).

Taylor, Charles. *Philosophical Papers*, 2 vols. (Cambridge: Cambridge University Press, 1985).

Taylor, Charles. "Understanding the Other: A Gadamerian View on Conceptual Schemes." In *Gadamer's Century: Essays in Honour of Hans-Georg Gadamer*. Ed. Jeff Malpas et al. (Cambridge, MA: MIT Press, 2002), pp. 279–297.

Wittgenstein, Ludwig. *Philosophische Untersuchungen* (Oxford: Basil Blackwell, 1958).

CHAPTER 13

PHILOSOPHY OF ART
With Special Regard to the Lectures on Aesthetics

HOLDEN KELM

13.1 INTRODUCTION

FRIEDRICH Schleiermacher's lifelong interest in art and culture was particularly focused on literature and music. Already in his youth, he read ancient classics like Homer, Hesiod, and Pindar, but also Goethe's *Werther* and Wieland's poems.[1] In his early Romantic period, he deepened his literary knowledge in a lasting way and he subsequently read authors such as Shakespeare, Schiller, Lessing, and Goethe's *Wahlverwandtschaften*.[2] During his time in Halle, he became friends with the composer Johann Friedrich Reichardt and his musically talented daughter Luise, and from 1808 he sang as a tenor in Zelter's *Singakademie* in Berlin. Between 1808 and 1834 Schleiermacher followed the cultural developments in his adopted home of Berlin, which included opera performances, the architectural works of Friedrich Schinkel, and visual art exhibitions held by the Academy of Arts.

Already during his student days in Halle, Schleiermacher occasionally dealt with the aesthetic problems of the late Enlightenment and "Empfindsamkeit" (sensitivity). In his essay *On the Naïve* (1789), he examined Moses Mendelssohn's writing *On the Sublime and Naïve in the Fine Sciences* (1771) and criticized his conception of the naïve character as indecisive, because it did not conclusively combine the general and individual characteristics of the naïve.[3] In his treatise *On Style* (1790/1791), Schleiermacher discussed the way in which language communicates feelings and thoughts in stylistic terms. He assumed that the communication

---

[1] Kurt Nowak, *Schleiermacher. Leben, Werk und Wirkung* (Göttingen: Vandenhoeck & Ruprecht, 2001), pp. 24–28.

[2] Wolfgang Virmond, "Schleiermachers Lektüre nach Auskunft seiner Tagebücher," in *Schleiermacher und die wissenschaftliche Kultur des Christentums*, ed. Günter Meckenstock (Berlin/New York: De Gruyter, 1991), pp. 74–76.

[3] Friedrich Daniel Ernst Schleiermacher, "Über das Naive," in *KGA* 1.1 ed. Günter Meckenstock (Berlin: De Gruyter, 1983), pp. 177–187.

of sensations is not possible directly, but only indirectly by means of natural, essential, and arbitrary signs. He concluded that the representations of the fine arts (*schöne Künste*) are also based on these types of signs.[4] Accordingly, Schleiermacher distinguished between an imitative (*mimisch*) and musical style (natural signs), a style in the visual arts (essential signs), and a linguistic style in rhetoric and poetry (arbitrary signs). In doing so, he referred back to the semiotic approach to the classification of arts, which his philosophical teacher in Halle, Johann August Eberhard, set out in his *Theory of Fine Sciences* (1786).[5] However, these scattered statements about art were made without detailed knowledge of Kant's *Critique of Judgment*, which Schleiermacher is not likely to have read until 1792 during his time as a private teacher in Schlobitten.[6]

After his move to Berlin in 1796, Schleiermacher became friends with Friedrich Schlegel and took part in the journal *Athenaeum*. In his *Vertraute Briefe* (1800) Schleiermacher met the numerous criticisms of Schlegel's novel *Lucinde* (1799) with a strong response, defending the early Romantic belief in the liveliness of poetry, and enthusiasm for reason and sociability. In his first monograph, *On Religion* (1799), Schleiermacher formulated a concept of "art as religion" (*Kunstreligion*), in which he connected art and religion as two "friendly souls" with "inner kinship" and equal sources of the "intuition of the infinite."[7] This connection led to the reproach, still circulating today, that Schleiermacher aestheticized religion.[8]

Schleiermacher's intention to follow in the footsteps of his early Romantic friends is evidenced by the poetic experiments he undertook, especially during his time in Stolp. However, apart from the poetic qualities of his early Romantic writings, Schleiermacher's plans did not go beyond a few poems, a draft novel, and later regularly written poetic riddles (*Charaden*).[9] Schleiermacher's connection with the composer Reichardt and his family in Giebichenstein near Halle was commemorated in the *Weihnachtsfeier* (1806), in which he made detailed reflections on works of early Romantic aesthetics.[10]

As a professor at the University of Halle and the University of Berlin, Schleiermacher successively developed a systematics of philosophical disciplines, in which aesthetics is conceived as a critical discipline of ethics. Schleiermacher gave his *Lectures on Aesthetics* in the semesters 1819, 1825, and 1832/1833, making aesthetics, after psychology (1818) and pedagogy (1813), the last philosophical discipline for which he developed a complete lecture series. In these lectures, Schleiermacher developed an approach to aesthetic productivity that differs from formal aesthetic approaches, such as Kant's *Critique of Judgement*,

---

[4] Friedrich Daniel Ernst Schleiermacher, "Über den Stil," in *KGA* 1.1, p. 365.

[5] Johann August Eberhard, *Theorie der schönen Wissenschaften* (Halle: Buchhandlung des Waisenhauses, 1786), pp. 5, 13.

[6] Cf. letter from Carl Duisburg to Schleiermacher, from December 4, 1792. *Brief* no. 204. In *KGA* 5.1, p. 274.

[7] *Reden¹*, p. 263.

[8] Cf. Ernst Müller, *Ästhetische Religiosität und Kunstreligion in den Philosophien von der Aufklärung bis zum Ausgang des deutschen Idealismus* (Berlin/New York: De Gruyter, 2004).

[9] Cf. Hermann Patsch, *Alle Menschen sind Künstler. Friedrich Schleiermachers poetische Versuche* (Berlin: De Gruyter, 1986).

[10] E.g. Reichardt's setting of the "Christmas Cantilena" by Matthias Claudius (1784), A. W. Schlegel's poem "Der Bund der Kirche mit den Künsten" (1800), and Novalis' sacred song "Wo bleibst du Trost der ganzen Welt" (1802). *WFG*, pp. 49–50, 59, 78–79. Cf. Gunter Scholtz, *Schleiermachers Musikphilosophie* (Göttingen: Vandenhoeck & Ruprecht, 1981), pp. 26, 37, 138.

by focusing less on the conditions of the reception of (beautiful) objects than on their production and their symbolic quality, based on human and especially artistic practice. In this respect, Schleiermacher's aesthetics represents an original position in classical German aesthetics.

Finally, Schleiermacher wrote his three treatises "On the Scope of the Concept of Art in Relation to the Theory of Art" (1831–1833). He presented two of these at the Prussian Academy of Sciences, while the third remained incomplete.[11] In these treatises, he focuses primarily on the conceptual foundations of his aesthetic theory, defining art as a mental activity similar to cognition. It is thereby self-referential and based not on general but individual knowledge. The formula, which Schleiermacher developed in the third treatise, that "all artistic activity is only self-manifestation" (of the artist), contains in a condensed manner the anthropological, psychological, and epistemological dimensions of his philosophy of art.[12]

Starting from this biographically founded sketch of Schleiermacher's engagement with art, aesthetics, and art theory, this chapter discusses his *Lectures on Aesthetics* in more detail. To consider the general sense of art in Schleiermacher's thinking, it begins with an overview of the meaning of art in his philosophical systematics. The content and development of his 1819, 1825, and 1832/1833 lectures will then be discussed from a historical-critical perspective. This presentation will be followed by an interpretation of Schleiermacher's late theory of poetry, with respect to the systematic position of poetry as the "art of the arts." Finally, Schleiermacher's philosophical-historical view of aesthetics will be examined, to discuss how he places himself in the field of classical German aesthetics.

13.2 THE MEANING OF ART IN SCHLEIERMACHER'S PHILOSOPHICAL SYSTEMATICS

Schleiermacher's aesthetics is of particular interest not only with regard to his engagement with art, poetry, and music, but also with regard to his philosophical systematics. Schleiermacher first reformulated the dynamic relationship between art and religion, originally presented in the *Speeches*, in his Halle *Brouillon zur Ethik* (1805/1806). As is well known, Schleiermacher connected and identified feeling with religion, which in his ethics means not only the religiosity of the individual but also the religiosity diffused in a community. In the context of ethical activities, art is determined as an "individual symbolization" that has the task of representing feeling, and in this respect "all humans are artists."[13] After Schleiermacher, feeling contains the fundamental relationship of the individual to the absolute. He condensed this, in his main theological work *The Christian Faith* (1821–1822), into the formula "the feeling of absolute dependence."[14] If feeling, and with it religiosity, is the

---

[11] Schleiermacher's three treatises "Über den Umfang des Begriffs der Kunst in Bezug auf die Theorie derselben" were first published in 1835 by Ludwig Jonas, in: *SW III/3*, pp. 179–224 (*AV*, pp. 725–742, 769–786, 787–794).
[12] *AV*, p. 792.
[13] *WA* Band 2, p. 184.
[14] *CG¹*, pp. 31–38.

essential component of a "mood" (*Stimmung*), as in Schleiermacher's *Lectures of Aesthetics*, and if the "organic expression of the mood" is artwork, then religiosity is also an important element of the artistic practice through which artwork is produced. Thus, art and religion are interwoven as individual forms of interpretation and representation of the relationship between the (artistic) subject and the absolute. In this respect, Schleiermacher could claim that "the true practice of art is religious."[15]

In his lecture manuscript on philosophical ethics (1812/1813), Schleiermacher concretized the relationship between art and religion: "If, accordingly, the forming of imagination in and with its emergence is art, and the rational content in peculiar knowledge is religion, then art relates to religion as language relates to knowledge."[16] As "language of religion," the ethical significance of art lies primary in its communicative function: Inasmuch as feeling cannot be communicated directly, art resembles an indirect, nonverbal communication. This means that artistic expressions can be received and understood by other individuals and also could become the trigger for new ones. Artistic expressions can thus be explained as a kind of social interaction that, as nonverbal (imitative and gestural) forms of communication, takes on an important function in the formation of a particular culture. In its general meaning, art appears as a representation of community life in its intersubjective activity, as a *symbol of sociability*, but at the same time as an individual force co-constituting and co-creating the ethical and cultural development, as a *practice of symbolizing*.

With regard to his theological systematics, it is obvious that Schleiermacher's lectures on practical theology and his lectures on Christian ethics also contain elements of art theory and references to art as a form of realization of the individual within a cultural community. Although Schleiermacher varied the position of the three types of action in his lectures on Christian ethics, art remained an essential component of "representing action" (*darstellendes Handeln*). Already in his lectures of 1809/1810, he stated, "All art in the higher sense is representation and proceeds directly from a feeling which is not posited as pleasure or displeasure. All art in the larger sense is always connected with religion. All worship (*Cultus*) seeks to form itself into art."[17]

Schleiermacher's development of dialectic from 1811 onwards gave ethics and aesthetics a new theoretical foundation. Although in ethics the philosophical search for truth as a general symbolization is opposed to the individual symbolization of art, philosophizing is not completely detached from artistic creation. Philosophizing shares with artistic creation not only the symbolizing relationship to nature as an activity of reason, but also the intellectual way of producing symbolic phenomena. Accordingly, in the dialectic lecture of 1811, Schleiermacher wrote, "Philosophizing is art because the application of the rules is not brought back under rules. It depends on one's attitude [*Gesinnung*] and talent."[18] According to Schleiermacher, artistic and philosophical creation could not be reduced to mechanical activities, nor could it be founded ultimately by a rational deduction. Rather, artistic and philosophical creation is the result of the peculiar way in which an individual realizes the original forms of reason in

---

[15] WA Band 2, p. 100. Cf. Anne Käfer, *"Die wahre Ausübung der Kunst ist religiös". Schleiermachers Ästhetik im Kontext der zeitgenössischen Entwürfe Kants, Schillers und Friedrich Schlegels* (Tübingen: Mohr Siebeck, 2006).
[16] *Ethik (Birkner)*, pp. 74–75, §228.
[17] *SW* I/12, supplement A, p. 29, §89.
[18] *Dial.*, p. 62.

confrontation with his life-world, because this confrontation shapes his mental activities—both imagination and reason—and his symbolic manifestations.

In addition to ethics and dialectic, Schleiermacher's psychology, developed from 1818 onwards, contains some concepts that are connected with his aesthetics in several respects, especially with regard to aesthetic feeling, an enthusiastic mood, the reflexive act of "Besinnung" (reflection), and dreaming.[19] Schleiermacher also made fundamental statements in his psychology lecture of 1818 about the difference between an everyday representation in accordance with art and a genuine artwork: "But we only call the expression art when a preconception of art in consciousness enters between the feeling and the expression."[20] While an individual in passionate states of desire or unwillingness expresses his feelings directly and can occasionally be artistic in these expressions, these expressions are nevertheless not artistic in the strict sense, because they are not caused by a reflexive act that Schleiermacher called in his aesthetics "Besinnung." This raises the question of exactly how the more general ethical and the more specific aesthetic sense of art is to be understood in Schleiermacher.

13.3 Schleiermacher's *Lectures on Aesthetics*

Unlike the precursors of aesthetic theory in classical German philosophy, like Schelling and K. W. F. Solger, Schleiermacher developed a philosophy of art that has its theoretical premises in ethics. On this ethical basis, art is defined as a symbolizing practice of the individual (artist), which on the one hand is involved in sociocultural developments, but on the other hand intends an emancipation from its external conditions by reflecting on them with the means of imagination (as individual reason) and thus emerges as a free productivity. According to Schleiermacher, aesthetic sensitivity, aesthetic feelings, and a judgement of taste are based on this productivity: art production and art reception are only different in degree, and are not mutually exclusive opposites.[21] In this productive-aesthetic approach lies the intrinsic significance of Schleiermacher's theory of art in the context of classical German aesthetics.

However, Schleiermacher gave his lectures at a time when aesthetics was only gradually establishing itself as a philosophical discipline and there was no generally accepted standard regarding its fundamentals. Schleiermacher's lectures are therefore an important component in the development of aesthetics as a philosophical discipline, especially with regard to the teaching of aesthetics at the philosophical institute of the Berlin University between 1811 and 1834. Here it was first Solger who gave six lectures on aesthetics or philosophical art theory from 1811 to 1819, in which he related classicist, early Romantic, and speculative motifs to one another.[22] After the unexpected death of Solger in 1819, Schleiermacher gave his lectures

---

[19] Cf. Thomas Lehnerer, *Die Kunsttheorie Friedrich Schleiermachers* (Stuttgart: Klett-Cotta, 1987), pp. 114–152.
[20] *Psychologie*, p. 89.
[21] Cf. *Ästhetik (Kelm)*, p. 39.
[22] Cf. Giovanna Pinna, "Einleitung," in K. W. F. Solger, *Vorlesungen über Ästhetik*, ed. Giovanna Pinna (Hamburg: Meiner, 2017), pp. xxvii–xxviii.

alternately with Georg Wilhelm Friedrich Hegel, who lectured on the philosophy of art four times in Berlin between 1820 and 1829.[23]

Similar to Hegel, Schleiermacher's philosophical work has come down to us almost exclusively in the form of lectures (with the exception of his early Romantic writings and the *Akademievorträge*). Of these lectures, a few lecture manuscripts by Schleiermacher and a number of transcripts by his listeners have been preserved, some of which have been published in posthumous editions. In contrast to the works published during his lifetime, these lectures pose a special task for interpretation, which not least concerns the *unity of the work* and the *question of the author*. Schleiermacher did not leave behind any coherent writing on aesthetics that could be considered a monograph. Rather, the situation of Schleiermacher's lecture manuscripts on aesthetics presents itself in a such a way that an uncompleted and very densely written manuscript on his 1819 lecture (*Kollegheft Ästhetik 1819*) is accompanied by a series of notes and marginalia, some of which were written at different times and in different contexts; in addition, the lectures of 1825 and 1832 are most extensively preserved in some (student) transcripts, which suggests that the textual explanations and notes from Schleiermacher's hand represent only a fraction of what he actually presented in his lectures.[24] This confirms the well-known view of Schleiermacher as a brilliant rhetorician, who often delivered his lectures (and sermons) freely, on the basis of only a few notes. Transcripts of lectures are therefore of special interest, but they appear to be a hybrid genre in terms of their authorship—an authorship that is distributed between Schleiermacher, who gave his lecture orally, and his different listeners who recorded it in writing.

Schleiermacher's lectures on aesthetics thus appear as a discourse handed down in different types of texts, which discuss, among other things, positions on the aesthetics of Kant, Schiller, Schelling, and Hegel. Schleiermacher intervened in the aesthetic discourse of his time especially with regard to the following five topics: (1) the actual significance of Kant's *Critique of Judgement* for aesthetic theory; (2) the concept of fine art as an imitation (mimesis) of the beauty of nature; (3) aesthetics as a philosophical science based on a concept of the unity of arts; (4) art as a reflexive and symbolizing activity of the individual; and (5) the historicity of art with special regard to the relationship between modern and ancient art.

13.3.1 The Lecture of 1819

In a letter to Joachim Christian Gaß at the turn of the year 1816/1817, Schleiermacher justified his first considerations about giving a lecture on aesthetics by a deficiency in his philosophical-theological systematics: "But unfortunately, I still lack whole disciplines that I cannot access, Introduction to the New Testament, psychology, aesthetics. I am still

---

[23] Cf. Walter Jaeschke, *Hegel-Handbuch. Leben–Werk–Wirkung* (Stuttgart: Metzler, 2016), p. 413.

[24] The material of Schleiermacher's *Lectures on Aesthetics*, preserved in various states, is divided as follows: A. Schleiermacher's manuscripts: 1. Notes on Aesthetics I, 2. Notes on Aesthetics II, 3. Kollegheft Ästhetik 1819, 4. Marginalia for the lecture of 1832/1833. B. Transcripts: 1819: Bluhme (fragment), Wigand (few extracts); 1825: Bindemann, Trendelenburg, Braune (few extracts), Anonymous (fragment); 1832/1833: Schweizer, Henke (fragment), Stern (fragment), Erbkam (few extracts), George (few extracts). Cf. *Ästhetik (Kelm)*, pp. l–lxxiv. These lectures will be published as digital scholarly edition on *Schleiermacher Digital* (https://schleiermacher-digital.de/).

very far from that."²⁵ A good two years later, in January 1819, Schleiermacher announced to his colleague, Immanuel Bekker, his first lecture of aesthetics for the summer semester of 1819.²⁶ However, his own unfinished scientific projects kept him very busy, especially the writing of his planned ethics and *The Christian Faith*, so he had little time for preparation. Nevertheless, on April 19, 1819, Schleiermacher began to give his first lecture.²⁷ The reason why Schleiermacher succeeded in developing an independent and conclusive conception of aesthetics can be attributed primarily to the fact that he already had a broad fund of systematically executed concepts on the philosophy of art, which he had sketched in particular in his lectures on philosophical ethics and psychology.

In Schleiermacher's lecture manuscript (*Kollegheft 1819*), after a short introduction, two main parts follow: (1) a general speculative part, in which Schleiermacher describes the concept of art and derives from it the classification of the particular arts, and (2) a special part, which contains the cycle of the particular arts. In the general part, aesthetics is derived from the principles of ethics, according to which the practice of art is an individual activity (similar to recognition), which has its basis in feeling. Insofar as feeling only enters into the production of art by means of reflection (*Besinnung*), Schleiermacher has to search for a new term and finds it in "mood," which he describes here as an "average of captured moments of affection," which also has an effect on the "free play of imagination."²⁸ He therefore assumes that the artistic representation contains "measure and change," which points to an inner type or "archetype" (*Urbild*) of the work of art that precedes its concrete shape. In this mental act the artistic subject creates a prototype of the artwork and in doing so reflects on an archetype, which has a general character: "So here art is the identity of enthusiasm, by virtue of which the expression arises from inner excitement, and deliberation, by virtue of which it arises from the archetype."²⁹ According to Schleiermacher, the external representation of the internally preformed artwork is based on the talent of the artistic subject, but it is still a rather mechanical work and therefore borders on the activities of organization (*organisierende Tätigkeiten*). Thus, the three essential moments of artistic activity are the enthusiastic mood (*begeisterte Stimmung*), the inner primal formation (*Urbildung*), and the external representation (*äußere Darstellung*). When a work of art emerges from this artistic activity, it also has a communicative and symbolic meaning for the recipients, which lies both in the productive mood and in the primal formation of the artist, who in a sense manifests himself in his work of art. Finally, such an artwork can be considered beautiful for Schleiermacher when the relations of its form contain a combination of elementary and organic completeness and appears as a "flawless existence" (*mangelloses Dasein*) that corresponds to the "ideal."³⁰

---

[25] Wilhelm Gaß, ed., *Fr. Schleiermacher's Briefwechsel mit J. Chr. Gaß: mit einer biographischen Vorrede* (Berlin: Reimer, 1852), p. 128.
[26] Heinrich Meisner, ed., *Briefwechsel Friedrich Schleiermachers mit August Boeckh und Immanuel Bekker* (Berlin: Litteraturarchiv-Gesellschaft, 1916), p. 102.
[27] Cf. Wolfgang Virmond, ed., *Die Vorlesungen der Berliner Universität 1810–1834* (Berlin: De Gruyter, 2011), p. 191. Schleiermacher presented the lecture in five weekly hours until August 7; 108 students were registered.
[28] *Ästhetik (Kelm)*, p. 54. Cf. Peter Grove, "Der Grundton aller unserer Gefühle. Schleiermachers Begriff der Stimmung," in *Der Mensch und seine Seele. Bildung-Frömmigkeit-Ästhetik*, ed. Arnulf von Scheliha and Jörg Dierken (Berlin: De Gruyter, 2017), pp. 533–552.
[29] *Ästhetik (Kelm)*, p. 47.
[30] *Ästhetik (Kelm)*, p. 71.

To define art speculatively as the "organic becoming of the mood" (*organisch werden der Stimmung*) and "free human production," which originates from a single source, finally enabled Schleiermacher to explain the particular arts uniformly: "Enthusiasm, however, is nothing other than the excitation of free production through mood. Thus, it is also in itself the same in all the arts, the becoming of the particular art itself, which is renewed each time, out of the general art drive [*Kunsttrieb*]."[31]

Schleiermacher apparently borrowed the term "art drive" here from the field of natural philosophy, where this term appears, for example, in the writings of Gottfried Reinhold Treviranus, Henrich Steffens, and Schelling, and is used for the instinctive and creative behavior of insects, such as bees or spiders and the combs or webs they produce.[32] According to Schleiermacher's transfer of this idea to art theory, the "art drive" refers to human beings' adaptability to their environment and the striving for perfection in their activities—practical or theoretical works can thus also be called beautiful as soon as they approach the ideal. With this turn of phrase, Schleiermacher's view that art is a formative and productive force similar to nature, which he received not least in Schelling's speech "On the Relation of the Visual Arts to Nature" (1807), is fulfilled to a certain extent.[33]

The speculative dimension of the "art drive" thus enabled Schleiermacher to trace the various fields of art back to a common principle. He developed the relationship of the particular arts to each other according to the direction of the art drive towards the enthusiastic mood of the artist (and with it to the organs by means of which an artwork can be produced and received). Accordingly, the specific enthusiasm for bodily movements and musical sounds is the beginning of the (subjective) arts of imitation (*Mimik*) and music, and the enthusiasm for regular or organic forms in the medium of inorganic matter is the beginning of the (objective) arts of architecture and sculpture. From this point, Schleiermacher divided the particular arts into three divisions. The first is the accompanying arts (*begleitende Künste*), including imitation (*Mimik*) and music. The second is the visual arts (*bildende Künste*), including architecture and sculpture. Since the *Kollegheft 1819* breaks off in the treatment of sculpture, the further course can only be concluded from later manuscripts. The transcripts of the lecture of 1825 clarify that the visual arts conclude with painting. And finally, the third division is the speaking arts (*redende Künste*), including poetry, in which the subjective and objective aspects of the first two departments are integrated. Schleiermacher finally finds an internal subdivision, which runs through all fields of art, in the difference between religious and sociable (*gesellig*) style and in the historical difference between antiquity and modernity.

---

[31] *Ästhetik (Kelm)*, pp. 68–69.

[32] Cf. Henrich Steffens, *Grundzüge der philosophischen Naturwissenschaft* (Berlin: Verlag der Realschulbuchhandlung, 1806), pp. 78–80, and Gottfried Reinhold Treviranus, *Biologie oder Philosophie der lebenden Natur für Naturforscher und Ärzte*, vol. 1 (Göttingen: bey Johann Friedrich Röwer, 1802), pp. 369–370.

[33] Friedrich Wilhelm Joseph Schelling, "Über das Verhältnis der bildenden Künste zu der Natur," in *Philosophische Schriften*, vol. 1 (Landshut: bei Philipp Krüll, 1809), p. 345. Cf. *Ästhetik (Kelm)*, p. 5.

13.3.2 The Lectures of 1825 and 1832/1833

Before beginning his second lecture on aesthetics, Schleiermacher deepened his knowledge of the arts, following his interest in music and continuing his singing lessons in the choir of the Berlin *Singakademie*. He also attended opera performances such as Weber's *Freischütz* (July 25, 1821), Gluck's *Iphigenie in Aulis* (February 11, 1822 and January 27, 1823), and Graun's *Der Tod Jesu* (March 28, 1823 and April 16, 1824).[34]

Schleiermacher's second lecture on aesthetics was then announced in the Berlin University lecture schedule for the summer semester of 1825.[35] The philosophical and theological projects with which he was busy during this period, mainly the revision of his *The Christian Faith* (1821/1822) and the ongoing work on his planned ethics, may have contributed to the fact that Schleiermacher presented his aesthetics in this semester without major changes from the 1819 lecture.[36]

Schleiermacher continued to develop his connoisseurship of art in the seven years following his second lecture. On March 11, 1829, together with prominent guests of the Prussian court as well as Carl Friedrich Zelter and Hegel, he experienced the revival of Bach's *St Matthew Passion*, arranged by Felix Mendelssohn Bartholdy, at the Berlin *Singakademie*. Schleiermacher also followed the construction of Berlin's neoclassical *Altes Museum*, designed by Friedrich Schinkel and opened in 1830. In 1832, he attended the 27th Art Exhibition of the Royal Academy of Arts. Finally, in 1831 and 1832, Schleiermacher presented his treatise "On the Scope of the Concept of Art" at the Prussian Academy of Sciences.

Schleiermacher gave his last lectures in the winter semester of 1832/1833.[37] The lecture manuscript (*Kollegheft 1819*) contains extensive marginalia for these lectures, which contain additional thoughts, schematizations, and some terminological changes and conceptual shifts in comparison to the 1819 and 1825 lectures. While Schleiermacher retained the basic three-part division of the lectures, he substantially expanded the historical introduction by a short history of aesthetics with regard to Kant, Schiller, Fichte, Schelling, and Hegel. As an important change in the general part can be mentioned the introduction of the term "immediate self-consciousness" (*unmittelbares Selbstbewusstsein*), which was now largely used synonymously with the term "mood" and thus referred in some respects to the conception of self-consciousness in *The Christian Faith*.[38] In addition, the ethical concept of "total consciousness" (*Gesamtbewusstsein*) replaced the term "art drive" as the general motivating ground of artistic practice. The development of the three moments of artistic practice was thereby examined less in a natural philosophical framework than in a sociocultural one—a terminological change that can be seen as a further consequence of the ethical foundation of art production. Finally, the arrangement of the visual arts changed slightly: the "garden art"

---

[34] Cf. *TK*.

[35] Cf. Wolfgang Virmond, ed., *Die Vorlesungen der Berliner Universität 1810–1834* (Berlin: De Gruyter, 2011), p. 383: "Aesthetics is presented by Prof. Schleiermacher five times a week from 6–7 a.m." The lectures ran from April 11 to September 9, 1825; eighty-one students were registered.

[36] Accordingly, there are only a few marginalia in the *Kollegheft* 1819 that can be clearly dated to the year 1825.

[37] Cf. Virmond, *Vorlesungen*, p. 712. Schleiermacher held the lectures five times a week from 7–8 a.m. from October 23, 1832 to March 29, 1833; seventy-one students were registered.

[38] CG^1, p. 26.

(mentioned in 1819 and 1825 only in the chapter on "architecture") was treated in 1832/1833 as an independent art form between "architecture" and "painting."

13.4 Schleiermacher's Theory of Poetry

In his aesthetic systematics, poetry is the last of the particular arts, and as such it has for Schleiermacher the function of interweaving the subjective and objective genres by containing both the moments arising from the enthusiastic mood and the determinations conveyed by the imagination (images and thoughts). Schleiermacher is not exceptional for this high esteem for poetry: In their lectures on the philosophy or art, Schelling, Solger, and Hegel also represent poetry as the highest and most complete art form.[39]

From a systematic point of view, Schleiermacher defined poetic art in contrast to and in connection with philosophical thinking: "All poetic art is activity in language."[40] Unlike philosophy, poetry is not about logical operations that allow *general* descriptions of reality, but rather about unique symbolic productions of the *individual*. As such, poetic language, as a result of the enthusiastic mood, originally arises in the practicing poet as an "inner speaking." Only when the poetic conception is internally complete does the poet express it, either in written or oral form.

According to Schleiermacher, the tonality of poetry based on the human voice is to be understood analogously to the tonality of music; in linguistic utterance there are high and low notes, rhythm, and melody. In music, however, the tones appear as measured, and in poetic language as unmeasured. The musical element of poetry therefore lies in a kind of "euphony" that moves beyond the "measuredness" (*Gemessenheit*) of musical tonality: "Poetry is the freely acquired productivity in relation to the musical element of language. Language should emerge in poetry as a totality of euphony [*Wohlklang*]."[41] But the musicality of poetry is determined not only by the euphony, but also by the rhythm of the poetic work, the meter. Schleiermacher therefore examined the metrical rules with which he had already dealt in his early Romantic phase. In this discussion Schleiermacher clarified in a general manner that poetic tonality can only be perceived if it is connected with words or linguistic content. This, in turn, brings poetry closer to thinking, which is for Schleiermacher essentially dependent on language.

But what is this individual (*Einzelne*) that poetry, as opposed to philosophy, is supposed to be able to describe? According to Schleiermacher, it is first of all something different from the imitation of nature. A poetic work about a person differs from a naturalistic description of this person, because poetry is more an invention of the poet than an imitation of reality. A poetic invention, Schleiermacher suggested, resembles more a symbolic representation or an image and differs therefore as well from philosophical deduction, because poetry is less concerned with general terms than with concrete representations of something (i.e. the peculiarity of a person). As we read in the Schweizer transcript, "The more the poet compels

---

[39] Because Schleiermacher's treatment of poetry is detailed in the transcript of Schweizer (1832/1833), the following reconstruction is largely based on this text.

[40] *Ästhetik (Kelm)*, p. 877.

[41] *Ästhetik (Kelm)*, p. 879.

and enables me to form a complete picture of the person, the more complete is his representation to me."[42] The individual negotiated by poetry is thus a linguistic and symbolic construct which, like a picture, must be determined in its elements throughout. According to Schleiermacher, this poetic construct should result in a complete whole in the imagination of the recipient, which—although it is fiction—could just as well be real. Thus, if the specific symbolic content of a poetic work cannot be defined in general terms, the understandability (*Verständlichkeit*) of a poetic work is something that language can only produce indirectly. Schleiermacher assumed that the continuous, frequent changing and altering movements of a mood (which are actually the element of music), could only be "captured" in the symbolic medium of language because of its creative mastery by the poet. Poetry thus enables the talented poet, in a general medium that fixes content by words and puts it in a fixed order, to symbolically represent something as changeable as the mood. This allows poetry to find an understanding perception in the recipients. By doubting the determinability of the individual by philosophy, however, Schleiermacher adopted a skeptical position that can be traced back to his general skepticism towards philosophical systems in which the final ground of human knowledge is regarded as accessible to philosophical reflection and not as a pre-reflective instance.[43]

In addition to these systematic discussions, Schleiermacher examined the division of literary genres into epic, dramatic, and lyrical poetry, which had been established at the "Goethezeit," by showing that this division presupposes the study of ancient mythology and languages, and therefore cannot be easily transferred to modern poetry and languages. Against the background of ancient epic poetry, Schleiermacher pointed out that the mythological and linguistic basis of ancient epics had changed with Christianity and the emergence of modern national languages. This is why epic genres like the novel could no longer have such a commonly known basis as Homer's *Iliad* or *Odyssey*. On the other hand, modern epic poems such as Klopstock's *Messiah* would build on ancient epic poetry, attempting to transpose its means into modern language. In modern drama, according to Schleiermacher, the division of labor had changed fundamentally: Whereas in ancient times the poet and the director of a drama were often one and the same person, in modern drama poets are only very rarely involved in the conception of the performance of their work. Finally, Schleiermacher addressed modern lyric poetry, noting that the metrical rules were partially overcome by poets such as Goethe, Schiller, and Klopstock.[44]

Schleiermacher's theory of poetry thus contains a thoroughly critical view of modern poetry, especially with regard to the lack of a commonly known mythology, which Christianity is apparently no longer able to provide. It is remarkable that Schleiermacher did not recapitulate the early Romantic demand for a "new mythology" at this point—he did not mention early Romantic aesthetics at all, nor anywhere else in his later writings on aesthetics—but left it at this critical juncture. His theory of poetry thus gives the impression of a philologically advanced, aesthetically classicist, and ethically oriented conception of literature.

---

[42] *Ästhetik (Kelm)*, p. 881.
[43] Cf. Andreas Arndt, "Unmittelbarkeit als Reflexion. Voraussetzungen der Dialektik Friedrich Schleiermachers," in *Schleiermacher als Philosoph* (Berlin/Boston: De Gruyter, 2013), pp. 198–212.
[44] *Ästhetik (Kelm)*, p. 889.

13.5 Schleiermacher's Sketch of a History of Aesthetics

Schleiermacher's introductions to his lectures address mainly the history of aesthetics. He discussed both the beginnings of artistic reflection with Plato and Aristotle, and the more recent developments in this discipline since Baumgarten and Kant. In the lecture of 1832/1833, Schleiermacher expanded this introduction extensively, beginning the history of aesthetics with Plato's remarks on the distinction between producing and imitating arts in the *Politeia* and the concept of mimesis in the *Poetics* of Aristotle. The more recent history of aesthetics is examined based on the "scholastic philosophy" of Leibniz and Wolff, the art theory of the Enlightenment, "Empfindsamkeit," and the concept of aesthetic autonomy. In his marginal notes to the lecture of 1832/1833, as well as in the corresponding passages of the preserved Schweizer transcript, Schleiermacher developed a theory of the "three advancements of aesthetics" in relation to the most recent history, in which he traced the most important positions in the genesis of his own productive-aesthetic approach.

The "first advancement" is attributed to Kantian aesthetics, whose outstanding characteristic for Schleiermacher was that it established art as a "purposiveness without purpose" and as a "means of connection" between theoretical and practical reason."[45] Kant's *Critique of Judgement*, for Schleiermacher, represents the paradigm of a passive or "pathematic" (*pathematisch*) conception of art that amounts to the psychological effects of beautiful objects and the formal categories of their judgement. Schleiermacher criticized and reversed this perspective by considering the relation between productivity and passivity as a reciprocal relation, so that he could state in his lecture manuscript (*Kollegheft 1819*) that "taste judgement" is already a "dark approach to production."[46] This perspective is based on the grounding of artistic receptivity and free productivity in the spontaneity of the human mind (imagination). Finally, Schleiermacher criticized Kant's analogy of the beautiful and the sublime as not adequate with respect to the opposition of nature and freedom. However, Schleiermacher largely shared the high value that Kant gives to aesthetics (and sensuality) as a connecting link between theoretical and practical reason.

Along with Kant, Schleiermacher also counted Schiller's aesthetics with the distinction of the "naïve and sentimental" to his "first advancement." Schiller was here portrayed as a pioneer of the productive-aesthetic approach on account of his concept of art as "free play": "As a poet, he had a special job in this respect and his speculative nature had to ask about the reason for productivity in this area, and that was the turning point for aesthetics."[47] Schleiermacher referred here to Schiller's letters *On the Aesthetic Education on Man* (1795) as well as to the treatise *On Naïve and Sentimental Poetry* (1795). With regard to Schiller's distinction between naïve and sentimental poetry and its application to ancient and modern art, Schleiermacher criticized Schiller for failing to define the common ground of this contrast more precisely.

---

[45] *Ästhetik (Kelm)*, p. 133.
[46] *Ästhetik (Kelm)*, p. 39.
[47] *Ästhetik (Kelm)*, p. 543.

In the sketch of 1832/1833, Schleiermacher attributed the "second advancement" of aesthetics to Fichte's positioning of art as a profession and means of education. After Schleiermacher, Fichte modified the Kantian approach in such a way that his investigation also focuses on the productive approach of art, even though this is only marginally discussed in the *System of Ethics* (1798), to which Schleiermacher mainly referred. The profession of the aesthetic artist is there given a relatively high status and its ethical significance is examined, which would mean progress in the theory of art. At the same time, however, art in Fichte's theory tends to abolish itself, because the treasury of art, as a quantum necessary for the formation of the aesthetic sense, is subjected to a purpose and is not thought in terms of historicity: "There should therefore only be one single artistic epoch in humanity, as a treasury from which this formation of the aesthetic sense can always be drawn."[48]

After Fichte, Schelling was counted as the "second advancement" in art theory with the brief remark that he has "mere tendency to construct the visual arts from natural science."[49] Schleiermacher thus concealed the significance that Schelling's speech "On the Relation of the Visual Arts to Nature" (1807) had for him; at the very least, numerous excerpts from this speech can be found in the notes he had prepared for his first lecture on aesthetics in 1819.[50] Moreover, Schleiermacher probably had a transcript of Schelling's *Lectures on the Philosophy of Art* (Jena 1802/1803, Würzburg 1804/1805), which has unfortunately not been preserved in his estate.[51] Schelling's reference to the philosophy of nature seems to be groundbreaking for Schleiermacher. At the same time, however, he deemed it not consistent enough, insofar as Schelling focused on the visual arts while neglecting the relation to nature of the other arts like music or imitation (*Mimik*): "And if one asks if the other arts should also be understood from natural sciences, this is not at all appropriate."[52]

Finally, the "third advancement" concerns Hegel, whose philosophy of art Schleiermacher treated in 1832/1833 for the first time in his aesthetics. With Hegel, art becomes "the absolute spirit" (*absoluter Geist*), as the sketch in the marginalia from 1832/1833 states. The inner unit of "absolute spirit," however, does not emerge in the form of art, but falls apart into different perspectives: "But it does not enter, it breaks down into indeterminate polytheism, enthusiasm into unfree pathos."[53] Schleiermacher clearly quoted the two expressions, "indeterminate polytheism" (*unbestimmte Vielgötterei*) and "unfree pathos" (*unfreies Pathos*), verbatim from the introductory paragraphs on the chapter on "art" in Hegel's *Encyclopedia of the Philosophical Sciences* (1827/1830).[54] The corresponding remarks in the Schweizer transcript suggest that Schleiermacher shared Hegel's criticism of empirical aesthetics, according to which art must imitate the beauty of nature. Rather, works of art receive their special value from the fact that they are consciously produced and thus differ from the randomness of

---

[48] *Ästhetik (Kelm)*, p. 544.
[49] *Ästhetik (Kelm)*, p. 39.
[50] Cf. *Ästhetik (Kelm)*, pp. 5–8.
[51] Cf. Friedrich Wilhelm Joseph Schelling, *Philosophie der Kunst und weitere Schriften (1796–1805)*, in *Historisch-kritische* Ausgabe, Dep. II, vol. 6.1, ed. Christoph Binkelmann and Daniel Unger (Stuttgart: Frommann-Holzboog, 2018), p. 64.
[52] *Ästhetik (Kelm)*, p. 545.
[53] *Ästhetik (Kelm)*, p. 134.
[54] Georg Wilhelm Friedrich Hegel, *Enzyklopädie der philosophischen Wissenschaften im Grundrisse (1827)*, in *Gesammelte Werke*, vol. 19, ed. Wolfgang Bonsiepen and H.-Chr. Lucas (Hamburg: Meiner, 1989), §§558, 560. Cf. *Bibliothek*, p. 732.

nature's productivity. It is remarkable that Hegel's aesthetics was described here as a "continuation of our line," that is, as a follow-up project to an aesthetical tradition in which Schleiermacher located his own conception.[55]

Obviously, this historical sketch is selective with regard to the positions and texts dealt with: Schleiermacher neither explicitly addressed early Romanticism, which would have been possible on the basis of Fichte's conception of imagination (*Einbildungskraft*), nor Schelling's *System of Transcendental Idealism (1800)*. However, the fact that Schleiermacher critically and strategically engaged with concepts of Kantian and post-Kantian aesthetics in his last lecture makes it clear that the significance of his aesthetics can be examined not only in the context of early Romanticism, but above all against the background of classical German aesthetics.

13.6 Conclusion

Schleiermacher's *Lectures on Aesthetics* were set in the context of the emergence of aesthetics as a philosophical discipline at the University of Berlin between 1811 and 1834. In his lecture of 1819, Schleiermacher developed a productive-aesthetic approach that contrasts with formal-aesthetic approaches (such as Kant's *Critique of Judgement*) by tracing the theory of art back to the artistic practice motivated by a general "art drive." In his lecture of 1832/1833, Schleiermacher slightly changed his conception by integrating concepts from his philosophy of "immediate self-consciousness" and his late ethics. By doing so, this last lecture can be seen as an extension of the sociocultural dimension and an emancipation from the natural philosophical founding of art production. In this respect, his aesthetics contains preliminary forms of the sociology of art.

Schleiermacher's sketch of the history of aesthetics is primarily oriented towards positions in classical German philosophy. The line Kant–Schelling–Hegel, in which Schleiermacher located his own conception, is still relevant for today's discussions, for example with regard to the concept of "aesthetic experience." Although Schleiermacher took a differentiated view of the close relationship between religion and art in his philosophical ethics, he adopted a distanced relationship to early Romanticism in his later years, which is clearly expressed in his theory of poetry, wherein the concept of a "new mythology" or a "progressive universal poetry" is nowhere mentioned. Nevertheless, there are some concepts that refer back to early Romanticism, especially that of the "enthusiastic mood" as the impulse-giving moment of artistic practice. Finally, Schleiermacher's aesthetics represents an original position within the framework of classical German philosophy, because of his productive-aesthetic approach, on the basis of which art is regarded in ethical terms as a kind of nonverbal and symbolic communication.

---

[55] *Ästhetik (Kelm)*, pp. 546–547.

Suggested Reading

Käfer, Anne. *"Die wahre Ausübung der Kunst ist religiös". Schleiermachers Ästhetik im Kontext der zeitgenössischen Entwürfe Kants, Schillers und Friedrich Schlegels* (Tübingen: Mohr Siebeck, 2006).
Kelm, Holden, and Dorothea Meier, eds. *Der Mensch und die Kunst bei Friedrich Schleiermacher. Beiträge zur Anthropologie und Ästhetik* (Berlin: De Gruyter, 2023).
Lehnerer, Thomas. *Die Kunsttheorie Friedrich Schleiermachers* (Stuttgart: Klett-Cotta, 1987).
Mädler, Inken. "Ästhetik." In *Schleiermacher Handbuch*, ed. Martin Ohst (Tübingen: Mohr Siebeck, 2017), pp. 295–299.
Müller, Ernst. *Ästhetische Religiosität und Kunstreligion in den Philosophien von der Aufklärung bis zum Ausgang des deutschen Idealismus* (Berlin/New York: De Gruyter, 2004).
Scholtz, Gunter. *Schleiermachers Musikphilosophie* (Göttingen: Vandenhoeck & Ruprecht, 1981).

Bibliography

Arndt, Andreas. "Unmittelbarkeit als Reflexion. Voraussetzungen der Dialektik Friedrich Schleiermachers." In *Schleiermacher als Philosoph* (Berlin/Boston: De Gruyter, 2013), pp. 198–212.
Eberhard, Johann August. *Theorie der schönen Wissenschaften* (Halle: Buchhandlung des Waisenhauses, 1786).
Gaß, Wilhelm, ed. *Fr. Schleiermacher's Briefwechsel mit J. Chr. Gaß: mit einer biographischen Vorrede* (Berlin: Reimer, 1852).
Grove, Peter. "Der Grundton aller unserer Gefühle. Schleiermachers Begriff der Stimmung." In *Der Mensch und seine Seele. Bildung–Frömmigkeit–Ästhetik*, ed. Arnulf von Scheliha and Jörg Dierken (Berlin: De Gruyter, 2017), pp. 533–552.
Hegel, Georg Wilhelm Friedrich. *Enzyklopädie der philosophischen Wissenschaften im Grundrisse* (1827). In *Gesammelte Werke*, vol. 19, ed. Wolfgang Bonsiepen and H.-Chr. Lucas (Hamburg: Meiner, 1989).
Jaeschke, Walter. *Hegel-Handbuch. Leben–Werk–Wirkung* (Stuttgart: Metzler, 2016).
Käfer, Anne. *"Die wahre Ausübung der Kunst ist religiös". Schleiermachers Ästhetik im Kontext der zeitgenössischen Entwürfe Kants, Schillers und Friedrich Schlegels* (Tübingen: Mohr Siebeck, 2006).
Lehnerer, Thomas. *Die Kunsttheorie Friedrich Schleiermachers* (Stuttgart: Klett-Cotta, 1987).
Meisner, Heinrich, ed. *Briefwechsel Friedrich Schleiermachers mit August Boeckh und Immanuel Bekker* (Berlin: Litteraturarchiv-Gesellschaft, 1916).
Müller, Ernst. *Ästhetische Religiosität und Kunstreligion in den Philosophien von der Aufklärung bis zum Ausgang des deutschen Idealismus* (Berlin/New York: De Gruyter, 2004).
Nowak, Kurt. *Schleiermacher. Leben, Werk und Wirkung* (Göttingen: Vandenhoeck & Ruprecht, 2001).
Patsch, Hermann. *Alle Menschen sind Künstler. Friedrich Schleiermachers poetische Versuche* (Berlin: De Gruyter, 1986).
Pinna, Giovanna. "Einleitung." In K. W. F. Solger, *Vorlesungen über Ästhetik*, ed. Giovanna Pinna (Hamburg: Meiner, 2017), pp. vii–lii.

Schelling, Friedrich Wilhelm Joseph. *Philosophie der Kunst und weitere Schriften (1796–1805)*. In *Historisch-kritische* Ausgabe, Dep. II, vol. 6.1, ed. Christoph Binkelmann and Daniel Unger (Stuttgart: Frommann-Holzboog, 2018).

Schelling, Friedrich Wilhelm Joseph. "Über das Verhältnis der bildenden Künste zu der Natur." In *Philosophische Schriften*, vol. 1 (Landshut: bei Philipp Krüll, 1809), pp. 341–396.

Schleiermacher, Friedrich Daniel Ernst. *Ästhetik 1832/33*. Ed. Holden Kelm (Hamburg: Meiner, 2018).

Schleiermacher, Friedrich Daniel Ernst. "Über das Naive." In *KGA* 1.1, pp. 177–187.

Schleiermacher, Friedrich Daniel Ernst. "Über den Stil." In *KGA* 1.1, pp. 365–390.

Schleiermacher, Friedrich. *Briefwechsel 1774-1796, KGA* 5.1, ed. Andreas Arndt and Wolfgang Virmond (Berlin: De Gruyter, 1985).

Scholtz, Gunter. *Schleiermachers Musikphilosophie* (Göttingen: Vandenhoeck & Ruprecht, 1981).

Steffens, Henrich. *Grundzüge der philosophischen Naturwissenschaft* (Berlin: Verlag der Realschulbuchhandlung, 1806).

Treviranus, Gottfried Reinhold. *Biologie oder Philosophie der lebenden Natur für Naturforscher und Ärzte*, vol. 1 (Göttingen: bey Johann Friedrich Röwer, 1802).

Virmond, Wolfgang. "Schleiermachers Lektüre nach Auskunft seiner Tagebücher." In *Schleiermacher und die wissenschaftliche Kultur des Christentums*, ed. Günter Meckenstock (Berlin/New York: De Gruyter, 1991), pp. 74–76.

Virmond, Wolfgang, ed. *Die Vorlesungen der Berliner Universität 1810–1834* (Berlin: De Gruyter, 2011).

CHAPTER 14

PSYCHOLOGY AND ANTHROPOLOGY

DOROTHEA MEIER

14.1 INTRODUCTION

THIS chapter surveys Schleiermacher's psychology in order to take a look at it from different perspectives. I will examine the ways in which it integrates the doctrine of the soul into the context of the time (1), describe the relationship of psychology and anthropology (2), outline the characteristics, content, and method of Schleiermacher's psychology lectures (3), examine their location within the system of the philosophical sciences (4), and finish with some remarks on reception and appreciation (5).

What ground does the term "psychology" cover at the beginning of the nineteenth century? May psychology already be spoken of as a distinct discipline at that time?[1] The situation regarding psychology that Schleiermacher engaged was not at all clear; there was neither a broad consensus about its position and significance nor a consistent nomenclature. The segmentation of psychology into rational and empirical branches implemented by Christian Wolff had caused a momentous split in thinking about psychology. This division attained a wide reception through the works of Immanuel Kant, and developed into a fission that contrasted a metaphysically oriented doctrine of the soul with an empirical psychology of faculties. According to Kant, metaphysical psychology could not be pursued scientifically due to the unprovability of the self-awareness of the soul. Therefore, it is no wonder that around 1800 there are signs of the development of empirical psychology, such as the clarification of its aims and methodology, the beginning of an institutionalization, the

---

[1] Most certainly, the modern understanding of psychology as a science that was established around 1900 cannot be assumed here. Psychological phenomena were intensively discussed one hundred years earlier by philosophers, teachers, doctors, and clergy. It has been argued that psychology developed at that time out of its "mother science" (Georg Eckardt, *Kernprobleme in der Geschichte der Psychologie* (Wiesbaden: Springer-Verlag, 2010), p. 75), that is, philosophy. Another proposition is that the two disciplines differentiated themselves from each other as different ways of thinking, "explaining" versus "understanding" (Nicole D. Schmidt, *Philosophie und Psychologie. Trennungsgeschichte, Dogmen und Perspektiven* (Reinbek: Rowohlt, 1995)).

establishment of relevant journals and of a "scientific community," and the implementation of psychological courses at universities.[2]

Of course, Schleiermacher took note of psychological debates at that time. He was inspired by exponents like Johann Christian August Heinroth, Henrik Steffens, Christian Weiß, Friedrich August Carus, Johann Christian Reil, Friedrich Wilhelm Schelling, Franz Anton Mesmer, or Ernst Platner, and wrote critically about Carl August Eschenmayer, Immanuel Kant, and Johann Friedrich Herbart. With his profound knowledge of ancient philosophy, however, he mainly drew conceptually on Aristotle and Plato. And yet his doctrine of the soul followed a very autonomous path.[3] Given that Schleiermacher was a pastor, a father of a family, and a friend, a crucial reason for devoting himself to psychology may have been a very practical interest in understanding psychological phenomena pertaining to everyday life. His biographical and conceptual closeness to the Romantics, which can be traced in detail, provided fertile ground for Schleiermacher's doctrine of the soul. Valorizing nature, emotion, instincts, and drives toward reason, Romanticism had created an image of humanity that recognized the individual as both unique and cosmically linked to totality, and that increased the awareness of the psyche. From these sources later arose the branches of developmental, social, personality, animal, and differential psychology. All of these are discernible in Schleiermacher. Beyond this, he attended to reports on physiology, semiotics, pathology, and the dietetics of the soul, as these appeared in Carl Philipp Moritz's journal *Magazin zur Erfahrungsseelenkunde* and Johann Christian Reil's *Beyträge zur Beförderung einer Kurmethode auf psychischem Wege*.[4] At the same time, his spiritual home was in German Idealism, and his perpetual search for scientificity, systematization, and encyclopedism was essential to the conception of his psychology. The result was a philosophical doctrine of the soul that amalgamates empirical and rational perspectives in specific ways. Most appropriately, it can be termed as a descriptive, analytic, and systematizing hermeneutics of mental processes on the basis of holistic and unmediated experiencing.[5]

Not only was the concept of Schleiermacher's psychology to a large extent independent from the works of others within this burgeoning discipline, it also remained peculiarly isolated within its own conceptual space in his own corpus. Even though many principles of his thinking, as well as logical links to other branches of his scientific system, are evident in the psychology lectures, his theological and philosophical texts have always been read and interpreted well without direct involvement of psychology. Also, Schleiermacher himself discussed psychology beyond the actual lectures only sparsely and incoherently. An early remark on the general nature of rational psychology in the *Dialektik* (1814/1815) says that it should contain the development of the idea of knowledge and of the idea of acting, since both lead to the ideas of God and World as constituent principles of human existence.[6] In his philosophical ethics Schleiermacher systematically classified the discipline by saying

---

[2] Georg Eckardt, Matthias John, Temilo Van Zantwijk, and Paul Ziche, eds., *Anthropologie und empirische Psychologie um 1800. Ansätze einer Entwicklung zur Wissenschaft* (Köln: Böhlau, 2001), p. 3.
[3] Schleiermacher wrote in a letter to Brinckmann on December 31, 1818 that he had set forth a psychology in his own way (*Br IV*, p. 241).
[4] Schleiermacher was personally acquainted with both Moritz and Reil.
[5] Dorothea Meier, *Schleiermachers Psychologie. Eine Phänomenologie der Seele* (Baden Baden: Ergon, 2019).
[6] *Dial.* 1, pp. 152–153.

that psychology would correspond with natural doctrine and the description of nature, that it would be empirical knowledge on the acting of the spiritual, and that empirically treated logic would belong to psychology.[7] In the second edition of *The Christian Faith* (1830), he wrote that dealing with religiosity was "something borrowed" from the doctrine of the soul without giving a more precise elaboration.[8] Since it was within psychology that he theoretically derived religion as a feeling belonging to the category of self-awareness, he could identify religiosity as a phenomenon on loan from psychology.

14.2 Why "Psychology" Rather than "Anthropology"?

Already in 1799, Schleiermacher anonymously published a seven-page review of Immanuel Kant's *Anthropologie in pragmatischer Hinsicht* in the *Athenaeum*, a journal edited by the Schlegel brothers.[9] There he termed Kant's anthropology a "collection of trivia" and even a "negation of all anthropology."[10] In particular he criticized Kant's contrast between physiological and pragmatic anthropology, because on his own view anthropology had to be the unification of both sides. Here Schleiermacher's broad understanding of this discipline is already clearly recognizable. However, his utterances on the nature of anthropology altogether remained restricted and inconclusive. In his ethics, Schleiermacher wrote that anthropology, whether considered in general or as divided into the physical and the psychical, was not to be regarded as a science. Nevertheless, somewhere and somehow the material sciences might raise the conception of human nature to scientificity.[11]

According to his holistic approach, the doctrine of what makes a person human necessarily contains the unity of physique and psyche. A human being is both being and thinking. Within a human being, nature is coextensive with spirit. Anthropology should be the location where both are brought together: "Anthropology as empirical description of nature, and logic as empirical description of the intellectual process, mediates the contrast between physics and ethics as belonging to both in different ways."[12] Since Schleiermacher did not develop his own natural philosophy, he relied on the field of human spirit, or psychology. He could not call it anthropology because, according to contemporary thinking, this would have required an empirical approach, whereas he started from the unconditional correlation of spirit and nature. However, from a present-day perspective the discipline that Schleiermacher called psychology constitutes a broad anthropological approach, one that draws an image of man with a claim to completeness.

"Probably, I have to start with imposing boundaries against anthropology; on the side of cognition excluding the physiological beginning, on the side of will the physiological

---

[7] Friedrich Schleiermacher, *Entwurf eines Systems der Sittenlehre*, in SW 3.5, p. 37.
[8] CG^2, v. 1, p. 24.
[9] Friedrich Schleiermacher, *Schriften aus der Berliner Zeit 1796–1799*, in KGA 1.2, pp. 365–369.
[10] KGA 1.2, pp. 365–366.
[11] Schleiermacher, *Entwurf eines Systems der Sittenlehre*, p. 50.
[12] Schleiermacher, *Entwurf eines Systems der Sittenlehre*, p. 50.

ending."[13] This was an intention Schleiermacher phrased in a brief note preceding the 1818 lecture. Drawing a line between psychology and anthropology means separating them theoretically. The doctrine of the soul leaves the purely empirical field in order to examine the spiritual at the only given point—the living human being. Schleiermacher incidentally concluded, "Therefore, psychology is on the one side a break [*Bruch*] (not an organic part) of anthropology."[14] This, however, seems to conflict with the earlier note in the same manuscript: "Psychology is on the one side only a break [*Bruch*] (namely part of anthropology)."[15] The words "namely" and "not" used in the same context generate some uncertainty, but do not necessarily have to be contradictory. Rather two slightly different perspectives come to light. On the one hand, anthropology in Schleiermacher's understanding undoubtedly comprises both physiology and psychology because the spiritual only exists in inextricable union with the physical, and can only be examined in the context of this union. The doctrine of the soul is "initially together with anthropology."[16] On the other hand, psychology parts with anthropology in order to develop its own focus on the spiritual, though not without acknowledging this fundamental inseparability.[17] Thus psychology is at the same time a part and a break. In correspondence with this understanding, in its methodology the doctrine of the soul begins empirically, and progresses on its way to further cognition by trying a connection with "speculative views."[18] Thus it is no wonder that in the 1818 lectures psychology is positioned as a "link in the whole chain of pneumatology."[19] A note in the same manuscript goes so far to characterize psychology as infinite in its compass, as a "theory of plants, animals, humans, earth, and world soul."[20] Just as the anthropological approach is oriented toward the empirical, Schleiermacher's psychology is oriented toward the metaphysical.

Crucial to the delineation of psychology (as well as physiology) in relation to anthropology is the premise of their fundamental togetherness.[21] Of course, physiology examines organic processes, just as psychology examines the spiritual. However, both actions form a unity, an interplay, a transition into each other. If psychology is conducted as one possible perspective on human life, physiology would be the other feasible approach. Every human is a particular version of the union of the material and the spiritual. Psychology is the science that views human life from the perspective of the spiritual, whereas physiology does so from the organic vantage point. Each angle includes the other one at least to a minimal degree. A possible separation under the precondition of the togetherness of its parts can be explained by Schleiermacher's dynamic and dialectical thinking. He only pursued the

---

[13] *Psychologie*, p. 15; manuscript 1818, folio 5 verso. Hereafter, *ms. 1818*, fol. 5v.
[14] *Psychologie*, p. 16; *ms. 1818*, fol. 6v.
[15] *Psychologie*, p. 7; *ms. 1818*, fol. 2v.
[16] *Psychologie*, p. 15; *ms. 1818*, fol. 5v.
[17] The reliable Hamburg postscript (1818) puts the point as follows: "However, in wanting a psychology, we want an aggregate of individual fractions from the knowledge that constitutes anthropology. From anthropology we only want to extract the psychic, which, therefore, is nothing but a fraction [*Bruch*] of the same because it is not a part [*Theil*] of it" (*Psychologie*, p. 211).
[18] *Psychologie*, p. 16; *ms. 1818*, fol. 6 recte. Hereafter: *ms. 1818*, fol. 6r.
[19] *Psychologie*, p. 16; *ms. 1818*, fol. 6v.
[20] *Psychologie*, p. 7; *ms. 1818*, fol. 2v.
[21] "The original that is presented here is originally anthropology; not as if it consisted of physiology and psychology, but rather without this division" (*Psychologie*, p. 632).

mental part because his primary interest was in the spiritual as the "most highly human."[22] His psychology is anthropology from the spiritual point of view. Within his system psychology occupies the place of anthropology, even though it parts ways with the latter theoretically. Only in this way can psychology realize the announced "notional glances."

14.3 THE LECTURES ON PSYCHOLOGY

Schleiermacher started with the actual elaboration of the doctrine of the soul comparatively late, first in the summer of 1818 and later in three more lectures: in the summers of 1821 and 1830, and finally—until one week prior to his death—in the winter of 1833/1834. These courses were very popular; indeed, the lectures of 1830 were Schleiermacher's best attended philosophical lectures, with 229 listeners.[23] Schleiermacher did not publish a work of psychology during his lifetime, but an impressive wealth of textual witnesses are extant. Firstly, manuscripts in Schleiermacher's own hand have survived, containing records, written down right after delivery, of the lectures of 1818, 1830, and 1833/1834. Though they provide authorized versions of the discourse, they do not document the whole of the delivered speech. Secondly, tiny autographic slips of paper provide the basis for lectures of the year 1821. Finally, twelve transcripts in all from listeners of the four courses exist: two from 1818, four from 1821, and three each from 1830 and 1833/1834.[24]

Each of the four lectures is structured in three main parts: an introduction, an elementary part, and a constructive part. While the introduction comprises between ten and fourteen lessons, the elementary part covers by far the most extensive number—forty-five to sixty-seven lessons. The constructive part is less comprehensive (five to eighteen lessons) and is structured differently in the different lecture series. The development between the first and the last course is far smaller than might be expected. Except for some terminology and for an obvious maturation, a more systematic linkage of thoughts, an increasing theoretical certainty, and some changes in detail, the concepts and the main thoughts of all four lectures do not differ greatly. In every case the introduction provides basics: the integration of psychology in the system of sciences, its relationship to anthropology, and methodological considerations. In the elementary part, Schleiermacher theorizes the nature of the human soul as an interaction between consciousness and basic mental processes. The constructive part transfers these general conclusions to special features. The individual person is portrayed in his or her singularity as representative of the being of humanity. Furthermore, social-psychological ideas appear, as when humans who form a nation or a people are described as constituting a singular entity with its own psychological characteristics.

---

[22] *Psychologie*, p. 635.
[23] Wolfgang Virmond, ed., *Die Vorlesungen der Berliner Universität 1810–1834 nach dem deutschen und lateinischen Lektionskatalog sowie den Ministerialakten* (Berlin: Akademie Verlag, 2011), p. 588.
[24] *KGA* 2.13 contains all of Schleiermacher's handwritten textual witnesses as well as one selected listener's transcript per course.

14.3.1 Philosophy of Life

"Thus we take life as our point of departure."[25] This statement, with which Schleiermacher opened his lectures on psychology, has multiple dimensions. Firstly, the sentence points out that the human soul shall be examined as it actually appears, not isolated from but in its union with the body, and dependent on anthropological data. Secondly, the sentence implies an intention to examine humans in their activity, in individual and collective exchange and togetherness within their material, historical, and social environments. Thirdly, the plan entails an acknowledgement of the laws of nature such as growth, alteration, and passing away. Above all, however, the starting point "life" intends to develop a hermeneutic explication of the soul. Each human deals with his or her objectifications of the spirit, both internal and external. His or her life accomplishes the realization of spirit in nature in both individual and collective form. Wilhelm Dilthey expressed this position later on in saying that life was an elementary fact that had to be the starting point of philosophy. According to Dilthey, "life is what is known from the inside; it is the very thing back behind which one cannot go."[26] Schleiermacher's psychology—after the manner of a philosophy of life—ventures a hermeneutic investigation into the spiritual as it actually emerges.

In order to satisfy the philosophy of life, the doctrine of the soul can only start from a point that precedes all interpretation. It has to presume that there is something internal that is the same for everybody.[27] The basis has to be factual, and, thus, has to be collective as well as individually different, or—with Dilthey—something back behind which we cannot go. This starting point Schleiermacher finds in "I." Whoever says "I" feels and knows that he or she has consciousness and is, therefore, part of a general consciousness.[28] Each human knows about his or her "self," the empirical, the reliable, the premised, the given. It provides the basis for jointly recognizing the soul. A progression in the knowledge of the person about him- or herself, and thus the development of a lower consciousness (intuitive knowledge) into a higher consciousness (volitional knowledge), is always given because of the identical and divergent being as well as the givenness of reflexivity in "self."

"I" can never be thought of as isolated. "I" acts lively within the general context of interrelations with the environment. The simple awareness of the self always implies a counterpart, "you." Put differently: "Consciousness is not self-consciousness without consciousness of someone else."[29]

The vivid "self" is bound to a bodily appearance. From the union of body and soul in "I" as the starting point of psychology, it follows that speculative reflections on a potential existence of the soul before, after, or outside human life become obsolete. The body is the requirement of the possibility that the soul appears vividly and acts. All interactions between the "I" and the environment are ensured by the body.

---

[25] *Psychologie*, p. 20; *ms. 1818*, fol. 8r.
[26] Wilhelm Dilthey, *Gesammelte Schriften*, vol. 7 (Göttingen: Vandenhoeck & Ruprecht, 1992), p. 261.
[27] *Psychologie*, p. 620.
[28] "The self is given a priori. It has to be given a priori because there cannot be an individual consciousness without the collective consciousness" (*Psychologie*, p. 208).
[29] *Psychologie*, p. 135; *ms. 1830*, fol. 2v.

14.3.2 Theory of Operations of the Soul

The elementary part of the lectures on psychology outlines a theoretical system of all human mental activities in the shape of a quadruplicity whose components are dialectical polarities within the human consciousness and in the self–world relationship.[30] According to the nature of "I," to be at the same time individuality and in identity with other human beings, the continuous and dynamic human consciousness splits into subjective (self-)consciousness and objective (joint) consciousness. The other polar opposition is that of receptivity (internalizing the world) and spontaneity (self-activity). By crossing both polarities, Schleiermacher produces a division of potential movements of the soul into quarters. Predominant receptivity of the subjective consciousness generates sentience (*Empfindung*). Receptive action of the objective consciousness produces perception (*Wahrnehmung*). Predominant spontaneity of the subjective consciousness expresses itself as representation (*Darstellung*). Spontaneous activity of the objective consciousness creates achievement (*Werkbildung*).[31] Schleiermacher's psychology consistently follows this scheme. Everything that can happen in the human soul is assimilable into the system. Figure 14.1 illustrates this structure.[32]

Schleiermacher's doctrine of the soul is an ambitious attempt at a highly complex system of all human mental activities. No wonder there are intriguing connections with other disciplines:[33] the explanation of sentience, especially of religious consciousness,[34] is reminiscent of the concepts of consciousness of God and the feeling of absolute dependence in religious faith, while the presentation of perception[35] matches ideas within Schleiermacher's dialectic. The spontaneously subjective and spontaneously objective operations of the soul correspond to the organizing and symbolizing actions described in his philosophical ethics. Further discussions on these relationships have been a desideratum.

14.3.2.1 *Predominantly Receptive Activities of the Soul*

The impulses for receptive activities lie outside the human being, who absorbs them with the help of the organic functions. To the senses of hearing, of sight, of taste, of smell, and of touch, Schleiermacher adds a sixth sense: the susceptibility of skin to the whole of the surrounding atmosphere. As such, receptivity is physically induced; however, it always has a

---

[30] In this chapter, only a short summary of the theory of the operations of the soul (outlined in the "elementary" part of the lectures) can be given. For more detailed information see Meier, *Schleiermachers Psychologie*, pp. 136–184.

[31] In the 1818 course, the respective actions are named feeling (*Empfinden*), contemplating (*Betrachten*) recognition (*Erkennen*), drive for acting (*Drang zur Tätigkeit*), and production of objects (*Hervorbingen von Gegenständen*).

[32] cf. Meier, *Schleiermachers Psychologie*.

[33] Presumably, Leopold George had these interrelations in mind when he wrote that psychology would "provide the key not only for the philosophical system but also for the theological foundational view" of Schleiermacher (Friedrich Schleiermacher, "Psychologie," in *SW* 3.6, p. vii).

[34] Cf. *Psychologie*, manuscripts: pp. 79–81, 161–163, 188–189; postscripts: pp. 315–321, 538–540, 734–748, 991–999.

[35] Cf. *Psychologie*, manuscripts: pp. 66–72, 156–160, 182–185; postscripts: pp. 284–302, 522–530, 700–725, 962–975.

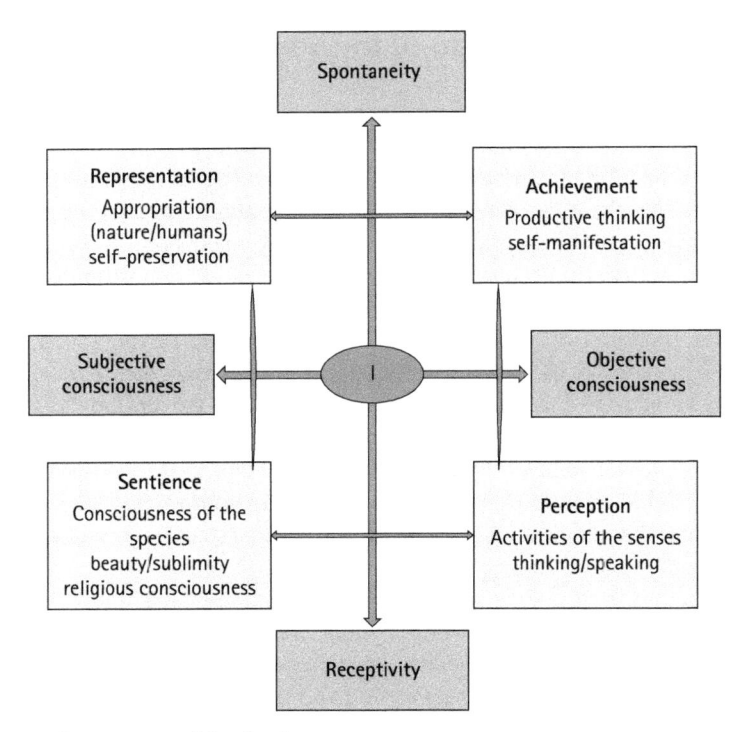

FIGURE 14.1 Operations of the Soul.

spiritual tendency, because object- and self-consciousness have been in the "I," thus also in the senses, from the beginning. The desire to turn each organic sensation into a conscious moment is a factual feature of the human soul. If this consciousness is more subjective it becomes feeling, and displays individual awareness in its variability. Out of this affective condition, a specific subjective self-consciousness arises, which will seek expression. If it is more objective, it will end up as perception that is based on the individual communal identity. Perceptions form the individual worldview.

Thinking is a higher mental activity that extends the lower receptive sensual operations. Worldview is heightened to a concept of the world. Humans have a naturally given need to research. Thinking finds its origin in the consciousness of the species, in the associated acknowledgement of other people, and in the urge to communicate. Thinking emerges along with speaking. Speaking reveals both the objective consciousness of communal identity and the subjective consciousness of individuality. Thinking aims at conceiving the existence as a whole that reproduces itself as a divided being in the individual process of thinking. Each individual can comprehend only part of the whole in his or her thinking. The concept of the world refers to the totality of the consciousness of individuals. In the individual process of thinking, the collective concept is converted into an idea that mirrors the existence in general. Because consciousness itself is a special kind of being, the concept of the world may be the same in different languages.

On the side of receptive subjective consciousness, the higher forms are consciousness of the species (*Gattungsbewusstsein*), feeling of the beautiful and the sublime, and religious consciousness.

The consciousness of the species is a peculiar human principle in which the individual confronts him- or herself with the generally human. He or she is an individual because his or her nature can be explained through the consciousness of the species. The principles of species-identity and individuality are obtained through this consciousness. Reciprocal communication on the one hand, and mutual recognition on the other, are the scaffolding of living together. Different emotions cause various forms of consensus and controversy in social intercourse.[36]

Feelings of the beautiful arise directed at single objects, natural phenomena, or people, as long as they satisfy the proper conditions. They emerge if these relate to the human, the living, and lead to an identification with the existence. Collections of several objects, impressive natural phenomena, or groups of people may arouse sublime feelings as long as they transcend human works. Looking sympathetically at such extraordinary occurrences, the individual becomes aware of him- or herself as finite and limited being.[37]

Consciousness of God is the necessary and logical extension of self-consciousness into the transcendental. In the absolute feeling of dependence, the individual senses their identity with all being. Immediate self-consciousness increases within the human being, gives spiritual depths, and overcomes all division; and thereby the contrast between the subjective and the objective is also abolished. While living, humans experience objective and subjective consciousness as parts. Only in religious faith do both parts unite. Being conscious of God, the human being feels his or her identity with totality.[38]

14.3.2.2 *Predominantly Spontaneous Activity of the Soul*

Spontaneous self-activity is inherent in the living soul. Initially small and partly unconscious, it is constantly growing. Spontaneous activities divide into those belonging to the subjective and objective consciousness respectively. Spontaneous-subjective actions end in representation (*Darstellung*) and belong to the real or outward side, whereas spontaneous-objective operations are realized in achievements (*Werkbildung*) and lie on the ideal or inward side.

Representations occur through the appropriation of nature—including the human beings—and through self-preservation. The principle of taking possession of things and people in the surrounding environment is inherent in human existence. At first, the individual adopts their body; at the opposite end of this type of activity stand the domination of nature and, ultimately, the creation of regulated civil relations in a state. In order to constitute sociable life and culture, the appropriation of other humans is essential. Each individual is given a self-consciousness and a consciousness of the species. The interplay of the two forms the basis for the active subjective operation of the soul in acknowledging and accepting fellow beings. Appropriating the external aims at creating culture.

---

[36] Cf. *Psychologie*, pp. 979–985.
[37] Cf. *Psychologie*, pp. 986–991.
[38] Cf. *Psychologie*, pp. 992–997.

The phenomenon of self-preservation means the psychic activity of ensuring that life can persist, and represents the pure nature of the living self. Schleiermacher refuses to call this a "drive" because as such it would refer only to the self, and thus would contradict the consciousness of the species.

Achievements subsume productivity in thinking and self-manifestation. Each individual has the drive to fulfil its consciousness, a need for knowledge. Objectification in productive thinking consists in transforming existence into consciousness. Individual attainment and merit can only be solidified in knowledge and science through communication and understanding, through the use of language.

Beginning with facial and gestural expressions, self-manifestation is the higher externalization of inner psychic processes. The drive of self-manifestation shows that, and in what ways, the human person wants to be an individual and part of the community simultaneously. The objectification of this consciousness reveals itself in all kinds of artistic production.

The appropriation of nature and fellow humans on the one side, and self-manifestation and productivity in thinking on the other, recall in their functions the organizing and symbolizing activities in which spirit appropriates matter. In the lectures on psychology, Schleiermacher thus derives crucial cultural performances theoretically from the operations of the human soul.

14.3.3 Individual Aspects of the Soul

The constructive part of the lectures tries to individualize Schleiermacher's general scheme on the basis of his theory of the soul. In detail, Schleiermacher discusses the psychic differences of genders, temperaments, characters, significance, and of mental variations resulting from temporal sequences of life.

Differences in the psychic modes of the soul may be observed between the two genders. Whether these are inherent or acquired remains undecided. According to Schleiermacher, such differences do not mean a hierarchy in worthiness. The strength of the female gender he discovers predominantly in the fields of subjective consciousness—for example in religion, in social life, in the insight into human nature, and in domains like education and household matters. Accordingly, males achieve more success in the fields of objective consciousness—in politics, science, art, and complex connections.

Schleiermacher develops a theory of temperaments grounded in the fundamental psychic categories of receptivity and spontaneity. This contrastive pair is crossed with a line representing the speed of the alternating mental moments and their content. Consequently, a quadrinomial system accrues: receptive and fast (sanguineous), receptive and slow (melancholic), spontaneous and fast (choleric), spontaneous and slow (phlegmatic).

Character is a product of the relationship of personal and social consciousness. In the interplay with physical preconditions, it is a predominantly spiritual corrective against imbalance and extremes. A personality displays character in the way they accomplish their portion of a shared task, and in a way, this has become the dominant idea. Thus character, so to speak, comprises a scale of individuals' contribution to their society, relative to the idea of the good and to their personal abilities.

People possess different grades of significance regarding their impact on communal life. The lowest level is indifference and passivity, the next higher one is marked by predominant receptivity. Above this are persons who act spontaneously, who display talent and initiative. Those who show a higher degree of development and who exercise influence over the community are the most productive and excellent. The reason for this is grounded in the nature of spirit. In line with the classifications of spontaneous activity, excellence shows itself on the real side (state, domination of nature, church) as heroism; on the ideal side (science, art), as ingenuity.

Because Schleiermacher understands human communities as compounded personalities, he extends phenomena such as character or temperament to peoples and nations.

Each individual develops different mental processes depending on the course of their life. These occur in all humans in similar ways. In this connection, Schleiermacher examines changing psychic operations while being awake and sleeping, making highly interesting observations concerning dreams and hypnosis. He also attends quite extensively to the course of life through different periods, describing the prenatal phase and birth, infancy, early childhood, boyhood, adolescence, the age of maturity, old age, and death.

14.3.4 Method

Schleiermacher's dynamic and dialectical delivery also applies to the lectures on psychology. Typically, he first presented his listeners with a hypothesis, immediately offered a counterargument, and discussed the subject meandering between the opposites. The results were normally unconventional, and often open-ended. In this way Schleiermacher wove a net of all possible thoughts and laid out his doctrine of the soul in a living manner.

According to the character of Schleiermacher's psychology, only a close correlation of empirical and speculative methods can lead to theoretical knowledge. The inductive way—beginning with the simple and proceeding to the general—predominates in the lectures on psychology, and this corresponds with his initial principle of starting from empirical evidence and venturing speculative proposals. From this perspective, Schleiermacher takes an intermediate position between empirical and rational psychologists.

As I observed above, psychology as knowledge of humans about themselves occupies a special position in Schleiermacher's scientific system. Since it is nurtured by other scientific branches, especially by dialectic, physics, and ethics, the doctrine of the soul makes use of dialectical rules, ethical perspectives, and natural scientific knowledge respecting the physical world. Psychology "is in the results of those three: the essence of the soul is regarded as part of nature, then as the essence of freedom in ethics, and the essence of the soul is also understood in relation to the antithesis between cognition and recognition in dialectic."[39]

Since the lectures on psychology explore the functioning of thinking in general, and the character of productive science in particular as matters of human mental operations, Schleiermacher accomplished more than theoretically exploring recognition by means of truth and misapprehension. His doctrine of the soul also has an epistemological dimension because the development of knowledge takes place in its own sphere.

---

[39] *Psychologie*, p. 206.

14.4 THE POSITION OF PSYCHOLOGY IN SCHLEIERMACHER'S SCIENTIFIC SYSTEM

Several presumptions on the systematic position of psychology exist. Herms[40] considers psychology to be the supreme discipline, whereas Arndt[41] suggests a quadrinomial order of the lines between physics and ethics with respect to dialectics and psychology. The textual sources do not allow an unequivocal placement. Matters are further complicated by the fact that there is a discrepancy between Schleiermacher's description of psychology's theoretical location and the actual character of the lectures. The 1821 lectures (which have only been known since the publication of *KGA* 2.13 in 2018) contain a particularly elaborate treatment of the classification of psychology as a science.

Schleiermacher began the lectures by pointing to the peculiar character of psychology: "on the one hand the doctrine of the soul is presupposed by all other parts of knowledge, and on the other hand it can only be the result of the completion of all other branches of knowledge."[42] This refers to psychology's important function. Accordingly, he explicitly described the ways in which the three classical disciplines—dialectic, physics, ethics—both presuppose psychology and contribute to it. His conclusion: "We have to consider the doctrine of the soul on the one side as the culmination, and on the other side as the general foundation of all knowledge."[43] Therefore, the doctrine of the soul cannot merely be an empirical science feeding into dialectic, ethics, and physics. The main concern would rather be the "speculative views."[44] Indeed, psychology lays the empirical foundation for the other disciplines. Then, further developing, it comes to the point where it ventures speculative proposals for the other branches. Ethics, physics, and dialectic start at this very point, appropriating these proposals and carrying them on in their own directions. Each of these three sciences circulates information with psychology in its own way.[45] Through this

---

[40] Eilert Herms, *Die Bedeutung der Psychologie für die Konzeption des Wissenschaftssystems beim späten Schleiermacher*, in *Schleiermacher und die wissenschaftliche Kultur des Christentums*, ed. Günter Meckenstock and Joachim Ringleben (Berlin: De Gruyter, 1991), pp. 369–401.

[41] Andreas Arndt, *Spekulative Blicke auf das geistige Prinzip. Friedrich Schleiermachers Psychologie*, in *Dialogische Wissenschaft. Perspektiven der Philosophie Schleiermachers*, ed. Dieter Burdorf and Reinold Schmücker (Paderborn: F. Schöningh, 1998), pp. 147–161.

[42] Anonymous, *Nachschrift zur Psychologie Schleiermachers 1821*, Cod. Ms. F. Frensdorf 1:1, Niedersächsische Staats- und Universitätsbibliothek Göttingen (Göttinger Nachschrift, 1821), p. 1.

[43] *Nachschrift zur Psychologie Schleiermachers 1821*, p. 5.

[44] *Psychologie*, p. 16; *ms. 1818*, fol. 6r.

[45] The lectures on psychology, firstly, provide a theory for the explanation of the processes that happen in the knowledge-attaining soul. Psychology leaves discussions of the internal nature of knowledge, and of its conditions and possibilities, to dialectic.

Secondly, the situation is similar with the relationship between psychology and ethics. Ethics realizes itself by the action of reason toward nature; concretely, in every individual conscious action that is ethically motivated and strives toward the highest good. The lectures on psychology, based as they are on the continual interaction of nature and reason, show how all human activity originates in the soul, and finds its equivalent in organizing and symbolizing operations. The doctrine of the soul keeps silence about the ways in which human action shall be formed in order to be morally significant. This is the point where ethics connects.

circulation, something happens with psychology. It evolves into a discipline that unites empiricism and speculation, and embodies the progression of human self-knowledge: "Thus, we have got two kinds of knowledge of man about himself. We think of the one as the beginning, and of the other as the end of all knowledge."[46]

For a vivid depiction of the relationship of the disciplines in relation to each other, a description by means of quadrinomial arrangements would be insufficient.[47] Only a spatial form (such as an upwardly open pyramid) would be worth considering, the base of which are the empirical disciplines. The technical disciplines would be located further up, then the critical, and on top the speculative sciences. Only in this way can the upward movement from empiricism to speculation be imagined as a perpetual, spiral-shaped process of interaction. Beyond this, it becomes possible to conceive contacts between disciplines of the same level (empirical, critical, or speculative) not as fixed, but as likewise in process through interactive inspiration and supplementation. Knowledge cannot reach a final state. Just as little could it culminate within a single discipline, because the preliminary sciences themselves do not come to an end; they repeatedly contribute new empirical data, and all branches of knowledge get involved again.

Because the doctrine of the soul involves the formation of knowledge itself, it is virtually situated on all of the levels of the system. The role of psychology does not exhaust itself empirically, and neither can it be understood as the supreme discipline. Rather, it provides the required space for humans to gain dynamic knowledge about themselves. In the process of the formation of knowledge, psychology, in interaction with the other disciplines, functions as the driving force, because it examines human consciousness itself. Since the human being is both natural and spiritual, and the human soul can only be portrayed in this connection, thinking psychologically means supervising the formation of knowledge of humans about themselves, starting organically and ending in abstractions. However, Schleiermacher's approximate "knowledge of man about himself as the result of all other branches" refers neither to psychology nor to any other discipline.[48] Although the doctrine of the soul is enriched by speculative elements, it would essentially dissolve in any complete knowledge; but since such knowledge is not conceivable, psychology retains its function. The term "peak of all knowledge" is only a heuristic device that facilitates understanding of the spiral path of the developing knowledge. Psychology cannot be given a clear position because it realizes itself in this process and thus cannot be separated from the other disciplines. The doctrine of the soul has a special status. As a theory of consciousness, it is not only closely connected with the other parts of knowledge, but is also the vehicle of the process of cognition.

So much for the theoretical interpretation. But critically surveyed, the actual lecture texts on psychology cannot satisfy this ambitious aspiration. Schleiermacher offers a preliminary

---

Schleiermacher meant "physics" to comprise the natural sciences. Their relationship toward psychology is obvious, too. Their topic is the knowledge of nature and its relationship to the humans who are only existent in their constant union of body and soul. As such, they are part of nature, and thus an object of physics, which provides natural scientific knowledge to psychology. On the other side, humans acquire knowledge of nature while thinking. Since psychology examines the actions of the cognitive consciousness, physics cannot be sufficient without psychology. Physics engages psychology at the point where knowledge of the human as the most highly developed part of nature starts.

[46] *Nachschrift zur Psychologie Schleiermachers 1821*, pp. 5–6.
[47] Arndt, *Spekulative Blicke auf das geistige Prinzip*.
[48] *Psychologie*, p. 479.

account of psychology. Beginning with the simplest and proceeding to the more complex, he develops a theory of all human actions of thinking, feeling, and acting. With speculative additions, he reaches points where other disciplines (ethics, dialectic, and physics) can connect. Although psychology is also described as the summit of all knowledge, the available texts do not support such a utopian claim. Rather, the lectures are propaedutic; this is the sense in which Schleiermacher's remark "Here, only the preliminary" is to be understood.[49] Regardless, psychology is of particular importance. It offers explanations for all processes within the human soul and serves as the foundations for all connecting disciplines: "Our studies are the indispensable condition of the validity of thinking and living, and therefore are the access to all clear cognition and all clear acting."[50]

14.5 Reception and Appreciation

Schleiermacher's psychology was published as the last volume of the *Sämmtliche Werke* in 1862, nearly thirty years after the final lecture on February 6, 1834. The editor, Leopold George, who himself had attended the course in the summer of 1830, conceded that Schleiermacher's doctrine of the soul was no longer current when the volume appeared. After this first publication no complete edition would appear until 2018, in KGA 2.13, although two extracts were published in the interim.[51]

Immense popularity with contemporary listeners on the one hand, and rather small attention by later recipients on the other—this is the discrepancy Schleiermacher's psychology has had to cope with until the present. The list of works dealing explicitly with the psychology is quite short. George was still confident that the lectures on psychology, "which, virtually, provide the key not only for the philosophical system but also for the theological foundational view [*Grundanschauung*] of the venerated master," would have a rich influence on the understanding of Schleiermacher's philosophy as well as on the emerging discipline itself.[52] This hope has not been realized. The idiosyncratic strategy of Schleiermacher's philosophical doctrine of the soul, based as it is on classical sources, did not satisfy the spirit of the time. Psychology had moved past Schleiermacher's position, toward empirical rather than rational concepts. Attention to his psychology has primarily been the product of historical interest or sidelights from other fields of research. After nearly 100 years of approximate silence, an obvious renaissance of the reception of the psychology becomes evident beginning in the 1980s.

The doctrine of the soul represents a fundamental discipline in Schleiermacher's conceptual space. Its concern is broad, its realization rich in detail. The constructive part in particular contains remarkable developmental-, social-, and personality-psychological ideas.

With the lectures on psychology, Schleiermacher presented a phenomenology of the human soul. A deep understanding of life in process created a real knowledge about the

---

[49] *Psychologie*, p. 15; *ms. 1818*, fol. 6r.
[50] *Psychologie*, p. 898.
[51] WA, pp. 1–80; Schleiermacher, *Schriften*, ed. Andreas Arndt (Frankfurt/Main: Deutscher Klassiker Verlag, 1996), pp. 845–944.
[52] Schleiermacher, "Psychologie," p. vii.

procedures that go on deep inside the human soul. Schleiermacher restricted himself to the soul in union with its given body. In this way, he excluded metaphysical assumptions.

The doctrine of the soul, resting as it does on receptive and spontaneous activities and their relationship with the different kinds of consciousness, relies on three things: firstly, on the acting individual; secondly, on the surrounding world in a certain historical situation and with natural, social, and interpersonal relationships; and thirdly, on the lively interchange between these two. In the sense of vivid, general, and at the same time individual interaction between subject and world, the psychology also represents a theory of formation. All of the activities of the soul—sentience, perception, representation, and achievement—embody components that constitute education and formation because they originate in the processes of exchange between the "I" and the world, which are regulated by spontaneity and receptivity. Each person, combining individuality and communal identity, proceeds most effectively on their path of formation through self-development according to their own characteristic features, and in constant communication with the ethical spheres (state, church, science, sociality) in a process of interacting reassurance.

By ascending from the individual human soul to collective dimensions of mental processes, and by expanding all kinds of thinking, feeling, and acting into collective spiritual procedures, Schleiermacher eventually describes the functioning of the society as a whole. The lectures on psychology may also be read as sociological theory, because the necessary sociality of human life is a premise. In the interplay of individual and supra-individual processes in the consciousness of the species, Schleiermacher explicates the conditions and possibilities, and even the operating principle, of human coexistence as such. Since each individual can only incorporate several parts of the existence in his or her consciousness, and since singular thinking and researching is at the same time dependent on the receptive and spontaneous activities of the others, Schleiermacher states that even individual worldviews have to be transferred into collective worldviews in order to become conscious.

Beyond this, Schleiermacher's psychology contains an epistemic dimension. On the one hand, behind his derivation of thinking out of the receptive actions of the objective consciousness there lies the question of how knowledge and recognition are gained. On the other hand, the doctrine of the soul itself forms a resonant space within which all other knowledge develops—a space where, between the poles of the particular individual and their potentially unlimited self-knowledge, increasing degrees of certainty can be attained.

Even if Schleiermacher's understanding of psychology and many of his explanations of mental processes have long since become outdated, his copious and detailed observations testify to a deep psychological insight. The large-scale formation of theoretical, sociological, and philosophical ideas prove the broad framework his doctrine of the soul embraces. Schleiermacher's psychology has not formed a recognized or influential school. It is, however, beyond doubt that the doctrine of the soul occupies an important place in his own cosmos.

Suggested Reading

Arndt, Andreas. *Schleiermachers Philosophie* (Hamburg: Felix Meiner, 2021).
Herms, Eilert. *Leibhafter Geist—beseelte Organisation. Schleiermachers Psychologie als Anthropologie. Ihre Stellung in seinem theologisch-philosophischen System und ihre*

Gegenwartsbedeutung. In *Der Mensch und seine Seele. Bildung–Frömmigkeit–Ästhetik. Akten des Internationalen Kongresses der Schleiermacher-Gesellschaft in Münster, September 2015*, ed. Arnulf von Scheliha and Jörg Dierken (Berlin: De Gruyter, 2017).

Herms, Eilert. *Philosophie und Theologie im Horizont des reflektierten Selbstbewußtseins.* In *Schleiermachers Dialektik. Die Liebe zum Wissen in Philosophie und Theologie*, ed. Christine Helmer, Christiane Kranich, and Birgit Rehme-Iffert (Tübingen: Mohr Siebeck, 2003).

Huxel, Kirsten. *Psychologie.* In *Schleiermacher Handbuch*, ed. Martin Ohst (Tübingen: Mohr Siebeck, 2017), pp. 285–290.

Schmidt, Sarah. *Die Konstruktion des Endlichen: Schleiermachers Philosophie der Wechselwirkung* (Berlin: De Gruyter, 2005).

Schönpflug, Wolfgang. *Geschichte und Systematik der Psychologie* (Weinheim: Beltz, 2004).

Tice, Terrence. *Schleiermacher's Psychology: An Early Modern Approach, a Challenge to Current Tendencies.* In *Schleiermacher und die wissenschaftliche Kultur des Christentums*, ed. Günter Meckenstock and Joachim Ringleben (Berlin: De Gruyter, 1991), pp. 509–521.

Bibliography

Arndt, Andreas. *Spekulative Blicke auf das geistige Prinzip. Friedrich Schleiermachers Psychologie.* In *Dialogische Wissenschaft. Perspektiven der Philosophie Schleiermachers*, ed. Dieter Burdorf and Reinold Schmücker (Paderborn: F. Schöningh, 1998), pp. 147–161.

Dilthey, Wilhelm. *Gesammelte Schriften, Bd. 1–26* (Leipzig/Berlin: Teubner; Göttingen: Vandenhoeck & Ruprecht, 1914–2006).

Eckardt, Georg. *Kernprobleme in der Geschichte der Psychologie* (Wiesbaden: Springer-Verlag, 2010).

Eckardt, Georg, Matthias John, Temilo Van Zantwijk, and Paul Ziche, eds. *Anthropologie und empirische Psychologie um 1800. Ansätze einer Entwicklung zur Wissenschaft* (Köln: Böhlau, 2001).

Herms, Eilert. *Die Bedeutung der Psychologie für die Konzeption des Wissenschaftssystems beim späten Schleiermacher.* In *Schleiermacher und die wissenschaftliche Kultur des Christentums*, ed. Günter Meckenstock and Joachim Ringleben (Berlin: De Gruyter, 1991), pp. 369–401.

Ludwig, Jonas, and Wilhelm Dilthey, eds. *Aus Schleiermacher's Leben. In Briefen*, 4 vols. (Berlin: G. Reimer, 1860–1863).

Meier, Dorothea. *Schleiermachers Psychologie. Eine Phänomenologie der Seele* (Baden: Ergon, 2019).

Moritz, Karl Philipp, ed. *Magazin zur Erfahrungsseelenkunde.* 10 vols. (Berlin, 1783–1793).

Nachschrift zur Psychologie Schleiermachers 1821, Cod. Ms. F. Frensdorf 1:1, Niedersächsische Staats- und Universitätsbibliothek Göttingen (Göttinger Nachschrift, 1821). [Anonymous source]

Reil, Johann Christian, and Johann Christoph Hoffbauer, eds. *Beyträge zur Beförderung einer Kurmethode auf psychischem Wege.* 2 vols. (Halle: Curt, 1808, 1812).

Schleiermacher, Friedrich. *Entwurf eines Systems der Sittenlehre.* In *SW* 3.5.

Schleiermacher, Friedrich. "Psychologie." In *SW* 3.6.

Schleiermacher, Friedrich. *Rezension von "Immanuel Kant: Anthropologie in pragmatischer Hinsicht"*, Königsberg 1798. In *Athenaeum* 2/2. Ed. August Wilhelm Schlegel and Friedrich Schlegel (Berlin, 1799), pp. 300–306.

Schleiermacher, Friedrich. *Schriften*. Ed. Andreas Arndt (Frankfurt/Main: Deutscher Klassiker Verlag, 1996).

Schmidt, Nicole D. *Philosophie und Psychologie. Trennungsgeschichte, Dogmen und Perspektiven* (Reinbek: Rowohlt, 1995).

Virmond, Wolfgang, ed. *Die Vorlesungen der Berliner Universität 1810–1834 nach dem deutschen und lateinischen Lektionskatalog sowie den Ministerialakten* (Berlin: Akademie Verlag, 2011).

CHAPTER 15

THEORY OF THE STATE

MIRIAM ROSE

Scholars had high expectations when Friedrich Daniel Ernst Schleiermacher's lectures on the theory of the state were first published as part of the critical edition (*KGA*) in 1998. Since Schleiermacher had been an innovative thinker in many areas of science, a similarly novel approach was expected from his hitherto little-known theory of the state. There were initially two main responses to the work. One regards Schleiermacher as a remarkable theologian and one of the first to seriously consider the matter of civil society and recognize the central role of democratic public opinion,[1] and affirms Schleiermacher as an important thinker in the history of democratic ideas.[2] The other thread within Schleiermacher scholarship, which draws on German Idealism and Prussian history as the primary framework for interpretation of Schleiermacher's thinking, leads to a comparison of Schleiermacher's doctrine of the state with that of Hegel and Fichte.[3] More recently, a less polarized approach has developed among Schleiermacher scholars, which emphasizes the importance of a more general historical context of his work.

In the following pages, Schleiermacher's thematic and biographical approaches to political theory will be outlined (§§15.1 and 15.2), followed by a presentation of their main content and features (§§15.3 to 15.5), in order then to reveal their relationship to the French Revolution (§15.6) and to the present time (§15.7).

---

[1] See Arnulf von Scheliha, "Religion, Gemeinschaft und Politik," in Andreas Arndt, Ulrich Barth, and Wilhelm Gräb, eds., *Christentum–Staat–Kultur: Akten des Kongresses der Internationalen Schleiermacher-Gesellschaft in Berlin, März 2006* (Berlin: Walter de Gruyter, 2008), pp. 317–336, pp. 332–336.

[2] See Matthias Wolfes, "Sichtweisen. Schleiermachers politische Theorie zwischen dem autoritären Nationalstaatsethos der Befreiungskriegszeit und dem deliberativen Konzept einer bürgerlichen Öffentlichkeit," in *Christentum–Staat–Kultur*, pp. 375–393; pp. 383–385.

[3] See Dankfried Reetz, *Schleiermacher im Horizont preußischer Politik: Studien und Dokumente zu Schleiermachers Berufung nach Halle, zu seiner Vorlesung über Politik 1817 und zu den Hintergründen der Demagogenverfolgung* (Waltrop: Hartmut Spenner, 2002).

15.1 POLITICAL THEORY IN THE WORK OF SCHLEIERMACHER

Schleiermacher conceives political theory as a theory of the state. He represents this theory mainly in lectures and in essays. But ideas regarding the state and political issues are present in many of Schleiermacher's writings. According to context, Schleiermacher takes five different approaches to the state, and arrives at surprisingly similar conclusions.

Schleiermacher first approaches a theory of the state through his ethics, which in fact represents a cultural theory. He addresses the subject of ethics in various lectures, in a few treatises and in some presentations to the Royal Prussian Academy of Sciences. The development of the state is here seen as part of the entire process of history. According to Schleiermacher, this process is directed toward an ever-increasing interrelation of nature and reason. This process takes place within the four or five spheres of human culture, of which the state is one. These spheres of human culture are based on four elementary types of human action, from which Schleiermacher develops his entire ethical system. Schleiermacher distinguishes between organizing and symbolic actions (*organisierendes und symbolisierendes Handeln*). He also distinguishes between action focused on human individuality and action focused on the sameness of all human beings. Combining these, Schleiermacher proposes four types of actions: organizing individuality, organizing sameness, symbolic individuality, and symbolic sameness. The state consists of actions that organize the lives of human beings taken as equal without specific regard to their individuality.

Schleiermacher's second approach to a theory of the state is based on the formation of theories within religion, which has philosophical roots in the area of ethics. These reflections are particularly detailed and extensive within his philosophy of religion and his theology, including his theological ethics. In both of these, he considers the relationship between religion and the state with a view to achieving the greatest possible degree of independence of one from the other. Above all, it is his concern to protect religion from access by the state, and even from state support. He criticizes strongly the current mixing of church and state that began in the fourth century.[4]

Schleiermacher opens up the third approach to the theme of politics through his sermons, which often take up political aspects or topics that can be interpreted in a political sense.[5] Since he was also pastor at the *Dreifaltigkeitskirche* (Holy Trinity Church) in Berlin during his time as a professor at the University of Berlin (1810–1834), preaching was one of his regular tasks. Schleiermacher emphasizes the Christian duty to take part in political affairs and to support the government.[6]

---

[4] *KGA* 1.2, pp. 280–283.

[5] See Johannes Bauer, *Schleiermacher als patriotischer Prediger: Ein Beitrag zur Geschichte der nationalen Erhebung vor hundert Jahren* (Gießen: Töpelmann, 1908); and Nottmeier, "Zwischen Preußen und Deutschland: Nation und Nationalstaat bei Friedrich Schleiermacher," in *Christentum–Staat–Kultur*, pp. 337–354.

[6] *KGA* 3.4, pp. 3–15; *KGA* 3.4, pp. 680–692; and *KGA* 3.12, pp. 500–510.

In his fourth approach, concerned with development of his pedagogical theory, Schleiermacher devotes himself in detail to the relationship between education and the state.[7] Schleiermacher argues in favor of a strong responsibility of the state for education and schools, but with the constant involvement of scientific pedagogy and public discourse. Education's concern should be how future citizens are being prepared to participate in the state and how they can develop an orientation toward the common good (*Gemeinwohl*). A liberal education and the formation of a civic public belong together. This part of Schleiermacher's work is receiving more and more attention from educational studies (especially Jens Brachmann, Christiane Ehrhardt, Birgitta Fuchs, and Michael Winkler).

The fifth approach is more directly scientific and concentrates on the theory of the state. Here, Schleiermacher reflects on the state and statehood as a subject in itself and emphasizes the cultural and historical individuality of each state. He rejects Enlightenment theories of the state, and in particular social contract theories and the normative universality of the theories of the eighteenth century. However, positive reference to and consideration of ancient theories play an important role for Schleiermacher, especially the theories of Plato and Aristotle as they were discussed in the circle of the early Romantics. Schleiermacher presented his detailed reflections in lectures on politics and political theory held at the University of Berlin, which was newly founded in 1810, and also in lectures at the Academy of Sciences. Details of political measures are of particular interest to him, along with European and global history, and practical questions of administration. He also includes, at least in part, the contemporary knowledge of administration, the military, and diplomacy which was accessible to him.

15.2 Stations of Engagement with Political Theory

Schleiermacher experienced the French Revolution as a 21-year-old student of theology and philosophy in Halle as it was happening in neighboring France. His letters reveal an intense interest in philosophical ideas, but not so much in political events. In fact, Schleiermacher writes about the French Revolution only to his father in 1793.[8] Since intellectual discourse in Germany blamed the doctrine of natural law for the escalation of violence in the further course of the French Revolution, it is understandable that Schleiermacher also studied natural law at this time.

The subsequent stages of his theoretical examination of political theory are well documented by his writings. In 1796/1797, Schleiermacher studied the doctrine of natural law as developed in the Age of Enlightenment.[9] Schleiermacher's interest in Aristotle's Nicomachean ethics goes back to 1788/1789;[10] later, he studied the "Politics" of Aristotle, and also wrote a Latin text comparing Aristotle and Plato with regard to their political

---

[7] *KGA* 1.11, pp. 125–146.
[8] *KGA* 5.1, pp. 280f.
[9] *KGA* 1.2, pp. 51–69, 71–74.
[10] *KGA* 1.1, pp. 1–43.

philosophy.[11] These basic points of reference, namely, a negative view of the political theories of the Enlightenment, positive links to Plato and Aristotle, and also his complex perception of the French Revolution, shape Schleiermacher's theoretical arguments about the state in all its phases of development.

As a preacher at the Charité in Berlin from 1796 to 1802, Schleiermacher moved in the circle of the early Romantics, where political perspectives and political utopias were also under discussion. One example is the essay by the Romantic poet Friedrich von Hardenberg (known as Novalis) entitled *Die Christenheit oder Europa* (1799; "Christianity or Europe"). This political utopia is intended as a continuation and expansion of Schleiermacher's ideas, but in opposition to Schleiermacher, Novalis suggests a close relation between religion and politics.

During his professorship in Halle (1804–1807), Schleiermacher was concerned with the foundations of ethics as such, and twice gave a lecture on the subject of philosophical ethics. The detailed work *Brouillon zur Ethik* (1805/1806; "Notes on Ethics") came into being at this time, and describes the fourfold forms of action mentioned above, namely the state, free sociability (*freie Geselligkeit*), the church and science, and the areas where they are expressed institutionally. Here Schleiermacher took an interest mainly in the relationships between the four spheres and their relative independence. Following the closure of the University of Halle in 1807 by Napoleon, Schleiermacher gave private lectures in Berlin. The first series of these on the doctrine of the state, entitled *Theorie des Staates* (Theory of the State), took place in 1808/1809; unfortunately, there is no surviving manuscript. Following the establishment of the University of Berlin in 1810, Schleiermacher discussed political science in a total of five academic lectures, which took place in 1813, 1817, 1817/1818, 1829, and 1833. These lectures were held at the philosophical faculty where Schleiermacher, as a member of the Academy of Sciences, was entitled to teach. The most intensive period of political theory formation for Schleiermacher thus dates to the years 1813–1818. In 1814, Schleiermacher also presented two Academy lectures on topics related to the philosophy of the state.[12]

Unfortunately, the situation as regards material available from this time is extremely inconsistent. There are no records that can be clearly assigned to the lecture of 1813. At least one student transcript of the lecture of 1817 has survived. Finally, some notes made by Schleiermacher himself for the lectures of 1817/1818 are extant, as well as a student transcript. The lecture that took place in 1829 offers the best textual basis, as a detailed manuscript by Schleiermacher himself as well as student transcripts are available. For the lecture in 1833, Schleiermacher used the lecture notes from 1829 and made some additional notes. Student transcripts of this lecture are also available. The various lectures on politics reveal a high degree of continuity in Schleiermacher's political thinking.

The practical and political commitment of Schleiermacher has been extensively recognized by the church historian Matthias Wolfes.[13] Schleiermacher's activities in 1813 provide an excellent example: at this crucial time in the relationship between Prussia and France, Schleiermacher acted as an editor and contributor for the newspaper *The Prussian Correspondent*. From July to August, Schleiermacher was the editor in charge of this

---

[11] *KGA* 1.1, pp. 499–509.
[12] *KGA* 1.11, pp. 95–124, 125–146.
[13] See Matthias Wolfes, *Öffentlichkeit und Bürgergesellschaft: Friedrich Schleiermachers politische Wirksamkeit* (Berlin, New York: Walter de Gruyter, 2004).

newspaper, which was published four times a week, mainly focusing on the reporting of political events from a liberal and national point of view. Schleiermacher directed his work against the armistice negotiated between Prussia and Russia, on the one hand, and France, on the other. As the result of an editorial in 1813 regarding an upcoming peace congress in Prague, Schleiermacher was in fact accused of high treason by the censorship authority. However, the dispute with the censorship authority did not prevent Schleiermacher from continuing to give lectures on the theory of the state. It can be assumed that his listeners paid sharp attention to any hidden criticism of the current Prussian government contained in the lectures and that they were able to understand subtle hints and references.

15.3 Structure of the Lectures and Approach to the Theory of the State

Structures and schemes play a central role in Schleiermacher's thinking. Often he displays considerable powers of innovation here, but without neglecting detailed aspects and individual considerations of the topic at hand. Therefore, in the following paragraphs, his lectures on the theory of the state are presented on the basis of their structure and some of their themes are described by way of examples.

The subject of "Formation and constitution of the State" (*Staatsbildung und Verfassung*),[14] is always discussed at the beginning of his lectures, followed by the themes of "State Administration" (*Staatsverwaltung*),[15] and finally "Defense of the State" (*Staatsverteidigung*).[16]

15.3.1 Formation of the State

As the basis for his theory of the state, Schleiermacher takes the transition from nonstate (*Nicht-Staat*) to state (*Staat*), which, in his view, has occurred at a point in history that can no longer be precisely determined. This transition should explicitly not be viewed as the conclusion of a contract, as was postulated in the social contract theories during the Enlightenment. It rather represents the moment in the history of a community when awareness dawns on that community that there is a difference between the sphere of the individual and the common sphere that unites all members of society and applies to all. At this time, usual behavior within society or, in Schleiermacher's words, the "custom" (*Sitte*) becomes the general law. With this clear awareness of the difference between the individual and society as a whole, awareness of the opposition between "authority" and "subject" (*Gegensatz von Obrigkeit und Untertanen*) also comes into being. The state therefore exists where there are laws that apply to all and therefore also where there is a difference between those who formulate and enforce these laws and those who recognize and obey them. The state itself consists

---

[14] *LvS*, pp. 75–114.
[15] *LvS*, pp. 114–164.
[16] *LvS*, pp. 164–169.

of the actions that are implemented in correspondence with the law. Therefore, the state is not a static entity, but a process, a network of actions, a dynamic development.

Another important element is still missing from the definition of the state: according to Schleiermacher, the state and its laws refer to the common relationship of people to the soil (*Boden*). Schleiermacher understands "soil" in the broadest sense: as a territory, as a concrete landscape, as an agrarian basis of life and as a living space.

For Schleiermacher, the subject of a state constitution is also associated with the formation of the state. The constitutional question plays a central role in the political debates taking place around 1800. In 1810, the Prussian king promised a constitution. He renewed this promise in 1815, but he did not fulfil it. Schleiermacher is cautious regarding this matter. He warns against overestimating the importance of the constitutional question. The decisive factor is the particular condition of the state, that is the particular form and design of the opposing roles of authorities and subjects. A written constitution gives expression to this condition. However, Schleiermacher ignores the fact that a constitution and the act of creating it could itself exercise a considerable influence on the condition of the state. Schleiermacher's second reservation as regards the importance of the constitutional question is that he considers the dynamic change of the state to be essential. A written constitution could have the tendency to codify and fix a specific condition of the state.

15.3.2 Administration of the State

Schleiermacher defines the administration of the state as "proper management of the law in order to transform the most complete form of natural human expression into an organism of intelligence."[17] Schleiermacher differentiates between various elements within the law as expressed here: elements subject to the administration of the state include property, trade, and transport, but also the political disposition of those who participate in the state. He then mentions institutionalized tasks, which are the administration of transport, education, and finance.

Schleiermacher is cautious about state intervention in economic life. Situations may arise in which the state must intervene, but this should never become a permanent solution. Schleiermacher is less cautious with regard to the education system. The family is primarily responsible for the education of children, followed in a broader sense by religious communities and scientific institutions. If these fulfil their educational tasks well, the state should withdraw from this area. However, it could also happen that inhibiting factors occur in any of these institutions. For example, parents may become impoverished. In this case, the state itself should play a role in upbringing and education. However, the state should not use this obligation as an excuse to intervene directly in religion or science. Here Schleiermacher makes it explicitly clear that this thesis stands in contradiction to the school and education system of the Prussian state as it was at the time.

Civil service or state administration are discussed as a separate topic. Schleiermacher takes a critical look at the organization of a civil service, which is regarded as a profession and is able to provide a livelihood to those working within it. He also sharp-sightedly observes

---

[17] *LvS*, p. 114.

that if performance of administrative tasks becomes a full-time profession, an accumulation of formalities and greater bureaucracy will result. With equal perception, he realizes that the civil service always acts as a delaying factor (in a negative sense) when it comes to government action.

15.3.3 Defense of the State

When it comes to defense of the state, Schleiermacher distinguishes between internal and external defense. External state defense involves military actions and diplomatic relations. The role of internal defense of the state is fulfilled by the judiciary.

The relationship of the state to science and religion, but also to free sociability, is a constant theme within Schleiermacher's political reflections. It plays a central role, especially with regard to defense of the state.

When it comes to science and religion, the state is not concerned with institutions or organizations as such, but with the activities of its citizens outside the state sphere. The fact that these other activities lead to the formation of institutional structures is initially of no relevance for the state. Schleiermacher develops his ideas on how the state should deal with the activities of its citizens, which are outside the state as such, based on the key concept of trust (*Vertrauen*). Mutual trust is necessary for the interaction of authority and subject. Possible mutual mistrust is not directed toward individuals in themselves, but toward the fact that individuals also allow themselves to be determined by their private interests when it comes to their political actions. Schleiermacher considers the mistrust to be quite appropriate, because political interests and private interests are both naturally inherent within human existence.

Schleiermacher identifies these private interests with religion, science, and free sociability. Surprisingly, there is no mention of economic or other interests here. For Schleiermacher, these interests are not private in today's sense of the term, because they involve communication and carry a natural tendency to express themselves in socially interactive terms. Schleiermacher develops a very neat and plausible argument here: The mistrust which arises from the fact that others within the state allow their political actions to be influenced by their private interests can only be kept within limits if these private interests can be expressed as freely as possible and therefore no conflict with political interests arises in the first place. According to Schleiermacher, undisturbed development of the state is only possible if it is based on the trust that follows when the religious, scientific, and social lives of its citizens can exist freely and the needs associated with them are met. Schleiermacher explicitly opposes establishing the state on the basis of Christianity. He is equally clearly in favor of the acceptance of atheism or of attitudes that would be considered atheistic. Nevertheless, Schleiermacher also points out the limits of religious freedom, which, if they are exceeded, endanger the state. Schleiermacher sees freedom for the private interests of individuals not only as beneficial to development of the state, but even as the "condition towards which everything strives."[18]

---

[18] *LvS*, p. 112.

Schleiermacher's position on "crimes against the state" (*Staatsverbrechen*), that is actions directed against the specific form of a state, is interesting.[19] He opposes the death penalty for "political crimes" (*politische Verbrechen*). All his considerations in this regard are aimed at relativizing the seriousness of such crimes: they could be actions that do not constitute crimes as such but rather consist of legitimate opposition to a government that is exceeding its powers. With regard to the individuals concerned, he concedes that they act out of courageous conviction. Schleiermacher does not touch more closely upon the idea of a possible right of resistance at any point.

In the following paragraphs, three central themes of each political theory are outlined as examples. Since Schleiermacher keeps returning to them at various times in his lecture, they are each presented separately.

15.4 CENTRAL POLITICAL THEMES: PROPERTY, LAW, AND WAR

15.4.1 Property

Schleiermacher sees property and the division of labor emerging and forming as the norm to coincide with the emergence of the state. He justifies this essential connection by referring to the fact that property implies both individual and collective awareness of the relationship between people and things. He distinguishes the concept of awareness from those of "habituation" (*Gewöhnung*) and "imitation" (*Nachahmung*).[20]

It is particularly interesting that Schleiermacher sees property as an enabler of geographical mobility and travel, and thus of trade and movement. Those who do not need to assert their right to land ("the soil," *Boden*) by means of their physical presence are able to move freely away from it. Schleiermacher assumes that with increasing trade and division of labor, everyone will wish for such mobility. Within the developed state, a differentiation occurs: those who possess their own land and therefore feel a certain "attachment" to it also feel an attachment to the state. However, those who do not own land are different. They are far less tied to their state and society. Those who are committed to the state by a formal position in state life form an exception.

Schleiermacher considers "the right to freely dispose of one's own property" to be justified.[21] If the state intervenes in this matter, it exceeds the bounds of its authority. The relationship of the state to individual property should consist only in the fact that it guarantees rights of ownership.

---

[19] *LvS*, pp. 168f.
[20] *LvS*, p. 116.
[21] *LvS*, p. 134.

15.4.2 Law

Although Schleiermacher equates statehood with the explicit expression of custom (*Sitte*) as effective law, he deals surprisingly little with legal theories and legal questions in his theory of the state. His efforts to set limits to the normativity of law by interpreting it as an expression of a custom that has become established over time are an obstacle to the establishment of a strong theory of law. Schleiermacher does not take into account the function of the law to protect the individual and to provide legal certainty. In general, the protection of individuals does not play any role. This is where Schleiermacher distances himself most from political concepts of the Enlightenment, and therefore from contractualism. The law serves the community, expresses its state of development, and strengthens the common spirit (*Gemeingeist*). In this way, Schleiermacher subordinates the law to the common spirit, and therefore to political conviction (*politische Gesinnung*).[22] This concept has nothing to do with a democratic rule of law.

Schleiermacher is well aware that "custom" (*Sitte*) and law do not develop in parallel: whilst custom changes gradually over time, changes in the law occur only rarely. The changes in legislation undertaken by the government should express custom as it is at any given time; the government can only gain access to what this entails by listening to many diverse individuals. Schleiermacher sees the guilds and the districts as vehicles in this regard. The law should not be used by the authorities primarily as an instrument of control, but should express custom as it continually changes. Schleiermacher does not maintain that law and legislation function as an instrument for change and progress.

Scholars agree that Schleiermacher's legal theory is strangely lacking in definition,[23] and is not at the highest level of the debates that were taking place at the time. Schleiermacher clearly aims to relativize the role of the law by understanding it as an expression of custom and emphasizing its origins in history. The law does not emerge as an instrument of state control. This part of Schleiermacher's theory is clearly the weakest. Philosophical scholars like Jaeschke or Arndt are critical about Schleiermacher's ideas, while theologians seem to be mostly very cautious with critics here. This theological attitude is rooted in the fact that in German systematic theology Schleiermacher functions still as a very important reference for current dogmatic argumentations.

15.4.3 War

Schleiermacher is optimistic that the frequency of wars will decrease in the course of further social development, whilst diplomacy will gain further importance. In this context, he paints a picture of the future development of relations between states that is born of his philosophy of history. Therefore, the different states are on a pathway toward perpetual peace.

---

[22] See Andreas Arndt, "Der Begriff des Rechts in Schleiermachers Ethik-Vorlesungen," in Andreas Arndt, Simon Gerber, and Sarah Schmidt, eds., *Wissenschaft, Kirche, Staat und Politik: Schleiermacher im preußischen Reformprozess* (Berlin: Walter de Gruyter, 2019), pp. 219–232, 231.

[23] See Arndt, "Der Begriff des Rechts in Schleiermachers Ethik-Vorlesungen"; and Miriam Rose, *Schleiermachers Staatslehre* (Tübingen: Mohr Siebeck, 2011), pp. 212–235.

Here, Schleiermacher relies on the following: He sees the unequal development of different states, which he considers to be the main cause of war, as balanced out by the development of public opinion. Public opinion applies a brake to those states that are developing too rapidly, while accelerating the rate of development of slower states. This is achieved through communication and lively exchanges in the areas of science, social intercourse, and religion. However, such communication requires the presence of a public sphere, a free press, and the freedom to travel. For Schleiermacher, communication and the public sphere are thus regarded as the decisive prerequisites for peace and as a universal means of preventing conflict. He also expects a general aversion to war, if only because prosperity in general will be seen as the overriding goal within society. In addition, economic interests promote peace by their very nature; they also support networks at an international level. Thirdly, Schleiermacher assumes that this results in reciprocal decisions on the part of individual states to be bound to arbitrational institutions that mediate any arising conflicts. Schleiermacher emphasizes that the state of peace cannot be secured by means of contracts or treaties, but only by the internal development of the different states and communicative networking between them.

15.5 Characteristics of the Lectures on the Theory of the State

How can Schleiermacher's political theory, its status, and its claims be characterized? The theory of state is in Schleiermacher's terms a "technical discipline" (*technische Disziplin*) as a derivation from the theory of ethics. Strangely enough, though, the lectures regarding the theory of state do not refer explicitly to a theory of ethics.

Schleiermacher's theory of the state is decidedly philosophical. He completely dispenses with explicitly theological argumentation. This philosophical approach can initially be understood in terms of its boundaries. First of all, Schleiermacher rules out designing an ideal state. This is out of the question, as it would mean that justice would not be done either to the particularity or the historicity of each state. In addition, Schleiermacher is not in favor of presenting practical rules for future politicians—although he, in fact, does so. Thirdly, rather than describing the specific conditions of Prussia obtaining in his own time, he attempts to design an abstract history of statehood in general, which can be used to analyze the history of a specific state so that its present condition can be understood in such a way that political action is possible within it. Schleiermacher assumes that there is not a single best form for the state or a single best state system or structure, but only a particularly appropriate form related to the historical development of any particular state.

Because of this approach to statehood, Schleiermacher often illustrates his reflections with concrete examples taken from the history of individual European states, with a particular focus on England and France. Schleiermacher's horizon, however, is in fact considerably broader than this: he also includes examples from Mexico and Canada.

Schleiermacher always designs political theory from the guiding perspective of how the state could act. A certain dichotomy appears in this context: on the one hand, state and government are identified in such formulations, although Schleiermacher otherwise constantly emphasizes that the state is constituted by the opposition (and thus the relationship) of authority and subject. As far as politics is concerned, he identifies the state and those in authority as being one and the same. It is also noteworthy that he adopts the perspective of those who form the government within the state. Within all his considerations and recommendations, the most important factor is what lies in the (long-term) interest of the state in terms of stable development. Schleiermacher formulates his ideas in these terms for students who will assume responsibilities within government at a later stage. In some places it becomes clear that Schleiermacher above all is thinking of the civil service in this context. According to Schleiermacher, good work on the part of the civil service is "mostly based on the enacted effectiveness of the idea of the state and on sound judgment."[24] Schleiermacher does not comment on other decidedly political action in the state. The theory of the state and the theory of the political coincide with Schleiermacher.

The lectures are deliberative in terms of their approach. Schleiermacher describes possible options and draws their consequences in the context of different starting points. In this way, the historical uniqueness of the development of the specific state is always linked to figurations that can be comprehended in schematic terms. Schleiermacher assumes that, when considered objectively, the effects of state intervention can be clearly predicted. He carefully weighs up their advantages and disadvantages, with the possible consequences. The aim of political consideration is not to identify the ideal action, or the ideal form of government, but the most appropriate action possible within a given historical situation.

The style of the lectures on the theory of the state is—perhaps contrary to expectations—precisely not programmatic. Schleiermacher is clearly striving to present the field of political theory, which was so highly charged at this time, as a normal topic of scientific consideration. The shortcomings of Schleiermacher's political ideas in comparison to other philosophers of his time might stem from his entanglement with ancient political theory, especially Plato and Aristotle. There are hints in current research[25] but no thorough examination.[26] The anti-pragmatic nature of Schleiermacher's political theory might as well be interpreted as a special feature of a political theory of a second order,[27] meaning a theory of possible political theories.

These lectures can be pointedly summarized in terms of three characteristics, as follows.

---

[24] *LvS*, p. 156.

[25] See Walter Jaeschke, "Schleiermacher als politischer Denker," in *Christentum–Staat–Kultur*, pp. 303–315, at p. 311; Andreas Arndt, *Die Reformation der Revolution: Friedrich Schleiermacher in seiner Zeit* (Berlin: Matthes & Seitz, 2019), p. 209.

[26] On the intense relationship between German Romanticism and ancient philosophy, see Dorit Messlin, *Antike und Moderne. Friedrich Schlegels Poetik, Philosophie und Lebenskunst* (Berlin: Walter de Gruyter, 2011), pp. 145–169.

[27] See Werner Stegmaier, "Eigentlich das Gebiet der persönlichen Reibungen: Schleiermachers bewegliche Konzeption eines beweglichen Staates," in *Schleiermacher und Kierkegaard: Subjektivität und Wahrheit. Akten des Schleiermacher-Kierkegaard-Kongresses in Kopenhagen, Oktober 2003*, ed. Niels Jørgen Cappelørn et al. (Berlin: Walter de Gruyter, 2006), pp. 479–502 (490).

15.5.1 State Theory as a Prosaic Theory Intending Prosaic Minds

Schleiermacher develops a sober and prosaic view of the state that avoids mystification but also minimizes the role of the state. This reveals the essence of politics, because Schleiermacher never wants the state to be more than the political—but also not less. The task of politics is to regulate the common relationship of the people to the soil, that is to the basis of life, in accordance with shared custom. Politics should only be concerned with this area. In this way, Schleiermacher relieves the state of the obligation to design society as a whole, and above all of its obligation to be a provider of meaning.

15.5.2 State Theory as a Theory of the Normal, Not as a Conflict Theory

Schleiermacher is hardly interested in the settlement of possible conflicts.[28] He considers the occurrence of hard conflicts to be an aberration. His theory of the state demonstrates, with the intention of offering orientation, how hard conflicts cannot even occur if states develop naturally. From today's perspective, this deliberate disregard of situations involving conflict strikes a discordant note. From Schleiermacher's point of view, however, raising the question of conflict resolution at all is already a first indicator of a problematic attitude toward the state. The most important reason why Schleiermacher works from a perspective that tends to suppress the possibility of conflict is the fact that the individual in their physical, mental, and moral existence is thought to be so dependent on the community as a whole that hard conflicts do not occur or only occur as an exception. He is most likely to think of conflicts as possibly occurring between different common spheres, for example, between the state and the church. He expresses a certain understanding for the fact that a government that acts outside the boundaries of its appropriate sphere of action will be replaced by means of revolution. However, he provides neither a recommendation for action in such cases, nor for political mechanisms aimed at conflict resolution. Therefore, Schleiermacher's theory refuses to be normative; it is explicitly non-normative.[29] The term "regulatory"[30] suits very well.

15.5.3 Politics as a Means of Shaping the Speed of Development of a State

Because the state is to be understood in terms of its development, the speed of development is of central importance. Schleiermacher assigns normative and definitive importance to

---

[28] See Denis Thouard, "Gefühl und Freiheit in politischer Hinsicht: Einige Überlegungen zu Humboldt, Constant, Schleiermacher und ihrem Verhältnis zum Liberalismus," in *Christentum-Staat-Kultur*, pp. 355–374 (369).
[29] See Jaeschke, "Schleiermacher als politischer Denker," p. 312; and Rose, *Staatslehre*, p. 298.
[30] See Wolfes, "Sichtweisen," p. 392.

this speed and its appropriateness, in so far as exceeding or falling below the appropriate speed of development eradicates the statehood of the state. Thus Schleiermacher rejects both restorative and revolutionary tendencies. The further development of the state in terms of substance, on the other hand, seems to him to be clearly determinable from the course of development to date. That all European states will introduce constitutions, that they will grant freedom of religion and freedom of the press, that there will be an elected legislative body: all of this is not subject to doubt. For Schleiermacher, the only open question concerns the speed at which this will occur.

15.6 SCHLEIERMACHER'S THEORY OF THE STATE AGAINST THE BACKDROP OF THE FRENCH REVOLUTION

As was the case for many thinkers of his time, the study of the French Revolution and its subsequent history is at the core of Schleiermacher's political thinking. As a reflection of this, a recent monograph on Schleiermacher's work is entitled *Die Reformation der Revolution*.[31]

The research into Schleiermacher's political theory is mainly interested in determining the political stance Schleiermacher takes in the political struggles of his time. This task is very difficult because Schleiermacher balances all arguments in such a complex manner that he never takes strong sides or displays clear solidarity with a specific political group. Because of this, most scholars find paradoxical expressions to define Schleiermacher's political identity: "liberaler Kommunitarismus,"[32] or "Liberaler ohne liberale Theorie."[33] In the last decade the research has left this approach behind and shifted the interest more and more to comparisons with contemporary theories and to the history of theology and of ideas. The comparison with Hegel plays here the central role.[34]

Schleiermacher's perspective on the French Revolution sharpens and relativizes the difference between political options, which, according to him, are not controversial in themselves; it is only the speed of change that is controversial. Schleiermacher sees the changes

---

[31] See Arndt, *Die Reformation der Revolution*.

[32] Friedrich Wilhelm Graf, "Lob der Differenz: Die Bedeutung der Religion in der demokratischen Kultur," in *Die herausgeforderte Demokratie: Recht, Religion, Politik, Beiheft zur Berliner Theologischen Zeitschrift*, ed. Christof Gestrich (2003), p. 25.

[33] Rose, *Staatslehre*, p. 292.

[34] See Walter Jaeschke, "Schleiermachers Lehre vom Staat im philosophiegeschichtlichen Kontext," in *Wissenschaft, Kirche, Staat und Politik*, pp. 207–218; Jörg Dierken, "Staat bei Schleiermacher und Hegel: Staatsphilosophische Antipoden?," in *Christentum-Staat-Kultur*, pp. 395–410; and Rochus Leonhardt, "Staat und Religion: Zur theologie- und zeitgeschichtlichen Einordnung sowie zur Gegenwartsrelevanz der Position Schleiermachers," in *Reformation und Moderne: Pluralität-Subjektivität-Kritik. Akten des Internationalen Kongress der Schleiermacher-Gesellschaft in Halle (Saale), März 2017*, ed. Jörg Dierken, Arnulf von Scheliha, and Sarah Schmidt (Berlin, Boston: Walter de Gruyter, 2018), pp. 229–231.

imposed by the Revolution as positive and natural changes. In this respect, revolution further promotes progress that is in any case imminent or overcomes a condition of decay caused by the rulers of the state. However, as a way of overthrowing the state, Schleiermacher considers revolutions to be reprehensible.

Schleiermacher concludes that governments must act in such a way that revolutions do not occur, because the necessary changes that are due in terms of the history of the state are implemented by the government itself. He does not formulate a perspective for citizens of the state; there is no talk of the right to instigate revolution. Schleiermacher attempts to relativize the positioning and to integrate the theme of revolution into more comprehensive theoretical contexts.

An even more far-reaching thesis is attached to this: The revolutionary impulse is considered inherent by Schleiermacher, insofar as change is included in the concept of the essence and existence of the state. This also makes the revolutionary impulse less urgent. His experience of revolution determines his approach on a formal level and state theory works as a theory of the changing state.

The fact that three terms play a central role in Schleiermacher's reflections can be linked to this formative experience of the French Revolution. When the concepts of freedom, equality, and common spirit/political disposition (*Gemeingeist*) are used, they can be read as a response to the programmatic concepts of the French Revolution, in other words Liberty, Equality, and Fraternity.

15.6.1 Freedom

Schleiermacher already addresses freedom, at least indirectly, in his reflections on the transition from nonstate to state. Only where people have the freedom to act on their own impulses, that is, where they are not slaves or servants, can they form a state and be part of a state. This freedom for the individual to act out of their own initiative forms the basis of the state in natural law, but for Schleiermacher this does not limit the state in its approach to its citizens. Within the state, individual citizens may act freely in relation to the cultural spheres of religion, science, and free sociability, and Schleiermacher demands that freedom be present in these areas. Schleiermacher rejects state intervention in religious affairs particularly strongly.

With regard to basic principles, he occasionally expresses himself clearly, but when it comes to specific questions he holds back or weighs freedom for religion and science against other current state interests. So why, from Schleiermacher's point of view, is it possible for freedom of religion, science, and trade to contradict the interests of the state? This is mainly due to the fact that religion, science, and trade align individuals with a cosmopolitan and transnational way of life, whilst political attitudes require a special bond with the state. Schleiermacher always argues that the state should act solely based on its own political self-interest. However, it is also important to consider consequences for the short and medium term. Schleiermacher brings the individual's need for freedom into play, but only as a description of the real factors that the state has to deal with. Here the distance between Schleiermacher's thinking and the ideas of the French Revolution is particularly marked.

15.6.2 Common Spirit or Political Disposition

Schleiermacher defines political disposition (*politische Gesinnung*) as "the will of all individuals to form a State with others."[35] Schleiermacher also uses the terms "civic disposition" (*bürgerliche Gesinnung*), "civic honor" (*bürgerliche Ehre*), and "the common spirit" (*Gemeingeist*) almost synonymously. They not only refer to recognition of the state as it exists per se, but also mean that skills and talents of individual citizens should be geared toward the state. Here, too, Schleiermacher thinks dialectically: Talents enable the individual to align with the state but they also lead to an individual relationship with the state, so that everyone has a different relationship with the state.[36] It is also precisely in the interest of the state that everyone carry out the activity for which they have the ability and inclination. The fact that women have very limited opportunities and that this limitation also applies to other sections of society is not discussed by Schleiermacher.

Schleiermacher also sees the activities of the individual as the source of a political disposition, provided that they are recognized as an effective contribution to the development of the state. In modern terms: self-realization results in a common spirit and a political disposition. It is not the awareness of one's own dependence on others or gratitude toward others—which are in themselves rather passive or receptive attributes—but the actual activity of the individual that forms the foundation for common consciousness and a focus on the common good. Taken further, this reasoning means that the state must ensure that every citizen is able to perform an activity that offers the possibility of self-realization as the basis of political awareness.

The various activities that are carried out within a society based on the division of labor also result in different experiences. According to Schleiermacher, in order to be able to deal with these differences, "empathy" is required.[37] This understanding must also find practical expression in the redistribution of wealth and resources.

Overall, he emphasizes that a prerequisite for awareness of the whole of society on the part of each individual, that is, the full development of a political disposition in the individual, is communication. By this he means organized communication that goes beyond the private. Schleiermacher discusses whether a political disposition as a consciousness of the common feeling of the citizens among themselves can be in opposition to citizens' loyalty to the state. According to Schleiermacher, such a contradiction can only occur if the political will of the citizens and the political direction of the authorities differ and therefore come into conflict with one another. Such a misalignment would then always be the fault of the authorities. It is particularly noteworthy that Schleiermacher sees the cause of the French Revolution only in terms of failures on the part of the rulers.

Schleiermacher subsumes the elements of solidarity of the citizens with each other, loyalty to the state, and orientation toward the common good within the concept of a political disposition. It is remarkable that he allows such great importance to be attached to the political disposition in connection with the actions of the state. This also offers a basis for further development of political ideas today.

---

[35] *LvS*, p. 146.
[36] *LvS*, p. 116.
[37] *LvS*, p. 124.

15.6.3 Equality

Equality is central to Schleiermacher's concept of a political disposition. Schleiermacher addresses many aspects of this part of the triad. Here, by way of example, equality with regard to financial resources will be discussed. As far as the distribution of wealth is concerned, Schleiermacher generally recommends the greatest possible equality for the sake of the overall development of national wealth. In order to promote equality of wealth rather than inequality, the state should intervene in legal relationships, but under no circumstances in matters of property. However, equality must not go too far for the sake of the development of the state. For example, access to higher education for all must be prevented, because activities at the base of society—he is probably thinking above all of farm and agricultural work—would not be compatible with such education. In this respect, but only in this respect, the state must allow and promote inequality. Schleiermacher clearly sees that the educational ideal he generally propagates cannot apply to all people as a matter of principle. However, his reasoning is interesting: Universal provision of (higher) education does not fail because of unequal talent, its failure must rather be ensured to enable the functioning of society. In terms of this insight, Schleiermacher's argument is solely focused on the state and prioritizes the community over the individual. There is not even a hint of reflection on its impact in anthropological, educational, or religious terms. This aspect is also a good example of the objectivity with which Schleiermacher presents his theory of the state.

15.7 On the Current Relevance of Schleiermacher's Doctrine of the State

The original expectation that Schleiermacher's newly edited lectures would offer a sustainable (theological) approach on Schleiermacher's part in terms of political theory has not in fact been fulfilled. If one starts from the perspective of political theories of the twentieth century, elements of an understanding of politics that is compatible with the present day are rather to be found in other areas of Schleiermacher's work. When Hannah Arendt thinks of politics as expressing the essential plurality of human action—as ensuing from human individuality—it is reminiscent of Schleiermacher's understanding of free sociability. In general, Arendt's understanding of politics and Schleiermacher's theory of free sociability coincide in surprisingly many respects.

There are individual insights or specific focus points within Schleiermacher's body of thought that are still compatible with present-day thinking, but they would have to be torn out of their context, both in terms of history and of Schleiermacher's work as a whole. Some of these are particularly worthy of mention.

Schleiermacher emphasizes humanity's common relationship with nature, more closely defined as a shared relationship with the land and its cultivation, as the essence of the state. Following a certain level of transformation, this can be linked with nature conservation along with the need to protect biodiversity and the climate and adapt to climate change—including protection against natural disasters—which are recognized as vital tasks today.

The issue of the speed of political change, especially in connection with acceleration of social change, is certainly one of the most controversial issues of our time. Here, Schleiermacher's ideas could play a useful role in mediating between polarized positions.

According to Schleiermacher, the more division of labor takes place within society, the more important communication between citizens becomes in order to balance out the one-sidedness of individual perspectives and experiences and to strengthen the common spirit. The media and different political parties as they exist today no longer fulfil this task to the extent necessary. Schleiermacher's questions and findings can be linked to the political debate as to how political communication can be shaped in the future. Here, too, German-language Schleiermacher scholarship could benefit significantly from the English-language research in the field. Inclusion of Schleiermacher's political thought into contemporary political philosophy and into the history of political thought, currently still in its infancy, promises to open up new perspectives with regard to this area of Schleiermacher's work.

Suggested Reading

Arndt, Andreas. *Die Reformation der Revolution: Friedrich Schleiermacher in seiner Zeit* (Berlin: Matthes & Seitz, 2019).

Arndt, Andreas, Ulrich Barth, and Wilhelm Gräb, eds. *Christentum–Staat–Kultur: Akten des Kongresses der Internationalen Schleiermacher-Gesellschaft in Berlin, März 2006* (Berlin: Walter de Gruyter, 2008).

Crouter, Richard. *Friedrich Schleiermacher: Between Enlightenment and Romanticism* (Cambridge: Cambridge University Press, 2005).

Rose, Miriam. *Schleiermachers Staatslehre* (Tübingen: Mohr Siebeck, 2011).

Vial, Theodore. "Schleiermacher and the State." In *The Cambridge Companion to Friedrich Schleiermacher*, ed. Jacqueline Mariña (Cambridge: Cambridge University Press, 2005), pp. 269–286.

Bibliography

Arndt, Andreas. *Die Reformation der Revolution: Friedrich Schleiermacher in seiner Zeit* (Berlin: Matthes & Seitz, 2019).

Arndt, Andreas, Ulrich Barth, and Wilhelm Gräb, eds. *Christentum–Staat–Kultur: Akten des Kongresses der Internationalen Schleiermacher-Gesellschaft in Berlin, März 2006* (Berlin: Walter de Gruyter, 2008).

Arndt, Andreas, Simon Gerber, and Sarah Schmidt, eds. *Wissenschaft, Kirche, Staat und Politik: Schleiermacher im preußischen Reformprozess* (Berlin: Walter de Gruyter, 2019).

Bauer, Johannes. *Schleiermacher als patriotischer Prediger: Ein Beitrag zur Geschichte der nationalen Erhebung vor hundert Jahren* (Gießen: Töpelmann, 1908).

Graf, Friedrich Wilhelm. "Lob der Differenz: Die Bedeutung der Religion in der demokratischen Kultur." In *Die herausgeforderte Demokratie: Recht, Religion, Politik, Beiheft zur Berliner Theologischen Zeitschrift*, ed. Christof Gestrich (Berlin: De Gruyter, 2003), pp. 14–29.

Graf, Friedrich Wilhelm. "Theologische Staats- und Kirchendiskurse der 'Sattelzeit.'" In *Die Säkularisation im Prozess der Säkularisierung Europa*, ed. Peter Blickle and Rudolf Schlögel (Epfendorf: bibliotheca academica Verlag, 2005), pp. 431–452.

Leonhardt, Rochus. "Staat und Religion: Zur theologie- und zeitgeschichtlichen Einordnung sowie zur Gegenwartsrelevanz der Position Schleiermachers." In *Reformation und Moderne: Pluralität–Subjektivität–Kritik. Akten des Internationalen Kongresses der Schleiermacher-Gesellschaft in Halle (Saale), März 2017*, ed. Jörg Dierken, Arnulf von Scheliha, and Sarah Schmidt (Berlin, Boston: Walter de Gruyter, 2018), pp. 229–231.

Messlin, Dorit. *Antike und Moderne. Friedrich Schlegels Poetik, Philosophie und Lebenskunst* (Berlin: Walter de Gruyter, 2011).

Reetz, Dankfried. *Schleiermacher im Horizont preußischer Politik: Studien und Dokumente zu Schleiermachers Berufung nach Halle, zu seiner Vorlesung über Politik 1817 und zu den Hintergründen der Demagogenverfolgung* (Waltrop: Hartmut Spenner, 2002).

Rose, Miriam. *Schleiermachers Staatslehre* (Tübingen: Mohr Siebeck, 2011).

Schleiermacher, Friedrich. *Predigten 1809-1815, KGA 3.4*, ed. Patrick Weiland and Simon Paschen (Berlin: De Gruyter, 2011).

Schleiermacher, Friedrich. *Predigten 1830-1831, KGA 3.12*, ed. Dirk Schmid (Berlin: De Gruyter, 2013).

Schleiermacher, Friedrich. *Briefwechsel 1774-1796, KGA 5.1*, ed. Andreas Arndt and Wolfgang Virmond (Berlin: De Gruyter, 1985).

Stegmaier, Werner. "Eigentlich das Gebiet der persönlichen Reibungen: Schleiermachers bewegliche Konzeption eines beweglichen Staates." In *Schleiermacher und Kierkegaard: Subjektivität und Wahrheit. Akten des Schleiermacher-Kierkegaard-Kongresses in Kopenhagen, Oktober 2003*, ed. Niels Jørgen Cappelørn et al. (Berlin: Walter de Gruyter, 2006), pp. 479–502.

Wolfes, Matthias. *Öffentlichkeit und Bürgergesellschaft: Friedrich Schleiermachers politische Wirksamkeit* (Berlin, New York: Walter de Gruyter, 2004).

B

SCHLEIERMACHER THE THEOLOGIAN

CHAPTER 16

THE *BRIEF OUTLINE*

PAUL T. NIMMO

16.1 INTRODUCTION

THE *Brief Outline* of Friedrich Schleiermacher is a remarkable text in the history of theology. Written as a textbook to accompany lectures introducing the discipline of theology, the work offers an innovative vision of the subject, its structure, and its purpose, and its signal influence on the later development of the field echoes down the intervening years to the present day. Such significance may at first seem unlikely for the work, given its concision and complexity, as well its highly radical and seldom imitated content. Yet the coming together of a unique constellation of contextual circumstances with Schleiermacher's own ineffable talent has led to this slim publication becoming one of the most influential of all his works.

This chapter explores the *Brief Outline* from a number of perspectives. First, it surveys the contexts within which it arose, with reference both to Enlightenment challenges to theological education and to Schleiermacher's own teaching career. Second, it considers the content of the *Brief Outline*, offering an account of its four principal sections. Third, it attends to the reception of the work, exploring its historic influence and indicating some critical responses. The conclusion reflects upon the contemporary relevance of the *Brief Outline*.

16.2 THE CONTEXT OF THE *BRIEF OUTLINE*

The early nineteenth century represented a remarkable and challenging period for theological education in Germany. A series of developments in Enlightenment thinking had significantly undermined the status and authority of the discipline of theology, which at that time was taught in separate Protestant and Catholic faculties in the universities. The classical beliefs common to both churches had increasingly come under the scrutiny of approaches guided by the critical use of human reason and encouraged by the steady advances of natural science. At the same time, increasing awareness of the historical dimension of all knowledge had led to a significant relativization of the status of the founding Scriptures of Christianity and of the subsequent tradition. The result was a series of problematic issues for the study of theology, among which Terrence Tice highlights four: the applicability of historical criticism to theology, the relationship between theology and the unity of knowledge, the particularity of theology in its relation to revelation, and the internal organization of the discipline of theology.[1]

Related to these developments, the higher education system in Germany, which had endured significant criticism late in the eighteenth century, was increasingly attracted to a bold vision of *Wissenschaft*, or "science," to ground its enterprise. The translation "science" should not mislead here: it refers not to natural science in itself, but to a rigorous and critical approach to study that seeks to acquire knowledge by way of demonstration from starting principles. Each individual science has its own subject area, structure, first principles, sources, methods, and aims, and is connected to the other sciences in an organic web of knowledge. The university was to provide a suitable home for this *wissenschaftlich* study of human knowledge, and the new University of Berlin, founded in 1810, was to be a flagship for this approach. The tricky questions for theology in light of this new intellectual ideology were whether it counted as such a science, and thus whether it belonged in a university at all.

It is within this academic context that the rise of works of theological encyclopedia in general—and the *Brief Outline* in particular—must be understood. These works, depicting the nature, divisions, and purpose of the discipline of theology, were primarily pedagogical. They paralleled similar works of introduction in other fields of study, but also had long-standing roots in the Christian tradition. Their task received a new sense of urgency and purpose in the intellectual environs of the Enlightenment, in which context theologians were seeking to demonstrate to students and skeptics alike the thematic unity, scientific quality, and disciplinary relatedness of their subject—and thus, ultimately, to justify its place within the university. And the corollary of this, as Thomas Albert Howard identifies, was "a decisive, if gradual, movement away from a sapiential, hortatory understanding of theological education . . . in the direction of a more scientific, critical theological pedagogy."[2] The *Brief Outline* is perhaps the most significant and influential of these critical scientific introductions.

Within the context of Schleiermacher's own work, attention to theological encyclopedia arose at the outset of his teaching career, when he faced what Zachary Purvis describes as "the same nexus of problems facing European scholars in earnest especially since the early years of Enlightenment: the nature of the university, the organization of knowledge, and the unity of theology's various parts."[3] Schleiermacher was convinced that these problems presented both challenge and opportunity, and that their solution depended upon integrating the best of historical science and critical method with the essence of Christianity. It is with this consistent vision in mind that Schleiermacher lectured on theological encyclopedia eleven times in the course of his academic work.[4] The first occasion was in his first semester teaching at the University of Halle in 1804–1805. Dissatisfied with existing works in theological

---

[1] Terrence Tice, "Editor's Postscript," in *BO*, pp. 141–142.

[2] Thomas Albert Howard, *Protestant Theology and the Making of the Modern German University* (Oxford: Oxford University Press, 2006), pp. 307–308.

[3] Zachary Purvis, *Theology and the University in Nineteenth-Century Germany* (Oxford: Oxford University Press, 2016), p. 2.

[4] For full details of these lectures, see Martin Rössler and Dirk Schmid, "Einleitung der Bandherausgeber," in Friedrich Schleiermacher, *Vorlesungen über die Theologische Enzyklopädie*, in *KGA* 2.2, pp. xvii–xxxi.

encyclopedia, Schleiermacher considered making his innovative lectures a standing offering in the Halle curriculum, and his thoughts and labors quickly turned toward their swift publication. However, the actual publication of the first edition of the *Brief Outline* was delayed until 1811: first, by the Napoleonic intervention in Prussia in October 1806, which closed the University and interrupted Schleiermacher's teaching, and then by a combination of working toward the new University in Berlin, setting up his married household, and undertaking parish work at the *Dreifaltigkeitskirche*.[5] By 1811, Schleiermacher had given his course on theological encyclopedia on three further occasions: again at Halle (in 1805–1806), privately in Berlin prior to the University opening (in 1808), and in his inaugural semester in the opening year of the University of Berlin (1810–1811). Over the next two decades, with the published work serving as a textbook to accompany his lectures, Schleiermacher offered the course in 1811–1812, 1814–1815, 1816–1817, 1819–1820, 1827, and 1829—testimony to its ongoing significance for his students and for himself. After the second, revised edition of the *Brief Outline* was published in 1831, it served as the textbook for his final delivery of the course in 1831–1832. Although none of Schleiermacher's lecture manuscripts survives, some student transcripts do exist.[6]

Both published editions of the textbook are slim volumes, consisting of a series of numbered propositions that are aphoristic in nature. The differences between the editions are in some ways significant, yet in other ways modest. The awkward numbering of the 392 propositions in the first edition, in which each section restarted with §1, is replaced in the second edition by sequential numbering of the now 338 propositions. The stringent concision of the earlier outing is slightly eased by the addition of brief elucidations of each proposition in the later work. And as Schleiermacher increasingly conceived of an audience also outwith the lecture hall, the readability of the work is improved by way of a rhetorical overhaul of every proposition, a careful reordering of some sections, and the provision of a table of contents. Yet in respect of the substantive content, little of significance has changed. Indeed, Schleiermacher himself recounts in the preface to the second edition that although he has added short explanatory adumbrations and made changes in respect of "expression and position [*Ausdruck und Stellung*]," yet "the view and the manner of treatment [*Ansicht und Behandlungsweise*] have on the whole remained absolutely the same."[7]

The aims of these published editions were manifold. The primary purpose is indicated already in the full title of the volume in both editions: *Brief Outline of Theological Study for the Purpose of Introductory Lectures*. Schleiermacher sought to provide a textbook for his students, offering them a concise account of the subject area of theology to accompany his lectures. But, as Purvis notes, the work also "represented [Schleiermacher's] programmatic statement on religion and pedagogical manifesto on the future of academic theology in the

---

[5] Dirk Schmid, "Einleitung des Herausgebers," in KD^1/KD^2, pp. 5, 10–11.

[6] For the details of these *Nachschriften*, see Rössler and Schmid, "Einleitung," pp. xxxi–xxxviii. On their value, see Richard Crouter's positive adjudication in *Friedrich Schleiermacher: Between Enlightenment and Romanticism* (Cambridge: Cambridge University Press, 2005), pp. 211–212, and compare Tice's more cautious view in "Bibliographical Note," in *BO*, p. 158.

[7] KD^2, p. 136; cf. *BO*, p. xxi. Translations in this chapter are the author's own; further citations of the *Brief Outline* appear inline, similarly refer to the second edition (unless otherwise noted), and indicate simply the paragraph number in KD^2, with an "A" where the material relates to Schleiermacher's *Andeutungen* (explanations).

highly transitional, post-Enlightenment, post-revolutionary world."[8] Close to the center of Schleiermacher's intentions was thus a desire to demonstrate that theology is appropriately conceived as *wissenschaftlich* and hence belongs within the context of a modern university.

16.3 THE CONTENT OF THE *BRIEF OUTLINE*

The *Brief Outline* sets out a statement of the practical purpose and corresponding unity of the discipline of theology, including an outline of its constituent subdisciplines and their organic relationships. In both editions the work falls into four principal parts: an introduction, followed by sections on the three subdisciplines of philosophical theology, historical theology, and practical theology. In this threefold structure, Schleiermacher was already being—in Howard's phrase—"somewhat idiosyncratic," departing from the traditional division of the field into exegesis, dogmatics, history, and practical theology.[9] However, he repeatedly emphasizes that for all their discrete areas of study and particularities of method, these subdisciplines share a united orientation and purpose, and are related in an organic fashion. In what follows, the contents of the introduction and then each of these three subdisciplines will be outlined, with the exclusive focus throughout being on the second edition of the *Brief Outline* from 1831.

16.3.1 Introduction

The first proposition of the introduction is particularly important for understanding Schleiermacher's conception of theology and thus the *Brief Outline* as a whole. It runs,

> Theology... is a positive science, whose parts are connected to the whole only by their common reference to a particular mode of faith, that is, a particular form of God-consciousness; the parts of Christian theology are thus connected by their relationship to Christianity. (§1)

Schleiermacher explains that the term "positive science," which he borrows from Schelling,[10] refers to a discipline whose unity does not follow from the conceptual organization of the sciences according to some necessary overarching idea of knowledge; instead it indicates that its distinct elements are "necessary for the addressing [*Lösung*] of a practical task" (§1A). The coherence of the discipline of theology thus does not depend on a first principle of thought, speculative or revealed, but on the common practical telos of its constituent academic studies. The goal of Christian theology—that which would not be possible *without* theology—Schleiermacher identifies as the "harmonious leadership [*zusammenstimmende Leitung*] of the Christian church, that is, Christian church government [*ein christliches Kirchenregiment*]" (§5). Given his academic and ecclesial setting, he is doubtless thinking here specifically of Protestant church government. And as Kurt Nowak observes, this term

---

[8] Purvis, *Theology and the University*, p. 140.
[9] Howard, *Protestant Theology*, p. 202.
[10] Schmid, "Einleitung," p. 33.

bears an expansive meaning in the *Brief Outline*: "Schleiermacher's understanding of 'church leadership' encompassed: the clarification of the life of faith and of the doctrinal position, the design of the sermon, of church organization, of liturgy, of church buildings, and much else."[11] Without this common ultimate purpose in view, Schleiermacher observes, the various distinct studies assembled for the study of theology would simply fragment and revert to other disciplines (§6).

At the outset of the *Brief Outline*, Schleiermacher thus indicates the ineradicable relationship between the academic study of theology and the historical reality of the Christian faith in its forms of appearance in history. In Schleiermacher's conception, the discipline of theology is an *ec-centric* discipline: as Richard Crouter notes, its "center lies outside itself in the practical tasks for which the science exists."[12] On this basis, Schleiermacher explicitly rules out both rational theology and its speculative approach to the discipline (§1A). By contrast, a person who combines the appropriate attendant interests—the scientific in the university sense and the practical in the religious sense—"to the highest degree and in the proper balance of theory and practice" conforms to Schleiermacher's "idea of a prince of the church [*Kirchenfürsten*]" (§9). Yet even if one is unable to attain such academic-ecclesial perfection, to be a theologian and to be existentially involved in the church are mutually invoking: one cannot be the one without the other (§12A). Yet the study of theology is not here simply reducible to the study of history. This is signaled already by Schleiermacher's denial of the idea that there can be any knowledge of Christianity "if one is satisfied only with an empirical conception" (§21). In the background here is Schleiermacher's conviction that even the flourishing of church leadership is only a proximate end of theology: the ultimate end is the advance of the Kingdom of God, and thus the spreading of faith, the increasing of the church, and the creating and deepening of corporate and personal communion with Jesus Christ.[13] The academic discipline that considers in general the way in which religious communities are "a necessary element for the development of the human spirit" and thus explores in what way and to what extent such communities can be distinguished and how this relates to their historical appearances is, in Schleiermacher's novel conception, philosophy of religion (§§22, 23). Within theology, and thus in relation to Christianity in particular, this task falls to philosophical theology.

16.3.2 Philosophical Theology

Philosophical theology, as Schleiermacher defines it, is a newly construed subdiscipline of theology, which, he declares, "has not yet been established or recognized as a unity" (§24A). For this reason, its portrayal here merits close attention. The principal task of the subdiscipline is to present "both the essence of Christianity, that by virtue of which it is a

---

[11] Kurt Nowak, *Schleiermacher: Leben, Werk, und Wirkung* (Göttingen: Vandenhoeck & Ruprecht, 2001), p. 232.

[12] Crouter, *Friedrich Schleiermacher*, p. 210.

[13] Though Schleiermacher nowhere reverts to such language in the *Brief Outline*, it is basic to his understanding of grace and providence in the *Christian Faith*, in which "the planting and extension of the Christian Church" is conceived as "the object of the divine government of the world," *CF (1928)*, §164. thesis.

particular mode of faith, and the form of the Christian community, and at the same time the way in which both of these are divided and differentiated" (§24). However, Schleiermacher insists, the particular essence of Christianity can neither be scientifically constructed nor empirically comprehended. Instead, it must be critically or dialectically determined, by "a juxtaposition of that which is historically given in Christianity and the contrasts by virtue of which religious communities can be distinguished from one another" (§32). This task requires one in turn to "take a starting point above Christianity in the logical sense of the word, that is, in the general concept of the religious [*fromme*] or faith community" (§33).

It might seem here as if Schleiermacher risks opening the door to speculative or rational approaches to Christianity, in spite of his earlier rejection of both. However, the object upon which philosophical theology reflects is already given by historical theology and is thus always presupposed—namely, the Christian mode of faith and its historical manifestations in religious communities (cf. §65), and, therefore, as the origin of this, the appearance of the Redeemer in the flesh in the person of Jesus of Nazareth. As Crouter observes, then, what philosophical theology achieves is "philosophical reflection on the form and content of a religion in its givenness," in order to undertake "the crucial task of locating and defining the 'religious consciousness' and 'church community' that are the bedrock of Christian existence."[14] And Schleiermacher correspondingly insists that in line with this scientific content it is a critical discipline, and in line with the nature of its object it is a historical-critical discipline (§37).

Philosophical theology has two principal parts. First, it has to clarify the "particular essence of Christianity" for a given church community, a task Schleiermacher (rather idiosyncratically) labels "apologetics" (§41). This outward-facing task expounds the distinctive nature of the Christian faith with reference to the historical manner of its formation, in relation both to other religious communities, and to its own perduring internal norms and institutional aspects (§§45–48). Apologetics is a necessary task for every religious community, and Schleiermacher even hopes that it might eventually lead to the disappearance of radical divisions between different Christian—or, at least, Protestant—communities (§53). Second, philosophical theology has to identify the "unhealthy deviations [from the essence of Christianity] arising in the community," and this task Schleiermacher (again idiosyncratically) labels "polemics" (§41). This inward-facing task identifies in the community negative tendencies such as "indifferentism" and "separatism," and extraneous elements such as "heresy" and "schism" (§§55–58), none of which comports with the essence of Christianity or its historical mode of development (§60). Here Schleiermacher seeks a balance—to be on guard for any "false toleration of that which is unhealthy," but also to preserve free space for fresh conceptual developments (§62A).

What is again remarkable in this innovative conception of philosophical theology, apart from its unconventional use of terms, is its consistent historical purchase. As Crouter recognizes, Schleiermacher affirms that "The primary spiritual datum is the reality of the church in empirical history, a claim that is both normative and demonstrable through the study of history."[15] At the same time, theology is more than simply empirical or historical, hence for Schleiermacher the work of philosophical theology is only possible "critically"

---

[14] Crouter, *Friedrich Schleiermacher*, p. 212.
[15] Crouter, *Friedrich Schleiermacher*, p. 213.

(§35). Again, the fine line between the rational-scientific and the historical-empirical emerges here.

16.3.3 Historical Theology

Historical theology represents for Schleiermacher the central theological discipline—"not only the foundation of practical [theology], but also the affirmation of philosophical theology" (§27). Perhaps correspondingly, it is also by far the longest part of the *Brief Outline*. At this point, as Ulrich Barth observes, what changes is "the direction of the question": the goal is no longer to determine the essence of Christianity, but "rather to grasp—on that basis and out of it—the 'course [*Verlauf*] of Christianity' (§79), indeed [to grasp this course] as a 'complete course [*Gesamtverlauf*]' (§72)."[16] This understanding yields three coordinate subdivisions of historical theology, respectively studying the earliest period of Christianity (exegetical theology), its course over time (church history), and its present situation (dogmatics and church statistics). Each of these studies, Schleiermacher recognizes, requires the use of *wissenschaftlich* techniques, in particular, historical criticism—"the universal and essential tool [*Organon*]" of historical theology and history in general (§102). Yet these studies also have a more-than-historical telos: their results are conceived first of all as "the necessary condition of every considered influence on the further advancement [of Christianity]" (§70). There is thus no history for history's sake.

Schleiermacher turns first to exegetical theology, the principal resource of which is "the collection of writings bearing within themselves the normative [*das normale*] presentation of Christianity"—in other words, the New Testament canon (§104). These first texts of Christianity are of particular significance because it is in the earliest history of any historical process that "its particular essence comes most purely to expression" (§83). In this conception, as Hans-Joachim Birkner notes, exegesis is no longer simply auxiliary to dogmatics but is "conscious as a historical science of its independent role and task."[17] The ongoing task of determining the New Testament canon belongs to the work of higher criticism (§110), while the task of determining the original text is the work of lower criticism (§118). To gain a full understanding of the texts also requires hermeneutical work and historical contextualization. In these activities, the exegete relies upon the general principles of a series of technical disciplines: there is no exclusively biblical hermeneutics or biblical philology, for example.

Within exegetical theology, Schleiermacher's focus is on the writings of the New Testament, those documents of primitive Christianity on which basis "the pure concept of Christianity can be presented" (§84A). The writings of the Old Testament, by contrast, do not present any "standard presentation of specifically Christian statements of faith" (§115A). At the same time, Schleiermacher insists that they should nonetheless be included in the Christian Bible (§115A), and that they have an auxiliary role in theology: their study, along with that of earlier and later Judaism and its texts and writers (§141), remains necessary for theology (§128).

---

[16] Ulrich Barth, "Theorie der Theologie," in *Schleiermacher Handbuch*, ed. Martin Ohst (Tübingen: Mohr Siebeck, 2017), p. 322.

[17] Hans-Joachim Birkner, *Schleiermacher-Studien*, ed. Hermann Fischer (Berlin/New York: Walter de Gruyter, 1996), p. 297.

Following exegetical theology, Schleiermacher turns to church history itself, the study of "the complete development of Christianity since it established itself as a historical phenomenon" (§149). This work also depends, for Schleiermacher, on the application of general historical principles, yet under the condition that "the whole course [of its history] is at the same time conceived as the presentation of the Christian spirit in motion, and thus everything is related to one inner [principle]" (§188). The two "most easily distinguishable features [*Functionen*]" in the development of Christianity' are "the formation [*Bildung*] of teaching" and "the shaping [*Gestaltung*] of the common life" (§166), and these together comprise the subject matter of church history. The latter includes worship and ethics, with ethics including questions of church polity (§§168, 174); the former relates to the continual effort to express ever more harmoniously and precisely "the Christian self-consciousness" (§177). Here in particular Schleiermacher emphasizes that church history must have a practical goal, relating to the purposes of church leadership, and that its work is unfruitful if it is merely self-serving (§191A). At the same time, this ecclesial telos should not get in the way of its academic approach. For Schleiermacher, the Protestant church and its leadership simply have nothing to fear from the results of honest scientific enquiry: "in the worst case, such can only provide it with the impulse to contribute to the elimination of recognized imperfections" (§193A).

The final section of historical theology relates to the present state of Christianity, and covers the disciplines of dogmatics and church statistics. Under dogmatics, Schleiermacher includes both Christian doctrine and Christian ethics: between them there is no "essential" separation (§223), even though there are justifiable grounds to distinguish them (§226). The inclusion of both these subjects under the rubric of historical theology, as well as the extensive attention here to church statistics, represents highly innovative moves on the part of Schleiermacher.

Dogmatics, or dogmatic theology, is for Schleiermacher "the coherent presentation of the teaching prevailing [*geltend*] at a given time, either in the church in general ... or in an individual church party" (§97). He thus criticizes the alternative term "systematic theology" for obscuring this historical dimension—and the connection to church leadership (§97A). In this way, he moves decisively beyond what Birkner characterizes as "the current conception ... of dogmatics" as "the systematization of biblical teachings": By contrast, dogmatics has its own particular area of study, namely, the doctrine asserted and effective in a specific context.[18] Schleiermacher begins by claiming that "A dogmatic treatment of [Christian] teaching is not possible without personal conviction" (§196), yet immediately qualifies that any treatment presenting only "the statements expressing the conviction of the individual" could not truly be called dogmatics (§197). Determinative for Schleiermacher is thus the ecclesial dimension of dogmatics, both in terms of its purpose, serving the leadership of the church, and with regard to its ascription to a specific community as the sphere of its influence and acceptance.

It is against this ecclesial backdrop that Schleiermacher's statements regarding philosophy must be viewed: for example, when he writes that "the development of doctrine ... is co-determined by the overall scientific situation, and above all by the reigning philosophical paradigm [*Philosopheme*]" (§167), or when he avers that the form of dogmatic statements is

---

[18] Birkner, *Schleiermacher-Studien*, p. 300.

"dependent on the current condition of the philosophical disciplines" (§213). The risk that dogmatics be considered to be subordinate to philosophy arises here: but in truth the relationship is—in the technical sense—accidental, such that regardless of the philosophical scheme to which any given Christian dogmatics is related, the Christian substance of the dogmatics remains the same, and is not adulterated by its mode of philosophical expression.

The task of church statistics is related to that of dogmatics in so far as it too seeks to contribute toward "knowledge of [Christianity's] situation in the present moment" (§85). In Schleiermacher's time, this was a very new area of study. As he conceives it, the subject attends to a given Christian community, and explores its "internal condition," including its polity, and its "external relations," including to other Christian communities and religious organizations as well as to the state and to the academy (§§237–238). There is also no basis for a purely parochial interest in the status of either the Protestant community or one's own immediate context; rather, Schleiermacher insists upon "knowledge of the situation of Christianity as a whole" (§244). As Nowak notes, however, a mere report would only give rise to a "meaningless compilation," hence the "internal" and "external" must be conceived in relation to each other,[19] such that the ecclesial interest of the work be kept in mind (§247).

The prominence given to history across this array of theological studies is again striking. Of particular note are the willingness to consider the normative texts of the Christian community to be fundamentally historical artefacts and the Christian teaching of the present community to be temporally specific, as well as the assumption that the course of Christian history is one of continuous and ongoing development. Indeed, Howard describes theological historicism as "a hallmark of nineteenth-century German Protestant thought."[20] Yet given the governing assumption of theology as a whole—its foundation in a specific mode of faith and its purpose in serving the church—what is at stake in this conception of theology is not simply (empirical) history. Instead, at its heart there lies the particular essence of Christianity, and thus the particular God-consciousness that founds and preserves the Christian community in human history, a history in which "the appearance of Christianity is . . . a turning-point" (§165A).

16.3.4 Practical Theology

The third major part of the discipline of theology is practical theology. This subdiscipline relates to the activities of church leadership, in so far as the latter is engaged "both extensively and intensively in holding together and developing further" the life of the Christian community (§25). The correct theoretical conception of these tasks of church leadership depends for Schleiermacher on knowledge of both the current situation of the church (from historical theology) and the essence of Christianity (from philosophical theology). The particular work of practical theology itself relates to "the correct mode of proceeding in carrying out all of the[se] tasks" (§260), and thus, Barth explains, to "classifying and grouping [of these tasks] in order to transform their procedures by way of 'rules' [§261]"—that is, by way of suitable methods (§263).[21] Yet knowing these rules and methods is not quite enough, for

---

[19] Nowak, *Schleiermacher*, p. 230.
[20] Howard, *Protestant Theology*, p. 318.
[21] Barth, "Theorie der Theologie," p. 326.

"the mode of their application to individual cases is not yet determined" (§265). What is in view here is thus a particular praxis that requires "a particular talent" and "inner constitution [*Beschaffenheit*]" (§§265A, 266). Referencing the antique concept of *techne*, Crouter observes that "practical theology is *technical*, an art or skillful craft . . . that links thought to practice."[22]

As a rubric under which to gather the tasks of church leadership, Schleiermacher uses the term "direction of souls [*Seelenleitung*]" (§263). Yet given the different forms of church leadership in different Christian communities, such direction is once again a community-specific affair, covering two distinct areas: "church government [*Kirchenregiment*]," directed toward the whole church, and "church service [*Kirchendienst*]," directed toward the individual community (§274). Here, church service refers to consideration of the tasks of edifying and governing the congregation and its members, and hence the areas of Christian worship, pastoral work, and ethical direction. Church government, meanwhile, relates to consideration of church polity, and particularly to the appropriate balance of the organized institutional features of the church and its free spiritual aspects. The last-named, Schleiermacher notes, includes the activity "of the academic theologian and of the ecclesiastical writer" (§328).

This detailed consideration of practical theology is the inevitable outcome of Schleiermacher's insistence upon the church community and church leadership as the essence and goal of theology. It is in connection with this part of the encyclopedia, Crouter notes, that "the theologian's gifts yield fruit and exert leadership within the life of a congregation, the larger church body, and the world of human affairs."[23] Yet successful conception of its tasks and methods, for Schleiermacher, depends on the foregoing work of philosophical and historical theology (§336). And conversely, both philosophical theology and historical theology share with practical theology the aim of the successful exercise of church leadership, and thus, ultimately, the telos of serving the increase of the church and the spread of redemption.

16.4 THE RECEPTION OF THE *BRIEF OUTLINE*

Dirk Schmid observes that to write the reception history of the *Brief Outline* would be "to write the history of the academic discipline of theological encyclopedia in the nineteenth and twentieth century."[24] Yet this influence was not evident or effective immediately. Indeed, as Birkner notes, "The writing of 1811 was anything but a literary success. It went practically unnoticed by the theology of the time."[25] Schleiermacher himself found the published version of his material to be an invaluable teaching aid, noting that with its support, "the lectures certainly become more comprehensible."[26] The first edition thus represents a success in its own terms, and was even received at court. The king, however, expressed the desire that educated people at the university should write more intelligibly; this was a criticism that

---

[22] Crouter, *Friedrich Schleiermacher*, p. 221.
[23] Crouter, *Friedrich Schleiermacher*, p. 221.
[24] Schmid, "Einleitung," p. 41.
[25] Birkner, *Schleiermacher-Studien*, p. 289.
[26] Quoted in Schmid, "Einleitung," p. 13.

Schleiermacher seems to have viewed almost as a badge of honor, insisting upon the importance of attending his lecture courses to receive the necessary clarifications.[27]

The king's concern, however, is also echoed in some of the few reviews of the first edition.[28] A number of reviewers lamented its lack of clarity, with both the aphoristic form and elaborate style of the work causing problems. It was further observed that the *Brief Outline* was purely formal and regrettably brief, and thus unsuited for orienting and instructing beginners. And beyond these rather general points, there were a series of specific formal concerns, notably that the *Brief Outline* lay wide open to the dangers of clericalizing, subordinating theology to the church in a distinctly un-Protestant way, and that the work was underdeveloped in its philosophical aspects, which led to it being less ecclesially valuable, even to the point of being not even Christian, let alone Protestant. At the same time, the *Brief Outline* was lauded for the ordering, uniformity, and unity of its material, as well as for its originality, and it was very well received among Schleiermacher's friends and students.

The second edition addressed some of the stylistic concerns of reviewers noted above regarding the first edition, yet it too provoked little by way of direct reviews or immediate reaction. Schmid suggests, however, that rather than this evidencing a lack of significance or attention, it indicates "that this book earned the position of a universally respected, almost already classic contribution to theological encyclopedia,"[29] and as Birkner relates, it is only with this second edition that the great history of its influence really begins.[30]

Among many later works greatly influenced by the *Brief Outline* there stands the enormously successful theological encyclopedia of Karl Rudolf Hagenbach (1801–1874), the first of ten editions of which was published in 1833, and which was thoroughly indebted to the form of Schleiermacher's vision.[31] Indeed, this volume's remarkable success easily eclipsed at the time that of the *Brief Outline*.[32] Given its attempt to balance the scientific and the ecclesial, the *Brief Outline* was also highly influential on the encyclopedias of Protestant mediating theology in the mid-nineteenth century.[33] On the Roman Catholic side, the *Brief Outline* was markedly significant for the work of Johann Sebastian Drey (1777–1853), who explicitly cited and regularly alluded to Schleiermacher in his own theological encyclopedia, first published in 1834.[34] And the *Brief Outline* was deployed as a textbook by some of Schleiermacher's contemporaries and associates, including Joachim Christian Gaß (1766–1831) and August Twesten (1789–1876), who respectively used the first and the second editions.[35]

As the nineteenth century progressed, the prominence and status of theological encyclopedia slowly diminished. Howard identifies three particular reasons for this decline: the increasing fragmentation of the discipline of theology and the corresponding threat to its unity; the ongoing problem of the relationship between academic theology and the church;

---

[27] Schmid, "Einleitung," p. 15.
[28] For full details of the relevant reviews, see Schmid, "Einleitung," pp. 16–33.
[29] Schmid, "Einleitung," p. 41.
[30] Hans-Joachim Birkner, "Vorwort," in Friedrich Schleiermacher, *Theologische Enzyklopädie: (1831/32). Nachschrift David Friedrich Strauss* [SchlA 4], ed. Walter Sachs (Berlin/New York: De Gruyter, 1987), p. viii.
[31] Howard, *Protestant Theology*, p. 313.
[32] Purvis, *Theology and the University*, p. 160.
[33] Purvis, *Theology and the University*, pp. 160, 165.
[34] Purvis, *Theology and the University*, pp. 161–162.
[35] Schmid, "Einleitung," p. 43.

and the emerging problem of the distinction between academic theology and the new discipline of religious studies.[36] Such problems attended theology as a whole, but the task of theological encyclopedia especially. In the early twentieth century, further blows were dealt to the genre, among which might be named the devastating impact of the First World War upon notions of historical progress and scientific confidence, and the rise on the one hand of dialectical theology and on the other hand of positivist approaches. In face of these onslaughts, Purvis recounts, the "particular idealist superstructure [of theological encyclopedia], committed to the unity of knowledge, sank under their cumulative weight, and consequently disintegrated."[37]

However, Purvis continues, even as theological encyclopedia fell away, so their impact and form have persisted in shaping the discipline and its curriculum in Germany and beyond.[38] Within this trajectory of influence, the *Brief Outline* itself has retained signal import. As Birkner observes, in so far as twentieth-century attempts "have engaged with the working conditions and problematic aspects of scientifically organized theology . . . the *Brief Outline* has always emerged as that conversation partner [*Bezugstext*] that has maintained its position as the seminal outline and as the basic scientific-theoretical document of modern theology."[39]

This seminal influence arises partly from the innovative features of the *Brief Outline*: the threefold arrangement of the discipline, the classification of philosophical theology as a distinct branch of enquiry, the positioning of dogmatics within historical theology, the insistence upon the inclusion of the study of church statistics, the exposition of practical theology as itself a scientific discipline, as well as the overarching insistence that the unity of theology lies in its definition as a positive science for the church. So innovative was his particular construal of the discipline that, as Schleiermacher frequently laments, the material content to fill it satisfactorily had not yet been developed (see at the outset, for example, §§24, 25A, 29A).

Yet the remarkable influence of the *Brief Outline* arguably arises principally from its attempt to hold together the scientific aspects and the ecclesial interests of the discipline. Howard observes that "defining the relationship of the new spirit of *Wissenschaft* to theology became one of the most worrisome, controversial, celebrated, and extensively discussed issues of the times."[40] Schleiermacher was entirely confident that the right balance of the two could be struck, writing that "a harmonious organization of the church"—which is, after all, the entire purpose of theology—"can . . . only proceed from a very developed historical consciousness"; but to be fruitful this must be accompanied by "a clear knowledge of the relationships between religious states [of being] and all others" (§8A). Indeed, in the view of Purvis, "The *Kurze Darstellung* [Brief Outline] became so successful in part because it held together the theory and practice of theology in the institutional setting of the modern scientific university."[41]

---

[36] Howard, *Protestant Theology*, p. 320.
[37] Purvis, *Theology and the University*, p. 227.
[38] Purvis, *Theology and the University*, p. 227.
[39] Birkner, "Vorwort," p. ix.
[40] Howard, *Protestant Theology*, p. 210.
[41] Purvis, *Theology and the University*, p. 165.

The extent to which Schleiermacher manages to hold the ecclesial and the academic together is not susceptible of easy adjudication. To satisfy all the relevant parties of his day—indeed, of any day—on the appropriate relation between the scientific and the ecclesial would seem to be impossible. Two particular trajectories of critical evaluation arose at this point.

From the one side, it was feared that with its purpose explicitly lying outwith its scientific study, theology is subordinated to the work of the church and, particularly, to the church leadership. If that were true—as David Friedrich Strauß, who attended Schleiermacher's lectures in 1831–1832, believed—it would be in danger of losing its academic credibility, as well, potentially, as its organic unity.[42] However, as Barth observes, while the reference to the church gives the discipline its unity, it is not for Schleiermacher this reference that grounds the scientific character of the discipline; the latter is grounded rather in the independent *wissenschaftlich* nature of those subdisciplines that are drawn into the work of theology, and that are the professional business of a circle of educated scholars.[43] Moreover, Schleiermacher frequently insists upon flexibility and freedom of enquiry in theology, championing the "free spiritual" labors of academic theologians and ecclesiastical writers, both of whom should be able to work without oppressive ecclesiastical authority (§328). That all said, his view that the ultimate aim of the discipline of theology lies in the advance of a particular religious community has never sat entirely easily in any modern university.

From the other side, as noted above, it was feared that in seeking to justify its home in the university, theology would risk sacrificing its core Christian principles. As Howard notes, most theological encyclopedias in Germany sought "to reconcile theology with modern forms of consciousness, whether speculative, historical, or scientific."[44] But for Schleiermacher, this reconciliation was not an act of compromise but of opportunism. Johannes Zachhuber writes that figures such as Schleiermacher "were inspired by the conviction that the new tools of historical and philological methodology as well as new philosophical insights would yield a better theology than had been possible in the past."[45] Schleiermacher thus advocated "continuing inward receptivity to new [scientific] investigations" as "essential to the spirit of the church" (§219A). It might be contended that Schleiermacher was optimistic at this point in respect of the compatibility of such academic investigations with the religious spirit of the church. And certainly he never launched any meaningful critique of the status or claims of modern *Wissenschaft* from a Christian perspective. Instead, he simply and consistently emphasized that to adopt a *wissenschaftlich* approach was not to turn away from the church and its essential teachings, and to recognize the central place of history in theology and in Christianity was not to denigrate the import and substance of Christian faith. This claim to the comportability of academic enquiry and Christian faith remains a disputed matter.

---

[42] Schmid, "Einleitung," pp. 44–45.
[43] Barth, "Theorie der Theologie," pp. 317–318.
[44] Howard, *Protestant Theology*, pp. 306, 319.
[45] Johannes Zachhuber, *Theology as Science in Nineteenth-Century Germany: From F.C. Baur to Ernst Troeltsch* (Oxford: Oxford University Press, 2013), p. 5.

16.5 Conclusion

In his eulogy for Schleiermacher, his friend Friedrich Lücke wrote that in the *Brief Outline* "theology appears for the first time as an organic whole . . . taking up, separating, connecting, arranging . . . the religious and the scientific, the practical and the theoretical, the positive and the philosophical," thereby rendering it "a theology of the future . . . a truly prophetic work."[46] For all the hyperbole, Lücke captures well the basic features of Schleiermacher's work in its attempts to navigate different constituencies and satisfy distinct interests. In a remarkably innovative way, it charts a new path beyond the previous approaches of Kantian practical theology, speculative idealist theology, traditional revealed theology, and rationally formed neology. And it does so in a highly systematic and rigorous manner, designed to assure readers of the viability of the discipline of theology within the context of the modern university.

While the genre of theological encyclopedia is seldom encountered today, the questions it—and the *Brief Outline* in particular—addresses are still as topical and contested as ever. Questions concerning the institutional home of theology, the curricular relationship between its constituent subdisciplines, and the interdisciplinary connections between theology and other sciences all continue to be topics of theological debate. The material contained in the *Brief Outline* will give any serious thinker ample grounds for reflection, even if they do not share Schleiermacher's confidence that scientific objectivity and personal faith can be reconciled. And even if they do share this optimism, questions will arise as to whether such a reconciliation can be transferable and applicable to very different times and contexts in which different relationships between the three actors of church, state, and academy prevail. Moreover, other questions relevant for the construal of the discipline of theology today doubtless require more attention than Schleiermacher was able to devote to them, particularly as they pertain to rapidly evolving areas such as technology, culture, and mission, and where they might be located within the structure of a theological encyclopedia.

Beyond these questions, one final legacy of the *Brief Outline* might be noted, and that is its conception of the students it is seeking to inform. On the one hand, the theologian is expected by Schleiermacher to be a person of faith, committed to both the religion of Christianity and the service of the church. On the other hand, the theologian is also expected to be an accomplished academic, knowing "the basic features of all the theological disciplines" (§16) while also being ready to engage in "purifying and expanding the existing achievements [of the discipline]" (§19). This ideal of the theological student may be laudable, but the question arises as to whether it, or the idea of a "prince of the church" that is its telos, has ever truly been anything more than aspirational. In this connection, perhaps one might simply conclude that it is far better to have such high ambitions for one's students than not.

---

[46] Friedrich Lücke, "Erinnerung an Dr. Friedrich Schleiermacher," *TSK* 7 (1834), p. 772, quoted in Purvis, *Theology and the University*, p. 160.

Suggested Readings

Howard, Thomas Albert. *Protestant Theology and the Making of the Modern German University* (Oxford: Oxford University Press, 2006).
Purvis, Zachary. *Theology and the University in Nineteenth-Century Germany* (Oxford: Oxford University Press, 2016).
Schmid, Dirk. "Einleitung des Herausgebers." In KD^1/KD^2, pp. 1–55.

Bibliography

Barth, Ulrich. "Theorie der Theologie." In *Schleiermacher Handbuch*, ed. Martin Ohst (Tübingen: Mohr Siebeck, 2017), pp. 316–327.
Birkner, Hans-Joachim. *Schleiermacher-Studien*. Ed. Hermann Fischer (Berlin/New York: Walter de Gruyter, 1996).
Birkner, Hans-Joachim. "Vorwort." In Friedrich Schleiermacher, *Theologische Enzyklopädie: (1831/32). Nachschrift David Friedrich Strauss* [SchlA 4], ed. Walter Sachs (Berlin/New York: De Gruyter, 1987), pp. vii–xii.
Crouter, Richard. *Friedrich Schleiermacher: Between Enlightenment and Romanticism* (Cambridge: Cambridge University Press, 2005).
Howard, Thomas Albert. *Protestant Theology and the Making of the Modern German University* (Oxford: Oxford University Press, 2006).
Nowak, Kurt. *Schleiermacher: Leben, Werk, und Wirkung* (Göttingen: Vandenhoeck & Ruprecht, 2001).
Purvis, Zachary. *Theology and the University in Nineteenth-Century Germany* (Oxford: Oxford University Press, 2016).
Rößler, Martin, and Dirk Schmid. "Einleitung der Bandherausgeber." In *KGA* 2.2, pp. xvii–l.
Schleiermacher, Friedrich. *Vorlesungen über die Theologische Enzyklopädie*, KGA 2.2, ed. Martin Rößler and Dirk Schmid (Berlin: De Gruyter, 2019).
Schmid, Dirk. "Einleitung des Herausgebers." In KD^1/KD^2, pp. 1–55.
Tice, Terrence. "Editor's Postscript" and "Bibliographical Note." In *BO*, pp. 127–156 and 157–165.
Zachhuber, Johannes. *Theology as Science in Nineteenth-Century Germany: From F.C. Baur to Ernst Troeltsch* (Oxford: Oxford University Press, 2013).

CHAPTER 17

INTRODUCTION TO THE *GLAUBENSLEHRE* AND *ON THE GLAUBENSLEHRE*

DANIEL PEDERSEN

17.1 INTRODUCTION

THE Introduction to *The Christian Faith* (*CG2* §§1–31) is one of the most important and controversial texts in the history of doctrine. It has been regarded as epoch-making by friend and foe alike.[1] The Introduction is a crucial text for students and scholars to be familiar with not only if they hope to understand Schleiermacher's thought, but also to understand the history of theology since.

However, the Introduction is a particularly difficult text to understand, let alone master. And its opacity has exposed Schleiermacher to misunderstanding—both from critics and admirers—even in his own day. In hopes of remedying this confusion, Schleiermacher wrote two open letters to his friend, Dr. Lücke, explaining himself further. Many of the objections and confusions addressed in the *Letters to Lücke* (hereafter *Letters*) center on the Introduction. Accordingly, best practice is to read the Introduction in light of what Schleiermacher claims in the *Letters*.

In what follows I examine the Introduction closely through a selection of central themes that have generated scholarly debate from Schleiermacher's day to the present. I do so in a way that is informed by the *Letters*, and also, where possible and fitting, draw some of these themes and claims together from both works explicitly.

I do so in the following order. First, I give an interpretative sketch of the Introduction to orient new readers, as well as to offer a view of the whole. Second, I take up the central topic of the Introduction: piety—that modification of feeling which is the consciousness of God. Third, I turn to the controversial question of the immediacy of this feeling with an

---

[1] See Karl Barth, *The Theology of Schleiermacher*, trans. Geoffrey Bromiley (Grand Rapids, MI: Eerdmans, 1982 [1923/24, 1978]), p. 193; Ernst Troeltsch, *The Christian Faith*, trans. Garrett E. Paul (Minneapolis: Fortress Press, 1991 [1912, 1913]), p. 9.

eye to ongoing debates about how immediacy might be understood and defended. Fourth, I look at Schleiermacher's influential but controversial account of non-Christian religious communions. And, finally, I shift emphasis from the Introduction to an important theme from the *Letters*—Schleiermacher's call for an "eternal covenant" between faith and science—which also serves to unify my previous interpretation of the God-consciousness with which I began.

By the end, I hope to not only clarify some important claims and concepts, and to say something about the scholarly conversation regarding them, but also to offer a characterization of the whole of the Introduction for readers to use as a pattern in their own further reading.

17.2 THE INTRODUCTION IN OUTLINE

The Introduction, Schleiermacher writes, clarifies the task of dogmatics so that we do not confuse it with some other, related task.[2] The clarification of the task of dogmatics means both a clarification of its ends and of its means.

For Schleiermacher, dogmatics is a function of the Christian church.[3] It has its source in Christian piety, and it has its term (i.e. its end) in Christian teaching and preaching[4]— the latter being itself ordered to the further propagation and reinforcement of piety. Being concerned with Christian piety from beginning to end, it is natural that readers of *The Christian Faith* would be concerned to learn what that piety is, how it is possible to begin from it, and why it is good to act for the sake of it.

It is to begin to satisfy these questions that Schleiermacher famously describes piety as a modification of *feeling* (*Gefühl*), in contrast to either knowing or doing.[5] This is to say, piety is a form of immediate self-consciousness,[6] which issues in thoughts and deeds, as well as which mediates between thinking and doing, between intellect and will.[7] The common element of all piety, Schleiermacher claims, is "the consciousness of being absolutely dependent on, or, which is the same thing, of being in relation with God."[8] Schleiermacher will call this feeling of absolute dependence the "God-consciousness" or the "consciousness of God"— the two are synonymous.[9]

Schleiermacher means to hold two things simultaneously in this account of piety. First, he holds that feeling is not a form of either thinking or doing.[10] And second, he holds that, although feeling is neither thinking nor doing, it is susceptible of, and naturally leads to, both (1) explanation and (2) action.[11] That means that something which is not, in itself, either

---

[2] *CG²*, §1; *CF (1928)*, pp. 1–2.
[3] *CG²*, §2; *CF (1928)*, pp. 3–4.
[4] *CG²*, §19, postscript; *CF (1928)*, pp. 92–93.
[5] *CG²*, §3; *CF (1928)*, pp. 5–12.
[6] *CG²*, §3.2; *CF (1928)*, pp. 6–7.
[7] *CG²*, §3.4; *CF (1928)*, pp. 8–11.
[8] *CG²*, §4; *CF (1928)*, p. 12.
[9] *CG²*, §4.4; *CF (1928)*, pp. 17–18; *OG*, p. 46.
[10] *CG²*, §3.3; *CF (1928)*, pp. 7–8.
[11] *CG²*, §3.4; *CF (1928)*, pp. 8–11.

thinking or doing nevertheless inevitably results in both determinate cognitive content and determinate action, in both particular thoughts and deeds. Feeling is neither thinking nor doing, but it is a source of both.

Feeling is susceptible of modification, and the communities of piety that naturally form around feeling reflect various modifications in their teaching and practice. Though there are both Christian and non-Christian communities of piety,[12] it would, however, be an error to think that the diverse modifications are equal. Rather, according to Schleiermacher, they stand in a hierarchical relationship with one another, ranked from least perfect to most perfect.[13]

First, the non-monotheistic communions reflect more or less *confused* modifications of the true consciousness of absolute dependence.[14] This is to say, they err either in falling short of the absoluteness of dependence required by true piety or by mistakenly identifying the cause upon which they depend. These include communions that assign divinity to statues, totems, or other created objects, as well as polytheistic communions that think there are a plurality of sources of ultimate dependence, even if those sources are held to be extra-mundane.

Second, even other communions that share the true consciousness of *absolute* dependence (i.e. the monotheistic communions of Judaism and Islam) suffer a greater or lesser deficit in whether their piety issues in action, and how well they characterize that upon which they depend absolutely.[15] According to Schleiermacher, the Christian communion, reflecting the distinctive Christian consciousness of redemption by Christ, alone enjoys the best kind of piety that is reflected in the unity of true first principles (absolute dependence on God) and determinate content (redemption by God in Christ).[16]

In all cases, the enjoyment of unsurpassable piety does not, however, guarantee the ability to *explain* such piety well. And, as Schleiermacher charges, it is the distinctive task of Christian dogmatics to give careful accounts of the Christian consciousness of redemption.[17] This is to be done clearly, coherently, and comprehensively (in short, *scientifically*),[18] all the while retaining the distinctiveness and diversity reflective of Protestant theology,[19] the generosity and critical eye required of modernity,[20] and the relation of the resulting explanation to piety as beginning and end—the end which is the reason-for-being of dogmatics in the first place.[21]

In sum, the Introduction delineates the task of Christian dogmatics that the remainder of *The Christian Faith* carries out. The Introduction specifies the inquiring subject (i.e. the church) and subject matter (i.e. piety and its corollary, God), specifies the ends that make this task desirable and the means that make it possible, and carefully distinguishes the specifically Christian task of ecclesial dogmatics from its semblances (like the work of another

---

[12] CG^2, §6.4; *CF (1928)*, pp. 28–29.
[13] CG^2, §7; *CF (1928)*, pp. 31–34.
[14] CG^2, §8; *CF (1928)*, pp. 34–39.
[15] CG^2, §9; *CF (1928)*, pp. 39–44.
[16] CG^2, §§9.2, 11, 14.1; *CF (1928)*, pp. 42–44, 52–60, 68–69.
[17] CG^2, §15; *CF (1928)*, pp. 76–78.
[18] CG^2, §§16–18, 28; *CF (1928)*, pp. 78–88, 118–123.
[19] CG^2, §§23–24; *CF (1928)*, pp. 101–108.
[20] CG^2, §§20–22, 25; *CF (1928)*, pp. 94–101, 108–111.
[21] CG^2, §19; *CF (1928)*, pp. 88–93.

communion, or of philosophy, etc.) in several respects. So much, but only so much, I take it, is the aim of the Introduction.

If correct, this correlates Schleiermacher's Introduction well with a long line of theological prolegomena. It is typical in theology from the Middle Ages, through the post-Reformation period, to the present, to begin a work of theology by delineating the theological aims at hand and by specifying sources and norms. Schleiermacher is simply putting his own twist on this perennial task.

17.3 Feeling and the God-consciousness

If Schleiermacher's account of feeling, the God-consciousness, modifications of piety, and so on, are all in service of a well-ordered Christian dogmatics itself ordered to Christian piety, a reader would be justified in wondering how these notions might be understood, and understood in a recognizably Christian way. Therefore, we start by examining piety itself, that modification of feeling Schleiermacher calls the consciousness of God.

Both in Schleiermacher's day and since, the notion of the God-consciousness has puzzled interpreters. Feeling (*Gefühl*) is *not* thought or action, but something else; and the God-consciousness is a modification of feeling.[22] Nonetheless, feeling is supposed to be a source of Christian dogmatics. In fact, the whole of *The Christian Faith* is meant to be a reflection on that feeling.[23] So whatever feeling is, it must be the sort of thing that is at least liable to being thought about, even if it is not thought itself. This has led to scholarly debates about how to understand the relation of the God-consciousness to the content it includes or implies.

Schleiermacher gives some examples that help to outline what he thinks consciousness in general is. First, he thinks we are conscious of ourselves and that we are conscious of being in a world.[24] So whatever consciousness means, Schleiermacher thinks consciousness is contentful in that we are (minimally) conscious of being selves in a world with all that being a self and being in a world entails. In fact, Schleiermacher writes in the *Letters*, "that a large part of my *Glaubenslehre* is nothing other than a description of this world view."[25]

In addition to such different kinds of consciousness (consciousness of self, world, and God), consciousness comes in different degrees for Schleiermacher. For example, he describes the kind of consciousness that animals have as less than fully self-conscious, but not simply unconscious. Schleiermacher compares this "confused animal grade"[26] of consciousness to that of very young children who have not yet learned to use language, as well as to adults in "the transition from waking to sleeping."[27] When consciousness is not confused (i.e. when children learn to speak and when adults awaken fully), we come to enjoy "sensible self-consciousness."[28] By sensible self-consciousness, Schleiermacher means the

---

[22] CG^2, §3; *CF (1928)*, pp. 5–12.
[23] CG^2, §31; *CF (1928)*, pp. 127–128.
[24] CG^2, §4; *CF (1928)*, pp. 12–18.
[25] *OG*, p. 44.
[26] CG^2, §5.1; *CF (1928)*, p. 19.
[27] CG^2, §5.1; *CF (1928)*, p. 19.
[28] CG^2, §5.3; *CF (1928)*, p. 21.

consciousness of sensible things, which is to say, the world we can touch and see, including ourselves as agents.

A further aspect of consciousness arises as a corollary to the sensible self-consciousness, from our awareness that our freedom, even in the sensible world, is not absolute. The corollary is our feeling—that is, consciousness—of being absolutely dependent on something that is neither ourselves, nor any other member of the world, nor the world as a whole.[29] This feeling—the feeling of absolute dependence—is the consciousness of God.[30]

Readers have often been perplexed by Schleiermacher's claims about the sensible self-consciousness and the God-consciousness. But even in this early light, Schleiermacher's account has a basic plausibility to it. Historically, nearly all Christian theologians have denied (1) that God is an object in the world, (2) that God is something that can be known by the senses, and (3) that God is the sort of thing we can act upon. At the same time, they have affirmed (1) that God exists, (2) that God is what explains the sensible world, and (3) that God acts upon us. Schleiermacher is in good company on all six counts, and whatever else his theory implies, it includes these basic commitments.

Nevertheless, while these commitments help us to outline what Schleiermacher means by the God-consciousness, they are still only parameters. For further help, scholars often look to fill out Schleiermacher's meaning from material beyond the Introduction. For example, the God-consciousness seems very similar to what Schleiermacher calls "intuition" in his *Speeches*. To my knowledge, no one before Schleiermacher used the compound word "God-consciousness" (though, as we will see, at least one thinker, Spinoza, writes about being conscious of God). However, many thinkers before Schleiermacher gave accounts of intuition—often linked to God—and we know that many of these thinkers directly influenced Schleiermacher. In consequence, scholars also sometimes use these other thinkers' notions of intuition to help illuminate Schleiermacher's account.

The idea that other thinkers, philosophers included, might help explain Schleiermacher's theology raises the controversial issue of the role of philosophy in the Introduction. The effort to *reduce* Schleiermacher's theology to philosophy has historical precedent,[31] and Schleiermacher directly addresses the charge in his *Letters*.[32] There he claims that his theology is not reducible to philosophy or to philosophical sources. But in the *Letters* he also writes that he makes free use of philosophy, particularly when the philosophers he makes use of are tacitly doing theology.[33] Most Schleiermacher scholars today take him at his word. In either case, in the Introduction he plainly acknowledges borrowing from philosophy (among other disciplines) for theological purposes.[34]

At the top of many lists of Schleiermacher's philosophical influences is Immanuel Kant.[35] If Schleiermacher was mainly following Kant, Kant's notion of intuition might help explain the God-consciousness. Kant is notoriously vague on what he means by intuition, however,

---

[29] CG^2, §4.3; *CF (1928)*, pp. 15–16.
[30] CG^2, §4.4; *CF (1928)*, pp. 16–18.
[31] See Barth, *The Theology of Schleiermacher*, p. 275.
[32] *OG*, pp. 38–39, 80–81.
[33] *OG*, pp. 81–82.
[34] CG^2, §§3–10; *CF (1928)*, pp. 5–52.
[35] See, for example, Colin E. Gunton, *The Actuality of Atonement: A Study of Metaphor, Rationality, and the Christian Tradition* (London: T&T Clark, 2004 [1988]), pp. 9–16; Theodore Vial, "Anschauung and Intuition, Again, (Or, 'We Remain Bound to the Earth')," in *Schleiermacher, the Study of Religion,*

and it seems that he uses the word in at least two ways. One thing Kant means by an intuition is a kind of representation. It is, at least in some cases, a conceptually unmediated representation.[36] The importance of something being conceptually unmediated will become clear when we look at debates around the God-consciousness and immediacy below. However, other readings making use of Kant have been offered as well. Vial argues that Kant is the source of Schleiermacher's notion of intuition but thinks "intuition" should be taken in another sense used by Kant: as a kind of direct causal influence that gives rise to a perception.[37]

Besides Kant there are yet more accounts of intuition that are, in my view, at least as likely as Kant's to have influenced Schleiermacher. These sources are much less commonly appealed to, and any explanation that makes use of them will likely be in at least some tension with explanations that appeal to Kant on related points. Therefore, the reader should be aware that the view I advance in what follows is a controversial one insofar as I claim that non-Kantian sources, especially traditional theological notions, traced back to Plato, provide the best explanatory power. So far as I know, however, although my view on these matters is unique as a whole, it is not unique in all its parts; and others' scholarship supports these contentions.

Spinoza is one other source for Schleiermacher's thinking,[38] and Spinoza also has an account of intuitive knowledge of God. Spinoza thinks that we can know God by what he calls the "third kind of knowledge": an immediate knowledge by intuition that entails determinate, even necessary, conclusions, yet which is non-inferential in nature (meaning, we do not arrive at this knowledge by inference from premises to conclusions).[39] Like Schleiermacher, Spinoza thinks that intuition of God not only results in true or adequate thoughts, but also freedom, blessedness, and love in the one who comes to understand God in this way.[40] It is, according to Spinoza, by this third kind of knowledge, that "we feel and know by experience that we are eternal. For the mind feels those things that it conceives in understanding no less than those it has in memory. For the eyes of the mind, by which it sees and observes things, are demonstrations themselves."[41] To know God by virtue of intuitive knowledge, Spinoza tells us, is the highest perfection of human being, and is accordingly accompanied by joy.[42] In fact, Spinoza claims that "the more each of us is able to achieve in this kind of knowledge, the more he is conscious of himself and of God, i.e., the more perfect and blessed he is."[43] And, most importantly of all, because God is the cause of this knowledge, an intellectual love of God arises as one of its necessary effects.[44] This intellectual

and the Future of Theology, ed. Brent W. Sockness and Wilhelm Gräb (Berlin: Walter de Gruyter, 2010), pp. 41, 44.

[36] See the discussion in Andrew Janiak, "Kant"s Views on Space and Time," *Stanford Encyclopedia of Philosophy* (2016), https://plato.stanford.edu/entries/kant-spacetime/.

[37] Vial, "Anschauung and Intuition, Again," pp. 44–46.

[38] Julia A. Lamm, *The Living God: Schleiermacher's Theological Appropriation of Spinoza* (University Park, PA: Pennsylvania State University Press, 1996); Daniel J. Pedersen, *The Eternal Covenant* (Berlin: Walter de Gruyter, 2017).

[39] Benedict Spinoza, "Ethics," in *The Collected Works of Spinoza*, vol. 1, ed. and trans. Edwin Curley (Princeton: Princeton University Press, 1985), IIP40S2.

[40] Spinoza, *Ethics*, VP20S.

[41] Spinoza, *Ethics*, VP23S, pp. 607–608, translation revised.

[42] Spinoza, *Ethics*, VP27.

[43] Spinoza, *Ethics*, VP31S, p. 610.

[44] Spinoza, *Ethics*, VP32.

love of God, caused by our intuitive knowledge of God, is not different than God's self-love. Therefore, the love by which we love God "is the very love of God by which God loves himself."[45] And it is our sharing in the self-love of God, through intuitive knowledge, in which salvation or blessedness consists.[46] Schleiermacher's account of the God-consciousness is remarkably close to Spinoza's account of intuitive knowledge of God on all counts.

This is no accident. Spinoza's account itself follows a long tradition in Christian theology of thinking about knowledge of God by vision ("intuition" comes from the medieval Latin *intuitio*: to see). Any number of ancient, medieval, or post-Reformation accounts could also be cited as possible sources,[47] but they all share the same basic idea: because of the uniqueness of God, we cannot know God in the same way that we can know an object in the world. Therefore, the way we come to know God is by coming to share in God's intuitive, that is non-inferential, self-understanding. The perfected fullness of this intuitive self-understanding of God is the beatific vision enjoyed by the blessed in heaven. My own view is that *this* traditional theological understanding of intuition, not Kant's, best explains what Schleiermacher thinks about the immediate consciousness of God.

In fact, Schleiermacher himself describes the beatific vision later in *The Christian Faith* in these exact terms: as the "completest fullness of the most living God-consciousness."[48] He explains that in that perfected consciousness of God,

> we should have an unimpeded knowledge of God in all and along with all; and also, so far as finite nature allows it, . . . we should steadily have knowledge of all that wherein and whereby God makes [Godself] known; and this without conflict arising between this desire in us and any other, or between the steady God-consciousness and consciousness in any other of its aspects. This surely would be pure and assured vision; and it would render us completely at home with God.[49]

Though couched in his own terms, Schleiermacher's description of the beatific vision is recognizably traditional. It is understanding by vision—that is, by intuition in the traditional sense—that yields thoughts and deeds (hence the references to knowledge and desire), but is itself neither, and is brought about by neither. This suggests that Schleiermacher worked backwards from the beatific vision when developing his account of the God-consciousness.

Along with the theological tradition of knowledge by vision there is a final, related, source of influence to consider: Plato, the thinker who, perhaps, formed Schleiermacher's thought most of all.[50] For Plato, God is the Good. Schleiermacher, too, explicitly writes that (for Protestants at least) the consciousness of God is not different than the idea of the Good.[51] In claiming this, Schleiermacher seems to be joining Plato, and a long line of Christian

---

[45] Spinoza, *Ethics*, VP36, p. 612.

[46] Spinoza, *Ethics*, VP36S.

[47] See, for example, Thomas Aquinas, *Summa Theologiae*, trans. the Fathers of the English Dominican Province (New York: Benziger Bros., 1947), Suppl. III, Q. 92, a. 1, resp.; Petrus van Mastricht, *Theoretico-Practica Theologia*, vol. 2: *Faith in the Triune God*, ed. Joel R. Beeke, trans. Todd M. Rester (Grand Rapids: Reformation Heritage Books, 2019 [1724]), I.2.13.v, I.2.23.v.

[48] CG^2, §163.2; *CF (1928)*, p. 719.

[49] CG^2, §163.2; *CF (1928)*, pp. 719–720.

[50] See Friedrich Schleiermacher, *Introductions to the Dialogues of Plato*, trans. William Dobson (London, 1836).

[51] CG^2, §83.1; *CF (1928)*, p. 342.

theologians following Plato, in *identifying* God and the Good. If so, consider how what Plato thinks about knowledge of the Good might help further clarify the God-consciousness.

Plato famously explains how knowledge of ordinary things relates to knowledge of the Good in Book VI of the *Republic*. Comparing the Good to the sun as that by which we understand all other things, Plato calls the Good an "unhypothetical first principle."[52] By that he means that the Good is a source or starting point that itself has no higher source—unlike all other principles that are not true first principles, but that are only assumptions treated as if they were starting points when thinking about specific matters.[53] The Good (God, for Schleiermacher) is not something sensible. But it arises as the corollary to all sensible things as the ultimate explanation for their existence and the cause of their intelligibility. This is likely what Schleiermacher has in mind when he says that the sensible self-consciousness gives rise to the God-consciousness and is, in turn, perfected by the God-consciousness.[54]

A few more details are important for comparison. The first is that, although, for Plato, the Good makes all things intelligible, it cannot be reached by means of thought because it is above all thought.[55] The second is that light, sight, and illumination are dominant terms.[56] What they help Plato describe is a kind of non-inferential understanding on analogy with vision. Third and finally, the intelligibility that the Good brings by illumination is, according to Plato, the same kind of intelligibility the God-consciousness brings in the beatific vision Schleiermacher describes above: namely, the perfect understanding of the necessity and intelligibility of all things as they follow from the Good as ultimate first principle.[57] In the following book of the *Republic*, Book VII, Plato characterizes this kind of illumination as redemptive. Therefore, like the Christian theological tradition, and like Spinoza, but unlike Kant, intellectual vision (i.e. intuition) of the Good (i.e. God) results, for Plato, in a non-inferential intelligibility that brings about redemption and blessedness.

These accounts of intuition might help us understand better what Schleiermacher means by the God-consciousness as a modification of feeling that is not thinking or doing, but issues in thoughts and deeds. But, if so, why call intuition "feeling" in the first place? What makes this an apt word to describe the immediate consciousness of God?

Vial's reading of Kant on intuition helps in this respect by emphasizing the reactive nature of intuition. On this reading, intuitions are the subjective result of causal influence on us.[58] Because they are the internal effects of extrinsic causes, intuitions are best described as "felt."

The theological tradition of understanding by vision would likewise explain the connection between consciousness and feeling by appeal to the way intellectual vision is passively received. As we saw above, Spinoza specifically speaks of this knowledge by vision in terms of feeling, as well as in terms of consciousness of self and God. And all in this tradition agree that we cannot understand God in the same way that we know objects in the world because God is the absolute and unique First Principle. Accordingly, God cannot be *comprehended* in the technical sense of being cast under a higher principle. We can never

---

[52] Plato, *Republic* VI, 511b.
[53] Plato, *Republic* VI, 511c–d.
[54] *CG²*, §34; *CF (1928)*, pp. 137–140.
[55] Plato, *Republic* VI, 511a.
[56] Plato, *Republic* VI, 508–509.
[57] See Schleiermacher, *Introduction to the Dialogues of Plato*, pp. 383–385.
[58] Vial, "Anschauung and Intuition, Again," pp. 45–46.

arrive at an acquaintance with the unhypothetical First Principle through dianoetic reasoning. Instead, consciousness of God must be passively implanted or bestowed as a source or beginning—a "disposition," as Schleiermacher writes in the *Letters*, "from which corresponding ways of thinking and acting develop."[59] And the way human agents begin to think we are agents and to act from the consciousness that we ourselves are a sort of unity is the same in kind as the way Christians begin to think and act from the consciousness that there is one and only one source upon which we depend absolutely.[60] Because consciousness of God is a non-inferential starting point, it is best described as "felt," but a feeling that, nevertheless, is the beginning of cognitive content.

17.4 IMMEDIACY AND THE GOD-CONSCIOUSNESS

Building on the above discussion, the next topic of focus is the closely related question of immediacy and the God-consciousness. This topic connects controversies in the *Letters* to current and ongoing debates about the plausibility of Schleiermacher's account.

One important specification of the God-consciousness that connects it to feeling is that it is *immediate*. In fact, the immediacy of the God-consciousness is likely the most important feature of all in marking it as a kind of feeling. But there have been, from Schleiermacher's day to the present, both criticisms of immediacy and disagreements over how to understand Schleiermacher's use of the term. In this section we will investigate the controversy with respect to the force of the objection and possible replies as well as to the way we might understand Schleiermacher's account of feeling in light of possible accounts of immediacy.

In his book *Religious Experience*, Proudfoot criticizes Schleiermacher for trying to have things both ways.[61] Schleiermacher claims the God-consciousness is immediate, but also that it has content and an intentional object, something it is about. But content and subject-matter specificity require the employment of concepts. And, Proudfoot argues, concepts are incompatible with immediacy. He thus concludes that Schleiermacher's account is incoherent. Although this argument rides on a meaning of "immediacy" and other assumptions that Schleiermacher's defenders have disputed, and although Proudfoot has since moderated his criticism, the basic challenge remains potent.[62]

Schleiermacher's defenders have given at least two kinds of replies to Proudfoot's critique. The first is to emphasize the conceptual content of the God-consciousness and thus deny the idea that immediacy is non-conceptual. The second is to grant that Schleiermacher's notion of immediacy is non-conceptual but deny that this is a problem. I will briefly say a little about both strategies before proposing a third option that lies between these two.

---

[59] *OG*, p. 39. See Aquinas, *Summa Theologiae*, I. Q. 97, a. 12, resp.

[60] Cf. Hegel's discussion of Jacobi on immediacy on exactly these points. G. F. W. Hegel, *Lectures on the Philosophy of Religion* (1824), vol. 1, ed. Peter Hodgson, trans. R. F. Brown, P. C. Hodgson, and J. M. Stewart (Berkley: University of California Press, 1984), p. 261.

[61] Wayne Proudfoot, *Religious Experience* (Berkeley: University of California Press, 1985), p. 32.

[62] See Wayne Proudfoot, "Immediacy and Intentionality in the Feeling of Absolute Dependence," in *Schleiermacher, the Study of Religion, and the Future of Theology*, ed. Brent W. Sockness and Wilhelm Gräb (Berlin: Walter de Gruyter, 2010), pp. 27–28, 37.

The first kind of reply is to counter that Schleiermacher does not think the God-consciousness is immediate in the sense of being non-conceptual because Schleiermacher thinks the God-consciousness is activated, mediated, and explained by language. Hector and Vial have both argued that this is true in different respects.[63] And both agree in general that, because language is intrinsically conceptual, and because the God-consciousness is connected to language, the consciousness of God is intrinsically conceptual. And, in different ways, this is purportedly compatible with immediacy. Schleiermacher's investment in the unity of thought and speech recommends this first kind of account.

A second kind of reply is exemplified by Adams who, while acknowledging that the consciousness of God for Schleiermacher is not contentless, throws doubt on Proudfoot's assumptions.[64] Adams counters that there might well be "a feeling of how it is with us, that is not conceptually structured but which we can express by assimilating it to conceptually structured claims about how it is with us; and some may find that quite plausible."[65] In other words, Adams grants that we could never explain this feeling without using concepts, but that there might be some form of consciousness that is experienceable *as feeling* prior (at least logically prior) to being understood and explained conceptually. Schleiermacher's placement of feeling prior to thought and deed recommends this second kind of account.

Despite their virtues and their differences, however, both sorts of replies seem to share an assumption with Proudfoot's critique: namely, that something is *either* pre- or non-conceptual, *or* it is conceptually structured. That is, either something does not fall *under* some concept, or it does. But what about the absolute First Principle itself? Under what other concept could God fall?

This question circles back to the notions of intuition linked to feeling in the Christian theological tradition. Recall that, according to that tradition, it is not possible to understand or comprehend God in the sense of casting God under a higher concept. It is not possible because there is no higher concept than the unhypothetical First Principle itself. In that sense, Schleiermacher agrees with the majority theological report: knowledge of God cannot be conceptually mediated—again, where conceptual mediation means casting God *under* an ostensibly higher concept. At the same time, however, God, the absolute First Principle, is not *non*-conceptual either, but rather is itself that by which all else is rendered intelligible. Because God is an illuminating or explaining principle, the language of God can be applied in better or worse ways. By way of application of our concept of God, we can continue to make many of the linguistic claims scholars have rightly noted were so important to Schleiermacher without, at the same time, diluting his claims about the immediacy of the God-consciousness. And because the First Principle is itself a kind of concept, God can *self*-mediate the determinate content that the divine essence latently contains.

On this latter reading, Schleiermacher might even offer a classic counter to Proudfoot's charge. God is the one unhypothetical First Principle that renders all else intelligible. Therefore, to paraphrase St. Augustine, if we think we have comprehended God under

---

[63] See Kevin W. Hector, *Theology without Metaphysics: God, Language, and the Spirit of Recognition* (Cambridge: Cambridge University Press, 2011); Vial, "Anschauung and Intuition, Again."

[64] Robert Merrihew Adams, "Faith and Religious Knowledge," in *The Cambridge Companion to Friedrich Schleiermacher*, ed. Jacqueline Mariña (Cambridge: Cambridge University Press, 2005), pp. 38–39.

[65] Adams, "Faith and Religious Knowledge," p. 39.

another concept, we can be sure it is not God we have comprehended. The only way we could come to a true acquaintance with God is, then, not through the mediation of higher concepts—for *there are no higher concepts*—but by the immediate consciousness of God, which is to say, by blessed vision.

17.5 OTHER RELIGIOUS COMMUNIONS

In the Introduction to *The Christian Faith* Schleiermacher not only describes Christian piety as a modification of the God-consciousness, but also claims that other religious communions also have a consciousness of God, albeit differently modified. What Schleiermacher means by this is my third topic of focus.

One line of interpretation emphasizes Schleiermacher as a theorist of the human phenomenon of religion. Whether or not this is correct, the idea has been very influential.[66] At the same time, however, Schleiermacher ranks other religious communions as better or worse, and ranks all as less perfect than the Christian communion. This is a controversial approach, but it is defensible, provided: (1) that we read Schleiermacher as a Christian theologian standing in a long tradition of thinking about non-Christian communions from the explicit vantage of his own faith; and (2) that we understand the God-consciousness as a first principle, and its modifications as different descriptions of what that principle contains or implies. Let me explain.

Schleiermacher thinks that there are various categories into which other, non-Christian, forms of piety fall. The most important is the distinction between monotheistic forms and all other forms of piety. Monotheistic forms of piety "express the dependence of everything finite upon one Supreme and Infinite Being,"[67] whereas all others divide their dependence among a plurality of gods or idols, with idol worship as "the lowest condition of humanity."[68] His description of other forms of piety is unabashedly normative and there is, according to Schleiermacher, a clear hierarchy of them.

It is important to note here that Schleiermacher's particular descriptions of other forms of piety would almost certainly not be countenanced by their adherents. Muslims and Jews especially might, with ample justification, resist Schleiermacher's description of their traditions and beliefs. However, even if Schleiermacher misunderstood Judaism and Islam, the notion of a normative ranking *as such* is a different matter. Provided Schleiermacher intends to offer a description of other forms of piety as a Christian theologian, normative description is arguably necessary.

That standard in relation to which Schleiermacher ranks all other forms of piety is, first, monotheism itself: the consciousness that we and everything else are absolutely dependent upon one and only one "Supreme and Infinite Being."[69] The commitment that everything

---

[66] See Troeltsch, *The Christian Faith*; Andrew Dole, "Schleiermacher and Otto on Religion," *Religious Studies* 40, no. 4 (2004), pp. 389–413; James K. Graby, Reflections on the History of the Interpretation of Schleiermacher," *Scottish Journal of Theology* 21, no. 3 (1968), pp. 283–299; Wilfred Cantwell Smith, "On Mistranslated Book Titles," *Religious Studies* 20 (1984), pp. 27–42.

[67] CG^2, §8; *CF (1928)*, p. 34.

[68] CG^2, §8.2; *CF (1928)*, p. 35, translation revised.

[69] CG^2, §8; *CF (1928)*, p. 34.

is explained by one unhypothetical first principle is here equated with a being upon which everything depends in fact. In contrast, the problem with what Schleiermacher calls "fetishism" and "polytheism" is their divided sense of dependence.[70] Their feeling of dependence is insufficiently absolute. It is the inadequacy of their consciousness to a fact of the matter that makes the description of other forms of piety imperfect. And this is correlated with their other states of consciousness. They suffer from a confusion and multiplication of first principles.

Schleiermacher claims that the monotheistic forms of Christianity, Judaism, and Islam stand in contrast to the confusion of idol worship and polytheism. All monotheisms agree on the absoluteness of our dependence, and therefore on the uniqueness of God. The three differ, Schleiermacher claims, according to whether this consciousness of absolute dependence issues in passive or active states. The former he calls "aesthetic" piety, and he thinks Islam belongs to this category. The latter he designates "teleological" piety. Judaism and Christianity are grouped together in this category as, respectively, less and more perfect versions of teleological piety. What finally makes Judaism and Christianity better or worse, more or less perfect, in relation to one another is their ends: in the first place by the kind of end, and in the second place by their adequacy to their ends. The distinguishing role of ends explains why Christianity's unique claim that God is *love*, advanced at the climactic end of *The Christian Faith*, proves so important to Schleiermacher.[71] Redemption as divine end renders the act of the "Supreme and Infinite Being" determinate, thus uniquely perfecting our description of God as *love*.[72]

The relative deficiency of other forms of piety does not, however, mean that they are simply bad. On the contrary, other forms of piety are never wholly false.[73] That makes Schleiermacher's account a generous analog of older "pagan virtue" accounts:[74] other religions can be compared to Christianity because non-Christians possess an incomplete, but genuine, share in Christian truth and goodness. What distinguishes Schleiermacher's account is that it assimilates the history of religions into this explicitly normative, Christian theological account of non-Christian forms of piety. In this sense these sections are "borrowed" (from ethics, philosophy of religion, etc.), but borrowed under explicitly Christian dogmatic auspices. Schleiermacher's account of the God-consciousness provides a way of distinguishing better and worse in various respects within this arrangement: first, by the relative adequacy of first principles; second, by the relative adequacy of determining ends.

17.6 The Eternal Covenant

Schleiermacher thinks we are conscious not only of God, but of ourselves and of the world. He also thinks all three are related, and indeed mutually informing.[75] The most perfect

[70] CG^2, §8; *CF (1928)*, pp. 34–37.
[71] CG^2, §§166–167.
[72] CG^2, §167.2; *CF (1928)*, p. 730–731.
[73] CG^2, §7.3; *CF (1928)*, p. 33.
[74] See, for example, David Decosimo, *Ethics as a Work of Charity: Thomas Aquinas and Pagan Virtue* (Stanford, CA: Stanford University Press, 2014).
[75] CG^2, §5.3; *CF (1928)*, pp. 20–22.

God-consciousness would result in the most perfect consciousness of the world.[76] What Schleiermacher thinks about the form and contents of the world is tied up with science, especially natural science, though also history, and more. Accordingly, Schleiermacher thinks that Christian piety has a stake in science. This is my fourth and final topic of focus.

In his *Letters*, Schleiermacher famously proposed an "eternal covenant" between the Christian faith and science, "so that faith does not hinder science and science does not exclude faith."[77] In so doing he alludes to another feature of the Introduction where he denounces Christian appeals to miracles to generate or sustain piety. There is a lively discussion about how best to understand the eternal covenant and its relation to claims about miracles and divine action in *The Christian Faith*.

Historically, the most commonly accepted reading of Schleiermacher's proposal for an eternal covenant between faith and science interpreted him as proposing an end to intellectual and cultural competition between faith and science by calling for a division of intellectual territory. Brandt exemplifies this reading,[78] which Dole calls the "segregation model."[79] On this interpretation, science and faith are simply about two different things. Therefore, so long as each keeps to its proper subject matter, there can be no conflict. One weakness of this account is that it implies that this sort of non-interference runs both ways, such that Christians should never, in principle, expect to alter their claims on the basis of science. But it seems that Schleiermacher calls for Christians to do just that in the Introduction. Therefore, it seems the "segregation" interpretation of the eternal covenant does not fully capture what Schleiermacher is doing.

To improve on this reading, Dole has proposed an alternative: the "accommodation model."[80] On this interpretation, the eternal covenant is not an agreement that faith and science have nothing to do with one another, but is, rather, an arrangement that would require faith to accommodate itself to the findings of science in cases where the two conflict. What the "accommodation model" takes into account that the "segregation model" does not is those cases in *The Christian Faith* where Schleiermacher calls for the emendation or abandonment of beliefs that seem to conflict with science and their replacement with beliefs that cohere with the best science of the day.

In addition, I have argued for a third line of interpretation.[81] Importantly, my account does not disagree entirely with either the "accommodation model" or the "segregation model." In fact, my account is compatible with both accounts in key respects—though it is closer to Dole's reading. However, in contrast to either "model," I do not read Schleiermacher's proposal for an eternal covenant as a political or methodological starting point but, instead, as an *entailment* of Schleiermacher's prior theological claims and commitments about the way God and the world actually are. Chief among those claims is that God's act in creation is so perfectly ordered to its intended end that God never acts in the world in a way that

---

[76] CG^2, §168; *CF (1928)*, pp. 732–735.
[77] *OG*, p. 64.
[78] See Richard Brandt, *The Philosophy of Schleiermacher* (New York: Harper, 1941), pp. 261–262.
[79] Andrew Dole, *Schleiermacher on Religion and the Natural Order* (Oxford: Oxford University Press, 2010), p. 140.
[80] Dole, *Schleiermacher on Religion and the Natural Order*, p. 144.
[81] See Pedersen, *The Eternal Covenant*.

could be characterized as an absolute miracle. Because of what Christians believe about God, Schleiermacher argues, we should deny miracles understood in this way.

Importantly, the eternal covenant relates to how we understand the consciousnesses of God and the world. On my reading, the consciousness of God and the world are not conclusions, but beginnings. Therefore, they set parameters within which all content must be understood. This comports well with Dole's "accommodation model" insofar as that model sets much the same rules for Christian claims about what the world is like. And yet it also comports well with the "segregation model" insofar as it agrees that genuine content cannot contradict the principles that yield it. But, in addition, principles in this sense, including the God-consciousness, should be understood as true sources of their content: not only regulative limits, but the genuine reasons for or causes of their content. Schleiermacher's motivation in the eternal covenant is, on my reading, not foremost methodological propriety or political savvy, but the coherence of claims about God's agency and activity with claims about the structure and contents of the world as the perfectly ordered means to God's good ends.

17.7 CONCLUSION

The Introduction to *The Christian Faith* has been the subject of almost uninterrupted interest since Schleiermacher's day. But the Introduction is dense and frequently unclear. This has generated energetic debate as well as lamentable misunderstanding.

In his *Letters*, Schleiermacher attempted to clarify his thought in the Introduction. There he claims that the Introduction contains material, legitimately borrowed, for already formed theological purposes and put in theological form. He insists that the Introduction is nothing but an introduction of the content that lies beyond.[82] To understand the Introduction well, one must do so in light of the whole of *The Christian Faith*.

In an attempt to show how this might make Schleiermacher's Introduction more understandable, I have made a beginning of this task across a range of some of the most important topics found in those sections. Some have been explained in light of philosophical borrowings and theological traditions. Some have had to do with history and natural science. All show Schleiermacher's self-conscious practice of interdisciplinary friendship. At the same time, each account Schleiermacher gave of these topics takes a definite form—specific theories are borrowed for specific purposes—and the form of each account is always well ordered to an already-assumed theological end. Whatever the difficulty and complexity of the Introduction, this is its organizing superstructure. And Schleiermacher's opaque claims become clearer in the light of his Christian theological vision.

SUGGESTED READING

Kelsey, Catherine L. *Thinking about Christ with Schleiermacher* (Louisville, KY: Westminster John Knox, 2003).

---

[82] *OG*, pp. 77–78.

McCormack, Bruce L. "What Has Basel to Do with Berlin? Continuities in the Theologies of Barth and Schleiermacher." In *Orthodox and Modern: Studies in the Theology of Karl Barth* (Grand Rapids: Baker, 2008), pp. 63–88.

Nimmo, Paul T. "Schleiermacher on Scripture and the Work of Jesus Christ." *Modern Theology* 31, no. 1 (2015), pp. 60–90.

Pedersen, Daniel J. *Schleiermacher's Theology of Sin and Nature: Agency, Value, and Modern Theology* (Abingdon: Routledge, 2020).

Poe, Shelli M. *Essential Trinitarianism: Schleiermacher as Trinitarian Theologian* (London: Bloomsbury T&T Clark, 2017).

Tice, Terrence N. *Schleiermacher* (Nashville, TN: Abingdon Press, 2006).

Bibliography

Adams, Robert Merrihew. "Faith and Religious Knowledge." In *The Cambridge Companion to Friedrich Schleiermacher*, ed. Jacqueline Mariña (Cambridge: Cambridge University Press, 2005), pp. 35–51.

Aquinas, Thomas. *Summa Theologiae*. Trans. the Fathers of the English Dominican Province (New York: Benziger Bros., 1947).

Barth, Karl. *The Theology of Schleiermacher*. Trans. Geoffrey Bromiley (Grand Rapids, MI: Eerdmans, 1982 [1923/24, 1978]).

Brandt, Richard. *The Philosophy of Schleiermacher* (New York: Harper, 1941).

Decosimo, David. *Ethics as a Work of Charity: Thomas Aquinas and Pagan Virtue* (Stanford, CA: Stanford University Press, 2014).

Dole, Andrew. "Schleiermacher and Otto on Religion." *Religious Studies* 40, no. 4 (2004), pp. 389–413.

Dole, Andrew. *Schleiermacher on Religion and the Natural Order* (Oxford: Oxford University Press, 2010).

Graby, James K. "Reflections on the History of the Interpretation of Schleiermacher." *Scottish Journal of Theology* 21, no. 3 (1968), pp. 283–299.

Gunton, Colin E. *The Actuality of Atonement: A Study of Metaphor, Rationality, and the Christian Tradition* (London: T&T Clark, 2004 [1988]).

Hector, Kevin W. *Theology without Metaphysics: God, Language, and the Spirit of Recognition* (Cambridge: Cambridge University Press, 2011).

Hegel, G. F. W. *Lectures on the Philosophy of Religion* (1824), vol. 1. Ed. Peter Hodgson. Trans. R. F. Brown, P. C. Hodgson, and J. M. Stewart (Berkley: University of California Press, 1984).

Janiak, Andrew. "Kant's Views on Space and Time." *Stanford Encyclopedia of Philosophy* (2016), ed. Edward N. Zalta. https://plato.stanford.edu/entries/kant-spacetime/.

Lamm, Julia A. *The Living God: Schleiermacher's Theological Appropriation of Spinoza* (University Park, PA: Pennsylvania State University Press, 1996).

Pedersen, Daniel J. *The Eternal Covenant* (Berlin: Walter de Gruyter, 2017).

Proudfoot, Wayne. "Immediacy and Intentionality in the Feeling of Absolute Dependence." In *Schleiermacher, the Study of Religion, and the Future of Theology*, ed. Brent W. Sockness and Wilhelm Gräb (Berlin: Walter de Gruyter, 2010), pp. 27–37.

Proudfoot, Wayne. *Religious Experience* (Berkeley: University of California Press, 1985).

Schleiermacher, Friedrich. *Introductions to the Dialogues of Plato*. Trans. William Dobson (London, 1836).

Smith, Wilfred Cantwell. "On Mistranslated Book Titles." *Religious Studies* 20 (1984), pp. 27–42.

Spinoza, Benedict. "Ethics." In *The Collected Works of Spinoza*, vol. 1. Ed. and trans. Edwin Curley (Princeton: Princeton University Press, 1985), pp. 407–617.

Troeltsch, Ernst. *The Christian Faith*. Trans. Garrett E. Paul (Minneapolis: Fortress Press, 1991 [1912, 1913]).

van Mastricht, Petrus. *Theoretico-Practica Theologia, vol. 2: Faith in the Triune God*. Ed. Joel R. Beeke. Trans. Todd M. Rester (Grand Rapids: Reformation Heritage Books, 2019 [1724]).

Vial, Theodore. "Anschauung and Intuition, Again, (Or, 'We Remain Bound to the Earth')." In *Schleiermacher, the Study of Religion, and the Future of Theology*, ed. Brent W. Sockness and Wilhelm Gräb (Berlin: Walter de Gruyter, 2010), pp. 39–50.

CHAPTER 18

THE CHRISTIAN FAITH AS LIBERAL THEOLOGY

WALTER E. WYMAN JR.

Schleiermacher's *Glaubenslehre* is an intricate work. Not only is the structure (with its three parts and three forms of dogmatic proposition in each part) complex, the discussion of the individual doctrinal loci is complicated. It is a challenge to grasp the big picture: What is the center of Schleiermacher's understanding of Christian doctrine? What is the overarching vision that informs the details? One can, of course, march through the system from front to back, summarizing in order Part I and then the First and Second Halves of Part I.[1] But such a procedure is inadequate to answer the question, What is the overarching theological vision? What is the red thread that runs through all the details and constitutes the work as a theological whole rather than an assemblage of discrete parts?

In coming to terms with Schleiermacher's theology one is, of course, wrestling with a two-hundred-year-old text. *The Christian Faith* is shaped by the historical context in which Schleiermacher lived and worked. As diagnosed by Richard Crouter, that context is "between Enlightenment and Romanticism."[2] As post-Enlightenment, specifically post-Kantian, Schleiermacher had to confront the epistemological problem posed by the critical philosophy's denial of the possibility of knowledge of transcendent realities. The ecclesiastical situation in Prussia had changed by the union of the Reformed and Lutheran churches in 1817; *The Christian Faith* was intended to serve this new situation. The context of theological discussion was further constituted by many competing (and now for the most part forgotten) voices.[3] Schleiermacher positioned himself at a distance from the live options of his day: rationalism, supernaturalism, and speculative theology. Andrew C. Dole argued the case that he accomplished this through a naturalistic theory of religion and an "enhanced naturalism" in Christian doctrine.[4] Yet Schleiermacher called himself a "real supernaturalist";[5]

---

[1] Martin Redeker, *Schleiermacher: Life and Thought*, trans. John Wallhausser (Philadelphia: Fortress Press, 1973), pp. 109–151 offers such a seriatim summary.

[2] Richard Crouter, *Between Enlightenment and Romanticism* (Cambridge: Cambridge University Press, 2005).

[3] See James Duke and Francis Fiorenza's sketches of Schleiermacher's conversation partners in *OG*.

[4] Andrew Dole, *Schleiermacher on Religion and the Natural Order* (Oxford: Oxford University Press, 2010), p. 138 and *passim*.

[5] *OG*, pp. 88–89.

what did he mean by that phrase? Where should Schleiermacher be located on the spectrum of theological options?

Among many interpreters, Schleiermacher is associated with theological liberalism.[6] Some directly call him a liberal without exploring what they mean by that term.[7] More often, he is called the "father" or "forerunner" of liberal theology. In his introductory textbook of selections from Schleiermacher's writings, Keith Clements summarizes the view of many: "Over a whole range of issues Schleiermacher foreshadows approaches which we recognize as distinctively 'modern' or, as some may prefer, 'liberal.'"[8] B. A. Gerrish, in *A Prince of the Church: Schleiermacher and the Beginnings of Modern Theology*, suggests the term "Liberal Evangelical" as an appropriate designation. What Gerrish meant by that term he explains succinctly: "The program was 'evangelical' because it was the distinctively evangelical consciousness (his own) that Schleiermacher made the object of his inquiry; it was 'liberal' because he did not consider himself tied to the old expressions of it."[9] That single sentence succinctly defines in what sense Schleiermacher's dogmatics might be considered liberal: because of its distinctive method (it takes consciousness rather than Scripture or dogma as its immediate object) and its openness to revising the tradition.

Of course it is entirely possible to discuss Schleiermacher's theology in depth without using the term "liberal theology." In his extensive critical discussion of Schleiermacher in his 1938 textbook, Horst Stephan never uses the term.[10] As is well known, Karl Barth regarded Schleiermacher's whole program, both method and execution, as a disastrous dead end for Protestant theology. But some of his most important discussions of Schleiermacher do not call him liberal.[11]

In his informative historical study of the term "liberal theology," Hans-Joachim Birkner points out that Schleiermacher's theology was not called "liberal" in the nineteenth century.[12] The term was used for some of the speculative theologians (such as A. E. Biedermann), and, as Friedrich Wilhelm Graf points out, for the Halle Neologists.[13] The later Ritschlian theologians (Ritschl, Herrmann, Troeltsch) were called "liberals." The dialectical theologians after World War I gave currency to the term "liberal theology," using the term

---

[6] My discussion here agrees with Arnulf von Scheliha's analysis in Chapter 32 of this volume, "Schleiermacher and Protestant Liberalism" of Schleiermacher's six "basic theological insights" that warrant seeing him as "the father of Protestant Liberalism" but focuses more narrowly on his dogmatics. See pp. 534–536 below.

[7] H. R. Mackintosh, *Types of Modern Theology, Schleiermacher to Barth* (London: Nisbet, 1937/1952), p. 36.

[8] Keith W. Clements, *Friedrich Schleiermacher: Pioneer of Modern Theology* (London: Collins, 1987), p. 7.

[9] B. A. Gerrish, *A Prince of the Church: Schleiermacher and the Beginnings of Modern Theology* (Philadelphia: Fortress Press, 1984), pp. 31–33.

[10] Horst Stephan and Martin Schmidt, *Geschichte der evangelischen Theologie in Deutschland seit dem Idealismus*, Dritte Auflage (Berlin: Walter de Gruyter, 1973), pp. 55–70, pp. 111–132.

[11] Karl Barth, *Protestant Theology in the 19th Century* (Valley Forge, PA: Judson Press, 1973), pp. 425–473; Barth, "Concluding Unscientific Postscript on Schleiermacher," in *The Theology of Schleiermacher*, ed. Dietrich Ritschl (Grand Rapids: Eerdmans, 1982), pp. 261–279.

[12] Birkner, "Liberale Theologie," pp. 51–62.

[13] Graf, "Liberale Theologie," pp. 86–98.

pejoratively to designate the theological error that they were seeking to overcome.[14] The works of Birkner and Graf make a strong implicit case that one uses the term "liberal theology" for Schleiermacher at the risk of anachronism.

Despite this risk, of which he is well aware, Gary Dorrien, in his ambitious *Kantian Reason and Hegelian Spirit: The Idealistic Logic of Modern Theology*, places "liberal theology" at the center of his analysis, which runs from Kant to Tillich. Admitting that "there never was a homogeneous tradition of liberal theology in Germany," he finds "core affinities that passed from Kant and Schleiermacher to Ritschl and Harnack."[15] Crucially for my argument, he boldly claims Schleiermacher for liberal theology. He concludes his discussion of Schleiermacher with the claim, "These were the keynotes of the first full-orbed liberal theology, which surpassed in influence all the liberal theologies that followed it, and which eventually was recognized as the quintessential liberal theology, long after Schleiermacher was gone."[16]

How does Dorrien understand liberal theology? He finds it to be a "three-layered phenomenon":

> Firstly it is the idea that all claims to truth, in theology and other disciplines, must be made on the basis of reason and experience, not by appeal to external authority.... Second, liberal theology argues for the viability and necessity of an alternative to orthodox over-belief and secular disbelief.... The agenda of modern theology was to develop a credible form of Christianity before the "cultured despisers of religion" routed Christian faith from intellectual and cultural respectability.... The third layer consists of specific things that go with overthrowing the principle of external authority... The liberal tradition reconceptualizes the meaning of Christianity in light of modern knowledge and values. It is reformist in spirit and substance, not revolutionary. It is open to the verdicts of modern intellectual inquiry, especially historical criticism and the natural sciences.[17]

Dorrien's three characteristics are persuasively presented, and arguably Schleiermacher fulfills all three. But they are all very general. Given the generality of the term and the possible objection to anachronism, further specification is desirable. In his later writing B. A. Gerrish privileges the term "revisionary."[18] That Schleiermacher's intentions are revisionist comes clearly to the fore in his open letters (*Sendschreiben*) on his *Glaubenslehre* to his friend Friedrich Lücke. "Every dogma that truly represents an element of our Christian consciousness can be so formulated that it remains free from entanglements with science." As his discussion makes clear, by "science" Schleiermacher is thinking of both natural science and historical research. In the *Sendschreiben* he specifically mentions "the doctrines of creation and preservation," the "account of miracles," and the "appearance of the redeemer" as places

---

[14] Hans-Joachim Birkner draws attention in particular to Rudolf Bultmann's 1924 essay, "Liberale Theologie und die jüngste theologische Bewegung," *Glauben und Verstehen*, vol. 1 (Tübingen: Mohr Siebeck, 1933), pp. 1–25.

[15] Gary Dorrien, *Kantian Reason and Hegelian Spirit: The Idealistic Logic of Modern Theology* (Chichester: Wiley-Blackwell, 2012), p. 10.

[16] Dorrien, *Kantian Reason and Hegelian Spirit*, p. 105.

[17] Dorrien, *Kantian Reason and Hegelian Spirit*, pp. 4–5.

[18] B. A. Gerrish, *Continuing the Reformation* (Chicago: The University of Chicago Press, 1993), pp. 10, 13. Later, Gerrish expresses doubts about the utility of "party badges" such as "liberal." Gerrish, *Christian Faith: Dogmatics in Outline* (Louisville: Westminster John Knox Press, 2015), pp. x–xi.

where traditional interpretations will have to be revised in the light of modern science.[19] "We must learn to do without what many are accustomed to regard as inseparably bound to the essence of Christianity."[20] To be more precise, Schleiermacher's revisionism, while never crossing the line into a fully developed religious naturalism or radical theology, departs from supernaturalism: he does not believe in supernatural causation, or divine interventions into nature, history, or the human consciousness, and anticipates to a remarkable degree the demythologizing of the Christian mythos. We will return to this issue below.

This chapter addresses two main questions: (1) What is Schleiermacher's overarching theological vision? and (2), In what sense is *The Christian Faith* liberal or revisionist theology? The following discussion is divided into three parts. Part I assembles some examples of Schleiermacher's liberal doctrinal moves or revisionism. Part II explores the shifts in method, conceptuality, and historical consciousness that underlie Schleiermacher's sometimes radical revisionism. Part III addresses the question posed at the outset: What is Schleiermacher's overarching vision of Christian dogmatics?

18.1 PART I

In the very first doctrine discussed in the *Glaubenslehre*, the doctrine of Creation, one already sees indications of the ways in which Schleiermacher's approach is modern and liberal. After noting that the New Testament passages that he has cited do not warrant "any more definite conception of the Creation," Schleiermacher goes on to observe:

> The further elaboration of the doctrine of Creation in Dogmatics comes down to us from times when material even for natural science was taken from the Scriptures and when the elements of all higher knowledge lay hidden in theology. Hence the complete separation of these two involves our handing over this subject to natural science.... We may patiently await the result.[21]

A bit further on, after observing that the Reformers (Luther and Calvin) viewed the "Mosaic account" (Genesis 1–2) as "a genuinely historical narrative," Schleiermacher goes on to argue that the ancient world did not take it literally. As far as the doctrine of creation is concerned, both respect for the integrity and independence of natural science and a nonliteral reading of the biblical narrative underwrite a revisionist approach.

What does the doctrine of creation mean if it does not mean a literal six-day creation with the sudden appearance of separate distinct species? It, along with the doctrine of preservation, means "that the world exists only in absolute dependence on God."[22] "The origin of the world must, indeed, be traced entirely to the divine activity, but not in such a way that this activity is thought of as resembling human activity; and . . . not so as to make the divine activity itself a temporal activity."[23] This formulation points to a large theological question: How is

[19] *OG*, p. 64.
[20] *OG*, p. 60.
[21] *CF (1928)*, §40.1, p. 150.
[22] *CF (1928)*, §36, p. 142.
[23] *CF (1928)*, §41, p. 152.

the divine activity properly conceived? Before turning to that question, it is instructive to turn to the two appendices to the doctrine of creation.

The two appendices take up the subjects of angels and the devil, where once again we can see Schleiermacher's revisionist thinking. While not outright rejecting the idea of angels (Schleiermacher finds nothing intrinsically impossible in the idea or contradictory to the Christian consciousness), he develops several lines of reasoning that cast doubt on it. He appeals to the literary genre of the biblical narrative, the role of human imagination, and various theological considerations. A vivid awareness of historicity delivers the *coup de grâce*: "that this conception is losing its influence among Christians follows naturally from the fact that it belongs to a time when our knowledge of the forces of nature was very limited, and our power over them at its lowest stage. In every such situation our reflections now instinctively take another direction, so that in active life we do not easily turn to angels." In short, for dogmatics "the subject remains wholly problematic." As for the Devil, "the idea . . . is so unstable (*haltungslos*) that we cannot expect anyone to be convinced of its truth."[24]

The second doctrine discussed in Part I, Preservation (*Erhaltung*), turns largely into a discussion of miracles. Martin Redeker has correctly pointed out that "the main problem of the first part of *The Christian Faith* is the relation of the creative power of God to the natural order as it is viewed in scientific research."[25] Schleiermacher's solution to that problem supports a skeptical or liberal position on the miracle stories of the Bible. Two propositions and their supporting argumentation establish the theological basis for Schleiermacher's revisionist moves: "The religious self-consciousness, by means of which we place all that affects or influences us in absolute dependence on God, coincides entirely with the view that all such things are conditioned and determined by the interdependence of Nature [*Naturzusammenhang*]."[26] This is a crucial proposition for understanding many of Schleiermacher's liberal or revisionist positions, for it lays the groundwork for conceiving, as Redeker says, "the relation of the creative power of God to the natural order." "It has been always acknowledged by the strictest dogmaticians that divine preservation, as the absolute dependence of all events and changes on God, and natural causation, as the complete determination of all events by the universal nexus, are one and the same thing, simply from different points of view."[27] Schleiermacher is here taking a stand on supernaturalism: "The Absolute Causality to which the feeling of absolute dependence points back can only be described in such a way that, on the one hand, it is distinguished from the content of the natural order and thus contrasted with it, and on the other hand, equated with it in comprehension."[28] What does this mean? The divine causality is "absolute causality." It is, he argued in §41 (cited above) not like human causality—that is, not episodic, directed to single effects, and not temporal. Yet the feeling of absolute dependence points to its reality. Schleiermacher is saying that divine causality underlies the creation (and, he will argue in the christological section, the mission of Christ), but it is not conceived of as intervention in the causal order (such as the sudden creation of human beings).

---

[24] *CF (1928)*, §43.1, p. 159; §43.2, p. 160; §44, p. 161.
[25] Redeker, *Schleiermacher*, p. 119.
[26] *CF (1928)*, §46, p. 170.
[27] *CF (1928)*, §46.2, p. 174.
[28] *CF (1928)*, §51, p. 200.

To be sure contemporary theologians and philosophers will have many questions to ask at this point. If God does not do anything in particular, is it meaningful to still talk about divine causality? This is not the place to solve this problem; rather, the task is to understand what Schleiermacher means when he calls himself a "real supernaturalist." He does not mean that he thinks that God intervenes in the causal nexus, inserting a causality to make something happen that would not otherwise occur. In the second open letter to Lücke he attempts to clarify what he means:

> Whenever I speak of the supernatural, I do so with reference to whatever comes first, but afterwards it becomes something natural. Thus creation is supernatural, but it afterwards becomes the natural order. Likewise, in his origin Christ is supernatural, but he also becomes natural, as a genuine human being. The Holy Spirit and the Christian church can be treated in the same way.[29]

With respect to miracles, "We should abandon the idea of the absolutely supernatural because no single instance of it can be known by us." An absolute miracle would presumably be an event that cannot be accounted for in any way by natural causality. Without passing judgment on the "inherent possibility" of miracles, Schleiermacher finds that the Christian consciousness does not require the facticity of the biblical miracles, that any absolute miracle destroys the coherence of the system of nature (*Naturzusammenhang*), and that the various arguments put forth in defense of miracles are unpersuasive.[30]

How should the revisionist thinking about God that underlies these statements be understood? In her detailed technical study of the issues, *The Living God: Schleiermacher's Appropriation of Spinoza*, Julia Lamm argues persuasively that Schleiermacher's thinking about God is best understood as "post-Kantian Spinozism." She singles out four characteristics as determinative: causal monism, complete determinism, higher realism (or critical realism), and a non-anthropomorphic image of God. When he calls himself a "real supernaturalist," then, Schleiermacher does not mean anything like the supernaturalism of his—or our—day. Rather, he was thinking of a "complete coincidence between natural and divine causality."[31] The question remains: Has he solved the problem?

Based on this revisionist theism, Part I of the *Glaubenslehre* proposes revisions to the way creation and preservation are thought about and criticizes conventional beliefs about angels, the Devil, and miracles. Part II extends Schleiermacher's theological revisionism into other doctrines. As he analyzes the consciousness of sin and works out his modern interpretation of the doctrine of Original Sin, Schleiermacher criticizes and rejects the idea of the Fall of Adam and Eve. "The idea of a change in human nature entailed by the first sin of the first pair has no place among propositions which rank as utterances of our Christian consciousness." Accordingly, "we must depart from" the Protestant creeds ("our symbolical books").[32] Schleiermacher seeks to retrieve and reformulate the doctrine of Original Sin independently of the Fall story (see §§70–72) because he finds that an analysis of the Christian

---

[29] *OG*, p. 89.

[30] *CF* (1928), §47.3, p. 183; §47.1, p. 178; §47.2, pp. 181–183.

[31] Julia Lamm, *The Living God: Schleiermacher's Theological Appropriation of Spinoza* (University Park: Pennsylvania State University Press, 1996), pp. 159, 162, 175–176, 185–187, 194–197.

[32] *CF* (1928), §72.3, pp. 298, 296. See also §72.4 (p. 299) for the claim that contemporary Christians are not obligated to follow the "confessional books."

consciousness warrants the notion of "sinfulness that is present in an individual prior to any action of their own."[33]

Turning to Christology, Schleiermacher's basic position is that "the ecclesiastical formulae concerning the Person of Christ need to be subjected to continual criticism." While agreeing with the intentions of the formula "in Jesus Christ divine nature and human nature were combined into one person," Schleiermacher judges that "there is almost nothing in the execution of this aim against which protest must not be raised." The traditional formula "has given scope for subtle inanities." Some antiquated ideas must be "banished from the system of doctrine, and handed over to the history of doctrine."[34]

Schleiermacher's revisionist formula is, "The Redeemer . . . is like all people [Menschen] in virtue of the identity of human nature, but distinguished from them all by the constant potency of His God-consciousness, which was a veritable existence of God in Him." Schleiermacher will still use the language of two natures (see, for example, §96), but his revisionist conceptuality in which his Christology is cast (the divine in Christ is the perfection of his God-consciousness) has rendered it problematic. Although "the general idea of a supernatural conception remains . . . essential and necessary," "the assumption of a Virgin Birth is superfluous." The problem to be solved is how can the perfection of Christ's God-consciousness be made intelligible? The revisionist conceptuality alone cannot solve the problem, because according to Schleiermacher's understanding of the corporate nature of sin, Jesus, born into human society, would have a defective God-consciousness. Hence Schleiermacher must have recourse to "an initial divine activity which is supernatural, but at the same time a vital human receptivity in virtue of which alone that supernatural can become a natural fact of history."[35] Once again contemporary thinkers will ask whether Schleiermacher has solved the problem.

Finally, a brief consideration of eschatology serves further to exemplify Schleiermacher's theological liberalism. Eschatology, dealing with the "consummation of the Church," is methodologically problematic for Schleiermacher, because "strictly speaking . . . we can have no doctrine of the consummation of the Church, for our Christian consciousness has absolutely nothing to say regarding a condition so entirely outside our ken." The eschatological doctrines "are not doctrines of faith, since their content (as transcending our faculties of apprehension) is not a description of our actual consciousness." Hence, he terms them "prophetic doctrines" to signal their difference in kind from the other doctrines. They have a place in the *Glaubenslehre* as representing two crucial points that are securely anchored in the Christian consciousness, personal survival of death and the consummation of the church, "in a picture appealing to the sensuous imagination." "We teach a return of Christ for judgment," but this is not a literal, bodily return. All attempts to think it through consistently end in aporiae: "all that might go to form a definite picture falls asunder." The "essential content" of this idea is that "the consummation of the church . . . is possible only through a sudden leap to perfection."[36] Schleiermacher affirms two basic convictions, the consummation of the church and the survival of the human personality after death, but "no firmly outlined or really lucid idea [*wahrhaft anschauliche Vorstellung*] is possible."[37] He goes

---

[33] *CF (1928)*, §70, p. 282 (translation slightly revised).
[34] *CF (1928)*, §95, p. 389; §96, p. 391; §96.1, p. 391; §96.3, p. 398; §97.4, p. 411.
[35] *CF (1928)*, §94, p. 385, translation slightly revised; §97.2, p. 405; §88.4, p. 365.
[36] *CF (1928)*, §157.4, p. 697; §157.2, p. 697; §159.3, p. 706; §160, p. 707; §160.2, p. 708.
[37] Postscript to the Prophetic Doctrines, *CF (1928)*, p. 722.

on to treat three remaining eschatological doctrines (the resurrection of the flesh, the Last Judgment, and eternal blessedness; an appendix treats another, eternal damnation). His approach is similar; he retains the traditional language, but reinterprets it (one might even say demythologizes it).[38] Eternal damnation he dispenses with entirely.

To summarize: Schleiermacher's theology is liberal in that it rejects a literal reading of the Genesis creation narratives, finds absolutely supernatural events and thus miracles untenable, rejects the Fall of Adam and Eve as explaining the human condition, finds the two-natures doctrine and vicarious satisfaction to be in need of revision, and does not accept a literal return of Christ or eternal damnation. These theological moves presuppose the kinds of general considerations analyzed by Dorrien and von Scheliha. Throughout his dogmatics Schleiermacher rigorously comes to terms with and revises the theological tradition. His criticism extends to seminal theologians of the past and even to the Protestant confessions.[39] Yet his approach remains liberal rather than radical: he wrestles with the doctrinal tradition in order to make it credible, not reject it.

18.2 Part II

Underlying these sometimes quite radical revisions in traditional Christian doctrines are three major presuppositions. They are dimensions of Schleiermacher's thinking occasioned by his post-Enlightenment context: a distinctive method, a distinctive conceptuality, and a historical consciousness.

18.2.1 Dogmatic Method

Although the formal definition of dogmatic theology is given in §19 ("dogmatic theology is the science which systematizes the doctrine [*Lehre*] prevalent in the Christian Church at a given time"),[40] it is the definition of a dogmatic proposition that is crucial for Schleiermacher's distinctive method. "Dogmatic propositions [*dogmatische Säze*] are doctrines [*Glaubensäze*] of the descriptively didactic type, in which the highest degree of definiteness is aimed at."[41] First, a philological note: as a translation for *Glaubensäze*, Mackintosh and Stewart's "doctrines" is problematic, for it obscures the difference between doctrine (*Lehre*) and *Glaubenssaz*. Tice, Kelsey, and Lawler are on target with the more literal translation, "statements regarding faith."[42] "Statements regarding faith," §15 asserts, are "accounts of Christian religious affections [*christlich frommen Gemützustände*]

---

[38] See Walt Wyman, "How Critical Is Schleiermacher's Revisionist Dogmatics?," in *Reformation und Moderne*, ed. Jörg Dierken, Arnulf von Scheliha, and Sarah Schmidt, Schleiermacher Archiv 27 (Berlin: Walter de Gruyter, 2018).

[39] See Walter E. Wyman Jr., "The Role of the Protestant Confessions in Schleiermacher's *The Christian Faith*," *Journal of Religion* 87, no. 3 (July, 2007), pp. 355–385.

[40] *CF (1928)*, p. 88.

[41] *CF (1928)*, §16, p. 78.

[42] *CF (2016)*, 1:116.

set forth in speech."⁴³ This definition is the key to Schleiermacher's revisionist dogmatic method. Statements regarding faith arise from pious emotions (*Erregungen*) or affections (*Gemüthzustände*) when they come to expression in words. Such statements can be poetic or rhetorical. They become dogmatic (and thus doctrines) only when cast in "descriptively didactic" form. Dogmatic propositions arise "solely out of logically ordered reflection upon the immediate utterances of the pious self-consciousness."⁴⁴ Hence Schleiermacher prefers the term *Glaubenslehre*, doctrine of faith, for his revisionist dogmatics. Dogmatics conceived as *Glaubenslehre* arises from and gives an account of the subjective pious consciousness. Doctrine "all rises out of the religious consciousness itself and is its direct expression."⁴⁵ Schleiermacher's is a "theology of consciousness" where doctrines have their origin in subjective experience and awareness.

This revisionist method is a solution to the epistemological problem posed for theology by the critical philosophy. Kant had argued powerfully that there can be no knowledge of transcendent reality. How, then, is theology possible? Kant's solution in the first critique is to permit the concepts of God, the World, and the soul as regulative ideas, and then in the second critique to treat them as postulates of practical reason. Schleiermacher's alternative solution was to turn to the subjective consciousness. Doctrinal theology was possible as an account of subjective states. Statements about the constitution of the World and divine attributes are allowed a place only if they can be derived from "descriptions of human states."⁴⁶

The task of dogmatic theology is to "purify" and "perfect" doctrines,⁴⁷ and this understanding points to Schleiermacher's construal of dogmatic criticism. He characterizes "the critical process" in the context of his discussion of Christology:

> The task of the critical process is to hold the ecclesiastical formulae to strict agreement with the foregoing analysis of our Christian self-consciousness, in order, partly, to judge how far they agree with it at least in essentials, partly (with regard to individual points) to inquire how much of the current form of expression is to be retained, and how much, on the other hand, had better be given up, either because it is an imperfect solution of the problem or because it is an addition not in itself essential, and harmful because the occasion of persistent misunderstandings.⁴⁸

This passage clarifies Schleiermacher's procedure in structuring his discussion of doctrines. In the introductory propositions to the various doctrines Schleiermacher develops his own analysis of the Christian pious consciousness, utilizing his distinctive conceptuality. Then he takes up the traditional doctrines, usually quoting the Protestant confessions. In these sections he develops his criticism. For example, in the introduction to the doctrine of sin (§§66–69) Schleiermacher uses his characteristic conceptuality to analyze the consciousness of sin. Then, in the doctrinal section (§§70–74) he engages critically the doctrines of original and actual sin. In the discussion of Christology, first in the introduction (§§86–95)

---

[43] *CF (1928)*, p. 76.
[44] *CF (1928)*, §16, Postscript, p. 81. Translation slightly altered.
[45] *CF (1928)*, §19, Postscript, p. 92.
[46] *CF (1928)*, §30, p. 125.
[47] *CF (1928)*, §19 Postscript, p. 92.
[48] *CF (1928)*, §95.2, p. 390.

he works out his own analysis of the deliverances of the pious consciousness, then in the "theorems" (*Lehrsäze*) he engages in doctrinal criticism. The same structure is evident in eschatology: the introduction (§157–159) where Schleiermacher establishes the two points that matter to him (the consummation of the church and the human survival of death) is followed by the "prophetical doctrines" (§§160–163) where he critically analyzes the four traditional eschatological doctrines.[49]

Schleiermacher's revisionism or liberal interpretations of doctrines sketched in Part I presuppose his conception of dogmatics (as the analysis and description of the pious Christian consciousness) and his conception of doctrinal criticism (as the holding of traditional doctrinal formulations to account, judging them by the norm of his analysis of the pious consciousness).

18.2.2 Conceptuality

Schleiermacher's analysis of Christian doctrines is articulated in terms of his distinctive conceptuality. That conceptuality is introduced in the "propositions borrowed from Ethics" in the Introduction. The "essence of piety" is "the consciousness of being absolutely dependent." This "highest grade of human consciousness" is an abstraction; it combines with the "lower" (the sensible self-consciousness) to form an actual moment of experience or concrete, actual state of consciousness.[50]

This philosophical anthropology provides the conceptuality that Schleiermacher makes use of when he turns to the actual Christian consciousness in his dogmatics. Already under §11 (which is not yet dogmatics but a proposition borrowed from apologetics, that is, philosophical theology), Schleiermacher explains what redemption means utilizing this conceptuality. Redemption is "a passage from an evil condition [*schlechten Zustand*], which is represented as a state of captivity or constraint, into a better condition." What is that "evil condition"? It is "an obstruction or arrest of the vitality of the higher self-consciousness, so that there comes to be little or no union of it with the sensible self-consciousness, and thus little or no religious [*fromme* (pious)] life." Redemption is necessary in order to fulfill "the impulse towards the God-consciousness."[51]

Thus when it comes to the dogmatics proper, deploying this conceptuality provides the language for and the direction to Schleiermacher's liberal revisions. Sin is explained as "an arrestment of the determinative power of the spirit, due to the independence of the sensuous functions."[52] This analysis, that sin is the inhibition of the God-consciousness, runs throughout the following discussion, locating sin as a flaw in consciousness rather than as a disobedient will, concupiscence, or other alternative. Another example, in Christology, has already been noted above: "the Redeemer ... is like all people in virtue of the identity of human nature, but distinguished from them all by the constant potency of His God-consciousness, which was a veritable existence of God in Him."[53] By utilizing

---

[49] See my discussion of both doctrinal criticism and the eschatological doctrines in Wyman, "How Critical Is Schleiermacher's Revisionist Dogmatics?," pp. 626–644.

[50] *CF (1928)*, §4, p. 12; §5, p. 18.

[51] *CF (1928)*, §11.2, pp. 54–55.

[52] *CF (1928)*, §66.2, p. 273.

[53] *CF (1928)*, §94, p. 385. Translation slightly revised.

this conceptuality Schleiermacher's revision of the two-natures doctrine turns away from a metaphysical claim about "two natures" and about the eternal Son of God become incarnate to a descriptive statement about the perfection of the Redeemer's God-consciousness.

18.2.3 Historical Consciousness

A third presupposition of Schleiermacher's liberal revisionism may be termed historical consciousness. This is in part a vivid awareness of temporality. Previous formulations of Christian doctrines must be open to revision because of the changed circumstances that occur through the passage of time. Previous formulations served the needs of their time (well or poorly), but may no longer meet the needs of the present.

Evidence of Schleiermacher's historical consciousness is found throughout *The Christian Faith*; three examples will suffice to illustrate the point.

> That each presentation [of doctrine] confines itself to the doctrine existing at a certain time, is indeed seldom expressly avowed, but it nevertheless seems to be a matter of course.... It is obvious that the textbooks of the seventeenth century can no longer serve the same purpose as they did then, but now in large measure belong merely to the realm of historical presentation.[54]

In this first example Schleiermacher's awareness of shifting context and (we may say) the historical relativity of doctrinal formulations is clear.

In the discussion of the "subsistence of the Church alongside the world" Schleiermacher takes up the two issues, of identifying "the essential and invariable features of the Church" and "the mutable element characteristic of the Church." The necessity of this division of the material in the doctrine of the church rests upon the historical consciousness as the awareness of "the historical reality of the Christian Church throughout its whole career."[55]

Finally, Schleiermacher's awareness of temporality is explicitly applied to Christian doctrine: "No definition of doctrine, then, even when arrived at with the most perfect community of feeling, can be regarded as irreformable and valid for all time.... The revision of the Church's public doctrine is a task in which every individual is bound to take a share, testing the established ideas and propositions."[56]

It is Schleiermacher's historical consciousness that undergirds and justifies his program of liberal revision of church doctrine. As pointed out in my introduction, it is Schleiermacher's place in history, "between Enlightenment and Romanticism," a time decisively shaped by Kant's critical philosophy, characterized by developments in natural science (anticipating Darwin), the emergence of historical criticism, the formation of the Protestant church union in Prussia, and the conflict between rationalist and supernatural Protestants, that provides the context for his theological thinking and calls forth a new theological method and revisions in doctrines.

---

[54] *CF (1928)*, §19.2, p. 89.
[55] *CF (1928)*, p. 586; p. 676; §126.2, pp. 584–585. The same historical consciousness as an awareness of temporality and change in the conditions of thought over time is reflected in Schleiermacher's location of dogmatics within historical theology.
[56] *CF (1928)*, §154.2, p. 690.

18.3 PART III

The examples of theological liberalism discussed in Part 1 and the three presuppositions analyzed in Part II do not answer the question posed at the outset: What is the overarching theological vision of *The Christian Faith*? How does Schleiermacher recast the understanding of Christian faith for Prussian Protestantism in the opening decades of the nineteenth century? This part is constructed around two approaches to answering this large question: beginning at the beginning, with the definition of the essence of Christianity in §11, and beginning at the conclusion, with the divine government of the world defined in §164.

18.3.1 The Essence of Christianity

"Christianity is a monotheistic faith, belonging to the teleological type of religion (*Frömmmigkeit*), and is essentially distinguished from other such faiths by the fact that in it everything is related to the redemption accomplished by Jesus of Nazareth."[57]

"The Redemption accomplished by Jesus of Nazareth" constitutes the essence of Christianity. Redemption from what? The "evil condition" introduced in §11.2. This foundational thought serves to structure Part II of the *Glaubenslehre*, the "explication of the facts of the religious [*frommen*, more literally 'pious'] self-consciousness as they are determined by the antithesis of sin and grace." Why "sin and grace" rather than "sin and redemption"? Schleiermacher explains in §63:

> The distinctive feature of Christian piety lies in the fact that whatever alienation from God there is in the phases of our experience, we are conscious of it as an action originating in ourselves, which we call Sin; but whatever fellowship with God there is, we are conscious of it as resting upon a communication from the Redeemer, which we call Grace.[58]

Reading the *Glaubenslehre* forwards, then, the "big picture" is that the Christian faith for Schleiermacher is the consciousness of sin and of redemption or, to use the more general word, grace. Is this construction of Christian doctrine a liberal revision?

From one perspective, it is a remarkably conservative or traditional interpretation. Consider, by way of comparison, the Reformed Heidelberg Catechism of 1563. Parts I and II are structured around sin and redemption, just as is Schleiermacher's *Glaubenslehre*.[59] From another perspective, however, Schleiermacher's construction is revisionist or liberal. Consider just two representative questions and answers from the Catechism:

> Question 7: From where, then, does this corrupt nature of human beings come?
> From the fall and disobedience of our first parents, Adam and Eve, in the Garden of Eden. Through this our nature became so corrupted that we are all conceived and born in sin.[60]

---

[57] *CF* (1928), §11, p. 52.
[58] *CF* (1928), p. 262.
[59] Lee C. Barrett, *The Heidelberg Catechism: A New Translation for the 21st Century* (Cleveland: The Pilgrim Press, 2007), pp. 33, 39.
[60] Barrett, *The Heidelberg Catechism*, p. 35.

> Question 15 What sort of mediator and redeemer must we seek then?
> One who is a true and righteous human being, and yet stronger than all creatures; in other words, one who is simultaneously true God.[61]

Where the Catechism holds a historical Fall into sin and the two natures of Christ, Schleiermacher uses the conceptuality of the consciousness of God, its defects and restoration, to reinterpret sin and redemption. Schleiermacher's theology is simultaneously conservative, retaining the structure and doctrine of classical Protestantism, and liberal, revising the explanation of the doctrinal claims.

18.3.2 The Divine Government of the World

Schleiermacher introduces the third section of Part II, "the divine attributes which relate to redemption," with this proposition:

> When we trace to the divine causality our consciousness of fellowship with God, restored through the efficacy of redemption, we posit the planting and extension of the Christian Church as the object of the divine government of the world.[62]

From the consciousness of redemption a conclusion is drawn about the divine governance (because, of course, there is no direct consciousness of the divine governance). This proposition is further explained in the first sentences of §164.3:

> In the divine causality there is no division or opposition anywhere, nor can we regard the government of the world as other than a unity, directed towards a single goal. Hence the Church, or the Kingdom of God in its whole extent as well as in the whole course of its development, forms the one object of the divine world-government.[63]

It is notable that here Schleiermacher equates the Christian church and the Kingdom of God. "The Kingdom of God is actually present in the fellowship of believers."[64] What is the significance of the claim that the church/Kingdom of God is "the one object of the divine world government"?

This conception of the divine world government is another way of answering the question, What is the overarching theological vision of *The Christian Faith*? It provides a sweeping vision of the place of the Christian church in the world, indeed, in the creation, and of God's plan and intention for the creation. The creation, the mission of Christ, and the redemption of human beings are all linked together as components of the divine government or, as is made clear in §164.3, divine providence (*Vorsehung*). Consider the following claims:

> The appearance of Christ and the institution of this new corporate life would have to be regarded as the completion, only now accomplished, of the creation of human nature.[65]

---

[61] Barrett, *The Heidelberg Catechism*, p. 41.
[62] *CF (1928)*, §164, p.723.
[63] *CF (1928)*, §164.3, p. 725.
[64] *CF (1928)*, §113.4, p. 528.
[65] *CF (1928)*, §89, p. 366.

> For, the entrance of Christ into humanity being its second creation, humanity has become a new creature, and we may regard this entrance as also the regeneration of the human race.[66]
>
> There is only one eternal and universal decree justifying human beings for Christ's sake. This decree, moreover, is the same as that which sent Christ on his mission.... The decree that sent Christ forth is one with the decree creating the human race.[67]

Based on the Christian consciousness of grace Schleiermacher concludes that there is a single divine decree to create and redeem. Creation and Redemption are linked in a single, overarching divine plan; Providence and Divine Government of the world are identical.

Despite the religious pluralism that is explicit in the first edition of the *Speeches* and implicit in the propositions borrowed from the philosophy of religion in the Introduction to the *Glaubenslehre*, in the end there is no room in Schleiermacher's understanding of the creation and redemption of the world for the ongoing vitality and legitimacy of the other religions. "He [Christ] alone is destined gradually to quicken the whole human race into higher life."[68] "All other religious communities are destined to pass over into this one [the Christian Church]."[69] This conclusion regarding the religions is consistent with the preceding claims about the divine government. At the same time it exemplifies the limit to Schleiermacher's revisionism or liberal theology. It is a strikingly illiberal position. Schleiermacher's overarching vision is anything but modest or limited to an interpretation of how Christians view the world in comparison to other competing visions. It advances a bold claim about the purpose of the creation itself that centers on the redemption of the entirety of humanity through Christ. The difficult question for those living in another century shaped by radically different sensitivities is whether such bold and expansive claims can or should be sustained, and whether they are indispensable to the Christian consciousness.

18.4 CONCLUSION

Schleiermacher's *The Christian Faith* belongs in the august company of the great Christian theologies. For all of its profundity and transcendent excellence, it is a work of its time. Schleiermacher addressed the issues of his day employing a conceptuality with roots in the unique post-Kantian context of the early nineteenth-century German discussion.

This chapter has argued that Schleiermacher's work is best understood as liberal or revisionist theology. By "liberal" I mean that it was crafted with the determination to be compatible with the knowledge of the world generated by the natural sciences and with the knowledge of the past uncovered by historical research. This commitment to not contradicting the sciences entailed the rethinking and, where necessary, the reformulation of traditional doctrines and understandings of the Christian faith. Schleiermacher sought to meet the needs of his time. Schleiermacher's overarching theological vision can be articulated in several different ways. The very structure of the *Glaubenslehre* turns on the

---

[66] *CF (1928)*, §106.2, p. 477.
[67] *CF (1928)*, §109.3, p. 501.
[68] *CF (1928)*, §13.1, p. 63.
[69] *CF (1928)*, §93.1, p. 377.

antithesis of sin and grace. From another perspective that vision turns on the divine governance of the world: the divine project of creation and redemption.

Already in the nineteenth century Schleiermacher's masterpiece had been criticized from opposite directions: from perspectives more conservative than his own who thought that he had gone too far in his revisions (Claus Harms), and by those who thought he had not gone far enough (D. F. Strauss). At the beginning of the twentieth century Ernst Troeltsch, who claimed to be following his example, joined those who found that Schleiermacher had not gone far enough: "Schleiermacher bogged down in accommodations to the ecclesiastical tradition; the result was a travesty in the shape of an ecclesiastical, biblicistic dogmatics." Troeltsch thought it was a mistake to try to permit "an alien dogmatic tradition laboriously to speak, as though it possessed the secret of how to speak with the voice of the present."[70] Theologians seeking to construct contemporary revisionist theologies along the paths that Schleiermacher first explored will have to judge which problems he solved inadequately (divine causality?) and where he had not gone far enough in his revisionist thinking (eschatology? Christian exclusivism?).

SUGGESTED READING

Crouter, Richard. *Between Enlightenment and Romanticism* (Cambridge: Cambridge University Press, 2005).

Dorrien, Gary. *Kantian Reason and Hegelian Spirit: The Idealistic Logic of Modern Theology* (Chichester: Wiley-Blackwell, 2012).

Gerrish, B. A. *A Prince of the Church: Schleiermacher and the Beginnings of Modern Theology* (Philadelphia: Fortress Press, 1984).

Hagan, Anette. *Eternal Blessedness for All? A Historical Systematic Examination of Schleiermacher's Understanding of Predestination* (Eugene, OR: Pickwick Publications, 2013).

Lamm, Julia. *The Living God: Schleiermacher's Theological Appropriation of Spinoza* (University Park: Pennsylvania State University Press, 1996).

Nowak, Kurt. *Schleiermacher: Leben, Werk, und Wirkung* (Göttingen: Vandenhoeck und Ruprecht, 2001).

Redeker, Martin. *Schleiermacher: Life and Thought*, trans. by John Wallhausser (Philadelphia: Fortress Press, 1973).

Vander Schel, Kevin. *Embedded Grace: Christ, History and the Reign of God in Schleiermacher's Dogmatics* (Minneapolis: Fortress Press, 2013).

BIBLIOGRAPHY

Adams, James Luther, and Walter F. Bense. *Ernst Troeltsch: Religion in History*. Fortress Texts in Modern Theology (Minneapolis: Fortress Press, 1991).

Barrett, Lee C. *The Heidelberg Catechism: A New Translation for the 21st Century* (Cleveland: The Pilgrim Press, 2007).

---

[70] James Luther Adams and Walter F. Bense, *Ernst Troeltsch: Religion in History*, Fortress Texts in Modern Theology (Minneapolis: Fortress Press, 1991), pp. 92, 106.

Barth, Karl. "Concluding Unscientific Postscript on Schleiermacher." In *The Theology of Schleiermacher*, ed. Dietrich Ritschl (Grand Rapids: Eerdmans, 1982), pp. 261–279.

Barth, Karl. *Protestant Theology in the 19th Century* (Valley Forge, PA: Judson Press, 1973).

Birkner, Hans-Joachim. "Liberale Theologie." In *Schleiermacher-Studien*, ed. Herrmann Fischer (Berlin: Walter de Gruyter, 1996). pp. 51–62.

Clements, Keith W. *Friedrich Schleiermacher: Pioneer of Modern Theology* (London: Collins, 1987).

Crouter, Richard. *Between Enlightenment and Romanticism* (Cambridge: Cambridge University Press, 2005).

Dole, Andrew. *Schleiermacher on Religion and the Natural Order* (Oxford: Oxford University Press, 2010).

Dorrien, Gary. *Kantian Reason and Hegelian Spirit: The Idealistic Logic of Modern Theology* (Chichester: Wiley-Blackwell, 2012).

Gerrish, B. A. *Christian Faith: Dogmatics in Outline* (Louisville: Westminster John Knox Press, 2015).

Gerrish, B. A. *Continuing the Reformation* (Chicago: The University of Chicago Press, 1993).

Gerrish, B. A. *A Prince of the Church: Schleiermacher and the Beginnings of Modern Theology* (Philadelphia: Fortress Press, 1984).

Graf, Friedrich Wilhelm. "Liberale Theologie." *Evangelisches Kirchenlexikon* 3 (1992), pp. 86–98.

Lamm, Julia. *The Living God: Schleiermacher's Theological Appropriation of Spinoza* (University Park: Pennsylvania State University Press, 1996).

Mackintosh, H. R. *Types of Modern Theology, Schleiermacher to Barth* (London: Nisbet, 1937/1952).

Redeker, Martin. *Schleiermacher: Life and Thought*. Trans. John Wallhausser (Philadelphia: Fortress Press, 1973).

Stephan, Horst, and Martin Schmidt. *Geschichte der evangelischen Theologie in Deutschland seit dem Idealismus*. Dritte Auflage (Berlin: Walter de Gruyter, 1973).

Wyman, Walt. "How Critical Is Schleiermacher's Revisionist Dogmatics?" In *Reformation und Moderne*, ed. Jörg Dierken, Arnulf von Scheliha, and Sarah Schmidt. Schleiermacher Archiv 27 (Berlin: Walter de Gruyter, 2018).pp. 627–644.

Wyman, Walter E., Jr. "The Role of the Protestant Confessions in Schleiermacher's *The Christian Faith*." *Journal of Religion* 87, no. 3 (July, 2007), pp. 355–385.

CHAPTER 19

SIN AND REDEMPTION

KEVIN M. VANDER SCHEL

Among the areas of modern Christian thought where Friedrich Schleiermacher is credited with a foundational influence, the doctrines of grace and sin often find little mention. Schleiermacher's theology has been rightly recognized for its pioneering treatments of modern theological method, consciousness and religious subjectivity, and the concept of God. His work is also hailed by admirers and critics alike for breaking new ground in the domains of Christology and the understanding of the Trinity.[1] By contrast, the specific features of Schleiermacher's account of redemption in the interrelated doctrines of sin and grace have been frequently overshadowed by broader considerations of his overall approach, particularly in its discussions of feeling (*Gefühl*) and religious self-consciousness. Among his own contemporaries, Schleiermacher was charged with subordinating the historical dimensions of Christianity to an archetypal or "ideal" understanding of Christ, such that Christ's crucifixion and historical ministry appeared as superfluous, mere ornamentation for an account of general piety or religious experience.[2] This characterization of Schleiermacher's understanding of redemption as centered on a generalized depiction of religious subjectivity also finds consistent echoes in the writings of dialectical or "neo-orthodox" theologians, whose criticisms played a prominent role in the Anglophone reception of Schleiermacher's thought. In the influential critique of Emil Brunner, for example, the question of the historical connection to Christ signals a "disturbance" in Schleiermacher's system, one that is incidental to the universal mysticism of religious experience that lies at its core.[3]

Yet nestled at the center of Schleiermacher's *Christian Faith*, or *Glaubenslehre*, is a scrupulously crafted treatment of grace (§§86–91, 106–112). As Julia Lamm notes, Schleiermacher's "treatise on grace" is the first modern systematic treatment of the subject, which develops a uniquely "incarnational view" of grace that presents the communication of grace as the historical extension and continuation of the incarnation of Christ.[4]

---

[1] See, for example, Chapters 16, 18, 20, and 21 in this volume.
[2] Such was the view of F. C. Baur, whose criticisms were particularly influential. See *OG*, pp. 33–37, 102.
[3] See Emil Brunner, *Die Mystik und das Wort* (Tübingen: J. C. B. Mohr, 1924), p. 121; also pp. 6–10, 29–30; and Brian A. Gerrish, *Tradition and the Modern World: Reformed Theology in the Nineteenth Century* (Chicago: University of Chicago Press, 1977), pp. 22–39.
[4] Julia A. Lamm, "Schleiermacher's Treatise on Grace," *Harvard Theological Review* 101, no. 2 (2008), p. 137.

And closely coordinated with this is a careful reframing of the doctrines of original sin and actual sin (§§65–85), an account that develops what is among the first modern conceptions of social sin.

Schleiermacher's innovative and carefully structured analyses of sin and grace outline a treatment of redemption that seeks at once to remain faithful to the Protestant tradition and to more adequately meet the critical challenges of modernity and post-Enlightenment thought.[5] In so doing, his work presents a striking reinterpretation of these doctrines, which both influences and anticipates later theological discussions in moving beyond older confessional categories to uncover more comprehensive, vital, and interpersonal dimensions of the Christian teachings of sin and salvation.[6] His *Christian Faith* presents a thoroughgoing de-regionalization of the concept of redemption, according to which redemption no longer constitutes a specific locus of theological reflection but the organizational center around which the entire presentation of doctrine turns. Christianity is "distinguished essentially" from other comparable modes of faith in that within it "everything is referred to the redemption accomplished through Jesus of Nazareth."[7] Moreover, within his discussions of sin and grace, Schleiermacher places distinct emphasis upon the social mediation of human sinfulness and carefully attends to the manner in which the redemptive activity of Christ is communicated to believers within history.

This chapter inquires into Schleiermacher's distinctive understanding of redemption and argues that a narrow interpretative focus on individual religious subjectivity obscures some of the most salient features of his treatment of sin and grace. The analysis here centers on two claims. The first is that sin and grace stand inextricably linked in Schleiermacher's theology, reflecting the basic antithesis of Christian self-consciousness in its connection with the redeemer, and furthermore that this relation determines the contours of each doctrine. It is only through the liberating fellowship with Christ that the distorting nature of sin is known, as we recognize the fault of the old Adam through the perfection of the new. The second claim is that Schleiermacher's treatment of both doctrines is throughout distinguished by an emphasis on the historical and social character of redemption. The redemptive work of Christ brings "a complete transformation of human affairs," yet it operates within existing historical and cultural structures and takes shape only in the gradual passage from the collective life of sin to the collective life of grace.[8] While the particular features of these doctrines often attract less focus than other aspects of his theology, this antithesis of sin and grace and the manner of its historical expression lies at the center of Schleiermacher's theological vision.

---

[5] On the importance of reinterpreting understandings of sin and redemption to meet modern challenges, see Gerrish, *Tradition*, pp. 13–39.

[6] Schleiermacher's discussions of sin and grace unfold through an extended critical engagement with existing Reformed and Lutheran confessions. On Schleiermacher's careful engagement with these creeds, see Walter E. Wyman, Jr., "The Role of Protestant Confessions in Schleiermacher's *The Christian Faith*," *The Journal of Religion* 87, no.3 (2007), pp. 355–385.

[7] *CF* (2016), §11, p. 79. Hereafter citations from this volume are given parenthetically in the text.

[8] Friedrich Schleiermacher, *Christmas Sermons: Displays of Development in a Theology of Christian Faith and Life (1790–1833)*, ed. Terrence N. Tice, trans. Terrence N. Tice and Edwina G. Lawler (Eugene, OR: Cascade Books, 2019), p. 127.

19.1 The Opposition of Sin and Grace

In composing the second edition of his *Christian Faith*, Schleiermacher devoted a significant portion of the work's introduction to the problem of adequately establishing its complex organization and method. As his letters to Friedrich Lücke indicate, he took particular care with regard to the placement of the doctrines of sin and grace within the larger architectonic of the work and noted that many criticisms of the first edition resulted from a misunderstanding of its careful structure.[9] In particular, he lamented that critics failed to grasp the governing logic that fixes the shape of the work overall and its treatment of particular doctrines: "Christians have their complete consciousness of God only as it is produced in them through Christ."[10]

The opposition between the consciousness of sin and grace stands at a crucial juncture in this system. The understanding of sin arises neither from an antithesis of sensations of pleasure and pain, nor does it simply follow from Christianity's moral orientation as a "teleological" religion. The meaning of sin is determined in relation to redemption, which unites and gives common meaning to diverse Christian communions. "Redemption" (*Erlösung*), Schleiermacher notes in the introduction to his *Christian Faith*, is a figurative term, which connotes deliverance or liberation from a constrained condition rather than atonement for particular wrongful actions. It suggests a release from the "wretched state" of bondage in which the consciousness of God is obstructed. Schleiermacher describes this condition as one that approaches a "God-forgetfulness" or "obliviousness as to God" (*Gottvergessenheit*) (§11.2, p. 82), alluding to the Pauline discussion of godlessness in Romans 1:18–32. Indications of such a condition may be found across the world's religious traditions, reflected in practices of penance, spiritual disciplines, and ritual purifications. Yet within Christianity the interconnection of this "incapacity" and the redemption from it plays a determinative role, as "all other religious stirrings" and moments are referred to it and organized around it (§11.3, p. 84).[11] While the "need for redemption" is operative everywhere in human living, the nature of sin is neither knowable in itself nor through a comparative treatment of natural piety in general. It is recognized in its enduring opposition to grace, in the confrontation with the work of the redeemer.

Accordingly, the treatments of sin and grace in Schleiermacher's *Christian Faith* fall at the beginning of the work's longer second part (§§62–85, 86–112), following the preparatory discussions of piety, the doctrine of creation, and the divine attributes in the introduction and first part. Where these initial discussions establish basic categories of religious self-consciousness in general, the enduring opposition of sin and grace forms the essential character of Christian self-consciousness through descriptions of the person and work of Christ, the regeneration of believers and communication of the Spirit, and the election of the church from the world.

---

[9] *OG*, pp. 70, 55–60.
[10] *OG*, p. 55.
[11] On this "incapacity," cf. also *BzE*, p. 82; and Matthew R. Robinson, "Sin and Evil in Schleiermacher," *Itinerari* (2017), pp. 233f.

Significantly, Schleiermacher follows a parallel procedure in his lectures on Christian ethics, or *christliche Sittenlehre*, a discipline that comprises the complementary piece of his dogmatic work and treats the forms of distinctively Christian action.[12] Though these lectures offer no sustained or independent treatment of sin and grace as such, they are likewise oriented around the new "principle of life" (*Lebensprinzip*) introduced through the redeemer, and they center on the "great contradiction" between the "force of sin"—as a "resistance against the higher life"—and the gradual elevation of the forms of human activity through divine grace.[13]

Throughout his dogmatic writings, then, the abiding opposition of sin and grace forms the center point that anchors Schleiermacher's description of distinctively Christian piety:

> Thus, what is distinctive in Christian piety consists in the following. We are conscious that whatever turning away from God might exist in the situations of our lives is a deed originating in ourselves, and this we call *sin*. However, we are conscious that whatever communion with God might exist there rests upon a communication from the Redeemer, and we call this *grace*. (§63, p. 385)

19.2 THE REIGN OF SIN

We are conscious of sin, in part, as grounded in ourselves, and, in part, as having its ground somewhere beyond our individual existence.[14]

This interdependence of sin and grace in Schleiermacher's thought yields a novel approach to the doctrine of sin. As Brian Gerrish notes, "we can speak of the consciousness of sin only as an abstraction from the consciousness of redemption."[15] Accordingly, Schleiermacher's writings neither provide a fixed definition of sin nor do they treat sin as an isolated feature of human experience. Sin has no independent or "self-contained mode of existence" and is it not "a self-contained process" that could be traced back to a specific cause (§81.1, p. 498). Sin is recognized instead in its intractable opposition to grace, as the active resistance or turning away from God that imprints Christian living with an abiding incompleteness and ongoing need for redemption.

This state of sin reflects a "definite conflict of flesh against spirit" (§66, p. 401) as each person finds themselves already hampered by an inner susceptibility and readiness to sin that exists prior to any particular action. In the gradual progression of conscious human life, the lower sensory functions do not advance in harmony with the higher spiritual consciousness, by which one becomes aware of the dependence upon God (§§3–5), but develop in an

---

[12] See Chapter 22 in this volume.

[13] CS (Peiter), pp. 65, n. 2; 96–97; and 104–105. In his *Christian Ethics*, the consciousness of sin is treated in connection with purifying action (*reinigendes Handeln*), whereas the consciousness of grace corresponds to propagative action (*verbreitendes Handeln*). See Kevin M. Vander Schel, *Embedded Grace: Christ, History, and the Reign of God in Schleiermacher's Dogmatics* (Minneapolis, MN: Fortress Press, 2013), pp. 190–215.

[14] *CF (2016)*, §69, p. 413.

[15] Brian A. Gerrish, *Christian Faith: Dogmatics in Outline* (Louisville, KY: Westminster John Knox, 2015), p. 102.

irregular and disordered manner. Thus, over against the nascent awareness of God in human living is the unruly and recalcitrant activity of the "flesh," and there exists in each "a living seed of sin . . . constantly at the point of bursting forth" as soon as it is awakened by a suitable outward temptation (§66.1, p. 403).

This sinful condition, though rooted in natural and created origins, pervades the entirety of human living as a "distortion of nature" (§68, p. 407).[16] However, Schleiermacher resists the speculative temptation to tie the ubiquity of sin to any one specific historical event or natural process. Human sinfulness is thus not the result of a tragic historical misstep or the loss of an original purity. The Mosaic narrative of humanity's "Fall" in the Garden of Eden instead illustrates the elusive manner in which sin arises in all (§72.4).[17] Likewise, the beginnings of sin and evil do not stem from the encumbrance of physical matter, a position Schleiermacher likens to Manicheanism.[18]

Instead, Schleiermacher describes sin in conspicuously social terms, a point commonly emphasized albeit variously interpreted in recent treatments of his thought.[19] Sin is "of a thoroughly collective nature" (*ein durchaus Gemeinschaftliches*) (§71.2, p. 428), and the reign of sin in human action is mediated historically, implanted within the progressive unfolding of human living over countless generations. Every individual is born into communities and forms of social living already long fractured by the effects of sin, and the sinful condition of each has its roots both in one's self and in something existing prior to and "above and beyond one's own existence" (§69.1, p. 414). In this respect, sin is an enduring feature of the historical development of human beings, a distorted condition, yet one that is universally inherited and appropriated as one's own. By consequence, the true character of sin is not found in the wayward dispositions or acts of lone individuals but in the reciprocal and communal life of human beings overall: "in each individual susceptibility to sin is the work of all and in all individuals it is the work of each" (§71.2, p. 428).

19.2.1 Original and Actual Sin

This collective dimension of sin entails a significant reimagining of the traditional categories of original and actual sin, as well as a revised understanding of the place of sin in the created order. Schleiermacher describes original sin (*Erbsünde*) in innovative fashion, as "the

---

[16] On Schleiermacher's distinctive claim of the "unnaturalness of sin," despite its natural and created origins, see Daniel Pedersen, *Schleiermacher's Theology of Sin and Nature: Agency, Value, and Modern Theology* (London: Routledge, 2020), pp. 86–114.

[17] As Marjorie Suchocki notes, Schleiermacher's conception of original sin breaks from the "myth of Adam." See Marjorie Suchocki, "Original Sin Revisited," *Process Studies* 20, no. 4 (1991), p. 234.

[18] See §§80–82, and §§59–61.

[19] Robinson's instructive essay "Sin and Evil in Schleiermacher" highlights the significant connections between the treatment of sin in Schleiermacher's *Christian Faith* and the conception of social evil developed in his philosophical ethics. By contrast, Pedersen's *Schleiermacher's Theology of Sin and Nature* de-emphasizes this social dimension (pp. 7, and 101–102). Similarly, Derek R. Nelson's *What's Wrong with Sin?* adopts Albrecht Ritschl's judgment that while Schleiermacher indicates social aspects of sin, his treatment overall remains too individualistic (*What's Wrong with Sin? Sin in Individual and Social Perspective from Schleiermacher to Theologies of Liberation* [Edinburgh: T&T Clark, 2009], pp. 15–48). Cf. here also Suchocki, "Original Sin," pp. 233–37.

collective act and collective fault of the human race" (§71, p. 425). The designation of this underlying sinful condition as "original" (*Erb-*) highlights its inherited (*erblich*) character, as the lives of those in later generations remain imprinted and conditioned by the communal action of those who have gone before. In this sense, original sin designates "something received and brought along prior to any deed" (§69 p.s., p. 416), an abiding readiness to sin in the acting subject that precedes all specific acts as a "complete incapacity" for good (§70, p. 418).

Such a corrupted condition has no precise beginning in an individual's life but is present from the outset. It indicates an inborn tendency or "susceptibility to sin from birth" (§71.1, p. 427) that functions as the active and sufficient ground of all particular sins, so that what is required for the actual expression of sin is not any further inward change but simply the presence of a suitable outward occasion. And as the exercise of sin gradually increases and takes on the force of habit, one succumbs to sin almost irresistibly, multiplying further sins both in oneself and others. Thus "everywhere that human life is present," the force of sin operates as an active principle of human life, so that it can be said even of young children and infants that "they will be sinners by means of that tendency which already exists in them" (§71.1, p. 428). Given time and suitable occasion, all persons repeat Adam's fall.

Once again, however, original and actual sin find their proper form not in solitary individuals but in the shared reciprocity of communal life. The distinctive shape that sin takes in an individual's life is molded by and reacts to the sins of others, as it participates in the larger webs of sinfulness reigning in one's broader social sphere. The sway of sin is thus operative in the full network of human relationships and human communities. It is a "collective force of the flesh," which develops over generations through the cumulative interactions, attitudes, and conflicts that distinguish persons according to family, class, race, and nation (§71.2, p. 429). And in each of these particular social groupings sin finds particular forms of expression. Beyond the focus on individual moral failings or distortions of desire, then, the rise of sin in each individual is representative of recurring patterns of sin in their larger communities and ultimately of the whole human race: "the susceptibility to sin in each individual refers back to the collective susceptibility to sin of all" (§71.2, p. 430).

With this novel approach to the doctrine of sin, Schleiermacher takes up and modifies many of the symbolic descriptions of original sin offered in Reformed and Lutheran creeds, such as "original disease," "original fault," "natural corruption," and "original defect" (§71, p. 425; and §71.2, p. 430). Yet he also substantially departs from many of the traditional classifications of sins, which differentiate sins according to desire or idolatrous error, inner or outer, intentional or unintentional, and mortal or venial. The only essential distinction falls between sin and redemption: whether the force of sin is progressively increasing in human living or passing away through the redemptive influence of Christ (§74.1–4).

19.2.2 Evil as Natural and Social

It is in light of this account of collective human sinfulness that Schleiermacher develops one of the more innovative features of his treatment of the doctrine of sin: a creative reframing of the relationship between sin and evil. In contrast to more customary accounts in which the prior existence of evil gives rise to sin in human beings, Schleiermacher maintains that the relationship must be reversed: "sin is, above all and overall, the first and original feature, but evil is the derived and secondary feature" (§76.1, p. 479). Evil emerges as the byproduct and consequence of sin, grounded not in the natural order of creation but in the corruption and deterioration of human living that follows the workings of sin. Where the susceptibility to sin reigns in human living, the growth of evil follows without fail.

Schleiermacher distinguishes two general classes of the evils encountered in human living. The first of these describes those "hindrances to life" that afflict all persons yet are relatively independent of human action, as a kind of "natural evil" (*natürliches Übel*). These evils involve no actual change in one's life or outward circumstance but reflect the recognition that "the world with sin appears to be different to human beings than it would have seemed without it" (§75.1, pp. 474–475). In this respect, unavoidable physical ills and limitations that are not intrinsically opposed to the consciousness of God—such as weakness, hunger, sickness, and bodily death—are in view of sin reckoned as miseries that torment human life. However, Schleiermacher further indicates a second class of afflictions and sufferings that proceed directly from human action as "social evil" (*geselliges Übel*).[20] These forms of evil result from the ongoing conflict and opposition among human beings and the innumerable ways in which persons and communities hinder, oppress, and struggle against others in pursuit of private gain. Such social injustices often yield immediate and unambiguous effects, such as violence, destruction, alienation, abuse, and exploitation. But they also exercise a continuing influence in future generations, shaping and misshaping social structures, traditions, and political and civic institutions. Considered in this way, Schleiermacher contends that apart from sin nothing in the finite and natural world could rightly be considered an evil. Yet given the presence of sin, the growth of evil in the world invariably follows: "evil is first introduced with the advent of sin, but once sin has appeared it arises inevitably" (§75.1, p. 475).

This novel portrayal of the link between sin and evil carries important implications for reimagining the role of evil in the orders of creation and redemption. It first entails a notably modified understanding of the claim that evil serves as punishment for sin. Schleiermacher rejects the view that would trace the punishment of specific sins to the righteous wrath of God. Indeed, his forthright assessment of the notion of divine wrath is unmistakable: "there is no such thing" (§109.4, p. 721). While maintaining that all evil in its connection with divine causality "is to be regarded as punishment for sin," he argues that it represents such a penalty only in the limited sense that evil enters the world as the inevitable byproduct and consequence of sin (§76, p. 478). Social evils exhibit this punishment in more direct and lasting fashion, through the expanding and deepening "deterioration of the world" that follows in the wake of human sin (§76.3, p. 482). Natural evils, by contrast, reflect this penalty only indirectly, as it is only through sin that natural imperfections, pain, and the limitations of finite existence are experienced as evil. Yet in neither case can one regard evils as punishment for a single individual's sin. Rather, evil is the "collective punishment" consequent to the "collective fault" of sin (§84.2, p. 527). All suffer the consequences of one another's sins.

Additionally, this treatment of sin and evil leads to revised conceptions of divine holiness and justice, and it significantly complicates the question of the relation of sin to the divine will. Here Schleiermacher establishes a clear contrast to the language of the creeds,

---

[20] Here, then, Schleiermacher's description signals a notable modification of the more traditional categories of "natural evil" and "moral evil." See also Gerrish, *Christian Faith*, pp. 92–94.

which hold that God must in no way be regarded as the author of sin and evil. As "without exception, all that is real" and all that happens is wholly dependent upon God (§48.3, p. 271), he argues that in a specific and limited sense God is also the author of sin (§79). That is, insofar as the unceasing "consciousness of sin belongs to the truth of our existence," sin is "ordained by God, itself being viewed as that which makes redemption necessary" (§81.3, p. 505). In regards to the existence of sin and evil, then, Schleiermacher proposes a unique form of supralapsarianism. God does not will redemption in response to sin but everything in the created order, including humanity's intractable susceptibility to sin, is arranged towards redemption through Christ: "God has ordained sin for human beings in relation to redemption" (§89.3, p. 556).

Schleiermacher's innovative reinterpretation of the doctrine of sin has been a frequent target of criticism for later theologians. Influential critiques from Karl Barth and Reinhold Niebuhr, in particular, fault its emphasis on religious subjectivity and its optimism about the human condition.[21] Yet his treatment has also exercised a subtle influence in modern theology. Schleiermacher's analysis of sin proved an ongoing and fruitful source of inspiration for Kierkegaard's discussions of repentance. It likewise provided important impetus for Walter Rauschenbusch's later development of the social gospel and informed John Hick's later descriptions of "Irenaean" approaches to theodicy.[22]

Furthermore, Schleiermacher's understanding of sin marks a distinctly forward-looking position, anticipating themes of more recent social and developmental treatments of sin in the latter twentieth century. Departing from more customary Augustinian interpretations of original sin, it describes the transmission of human sinfulness in social terms, set within the context of reciprocal human relationships and the ongoing process of creation.[23] In this respect, as scholars such as Marjorie Suchocki and Shelli Poe have more recently noted, Schleiermacher's conception of sin as a collective and ongoing distortion of human living finds notable and surprising points of connection in the critical analyses of social and structural sin emerging from liberation and feminist theologies.[24]

---

[21] See Karl Barth, *Church Dogmatics*, vol. 3, ed. G. W. Bromiley and T. F. Torrance (Edinburgh: T&T Clark, 2000), pp. 319–334; and Reinhold Niebuhr, *The Nature and Destiny of Man*, vol. 1 (Louisville, KY: Westminster John Knox Press, 1996), pp. 245–248.

[22] See Richard E. Crouter, "Schleiermacher: Revisiting Kierkegaard's Relationship to Him," in *Kierkegaard and His German Contemporaries*, vol. 2, ed. Jon Stewart (London: Ashgate, 2007), pp. 197–232, especially pp. 215–218; Walter Rauschenbusch, *Theology for the Social Gospel* (Louisville, KY: Westminster John Knox Press, 1997), pp. 27, 92–93; and Walter E. Wyman, Jr., "Rethinking the Christian Doctrine of Sin: Friedrich Schleiermacher and Hick's 'Irenaean Type,'" *The Journal of Religion* 74, no. 2 (April 1994), pp. 199–217. As Xiaolong Zhou has more recently demonstrated, however, the characterization of Schleiermacher's treatment of sin as "Irenaean" is misleading, as Schleiermacher regarded Augustine as a serious interlocutor and sought to retrieve central elements of his position. See Zhou, "Schleiermachers Kritik an der Hamartiologie Augustins: Eine philosophische Erklärung", *Neue Zeitschrift für Systematische Theologie und Religionsphilosophie* 65, no. 2 (2023), pp. 157–185.

[23] Walter E. Wyman, Jr., "Sin and Redemption," in *The Cambridge Companion to Friedrich Schleiermacher*, ed. Jacqueline Mariña (New York: Cambridge University Press, 2005), p. 145.

[24] See Suchocki, "Original Sin," pp. 233–243; and Shelli M. Poe, *The Constructive Promise of Schleiermacher's Theology* (Edinburgh: T&T Clark, 2021), ch. 2.

19.3 The Reign of Grace

> But if we are to see everything that can develop out of such original perfection all together in a single human instance, it is not to be sought in Adam, in whom it would again have to be lost, but rather in Christ, in whom it has brought benefit to all.[25]

The close interconnection of sin and redemption also determines the character of Schleiermacher's original treatment of grace. The transition from the old life under sin to the new life in Christ marks the pivot on which his descriptive analysis of Christian self-consciousness turns. The misery of the collective life of sin is known as it is gradually overcome by the blessedness of the new and divinely effected collective life in Christ, which inaugurates the reign of God in human history.[26] The distinctive strength of Schleiermacher's treatment of grace in his *Christian Faith* lies in the careful coordination of two emphases: the character of the new life in Christ, and the manner in which it emerges in the midst of human historical living.

19.3.1 New Life in Christ

As with his analysis of sin, Schleiermacher does not provide a strict definition of grace. Instead, he develops a rich and suggestive vocabulary of the workings of grace.[27] He describes grace as "a particular divine communication" (§80.1, p. 491) and a "communication from the Redeemer" (§63, p. 385), which removes sin's misery or "lack of blessedness" (*Unseligkeit*) (§86 p. 539) and brings peace and "blessedness" (*Seligkeit*) (§87, p. 544) in its place. Yet he also speaks of the consciousness of grace as the state of "being united with Christ" (§101.2, p. 631), and the "divine life within us" as human beings (§108.6, p. 709). This gift of grace is not the imparting of any one particular facet or effect of Christ's activity but "Christ's self-communication" (§108.6, p. 710). Most fundamentally, as Schleiermacher puts it in an 1831 Christmas sermon, the gift consists in the fact that "the redeemer is given to the world."[28] Christ is distinguished from all others by his "essential sinlessness" (§98, p. 608), the perfect presence of God to human nature within him. And the "new implanting of God-consciousness" (§94.3, p. 579) that extends from his redeeming influence transforms the entirety of human living, bringing a new and distinctive manner of apprehending, perceiving, and acting.

Outside of this redeeming influence, the consciousness of God in each remains "weak and suppressed," emerging only intermittently in "occasional sparks" that do not take hold in one's life (§106.1, p. 683). Through the connection to Christ, however, the consciousness

---

[25] *CF* (1928), p. 387.

[26] See §§87–88. See also Gerrish, *Christian Faith*, pp. 119–136.

[27] Nadia Marais carefully traces this vocabulary in her essay "Contaminated by Grace? Salvation, Sociability, and the Church as Collective Life," in *Beyond Tolerance: Schleiermacher on Friendship, Sociability, and Lived Religion*, ed. Matthew R. Robinson and Kevin M. Vander Schel (Berlin: De Gruyter, 2019), pp. 129–144, especially pp. 130–133.

[28] Schleiermacher, *Christmas Sermons*, p. 131.

of God emerges as the organizing principle of human thought and action, which reorders all other conscious impulses and activities: a new form of human historical living "engrafted" onto the old (§106.1, p. 683). In this respect, Schleiermacher finds the New Testament affirmations of a new birth and new creation appropriate (2 Cor. 5:17). Redemption marks the emergence of a "new human being" and a "new creature": "one's life stands under a different formulation and is consequently a new life" (§106.1, p. 683).

Taken in this sense, the communication of grace is not limited to the forgiveness of particular sins but constitutes a continuation of the union of God with human nature begun in the incarnation. The entrance of the redeemer into the world yields a higher influence that transforms human activity and inaugurates a new community of grace. The effect of Christ's work, then, is both person-forming and world-forming. In the same measure that "creation did not have an orientation toward individuals" but "on the contrary, the world was created," so too "the activity of the Redeemer is also world-forming [weltbildend], and its object is human nature, in the entirety of which a powerful God-consciousness is to be planted as a new principle of life" (§100.2, pp. 624–625). Accordingly, as Schleiermacher argues, this new life in Christ is not an additional divine action but discloses the fundamental unity of all divine activity in the world. Creation, the incarnation, and the communication of grace together comprise "one divine act for the purpose of altering our relationship with God, the temporal manifestation of which is begun in the incarnation of Christ and from which the collective new creation of humanity proceeds" (§109.3).[29]

Schleiermacher recognized that this incarnational understanding of grace necessitated a thorough reframing of Lutheran and Reformed confessional formulas. As Walter Wyman and Julia Lamm have noted, his treatment presents a painstaking engagement with the language of these confessions, reorganizing the traditional Protestant categories of grace around the two concepts of regeneration and sanctification (§106).[30] Under the heading of regeneration (§§107–109), he gathers together and systematizes central Protestant teachings dealing with justification and conversion, repentance, and the forgiveness of sins. Each of these central Protestant affirmations, he argues, deals with one facet of the same dawning reality: the "turning point" by which a person begins to pass from the collective life of sin to the "community of life with Christ" (§108.2, pp. 694–695). Within his discussion of sanctification (§§110–112), he describes the progressing aspect of this redeemed life, as a continuing process of becoming that is distinguished by the gradually decreasing activity of sin and the "growing dominion of the life with Christ over the flesh" (§111.1, p. 734). At every point, then, this higher form of life proceeds not as a result of any particular human action but through faith's "taking hold of Christ" (§109.4, p. 721). Yet at each point Schleiermacher also insists that this foundational influence of Christ is not a change within individual persons alone but consists in the new collective life that is founded by him (§100.3).

---

[29] CG^2, §109.3, p. 198; translation amended by author. Cf. *CF (2016)*, p. 719. On the unity of divine action in creation and redemption, see also Paul T. Nimmo, "The Mediation of Redemption in Schleiermacher's *Glaubenslehre*," *International Journal of Systematic Theology* 5, no. 2 (2003), pp. 187–199.

[30] See Lamm, "Schleiermacher's Treatise," pp. 144–145, 155–156, 163; and Wyman, "The Role of Protestant Confessions," pp. 377–382. Within Schleiermacher's Christian ethics, the categories of regeneration and sanctification play a similarly determinative role in propagative action, which proceeds from the consciousness of grace. See Kevin M. Vander Schel, "Grace and Human Action: Distinctively Christian Action in Schleiermacher's Christian Ethics," *The Journal of Religion* 96, no. 1 (2016), pp. 15–22.

Furthermore, in addition to the liberation from sin, the communication of grace holds significant implications for the place of evil in the created order. Christ's redemptive activity, as the "taking away of sin" (§100.3, p. 628), brings not only release from the constraint of human sinfulness but also "reconciliation" (*Versöhnung*), which "removes the interconnection between evil and sin" (§101.2. p. 630). Though pain and suffering remain as the product of ongoing natural limitations and social ills, in the vital connection with Christ such sorrows no longer serve to obstruct the consciousness of God as "evil" but coexist with it to better indicate the path of faithfulness. In bringing forgiveness of sin, Christ's work interrupts the punishment of sin through evil, setting believers free from the misery of sin and gathering them into his own "unclouded blessedness" (§101, p. 629).

It is within this redemptive and reconciling activity as a whole that the scandal of the cross, the "greatest element [*Moment*] in the work of redemption," finds its place (§104.4, p. 660). The reconciling death of Christ manifests perfect sympathy for humanity's weakness (§101.4) and reflects the character of his life overall, in his "unfailing perseverance" in suffering and redressing the evil that follows sin. This "absolutely self-denying love" reveals "in utmost clarity how it was that God was in him reconciling the world to Godself" (§104.4, p. 661).[31]

19.3.2 The Historical Mediation of Grace

This dual accent on the ubiquity of sin and the thoroughgoing consciousness of grace sets Schleiermacher's account apart from more Pelagian or Socinian trajectories, which would lessen the need for redemption or reduce the importance of Christ's work to an exemplary spiritual dignity or representative moral sacrifice. Christ's exclusive dignity follows from the absolute perfection and strength of his consciousness of God, which was "an actual being of God in him" (§94, p. 574). And the unique redemptive activity of Christ consists not merely in noble teachings or moral deeds but in a new and higher form of communal living that incorporates believers into fellowship with God.

Equally notable, however, is the manner by which this founding of new life emerges in the midst of human historical living and becomes enmeshed in human communities. Schleiermacher rejects those views of redemption that would posit Christ's influence as operating above or outside the conditions of the historical world. He also criticizes "magical" views of redemption, by which Christ's work might yield a direct personal influence on an individual independently of the community of believers or any historical or natural mediation.[32] Neither the later *Christus Victor* model of evil's triumphant defeat through divine command nor Zinzendorf's devotion to the blood and wounds of Christ find a place in his system.[33] He maintains by contrast that redemption effects a gradual but decisive transformation of human living through the transition from the collective life of sin to the collective life of grace. Accordingly, redemption is properly manifested not in discrete individuals but in the reciprocal life of the community of faith. Just as "sin is essentially something communal"

---

[31] On the suffering of Christ in Schleiermacher's treatment of redemption, see Poe, *The Constructive Promise*, ch. 2.

[32] See §§100.3 and 101.3. On this manner of this mediation, see also Nimmo, "The Mediation of Redemption," pp. 189–192.

[33] Cf. §104.4.

(§78.3, p. 488), so too the transforming and liberating work of the redeemer extends to all: "redemption through Christ is ordained for the entire human species" (§83.2, p. 518).

The emphasis on the historical connection to Christ demystifies an important but elusive aspect of Schleiermacher's treatment of grace and redemption: redemption in all cases proceeds from the divine activity of Christ yet is everywhere contingent upon ongoing natural and historical development. The beginnings of redemption and the emerging reign of God thus do not constitute a second, supernatural order fitted atop the natural world but signal the divinely ordained liberation and elevation of historical living that bring creation to its completion.[34]

Such an accent on the historical embeddedness of redemption lends Schleiermacher's treatment of grace its distinctive character. The appearance of Christ and redemption from the general condition of human sinfulness reveal a gracious divine power at work in human living, which is irreducible to natural operations and occurrences yet communicated in and through the structures of the natural and historical world. In Christ, the supernatural becomes natural, as his originative redemptive influence operates within the historical world to resist the contagion of sin and bring creation to its fulfillment in the reign of God.[35]

In this regard, the often-repeated criticism that Schleiermacher's understanding of redemption in Christ remains too closely tied to religious subjectivity and interiority carries a certain irony.[36] The genuine work of Christ is the entire collective life of the Christian community, and the liberation from the force of sin is expressed in this corporate life. While departing from certain traditional Augustinian and Reformed theological emphases, then, his account of grace resonates in important ways with more recent discussions of grace in history and the manner in which the work of Christ is received and becomes operative within the community of faith.[37]

19.4 CONCLUSION

As the above overview indicates, Schleiermacher's bold refashioning of the doctrines of sin and grace offers an account of redemption that is remarkable in its originality and scope and which, contrary to long-standing interpretations of his work, places notable emphasis

---

[34] The prominence of the historical connection to Christ is also reflected in Schleiermacher's lectures on Christian ethics, which describe a gradual elevation of human living that begins with Christ and continues under the "lordship of the Spirit." See *CS (Peiter)*, pp. 260–261, 560–561; and Vander Schel, "Grace and Human Action," pp. 27–32.

[35] See §§88.4, 94.3, and 100.3. On the theme of the supernatural-becoming-natural in Schleiermacher's theology, see Vander Schel, *Embedded Grace*, pp. 83–86, 176–179.

[36] Among the most prominent of these critics is again Karl Barth, who regards Schleiermacher's depiction of the opposition of sin and grace as a mere psychological antithesis that fails to capture the genuine Protestant teaching of sin and justification. On Barth's criticism, see Paul T. Nimmo, "Schleiermacher on Justification: A Departure from Tradition?," *Scottish Journal of Theology* 66, no. 1 (2013), pp. 50–73.

[37] Curiously, Schleiermacher's incarnational understanding of grace places his treatment in the somewhat unexpected company of twentieth-century Catholic theology, which develops the understanding of grace as a continuation of the union of divine and human nature found in the appearance of Christ. See Lamm, "Schleiermacher's Treatise," pp. 166–168.

on human sociality. As Brian Gerrish notes, "sin and redemption are about the individual's relation not to God or Christ only, but also to *the world*."[38] As such, it is also a challenging treatment, which holds together a number of persistent tensions. It maintains dual emphases on self-consciousness and the collective life of community; it insists both upon the universality of redemption and its exclusive origin in Christ; and it upholds both the finality of Christ's redemptive activity and its contingency upon historical progress.

In each of these respects, Schleiermacher's theology confronts its readers with a peculiar combination of historical-sensitivity and christocentrism. On one hand, the historical appearance of the redeemer stands at the center of his system as the principal instance of grace, and the shape and content of every aspect of Christian faith—from doctrines of creation and election to the broader contrast between nature and the supernatural—is illuminated by "thinking in reverse order" (§94.2, p. 578) from this fundamental relation to Christ. As Schleiermacher notes, "everything is created with a view to the Redeemer," and "the entire ordering of nature would have been different from the beginning onward if redemption through Christ had not been destined for the human race after sin had occurred" (§164.1, pp. 999–1000). On the other, Christ's decisive influence is entirely mediated by ordinary and unremarkable social relationships, and it is conditioned at every point by natural and historical development.

In many regards, this dynamic underscores an enduring strength of Schleiermacher's approach: his theology presents an analysis of the redemptive work of Christ that is deeply historically minded without being reductively historicist. Yet in other respects this historically conscious christocentrism brings its own particular set of limitations. As with other christocentric views, it significantly complicates the task of inter-religious dialogue by considering all genuine religious developments outside Christianity as subordinate steps towards the superior fulfillment of religious living in the fellowship with Christ. It also introduces a more fundamental difficulty. As any theological articulation of the content of Christ's new and decisive influence invariably assumes a particular set of values, social forms, and intellectual genealogies, it risks privileging certain cultural traditions as normative developments of humanity while devaluing others as incomplete or distorted. As Joerg Rieger notes, for example, while Schleiermacher's theology displays some notable and significantly anticolonial tendencies—particularly in his Christian ethics—his overall project at points reflects a modern colonial mindset that tethers understandings of Christianity to the attitudes of the emerging European middle class.[39] Likewise, as Ted Vial has argued, appreciation of Schleiermacher's pioneering account of religion must be counterbalanced with a sober awareness of interconnectedness of the modern concepts of religion and race.[40]

Yet amidst these tensions and limitations, Schleiermacher's treatment of sin and redemption offers considerable theological promise. His innovation in highlighting the social and historical dimensions of redemption charts a path beyond older confessional disputes of grace and sin and introduces new and important lines of thinking in modern and contemporary theology. In particular, his revisionary account broadens discussion of redemption beyond privatized conceptions of individual atonement to explore questions of the historical

---

[38] Gerrish, *Christian Faith*, p. 91, emphasis in text.
[39] See Joerg Rieger, *Christ and Empire* (Minneapolis, MN: Fortress Press, 2007), pp. 197–236.
[40] Theodore Vial, *Modern Religion, Modern Race* (New York: Oxford University Press, 2016), pp. 155–187.

mediation of sin and grace and the resultant patterns of thought and action that imprint cultural practices, social identities, and political institutions. In this respect, Schleiermacher's understanding of sin and redemption outlines a prototypical treatment of a recurring challenge of modern Christian thought: that of depicting the liberation from sin beyond the interiority of faith as it takes shape amidst the diverse social forms and structures of historical human living.

Suggested Reading

Gerrish, Brian A. *Christian Faith: Dogmatics in Outline* (Louisville, KY: Westminster John Knox, 2015), pp. 77–106, 119–136.

Lamm, Julia A. "Schleiermacher's Treatise on Grace." *Harvard Theological Review* 101, no. 2 (2008), pp. 134–168.

Nimmo, Paul T. "The Mediation of Redemption in Schleiermacher's *Glaubenslehre*." *International Journal of Systematic Theology* 5, no. 2 (2003), pp. 187–199.

Wyman, Jr., Walter E. "Sin and Redemption." In *The Cambridge Companion to Friedrich Schleiermacher*, ed. Jacqueline Mariña (New York: Cambridge Univ. Press, 2005), pp. 129–149.

Bibliography

Barth, Karl. *Church Dogmatics*, vol. 3. Ed. G. W. Bromiley and T. F. Torrance (Edinburgh: T&T Clark, 2000).

Brunner, Emil. *Die Mystik und das Wort* (Tübingen: J.C.B. Mohr, 1924).

Crouter, Richard E. "Schleiermacher: Revisiting Kierkegaard's Relationship to Him." In *Kierkegaard and His German Contemporaries*, vol. 2, ed. Jon Stewart (London: Ashgate, 2007), pp. 197–232..

Gerrish, Brian A. *Christian Faith: Dogmatics in Outline* (Louisville, KY: Westminster John Knox, 2015).

Gerrish, Brian A. *Tradition and the Modern World: Reformed Theology in the Nineteenth Century* (Chicago: University of Chicago Press, 1977).

Lamm, Julia A. "Schleiermacher's Treatise on Grace." *Harvard Theological Review* 101, no. 2 (2008), pp. 134–168.

Marais, Nadia. "Contaminated by Grace? Salvation, Sociability, and the Church as Collective Life." In *Beyond Tolerance: Schleiermacher on Friendship, Sociability, and Lived Religion*, ed. Matthew R. Robinson and Kevin M. Vander Schel (Berlin: De Gruyter, 2019), pp. 129–144.

Nelson, Derek R. *What's Wrong with Sin? Sin in Individual and Social Perspective from Schleiermacher to Theologies of Liberation* (Edinburgh: T&T Clark, 2009).

Niebuhr, Reinhold. *The Nature and Destiny of Man*, vol. 1 (Louisville, KY: Westminster John Knox Press, 1996).

Nimmo, Paul T. "The Mediation of Redemption in Schleiermacher's *Glaubenslehre*." *International Journal of Systematic Theology* 5, no. 2 (2003), pp. 187–199.

Nimmo, Paul T. "Schleiermacher on Justification: A Departure from Tradition?" *Scottish Journal of Theology* 66, no. 1 (2013), pp. 50–73.

Pedersen, Daniel. *Schleiermacher's Theology of Sin and Nature: Agency, Value, and Modern Theology* (London: Routledge, 2020).

Poe, Shelli M. *The Constructive Promise of Schleiermacher's Theology* (Edinburgh: T&T Clark, 2021).

Rauschenbusch, Walter. *Theology for the Social Gospel* (Louisville, KY: Westminster John Knox Press, 1997).

Rieger, Joerg. *Christ and Empire* (Minneapolis, MN: Fortress Press, 2007).

Robinson, Matthew R. "Sin and Evil in Schleiermacher." *Itinerari* (2017), pp. 225–246.

Schleiermacher, Friedrich. *Christmas Sermons: Displays of Development in a Theology of Christian Faith and Life (1790-1833)*. Ed. Terrence N. Tice, trans. Terrence N. Tice and Edwina G. Lawler (Eugene, OR: Cascade Books, 2019).

Suchocki, Marjorie. "Original Sin Revisited." *Process Studies* 20, no. 4 (1991), pp. 233–243.

Vander Schel, Kevin M. *Embedded Grace: Christ, History, and the Reign of God in Schleiermacher's Dogmatics* (Minneapolis, MN: Fortress Press, 2013).

Vander Schel, Kevin M. "Grace and Human Action: Distinctively Christian Action in Schleiermacher's Christian Ethics." *The Journal of Religion* 96, no. 1 (2016), pp. 3–28.

Vial, Theodore. *Modern Religion, Modern Race* (New York: Oxford University Press, 2016).

Wyman, Walter E., Jr. "Rethinking the Christian Doctrine of Sin: Friedrich Schleiermacher and Hick's 'Irenaean Type.'" *The Journal of Religion* 74, no. 2 (April 1994), pp. 199–217.

Wyman, Jr., Walter E. "The Role of Protestant Confessions in Schleiermacher's *The Christian Faith*." *The Journal of Religion* 87, no.3 (2007), pp. 355–385.

Wyman, Jr., Walter E. "Sin and Redemption." In *The Cambridge Companion to Friedrich Schleiermacher*, ed. Jacqueline Mariña (New York: Cambridge University Press, 2005), pp. 129–149.

Zhou, Xiaolong. "Schleiermachers Kritik an der Hamartiologie Augustins: Eine philosophische Erklärung". *Neue Zeitschrift für Systematische Theologie und Religionsphilosophie* 65, no. 2 (2023), pp. 157–185.

CHAPTER 20

PERSON AND WORK OF CHRIST

MAUREEN JUNKER-KENNY

20.1 INTRODUCTION

THE publication of Schleiermacher's *The Christian Faith* in 1821/1822 inaugurated within theology the anthropological turn of modernity that resulted from the changed conditions of knowledge outlined by Kant in his *Critique of Pure Reason* (1781). The starting point of Schleiermacher's material dogmatics is the Christian consciousness of redemption. Statements about God are no longer justified by arguing from the exterior world to a creator God as the cause of its existence, but by an analysis of human self-consciousness. The possibility of reaching knowledge of God by way of theoretical, object-related reason is dismissed and replaced with a reflection on the constitution of human subjectivity as the anchor-point of knowledge and agency. For Schleiermacher, dogmatics could no longer begin with either the authority of the Bible or with objectivizing truth claims about the world and its origin. Any systematic account of the Christian faith had to begin by examining the ability of the human person to be addressed by God based on a different method, namely, a transcendental enquiry into the internal conditions of the possibility of speaking of God.

In its architecture, the *Glaubenslehre* documents how the new requirement of relating a truth claim to the subject's capacities of knowing has been taken on board. It consists of an "Introduction" that combines different disciplines—such as philosophy, comparative history of religions, and hermeneutics—to establish the definitions of the essences of religion and of Christianity, and of a two-part material dogmatics. In Part II, which begins with the "Consciousness of Sin," Christology is treated under the "Consciousness of Grace." This specifically Christian part follows Part I, which examines the concepts of God and of the human creature that are presupposed in the doctrines of Part II, abstracting from their concretization in the Christian experience of redemption. *The Christian Faith* thus displays an elliptical structure with two focal points: a philosophical principle consisting in the concept of religion that is reached from an analysis of human subjectivity, and, through its further determination in Christianity as one of the positive, historical religions, a theological or dogmatic principle consisting in the definition of the essence of Christianity. With these two enquiries, the "Introduction" establishes a link to the general consciousness of truth. It justifies religion as an irreducible dimension of the human constitution and the specific historical traditions of faith as communities centered on this element, thus, as regular or even "necessary" formations in human life and not as "aberrations" (BO, ²§22).

The framework for Christology within this architecture and its propositions will be treated in the following steps of analysis: (1) the original argumentation developed in the first edition; (2) the key critique by F. C. Baur; (3) the corrections and new emphases in the Christology of the second edition;[1] and (4) ongoing debates.

20.2 THE ORIGINAL OUTLINE 1821/1822

In the ordering of religions that Schleiermacher takes over from the Enlightenment, monotheism is seen as the highest stage. Comparing Judaism, Christianity, and Islam at a formal level, he finds the connection between the core religious content and the founding figure to be closest in Christianity. The fact that "redemption" as the organizing center of the Christian faith is uniquely attributed to the person of Jesus allows Schleiermacher to draw out some of the implications set by this definition of its essence. Already in the Introduction he indicates the boundaries of this faith tradition by outlining "natural heresies" (2.1). In Part II of the material dogmatics, the theological effort to present the Christian self-consciousness in the most adequate and consistent categories possible takes the form of examining and identifying problems with the two-natures terminology of the early christological councils (2.2). Their concepts are replaced by a new conception of Christ that avoids both the extrinsic nature of a supernaturalist starting point that begins with the sheer authority of divine revelation without any reflection on the human capacity of understanding that revelation, and also a rationalist reduction of the Redeemer to a moral exemplar. Jesus Christ's "dignity" is expressed by designating him as the "archetype" of the God-consciousness and his "work" is defined as effecting redemption by communicating its strength to the faithful, taking them up into the circle of his life (2.3).

20.2.1 The "Natural Heresies" Derived from the Essence Definition of Christianity in the "Introduction"

Schleiermacher begins his enquiry into the essence of Christianity with the observation that the limits beyond which a belief is deemed no longer Christian have been a matter of dispute among the theological schools of his era. Having established the consciousness of redemption by Jesus of Nazareth as the typical self-understanding of the Christian religion, he clarifies the implications of the concept of redemption for the interpretation of the terms "nature," "reason," and "revelation." Statements that either undermine the human ability to

---

[1] For brevity's sake, I will use ¹§ for quotations from the first (CG^1) and ²§ for quotations from the second edition (CG^2). Translations from CG^1 are my own, CG^2 is quoted either in the ET of 1928 or of 2016. "LS" stands for the "lead sentence" or thesis of each paragraph.

be redeemed or the ability of the Redeemer to redeem, are judged to be deficient. It is possible to identify the "natural heresies" of Christianity (^{1}§25) well in advance of the two doctrinal parts of the material dogmatics on a conceptual basis. The ways in which the essence can be missed in the two respects, relating either to human nature or to the Redeemer, are marked by alternatives that are named after historical heresies. The "soteriological" or "anthropological" heresies relate to human beings as the addressees of the work of redemption, making redemption either unnecessary or impossible: in "Pelagianism," the human need for redemption is interpreted as a gradual process so that redemption appears to be achievable by mutual support among humans. In "Manicheism," by contrast, humans are not capable of receiving redemption without first requiring "absolute transformation." The "christological" heresies relate to the person and dignity of the Redeemer and consist in two ways of rendering him incapable of accomplishing redemption. "Docetism" results from assuming Christ's "unlimited difference" from humanity, denying his "human embodiment and nature," whereas the "Ebionite" or "Nazarean" heresy overemphasizes his "essential likeness" to humanity to a degree that one can no longer speak of "redemption." The contrasts within the anthropological heresies and the christological heresies complement each other: Manicheism corresponds with Docetism, and Pelagianism with the Ebionite heresy.[2] Having charted these positions as contravening the core of the Christian confession, it becomes clear that in Schleiermacher's dogmatic system, theological anthropology and Christology must be determined in ways that avoid both the supernaturalist and rationalist extremes of his era.

20.2.2 The Problems of the Two-Natures Terminology in the Christological Tradition

One key concern for Schleiermacher in his attempt to transform the doctrine of Christ from the substance ontological thought form inherited from the christological councils, is to reconnect systematically the "person" and the "work" of Christ. The dignity and the accomplishment of the Redeemer need to be interpreted as mutually implying each other. Thus, the "person" and "work," "dignity," and "activity" of Christ "completely match each other and each is the measure for the other" (^{1}§113,1. II,18). The categories used by the Council of Chalcedon to capture as well as rule out inadequate ways of formulating the being of God in Christ must be superseded by concepts that express what is given in the Christian self-consciousness, namely, the foundational experience of redemption. Therefore, the observation is true that Christology is being accessed from Jesus Christ's activity,[3] in other words, from soteriology. However, as Schleiermacher argues already in the first edition, even before F. C. Baur's critique of an "ideal Christ" replacing the historical Redeemer, his Christology is kept from being a projection of human beings in their need by locating

---

[2] Cf., for example, Hans Küng, "Friedrich Schleiermacher: Theology at the Dawn of Modernity," in Küng, *Great Christian Thinkers* (New York: Continuum, 1994), pp. 155–184.

[3] Gerhard Ebeling, "Interpretatorische Bemerkungen zu Schleiermacher Christologie," in *Schleiermacher und die wissenschaftliche Kultur des Christentums*, ed. Günter Meckenstock (Berlin/New York: De Gruyter, 1991), p. 136. Ebeling already sees the two-natures doctrine of the old church as expressing "two aspects of a single matter, not as an addition of two factors" (138).

the origin of redemption in the full, unprecedented, and unsurpassable strength of Jesus' God-consciousness.

What, then, is problematic about the two-natures terminology of the christological tradition? Apart from its conceptual inconsistencies, Schleiermacher argues that it fails to convey the unity of Jesus Christ's person, which is decisive for the relationship of believers to the Redeemer. Several difficulties are identified: the "equivocation" regarding the subject of agency between the divine Logos and the human nature, reason, and will of Jesus; the extension of the term "nature" from an already existing meaning in the human realm, and especially the incongruity of using it to comprise the divine, which is infinite; the contradiction of the general meaning in which the same nature is attributed to a variety of persons; and a divergent use of the same term in the doctrine of the Trinity which, if applied consistently, would add a finite element to all three divine persons.[4] Since these concepts have only opened up a space of "hair-splitting vacuity" (*spitzfindigen Leerheit*) (^{1}§117,3. II,38), a different way must be found to express the uniqueness of the Redeemer, one in which neither the human nor the divine aspect are diminished.

Lori Pearson is among those who positively assess Schleiermacher's critical christological achievement, after examining its correspondence to the alternatives of the patristic era prior to Chalcedon: "Schleiermacher is working with a 'high' soteriological orientation and relating it in a new way to a strongly historicized and naturalized view of Christ's human nature."[5] Jacqueline Mariña equally concludes that Schleiermacher "preserves the upshot of the insights of Chalcedon while at the same time rejecting the language in which those insights were framed."[6] Which alternative conception does he propose to avoid the impasses into which the substance ontological categories have led?

20.2.3 Jesus as the Archetype of the God-consciousness

Schleiermacher's critique of the terminology in which Christology had been developed is based on a positive counterproposal. His objections are oriented toward a content that has been obscured and needs to be made accessible to believers of his era: Jesus Christ is the historical instantiation of the complete realization of the human God-consciousness and is thus its "archetype." Each believer's realization of their God-consciousness continues to draw on his mediation.

In their method of inference, the lead propositions of the material parts of *The Christian Faith* reflect the need to name the epistemological subject. Their form of inferring from the effect back to its cause makes the connection visible to the *principium cognoscendi* of dogmatics, the Christian pious self-consciousness: "Since the promotion [*Förderung*] of the higher life is traced back to the Redeemer in the consciousness of the Christian, this refers

---

[4] Cf., for example, Karl-Heinz Menke, *Jesus ist Gott der Sohn. Denkformen und Brennpunkte der Christologie* (Regensburg: Pustet, 2008), pp. 341–343.

[5] Lori Pearson, "Schleiermacher and the Christologies behind Chalcedon," *Harvard Theological Review* 96 (2003), p. 367.

[6] Jacqueline Mariña, "Christology and Anthropology in Friedrich Schleiermacher," in *The Cambridge Companion to Friedrich Schleiermacher*, ed. J. Mariña (Cambridge: Cambridge University Press, 2005), p. 153.

to the historical and the archetypal as inseparably united in his person" (¹§114 LS; II,19). The "spiritual outcome" must have its source in the specificity of the Redeemer; otherwise it would be more accurate to assume "redeeming eras and events than a Redeemer in the proper sense, and see the cause in favorable circumstances owed to chance" (¹§113,1. II,17).

Schleiermacher's model for interrelating a Christology from below and one from above in one consistent framework begins with the earthly Jesus. His "sinlessness" is unique but nevertheless constitutes a conceptual possibility of human nature. At the same time, his existence cannot be explained from his human context. The element "from above" retains what is divine, without splitting the unity of his self-consciousness in two. The divine is the initiating and integrating element, while the human side receives and represents it:

> Once the difference between the Redeemer and all other human beings is stated as having in him a pure being of God under the form of consciousness and conscious activity, instead of our impure and darkened [*verunreinigten und verdunkelten*] God-consciousness: then the divine in the Redeemer is the innermost fundamental power [*Grundkraft*] from which every activity proceeds, and which holds every element together; everything human is in every moment the receiving and representing organism of the former. (¹§117,3. II, 37; cf. ²§96,3; CF (1928), 397)

As Richard R. Niebuhr summarizes, the inherited terminology of a "divine nature conjoined to a human nature" is replaced by the "constant potency" of Jesus' God-consciousness[7] in his self-understanding, thoughts, and acts. Moving to modern concepts of subjectivity and history, however, introduces challenges of a different kind to Christology. How was this transformation of Christology into an outline that corresponds to the new anthropological conditions of knowledge received by his contemporaries, and which questions did they raise?

20.3 A CRITIQUE THAT RESULTED IN REVISIONS: F. C. BAUR ON THE FIRST EDITION'S CHRISTOLOGY

The final elaboration of Schleiermacher's Christology that is found in the second edition of *The Christian Faith* gains its specific contours when it is read against the backdrop of the critiques the original version encountered. The key objection that would be met by making substantial changes to the structure of the Introduction and to the Christology came from a member of the then supernaturalist Tübingen School, Ferdinand Christian Baur. He became the leading figure of the Tübingen School's subsequent reorientation after his turn to Hegelian Idealism. In Baur's reading, Schleiermacher posits an "ideal Christ" arising from the Christian self-consciousness, eschewing the historical foundation that the Bible represents (3.1). Despite the substantial changes to the second edition, Baur's critique has been reiterated throughout the history of *The Christian Faith*'s reception. Within the past one hundred years, Karl Barth and his school have pitted Schleiermacher's approach as the

---

[7] Richard R. Niebuhr, *Schleiermacher on Christ and Religion* (New York: Ch. Scribner's Sons, 1964), p. 225.

alternative to a theology based on the Word of God; this "impasse" has since been addressed from different angles.[8] Alister McGrath's reconstruction of the *Glaubenslehre*, which is based on Baur and his own judgement along Barthian lines (3.2), will be compared with other assessments regarding the relevance of history for Schleiermacher's christological argumentation (3.3).

20.3.1 Ferdinand Christian Baur: An "Ideal" Christ Constructed Independently of History

From his first account of the new work in a letter to his brother in 1823,[9] to his two published reviews in 1827[10] and 1828, and his subsequent books, Baur's questions concern the foundations of the Christology that *The Christian Faith* puts forward. He interprets its designation of Jesus Christ as "archetype" as proposing an "ideal Christ," developed without reference to history. Not distinguishing between the Introduction and the dogmatic system, Baur diagnoses the essence definition of Christianity to be lacking validation by the New Testament. Overlooking also the different levels of the God-consciousness attributed to the immediate self-consciousness of every human being, and its different concretization in each positive religion through which it comes to historical experience, Baur concludes that Schleiermacher's account of the Redeemer is a creation of reason. For Baur, the method of inference reveals Christ's origin in the "religious self-consciousness." The decisive question is, does "the concept of the Redeemer coincide fully with the concept of redemption so that he is actually only the idea of redemption conceived personally," or is it itself "historically given in the true sense"?[11] He regards the first option to be the case. Since the historical ground

> is absent from the deepest structure of Schleiermacher's theology..., Schleiermacher's dogmatics is included in the "gnosis" typology. Its theological substance, precisely because the historical element is lacking..., is ultimately led back to a cognitive content qualified by reason, not by revelation. Indeed, revelation is irreducibly constituted by a *factual event*. That is why Baur maintains that Schleiermacher's dogmatics belongs to the typology of rationalism... defined as "that system that presents human reason as the highest cognitive principle

---

[8] Stephen Sykes, "Schleiermacher and Barth on the Essence of Christianity—An Instructive Disagreement," in *Barth and Schleiermacher: Beyond the Impasse?*, ed. James O. Duke and Robert F. Streetman (Philadelphia: Fortress Press, 1982), pp. 88–107. Robert J. Sherman, *The Shift to Modernity. Christ and the Doctrine of Creation in the Theologies of Schleiermacher and Barth* (New York/London: T&T Clark, 2005).

[9] The letter to his brother Friedrich August from July 27, 1823 has been edited by Heinz Liebing, "Ferdinand Christian Baurs Kritik an Schleiermachers Glaubenslehre," *Zeitschrift für Theologie und Kirche* 54 (1957), pp. 225–243.

[10] Ferdinand Christian Baur, *Primae Rationalismi et Supranaturalismi historia capita potiora, Pars II: Comparatur Gnosticismus cum Schleiermacherianae theologiae indole.* (Tübinger Osterprogramm) (1827); partly reprinted in *KGA* 1.7.3, pp. 243–256.

[11] Ferdinand Christian Baur, "Anzeige der beiden academischen Schriften," *Tübinger Zeitschrift für Theologie* 1 (1828), pp. 220–264, 241; partly reprinted as Baur, "Selbstanzeige," in *KGA* 1.7.3, pp. 256–277, 266.

in religion" and as "that system which, as concerns divine things, never exceeds the sphere, enclosed in itself, of human reason and consciousness."[12]

This result has been reached in a reconstruction that ignores the architecture of the *Glaubenslehre*. Summarizing Baur's critique as that of having attempted "to demonstrate Christianity a priori,"[13] in the second edition Schleiermacher reordered the Introduction and clarified its function and steps with new subheadings. Baur took the pious self-consciousness—which became the *principium cognoscendi* of Christian dogmatics only due to its historical determination—as competing with the historical source of Christology, that is, the New Testament. From Baur's supernaturalist stance, the Introduction should have started from biblical revelation. Schleiermacher's intentions to give justified accounts both of the concept of piety and of the location of Christianity among other positive religions are not registered. Yet despite the inaccuracies and misinterpretations, the question Baur was the first to pose will have to be returned to: Does "the concept of the Redeemer coincide fully with the concept of redemption so that he is actually only the idea of redemption conceived personally"?

20.3.2 Alister McGrath's Renewal of Baur's Critique

In the history of reception of Baur's key point, Alister McGrath follows his reconstruction and links it with the judgement that taking "feeling" as one's anthropological point of departure will end in Feuerbach's projection theory. The only way to avoid this descent is to take the Word of God as one's theological starting point: "Feuerbach's critique of religion may indeed lose much of its force when dealing with non-theistic religions, or theologies (such as that of Karl Barth) which claim to deal with a divine encounter with man from outside him; when applied to a theistic construction or interpretation of man's emotional or psychological states, however, it is in its element." Also for McGrath, the method of inference "from religious feeling" to the person of Jesus points to an "ideal" instead of a historical Redeemer. The outcome is not an "ideal rationalism" as for Baur in 1823, but the uncovering of religion as an illusion. McGrath concludes, "The possibility that the . . . relation between the 'archetypal Christ' and the Jesus of history was purely illusory, resulting from the erroneous objectification and externalisation of man's aspirations, could no longer be ignored. The unsatisfactory foundation which Schleiermacher established for this relation was thus cruelly exposed, its inadequacy obvious to all."[14]

McGrath attributes the failure of Schleiermacher's theory of Christ as archetype to a more fundamental deficit: "Much more serious, however was the apparent disinclination of Schleiermacher to come to terms with the irreversible trend towards historicisation

---

[12] Sergio Sorrentino, "History and Temporality in the Debate between F. Ch. Baur and Schleiermacher," in *Schleiermacher's Philosophy and the Philosophical Tradition*, ed. S. Sorrentino, Schleiermacher: Studies and Translations Vol. 11 (Lewiston, NY: Edwin Mellen Press, 1992), pp. 111–132, p. 112, with reference to the "Selbstanzeige," KGA 1.7.3, pp. 257, 259.

[13] Schleiermacher, *On the Glaubenslehre. Two Letters to Dr. Lücke*, trans. James Duke and Francis Fiorenza (Atlanta: Scholars Press, 1981), p. 76.

[14] Alister McGrath, *The Making of Modern German Christology: From the Enlightenment to Pannenberg* (Oxford: Oxford University Press, 1986), p. 47.

initiated by the *Aufklärung*."[15] This conclusion will have to be examined in relation to other views. The overall critique is that Schleiermacher failed to express the distinctiveness of the Christian faith and took over rationalist premises: He "avoided concepts and values that were ... objectionable to the Enlightenment."[16] For the author of the *Speeches* with his ardent critique of "an age whose hobbyhorse was a lamentable generality and an empty sobriety, which ... works against true cultivation,"[17] a more nuanced judgement than McGrath's is required. In defending religion as a valid human pursuit through a theory of subjectivity, Schleiermacher combines insights both from the Enlightenment and from Romanticism in his reconstruction of faith in Jesus Christ as Redeemer.

20.3.3 Examining the Relevance of History for the First Edition's Christology

Before analyzing how Schleiermacher responds to Baur's critique in his revisions for the second edition of his *Glaubenslehre*, the assumptions contained in Baur and McGrath's negative assessments need to be compared with other views. One of the key reasons for Schleiermacher's new departure in dogmatic theology was the rise of the historical and natural sciences that he wanted theology to take on board and not contradict. The following four comments correct the judgement of an "ideal Christ," and open up a different direction of enquiry. While agreeing that some formulations in the *Glaubenslehre* can cause misunderstandings, Gerhard Ebeling clarifies against Baur's impression "of an introverted subjectivism" that "already the feeling of absolute dependence as such is in its essence an external relationship [*Externbeziehung*]." As the cause of the human subject's existence, God is external to human self-consciousness. He goes on: "*A fortiori*, the Christian pious self-consciousness ... can only exist based on the appearance of Jesus." Against Baur's premise that "the historical Christ is only a secondary appearance of an idea," which is "given independently of it," he recalls Schleiermacher's "resolute will to be accountable for connecting to the historical Jesus."[18]

Christine Helmer points to the historical and text-critical investigations into the New Testament of his exegetical teaching both in Halle and Berlin. Besides being

> the first theologian to offer public lectures on the life of Jesus ..., Schleiermacher was considered to be at the forefront of New Testament scholarship in his time. In conversation with the nascent early nineteenth-century research on the Synoptics, Schleiermacher proposed a theory of Synoptic dependence resting on orally transmitted stories about Jesus prior to their redaction by the New Testament authors. In regard to 1 Timothy, Schleiermacher showed that the apostle Paul was not its author, thereby paving the way for critical deuteropauline scholarship. Similarly, Schleiermacher's research on the parallel structure of Colossians 1:15–20 set the literary parameters for research on this text well into the late twentieth century.[19]

---

[15] McGrath, *The Making of Modern German Christology*, p. 31, n. 55.
[16] Alister McGrath, ed., *The Christian Theology Reader* (Oxford: Blackwell, 2007, 3rd ed.), pp. 372–374.
[17] *Speeches¹*, p. 207.
[18] Ebeling, "Interpretatorische Bemerkungen," pp. 127, 128, 129.
[19] Christine Helmer, "Schleiermacher's Exegetical Theology and the New Testament," in *The Cambridge Companion to Friedrich Schleiermacher*, ed. Jacqueline Mariña (Cambridge: Cambridge University Press, 2005), p. 229.

Richard R. Niebuhr highlights how against the

> demand that the sinlessness of Jesus be proved, that Jesus of Nazareth be demonstrated to be the Christ . . ., Schleiermacher replied that such proof cannot be given. However, what theology can and must do is to describe how Christian faith originated and how it is experienced in the present. . . . [F]aith is elicited by the persuasiveness of its object . . . . Hence, Christ completes the creation of faith; faith does not create Christ.[20]

Roger Haight characterizes his approach as "a Christology from below. His *The Life of Jesus* shows that he had an interest in the earthly life and ministry of Jesus. His Christology has Jesus of Nazareth, the earthly figure, as its initial imaginative focus of attention."[21] Thus, it appears that a reference to "history" can be called for from different understandings of its function and methods, depending on the theological program in question. A constitutive limit, however, should be admitted: Historical research cannot reach the internal thoughts and motivations of agents. A different issue emerges for theological enquiry, namely, the evidence claimed for the founder within his original community of disciples and ever since.

20.4 THE CORRECTIONS AND NEW ACCENTUATIONS OF THE SECOND EDITION

The first point to be addressed is the relevance of the historical experience of Jesus as Redeemer (4.1). A substantial revision is carried out regarding the connection between the higher and the lower consciousness in the Redeemer and the believers (4.2). A further change consists in now permitting a new, overarching perspective to be included, a view from the one divine decree from which his appearance—that for human insight is a historical turning point—is understood as the always intended "perfection of creation" (4.3). Fourth, to explain the effect of the Redeemer both on the original and on all subsequent disciples, the concept of the "total impression" of Christ is developed, taking up Baur's unfeasible demand to prove the essence definition of Christianity historically (4.4).

20.4.1 Not to be Replaced by the Idea: The Historical Existence of the Archetype

The revisions carried out in the second edition serve two key purposes: to justify the elliptical structure by anchoring the thesis of a natural God-consciousness in a philosophical analysis of subjectivity with a claim to "necessity" (^{2}§4,1); and to elaborate more clearly how the "archetypal" and the "historical" coincided completely in the person of Jesus. By distinguishing the disciplines employed in the Introduction to reach a general concept of religious community as the social formation arising from piety, defined as an essential

---

[20] Niebuhr, *Schleiermacher on Christ and Religion*, pp. 217–218, with reference to ^{2}§88,2.
[21] Roger Haight, "Take and Read: The Christian Faith," *National Catholic Reporter*, May 23, 2016, accessed March 1, 2020, https://www.ncronline.org/blogs/ncr-today/take-and-read-christian-faith.

human pursuit, and its specification in Christianity, the distinct tasks and methods of the Introduction are clearly set off from the body of doctrines, including Christology.

By reformulating the lead propositions and forging ^{1}§§114 and 115 together into ^{2}§93, the misinterpretation that Christology is owed to a construction, as held by F. C. Baur, is countered:

> If the spontaneity of the new corporate life is original in the Redeemer and proceeds from him alone, then as an historical individual He must have been at the same time ideal [*urbildlich*] (i.e. the ideal must have become completely historical in Him), and each historical moment of His experience must at the same time have borne within it the ideal. (^{2}§93 LS; *CF (1928)*, 377).

Thus, the union of the historical and the archetypal (which *CF (1928)* translates as "ideal," *CF (2016)* as "prototypical") in the person of Jesus could only be grasped from his life.

Schleiermacher also revised his previous alignment of Jesus Christ's own proclamation with the subsequent development of theological doctrine. In the second edition he clearly distinguishes "Christ's self-proclamation [*Selbstverkündigung*]" as the "only *one* source from which all Christian doctrine is derived" from the "one way in which Christian doctrine is pursued,... based on [*entsteht*] religious [*frommen*] consciousness itself and on the immediate expression of it" (^{2}§19. *CF (2016)*, 138). The original version had allocated theological doctrines and Christ's own teaching to the same level: "In the area of Christianity there cannot be two but only one way in which doctrine originates as the expression of piety and of faith: and the ecclesial doctrines are completely similar [*ganz gleichartig*] to the doctrines of Christ and the Apostles also in their origin [*Entstehung*], only different through their scientific presentation" (^{1}§1,4. I, 12).

20.4.2 From Fusion to Determination: A Different Account of the Relation between the Higher and the Lower Consciousness

The second edition's revised analysis of subjectivity in ^{2}§§3 and 4 establishes the irreducible function of religion as a modification of the immediate self-consciousness from which the theoretical concept of God is held to originate. The stringency of this new transcendental, no longer just phenomenological, analysis leads to a change regarding the interaction of the God-consciousness with the sensible self-consciousness. In the first edition, the relationship between the God-consciousness and sensible self-consciousness was envisaged as a "fusion." The first edition held that the sensible feelings "melted" (*verschmelzen*) (I, 37.39) with the pious affections. The second edition, in contrast, states that "this conjunction cannot be regarded as a fusion" but "rather a co-existence of the two in the same moment." The function inherent in human embodiment is therefore no longer seen as disappearing into a synthesis with the "higher self-consciousness" (^{2}§5,3; *CF (1928)*, 21). In other words, the lasting function of the sensible self-consciousness is now recognized. When it comes to the relationship between the sensible self-consciousness and the God-consciousness, the question is how the first can become transparent for the latter. What was a latent contradiction in Schleiermacher's first anthropological theory is thus revised by the second edition. In the first version, the sensible self-consciousness first seems to be acknowledged as that which carries the subject's irreducible, original relationship to the world. Yet in the "higher" consciousness it is set to disappear. In the second edition, it becomes clear that the sensible self-consciousness that makes it possible for the human person to relate to the world is given an abiding function in a life oriented by the "higher" or God-consciousness.

In both editions, the archetypal character of Jesus Christ consists in the steady, effortless, or "unstruggling" *(kampflos)* superiority of his God-consciousness over his sensible self-consciousness. This is what is unique or "miraculous... in the person of the Redeemer" (^{1}§114,2. II, 20). However, the first edition had concluded from the finding that in Jesus Christ "no hindrance can be found between them" that in him the God-consciousness and the sensible self-consciousness must be "totally the same" *(völlig dasselbe)*. The reason given in the first edition is that "where there is difference, there still is also reciprocal hindrance" (^{1}§18,4. I,66). The second edition, in contrast, explains the absolute strength of the God-consciousness as giving the "impulse to every moment" of the sensible self-consciousness that retains its independent status; the relationship is one of determination, not absorption.

20.4.3 From Historical Turning Point to Completion of Creation: Christ as the Second Adam

Both editions had concluded that since Jesus Christ's appearance represents the "reality of the purely sinless development which was conceived of as only possible before" (^{1}§115,2. II, 25), the creation of human nature has been completed in him. But the second edition, justified by an enlargement of the Christian self-consciousness to encompass also the perspective of the original divine decree, advances the Pauline term of the "Second Adam" as the guiding perspective. The "creative divine act" to which this completion is owed is evoked in a specification in the second edition: Jesus Christ's

> distinctive spiritual content cannot be accounted for based on the content of the circle of human beings to which he belonged. Rather, it can be accounted for based only on the general source of spiritual life through a creative divine act, in which act the concept of the human being as the subject of the God-consciousness is completed to an absolutely greatest extent. (^{2}§93,3; *CF (2016)*, II. 569, slightly amended)

Yet, as also Gerhard Ebeling points out, there is a tension or "competition" between the "two soteriological conceptions": " 'redemption' and 'perfection' [*Vollendung*] in history, ... one accentuating the restitution of a pure creation, the other the transcending of creation towards a goal that is still outstanding."[22] What Ebeling identifies as restitution is reached by a redemption that constitutes a historical turning point. The completion of creation, with its extension toward the future in which all of humanity is foreseen to eventually become Christian (cf. ^{2}§120,4; *CF (1928)*, 558), however, is not a reversal but a linear continuation of what was intended by God from creation onwards.[23] The question is whether this

---

[22] Ebeling, "Interpretatorische Bemerkungen," p. 134.
[23] In "Christ and the Perfection of Creation in Schleiermacher's Dogmatic Theology" (*Roczniki Teologiczne* 64 [2017], p. 48), Kevin Vander Schel summarizes succinctly: "Schleiermacher thus depicts Christ's influence as bringing about a gradual transformation of human history from within,

understanding, developed already in the Introduction, that the "supernatural" is destined to become "natural," is enough to ground the unsurpassable significance of Jesus Christ and his ongoing mediating role.

20.4.4 The "Total Impression" of the Historical Person of Jesus Engaging the Freedom of Believers

While the first edition referred to "the person himself and his immediate power" (¹§21,1. I, 83), the second in its response to Baur's critique of an "ideal Christ" develops the concept of the "total impression"(*Eindruck*) of Jesus (²§14 Postscript; *CF (2016)*, I, 115 and ²§99 Postscript; *CF (2016)*, II, 619). The method of inference from the Christian pious self-consciousness is retained but specified through this term. The historical person of Jesus communicated redemption by freely attracting disciples. Baur's question about the historical foundation of the first edition's Christology is thus answered with an evidence claim: Jesus' "total impression" is to account for the original gathering of his community as well as its spread in all subsequent eras.

This concept also helps address a further question that arose about the role of human freedom in Schleiermacher's concept of religion as the feeling of absolute dependence, within the nexus of nature and in the process of redemption. The second edition emphasizes the active receptivity of believers in their freedom:

> the creative activity of Christ ... is entirely concerned with the sphere of freedom ... what it produces is altogether free ... He can influence what is free ... only in accordance with the nature of the free. The activity by which He assumes us into fellowship with Him is, therefore a creative production in us of the will to assume Him into ourselves. (²§100,2; *CF (1928)*, 426)

The freedom of the relationship offered by Jesus Christ is also illustrated by a revision of the theorem of his kingly office (¹§126) that includes a critique of the Prussian king. Having struggled for the freedom of the church from the state in the Agenda controversy, Schleiermacher sets off Christ's fulfilment of the kingly office from temporal rulers:

> we must keep to the recollection, not yet extinct, that the conception of king was opposed ... to that of a tyrant, whose power was just as unlimited but not natural; and ... to that of the authorities of a society, who possessed only a limited and delegated power, conferred on them by the governed themselves ... tyranny ... might have other aims than the free development and the natural prosperity of those over whom it was exercised ... In contrast with both, ... [i]ndividuals ... submit voluntarily to the Lordship of Christ. (²§105,1; *CF (1928)*, 466)

Yet, even if the *Glaubenslehre* succeeds in explaining the attraction of the person of Jesus in terms of the "total impression" on his followers in all eras, this is not spelled out any further regarding the unique insights his life and proclamation offers into the being of God.

The reasons for the missing connection from his Christology to his doctrine of God will now be examined in conclusion.

---

inaugurating the reign of God that does not destroy or oppose the created and historical world but draws it to completion."

20.5 ONGOING QUESTIONS

By replacing the "divine nature" of the Chalcedonian formula with the unique strength of Jesus' God-consciousness, his distinction from humanity has been expressed in the new categories of modernity, that is, "freedom" and "history." Schleiermacher thus opened up a new era of theological reflection. Yet, this breakthrough is affected by an underdetermination of Jesus' concrete relationship to God. The two final aspects to be treated are, first, the observation made at different stages in the history of reception of the *Glaubenslehre*, that no new content about God is disclosed in Jesus' historical proclamation and praxis;[24] and, second, as its backdrop, the insistence on a single divine decree encompassing creation and redemption.

20.5.1 The Lack of a New Disclosure of God in Jesus Christ

Even if the whole approach of the *Glaubenslehre* is programmatically based on the experience of the Redeemer, this does not lead to a new view of God. R. R. Niebuhr judges, "Schleiermacher's weakness is that he does not give to Christ, in his thinking about God, nearly the same power of reforming the mode of thought that he allows him, in his thinking about man."[25] Matthias Gockel concludes as follows:

> Christ is the universal redeemer and mediator of salvation but his appearance does not contribute specifically to the determination of the divine will and decree. Despite the christologically motivated affirmation of general redemption and rejection of eternal damnation, the overall reconstruction remains theocentric; it is grounded in the belief in God the almighty creator, even though ecclesiology is its context and christology its background.[26]

Thus, the one point where F. C. Baur is right is in his content diagnosis. There is no new, unprecedented insight in what Christ mediates but only the full strength of the actualized God-consciousness everyone is supposed to possess. The problem at the root of Schleiermacher's Christology is the overextension of the result of the philosophical analysis of self-consciousness, contingency. The finding that self-consciousness is unable to ground itself was named a "feeling of absolute dependence"; added to this was the positing of a "Whence" in ²§4,4, a ground of human existence already perceived as benevolent and reliable. This result of the philosophical enquiry into self-consciousness can only be confirmed, but not revealed by Jesus Christ. Regarding the concept of revelation, Hans-Joachim Birkner observed, "only in feeling, the feeling of absolute dependence, is there a relationship between God and the human person, only *there* and there *actually* [*wirklich*]. This is the central statement of Schleiermacher's theological program . . . yet it is not evident at first in

---

[24] For an overview, cf. Maureen Junker-Kenny, *Self, Christ and God in Schleiermacher's Dogmatics: A Theology Reconceived for Modernity* (Berlin/Boston: De Gruyter, 2020), pp. 184–207.
[25] Niebuhr, *Schleiermacher on Christ and Religion*, p. 212.
[26] Matthias Gockel, *Barth and Schleiermacher on the Doctrine of Election: A Systematic-Theological Comparison* (Oxford: Oxford University Press, 2006), p. 103.

which sense Schleiermacher can say that God 'reveals God's self to him and through him'" (²§103,2).[27]

This lack of a genuine content—such as the revelation of God's love—and the role of substitution played by the doctrine of sin, supplying the reason for humanity's need for Christ, leads Thomas Pröpper to judge the *Glaubenslehre* as offering "the classical example for the role of sin as a dogmatic helper in need [*Nothelferrolle*]."[28] Magnus Lerch sees the unique dignity of Christ as merely being "secured hamartiologically," and otherwise dissolving into human reason.[29] If the "unhindered strength" of Jesus' God-consciousness had been elucidated as his free acceptance of God's invitation, then his proclamation would have been the clue to God's being as love. While "love" remains the one divine attribute credited with expressing God's essence (²§166), despite all anthropomorphic restrictions, what Jesus' life reveals is that human nature has now reached the perfect state that was always intended. Thus, his particularity disappears in what is generally human, an already shared God-consciousness. The meaning of salvation history is the ultimate realization of the essence of the human person.

20.5.2 Creation and Redemption as One Divine Decree

In the second edition, the perfection of human nature becomes the ultimately guiding perspective. It is no longer stated as a connecting doctrine but as directly drawn from the Christian pious self-consciousness. The perfection of human nature is reached as an aspect of the single divine decree governing God's whole relationship to the world. Why is the unity of this pretemporal decree so ardently defended? It is not the supralapsarian position presupposed by it that is the problem, but the concept of God that it originates from: a God whose agency can only be eternal and never within history, for whom no new action but only preservation is conceivable, and who cannot be referred to in personalistic or anthropomorphic terms. Behind this prohibition of ascribing "change" to God—such as creation, in contrast to the continuity of preservation,[30] or the new initiative of redemption, or any action in history—is an idea of perfection that can scarcely be attributed to the biblical heritage. This metaphysical concept is the reason that the *Glaubenslehre* is unable to spell out the freedom of God, of Jesus Christ, and of the human subject as the origin of their unique agencies. The single divine decree encloses creation, redemption as a turning point in the history of humanity as well as the unpredictable human reaction to it. Schleiermacher regarded John 1:14 as the core Christian message that he strove to express. Yet the framework—universal causality as the guiding category for God, divine omnipotence limited by tying its expression completely to the world (¹§68.a. and ²§54), and identifying "can" and "do" in God—does not

---

[27] Hans-Joachim Birkner, "'Offenbarung' in Schleiermachers Glaubenslehre [1956]," in Birkner, *Schleiermacher-Studien*, ed. Hermann Fischer, Schleiermacher-Archiv 16 (Berlin/New York: De Gruyter, 1996), pp. 83, 85.
[28] Thomas Pröpper, *Theologische Anthropologie*, 2 vols. (Freiburg: Herder, 2011), vol. II, p. 677.
[29] Magnus Lerch, *Selbstmitteilung Gottes. Herausforderungen einer freiheitstheoretischen Offenbarungstheologie* (Regensburg: Pustet, 2015), p. 143.
[30] Wolfhart Pannenberg, *Schleiermachers Schwierigkeiten mit dem Schöpfungsgedanken* (Munich: Verlag der Bayerischen Akademie der Wissenschaften, Sitzungsberichte, 1996, Heft 3).

leave any scope for eschatological action and curtails what Christology can add. As Susanne Schaefer concludes,

> Well before any revelation—something that would actually be able to give insight into the essence of God—, it has already been decided in the logic of the *Glaubenslehre how* God is in relation to the world . . . Due to the overall design . . ., the event of revelation [*Offenbarungsgeschehen*] in which God first becomes known as love could no longer be of constitutive significance for the teaching on divine attributes.[31]

The decisiveness and coherence of Schleiermacher's reworking of Christian dogmatics for a new age remain impressive, inaugurating horizons, categories, and tasks that also enable its internal critique.

Suggested Reading

Clements, Keith W. *Friedrich Schleiermacher. Pioneer of Modern Theology* (London: Collins, 1987), pp. 7–65.

Duke, James O., and Francis Fiorenza. "Translators' Introduction" and "Notes" to Schleiermacher, in *On the Glaubenslehre. Two Letters to Dr. Lücke*, trans. Duke and Fiorenza (Atlanta: Scholars Press, 1981), pp. 1–32, 95–130.

Fischer, Hermann. *Friedrich Daniel Ernst Schleiermacher* (Munich: Beck, 2001).

Lamm, Julia. "Schleiermacher's Treatise on Grace." *Harvard Theological Review* 101 (2008), pp. 133–168.

Sorrentino, Sergio. "Feeling as a Key Notion in a Transcendental Conception of Religion." In *Schleiermacher, the Study of Religion, and the Future of Theology: A Transatlantic Dialogue*, ed. Brent W. Sockness and Wilhelm Gräb (Berlin/New York: De Gruyter, 2010), pp. 97–108.

Bibliography

Birkner, Hans-Joachim. "'Offenbarung' in Schleiermachers Glaubenslehre [1956]." In Birkner, *Schleiermacher-Studien*, ed. Hermann Fischer. Schleiermacher-Archiv 16 (Berlin/New York: De Gruyter, 1996), pp. 81–98.

Ebeling, Gerhard. "Interpretatorische Bemerkungen zu Schleiermacher's Christologie." In *Schleiermacher und die wissenschaftliche Kultur des Christentums*, ed. Günter Meckenstock (Berlin/New York: De Gruyter, 1991), pp. 125–146.

Gockel, Matthias. *Barth and Schleiermacher on the Doctrine of Election: A Systematic-Theological Comparison* (Oxford: Oxford University Press, 2006).

Haight, Roger. "Take and Read: The Christian Faith." *National Catholic Reporter*, May 23, 2016, accessed March 1, 2020. https://www.ncronline.org/blogs/ncr-today/take-and-read-christian-faith.

---

[31] Susanne Schaefer, *Gottes Sein zur Welt. Schleiermachers Subjektanalyse in ihrer Prinzipienfunktion für Glaubenslehre und Dialektik* (Regensburg: Pustet, 2002), pp. 212–213.

Helmer, Christine. "Schleiermacher's Exegetical Theology and the New Testament." In *The Cambridge Companion to Friedrich Schleiermacher*, ed. Jacqueline Mariña (Cambridge: Cambridge University Press, 2005), pp. 229–247.

Küng, Hans. "Friedrich Schleiermacher: Theology at the Dawn of Modernity." In Küng, *Great Christian Thinkers* (New York: Continuum, 1994), pp. 155–184.

Lerch, Magnus. *Selbstmitteilung Gottes. Herausforderungen einer freiheitstheoretischen Offenbarungstheologie* (Regensburg: Pustet, 2015).

Liebing, Heinz. "Ferdinand Christian Baurs Kritik an Schleiermachers Glaubenslehre." *Zeitschrift für Theologie und Kirche* 54 (1957), pp. 225–243.

Junker-Kenny, Maureen. *Self, Christ and God in Schleiermacher's Dogmatics: A Theology Reconceived for Modernity* (Berlin/Boston: De Gruyter, 2020).

Mariña, Jacqueline. "Christology and Anthropology in Friedrich Schleiermacher." In *The Cambridge Companion to Friedrich Schleiermacher*, ed. J. Mariña (Cambridge: Cambridge University Press, 2005), pp. 151–170.

McGrath, Alister. *The Making of Modern German Christology: From the Enlightenment to Pannenberg* (Oxford: Oxford University Press, 1986).

McGrath, Alister, ed. *The Christian Theology Reader* (Oxford: Blackwell, 2007, 3rd ed.).

Menke, Karl-Heinz. *Jesus ist Gott der Sohn. Denkformen und Brennpunkte der Christologie* (Regensburg: Pustet, 2008).

Niebuhr, Richard R. *Schleiermacher on Christ and Religion* (New York: Ch. Scribner's Sons, 1964).

Pannenberg, Wolfhart. *Schleiermachers Schwierigkeiten mit dem Schöpfungsgedanken* (Munich: Verlag der Bayerischen Akademie der Wissenschaften, Sitzungsberichte, 1996, Heft 3).

Pearson, Lori. "Schleiermacher and the Christologies behind Chalcedon." *Harvard Theological Review* 96 (2003), pp. 349–367.

Pröpper, Thomas. "Schleiermachers Bestimmung des Christentums und der Erlösung. Zur Problematik der transzendental-anthropologischen Hermeneutik des Glaubens" (1988). In Thomas Pröpper, *Evangelium und freie Vernunft* (Freiburg: Herder, 2001), pp. 129–152.

Pröpper, Thomas. *Theologische Anthropologie*, 2 vols. (Freiburg: Herder, 2011).

Schaefer, Susanne. *Gottes Sein zur Welt. Schleiermachers Subjektanalyse in ihrer Prinzipienfunktion für Glaubenslehre und Dialektik* (Regensburg: Pustet, 2002).

Schleiermacher, Friedrich. *Der christliche Glaube nach den Grundsätzen der evangelischen Kirche im Zusammenhange dargestellt (1821/22): Marginalien und Anhang*, KGA 1.7.3, ed. Ulrich Barth in collaboration with Hayo Gerdes and Hermann Peiter (Berlin: De Gruyter, 1983).

Sorrentino, Sergio. "History and Temporality in the Debate between F. Ch. Baur and Schleiermacher." In *Schleiermacher's Philosophy and the Philosophical Tradition*, ed. S. Sorrentino. Schleiermacher: Studies and Translations Vol. 11 (Lewiston, NY: Edwin Mellen Press, 1992), pp. 111–132.

Sherman, Robert J. *The Shift to Modernity: Christ and the Doctrine of Creation in the Theologies of Schleiermacher and Barth* (New York/London: T&T Clark, 2005).

Sykes, Stephen. "Schleiermacher and Barth on the Essence of Christianity—An Instructive Disagreement." In *Barth and Schleiermacher: Beyond the Impasse?*, ed. James O. Duke and Robert F. Streetman (Philadelphia: Fortress Press, 1982), pp. 88–107.

Vander Schel, Kevin. "Christ and the Perfection of Creation in Schleiermacher's Dogmatic Theology." *Roczniki Teologiczne* 64 (2017), pp. 47–67.

Vander Schel, Kevin M. *Embedded Grace: Christ, History, and the Reign of God in Schleiermacher's Dogmatics* (Minneapolis: Fortress, 2013).

CHAPTER 21

TRINITARIAN THOUGHT

SHELLI M. POE

SCHLEIERMACHER'S position on the doctrine of the Trinity has been a source of controversy since he first published his masterwork, *Der christliche Glaube* (*Christian Faith*, also known as the *Glaubenslehre*), in 1820/1821 and the second edition in 1830/1831. The spectrum of scholarly argument ranges from the oft-heard accusation that Schleiermacher relegates the doctrine of the Trinity to an appendix as a mere afterthought to his systematic theology, to the much less cited argument that he actually upholds the dominant form of the doctrine. Schleiermacher's faithfulness to the doctrine of the Trinity as a distinctively Christian doctrine is at stake in this research. Given the importance of the doctrine of the Trinity for many contemporary theologians, the debate will contribute substantially within academic theology to either the firm placement of Schleiermacher's theology exclusively on the shelves of historical study, or a continued resurgence of Schleiermacher studies based on the assessment that his theological work is only beginning to receive an appropriate hearing amongst and could be of benefit to contemporary theologians. This chapter is divided into three sections. The first section provides a critical review and analysis of the significant debates surrounding Schleiermacher's trinitarian thought. The second section advances the argument that Schleiermacher is an original trinitarian thinker whose work on the subject is in the early stages of recognition among scholars. The third section offers directions for further research on Schleiermacher's trinitarian thought.

21.1 CRITICAL REVIEW OF CURRENT RESEARCH

Scholars who tread into the waters of Schleiermacher's trinitarian thought will be faced with at least three questions. First, does Schleiermacher relegate the doctrine of the Trinity to an appendix to his *Christian Faith*? Second, does he offer a Sabellian form of trinitarian doctrine? And third, does Schleiermacher make any significant contributions to the development of trinitarian thought? Scholarly consensus regarding the answers to these three questions will shape Schleiermacher's legacy vis-à-vis trinitarian thought and is also likely to wield substantial influence over an assessment of his work more broadly as the progenitor of modern Protestant theology.

21.1.1 Importance of the Doctrine

Schleiermacher's brief discussion of the doctrine of the Trinity, which he placed at the end of his *Christian Faith* in paragraphs 170–172, has been routinely understood as an appendix to his dogmatic theology.[1] Many interpreters have supposed that the doctrine of the Trinity is treated at the end of the text because it is unimportant to his theology, a mere afterthought. Already in the middle of the nineteenth century, Ferdinand Christian Baur criticized Schleiermacher's view of the doctrine of the Trinity by stating that for him, the doctrine of the Trinity "can only be established indifferently and negatively."[2] Fred Sanders summarizes the prevailing scholarly opinion when he writes that for Schleiermacher the doctrine is "something of an appendix to the main work," that he "did in fact push it to the margin of his system," and that "for well over a century, the doctrine remained dormant wherever Schleiermacher's influence was felt."[3] Sanders highlights the "oft-told tale of how the doctrine of the Trinity was marginalized in the modern period, until a heroic rescue was performed by one of the Karls (Barth or Rahner)."[4] In truth, however, the reception history of Schleiermacher's work on the doctrine of the Trinity is more complicated. For even those who criticized Schleiermacher's treatment of the doctrine of the Trinity "exhibited a commitment to Schleiermacher's insight that every authentic doctrine is rooted in the Christian experience of God's redemptive activity."[5] That is a commitment that would change the landscape of trinitarian thought dramatically from his time to the present. Remaining within the nineteenth century, theologians were divided in their treatment of the doctrine of the Trinity following Schleiermacher's work. On the one hand, theologians like Philip Marheineke, Isaac August Dorner, Johann von Hofmann, and Moses Stuart made the doctrine of the Trinity central to their theological projects while also recognizing the new theological landscape ushered in by Schleiermacher. On the other hand, theologians like Albrecht Ritschl, Wilhelm Hermann, Adolf von Harnack, Ernst Troeltsch, and Horace Bushnell built on Schleiermacher's criticisms of the doctrine of the immanent Trinity.[6] Given the ubiquity of the Barthian or Rahnerian rescue tale, however, Schleiermacher's

---

[1] Claude Welch, *In This Name: The Doctrine of the Trinity in Contemporary Theology* (New York: Scribner's, 1952), p. 4.

[2] Ferdinand Christian Baur, *Die Christliche Lehre von der Dreieinigkeit und Menschwerdung Gottes*, vol. 3 (Tübingen: Osiander, 1843), p. 852. Cited in Walter, "Trinity as Circumscription of Divine Love according to Friedrich Schleiermacher," Neue Zeitschrift für Systematische Theologie und Religionsphilosophie 50/1 (2008), p. 63.

[3] Fred Sanders, "The Trinity," in *Mapping Modern Theology: A Thematic and Historical Introduction*, ed. Kelley M. Kapic and Bruce L. McCormack (Grand Rapids: Baker Academic, 2012), pp. 31, 32, 33.

[4] Sanders, "The Trinity," p. 44.

[5] Samuel M. Powell, "Nineteenth-Century Protestant Doctrines of the Trinity," in *The Oxford Handbook of the Trinity*, ed. Gilles Emery and Matthew Levering (Oxford/New York: Oxford University, 2011), p. 272.

[6] For a summary of these German thinkers' views and their relation to Schleiermacher, see Powell, "Nineteenth-Century Protestant Doctrines of the Trinity." For the Americans, see Jeffrey A. Wilcox, "A More Thorough Trinitarian," in *Schleiermacher's Influences on American Thought and Religious Life, 1835–1920*, vol. 1, ed. Jeffrey A. Wilcox, Terrence N. Tice, and Catherine L. Kelsey (Eugene, OR: Pickwick, 2013); Welch, *In This Name*, pp. 23–29; and David Hadddorff, "Schleiermacher and Horace Bushnell: Is There a Missing Link?," in *Schleiermacher's Influences on American Thought and Religious Life, 1835–1920*, vol. 1, ed. Jeffrey A. Wilcox, Terrence N. Tice, and Catherine L. Kelsey (Eugene, OR: Pickwick, 2013).

relationship to trinitarian thought has been sparsely treated in scholarly works, both within Schleiermacher studies and in wider appraisals of modern theology.

In contrast to the widely circulated report that Schleiermacher's discussion of the doctrine of the Trinity appears as an appendix to his *Christian Faith*, that discussion actually appears in its "Conclusion" (*Schluß*), which both the Mackintosh/Stewart and Tice/Kelsey/Lawler English translations make clear.[7] Moreover, Schleiermacher claims that the doctrine of the Trinity is the "copestone [*Schlußstein*] of Christian doctrine" within his own dogmatics.[8] A copestone is a stone that covers the top of a wall or roofline. Catherine Kelsey and Terrence Tice accurately note that Schleiermacher's "concluding discussion is intended to 'cap,' or draw together synthetically the entire system in summative fashion, not to produce a merely inconclusive addendum."[9] In fact, Schleiermacher goes even further than the word "copestone" would suggest, when he claims that his explication of the Christian consciousness of grace "stands or falls" with what is essential to the doctrine of the Trinity, namely, the union of the divine with humanity in Christ and subsequently in the church.[10] As such, the doctrine does not simply serve as a synthetic summary of his *Glaubenslehre*, but could aptly be regarded as the "keystone" of Schleiermacher's systematic theology. A "keystone" is the center stone in an arch, without which the arch would fall apart. This alternative architectural metaphor highlights the indispensable quality of the doctrine of the Trinity for the construction and analysis of Schleiermacher's systematic theology, in addition to the summative function his treatment of the doctrine performs at the conclusion of his work.

A handful of recent interpreters have commented on the importance of Schleiermacher's treatment of the doctrine of the Trinity within his *Glaubenslehre*. The minority report has a strong proponent in Robert R. Williams, who adds yet another architectural metaphor to the mix in arguing that the doctrine of the Trinity is, for Schleiermacher, "the very cornerstone of Christian doctrine, including the doctrine of God."[11] Likewise, Powell calls the popular idea that Schleiermacher relegated the doctrine of the Trinity to an appendix "perfectly absurd."[12] He reiterates the claims of Schleiermacher himself when he maintains that "the doctrine of the Trinity occupies the conclusion, not because it is unimportant, but because it is the logical culmination of his doctrine of God, which spans the entire second part of *The Christian Faith*."[13] More recently, Francis Schüssler Fiorenza and Paul J. DeHart have also offered brief analyses of Schleiermacher's trinitarian thought.[14] DeHart highlights the

---

[7] Friedrich Schleiermacher, *The Christian Faith*, ed. H. R. Mackintosh and J. S. Stewart (London/New York: T&T Clark, 1999); Schleiermacher, *Christian Faith: A New Translation and Critical Edition*, 2 vols., ed. Catherine L. Kelsey and Terrence N. Tice, trans. Terrence N. Tice, Catherine L. Kelsey, and Edwina Lawler (Louisville, KY: Westminster John Knox, 2016). Hereafter, references to *Christian Faith* (2016) will be cited as *CF (2016)*.

[8] *CF (2016)*, §170.1, p. 1021.

[9] *CF (2016)*, p. 1021, n.12.

[10] *CF (2016)*, §170.1, p. 1020.

[11] Robert R. Williams, *Schleiermacher the Theologian: The Construction of the Doctrine of God* (Philadelphia, PA: Fortress, 1978), p. 139.

[12] Samuel M. Powell, *The Trinity in German Thought* (Cambridge/New York: Cambridge University, 2001), p. 90.

[13] Powell, *The Trinity in German Thought*, p. 90.

[14] Francis Schüssler Fiorenza, "Understanding God as Triune," in *The Cambridge Companion to Friedrich Schleiermacher*, ed. Jacqueline Mariña (Cambridge/New York: Cambridge University, 2005), pp. 171-188. I return to his view below.

fact that "Schleiermacher's dogmatics does indeed contain a quite detailed, though highly compressed, discussion of the doctrine of the Trinity, clearly labeled as such and showing evidence of exceedingly careful thought."[15]

Although a groundswell of interest in Schleiermacher as a trinitarian thinker has yet to emerge, the tide is certainly turning from the old "appendix" thesis toward something that resembles Schleiermacher's own estimation of the significance of the doctrine of the Trinity in his *Glaubenslehre*. Recent interpreters confirm that Schleiermacher's trinitarian thought is not marginal within his work but expresses the central features of his theology as a whole.

21.1.2 The Doctrine vis-à-vis Sabellianism

Interpreters who overcome the obstacle that has been the placement of the doctrine of the Trinity have a second hurdle to clear: Schleiermacher's comments on the doctrine of the Trinity in paragraphs 170–172 are highly critical of the dominant ecclesial form of the doctrine. Worse, for many readers, he also mentions Sabellianism in a positive light. The assessment, now typical, is that Schleiermacher is a modalist. As Claude Welch understands it, Schleiermacher "does not see any real distinction between the presence of God in Christ and God in the Church. For him, there is no difference which is significant for the nature of God, between the *forms* of union."[16] This influential interpretation and others like it have led to a verdict of simple equivalency between Sabellianism, as students of Christian theology have typically learned it, and Schleiermacher's trinitarian thought.

In 1822, after the publication of the first edition of his *Christian Faith*, Schleiermacher published an essay that compares portions of the Athanasian and Sabellian understandings of the doctrine of the Trinity, namely "Über den Gegensatz zwischen der Sabellianischen und der Athanasianischen Vorstellung von der Trinität," published in English as "On the Discrepancy between the Sabellian and Athanasian Method of Representing the Doctrine of the Trinity." He investigates Sabellianism in that understudied work because he believes that "what is unsatisfactory and obscure in our creeds, with regard to the doctrine of the Trinity, was occasioned by going too far in opposition to Sabellianism."[17] In the essay, Schleiermacher understands Sabellianism as the view that the doctrine of the Trinity ought to be restricted to what can be said about the economic Trinity. The Trinity is "God revealed," and the Godhead "is never revealed to us as it is in itself."[18] On Schleiermacher's reading of Sabellius, the three persons of the Trinity are distinguished by the different objects with which the Godhead unites itself and God's special operations upon those different objects: "In governing the world in all its various operations on finite beings, the Godhead is Father. As redeeming, by special operations in the person of Christ and through him, it is Son. As sanctifying, and in all its operations on the community of believers, and as a Unity in the same, the Godhead is Spirit."[19] In other words, for Sabellius, God is revealed as Father when God governs creation,

---

[15] Paul J. DeHart, "Ter mundus accipit infinitum: The Dogmatic Coordinates of Schleiermacher's Trinitarian Treatise," *Neue Zeitschrift für Systematische Theologie und Religionsphilosophie* 52, no. 1 (2010), p. 17.
[16] Welch, *In This Name*, pp. 6–7.
[17] *ODSA*, part 1, p. 329.
[18] *ODSA*, part 2, p. 61.
[19] *ODSA*, part 2, p. 70.

as Son when God redeems in and through Christ, and as Holy Spirit when God sanctifies and unifies the Church.

In Schleiermacher's estimation, the restriction of the doctrine of the Trinity to the economic Trinity does not make Sabellius a modalist. He writes, "Sabellius did not regard the personality of the Godhead as a transitory phenomenon."[20] Rather, for Sabellius as Schleiermacher interprets him, once the Godhead simultaneously creates and unites with creation, and then with the person of Christ, and then with the community of Christians, "the state or condition that ensues is abiding."[21] Before creation, the Godhead "was not Father, strictly speaking, but the pure divine Unity, not yet developed, but existing in and by himself."[22] By creating and uniting with creation, God "becomes the first person or the Father, manifested by all the powers of life and animation which form the organic structures of the universe; and these stand related to him as their Father."[23] Likewise, for Sabellius, God becomes the Son only by simultaneously creating and uniting with Christ, where "the person itself sprung from the union."[24] Schleiermacher leaves it up in the air whether, for Sabellius, the Godhead was Spirit before creating and uniting with the community of Christians. He maintains that this depends on "whether [Sabellius] acknowledged a true church under the Old Testament."[25] After each of the unions, however, Schleiermacher thinks it is clear that for Sabellius, the Godhead is and remains Father, Son, and Holy Spirit. Schleiermacher notes that this way of conceiving the doctrine of the Trinity stands in opposition to the Athanasian method, whereby it is maintained

> that there is a Trinity in the Godhead which is purely internal; that there is something that was originally distinct and separate, independently of all the operations of the Godhead; that the Godhead was Father and Son and Holy Ghost, in itself and from eternity, and would have been such had there been no creation, or had it never united itself with our nature, nor ever dwelt in the community of believers.[26]

In short, Schleiermacher takes the doctrine of the immanent Trinity to be "all the difference between the two systems."[27]

At the end of his 1822 essay, Schleiermacher does not wholly endorse the claims laid out in his interpretation of Sabellianism. Rather, he states more cautiously that "to the Sabellian views we cannot refuse at least to yield our testimony, that they are the result of originality of thought and independence of mind."[28] In his *Christian Faith* (1830/1831), it can be seen just how far Schleiermacher agrees with the contents of his interpretation of Sabellianism. There can be no doubt that, like Sabellianism, Schleiermacher dispenses with the doctrine of the immanent Trinity. He rejects the view that there are three eternal "persons" (*hypostases*) that exist "eternally in Supreme Being."[29] His rejection of the doctrine of the immanent Trinity

---

[20] *ODSA*, part 2, p. 54.
[21] *ODSA*, part 2, p. 59.
[22] *ODSA*, part 2, p. 60.
[23] *ODSA*, part 2, p. 60.
[24] *ODSA*, part 2, p. 60.
[25] *ODSA*, part 2, p. 59.
[26] *ODSA*, part 2, p. 70.
[27] *ODSA*, part 2, p. 70.
[28] *ODSA*, part 2, p. 80.
[29] *CF (2016)*, §170.2, p. 1021.

can be understood in both a modest and strong form. In the modest form, Schleiermacher rejects the view that the doctrine of the immanent Trinity is needed for genuine Christian piety. He does not think that the doctrine of the immanent Trinity is entailed by the affirmation of a divine union with humanity in Christ and the church.[30] As such, he claims that "our faith in Christ and our living communion with him would be the same even if we had no knowledge of this transcendent fact [of the immanent Trinity] or if this fact were different."[31] In the strong form, Schleiermacher rejects the doctrine of the immanent Trinity because of its tendency toward the dangers of tritheism and subordinationism. He thinks Sabellius is right to refrain from deriving the Son and Spirit from the first and/or second persons, respectively. For were this to be the case, there would be a "relationship of dependency" between the Father, Son, and Spirit, which would indicate their inequality with one another.[32] Schleiermacher's discussion of the doctrine of the Trinity in the Conclusion of his *Christian Faith* makes it clear that he rejects the doctrine of the immanent Trinity in both the modest and strong forms noted here, but not for the purpose of dispensing with trinitarian thought altogether. Rather, his rejection of the doctrine of the immanent Trinity is meant to motivate a Protestant reformulation of trinitarian doctrine that is both related to Christian piety and avoids the dangers of tritheism and subordinationism.[33] At this point we might pause simply to note that one could appreciate Schleiermacher's call for a revitalization of the doctrine of the Trinity without following his own preliminary steps toward a reformulation of that doctrine, which will be treated below.

Beyond Schleiermacher's rejection of the doctrine of the immanent Trinity, his trinitarian thought differs from that of Sabellius in at least two ways. First, Schleiermacher asserts in his *Christian Faith* that the Holy Spirit does not exist temporally prior to the existence of the community of Christians. The Spirit, for Schleiermacher, is specifically Christ's Spirit, which is "the unity of life that is inherent in Christian community, viewed as a moral person."[34] "Once particular influences were no longer proceeding directly from Christ," Schleiermacher explains, "a divine presence had to be in the Christian church, which we can just as well call the being of God within it, provided that communication of Christ's perfection and blessedness is continually to persist in it."[35] This view of the Spirit is, as Francis Schüssler Fiorenza explains, "closer to the traditional *filioque* than it is to [the traditional interpretation of] Sabellian modalism."[36] I would hasten to add, however, that for Schleiermacher it is nonetheless important for the avoidance of subordinationism that neither the Son nor the Spirit are genetically dependent upon the Father. The second difference between Schleiermacher's trinitarian thought and his interpretation of Sabellius is that Schleiermacher maintains that while the realization of the divine decree of salvation in creation, Christ, and the church is temporal, the decree itself is eternal. This means divine causality cannot be divided among

---

[30] *CF (2016)*, §170.2, p. 1022.

[31] *CF (2016)*, §170.3, p. 1023.

[32] *CF (2016)*, §171.2., p 1026.

[33] Schleiermacher notes that the dominant doctrine of the Trinity derives "from a time when Christianity was still spreading extensively across heathendom" (*CF (2016)*, §172.1, p. 1031) and "did not receive any fresh treatment when the Evangelical church was established" (*CF (2016)*, §172, p. 1031). Compare with a similar statement in §96.3 regarding the doctrine of Christ.

[34] *CF (2016)*, §116.3, p. 765.

[35] *CF (2016)*, §116.3, p. 766.

[36] Schüssler Fiorenza, "Understanding God as Triune," p. 186.

the Father, Son, and Holy Spirit, such that the Father creates, the Son redeems, and the Spirit sanctifies, while the unity of God remains unrevealed. Rather, for Schleiermacher, the unity of God is revealed within the economy of salvation insofar as redemption and sanctification are part of the process of God's temporally progressive activity of creation.

21.1.3 Contributions to the Development of Trinitarian Thought in Christian Faith

Schleiermacher believes his *Christian Faith* provides preliminary steps toward a new formulation of the doctrine of the Trinity, which Schüssler Fiorenza aptly notes "goes beyond the contrast between Athanasius and Sabellius."[37] In paragraph 172, Schleiermacher indicates that to rethink trinitarian doctrine, "the question would be whether formulations could not be found that did not predicate eternal distinctions in Supreme Being but were still capable of presenting in their true light both unitings of Supreme Being with human nature and in an equal manner."[38] Schleiermacher would require two conditions: first, that the Godhead remain immutable; and second, that it be recognized that "we are able to conceive the divine causality in its eternity only as decree but to represent its realization only as temporal."[39] By describing the union of the divine being and humanity in the person of Christ and the church in the second part of his *Christian Faith*, Schleiermacher has already provided formulations that satisfy those two conditions. In paragraph 172, Schleiermacher goes on to suggest that when the Bible refers to God as "Father," it makes no distinction between "Father" and the unity of the Godhead; and when the Bible refers to the "Son of God," it makes no distinction between "Son" and the whole Christ.[40] He leaves it open whether a similar statement could be made with regard to the "Spirit." If such a statement could be made, the claim would likely be that when the Bible generally refers to the "Spirit," it does not typically distinguish between the "Spirit" and the unity of the Godhead. When a distinction is made in the New Testament, "Spirit" is attached to "Christ" and refers to the unity found within the church. Schleiermacher concludes his *Christian Faith* by asking his readers to decide whether his suggested answers to these considerations could hold together, that is, whether one could exclusively maintain a doctrine of the economic Trinity while upholding divine immutability and eternity, and whether one could understand the Father, Son, and Holy Spirit as the Godhead, Christ, and the Spirit of Christ in the church, respectively, while retaining the equality of these three with one another.

Of the relatively few number of scholars who have written about the nuances of Schleiermacher's trinitarian thought in his *Christian Faith* and subsequent 1822 essay, there is a spectrum of argumentation regarding the extent to which Schleiermacher maintains the Athanasian doctrine or re-envisions trinitarian doctrine more in line with Sabellius' thought as he interprets it. Robert R. Williams stands at the opposite end of the spectrum to the popular view that Schleiermacher entirely rejects the Athanasian doctrine. Williams

---

[37] Schüssler Fiorenza, "Understanding God as Triune," p. 174.
[38] *CF (2016)*, §172.3, p. 1036.
[39] *CF (2016)*, §172.3, p. 1036.
[40] *CF (2016)*, §172.3, pp. 1036–1037.

maintains that "there is no cognitive difference" between Schleiermacher's thought and the doctrine of the immanent Trinity, as long as one also recognizes that Schleiermacher maintains the complete coinherence of the hidden and revealed God.[41] For Williams, such coinherence refers to Schleiermacher's coupling of negative and positive divine attributes in his doctrine of God (e.g. eternal-omnipotence), and his refusal to conceive of a hidden God behind the revealed God. Granting that Schleiermacher rejects the notion of three eternal *hypostases*, Williams nonetheless thinks that "it seems possible and appropriate to speak of the hiddenness and revealedness of the Father, the Son, and the Spirit" in such a way that "trinity as a collective whole ceases to be identified with merely . . . God revealed."[42] This is a surprising conclusion, given the explicit and clear argumentation Schleiermacher offers against the Athanasian doctrine of the Trinity, and Williams does not convincingly demonstrate how the Father, Son, and Spirit are hidden and revealed in a way that warrants his conclusion.[43]

Most current scholarship has reached consensus that interpreters should both avoid Williams' conclusion and also the appendix thesis. Within the ground that exists between these two positions, most contemporary scholarship has offered only brief and somewhat critical evaluations of Schleiermacher's trinitarian thought. Powell, for example, argues that Schleiermacher laid a foundation for a comprehensive and coherent doctrine of the Trinity, but nothing further, and that Schleiermacher has "no excuse" for not providing "something better than he did."[44] Moreover, he criticized Schleiermacher's *Christian Faith* for its "lack of a substantial doctrine of the Father," which "mars the architectural balance of his work and fails to address one of the fundamental topics of theology."[45] Francis Schüssler Fiorenza is more positive. He argues that Schleiermacher transforms the neo-Platonic Proclean triad of power, eternal life, and knowledge so that instead of focusing on abstract divine power, "the consciousness of God as love perfected in wisdom is the heart of the Christian faith."[46] Schüssler Fiorenza leaves it open whether Schleiermacher's work "is sufficiently Trinitarian," but rightly insists on the importance of his continuing influence on the question.[47] Moving further toward a positive view, Paul J. DeHart judges Schleiermacher's preliminary sketch of a reformulated doctrine of the Trinity to be both brilliant and insightful because of its central focus on the economy of salvation and its maintenance of divine transcendence. Nonetheless, he criticizes Schleiermacher's "flat rejection of any notion of triune personhood immanent within the eternal being of the creator."[48] The attention these and other scholars have paid to Schleiermacher's trinitarian thought amounts to a real shift in treatments of his theology, at least among the Schleiermacher guild, and that shift is arguably making its way into the wider academy as well.

---

[41] Williams, *Schleiermacher the Theologian*, p. 154.
[42] Williams, *Schleiermacher the Theologian*, p. 156.
[43] See also Robert F. Streetman, *Friedrich Schleiermacher's Doctrine of Trinity and Its Significance for Theology Today* (PhD dissertation. Drew Gateway 46, 1975–1976); Carol Jean Voisin, *A Reconsideration of Friedrich Schleiermacher's Treatment of the Doctrine of the Trinity* (PhD dissertation. Graduate Theological Union, 1981).
[44] Powell, "Nineteenth-Century Protestant Doctrines of the Trinity," p. 271.
[45] Powell, *The Trinity in German Thought*, p. 101.
[46] Schüssler Fiorenza, "Understanding God as Triune," p. 176.
[47] Schüssler Fiorenza, "Understanding God as Triune," p. 187.
[48] DeHart, "Ter mundus accipit infinitum," pp. 36–37.

21.2 FUTURE DIRECTIONS

My own sense is that the discussion needs to move beyond Schleiermacher's explicitly stated "preliminary steps" regarding a reformulation of the doctrine of the Trinity, toward a consideration of how his mature theology implicitly provides more than a preliminary reconstruction. Schleiermacher placed his discussion of the Trinity at the end of the *Glaubenslehre* because he wanted to demonstrate that an appropriately triune understanding of God could be provided without affirming a doctrine of the immanent Trinity.[49] As such, it is an important interpretive move to read the *Glaubenslehre* again, only this time beginning from its conclusion.[50] Scholars have begun to do so whenever they address Schleiermacher's discussion of the doctrine of the Trinity in the context of his entire system of doctrine, and especially the second part of his *Christian Faith*.

21.2.1 Schleiermacher on Love, Wisdom, and Universal Causality

The ending of part two (§§164–169) of Schleiermacher's *Christian Faith* discusses the divine attributes that relate to redemption: divine love and divine wisdom. In paragraphs 50–56 and 79–85, Schleiermacher affirms that God is eternal, omnipresent, omnipotent, omniscient, holy, and just. These attributes are no less important, as they discuss divine causality prior to the union of divinity and humanity in the person of Christ. The difference between these earlier paragraphs and paragraphs 164–169, however, is important. In part 1 and the first aspect of part 2, Schleiermacher presents the divine attributes as just so many ways that the divine causality can be described. In the final section of part 2, however, Schleiermacher identifies divine love and wisdom as the only attributes that are "expressions for the very being of God."[51] Further, although divine love and wisdom can be separated in human life and understanding, in God they are "so totally one that one can also view each attribute as already contained in the other one."[52] In other words, divine love and wisdom are perichoretic or coinhering. Schleiermacher describes divine love as that by which "the divine being communicates itself,"[53] and divine wisdom as that by which the divine being "orders and determines the world for the divine self-communication that is carried out in redemption."[54] Other attributes, like "eternity" or "omnipotence," could not be equated with the being of God in the way that love and wisdom could be.

Although Schleiermacher does not identify divine causality as a third description of the very essence of the divine being, he uses the phrase "divine causality" (*die göttliche*

---

[49] *CF (2016)*, §172.3, p. 1035.

[50] For a sustained treatment of Schleiermacher's doctrine of the Trinity that takes this backward-reading approach, see Shelli M. Poe, *Essential Trinitarianism: Schleiermacher as Trinitarian Theologian* (New York/London: Bloomsbury, 2017).

[51] *CF (2016)*, §167.2, p. 1009.
[52] *CF (2016)*, §165.2, p. 1004.
[53] *CF (2016)*, §166, p. 1004.
[54] *CF (2016)*, §168, p. 1010.

Ursächlichkeit),[55] "absolute causality" (*die schlechthinnige Ursächlichkeit*),[56] or "universal causality" (*die allgemeine*)[57] throughout the *Glaubenslehre* when he refers to the divine being. The attributes described in the first part of the *Glaubenslehre* emphasize how absolute causality is different from finite causality. Divine causality is not partial or temporal, but is that universal causality by which God creates-preserves-governs-redeems the world as a whole by the "planting and spreading of the Christian church."[58] In this way, divine causality is implicitly woven into the fabric of Schleiermacher's conceptions of divine love and wisdom.

I would argue that within Schleiermacher's theology, the divine attributes of love, wisdom, and causality are consubstantial, coequal, and coinhering expressions of the very being of God, even though Schleiermacher himself does not explicitly conceive of God in this way. Elsewhere, I have called this reinterpretation of Schleiermacher's trinitarian thought "the doctrine of the essential Trinity." This is meant to indicate that in addition to the doctrine of the economic Trinity, Schleiermacher's theology implicitly affirms that God creates the world and unites with humanity for its redemption because God's very being (*Wesen*) is love, wisdom, and universal causality. Developing the idea constructively, I would suggest that these three contours of the divine life describe the divine being non-speculatively by focusing on the divine *Wesen* that motivates redemption history.

These contours of the divine life do not correlate in a one-to-one fashion with the three persons set forth in the doctrine of the economic Trinity; the Father/Creator, Son/Redeemer, and Spirit/Sustainer are not correlated respectively with causality, love, and wisdom in Schleiermacher's theology. First, such a correlation could suggest that the persons of the immanent Trinity are simply being affirmed under different names, a move with which Schleiermacher would no doubt take issue because of his concern for divine unity and the equal divinity of the unions of the divine being with human nature in Christ and the church. Second, Schleiermacher's theology makes it impossible to assign causality, love, and wisdom to each of the traditional "persons" of the doctrine of the economic Trinity. Although he identifies love with the redemption accomplished in and through Christ, he also emphasizes that creation as a whole is created and preserved in order to bring about Christ's person and work, such that he can say that "already Christ was also always coming into being, even as a human person, at the same time as the world was coming into being."[59] This makes a correlation between Christ and divine love apart from divine wisdom and causality impossible. In addition, his theology makes individuals' engagement with the Christian community essential to the process of redemption. As such, a correlation between the Spirit and divine love apart from divine wisdom and causality impossible. Even though Schleiermacher's thought would not allow for easy correlations between the three contours of the divine being and the three phases of redemption history, the former are nonetheless revealed by the economy of salvation. Divine love dwells in Christ and the church, which indwelling is prepared for and carried out by divine wisdom in relation to the entire universe. As such, divine love, wisdom, and absolute causality are equally present in each phase of the economy of salvation.

---

[55] *CG (Redeker)*, §51, p. 264.
[56] *CG (Redeker)*, §51, p. 263.
[57] *CG (Redeker)*, §46, p. 230.
[58] *CF (2016)*, §164, p. 999.
[59] *CF (2016)*, §97.2, p. 595.

I would suggest that the core function of the doctrine of the Trinity, as Schleiermacher sees it, which is, namely, to indicate the equal unions of the divine being with human nature in Christ and the church, is only adequately carried out by affirming both the doctrine of the economic Trinity and what I am calling the doctrine of the essential Trinity together. In the economy of salvation, the divine *Wesen* unites with humanity in Christ and the church, and this divine activity is motivated and constituted by divine love and wisdom in causal relation to the entire universe. As I see it, Schleiermacher's treatment of trinitarian doctrine has been widely criticized in part because he did not make explicit what I have identified as an implicit doctrine of the essential Trinity that can be teased out of his thought.

In light of Schleiermacher's critics, whether this constructive interpretation of Schleiermacher's theology could amount to a doctrinal development within trinitarian thought that is worth pursuing further depends, in part, on the criteria one uses to assess whether a theological proposal might be counted as "faithful" to the doctrine of the Trinity or "sufficiently Trinitarian." Claude Welch's discussion of both trinitarian theology and Schleiermacher's view of the doctrine is instructive on this matter.[60] He observes that, strictly speaking, there is nothing in the doctrine of the economic Trinity to guard against modalism. In some theological texts like Tertullian's, however, "eternity," "essentiality," the generation of the Son, and the procession of the Spirit are all included in the doctrine of the economic Trinity. In addition, Welch notes that further ambiguity is introduced when, in the doctrine of the immanent Trinity, some theologians maintain the eternity and essentiality of the distinctions but do not affirm a doctrine of internal relations. As a means of clarifying various theologians' perspectives, Welch proposes three doctrines of the Trinity rather than the customary two by adding a doctrine of the essential Trinity. The doctrine of the economic Trinity affirms only the threefoldness of God in God's historical revelation. The doctrine of the essential Trinity, as Welch constructs it, affirms the doctrines of *homoousios*, coeternity, and coequality, along with terms like *hypostasis* and *persona* as indications of the "essential" character of the divine distinctions. The doctrine of the immanent Trinity affirms the internal relations of generation and procession along with coinherence.

While these distinctions, Welch thinks, are helpful for parsing various theologians' views, he does not substitute them for the two traditional categories because, as he explains, "I quite agree with Schleiermacher that there can be no doctrine worthy of the name Trinity which does not affirm the 'essential' character of the distinctions ... and I should also hold that there can be no doctrine of an 'essential' Trinity that does not include the doctrine of relations."[61] For Welch, the doctrine of the Trinity is not sufficiently trinitarian without the doctrine of relations by which the Father generates the Son, and the Spirit proceeds from the Father (and Son). Thus, although he recognizes that there is more diversity in trinitarian theological history than the primary use of the doctrines of the economic Trinity and of the immanent Trinity would suggest, he rejects that diversity. For Welch, any trinitarian thought that does not include an affirmation of the doctrine of the immanent Trinity is not sufficiently trinitarian. I would surmise that this is also the case for most of Schleiermacher's critics.

Against Welch's estimation, as my constructive interpretation of Schleiermacher's trinitarian thought has already indicated, I think Welch's three categories for analyzing various

---

[60] Welch, *In This Name*, pp. 4–9, 293–294.
[61] Welch, *In This Name*, p. 294.

theologians' trinitarian doctrines are insightful. Indeed, I have adopted and adapted his description of "the doctrine of the essential Trinity" to describe my own interpretation of Schleiermacher's theology outlined above, except that the doctrine as I have adapted it includes coinherence, and excludes the terms *hypostases* or persons along with the doctrine of relations.

With this background in mind, we can return to the question whether the doctrine of the essential Trinity, as outlined in my constructive reinterpretation of Schleiermacher's thought, counts as "faithful" to the doctrine, or "sufficiently Trinitarian." It certainly seems to me that an affirmation of three coequal, coessential, perichoretic distinctions within the very being of God (love, wisdom, and absolute causality), which are revealed in the economy of salvation (creation, redemption, sanctification), is authentically trinitarian. At the very least, however, Schleiermacher's discussion of the classical trinitarian doctrine and his efforts to constructively engage the tradition ought to be recognized as an invitation to ongoing creative engagement, for the purpose of retrieving formulations that are more adequate to developments in the Christian faith.

Although Schleiermacher did not explicitly discuss the doctrine of the essential Trinity as I have formulated and drawn it out of his text, there can be no doubt that the *Glaubenslehre* shows a deep concern to reinvigorate and reformulate a doctrine of the Trinity that would be tethered to Scripture, relevant for Christian faith and life, and based on a faithful reception of redemption in and through Christ and the Spirit in the church. Explorations of Schleiermacher's mature theology that go beyond a restatement of his brief comments on the doctrine of the Trinity and attempt to understand how Schleiermacher's theology as a whole could actually shift the trinitarian discussion in significant ways is an area of Schleiermacher studies that is rich with potential for emerging scholarship.

21.2.2 Defining Issues

Other future directions for scholarship include treatments of Schleiermacher's understanding of the Trinity in relation to pneumatology as well as sexuality and gender. Karl Barth famously wondered whether Schleiermacher's project could be conceived as a theology of the third article of the Nicene Creed.[62] Although Barth's assessment of Schleiermacher needs revision in many respects, he has here identified an area of research that remains to be fully explored. Some have begun to take Barth's suggestion seriously as it relates to Schleiermacher's understanding of the Trinity. Kevin W. Hector, for instance, offers an argument regarding how the Spirit works, on the basis of a novel reading of Schleiermacher's pneumatology. He argues that the Spirit mediates Christ's activity to the church by means of a chain of disciples that reaches back to Christ himself, through which congregants receive and internalize Christ's instruction and so become competent judges and teachers of Christian behavior and ideas.[63] Taking another example, Ralph Del Colle offers an analysis

---

[62] Karl Barth, "Concluding Unscientific Postscript," in *The Theology of Schleiermacher, Lectures at Göttingen, Winter Semester of 1923/4*, ed. Dietrich Ritschl, trans. George Hunsinger (Grand Rapids: Eerdmans, 1982), pp. 278–279.

[63] Kevin W. Hector, "The Mediation of Christ's Normative Spirit: A Constructive Reading of Schleiermacher's Pneumatology," *Modern Theology* 24, no. 1 (January 2008), pp. 1–22.

of Schleiermacher's trinitarian thought that highlights its conceptual links to the doctrines of Christology and pneumatology. He argues that although Schleiermacher does not describe the divine indwelling in Jesus as Spirit, his Christology is structured similarly to Spirit Christologies "by fulfilling the requirement that what was present in Jesus via his God-consciousness is present in believers via their self-consciousness as Christians participating in the corporate life of the church."[64] Del Colle himself endorses a classical trinitarian Spirit Christology that stands in contrast to Schleiermacher's own view. Nonetheless, he argues that Schleiermacher's trinitarian thought can contribute to his own project insofar as for Schleiermacher "the divine self-disclosure in Christ and the Spirit each bear their own proper characteristics relative to the created order,"[65] and "Schleiermacher's correspondence between living fellowship with Christ and participation in the Holy Spirit as the common spirit of the community... affords a dynamic and nuanced sense of presence to the theology of grace."[66] The third article of the creed will no doubt gain further attention in future scholarship because of the exponential rise and growth of global Pentecostal and Charismatic movements. Given the relatively undeveloped character of the Spirit in systematic theology, scholars interested in pneumatology as it relates to trinitarian thought may find an innovative interlocutor in Schleiermacher.

A second direction for future scholars who are interested in exploring Schleiermacher's trinitarian thought is the role that sexuality and gender play in constructing doctrines of the Trinity. In *God and Difference*, Linn Marie Tonstad critically analyzes a number of leading trinitarian theologies, including those of Hans Urs von Balthasar, Graham Ward, Sarah Coakley, and Kathryn Tanner, with special attention to the role that sexuality plays in the doctrines of the Trinity they each construct. In the constructive portion of her work, Tonstad admits that Schleiermacher was a "significant, albeit subterranean" influence on her theology.[67] She argues with Schleiermacher that although paternity and filiation within the doctrine of the immanent Trinity were originally meant to counter subordinationism, they now advance it. Trinitarian theologians, Tonstad states, need to learn from feminists, womanists, and queer theorists who "have taught us the futility of dislodging subordination and hierarchy by striking through the greater than sign and replacing it with the equals sign when the very relationship between the terms is constitutive inequality."[68] For Tonstad, the doctrine of the Trinity should not be about sexuality, but needs to be focused on "the for-us character of divine action and the *vere deo* that is Christ."[69] Janet Martin Soskice also takes up Schleiermacher's trinitarian thought by developing his argument about divine love and wisdom.[70] She claims that Love (which is inseparable from Wisdom) and Being-Itself ought to be raised to the level of divine names rather than attributes.[71] The attention that

---

[64] Ralph Del Colle, "Schleiermacher and Spirit Christology: Unexplored Horizons of *The Christian Faith*," *International Journal of Systematic Theology* 1, no. 3 (November 1999), p. 306.

[65] Del Colle, "Schleiermacher and Spirit Christology," p. 306.

[66] Del Colle, "Schleiermacher and Spirit Christology," p. 307.

[67] Linn Marie Tonstad, *God and Difference: The Trinity, Sexuality, and the Transformation of Finitude* (New York/London: Routledge, 2016), p. 287.

[68] Tonstad, *God and Difference*, p. 289.

[69] Tonstad, *God and Difference*, p. 290.

[70] Janet Martin Soskice, "Being and Love: Schleiermacher, Aquinas and Augustine," *Modern Theology* 34, no. 3 (July 2018), pp. 480–491.

[71] While Soskice neither directly links these divine names to sexuality nor develops a fully formed doctrine of the Trinity in "Being and Love," her work in the *Kindness of God* fills in some of those

thinkers like Tonstad and Soskice pay to Schleiermacher's trinitarian thought will continue to be significant as feminism, womanism, *mujerista* theology, queer theology, and other constructive forms of theology that attend to sexuality and gender exert their growing influence on Christian systematic theology.[72]

21.3 Conclusion

One hundred years ago, including a chapter on Schleiermacher's trinitarian thought in a volume like the present one would be almost unthinkable. Yet today there is growing consensus among Schleiermacher scholars and the wider academic community that Schleiermacher might yet have something to contribute to contemporary discussions of the doctrine of the Trinity. At stake in this debate is not simply whether and how Schleiermacher should be included in accounts of the historical development of the doctrine of the Trinity, but whether and how his treatment holds potential to contribute to contemporary discussions within systematic theology and to point in new theological directions. Schleiermacher clearly rejects the doctrine of the immanent Trinity, primarily because he thinks that it is not entailed by or helpful for a faithful reception of divine activity in Christ and the Spirit. Even so, he maintains what he identifies as the essential portions of the doctrine of the Trinity and calls for its reformulation. Arguably, his work points to a "doctrine of the essential Trinity" that would expand the current trinitarian discussion. The future of that discussion could also include inquiry that treats Schleiermacher's trinitarian thought vis-à-vis the development of pneumatology, and analyses and development of the doctrine of the Trinity in light of its relation to sexuality and gender.

Although, as Brian Gerrish notes, "Schleiermacher is not in vogue among trinitarian thinkers these days,"[73] perhaps he should be. His thought has been a catalyst for the reformulation of many doctrines following the Enlightenment and Romanticism, and current scholarship on his treatment of the doctrine of the Trinity has only scratched the surface of his rich theological texts. If the potential of his trinitarian thought is recognized, it could accommodate further doctrinal development and more diverse expressions of Christian practice.

Suggested Reading

DeHart, Paul J. "Ter mundus accipit infinitum: The Dogmatic Coordinates of Schleiermacher's Trinitarian Treatise." *Neue Zeitschrift für Systematische Theologie und Religionsphilosophie* 52, no. 1 (2010), pp. 17–39.

---

gaps. Janet Martin Soskice, *The Kindness of God: Metaphor, Gender, and Religious Language* (Oxford/New York: Oxford University, 2007), pp. 50–51.

[72] See Shelli M. Poe, "Trinity," in *Schleiermacher's Promise for Constructive Theologies* (New York/London: Bloomsbury, 2021), pp. 39-77.

[73] B. A. Gerrish, "Conversation with My Reviewers," *International Journal of Systematic Theology* 18, no. 3 (July 2016), p. 333.

Poe, Shelli M. *Essential Trinitarianism: Schleiermacher as Trinitarian Theologian* (New York/London: Bloomsbury, 2017).
Powell, Samuel M. *The Trinity in German Thought* (Cambridge/New York: Cambridge University, 2001).
Schüssler Fiorenza, Francis. "Understanding God as Triune." In *The Cambridge Companion to Friedrich Schleiermacher*, ed. Jacqueline Mariña (Cambridge/New York: Cambridge University, 2005), pp. 171–188.

Bibliography

Barth, Karl. "Concluding Unscientific Postscript." In *The Theology of Schleiermacher, Lectures at Göttingen, Winter Semester of 1923/4*, ed. Dietrich Ritschl, trans. George Hunsinger (Grand Rapids: Eerdmans, 1982), pp. 278–279.
DeHart, Paul J. "Ter mundus accipit infinitum: The Dogmatic Coordinates of Schleiermacher's Trinitarian Treatise." *Neue Zeitschrift für Systematische Theologie und Religionsphilosophie* 52, no. 1 (2010), pp. 17–39.
Del Colle, Ralph. "Schleiermacher and Spirit Christology: Unexplored Horizons of *The Christian Faith*." *International Journal of Systematic Theology* 1, no. 3 (November 1999), pp. 286–307.
Gerrish, B. A. "Conversation with My Reviewers." *International Journal of Systematic Theology* 18, no. 3 (July 2016), pp. 329–334.
Hadddorff, David. "Schleiermacher and Horace Bushnell: Is There a Missing Link?" In *Schleiermacher's Influences on American Thought and Religious Life, 1835–1920*, vol. 1, ed. Jeffrey A. Wilcox, Terrence N. Tice, and Catherine L. Kelsey (Eugene, OR: Pickwick, 2013), pp.190–216.
Hector, Kevin W. "The Mediation of Christ's Normative Spirit: A Constructive Reading of Schleiermacher's Pneumatology." *Modern Theology* 24, no. 1 (January 2008), pp. 1–22.
Poe, Shelli M. *Essential Trinitarianism: Schleiermacher as Trinitarian Theologian* (New York/London: Bloomsbury, 2017).
Poe, Shelli M. *Schleiermacher's Promise for Constructive Theologies* (New York/London: Bloomsbury, 2021).
Powell, Samuel M. "Nineteenth-Century Protestant Doctrines of the Trinity." In *The Oxford Handbook of the Trinity*, ed. Gilles Emery and Matthew Levering (Oxford/New York: Oxford University, 2011), pp. 267–280.
Powell, Samuel M. *The Trinity in German Thought* (Cambridge/New York: Cambridge University, 2001).
Sanders, Fred. "The Trinity." In *Mapping Modern Theology: A Thematic and Historical Introduction*, ed. Kelley M. Kapic and Bruce L. McCormack (Grand Rapids: Baker Academic, 2012), pp. 21–45.
Schleiermacher, Friedrich. *Christian Faith: A New Translation and Critical Edition*, 2 vols. Ed. Catherine L. Kelsey and Terrence N. Tice, trans. Terrence N. Tice, Catherine L. Kelsey, and Edwina Lawler (Louisville, KY: Westminster John Knox, 2016).
Schleiermacher, Friedrich. *The Christian Faith*. Ed. H. R. Mackintosh and J. S. Stewart (London/New York: T&T Clark, 1999).

Schüssler Fiorenza, Francis. "Understanding God as Triune." In *The Cambridge Companion to Friedrich Schleiermacher*, ed. Jacqueline Mariña (Cambridge/New York: Cambridge University, 2005), pp.171–188.

Soskice, Janet Martin. "Being and Love: Schleiermacher, Aquinas and Augustine." *Modern Theology* 34, no. 3 (July 2018), pp. 480–491.

Soskice, Janet Martin. *The Kindness of God: Metaphor, Gender, and Religious Language* (Oxford/New York: Oxford University, 2007).

Streetman, Robert F. *Friedrich Schleiermacher's Doctrine of Trinity and Its Significance for Theology Today* (PhD dissertation. Drew Gateway 46, 1975–1976).

Tonstad, Linn Marie. *God and Difference: The Trinity, Sexuality, and the Transformation of Finitude* (New York/London: Routledge, 2016).

Voisin, Carol Jean. *A Reconsideration of Friedrich Schleiermacher's Treatment of the Doctrine of the Trinity* (PhD dissertation. Graduate Theological Union, 1981).

Welch, Claude. *In This Name: The Doctrine of the Trinity in Contemporary Theology* (New York: Scribner's, 1952).

Wilcox, Jeffrey A. "A More Thorough Trinitarian." In *Schleiermacher's Influences on American Thought and Religious Life, 1835–1920*, vol. 1, ed. Jeffrey A. Wilcox, Terrence N. Tice, and Catherine L. Kelsey (Eugene, OR: Pickwick, 2013), pp. 159–189.

Williams, Robert R. *Schleiermacher the Theologian: The Construction of the Doctrine of God* (Philadelphia, PA: Fortress, 1978).

CHAPTER 22

CHRISTIAN ETHICS

JAMES M. BRANDT

22.1 INTRODUCTION

FRIEDRICH Schleiermacher's *Christian Ethics*, known in German as *Die Christliche Sitte* or *Christliche Sittenlehre*,[1] occupies an important place in his oeuvre. Above all, *Christian Ethics* is the indispensable complement to Schleiermacher's much better-known *Christian Faith*, *Glaubenslehre* in German.[2] Together the *Christian Faith* and *Christian Ethics* comprise Schleiermacher's theological vision, including analyses of the content of Christian faith and of how faith is lived.

Christian Faith, together with the *Speeches* and the *Brief Outline*, are credited with inaugurating a new epoch in Protestant theology by coming to terms with the modern worldview.[3] Together these works overcome the impasse in early nineteenth-century theology created by the conflict between rationalism and supranaturalism, putting theology on a new footing. Many scholars would argue that Protestant theology is still in the epoch inaugurated by Schleiermacher, an epoch marked by critical engagement with inherited theology and resulting in diverse approaches that reinterpret and revise what has gone before.

Our thesis is that *Christian Ethics* accomplishes something comparable to what the *Speeches*, *Christian Faith*, and *Brief Outline* achieve. *Christian Ethics* provides a new grounding and approach that, similarly, moves beyond the rationalist/supernaturalist conflict in theological ethics. Like the *Christian Faith*, the *Christian Ethics* conceives of the relation between the natural and the supernatural in a new and distinctive way. The work lays out the way that the natural processes of the faith work. Similarly, it develops a vision that encompasses the important forms of historical life and demonstrates how the Christian church relates to the overall moral process of ensouling nature with reason. This comprehensive vision transcends contemporary theological ethics dominated by Kantian-influenced emphasis on duty.

---

[1] See F. D. E. Schleiermacher, *Die christliche Sitte nach den Grundsätzen der evangelischen Kirche im Zusammenhange dargestellt*, ed. Ludwig Jonas (Berlin: G. Reimer, 1843), and *CS (Peiter)*.

[2] See *CG2*.

[3] See *Speeches¹* and *BO*.

An important element in moving beyond what had gone before is Schleiermacher's turn to history. *Christian Ethics* continues Schleiermacher's explicit, self-conscious incorporation of historical awareness. Schleiermacher is among the first to bring the newly emerging historical consciousness into theology. *Christian Ethics* is thoroughly historicized in recognizing that all ethical claims are historically relative; no final or absolute statement of ethics or theology is possible. In addition, human historical life becomes the subject matter of ethics. *Christian Ethics* attends to the life of the church in its historical passage and to the diverse forms of activity and community which constitute human life. This results in history being valorized in a new way. In addition, the theological system culminates in the *Christian Ethics* with its description of the this-worldly task of furthering the Reign of God on earth.

In *Christian Ethics* Schleiermacher continues the approach of the *Speeches* and *Christian Faith*, grounding his theology in Christian religious self-consciousness or piety. Fundamental to Schleiermacher's understanding is his distinction between piety as the experienced and lived reality of the Christian community, and theology as a form of knowing that thematizes piety. Christian piety is the reception of redemption in Christ, a new and higher form of life. Piety is also the ground for activity as it impels the individual believer and the whole Christian community to live toward the Reign of God. Christian ethics, then, identifies and describes the forms of activity that flow from piety.

This essay provides an analysis of *Christian Ethics* and substantiates our thesis, showing how it transcends contemporary theological ethics. The essay is divided into six sections: the place of *Christian Ethics* in Schleiermacher's overall system of thought and in his theological system; the character and content of *Christian Ethics*; how *Christian Ethics* overcomes the rationalist/supranaturalist conflict and transcends contemporary version of ethics; the composition and publication of the lectures which became *Christian Ethics*; reception and criticism of the *Christian Ethics*; and concluding remarks.

22.2 *Christian Ethics* in the Architectonic of Schleiermacher's Thought

The mature Schleiermacher developed a sophisticated philosophical and theological system grounded in an understanding of the nature of knowledge, giving particular attention to questions of ethics. Insight into the character of *Christian Ethics* can be gained by indicating its place in Schleiermacher's overarching system of thought and where it stands in relation to other forms of knowledge. The Dialectic [*Dialektik*] lays out his epistemological understanding and distinguishes various kinds of knowledge, even while it asserts that all forms of knowledge and all processes by which knowledge is sought are interdependent.[4] Philosophical ethics is the other essential component of the mature philosophical system.[5] This work investigates human historical life and identifies various forms of reason and the varieties of human activity in which they are embodied. Identifying major themes in the

---

[4] See *Dial.*
[5] See *PE*.

Dialectic and philosophical ethics provides insight into the relation of *Christian Ethics* to other forms of thought and into its distinctive character.

An important intellectual current in which Schleiermacher participated and which stamped his philosophical-theological system was the movement of *Wissenschaftsideologie*. This movement set forth a scholarly ideal that promoted the pursuit of knowledge for its own sake and exercised great influence on the German intellectual landscape. "Wissenschaft," usually and inadequately translated as "science," affirms the ongoing process of investigation in which research and learning are united seamlessly. All disciplines and investigative methodologies were to contribute to the overall enterprise, but the significance of each can be seen only in relation to the whole.[6]

Schleiermacher's philosophical-theological system is imbued with the principles and spirit of *Wissenschaft* and can be said to rival the systems of the great critical Idealists of his day. The Dialectic does not provide a supreme principle that is outside of real human knowing. Schleiermacher begins with actual human knowing, taking a "finite" approach.[7] The Transcendental part of the Dialectic lays out the conditions for the production of knowledge. Actual knowledge is possible for Schleiermacher only as an unending quest that can be characterized as both artistic and dialogical. The quest for knowledge does not follow strict rules, but involves genuine investigation and creativity, continually sorting out truth and error by means of actual conversation and disputation by human beings. For Schleiermacher, knowledge is grounded in an immediate awareness of Absolute Being. This awareness, which accompanies all actual knowing, is without object and is non-reflexive; it happens by means of "feeling" (*Gefühl*) or immediate self-consciousness. Here is a point of contact between Dialectic and theology for both include attention to this immediate consciousness of the absolute. Immediate consciousness of Absolute Unity provides the grounding for knowledge. The world, an inexhaustible multiplicity, an internally differentiated unity, is the goal of knowledge.[8] Real knowing emerges from the ongoing process of dialogue and disputation among human beings. As such, knowledge is historical and relative, and recognition of this historicity and relativity is essential for knowledge to move forward and to have a proper assessment of its capabilities and limits. Dialectic provides an account of the operations of knowing that are presupposed by and operative in actual knowing.

Important for our purposes is Dialectic's identification of the two real sciences: physics, which attends to nature; and ethics, which considers reason's quest and shape nature. Ethics, in Schleiermacher's understanding, gives attention to reason's quest to shape nature and is manifest in all forms of human historical life. Also important for our purposes is the distinction made in the Dialectic between pure thinking, artistic thinking, and practical thinking. Although in reality these forms of thinking are inseparable, it is important to distinguish them for purposes of reflection since each form of thinking represents a distinctive form of rational activity. Pure thinking is directed to knowledge and corresponds to the rational activity of thinking. Artistic thinking is free association or fantasy and corresponds to the rational activity of feeling. Practical thinking aims to change something in the world. It

---

[6] B. A. Gerrish, *Continuing the Reformation: Essays on Modern Religious Thought* (Chicago: University of Chicago Press, 1993), pp. 251–255; and Kevin M. Vander Schel, *Embedded Grace: Christ, History and the Reign of God in Schleiermacher's Dogmatics* (Minneapolis: Fortress Press, 2013), pp. 49–55.

[7] On the development of Schleiermacher's *Dialektik*, see Chapter 9 in this volume.

[8] Cf. *Dial.* 1, pp. 117f., §179.2.

requires cognition, but it aims at transformation and corresponds to the rational activity of acting.[9] As ethics analyzes particular forms of human historical life, it is primarily concerned with the practical thinking that seeks to make a change in the world. Ethics also attends to artistic thinking as an expression of reason's imaginative symbolization of nature.

Schleiermacher's lectures on philosophical ethics provide ethical analysis in his distinctive use of the term—examination of the work of reason in human historical life. These lectures bring to culmination a lifetime of scholarly engagement with ethical themes and issues. From his youthful essays, particularly "On Freedom," through the *Monologues* of 1800 to the *Brouillon zur Ethik*, lectures delivered in 1805–1806, Schleiermacher develops his thoughts on ethics in conversation with thinkers from Plato to Kant and Fichte. All of this effort informs his philosophical ethics, work which Hans-Joachim Birkner identifies as representing Schleiermacher's "most important achievement, and in the history of ethics constitutes a completely original project."[10]

Philosophical ethics has as its object the whole range of human historical life that manifests the human vocation to ensoul nature with reason. Practical thinking, the drive to effect change, is a crucial presupposition of philosophical ethics. In Schleiermacher's view, ethics provides a description of all manner of human living, with analysis at two different levels. Speculative ethics seeks to determine the essence of things and develops concepts and categories for use in describing a particular realm of human life. Empirical ethics concerns the particular manifestations of reason in history. In Schleiermacher's system the philosophical ethics is speculative and develops concepts, while the *Christian Ethics* (along with dogmatics) is a form of empirical ethics, attending to the particular way Christian spirit is active in history.[11]

In Schleiermacher's view the process of reason appropriating and forming nature is already underway. Providing understanding of the structure and dynamics by which this happens, ethics brings this process to self-consciousness and evokes further participation in it. Schleiermacher had wrestled with ethics from early on and he came to distinguish three forms: ethics of duty, ethics of virtue, and ethics of the good. All three approaches are necessary for a comprehensive view of ethics, but Schleiermacher has a decided preference for an ethics of the good. The most important part of philosophical ethics is the reflection on the highest good, where Schleiermacher develops his understanding of the crucial communal aspects of ethical life.[12]

As Schleiermacher considers the drive of reason toward the highest good, he analyzes reason itself. He says that reason has both an organizing and a symbolizing function. The organizing function of reason involves shaping nature. Nature then becomes an organ of reason. For example, a vegetable garden is reason imprinting itself on nature and forming nature as its organ. Reason also has a symbolizing function; it develops a system of signs and symbols whereby reason itself can be represented and communicated. So the various vegetables in the garden are catalogued and their characteristics understood; language is used to express and communicate understanding of nature, and, reflexively, of reason itself.

---

[9] Cf. *Dial.* 1, p. 418., §4.3; and Hans-Joachim Birkner, *Schleiermachers Christliche Sittenlehre im Zusammenhang seines philosophisch-theologischen Systems* (Berlin: Töpelmann, 1964), pp. 31–38.
[10] Birkner, *Schleiermachers Christliche Sittenlehre*, p. 37.
[11] WA 2, pp. 531–540; Birkner, *Schleiermachers Christliche Sittenlehre*, p. 33.
[12] WA 2, pp. 536–537; Birkner, *Schleiermachers Christliche Sittenlehre*, pp. 33–34.

Schleiermacher also names identical and individual aspects of reason. Some expressions of reason, for example mathematical computation, need to be identical for all persons. Crucial to Schleiermacher's view in which the notion of "individuality" plays a key role, there are also expressions of reason, such as artistic expression and the use of language, marked by individuality. These manifestations of reason are not identical in all persons. There are, for example, an infinite variety of ways to create art. Schleiermacher then crosses these two sets of polar opposites and identifies four forms of human reason: the identical organizing, the individual organizing, the identical symbolizing, and the individual symbolizing. These forms of reason correspond to four great forms of human community. The identical organizing form pertains to economics and politics; its form of community is the state. Individual organizing concerns social relations and hospitality; its form of community is "free sociality" (*freie Geselligkeit*). The identical symbolizing form involves knowledge expressed in communities of the school and academy. And the individual symbolizing is the arena of art and religion with its social form being the church.[13]

Schleiermacher identifies his approach to ethics as "descriptive," and clearly it includes much description and analysis of the operations of reason. At the same time his ethics includes a normative element. This is so because the drive of reason can never be satisfied with former products. Reason's work is always in need of improvement. Ethical reflection seeks to identify current deficiencies and chart a way forward. Similarly, to be true to itself, the drive of reason always seeks a common life in which the interdependence of individuals and communities is manifest. Truly ethical action is always action for the human species, even while individuality and particularity are to be recognized and affirmed. Ethics has the normative task of identifying the incompleteness of what is, calling for further development, and orienting human action toward an interdependent common life in which persons and communities are bound together even while individuality is respected.[14]

In terms of Schleiermacher's schema Christian ethics is an expression of empirical ethics setting forth the life of a particular community of the individual symbolizing type. By seeing *Christian Ethics* within the larger scheme of Schleiermacher's thought, we can see its character and how it participates in reason's project of ensouling nature, even while maintaining its own distinctiveness.

Christian Ethics also occupies a particular place in Schleiermacher's view of theology. He lays out his vision of theology in his 1811 work, *Brief Outline of the Study of Theology*. This work understands all theological disciplines sharing a common practical goal: furthering the life of the church. Schleiermacher distinguishes three forms of theology. Philosophical theology is a "critical discipline" that starts from a place "above" Christianity. It mediates between speculative and empirical forms of knowledge and seeks to identify the distinctive essence of Christianity and to generate concepts that can be employed and evaluated in the next moment, historical theology. This middle moment of theology comprises biblical exegesis, the history of the church, and doctrinal theology. Doctrinal theology is historical in that it deals with the present moment of history and sets forth the theology (dogmatics and ethics) currently valid in the church. The third form of theology, practical theology, the "crown and goal" of the whole, builds on what has been gained from philosophical

---

[13] WA 2, pp. 567–568.

[14] On the aims and orientation of Schleiermacher's philosophical ethics, see Chapter 10 in this volume.

and historical theology and considers how these insights are best embodied in the life of the church. This vision of theology conforms to the *wissenschaftlich* canons of knowledge to which Schleiermacher subscribed, seeing theology as a thoroughly historical and human enterprise, which has its place in an overarching vision of human knowledge. Theology is at once an academic discipline engaging current thought and an ecclesial discipline providing direction for the life of the church.

Christian ethics is included under historical theology as it considers not the past, but the present. Together with dogmatics it comprises doctrinal theology. Schleiermacher is at pains to show that doctrinal theology comprises dogmatics and ethics, and only these two. He grounds this claim in his view of Christian piety. Piety, or Christian self-consciousness, is neither thought nor activity. At the same time, Schleiermacher avers, piety includes an element of interest and an element of impulse to activity. Dogmatics deals with naming conceptually the object of piety's interest—God. Ethics concerns itself with the activities that arise from piety's impulse. Schleiermacher formulates the tasks of the two disciplines, saying that dogmatics considers what must *be* the case on the basis of religious self-consciousness, while ethics deals with what must *come to be* based on the same religious self-consciousness. Schleiermacher asserts that dogmatics and ethics are complementary, that together they comprise an organic unity. He also addresses the fact that he and other theologians offer separate treatments of the two disciplines. He argues that separate treatments of dogmatics and ethics allow both to be seen in their own interconnectedness, and that the separation has allowed for Christian ethics to be more completely developed. When ethics is subsumed under dogmatics, however, it is swallowed up and does not appear as an interconnected whole. In the end, Schleiermacher justifies his own separate treatment in the interests of a fuller and more complete presentation of ethics.

For Schleiermacher, Christian ethics is primarily descriptive, providing a phenomenological analysis of the moments of Christian piety and the corresponding actions that arise from each moment. The purpose of ethics is to map out the manifestations of Christian spirit, indicating their teleological drive. Herein lies Christian ethics' normative element, its audience being leaders in the church. The point is to share a conceptually rigorous view of Christian ethics so that those leaders can return to their tasks with fuller understanding. They can then participate more consciously and fully in the drive of Christian spirit that is already in process and which they are to further.

22.3 Composition and Publication of the Lectures on *Christian Ethics*

Despite its importance within his theological program, however, it is not surprising that the *Christian Ethics* was relatively unknown throughout the nineteenth century. The work as we have it is a compilation based on lectures only published after Schleiermacher's death. Schleiermacher devoted himself to the field of ethics for the whole course of his academic career and gave twelve semester-long courses on the topic of Christian ethics. Knowing he would not be able to get this material into a publishable form before his death, he commissioned his student, Ludwig Jonas, to publish the work. Jonas did so in 1843. He based his edition on Schleiermacher's lectures from 1822/1823 because he had five student transcriptions from that year and some lecture notes from Schleiermacher's own hand. Jonas also included materials from other years: long footnotes and four lengthy appendices of lecture material. In 2010 Hermann Peiter published a new version of the *Christian Ethics* based on the lectures of 1826/1827, drawing on student notes and manuscripts from Schleiermacher, some of which had not been previously published.[15] Peiter's is a critical edition that includes a detailed apparatus showing the sources he utilized to construct the text.

The three forms of action—purifying, broadening, and presentational—provide the organizational principle around which the *Ethics* is structured in the lectures of 1822/1823. Schleiermacher also worked with a distinction between activity that constitutes the inner life of the Christian community and activity directed outward that engages the larger society. In the 1826/1827 lectures, he retains the three forms of action but deemphasizes the inner/outer distinction, instead giving central place to formation of both disposition and talent. Formation of disposition is identified with the theological theme of regeneration and formation of talent with sanctification. Thereafter the three forms of action and the formation of disposition and talent are the crucial concepts structuring his thought.

22.4 Character and Content of Christian Ethics

From a subjective perspective, piety is the ground for Christian ethics (and dogmatics). This is so because piety or Christian self-consciousness is the reception of the new and higher life of communion with God in Christ. Objectively, then, the ground for ethics and dogmatics is redemption brought about by Christ. This is born out in Schleiermacher's thinking about the nature of Christian ethics. For Schleiermacher, "the instructions [*Vorschriften*] of Christian ethics must be descriptions of the actions of Christ."[16] The new life of believers is given in Christ, and through Christ's spirit, the community carries on the work of Christ.

> All actions of Christians are either completions of the church-forming action of Christ, the reception of Christ's action, or continuations of it; in either case therefore they are a continuous realization of the relationship established between Christ as the redeemer and the human race as the redeemed.[17]

Here we see the distinctively Christian character of *Christian Ethics*, which is grounded in redemption and tasked with naming and analyzing the ongoing the work of Christ, which happens now through the Christian community. Christian self-consciousness comes to be as persons are drawn into the new and higher form of life—communion with God through Christ.

For Schleiermacher, then, all Christian activity is grounded in the pious apprehension of redemption in Christ, which he characterizes as "blessedness" or "joy in the Lord." This

---

[15] CS (Peiter).
[16] Schleiermacher, *Die christliche Sitte*, p. 75.
[17] Schleiermacher, *Die christliche Sitte*, pp. 74–75.

sense is basic to Christian self-consciousness and is at the root of all Christian activity. All Christian self-consciousness includes this sense of blessedness. Blessedness gives rise to what Schleiermacher calls "presentational action," action that seeks to express an inner state in an outer way. At the same time consciousness may be determined by the antithesis between spirit and flesh. Moments that include the dominion of spirit over flesh are experienced as pleasure (*Lust*). Moments in which there is a sense of resistance to the spirit's dominion are experienced as a lack of pleasure (*Unlust*). Self-consciousness determined as pleasure gives rise to activity that intends to expand the sway of spirit over flesh, hence a broadening action. Self-consciousness determined as lack of pleasure gives rise to restoration or purification, activity that seeks to restore the dominion of spirit over flesh. The basic sense of blessedness both precedes and follows after the other two moments that can characterize consciousness, so blessedness is basic to Christian consciousness and recurs amid the fluctuations of consciousness as pleasure or lack of pleasure. This blessedness is relative, not yet perfected, but as communion with Christ, it receives and participates in Christ's perfection. Blessedness points to "the perfected dominion of the spirit in everything that can in any way be recognized as a combining of spirit with flesh."[18] Because of its sense of completion, actions that flow from blessedness seek no outer change or result. Presentational action is the totality of all actions by which believers represent themselves as organs of God. By virtue of these actions of self-presentation, individual members of the community make themselves known to one another and community comes to be.

In addition to presentational action, the *Christian Ethics* identifies restorative and broadening actions as actions that arise from Christian self-consciousness. These two forms of action are efficacious actions because they do seek to effect a change. While broadening action corresponds to what Schleiermacher calls "organizing action" in his philosophical ethics, there is nothing in the latter work that corresponds to restoring action. This is so because restoring action is based on the opposition between sin and grace that is constitutive of Christian consciousness. While redemption brings new life and the spirit's dominion over flesh, this dominion is not yet complete, providing for the possibility of resistance and the need for restoring action.

Presentational (*darstellende*) activity, arising from Christian self-consciousness, is basic to Christian community. Presentational activity both re-creates the church and presupposes its existence. Schleiermacher speaks of the church and presentational activity as being "equally original."[19] Presentational action is the way that Schleiermacher understands worship. Worship happens when believers gather and express their inner sense of communion with God in an outward way. In the give and take of such sharing the church comes to be. Schleiermacher differentiates two forms of worship: worship "in the narrow sense" (*engeren Sinn*), which is the public worship life of the community, and worship "in the broad sense" (*im weiteren Sinn*), which happens in the everyday life of believers. By means of presentational activity, the community and individual believers represent themselves as organs of the Spirit. The church, considered both generically and in its Christian particularity, is a community of symbolization.

---

[18] *CE (Brandt)*, p. 139.
[19] *CE (Brandt)*, p. 144.

In thinking about restoring action, Schleiermacher works with a distinction between the individual and the whole (or community) and conceives of the whole working restoratively on the individual and the individual doing the same on the community. When the individual is in need of restoration, Schleiermacher proposes a spiritual "gymnastic," works of mercy, especially service to those who are sick or in poverty. Providing this gymnastic is the work of the community on the individual. Schleiermacher affirms such gymnastics because they are productive of something positive, as distinct from works of privation, which have no positive result. In terms of individual working restoration on the whole, he has in mind the church's ongoing need for betterment. The prime historical example is the Protestant Reformation of the sixteenth century with Luther leading efforts to better the church. While the church is perfect in an "eternal way," it is never perfect in its appearance in history, so place for criticism and reform must be allowed.

Broadening action is based on the dominion of spirit over flesh and seeks to expand the sway of spirit. In the lectures of 1822/1823, he asserts that "the whole saving action of Christ can be comprehended under the form of broadening action."[20] This is so because salvation begins with the person and life of Christ and then expands as others are drawn in. Broadening action is bounded by two points, beginning with the person of Christ and having as its goal the perfection of all human beings in Christ. Broadening action is of two types: an intensive broadening, which involves the formation of persons already within the Christian community, and extensive expansion as the Gospel is taken to new peoples. Intensive broadening aims at developing the disposition, both of understanding and of will, and of talent that can be employed in fulfilling the general human vocation and the particular Christian vocation. Intensive broadening emerges from the life of the community as the Spirit is active therein and aims to deepen the sense of communion with God that is the basic mark of Christian faith. Such broadening is not automatic. To prevent the church from falling into a false estimate of its perfection, the life of the community must be marked by public and open exchange, which can lead to genuine discernment as to direction of the church's life. Schleiermacher's reflection on extensive broadening, evangelistic expansion, is not as fully developed as his thinking about intensive broadening, but he does note that such witness requires a catholic and pastoral spirit to be genuinely faithful.

The church is a natural human community like any other, different only in that it continues the presence and work of Christ through its ongoing life. This ongoing life includes engagement with the larger culture in which the church exists. In thinking about such cultural expressions as political and economic organization (the state), communal forms of life (the family and free sociality), language and knowledge (the academy and schools), and artistic expression (all manner of artistic groups), Schleiermacher consistently acknowledges that these life forms preexist Christianity, and Christianity has no need to raze them and start over. Rather, the Christian spirit affirms the contributions to human life made by the *koinos logos* (common human reason) and considers how Christians are to relate to them. Schleiermacher affirms that Christians are to participate in all manner of social groups and organizations, and in so doing, "work at the same time so that the communal feeling in each totality to which one belongs is ever more in agreement with the claims of the Christian principle."[21]

---

[20] *CE (Brandt)*, pp. 99–100.
[21] *CE (Brandt)*, p. 173.

Schleiermacher conceives of the church's engagement with its larger context in terms of the three forms of action that derive from Christian self-consciousness. As restoring, broadening, and presentational action constitute the life of the church itself, so these forms of action are employed to identify activities in the larger social and cultural world.

Although Schleiermacher recognizes and affirms the goodness of all forms of cultural life, he also asserts that sin remains an active force in the world. Sinful distortions of human life require identification and restoration in order to become constructive again. As part of his analysis of restoring action, Schleiermacher offers a sweeping condemnation of violence, corporeal punishment, and coercion as unchristian. In the 1822/1823 lectures, he rejects wars of aggression, the death penalty, violent revolution, and colonization by means of force. In addition, he renounces divorce, dueling, slavery, and dehumanization in labor. The Christian task is to identify such distortions and contribute to transformation. In relation to the state, Schleiermacher is particularly trenchant in his opposition to any form of selfish nationalism, "because the self-interest of the state is the most powerful force that can oppose Christianity."[22] Conversely, when the Christian spirit transforms nationalism and brings it into service of the Reign of God, "it is the highest high of political life and the most lordly triumph of the Christian spirit."[23]

In the lectures from 1826, Schleiermacher develops broadening action in terms of the distinction between cultivation of the disposition and cultivation of talent. Regeneration, whereby the union between the Spirit and human reason occurs, establishes the Christian disposition. The expansion of the Christian disposition is the task of the Christian community and, importantly, of the family. He sees the family as the most basic human community, and it is imprinted with the Christian spirit as it brings together the tasks of propagation and formation. The family is a prime example of a form of human community that pre-exists the church and is appropriated and transformed by the Christian spirit. Cultivation of talent refers to the process of sanctification, whereby a believer's organic functions and particular capabilities develop to be organs of the Spirit. Christ brings a higher form of human life, which is always oriented to human cultivation of nature, the overarching vocation of humanity. This vocation is enacted in the particular forms of human community and practice that pre-exist the church, especially the state. The state is the "form of a people," a basic human community and not merely a necessary evil.[24] It has a central role as custodian of the broadening process, notably in educational, civic, and economic life. The Christian community seeks to bring the state into service of the highest good, the Reign of God. As talents are formed and imbued with the Christian spirit the particularities of a given community (its language, culture, and customs) are taken up and become organs of the divine Spirit. Sanctification, the formation of talents under the sway of the Spirit, works through these ordinary, natural means. We have here a marked affirmation of natural human processes as the domain of Christian ethics.

Presentational action in the outer sphere includes all forms of artistic expression from music and drama to painting and sculpture. The goal of Christian participation in presentational action that occurs in the outer sphere is "to manifest the presentational Christian virtues in all social relationships with all individuals."[25] In the context of

---

[22] *CE (Brandt)*, p. 135.
[23] *CE (Brandt)*, p. 135.
[24] Schleiermacher, *Die christliche Sitte*, p. 455.
[25] *CE (Brandt)*, p. 173.

reflecting on presentational action, Schleiermacher identifies the "Christian principle" as "brotherly love." He defines brotherly love as the "inner necessity for the continual joining of self-consciousnesses separated by personal existence."[26] This joining together of self-consciousness is characterized by equality and mutuality. Christian equality is grounded in the equal need all have for Christ and the fact that the Spirit is given to all. Mutuality derives from the fact that in Christian community all members are to both give and receive, be both active and receptive. In relation to presentational action, Schleiermacher affirms engaging the given forms of human community and practice, transforming them by permeation with the Christian spirit of love, embodied in equality and mutuality.

22.5 OVERCOMING THE RATIONALIST/SUPRARNATURALIST DIVISION AND TRANSCENDING CONTEMPORARY THEOLOGICAL ETHICS

Our thesis is that Schleiermacher's *Christian Ethics* transcends the theological ethics of the day in a way similar to the way *Christian Faith* transcends contemporary theology. *Christian Faith* is credited with inaugurating a new era in Protestant theology, with launching the New Protestantism. Since *Christian Ethics* was not known, it did not have the influence in the world of theological ethics that the *Christian Faith* did in theology. Nonetheless, we will show how the *Christian Ethics* forges into new territory and needs to be seen as something genuinely new and distinctive, going beyond what had been in theological ethics.

The crucial element in the theological context in which Schleiermacher found himself was the deep division between supranaturalists and rationalists. The issues between rationalists and supranaturalists had been brewing at least since the posthumous publication of Hermann Reimarus' *Wolfenbüttel Fragments* by G. E. Lessing.[27] Reimarus brings the tools of historical criticism to bear on the Gospels and concludes that Jesus was not divine, but a moral teacher of a high order. The work of Reimarus and Lessing sparked a strong counter-reaction and conflict persisted to the end of the eighteenth century. In the early nineteenth century, with the emergence of self-identified rationalist thinkers the divide with the supranaturalists becomes deep and unbridgeable.

Important rationalist theologians of the early nineteenth century include Heinrich Henke and Julius Wegschneider. Like other rationalist theologians they shared a common concern for reason and critical thought. They sought to provide a rational foundation for faith in a way that could coexist with the growth of scientific and historical understanding. To be rational required that the miraculous and supernatural elements of the New Testament be minimized or excluded altogether. Rationalists examined the historical development of Christianity and concluded that the teaching and example of Christ were central and the dogma that developed subsequently deviated from his simple witness. Many saw the

---

[26] *CE (Brandt)*, p. 148.
[27] See Hermann Reimarus, *Reimarus: Fragments*, ed. Charles H. Talbert, trans. Ralph S. Fraser (Philadelphia: Fortress Press, 1970).

universal truth of rational religion as the goal of historical development. Christ then was seen as a step that led to true and rational religion.

The supranaturalists rejected the rationalist exclusion of the miraculous and the supernatural and their view of Christ as merely a moral teacher, a step on the way to a universal rational religion. Among the important supranaturalist theologians were Gottlob Christian Storr and Johann Flatt at Tübingen and Christian Zollich at Göttingen. Most supranaturalist theologians were not completely opposed to critical reason. Storr, for example, was the first to argue for the Markan priority of the Synoptic Gospels. Among the ideas at stake for the supranaturalists were the importance of revelation, the authority of the Bible, and recognition of God's ongoing and mysterious activity in the world. In the early nineteenth century the rationalists and suprarationalists were at complete loggerheads, and there seemed no way forward for theology.

Casting his shadow over all theological and philosophical developments in this period was Immanuel Kant. His *Critique of Pure Reason* identifies strict limitations on what can be known and calls into question the possibility of any metaphysical claims. Kant's second critique, *The Critique of Practical Reason* (1788), examines humanity's universal and self-certifying moral sense. Here the claims for the existence of God, human freedom, and immortality of the soul, seen as beyond the ken of pure theoretical reason, are allowed the status of postulates necessary for human moral sense to be coherent. Thus, we have in Kant the moral sense as given and primary, with religious claims about freedom, immortality, and God established only as secondary postulates. Kant's ethic is an ethic of duty, the categorical imperative before which all humans stand. Both the rationalists and the supranaturalists take up this ethics of duty and make it central to their ethical positions. The imperative mode that affirms following one's duty and obedience to law are the hallmarks of ethics for both rationalists and supranaturalists.[28]

Our thesis is that *Christian Ethics* moves beyond that impasse and provides a new and distinctive vision of theological ethics. *Christian Ethics* does this in two ways. The first is that *Christian Ethics* continues and completes the theme of the supernatural becoming natural, which was a crucial element of the theology of *Christian Faith*. The central fact around which Schleiermacher's theology revolves is Christ as the redeemer, and Christ is "supernatural" in Schleiermacher's distinctive understanding of the term. Christ possesses perfect consciousness of God. This perfect sense of communion with God is communicated by Christ to his followers and subsequently to others. As Schleiermacher says, the actions of the church are "continuations of the relationship between Christ as the Redeemer and the human race as the redeemed."[29] *Christian Ethics* describes and analyzes the ways the supernatural-become-natural finds expression through the actions that constitute the church. By means of the actions of this human and natural community, the saving action of Christ is continued and mediated to the world. So *Christian Ethics* has the crucial role in setting forth in detail the natural processes that constitute the life of the church. Similarly in relation to the larger society and culture, the church is to engage the institutions, customs, and mores that preexist it; it is not to raze social and cultural forms and start over.[30] Here again the natural, human forms of life are affirmed. *Christian Ethics* completes the theme of the supernatural-become-natural

---

[28] Vander Schel, *Embedded Grace*, pp. 183–184.
[29] Schleiermacher, *Die christliche Sitte*, p. 74.
[30] Cf. Schleiermacher, *Die christliche Sitte*, p. 441.

begun in *Christian Faith* and demonstrates how Schleiermacher's theological system creatively overcomes the supernaturalism/rationalist impasse.

Secondly, *Christian Ethics* moves beyond the dominant theological ethics of the day with its narrow focus on duty to an ethics of the Reign of God as the highest good and an ecclesial ethics that fulfills the goal of providing direction for the life of the church. *Christian Ethics* provides a rich description and analysis of the life of the community of faith and its engagement with the larger society and culture. The actions that constitute the life of the community and of individual believers are set forth together with their grounding in the pious reception of redemption. The "outer sphere" also receives careful attention. Schleiermacher analyzes forms of community from family and "free sociality" to the economic realm and the state, indicating appropriate ways for the church and individual believers to engage these diverse expressions of human reason and community. Schleiermacher's ethical vision is at once deeply grounded in the higher life of redemption in Christ and broad in its comprehension of the wide variety of cultural goods that constitute human life—all this with the goal of manifesting the highest good, the Reign of God. In this way *Christian Ethics* moves beyond the Kantian-influenced ethics of the day. Had the work been more widely known it might have reoriented theological ethics as *Christian Faith* did theology.

22.6 Reception and Critique of Schleiermacher's Ethics

A long trajectory of critique has been directed at *Christian Faith*, even as it is seen as inaugurating a new epoch in Protestant theology. Given its long obscurity, little criticism has been directed at the *Christian Ethics*. However, there has been a smaller chorus of those who leveled significant critique at Schleiermacher's ethical position. Albrecht Ritschl claims that Schleiermacher fails to grasp the ethical moment with a firm hand.[31] However, Ritschl makes no reference to *Christian Ethics*, thereby blunting his criticism.[32] H. Richard Niebuhr identifies Schleiermacher with the "Christ of culture" type in his classic work, *Christ and Culture*. Schleiermacher is accused of selling out the Christian faith for the sake of cultural relevance. The Christ of culture type is clearly Niebuhr's least favorite, and he identifies its shortcomings in ways the other types are spared.[33] Niebuhr misses the strong affinity *Christian Ethics* has for the "Christ transforming culture" type.[34]

A more recent critic has indicated how *Christian Ethics* exhibits chauvinism in relation to non-Western cultures. Joerg Rieger has correctly shown how the *Ethics* affirms the colonial enterprise (although rejecting the use of force) and asserts the superiority of Western culture. The lectures understand colonization as the spread of "civilization" to those who

---

[31] Albrecht Ritschl, *A Critical History of the Christian Doctrine of Justification and Reconciliation*, trans. John S. Black (Edinburgh: Edmonston and Douglas, 1872), pp. 454–474.

[32] See James M. Brandt, "Ritschl's Critique of Schleiermacher's Theological Ethics," *Journal of Religious Ethics* 17, no. 2 (Fall 1989), pp. 51–72.

[33] H. Richard Niebuhr, *Christ and Culture* (New York: Harper & Row, 1951), pp. 83–115.

[34] See James M. Brandt, *All Things New: Reform of Church and Society in Schleiermacher's Christian Ethics* (Louisville, KY: Westminster John Knox Press, 2001), pp. 109–134.

are "uncivilized."[35] Here Schleiermacher's thought endorses the Western colonial project and the dark underside of the alliance between Christianity and Western culture. As Reiger recognizes, there are resources in Schleiermacher's *Christian Ethics* for overcoming this chauvinism. And in this context Schleiermacher himself affirms the need for ongoing critical reflection because distortions, in this case the use of force, are always at work and need to be identified and halted.[36]

22.7 Concluding Reflection

Schleiermacher's philosophy and theology are suffused with a deep sense of historical consciousness. This includes a recognition that Christian ethics exists as part of an ongoing tradition that never reaches a fixed and final expression. Schleiermacher also makes history the locus of his ethical reflection, attending to actions that constitute the faith community and to how Christians engage the larger society and culture. He provides both his *Christian Ethics* and his philosophical ethics and wrestles with the commonalities and differences between these two approaches. The former is deeply grounded in Christian faith and the latter provides a comprehensive vision of the processes and goals of the human venture. Schleiermacher's creativity and depth of insight inspire and provoke those who wrestle with similar issues today and into the future.

Suggested Reading

Bigler, Robert. *The Politics of German Protestantism: The Rise of the Protestant Church Elite in Prussia, 1815–1848* (Berkeley: University of California Press, 1972).
Crossley, John P. "Schleiermacher's Christian Ethics in Relation to his Philosophical Ethics." *Annual of the Society of Christian Ethics* 18 (1998), pp. 93–117.
Gerrish, B. A. *Christian Faith: Dogmatics in Outline* (Louisville, KY: Westminster John Knox Press, 2015).
Herms, Eilert. *Menschen im Werden: Studien zu Schleiermacher* (Tübingen: Mohr Siebeck, 2003).
Herms, Eilert. "Schleiermacher's Christian Ethics." In *The Cambridge Companion to Friedrich Schleiermacher*, ed. Jacqueline Mariña (Cambridge: Cambridge University Press, 2005), pp. 209–228.
Peiter, Hermann. *Christliche Ethik bei Schleiermacher—Christian Ethics according to Schleiermacher: Gesammelte Aufsätze und Besprechungen—Collected Essays and Reviews.* Ed. Terrence N. Tice (Eugene, OR: Wipf and Stock, 2010).
Poe, Shelli M., ed. *Schleiermacher and Sustainability: A Theology for Ecological Living* (Louisville: Westminster John Knox Press, 2018).

---

[35] Schleiermacher, *Die christliche Sitte*, pp. 286–290.
[36] Schleiermacher, *Die christliche Sitte*, p. 290.

Bibliography

Birkner, Hans-Joachim. *Schleiermachers Christliche Sittenlehre im Zusammenhang seines philosophisch-theologischen Systems* (Berlin: Töpelmann, 1964).

Brandt, James M. *All Things New: Reform of Church and Society in Schleiermacher's Christian Ethics* (Louisville, KY: Westminster John Knox Press, 2001).

Brandt, James M. *Die Christliche Sittenlehre: A Reassessment of Schleiermacher's Theological-Ethical Vision* (PhD dissertation. University of Chicago, 1991).

Brandt, James M. "Ritschl's Critique of Schleiermacher's Theological Ethics." *Journal of Religious Ethics* 17, no. 2 (Fall 1989), pp. 51–72.

Brandt, James M. *Selections from Schleiermacher's Christian Ethics* (Louisville, KY: Westminster John Knox Press, 2011).

Gerrish, B. A. *Continuing the Reformation: Essays on Modern Religious Thought* (Chicago: University of Chicago Press, 1993).

Herms, Eilert. "Encyclopedia, Philosophical Ethics, Anthropology, and Dogmatics." In *Schleiermacher, the Study of Religion, and the Future of Theology*, ed. Brent W. Sockness and Wilhelm Gräb (Berlin: Walter de Gruyter, 2010), pp. 361–374.

Kant, Immanuel. *Critique of Practical Reason*. Trans. Werner S. Pluhar (Indianapolis, IN: Hackett, 2002).

Niebuhr, H. Richard. *Christ and Culture* (New York: Harper & Row, 1951).

Reimarus, Hermann. *Reimarus: Fragments*. Ed. Charles H. Talbert, trans. Ralph S. Fraser (Philadelphia: Fortress Press, 1970).

Rieger, Joerg. *Christ and Empire: From Paul to Postcolonial Times* (Minneapolis: Fortress Press, 2007).

Ritschl, Albrecht. *A Critical History of the Christian Doctrine of Justification and Reconciliation*. Trans. John S. Black (Edinburgh: Edmonston and Douglas, 1872).

Schleiermacher, F. D. E. *Die christliche Sitte nach den Grundsätzen der evangelischen Kirche im Zusammenhange dargestellt*. Ed. Ludwig Jonas (Berlin: G. Reimer, 1843).

Vander Schel, Kevin M. *Embedded Grace: Christ, History and the Reign of God in Schleiermacher's Dogmatics* (Minneapolis: Fortress Press, 2013).

CHAPTER 23

THE LIFE OF JESUS

CHRISTIAN DANZ

FRIEDRICH Schleiermacher's lectures on "The Life of Jesus," held for the first time in the winter term of 1819/1820, presuppose the European enlightenment. His own approach in the quest for the historical man from Nazareth becomes understandable only against the background of the eighteenth-century debates about Jesus and the origins of Christianity. The Berlin theologian took up the Enlightenment's criticism of the traditional image of Jesus while also criticizing the Enlightenment approach. Schleiermacher was not the first theologian who gave public lectures at the university on the life of Jesus, contrary to what Albert Schweitzer claimed in his well-known book about the history of historical Jesus research.[1] Schweitzer followed a statement by David Friedrich Strauß. Strauß wrote that lectures on the life of Jesus were new at the time in which Schleiermacher offered his own lectures on this matter.[2] But this is not the case. During the 1790s Johann Wilhelm Schmid, a theologian from the University of Jena, had already offered lectures on the life of Jesus. The title of his final course of lectures, from the summer term of 1797, was *historiam vitae Iesu Christi critice et pragmatice enarrabit tractandus fit, demonstrabit*.[3] Around 1819 there was a boom of such lectures. During the summer term of 1819 Heinrich Gottlob Eberhard Paulus offered lectures on the life of Jesus in Heidelberg, and in 1823 Karl von Hase, on the theological faculty of the University of Tübingen, did so as well.[4]

---

[1] Cf. Albert Schweitzer, *Geschichte der Leben-Jesu-Forschung*, vol. 1 (München/Hamburg: Siebenstern Taschenbuch Verlag, 1966), p. 100.

[2] David Friedrich Strauß, *Der Christus des Glaubens und der Jesus der Geschichte. Eine Kritik des Schleiermacher'schen Lebens Jesu* (Berlin: Franz Duncker, 1865), p. 1.

[3] [Anonymous], *Praelectionum publice privatimque in academia Ienensi, summer curese 1797* (Jena, 1797).

[4] Cf. Martin Ohst, "Der theologie- und kirchengeschichtliche Hintergrund des Atheismusstreits," in *Fichtes Entlassung. Der Atheismusstreit vor 200 Jahren*, ed. Klaus-Michael Kodalle and Martin Ohst (Würzburg: Königshausen & Neumann, 1999), p. 32.

23.1 THE SEARCH FOR THE HISTORICAL JESUS IN THE THEOLOGY OF ENLIGHTENMENT

The historical Jesus research that began with the investigations of Hermann Samuel Reimarus was motivated by two developments in Enlightenment scholarship. The first is the historical criticism of the biblical writings in the eighteenth century.[5] With the implementation of historical criticism within Protestant theology, the position on Scripture held by old Lutheran theology fell apart. The reason for this is that biblical Scriptures were now regarded as documents from an ancient time. But with the new understanding of Scripture through the lens of historical criticism, the biblical texts were to be understood in their own historical context. What followed is that interpreters came to be aware not only of contradictions within the biblical text, but also of the difference between the Old and the New Testaments. For example, in a historical view, the prophetic predictions of the Old Testament do not find their fulfilment in the New. But in addition, the difference between the church's dogmatic image of Jesus Christ and the historical material was becoming increasingly clear. One new condition of Christianity at this time, then, is the tension between faith and history. The second condition consists of the critique of knowledge by David Hume and Immanuel Kant. When subjected to this critique the classical doctrine of Jesus Christ as a God-man loses its plausibility for contemporaries.

As a result of these new conditions, there was now a task to find a new foundation both for Christianity and theology. The search for the historical Jesus was one answer; another was the concept of religion as the methodological basis for theology. Both answers are related. One of the first researchers who made a sharp distinction between the historical Jesus and the Christian image of the Christ, or between the religion of Jesus and the Christian religion, was Reimarus.[6] For him Jesus belonged entirely to Second Temple Judaism, and Christianity was an invention of his disciples, who stole the dead body of Jesus and told others that he had risen from the dead. Through this they created a spiritual interpretation of Jesus. But this interpretation, and therefore Christianity, is different from the aims of Jesus himself, as Reimarus worked out in his fragments. Jesus took himself to be a messiah in the political sense of ancient Judaism, and not a spiritual redeemer. When Gotthold Ephraim Lessing published these so-called fragments from an unknown author, they generated a huge controversy. Many theologians like Johann Salomo Semler wrote books against the theses of Reimarus.[7] Yet Semler shared with Reimarus the new historical conditions of biblical research.

A new understanding of history was established during the Enlightenment. This understanding leads to a contrast between history and the idea of Christianity, so that the image

---

[5] For an overview see Henning Graf Reventlow, *History of Biblical Interpretation, vol. 4: From Enlightenment to the Twentieth Century* (Atlanta: Society of Biblical Literature, 2010), pp. 23–229.

[6] Hermann Samuel Reimarus, *Vom Zwecke Jesu und seiner Jünger. Noch ein Fragment des Wolfenbüttelschen Ungenannten*, ed. Gotthold Ephraim Lessing (Braunschweig, 1778); cf. Reventlow, *History*, pp. 155–165.

[7] Johann Salomo Semler, *Beantwortung der Fragmente eines Ungenannten insbesondere vom Zweck Jesu und seiner Jünger* (Halle: Verlag des Erziehungsinstituts, 1779); cf. Reventlow, *History*, pp. 175–190; Christian Danz, *Grundprobleme der Christologie* (Tübingen: Mohr Siebeck, 2013), pp. 106–118.

of the Christ of faith can no longer be traced back to the Jesus of history. What is historical is unique and contingent; but the idea, which alone is general, has no history. Two strategies are possible for dealing with this new gap.[8] First, theology can stress the idea of Christianity. This was the position of Lessing.[9] It is the idea of Christianity and not its history that is fundamental, because only the idea is universal. Or in Lessing's own words, "*accidental truths of history can never demonstrate the necessary truth of reason.*"[10] And second, Jesus can be understood as the historical founder of the true religion of reason. This was the position of Semler. For him Jesus brings a new religion into history, namely the autonomous religion of morality, which is totally different from the religion of the old Hebrews. The first of these solutions gives history no role, while for the second Jesus is merely the beginning of a development. What is not really clear in either position is the significance of the Jesus of the history for contemporary Christianity. In one view he is a historical image for the idea, and in the other the accidental starting point of a history.

The importance of Schleiermacher's view of Jesus both within his Christology and his lectures on *The Life of Jesus* becomes obvious in view of this gap between history and idea. Namely, he brings both dimensions together against the backdrop of the Enlightenment debates.

23.2 The Lectures on the Life of Jesus

23.2.1 Schleiermacher's Lectures on the Life of Jesus

Schleiermacher offered his lectures on the life of Jesus five times at the university of Berlin. The first course began in the winter term of 1819/1820 on October 19, 1819 and ended on March 25, 1820.[11] The title of the first course of lectures is not "The Life of Jesus," but the older phrasing "The Life of Christ." It is also important to note that Schleiermacher differentiated these lectures from his others, giving them the title "The Life of Christ narrated by Mr. Prof. Dr. Schleiermacher" in the university calendar.[12] The second course began on April 14, 1823. After giving over seventy lectures Schleiermacher concluded on August 1, 1823. But by that point the title of the lectures had changed: for the first time in the summer of 1823, Schleiermacher used the title "The Life of Jesus," and in the university calendar "The Life of Jesus narrated by Schleiermacher." The third course ran between October 26, 1829 and March 26, 1830, and the fourth during the summer term of 1831. Schleiermacher offered his last lectures on the life of Jesus between May 14, 1832 and August 29, 1832. But for these lectures he changed the entry in the university calendar. His announcement no longer promised a

---

[8] Cf. Christian Danz, *Jesus von Nazareth zwischen Judentum und Christentum. Eine christologische und religionstheologische Skizze* (Tübingen: Mohr Siebeck, 2020), pp. 92–99.
[9] Gotthold Ephraim Lessing, "Über den Beweis des Geistes und der Kraft," in *Freimäurergespräche und anderes. Ausgewählte Schriften* (München: Beck, 1981), pp. 29–34, emphasis in the original.; cf. Reventlow, *History*, pp. 165–175.
[10] Lessing, "Über den Beweis," p. 32.
[11] *VLJ*, p. xx.
[12] *VLJ*, p. xxi.

narration of "The Life of Jesus." As in his other lectures he announced the lecture "The Life of Jesus executed by Schleiermacher."[13]

During each course, Schleiermacher lectured from Monday until Friday for one hour. His lectures on the life of Jesus were very successful, attracting more students than his other lectures at the University of Berlin—between 137 and 251 students across the different courses.

23.2.2 The Material of Schleiermacher's Lectures on the Life of Jesus

We do not know very much about the background and formation of Schleiermacher's lectures on the life of Jesus. In his letters he hardly mentions his lectures. In a letter from November 28, 1819, Schleiermacher's friend Joachim Wilhelm Gaß inquired about the lectures and expressed a desire to discuss the subject, since he had announced a similar lecture. Schleiermacher answer to his friend's question has not been preserved.[14] Neither has a response to a later letter from Gaß on April 12, 1820, in which he asked Schleiermacher to send him the lecture notebooks.[15] Schleiermacher only mentioned his lectures about the life of Jesus in a letter to Gaß from November 12, 1829:[16] "Unfortunately, my two lectures [*Collegia*] also occupy me more than a little bit; but since I last attended to the first Epistle to the Corinthians a couple of new commentaries have appeared, and from the life of Jesus I have only notes and bits of paper."[17] His diaries contain some entries pertaining to the different lectures between 1819 and 1832.

In preparation for his lectures in 1819 Schleiermacher drafted notes and excerpts from the contemporary literature on the New Testament and the beginning of Christianity for himself. These manuscripts are persevered in his posthumous papers and are now published in the volume 15 of the *Schleiermacher Kritische Gesamtausgabe* under the title *To the life of Jesus* (*Zum Leben Jesu*) and *Omnibus volume to the life of Jesus* (*Konvolut zum Leben Jesu*).[18] These manuscripts date from 1819 to 1829.[19] In them we find excerpts from the contemporary literature about the life of Jesus—for example, Heinrich Gottlob Eberhard Paulus' commentary on the New Testament (1800–1804). Besides the commentary from Paulus, Schleiermacher worked with the book *Geschichte der drey letzten Lebensjahre Jesu* from Johann Jakob Heß (1773), and also with classical books from Hugo Grotius or from early Christian theologians including Origen, Eusebius, and others.

In addition to these notes, eight slips of paper, with an outline for his several lectures on the life of Jesus from the summer term of 1832, are preserved in Schleiermacher's posthumous papers. Karl August Rütenik used these for his first edition of Schleiermacher's lectures

---

[13] *VLJ*, p. xxiii.
[14] *VLJ*, p. xx.
[15] Ibid.
[16] Ibid.
[17] Wilhelm Gaß, ed., *Fr. Schleiermacher's Briefwechsel mit J. Chr. Gaß: mit einer biographischen Vorrede* (Berlin: Reimer, 1852), p. 220.
[18] These are found in *VLJ*, pp. 5–82 and 82–100.
[19] *VLJ*, pp. xxvii–xxxi.

in 1864, placing Schleiermacher's notes at the beginning of each lecture. Schleiermacher's outline for the lectures from 1832 is now published in the critical edition of his works.[20]

The first edition of Schleiermacher's lectures on the life of Jesus was edited by Rütenik in 1864. He published the lectures in the series of Schleiermacher's complete works thirty years after Schleiermacher's death. The reason for this late publication of the lectures was the publication, in 1835/1836, of David Friedrich Strauß' book *The Life of Jesus*. Against the backdrop of this book and its critical results it was not possible to publish Schleiermacher's lectures on the same topic. Strauß only one year after the publication of Schleiermacher's lectures wrote a very critical book against *The Life of Jesus* from Schleiermacher.[21] His main objection, that the historical Jesus portrayed by the Berlin theologian was not historical, determined the reception history of Schleiermacher's lectures on the life of Jesus with lasting effect.[22]

Rütenik's edition was for a long time the only source for Schleiermacher's understanding of the historical Jesus. But the edition is very problematic. Rütenik used different student transcripts from Schleiermacher's lecture from the summer term of 1832.[23] What he presented to us is a compilation. He did not identify his sources. Strauß himself criticized the poor quality of the edition in *Der Christus des Glaubens und der Jesus der Geschichte*.[24] Originally Rütenik had planned a second volume with supplements to the lectures, but the plan was never realized. An English translation of Rütenik's edition was published in 1975.

A critical edition with Schleiermacher's lectures on the life of Jesus was published in 2018 in the *Schleiermacher Kritische Gesamtausgabe*, edited by Walter Jaeschke, who applied the methods of critical scholarship to all of Schleiermacher's manuscripts.[25] The edition also reproduces a manuscript from the 1823 lectures by Karl Wolff, who was a student on the theological faculty at the University of Berlin between October 18, 1828 and April 14, 1829.[26] Wolff claimed that his manuscript was derived from a manuscript written by Schleiermacher during the summer term of 1823.[27] Besides the lecture from 1823, the volume offers a transcript of the lectures from the summer term of 1832 from Ernst Collin, who was a student at the theological faculty of the University of Berlin between May 4, 1830 until September 25, 1834.[28]

There are eight known student transcripts from Schleiermacher's lectures on the life of Jesus between 1819 and 1832.[29] One of the most well known is from David Friedrich Strauß. During his studies in Berlin in 1831 Schleiermacher did not offer his lectures on the life of Jesus. So Strauß copied two student transcripts of the lectures, from the summer term of 1823 and the winter term of 1829/1830. He would then use these transcripts for his own project on the life of Jesus.

---

[20] *VLJ*, pp. 101–133.
[21] Cf. Schweitzer, *Geschichte*, p. 101.
[22] Cf. Strauß, *Der Christus des Glaubens*, pp. 209–223.
[23] *SW* 1.6, pp. vi–xiv.
[24] Strauß, *Der Christus des Glaubens*, pp. 1–19.
[25] *VLJ*.
[26] *VLJ*, pp. 136–306.
[27] Cf. *VLJ*, pp. xxxii–xl.
[28] *VLJ*, pp. l–li. Collin's transcript is found in *VLJ*, pp. 311–508.
[29] Cf. *VLJ*, pp. xl–lii.

23.2.3 The Intention of Schleiermacher's Lectures on the Life of Jesus

All of the extant lectures from Schleiermacher on the life of Jesus have a similar structure. Schleiermacher begins with an introduction and then explains the life of Jesus. The structure of his explanation is threefold. Schleiermacher distinguishes between the public ministry of Jesus, beginning with his baptism, and the time of the passion of Jesus, beginning with his arrest.[30] These are the two main periods of the life of Jesus. A third period is the time before the public ministry of Jesus, the time of Jesus' youth and development. What Schleiermacher intended with his lectures was to give a description of the life or a biography of Jesus Christ. "The task is to find the interior of its development as a unity in such a way that one can also determine results under the assumption of other coefficients."[31]

Schleiermacher's lectures on the life of Jesus have repeatedly attracted criticism since their publication in 1864. Strauß raised the main objection against Schleiermacher's image of Jesus in his book of 1865. The historical Jesus whom Schleiermacher presented is a doctrinal construction: "Schleiermacher's Christ is as little a real person as the Christ of the Church; in a truly critical treatment of the Gospels one comes as little to Schleiermacher's Christ as to the Church's Christ."[32] This is the same objection as in *The Life of Jesus* thirty years earlier—namely, that Schleiermacher's historical Jesus is a back-projection from the consciousness of redemption.[33] In the scholarly literature on Schleiermacher's historical image of Jesus, Strauß' criticism has prevailed. Albert Schweitzer also took up this criticism in his research on the historical Jesus. Schleiermacher's life of Jesus "is not a historical but a dialectical achievement. Nowhere else is it so clear that the great dialectician was actually an unhistorical thinker, as precisely in his treatment of the story of Jesus."[34] The argument is simply that Schleiermacher transfers the image of Jesus Christ from *The Christian Faith* to history. Since he gave his first lectures on the Life of Jesus while at the same time working on *The Christian Faith*, this assumption arises naturally.[35]

But was Schleiermacher really concerned with the historical Jesus, who is to function as the foundation of the Christian faith, as the history of research has assumed so far? The outline of Schleiermacher's lectures already makes it clear that the public proclamation of Jesus is the focus of his interest. Jesus Christ is above all a public teacher. What he proclaims is the kingdom of God, and this is one with himself. If we have this in mind, we can see another dimension of Schleiermacher's lectures. What Schleiermacher presented to his audience is not so

---

[30] Cf. *VLJ*, pp. 102 (Schleiermacher 1832), 148f. (Wolff 1823), 327 (Collin 1832).

[31] *VLJ*, p. 10 (Schleiermacher 1832).

[32] Strauß, *Der Christus des Glaubens*, p. vii.

[33] David Friedrich Strauß, *Das Leben Jesu, kritisch bearbeitet*, 2 vols. (Tübingen: Osiander, 1835/1836), vol. 2, pp. 711–720. Ferdinand Christian Baur criticizes Schleiermacher's Christology in the same manner; Baur, *Lehrbuch der Dogmengeschichte* (Stuttgart: Ad. Becher's Verlag, 1847), pp. 253–256, 273f. Cf. Maureen Junker-Kenny, *Self, Christ and God in Schleiermacher's Dogmatics: A Theology Reconceived for Modernity* (Berlin/Boston: De Gruyter, 2020), pp. 109–125.

[34] Schweitzer, *Geschichte*, p. 100.

[35] For a more differentiated picture of the relationship between *The Life of Jesus* and *The Christian Faith*, Dietz Lange pleads and elaborates the historical claim of Schleiermacher's lectures. Cf. Lange, *Historischer Jesus und mythischer Christus. Untersuchungen zu dem Gegensatz zwischen Friedrich Schleiermacher und David Friedrich Strauß* (Gütersloh: Gütersloher Verlagshaus Mohn, 1975), pp. 57–172.

much an empirical image of the historical Jesus as it is an exemplary religious biography. This becomes clear when one takes care to emphasize the religious viewpoint of the representation throughout. In this respect Schleiermacher was concerned less with an image of the historical Jesus than with a religious image of the man from Nazareth. This is because the religious consciousness is a historical consciousness. It is attached to the history of Jesus, to which it traces itself. There is also another aspect. As Halvor Moxnes has shown, in his portrayal of the life of Jesus, the Berlin theologian also portrayed his own time in Germany.[36] This becomes visible in the way Schleiermacher presented Jesus as a public teacher for his people in his lectures. Against the background of the debates about the national unity of Germany after the Napoleonic wars, Jesus comes into view, as it were, as a teacher of the nation.

> Schleiermacher's presentation of Jesus was part of Schleiermacher's ongoing attempt to form a new subjectivity, to provide an image of Jesus as human person, as a model to be imitated. The challenge that Schleiermacher faced was to explain how a person who belonged to "his time, age and people" could have exemplary character, so that the knowledge of Jesus in his historical setting could be of practical value in the present.[37]

23.3 Schleiermacher's Interpretation of the Life of Jesus

23.3.1 The Introduction to the Life of Jesus

Schleiermacher opened each introduction to his lectures with methodological investigations. Here he discussed three themes. The first is the problem of a life-story characterized with a tension between history and chronicle; the second is the dilemma of a historical view of Jesus Christ; and the third is the difficulty of the sources for a life of Jesus. Schleiermacher concluded his introductions with a presentation of the structure of the life of Jesus. Thus there are two important things in the introductions: the insight that every history of Jesus is a construction and the religious point of view on the history of Jesus. As we will see, Schleiermacher's life of the historical Jesus is a religious interpretation of the history of Jesus and not a mere historical interpretation.

A life-story is not a chronicle, but a history or a narration of a life in its unity. For this reason, a life-story of Jesus of Nazareth must be more than a mere chronicle, but must seek to present the unity of his life, as Schleiermacher explained at the beginning of his lectures. But the unity of a life-story does not lie on the surface of biographical data and actions. Our sources are stories about Jesus recorded in the Gospels. But the Gospels differ from each other, as they tell their stories from different perspectives. So there are many methodological and hermeneutical problems for the project of telling the story of the life of Jesus. Schleiermacher was well aware of these problems; but the task remains to give a life-story

---

[36] Halvor Moxnes, *Jesus and the Rise of Nationalism: A New Quest for the Nineteenth-Century Historical Jesus* (London/New York: I.B. Tauris, 2012), pp. 61–93.
[37] Ibid., 69.

of Jesus, and this requires searching out the inward unity of his development,[38] for this is what constitutes the idea of a life-story. This task requires more than exegetical investigation. As Schleiermacher explained, exegetical research into the Gospels during his time had still not yet arrived at its final conclusion.[39] Furthermore, exegetical investigation leads only to narrow results and not to a complete image of Jesus in his time.[40] The image of the life-story of Jesus is a construction, and this is exactly the task of the lectures. Schleiermacher was convinced that "a real lively unity of the person and of the character of Jesus" underlies all the Gospel stories about the life of Jesus.[41] This unity does not arise through exegetical investigation alone. It is a historical construction, and at the same time the criterion of correct exegesis.[42]

But the project of telling a life-story of Jesus is confronted by two further difficulties. Jesus is a historical person and at the same time a part of his own time and his nation and people. Here Schleiermacher used terms like "Volksthümlichkeit" and "Gesamtleben."[43] In using these terms from contemporary debates about the German nation, Schleiermacher portrayed Jesus as part of his people. Understanding this relationship correctly is a problem in itself. But this problem is further compounded by an additional issue. Jesus is not only a part of his nation, he is also at the same time the founder of the Christian religion. In the Christian religion Jesus Christ is the redeemer, and this means that he is more than a mere human. For the Christian faith, Christ as redeemer is "übermenschlich."[44] But for a *übermenschliches* being history is not possible. A historical understanding leads to an image of a Jesus who is not different from other humans. Yet, as a mere historical being, Jesus could only be the accidental beginning of the Christian religion. The project of offering a life-story of Jesus thus faces a dilemma: the historical understanding of Jesus leads to a rejection of the *übermenschlichen* elements, and from the point of view of Jesus as *übermenschlich*, no historical image of the founder of the Christian religion is possible.

Schleiermacher's solution to this dilemma derives from his theory of religion. The consciousness of God, which is universally present in all humans, is also in Jesus Christ. But it is in him in a particular way—"not in the general way as it is in us."[45] In Jesus, God-consciousness is constant; therefore the high point of religion in history is realized in him. What follows from this is that Jesus Christ is at the same time both a true human being and different from all other humans. The consciousness of God, or the higher self-consciousness, is the inner life of Jesus, and all outer acts and expressions of Jesus are human. Furthermore,

---

[38] Cf. *VLJ*, p. 101 (Schleiermacher 1832).

[39] Schleiermacher engages the Gospel scholarship of his time extensively in *Ueber die Schriften des Lukas. Ein Versuch*, KGA I.8, pp. 5–180.

[40] *VLJ*, p. 138 (Wolff 1823); cf. Ulrich Barth, "Hermeneutik der Evangelien als Prolegomena zur Christologie," in *Zwischen historischem Jesus und dogmatischem Christus. Zum Stand der Christologie im 21. Jahrhundert*, ed. Christian Danz and Michael Murrmann-Kahl (Tübingen: Mohr Siebeck, ²2011), pp. 279–282.

[41] *VLJ*, p. 139 (Wolff 1823).

[42] Cf. Simon Gerber, *Schleiermachers Kirchengeschichte* (Tübingen: Mohr Siebeck, 2015), pp. 63–184; Hermann Patsch, "Schleiermachers Berliner Exegetik," in *Schleiermacher Handbuch*, ed. Martin Ohst (Tübingen: Mohr Siebeck, 2017), pp. 327–340.

[43] *VLJ*, pp. 314 (Collin 1832), 101 (Schleiermacher 1832).

[44] *VLJ*, p. 140 (Wolff 1823).

[45] *VLJ*, p. 143 (Wolff 1823).

it is here in the lectures regarding the historical Jesus that the theory of religion replaces the old doctrine of the two natures of Christ.[46] In presenting his own account Schleiermacher stresses the analogy with the Holy Spirit: just as the Spirit is in humans who are reborn, so is the consciousness of God in Jesus Christ. Both the reborn and Jesus remain human, because both cases describe the emergence of religion. This gives Schleiermacher the possibility for a solution to the main problem of contemporary theology, which is to satisfy both "the practical need to understand Christ in a purely human way and the interest of faith to put the divine into him."[47] From this results a more precise formulation of the task of giving a life-story of Jesus Christ. To search for the living inward unity of the life-story of Jesus means to describe his inner consciousness of God on the basis of the outer expressions recorded in the Gospels.

Another difficulty arises with the sources for a life-story of Jesus. The New Testament Gospels are the only sources for this project; but in fact they are "inauspicious" for the task.[48] To be sure, the Gospels tell a story of Jesus; but what is missing is a continuous story. Schleiermacher's solution to this difficulty is twofold. On the one hand, he declared that it is not necessary to give a continuous story of the life of Jesus: it is more important to explain the historical continuity between Jesus and the Christian religion. And on the other hand, Schleiermacher preferred the Gospel of John to the Synoptic Gospels. He regarded John as an eyewitness of the story of Jesus, because John is the disciple whom Jesus loved (John 21:20). Both John and Matthew are regarded as eyewitnesses in the church tradition. But for Schleiermacher, in contrast to the old tradition, Matthew is not really an eyewitness to the story of Jesus. Thus Schleiermacher's own story of the life of Jesus depends primarily on John. This position is not without its consequences, and its implications for the image of the life of Jesus have often been noted.[49] For Schleiermacher, Jesus travels repeatedly between Jerusalem and Galilee, whereas in the Synoptic Gospels he comes to Jerusalem only once.

Schleiermacher's preference for the Gospel of John is one of the main points on which his life of Jesus was criticized. By the time the book was published in 1864, New Testament research had rejected the Gospel of John as a source of history. But there are other reasons for Schleiermacher's preference for the fourth evangelist. They are related to his idea of the life of Jesus but also with his hermeneutic.[50] First of all, he believed that John offers a continuous account of the life of Jesus and not only chronicles like the Synoptics. He was also convinced that Jesus cannot be understood apart from his people and his nation. And it is exactly this connection that Schleiermacher finds in John: "*Concerning the development of relationships with the nation. Here again John must be the guide. The others [sc. the Synoptics] too little order in the temporal relations, that one can hardly use them where it depends on*

---

[46] Cf. *VLJ*, pp. 104 (Schleiermacher 1832), 143 (Wolff 1823).
[47] *VLJ*, p. 104 (Schleiermacher 1832).
[48] *VLJ*, p. 146 (Wolff 1823).
[49] Cf. Schweitzer, *Geschichte*, pp. 103–105.
[50] Cf. Daniel Weidner, *Bibel und Literatur um 1800* (München: Wilhelm Fink, 2011), pp. 317–337; Christian Danz, "Empfänglichkeit und Selbsttätigkeit. Friedrich Schleiermachers Deutung des Johannes-Evangeliums und ihre religionsphilosophischen, theologischen und hermeneutischen Grundlagen," in *Schleiermacher und das Neue Testament. Expeditionen in die Welt seiner exegetischen Vorlesungen*, ed. André Munzinger, Enno Edzard Popkes, Ralph Brucker, and Dirk Schmid (Berlin/Boston: De Gruyter, 2023), pp. 145–159.

finding an increase. Whereas with Johannes a pragmatic tendency is unmistakable."[51] For Schleiermacher Jesus is primarily the public teacher of his nation. Because the Nazarene teaches publicly, he cannot have any esoteric doctrine. This also rules out the assumption, found in the research of the time, that Jesus had contact with the Essenes.

23.3.2 The History of Jesus from his Birth until the Begin of his Public Ministry

Every biography begins with the birth of its hero. So does that of Jesus Christ. But sources for his birth and the history of his youth are scarce. John does not mention this period. In his depiction of the childhood story of Jesus, Schleiermacher drew on Luke and the Gospel of Matthew to discuss the stories of Jesus' birth and of the twelve-year-old in the temple.

In addition, Schleiermacher's life of Jesus aspires to a religious, and not merely a historical, point of view on Jesus' birth and youth. "When Christ was born, how old he was when he took up his magisterium, whether he was exactly 30 years old or older, is of little interest to us. It is a matter for the chronologist, not the theologian."[52] What is important is the consciousness of God in Jesus as this does not depend on specific historical details, so too it does not depend on the precise manner of his birth. The sinlessness of Jesus is the particular kind of God-consciousness that he possesses. The claim that Jesus is, from the beginning of his life, the fullest realization of religion in history is found in both Schleiermacher's lectures on *The Life of Jesus* and *The Christian Faith*, and for both texts this is a miracle.[53] In his lectures Schleiermacher discussed the stories about the birth of Jesus from Luke and Matthew. He regarded Matthew as preferable to Luke, on the grounds that the latter offered a poetic presentation of the story with the aim of bringing Jesus and John the Baptist together. Schleiermacher pointed out that the stories from Matthew and Luke about the birth of Jesus have a historical core, but he regarded the absence of a human father in Jesus' immaculate conception superfluous.

With the birth of Jesus, his human development begins. The basis and foundation of his development is his consciousness of God. From this it follows that Jesus' development is a matter of his becoming progressively aware of this consciousness. His is a development like all other humans, with the exception that it is a development without sin, guilt, or error. The completion of the education of Jesus is represented by the story of the twelve-year-old Jesus in the Temple in Jerusalem.[54] By this time Jesus is aware of his inner unity with God, so that his higher self-consciousness constantly determines his lower self-consciousness. But what then does education mean for Jesus? For Schleiermacher, Jesus received a common education and read the Scriptures. Each "boy was instructed in the law to a certain degree, he had to know the customs and holy signs, and the dignity of the holy persons"; in addition, there was "the study of the language in which the holy books were written."[55] But all of

---

[51] *VLJ*, p. 131 (Schleiermacher 1832); cf. p. 457 (Collin 1832), and also Moxnes, *Jesus*, pp. 67f.
[52] *VLJ*, p. 150 (Wolff 1823).
[53] Cf. CG^2, pp. 47f. (§94.3).
[54] Cf. *VLJ*, p. 167 (Wolff 1823).
[55] *VLJ*, p. 353 (Collin 1832).

Jesus' religious knowledge derived from himself, and not from external sources, including the Scriptures. His knowledge was without error. In virtue of this knowledge Jesus understood the prophets of the Old Testament better than they understood themselves.[56] Jesus did not receive his idea of the Messiah from the Old Testament, but rather he received this idea from himself like all other religious notions. Although "the view of the messianic idea, [and of] the shape of the outlines of the Kingdom of God" developed "gradually" in him, these differed from the Jews' secular-political conception of the Messiah and his work from the very beginning.[57]

It is crucial that Jesus' development, from his birth until the beginning of his public ministry, is continuous. There is no breakthrough of a higher inspiration or anything similar, because the basis for the life of Jesus from its beginning is his unity with God in his inward self-consciousness. This constitutes the personality of Jesus and the basis of his actions.

23.3.3 The Public Ministry of Jesus

The story of the twelve-year-old Jesus in the Temple represents for Schleiermacher the culmination of his development. By this time Jesus had become aware of his own self-consciousness of God, and therefore his unity with God was the inward basis of all his actions. Prior to his public ministry Jesus studied the Scriptures for himself, and not as a member of a school for interpretation of the Scriptures, and by the start of his public teaching his development was complete. In this respect the transition to public proclamation consisted in the fact that Jesus' inner God-consciousness passed over into external communication.[58] In his presentation Schleiermacher distinguishes between an inner and an outer dimension of the public ministry of Jesus up to his arrest. The outer dimension includes the localities and circumstances of Jesus' public teaching and acting, while the inner dimension Schleiermacher understood as Jesus' teaching and his establishment of the church. Precisely this—the relationship of the public preaching of Jesus to his people, which serves as a model for Schleiermacher's own time—is the focus of interest of the lectures.[59]

Because Schleiermacher preferred the Gospel of John, Jerusalem is the center of Jesus' activities. Similar to Johann Gottlieb Fichte, Jesus held his public speeches in the Temple of the capital.[60] Galilee, which is the main place of Jesus' activity for the Synoptics, retreats into the background. According to Schleiermacher Jesus was not poor, for he was a public teacher: "teachers and scribes formed the excellent part of the nation, and therefore they enjoyed excellent respect."[61] Jesus taught in synagogues, gave occasional public speeches, spoke about doctrinal things, and in the private sphere spoke with his disciples. His baptism by John the Baptist represented the beginning not of his own teaching, but rather his own baptizing.[62] For the theological tradition, as for Schleiermacher, the baptism of Jesus is

---

[56] Cf. *VLJ*, pp. 182f. (Wolff 1823).
[57] *VLJ*, p. 183 (Wolff 1823).
[58] Cf. *VLJ*, p. 363 (Collin 1832).
[59] Cf. Moxnes, *Jesus*, p. 69.
[60] *VLJ*, p. 203 (Wolff 1823).
[61] *VLJ*, p. 353 (Collin 1832); cf. Moxnes, *Jesus*, p. 83.
[62] Cf. *VLJ*, pp. 109f. (Schleiermacher 1832), 187–194 (Wolff 1823), 362–366 (Collin 1832).

a problem, because Jesus is without sin. Why then the baptism? But a further problem arose for Schleiermacher. If Jesus knows himself as the Messiah from the beginning of his public ministry, why then are there miracles, and the Holy Spirit descending as a dove on Jesus? Schleiermacher argued that this is all for the sake of John the Baptist, so that he would receive the conviction that Jesus was the Messiah. Furthermore, the baptism of Jesus is an act of duty. With his own baptism Jesus confessed that he was a part of his national community. "Like every human being, Christ was both an individual and a member of his people; i.e. he was put under the law, i.e. under the association of the Jewish people."[63] Being a part of the community of his own people is a necessary element in the realization of the kingdom of God.

The public teaching of Jesus and his establishment of the church are interrelated. The miracles of Jesus are also a part of this task.[64] Schleiermacher downplayed the miracles, arguing that belief in their occurrence is not necessary for Christian faith. These miracles are strictly related to Jesus' teaching and his task of founding a community, which means that they are outer expressions of his inward unity with God. They have a spiritual effect and therefore a common moral significance as a part of Jesus' teaching. The content of Jesus' teaching is the kingdom of God. But the content of his doctrine is Jesus himself. His ministry and teaching is the interpretation of the Scriptures of the Old Testament.[65] Because the consciousness of God is the basis of all of Jesus' actions, and because this self-consciousness is perfect, it is not possible that Jesus could give an incorrect interpretation of the Old Testament. His interpretation of the Scriptures is not allegorical, and yields their true sense. "So he considers himself to be the fulfillment of the messianic idea laid down in the Old Testament. The Jewish idea was admittedly strongly political, which was dropped with Christ."[66] With his interpretation of the Jewish religion as well as its messiah idea Schleiermacher follows those of his time.

Schleiermacher discusses several aspects of Jesus' teaching—for example, his doctrines of God and the Spirit, and his eschatology. All these themes are expressions of his inner self-consciousness. But Jesus' teaching is connected with the foundation of the church. As in *The Christian Faith*, in the lectures the person of Jesus Christ is intertwined with his "vocation."[67] So Jesus' communication of the kingdom of God is the communication of his person and at the same time of the community of life with him. Therefore in his teaching he takes up the people in the new community of life that he founded. Thus faith, or unity with Jesus, is a matter of receiving the communication of his higher self-consciousness. Jesus communicates his consciousness of God, and the higher self-consciousness of others, beginning with his disciples, arises from this communication. The divine element in Jesus is his higher self-consciousness, which forms the new community. It connects members with Christ and with each other. Thus the center of the new community of life is Jesus Christ.

The new community established by Christ contrasts sharply with the Old Testament one. The latter is a theocracy of which the opposition of priests and laity is constitutive. Christ, on the other hand, establishes a community of equals, in which the opposition of priests

---

[63] *VLJ*, p. 193 (Wolff 1823).
[64] Cf. *VLJ*, pp. 207–229 (Wolff 1823), 391–406 (Collin 1832). Cf. Lange, *Historischer Jesus*, pp. 105–109.
[65] Cf. *VLJ*, pp. 243–249 (Wolff 1823).
[66] *VLJ*, p. 245 (Wolff 1823).
[67] *VLJ*, p. 120 (Schleiermacher 1832).

and laity is abolished. "Furthermore, his vocation was not at all to create a community of a political nature with an external sanction . . . But he teaches in this conviction a perfect equality of all among him."[68] Of course, the community founded by Jesus is not political, but this community model has political consequences. It also functions as an ideal image for Schleiermacher's own time.[69]

23.3.4 The History of the Passion of Jesus Christ

Schleiermacher concluded his presentation of the life of Jesus with the history of his passion. Distinct from the public ministry, the passion, which starts with his arrest, is the second section of the life of Jesus. Whereas during his public ministry Jesus is predominantly active, he is now predominantly passive. In this part of his lectures Schleiermacher discussed the Pharisees' opposition to Jesus; Jesus' captivity, trial, crucifixion, and death; his resurrection; and, finally, his ascension.

The new community founded by Jesus was opposed to the Jewish form of community, as it dissolved its hierarchical foundations. This is indicated in the proclamation of Jesus, which has the latter as its content and is fundamentally directed against Jewish religiosity.[70] This aroused the opposition of the Pharisees, which eventually led to Jesus' trial and the sentence of death. In general the theologian from Berlin discussed the betrayal of Judas against the background of the scholarship of his day. Judas was not a member of the inner circle of the disciples of Jesus—the apostles—but was rather part of the broader circle. The reason for this is that Jesus had a perfect knowledge of people. So it is impossible that Jesus would have included Judas among the apostles. The source for the reports of Jesus' trial, his questioning by the Sanhedrin, his discourse with Pontius Pilate, and the crucifixion is John, because the other disciples had fled. Just as in his dogmatics, in the lectures the death of Jesus Christ has no special significance for the life of Jesus. "[That] the death was absolutely necessary is an untenable claim. Here the historical and the dogmatic intertwine."[71] What is decisive is the unity of divine and human in the continuity of his life. "Everywhere, therefore, death not as something special but as a consequence of life activity, or as a condition of expected fertility."[72] Thus Schleiermacher replaces the traditional doctrine of atonement for which Christ died vicarious for the sins of the world with the consciousness of God as the inner unity of the life of Jesus Christ. Since for Schleiermacher the inner continuity of Jesus' life, that is the constant God-consciousness, is decisive, the Gethsemane narrative can just as little have historicity as can a God-forsakenness of Jesus Christ on the cross.

---

[68] *VLJ*, p. 124 (Schleiermacher 1832); cf. pp. 264–273 (Wolff 1823), 432–435 (Collin 1832), and also Moxnes, *Jesus*, pp. 84–90.

[69] Cf. Moxnes, *Jesus*, p. 88.

[70] Cf. Hermann Fischer, "Jesus und das Judentum nach Schleiermachers 'Leben-Jesu'-Vorlesung," in *Christentum und Judentum. Akten des Internationalen Kongresses der Schleiermacher-Gesellschaft in Halle, März 2009*, ed. Roderich Barth, Ulrich Barth, and Claus-Dieter Osthövener (Berlin/Boston: De Gruyter 2012), pp. 309–324.

[71] *VLJ*, p. 274 (Wolff 1823); cf. Lange, *Historischer Jesus*, pp. 109–111.

[72] *VLJ*, p. 127 (Schleiermacher 1832).

It also follows that the resurrection of Jesus is neither the highpoint of his history nor the starting point of Christianity, as in the later Protestant theology. In his interpretation of the resurrection of Jesus Schleiermacher presented an alternative: on the one hand, if Jesus was dead he could not be resurrected, and on the other, if he was not dead he could be resurrected. For Schleiermacher the latter is "perfectly compatible with the Christian faith."[73] There are two things behind these considerations. First, for Schleiermacher the criterion of death is decay; but this "was not there" with Jesus.[74] And second, in his interpretation of Christ's death and resurrection, what is decisive is the religious point of view, namely "the continuity of the image we have made of Christ, that this remains purely the same until the last moment."[75]

At the end Schleiermacher discussed the ascension of Jesus Christ, which according to him is not a historical fact.[76] The Christian faith begins with the public ministry of Jesus. But for Christianity to become an independent religion, the second death of Jesus (his ascension) was just as necessary as his first death and resurrection. The self-acting religious productivity of the disciples and the church begins with Jesus' departure from this world, and with his spiritual presence in the world through the Holy Spirit.[77]

Suggested Reading

Fischer, Hermann. "Jesus und das Judentum nach Schleiermachers 'Leben-Jesu'-Vorlesung." In *Christentum und Judentum. Akten des Internationalen Kongresses der Schleiermacher-Gesellschaft in Halle, März 2009*, ed. Roderich Barth, Ulrich Barth, and Claus-Dieter Osthövener (Berlin/Boston: De Gruyter 2012), pp. 309–324.

Lange, Dietz. *Historischer Jesus und mythischer Christus. Untersuchungen zu dem Gegensatz zwischen Friedrich Schleiermacher und David Friedrich Strauß* (Gütersloh: Gütersloher Verlagshaus Mohn, 1975).

Moxnes, Halvor. *Jesus and the Rise of Nationalism: A New Quest for the Nineteenth-Century Historical Jesus* (London/New York: I.B. Tauris 2012), pp. 61–93.

Strauß, David Friedrich. *Der Christus des Glaubens und der Jesus der Geschichte. Eine Kritik des Schleiermacher'schen Lebens Jesu* (Berlin: Franz Duncker, 1865).

Bibliography

[Anonymous] *Praelectionum publice privatimque in academia Ienensi, summer curese 1797* (Jena, 1797).

Barth, Ulrich. "Hermeneutik der Evangelien als Prolegomena zur Christologie." In *Zwischen historischem Jesus und dogmatischem Christus. Zum Stand der Christologie im 21.*

---

[73] *VLJ*, p. 299 (Wolff 1823). Cf. pp. 487–505 (Collin 1832), and also Schleiermacher, *Vorlesungen über die Leidens- und Auferstehungsgeschichte (1821)*, in *KGA* 2.15, pp. 511–653.
[74] *VLJ*, p. 481 (Collin 1832).
[75] Ibid.
[76] Cf. *VLJ*, p. 301 (Wolff 1823).
[77] Cf. Schleiermacher's doctrine of the *Gemeingeist*: CG^2, pp. 248–259 (§§121f.).

Jahrhundert, ed. Christian Danz and Michael Murrmann-Kahl (Tübingen: Mohr Siebeck, ²2011), pp. 275–305.

Baur, Ferdinand Christian. *Lehrbuch der Dogmengeschichte* (Stuttgart: Ad. Becher's Verlag, 1847).

Danz, Christian. "Empfänglichkeit und Selbsttätigkeit. Friedrich Schleiermachers Deutung des Johannes-Evangeliums und ihre religionsphilosophischen, theologischen und hermeneutischen Grundlagen." In *Schleiermacher und das Neue Testament. Expeditionen in die Welt seiner exegetischen Vorlesungen*, ed. André Munzinger, Enno Edzard Popkes, Ralph Brucker, and Dirk Schmid (Berlin/Boston: De Gruyter, 2023), pp. 145–159.

Danz, Christian. *Grundprobleme der Christologie* (Tübingen: Mohr Siebeck, 2013).

Danz, Christian. *Jesus von Nazareth zwischen Judentum und Christentum. Eine christologische und religionstheologische Skizze* (Tübingen: Mohr Siebeck, 2020).

Fischer, Hermann. "Jesus und das Judentum nach Schleiermachers 'Leben-Jesu'-Vorlesung." In *Christentum und Judentum. Akten des Internationalen Kongresses der Schleiermacher-Gesellschaft in Halle, März 2009*, ed. Roderich Barth, Ulrich Barth, and Claus-Dieter Osthövener (Berlin/Boston: De Gruyter 2012), pp. 309–324.

Gaß, Wilhelm, ed. *Fr. Schleiermacher's Briefwechsel mit J. Chr. Gaß: mit einer biographischen Vorrede* (Berlin: Reimer, 1852).

Gerber, Simon. *Schleiermachers Kirchengeschichte* (Tübingen: Mohr Siebeck, 2015).

Heß, Johann Jakob. *Geschichte der drey letzten Lebensjahre Jesu*, 2 vols. (Zürich: Orell, 1773).

Junker-Kenny, Maureen. *Self, Christ and God in Schleiermacher's Dogmatics: A Theology Reconceived for Modernity* (Berlin/Boston: De Gruyter, 2020).

Lange, Dietz. *Historischer Jesus und mythischer Christus. Untersuchungen zu dem Gegensatz zwischen Friedrich Schleiermacher und David Friedrich Strauß* (Gütersloh: Gütersloher Verlagshaus Mohn, 1975).

Lessing, Gotthold Ephraim. "Über den Beweis des Geistes und der Kraft." In *Freimäurergespräche und anderes. Ausgewählte Schriften*, ed. Claus Träger (München: Beck, 1981), pp. 29–34.

Moxnes, Halvor. *Jesus and the Rise of Nationalism: A New Quest for the Nineteenth-Century Historical Jesus* (London/New York: I.B. Tauris, 2012).

Ohst, Martin. "Der theologie- und kirchengeschichtliche Hintergrund des Atheismusstreits." In *Fichtes Entlassung. Der Atheismusstreit vor 200 Jahren*, ed. Klaus-Michael Kodalle and Martin Ohst (Würzburg: Königshausen & Neumann, 1999), pp. 31–47.

Patsch, Hermann. "Schleiermachers Berliner Exegetik." In *Schleiermacher Handbuch*, ed. Martin Ohst (Tübingen: Mohr Siebeck, 2017), pp. 327–340.

Paulus, Heinrich Eberhard Gottlob. *Philologisch-kritischer und historischer Commentar über das Neue Testament*, vols. I–IV (Lübeck: Johann Friedrich Bohn, 1800–1804).

[Reimarus, Hermann Samuel.] *Vom Zwecke Jesu und seiner Jünger. Noch ein Fragment des Wolfenbüttelschen Ungenannten*, ed. Gotthold Ephraim Lessing (Braunschweig, 1778).

Reventlow, Henning Graf. *History of Biblical Interpretation, Vol. 4: From Enlightenment to the Twentieth Century* (Atlanta: Society of Biblical Literature, 2010).

Rütenik, Karl August, ed. *Das Leben Jesu: Vorlesungen an der Universität zu Berlin im Jahr 1832* (Berlin: Reimer, 1864).

Schleiermacher, Friedrich. *Exegetische Schriften*, KGA 1.8, ed. Hermann Patsch and Dirk Schmid (Berlin: De Gruyter, 2001).

Schleiermacher, Friedrich. *Vorlesungen über das Leben Jesu, Vorlesung über die Leidens- und Auferstehungsgeschichte*, KGA 2.15, ed. Walter Jaeschke (Berlin: De Gruyter, 2018).

Schweitzer, Albert. *Geschichte der Leben-Jesu-Forschung*, vol. 1 (München/Hamburg: Siebenstern Taschenbuch Verlag, 1966).

Semler, Johann Salomo. *Beantwortung der Fragmente eines Ungenannten insbesondere vom Zweck Jesu und seiner Jünger* (Halle: Verlag des Erziehungsinstituts, 1779).

Strauß, David Friedrich. *Der Christus des Glaubens und der Jesus der Geschichte. Eine Kritik des Schleiermacher'schen Lebens Jesu* (Berlin: Franz Duncker, 1865).

Strauß, David Friedrich. *Das Leben Jesu, kritisch bearbeitet*, 2 vols. (Tübingen: Osiander, 1835/1836).

Weidner, Daniel. *Bibel und Literatur um 1800* (München: Wilhelm Fink, 2011).

CHAPTER 24

SCHLEIERMACHER AS A SCRIPTURAL EXEGETE

HERMANN PATSCH

Friedrich Schleiermacher was a universal genius. Whatever scientific discipline he tackled—be it theological disciplines (with the exception of the Old Testament), philosophy, Greek studies, pedagogy and psychology, or translation studies—his results were formative, and still capture attention in the present day. This also applies to his work as a New Testament scholar, even if the number of his publications, with two monographs and two essays, is itself modest. He lectured on the New Testament at Halle and Berlin for forty-two semesters; the impact of all this instruction has been chronicled in the history of the discipline.[1] When he took over his professorship in Berlin in 1812, he was appointed head of the department for New Testament exegesis. One can only guess at the extent of his work in that position; its influence on students can hardly be overestimated. And one must not forget that this work coincided with his preaching on New Testament texts in his vicarage. His academic work as a university teacher was never an end in itself.

When he was appointed associate professor of theology and philosophy at the University of Halle in 1804, Schleiermacher had not yet acquired a single academic title and was not recognized by a single scientific work, in the strict sense of the term, on academic theological subjects. As early as the winter semester 1805/1806 he dared to offer public (i.e. unpaid) exegetical lectures on Paul's letter to the Galatians in front of an unusually large audience, and as a hermeneut he set his own standards from the start.[2] In addition to his academic success, these lectures were so important for his own understanding of Paul as an author that they were the occasion for a continuous course, "Interpretationis Librorum Novi Testamenti," which he taught over several semesters. There followed in the summer semester of 1806 a

---

[1] See Werner Georg Kümmel, *Das Neue Testament. Geschichte der Erforschung seiner Probleme* (Freiburg: Karl Alber, 1958); Hermann Patsch, *Schleiermachers Berliner Exegetik*. Schleiermacher Handbuch, ed. Martin Ohst (Tübingen: Mohr Siebeck, 2017), pp. 327–340; and Eckart David Schmidt, *Jesus in Geschichte, Erzählung und Idee. Perspektiven der Jesusrezeption in der Bibelwissenschaft der Aufklärung, der Romantik und des Idealismus* (Tübingen: Mohr Siebeck, 2022).

[2] See Hermann Patsch, "'. . . mit Interesse die eigentliche Theologie wieder hervorsuchen.' Schleiermachers theologische Schriften der Hallenser Zeit," in *Friedrich Schleiermacher in Halle*, ed. Andreas Arndt (Berlin: De Gruyter, 2013), pp. 31–54.

course on the greater letters of Paul, during which he wrote self-confidently to his friend J. C. Gass that "I hope soon to understand the apostle Paul as well as I understand Plato himself."[3]

This sentence reveals an important indication of Schleiermacher's way of working. With the ongoing work of his Plato translation (beginning in 1804), inherited from the early Romantic beginnings with Friedrich Schlegel, he was familiar with questions of authenticity and historical classification. This work required the application of the historical-philological methods of textual explanation of the historical-grammatical school, as they had become mandatory through Christian Gottlob Heyne in Göttingen and Friedrich August Wolf in Halle, and which Schleiermacher would use with ease. However, it also required the hermeneutical search for the author's individuality, which could not be achieved solely through an editorial philology focused on grammatical structures, but rather only through the interaction of grammatical and psychological interpretation. The question of the author's personality had become pressing since Wolf, in his *Prolegomena ad Homerum* (1795), had divided the poetic figure of Homer, admired since antiquity, into individual figures of an entire Homeric school. The same claim was also asserted regarding some of Plato's works, not least by Schleiermacher's friend Schlegel. In any case, ascriptions of authorship accepted through long traditions were suddenly declared to be in need of justification. The mere reference to tradition as such was no longer sufficient. In the end, this also had to apply to the biblical writings. If Schleiermacher wanted to understand the Paul of the principal New Testament writings as a person like Plato, then he had to look for criteria beyond the mere ascriptions of Christian antiquity. And then, as with Plato, the decision could be made in such a way that there could be pseudonymous works. In view of the force of tradition and the theologically explosive nature of such claims, this was of course a courageous conclusion, which no one before him had drawn so forthrightly for the letters handed down under the name of Paul.

24.1 Schleiermacher's Monograph on the First Epistle to Timothy

Schleiermacher did not clearly find the Paul whom he had reconstructed from the Epistle to the Galatians, the Epistle to the Corinthians, and the Epistle to the Romans to be visible in the First Epistle to Timothy. This was the decisive realization that he had come to in his preparation for the lectures announced for the winter semester of 1806/1807 on the lesser Epistles of Paul and Hebrews.[4] When this became clear to him, and with the abolition of the University of Halle in 1806 by Napoleon having left him without employment or income, he must have decided to share this new conviction in print with a general, educated public rather than with his academic audience. His vehicle was of course not the Latin dissertation that should have identified him as a professor (this was never in fact produced), but a 239-page German "Sendbrief" sent to an unknown consistorial assessor and field preacher, which would be printed as a public circular: *On the so-called first Epistle of Paul to Timotheus. A Critical letter*

---

[3] *KGA* 5.9, p. 58.
[4] Andreas Arndt and Wolfgang Virmond, eds., *Schleiermachers Briefwechsel (Verzeichnis) nebst einer Liste seiner Vorlesungen*, Schleiermacher-Archiv 11 (Berlin: De Gruyter, 1992), p. 302.

to J [oachim] C [hristian] Gaß.[5] But with its myriad Greek quotations, the book was not written for a lay audience; it assumed a theologically and philologically educated reader.

The "so-called" in the title signals the work's hypothesis: The First Epistle to Timothy is a pseudonymous work. The form of this monograph is clearly a bit of Romantic cheek: it is an almost unstructured body of text that begins with "You remember, my dearest friend," and ends after 239 pages with "Farewell." There had never been anything like it before in biblical scholarship, and neither has there been anything like it since. And it created the "fear of Deuteropaulinism"; that is, the fear that through historical-theological methodology all religious security that results from the examination of the Holy Scriptures will be lost.[6] Schleiermacher was enough of a theologian to comment on this fear in advance in his book.

What did his philological-hermeneutic skill look like? Schleiermacher made use of all the philological and historical implements of available scholarship, as is also known from the surviving notes from his lectures, and these were extensive. In the end, he was amused by the glossators, lexicographers, and interpreters with their "castigations" or learned chastisements, but he knew them all.[7] What was important to him was not at all to introduce new historical-philological material to the biblical text—apart from occasional observations (Plato, perhaps Plutarch), it came from secondhand—but rather to ask new questions about the text with the help of this material. These new questions required new answers.

The biblical text that Schleiermacher quotes in the *Sendbrief* is the *textus receptus* according to what at the time was the latest status of the New Testament textual criticism, as it had just been presented to the scholarly public in the new edition by Johann Jakob Griesbach.[8] We know from biographical remarks that Schleiermacher familiarized himself with the Greek vocabulary through the cursory reading of the native speakers; that is, through the commentaries of the Church Fathers, here through Chrysostom, Oecumenius, Theodoret, and Theophylact. He owned some of these commentaries in his private library and quoted them in the course of his argument. Further evidence from the Church Fathers was provided by the annotations in Hugo Grotius' *Novum Testamentum* of 1646; Schleiermacher found the classical ancient material in the exemplarily learned comments in the 1752 edition of the New Testament by Johann Jakob Wettstein. Schleiermacher was not, however, interested in rabbinics. The excellent lexicon on the Greek New Testament by Johann Friedrich Schleusner in the second edition of 1801, which he consulted for every word, was extremely important to him. Schleusner drew attention to the *hapax legomena* with a "*saepius non legitur*" and thus provided Schleiermacher with one of his main arguments. Whether he used Erasmus Schmid's New Testament concordance from 1717 or Abraham Tromm's LXX concordance from 1718 cannot be established with certainty. Schleusner also referred him to the earlier encyclopedias by Johann Caspar Suicer (1682), Julius Pollux (1706), and Johann Christian Biel (1779/1780), which Schleiermacher

---

[5] Friedrich Schleiermacher, *Ueber den sogenannten ersten Brief des Paulos an den Timotheos. Ein kritisches Sendschreiben an J. C. Gaß* (Berlin: Reimer, 1807); *KGA* 1.5, pp. 157–242.

[6] See Hermann Patsch, "The Fear of Deutero-Paulinism: The Reception of Friedrich Schleiermacher's 'Critical Open Letter' concerning 1 Timothy in the First Quinquenium," trans. Darrell J. Doughty, *The Journal of Higher Criticism* 6, no. 1 (Spring 1999), pp. 3–31.

[7] *KGA* 1.5, p. 241; cf. pp. xcvii–c.

[8] See Johann Jacob Griesbach, *Novum Testamentum Graece*, Volumen II, *Epistolas omnes et apokalypsin complectens*, Editio secunda (London: Impensis J. Mackinlay, et Cuthell et Martin, 1806).

then cited several times. In exegetical monographs on the pastoral letters, he consistently used the work of his contemporary Johannes Heinrich Heinrichs, *Paulli Epistolae ad Timotheum Titum et Philomenum Graece* from 1798, which was designed as a line-by-line commentary. He also made occasional use of George Benson's *Paraphrastic Explanation and Notes on some Books of the New Testament* of 1761 and Johann Lorenz von Mosheim's *De rebus christianorum ante Constantinum magnum commentarii* of 1753, while expressing reservations about both works. At the end of the work, Schleiermacher makes use of church-historical evidence pertaining to the office of deaconess from Joseph Bingham's *Origines sive antiquitates ecclesiasticae* of 1724 and 1751, respectively. Schleiermacher thus proved to be thoroughly well read and learned in the old philological sense. However, the decisive factor was not this knowledge, which others also had and which was assumed by all in scientific exegesis, but rather the new conclusions he drew.

Schleiermacher's "epistolary" work (as he described it), which appeared without any textual divisions, can be divided into a semantic-linguistic part and a genre-analytical part, in addition to preliminary and the concluding remarks.[9] In his survey of the vocabulary (*Sprachschätze*) of the epistles,[10] Schleiermacher immediately emphasizes the quite disproportionate peculiarity of the language of the first letter to Timothy compared to the other Pauline Epistles. Already in verse 3 the exegete classifies "strange" ἑτεροδιδασκαλεῖν, which occurs twice in this letter, as non-Pauline. This does not contradict the fact that the Church Fathers know the verb. And so it goes word for word up to the end of the sixth chapter, fifty printed pages long, with the conclusion that the presence of "completely foreign words" instead of the Pauline "favorite expressions" suggest a "clumsy compiler" who must have worked at a later time than the apostolic.[11] This is also confirmed for him in comparison with the Epistles of Titus and 2 Timothy. Here Schleiermacher sees semantic similarities between the first half of 1 Timothy and the letter of Titus, and between the second half and 2 Timothy. He interprets these as literary dependencies, with a "suspicious scent of later times."[12] In contrast, the historical difficulties could not be resolved if Pauline authorship were accepted.

Schleiermacher began again, however, by examining the style of the letter in comparison with the recognized Pauline epistles. This is certainly the most creative part of the investigation, in that, unlike semantic analysis, it could not rely on secondary literature at any point. Perhaps Schleiermacher can be called a pioneer of the epistolographic history of forms. For him, 1 Timothy is neither an instructional letter nor a familiar letter, but rather a "rather poorly fictitious script" that is "completely unworthy of the apostle."[13] What it lacks is "an object ... that forms a unity, such that the whole can, with all expression of confidence, be regarded at the same time as a representation of the religious attitude [*Gesinnung*] itself under these circumstances."[14] According to the general characterization of the types of letters, Schleiermacher finds no "comprehensible connection" in the first letter in comparison with the letter to Titus and the letter of 2 Timothy.[15] Schleiermacher does not find what he will

---

[9] *KGA* 1.5, p. xcvi.
[10] *KGA* 1.5, p.165.
[11] *KGA* 1.5, pp. 186f.
[12] *KGA* 1.5, p. 200.
[13] *KGA* 1.5, p. 204.
[14] *KGA* 1.5, p. 205.
[15] *KGA* 1.5, p. 211.

call the "unity of the work as a fact of the author" in his hermeneutics.[16] Somewhat laboriously, and in constant conversation with the Church Fathers and the church-historical evidence in Joseph Bingham, he locates the meaning of the pseudepigraphic creation, which he dates to the end of the first century, among other things, in the strengthening of the office of deaconess.

The impact of Schleiermacher's monograph grows from the abundance of linguistic observations, especially the *hapax legomena*, and the evidence of the unstructured nature of the literary "will." He could not find the personality of the author, as he had been able to do, through the psychological method, in Plato and in the great Pauline letters. In the end he was only able to state that the search for a historical development of such an author was to be regarded as "ridiculous" and was consequently ultimately superfluous.[17]

Schleiermacher did not write this monograph only as a historian who wanted to understand a work of the past, nor simply as a politically engaged scholar—in the closing sentences he interpreted his choice of the German language for a scientific work after the fall of Halle in a nationalist and anti-Napoleonic way[18]—he of course also wrote as a theologian. He was well aware that the criticism of his radical hypothesis of pseudo-Paulinism at the end of the first century was bound to cause offense in church circles. He immediately commented on this at the beginning of the book. Since he was confident of his approach, he could directly deal with the theological problem before he began with the historical-critical work.

In these prolegomena (if one may so call them), Schleiermacher referred to a principle of his general hermeneutics, in not wanting the books of the New Testament to be subject to any rules other than those established by the "old grammarians," and also in not wanting to include any of them as part of a collection but treating each rather as a standalone whole.[19] He believed that adherents of the doctrine of inspiration should also be able to agree with this position. But with this invitation he had already lured them into the trap: If it then becomes evident that a book deviates completely, both in the use of the words and idioms as well as in the phrase and the context of the thoughts of the other writings of the same writer—in this case, Paul—one could not assume "almost foolishly" that the Holy Spirit was responsible for this. For Schleiermacher this would be a "limited view of the holy letter that I cannot contemplate without partly complaining about it and partly becoming agitated about it."[20] The "divine prestige" of the holy books could ultimately not be derived from the collection of biblical books, because then the divinity of Christianity itself would be merely derivative; rather, it derives from the divinity of Christianity itself. He called this the "higher insight," according to which a pseudonymous but "genuinely Christian writing" could then be used in preaching without hesitation.[21] In the end that was important to the lifelong preacher Schleiermacher.

The focus on the individuality of Paul, which Schleiermacher pursued to the establishment of pseudo-Paulinism, gave rise to a plan for a Latin critical edition (including commentary) of the "real" letters of Paul, which he intended to supercede the *textus receptus*: *Divi*

---

[16] VHK, pp. 171–172.
[17] KGA 1.5, p. 240.
[18] KGA 1.5, pp. 241–242.
[19] KGA 1.5, p. 158.
[20] KGA 1.5, p. 159.
[21] KGA 1.5, p. 159.

Pauli quae exstant—Denuo recensuit et commentario instruxit DF Schleiermacher. This focus on Paul as a writer-subject would have been innovative in any case if he had been able to execute this plan, from which a partial manuscript has been preserved.[22] To this day there is no such special edition. Such a work perhaps would have been similar to his contributions to the Plato edition by Ludwig Heindorf.[23]

24.2 On the Writings of Luke

Schleiermacher also influenced research on Synoptics. With the opening of the Berlin University and thus the theological faculty, of which he was appointed dean, he immediately began to lecture on Luke-Acts in the first winter semester of 1810/1811. That was the beginning of his research on Luke, which led to a critical attempt at a monograph.[24] He worked out this material in parallel with his lecture of 1816/1817. A second part on Acts, the introduction to which was prepared for printing and has been preserved,[25] and a third part on the language of Luke would have followed, but the overworked Schleiermacher never completed these works. This plan for a work on Gospel linguistics also pointed to the future.

Schleiermacher's introduction to the Acts of the Apostles reveals the development process of his exegetical approach more clearly than does the monograph on Luke's Gospel. What he first saw in Acts, he later saw in the author's earlier work. Schleiermacher hypothesized that the evangelist Luke, who was not a disciple but belonged to a second generation of Christians, combined originally independent eyewitness accounts without further redaction.[26] Schleiermacher came up with this theory because when he examined the Acts of the Apostles in his lectures on the Lukan writings, the work appeared to him to be incoherent: it did not display a uniform plan, and therefore could not have been written according to one idea and by one author. From this he concluded that the collector and compiler Luke had put together a collection of independent parts by unknown authors. He applied this procedure analogously to the Gospel. In doing this he wanted above all to surmount the dispute between the exegetes of the time, who fluctuated in Gospel research among three positions: (1) the so-called Eichhorn hypothesis, originated by Lessing, of an original Gospel (now lost) in Hebrew or Aramaic; (2) the usage hypothesis of J. L. Hug, according to which Matthew was the oldest Gospel, which Mark copied, and with Luke then depending on both; and finally (3) the Griesbach hypothesis, toward which Schleiermacher himself leaned, that Mark borrowed from Matthew and Luke (which is why he did not give a lecture on the Gospel of Mark). As a result, Schleiermacher dispensed with synoptic comparison for his work,

---

[22] *KGA* 1.5, p. xcix.
[23] Wolfgang Virmond, "*interpretari necesse est*. Über die Wurzeln von Schleiermachers 'Hermeneutik und Kritik,'" in *Friedrich Schleiermacher in Halle*, ed. Andreas Arndt (Berlin: De Gruyter, 2013), pp. 67–76.
[24] See Friedrich Schleiermacher, *Ueber die Schriften des Lukas ein kritischer Versuch. Erster Theil* (Berlin: Reimer, 1817), in *KGA* 1.8, pp. 2–180; Schleiermacher, *A Critical Essay on the Gospel of St. Luke*, trans. Connop Thirlwall (London: John Taylor, 1825).
[25] *KGA* 1.8, pp. 183–193.
[26] This is the so-called *diegesen* hypothesis (Kümmel, *Das Neue Testament*, pp. 99–100). Schleiermacher did not use the term himself; he spoke of *apomnemoneumata*—collections or essays.

and concentrated on delimiting the individual pieces from a literary-critical point of view by working out the fugues and narrative formulas, as form criticism would begin anew a century later. The individual pieces, discovered in this way, which the collector Luke put together unaltered, would need to be investigated for their authenticity.

Schleiermacher obtains these "pieces" from four "main divisions,"[27] into which the whole Gospel is broken down. These are Luke 1 and 2; 3:1–9:50; 9:51–19:42; and 20:1–24:53. He considers Luke 1:5–50 to be an independent poem, which the collector placed unchanged at the beginning of his Gospel. He divides Luke 2, which he considers incompatible with Matt. 1–2, into three parts, to which he assigns different degrees of historical weight. In Luke 3–9 Schleiermacher distinguishes seven units recognizable by their closing formulas, which have already been partly put together themselves and can occasionally be combined with local traditions. He lets the Lukan travelogue extend to 19:48 and considers it to be an inserted, independent script, which, however, already consists of fourteen individual pieces. In Luke 20–24 he sees three different interwoven units. Since he did not develop this position very far—not even in his first lecture on the life of Jesus from 1819/1820—it is understandable that he sought to achieve greater clarity in his lectures from 1821 on the Passion and Resurrection of Jesus.[28] This was necessary because his dogmatics needed to present a Christology.[29] His exegetical and dogmatic considerations were thus interlocking. This interconnection could not be inferred from the printed dogmatics alone, which has often been accused of lacking biblical justification; rather, its full import is evident only in the lectures on the life of Jesus, which remained unpublished during his lifetime.

24.3 SCHLEIERMACHER'S LATER ESSAYS ON COLOSSIANS 1:15–20 AND PAPIAS' TESTIMONIES

Schleiermacher also made research history with two essays published in 1832. In doing so, he once again demonstrated an usually high level of historical-philological workmanship. Schleiermacher's comprehensive work on the Colossians hymn 1:15–20—though Schleiermacher does not yet speak of a "hymn" as such—inaugurates the historical-critical exegesis of this text.[30] Schleiermacher paid particular attention to its formal structure and thus brought a completely new point of view into play. He works out the "decidedly biarticulate structure" of the text in structural parallelism (Col. 1:15–16; 1:18b–19; though such indications of hymns were not recognizable in the editions of the New Testament texts at that time),[31] with intermediate links as parallel double clauses (Col. 1:17–18a) and

---

[27] Friedrich Schleiermacher, *Luke: A Critical Study*, trans. Connop Thirlwall, with Further Essays, Emendations, and Other Apparatus by Terrence N. Tice, Schleiermacher: Studies and Translations 13 (Lewiston, NY: Edwin Mellen Press, 1993), p. 19.

[28] *VLJ*, pp. 559–653.

[29] See *CG1*.

[30] *KGA* 1.8, pp. 177–226: ET: Friedrich Schleiermacher, *On Colossians 1: 15–20 (1832)*, trans. Esther D. Reed and Alan Braley, in *Schleiermacher on Workings of the Knowing Mind*, ed. Ruth Drucilla Richardson, New Athenaeum / Neues Athenaeum 5 (Lewiston, NY: Edwin Mellen Press, 1998), pp. 33–80.

[31] *KGA* 1.8, p. 201; Schleiermacher, *On Colossians 1: 15–20 (1832)*, p. 53.

introduction (from v. 9) and continuation (up to v. 23). He became conscious of the contrast in composition and writing style in this part of text of the letter as compared with the other Pauline letters. He also noticed the "remarkable assertions about Christ."[32] But in contrast to his interpretation of the first epistle to Timothy, here he does not conclude a non-Pauline origin or an adoption of structured material from earlier texts—that is, he is not yet working methodically in the criticism of religion and tradition—rather, he tries to understand the formulations on the basis of Paul's patterns of thinking and speaking, with recourse to commentaries of the Church Fathers on Colossians, among other sources. The mythical references, as for example to Christ's mediation in creation (v. 16), are interpreted away as not yet conceivable by Paul. This conclusion is denounced as a "wish": "Where the seed of the lust for discovery falls on this ground of perplexity, it usually produces a rich crop of hermeneutical weeds."[33] Ultimately, only a political-moral interpretation, with a view to the community of reconciliation founded indirectly by him from Jews and Gentiles, seems to him to be factually appropriate. The congregation from Colossae, "at least indirectly of Pauline origin" was used to Paul's type of teaching and could not have misunderstood him.[34] For Schleiermacher, "dark" expressions or "obscure sayings" are about civic offices and activities of powerful persons that are related to Christ.[35]

Schleiermacher did not prevail with this "ethical" interpretation. But his formal analysis stimulated future research, right down to the printing system in the modern editions of the New Testament—including, for example, the visual discrimination between poetry and prose within the text—which cannot be found in earlier *scriptio continua* editions and consequently could not have been in the original at the time.

The essay on Papias' testimony to the Gospels of Mark and Matthew in the *Historia Ecclesiastica* of Eusebius from the beginning of the fourth century was little noticed at the time, but it has brought the term "Logienquelle" (*logia* source) to source criticism for the Gospels.[36] The investigation evidently arose from Schleiermacher's lectures on the introduction to the New Testament of 1831/1832. The sources he researched have arguably not improved much since then.[37]

The essay refers to the short quotations that Eusebius gives in his church history from the λογίων κυριακῶν ἐξηγήσεις ("analysis of the sayings of the Lord") of Papias from Hierapolis in Phrygia, a Christian of the third generation (around 130). It says there, Περὶ δὲ τοῦ Ματθαίου ταῦτ᾽ εἴρηται. Ματθαῖος μὲν οὖν ἑβραΐδι διαλέκτῳ τὰ λόγια συνεγράψατο ("About Matthew he said as follows: Matthew collected the sayings (of the Lord) in the Hebrew language"). Schleiermacher begins with the philological observation that the ordinary meaning of *logion* is "divine prophecy" and that its meaning in the Septuagint is "God's commandments," and that consequently *logia* in the note of Papias should be translated as "sayings of Christ." This could not be a reference to the Gospel of Matthew that

---

[32] Schleiermacher, *On Colossians 1: 15–20 (1832)*, p. 48; *KGA* 1.8, p. 197.
[33] Schleiermacher, *On Colossians 1: 15–20 (1832)*, p. 57; *KGA* 1.8, p. 204.
[34] Schleiermacher, *On Colossians 1: 15–20 (1832)*, p. 80; *KGA* 1.8, p. 226.
[35] Schleiermacher, *On Colossians 1: 15–20 (1832)*, p. 68; *KGA* 1.8, p. 215.
[36] *KGA* 1.8, pp. 229–254.
[37] Ulrich H. J. Körtner, "Papiasfragmente," in *Papiasfragmente. Hirt des Hermas*, ed. Ulrich H. J. Körtner and Martin Leutzsch, Schriften des Urchristentums III (Darmstadt: Wissenschaftliche Buchgesellschaft, 1998), p. 58, on Eusebius of Caesarea, *Historia Ecclesiastica* III, ch. 39.

has been handed down to us, because this by no means contains only the words of Jesus but encompasses the whole life of Jesus. And when Eusebius summarizes that this collection has been explained by everyone as he was able, Schleiermacher concludes from this that there are several such attempts in apocryphal gospels—today we could add, for example, the Gospel of Thomas—and calls the heading "Gospel according to Matthew" a "family name," and so as it were a generic name. Schleiermacher then interprets the Gospel writing of the New Testament as such an attempt by an unknown author of the second generation, in which this collection of speeches, the *logia* of the apostle Matthew, originally in Hebrew (i.e. Aramaic), must still be contained in a Greek translation.

It is quite astonishing how Schleiermacher then, as he had in his monograph on Luke, roughly determined the limits of the so-called *logia* source, which was later developed in a completely different way, with the help of the redaction formulas. He even suspected that the author of the Gospel of Luke also knew this collection but did not need it (cf. Luke 1:1) because he found a different historical context in his historical materials. Here Schleiermacher's prejudice about the Gospel of Luke prevailed. With this he stopped in the forecourt the identification of the source of the sayings "Q." But his insistence on the meaning of the word *logion* in Papias has given synoptic research the term "*logia* source" (a term which he himself did not use).

As far as the Gospel of Mark is concerned, Schleiermacher considers the tradition that this was the ἑρμηνευτής (interpreter) of Peter, which is also found in Papias, to be sustainable. Its collection is the basis of the Gospel "according to Mark." Schleiermacher considers the Synoptic problem to be still unresolved; all different relationships of dependence are conceivable. The substantiation of the Markan hypothesis, advanced by his friend Karl Lachmann, shortly after his death (1835) and the development of the two-source theory by Christian Hermann Weisse and Christian Gottlob Wilke (1838) would have astonished him.

24.4 THE EXEGETICAL LECTURES

As a professor of "the knowledge of God" ("Gottes Gelahrtheit"; the title given on the cover of the monograph on the Gospel of Luke), Schleiermacher offered lectures on the subject of the New Testament throughout his life as a professor. In doing so, he only ignored the Gospel of Mark because, according to the Griesbach hypothesis, he considered it to be an excerpt from Matthew and Luke; and the Revelation of John, which for him stood on the border with the apocryphal writings. The handwritten lecture notes and hearers' transcripts (*Nachschriften*) that have been preserved in his estate have not yet been published. In his "Introduction to the New Testament" in 1829 and 1831/1832 he gave a summary of his overall understanding of the New Testament writings, which reflects the legacy of the later Schleiermacher's interpretation of the Scriptures under historical-critical aspects. In 1845 these lectures were published in the *Sämmlichen Werken* by G. Wolde, with a preface by Friedrich Lücke, based on the transcripts of the 1831/1832 series, with valuable additions from Schleiermacher's handwritten notes from 1829.[38] A critical edition in the *KGA* is still missing.

---

[38] See *SW* 8.

It is characteristic of Schleiermacher that he begins with a methodological reflection on the genre of the "Introduction." He denies it the status of a science, since it only compiles materials from the previous hermeneutics and criticism of the texts. But for the researcher just setting out, it is necessary to the formation of judgment. The beautiful quote reads, "But it is not worthy of a Protestant theologian to be dependent; he must be in a position always to justify his judgments himself."[39] Consequently, the introductory lecture should position the hearer in the place of the original reader as much as possible. This takes place in constant conversation with the textbook of his friend and former colleague Wilhelm Martin Leberecht de Wette, *Textbook of the Historical-Critical Introduction to the N.T.* (1826, ²1830), which de Wette had delivered as lectures during his time in Berlin.[40] Of course Schleiermacher had mastered the material and the scientific discussion with ease. After the presentation of the history of the canon, the history of the text and the history of printing, there is a special introduction to the individual parts of the New Testament. One can read this part as the historical literary history of the New Testament Scriptures. Schleiermacher begins with Paul and the Paulines, then moves on to the four Gospels, followed by the Acts of the Apostles and the Catholic epistles, and finally by the Epistle to the Hebrews and Revelation. From Paul's epistles as the oldest collection, he obtains not only an absolute and comparative chronology, but also a classification of content. For him, inner characteristics determine the authenticity of a text. Schleiermacher sees the Epistles to the Romans, Galatians, 1 and 2 Thessalonians as well as 1 and 2 Corinthians as the core of the decision for authenticity, from which Paul's teaching must also be reconstructed. 1 Timothy is still a pseudonymous work for him; in the case of 2 Timothy and the Epistle of Titus he admits his uncertainty, but he does not want to follow Eichhorn's radical hypothesis for the inauthenticity of both. In his judgment the Epistle to the Colossians is genuine, while the Epistle to the Ephesians is a letter approved by Paul. Schleiermacher sees the divergent style of language as a historical criterion and appeals for a gradation in judgments of authenticity and inauthenticity. The same must apply to the interpretation of the epistles.

Schleiermacher's most difficult problems are the Gospels, the assessment of which is the largest portion of his analysis. With the Synoptic Gospels he remains true, albeit with hesitation, to Griesbach's usage hypothesis, that the author of Mark had the other two Synoptic Gospels before him. He lectures on the testimonies of the early Church Fathers, revealing the results of his Papias studies before they were printed. As in his monograph on Luke, he rejects the hypothesis of a primordial Gospel by Eichhorn, because it only provides a "lean skeleton" and the nature of the Gospel of John cannot be explained.[41] The Synoptics give him the outer framework of the life of Jesus with significant historical weight, and they provide him with the individual "aggregates"—just like in his lectures on the life of Jesus. He looks for natural reasons, for example didactic reasons, for differences between parallel passages. When in doubt, Schleiermacher adheres to the Gospel of John—especially in the Passion story—which is the only one to reproduce the authentic Jesus.

---

[39] *SW* 8: pp. 4–5.
[40] See ET: Martin Leberecht de Wette, *An Historico-Critical Introduction to the Canonical Books of the N. T.*, translated from the fifth, improved and enlarged edition (1848) by Frederick Frothingham (Boston, 1858).
[41] *SW* 8, p. 225.

The Gospel of John is crucial for Schleiermacher. He knows the counter-arguments, but concerning this Gospel he has the "total impression" that, with the exception of a few additions, it relates "nothing but the self-experience" of Jesus' disciple John,[42] which means that the evangelist conveyed the *ipsissima vox* of Jesus. He considers the doubt about this to be biased. Even the confession of the Baptist (John 1:29–36) goes back to John as an ear-witness.[43] In this Gospel, especially in the I-am speeches, the hermeneut Schleiermacher finds the inner life of Jesus, which he developed more comprehensively in his lectures on the life of Jesus and in his homilies on this Gospel.[44] The exegete justifies this historically, but the dogmatic interest in this result cannot be overlooked in view of his dogmatics.

In treating the Acts of the Apostles, Schleiermacher insists that it contains individual pieces edited by Hellenistic Christians, which the compiler has merely combined.[45] With regard to the Catholic epistles, Schleiermacher judges the first epistle of John as apostolic and the other two as "deuterocanonical."[46] Despite some reservations, Schleiermacher considers the first epistle of Peter to be a letter from the apostle, whereas the second epistle of Peter and the epistle of Jude are pseudonymous. With the equally pseudonymous epistle of James Schleiermacher agrees with Luther, who called it a "letter of straw"; he does not need it for Christian teaching.[47] The epistle to the Hebrews is important to him; he regarded it as the work of a second-generation apostle, and as important as the epistles of Paul because of its "purely Christian content."[48] He considers the apocalypse of John, which had never been the subject of his lectures, to be pseudonymous (that is, not written by the evangelist) and calls it "a boundary point between the canonical and the apocryphal"; it is of little use for the normal representation of Christianity.[49] It is only logical that he preached on this book only four times in a long life as a minister.

It is notable that Schleiermacher draws up a kind of double table of ranked values, which proceed in three stages: In the Gospels, he prefers the Gospel of John, which relates to the Synoptics like the real Pauline Epistles relates to those of other authors (e.g. the epistle to the Hebrews). To this extent, they each have the same weight for determining what is Christian. But on the other hand, Schleiermacher judges the pseudonymous epistles and Revelations to be subordinate to the others, existing on a third level, with the result that he has to distinguish between proto- and deuterocanonical writings in the New Testament.[50] It is obvious that this is not a historical-exegetical but a dogmatic judgment.

Schleiermacher had the strongest influence on the future history of exegesis through his lectures on the life of Jesus. In this work he founded a new academic discipline. He gave these lectures five times between 1819/1820 and 1832.[51] He justified the necessity of this new

---

[42] *SW* 8, p. 318.
[43] *SW* 8, p. 320.
[44] See Hermann Patsch, "Schleiermachers Homilien zum Johannes-Evangelium," in *Geist und Buchstabe. Interpretations- und Transformationsprozesse innerhalb des Christentums*, ed. Michael Pietsch and Dirk Schmid, Festschrift für Günter Meckenstock zum 65, Geburtstag, Theologische Bibliothek Töpelmann 164 (Berlin: De Gruyter, 2013), pp. 131–154.
[45] *SW* 8, p. 359.
[46] *SW* 8, p. 400.
[47] *SW* 8, p. 425.
[48] *SW* 8, p. 446.
[49] *SW* 8, p. 471.
[50] *SW* 8, p. 473.
[51] Cf. *VLJ*.

type of lecture for Christian ministry by saying that (following the recent dismissal of de Wette in 1819) he now lacked competition in the area of New Testament studies, and that consequently he would lecture on all four Gospels "in a slightly different form."[52] This external justification, which can be read politically, also had an internal purpose, in that at that time he began work on his dogmatics, and needed to become clear on the historical basis of Christianity for the purposes of Christology.[53] Similarly, the lectures of 1829/1830 and 1831 did the preparatory work for the second edition of his *Christian Faith* in 1830/1831, the material for which returns with further reflections in the lecture of 1832. The middle lecture from 1823 has become significant for intellectual history in that a copy (not yet published) served as the basis for David Friedrich Strauss's engagement with Schleiermacher in his monograph *The Life of Jesus* from 1835/1836.[54]

In each of the edited lectures Schleiermacher prefaced his presentation of the life of Jesus with detailed scientific theoretical considerations on historiography, which reveal a development of the systematic approach.[55] Here historical and theological-dogmatic principles are linked in order to combine the human and the divine in Christ in thought. In his lecture from 1823 he apparently clears away all difficulties: "Thus in our whole undertaking, we will consider every action of Christ in a purely human way, and the divine in the action not as more in some and less in others, but rather we view that same rationale as equally underlying all—and this is the inner principle of our entire process."[56] In 1832 he regrets the separation of the dogmatic and the historical and refers the solution to the problem to dogmatics, "in which it is still understood."[57] That the historical-critical investigation is preceded by a systematic-theological foundation is clearly stated here and is not hidden.

That Schleiermacher divides the life of Jesus into three periods of time—his life before appearing in public, his public life up to his capture, and from capture to ascension—is conventional. A harmony of the Gospels is of course not established. All judgments arise from precise exegetical work, with Schleiermacher keeping pace with contemporary debates. Like most of his exegetical colleagues Schleiermacher is quite enlightened in his historical judgments, even if he tried to distance himself from radical points of view such as those represented by Heinrich Eberhard Gottlob Paulus or from new conservatives such as his colleagues Ernst Wilhelm Hengstenberg and Friedrich August Gottreu Tholuck. His reservations about the birth stories and the healing miracles are both critically justified,[58] as are the (very carefully formulated) apparent-death hypothesis as an interpretation of the crucifixion of Jesus.[59] These judgments were annoying to many, as were his skepticism in the

---

[52] Wolfgang Virmond, ed., *Die Vorlesungen der Berliner Universität 1810–1834 nach dem deutschen und lateinischen Lektionskatalog sowie den Ministerialakten* (Berlin: De Gruyter, 2011), p. 780.
[53] The first edition of his *Glaubenslehre* appeared in 1821/1822. See CG¹.
[54] Hermann Patsch, [Review] "Friedrich Schleiermacher, Vorlesungen über das Leben Jesu. Vorlesung über die Leidens- und Auferstehungsgeschichte (KGA II/15), hg. von Walter Jaeschke," *Journal for the History of Modern Theology / Zeitschrift für Neuere Theologiegeschichte* 26, no. 1 (2019), pp. 147–156.
[55] VLJ, pp. 137–149, 311–330; Matthias Hofmann, "Schleiermachers Vorlesungen über das Leben Jesu—Die Einleitungen der Kollegien von 1819/20 und 1829/30. Zwei Teileditionen von Hörernachschriften," *Journal for the History of Modern Theology / Zeitschrift für Neuere Theologiegeschichte* 27, no. 2 (2020), pp. 270–310.
[56] VLJ, p. 146.
[57] VLJ, p. 322.
[58] VLJ, pp. 103–104, 156, 333–336.
[59] VLJ, pp. 299, 481.

treatment of the Satan tradition[60] and his reluctance to portray the Ascension,[61] which consequently had to be considered about the second death of Jesus.[62] In the same context, however, Schleiermacher could also refer very conservatively to the credibility of the disciples, on which the credibility of the New Testament depends.[63] The nature of the sources—on the one hand the Synoptics, on the other hand the peculiar Gospel of John—does not permit a really chronologically coherent presentation of the life of Jesus,[64] but it does allow an approximation to this. Schleiermacher obtains the external historical events (somewhat abbreviated) from the investigation of the Synoptics, but the inner life of Jesus, his "character" and the "exposition of his consciousness,"[65] from the Gospel of John, whose author he regards as an immediate disciple. John gave him (in Greek) the *ipsissima vox* of the "Redeemer." From both strands of tradition he was then able to develop in an exciting way the "ethical way of the teaching Christ," the "teaching activity of Christ,"[66] in which his actual systematic interest lay. Schleiermacher presupposed this personal, internally unified image of the historical Jesus in his two editions of *Dogmatics*.

"Christ is an *ens sui generis*, and all attempts to reount his whole life naturally are purely in vain. The task of resolving this can only be regarded as a purely theological one."[67] With this final sentence of the lecture of 1832 Schleiermacher left the question of a life of the historical Jesus of Nazareth and entered the Christology of his dogmatics.

24.5 Conclusion

For Schleiermacher, contra Lessing, there was no "broad ugly ditch" running between the historical-philological and theological interpretation of the Scriptures. Both are linked to him for his entire life in a dialectical unity. This is why historical research did not create any lasting uncertainty for him. And thus, particularly impressively at the end of his lecture on the introduction to the New Testament of 1832, he was able to view the assertion that in comparison to the Jewish "national literature," including the Old Testament, the New Testament represents something new that cannot be derived from the existing religious environment, as well grounded not only in terms of systematic theology but also historically. Christianity and its teachings are not "modified Judaism" for him.[68] Any attempt to reduce the "distinctively Christian" by imposing a foreign origin on it, says the New Testament scholar at the end of a long exegetical life, "cannot stand" before the forum of historical criticism.[69]

---

[60] *VLJ*, pp. 125–126, 437–441.
[61] *VLJ*, pp. 301, 502–503, 653.
[62] *VLJ*, pp. 507–508.
[63] *VLJ*, pp. 299, 301.
[64] *VLJ*, p. 327.
[65] *VLJ*, pp. 326, 252.
[66] *VLJ*, pp. 259, 406.
[67] *VLJ*, p. 508.
[68] *SW* 1.8, p. 481.
[69] *SW* 1.8, p. 482.

Suggested Reading

Helmer, Christine. "Schleiermacher's Exegetical Theology and the New Testament". In *The Cambridge Companion to Schleiermacher*, ed. Jacqueline Mariña (Cambridge: Cambridge University Press, 2005), pp. 229–248.
Kelsey, Catherine. "A reading of Schleiermacher's *Life of Jesus Lectures*: A Historian at Work." In *Schleiermacher, Romanticism, and the Critical Arts. A Festschrift in Honor of Hermann Patsch*, ed. Hans Dierkes, Terrence N. Tice and Wolgang Virmond (Lewiston: Edwin Mellen Press Lewiston, Queenston, Lampeter 2007, 2008), pp. 209–226.
Schmidt, Eckart David. *Jesus in Geschichte, Erzählung und Idee. Perspektiven der Jesusrezeption in der Bibelwissenschaft der Aufklärung, der Romantik und des Idealismus* (Tübingen: Mohr Siebeck, 2022).

Bibliography

Arndt, Andreas, and Wolfgang Virmond, eds. *Schleiermachers Briefwechsel (Verzeichnis) nebst einer Liste seiner Vorlesungen*. Schleiermacher-Archiv 11 (Berlin: De Gruyter, 1992).
de Wette, Martin Leberecht. *An Historico-Critical Introduction to the Canonical Books of the N. T.* Translated from the fifth, improved and enlarged edition (1848) by Frederick Frothingham (Boston, 1858).
Griesbach, Johann Jacob. *Novum Testamentum Graece. Volumen II. Epistolas omnes et apokalypsin complectens*. Editio secunda (London: Impensis J. Mackinlay, et Cuthell et Martin, 1806).
Hofmann, Matthias. "Schleiermachers Vorlesungen über das Leben Jesu—Die Einleitungen der Kollegien von 1819/20 und 1829/30. Zwei Teileditionen von Hörernachschriften." *Journal for the History of Modern Theology / Zeitschrift für Neuere Theologiegeschichte* 27, no. 2 (2020), pp. 262–310.
Kelsey, Catherine. "A reading of Schleiermacher's *Life of Jesus Lectures*: A Historian at Work." In *Schleiermacher, Romanticism, and the Critical Arts. A Festschrift in Honor of Hermann Patsch*, ed. Hans Dierkes, Terrence N. Tice and Wolgang Virmond (Lewiston: Edwin Mellen Press Lewiston, Queenston, Lampeter 2007, 2008), pp. 209–226.
Körtner, Ulrich H. J. "Papiasfragmente." In *Papiasfragmente. Hirt des Hermas*, ed. Ulrich H. J. Körtner and Martin Leutzsch. Schriften des Urchristentums III (Darmstadt: Wissenschaftliche Buchgesellschaft, 1998), pp. 3–106.
Kümmel, Werner Georg. *Das Neue Testament. Geschichte der Erforschung seiner Probleme* (Freiburg: Karl Alber, 1958).
Patsch, Hermann. "Die Angst vor dem Deuteropaulinismus. Die Rezeption des 'kritischen Sendschreibens' Friedrich Schleiermachers über den 1. Timotheusbrief im ersten Jahrzehnt." *Zeitschrift für Theologie und Kirche* 88, no. 4 (1991), pp. 451–477.
Patsch, Hermann. "The Fear of Deutero-Paulinism: The Reception of Friedrich Schleiermacher's 'Critical Open Letter' concerning 1 Timothy in the First Quinquenium." Trans. Darrell J. Doughty. *The Journal of Higher Criticism* 6, no. 1 (Spring 1999), pp. 3–31.
Patsch, Hermann. "'. . . mit Interesse die eigentliche Theologie wieder hervorsuchen.' Schleiermachers theologische Schriften der Hallenser Zeit." In *Friedrich Schleiermacher in Halle*, ed. Andreas Arndt (Berlin: De Gruyter, 2013), pp. 31–54.

Patsch, Hermann. [Review]. "Friedrich Schleiermacher, Vorlesungen über das Leben Jesu. Vorlesung über die Leidens- und Auferstehungsgeschichte (KGA II/15), hg. von Walter Jaeschke." *Journal for the History of Modern Theology / Zeitschrift für Neuere Theologiegeschichte* 26, no. 1 (2019), pp. 147–156.

Patsch, Hermann. "Vom Pseudo-Paulus über den Sammler Lukas zum johanneischen Erlöser—Zur Philologie und theologischen Exegese bei Schleiermacher." In *Reformation und Moderne. Pluralität–Subjektivität–Kritik*, ed. Jörg Dierken, Arnulf von Scheliha, and Sarah Schmidt. Schleiermacher-Archiv 27 (Berlin: De Gruyter, 2018), pp. 749–769.

Patsch, Hermann. "Schleiermachers Berliner Exegetik." In *Schleiermacher Handbuch*, Ed. Martin Ohst (Tübingen: Mohr Siebeck, 2017), pp. 327–340.

Patsch, Hermann. "Schleiermachers Homilien zum Johannes-Evangelium." In *Geist und Buchstabe. Interpretations- und Transformationsprozesse innerhalb des Christentums*, ed. Michael Pietsch and Dirk Schmid. Festschrift für Günter Meckenstock zum 65. Geburtstag. Theologische Bibliothek Töpelmann 164 (Berlin: De Gruyter, 2013), pp. 131–154.

Schleiermacher, Friedrich. *Briefwechsel 1806–1807 (Briefe 2173–2597). KGA 5.9*. Ed. Andreas Arndt and Simon Gerber (Berlin: De Gruyter, 2011).

Schleiermacher, Friedrich. *On Colossians 1: 15–20 (1832)*. Trans. Esther D. Reed and Alan Braley. In *Schleiermacher on Workings of the Knowing Mind*. Ed. Ruth Drucilla Richardson. New Athenaeum / Neues Athenaeum 5 (Lewiston, NY: Edwin Mellen Press, 1998), pp. 33–80.

Schleiermacher, Friedrich. *A Critical Essay on the Gospel of St. Luke*. Trans. Connop Thirlwall (London: John Taylor, 1825).

Schleiermacher, Friedrich. *Ueber den sogenannten ersten Brief des Paulos an den Timotheos. Ein kritisches Sendschreiben an J. C. Gaß* (Berlin: Reimer, 1807).

Schleiermacher, Friedrich. *Ueber die Schriften des Lukas ein kritischer Versuch. Erster Theil* (Berlin: Reimer, 1817).

Schleiermacher, Friedrich. *Ueber die Zeugnisse des Papias von unsern beiden ersten Evangelien*. Theologische Studien und Kritiken 4 (1832), pp. 735–768.

Schleiermacher, Friedrich. *Schriften aus der Hallenser Zeit 1804-1807, KGA 1.5*, ed. Hermann Patsch (Berlin: De Gruyter, 1995).

Schleiermacher, Friedrich. *Exegetische Schriften, KGA 1.8*, ed. Hermann Patsch and Dirk Schmid (Berlin: De Gruyter, 2001).

Schleiermacher, Friedrich. *Ueber Kolosser 1, 15–20*. Theologische Studien und Kritiken 3 (1832), pp. 497–537.

Schleiermacher, Friedrich. *Luke: A Critical Study*. Trans. Connop Thirlwall. With Further Essays, Emendations, and Other Apparatus by Terrence N. Tice. Schleiermacher: Studies and Translations 13 (Lewiston, NY: Edwin Mellen Press, 1993).

Schleiermacher, Friedrich. *Schriften aus der Hallenser Zeit 1804-1807. KGA I.5*. Ed. Hermann Patsch (Berlin: De Gruyter, 1995).

Schleusner, Johann Friedrich. *Novum Lexicon Graeco-Latinum in Novum Testamentum congessit et variis observationibus philologicis illustravit*. Tomus I.II. Editio altera emendatior et auctior (Leipzig: Apud A. et. J.M. Duncan, 1801).

Schmidt, Eckart David. *Jesus in Geschichte, Erzählung und Idee. Perspektiven der Jesusrezeption in der Bibelwissenschaft der Aufklärung, der Romantik und des Idealismus* (Tübingen: Mohr Siebeck, 2022).

Virmond, Wolfgang. *"interpretari necesse est. Über die Wurzeln von Schleiermachers 'Hermeneutik und Kritik.'"* In *Friedrich Schleiermacher in Halle*, ed. Andreas Arndt (Berlin: De Gruyter, 2013), pp. 67–76.

Virmond, Wolfgang, ed. *Die Vorlesungen der Berliner Universität 1810–1834 nach dem deutschen und lateinischen Lektionskatalog sowie den Ministerialakten* (Berlin: De Gruyter, 2011).

CHAPTER 25

PRACTICAL THEOLOGY

BIRGIT WEYEL

25.1 Practical Theology in the Context of a New Definition of Theology

FRIEDRICH Schleiermacher is quite rightly considered the founder of practical theology.[1] Within German-speaking and Protestant theology, many of the textbooks on the individual disciplines within practical theology,[2] as well as on practical theology as a whole,[3] introduce Schleiermacher on the first page. This recognition is due to his novel conception of a program of theological study, which introduced practical theology as a distinct theological discipline with a fully scientific character. Before Schleiermacher (and beyond him), practical theology was predominantly an appendage to exegetical and dogmatic lectures and represented only the application reference in the form of hints. At the same time, practical theology remains closely related to its theological sister disciplines, philosophical and historical theology. The basic sketches of Schleiermacher's conception of theology can be found in his *Brief Outline of the Study of Theology*, which presents an encyclopedia of theology and includes the propaedeutic aim of serving as an introduction to the study of theology overall.[4]

Against the background of this encyclopedic definition, it has been pointed out that practical theology's scientific self-understanding rests on multilayered presuppositions. Both the subject matter of practical theology and the theoretical perspectives on its perceived place and role in the university relate to its constructed character, which oscillates between

---

[1] Cf. Wilhelm Gräb, "Praktische Theologie," in *Schleiermacher Handbuch*, ed. Martin Ohst (Tübingen: Mohr Siebeck, 2017), p. 399.

[2] Cf. Friedrich Wintzer, *Die Homiletik seit Schleiermacher bis in die Anfänge der "dialektischen Theologie" in Grundzügen* (Göttingen: Vandenhoeck & Ruprecht, 1969).

[3] Cf. Christian Grethlein and Michael Meyer-Blanck, eds., *Geschichte der Praktischen Theologie. Dargestellt anhand ihrer Klassiker* (Leipzig: Evangelische Verlagsanstalt, 1999).

[4] Cf. Martin Fritz, "Schleiermachers Idee theologischer Bildung. Zur Aktualität der 'Kurzen Darstellung des theologischen Studiums'," in *Fremde unter einem Dach? Die theologischen Fächerkulturen in enzyklopädischer Perspektive*, ed. Markus von Buntfuß and Martin Fritz (Berlin/Boston: De Gruyter, 2014), pp. 167–203.

theory-building and object reference.⁵ Certainly, every academic discipline is challenged with continually (re-)formulating its own self-conception. The fact that the sciences and humanities deal with critical questions via the medium of methodical self-reflection should also be the rule. But the challenge of teaching practical theology within a university setting is twofold: first, to prove its properly scholarly or "scientific" (*wissenschaftlich*) character and thus its *raison d'être* in the university; and second, to effectively show its relevance to contemporary church practice. In this respect, the field of practical theology must always navigate the tensions between critical scholarship and practice, between neighboring theological and academic disciplines and the demands of a pluralistic religious culture. In view of these challenges, Schleiermacher's conception of theology remains an important point of reference for pursuing these questions of self-understanding.

Schleiermacher's division of theological study into the areas of philosophical, historical and practical theology represents a significant reorganization,⁶ because within this scheme practical theology is not only placed alongside these other fields as an independent discipline but it is also indispensable to the broader conception of theology-as-science. Schleiermacher defines theology as a "positive science," which refers to its subject matter, Christianity, in an action-oriented manner, with a view towards competently leading the Christian church.⁷ He offers an important formulation of this point in the *Brief Outline*: "Christian theology, accordingly, is that assemblage of scientific knowledge and practical instruction [*Kunstregeln*] without the possession and application of which a united leadership of the Christian Church, that is, a government of the Church in the fullest sense, is not possible."⁸

Theology as an academic discipline is thus oriented towards one purpose: the leadership of the church. Accordingly, its takes up its characteristic shape against the background of the complex historical situation in which Schleiermacher developed his understanding of theology: the separation of the church and Christianity, the development of a concept of religion that entails a distinction between religion and theology, and the increasing relativization of claims to absolute validity in light of growing historical awareness.⁹

Viewed in this light, the move to classify church leadership as a practical manifestation of theology signals an important theological shift towards reckoning with the sociocultural environment of the Christian religion.¹⁰ Within this context of an increased need for reflection, and a practical need for guiding and cultivating concrete religious activities, religious practice itself is elevated to the rank of a proper object for scientific or scholarly study. Presupposed here is a distinction between theology as a form of reflection on religious

---

⁵ Cf. Volker Drehsen, *Neuzeitliche Konstitutionsbedingungen der Praktischen Theologie. Aspekte der theologischen Wende zur sozialkulturellen Lebenswelt christlicher Religion* (Göttingen: Gütersloher Verlagshaus, 1988), pp. 4f.

⁶ Cf. Christian Albrecht, *Enzyklopädische Probleme der Praktischen Theologie* (Tübingen: Mohr Siebeck, 2011), p. 13.

⁷ Cf. Gräb, "Praktische Theologie," p. 399.

⁸ *BO* §5, p. 3; cf. *KGA* 1.6, §5, p. 328.

⁹ Cf. Martin Laube, "Zur Stellung der Praktischen Theologie innerhalb der Theologie—Aus systematisch-theologischer Sicht," in *Praktische Theologie. Eine Theorie- und Problemgeschichte*, ed. Christian Grethlein and Helmut Schwier (Leipzig: Evangelische Verlagsanstalt 2007), pp. 64–68.

¹⁰ Cf. Drehsen, *Neuzeitliche Konstitutionsbedingungen*.

practice and religion itself.[11] For Schleiermacher, religious practice becomes a foundational reference point for theology, which grounds the connections between various theological disciplines: "Theology is a positive science, the parts of which join into a cohesive whole only through their common relation to a distinct mode of faith, that is, a distinct formation of God-consciousness. Thus, the various parts of Christian theology belong together only by virtue of their relation to Christianity. This is the sense in which the word 'theology' will always be used here."[12] In view of religious pluralism in the present time, one should also emphasize that this theological model claims validity not only for Christianity but also for other religions.[13] According to Schleiermacher, the understanding of theology as a form of reflection emerging from the religious practice of a community does not need to be an explicitly Christian nor even a Protestant model. It presupposes only the formation of a given community and an interest in self-reflection and orientation. The relationship of theological reflection to Christianity includes not only a functional aspect but also a substantive one, which consists in determining the material essence of Christianity. The unity of theology consists in a dual constitution that joins these substantial and functional aspects into a discipline that studies Christianity for the sake of the promotion of Christianity.[14] The task of defining the essence of Christianity should not be understood as a speculative procedure that is critically opposed to empiricism. In Schleiermacher's view, Christianity is instead a historical phenomenon, whose essence is determined by historical analysis not by metaphysical or supernatural principles.[15] It consists of a reflective historicity.[16] The essence of Christianity is not located outside of history but is instead woven into it. "It is this shift of Schleiermacher's course [*Weichenstellung*] from the dogmatic to the historical definition of essence that is to ensure scientific communicability for Christianity under the conditions of modern historical consciousness."[17]

Schleiermacher's reconceptualization of church leadership as a task of theology is as fundamental as it is far-reaching. Against the background of the common ground of theology as a whole, the three subdisciplines of philosophical, historical, and practical theology take on their own life. All three remain closely linked yet each is assigned specific tasks. Philosophical theology constitutes a fundamental research discipline,[18] which works critically, insofar as it compares the ideal definition of Christianity with its historical

---

[11] Cf. Bodo Ahlers, *Die Unterscheidung von Theologie und Religion. Ein Beitrag zur Vorgeschichte der Praktischen Theologie im 18. Jahrhundert* (Gütersloh: Gütersloher Verlagshaus, 1980).

[12] *BO* §1, p. 1; *KGA* 1.6, §1, p. 325.

[13] "Whether any distinct mode of faith will give shape to a definite theology depends on the degree to which it is communicated by means of notions rather than symbolic actions, and at the same time on the degree to which it attains historical importance and autonomy. Theologies, moreover, may differ for every mode of faith, in that they correspond to the distinctiveness of each both in content and in form." *BO* §2, p. 2; *KGA* 1.6, §2, p. 326.

[14] Cf. Laube, "Zur Stellung der Praktischen Theologie," p. 81.

[15] Cf. Markus Schröder, *Die kritische Identität des neuzeitlichen Christentums. Schleiermachers Wesensbestimmung christlicher Religion* (Tübingen: Mohr Siebeck, 1996), p. 124.

[16] Schröder, *Die kritische Identität*, p. 124.

[17] Schröder, *Die kritische Identität*, p. 124. All translations from German sources are the author's unless indicated otherwise.

[18] Cf. Gräb, "Praktische Theologie," p. 399, and *BO* §37, p. 17. See in detail the lucid analysis of Ulrich Barth, "Theorie der Theologie," in *Schleiermacher Handbuch*, ed. Martin Ohst (Tübingen: Mohr Siebeck, 2017), pp. 316–327.

manifestations. "Thus, two aspects of its work are to be kept in mind: a) that, in accordance with its scientific contents, it operates as criticism; and b) that, in accordance with the nature of its object, it operates as historical criticism."[19] Historical theology reflects upon the historical course of Christianity and has always been intertwined with philosophical theology, because it reveals the historical material with which philosophical theology works to define its concepts through criticism, polemics, and apologetics. Against the background of church leadership, which has to be approached as joint labor, methods of church leadership ultimately fall under the responsibility of practical theology.[20] These methods are "rules of 'art'" (*Kunstregeln*) (§265). Practical theology does not impart knowledge, a role that is assigned to the other two subdisciplines of theology, but it is a "fine art" (§265) or "technique" (§25), in the sense of the Aristotelian distinction between τέχνη and ἐπιστήμη. Such "rules of art" belonging to practical theology must be explicitly distinguished from the rules of a mechanical technique, insofar as the rules of the fine arts do not include instructions for their own application. They are rules "in which the nature and manner of its application to particular instances is not predetermined" (§265). Accordingly, the common, and recurring, misunderstanding that Schleiermacher's practical theology is comprised of the guidance and knowledge of rules must be expressly rejected. The discipline of practical theology, in maintaining the vital connection with active Christian life, does not lose its methodological character and independence as scientific discipline, nor does it mutate into a mere *theologia applicata*. It has a specific task and a distinct style that distinguishes it from philosophical and historical theology.

Yet, while distinct, all three forms of theological inquiry belong together. They form mutual points of reference and interconnections. Schleiermacher illustrates these connections using the metaphor of the tree.[21] It is obvious that the roots (philosophical theology), trunk or body (historical theology), and the crown (practical theology) of the tree cannot exist independently. They form parts of a living organism that belong together. Regrettably, later interpretations of Schleiermacher's theological encyclopedia frequently mistook the meaning of this metaphor. Over the course of the nineteenth century, the crown of the tree was at several points interpreted and reinterpreted as a royal crown. However, a royal crown would not illustrate the unity of and vitality of theology but rather suggests rivalry or at least competition between these theological disciplines.[22] On such a view, it becomes easy to overlook the point that Schleiermacher's tripartite arrangement cannot be represented by the descriptions of individual professorships or faculty positions commonly used today. In the context of Wilhelm von Humboldt's reorganization of the new university in Berlin, therefore, independence of theological disciplines and the distinct description of the tasks of theological positions do not coincide. Schleiermacher did not intend professorships in the

---

[19] *BO* §37, p. 17; *KGA* 1.6, p. 340.

[20] Cf. *BO* §260, p. 98.

[21] In the first edition of the *BO*.

[22] Examples for the metaphor of the crown of a king are: Karl Ludwig Nitzsch, "Gemeinschaftliche Vorschläge zu dem in Wittenberg zu errichtenden Prediger-Seminario vom 28. November 1816," in *Archiv des Predigerseminars Wittenbergs*, Akte 135, pp. 17–44 (unpublished archive), p. 17 (cited in Birgit Weyel, *Praktische Bildung zum Pfarrberuf. Das Predigerseminar Wittenberg und die Entstehung einer zweiten Ausbildungsphase evangelischer Pfarrer in Preußen* [Tübingen: Mohr Siebeck, 2006], p. 91); Martin von Nathusius, *Der Ausbau der praktischen Theologie* (Leipzig, 1899), p. 49: "'Practical theology is the crown of theological studies,' says Schleiermacher. But nowadays it is more like a train [*Schleppe*]."

new theological faculty in Berlin to have a monodisciplinary specialization.[23] Further, the encyclopedic presentation of theology in the *Brief Outline* not only aims at an interpretation of distinct theological disciplines but carries a clear didactic intention of serving as an introduction to the study of theology itself. Statements about the order of the disciplines in the course of study are then best understood as propaedeutic indications, offered with the aim of organizing and clarifying the educational process for students. Certainly, it makes sense to deal with the requirements of practical theology only after knowledge in philosophical and historical theology has been acquired. In this way, Schleiermacher's program of theological study reveals an inner sense of direction.[24] Indeed, the inquiries that structure each subdiscipline are actually circular thought processes.

The study of theology as a whole, then, is ultimately geared towards practice. Theology is a positive and not a speculative science. It forms a theory of religious practice, and with regard to providing a proper orientation for this practice, it has a function that is both critical and constructive. In this context, practical theology takes on the task of developing procedures.[25] In his own recent encyclopedia of practical theology, Christian Albrecht notes that

> Practical theology … has the task of grasping the independence of lived religion in a theological way—but not in such a way that it primarily aims at religious-theoretical or religious-sociological phenomena, but rather that as a theological subdiscipline it represents the action-oriented practical relevance of theology as a whole, and indeed does so as a dimension originating from the interior of theology as a whole.[26]

The fact that a contemporary textbook on practical theology would take Schleiermacher's conception of practical theology as its starting point reflects the influential character of Schleiermacher's refashioned understanding of the study of theology, which emphasizes the inquiry into religious practice as an independent area of study. Implications for practical theology's understanding of itself will be considered further below.

Schleiermacher forms an important reference for almost all practical theological textbooks in the present. For some, Schleiermacher's conception of the church, which is explored in the next section, is the crucial theoretical reference. However, some narrowness can be observed: For example, one can ask whether the concentration on the profession of the pastor (and, in addition, the teacher) does not obscure the view of the plurality and diversity of religious actors. While it is a misunderstanding to accuse Schleiermacher of being pastor-centric, there is a strong orientation to the pastoral profession inscribed in practical theology. The focus on the church must at least be extended to religious practice inside and outside the church.

Based on his reconceptualization of practical theology, the following two sections trace the unfolding of his practical theology. Section 25.2 explores the differentiation between church ministry and church the government in church, which is important for Schleiermacher's

---

[23] Cf. Gräb, "Praktische Theologie," p. 401.
[24] Cf. Laube, "Zur Stellung der Praktischen Theologie," p. 74.
[25] For further details, see Schröder, *Die kritische Identität*, pp. 142ff.
[26] Christian Albrecht, "Die Praktische Theologie im Kreis der theologischen Fächer. Theorie der religiösen Praxis des Christentums," in *Fremde unter einem Dach? Die theologischen Fächerkulturen in enzyklopädischer Perspektive*, ed. Markus Buntfuß and Martin Fritz (Berlin/Boston: De Gruyter, 2014), p. 152.

concept of the church. Section 25.3 introduces the fields and subjects of practical theology and presents his concept of church. Finally, section 25.4 reflects on Schleiermacher's impulses for the current practical theological discourse.

25.2 Practical Theology and the Concept of the Church

Schleiermacher's *Brief Outline* sketches a formal encyclopedia of theology, which unlike more contemporary introductory textbooks does not provide an overview of the contents of individual theological disciplines or a survey of traditional theological sources but rather treats the methodological organization and structure of theological inquiry.[27] However, in the later volume *Practical Theology* published in 1850 by Jacob Frerichs as part of a larger edition of Schleiermacher's writings, the concrete implementation of the program of practical theology could be said to take the form of a textbook. Among its 850 pages is included a posthumous compilation of lecture notes, which are further complemented by supplemental material from Schleiermacher's estate. The volume was reprinted in 1983 and is the source on which the following presentation is based.[28]

Schleiermacher offered lectures on practical theology nine times between 1812 and 1833, at first for four semester periods a week (1812) and then for five semester periods a week. As was his habit with academic lectures, he presented his lectures on practical theology spontaneously based on an outline of compact thesis-like notes.[29] In addition to a general introduction (of about 60 pages), the lectures are divided into two main parts, which follow the systematic division of practical theology he indicates in the *Brief Outline*. The first and largest part considers church ministry (*Kirchendienst*) (pp. 64–520). The second part is dedicated to the government of the church (*Kirchenregiment*) (pp. 521–730). Although the church is an organic whole, in favor of the systematic division of practical theology, Schleiermacher distinguishes between local and general church leadership, that is between the ministry and the governance of churches. "We can nevertheless distinguish between these two, although it always remains a relative opposition.... For the local effect, to grasp the opposition as strongly as possible, we take the smallest part as an organic norm and say, it is the effect on a Christian community, or what we call church ministry [*Kirchendienst*]."[30]

This first part on church ministry is directed towards the local community and includes an exploration of the various activities in the local congregation that are led by the church.[31]

---

[27] Cf. Hans-Joachim Birkner, "Schleiermachers 'Kurze Darstellung' als theologisches Reformprogramm," in *Schleiermacher-Studien*, ed. Hans-Joachim Birkner (Berlin/New York: Walter de Gruyter, 1996), p. 291.

[28] *PrTh*. The edition of *Practical Theology* that is expected to be published as part of the *KGA* is still pending.

[29] Andreas Arndt and Wolfgang Virmond, *Schleiermachers Briefwechsel (Verzeichnis) nebst einer Liste seiner Vorlesungen*, Schleiermacher-Archiv 11 (Berlin/New York: De Gruyter, 1992), pp. 293–330. The supplements (Schleiermacher's manuscripts) printed in the appendix of *PrTh* give an impression of the form of his own lecture theses and notes.

[30] *PrTh*, p. 34.

[31] Cf. Gräb, "Praktische Theologie," pp. 404–407.

It gives detailed descriptions about the worship service,[32] then about the duties of clergy outside of service, such as religious education and pastoral care (pp. 327–488), and concludes with an appendix on the topic of pastoral wisdom (pp. 488–520). The second part, concerning the government of the church, is dedicated to general church leadership. Here the focus is primarily on questions of church constitution and church organization. The governance of the church concerns itself with the general impact of church leadership upon church affairs (p. 522) and consequently is more difficult to grasp. With regard to this broader impact, the lectures note, "The more it really makes the whole its object, the more fragmentary it is, because the whole is not given in a definitive way but refers back to what is individual."[33]

Within this theory of the church government, the church is conceived as an independent system within the state, whose internal and external affairs are its own responsibility. Against the background of the sovereign church government and the episcopate of the king, an eminently ecclesiastical position becomes clear at this point in the lectures, which demands the independence of the church from state government. Wilhelm Gräb notes that Schleiermacher's treatment is groundbreaking in this regard.[34] Martin Doerne also attests to the originality of Schleiermacher's analysis, underlining the fact that besides the church service, the governing body of the church must also have its own place in the theory of church practice. And indeed, this is one of the insights with which Schleiermacher enriched the discipline of practical theology.[35] While the lectures admittedly devote more space to considerations of church service than to the government of the church, altogether a theory of the church is present throughout, in the form of a carefully considered assessment of the church as a whole (specifically the Protestant regional church), which had distanced itself both from the idea of a self-sufficient individual parish and from the hierarchical and bureaucratic superordination of the church over the local parish.[36]

According to Schleiermacher, church and religion emerge simultaneously. "Once there is religion, it must necessarily also be social. That not only lies in human nature but also is preeminently in the nature of religion."[37] The religious interest of humanity, which is an anthropological constant, urges communication with others, which takes on a social form through the church. "The real purpose of the religious community is therefore the circulation [*Circulation*] of religious interest."[38] Church-governing action aims at promoting this exchange and is essentially prompted by an existing inequality in communication, which however is only an issue of transition.[39] The lectures read,

> If we presuppose that inner equality and at the same time presuppose that the direction towards the community forms a common life for sharing [*Mittheilung*] in relation to Christianity, and thereby consider this community as encompassing the whole area of Christianity, then here we postulate the possibility of sharing all with all [*eine Mittheilung aller an alle*]. For this is the

---

[32] *PrTh*, pp. 68–326.
[33] *PrTh*, p. 34.
[34] Cf. Gräb, "Praktische Theologie," p. 407.
[35] Martin Doerne, "Theologie und Kirchenregiment. Eine Studie zu Schleiermachers praktischer Theologie," *Neue Zeitschrift für Systematische Theologie und Religionsphilosophie* 10 (1968), p. 372.
[36] Ibid., p. 373.
[37] *Speeches¹*, p. 73.
[38] *PrTh*, p. 65. Highlighted in the original.
[39] Cf. Gräb, "Praktische Theologie," p. 405.

original form and common life in equality. If we all think alike in relation to the possession and use of the means necessary for such sharing, and all in the same position, then equality will remain complete, and there would be no question of a guiding activity.[40]

Against the background of the ideal of equality, the distinction between clergy and laity, as indicated in the *Brief Outline* (§267), is to be understood provisionally. It concerns assigning roles according to the capacity for competently performing leadership tasks[41] and arises from the fact that different religious persons have different dispositions: "this is not at all a distinction between people, but merely a distinction of situation and functions. Each person is a priest to the extent that he draws others to himself in the field that he has specially made his own and in which he can present himself as a virtuoso [*als Virtuosen*]; each is a layperson to the extent that he follows the art and direction of another where he himself is a stranger in religion."[42] In the end, everyone works and lets themself be affected by the work of everyone else. Productivity and receptivity create a relative tension that in turn creates a dynamic that promotes the exchange of religious interest.[43]

Further specific themes of practical theology, such as worship and preaching, and pastoral care and teaching are embedded harmoniously in this guiding conception of theology and church, church leadership, and the exchange of religious interest. The remainder of this chapter outlines several material considerations from Schleiermacher's innovative contributions to these areas.

25.3 Practical Theology and Religious Practice

25.3.1 Worship and Sermon

Within the framework of the lecture notes, and in accordance with the *Brief Outline*, only the rules of art for the organization of the worship service are discussed. Reflections on the nature of Christian worship form a part of philosophical theology. The descriptive and evaluative depiction of given forms of Christian worship belongs to the subdiscipline of historical theology.[44] In this regard the theory of worship and preaching, as well as the other objects of practical theology, cannot be developed without reference to the other areas of Schleiermacher's work, such as the *Brief Outline*, his Christian ethics (*Christliche Sittenlehre*), the *Speeches* on religion, and his *Christian Faith*. What follows below is thus based on a

---

[40] *PrTh*, pp. 14f.
[41] Cf. Gräb, "Praktische Theologie," p. 405.
[42] *Speeches¹*, pp. 75f.
[43] Cf. Henning Luther, "Praktische Theologie als Kunst für alle. Individualität und Kirche in Schleiermachers Verständnis Praktischer Theologie," *Zeitschrift für Theologie und Kirche* 84 (1987), pp. 384f. According to *PrTh*, p. 50, "Thus all work and allow themselves to be worked upon; practical theology would therefore be an art for all."
[44] Cf. Ralf Stroh, *Schleiermachers Gottesdiensttheorie. Studien zur Rekonstruktion ihres enzyklopädischen Rahmens im Ausgang von "Kurzer Darstellung" und "Philosophischer Ethik"* (Berlin/New York: Walter de Gruyter, 1998), p. 30.

systematic interpretation,[45] but one nevertheless focused on the rules of art outlined in the lectures in *Practical Theology*. The practical-theological theory of worship begins with the relationship between individual piety and public worship. The worship service is "an association of individuals which forms a Christian community and which occupies a certain place."[46] Its purpose, however, unlike other communal activities, is to be determined by a religious interest. It has "nothing other than a religious purpose and content."[47] Associations that pursue a religious purpose are "interruptions in the rest of life,"[48] which inhibit the ordinary hustle and bustle, and especially the bourgeois business-as-usual mindset. Yet this inhibition or interruption yields a positive effect: "Activity is interrupted and self-awareness [*Selbstbewußtsein*] is released."[49] The self-awareness of the Christian faith community is presented in such service; worship is by its very nature a shared religious experience: "When people, by suspending work and business, unite in larger masses in a common activity, it is a celebration."[50] The fine arts are an appropriate form of representation in religion, because "all art has its essence in representation, and everything that wishes to be nothing other than representation is art."[51] Thus, the purpose of the service lies in the representative communication of religious consciousness.[52] Several important insights in this innovative understanding of worship deserve further emphasis.

   a. Worship serves the religious interests of the individual while remaining an inherently social activity. The church and liturgical service are expressions of the socialization of individual religiousness. Dietrich Rössler explains that according to Schleiermacher, the community is the medium in which the inwardness of self-consciousness can emerge, and it is at the same time the forum in which this emergent self-consciousness is communicated and able to be subjectively appropriated by others.[53]
   b. With reference to Schleiermacher's analysis of distinctively Christian action in his Christian ethics, worship is assigned to *representational* (*darstellende*) and not to effective (*wirksame*) action.[54] By its very nature, it is a celebration that must be protected against any instrumentalization.[55]

---

[45] Cf. Christian Albrecht, "Schleiermachers Predigtlehre. Eine Skizze vor dem Hintergrund seines philosophisch-theologischen Gesamtsystem," in *Klassiker der protestantischen Predigtlehre*, ed. Christian Albrecht and Martin Weeber (Tübingen: Mohr Siebeck, 2002), pp. 93–96.
[46] *PrTh*, p. 69.
[47] *PrTh*, p. 69.
[48] *PrTh*, p. 70.
[49] *PrTh*, p. 72.
[50] *PrTh*, p. 70.
[51] *PrTh*, p. 71.
[52] *PrTh*, p. 75.
[53] Dietrich Rössler, "Unterbrechungen des Lebens. Zur Theorie des Fests bei Friedrich Schleiermacher," in *In der Schar derer, die da feiern. Feste als Gegenstand praktisch-theologischer Reflexion*, ed. Peter Cornehl, Martin Dutzmann, and Andreas Strauch (Göttingen, 1993), p. 36.
[54] *Sitte*, pp. 537ff.; Beil. A, pp. 23f.; Beil. B, pp. 149f.
[55] Cf. Ursula Roth, *Die Theatralität des Gottesdienstes* (Gütersloh: Gütersloher Verlagshaus, 2006), p. 169.

c. The form of representation (*Darstellung*) as art is a symbolic activity. In particular, oratory and music are essential to worship as especially appropriate mediums of this representation.[56]

Schleiermacher's treatment of homiletics also forms an integral part of this theory of worship. Preaching and liturgy exist in mutual and reciprocal relationship.[57] The sermon refers to the Christian-religious interest of the listeners. Its task is to expose, reinforce, and promote the traces of listeners' Christian-religious consciousness.[58]

The sermon plays an important role in cultivating and circulating religious interest, aiming "to enliven the religious consciousness of those present."[59] The sermon thus seeks to edify listeners, going beyond an instructive or didactic form of communication. The centrality of peaching also again underscores the importance of developing "rules of art" (*Kunstregeln*) in practical theology. Schleiermacher devotes a large portion of his remarks on the development of the sermon to rhetorical considerations, such as the conceptual structure of the sermon, its disposition, the role of meditation in preparing for the production of the sermon, and questions of style. These rules of art by no means only concern external or minor qualities of preaching but underline the edifying character of the sermon itself. The preacher's role in homiletics is expansive. The sermon is at once an expression of the preacher's own individual piety and an exposition of church teaching. Each preacher will freely appropriate church teaching for themselves, in order to produce an individual understanding of faith that can be shared with others:

> It is presupposed that the clergyperson stands in harmony with the doctrinal type [*Lehrtypus*] of his Church, naturally with lively Protestant freedom; for since he lives in history and relates the particular always to the general, the spirit of his Church must have permeated him in such a way that everything that affects this spirit affects him. He is religiously affected; never will he believe that he has satisfied his calling unless the totality of his ministry is also the totality of his religious self-expression.[60]

Of interest here also is the way in which politics enters the sermon. Schleiermacher is critical of "applying politics to the pulpit."[61] He gives the example of a victory sermon in the context of military conflicts. Here it becomes clear that his criticism of the appropriation of religion by politics is directed against the sovereign church regiment. Politics are outside the religious sphere, and the religious interests of the preacher should give way to individual biases within the sermon. Yet while sermons should not depart from the field of religion, political topics at times make their way to the fore such that the preacher cannot responsibly ignore them but must instead make them the subject of the sermon to address his listeners' interests. His listeners should not then get the impression that the political is gaining the

---

[56] *PrTh*, p. 80.
[57] Wilhelm Gräb, *Predigt als Mitteilung des Glaubens* (Gütersloh: Gütersloher Verlagshaus, 1993), pp. 191f.
[58] Cf. Albrecht, "Schleiermachers Predigtlehre," p. 113.
[59] Albrecht, "Schleiermachers Predigtlehre," p. 115.
[60] Cf. also *PrTh*, pp. 116, 205.
[61] *PrTh*, p. 209.

upper hand, but rather that the preacher "will establish religious maxims to which the political only joins by way of example."[62]

Finally, these homiletic rules of art also serve an important and substantive role in preachers' individual self-reflection. Wilhelm Gräb notes in his own homiletic textbook that according to Schleiermacher,

> Preaching is not a craft, and the desk where it is created is not a workshop. Preaching is a hermeneutic-communicative act . . . A theory of preaching that seeks to lead to this hermeneutic-communicative act therefore does not formulate rules of thumb and does not give tips, but accompanies preachers on the path of self-reflection on their own multi-faceted actions.[63]

25.3.2 Pastoral Care

Beyond worship and preaching, Schleiermacher's practical theology also treats pastoral teaching as an exemplary field of Christian action. Here, the concept of freedom finds a prominent place.[64] The idea of freedom is constitutive for Schleiermacher's understanding of pastoral care (*Seelsorge*), which was developed against the background of civic and emancipatory ideas advanced during the Enlightenment period. The essential task of pastoral care is to increase the spiritual freedom of the people.[65] In the *Brief Outline*, Schleiermacher assigns pastoral care to worship service (*Gottesdienst*), that is to the parochial demands on the clergy, in activities of church governance. This contrasts with the edifying activity of the clergy, which instead aims at eliminating gradual differences between minors and adults in religious matters by leading minors to a state of maturity.[66] The aim of pastoral care is integration into the community, which is characterized by religious independence.[67] While general pastoral care is directed towards the ruling activities within the parish as a whole, particular pastoral care is aimed at the individual who is temporarily disturbed by crisis-like living conditions.[68] Pastoral care, both general and special, works towards the religious independence of all, which essentially consists in the capacity of all members to directly consult the divine word themselves within the framework of the service: "In that members of the community are here placed in an immediate relationship with the divine word, we concede to them that they themselves can advise their conscience from the divine word."[69] The

---

[62] *PrTh*, p. 211.
[63] Wilhelm Gräb, *Predigtlehre. Über religiöse Rede* (Göttingen: Vandenhoeck & Ruprecht, 2013), p. 82.
[64] Cf. Birgit Weyel, "Seelsorge als Praxis der Freiheit. Eine praktisch-theologische Konturierung gelebter Freiheit," in *Bestimmte Freiheit. Festschrift für Christof Landmesser*, ed. Martin Bauspieß, Johannes U. Beck, and Friederike Portenhauser (Leipzig: Evangelische Verlagsanstalt, 2020), pp. 325–340.
[65] *PrTh*, p. 431.
[66] See also Christian Albrecht, "Schleiermachers Programm der Seelsorge als Wiederherstellung religiöser Autonomie," in *Der Mensch und seine Seele. Bildung–Frömmigkeit–Ästhetik. Akten des internationalen Kongresses der Schleiermacher-Gesellschaft in Münster September 2015*, ed. Arnulf von Scheliha and Jörg Dierken (Berlin/Boston: De Gruyter, 2017), p. 280.
[67] Ibid., p. 281.
[68] *BO* §299, p. 112.
[69] *PrTh*, p. 430.

autonomy of the individual enjoys the highest priority in questions concerning the orientation of their own life. Again, as the lectures note, "We proceed from the presupposition that each member of the community stands in an immediate relationship with the divine Word, can advise himself from the Word, and may or may not have confidence in his understanding of the divine Word."[70]

Individual pastoral care in the sense of a conversation between the clergy and a member of the congregation constitutes the special case, because there is no longer a capacity for the individual to regularly consult with the divine Word. The need for the clergyperson to turn to the individual stems from the fact that independent participation in the edifying activities of the Christian community is no longer a given. In such a situation, the individual has "fallen out of identity with the community due to *external circumstances*";[71] their confidence is in pieces. Pastoral care is therefore always to be thought of as an expression of church leadership. Yet the converse also holds: church leadership is understood as forming part of pastoral care.[72] Particular pastoral care is offered in discrete cases of need and is limited in time. It is no longer necessary when the individual returns to a state of independence. This indeed must be the purpose of pastoral care: "From this arises the canon: wherever such demands are made on the clergyperson, they must use these demands to increase the spiritual freedom of the community member and to give them such clarity that the demand no longer arises in them."[73]

The idea of freedom also guides the initiation of the pastoral conversation. Although the initiative can come either from the individual in need or from the clergy, it is in every case the individual community member who decides whether to enter into this pastoral relationship. This is where their irreducible freedom comes into play, which is not called into question even by the crisis of their current situation. The principle of autonomy is valid here, because it is rooted in the individual's relationship with God. It follows by consequence that the member of the congregation is free to call upon the clergy but equally free to refrain from doing so: "The establishment of the relationship of special pastoral care as a duty of community members cannot exist in the Protestant Church."[74] Here then Schleiermacher sets a clear contrast with the Roman Catholic practice of confession. Pastoral care is genuinely treated as a special case and should always be thought of as a temporary relationship in order to ensure that its actual goal, the recovery of self-care, is achieved. Accordingly, the difference between the spiritually mature and immature is not to be understood categorically; rather, spiritual development admits of gradual differences and smooth transitions. The lectures describe the note:

> Every individual who is a member of the congregation has shortcomings and infirmities, in relation to which an engagement with the clergy can be of benefit. If one wished to conclude from this that the clergyperson should have such a special relationship with everyone, then this would be something impossible. It would not be appropriate to the spirit of the Protestant Church; indeed, it would result in such a guardianship as in the Catholic Church, the relationship of the confessor to the penitent child.[75]

---

[70] PrTh, p. 430.
[71] PrTh, p. 459, italics in the original.
[72] Cf. BO §263, p. 99.
[73] PrTh, p. 431, italics in the original.
[74] PrTh, p. 430.
[75] PrTh, p. 442.

Paternalism therefore has no place within this kind of pastoral care, as it would contradict the maturity of the individual believer. Neither should special pastoral care be conceived of as a merely temporary form of spiritual guardianship. In such cases, it would not be incorrect to speak of an asymmetry in the relationship between the pastor and a person seeking pastoral care.[76] However, a deficiency model[77] that focuses on a strong asymmetry and the need for help of the person seeking pastoral care cannot be perceived in Schleiermacher's conception of pastoral care. Instead, in situations of crisis where external support is required outside of oneself, there is a reason for pastoral care, but the autonomy of the individual is at no time suspended. The final and regulatory authority in each case remains the freedom and personal responsibility of conscience. Therefore, the aim of special pastoral care is to facilitate the proper orientation and regulating function of the individual's conscience.

We are therefore dealing with a concept of freedom that seeks to defend the maturity of the individual against claims to power by others. For Schleiermacher, freedom is always concrete. On the one hand, it manifests itself in crisis situations via the sovereignty to claim special pastoral care or to refrain from doing so. Those seeking pastoral care also freely determine the contents and limits of the conversation themselves. On the other hand, freedom is lived out continuously in the community, in that individuals regularly participate in the religious life. The freedom of the individual to be protected from paternalism in this way is the standard for pastoral care, which must be measured by the extent to which it succeeds not only in winning the trust of the individual, but also in making room for their individuality in the shaping of the conversation.

25.4 Practical Theology Reconsidered

Against the background of Schleiermacher's broader program for theological study, several aspects of his practical theology merit further emphasis in connection to contemporary theological discussions.

First, practical theology is a theory of religious practice. Schleiermacher has been criticized in various quarters on the charge that his practical theology ultimately aims only at application and does not correspond to the demands on the theoretical level of an academic discipline. The question about the relationship between theory and practice, or speculation and empiricism, is a methodological question that is an enduring concern in practical theology. The reference to its character of its "rules of art" (*Kunstregeln*) as well as its character of technology (in the sense of τέχνη), holds a constructive object orientation. His practical theology thus does not aim at a rule-guided application in the sense of a deduction of action orientations, for example from philosophical theology. In recent years, practical theology has absorbed impulses from qualitative empirical research in the social sciences, especially

---

[76] Cf. Jürgen Ziemer, "Die Beziehung zwischen Ratsuchendem und Seelsorge," in *Handbuch der Seelsorge. Grundlagen und Profile*, ed. Wilfried Engemann (Leipzig: Evangelische Verlagsanstalt, 2007), p. 157.

[77] Cf. Friedrich Wintzer, ed., *Seelsorge. Texte zum gewandelten Verständnis und zur Praxis der Seelsorge in der Neuzeit* (München: Kaiser, 1999), p. xviii; Jürgen Ziemer, *Seelsorgelehre. Eine Einführung für Studium und Praxis*, 2nd ed. (Göttingen: Vandenhoeck & Ruprecht, 2004), p. 73.

from sociology, practice theory, and ethnography, which can be summarized as Grounded Theory. Grounded Theory means a research style based on scientific philosophy, and at the same time a coordinated ensemble of individual techniques with the help of which a theory grounded in the data can be developed step by step from interviews, field observations, documents, and statistics.[78] In my view, Schleiermacher's concept of theology shows a proximity to Grounded Theory, which develops its theory from empiricism via a systematic and controlled qualitative-interpretive procedure. In doing so, as is the case with the theory variant of Glaser and Strauss, previous knowledge is also included.[79] This knowledge can be fed from a variety of sources, including other academic disciplines. In view of the reception of Schleiermacher's thought, the reference to the task of defining the essence of Christianity seems to emerge as central. However, a style of work results that can be adapted to the situation and which is neither deductive nor inductive. The formation of theory always processes and integrates empirical components. And the perception, or rather the data-collection of empiricism is always already formed and structured in a way that can be reflected upon. A position that would naïvely juxtapose or flatly oppose theory and empiricism would therefore be untenable. An empirical mindset, and with it the reference of theology as a positive rather than speculative science, is constitutive for theology as a whole. Practical theology would have a special hinge function here, insofar as it reflects the theoretical content of empirical perception and the empirical content of theory. This aspect reflects Schleiermacher's overall conception of theology as an "assemblage of scientific knowledge and practical instruction."[80]

A second point deserving further consideration is Schleiermacher's understanding of the place of practical theology within the university. Over the course of its history as an academic discipline, the proper institutional location of practical theology has often been the subject of discussion, though it is seldom problematized. The conception of practical theology presented by Schleiermacher is essentially related to the early nineteenth-century reform of Berlin university. In this context, academic studies were not primarily conceived as training for professional practice on the basis of their expectations of usefulness. Rather, the neo-humanist ideal of education (*Bildung*) corresponds to the principle of an openness to processes of further social development and a reflective distancing from traditional routines. Such aims can only be realized through disciplined academic thinking. Schleiermacher contributed to this idea of the university not only through his encyclopedic draft of theology, but also through offering his own expert opinion on the tasks and organization of the university.

In his *Gelegentliche Gedanken* Schleiermacher defines the university as a unique institution that serves as a transition between school and academy. Thus, it exists "between the time when, through a foundation of knowledge and through actual learning, young persons are first shaped by science, and the time when, in the strength and fullness of scientific life, they themselves expand the field of knowledge and cultivate it more beautifully."[81] Here the

---

[78] Cf. Anselm Strauss and Juliet Corbin, *Grounded Theory. Grundlagen Qualitativer Sozialforschung* (Weinheim: Beltz, 1996), p. vii.

[79] Jörg Strübing, "Pragmatismus als epistemische Praxis. Der Beitrag der Grounded Theory zur Empirie-Theorie-Frage," in *Theoretische Empirie. Zur Relevanz qualitativer Forschung*, ed. Herbert Kalthoff, Stefan Hirschauer, and Gesa Lindemann (Frankfurt am Main: Suhrkamp Verlag, 2008), p. 284.

[80] *BO* §5, p. 3; *KGA* 1.6, §5, p. 328.

[81] *Gedanken*, p. 238.

university is given the dual task of learning and carrying out critical academic thinking. "So the university is preeminently concerned with the initiation of a process, with the supervision of its first developments. But this is nothing less than an entirely new spiritual life process."[82] Practical theology, which has its place at the university, is also understood in this sense as encompassing a particular style of academic thinking. Schleiermacher spoke out critically against the theological seminaries (*Predigerseminare*) that were emerging at the same time and which offered practical training for graduates who would go on to receive qualifications for ministry, because they were a learning practice that fell short of this academic style of thinking. Such an approach in the theological seminary rather leads to "one-sidedness" (*Einseitigkeit*), an attitude of "patronizing" (*Gängelei*), and the imitation of a certain affected "manner" (*Manier*),[83] because the educational institution at once restricts academic freedom and promotes a mechanical application of pastoral prudence rules.[84] In this regard, the question of the place and function of practical theology in the university, and its relation to other institutions offering practical-theological training, remains an enduring point of consideration.

Suggested Reading

Doerne, Martin. "Theologie und Kirchenregiment. Eine Studie zu Schleiermachers praktischer Theologie." *Neue Zeitschrift für Systematische Theologie und Religionsphilosophie* 10 (1968), pp. 360–386.
Gräb, Wilhelm. "Praktische Theologie." In *Schleiermacher Handbuch*, ed. Martin Ohst (Tübingen: Mohr Siebeck, 2017), pp. 399–410.
Weyel, Birgit. "Practical Theology and Religion." In *International Handbook of Practical Theology*, ed. Birgit Weyel, Wilhelm Gräb, Emmanuel Lartey, and Cas Wepener (Berlin/Boston: Walter de Gruyter, 2022), pp. 219–231.

Bibliography

Ahlers, Bodo. *Die Unterscheidung von Theologie und Religion. Ein Beitrag zur Vorgeschichte der Praktischen Theologie im 18. Jahrhundert* (Gütersloh: Gütersloher Verlagshaus, 1980).
Albrecht, Christian. *Enzyklopädische Probleme der Praktischen Theologie* (Tübingen: Mohr Siebeck, 2011).
Albrecht, Christian. "Die Praktische Theologie im Kreis der theologischen Fächer. Theorie der religiösen Praxis des Christentums." In *Fremde unter einem Dach? Die theologischen Fächerkulturen in enzyklopädischer Perspektive*, ed. Markus Buntfuß and Martin Fritz (Berlin/Boston: De Gruyter, 2014), pp. 149–165.

---

[82] *Gedanken*, p. 238, translation amended.
[83] Friedrich Daniel Schleiermacher and Wilhelm Martin Leberecht de Wette, "Gutachten der theologischen Facultät zu Berlin, über die zweckmäßige Anlegung von Prediger Seminarien vom 6. Mai 1816," in *Archiv der Humboldt University of Berlin, Bestand Theologische Fakultät*, Repertorium 47, pp. 2–8 (unpublished archive, handwritten by Schleiermacher and co-signed by de Wette), p. 4.
[84] Weyel, *Praktische Bildung*, pp. 68ff.

Albrecht, Christian. "Schleiermachers Predigtlehre. Eine Skizze vor dem Hintergrund seines philosophisch-theologischen Gesamtsystem." In *Klassiker der protestantischen Predigtlehre*, ed. Christian Albrecht and Martin Weeber (Tübingen: Mohr Siebeck, 2002), pp. 93–119.

Albrecht, Christian. "Schleiermachers Programm der Seelsorge als Wiederherstellung religiöser Autonomie." In *Der Mensch und seine Seele. Bildung–Frömmigkeit–Ästhetik. Akten des internationalen Kongresses der Schleiermacher-Gesellschaft in Münster September 2015*, ed. Arnulf von Scheliha and Jörg Dierken (Berlin/Boston: De Gruyter, 2017), pp. 277–291.

Arndt, Andreas, and Wolfgang Virmond. *Schleiermachers Briefwechsel (Verzeichnis) nebst einer Liste seiner Vorlesungen*. Schleiermacher-Archiv 11 (Berlin/New York: De Gruyter, 1992).

Barth, Ulrich. "Theorie der Theologie." In *Schleiermacher Handbuch*, ed. Martin Ohst (Tübingen: Mohr Siebeck, 2017), pp. 316–327.

Birkner, Hans-Joachim. "Schleiermachers 'Kurze Darstellung' als theologisches Reformprogramm." In *Schleiermacher-Studien*, ed. Hans-Joachim Birkner (Berlin/New York: Walter de Gruyter, 1996), pp. 285–305.

Doerne, Martin. "Theologie und Kirchenregiment. Eine Studie zu Schleiermachers praktischer Theologie." *Neue Zeitschrift für Systematische Theologie und Religionsphilosophie* 10 (1968), pp. 360–386.

Drehsen, Volker. *Neuzeitliche Konstitutionsbedingungen der Praktischen Theologie. Aspekte der theologischen Wende zur sozialkulturellen Lebenswelt christlicher Religion* (Göttingen: Gütersloher Verlagshaus, 1988).

Fritz, Martin. "Schleiermachers Idee theologischer Bildung. Zur Aktualität der 'Kurzen Darstellung des theologischen Studiums.'" In *Fremde unter einem Dach? Die theologischen Fächerkulturen in enzyklopädischer Perspektive*, ed. Markus von Buntfuß and Martin Fritz (Berlin/Boston: De Gruyter, 2014), pp. 167–203.

Gräb, Wilhelm. "Praktische Theologie." In *Schleiermacher Handbuch*, ed. Martin Ohst (Tübingen: Mohr Siebeck, 2017), pp. 399–410.

Gräb, Wilhelm. *Predigt als Mitteilung des Glaubens* (Gütersloh: Gütersloher Verlagshaus, 1993).

Gräb, Wilhelm. *Predigtlehre. Über religiöse Rede* (Göttingen: Vandenhoeck & Ruprecht, 2013).

Grethlein, Christian, and Michael Meyer-Blanck, eds. *Geschichte der Praktischen Theologie. Dargestellt anhand ihrer Klassiker* (Leipzig: Evangelische Verlagsanstalt, 1999).

Laube, Martin. "Zur Stellung der Praktischen Theologie innerhalb der Theologie—Aus systematisch-theologischer Sicht." In *Praktische Theologie. Eine Theorie- und Problemgeschichte*, ed. Christian Grethlein and Helmut Schwier (Leipzig: Evangelische Verlagsanstalt 2007), pp. 61–136.

Luther, Henning. "Praktische Theologie als Kunst für alle. Individualität und Kirche in Schleiermachers Verständnis Praktischer Theologie." *Zeitschrift für Theologie und Kirche* 84 (1987), pp. 371–393.

Nitzsch, Karl Ludwig. "Gemeinschaftliche Vorschläge zu dem in Wittenberg zu errichtenden Prediger-Seminario vom 28. November 1816." In *Archiv des Predigerseminars Wittenbergs*, Akte 135, pp. 17–44 (unpublished archive).

Rössler, Dietrich. "Unterbrechungen des Lebens. Zur Theorie des Fests bei Friedrich Schleiermacher." In *In der Schar derer, die da feiern. Feste als Gegenstand praktisch-theologischer Reflexion*, ed. Peter Cornehl, Martin Dutzmann, and Andreas Strauch (Göttingen, 1993), pp. 33–40.

Roth, Ursula. *Die Theatralität des Gottesdienstes* (Gütersloh: Gütersloher Verlagshaus, 2006).

Schröder, Markus. *Die kritische Identität des neuzeitlichen Christentums. Schleiermachers Wesensbestimmung christlicher Religion* (Tübingen: Mohr Siebeck, 1996).

Strauss, Anselm, and Juliet Corbin. *Grounded Theory. Grundlagen Qualitativer Sozialforschung* (Weinheim: Beltz, 1996).

Stroh, Ralf. *Schleiermachers Gottesdiensttheorie. Studien zur Rekonstruktion ihres enzyklopädischen Rahmens im Ausgang von "Kurzer Darstellung" und "Philosophischer Ethik"* (Berlin/New York: Walter de Gruyter, 1998).

Strübing, Jörg. "Pragmatismus als epistemische Praxis. Der Beitrag der Grounded Theory zur Empirie-Theorie-Frage." In *Theoretische Empirie. Zur Relevanz qualitativer Forschung*, ed. Herbert Kalthoff, Stefan Hirschauer, and Gesa Lindemann (Frankfurt am Main: Suhrkamp Verlag, 2008), pp. 282–285.

von Nathusius, Martin. *Der Ausbau der praktischen Theologie* (Leipzig, 1899).

Weyel, Birgit. "Practical Theology as a Hermeneutical Science of Lived Religion." *International Journal of Practical Theology* 18 (2014), pp. 150–159.

Weyel, Birgit. *Praktische Bildung zum Pfarrberuf. Das Predigerseminar Wittenberg und die Entstehung einer zweiten Ausbildungsphase evangelischer Pfarrer in Preußen* (Tübingen: Mohr Siebeck, 2006).

Weyel, Birgit. "Seelsorge als Praxis der Freiheit. Eine praktisch-theologische Konturierung gelebter Freiheit." In *Bestimmte Freiheit. Festschrift für Christof Landmesser*, ed. Martin Bauspieß, Johannes U. Beck, and Friederike Portenhauser (Leipzig: Evangelische Verlagsanstalt, 2020), pp. 325–340.

Wintzer, Friedrich. *Die Homiletik seit Schleiermacher bis in die Anfänge der "dialektischen Theologie" in Grundzügen* (Göttingen: Vandenhoeck & Ruprecht, 1969).

Wintzer, Friedrich, ed. *Seelsorge. Texte zum gewandelten Verständnis und zur Praxis der Seelsorge in der Neuzeit* (München: Kaiser, 1999).

Ziemer, Jürgen. "Die Beziehung zwischen Ratsuchendem und Seelsorge." In *Handbuch der Seelsorge. Grundlagen und Profile*, ed. Wilfried Engemann (Leipzig: Evangelische Verlagsanstalt, 2007), pp. 143–157.

Ziemer, Jürgen. *Seelsorgelehre. Eine Einführung für Studium und Praxis*, 2nd ed. (Göttingen: Vandenhoeck & Ruprecht, 2004).

C

SCHLEIERMACHER'S PASTORAL AND OCCASIONAL WRITINGS

CHAPTER 26

EARLY WRITINGS ON ETHICS
Monologen, Vertraute Briefe, *and* Grundlinien

OMAR BRINO

MONOLOGEN (*Soliloquies*), *Vertraute Briefe über Friedrich Schlegels* Lucinde (*Confidential Letters on Friedrich Schlegel's* Lucinde) and *Grundlinien einer Kritik der bisherigen Sittenlehre* (*Outlines of a Critique of Previous Ethical Theory*) are the first and most important books published by Schleiermacher on ethical themes. Despite the difference in style between the systematic and "scientific" approach of the broad *Outlines* (1803) and the "effusive" writing of the short *Soliloquies* (1800), the two works share the same basic perspective, as the author himself explicitly says.[1] The *Outlines* develop this common perspective at a theoretically deeper level, detailing an explicit confrontation with ancient, modern and contemporaneous philosophers, whereas such confrontation remains implicit in the more "evocative" *Soliloquies*. Although the *Confidential Letters* (1800) are of more occasional nature and limited to a specific theme, that of conjugal love, even this work is inscribed in a single argumentative arc with the other two.

In the first section of this chapter I will briefly make reference to the emergence of significant elements in Schleiermacher's ethical perspective that were already apparent in the manuscripts written before his earliest publications. In the second, central section of the chapter I will analyze the main aspects of the ethical proposal that Schleiermacher achieved in *Soliloquies*, *Confidential Letters*, and *Outlines*. In the third section, I will end with some indication of how the positions found in Schleiermacher's first important books on ethics would remain in his subsequent thought, while in contrast, other aspects would be emphasized differently or even changed.

---

[1] *GKS*, p. 29, lines 18–21.

26.1 Starting Points of Schleiermacher's Ethical Thought in the Manuscripts Written in His Youth

The notes that the 21-year-old Schleiermacher wrote in 1789 on Kant's *Critique of Practical Reason*, a year after its publication in 1788, are already significant for his future ethical thought. In particular, here Schleiermacher analyzed what Kant had said about "respect" (*Achtung*) as a moral incentive (*Triebfeder*). According to Kant, this incentive comprises a humiliation of the underlying pathological inclinations of self-conceit (*Eigendünkel*).² Commenting on this Kantian position, the young Schleiermacher wrote, "Only a negative feeling originates directly from the relation of practical reason to self-conceit . . ., an inhibition of the causality of a pathologically driven feeling . . .; it is still, however, not an incentive."³ Already in the first manuscripts Schleiermacher was also unconvinced by the approach of the *Critique of Practical Reason*, for which actions are absolutely free from "natural" and "pre-rational" human components. In his studies at the University of Halle, Schleiermacher had the opportunity to explore other theories of action—in particular the Aristotelian one that he studied at firsthand, and the Leibnizian-Wolffian one of his teacher Johann August Eberhard.

In the manuscript *On Freedom* of ca. 1790–1792, Schleiermacher thus sought a sort of mediation between a pre-Kantian natural teleological approach and the Kantian critical one. According to this manuscript, in the natural world and in the pre-rational component of the person there are laws of specific production, and strictly rational human action is established in relative but not absolute autonomy with respect to these laws, according to its own distinct characteristics of specifically moral production.⁴

This specifically moral production, however, does not at all have the happiness of individuals as its own aim.⁵ Rather, Schleiermacher asserted that the purpose of ethics for each individual is to contribute to a common spiritual culture. There are already indications on this view in the manuscript *On What Gives Value to Life* of 1792/1793,⁶ in the pages of which many points foreshadow the *Soliloquies*. Already terms like *Kultur* and *Bildung* are intensely associated with ethics, referring to the common goods of science, art, friendship, and civil values.⁷ It is precisely in this direction that Schleiermacher would constitute his own conception of the highest good as a social idea of humanity to which each individual can make a specific contribution. Indeed, from the beginning Schleiermacher was critical

---

² Cf. Immanuel Kant, *Gesammelte Schriften*, ed. the Royal Prussian (later German, then Berlin-Brandenburg) Academy of Sciences (Berlin: Reimer [then de Gruyter], 1900–), vol. 5, p. 73 (Kritik der praktischen Vernunft, A 129–130).

³ *KGA* 1.1, p. 132; *NK*, p. 27. Cf. Jackeline Mariña, *Transformation of the Self in the Thought of Schleiermacher* (Oxford: Oxford University Press, 2008), pp. 15–42.

⁴ See *UF*; *OF*.

⁵ See e.g. *KGA* 1.1, pp. 100, 460.

⁶ *UWL*; *WGVL*.

⁷ See *UWL* pp. 446, 449. On the relation between ethics and *Bildung*, which is a structural character of Schleiermacher's thought from its beginning, cf. recently Arnulf von Scheliha and Jörg Dierken, eds., *Der Mensch und seine Seele. Bildung–Frömmigkeit–Ästhetik* (Berlin/Boston: De Gruyter, 2017), pp. 35–215.

of the conception of the highest good of the *Critique of Practical Reason*, in which Kant reintroduced in a transcendent dimension the individual happiness that he had previously excluded from ethics.[8]

26.2 THE BASIC POSITIONS OF SCHLEIERMACHER'S ETHICAL THOUGHT IN *SOLILOQUIES*, *CONFIDENTIAL LETTERS*, AND *OUTLINES*

26.2.1 *Soliloquies*

When Schleiermacher came to Berlin as a preacher at the Charité Hospital in 1796, he also had already under his belt intense meditations on ethical problems, conducted both in the "scholastic"-systematic style, as in *On Freedom*, and in the more direct style of popular philosophy, as in *On What Gives Value to Life*. In participating in the rich cultural world of Berlin and in the Schlegel brothers' magazine *Athenaeum*, Schleiermacher had the opportunity to develop his positions further.[9] Quickly written at the end of 1799 and published anonymously in January 1800, the *Soliloquies* represent Schleiermacher's attempt to set out the main points of his own ethical thought in an incisive but not pedantic form.[10]

The five short *Soliloquies* are presented as a reflection occasioned by the passage of one year to another. From the beginning to the end of the book, Schleiermacher warns against an ethical subjectivity based only on competition and its regulation. This perspective leads not only to the degradation of community relations, but also to an ultimate dissatisfaction of individuals: at the end, one feels "disillusionment and disgust with all this useless pursuit of novel enjoyments, perceptions and activities."[11]

If in the fourth speech of *On Religion* of 1799 Schleiermacher had dealt with religious communities, in the *Soliloquies* reflection on community relations extends to friendship,

---

[8] See *UHG*; *OHG*. Since the critical edition of 1984 (*KGA* 1.1), Schleiermacher's early manuscripts have been intensively studied and translated. Some interpreters have emphasized more the "communitarian" elements in them (e.g. Bernd Oberdorfer, *Geselligkeit und Realisierung von Sittlichkeit. Die Theorieentwicklung Friedrich Schleiermachers bis 1799* [Berlin/New York: De Gruyter, 1995]); others have focused instead on their theory of acting, in critical debate with Kant (e.g. Günter Meckenstock, *Deterministische Ethik und kritische Theologie. Die Auseinandersetzung des frühen Schleiermacher mit Kant und Spinoza 1789-1794* [Berlin/New York: De Gruyter, 1988]). Even if in contact with multiple sources, the manuscripts in any case show the maturation of a specifically determined proposal (cf. Gunter Scholtz, *Ethik und Hermeneutik. Schleiermachers Grundlegung der Geisteswissenschaften* [Frankfurt am Main: Suhrkamp, 1995], pp. 18-34; Denis Thouard, *Schleiermacher. Communauté, individualité, communication* [Paris: Vrin, 2007]; and more recently Emanuela Giacca, *La formazione del pensiero etico di Schleiermacher* [Roma-Pisa: Fabrizio Serra, 2015], and Davide Bondì, *Il giovane Schleiermacher. Etica e religione* [Brescia: Morcelliana, 2018]).

[9] On this period in the development of Schleiermacher's thought cf. Andreas Arndt, ed., *Wissenschaft und Gesellschaft: Friedrich Schleiermacher in Berlin 1796-1802* (Berlin/New York: De Gruyter, 2009).

[10] On the history of the text and the first reception, cf. *KGA* 1.3, pp. vii-cxxvi (Günter Meckenstock's editorial introduction to the volume).

[11] *Monologen*[1], p. 7; *Solil.*, p. 13.

marriage, and politics. In this "present generation,"[12] such communities are often narrowed to the mere purpose of limiting selfishness, reducing the most obvious conflicts. Marriage is degraded to conformist utility;[13] the state has ceased to be a primary public reference for the life of all citizens, as in antiquity, and "all believe that the best of states is one that gives least evidence of its existence . . ., nothing but a necessary evil, as an indispensable mechanism for covering up crime and mitigating its effects . . ., nothing but a limitation."[14]

Faced with such individual and private egoism that not only has imposed itself on political relations, but also extends to the ethical ones such as friendship and family, the *Soliloquies* defend an alternative conception of individual subjectivity as a constructive and peculiar participation in a common whole. What Schleiermacher calls his "highest intuition" consists of seeing that "each man is meant to represent humanity [*Menschheit*] in his own way, combing its elements uniquely."[15] Peculiar and individual historicity, already appreciated in *On Religion* with regard to religious feelings, is thus valued in the *Soliloquies* as an ethically relevant dimension that does not deserve to be considered only as something potentially harmful and conflicting, but can also be appreciated because of what specifically it can provide to the community with others.[16]

The conflicts and dangers of individuals for other individuals do not arise, therefore, from individual subjectivity as such, but from the fact that it is emptied and schematized in an abstract selfish arbitrariness in which communication with others is totally replaced by a generic desire to prevail. Once individual specificity has been reduced to this generic conflictual arbitrariness that ought to be limited, the supreme ethical goal would be a generic uniformity resulting from reciprocal limitation. But in contrast, when individuality is appreciated as a constructive ethical dimension, even the various associations—from the smallest ones, such as marriage and friendship, to the larger ones such as states and religious communities—can be ethically appreciated in their historical interactions. "Imagination" (*Fantasie*), already defended in *On Religion*, represents the specific faculty of such formative interactions even more in the *Soliloquies*.

---

[12] *Monologen¹*, p. 35; *Solil.*, p. 62.
[13] *Monologen¹*, pp. 32–33, 47–48; *Solil.*, pp. 57–58, 78–81.
[14] *Monologen¹*, p. 33; *Solil.*, p. 59.
[15] *Monologen¹*, p. 18; *Solil.*, p. 31. Cf. on this point Georg Simmel, "Das Individuum und die Freiheit," in G. Simmel, *Brücke und Tür. Essays des Philosophen zur Geschichte, Religion, Kunst und Gesellschaft*, ed. M. Landmann (Stuttgart: Koehler, 1957), p. 267; English translation: Simmel, "Freedom and the Individual," in G. Simmel, *On Individuality and Social Forms. Selected Writings*, edited with an introduction by D. N. Levine (Chicago/London: University of Chicago Press, 1971), p. 224.
[16] Brent W. Sockness, in "Schleiermacher and the Ethics of Authenticity: The '*Monologen*' of 1800," *Journal of Religious Ethics* 32 (2004), pp. 477–517, speaks of a specific ethics of individual authenticity in the *Soliloquies*, also referring to what Charles Taylor calls an "expressivist" understanding of human selfhood. Such expressive interpretation of individual authenticity is only possible, as Thouard has efficiently underlined, in mutual communication with others: "Schleiermacher's originality . . . is to set up places for self-invention within the ways in which the human community is organized" (Denis Thouard, "L'éthique de l'individualité chez Schleiermacher," *Archives de Philosophie* 77 [2014], p. 299). On this specific intersubjective view of individuality in the *Soliloquies* cf. also Matthew R. Robinson, "Vollendet: The Completion of Humanity, the Gospel of John, and the Intersubjective Soul of Schleiermacher's *Monologen*," in *Der Mensch und seine Seele. Bildung-Frömmigkeit-Ästhetik*, ed. Arnulf von Scheliha and Jörg Dierken (Berlin/Boston: De Gruyter, 2017), pp. 405–419.

In this direction, Schleiermacher continues with a heartfelt prophetic tone, the relationship with other individuals depends no longer on the pleasures or sorrows that can be obtained from the changing cases of life, at the mercy of "destiny," but on the awareness of participating with one's entire unique individuality in a common whole: in this awareness consists the authentic "assurance of freedom"[17] (the author reformulates here a contrast between freedom and destiny typical in much eighteenth-century literature and widely used already in *On What Gives Value to Life*). Social manners or customs (*Sitten*), far from constituting only a conformist or hypocritical adjustment to set rules of mere coexistence, can become thus the peculiar form of a participatory interaction with others.[18] Language has a fundamental importance in this context.[19]

This participatory relationship by individuals, in their fullest peculiarity, to the whole of humanity is heartily depicted in the last *Soliloquy* with the tones of an eternal youth,[20] similar to an ethical counterpart of what is said in the second speech *On Religion* about the opening to immortality in the finite.[21]

Schleiermacher emphasizes that this participatory inspiration does not exclude but stimulates "sober wisdom" and the "cold weighing" of "means and ends";[22] once the inner serenity of one's own peculiar participation in humanity has been reached, such serenity translates into an effective and concrete action, into thoughtful and mature choices, and does not remain enclosed within itself.

In the following years, Schleiermacher would come to think of the *Soliloquies* as a perhaps too "idealized"[23] but vivid and spontaneous presentation of his own ethical basic positions. He published three other editions, in 1810, 1822, and 1829, introducing small but numerous and nuanced variations.[24] The 1810 and later editions were published under his own name.

---

[17] *Monologen¹*, p. 42; *Solil.*, p. 70.

[18] *Monologen¹*, pp. 38–39; *Solil.*, pp. 65–66. Schleiermacher had already written an essay on sociability that was anonymously published in a Berlin periodical in 1799, remaining unfinished (*VTB*; *TSC*). On the origins and development of Schleiermacher's reflections on sociability (*Geselligkeit*), cf. Thouard, *Schleiermacher*, pp. 21–76.

[19] *Monologen¹*, pp. 37–38; *Solil.*, pp. 64–65.

[20] *Monologen¹*, pp. 56, 61; *Solil.*, pp. 94, 103.

[21] The relationship between the *Soliloquies* and *On Religion* has also been discussed recently. According to Christiane Ehrhardt, in *Religion, Bildung und Erziehung bei Schleiermacher: Eine Analyse der Beziehungen und des Widerstreits zwischen den "Reden über die Religion" und den "Monologen"* (Göttingen: Vandenhoek & Ruprecht, 2005), there are some contrasts between the two works. For a "complementary" reading of them, see instead Robinson, "Vollendet," and Bondì, *Il giovane Schleiermacher*, esp. pp. 185–194. In accord with these complementary readings, I think that the differences between the two works should not be exaggerated, because they deal with distinct but compatible issues: in *On Religion*, the focus is on the one, infinite origin of both human subjectivity and the natural world; in the *Soliloquies*, the focus is on the relationships of human subjectivities among themselves.

[22] *Monologen¹*, p. 59; *Solil.*, p. 100.

[23] *KGA* 5.10, p. 251.

[24] Cf. *Monologen²* and *KGA* 1.12, pp. lxiii–lxix.

26.2.2 *Confidential Letters*

Marriage and conjugal love, included with other community spheres such as friendship and explored in some heartfelt pages of the *Soliloquies*, became the central theme of the *Confidential Letters on Friedrich Schlegel's* Lucinde, published anonymously in June of 1800.[25]

Schlegel's book exalted a life based on passion and imagination, to the point of defending a contemplative "idleness" (*Müßigang*) and a "boldness" (*Frechheit*) about the fusion of sensuality and love, and of nature and spirit, in a marked antithesis to the industriousness and moderation of Enlightenment ethics. The novel deliberately sought the scandal that punctually arrived. The late Enlightenment popular philosophers increased their attacks on and their satirical derision against Schlegel himself, his writings, and his circle of friends.

In the face of controversy, Schleiermacher decided to defend some of the contents advanced by his friend's novel, seizing the opportunity for a broader reflection on love and marriage. For his literary genre he chose the epistolary novel, which throughout the eighteenth century had been the most commonly used form of literary communication on the themes of love and family.

The primary intent of *Lucinde*, Schleiermacher argued, was not to describe sensuality as such, like the widespread eighteenth-century erotic and libertine literature so often did, but rather to propose a vision of love that does not separate its spiritual and physical aspects. Indeed, for the *Confidential Letters*, "pleasure and joy and the intertwining of bodies and life" are "no longer the separate work of a distinct, powerful divinity, but all in one with the deepest and most sacred feeling, a fusion and union of the two halves of the human being in a mystical wholeness."[26]

Sensual libertinism, on the one hand, and marriage, as a mere juridical contract for social convention on the other, are two sides of the same degraded vision of the relationship between men and women. In this degraded vision, the natural component of love is lowered either to a mere animalistic enjoyment or to a mere reproductive function, without considering the deep union of physical and ethical aspects that characterize a love relationship. "Nothing of what is divine," Schleiermacher says, "can be broken down into its elements of spirit and flesh, will and nature, without being profaned."[27] The *Confidential Letters* identify in "decency" (*Schaamhaftigkeit*) the feeling that safeguards this deep unity of love, beyond external prudery, on the one hand, and vulgar shamelessness, on the other.[28]

Schleiermacher was well aware that such a "true marriage," one as an authentic ethical and physical union, was very rare in his own age, when compared to arranged marriages for social or economic reasons; the main victims of this situation were above all women, forced into an imposed family regime. A biographical element can also be seen here. Schleiermacher was then sentimentally linked to Eleonore von Grunow, wife of a Berlin preacher. Eleonore,

---

[25] Cf. *KGA* 1.3, pp. xlviii–lxxii.

[26] *Lucinde*, p. 194. Cf. Sarah Schmidt, *Die Konstruktion des Endlichen. Schleiermachers Philosophie der Wechselwirkung* (Berlin/New York: De Gruyter, 2005), pp. 94–98; Elisabeth Hartlieb, *Geschlechterdifferenz im Denken Friedrich Schleiermachers* (Berlin/New York: De Gruyter, 2006), pp. 122–129.

[27] *Lucinde*, p. 165.

[28] *Lucinde*, pp. 168–178.

represented in the homonymous character of the *Confidential Letters*, was married when an adolescent, by family imposition, to a much older man whom she did not love. (After some years of indecision and torment, she would nevertheless remain with her husband.[29])

Unlike the *Soliloquies*, the *Confidential Letters* would never be reprinted by the author after the first anonymous edition: they were linked to very determined circumstances. The defense of a "scandalous" novel as *Lucinde* was an act of conscious courage. Schleiermacher knew well that the anonymity of the *Confidential Letters* would eventually be seen through, and that there would be consequences from his ecclesiastical superiors. In January 1802, the young preacher was indeed ordered to leave Berlin and to move to the small and distant town of Stolp, in East Prussia, where he would remain for about two years.[30]

26.2.3 *Outlines*

The *Outlines of a Critique of Previous Ethical Theory* were written for the most part in Stolp between the spring of 1802 and that of 1803, and were published in September of the later year. Although the writing of the book took a relatively short time, all the remarkable study that Schleiermacher had devoted to the theory and history of ethics since his university years converged in it.

While Schleiermacher's previous publications conformed mostly to an oratorical or popular style, the *Outlines*, as already many of the early manuscripts of ethics, were written in the style of a scientific treatise, according to the criteria of university philosophy. Moreover, where the first editions of *On Religion* and of the *Soliloquies*, as well as the *Confidential Letters*, had been published anonymously, the *Outlines* were published under the author's name. The themes already presented in a freer, literary way in the *Soliloquies* received a more thorough treatment in the *Outlines*, closer and more deeply connected to the long history of moral philosophy, from the Socratic schools to Kant and Fichte.[31]

---

[29] Cf. Ruth D. Richardson, *The Role of Women in the Life and Thought of the Early Schleiermacher (1768-1806): An Historical Overview* (Lewiston, NY: Mellen, 1991).

[30] On the period of Stolp cf. *KGA* 1.4, pp. vii-xcii (Eilert Herms, G. Meckenstock and Michael Pietsch's introduction to the volume).

[31] The *Outlines* has often been too little considered in the literature on Schleiermacher, despite the fact that, in the second half of the nineteenth century, scholars of the caliber of R. Haym had already stressed its relevance. Breaking decades of long silence, Eilert Herms, in *Herkunft, Entfaltung und erste Gestalt des Systems der Wissenschaften bei Schleiermacher* (Gütersloh: Mohn, 1974), indicated in the *Outlines* the key work of Schleiermacher's philosophical development. Herms himself then edited the work with M. Pietsch in *KGA* 1.4 (2002), making explicit many textual references left implicit by the author. In the still fundamental article by Claudio Cesa, "Schleiermacher critico dell'etica di Kant e Fichte. Spunti dalle 'Grundlinien'," *Archivio di Filosofia* 53 (1984), pp. 19-34, the *Outlines* are defined as "one of the most important books of classical German thought" and are clearly identified as the decisive text for understanding Schleiermacher's theoretical relationship to Kant and Fichte. Similarly, some papers of the groundbreaking collective volume by André Laks and Ada Neschke, eds., *La naissance du paradigme herméneutique* (Lille: Presses Universitaires de Lille, 1990; 2nd augmented edition, Villeneuve d'Ascq: Presses Univ. du Septentrion, 2008), highlight the centrality of the *Outlines* for understanding Schleiermacher's interpretation of Plato (more recently, see André Laks, "Schleiermacher on Plato: From Form (Introduction to Plato's Works) to Content (Outlines of a Critique of Previous Ethical Theory)," in *Brill's Companion to German Platonism*, ed. Alan Kim [Leiden/Boston: Brill, 2019], pp. 146-164). Schmidt, in *Die Konstruktion*, esp. pp. 260-280, also argues for the importance of the *Outlines* in the

In fact, the book is a broad historical-critical analysis of ancient, modern, and current moral doctrines, which are evaluated according to their coherence and completeness. The coherence of a doctrine is a matter of its considering and directing human actions from specific principles, without adding elements contrary to them; the completeness of a doctrine is its ability to embrace all areas of human action without excluding any of them from ethical consideration.[32]

All principles develop through the specific ethical concepts, which the *Outlines* identify as goods, virtues, and duties, each with a respective opposite: evils, vices, and transgressions. Goods represent what can be achieved through ethical principles, and the systematic connection between goods constitutes the highest good. Virtues denote the inner forces that ethical principles intend to encourage in the individual agents; their consistent development is given by the ideal of the wise. And finally, duties express the formulas that ethical principles prescribe to address ethical actions; the overall direction from which particular duties derive is the moral law.

The more an ethical doctrine is coherent and complete, that is systematic, the more these three series of concepts (goods, virtues, and duties) and their respective overall configurations (highest good, wise, moral law) are harmoniously developed, without the exclusive prevalence of any of them. A doctrine that deals only with formulating directives/duties, without worrying about the achieved results/goods and the internal forces to be promoted/virtues, is therefore certainly deficient; and vice versa, the ethical goods cannot be simply described, without indicating the direction of actions to achieve them and the internal forces of the agent that must be incentivized for this purpose.[33]

The principles of ethical doctrines to date are then classified through specific differentiations among them. "Practical" (*praktisch*) and "eudemonistic" (*eudemonistisch*) principles are primarily differentiated: the former aim to determine actions or beings in themselves, while the latter aim at the subjective effects of actions or beings, that is happiness or pleasure.[34] Another crucial differentiation is made by Schleiermacher between "propositive" (*hervorbringend*), "formative" (*bildend*), and "constructive" (*erzeugend*) principles on the one hand, and "restrictive" (*beschränkend*) and "negative" (*negativ*) ones on the other. In formative, constructive doctrines the action is structured from the beginning on the basis of ethical principles, whereas in the restrictive doctrines the principles intervene only over previously assumed non-ethical dimensions.[35] On the basis of these criteria and classifications, the *Outlines* develop their evaluation of the different historical ethical doctrines.

Firstly, all the eudemonistic ethics are strongly criticized. The ancient Cyreniacs themselves admitted with unscrupulous frankness that it was impossible to build a coherent ethics

---

development of Schleiermacher's dialectics. For a broad structural analysis of the *Outlines* and for its central location in Schleiermacher' thought cf. Omar Brino, *L'architettonica della morale. Teoria e storia dell'etica nelle Grundlinien di Schleiermacher* (Trento: Editrice Università degli Studi di Trento, 2007). That the *Outlines* constitutes the point of arrival of Schleiermacher's philosophical maturity has also recently been underlined in Giacca, *La formazione*. Overall, more attention to the *Outlines* still represents, in my view, a decisive frontier for any future research on Schleiermacher.

[32] See *GKS*, pp. 37, 136–137.
[33] See *GKS*, pp. 100–102.
[34] See *GKS*, pp. 69–70.
[35] See *GKS*, pp. 83–84.

on the basis of mere pleasure. When Aristippus said that "pleasure is good even when it comes from shameful facts" or when Hegesias asserted that suicide was to be preferred in the instant when there was no pleasure, they highlighted the fundamental self-destructiveness of every eudemonistic perspective.[36] Modern eudemonists were certainly more moderate, but for this reason even more incoherent. Schleiermacher referred here mainly to the British moral-sense theorists—Shaftesbury, Hutcheson, Ferguson, and Smith—all united in one school.[37] In the first place, according to Schleiermacher, the British moral-sense perspective presupposes an egoistic interest in happiness as the main driving force behind all actions; and secondly, it presents a feeling—that is benevolence, *Wohlwollen*—that spontaneously limits that egoist basic interest in favor of living with others: "there is the comical situation that benevolence ultimately lies in the conservation of the selfish pleasure of others."[38]

A formal coherence is reached, on the contrary, by those whom Schleiermacher calls "restrictive practical" moral philosophers, ascribing to this group the ancient Stoics and the modern Kant. The problem, however, according to Schleiermacher, is that in these philosophers such coherence remains merely formal, leaving their doctrines "incomplete." The main function of a restrictive practical principle is, indeed, to oppose a potential conflict between individuals. Whatever is not potentially harmful in individual actions remains excluded from a properly ethical consideration: that is, it is "permitted," "licit" (*erlaubt*). In this way, important areas of human life—science, art, communities such as friendship or love—tend to be excluded from the configuration of ethical principles, which consider them only where conflicts can arise.[39]

According to Schleiermacher, Kant had shaped his moral law on the model of juridical private law, which is limited precisely to resolving the potential conflicts of self-interest. Certainly in Kant the moral law requires an inner intention, while the juridical law is satisfied with external action; both types of law, however, Schleiermacher continued, act in a similar way: they select, in a given arbitrariness (*Willkür*), what does not conflict with a universal law of a restrictive type, without being able to enter into the contents of that arbitrariness.[40] This proposal is ethically so incomplete that in the dialectic of practical reason Kant was forced to reintroduce, in a transcendent dimension, what he had categorically excluded from the moral law, that is subjective happiness, in order to have something to fill an emptied ethical act.[41]

To both eudemonistic and restrictive ethics, Schleiermacher opposes the constructive practical doctrines whose first exponents are considered to be Plato and Aristotle. According to Plato's philosophy, individuals participate with all their specific peculiarity in community spheres, which therefore arise not at all through mutual limitation, but through participation in a whole; all aspects of human life—friendship, love, political life, science, religiosity, and also art (despite the criticism of the latter in the *Republic*)[42]—are considered by Plato in

---

[36] See *GKS*, pp. 113–114.
[37] Cf. Andreas Arndt, *Friedrich Schleiermacher als Philosoph* (Berlin/Boston: De Gruyter, 2013), pp. 102–114.
[38] *GKS*, p. 112.
[39] See *GKS*, pp. 127–134, 161–164.
[40] See *GKS*, pp. 94–95, 128.
[41] See *GKS*, pp. 53, 124.
[42] See *GKS*, p. 305 and Plato, *Platonis Opera*, ed. John Burnet, 5 vols. (Oxford: Oxford University Press, 1900–1907), vol. 2, pp. 245a–c, where poetry is given by the gods.

their specific ethical meaning, without leaving them to mere empty arbitrariness. Aristotle, for his part, takes ethical contents to be realized in a specific and peculiar way, starting from the nature of man as a rational and social animal, and happiness results from this realization in the dianoetic and ethical virtues respectively. An eudemonistic perspective therefore cannot be ascribed to the Stagirite. For Aristotle happiness is only the result of actions that adhere to precise parameters to be realized; according to him happiness is not the parameter itself through which the morality of an action is to be judged.[43]

However, all ancient philosophy, even in its major exponents such as Plato and Aristotle, presents elements that appear to be completely outdated and ethically questionable. First of all, in antiquity there was an almost exclusive predominance of the political community over all other forms of association;[44] individual space was thus limited into a single social dimension and was less free than in the modern world, within which, starting from the crucial differentiation of state and church, more fields of social interaction have opened up.[45] In addition, in antiquity women were wholly subordinated to men[46] (from which an unbalanced view of love also derives).[47] Furthermore, certain political or ethnic distinctions such as Greeks vs. Barbarians, and free people vs. slaves—were widely considered, in antiquity, to be part of the universal nature of humanity. Participation in communities in the modern world is inscribed in a universal idea of humankind that goes beyond Plato, Aristotle, and all other ancient moralists with regard to such topics. If these limitations are common to Plato and Aristotle, the *Outlines* is more critical of the latter. The Platonic approach is considered more compact and coherent, whereas in Aristotle the ethical and dianoetic virtues are not organically connected to each other.[48]

Among the modern philosophers, Spinoza, according to the *Outlines*, is the one who had to date striven the most to build a consistent practical constructive ethics. He starts from the principle of knowledge and love of God and concretizes it in a correspondent knowledge and love for all his infinite modes, according to one's own particular singularity. The specific vital "conatus" of each individual is strengthened in this knowledge and love, and "laetitia" derives from this. Spinoza does not therefore envisage a mere contemplative quietism: on the contrary, he stimulates an active life of each individual in relation to other "*res particulares*, each of which expresses the Eternal 'in a certain and determined mode.'"[49] According to Schleiermacher, however, the value of individuality is more asserted than carried out by Spinoza: therefore, he is not completely able to work out his philosophy of individuality in an ethical consideration of historical concreteness as such.[50] A proof of this is that in Spinoza, artistic knowledge, which is linked to peculiar historicity and individuality, remains, not accidentally, too undervalued compared to scientific knowledge.[51]

[43] See *GKS*, pp. 73–74.
[44] See *GKS*, pp. 337–338.
[45] See *GKS*, p. 310.
[46] See *GKS*, p. 311.
[47] See *GKS*, p. 295.
[48] See e.g. *GKS*, p. 246.
[49] See *GKS*, p. 98 and Spinoza, *Ethica*, I 25 Cor.: "res particulares nihil sunt, nisi Dei attributorum affectiones, sive modi, quibus Dei attributa certo, & determinato modo exprimuntur" (Benedictus de Spinoza, *Opera*, ed. Carl Gebhardt, 4 vols. [Heidelberg: Winter, 1925], vol. 2, p. 68). See also *GKS*, pp. 88–89, 123.
[50] See *GKS*, p. 64.
[51] See *GKS*, p. 305.

Among the most recent philosophers, Fichte is particularly discussed in the *Outlines*; the same approach with which Schleiermacher evaluates the different ethics, focusing on their systematic consistency, clearly indicates a deep confrontation with him. Schleiermacher also admits that Fichte, more than Kant, strives to present a doctrine attentive to the content, and not just to the form, of action. In the third part of his *System of Ethics* of 1798, in particular, Fichte tries to articulate ethical contents in a systematic form, through diversified duties, with which each individual ought to contribute to an overall moral elevation according to his particular position. This Fichtean proposal is analyzed in detail in the *Outlines*; but for Schleiermacher it remains in the end unsatisfactory, because each individual and social activity is reduced to a mere "instrument" for the realization of a universal moral law, rather than being appreciated as a specific and peculiar good in itself.[52] Art, for example, according to the Fichtean ethical doctrine, would be exhausted in improving the relationships of individuals to the moral law, without constituting an autonomous ethical dimension in itself.[53] Political and religious communities would be restricted to a similar instrumental function.[54] Thus despite all efforts, according to Schleiermacher, the Fichtean ethical approach remains restrictive, like the Kantian one; a counter-proof of this is seen by Schleiermacher in the fact that the whole ethical activity is enclosed by Fichte in the sole concept of duties, depriving itself of goods—as ethical results—and of virtues, as formative inner ethical forces in individuals.

Schleiermacher's constructive proposal, in contrast, aspires to evaluate every specific community and spiritual area and every unrepeatable individual contribution not as means and instruments for an extrinsic goal, but ethically as such, as a peculiar and inalienable aspect of a whole. Universality (*das Allgemeine*) and peculiarity (*das Eigentümliche*) can only be correctly developed reciprocally.[55] In this context, for Schleiermacher, individual evil arises when a person encloses themself in a generic aggressiveness, without being able to make their own peculiarity purposeful for common goods; and similarly, social evil arises where a community—for example a political or a religious one—selfishly encloses itself and becomes aggressively noncooperative in the context of a wider interaction among the different human communities.[56]

Paying attention to the different communities, in their peculiar but not merely selfish dimensions, it is also possible to make proper use of an aspect that Fichte rightly emphasizes in an ethical doctrine: that is, that it should try to "improve" and not only to describe the historical and social conditions it finds.[57] Despite this correct emphasis, the improvement envisaged as a duty by Fichte still risks remaining unrealistic and isolated, as a supreme ideal unrelated to an overall recognition of the historical peculiarities through which it might be implemented; Schleiermacher, on the contrary, seeks a correlation between, on the one

---

[52] See *GKS*, pp. 92–93, 128–129.

[53] See *GKS*, pp. 306–307.

[54] See *GKS*, pp. 309, 313.

[55] See *GKS*, pp. 90–99. On the concept of "reciprocal interaction" or "mutual determination" (*Wechselwirkung*) in Schleiermacher cf. Schmidt, *Die Konstruktion*.

[56] See one of Schleiermacher's earliest university lectures on ethics (1805/06): "Evil is posited in both particular and large-scale acts partly as incapacity and partly as corruption. Incapacity is [when] something general does not come into existence in particular.... Corruption is [when] the particular refuses community.... An intolerant church is egoistic, as a closed state is" (*WA* vol. II, pp. 102–103; *NOE*, p. 55).

[57] See *GKS*, pp. 307–314, 328–334.

hand, the aspect of inquiry, which gives an account of the historical development of the current social spheres in their peculiar determinateness, and on the other hand, the "prophetic"[58] aspect, which indicates the directions of pursuing and reforming these spheres. He therefore conceives the idea of relating ethics to a series of investigative and applicative disciplines, in order to maintain a relationship between general ethical concepts—goods, virtues, and duties—and particular social and historical spheres. Of this "scientific cycle" of "practical sciences"[59] the *Outlines* offers the possible examples of politics, pedagogy, and economics; on the one hand these are autonomous disciplines when investigating particular areas, but on the other hand they are reconnected to ethics, both in order to reflect about the general moral parameters of human action and to translate and apply these parameters to historical concreteness.[60]

The comparison with Fichte, and more generally with the whole post-Kantian philosophical climate, is also evident in the way in which Schleiermacher deals with both the problem of the inclusion of ethics in a complete system of knowledge and the problem of the relationship ethics, as doctrine of human action, establishes within this system with respect to physics, as doctrine of the overall nature in which this action is exercised. Only in this general context can the theme of freedom of will be discussed.[61] The antinomic relationship established by Kant between moral law and natural law is strongly criticized. Here too, Schleiermacher sees an undue "judicialization": natural law would be conceived as a sort of universal law that can be avoided or resisted, whereas the relationship between universality and individuality in natural law cannot be at all oppositional—as it is in the juridical law—but must be one of reciprocal production.[62] For example, no natural body perceives the fact of being subjected to the universal law of gravitation as an imposition that can be avoided or resisted. Despite his complex doctrine of impulses, Fichte does not differ enough from Kant, according to Schleiermacher, even on these issues,[63] while Plato and Spinoza again offer a more productive solution, because they understand the ethical will and natural forces as two distinct aspects of a complex whole that finds its common origin above both aspects taken unilaterally.[64]

In light of this material we can understand the interest with which Schleiermacher looked at Schelling's systematics, both in the *Outlines* and in a detailed 1804 review of the *Lectures on the Method of Academic Study*. According to Schleiermacher, however, Schelling did not distinguish sufficiently between what is peculiarly human and ethical on the one hand, and what is natural and cosmic in general on the other;[65] therefore, Schelling did not succeed

---

[58] *GKS*, p. 332.

[59] *GKS*, pp. 333–334.

[60] On normativity and description in Schleiermacher's ethics cf. Scholtz, *Ethik und Hermeneutik*, and Arnulf von Scheliha, "Sources of Normativity in Schleiermacher's Interpretation of Culture," in *Schleiermacher, the Study of Religion, and the Future of Theology*, ed. Brent Sockness and Wilhelm Gräb (Berlin/New York: De Gruyter, 2010), pp. 285–298.

[61] *GKS*, p. 40.

[62] See *GKS*, pp. 50–51, 95–96.

[63] See *GKS*, pp. 53–62, 85–87. See also the criticism of Kant's and Fichte's positions on love and relationship between the sexes, *GKS*, pp. 293–302. Cf. Hartlieb, *Geschlechterdifferenz*, pp. 132–138.

[64] See *GKS*, pp. 63–66. In a contemporary letter, Schleiermacher says that, also in the "critical" *Outlines*, he remains the same "old mystic" of the previous works (*KGA* 5.6, p. 277). Cf. also *GKS*, p. 29, line 19.

[65] See *KGA*, 1.3, p. 320; *GKS*, p. 356; *KGA* 1.4, p. 479.

in delineating a proper moral philosophy—or rather, he did not want to, favoring instead a cosmic-tragic conception of an aesthetic kind. In this sense, the 1804 review explicitly saw some fascination in Schelling for "pagan" elements such as that of "destiny."[66]

26.3 EARLY AND LATE SCHLEIERMACHER WRITINGS ON ETHICS

Schleiermacher presented his main mature ethical ideas in a series of addresses at the Berlin Academy of Sciences, progressively published from 1820 to 1832 as papers in its annual *Proceedings*. Taken together, these papers develop basic positions that are in many respects in continuity with the *Outlines*. We therefore find: a relationship of non-antinomic specificity between ethics and physics;[67] the proposal of a practical and formative ethical perspective in place of only restrictive or only eudemonistic ones;[68] the elaboration of this practical and formative perspective in a doctrine of virtues,[69] a doctrine of duties,[70] and a doctrine of the highest good, where this last is understood as an overall social philosophy of culture open to the future.[71]

The references to the *Outlines* are explicit and precise in these late ethical papers,[72] and it is no coincidence that Schleiermacher was preparing a second edition of his primary ethical work that would be published posthumously the year of his death.[73] Above all, the basic idea remains consistent from the *Outlines* to the late papers: a reciprocal, "formative," "constructive" relationship between individuals on the one hand, and social and universal environments on the other, without an antagonistic prevalence of one pole over the other.[74]

Of course, there are also changes and different emphases in the late writings. An essential underlying reason for these different emphases is Schleiermacher's attempt to give a more "institutional" impact to his own positions.

If already in the *Outlines* there is thus a defense of scientific knowledge as a fundamental individual and community good, in later years we find Schleiermacher at the forefront of the renewal of Prussian university and scholastic institutions.

The increasingly "institutional" form assumed by Schleiermacher's ethics can also be seen by comparing the *Confidential Letters* of 1800 to the sermons *On the Christian Household* of 1820. Both texts affirm the centrality of a reciprocal conjugal love; but if the early work had been more focused on questioning the ancient patriarchal family, the mature work insisted

---

[66] See *KGA* 1.4, p. 475.
[67] See *AV*, pp. 429–451. Cf. Andrew C. Dole, *Schleiermacher on Religion and the Natural Order* (Oxford: Oxford University Press, 2009), pp. 64–69.
[68] See *AV*, pp. 491–513.
[69] See *AV*, pp. 313–335.
[70] See *AV*, pp. 415–428.
[71] See *AV*, pp. 535–553, 657–677. Cf. Scholtz, *Ethik und Hermeneutik*, pp. 35–63; Mariña, *Transformation*, pp. 146–163.
[72] See *AV*, pp. 315, 320, 512, 545, 547.
[73] Cf. *KGA* 1.4, pp. lxix–lxxi.
[74] Cf. Omar Brino, "Système et histoire dans l'éthique de Schleiermacher," *Archives de Philosophie* 77 (2014), pp. 237–258.

on confirming the formative nucleus of conjugal love at an institutional level. At the same time, the most innovative aspects of the relations between the sexes in the *Confidential Letters* were attenuated in the following years.[75] In a similar way, the small but numerous and detailed changes to the late editions of the *Soliloquies* substituted for the earlier positions a more "pragmatic," less "provocative," and less "ideal" perspective.[76]

In general, the mature Schleiermacher's increased emphasis on institutions is most evident in his deep commitment to a renewal of the Protestant church. Yet this intense theological-institutional application had a largely negative impact on the properly philosophical reception of his work. If Hegel already considered Schleiermacher's ecclesiastical and theological commitment as a sign of ambiguity and of antagonism to both the modern state and philosophy,[77] the harshest criticisms came from the revolutionary element in nineteenth-century German thought, which saw Schleiermacher's work of renewing institutions such as the university and, above all, the church as a sign of "conformism" or, worse, "hypocrisy." These kinds of assessments have had long-term effects and are among the reasons why not just "confessional" thinkers, but above all "secular" mainstream philosophers in the twentieth century, did not take Schleiermacher into consideration as fully as they did Kierkegaard; there is the fact that this latter had radical anti-institutional and anti-conformist positions, even if they were not seldom quite close to what we would call today "religious fundamentalism."

Even those between the nineteenth and twentieth centuries who had had a more positive consideration of Schleiermacher, first and foremost Wilhelm Dilthey, thus generally preferred to turn to his early writings, in which participation in cultural and spiritual communities was presented in a more spontaneous and less institutional way. In this direction, however, the differences between the "early" and the "late" Schleiermacher's philosophical works were perhaps accentuated more than is necessary. The 1803 *Outlines* and the 1820–1832 academic ethical papers, or the editions of *Soliloquies* between 1800 and 1829, attest instead to significant continuity with respect to some important deep-seated principles in his thinking. Dilthey's critique of historical reason, moreover, risked having a perspective turned only to the reconstruction of the past, while Schleiermacher intended the relationship between ethics and history in a dynamic sense that would lead from the past to the future.[78]

Even the great Dilthey thus risked solidifying a deficient representation, which attenuated Schleiermacher's articulated reciprocal correlation, in the context of a renewal of ethical and cultural institutions, between universalistic normativity on the one hand, and individual and socially unique historicity on the other. Compared to philosophers like Hegel, who tend

---

[75] See Sarah Schmidt, "Menschheit, Geschlecht und Liebe revised—Schleiermachers Briefwechsel mit seiner Braut (1808/1809)," in *Wissenschaft, Kirche, Staat und Politik*, ed. Andreas Arndt, Simon Gerber, and Sarah Schmidt (Berlin: De Gruyter, 2019), pp. 43–73. On the relationship of sexes in Schleiermacher's mature works cf. Hartlieb, *Geschlechterdifferenz*, pp. 156–231.

[76] Cf. *KGA* 1.12, p. lxvi.

[77] Cf. Richard Crouter, *Friedrich Schleiermacher: Between Enlightenment and Romanticism* (Cambridge: Cambridge University Press, 2005), pp. 70–97; Arndt, *Friedrich Schleiermacher*, pp. 213–247.

[78] About Dilthey and Schleiermacher cf. Scholtz, *Ethik und Hermeneutik*, pp. 235–257; Crouter, *Friedrich Schleiermacher*, pp. 21–38. On Schleiermacher's reflections on the future cf. Brent W. Sockness and Wilhelm Gräb, eds., *Schleiermacher, the Study of Religion, and the Future of Theology* (Berlin/New York: De Gruyter, 2010).

clearly to subordinate individual existence to social dimensions, or like Kierkegaard, who tend on the contrary to radically contrast singular existence with society, Schleiermacher, both in his early and late writings, although with different emphases, offers an articulated proposal of mutually "formative," "constructive" interaction between individuals and societies, and between historicity and universality.

Therefore, if there is certainly no shortage of underdeveloped points or excessively time-bound aspects in Schleiermacher's thought,[79] reading the main works on ethics that he decided to publish under his own name—*Soliloquies*, *Outlines*, and the academic papers—reading these today, in their systematic correlation, puts at our disposal an original moral philosophical thinker, who deals in his own specific way with issues that are still far from outdated.

Suggested Reading

Laks, André. "Schleiermacher on Plato: From Form (Introduction to Plato's Works) to Content (Outlines of a Critique of Previous Ethical Theory)." In *Brill's Companion to German Platonism*, ed. Alan Kim (Leiden/Boston: Brill, 2019), pp. 146–164.

Richardson, Ruth D. *The Role of Women in the Life and Thought of the Early Schleiermacher (1768–1806): An Historical Overview* (Lewiston, NY: Mellen, 1991).

Robinson, Matthew R. "Vollendet: The Completion of Humanity, the Gospel of John, and the Intersubjective Soul of Schleiermacher's *Monologen*." In *Der Mensch und seine Seele. Bildung-Frömmigkeit-Ästhetik*, ed. Arnulf von Scheliha and Jörg Dierken (Berlin/Boston: De Gruyter, 2017), pp. 405–419.

Sockness, Brent W. "Schleiermacher and the Ethics of Authenticity: The '*Monologen*' of 1800." *Journal of Religious Ethics* 32 (2004), pp. 477–517.

Thouard, Denis. *Schleiermacher. Communauté, individualité, communication* (Paris: Vrin, 2007).

Bibliography

Arndt, Andreas. *Friedrich Schleiermacher als Philosoph* (Berlin/Boston: De Gruyter, 2013).

Arndt, Andreas. *Die Reformation der Revolution. Friedrich Schleiermacher in seiner Zeit* (Berlin: Matthes & Seitz, 2019).

Arndt, Andreas, ed. *Wissenschaft und Geselligkeit: Friedrich Schleiermacher in Berlin 1796–1802* (Berlin/New York: De Gruyter, 2009).

Bondì, Davide. *Il giovane Schleiermacher. Etica e religione* (Brescia: Morcelliana, 2018).

Brino, Omar. *L'architettonica della morale. Teoria e storia dell'etica nelle Grundlinien di Schleiermacher* (Trento: Editrice Università degli Studi di Trento, 2007).

Brino, Omar. "Système et histoire dans l'éthique de Schleiermacher." *Archives de Philosophie* 77 (2014), pp. 237–258.

---

[79] Cf. Andreas Arndt, *Die Reformation der Revolution. Friedrich Schleiermacher in seiner Zeit* (Berlin: Matthes & Seitz, 2019).

Cesa, Claudio. "Schleiermacher critico dell'etica di Kant e Fichte. Spunti dalle 'Grundlinien.'" *Archivio di Filosofia* 53 (1984), pp. 19–34.

Crouter, Richard. *Friedrich Schleiermacher: Between Enlightenment and Romanticism* (Cambridge: Cambridge University Press, 2005).

Dole, Andrew C. *Schleiermacher on Religion and the Natural Order* (Oxford: Oxford University Press, 2009).

Ehrhardt, Christiane. *Religion, Bildung und Erziehung bei Schleiermacher: Eine Analyse der Beziehungen und des Widerstreits zwischen den "Reden über die Religion" und den "Monologen"* (Göttingen: Vandenhoek & Ruprecht, 2005).

Giacca, Emanuela. *La formazione del pensiero etico di Schleiermacher* (Roma–Pisa: Fabrizio Serra, 2015).

Hartlieb, Elisabeth. *Geschlechterdifferenz im Denken Friedrich Schleiermachers* (Berlin/New York: De Gruyter, 2006).

Herms, Eilert. *Herkunft, Entfaltung und erste Gestalt des Systems der Wissenschaften bei Schleiermacher* (Gütersloh: Mohn, 1974).

Kant, Immanuel. *Gesammelte Schriften*. Ed. the Royal Prussian (later German, then Berlin-Brandenburg) Academy of Sciences (Berlin: Reimer [then de Gruyter], 1900–).

Laks, André. "Schleiermacher on Plato: From Form (Introduction to Plato's Works) to Content (Outlines of a Critique of Previous Ethical Theory)." In *Brill's Companion to German Platonism*, ed. Alan Kim (Leiden/Boston: Brill, 2019), pp. 146–164.

Laks, André, and Ada Neschke, eds. *La naissance du paradigme herméneutique* (Lille: Presses Universitaires de Lille, 1990) (2nd augmented edition, Villeneuve d'Ascq: Presses Univ. du Septentrion, 2008).

Mariña, Jackeline. *Transformation of the Self in the Thought of Schleiermacher* (Oxford: Oxford University Press, 2008).

Meckenstock, Günter. *Deterministische Ethik und kritische Theologie. Die Auseinandersetzung des frühen Schleiermacher mit Kant und Spinoza 1789–1794* (Berlin/New York: De Gruyter, 1988).

Oberdorfer, Bernd. *Geselligkeit und Realisierung von Sittlichkeit. Die Theorieentwicklung Friedrich Schleiermachers bis 1799* (Berlin/New York: De Gruyter, 1995).

Plato. *Platonis Opera*. Ed. John Burnet, 5 vols. (Oxford: Oxford University Press, 1900–1907).

Richardson, Ruth D. *The Role of Women in the Life and Thought of the Early Schleiermacher (1768–1806): An Historical Overview* (Lewiston, NY: Mellen, 1991).

Robinson, Matthew R. "Vollendet: The Completion of Humanity, the Gospel of John, and the Intersubjective Soul of Schleiermacher's *Monologen*." In *Der Mensch und seine Seele. Bildung-Frömmigkeit-Ästhetik*, ed. Arnulf von Scheliha and Jörg Dierken (Berlin/Boston: De Gruyter, 2017), pp. 405–419.

Scheliha, Arnulf von. "Sources of Normativity in Schleiermacher's Interpretation of Culture." In *Schleiermacher, the Study of Religion, and the Future of Theology*, ed. Brent Sockness and Wilhelm Gräb (Berlin/New York: De Gruyter, 2010), pp. 285–298.

Scheliha, Arnulf von, and Jörg Dierken, eds. *Der Mensch und seine Seele. Bildung-Frömmigkeit-Ästhetik* (Berlin/Boston: De Gruyter, 2017).

Schleiermacher, Friedrich. *Briefwechsel 1802-03, KGA 5.6*, ed. Andreas Arndt and Wolfgang Virmond (Berlin: De Gruyter, 2005).

Schleiermacher, Friedrich. *Briefwechsel 1808, KGA 5.10*, ed. Simon Gerber and Sarah Schmidt (Berlin: De Gruyter, 2015).

Scholtz, Gunter. *Ethik und Hermeneutik. Schleiermachers Grundlegung der Geisteswissenschaften* (Frankfurt am Main: Suhrkamp, 1995).

Schmidt, Sarah. *Die Konstruktion des Endlichen. Schleiermachers Philosophie der Wechselwirkung* (Berlin/New York: De Gruyter, 2005).

Schmidt, Sarah. "Menschheit, Geschlecht und Liebe revised—Schleiermachers Briefwechsel mit seiner Braut (1808/1809)." In *Wissenschaft, Kirche, Staat und Politik*, ed. Andreas Arndt, Simon Gerber, and Sarah Schmidt (Berlin: De Gruyter, 2019), pp. 43–73.

Simmel, Georg. "Freedom and the Individual." In G. Simmel, *On Individuality and Social Forms. Selected Writings*, edited with an introduction by D. N. Levine (Chicago/London: University of Chicago Press, 1971), pp. 217–226.

Simmel, Georg. "Das Individuum und die Freiheit." In G. Simmel, *Brücke und Tür. Essays des Philosophen zur Geschichte, Religion, Kunst und Gesellschaft*, ed. M. Landmann (Stuttgart: Koehler, 1957), pp. 260–269.

Sockness, Brent W. "Schleiermacher and the Ethics of Authenticity: The '*Monologen*' of 1800." *Journal of Religious Ethics* 32 (2004), pp. 477–517.

Sockness, Brent W., and Wilhelm Gräb, eds. *Schleiermacher, the Study of Religion, and the Future of Theology* (Berlin/New York: De Gruyter, 2010).

Spinoza, Benedictus de. *Opera*. Ed. Carl Gebhardt, 4 vols. (Heidelberg: Winter, 1925).

Thouard, Denis. "L'éthique de l'individualité chez Schleiermacher." *Archives de Philosophie* 77 (2014), pp. 281–300.

Thouard, Denis. *Schleiermacher. Communauté, individualité, communication* (Paris: Vrin, 2007).

CHAPTER 27

ON RELIGION

DIETRICH KORSCH

27.1 How to Understand an Epoch-Making Book

SCHLEIERMACHER'S *On Religion* appeared in September 1799 as a small volume (329 pages in octavo), but it deeply changed understandings of (not only Christian) religion—and this in a double sense. First, the text brings about a shift in the center of theological discourse from "God" to "religion," considering the presuppositions of speaking about God in actual human communication. If we retranslate "On Religion"—a title that was still quite uncommon in German during that period—as *De religione*, we can see the title as an alternative to the more familiar *De Deo*, "On God."[1] And second, the mode of religious communication changes from deliberation on theoretical propositions to rhetorical exchange. This is why the style of *On Religion*, specifically its presentation in the form of "Speeches," is as fundamental as its conceptual content. The fact that the "Speeches" have never been performed underlines the point that the rhetorical theory animating the text is not accidental but is, rather, intrinsic to the theme itself, namely religion. The following survey presents an analysis of the Speeches focused on this element.

To read *On Religion* from this angle is not yet common. Schleiermacher's own revisions of the early text for the second edition in 1806 removed in a way, while retaining the basic ideas with minor modifications, its rhetorical impulses in favor of a more doctrinal attitude. I will return to the conceptual changes below. The third edition of 1821 added "explanations" that follow the same outline, whereas the fourth and final edition of 1831 only changed some stylistic details.[2]

The reception of the Speeches immediately after their first publication was ambivalent, determined above all by the standpoint of the reviewers. Philosophical and theological

---

[1] A predecessor is Johann Joachim Spalding, *Religion, eine Angelegenheit des Menschen* (1798), ed. Tobias Jersak and Georg Friedrich Wagner, *Schriften*, Abt. 1, Bd. 5 (Tübingen: Mohr Siebeck, 2001).

[2] The critical edition of the second through fourth editions is contained in *KGA* 1.12. An English translation of the Second Speech in the second edition of 1806 can be found in *CWS*. The 1821 edition has been translated by John Oman (*Speeches*²).

prejudices so dominated judgements at the time that the outstanding relevance of the text almost disappeared behind current controversies.[3] The reception of the later versions was dominated by doctrinal points of view, primarily focused on the relationship of this early work with Schleiermacher's later writings, trying to consider his actual professional status as professor of theology at Halle (second edition, 1806) or at Berlin (third edition, 1821). Nuanced investigations have been made into the changes in these editions.[4] These revisions determined the later reception of the text, and its revolutionary impetus was lost.

It was only the republication, in 1899, of the speeches "in their original form" ("in ihrer ursprünglichen Gestalt") by Rudolf Otto that opened readers' eyes to the religious revolution that had happened a century earlier—a revolution motivated by the search for a modern way of representing religion and, subsequently, theology. The rediscovery of the work's original significance, however, became entangled with the postwar reconstruction of theology after 1918; in this context assessments of the book were constrained by the battle against so-called subjectivist approaches in theology, mounted in particular by the dialectical theology. Only in the last thirty years, in parallel with the production of the great edition of the *KGA*, have the true dimensions of Schleiermacher's approach become visible.

In recent German scholarship there has emerged an interesting alternative, apparently grounded in a kind of dual aspect of Schleiermacher's work. On the one hand, Eilert Herms has reconstructed the system of a wide-reaching ontology on the basis of an empirically grounded phenomenology, according to which self-consciousness itself is full of realistic content.[5] And on the other, Wilhelm Gräb and Ulrich Barth have restricted the core of Schleiermacher's philosophy and theology to a type of self-conscious subjectivity that is historically and ethically mediated and for which religious interpretation gives a special and thorough, but not universal, sense.[6] The reading of Schleiermacher offered in this chapter tries to evade this alternative by starting from his linguistic practice, noting that both branches—ontology as well as a theory of subjectivity—presuppose a praxis of communication that makes the different aspects accessible without eliminating their importance. From this perspective, the changes in the conceptuality of the different editions can also be better understood: the contexts of communication change, and thereby the means of communicating as well.

Recent Anglophone Schleiermacher research, which has tended to focus on *The Christian Faith* and other (rather dogmatic) writings,[7] could inscribe itself in this categorial field without leaving behind the complexity of Schleiermacher's work.

---

[3] Cf. Günter Meckenstock, "Historische Einführung des Herausgebers," in *Reden (Meckenstock)*, pp. 12–50, and *KGA* 1.12, pp. xxvi–lxiii for more detail.

[4] Ruth Jackson Ravencroft, "Anonymity as a Strategy in Friedrich Schleiermacher's Early Work, and Its Theological and Social Implications," *Publications of the English Goethe Society* 88 (2019), p. 200; Andrew C. Dole, *Schleiermacher on Religion and the Natural Order* (New York: Oxford University Press, 2010), pp. 2–6.

[5] Eilert Herms, *Menschsein im Werden. Studien zu Schleiermacher* (Tübingen: Mohr Siebeck, 2013).

[6] Ulrich Barth, "Die Religionstheorie der 'Reden.' Schleiermachers theologisches Modernisierungsprogramm," in *Aufgeklärter Protestantismus* (Tübingen: Mohr Siebeck, 2004), pp. 259–289; Wilhelm Gräb, *Vom Menschsein und der Religion. Eine praktische Kulturtheologie* (Tübingen: Mohr Siebeck, 2018). Cf. Wilhelm Gräb, Review of *Menschsein im Werden*, by Eilert Herms. *Theologische Literaturzeitung* 130 (2005), pp. 811–816.

[7] As an example, see Christine Helmer, "Schleiermacher," in *The Blackwell Companion to Nineteenth Century Christian Theology*, ed. David A. Fergusson (Chichester: Wiley-Blackwell, 2010), pp. 31–57,

27.2 THE COMPOSITION AND THE CONTEXTS OF THE SPEECHES

Although in the end the Speeches became a written text, their composition in 1799 was deeply intertwined with Schleiermacher's vivid conversation with friends and colleagues at the time. His professional employment as health-care chaplain at the Berlin Charité brought him into intense contact with Friedrich Schlegel, with whom he also shared living quarters for a time, and with the whole Romantic movement in Berlin. In the spring of 1799, Schleiermacher moved out of the city in order to fill in for a colleague in Potsdam, and from letters to his Berlin friends we know quite a lot about his drafting of the Speeches during this time.[8] Schlegel and Henriette Hertz, in particular, followed the different stages of Schleiermacher's work, although of course without being able to survey the whole. But the most fraught issue of the period is the relation of Schleiermacher's conception to Johann Gottlieb Fichte. Fichte had been accused of atheism in the autumn of 1798, and he lost his professorship at Jena in March of 1799. In a way these events complicated Schleiermacher's primary aim of making the notion of God secondary to experience in religious discourse.

This leads us to the broader intellectual context of the period. It is worthwhile to note that important philosophical work of the time attempted to provide a solid foundation for human understanding, especially concerning science and morality, while critically relegating religion to a secondary range. Prevalent in journals as well as in the popular bourgeois "salon" culture was an attitude toward consciousness that can be called "enlightened," an attitude that claimed to assess and evaluate real human intellectual processes in a vivid and decided way, again oriented towards the future of science and morality—and dismissive of traditional forms of religion. Though inspired by such philosophical giants as Immanuel Kant and Johann Gottlieb Fichte, in the end this attitude toward consciousness was not a product of rigorous philosophical argumentation, but rather reflected common sentiments about what was regarded as the "cutting edge" philosophy of the day. Thus the speeches *On Religion* engaged common philosophical interests of the day without entering too deeply into philosophical subtleties because they were directed toward an audience that did not quite possess the level of philosophical acumen to which they aspired. Such persons are the "cultured despisers" to whom the speeches are addressed.

This aspiration required a two-sided approach. First, the theme of religion would need to be introduced in a manner accessible to an educated bourgeois audience who were not scientifically trained professionals. And second, the argumentation would need to refer to those important authors who formed the background of common opinion. This double challenge led Schleiermacher to a new kind of discourse on religion in the speeches. From this situation we already see that Schleiermacher's strategy for engaging relevant concepts was rooted in a specific historical situation, one that called for a common and universal understanding

---

where the Speeches do not play a role. The ambiguous, often misleading reception of Schleiermacher in the field of religious studies is critically discussed in Andrew C. Dole, "The Case of the Disappearing Discourse: Schleiermacher's Fourth Speech and the Field of Religious Studies," *The Journal of Religion* 88, no. 1 (2008), pp. 1–28.

[8] Meckenstock, "Historische Einführung," pp. 2–12.

not only of religion, but also of the basics of science and morality. Schleiermacher's historical situatedness thus provoked a new formulation of Christianity, one intended to establish a common and universal understanding of religion as basic to human consciousness.

Before looking to the details of Schleiermacher's procedure, we must first recall the main elements of the philosophical background. The culminating figure of the German Enlightenment was Immanuel Kant. His separation of theoretical philosophy from practical philosophy, as based on two different but complementary forces of consciousness, freed the capacity of conceptual knowledge about the states of the empirical world (in his 1781 *Critique of Pure Reason*) from the inner obligations to follow authoritative imperatives in conduct and behavior (as developed in the 1788 *Critique of Practical Reason*). For Kant, it was necessary to assert that these two capacities of reason—enabling scientific and technical mastery of the empirical world on the one hand, and promoting human morality by following the categorical imperative on the other—belong together. But due to the insuperable distance between pure self-reflection in obeying moral imperatives and the application of categories and forms of intuition (*Anschauungsformen*) to empirical impressions, it was not possible to unite the two basic forces of human reason. Only his *Critique of Judgement* (1790) offered hints as to the coherence of the two spheres, found in nature or in aesthetic contemplation. The notion of God, however, did not play a role in uniting human rational drives. In his *Religion within the Boundaries of Pure Reason* (1793), the concept of God was postulated as guarantee for a future unity of morality and beatitude—which was, apparently, a conceptual demotion of religion to an aspect, however necessary, of practical reason. It is significant that all important followers of Kant, including Fichte, Schelling, and Hegel, critically tried to overcome the split of human consciousness by construing a third element to represent its unity, whether by dialectical thinking or through arguments for various kinds of immediacy in (self-) consciousness.

Fichte, building on his *Science of Knowledge* (1794), regarded the "I" in its basic activity (*Tathandlung*) as a production of the human consciousness that united the representation of the empirical world with the self-legislating nature of human morality. It was but a consequence of this theoretical arrangement that he postulated the concept of God as the last and deepest basis of the free activity of the "I." But he strongly held the opinion that there was no knowledge of God as such; the notion of God only came to mind by following the moral imperatives. Thus Fichte deepened the basic function of the concept of God on the one hand, but banished it completely from all extra-moral intuition on the other. This is why he rejected the notion of a personal Deity as ultimately unable to provide a satisfactory foundation for human subjectivity and thus as superstitious (*Über den Grund unseres Glaubens an eine göttliche Weltregierung*, 1798)—hence the accusations of atheism against him.

The reproach of atheism triggered debates about Baruch de Spinoza, who had been polemically reintroduced to contemporary discussion by Friedrich Heinrich Jacobi in his denunciations of the late Lessing for being a pantheist (1785). In spite of this reproach, Spinoza's "*hen kai pan*" ("the one which is the whole") seemed to offer liberation from the Kantian bind that required both pure and practical reason but could not unify them. But at what cost? Was the price not that core Enlightenment accomplishment, namely, the autonomous self-consciousness?

Perhaps the Romantic impulse to reach out to the universe by immediate impressions of self-denial and self-assertion could be seen as analogous in spirit to Spinoza's holism, though the Romantics sought to deal with the problem in decidedly aesthetic, not to mention ironic, ways.

This is, roughly speaking, the intellectual situation to which Schleiermacher referred and within which he spoke. With regard to this constellation we can preview the issues he dealt with in seeking to establish the autonomy of religion and its basic function for human consciousness. Referring to Kant, Schleiermacher needed to seek a formula for and an insight in a "third," which surmounts the alternative of the theoretical or practical powers of the mind. With Fichte, he preserved divine immediacy in relation to human consciousness, but without restricting access to the divine or to morality. And as in Spinoza, from its first conception the universe, though schematized as an overwhelming One, must bear in itself a subjective counterpart.

27.3 Unifying Objectivity and Subjectivity by Communication: The Basic Idea of Religion as Part of Human Consciousness

If we combine these aspects, we can understand Schleiermacher's basic approach to describing the independence of religion and its function for human consciousness, namely, his recourse to "intuition of the universe" and "feeling" in the Second Speech. In both cases, we have to do, so to speak, with a structured immediacy. To begin with "intuition," we must recall that the German *Anschauung* is taken from the field of optical perception rather than from intellectual insight. When Schleiermacher speaks about *Anschauung des Universums* (intuition of the universe) as the core of religion, he is alluding to the fact that we see something that presents itself to our capacity for viewing. In this case, that which we intuit overcomes our subjective perspective by imprinting its reality into our consciousness. On the other hand, *nota bene*, this by no means eliminates our subjectivity. Immediacy happens in a movement from the whole, but toward the individual—so that the universe is present in the subjective mind. It is worth noting that all intuitions proceed in an individual manner, but refer altogether to the One, the universe.

"Feeling," however, the second subjective feature highlighted by Schleiermacher, is a merely internal relation. Being a relation (*something* is felt by *me* as a subject), feeling posits an internal difference, namely, the difference of body from mind. If feeling happens, there is an immediate contact of body and mind that supports human identity in the midst of the universe. The capacity of feeling is not derived from any human activity, but lies on the ground of all dimensions of human existence in the world—and this is the reason why "feeling" is a specifically religious phenomenon (and at the same time, this explains why it could be the later Schleiermacher's preferred topic when he develops the substance of religion). "Feeling" is thus the other, "internal" side of immediacy, correlated with intuition (*Anschauung*) as the "external" side. When religion happens, an externally and an internally structured immediacy are required to schematize its taking place.

Religion, therefore, posits humanity in a specific state in which individuals are united with the whole as well as with their own corporal and mental existence. This is why

Schleiermacher can assert both the individual human being's experience of the universe and the belonging of individuals and all humanity to the universe. In both perspectives, religion appears as the deepest basis of all human consciousness.

What are we doing by schematizing Schleiermacher's proceeding in this way? We are simply following the advice he himself gives in the Speeches. The discourse on religion does not refer to "intuition" or "feeling" as phenomena by themselves; what they mean for religion emerges from the linguistic practice Schleiermacher initiates. In other words, the attention must be focused on the words of the speaker him- or herself. We can observe this in detail by looking at the specific themes Schleiermacher deals with in the Speeches.

It is obvious that Schleiermacher's first step must be to assure both parties, the speaker and the listener(s), of the common ground on which the communication that follows will take place. Their positions vis-à-vis one another also must be established realistically. They find themselves interwoven in a process of understanding and of debate in which they take different starting points, but without being in complete disagreement (the First Speech). If this setting can be established, the explanation of the special character or essence of religion can proceed. We must expect the discussion to follow the guidelines of communication in general: that is, we assume that religion can be discussed, and thus is to be placed within the field of human understanding (the Second Speech). But it is not only the topical place of religion that needs to be specified; the ways of communicating religion must also be clarified. This highlights two characteristics of religion: first, the necessary conjunction of religion with individual learning, and particularly with linguistic capability (the Third Speech); and second, the institutional aspect of religious communication (the Fourth Speech).

Once Schleiermacher has plotted these two procedures of embedding religion in the field of human understanding—linguistic competence and the institutional context of communication—the concept of religion, even though assigned to its "own province in the mind,"[9] emerges definitively as the ground of all human understanding. Only once this ground-clearing work has been done can he turn (in Speech Five) to the empirical religions, that is, to the real appearance of religion within the boundaries of everyday experience.

Following this outline, it is easier to understand the way Schleiermacher builds his argument. Being involved in an actual process of communication, as Schleiermacher is in the Speeches, creates the hermeneutical space for coming to identify religion as fundamental to all human understanding—an insight that makes the concluding analysis of existing religions possible. Thus we find an interdependence of communication in general—which needs to be grounded in its competence of receiving the whole as objective (by intuition) and being in immediate contact with the whole (by feeling)—and religion as its specific ground and rationale.

It must be admitted that Schleiermacher's rhetorical strategy occasionally hides the logic of the progression he has in mind. But frankly, this seems intentional, for the process of becoming aware of the internal structure of understanding, and thereby of the operating modes of reason in general, must not be regarded as a kind of logical proof, which already presupposes too much ratified comprehension. This is why I seek to give an overview of the content of Schleiermacher's book by pointing out the conceptual background that his rhetorical strategy presupposes. It might be an advantage of reading Schleiermacher in English

---

[9] *Speeches*[1], p. 17.

that attention is drawn more to the conceptual structure of the text than to its poetic form, which creates more difficulties for German readers. In the following sections, I describe the five Speeches in sequence.

27.4 OUTLINE OF THE CONTENT OF THE SPEECHES

27.4.1 The First Speech: Apology

The First Speech is titled "Apology" and serves, as we noticed, to establish the common ground of understanding. Bearing in mind how deeply immersed Schleiermacher was in Plato's work, the term "Apology" raises an analogy to Plato's dialogue of the same name, which describes the arguments of the trial of Socrates. One explicit overlap between the two is particularly pertinent. In Plato's *Apology*, Socrates declared his competence to be the consequence of being driven by a divine *daimonion*, which enables him to secure difference from the outer world and to establish a connection with the Platonic ideas. So, too, the young Schleiermacher asserts that he is "convinced to speak by an inner and irresistible necessity that divinely rules me,"[10] referring to this as a "divine calling."[11]

The contexts of these affirmations, however—classical Athens and Enlightenment Berlin—are rather different. To cite only the most important fact, Plato's *Apology* is written from a retrospective point of view on Socrates' defense before his being sentenced to death by his judges, whereas Schleiermacher's perspective is directed toward a future of possible understanding. Socrates must presume that even his enemies can gain access to the ideas if they really want, but they can also refuse this step of insight. In contrast, Schleiermacher sees himself as engaged in a process of common understanding in which his interlocutors participate whether they want to or not. Being engaged in communication in the context of the Enlightenment means, first, that there is a striving to build up individual participation in the common sense or in reason in general. We find in this perspective a movement from individual conditions towards a unifying whole. And second, progress in self-formation (*Bildung*) necessarily requires the most developed means for promoting individual ambition. This is why Schleiermacher dares to present himself as an expert in religion. His specific formation and position make him an important member of the common discourse. But conversely, in a certain sense we also find here a mediation of communality with individuality.[12] With these two stipulations Schleiermacher opens his discourse on religion, presupposing that a certain culture of religion belongs to well-formed individual life. With this in mind, we may come back to the Platonic sense of apology: far from submitting one's own conviction to alien and potentially improper judgment, apology tends to communicate an as-yet-unknown meaning to listeners. Being persuaded of such an as-yet-unknown and thus new meaning, however, does not lead to an exchange of the old (i.e., previous meaning) for the new (i.e., the new meaning), but rather brings about an enrichment of one's own intellectual

---

[10] *Speeches¹*, p. 4.
[11] *Speeches¹*, p. 5.
[12] Dalia T. Nassar, "Immediacy and Mediation in Schleiermacher's 'Reden Über Die Religion,"' *The Review of Metaphysics* 59, no. 4 (2006), p. 838.

and emotional life. This appeals directly to the aspiration of the Enlightenment public to arrive at the pinnacle of self-formation with respect to the vigorous use of mental and social capacities. "I wish to show you from what capacity of humanity religion proceeds, and how it belongs to what is for you the highest and dearest."[13]

27.4.2 The Second Speech: On the Essence of Religion

The Second Speech "On the Essence of Religion" is, without any doubt, the core of Schleiermacher's book. "Essence," by the way, must not be understood in a Platonic sense; we could also say "theme" or "topic," the subject of what is under discussion. Indeed the definition of "religion" does not result from a kind of immediate insight, but from following the hermeneutical path and using the rhetorical strategies just indicated. Three main lines of argument require examination, to which I shall add one thought as an appendix. The first concerns the topical space assigned to religion within the complexity of human self-understanding. The second concerns the filling of this empty space with positive elucidations about what religion is in itself. And the third concerns the basic forms of empirical appearance that this space and elucidations generate. What follows as the "appendix" is a comparison of this result with two of the mostly widely used ideas about religion in Enlightenment discourses on religion: the notions of God and immortality.

To start with the first point, religion is located alongside metaphysics and morality and cannot be sufficiently explained by the use of either of them alone. Initially Schleiermacher adopts the Kantian distinction between the theoretical and practical capabilities of reason, as explained in the *Critique of Pure Reason* (1781) and the *Critique of Practical Reason* (1788). But as he proceeds, two differences appear in comparison to Kant. The first is the way Schleiermacher describes this distinction. He does not start with the internal capacities of reason in relation to the understanding of the outer world and to the inner regularity of acting, but regards both capacities as always connected with the results of reason's operation. The so-called metaphysical strategy assures humanity of understanding things in the world and fitting insights together into a coherent whole. But the so-called moral procedure places humanity in the context of a complex of activities by which a stable texture of acting is built up. This is a kind of Spinozian argumentation, departing from a whole and looking to the individual.

Noticing this way of arguing sheds light on the second feature of Schleiermacher's specific explanation. Both of the human capacities just named are rooted, as it were, in the human intention to dominate the world; in this way, both exhibit that uniquely practical aim of Enlightenment culture. This is why anything that hinders the conquest of the world, such as religion, is regarded as old-fashioned and incompatible with modernity. This insight into the hidden unity of both intellectual and social strategies behind the actual debate on religion is crucial for a new approach to understand the composition of Schleiermacher's "Speeches." We can apprehend that there is no such thing as "metaphysics" or "morals" existing anywhere in the world, aside from the kind of communicating about humanity's practical position within the whole of the world. The idea of the whole (or, as Schleiermacher often

---

[13] *Speeches¹*, p. 10.

prefers to say, the universe) is a function of human understanding. This is also important for Schleiermacher's use of "religion." For we do not need to seek any specific moment—psychological or emotional or immediately intellectual—that can be isolated to serve as a foundation for religion; even "religion" is a moment in the overall rhetorical process of describing and understanding humanity's position in the world: "all communication of religion cannot be other than rhetorical."[14]

This leads us to the second chain of arguments in the Second Speech. Let us consider the most famous formulation first: "religion is the sensibility and taste of the infinite."[15] How this formula can be elucidated by "intuition of the universe" on the one hand,[16] and by the insight that "every intuition is . . . connected with a feeling" on the other,[17] is well known. To recall our observations from above, "intuition" is located at the transition from outer experience to inner sensibility, connecting the direction from the intuited to the person intuiting, and refers in this way to a capacity of intuition that functions as a common ground of both outer experience and inner sensibility, of both intuited and intuiter. Such an analogy of religious intuition to intellectual intuition is striking but totally appropriate. "Feeling," on the other hand, represents "taste," the inner resonance of an outer experience, that is the sensible correspondence of body and mind—which is, in itself, only possible if the two spheres of the corporal and the intellectual are united in advance, not only consequently and accidentally. So both levels refer to a specific conjunction of the individual and the universe. And it must be considered whether both forms of unity could, perhaps, be united in a moment, placing the human individual at a point of intersection where the universe is encountered immediately. Schleiermacher speaks in a famous passage of the "first mysterious moment . . . before intuition and feeling have separated,"[18] comparing the evidence with "a maiden's kiss, a holy and fruitful nuptial embrace."[19] Factually, this moment must happen, but cannot be grasped, as reflection arises with the first articulation of what has happened.

Again, this twist of Schleiermacher's argumentation supports our hermeneutical and rhetorical reading of his ideas. We simply have to transpose the schemes of apprehension we have been considering from the psychological to the linguistic sphere. Neither "intuition" nor "feeling" exists without rhetorical manifestation and fixation. Only by specifying the relation of the individual act of speaking to spoken language in general (*parole* and *langue* in the sense of Ferdinand de Saussure) can we imagine what "the individual" and "the universe" could be. Certainly, both extremes, individuality and universality, do not come about only by speaking. On the contrary, they are ever present, but reach our consciousness only by means of the use of language. Considered in this perspective, we understand why religion is an indispensable ground of any use of reason. Indeed the use of language for certain purposes, especially in pursuit of the technical and practical aims of Enlightenment culture, presupposes the function of language, which must be then developed into ever-more detailed and nuanced forms of communication if the great and general human tendency toward self-assertion in the world is to succeed. This means that the essence of religion consists

---

[14] *Speeches¹*, p. 22.
[15] *Speeches¹*, p. 23.
[16] *Speeches¹*, p. 24.
[17] *Speeches¹*, p. 29.
[18] *Speeches¹*, p. 31.
[19] *Speeches¹*, p. 32.

in preparing the ground for all possible human communication. And this ground has to be thematized separately from the practical aim to dominate the world. For this, a sphere of imagination is required, which cannot be utilized only with strategic-practical intentions. To put it in another way, the domination of the world is only possible if we register the fact that the world is given to us as we experience it in language, and as we bring it to consciousness by imagination. Thematizing religion specifically, however, brings us to the next step in the reconstruction of the Second Speech: consideration of the historical forms of religious utterance.

From this perspective, Schleiermacher turns to the insight that religious communication always happens in relation to particular historical circumstances. The schematization of religion as a separate branch of human understanding has to do with practical attitudes humanity harbors toward the world under given conditions. This is why Schleiermacher distinguishes three possible fields or reference points for religious communication (and related types of religious imagination): nature, humanity, and history. It is not too difficult to associate the first two fields with different aspects of Enlightenment-period discourses. To take the first case, "nature," as we know it from Kant's third *Critique*, provides the impression of a whole before human apprehensions (both in the sense of "prior to" and "in front of"). In this way, nature is a field of religious communication and of the development of religious imagination. In nature "it is the spirit of the world that reveals itself in the smallest things just as perfectly and visibly as in the greatest; that is an intuition of the universe that develops out of everything and seizes the mind."[20]

But dealing with religion under such circumstances narrows the religious perspective, as it excludes the fact that nature is used as a project of human self-preservation. This is why the next horizon of religious articulation—the whole of humanity—arises. "Therefore, let us repair to humanity, that we may find the material for religion."[21] This alludes to the moral responsibility of human action in the world; to refer to humanity as the material for religion is to refer to another field of religious communication that is more idealistic and more dynamic than imaginations taken from the natural sphere, even though it nevertheless remains instrumental in its use. *Nota bene*: this does not make religion an unrealizable idea(l), as it might seem; this pretense can be overcome by making the specific nature of religion clearer. Thus, Schleiermacher calls to mind that theatre of religion called "history," hinting at a certain notion of progress in religion's self-presentation. "History, in the most proper sense, is the highest object of religion."[22] History is a combination of nature and humanity: Human beings act within nature as something given, trying to achieve their aims, and thereby bring about history. But they remain themselves embedded in the givenness and limitations of nature, and cannot treat the whole of the world as an object of instrumental activity. Thus, conversely, history also interferes with nature and (morally guided) human action by being excluded from becoming a possible object of action. This is why Schleiermacher directs attention to this field without actually highlighting history as the final dimension of religion. In a sophisticated manner, Schleiermacher presents a critique of Enlightenment optimism, directing the concentration of the public toward the unfinished status of the Enlightenment

---

[20] *Speeches¹*, pp. 36–37.
[21] *Speeches¹*, p. 38.
[22] *Speeches¹*, p. 42.

project and rhetorically arguing that it cannot be achieved without religion. This is, to say the least, a special form of apologetics.

At this stage in the argument, it suffices to have refuted false conceptions or prejudices against religion; and it may be helpful to correct inadequate articulations of religion, which I offer as the promised "appendix" to the three moments in Schleiermacher's argument just discussed. The Kantian (and Fichtean) way of conceiving religion by means of moral argumentation clearly fails, on Schleiermacher's account. But on the other hand, efforts to justify the concept of God and the idea of immortality as necessary for religion (presented in defenses of "natural religion" within Enlightenment discourses) also collapse. Religion is other and more than an amplification of moral laws for the purpose of convincing irresolute persons. And proclaiming a kind of independence of "God" besides and as a counterpart of human religion would make God a part of natural knowledge, failing to acknowledge the junction of the universe with the individual existence of humanity. Conversely, this is also why an insistence on the preservation of a particular individual's body, which is what immortality is commonly thought to refer to, is basically a nonreligious intention; it negates the permanent belonging of the individual to the universe, independent from the way of all life.

Schleiermacher's critical approach has cleared the ground for his constructive project, namely the analysis of religion in its most basic, elementary sense. The "essence" of religion in its forms of manifestation now allows progress toward that further determination. It may not be accidental that, as we know biographically, Schleiermacher's productivity declined for a time after he finished the Second Speech.[23] Indeed, the Third and Fourth Speeches explicate two important insights already included in the arguments of the Second (as well as in its performative way of arguing). Nevertheless, the aspects of communicability and of communality of religion will need to be presented in detail.

27.4.3 The Third Speech: On Self-Formation for Religion

"On Self-Formation for Religion" is the title of the Third Speech. Here the German *Bildung* can be difficult to be translate into English. The main traits, however, can be delineated so that the specific content of this keyword of the German Enlightenment and German Romanticism becomes visible. First, Schleiermacher returns to his initial conviction that only a religiously affected individual is able to communicate religion. "How often have I struck up the music of my religion in order to move those present . . . to the fullest harmony of religious feelings?"[24] Music does not convince by assertion, but searches for resonance and accord among the listeners present. This requires that the listeners have a certain level of musical competence. Religious competence, however, cannot be produced, but must be presupposed: "A person is born with the religious capacity as with every other, and if only his sense is not forcibly suppressed . . . religion would have to develop unerringly in each person."[25] In other words there is a basic capacity for religious communication, for the utterance and adoption of religious expressions. This is the elementary conviction of

---

[23] Cf. Meckenstock, "Historische Einführung," pp. 4–6.
[24] *Speeches¹*, pp. 55–56.
[25] *Speeches¹*, p. 59.

universal enlightenment: that all people are created equal—if the development of religious competence is not limited or contorted.

In keeping with our previous reading of the Speeches, there is one limitation above all in the development of religion in the individual: namely "the rage of the understanding,"[26] that is the fact that any maxim of action is determined by a practical outlook that seeks to subordinate everything to one's own benefit. This basic orientation distorts the free development of the human mind and hinders the real improvement of the world. Although it might seem integral to the process of enlightenment, it is in fact a betrayal of the Enlightenment ideal. Those who want to overcome this inner-worldly restriction of enlightenment are often misled either to construe a supernatural transcendent world or to negate the world's relevance in favor of a merely subjective mysticism. Both variations suffer from the negation of the real presence of the universe within individual existence.

A strong development of all human capacities is the best condition for inculcating religion. In this sense, religion is deeply connected with the Enlightenment movement's project and goals, provided that human self-limitations are overcome: "Everything, therefore, must begin by putting an end to the bondage in which human sense is held."[27]

27.4.4 The Fourth Speech: On the Social Element in Religion; or, On Church and Priesthood

Not unrelated to the presence of the universe in individual existence is the appearance of religion in institutional form. This theme is dealt with in the Fourth Speech, "On the Social Element in Religion; or, On Church and Priesthood." It might seem that the Fourth Speech is the weakest part of the book, as Schleiermacher's allusions remain somewhat structural and utopian, if we have in mind the actual status of existing state churches in Germany at the time. This impression is due above all to the historical situation around 1800, and this is why Schleiermacher tried to concretize his earlier critique in his later "explanations" to the Fourth Speech.[28] Clearly, the Enlightenment critique of religion was addressed in its sharpest form against the church as an organization, in which religious belief and social repression went hand in hand. Schleiermacher's counterargument to this reproach consists in presenting a utopian idea of religious communication based upon the free utterance of religious intuitions and feelings, a sort of domination-free communication in a sense very similar to that articulated later by Jürgen Habermas.[29] The actual, albeit utopian, exchange of religious intuitions and feelings, proceeding from the individual, represents the very core of the "church," in which speaking and listening are evenly distributed. Where the church contains people who are still seeking to complete religion, a distinction between "priests" and "laypersons" arises, a distinction that can only be justified by the aim to diminish the difference. This purpose, however, is frustrated by the actual composition of historical "churches," to which the state had assigned nonreligious duties, such as education or the

---

[26] Ibid.
[27] *Speeches¹*, p. 66.
[28] *KGA* 1.12, pp. 216–249.
[29] Cf. Axel Honneth and Hans Joas, eds., *Communicative Action: Essays on Jürgen Habermas's The Theory of Communicative Action* (Cambridge: Polity Press, 1991).

promotion of legal obedience. Within these existing churches, the duty of religiously affected individuals (in the role of "priests") is to promote the equality of all participants in religious communication in order to build up a more concrete "church," definitively free from state influence. The state-free churches in North America could have the potential of building up conditions for a more authentic religious communication. But this would require a change in their internal group-oriented structures.[30] In Germany, at least, this shape of the church was still far off (and remains far off today), and it might be asked whether future religious associations should even be called "churches": what Schleiermacher may have had in mind, after all, is the idea of a peculiar status of religious communication, comparable to the self-reference of religious communication in the work of Niklas Luhmann.[31]

27.4.5 The Fifth Speech: On the Religions

With this final speech we come back to the empirical level of considering religion. The basic insight is that religion is everywhere and always a historical phenomenon. We can easily grasp this point by keeping in mind that religion always starts with individuals articulating their intuitions of the universe and disclosing their accompanying feelings. Judged in light of this insight, the concept of a "natural religion" as it was promoted by Enlightenment thinkers to preserve religion from critique (and to be used to critique the historical churches) already appears insufficient. All historical religions start with single individuals who are able to perform a certain constellation of individual existence in relation to the universe. Any formulation of such a structural relationship happens of its own accord, and there is no real dependence of one on another. But particular communities only accept those formulations of religious insights that befit a specific historical situation. Thus, discovering authentic presentations of religion is a most creative act.

In these reflections, Schleiermacher offers a hermeneutical model to understand the historical religions, which have an equal status as phenomena in history.[32] The openness of Schleiermacher's conception to history in religious matters is as significant as it is impressive, and it can be made useful in promoting further reciprocal religious recognition. His proposal, nevertheless, is based on a clearly structured relation of the individual and the universe.

Schleiermacher's observations concerning historical religious formations appear, admittedly, idealistic due to their dependence on his structural model.

In this way Judaism and Christianity take a very special place within the wide range of possible historical religions. Judaism, for example, incorporates the distinction of the universe from the individual in the following manner: all religion is articulated by an individual that posits itself in contrast to the universe. The empirical demonstration of this contrast is the contradiction in morality, namely, that the actions of an individual always

---

[30] Cf. *KGA* 1.12, pp. 240f.

[31] Niklas Luhmann, *A Systems Theory of Religion*, ed. A. Kieserling (Stanford: Stanford University Press, 2013).

[32] A reappraisal from the side of religious studies can be found in Thomas E. Reynolds, "Religion within the Limits of History: Schleiermacher and Religion—A Reappraisal," *Religion* 32, no. 1 (2002), pp. 51–70.

fall short of the requirements of the universal. The response of the universe is retaliation against the individual. This religious content expresses itself in the form of confronting and being confronted by God, possibly in a very intense manner. Even retaliation is a kind of recognition.

Christianity, in contrast, overcomes the principle of retaliation with reconciliation or redemption. "The original intuition of Christianity . . . is none other than the intuition of the universal straining of everything finite against the unity of the whole and of the way in which the deity handles this striving, how it reconciles the enmity directed against it."[33] It is clear that this form of intuition must also be initiated by an individual person whose fate is tightly interwoven with the message—Jesus is that person, in whose history preaching, suffering, and being adopted by the universe coincide. His fate, on the other hand, represents a model that concerns all religious subjects: all can be understood (and appear as justified) by understanding themselves as following (from) his historical demeanor. This unites persons who form and lead religious groups as well as simple "laypersons." This unity of humankind despite all empirical differences is why Christianity, so understood, can be proclaimed as a "religion of religions"—a claim that is not meant to express any superiority, but to leave all religious phenomena their own place, understanding them in a purely structural manner, as oriented toward a finite aim in history. Schleiermacher did regard the Judaism of his day as on the way towards assimilation to Christianity, but the relation of Christianity overcoming Judaism in Schleiermacher's outline must be seen as a result of his theoretical construction of religion. And the ways his own argument affirms their coexistence should also be noted. The use of Schleiermacher's hermeneutical canon thus requires historical consciousness and responsibility. It is itself a product of history und must be judged following this condition.

27.5 SUMMARY

In summarizing Schleiermacher's achievement in the Speeches, we can say that he was able to face the Enlightenment challenge posed by the "cultural despisers of religion" in an apologetic way, revealing the specific contribution of religion to that wholeness to which Enlightenment period intellectuals aspired. He accomplished this by elaborating the place of religion within human consciousness as a basic function of its operation. Additionally, he described a close conjunction of religion with the self-formation of humanity under modern conditions, accentuating individual capabilities to live responsibly and confidently. His considerations include a hermeneutical rule to interpret religions as cultural and historical phenomena, which should lead to mutual acceptance without erasing differences. In these ways Schleiermacher contributed to a culturally responsible and religiously authentic self-presentation of Christianity.

The wide vista over the field of religion opened by the original Speeches is much more significant than are the later revisions of the text in the two following editions. For this reason, it makes sense to say the reception of the Speeches really recommended about 1900. The most specific alteration in a systematic sense is the nearly complete replacement of

---

[33] *Speeches¹*, p. 115.

"intuition" by "feeling" in the later editions. This seems to be a rather significant change, as it makes the inner resonance in the middle of consciousness more important than the always-codetermined outer impressions that played such an important role in the concept of "intuition." In fact this observation supports my claim that, in the end, the rhetorical strategy of the text is more important than its allusions to sensual intuitions and ontological constructions.

Suggested Reading

Barth, Ulrich. "Die Religionstheorie der 'Reden.' Schleiermachers theologisches Modernisierungsprogramm." In *Aufgeklärter Protestantismus* (Tübingen: Mohr Siebeck, 2004), pp. 259–289.
Crouter, Richard. "Introduction." In *Speeches¹*, pp. xi–xxxix.
Meckenstock, Günter. "Historische Einführung des Herausgebers." In *Reden (Meckenstock)*, pp. 1–52.
Vial, Theodore. *Schleiermacher: A Guide for the Perplexed* (London: Bloomsbury T&T Clark, 2013).

Bibliography

Barth, Ulrich. "Die Religionstheorie der 'Reden.' Schleiermachers theologisches Modernisierungsprogramm." In *Aufgeklärter Protestantismus* (Tübingen: Mohr Siebeck, 2004), pp. 259–289.
Dole, Andrew C. "The Case of the Disappearing Discourse: Schleiermacher's Fourth Speech and the Field of Religious Studies." *The Journal of Religion* 88, no. 1 (2008), pp. 1–28.
Dole, Andrew C. *Schleiermacher on Religion and the Natural Order* (New York: Oxford University Press, 2010).
Ferreira, M. Jamie. "Love and the Neighbor: Two Ethical Themes in Schleiermacher's *Speeches*." *The Journal of Religion* 84, no. 3 (2004), pp. 410–430.
Gräb, Wilhelm. *Vom Menschsein und der Religion. Eine praktische Kulturtheologie* (Tübingen: Mohr Siebeck, 2018).
Gräb, Wilhelm. Review of *Menschsein im Werden*, by Eilert Herms. *Theologische Literaturzeitung* 130 (2005), pp. 811–816.
Helmer, Christine. "Schleiermacher." In *The Blackwell Companion to Nineteenth Century Christian Theology*, ed. David A. Fergusson (Chichester: Wiley-Blackwell, 2010), pp. 31–57.
Herms, Eilert. *Menschsein im Werden. Studien zu Schleiermacher* (Tübingen: Mohr Siebeck, 2013).
Honneth, Axel, and Hans Joas, eds. *Communicative Action: Essays on Jürgen Habermas's The Theory of Communicative Action* (Cambridge: Polity Press, 1991).
Jungkeit, Steven R. *Spaces of Modern Theology: Geography and Power in Schleiermacher's World* (New York: Palgrave MacMillan, 2012).
Keesee, Neal K. "The Divine Purpose in 'On Religion.'" *The Journal of Religion* 78, no. 3 (1998), pp. 405–424.
König, Christian. *Unendlich gebildet: Schleiermachers kritischer Religionsbegriff und seine inklusivistische Religionstheologie anhand der Erstauflage der Reden* (Tübingen: Mohr Siebeck, 2016).

Lamm, Julia A. "The Early Philosophical Roots of Schleiermacher's Notion of *Gefühl*, 1788–1794." *Harvard Theological Review* 87, no. 1 (1994), pp. 67–105.

Luhmann, Niklas. *A Systems Theory of Religion*. Ed. A. Kieserling (Stanford: Stanford University Press, 2013).

Meckenstock, Günter. "Historische Einführung des Herausgebers." In *Reden (Meckenstock)*, pp. 1–52.

Nassar, Dalia T. "Immediacy and Mediation in Schleiermacher's 'Reden Über Die Religion.'" *The Review of Metaphysics* 59, no. 4 (2006), pp. 807–840.

Prozesky, Martin. "Friedrich Schleiermacher's Reden and the Problem of Religious Plurality." *HTS Teologiese Studies/Theological Studies* 75, no. 4 (2019), a5458.

Ravencroft, Ruth Jackson. "Anonymity as a Strategy in Friedrich Schleiermacher's Early Work, and Its Theological and Social Implications." *Publications of the English Goethe Society* 88 (2019), pp. 184–201.

Ravencroft, Ruth Jackson. *The Veiled God: Friedrich Schleiermacher's Theology of Finitude* (Leiden: Brill, 2019).

Reynolds, Thomas E. "Religion within the Limits of History: Schleiermacher and Religion—A Reappraisal." *Religion* 32, no. 1 (2002), pp. 51–70.

Robinson, Matthew Ryan. *Redeeming Relationship, Relationships That Redeem: Free Sociability and the Completion of Humanity in the Thought of Friedrich Schleiermacher* (Tübingen: Mohr Siebeck, 2018).

Spalding, Johann Joachim. *Religion, eine Angelegenheit des Menschen* (1798). Ed. Tobias Jersak and Georg Friedrich Wagner. *Schriften*, Abt. 1, Bd. 5 (Tübingen: Mohr Siebeck, 2001).

Vial, Theodore. *Schleiermacher: A Guide for the Perplexed* (London: Bloomsbury T&T Clark, 2013).

CHAPTER 28

SERMONS

CATHERINE L. KELSEY

> Just as I know of nothing more splendid to desire for my life than the uniting of the podium and the pulpit, so it would certainly be very apropos for you to be able to be effective in this twofold manner.
>
> —Friedrich Schleiermacher[1]

SCHLEIERMACHER'S theological academic work, associated here with a lecture podium, was intimately connected to his proclamation of Christ, associated here with his pulpit preaching in a worshipping community of faith. In 1810, when he wrote these sentences to a young colleague, Schleiermacher had been preaching weekly for eighteen months in his congregation at *Dreifaltigkeitskirche* and was about to begin twenty-three years of simultaneously preaching weekly and lecturing five days a week at the new university he was helping found in Berlin.[2] This twofold profession was rooted in Schleiermacher's understanding of the

---

[1] Schleiermacher, Letter 3402 to Johannes Karl Hartwig Schulze on February 26, 1810. *KGA* 5.11 (2015), p. 373. This is consistent with his letter to Eichstädt in December 1806 soon after the French occupation of Halle and the closing of the university and his appointment there. He indicated that he needed both a philosophy and theology professorship as well as a nearby pulpit, that is, an appointment as a pastor. Jena, because it was Lutheran and he was Reformed, could not offer him the pulpit, making it out of the question for future employment. Hermann Patsch, "Schleiermachers Briefwechsel mit Eichstädt," *Zeitschrift für Neuere Theologiegeschichte* 2 (1995), p. 289 or *KGA* 5.9, letter 2367, pp. 39–41.

[2] His appointment was made in 1808 and he began preaching weekly there in 1809. Details about Schleiermacher's responsibilities and leadership in this congregation and his earlier assignments can be found in Andreas Reich, *Friedrich Schleiermacher als Pfarrer an der Berliner Dreifaltigkeitskirche 1809–1834* (Berlin: Walter de Gruyter, 1992), the editor's introductions to each of the 14 volumes of sermons in *KGA* 3, and Part C of Martin Ohst, ed., *Schleiermacher Handbuch* (Tübingen: Mohr Siebeck, 2017). The most complete English account to date is in Catherine L. Kelsey, *Schleiermacher's Preaching, Dogmatics, and Biblical Criticism: The Interpretation of Jesus Christ in the Gospel of John* (Eugene, OR: Pickwick Publications, 2007), pp. 9–30, but see also Anette I. Hagen, *Eternal Blessedness for All? A Historical-Systematic Examination of Friedrich Schleiermacher's Reinterpretation of Predestination* (Eugene, OR: Pickwick Publications, 2013), pp. 159–163.

nature of Christian dogmatic theology, and in his understanding of proclamation, particularly preaching.[3] That is why he hoped his young colleague might join him in the double pursuit.

This chapter begins by arguing for the value of Schleiermacher's sermons alongside his dogmatic and ethical writing. It then introduces the kinds of sermons he preached and the variety of sources now gathered in *KGA* 3 that provide extensive access to his voluminous preaching. The typical form of his sermons is described, leading to a discussion of the way Schleiermacher interacted with the congregation through his preaching. His extensive use of Scripture is considered and then the chapter concludes with a brief reception history of Schleiermacher's sermons.

28.1 THE VALUE OF THE SERMONS

Schleiermacher's sermons are significant because they give us some access to a community of Christians at worship, a primary location in which faith is articulated in words. What is experienced in communal worship—relationship with God, with self, with neighbors (both present and absent)—is living faith itself. What is assumed in worship and what is known in worship is the very content that Christian doctrine and Christian ethics describe systematically. Dawn DeVries argues with precision, Schleiermacher understands "preaching as, in effect, an incarnational event that re-presents the person and work of the Jesus of history.... Schleiermacher held on firmly to the very understanding of the Word that the Reformers themselves treasured: the efficacious Word as sacrament, the Word that 'presents Christ.'"[4] The gathered community between them incarnates Christ, embodying Christ's Spirit, the Holy Spirit. The role of preaching in a community gathered to worship, then, is to articulate Christ's God-consciousness in such a way that it is recognized for what it is in that moment of the faith community's life together. Such recognition by a community strengthens and deepens the faith of individuals within it at whatever their growth point might be. As Iain G. Nicol and Allen Jorgenson indicate in their introduction to a translation of Passion sermons, it is common to misinterpret propositions in *Christian Faith* as focused on individual faith. Schleiermacher's preaching demonstrates his consistent understanding of salvation as an experience of the whole human community together.[5] Schleiermacher articulated that faith through his preaching so as to attract engagement with it and deepen participation in it in the context of community.

Scholars familiar with Schleiermacher's sermons offer at least four different kinds of reasons to read them in the twenty-first century. First, they can be read as an introduction to

---

[3] See *CF (2016)*, §14.1, p. 104 for a description of the witness to faith that constitutes proclamation, and §19.1 and 19P.S., pp. 133, 138 for the relationship between dogmatics and proclamation. See the index to *CF (2016)* for its extensive account of proclamation, woven through Part II and the Introduction.

[4] Dawn DeVries, *Jesus Christ in the Preaching of Calvin and Schleiermacher* (Louisville, KY: Westminster John Knox Press, 1996), pp. 2 and 4. The argument is made in detail in chapter 4.

[5] Friedrich Schleiermacher, *Jesus' Life in Dying: Friedrich Schleiermacher's Pre-Easter Reflections to the Community of the Redeemer*, trans. Iain G. Nicol and Allen G. Jorgenson (Eugene, OR: Cascade Books, 2020), pp. 2–4. See Theodore M. Vial, *Schleiermacher: A Guide for the Perplexed* (London: Bloomsbury, 2013), pp. 39–46 for how this emphasis on community is consistent with Schleiermacher's epistemology.

his theology and worldview.[6] The sermons directly express Christian faith without pausing to examine alternative historical doctrinal formulations of that faith, and yet do point out common ways of misunderstanding or avoiding implications of it. Terrence N. Tice demonstrates how effectively a sermon can introduce Schleiermacher's theology.[7]

A second reason for attending to Schleiermacher's sermons is that the nature of religious language itself requires both homiletical *and* doctrinal expressions in order to more adequately approach the mystery of Christ. As Buran Phillips argues,

> Thus, it becomes all the more important to engage Schleiermacher's sermons in order to apprehend the elements of his Christology fully. Christological doctrines, made difficult by the limitations of language itself, are a reaching out for or a grasping toward understanding the person of Jesus Christ. In the rhetorical language of preaching, it is Christ who reaches out to reveal himself, informing as well as transforming. Consequently, Schleiermacher's homiletical work, particularly with regard to Christology, does more than complement his doctrinal work. Rather, it becomes a necessary counterpart; for Schleiermacher's Christ is truly "made flesh" only through such actions and uses of words as preaching.[8]

In Phillips' argument, Schleiermacher's sermons are more than an introduction to his dogmatics; they are necessary in order to "'be grasped' by the object of faith," without which a reader has not fully understood his dogmatics.[9]

This leads directly to a third reason to attend to Schleiermacher's preaching: to come as close as it is possible to accomplish through a text to Christ's God-consciousness as Schleiermacher experienced it and sought to convey it.[10] In *Christian Faith* Schleiermacher described Christian proclamation as Christ's self-presentation. DeVries indicates that "Hearers of the preached Word, under the appropriate conditions, encounter not a feeble human speaker but the Redeemer himself. In this sense, preaching is a re-presentation of the self-presentation of Christ."[11] But the appropriate conditions she articulates are crucial to Schleiermacher and limit what can be accomplished through reading a sermon text. In Schleiermacher's understanding of the efficacy of preaching, the re-presentation of Christ only happens in the midst of a community of faith. Consequently, individual readers of Schleiermacher's preaching texts may be able to encounter traces of Christ's God-consciousness re-presented to another time, but will not encounter a living experience meant for us. We can approach recognizing Schleiermacher's experience of Christ's God-consciousness through sermon texts, approaching closer than through dogmatic texts, but

---

[6] Reiner Preul, "Schleiermacher als Prediger," in *Schleiermacher-Tag 2005: Eine Vortragsreihe*, ed. Günter Meckenstock (Göttingen: Vandenhoeck & Ruprecht, 2006), p. 420. "Nearly all thoughts which he expounds as a preacher, can be equivalent to his faith [*Glaube*] and his moral teaching [*Sitten*]. And vice versa, almost all the insights formulated there find their reflection in the sermons." Trans. Kelsey.

[7] Terrence N. Tice, *Schleiermacher: The Psychology of Christian Faith and Life* (Lanham, MD: Lexington Books/Fortress Academic, 2018).

[8] Buran F. Phillips, *Friedrich Schleiermacher's Interpretation of the Epistle to the Colossians: A Series of Sermons (1830-1831)* (Lewiston, NY: Edwin Mellen Press, 2009), pp. 69-70.

[9] Phillips, *Friedrich Schleiermacher's Interpretation of the Epistle to the Colossians*, p. 92.

[10] I suggest one way to think about the experience of Christ's God-consciousness in light of the experience of being a preacher, in *Schleiermacher's Preaching, Dogmatics, and Biblical Criticism*, pp. 75-78 and Catherine L. Kelsey, *Thinking about Christ with Schleiermacher* (Louisville, KY: Westminster John Knox, 2003), pp. 9-10.

[11] DeVries, *Jesus Christ in the Preaching of Calvin and Schleiermacher*, pp. 64-65.

God-consciousness still cannot grasp us through texts. That grasp requires encounter with living faith in the context of a faith community, in Schleiermacher's view.

Finally, I have shown that *Christian Faith* is constructed to provide a dogmatic theology that is consistent with core assumptions underlying Schleiermacher's preaching throughout his career.[12] The purpose of Schleiermacher's dogmatic theology is to offer an intellectual construct within which faith as it is preached and experienced in a community at worship coheres with itself and with the faith of Christ's first disciples. Thus, Schleiermacher's preaching and his dogmatic writing are closely linked. Study of sermons can facilitate interpretation of both Schleiermacher's dogmatics as well as his Christian ethics.

28.2 SOURCES AND KINDS OF SERMONS

Schleiermacher was a prolific preacher. He preached on over 3,556 documented occasions in his lifetime.[13] Since 2003 the third *Abteilung* of the *KGA* has almost tripled the number of sermon texts or outlines available to scholars—an unusual expansion of sources 175 years after Schleiermacher's death. Prior to this significant scholarly effort approximately 526 sermons were available in print, primarily in *SW*. Since completion of *KGA* 3 with the index volume 15 in 2018 there are 1,525 sources for 1,350 separate preaching occasions.[14] These range from Schleiermacher's first sermon in 1790 to his last just days before his death in 1834.

By the end of the 1790s Schleiermacher had trained himself to preach without a manuscript, though he often had an outline on paper and always had an outline in mind. As a result, we have several kinds of sources for his sermons: outlines in his own hand (written down before or after the sermon was delivered), manuscripts he wrote out and edited, and transcriptions taken down by listeners, a few of which Schleiermacher then edited. Only 258 sermons were published by Schleiermacher himself, primarily in seven collections that appeared across his lifetime. The rest of the sermons published in *SW* were from transcripts Schleiermacher never had the opportunity to correct. The fourteen volumes of sermons in *KGA* 3 include Schleiermacher's outlines, full manuscripts in Schleiermacher's hand, transcripts taken down by colleagues, corrections of those transcripts in Schleiermacher's hand, as well as all the sermons published by Schleiermacher and those published after his death in *SW*.

The topics for Schleiermacher's preaching include "patriotic" sermons offered during the invasion of Prussia by Napoleon's army from 1806 until the liberation of Berlin in a battle at its Halle Gate (at the south end of Schleiermacher's geographic parish) in 1813.[15] There

---

[12] Kelsey, *Schleiermacher's Preaching, Dogmatics, and Biblical Criticism*, pp. 73–96.

[13] "Kalendarum," *KGA* 3.1, p. 769. This 266-page appendix lists every preaching occasion noted in Schleiermacher's surviving calendars in addition to the sermons in transcription and published. Across the forty-three years of his preaching career this averages out to more than 1.5 times per week, but he wasn't preaching regularly until his appointment to Landsberg in 1794, nor was preaching possible for much of 1806–1807, so in many years the average was much higher.

[14] *KGA* 3.15 is a rich resource for examining the sermons. Even readers without much German can make use of the 213-page index of Scripture references in the sermons. It also contains a listing of all the sermon themes for main services, and a keyword index.

[15] Vial, *Schleiermacher*, pp. 110–113 is a helpful introduction to these in English.

are also multiple series of sermons that examine much of a particular New Testament book, including Mark, John, Acts, Galatians, Philippians, Colossians, 1 Thessalonians, James, 1 Peter, and 2 Peter.[16] Unpublished prior to the *KGA* are sermons for hundreds of ordinary-time Sundays as well as sermons for baptisms, weddings, funerals, confirmations, and Saturday preparatory services (when the focus was on confession and absolution in anticipation of Sunday eucharist).

The very first sermons that Schleiermacher himself published were not his own. He participated in translating two of the four volumes of the Scottish preacher Hugh Blair's widely influential preaching into German. The translations appeared in 1795 and 1802.[17] Blair was known for combining clever argumentation with edification. His sermons were moral and rational, expressing insight into human nature.[18] The experience of translating Blair helped Schleiermacher decide to publish the first collection of his own sermons in 1801.[19] A second collection appeared in 1808, the third in 1814, the fourth in 1820 (Christian household sermons), the fifth in 1826 (Christian festival sermons vol. 1), the sixth in 1831 (Augsburg sermons), and the seventh and final collection in 1833 (Christian festival sermons vol. 2).[20] Schleiermacher had reservations about publishing his sermons.[21] He chose to publish only those sermons that he thought had usefulness to a wide audience. As a result, his first collection included only three of the many sermons he preached at Charité Hospital, supplementing them with nine sermons preached in Landsberg an der Warthe, Potsdam, and elsewhere as a guest preacher in Berlin. The second sermon collection of 1808 intentionally published sermons from 1806, 1807, and January 1808 because they spoke to the reality under French military occupation.[22] The third collection contains sermons preached in 1812, but was not published until summer 1814, well after the spring 1813 freeing of Berlin from the French. The last four collections are each organized around a theme, as indicated.

The number and range of sermons available in English translation continues to expand. The first two volumes, published by Mary Wilson (1890) and Dawn DeVries (1987), are thoughtful selections of a variety of sermons. More recent translation volumes have provided a specific series, such as the Christian household sermons (1991)[23], the Augsburg

---

[16] Series based on both biblical texts and themes are listed in *KGA* 3.1, pp. l–lii.

[17] Critical edition is *KGA* 4.1.

[18] *KGA* 4.1, p. xxiv.

[19] See Christoph Meier-Dorken, *Die Theologie der frühen Predigten Schleiermachers* (Berlin: Walter de Gruyter, 1988), pp. 35–45 for an account of the influence of Blair on Schleiermacher's early preaching.

[20] Each of the first four collections appeared in second editions between 1806 and 1826. The last three collections appeared in only one edition. Schleiermacher did some corrections when new editions appeared. Changes are carefully noted in *KGA* 3.1 and 3.2.

[21] In the introduction to the second edition of his second sermon collection, Schleiermacher expressed his expectation that only his immediate hearers received the full value of the sermons published therein. *KGA* 3.1, p. 417. See also Bernhard Schmidt, *Lied–Kirchenmusik–Predigt im Festgottesdienst Friedrich Schleiermachers: Zur Rekonstruktion seiner liturgischen Praxis* (Berlin: Walter de Gruyter, 2002), pp. 439–440 n55.

[22] Günter Meckenstock, "Zeitgeschichtliche Bezüge in Schleiermachers Predigten 1808–1810," in *Wissenschaft, Kirche, Staat und Politik: Schleiermacher im preußischen Reformprozess*, ed. Andreas Arndt, Simon Gerber, and Sarah Schmidt (Berlin: Walter de Gruyter, 2019), p. 262.

[23] There is a post-Reformation tradition of "household sermons" addressing questions of how Christians live together. Schleiermacher used some of the "housetable" texts from Luther's smaller catechism, but not for all of his series. In this series Schleiermacher casts a vision of a household in which all roles are respected, and the responsibility of the master of the household is the growth of those who

sermons (1997) or the Colossians sermons (2009), or have been selected by season of the liturgical year, such as New Years (2003), Christmas (2019), and Passion (2020).[24]

We turn to four ways to characterize the sermons: what they generally assume or seek to achieve, their form, how they show the preacher seeking to interact with the congregation, and their uses of Scripture.

28.2.1 Emphases

There is striking consistency among twenty-first-century interpreters of Schleiermacher's sermons in identifying the emphases expressed in them. Three are particularly important to be familiar with: the role of community in relation to faith in Christ, the focus on Christ, and attention to Christ's proclamation of the Reign of God.

Examples of the role of community are abundant in the sermons. Günter Meckenstock draws attention to an 1810 sermon[25] that argues the first disciples saw faith as a community rather than as an individual God-and-I experience. Schleiermacher concluded there that had faith been only an individual thing it quickly would have grown cold. Similarly, an 1820 Christmas sermon states,

> We ... know that the reign of God does not consist in the relationship of individuals to the Redeemer, that the Redeemer has not descended simply to enter into the hearts of particular human beings and in that way to bless or save each individual. Rather, he also came to bless or save them in that he collected them within one greatly extended community.[26]

Later in that 1820 sermon assurance is also described with this communal aspect, as "assurance in the sacred bond of the community that he founded among those who acknowledge him." Redemption is also directly associated with incorporation into a community of Christians across Schleiermacher's preaching on John.[27] In her study of the sermon series on Acts Anette Hagen argues, "As Schleiermacher insists in his sermon on Acts: 4:5–14, 'the divine revelation in Christ and his Spirit do not dwell in any individual person.' It dwells in the Church as the totality of all who are related by faith in the Redeemer. Indeed, the preservation of God's grace depends on the continuation of the community among Christians."[28] Brian Gerrish argues that for Schleiermacher, Christian doctrines "are accounts of a particular community's faith, a faith that the individual comes to experience only through participation in the community."[29] Selective reading of *Christian Faith* can miss the essential role of community; any reading of the sermons makes this feature of Schleiermacher's dogmatics stand out clearly. Attentive readers of Schleiermacher's sermons are consistently

---

serve, with a goal that they might become independent. Thus, servitude, like childhood, is a transitory situation on the way to independence, rather than a permanent state for a human life.

[24] For additional volumes containing individual translated sermons, see the Bibliography.
[25] *KGA* 3.4, p. 104.
[26] Tice, *Schleiermacher: The Psychology of Christian Faith and Life*, p. 16.
[27] Kelsey, *Schleiermacher's Preaching, Dogmatics, and Biblical Criticism*, p. 70.
[28] Hagen, *Eternal Blessedness for All?*, p. 172.
[29] Brian Gerrish, "The Nature of Doctrine," *Journal of Religion* 68 (1988), pp. 87–92.

shown that faith community constitutes the environment within which faith is experienced in others, is evoked in individuals, and forms the Reign of God prior to its consummation.

A second clear emphasis in Schleiermacher's sermons is the complete focus on Jesus Christ. Everything in redemption is accomplished through Jesus of Nazareth and his God-consciousness and the faithful are actually transformed by the life of Christ in them.[30] There is no redeeming natural knowledge of God acknowledged in the sermons. Consistent with this view, there are very few sermons on anything other than New Testament texts.[31] The focus on Jesus Christ in sermons on New Testament texts is not to gain principles about him, but rather, is for the purpose of becoming more like him, particularly like him in his relationship to God and to other humans.

Reiner Preul notes that within the focus on Jesus of Nazareth seen in Schleiermacher's sermons, resurrection, ascension, and returning to judge are set aside as constituent parts of the doctrine of Christ's person.[32] Something about the way Jesus *lived* and proclaimed himself made redemption available to those who would accept the gift of it.[33] In the sermons, Schleiermacher drew a picture of Christ that made the experience of Christ's God-consciousness visible and he described the current experience of his hearer's experience of faith as consistent with that of the first disciples and the Redeemer's own experience of relationship with God. Schleiermacher rarely used the term "God-consciousness" in his preaching, instead he evoked and described the experience of it.

A third emphasis widely found in Schleiermacher's preaching concerns the Redeemer's proclamation of the Reign of God, part of his comprehensive view that "the world is the sphere of God's omnipotence." But in a narrower sense the Reign of God "is not so much a place where believers dwell but it is in fact in the believers themselves."[34] Schleiermacher was one of the persons who revived attention to this theme of the Synoptic Gospels in both his preaching and his university lectures on the New Testament and life of Jesus.[35] His focus on the Reign of God connected his reading of the Synoptic Gospels with his reading of the Gospel of John.[36]

28.2.2 Form

Description of the form of Schleiermacher's preaching to a congregation is complicated by the sermons that were published during his lifetime. We have known that Schleiermacher edited his sermons for publication, but until the *KGA* edition it was difficult to know in

---

[30] Preul, "Predigten," pp. 420–1.
[31] Less than 8 percent of all Schleiermacher's sermons used a Hebrew Bible main text. See *KGA* 3.15.
[32] Reiner Preul, "Predigten," in *Schleiermacher Handbuch*, ed. Martin Ohst (Tübingen: Mohr Siebeck, 2017), p. 421.
[33] Kelsey, *Schleiermacher's Preaching, Dogmatics, and Biblical Criticism*, pp. 67–68.
[34] Hagen, *Eternal Blessedness for All?*, pp. 173f. Her analysis of the 1820–1821 sermon series on Acts shows this especially clearly.
[35] See *CF (2016)* index entry "reign of God" for the extensive exposition of it there and compare to the sermons index *KGA* 3.15 "Reich Gottes" where it is a very common term throughout his career but particularly so in 1826–1827 sermons. See also Kelsey, *Schleiermacher's Preaching, Dogmatics, and Biblical Criticism*, pp. 88f, 110.
[36] Kelsey, *Schleiermacher's Preaching, Dogmatics, and Biblical Criticism*, p. 117.

what kind of editing he engaged. Comparison of a sermon preached on February 16, 1812 in the form published by Schleiermacher in his third sermon collection in 1820 with the transcription of that event created by his colleague Friedrich August Pischon is instructive: the published version has multiple changes that broaden the address from the particular day in the liturgical year, and both the introduction and conclusion are expanded for publication.[37] The sermon he published was thereby adapted for readers. *KGA* shows this process in facsimile of the autograph of a transcription manuscript by Pischon of another sermon, preached on December 26, 1814. The facsimile shows two paragraphs (constituting two pages in print) of introduction in Schleiermacher's own hand added to the manuscript after crossing out a portion of Pischon's original transcription.[38]

Schleiermacher preached in several kinds of worship contexts and his preaching adapted to those contexts, primarily in its length. For the twenty-five years that he preached at *Dreifaltigkeitskirche* in Berlin he alternated with the Lutheran pastor week by week between preaching the early service and the main service on Sunday mornings. The main service was advertised in 1825 as lasting about 1.5 hours, which explains why sermons preached in the main service tend to be longer by about 10 minutes than those preached in the early service.[39] Reading the transcripts aloud yields a sermon of 35 to 45 minutes duration, well within the principle articulated in his lectures on practical theology that sermons should be at least 30 minutes but an hour is too long.[40] Most of the sermon series that moved verse by verse through a New Testament book were preached at the early service. Though these sermons are often termed "homilies" to distinguish them from the main-service sermons, they are normally more than 30 minutes in length. What the *KGA* designates as "occasional" preaching—baptism, wedding, funeral, confirmation, and a few other occasions—are closer in length to a twenty-first-century homily. All these types of sermons were meant to be heard rather than read; it can help a reader find the cadence and meaning of the sentences, with their many clauses, to speak them aloud as if preaching.[41]

The sermons Schleiermacher published typically have a two-part introduction that moves from a general problem or season of the church year, to a particular aspect of it or perspective on it, leading to a biblical text that focuses a particular theme. The transcriptions of his preaching typically have a much shorter introduction or simply begin with the biblical text, suggesting that this introductory material was primarily added to benefit readers of published texts, who have not already been placed into the sermon's context through earlier portions of the worship service. The body of the sermon typically falls into two main sections, sometimes three. Often these sections are associated with a phrase in the biblical text. Then the conclusion draws to an affirmation, sometimes in the form of a choice that the preacher and congregation make together through the preacher's words.

---

[37] *KGA* 3.1, pp. 468–480 and *KGA* 3.4, pp. 449–457.

[38] *KGA* 3.4, pp. 614–620, facsimile 596. This sermon, on John 1:14, was on one of his favorite Scripture verses, frequently referenced in his preaching on other texts.

[39] *KGA* 3.9, p. xx.

[40] *SW* I.13, p. 214.

[41] This is true whether one is reading in English or German; in most translations the sentence cadences are quite similar, particularly the rhetorical strategy of multiple short clauses within a sentence building into a conclusion.

28.2.3 Interaction with Congregation

Readers may be surprised to find no stories or anecdotes in Schleiermacher's sermons, and yet in a relatively abstract discussion, how closely each sermon follows the chosen biblical text. Bernhard Schmidt suggests that the aesthetic tastes of Schleiermacher's time welcomed his allusive discourse. His listeners liked doing the work of going from his more general descriptive statements to identify who they had themselves seen doing just what he pointed toward. Schmidt quotes Schleiermacher suggesting that his more "veiled discourse" engaged the imagination of hearers: "The true exemplification is thus in the listener."[42] It would also have been a wise form of discourse in times when civil authority was dangerously suspicious of him, a circumstance Schleiermacher experienced several times in his career.[43] Schmidt suggests, "To the extent the hearer of a sermon was intellectually challenged as a listener, to that extent their cooperative thinking was also expected to make ideas concrete. At the same time, guessing allusions might also have had a welcome conversational effect."[44] What made this style of preaching work so effectively was that Schleiermacher was not reading his sermon; by 1800 he always preached entirely extemporaneously, sometimes with great emotion, directly to the congregation, using nonverbal rhetorical tools (his gaze, pauses, volume, speed) to grab their imagination and get them thinking alongside him. More than just instruction, the form and delivery of the sermon evoked and formed faith as an activity of engagement.

Hagen expresses an important point about the congregation: "He consistently addressed his sermons to an audience whose faith he programmatically presupposed."[45] This is demonstrable in his sermons and explained in *Christian Faith*.[46] Just as Christ's God-consciousness draws persons to itself and to him, preaching articulates faith in a community in order to affirm it in those who have it and, simultaneously, in order to attract those who do not. There is no reason to articulate anything else in preaching. Whereas readers of *Christian Faith* can get confused by positions that Schleiermacher lays out but ultimately rejects (if one reads far enough), the sermons avoid this problem. There is no doubt at the conclusion of each sermon what is being affirmed—a relationship with Christ shared in a community that receives from him, just as Christ receives from the Father.[47] Schleiermacher's preaching never explicitly distinguishes between an inner and outer circle, or the invisible and visible church; his preaching is addressed as if everyone present is, or is becoming, one who shares in Christ's God-consciousness.[48]

---

[42] Schmidt, *Lied-Kirchenmusik-Predigt im Festgottesdienst Friedrich Schleiermachers*, p. 440.

[43] Prussia under French occupation or hegemony in 1806–1813 and being under investigation by the Prussian government in 1822–1823 are two significant periods in which Schleiermacher could be sure that there were spies in the congregation.

[44] Schmidt, *Lied-Kirchenmusik-Predigt im Festgottesdienst Friedrich Schleiermachers*, p. 440.

[45] Hagen, *Eternal Blessedness for All?*, p. 176.

[46] See "proclamation" entries in the index, *CF (2016)*, p. 1122.

[47] Schleiermacher's understanding of *Mittheilung*/communication helps one recognize the close relationship between his Christology and his practice of preaching. With such an understanding, it can hardly be surprising that he found himself eager to preach. See Kelsey, *Schleiermacher's Preaching, Dogmatics, and Biblical Criticism*, pp. 79–80.

[48] Tice, *Schleiermacher: The Psychology of Christian Faith and Life*, p. 31 n4.

28.2.4 Use of Scripture

Schleiermacher's sermons are saturated in Scripture and structured by biblical texts. The only sermons he preached that were not structured by a biblical text were wedding and funeral sermons and some of the baptismal sermons. Even in the sermon series celebrating the anniversary of the handing down of the Augsburg Confession, "the normative and controlling element throughout the series is not the confession itself but the various New Testament passages and texts in relation to which the confession is assessed."[49] Schleiermacher's preaching makes very visible that he received the New Testament as the preeminent account of how faith evoked by Jesus Christ is experienced by those who follow Christ—from the first followers in Galilee until our own time.

As a Reformed preacher, Schleiermacher was free to select his texts for preaching. In the nineteenth century Berlin Protestants used an eighteenth-century lectionary called "Altkirchlichen Perikopen."[50] Schleiermacher used it selectively; for example, in 1828–1829 he used a portion of the prescribed text for a given Sunday about one-third of the time. The rest of the time he selected texts unrelated to the lectionary.[51] One strategy for selecting texts, employed by centuries of preachers, is to do a series of sermons on one book. Schleiermacher employed this strategy frequently for the Sundays he preached the early service. He preached three different series on Acts, in 1812, 1820, and 1832. After that first series in 1812 he turned to a short series on Galatians in 1816. Then in 1817 he began to preach *seriatum* through Philippians in fourteen sermons. That was such a success that he turned to preach *seriatum* through 1 Peter in 1819, James in 1820, returned to Philippians in 1822–1823, the Gospel of John in a series of ninety-five sermons 1823–1827, 1 Thessalonians in 1827–1828, Colossians in 1830–1831, and he began the Gospel of Mark in 1831. It was fifty-four sermons along when he died in February 1834.

The Scripture index for the *KGA* 3 sermons volumes shows a startling number of references to John 1:14—some part, usually the last half ("we have beheld his glory, as of the only son of the Father"), is referred to more than twice as frequently as any other verse in Scripture.[52] Though the text was the stated text for only three sermons (January and December 1814, and March 1829), it was referred to 380 times from 1814 through to the conclusion of his very last sermon days before his death in 1834. His next most frequent reference, only 177 times, was to Colossians 2:9 ("How can we thank God enough for you in return for all the joy that we feel before our God because of you?").[53]

Schleiermacher rarely preached from Hebrew Bible texts, with the notable exception of using Psalm texts extensively for sermons that were not the main Sunday service in 1800. This was one of the years of his service at the Charité Hospital in Berlin. Beginning with

---

[49] Friedrich Schleiermacher, "Editor's Introduction," in *Reformed but Ever Reforming: Sermons in Relation to the Celebration of the Handing Over of the Augsburg Confession (1830)*, trans. Iain G. Nicol (Lewiston, NY: Edwin Mellen Press, 1997), p. xiv.

[50] Republished in 1890 in the *Allgemeines Kirchenblatt für das evangelische Deutschland*, Jg. 39. 1890, pp. 576–599.

[51] *KGA* 3.11, pp. xi–xii.

[52] See *KGA* 3.15, pp. 225–227.

[53] Next frequently cited texts were: John 4:21–24 (124 times), John 5: 19–20 (119 times), Hebrews 1:3 (93 times), 1 John 4:16 (77 times), 2 Corinthians 12:9 (73 times), and John 1:12 (62 times). The most frequent reference to a Hebrew Bible text was Psalm 119:105 (20 times).

his call to *Dreifaltigkeitskirche*, Berlin in 1808, Hebrew Bible texts were the main preaching text less than 2 percent of the time; most of this total of fifteen sermons over twenty-five years were the specified text for a civil observance, such as a called day of prayer (*Buβtag*) or a New Year's observance. References to Hebrew Bible texts were more frequent, but still only approximately 10 percent of the total references. In almost all references to Scripture in his preaching, Schleiermacher assumed his listeners would catch the allusion and know its source so he did not provide the book, chapter, or verse.[54] Both his thought world and that of his listeners were steeped in scriptural language. But because his focus was on proclaiming Christ, most of that language was from the New Testament.

Schleiermacher was accused in his lifetime by Ferdinand Christian Baur of reading Scripture un-historically. Baur's student David Friedrich Strauss and thereafter Albert Schweitzer in the nineteenth century and Rudolf Bultmann in the twentieth century perpetuated and expanded the accusation. Their critiques of Schleiermacher's historical judgments depend, in large part, on unexamined theological assumptions they make about when and how the redeeming work of Christ occurred.[55] When those assumptions are examined the critiques of Schleiermacher based on them carry far less force. Schleiermacher's sermons assume continuity between the initial faith elicited by the Redeemer, held by his disciples during his lifetime, and the faith of all who experience redemption through him after his death until the present. This assumption was validated in Schleiermacher's community of faith at worship.

28.3 Reception

Reception of Schleiermacher's preaching has occurred with two very different audiences—the people who heard him preach in person and the people who read published sermon texts. Although a detailed account of congregational responses to his preaching remains to be written, any reader of sermon texts will do well to keep in mind the congregational context for which and in which each sermon was first created. A very brief summary here may help a reader ask relevant questions about context.

Schleiermacher was fully ordained in Berlin on April 6, 1794 and preached his first sermon under assignment on April 18, 1794 as the assistant to the ailing Reformed pastor of the concordat church in Landsberg an der Warthe. He preached regularly and eagerly there. When that pastor died in the summer of 1795 he was not allowed to remain in Landsberg and chose to return to Berlin and serve as the Reformed chaplain at Charité, the military and indigent hospital. In this context he preached in prayer services to persons who were quite likely to die, and the texts from which he preached reflect this setting. For three months in 1799 he substituted in Potsdam for the military chaplain there and preached more than once in the presence of the king. In 1802 he was reassigned as the senior pastor in Stolpe, where the small number of Reformed parishioners made preaching weekly and holding confirmation a light duty. In 1804 as the opportunity to become preacher to the university and professor of

---

[54] Schmidt, *Lied–Kirchenmusik–Predigt im Festgottesdienst Friedrich Schleiermachers*, p. 441.
[55] Kelsey, *Schleiermacher's Preaching, Dogmatics, and Biblical Criticism*, pp. 113–116.

philosophy and theology in Halle emerged in a new position, Schleiermacher moved eagerly. However, new university positions, even when created by the king, can encounter resistance. Though Schleiermacher preached elsewhere in Halle, it was summer of 1806 before the first planned university worship featuring the new position was held on campus. Then in October Halle was attacked by the French and the church was confiscated. Schleiermacher continued to preach in the *Domkirche* through Easter 1807. He moved to Berlin in May 1807 and did guest preaching. Then in early May 1808 the Reformed pastor at *Dreifaltigkeitskirche* died, and Schleiermacher was named to the position by the end of the month. He began service to the congregation in Fall 1808 and served formally from June 1809 to his death in 1834.[56]

By the 1820s the *Dreifaltigkeitskirche* was usually full at the main service; it had room for 1,600 people on a main floor with two balconies. The pulpit was very high, looking out directly at the second balcony and down on the first balcony and box seating on the main floor.[57] Among educated Berliners Schleiermacher's preaching was particularly appreciated, but his preaching attracted a variety of hearers, including Moravians, Jews, baptized and unbaptized Christians, young philosophers and philologists, and "elegant women."[58] Once assigned to *Dreifaltigkeitskirche*, Schleiermacher preached every Sunday there and rarely anywhere else, except for baptisms and weddings. He preached to his people, "my devout friends," "my beloved hearers."[59] The curious came to hear him there. Most who heard him came away impressed, if not moved.

Readers of Schleiermacher's sermon texts have had a more mixed response, in his time and in the twentieth century.[60] It has been common for a scholar to read only a small number of sermons and arrive at sweeping and often inaccurate generalizations. Karl Barth is a twentieth-century example. Dawn DeVries offers a convincing rebuttal of his "inaccurate and unfair" account of Schleiermacher's theology of preaching.[61] In Schleiermacher's lifetime his sermons were widely ready by laity and clergy. Theologians, however, tended to be critical because his sermons re-present faith rather than interpreting it rationally or supernaturally. Since Schleiermacher had created a third way that did not fall neatly into either rationalist or super-naturalist approaches, he was accused of being both. Then and today, theologians who assume that redemption occurs primarily at Christ's death or resurrection frequently misunderstand Schleiermacher's consistent view that redemption is a function of incarnation.[62]

---

[56] See *KGA* 3.1, pp. xxii–liii, for a detailed account by Günter Meckenstock.

[57] The building was largely destroyed in World War II bombing and was leveled after the war.

[58] Meckenstock, "Zeitgeschichtliche Bezüge in Schleiermachers Predigten 1808–1810," p. 270.

[59] Schleiermacher used about nine related names for the congregation as he addressed them, often left in abbreviated form when the sermons were published. Abbreviations can be found in *KGA* 3.1, p. 1039.

[60] The Schleiermacher bibliographies by Terrence N. Tice (1966, 1985) provide the best resource for finding reviews and uses of Schleiermacher's preaching, though there are far fewer assessments of his preaching than of his theology, hermeneutics, philosophical ethics, or pedagogy. See Terrence N. Tice, *Schleiermacher Bibliography (1784-1984), Updating and Commentary* (Princeton, NJ: Princeton Theological Seminary, 1985); *Schleiermacher Bibliography: With Brief Introductions, Annotations, and Index* (Princeton, NJ: Princeton Theological Seminary, 1966).

[61] DeVries, *Jesus Christ in the Preaching of Calvin and Schleiermacher*, p. 69 n51.

[62] See for example, Emanuel Hirsch, *Schleiermachers Christusglaube: Drei Studien* (Gütersloh: Mohn, 1968), pp. 92 and 59. Cf. Kelsey, *Schleiermacher's Preaching, Dogmatics, and Biblical Criticism*, pp. 63 and 71.

Several solutions to the problem of selective reading of Schleiermacher's sermons have been effectively demonstrated, including focusing on sermons from one period,[63] focusing on a sermon series,[64] or focusing on one liturgical season across many years.[65] The most detailed analyses of sermons in English can be found in Kelsey's *Schleiermacher's Preaching, Dogmatics, and Biblical Criticism* (2007), DeVries' *Jesus Christ in the Preaching of Calvin and Schleiermacher* (1996), and the extensive introductions to the recent translation volumes. The completion of *KGA* 3 makes possible further use of these strategies and the development of yet new ones. Furthermore, as Mary Streufert has shown in a feminist project, Schleiermacher's preaching and understanding of proclamation in community continues to offer useful tools for contemporary theological projects.[66]

The opportunity for further research using Schleiermacher's sermons is vast, wide-ranging, and deeply relevant to thinking about how Christian faith may be effectively communicated from one generation to the next. Attention to Schleiermacher's sermons is consistent with his own desire to hold his academic work and his proclamation in faith community together in practice. Furthermore, close attention to his preaching highlights the importance of Christian community in his thought, tempering the individualistic lens that readers might bring to portions of *Christian Faith*.

SUGGESTED READING

DeVries, Dawn. *Jesus Christ in the Preaching of Calvin and Schleiermacher* (Louisville, KY: Westminster John Knox Press, 1996).

Hagen, Anette I. *Eternal Blessedness for All? A Historical-Systematic Examination of Friedrich Schleiermacher's Reinterpretation of Predestination* (Eugene, OR: Pickwick Publications, 2013).

Kelsey, Catherine L. *Schleiermacher's Preaching, Dogmatics, and Biblical Criticism: The Interpretation of Jesus Christ in the Gospel of John* (Eugene, OR: Pickwick Publications, 2007).

Also note the nine translations of Schleiermacher's sermons listed in the Bibliography under his name. With the exception of Mary Wilson's volume, each translator offers an informative introduction to Schleiermacher's preaching in their volume.

---

[63] See Meier-Dorkin, *Die Theologie der frühen Predigten Schleiermachers*, on the early sermons before 1806, or Vial, *Schleiermacher*, pp. 110–113, on the political sermons.

[64] For John sermons, see Kelsey, *Schleiermacher's Preaching, Dogmatics, and Biblical Criticism*; for Colossians sermons, see Phillips, *Friedrich Schleiermacher's Interpretation of the Epistle to the Colossians*; for Acts sermons, see Hagen, *Eternal Blessedness for All?*

[65] For New Year's sermons, see Edwina Lawler, *Fifteen Sermons of Friedrich Schleiermacher Delivered to Celebrate the Beginning of a New Year* (Lewiston, NY: Edwin Mellen Press, 2003); for Christmas sermons, see Friedrich Schleiermacher, *Christmas Sermons: Displays of Development in a Theology of Christian Faith and Life (1790–1833)*, ed. Terrence N. Tice, trans. Terrence N. Tice and Edwina G. Lawler (Eugene, OR: Cascade Books, 2019); for Passion sermons, see Schleiermacher, *Jesus' Life in Dying*.

[66] Mary J. Streufert, "Reclaiming Schleiermacher for Twenty-first Century Atonement Theory: The Human and the Divine in Feminist Christology," *Feminist Theology* 15, no. 1 (2006), pp. 98–120.

Bibliography

DeVries, Dawn. *Jesus Christ in the Preaching of Calvin and Schleiermacher* (Louisville, KY: Westminster John Knox Press, 1996).

Gerrish, Brian. "The Nature of Doctrine." *Journal of Religion* 68 (1988), pp. 87–92.

Hagen, Anette I. *Eternal Blessedness for All? A Historical-Systematic Examination of Friedrich Schleiermacher's Reinterpretation of Predestination* (Eugene, OR: Pickwick Publications, 2013).

Hirsch, Emanuel. *Schleiermachers Christusglaube: Drei Studien* (Gütersloh: Mohn, 1968).

Kelsey, Catherine L. *Schleiermacher's Preaching, Dogmatics, and Biblical Criticism: The Interpretation of Jesus Christ in the Gospel of John* (Eugene, OR: Pickwick Publications, 2007).

Kelsey, Catherine L. *Thinking about Christ with Schleiermacher* (Louisville, KY: Westminster John Knox, 2003).

Lawler, Edwina. *Fifteen Sermons of Friedrich Schleiermacher Delivered to Celebrate the Beginning of a New Year* (Lewiston, NY: Edwin Mellen Press, 2003).

Lücke, Friedrich. "Erinnerungen an Dr. Friedrich Schleiermacher." *Theologische Studien und Kritiken* (1834), pp. 745–813.

Meckenstock, Günter. "Zeitgeschichtliche Bezüge in Schleiermachers Predigten 1808–1810." In *Wissenschaft, Kirche, Staat und Politik: Schleiermacher im preußischen Reformprozess*, ed. Andreas Arndt, Simon Gerber, and Sarah Schmidt (Berlin: Walter de Gruyter, 2019), pp. 257–275.

Meier-Dorken, Christoph. *Die Theologie der frühen Predigten Schleiermachers* (Berlin: Walter de Gruyter, 1988).

Ohst, Martin, ed. *Schleiermacher Handbuch* (Tübingen: Mohr Siebeck, 2017).

Patsch, Hermann. "Schleiermachers Briefwechsel mit Eichstädt." *Zeitschrift für Neuere Theologiegeschichte* 2 (1995), pp. 255–302.

Phillips, Buran F. *Friedrich Schleiermacher's Interpretation of the Epistle to the Colossians: A Series of Sermons (1830–1831)* (Lewiston, NY: Edwin Mellen Press, 2009).

Preul, Reiner. "Predigten." In *Schleiermacher Handbuch*, ed. Martin Ohst (Tübingen: Mohr Siebeck, 2017), pp. 411–425.

Preul, Reiner. "Schleiermacher als Prediger." In *Schleiermacher-Tag 2005: Eine Vortragsreihe*, ed. Günter Meckenstock (Göttingen: Vandenhoeck & Ruprecht, 2006), pp. 87–94.

Reich, Andreas. *Friedrich Schleiermacher als Pfarrer an der Berliner Dreifaltigkeitskirche 1809–1834* (Berlin: Walter de Gruyter, 1992).

Schleiermacher, Friedrich. *Predigten. Erste bis Vierte Sammlung (1801-1820) mit den Varianten der Neuauflagen (1806-1826)*, KGA 3.1, ed. Günter Meckenstock (Berlin: De Gruyter, 2012).

Schleiermacher, Friedrich. *Predigten 1809-1815*, KGA 3.4, ed. Patrick Weiland and Simon Paschen (Berlin: De Gruyter, 2011).

Schleiermacher, Friedrich. *Predigten 1825*, KGA 3.9, ed. Kristen Maria Christine Kunz and Brinja Maria Bauer (Berlin: De Gruyter, 2017).

Schleiermacher, Friedrich. *Predigten 1828-1829*, KGA 3.11, ed. Patrick Weiland (Berlin: De Gruyter, 2014).

Schleiermacher, Friedrich. *Register [Predigten]*, KGA 3.15, ed. Brinja Maria Bauer, Ralph Brucker, Britta Kunz, Michael Pietsch, Dirk Schmid, Patrick Weiland, and Günter Meckenstock (Berlin: De Gruyter, 2018).

Schleiermacher, Friedrich. *Hugo Blairs Predigten*, KGA 4.1, ed. Günter Meckenstock and Anette Hagan (Berlin: De Gruyter, 2019).

Schleiermacher, Friedrich. *Briefwechsel 1809–1810 (Briefe 3021–3560)*, KGA 5.11, Ed. Simon Gerber and Sarah Schmidt (Berlin: De Gruyter, 2015).

Schleiermacher, Friedrich. *Briefwechsel 1806-1807,* KGA 5.9, ed. Andreas Arndt and Simon Gerber (Berlin: De Gruyter, 2011).

Schleiermacher, Friedrich. *Briefwechsel 1809-1810,* KGA 5.11, ed. Simon Gerber and Sarah Schmidt (Berlin: De Gruyter, 2015).

Schleiermacher, Friedrich. *The Christian Household: A Sermonic Treatise.* Trans. Dietrich Seidel and Terrence N. Tice (Lewiston, NY: Edwin Mellen Press, 1991).

Schleiermacher, Friedrich. *Christmas Sermons: Displays of Development in a Theology of Christian Faith and Life (1790–1833).* Ed. Terrence N. Tice, trans. Terrence N. Tice and Edwina G. Lawler (Eugene, OR: Cascade Books, 2019).

Schleiermacher, Friedrich. *Jesus' Life in Dying: Friedrich Schleiermacher's Pre-Easter Reflections to the Community of the Redeemer.* Trans. Iain G. Nicol and Allen G. Jorgenson (Eugene, OR: Cascade Books, 2020).

Schleiermacher, Friedrich. "Pentecost Sunday (May 1825), I Corinthians 2:10–12: The Spirit from God and the Human Spirit." In *Schleiermacher: Christmas Dialogue, The Second Speech, and Other Selections*, ed. and trans. Julia A. Lamm (New York: Paulist Press, 2014), pp. 224–241.

Schleiermacher, Friedrich. *Die praktische Theologie nach den Grundsäzen der evangelischen Kirche in Zusammenhange dargestellt.* Ed. Jacob Frerichs *SW* 1.13 (Berlin: Reimer, 1850).

Schleiermacher, Friedrich. *Reformed but Ever Reforming: Sermons in Relation to the Celebration of the Handing Over of the Augsburg Confession (1830).* Trans. Iain G. Nicol (Lewiston, NY: Edwin Mellen Press, 1997).

Schleiermacher, Friedrich. "Second Sunday of Advent (December 1832), Hebrews 4:15: Christ Is Like Us in All Things but Sin." In *Schleiermacher: Christmas Dialogue, The Second Speech, and Other Selections*, ed. and trans. Julia A. Lamm (New York: Paulist Press, 2014), pp. 241–249.

Schleiermacher, Friedrich. *Selected Sermons.* Trans. Mary F. Wilson (New York: Funk and Wagnalls, 1890).

Schleiermacher, Friedrich. *Servant of the Word: Selected Sermons of Friedrich Schleiermacher.* Trans. Dawn DeVries (Philadelphia: Fortress Press, 1987).

Schleiermacher, Friedrich. "The Transformation That Has Begun from the Redeemer's Appearance upon the Earth: Christmas Sermon 1820." In *Schleiermacher: The Psychology of Christian Faith and Life.* Trans. Terrence N. Tice (Lanham, MD: Lexington Books/Fortress Academic, 2018), pp. 15–39.

Schmidt, Bernhard. *Lied–Kirchenmusik–Predigt im Festgottesdienst Friedrich Schleiermachers: Zur Rekonstruktion seiner liturgischen Praxis* (Berlin: Walter de Gruyter, 2002).

Streufert, Mary J. "Reclaiming Schleiermacher for Twenty-first Century Atonement Theory: The Human and the Divine in Feminist Christology." *Feminist Theology* 15, no. 1 (2006), pp. 98–120.

Tice, Terrence N. *Schleiermacher* (Nashville, TN: Abingdon Press, 2006).

Tice, Terrence N. *Schleiermacher Bibliography (1784–1984), Updating and Commentary* (Princeton, NJ: Princeton Theological Seminary, 1985).

Tice, Terrence N. *Schleiermacher Bibliography: With Brief Introductions, Annotations, and Index* (Princeton, NJ: Princeton Theological Seminary, 1966).

Tice, Terrence N. *Schleiermacher: The Psychology of Christian Faith and Life* (Lanham, MD: Lexington Books/Fortress Academic, 2018).

Vial, Theodore M. "Friedrich Schleiermacher on the Central Place of Worship." *Harvard Theological Review* 91, no. 1 (Jan. 1998), p. 59.

Vial, Theodore M. *Schleiermacher: A Guide for the Perplexed* (London: Bloomsbury, 2013).

CHAPTER 29

THE *CHRISTMAS EVE DIALOGUE*

ANDREW PACKMAN AND ANDREW C. DOLE

29.1 INTRODUCTION

A pert, immaculately decorated Prussian household, illumined from within by candlelight, cheerful conversation, and the warmth of a family's Christmas celebration—this is the scene that Schleiermacher sets for his perennially captivating *Christmas Eve Dialogue*. Within this scene, readers discover a delightful cast of characters representing various generations and religious temperaments who, in a manner that oscillates between playful irony and pious solemnity, celebrate Christmas by enacting many of the holiday's customary rituals in their own distinctive ways.

This chapter has two central aims. First, it offers an introduction to the *Christmas Eve Dialogue* by describing the context of its composition and summarizing its contents. And second, it engages important trajectories with the work's reception history. To what extent did Schleiermacher pattern the work after the Platonic dialogues, with which he was much engaged at the time? Are his characters purely fictional vehicles, or do their characteristics and utterances reflect actual persons in Schleiermacher's circles? Are their contributions to the evening's festivities representative of Schleiermacher's own thinking about Christmas, and Christology, or does he allow them to express views that he did not himself hold? What is the significance of the female characters in this work? Does their inclusion indicate some degree of proto-feminism in Schleiermacher's thinking, or does their presentation uncritically reflect the patriarchal culture of his day? After necessarily brief engagements with these questions the chapter will conclude with a modest proposal as to how the work might reflect Schleiermacher's early thinking on the dynamics of religious community.

29.2 BIOGRAPHICAL AND HISTORICAL BACKGROUND

Schleiermacher hurriedly composed the *Christmas Eve Dialogue* in a matter of weeks in December of 1805, submitting the final pages to the publisher on Christmas Eve morning. This meant that, despite his intention to distribute the work as a gift to his friends, it would not appear in print until the following month. Schleiermacher had recently begun teaching at the University of Halle, a move that came as a welcome intellectual and social reprieve from the rather dismal existence as a pastor in Stolp. His intellectual labors there included his lectures on philosophical ethics and hermeneutics, as well as his magisterial translation of Plato's works published in 1804. Several themes emphasized in the *Christmas Eve Dialogue* also figure prominently in these lectures, and his interest in dialogue as a literary and philosophical form has clear analogues in his study of Plato.

On the social scene, Schleiermacher's move to Halle came alongside the deterioration of two significant relationships. The first was to his friend and collaborator Friedrich Schlegel, whose partnership in the Plato translation project was called off in 1803. Second, and more proximate to the writing of the *Christmas Eve Dialogue*, was the broken engagement with Eleanore Grunow. After many years of anguished deliberation about the moral permissibility of divorce, Grunow finally elected to remain with her husband and to conclusively end her engagement with Schleiermacher. He received her letter communicating her decision in October of 1805, mere days before he began the Winter Semester at Halle. This was undoubtedly a time of great emotional distress for the now 37-year-old Schleiermacher, whose contemporary correspondence records an intense yearning for the rich, family life that he witnessed as a frequent guest in the homes of his friends.

By his own accounting, the explicit inspiration for *The Christmas Eve Dialogue* came on the evening of December 3, 1805 when Schleiermacher attended a performance by the flautist Friedrich Ludwig Dülon (1769–1826). Dülon was something of a celebrity in his time, playing to packed crowds throughout the German-speaking lands and eliciting strongly positive reviews of his "soulful" performance. These reviews frequently emphasized Dülon's visual impairment; he suffered from congenital sightlessness. Interpreters of *The Christmas Eve Dialogue* often propose that the pairing of extraordinarily "soulful" beauty with the performer's physical disability provided the "wonderful, sudden inspiration" for the work that Schleiermacher describes in his correspondence.[1] Neither human frailties nor the inscrutable forces that solicit and exacerbate them fully inhibit the glory and joy percolating just below the surface of reality, ready to burst forth for those properly attuned to it.

The larger political context of Schleiermacher's intellectual productions in Halle is marked by the looming threat of Napoleon's invasion of the German states. While Schleiermacher sat captivated by Dülon's arias, Third Coalition armies were surrendering to French forces at Austerlitz. The defeat of Russian and Austrian forces spurred Prussian leadership to sign a non-aggression treaty with Napoleon, a decision that Schleiermacher thought both imprudent and disgraceful. After months of fearful anticipation, his suspicions were confirmed

---

[1] See Hermann Patsch's editorial introduction in *KGA* 1.5, pp. xlv–xlvi.

when, in October of 1806, French troops finally descended violently on Halle. This occasioned the closure of the university, effectively putting Schleiermacher out of work. But it also threatened his Prusso-centric conception of Europe. For Schleiermacher, Napoleon symbolized a totalizing Catholic vision of Europe that sought to eradicate Protestantism and, with it, the rich diversity of Christianity's religious and political forms. Much of his future labors to reconcile the Lutheran and Reformed churches in Prussia can be understood as an effort to establish a unified, Teutonic Protestantism to ward off the ascendent Catholic threat.

These influences, ranging in scope from the deeply personal to the geopolitical, provide important contextual clues for understanding *The Christmas Eve Dialogue*. But the conditions occasioning the work's production do not exhaustively account for the work's thematic and formal features. To those we now turn.

29.3 CHARACTERS AND NARRATIVE CONTENT

As already noted, *The Christmas Eve Dialogue* opens with a vivid description of a German house immaculately prepared for the Christmas celebration. The home belongs to Ernestine and Eduard, a married couple who serve as hosts to the evening's events. Ernestine is a thoughtful mother and meticulous hostess, whose flair for the domestic arts and keen religious sensibility are responsible for setting the grand scene for the dialogue. These charisms draw the entire gathering's admiration, which, at moments, ascends to a form of religious adoration shimmering with explicit Marian allusions. Eduard exudes a playful warmth, though his penchant for philosophical speculation emerges as the evening progresses. Ernestine and Eduard's children make cameo appearances, although it is their young daughter Sophie, a precocious child with strong religious impulses, who figures most prominently.

The other characters are friends of this family at various life-stages and religious orientations. These are Leonhardt, a pugilistic lawyer and religious skeptic; Friederike and Ernst, a young couple on the verge of marriage; Agnes, a mother of two children who is expecting the birth of a third; and Karoline, who is apparently younger and unmarried. The dialogue concludes with the long-awaited arrival of the enigmatic Josef, who, after an evening of mirthful celebrating, playfully chides the gathering—and especially the men—for their sharing all-too-serious discourses as opposed to the joyful atmosphere of the season.

The work opens, not by introducing its character or foregrounding thematic elements, but by construing an evocative *mise en scène* with all the trappings of Christmas. Festive decorations, floral arrangements in the windows, snow glimmering outside, and an enchanting play of light and shadow give the scene a shimmering, inviting, and slightly mysterious air. Ernestine is introduced as the orchestrator of this scene, which serves as the backdrop for the exchange of gifts. The characters revel, half earnestly and half jokingly, in the activity as they gleefully discern the giver of each particular gift. The female characters prove much keener at this task than their male counterparts, and this occasions the dialogue's first of several reflections on gender difference and the apparent complementarity between men's inherently "direct" approach and the "many arts" of women. The exchange of gifts is punctuated by moments of pious silence as each of the characters turn their gaze admiringly upon Ernestine. "They gathered around her, as though everything else had been enjoyed and she were the giver of it all... all of them, as it befitted each one, demonstrated their most heartfelt love and devotion. She herself had to give the signal for them to claim their gifts."[2]

The focus then turns to the young Sophie who, exhibiting no interest in her own gift, chooses rather to survey the scene as a whole and takes great delight therein. When her father, Ernst, finally discloses that she has been given music, she exclaims, "Music!... O great Music! Christmas for a lifetime! Sing, children, the most wondrous things."[3] This introduces a central theme of the work, which returns frequently to music's fittingness as a form of religious expression as well as the centrality of children to the Christmas festival.[4] Sophie exhibits a lively talent for music, giving each note its proper value and attentively creating space for each voice. But the most remarkable display of her religious and artistic precociousness comes in the form of a Christmas panorama that Sophie has painstakingly constructed as a gift to the entire family. The remarkably complex piece depicts "the external history of Christianity" ranging from biblical scenes (Christ's baptism, crucifixion, ascension, and Pentecost) and the destruction of the Second Temple through pivotal events in medieval church history (Crusades, the martyrdom of John Hus, Luther's burning of the papal bull) and stretching all the way to Schleiermacher's contemporary setting with representations of the cemetery in Herrnhut and the orphanage in Halle. Hidden amongst these vignettes was the birth scene itself, which required careful attention:

> You had to follow the angels and shepherds, who were also gathered around a fire. You opened a door in the wall of the structure and caught sight of the holy family in a sort of room, which, because the house served only as decoration, really lay outside. Everything was dark in the meager hut, except for a powerful, concealed light that illumined the head of the child and formed a reflection on the downturned face of the mother. In contrast to the wild flames outside, this mild radiance acted as heavenly fire against the earthly.[5]

The panorama serves as a microcosm of the scene depicted in the house itself, with Sophie performing the role of Schleiermacher as author, carefully embedding Christianity's most ancient and confounding truth in the trappings of a contemporary historical episode.

Following a brief musical interlude, the adult characters engage in a lively conversation covering a variety of themes, each of which is to reappear later in the dialogue. They discuss the meaning of Christmas gift-giving, the significance of various life-stages—and especially childhood—to the celebration of Christmas, the relationship of music to religious feeling, and the complementarity of men and women for an adequate perception of the meaning of Christmas and its proper celebration. Again, Sophie figures centrally as both a topic of and participant in the dialogue. The skeptical Leonhardt raises concerns that the precocious child is perhaps too pious, indicating an unhealthy and potentially life-denying impulse that he attributes to both Moravian pietists and Catholics and counts as a distortion of proper, Enlightened religiosity. At one point, half-jokingly and half in earnest, he interrogates the child, pressing her to analyze the affective quality of her religious experience. When

---

[2] *CWS*, p. 102.

[3] *CWS*, pp. 104f.

[4] "And now, since Christmas is quite properly a children's holiday, and she [Sofie] lived in it in such a totally exceptional way, it followed that no more preferable present than this could have made an appearance." *CWS*, p. 105.

[5] *CWS*, p. 106.

she resists his analytical probes, the others interpret this as an admirable presentation of the "childlike sense, without which one cannot enter the kingdom of God"[6] and which is characterized by a tendency "to accept every mood and every feeling for itself, and to wish to have it purely and completely."[7] While most frequently found in children, there is general agreement that women exhibit this affective temperament more naturally than men, who are predisposed to exhibit Leonhardt's analytical spirit.

These generalizations about gender difference frame the dialogue's following two movements: the women's stories and the men's speeches. While both sets of discourses take the meaning of Christmas as their subject matter and are presented, ostensibly, as an exchange of gifts, Schleiermacher foregrounds the distinctive modes of presentation as essential and complementary features of these two genders.

The women offer their stories first, recounting vivid memories of Christmases past that prioritize Marian themes of motherly love. Ernestine recalls her feelings of enrapturement upon seeing a woman with her child sitting in an open choir stall amidst an otherwise stale and lifeless Christmas Eve service. Against the cold backdrop and the preacher's "squawking voice,"[8] she portrays "the noblest picture I have ever seen"[9] in which the child was "grasped in a half-unconscious dialogue of love and longing with his mother."[10] This "picture," in turn, motivates an exchange of gifts between the mother, Ernestine, and the infant.

Agnes tells of an impromptu Christmas baptism, in which a family's domestic Christmas celebration, replete with the exchange of gifts, is interrupted by the sudden decision to offer the infant child "the most beautiful gift" of Christ. Whereas the first story centered on the mother–child relationship, this vignette presents the mother and child surrounded by family and friends and engaged in a communal ritual, "according to the fine, old local custom" in which "we all laid hands on the child."[11] This renders an ecstatic quality to the tender domestic scene, and yet it is "only the mother, whose love sees the whole person in the child [that] sees the heavenly radiance flowing out from him."[12]

Finally, Karoline recalls the recent memory of a morbidly ill child's dramatic recovery last Christmas Eve. Driven to exhaustion from caring for the increasingly sick infant and preparing for the Christmas celebration, the child's mother finally lays down to rest, expecting never to see the boy alive again. And yet, upon waking, she finds quite the opposite—a child revivified and on its way to full recovery, "drawn forth through death and sanctified to a higher life."[13] Here again, the theme of gift-exchange is paramount. The mother's faithful relinquishing of her child to God's care is met with the gift of the healed and resuscitated boy, "immediately given by God."[14]

By contrast to these tender, evocative stories drawn from the women's lived experience, the men elect to offer speeches. Following the "English manner—not to mention the ancient

---

[6] *CWS*, p. 123.
[7] *CWS*, p. 123.
[8] *CWS*, p. 127.
[9] *CWS*, p. 127.
[10] *CWS*, p. 128.
[11] *CWS*, p. 132.
[12] *CWS*, p. 132.
[13] *CWS*, p. 135.
[14] *CWS*, p. 135.

one, which is not entirely foreign to us,"[15] they agree to reflect on the nature and meaning of the Christmas festival by extolling it in some way. Leonhardt begins, extolling the functional efficacy of the festival. Noting that "the remembrance of great events is secured and preserved through certain acts recurring at appointed times,"[16] he argues that the Christmas festival revives the memory of Christianity's origin more effectively than alternative methods such as the reading of Scripture or the teaching of doctrine. Displaying his nature as a religious skeptic, Leonhardt explicitly notes the dearth of reliable information about the historical Jesus: "for how little can be traced back to Christ himself, and most of that is, by far, of another and later origin!"[17] Thus the idea of Jesus as the founder of Christianity "has only a sketchy meaning"[18] and provides a weak "experiential, historical basis of the matter."[19] But this historical inscrutability places the festival's real significance in sharp relief. For it is the festival's ritual performance itself, not any particularly remarkable quality of its originator, that is most responsible for preserving Christianity itself: sometimes, he proposes, "through such customs, history itself is created."[20] And in the case of Christmas, the "children are primarily the ones who lift and carry [the festival]—and, in turn, through the holiday, life and carry Christianity itself."[21]

Ernst's speech amends, and to some degree, contests Leonhardt's position. His interest is drawn to the question of just what the Christmas festival commemorates. The universality of the spirit of the holiday is evidence that its inner basis must be "the cause for all joy that moves in waves among people"; and (with the exception of those unfortunates who "live only in the change" that the new year brings) "there is no other principle of joy than redemption, and for us, the initial point of redemption must be the birth of a divine child."[22] Properly understood, the inner basis for the holiday is that "we become conscious of the innermost ground and the uncreated power of the new, untroubled life."[23] Ernst acknowledges the distance between contemporary Christianity and the "divine child" ("when the matter is viewed critically . . . the historical traces may still be weak"), but argues that even weak historical traces suffice to anchor the reawakening of the necessary idea of a Redeemer: "The largest crystallization needs only the smallest crystal in order to trigger its formation."[24]

Speaking last, Eduard invokes the Gospel of John (which, it should be remembered, Schleiermacher regarded as an eyewitness account), expressing a preference for remembering Christ not as an infant, "formed and appearing such and so, born of this or that woman, here or there," but as the Word made Flesh. For him Christmas is the celebration of human nature "beheld and recognized from the divine principle."[25] Humans experience

---

[15] *CWS*, p. 137.
[16] *CWS*, p. 138.
[17] *CWS*, p. 139.
[18] *CWS*, p. 139. "In short, the experiential, historical basis of the matter is so weak that our holiday is exalted all the more, and its power closely borders on the aforementioned—namely, that sometimes, through such customs, history itself is created." *CWS*, p. 140.
[19] *CWS*, p. 140.
[20] *CWS*, p. 140.
[21] *CWS*, p. 141.
[22] *CWS*, pp. 143f.
[23] *CWS*, p. 144.
[24] *CWS*, p. 145.
[25] *CWS*, p. 147.

the "higher life and the peace of God" only in context of the communicative activity that defines the church; "and therefore we also seek one point from which this communication proceeded," which point "must already have been born as the human-in-itself, as the God-man."[26] Thus the true source of Christmas joy is the fact that "every one of us intuits in the birth of Christ our own higher birth."[27]

The speeches are brought to an abrupt close by the refusal of Josef, who has only just arrived, to continue in the same vein. Josef reports that he has been wandering the city, "everywhere taking part in all the trifles and games, and [I] have loved everything and laughed." When asked to offer a speech of his own, he protests: "all forms are too rigid for me," he demurs, "and all speech too tedious and cold."[28] The *Dialogue* ends with Josef calling for the gathering to shift from the mode of discourse to that of song: in the final sentence he invites the others to join him in singing "something pious and joyful," "and above all, if she is not already asleep, bring the child along, and let me see your splendors."[29]

29.4 Themes in the Interpretation of the *Dialogue*

The reception history of the *Christmas Eve Dialogue* (the earliest phase of which has been documented at length by Hermann Patsch)[30] makes it clear that the work rewards close attention from different angles. We will examine three prominent and interconnected approaches here: one that seeks a proper understanding of Schleiermacher's use of the dialogical form, a second that focuses on the *Dialogue*'s theological content, and a third that interrogates the views on women and gender that come to expression in the work.

29.4.1 The *Dialogue* as a Dialogue

Glossing Schleiermacher's use of the dialogical form requires confronting two separate questions. The first is what literary antecedents or prototypes most strongly informed Schleiermacher's own composition; the second concerns the relationship between Schleiermacher's own views and those expressed by the dialogue's characters.

The dialogical form had been employed by recent authors known to Schleiermacher (Patsch mentions works by Goethe, Friedrich Schlegel, and Schelling),[31] and the influence

---

[26] *CWS*, pp. 148f.
[27] *CWS*, p. 148.
[28] *CWS*, p. 150.
[29] *CWS*, p. 151.
[30] See Hermann Patsch, "Die esoterische Kommunikationsstruktur der *Weinhachtsfeier*. Über Anspielungen und Zitate," in *Schleiermacher in Context: Papers from the 1988 International Symposium on Schleiermacher in Herrnhut, the German Democratic Republic*, ed. Ruth Drucilla Richardson (Lewiston, NY: Edwin Mellen Press, 1991), pp. 132–156, and also Patsch's editorial introduction in *KGA* 1.5, pp. lv–lxiv.
[31] *KGA* 1.5, p. xlviii.

of the Romantic movement on this work is both indisputable and a rich topic for investigation.[32] Nevertheless scholarly consensus has favored the Platonic corpus as the weightiest antecedent for Schleiermacher's decision to cast his "Christmas gift" in the form of a dialogue. The question of whether Schleiermacher modeled his dialogue on one Platonic work—the *Symposium*, the *Phaedo*, and the *Phaedrus* have all been mooted[33]—is a trickier one. The most important recent engagement with this question is from Julia Lamm, who argues that Schleiermacher took as his prototype the Platonic corpus as a whole, in the organizational structure that resulted from his own researches. Schleiermacher regarded the Platonic corpus as a "trilogy of trilogies," with the *Phaedrus*, the *Symposium*, and the *Republic* each anchoring one trilogy. Juxtaposing these works with the three main sections of the *Dialogue* is illuminating: it highlights the important methodological role played by the opening discourses (corresponding with Schleiermacher's understanding of the *Phaedrus*), suggests that the women's discourses occupy the place of the *Symposium*, and juxtaposes the men's discourses with the *Republic*.[34] One interesting result of this work is that it gives the women's stories pride of place as the core of the *Dialogue* as a whole; Lamm notes the sharp contrast between this rendering and the judgment of earlier commentators such as David Schenkel, according to whom the women "say barely anything meaningful."[35]

Engaging the second question, in one of the first published reviews Schelling isolated his criticisms of the character's positions from any criticism of its author: "for who knows what thoughts are entertained by he who does not himself appear."[36] But this agnostic position is somewhat rare through much of the reception history. David Friedrich Strauss saw elements of Schleiermacher's own views in all three of the men's speeches—an appreciation of skeptical criticism as "purifying" religiosity (Leonhardt), the move from living Christian experience to an understanding of Christ (Ernst), and the preference for John's Jesus (Eduard); he also saw Schleiermacher in Josef's act of drawing the gathering back to "the subjectivity of feeling, in which, in [Schleiermacher's] view, all religion has its true home."[37] Nearly a century later, Karl Barth could cite as the consensus of Schleiermacher scholarship that "no single speaker, but in some sense, all three [male] speakers represent Schleiermacher's 'real opinion.'"[38] But Barth added a significant fillip to this principle by asserting, as a "rule" of interpretation, that while Josef may well represent Schleiermacher most directly, "we must not expect to hear from the lips of the other characters anything which is not also

---

[32] So, for example, in "Die 'mimische' *Weihnachtsfeier*. Überlegungen zu einer unsicheren Lesung," in *Schleiermacher, Romanticism, and the Critical Arts: A Festschrift In Honor of Hermann Patsch*, ed. Hans Dierkes, Terrence Tice, and Wolfgang Virmond (Lewiston, NY: Edwin Mellen Press, 2007), pp. 159–164, Hermann Patsch explores the (philologically uncertain) hypothesis that Schleiermacher described the text to Friedrich Schlegel as a "mimic representation," which choice of terminology would provide important clues to Schleiermacher's own sense of the dynamics of the text.

[33] Julia Lamm, "Schleiermacher's Christmas Dialogue as Platonic Dialogue," *The Journal of Religion* 92 (2012), p. 393.

[34] Lamm, "Schleiermacher's Christmas Dialogue," p. 400.

[35] Lamm, "Schleiermacher's Christmas Dialogue," p. 393.

[36] Patsch, Hermann. "Die Zeitgenössische Rezeption der 'Weihnachtsfeier'". In *Internationaler Schleiermacher-Kongreß Berlin 1984*, ed. Kurt-Victor Selge (Berlin: De Gruyter, 1985), p. 1227.

[37] David Friedrich Strauss, *Charakteristiken und Kritiken: eine Sammlung zerstreuter Aufsätze aus den Gebieten der Theologie, Anthropologie und Aesthetik* (Leipzig: O. Wigand, 1844), p. 43.

[38] Karl Barth, "Schleiermacher's 'Celebration of Christmas,'" in *Theology and Church: Shorter Writings, 1920–1928*, trans. Louise Pettibone Smith (New York: Harper & Row, 1962), p. 147.

Schleiermacher's own thinking."[39] Barth applies this rule in particular to Leonhardt's expression of skepticism regarding the importance of the historical Jesus: "for here Schleiermacher himself speaks, although naturally from the most extreme dialectical possibility"; and whatever the force of the other men's responses, for Barth Leonhardt's "speech was not given in order to be refuted."[40] It should be obvious that requiring Schleiermacher to agree with everything his characters say dramatically narrows the possibilities for understanding his intentions in drafting the dialogue (a point emphasized by Ruth Jackson Ravenscroft, as we will see shortly), and it should be noted that Barth offers no reasons to support his assertion of this rule of interpretation. But at the same time it cannot be denied that there are views with which Schleiermacher had little sympathy that do not appear in the *Dialogue*; as Richard R. Niebuhr noted, "no reader can overlook the silence of all voices that might represent a consistent biblicism or a really speculative idealism or a sterner moralism."[41]

One additional complication confronts any attempt to position the *Dialogue*'s characters firmly in relation to Schleiermacher himself. Schleiermacher based many of these characters on persons known to him; in Patsch's words, "the clues and hints that are still discernible reveal a dense network of references to persons and to contemporaneous events and thoughts."[42] Schleiermacher, it seems, intended that his friends should see themselves in the work (which, according to his student Adolph Müller, motivated him to initially publish the work anonymously).[43] To the extent that this is the case, to treat his characters as nothing more complex than reflections of aspects of Schleiermacher's own views would be to miss a crucial dimension of the work. But of course even though some of his intended references can be reconstructed,[44] Schleiermacher knew his characters' originals far better than we ever will; and for this reason a comprehensive and adequate grasp of this dimension of the work may never be possible.

29.4.2 The *Dialogue* as Dogmatics

The question of the relationship between Schleiermacher and his characters is intimately connected with the question of the theological content of the *Dialogue*. Patsch observes that the work has very often been treated by interpreters as a "theological treatise" rather than, as Schleiermacher intended, a literary creation; early on Friedrich Schlegel signaled this tendency when, after breaking off his relations with Schleiermacher, he referred disparagingly to the *Dialogue* as a "Calvinistic Nativity play [*Krippenspiel*]."[45] Patsch notes specifically that

---

[39] Barth, "Schleiermacher's 'Celebration,'" p. 142.

[40] Barth, "Schleiermacher's 'Celebration,'" p. 149. Compare what Barth would say on this point in the lectures on which this publication is based: "among the others, there is none who says things that are totally alien to Schleiermacher's own thinking—not even the often disturbing Leonhardt." Karl Barth, *The Theology of Schleiermacher: Lectures at Göttingen, Winter Semester of 1923/24*, ed. Dietrich Ritsch, trans. Geoffrey W. Bromiley (Grand Rapids: Eerdmans, 1982), p. 58.

[41] Richard R. Niebuhr, *Schleiermacher on Christ and Religion: A New Introduction* (New York: Charles Scribner's Sons, 1964), p. 40.

[42] *KGA* 1.5, p. l.

[43] Patsch, "Die Zeitgenössische Rezeption," p. 1218.

[44] See Patsch, "Die esoterische Kommunikationsstruktur."

[45] Patsch, "Die Zeitgenössische Rezeption," p. 1220.

the work has commonly been interpreted either "genetically, that is as a stage in the development of Schleiermacher's thinking, or as a theological and historical exemplar of the formation of speculative Christology in the nineteenth century."⁴⁶

Karl Barth represents both of these interpretive angles well, for his engagement with Schleiermacher's texts was controlled above all by his keen interest in reconstructing Schleiermacher's theological views as paradigmatic of a disastrous trajectory within the history of Protestant theology. His examination of the *Dialogue* was one moment in his assessment, in his Göttingen lectures of 1923–1924, of Schleiermacher's various writings on Christmas, and ultimately his project was that of identifying the position on Christmas—and in particular, his position on the extent to which Protestant theology needs to make strong historical claims about Jesus—that Schleiermacher held at the time of its composition. After a survey of the contents of the *Dialogue* Barth ventured the conclusion that it is not anything said by the male characters but rather "music and the eternal feminine" that are "the real theological substance" of the work. Departing from a long tradition of marginalizing the female characters, Barth opined that "it is the women with their stories, with their variations on the mother–child relationship, not the men with their Christology, who in Schleiermacher's mind say what is really essential about Christmas."⁴⁷ And his ultimate conclusion was that "the impressive reference to the direct communication of the divine which takes place in music and the eternal feminine is the decisive proof that for Schleiermacher, what Christmas imparts is, in fact, a human capability, 'the supreme triumph of human nature.'"⁴⁸ Barth found this position to be in continuity with Schleiermacher's earlier writing: "in his basic theme Schleiermacher has remained true to himself."⁴⁹

In case this is not sufficiently obvious, Barth's characterization was intended as a piece of criticism. Engaging Barth on his reading of the *Dialogue*, Ruth Jackson Ravenscroft carefully reconstructs the "damning analysis of Schleiermacher's Christology" that Barth undertakes.⁵⁰ Jackson Ravenscroft's interest is directed particularly at the ways in which Schleiermacher approaches the theme of difference in his various works, and this interest provides reason to resist the kind of harmonizing approach that Barth displays. "In Barth's view," she writes,

> Schleiermacher fails to attest to the glory and uniqueness of the Incarnation, which, ordained by God as a specific event in time, effects a radical transformation through human history as a whole. Instead, Schleiermacher appears to *domesticate* the Incarnation and its influence, and to depict the completion and exaltation of the human race as a process that can be realized by humans themselves.⁵¹

Jackson Ravenscroft calls critical attention to Barth's treatment of the *Dialogue* "as if it were a fully worked-out systematic theology—one which carries a linear trajectory, a single voice, and a unified purpose," and prefers a different approach: that "the dialogue's multiple voices

---

⁴⁶ Patsch, "Die Zeitgenössische Rezeption," p. 1215.
⁴⁷ Barth, *The Theology of Schleiermacher*, p. 71.
⁴⁸ Barth, *The Theology of Schleiermacher*, p. 71.
⁴⁹ Barth, *The Theology of Schleiermacher*, p. 72.
⁵⁰ Ruth Jackson Ravenscroft, *The Veiled God: Friedrich Schleiermacher's Theology of Finitude* (Leiden: Brill, 2019), p. 228.
⁵¹ Jackson Ravenscroft, *The Veiled God*, p. 227.

provide a constant and polyvalent witness to the specific difficulty of trying to reconcile the relationship . . . between the Jesus of history and the Christ of faith."[52] She also challenges Barth's proposed rule of interpretation: "to assert against Barth that Schleiermacher does not impose such a totalizing authorial grasp over the dialogue, then, means paying attention to the differences between the voices in the text, treating these voices as independent, and as being able to represent perspectives which lie beyond Schleiermacher's own."[53] And she sees the text as displaying a different type of continuity from the one identified by Barth: she sees the *Dialogue* echoing Schleiermacher's earlier ethical writings, particularly in the ways in which they develop the Pauline theme of "an ecclesial body made up of distinct but interdependent members."[54] We will return to this important proposal below.

29.4.3 Women and Gender

It is with good reason that the *Christmas Eve Dialogue* has been an important text for engagements with Schleiermacher on the topics of women and gender. Not only does Schleiermacher present both male and female characters in the work: gender is an explicit theme of discussion among them, with both male and female characters making statements about the characteristics of both men and women, and about the role the differences between men and women play in the dynamics of the Christmas festival.

Gender emerged as a prominent theme of academic discourse around the middle of the twentieth century; prior to this period it was occasionally seen as noteworthy that Schleiermacher's *Dialogue* seems to assign significance to women, but the topic received little sustained attention. As noted above, the historical tendency to focus attention on the men's speeches in the interpretation of the work sidelines the experiences and concerns of the female characters. And Karl Barth seems to have regarded it as a mark of the work's scandalous unsoundness that a celebration of "the divine in woman" seems to do real theological work.[55]

Engagements with the *Dialogue* on the topic of gender have for the most part taken place within a framework determined by two concerns. One of these we have encountered above: it is a concern to extract Schleiermacher's own position from his characters' portrayals and discourses. And the second has been to assess whether, and to what extent, the work's portrayal of gender differences is consonant with contemporary feminist positions.[56] Both of these concerns motivate the positioning of the *Dialogue* as one element within a larger body of textual evidence and tend to draw attention from the particularity of the different

---

[52] Jackson Ravenscroft *The Veiled God*, pp. 229, 232.
[53] Jackson Ravenscroft, *The Veiled God*, p. 233.
[54] Jackson Ravenscroft, *The Veiled God*, p. 233.
[55] Barth, "Schleiermacher's 'Celebration,'" p. 156. Michael Ryan follows Ruth Drucilla Richardson's judgment, in her unpublished dissertation, that Barth was "speaking ironically, with a demeaning intention" here; Michael D. Ryan, "Friedrich Schleiermacher's Reinvention of the Christian Faith: *Die Weihnachtsfeier* as a Vision of Christian Humanism," in *The State of Schleiermacher Scholarship Today: Selected Essays*, ed. Edwina Lawler, Jeffery Kinlaw, and Ruth Drucilla Richardson (Lewiston, NY: Edwin Mellen Press, 2006), p. 337.
[56] For a more extensive examination of the topic of gender in Schleiermacher's thought, see Ruth Jackson Ravenscroft's essay in the present volume [C37P01-C37P41].

pronouncements on women and gender that Schleiermacher puts into the mouths of his characters.

Schleiermacher's portrayal of gender roles and relations in the *Dialogue* has been reconstructed differently by different scholars, and in some cases condemnation and defense have hinged on reconstructive differences. Dawn DeVries has responded to charges levied by Marilyn Chapin Massey that in the *Dialogue* Schleiermacher suppressed "a new vision of feminine divinity and a new order based on that vision," informed by a general aim to "restrict both women and religion to the narrow domain of the bourgeois household."[57] In contrast to Massey's reading of the work, DeVries argues that "the definition of gender roles is subject to ruthless irony in Schleiermacher's hands," and that Schleiermacher portrays women as capable of engaging matters traditionally restricted to men, as when he presents the child Sophie as interested in dogmatics. DeVries argues further that, properly understood, the work indicates that Schleiermacher favored "a kind of androgyny or mutuality, in which both sexes participate in all of the qualities specified by gender distinctions."[58] This judgment differs from that of Elisabeth Hartlieb, according to whom the *Dialogue* presents "a model of egalitarian complementarity of the sexes."[59]

It is worth noting that however important Schleiermacher's relationship to feminism might be, it is not obligatory to engage the *Dialogue* on the topics of women and gender with that question in the forefront. The work by Julia Lamm mentioned above has produced results that are of considerable interest independently of the extent to which they support an assessment of Schleiermacher from the perspective of feminism. Lamm's reconstruction of the work as a Platonic dialogue has the distinction of closely examining the contributions made by Schleiermacher's female characters in their particularity. The stories they tell are the stories of different women, reflective of different life experiences, including experiences of motherhood; and if one of the purposes of the stories is "to present the incarnation in a vivid and accessible way so as to evoke an affective response," another is to "set forth a kind of progression and transformation" to which motherly love (*Mutterlieb*)—which thus figures as Schleiermacher's analogue to Plato's *Eros*—is central.[60] And on her structural reconstruction it is these stories that Schleiermacher places at the very heart of the *Dialogue*; Lamm suggests that the men's speeches, rather than "answering the questions raised by the women's stories" (as Richard R. Niebuhr had claimed), can be read as abstract companion pieces to the concrete life-experiences related by Schleiermacher's female characters.[61]

---

[57] Dawn DeVries, "Schleiermacher's 'Christmas Eve Dialogue': Bourgeois Ideology or Feminist Theology?," *The Journal of Religion* 69 (1989), pp. 169f.

[58] DeVries, "Schleiermacher's 'Christmas Eve Dialogue,'" p. 182.

[59] Elisabeth Hartlieb, *Geschlechterdifferenz im Denken Friedrich Schleiermachers* (Berlin: De Gruyter, 2006), p. 33, cited in Lamm, "Schleiermacher's Christmas Dialogue," p. 395.

[60] Lamm, "Schleiermacher's Christmas Dialogue," pp. 411f.

[61] Lamm, "Schleiermacher's Christmas Dialogue," p. 418.

29.5 CONCLUSION

In concluding this chapter we would like to venture a modest development of the theme explored by a number of the scholars cited above, that of the significance of the diversity of the characters Schleiermacher presents his readers in the *Dialogue*. We see at least one possibly interesting avenue, suggested above all by the interpretive line pursued by Jackson Ravenscroft, for applying this theme to the project of extracting theologically significant content from this work.

Only a few years before penning the *Dialogue* Schleiermacher had, in his *Speeches*, voiced a strong appreciation for internal diversity within religious communities. In that work, the discourse of a religious community is made vibrant by the distinctive contributions of its members, each of whom speaks from their own experience, their own "intuitions of the universe." And while it is undeniable that Schleiermacher came to view established religion in a more positive light as he aged, his dogmatics presents even orthodoxy as a phenomenon characterized by internal diversity. His mature view was that within any given religious community the effective transmission of Christian piety can take place via a range of formulations, which must of necessity change and develop with time and history. Theology's task is to make visible the boundaries of that range, indicating the points at which the diversification of expressions of piety introduces material that is incompatible with the essence of the tradition in question.[62] Viewed against the backdrop of this strand within Schleiermacher's thinking, the *Christmas Eve Dialogue* can be regarded as a portrayal of a moment in the life of a religious community—or, more precisely, of one form that religious community can assume.[63]

In our view, what is theologically significant about such a view of the *Dialogue* is that it illustrates Schleiermacher's understanding of the range of activities that figure in the transmission and collective formation of piety (to use language drawn from his later work). Schleiermacher's characters are all engaged in celebrating the Christmas festival, and arguably, their collective celebration comprises all of the actions that appear in the text, including Ernestine's arrangement of the setting, Sophie's musical performances, the women's stories, the men's speeches, Josef's concluding "unsaying," and of course the singing that is just about to break out when the curtain falls. This point is of theological significance for two reasons. One reason is that the setting of the *Dialogue* is, of course, not a church building but a home; this demonstrates the breadth of Schleiermacher's conception of religious community, of which formal "church" is only one variant. And the second reason is that not only are the discursive contributions of the different characters themselves very different in kind, only

---

[62] Andrew Dole, "Schleiermacher's *Glaubenslehre* and Its Immediate Reception," in *The Oxford Handbook of Modern German Theology*, vol. 1, ed. Grant Kaplan and Kevin Vander Schel (Oxford: Oxford University Press, 2023), p. 467.

[63] Shelli M. Poe has drawn attention to the importance of the theme of community in the *Dialogue*, citing Eduard's speech in praise of an appreciation of community as a pathway to "the higher life and the peace of God." Poe connects the theme of community to those of embodiment and diversity, arguing that the work presents the diversity of bodies within community as a positive good. See Shelli M. Poe, *The Constructive Promise of Schleiermacher's Theology* (London: T&T Clark, 2021), chapter 3, in particular pp. 146–151.

occasionally verging on the homiletical, Schleiermacher also went out of his way to flag one character's contribution to the celebration of the festival as in fact downright un-churchly. This is, of course, Leonhardt's speech. Leonhardt begins by remarking that since "tomorrow you will undoubtedly go to church," a repetition in that context of the present evening's discourse would be both annoying and boring for his listeners; and therefore "I will veer as far as possible away from this course."[64] And in case readers missed this first cue, when Leonhardt has finished, Schleiermacher has Ernestine commend him "for how sincerely he kept his word, as he promised, to stay as much as possible away from what we would perchance hear tomorrow in places of public worship."[65]

Thus Schleiermacher takes care to point out to his readers that this Christmastime gathering not only includes among the discourses celebrating the festival one that incorporates skepticism about the solidity of historical information about Jesus, it also includes among those gathered to devote themselves to this celebration a participant who, it seems, is not a churchgoer. And yet not only is Leonhardt's speech not refuted, as Barth's keen eye noted well, but the speech neither scandalizes nor seems particularly to trouble the other guests, none of whom find themselves in entire agreement with its content. The fact that Leonhardt distinguishes himself from those who will be attending church on the morrow passes without comment, and there is no indication that it makes any difference to his engagement in the evening's activities. Thus, for example, there is no sign at the end of the work that Leonhardt will fail to join with the others in singing "something pious and joyful."

We are inclined to see here a comment by Schleiermacher on the relatively capacious nature of Christian community. This comment can be understood in a more modest or stronger form, and we will conclude this chapter by sketching these without further elaboration. On the more modest reading, Leonhardt's inclusion in the *Dialogue* indicates that Schleiermacher thought that skepticism and, perhaps, rationalism in one's approach to Christianity were not incompatible with participation in the activity of generating collective joy through the remembrance of Jesus; that, as it were, the collective life of Christianity was robust and capacious enough to include the Leonhardts of the world without any diminishment of its efficacy for the circulation of what he would later term "blessedness" (*Seligkeit*). And on a stronger reading, the inclusion of Leonhardt's speech is pointed in a manner similar to Schleiermacher's presentation of women's stories about their own experiences as contributions to religious discourse. Perhaps the dramatic role played by Leonhardt's speech is not that of demonstrating the resilience of joyous Christian fellowship but in fact that of contributing to it; perhaps, in Schleiermacher's mind, Leonhardt's speech is no less an upbuilding expression of Christian piety than are the contributions of the other characters. That is, perhaps Schleiermacher thought that even discourses like Leonhardt's—and, indeed, persons like Leonhardt—could serve the purpose of promoting Christian blessedness, even if (as would surely have been the case with the stories of his female characters) such a thing could only happen outside of the established structures of the Prussian church.

---

[64] *CWS*, p. 137.
[65] *CWS*, p. 142.

Suggested Reading

DeVries, Dawn. "Schleiermacher's 'Christmas Eve Dialogue': Bourgeois Ideology or Feminist Theology?" *The Journal of Religion* 69 (1989), pp. 169–183.
Lamm, Julia. "Schleiermacher's Christmas Dialogue as Platonic Dialogue." *The Journal of Religion* 92 (2012), pp. 392–420.
Ryan, Michael D. "Friedrich Schleiermacher's Reinvention of the Christian Faith: *Die Weihnachtsfeier* as a Vision of Christian Humanism." In *The State of Schleiermacher Scholarship Today: Selected Essays*, ed. Edwina Lawler, Jeffery Kinlaw, and Ruth Drucilla Richardson (Lewiston, NY: Edwin Mellen Press, 2006), pp. 333–366.

Bibliography

Barth, Karl. "Schleiermacher's 'Celebration of Christmas.'" In *Theology and Church: Shorter Writings, 1920–1928*, trans. Louise Pettibone Smith (New York: Harper & Row, 1962), pp. 136–158.
Barth, Karl. *The Theology of Schleiermacher: Lectures at Göttingen, Winter Semester of 1923/24*, ed. Dietrich Ritsch, trans. Geoffrey W. Bromiley (Grand Rapids: Eerdmans, 1982).
DeVries, Dawn. "Schleiermacher's 'Christmas Eve Dialogue': Bourgeois Ideology or Feminist Theology?" *The Journal of Religion* 69 (1989), pp. 169–183.
Dole, Andrew. "Schleiermacher's *Glaubenslehre* and Its Immediate Reception." In *The Oxford Handbook of Modern German Theology*, vol. 1, ed. Grant Kaplan and Kevin Vander Schel (Oxford: Oxford University Press, 2023), pp.462–480.
Hartlieb, Elisabeth. *Geschlechterdifferenz im Denken Friedrich Schleiermachers* (Berlin: De Gruyter, 2006).
Jackson Ravenscroft, Ruth. *The Veiled God: Friedrich Schleiermacher's Theology of Finitude* (Leiden: Brill, 2019).
Lamm, Julia. "Schleiermacher's Christmas Dialogue as Platonic Dialogue." *The Journal of Religion* 92 (2012), pp. 392–420.
Niebuhr, Richard R. *Schleiermacher on Christ and Religion: A New Introduction* (New York: Charles Scribner's Sons, 1964).
Patsch, Hermann. "Die Zeitgnössische Rezeption der 'Weihnachtsfeier'". In *Internationaler Schleiermacher-Kongreß Berlin 1984*, ed. Kurt-Victor Selge (Berlin: De Gruyter, 1985), pp. 1215-1228.
Patsch, Hermann. "Die esoterische Kommunikationsstruktur der *Weinhachtsfeier*. Über Anspielungen und Zitate." In *Schleiermacher in Context: Papers from the 1988 International Symposium on Schleiermacher in Herrnhut, the German Democratic Republic*, ed. Ruth Drucilla Richardson (Lewiston, NY: Edwin Mellen Press, 1991), pp. 132–156.
Patsch, Hermann. "Die 'mimische' *Weihnachstfeier*. Überlegungen zu einer unsicheren Lesung." In *Schleiermacher, Romanticism, and the Critical Arts: A Festschrift In Honor of Hermann Patsch*, ed. Hans Dierkes, Terrence Tice, and Wolfgang Virmond (Lewiston, NY: Edwin Mellen Press, 2007), pp. 159–164.
Poe, Shelli M. *The Constructive Promise of Schleiermacher's Theology* (London: T&T Clark, 2021).
Quapp, Ernst. *Barth contra Schleiermacher? "Die Weihnachtsfeier" als Nagelprobe: mit einem Nachwort zur Interpretationsgeschichte der Weihnachtsfeier* (Marburg: K. Wenzel, 1978).

Ryan, Michael D. "Friedrich Schleiermacher's Reinvention of the Christian Faith: *Die Weihnachtsfeier* as a Vision of Christian Humanism." In *The State of Schleiermacher Scholarship Today: Selected Essays*, ed. Edwina Lawler, Jeffery Kinlaw, and Ruth Drucilla Richardson (Lewiston, NY: Edwin Mellen Press, 2006), pp. 333–366.

Strauss, David Friedrich. *Charakteristiken und Kritiken: eine Sammlung zerstreuter Aufsätze aus den Gebieten der Theologie, Anthropologie und Aesthetik* (Leipzig: O. Wigand, 1844).

Wittekind, Folkhardt. "Die Gespräch über *Die Weihnachtsfeier*." In *Schleiermacher Handbuch*, ed. Martin Ohst (Tübingen: Mohr Siebeck, 2017), pp. 178–188.

PART III
THINKING AFTER SCHLEIERMACHER

A RECEPTION HISTORY

CHAPTER 30

SCHLEIERMACHER'S WORK AND INFLUENCE ON CLASSICAL STUDIES

LUTZ KÄPPEL

30.1 SCHLEIERMACHER'S EARLY BEGINNINGS

In the second half of the eighteenth century, Latin and Greek were an integral part of higher education in Germany. Schleiermacher himself had studied ancient languages as a pupil at the Pädagogium of Niesky, starting in 1783.[1] There he acquired substantial skills in classical languages, so that he was soon able to read not only the Latin classics, but also Homer, Hesiod, Theocritus, Sophocles, Euripides, and Pindar. His youthful enthusiasm for ancient Greek authors was fostered in a close friendship with his classmate Johann Baptist von Albertini. The two boys both elatedly presented themselves as "Orestes and Pylades." As a student at the University of Halle (1787–1789), Schleiermacher's studies in theology were constantly supplemented by lectures on philosophy by Johann August Eberhard (1739–1809), by which he got to know Plato and especially Aristotle. His first translations spring from this context. In summer 1789 he even wanted to prepare a translation of Aristotle's *Nicomachaean Ethics*. A manuscript with notes and a draft of a full translation of books 8 and 9 exists, but it remained a first exercise in translating a Greek philosophical text and Schleiermacher never published it.[2] Schleiermacher also attended lectures in classics delivered by the leading classicist of his time, Friedrich August Wolf (1759–1824), who not only revolutionized Homeric scholarship, but also established the first strict methodology of philology in extremely close readings of Greek authors. Schleiermacher always treated Wolf with due respect, even though the two did not get along.

---

[1] W. Dilthey, "Schleiermachers Übersetzung des Platon," in *Leben Schleiermachers*, Erster Band, Zweiter Halbband (GesSchr. XIII/2), 3rd. ed., ed. Martin Redeker (Berlin/Göttingen: Walter de Gruyter and Vandenhoeckh & Ruprecht, 1970), 1.1, p. 19; Kurt Nowak, *Schleiermacher. Leben, Werk und Wirkung* (Göttingen: Vandenhoeck & Ruprecht, 2001), p. 24.

[2] *KGA* 1.1, pp.1–80; with pp. xxxii–xl.

Schleiermacher's further engagement with classical antiquity was focused almost exclusively on Greek philosophy. Manuscripts and articles include translations and notes on Aristotle, the pre-Socratics, Diogenes Laertius, and Xenophon.[3] Two contributions, however, were bound to become epoch-making steps not only with respect to the authors he was dealing with, but also with respect to the historiography of ancient philosophy as well as the history of the methodology of classical scholarship in general: the interpretation and translation of Plato's dialogues, and the philological reconstruction of Heraclitus' philosophy according to the fragments and testimonies. In order to situate Schleiermacher's philological work historically, the following sections will first outline the historical circumstances of the emergence and formation of these two main contributions, and then give an appraisal of the main systematic achievements that have influenced the development of classical studies until today.

30.2 Plato

30.2.1 The History of the Origin of the Plato Translation

Among Schleiermacher's diverse achievements, one particularly stands out from a literary and philosophical-historical point of view: the epoch-making translation of Plato.[4] This translation was suggested by Friedrich Schlegel as a collaborative project between the two of them. Schleiermacher came to Berlin in 1796, where he worked as a preacher at the Charité Hospital and also got to know Schlegel and thus early romanticism. The translation plan was drawn up in 1798. In retrospect, Schleiermacher reports in detail in a letter to August Boeckh from June 18, 1808 about the beginnings of the project:

> It was in 1798, when Friedrich Schlegel, in our philosophical conversations, in which Plato was not infrequent, at first very briefly expressed the idea that it was necessary to assert Plato in the state of philosophy at that time, and therefore to translate his work in its entirety. Already with the first statement it was clear that this must be our common work ... Friedrich began to read it; I ... did not hurry ... until he suddenly wrote to me: Wagner wanted to translate Plato, so we would have to announce our undertaking quickly and go to work.[5]

In March 1800 Schlegel had signed a contract with the publisher Frommann for the publication of a translation and published an announcement on March 21 in the *Intelligenzblatt der Allgemeine Literaturzeitung*: For the Easter Fair 1801, the first volume of a complete translation was to be available under Schlegel's name, with a special treatise by Schlegel as an introduction and—in addition to the translations—a "declaration of the train of thought and context" as well as "accompanying notes."[6] Despite slight annoyance at Schlegel's seemingly

---

[3] See the Bibliography below for an illustrative sampling of these works.

[4] For a more systematic treatment of Schleiermacher's Plato, see the contribution by Julia Lamm in Chapter 1 of this volume; see also Julia A. Lamm, *Schleiermacher's Plato* (Berlin and Boston: Walter de Gruyter, 2021).

[5] *KGA* 5.10, ed. Simon Gerber and Sarah Schmidt (Berlin: De Gruyter, 2015), no. 2701, pp. 24ff.

[6] See no. 43, 1800, col. 349f., in *PW(Käppel)*, p. xvii, n8.

arbitrary approach, Schleiermacher got to work on the condition that he be named as a co-author on the title when it appeared.

The correspondence in the following months mainly centered on the correct arrangement of the dialogues and the elimination of the spurious pieces. Schlegel's tardiness was increasingly causing upset. After Schleiermacher's vehement urging, Schlegel finally sent his arrangement of the Platonic oeuvre on December 8, 1800.[7] For Schleiermacher, this is the impulse to start with the *Phaedrus* in accordance with Schlegel's order. Between January and mid-March 1801 he translated the dialogue, annotated it,[8] and sent the result to Schlegel.[9] The *Protagoras* was translated between March and June 1801.[10] The philologist L. F. Heindorf, who was preparing a critical edition of the original Greek text, had been involved in the formulation of the translation from the very beginning. Schleiermacher even used the drafts of his edition as early as 1801, the first volume of which appeared in 1802.[11] The printing of the *Phaedrus* at the Frommann publishing house started,[12] and even the first royalties had been paid to Schlegel.[13] At the same time, Schlegel seems to have played fast and loose with Schleiermacher's work. In the context of his "Habilitation" at the University of Jena he apparently handed in Schleiermacher's manuscripts as his own work to prove his academic eligibility.[14] Schleiermacher did not know about that fraud, but the mood between the two was nevertheless deteriorating because of Schlegel's constant tardiness. As a result Schleiermacher began to withdraw from the project after repeated disappointments and asked Frommann to return the *Phaedrus* material.[15] The joint venture had failed. Schlegel provided neither the promised translations of *Parmenides* and *Phaedo* nor the general introduction to the new interpretation of Plato, which should theoretically justify the whole venture. Eventually, Schlegel retired from the project in 1803 and left the initiative to Schleiermacher.[16] Finally, Frommann cancelled the project completely.[17]

Schleiermacher quickly found a new publisher in G. A. Reimer to do the translation alone.[18] The material from Frommann's *Phaedrus* was also recovered,[19] so that the way was clear for a new beginning. After Schleiermacher had to give up his position in Berlin in 1802 and moved to Stolp (Pomerania) in order to become a court preacher, he accepted the challenge and, on July 29, 1803, announced the full translation of Plato's works.[20] From then on, the translation project moved quickly. The classical philologists L. F. Heindorf (1774–1816) and G. L. Spalding (1762–1811) actively supported Schleiermacher with corrections of the manuscripts and the proofs. Schleiermacher, who soon abandoned Schlegel's views

---

[7] *KGA* 5.4, no. 993, with pp. 353–59.
[8] *KGA* 5.5, no. 1008, no. 1017.
[9] *KGA* 5.4, no. 1030.
[10] *KGA* 5.4, no. 1030, no. 1066.
[11] See *KGA* 5.5, no. 1051.
[12] *KGA* 5.5, no. 1032.
[13] *KGA* 5.5, no. 1207.
[14] Incidentally, this handwritten first version (with Schlegel's corrections) is the copy that is preserved in the archive of the Berlin-Brandenburg Academy of Sciences (SN no. 154); see *PW(Käppel)*, pp. xix–xxi.
[15] *KGA* 5.6, no. 1476.
[16] *KGA* 5.6, no. 1490.
[17] *KGA* 5.6, no. 1503, no. 1517.
[18] *KGA* 5.6, no. 1507, no. 1511.
[19] *KGA* 5.7, no. 1607, no. 1616.
[20] See *Jenaische Allgemeine Literatur-Zeitung* (November 12, 1803), in *PW(Käppel)*, pp. xxviii–xxx.

about arrangement and authenticity of the dialogues, now followed his own ideas.[21] The first version of *Phaedrus*, which had been poorly annotated by Schlegel and had already been printed by Frommann,[22] was heavily revised for printing with Reimer.[23] Since mid-December 1803, Schleiermacher worked out a new version.[24] The first volume appeared in time for the Easter fair in May 1804, and four more followed up to 1809, supplemented by a sixth volume in 1828, after the publication of the second edition of the first five volumes in 1817–1826. Meanwhile Schleiermacher had returned to Berlin, where he became preacher at the Dreifaltigkeitskirche (Trinity Church) in 1809, professor of theology at the newly founded Friedrich-Wilhelms-Universität (now Humboldt University of Berlin) in 1810, and member of the Prussian Academy of Sciences Berlin in 1811. From mid-1803 he worked on Plato with great energy. The first five volumes appeared between 1804 and 1809 with most of the dialogues. From 1817 onwards the volumes appeared in a second edition, revised and expanded by Schleiermacher. As a new and final volume he added the *Politeia* in 1828.

30.2.2 Schleiermacher's Interpretative Method

Schleiermacher's new manner of dealing with Plato was his consideration of the individual in relation to the whole and the whole in its importance for the understanding of the individual. This was imposed as the guiding hermeneutic principle, which made it necessary to deal with the order of the entire corpus of dialogues. The focus was initially on the chronology of the dialogues, but a combination of systematics and chronology gradually emerged. W. G. Tennemann had already attempted to establish a chronology of the Platonic dialogues in his *System der Platonischen Philosophie*,[25] but this chronology had not become effective in Schleiermacher's interpretations of the dialogues at all. In his new project, a chronological approach should be combined with "one that would be more calculated to best and most quickly explore Plato to the present time."[26] On this point Schlegel and Schleiermacher initially agreed. From 1801 onwards, Schleiermacher became independent not only organizationally, but also conceptually. Philologists such as Spalding and, of course, Heindorf, who himself prepared a critical Plato edition, served as Schleiermacher's collaborators.

Schleiermacher's design focuses entirely on the dialogues. He (like Schlegel) rejected an "esoteric" oral teaching, such as that claimed by Plato reception from Neo-Platonism to Tennemann, following ancient evidence. Instead, the dialogues are viewed in their entirety. Like every dialogue in itself, the dialogues as a whole represent a development. To understand each dialogue, it is therefore necessary to grasp the "peculiar nature of the whole."[27] This was—without prejudice to Tennemann's attempts to systematize the dialogues, to which Schleiermacher also refers—a new approach, insofar as the corpus of the dialogues itself is

---

[21] See the contribution by J. Lamm in Chapter 1 pp. 17–21 of this volume.
[22] Cf. *KGA* 5.5, no. 1052, no. 1097.
[23] *KGA* 5.7, no. 1617.
[24] See, e.g., *KGA* 5.7, no. 1617.
[25] Wilhelm Gottlieb Tennemann, *System der Platonischen Philosophie*, 4 vols. (Leipzig: Johann Ambrosius Barth, 1792–1795), 1, pp. 115ff.
[26] Schleiermacher to Boeckh, June 18, 1808, in *KGA* 5.10, no. 2701, pp. 33–35.
[27] *PW(Käppel)*, p. 28.

regarded as an "organism," so that the initial question about the order of the dialogues gains hermeneutical relevance. Content and form are related to each other, and Plato appears as a "philosophical artist."[28]

The "natural sequence" of the dialogues, considered as a whole, represents a systematic development from the questionability and uncertainty of knowledge to the foundation and presentation of confirmed knowledge.[29] For Schleiermacher, the sequence of the dialogues is no longer based on chronological order, but on a systematic pedagogical or didactic program.[30] Schleiermacher developed this basic scheme for the first time in *Zum Platon*.[31] It also forms the framework for the presentation of the printed translation volumes with their sub-volumes. Large parts of the introduction serve not least to justify this presentation.[32]

Schleiermacher's approach to the interpretation of Plato continues to have an undiminished effect today—without prejudice to an abundance of opposing positions. With the late dating of *Phaedrus*, the sequence of dialogues propagated by Schleiermacher was soon criticized at a crucial point.[33] In the second half of the twentieth century, Schleiermacher's rejection of indirect tradition by the so-called Tübingen School (e.g. Krämer, Gaiser, Szlezák) was massively attacked. But this could do little to affect the power of the Schleiermacher paradigm. The emphatic inclusion of Schleiermacher's approach already begins in Boeckh's review of the Plato translation: "No one has ever fully understood Plato and taught others how to understand him except this man."[34] It continues to this day.

30.2.3 The Translation and Notes

Similar to Schleiermacher's new approach to the interpretation of Plato, the translation work itself was epoch-making. This translation is still canonical as *the* "German Plato." From the beginning, Schleiermacher (and already Schlegel) self-confidently had intended this. Even a comparison with the importance of the translation of Homer by Johann Heinrich Voss was already stated openly at the time of printing.[35] Jörg Jantzen recently pointed out that it was neither Schleiermacher's dialogue theory nor the learned comments that guaranteed the translation's durability, but that it was the special quality of the translation that was due to the overwhelming success of Schleiermacher's work on Plato: "It is the language that has made the translation part of German philosophical literature, as it were."[36] The translation was

---

[28] *PW(Käppel)*, pp. 19, 28, 29.
[29] *PW(Käppel)*, p. 33.
[30] For a more detailed discussion of this, see Chapter 1 [C1P20-23] in this volume.
[31] *KGA* 1.3, p. 373.
[32] *PW(Käppel)*, pp. 52–59.
[33] See Johann Gottfries Stallbaum, *Platonis Opera Omnia 4.1: Phaedrus* (Gotha: Hennings, 1832), pp. iii–xxv.
[34] Correspondence with Boeckh (1808), *KGA* 5.10, no. 2701, lines 3f.
[35] See Schleiermacher's letter to Reimer on January 7, 1804, in *KGA* 5.7, no. 1629.
[36] Jörg Jantzen, " . . . daß ich nämlich sterben will, wenn der Platon vollendet ist," in *Schleiermachers Übersetzung antiker Literatur, Funktionen und Konzeptionen im 19. und 20. Jahrhundert*, Transformationen der Antike 7, ed. Martin Harbsmeier, Josefine Kitzbichler, Katja Lubitz, and Nina Mindt (Berlin: Walter de Gruyter, 2008), pp. 41–45, citation 42.

something completely new up to that point. With its alien Greek-style syntactic structures, its abundance of particles, its sought-after (sometimes exhausting) German language, the reader actively took part in the dialogue, thoughtfully and co-philosophically, seemingly in the medium of a German translation, but actually just like in the Greek original. This corresponds to Schleiermacher's translation theory, which he later developed in 1813 in *The Different Methods of Translation*. It is—in modern terms—not specifically about target-language-oriented translation, but "the translator leaves the writer alone as much as possible and moves the reader towards him."[37] The German language adapts to the Greek in syntax and diction—not the other way round—and thereby gains a new quality both philosophically and aesthetically. This new revolutionary type of translation has, of course, also been ridiculed or criticized in the beginning: "Syrup periods," "gibberish," "illegible," "Greek with German script" (F.A. Wolf); "roaring with words like in Schlegel's School" (Charlotte von Schiller); "in this artificial and laborious replica by no means the beautiful, lively archetype" (Friedrich Ast) were early judgments about Schleiermacher's Plato translations.[38] With this language, however, Schleiermacher created the diction that we still intuitively recognize as the "German," that is, "Schleiermacher's" Plato.

This method—to bring the reader closer to Plato—was supported by the notes. They justify certain readings, discuss translation alternatives, and provide a certain background for understanding the text. It is noteworthy that the annotations are not placed as footnotes under the text like a scholarly apparatus, but are collected as endnotes at the end of each volume with the page number, line, and text lemma to which they refer. They are not referenced by footnote numbers in the text, but must be actively sought by the reader. As a result, the independent reading flow is not disturbed by the translator's comments. The reader has to work actively in order to understand the text.

Even more significant are the preliminary drafts and the communications on the understanding of the meaning of specific passages of the text, which took place between Schleiermacher, Heindorf, and Spalding. This "triangle dialogue" of the German translator (Schleiermacher) with the Greek author (represented by the editions) and the philological experts (Heindorf and Spalding) is well documented by the manuscripts collected in the archive of the Berlin-Brandenburgische Akademie der Wissenschaften (*Nachlass Schleiermacher*), which are—together with the two editions and the underlying Greek texts—currently being published in the *KGA* series for the first time.[39] This material shows how meaning and understanding gradually emerge in the feedback process between source language and target language. The hermeneutical "gap" between the two is filled by the dialogue between discussion partners. This "oscillating" method of translating and understanding (and vice versa) is definitely the most important legacy of Schleiermacher's translation of Plato.

---

[37] *KGA* 1.11, p. 74.

[38] Collected by Hermann Patsch in *Alle Menschen sind Künstler. Friedrich Schleiermachers poetische Versuche* (Berlin: Walter de Gruyter, 1986), p. 69.

[39] See *KGA* 4.3, ed. Lutz Käppel, Johanna Loehr, and Male Günther (2016) and *KGA* 4.5, ed. Lutz Käppel and Johanna Loehr (2020); the work on four more volumes is in progress.

30.3 Heraclitus

The other most notable work on ancient Greek philosophy by Schleiermacher is the treatise on Heraclitus. Schleiermacher wrote it for the *Museum der Alterthumswissenschaft*, published by Friedrich August Wolf and Philipp Buttmann. It appeared as a contribution to the first volume for the year 1807. The third section with Schleiermacher's *Heraclitus*, however, was delivered only towards the end of 1808. There the text covers pages 313 to 533 (220 pages). The work was probably written in the first half of 1808, that is, about at the same time as the third volume of the Plato translations,[40] namely of *Gorgias, Theaetetus, Menon*, and *Euthydemos*, a volume in which Heraclitus also plays an important role.[41]

The correspondence says nothing about why Schleiermacher wrote a treatise on Heraclitus. In any case, from a few letters from March 1808 it appears that Schleiermacher's treatise was intended specifically for the *Museum*, and that the work was deliberately designed and carried out as philological work. He wrote to Carl Gustav von Brinckmann on March 1, 1808,

> Now I am deep in ancient Heraclitus, whose fragments and doctrines I present for the *Museum der Alterthumswissenschaften*. What happens to people! A few years ago I would have thought it impossible to be in connection with Wolf in the field of philology. But the virtuosos in this field are so frugal with their work that the bunglers must also be fetched.[42]

A second—and perhaps the most important, because most intrinsic—impulse to reconstruct the doctrine of Heraclitus seems to have been Schleiermacher's own work on Plato's *Theaetetus*, which was finished in 1805. In a way, the *Heraclitus* can be seen as a continuation of his work on the *Theaetetus*, especially the epistemological problems discussed there, Heraclitus being a central figure in the discussion about the stability/non-stability of perception. Schleiermacher also, being freshly introduced to Halle as a professor, surprisingly starts a lecture about hermeneutics in the summer semester 1805, coinciding with the final editorial work of the *Theaitetos*. The conceptual interdependence of Schleiermacher's readings of Plato's *Theaitetos*, his reconstruction of Heraclitus' epistemology, and his own hermeneutics, seems evident but is not yet sufficiently recognized by research.[43]

Another—more external—occasion seems to have been Schleiermacher's first lecture on *The History of Ancient Philosophy* in Berlin in the summer of 1807. The presentation there does not go much beyond a general summary that can be found everywhere in the textbooks of the time. Schleiermacher apparently felt a certain dissatisfaction with his treatment of the philosophy of individual authors in this lecture. If one compares his presentation of Heraclitus in the edition of the lecture by Heinrich Ritter in 1838, this can be understood.

Already in this lecture Schleiermacher had formulated one of the principles of his history of philosophy, which applies to the reconstruction of the history of philosophy as a whole as

---

[40] See *KGA* 4.5.
[41] Schleiermacher's *Heraclitus* is available in the original edition from 1807 (1808) as a digital facsimile (Heidelberg University Library) and now as a critical edition by Dirk Schmid (*KGA* 1.6).
[42] *KGA* 5.10, no. 2650, pp. 44ff.
[43] Cf. *KGA* 4.5, pp. xxix–xxx.

well as that of the thinking of a single philosophical writing in particular. In Schleiermacher's view, there is a hermeneutic circle between systematics and historicity: There has to be a guideline of interpretative patterns in order to combine the disparate bulk of material to a senseful organism.[44]

And what applies between philosophy itself and the history of philosophy also applies at the author level. And that's exactly what Schleiermacher's Heraclitus treatise is about. The title alone reveals Schleiermacher's approach: *Heraclitus, the dark, of Ephesus, depicted from the debris of his work and the testimonies of the ancients.* The subject is, hence, the person, not one or more texts. The person is characterized by the epithet that has been common since antiquity, which, so to speak, justifies and motivates the investigation. The origin of Ephesus refers to the *historical* place. In addition to the object, the method of investigation is also indicated: The "debris" of his work, that is, the authentic fragments are the basis of the presentation. Different from these are the "testimonies of the old." This distinction also determines the examination methodically. The focus is on the fragments that have been preserved. But here the problem arises that even these are not directly available but have only been handed down by later authors such as Plutarch, Sextus Empiricus, and Clemens of Alexandria. These authors, in turn, sometimes quote fragments of Heraclitus that come from later writings and that only have been attributed to Heraclitus in the course of tradition. Schleiermacher therefore states, "Accordingly, all representations and conclusions that rested only on the fragments would not be free from suspicion and not sufficiently substantiated, that is, only insofar as they are held directly by the few passages that Plato and Aristotle have already handed down to us."[45]

This is where the "testimonies and reports from the ancients", as Schleiermacher calls them, come into play. Early testimonies should be separated from late ones, and Stoic sources in particular should be treated with caution, since they, so to speak, attached themselves to Heraclitus and subsequently modified him according to their own philosophy. For Schleiermacher only Plato and Aristotle can be regarded as early trustworthy witnesses for Heraclitus' fragments, but they, too, offer only sparse material, and even here the authenticity of the respective quotations of Heraclitus has yet to be checked:

> ... the correct procedure seems to be that, based only on these, the remaining fragments are ... identified and used to the extent that they relate to or at least agree with them, and that one does not attach more weight to later testimonials than they show a natural connection with the fragments thus recognized. Anyone who would thus be able to weave a wreath in a skillful and meaningful way out of both testimonies and fragments, without leaving aside a flower that belongs to it, we would have to believe him, that he was teaching us the truth and everything that we can still know about the wisdom of the Ephesian.[46]

Schleiermacher's methodological program for the reconstruction not only of Heraclitus, but also of the writings and teachings of all ancient philosophers, is both revolutionary and trendsetting at the same time. Schleiermacher's predecessors—if they are interested in the reconstruction of Heraclitus at all and do not use him as a vehicle for their own philosophical goals—either created lists of quotations of Heraclitus from Sextus Empiricus, Clemens, and

---

[44] SW III/4.1, p. 15. See below p. 22. XXX.
[45] KGA 1.6, pp. 108f.
[46] KGA 1.6, pp. 110f.

others together with the (spurious) letters handed down under Heraclitus' name or simply paraphrased the ancient accounts of Heraclitus' teaching. For Schleiermacher, in contrast, the use of the inner connection of both elements—the original words of Heraclitus and their reception in the form of the reports of later readers—is more than just a clever trick to uncover the real fragments. It is a multiply staggered circle: starting with the reports by Plato and Aristotle, a suitable first group of fragments is identified. In addition to that, matching reports with matching fragments are added, and so on, until the "wreath of truth" becomes denser and denser and braided more and more tightly, a process that is constantly recursive and takes place ad infinitum. What is being developed here as a philological method for creating a corpus of fragments is essentially nothing less than an applied theory of understanding. Schleiermacher developed the methodologically safe recourse to "truth," in this case: the real teaching of Heraclitus. Working on Heraclitus is first of all working on the method itself.

But Schleiermacher's interest in Heraclitus, it seems, goes beyond the methodological. If one follows the course of his investigation and compares it with earlier works on Heraclitus, it is striking that Schleiermacher did not develop Heraclitus' teaching like the earlier ones from his alleged thesis that fire is the principle of being. His treatment follows a completely different line: Schleiermacher begins with the question whether Heraclitus, who was called "the dark" by the tradition (ὁ σκοτεινός), deliberately wrote incomprehensibly in order to cover up the truth esoterically. He exposes this characterization of Heraclitus as a misunderstanding of tradition. On the contrary, according to Schleiermacher, Heraclitus stated in the relevant fragments that it was the thing itself that veils itself and that great methodical effort was required to unveil it. Schleiermacher perceives Heraclitus as an epistemologist in the first place, who is in search of truth. For him the corresponding fragments are central testimonies for the epistemologist Heraclitus, and therefore stand at the beginning of his edition, for example: "The King, who owns the Oracle at Delphi, does not explain, nor hides, but gives hints" (no. 10); "The One Wise alone does not want and does want to be spoken, the name of Zeus" (no. 11); "Owing to its incredibility it—the truth—slips away from being recognized" (no. 12).[47]

Schleiermacher interprets all these statements as philosophical principles. The truth is not there. It must—and can—be brought out of its hiddenness through philosophical activity, treated semantically ("it gives hints: σημαίνει") and brought up to the level of language. Then Schleiermacher lists a few fragments that condemn wrong practices: Being a know-it-all or relying on wrong authorities does not help.[48]

Schleiermacher then reconstructs the actual core of Heraclitus' teaching in the familiar sense, namely, the doctrine of the flow of all being. Schleiermacher interprets the famous phrase that *you cannot step into the same river twice* very innovatively from both sides. Schleiermacher first introduces the concept of flow as applying to the river you are stepping into and to the stepping person him- or herself.[49] However, he then combines this sentence again with fragments about perception and thus links the ontological problem with the epistemological one: "Heraclitus has expressed himself in such a way that [no. 24] if all beings

---

[47] KGA 1.6, pp. 119–121 = Frg. B 93, 33, 86 in *Die Fragmente der Vorsokratiker*, ed. Hermann Diels and Walther Kranz, 3 vols., 6th ed. (Berlin: Weidmann, 1951/1952) (hereafter D.-K.).

[48] KGA 1.6, pp. 129–134.

[49] KGA 1.6, pp. 134–138 (no. 20, 21) = Frg. B 91, 12 D.-K.

were smoke, the nose would distinguish them."⁵⁰ Only then do the well-known fragments dealing with natural philosophy (of fire, the sun, etc.) follow, which can be passed over here.⁵¹

The famous fragments of the unity of opposites, the παλίντονος ἁρμονίη,⁵² then occupy a large space again. These passages are characteristic: "Link perishable and non-perishable, coming together and diverging, matching and non-matching" and "From everything one, and from one everything" (no. 37.b.). Schleiermacher adds, "It is just as natural, of course, that the assertion and all that has been made so far that opposites everywhere necessarily belong together, perhaps even that no product of nature could exist without a peculiar contrast."⁵³

It is only towards the end of this discussion that Schleiermacher comes across the fragment, which is often regarded as the key to Heraclitus' work:

> People always find themselves without understanding of this existing relationship, both before they hear about it and after they first heard about it. Being ignorant of the things happening according to this relationship, they seem to be trying to make such speeches and works, such as I carry out, which, according to nature, divide everything up and determine how it is. But the rest of the people remain unconscious of what they are doing awake, just as they forget what they have done asleep. (No. 47)⁵⁴

Heraclitus is talking about the "logos," which people generally do not understand, but which is, in a sense, the essence of the world. Schleiermacher does not translate λόγος here, as is often the case, as reason or as (Heraclitus') doctrine or (divine) spirit or the like, but as a *Verhältnis*, that is proportion, relation, or relationship. For Heraclitus, the real insight into the world unfolds as a relationship between poles, as tension, harmony, as a unity of opposition. This logos as a relationship is the ξυνόν, the common: "One must therefore follow the common: notwithstanding the law [namely, of thinking, the same thing as the law of being] is a common thing, since most people live as having a peculiar insight" (no. 48).

Schleiermacher's interpretation summarizes these two fragments as follows:

> Apparently, the insight which each individual has differently for himself is rejected as wrong, and only the pure expression of the common law is praised as truth. But why there is so much cause to complain about the lack of this common principle of truth in people's imaginations, and where this lack comes from, is understood from the Ephesians with all previous closely related thoughts of the soul, which we have to present here.⁵⁵

The development of Heraclitus' doctrine of the soul then takes up the last part of the treatise. It cannot be treated with all its physiological details in here—this would be a separate study, to which Schleiermacher's lectures on psychology could certainly be compared in an instructive manner.⁵⁶ For that reason here only the final point will be mentioned, which Schleiermacher's reconstruction amounts to, namely that Schleiermacher comes back to the

---

⁵⁰ *KGA* 1.6, pp. 119–121 = Frg. B 93. 33. 86 D.-K.
⁵¹ *KGA* 1.6, pp. 142–165.
⁵² *KGA* 1.6, no. 34 = Frg. B 51 D.-K.
⁵³ *KGA* 1.6, pp. 168, 180f. (no. 34, 37b.) = Frg. B 51, 10 D.-K.
⁵⁴ *KGA* 1.6, p. 210 (no. 47) = Frg. B 1 D.-K.
⁵⁵ *KGA* 1.6, p. 211 (no. 48) = Frg. B 2 D.-K.
⁵⁶ On Schleiermacher's lectures on psychology, see *Psychologie*. See also Chapter 14 in this volume.

thought of the eternal river at the end: "We climb into and not into the same streams, are and are not."[57]

It is indeed remarkable that Schleiermacher fits this idea into the doctrine of the soul. It was already mentioned above that Schleiermacher did not refer to the metaphor of flowing—as it is usually done—or to the constant change of the physical world, but above all to the nature of the soul looking at it. In Schleiermacher's reconstruction of Heraclitus is thus not the philosopher of nature the tradition saw in him before, but an epistemologist in search of true knowledge, a "real" philosopher. This "real" knowledge does not lie in the knowledge of the individual, but of the ξυνόν, the "common" in the logos. In Schleiermacher's own words,

> Heraclitus may actually have said that he had searched for himself in this eternal river and had not found himself as being, persisting, but that it was only precisely from this that all knowledge had sprung to him. Everything explained so far very easily lines up here, so that in fact the germ of all his wisdom can only have been this losing himself and finding himself only in common reason.[58]

30.4 HERACLITUS AND PLATO: A SYNOPSIS

Schleiermacher picks out Heraclitus of all the early thinkers, who as "the dark one" had always been a philological and hermeneutic challenge, both to display a showpiece of methodology in classical scholarship and to undertake a philosophical analysis in order to formulate a genuine concept of epistemology. On the one hand, he developed a new method of reconstructing the history of philosophy by placing the traditional words of the philosopher in tension with their reception by later authors and in turn using them as an instrument to regain authentic words. On the other hand, for the first time he does not reconstruct Heraclitus as a conventional philosopher of nature, but rather as an ontologist and even more as an epistemologist. Schleiermacher interprets the "logos" in Heraclitus as the principle inherent in the world in the context of the idea of the unity of opposites, the παλίντονος ἁρμονίη: it is the relationship of the phenomena to one another. Access to its knowledge is not generated by following recognized authorities or direct individual sensory perception, but through an active methodical process of interaction between the soul (in flux) in its various physiological states and the world to be recognized, a process that takes place in a "common" leading to what can be called "the truth."

It is particularly sophisticated that Schleiermacher's philological method for the reconstruction of Heraclitus' doctrine is structurally inscribed in the content of this reconstruction. Schleiermacher reconstructs Heraclitus with the ancient philosopher's own philosophical method, which in turn is only the product of this reconstruction. This entangled structural self-similarity is what is actually a fascinating modernism in

---

[57] *KGA* 1.6, p. 239 (no. 72) = Frg. B 49a D.-K.
[58] *KGA* 1.6, p. 240.

Schleiermacher's reconstruction. Schleiermacher builds a new, "modern" concept from the debris of the ancient tradition.

The encounter with Plato operates along the same lines. If work on Heraclitus is a reconstruction from fragments, the method of approaching Plato is that of translation, and this is also a "philological" method. This method has been developed in lectures since 1805 and first systematically presented in the academic speeches of 1813. Here Schleiermacher explicitly presents his specific method, in which a given, defined content is not brought over from the other system, but in which the work of translation consists in the linguistic (and intellectual) approach to the other and ultimately leads to the "common." This method of modern understanding of ancient material, which is developed practically in the work on Plato and Heraclitus, also has its counterpart in the Platonic theory of dialogue, as Schleiermacher sees it. For Plato, according to Schleiermacher, philosophical knowledge does not arise from the fact that a person equipped with knowledge passes it on to someone who is ignorant as a specific entity, but rather from the fact that the ignorant enters into interaction with the other person in a dialectical process. There, too, we find the same self-similar structure that creates a modern concept from the ancient material: The methodological concept suggested by the ancient material is used in the modern reconstruction of this material and thereby inherent in the modern concept.

These two examples show that Schleiermacher's endeavors in ancient philosophy should not be seen as an antiquarian exercise, but rather as work on current concepts, concepts that have remained the basic paradigms of philology, philosophical hermeneutics, his own hermeneutics in the time between 1805 and 1808, and theology to this day.

30.5 ACADEMIC TEACHING BEYOND PUBLICATION PROJECTS

30.5.1 The Dates

Schleiermacher extensively dealt with the history of ancient philosophy in the context of his lectures. After Napoleon's closure of the University of Halle in autumn 1806, Schleiermacher decided to go to Berlin and offer lectures there, even before the Berlin University had opened. It was there that he gave the lecture "History of Ancient Philosophy" for the first time in 1807, followed in the summer of 1810 by "The History of Philosophy among Christians." After the university had opened, Schleiermacher finally moved to Berlin and gave lectures not only at the Faculty of Theology, but also from the summer semester in 1811 at the Faculty of Philosophy. There he repeated the lecture series three times until 1823.[59]

---

[59] Andreas Arndt and Wolfgang Virmond, *Schleiermachers Briefwechsel (Verzeichnis) nebst einer Liste seiner Vorlesungen*, Schleiermacher-Archiv 11 (Berlin: Walter de Gruyter, 1992), pp. 297, 303–330.

30.5.2 The Structure of the Lectures

According to the two lectures, the history of philosophy comprises two parts: "The history of ancient philosophy"[60] and "History of modern philosophy."[61] The latter was supplemented by a "Brief description of the Spinozist system."[62]

Schleiermacher's approach to the history of philosophy is evident in the first sentence of his introduction to the first part, which is also an introduction to both lectures: "Agreement on the task is difficult. For whoever lectures on the history of philosophy must possess philosophy in order to be able to separate out the individual facts that belong to it, and whoever wishes to possess philosophy must understand it historically."[63] For Schleiermacher, there is a hermeneutic circle, as it were, between systematics and historicity for philosophy. For the history of philosophy, this means that the (systematic) inner context must be its guiding principle, not the stringing together of incoherent facts. In this way, the division of the history of philosophy into periods and phases is also underpinned by content-related interpretative patterns, which on the one hand prevent the historical material from decaying into an amorphous smorgasbord of individual information, and on the other hand themselves gain a substance through the historical material, anchoring their speculative character in history.

Schleiermacher divides ancient philosophy into two periods: the first up to Socrates, the second from Socrates onwards. Modern philosophy also falls into two periods: a first, which encompasses medieval philosophy (nominalism-realism), a second, which encompasses the early modern period "except for Kant"; the lectures break off at Spinoza.

30.5.3 Philosophical Perspectives of the Presentation

In his introduction to the second part, Schleiermacher formulates the main difference between "old" and "new" philosophy as follows:

> The old philosophy is predominantly the realization of reason under the form of ideas, the new philosophy is mainly the realization of reason under the form of will . . . Therefore, according to ancient philosophy, man in general regards himself as a natural being. No opposition to fate, no philosophy about freedom from this point of view; whereas in the new philosophy this is the recurring task. Because as a will man opposes nature and sees fate as an intervention.[64]

Of course, this is said entirely from the perspective of modern philosophy, in which the old must appear as "not yet." However, ancient philosophy itself is also valued in its own right, namely in finding and losing the unity of life in science or knowledge:

> The basic fact is the division into logic, physics and ethics, which reveals a concept of the full scope of the field of knowledge and a developed sense for scientific treatment. The real side is

---

[60] Friedrich Schleiermacher, *Geschichte der Philosophie. Aus Schleiermachers handschriftlichem Nachlass herausgegeben von Heinrich Ritter*, SW III/4.1, pp. 13–141.
[61] *SW* III/4.1, pp. 143–282.
[62] *SW* III/4.1, pp. 283–311.
[63] *SW* III/4.1, p. 15.
[64] *SW* III/4.1, p. 147.

presented by physics and ethics. The higher life is nothing other than the being of things in man and the being of man in things. The awareness of this life is knowledge. The awareness of the former element is physics, the awareness of the latter is ethics. Dialectics represent the general element...[65]

For Schleiermacher, this is the core of ancient philosophy, which unfolds between a pre-rational, mythological beginning and an end in "language, artificiality and rhetoric." Central to this are the pre-Socratics, Socrates and Plato, and Aristotle. In the end, neo-Platonism is carried out only rudimentarily.

30.6 Schleiermacher as Organizer of Classical Studies and His Central Intellectual Role at the Beginning of German *Altertumswissenschaft*

More important than Schleiermacher's lectures themselves were his activities as a great organizer of scholarship at the university in Berlin and as a member of the Academy of Sciences. Among his manifold activities the most productive was his promotion of young classical scholars. Two of them stand out: Immanuel Bekker (1785–1871) and August Boeckh (1785–1864).

Bekker, a student of Schleiermacher's friend L. G. Spalding at the Gymnasium Zum Grauen Kloster in Berlin (until 1803) and of Friedrich August Wolf (and Schleiermacher) at the University of Halle (PhD 1806), initially worked (by placement of Schleiermacher) as a private tutor near Berlin (from 1807), was appointed to the newly founded Berlin University as professor for classical Philology (1809/1810), and worked as a member of the Prussian Academy of Sciences (1815). From May 1810 until December 1812 he undertook—at the academy's expense and with the support of Schleiermacher—research trips to Paris for the collation of manuscripts for a Plato edition (initially planned together with F. A. Wolf). In the course of 1811, he was able to collate and record manuscripts for the new edition, which became the epoch-making and still fundamental edition of the Platonic dialogues until today. The close connection of Bekker and Schleiermacher and the high appreciation of Schleiermacher by Bekker becomes clear in the dedication of his 1816 edition: "Friderico Schleiermachero Platonis restitutori d. Editor." Bekker's work on Plato, however, was only the beginning of the career of one of the most influential editors in classical scholarship, including Aristotle and more than fifty standard editions.

Boeckh, too, had studied with F. A. Wolf in Halle since 1803, where he also attended lectures given by Schleiermacher. His review of Schleiermacher's first two volumes of Plato was the most substantial and most approving ever written.[66] But, more important, after his

---

[65] *SW* III/4.1, p. 18.
[66] Correspondence with Boeckh (1808), *KGA* 5.10, no. 2701.

appointment as a professor in Berlin, he became the leading figure of German academics of the nineteenth century, organizing the German "Altertumswissenschaft" in the way it dominated classical studies in the nineteenth century. The framework for this endeavor was a concept that was based on Schleiermacher's hermeneutics: Boeckh's concept in *Encyklopädie und Methodologie der philologischen Wissenschaften* was the foundation of German "Altertumswissenschaft" and the dependence on Schleiermacher was explicit: "In my presentation Schleiermacher's ideas . . . are used. But in such a way, that I am not able any more to differentiate between my own and the foreign."[67]

30.7 Conclusion

Schleiermacher can be regarded as the intellectual and organizational founding father of modern German classical scholarship, as it was practiced from the nineteenth century onwards. His interpretation of Plato is still the landmark of Platonic studies for followers as well as detractors. His method of interpretation in the reconstruction of lost authors from fragments and testimonies is still the backbone of all modern editions of fragments. His theory of hermeneutics, which was systematically developed in the medium of translation and reconstruction, is still an integral standard approach to ancient texts. The concept of German "Altertumswissenschaft" goes back to his organization of scholarship in the academic environment in Berlin. One cannot overrate the contributions of this outstanding scholar in so many fields, especially for the history of classical studies.

Suggested Reading

Dilthey, W. "Schleiermachers Übersetzung des Platon." In *Leben Schleiermachers*. Erster Band, Zweiter Halbband (GesSchr. XIII/2). 3rd ed., ed. Martin Redeker (Berlin/Göttingen: Walter de Gruyter and Vandenhoeckh & Ruprecht, 1970), pp. 37–75.
Güthenke, C. *Feeling and Classical Philology. Knowing Antiquity in German Scholarship, 1770–1920* (Cambridge: Cambridge University Press, 2020).
Käppel, L. "Schleiermachers Platon-Übersetzungen" and "Geschichte der Philosophie." In *Schleiermacher Handbuch*, ed. Martin Ohst (Tübingen: Mohr Siebeck, 2017), pp. 157–165; 280–285.
Laks, André. "Schleiermacher on Plato: From Form (Introduction to Plato's Works) to Content (Outlines of a Critique of Previous Ethical Theory)." In *Brill's Companion to German Platonism*, ed. A. Kim (Leiden: Brill, 2019), pp. 146–164.
Lamm, Julia A. *Schleiermacher's Plato* (Berlin: Walter de Gruyter, 2021).

---

[67] August Boeckh, *Encyklopädie und Methodologie der philologischen Wissenschaften*, ed. E. Bratuscheck, 2nd ed. from Rudolf Lussmann (Leipzig: Teubner, 1886), p. 75.

Bibliography

Schleiermacher's Writings on Aristotle

Schleiermacher, Friedrich. *Anmerkungen und Übersetzung zu Aristoteles: Nikomachische Ethik 8–9 (1788/1789)*. In *KGA* 1.1, ed. Günter Meckenstock (Berlin: De Gruyter, 1983) pp. 1–80.

Schleiermacher, Friedrich. *Zu Aristoteles Ethik (1816/17)*. In *KGA* 1.14, ed. Eilert Herms, Günter Meckenstock, and Michael Pietsch (Berlin: De Gruyter, 2002) pp. 223–266.

Schleiermacher, Friedrich. *Aristoteles Metaphysik. Auszug*. In *KGA* 1.14, pp. 369–376.

Schleiermacher, Friedrich. *Citationes Aristotelicae (vermutlich 1802)*. In *KGA* 1.14, ed. Matthias Wolfes and Michael Pietsch ed. Martin Rößler and Lars Emersleben (Berlin: De Gruyter, 2003) pp. 69–71.

Schleiermacher, Friedrich. *Über die ethischen Werke des Aristoteles (1817)*. In *KGA* 1.11, ed. Martin Rößler and Lars Emersleben (Berlin: De Gruyter, 2002), pp. 271–308.

Schleiermacher, Friedrich. *Exzerpt aus Aristoteles: Metaphysik (mit Übersetzung und Anmerkungen) (1789)*. In *KGA* 1.1, pp. 165–175.

Schleiermacher, Friedrich. *Exzerpt aus Aristoteles: Physik*. In *KGA* 1.14, pp. 377–383.

Schleiermacher, Friedrich. *Über die griechischen Scholien zur Nikomachischen Ethik des Aristoteles (1816)*. In *KGA* 1.11, pp. 219–237.

Schleirmacher, Friedrich. *Notizen zu Aristoteles: Politik (1793/94)*. In *KGA* 1.14, pp. 25–47.

Schleiermacher, Friedrich. *Philosophische Sprache Aristoteles*. In *KGA* 1.14, pp. 383–389.

Schleiermacher, Friedrich. *Über die Scholien zur Nikomachischen Ethik A und B (1816)*. In *KGA* 1.14, pp. 185–211.

On Plato

Schleiermacher, Friedrich. *Philosophia politica Platonis et Aristotelis (1794)*. In *KGA* 1.1, pp. 499–509.

Schleiermacher, Friedrich. *Zum Platon (Vermutlich 1801–1803)*. In *KGA* 1.3, ed. Günter Meckenstock ed. Martin Rößler and Lars Emersleben (Berlin: De Gruyter, 1988), pp. 341–375.

Schleiermacher, Friedrich. *Zu Platon, Republik II. Bekker p. 72, 3 sq. (1826)*. In *KGA* 1.11, pp. 523–533.

Schleiermacher, Friedrich. *Über Platons Ansicht von der Ausübung der Heilkunst (1825)*. In *KGA* 1.11, pp. 459–478.

Schleiermacher, Friedrich. *Platons Werke I/1-2, II/1-3, III/1 (^{1}1804–1828), Platons Werke I/1-2, II/1-3 (^{2}1817–1826)*. In *KGA* 4.3-8, ed. Lutz Käppel, Johanna Loehr, and Male Günther (Berlin: De Gruyter, 2016-).

Schleiermacher, Friedrich. *Rezension von Friedrich Ast: De Platonis Phaedro (1802)*. In *KGA* 1.3, pp. 467–483.

On Heraclitus and Other Pre-Socratics

Schleiermacher, Friedrich. *Über Anaximandros (1811)*. In *KGA* 1.11, pp. 31–63.

Schleiermacher, Friedrich. *Über Diogenes von Apollonia (1811)*. In *KGA* 1.11, pp. 9–29.

Schleiermacher, Friedrich. "Herakleitos, der dunkle, von Ephesos, dargestellt aus den Trümmern seines Werkes und den Zeugnissen der Alten." In *Museum der*

Alterthums-Wissenschaft, vol. 1, ed. Friedrich August Wolf and Philipp Buttmann (Berlin: Realschulbuchhandlung, 1808), pp. 313–533.

Schleiermacher, Friedrich. *Herakleitos der dunkle, von Ephesos, dargestellt aus den Trümmern seines Werkes und den Zeugnissen der Alten (1808)*. In *KGA* 1.6, ed. Dirk Schmid (Berlin: De Gruyter, 1998) pp. 101–241.

Schleiermacher, Friedrich. *Über den Philosophen Hippon. Hippo Rheginus? Metapontinus? Melius?* In *KGA* 1.11, pp. 343–355.

Schleiermacher, Friedrich. *Text zu Demokrit (Vermutlich 1814/15)*. In *KGA* 1.14, pp. 119–124.

Schleiermacher, Friedrich. *Über das Verzeichnis der Schriften des Democritus bei Diogenes Laertius (1815)*. In *KGA* 1.11, pp. 147–171.

Miscellaneous Writings on Classical Topics

Schleiermacher, Friedrich. *Geschichte der Philosophie. Aus Schleiermachers handschriftlichem Nachlass herausgegeben von Heinrich Ritter*. SW III/4.1.

Schleiermacher, Friedrich. *Über den Wert des Sokrates als Philosophen (1815)*. In *KGA* 1.11, pp. 199–210.

Works Cited

Arndt, Andreas, and Wolfgang Virmond. *Schleiermachers Briefwechsel (Verzeichnis) nebst einer Liste seiner Vorlesungen*. Schleiermacher-Archiv 11 (Berlin: Walter de Gruyter, 1992).

Boeckh, August. *Encyklopädie und Methodologie der philologischen Wissenschaften*. Ed. E. Bratuscheck. 2nd ed. from Rudolf Lussmann (Leipzig: Teubner, 1886).

Dilthey, W. "Schleiermachers Übersetzung des Platon." In *Leben Schleiermachers*. Erster Band, Zweiter Halbband (GesSchr. XIII/2). 3rd. ed., ed. Martin Redeker (Berlin/Göttingen: Walter de Gruyter and Vandenhoeckh & Ruprecht, 1970), pp. 37–75.

D.-K. *Die Fragmente der Vorsokratiker*, 3 vols., 6th ed. Ed. Hermann Diels and Walther Kranz (Berlin: Weidmann, 1951/1952).

Jantzen, Jörg. " . . . daß ich nämlich sterben will, wenn der Platon vollendet ist." In *Schleiermachers Übersetzung antiker Literatur, Funktionen und Konzeptionen im 19. und 20. Jahrhundert*. Transformationen der Antike 7, ed. Martin Harbsmeier, Josefine Kitzbichler, Katja Lubitz, and Nina Mindt (Berlin: Walter de Gruyter, 2008), pp. 29–48.

Nowak, Kurt. *Schleiermacher. Leben, Werk und Wirkung* (Göttingen: Vandenhoeck & Ruprecht, 2001).

Patsch, Hermann. *Alle Menschen sind Künstler. Friedrich Schleiermachers poetische Versuche* (Berlin: Walter de Gruyter, 1986).

Schleiermacher, Friedrich. *Platons Werke I,1, Berlin 1804. 1817*, KGA 4.3, ed. Lutz Käppel, Johanna Loehr, and Male Günther (Berlin: De Gruyter, 2016).

Schleiermacher, Friedrich. *Platons Werke II,1, Berlin 1805. 1818*, KGA 4.5, ed. Lutz Käppel and Johanna Loehr (Berlin: De Gruyter, 2020).

Schleiermacher, Friedrich. *Briefwechsel 1774-1796*, KGA 5.1, ed. Andreas Arndt and Wolfgang Virmond (Berlin: De Gruyter, 1985).

Schleiermacher, Friedrich. *Briefwechsel 1800*, KGA 5.4, ed. Andreas Arndt and Wolfgang Virmond (Berlin: De Gruyter, 1994).

Schleiermacher, Friedrich. *Briefwechsel 1801-02*, KGA 5.5, ed. Andreas Arndt and Wolfgang Virmond (Berlin: De Gruyter, 1999).

Schleiermacher, Friedrich. *Briefwechsel 1802-03, KGA* 5.6, ed. Andreas Arndt and Wolfgang Virmond (Berlin: De Gruyter, 2005).

Schleiermacher, Friedrich. *Briefwechsel 1803-04, KGA* 5.7, ed. Andreas Arndt and Wolfgang Virmond (Berlin: De Gruyter, 2005).

Schleiermacher, Friedrich. *Briefwechsel 1808, KGA* 5.10, ed. Simon Gerber and Sarah Schmidt (Berlin: De Gruyter, 2015).

Tennemann, Wilhelm Gottlieb. *System der Platonischen Philosophie*, 4 vols. (Leipzig: Johann Ambrosius Barth, 1792–1795).

CHAPTER 31

SCHLEIERMACHER AND MEDIATING THEOLOGY

ANNETTE G. AUBERT

31.1 INTRODUCTION

IN an 1826 address at the Royal Academy of Sciences, Friedrich Schleiermacher noted that Frederick the Great "did not found a school, but an era."[1] Schleiermacher could have been talking about himself: he resisted efforts to label himself as a theological leader of an intellectual school,[2] yet he is forever linked with the school of mediating theology, for which he served as a central influence. Ernst Troeltsch (1865–1923), who praised Schleiermacher for instituting fundamental Protestant reforms, insisted that modern theology was best characterized as having a mediating characteristic, and he described Schleiermacher as the most important figure in what he referred to as the "program of mediation" that inspired nineteenth-century Protestant theologians.[3] Following Schleiermacher's lead, many of those theologians took on the twin tasks of researching the historical origins of Christianity and affirming their findings through modern scientific methods.

Scholars have expressed a broad range of opinions regarding Schleiermacher and his influence on mediating theology.[4] While some scholars acknowledge certain nineteenth-century professors at German university faculties as heirs of Schleiermacher's religious and

---

[1] Friedrich Schleiermacher, *Reden und Abhandlungen, der Königlichen Akademie der Wissenschaften vorgetragen von Friedrich Schleiermacher aus Schleiermachers handschriftlichem Nachlasse herausgegeben von Ludwig Jonas* (Berlin: Reimer, 1835), vol. 2, p. 83.

[2] Friedrich Schleiermacher, *Theologische-dogmatische Abhandlungen und Gelegenheitsschriften*, KGA 1.10, ed. Hans-Friedrich Traulsen in collaboration with Martin Ohst (Berlin: de Gruyter, 1990), p. 311.

[3] Ernst Troeltsch, "Protestantisches Christentum und Kirche in der Neuzeit," in *Die Kultur der Gegenwart: Ihre Entwicklung und Ziele*, ed. Paul Hinneberg (Berlin: Teubner, 1922), pp. 725–726.

[4] See Emanuel Hirsch, *Geschichte der neueren evangelischen Theologie im Zusammenhang mit den allgemeinen Bewegungen des europäischen Denkens*, vol. 5 (Gütersloh: C. Bertelsmann, 1954); Knut Ragnar Holte, *Die Vermittlungstheologie: Ihre theologischen Grundbegriffe kritisch untersucht*, trans. Björn Kommer (Uppsala: Almquist & Wiksells, 1965); Jörg Rothermundt, *Personale Synthese: Isaak August Dorners dogmatische Methode* (Göttingen: Vandenhoeck & Ruprecht, 1968); Friedemann Voigt, *Vermittlung im Streit* (Tübingen: Mohr Siebeck, 2006).

intellectual heritage,[5] others argue that, for narrowly defined reasons, Schleiermacher should not be described as having created a "school," despite his description by some as a forefather of the mediating school.[6] Karl Barth is among those who argue that Schleiermacher did not create a school,[7] notwithstanding Isaak Dorner's (1809–1884) description of mediating theology as the "school of Schleiermacher" in his *Geschichte der protestantischen Theologie*.[8] Since Schleiermacher's efforts were characterized by a mix of religious and scientific ideas that resist analysis as a complete system, scholars have concluded that there was no "Schleiermacher school."[9]

The purpose of this chapter is to clarify Schleiermacher's ideas and his relationship to mediating theology. If it is true that Schleiermacher was the school's forefather, then his nineteenth-century followers should be viewed as heirs who contributed to the advancement of his theological mediation. Schleiermacher and his students prevented the nineteenth century from becoming a time of sheer irreversible secularization and religious decline, and instead turned it into a period of revival for dogmatic theology and theological education.[10] The pedagogical and academic impact of his work on mediating theology was significant, with his ideas being expressed within the academic discipline of theology, especially at universities in Germany. The mediating theologians contributed to significant progress in all branches of theological science, including in biblical studies, church history, dogmatics, and practical theology. After his death, Schleiermacher's students influenced the next generation of theologians on both sides of the Atlantic through their works and translated texts.[11]

Although mediating theologians were preoccupied with topics similar to those addressed by Schleiermacher, they did not constitute a cohesive school. An analysis of their texts reveals considerable evidence of religious diversity among mediating theologians, as well as proof of their statuses as independent thinkers inspired by a variety of intellectual traditions. Although these and others can be divided into three categories—speculative, ecclesiastical, and revivalistic—they were all inspired by Schleiermacher and adopted ideas from G. W. F. Hegel.[12] This chapter will emphasize a historically and theologically oriented conceptualization of mediation in tracing some of its historical developments and core principles.

---

[5] Holte, *Vermittlungstheologie*, p. 9.

[6] George Cross, *The Theology of Schleiermacher: A Condensed Presentation of His Chief Work, "The Christian Faith"* (Chicago: University of Chicago Press, 1911), p. 299.

[7] Karl Barth, *Protestant Theology in the Nineteenth Century*, trans. Brian Cozens and John Bowden (Grand Rapids: Eerdmans, 2002), p. 411.

[8] Isaak A. Dorner, *Geschichte der protestantischen Theologie besonders in Deutschland* (Munich: J. G. Cotta, 1867), p. 813.

[9] Otto Lempp, "Schleiermachersche Schule," in *Die Religion in Geschichte und Gegenwart. Handwörterbuch in Gemeinverständlicher Darstellung*, vol. 5, ed. Hermann Gunkel, Otto Scheel, and Leopold Zscharnack (Tübingen: J. C. B. Mohr, 1913), p. 314.

[10] Annette G. Aubert, "Protestantism," in *The Oxford Handbook of Nineteenth-Century Christian Thought*, ed. Joel D. S. Rasmussen, Judith Wolfe, and Johannes Zachhuber (Oxford: Oxford University Press, 2017), pp. 504–523; Brian A. Gerrish, *Tradition and the Modern World: Reformed Theology in the Nineteenth Century* (Chicago: University of Chicago Press, 1978), p. 122.

[11] Annette G. Aubert, *The German Roots of Nineteenth-Century American Theology* (New York: Oxford University Press, 2013), pp. 32–34.

[12] Aubert, *German Roots*, p. 73.

31.2 THEOLOGICAL AND SCIENTIFIC MEDIATION

Schleiermacher never wrote a specific text on mediating theology, but there is considerable evidence showing his belief in the paramount importance of links between theology and modern education, as well as between theology and science. His balancing of scientific and theological arguments set the stage for the acceptance of mediating theology as a valid intellectual position and method.[13] An important mediator, Carl Ullmann (1796–1865), agreed with Schleiermacher's assertion that the scientific position, which "results from this mediation, is the true, healthy middle."[14] Schleiermacher's students portrayed mediation as a theological goal by "positioning themselves in the middle" and by joining "the conflicting forces of the time."[15]

Schleiermacher's interest in mediation can be traced back to his *Speeches on Religion* (1799), which can be viewed as a mediation manifesto. This collection of speeches and critiques of contemporary culture reveals his captivation with the idea of mediation.[16] Structured according to mediating methods and ideas, it particularly reveals Schleiermacher's early mediating concerns that included the expression of a twofold thematic mediation involving religion and redemption.[17] The fourth speech, and specifically the phrase "create it anew from the midpoint," gives some insights into his understanding of religion and the church.[18] According to Schleiermacher, the church of his day should be subject to "a new consideration" and rebuilt from its core.[19] The *Speeches* also underscores Schleiermacher's belief that mediation had theological significance in its emphasis on Christ's redemptive work.[20] He tried to establish a combination of redemption and mediation as "the center of religion"— that is, the "religion of Christ."[21] As part of his description of Christianity being distinct from other religions, Schleiermacher portrayed aspects of mediation between the finite and infinite as a key Christian characteristic.[22]

Schleiermacher's form of mediation was theological and scientific. Efforts to modernize human knowledge were in high gear at the end of the eighteenth century, with new scientific disciplines (including theology) replacing traditional mechanical models. By the second decade of the 1800s, German Protestantism was going through "a reorganization" process involving the new theology, philosophical idealism, and historical Romanticism.[23]

---

[13] Thomas Albert Howard, *Religion and the Rise of Historicism: W. M. L. de Wette, Jacob Burckhardt, and the Theological Origins of Nineteenth-Century Historical Consciousness* (Cambridge: Cambridge University Press, 2000), p. 55.

[14] Carl Ullmann, "Ueber Partei und Schule, Gegensätze und deren Vermittlung," *Theologische Studien und Kritiken* 9, no. 1 (1836), pp. 41, 45.

[15] Ullmann, "Ueber Partei und Schule," pp. 40–41, 58–59.

[16] John Clayton, "Theologie als Vermittlung—Das Beispiel Schleiermachers," in *Internationaler Schleiermacher-Kongreß Berlin 1984*, Teilband 2, ed. Kurt-Victor Selge (Berlin: de Grutyer, 1985), p. 901.

[17] *Reden²*, p. 293.
[18] *Reden²*, p. 182.
[19] *Reden²*, p. 182.
[20] *Reden²*, p. 293.
[21] *Reden²*, pp. 310–311.
[22] *Reden²*, pp. 120–122.
[23] Karl Heussi, *Kompendium der Kirchengeschichte* (Tübingen: J. C. B. Mohr, 1909), p. 552.

Schleiermacher was one of the first theologians to describe mediation as having a scientific characteristic, and his suggestion that theology be added to university curriculums as a scientific discipline is considered one of his greatest contributions. In his first academic sermon, given in 1806, Schleiermacher forcefully defended what he called a covenant between faith and science, and rejected the idea of inevitable conflict between religion and science.[24] He promoted mediation between religion and science, during an early stage of his university career. Linking new scientific concepts with theology was considered an important task among German scholars, and Schleiermacher enthusiastically endorsed modern science as a new authority for the modern university. Along with his students and other heirs of his ideas, Schleiermacher created a new scientific theological literature in the spirit of *Wissenschaft*. Acknowledging his efforts to establish theology as a genuine university discipline, other mediating professors of theology at German universities contributed to a large dogmatic and biblical literature that emphasized the scientization and historicization of theological studies.

The academic journal most strongly associated with the establishment of mediating theology is the *Theologische Studien und Kritiken*, the first issue of which appeared in 1828. For two decades, it helped shape the religious landscape in Germany and exerted an influence beyond German borders. The religious leitmotif of mediation was clearly spelled out in the journal's first issue, which was edited by Ullmann and Friedrich Wilhelm Carl Umbreit (1795–1860). Early supporters and contributors included Friedrich Lücke (1791–1855), Carl I. Nitzsch (1787–1868), and Johann Karl Ludwig Gieseler (1792–1854). As stated, the journal's main purpose was to support "true scientific theological research" and "true mediation."[25] Schleiermacher's students adopted his epistemological and scientific premises when preparing manuscripts for submission.[26]

The journal discussed Schleiermacher's positions in debates involving dogmatics and did much to influence how mediating theologians perceived him. He himself used it to engage with reviewers and critics and to publicize the second edition of *Christian Faith*, which appeared in 1831. The second issue of *Theologische Studien und Kritiken* (1829) contained two letters that Schleiermacher had sent to Lücke under the heading "Sendschreiben 'Über seine Glaubenslehre, an Dr. Lücke.'"[27] The revealing letters reviewed Schleiermacher's responses to Nitzsch and other members of the mediating school, including his opinion that Nitzsch provided the best critical review of *Christian Faith*. He noted that Nitzsch's primary observation was the inclusion of "what is particularly Christian into a general religious knowledge."[28] In response to Nitzsch's critique, Schleiermacher asserted that his description of knowledge was "nothing different than an abstraction of what is Christian."[29]

Through their texts and lectures, mediating theologians played an important role in Schleiermacher's reception history. In an 1869 Berlin lecture, August Detlev Christian Twesten reviewed some of the most important contributions that his teacher had made,

---

[24] *KGA* 3.3, p. 866.
[25] Alf Christophersen, *Friedrich Lücke (1791–1855)*, vol. 2: *Dokumente und Briefe* (Berlin: de Gruyter, 1999), pp. 421–422.
[26] Voigt, *Vermittlung*, p. 10.
[27] Schleiermacher, *Theologische-dogmatische Abhandlungen*, pp. 309–394.
[28] Schleiermacher, *Theologische-dogmatische Abhandlungen*, p. 333.
[29] Schleiermacher, *Theologische-dogmatische Abhandlungen*, p. 333.

paying particular attention to the *Glaubenslehre* and the *Christliche Sittenlehre*. Twesten described both works as supporting an understanding of Schleiermacher's approach of historical studies in relationship to religious consciousness. Twesten argued that Schleiermacher resisted both a "speculative theology" and a doctrine of God derived from philosophy, preferring instead to encourage the Christian church to consider a scientific connection with faith. Twesten regarded practical theology as a jewel in the crown of Schleiermacher's theology and concluded that Schleiermacher was ultimately "a man of the university" who used his lectures to disseminate his ideas.[30]

31.3 Theological System-Building: F. D. E. Schleiermacher, Isaak A. Dorner, Carl Liebner, and Karl Hagenbach

Starting with Schleiermacher's work, nineteenth-century theological systems tended to be based on the idea of a central dogma—a new approach that replaced the *loci* method by emphasizing Christology as the central dogmatic principle.[31] In his *Theologische Enzyklopädie* (1831/1832), Schleiermacher described the dogma linking all religious convictions as the "central point of Christianity."[32] Similar to other works written by mediators, Dorner emphasized a christocentric approach to dogma.[33] For mediating theologians such as Dorner, the dogma of the person of Christ should be considered the ultimate central dogma of all Christian doctrines. The list of other mediating theologians who focused on Christology in their dogmatic work included Carl Theodor Albert Liebner (1806–1871), a Professor at Göttingen, Kiel, and Leipzig who published *Die Christliche Dogmatik* (1849), which was established on a christological principle.

In their efforts to expand on Schleiermacher's new system, his students wrote dogmatic works that eventually replaced existing textbooks. The autonomy, uniqueness, and diversity of these dogmatic works attest to Schleiermacher's intellectual and analytical powers.[34] Those new texts reflect Schleiermacher's interest in combining religious consciousness with a scientific theology.[35] One of the most developed and respected works was Dorner's two-volume *System der Christlichen Glaubenslehre* (1879, 1881), which expanded on Schleiermacher's descriptions of faith and Christian experience as sources of knowledge.[36]

---

[30] August Twesten, *Zur Erinnerung an Friedrich Daniel Ernst Schleiermacher: Vortrag gehalten in der Königlichen Friedrich-Wilhelms-Universität zu Berlin* (Berlin: Buchdruckerei der Königlichen Akademie der Wissenschaften, 1869), pp. 26, 28, 31.

[31] Aubert, *German Roots*, p. 42.

[32] Friedrich Schleiermacher, *Theologische Enzyklopädie (1831/32)*, ed. Walter Sachs, Schleiermacher-Archiv 4 (Berlin: de Gruyter, 1987), p. 198.

[33] Isaak A. Dorner, *System der Christlichen Glaubenslehre*, vol. 1 (Berlin: Hertz, 1886), p. 36.

[34] Isaak A. Dorner, *History of Protestant Theology*, vol. 2, trans. George Robson and Sophia Taylor (Edinburgh: T&T Clark, 1871), p. 394.

[35] Revere Franklin Weidner, *An Introduction to Dogmatic Theology: Based on Luthardt* (Rock Island: Augustana, 1888), pp. 239–240.

[36] Dorner, *System*, vol. 1, pp. 1, 4–5.

However, unlike Schleiermacher, Dorner believed that faith, in its truest sense, moves toward knowledge.[37] Other books that show Schleiermacher's influence include Johann Peter Lange's *Christliche Dogmatik* (1849–1852), Liebner's *Die christliche Dogmatik aus dem christologischen Princip dargestellt* (1849), Nitzsch's *System of Christian Doctrine* (1829, 1853), Richard Rothe's *Zur Dogmatik* (1863), Alexander Schweizer's *Glaubenslehre der evangelischen reformirten Kirche*, and Twesten's *Vorlesungen über die Dogmatik* (1826, 1838). Several of these new dogmatic works based on Schleiermacher's mediating agenda and new methodology found their way to the shelves of university and theology school libraries on both sides of the Atlantic.

Schleiermacher also influenced theological encyclopedia research and writing through his *Brief Outline on the Study of Theology* (1811). His encyclopedia work far surpassed the much-lauded efforts of the German academics Johann August Nösselt (1734–1807) and Gottlieb Jakob Planck (1751–1833). Lücke credited Schleiermacher's encyclopedia theology as presenting an "organic whole," but expressed concern about the difference between scientific and historical interests from which Schleiermacher's theological system emerged.[38] Other mediating scholars expressed their own misgivings with Schleiermacher's work in their lectures and publications on topics associated with scientific theological encyclopedia. In his *Grundriss der theologischen Encyklopädie, mit Einschluss der Methodologie* (1877), Lange (one of Nitzsch's students and a Professor of Theology at the University of Bonn) described the emphasis of historical theology over dogmatics as the "greatest mistake in Schleiermacher's system."[39] After critically assessing Schleiermacher's theological encyclopedia, mediating figures published their own encyclopedic texts based on Schleiermacher's efforts. Examples include Philipp Marheineke's *Theologische Encyklopädie* (1832–1833), Philip Schaff's *Theological Propaedeutic* (1892), and August Tholuck's essay, "Theological Encyclopedia and Methodology" (1844).

Karl Hagenbach (1801–1874), a Swiss mediating theologian and Theology Professor at the University of Basel, who was one of Schleiermacher's students in Berlin, expanded Schleiermacher's theological encyclopedia work.[40] Hagenbach lectured on the topic of theological encyclopedia in the 1820s, and in 1833 published *Encyklopädie und Methodologie der theologischen Wissenschaften*, which he dedicated to W. M. L. de Wette and Schleiermacher. Like Schleiermacher, Hagenbach emphasized a historical understanding of theology based on his belief that for the church and theology to co-exist, "they must consent to undergo a new intellectual development . . . [by way] of a process of culture and humanity."[41] Also, similar to Schleiermacher, Hagenbach argued that a theological system must be established according to the religious spirit of the age, and that progress should be considered a central

---

[37] Claude Welch, *Protestant Thought in the Nineteenth Century*, vol. 1: *1799–1870* (New Haven: Yale University Press, 1972), p. 275.

[38] Friedrich Lücke, "Erinnerungen an Dr. Friedrich Schleiermacher," *Theologische Studien und Kritiken* 7 (1834), pp. 772, 775.

[39] Johann P. Lange, *Grundriss der theologischen Encyklopädie mit Einschluss der Methodologie* (Heidelberg: Carl Winter, 1877), p. 18.

[40] Aubert, *German Roots*, pp. 85–89.

[41] Karl R. Hagenbach, *History of the Church: In the Eighteenth and Nineteenth Centuries*, vol. 2., trans. John F. Hurst (New York: Scribner, 1869), p. 4; see also Thomas Albert Howard, *Protestant Theology and the Making of the Modern German University* (Oxford: Oxford University Press, 2006), p. 318.

characteristic of dogma. Positing that "the historical sense is an essential foundation of the theological character," Hagenbach believed that dogma should be protected from becoming a "rigid traditional orthodoxy," but with innovation not automatically serving as a guiding principle.[42]

Schleiermacher and Hagenbach disagreed on some important points. Schleiermacher described a threefold division of theology (historical, philosophical, and practical) in his *Brief Outline on the Study of Theology*, but Hagenbach believed in a fourfold division (exegetical, historical, systematic, and practical).[43] However, Hagenbach's descriptions of these categories share many similarities with *Brief Outline*. Like Schleiermacher, he defined systematic theology as a scientific process of identifying interrelationships within Christian doctrine. In his *Encyklopädie*, Hagenbach asserted that "the root of Christian doctrine is only one," and that individual teachings must be approached within the context of an organic whole.[44] Based on his belief that Christian dogmatics should hold a central position in theology, Hagenbach insisted that the topic be studied as "a historical-philosophical science" and believed that historical-exegetical methods could serve as the basis for an organically connected system. But in doing so he purposefully avoided an excessively historicized theology.[45] Based on his resistance to making dogmatics simply a "historical science," he criticized Schleiermacher's overemphasis of dogmatics as an example of *Wissenschaft*.[46]

By promoting scientific theology through his encyclopedic work in a university context, Schleiermacher brought new insights to practical theology. In his *Brief Outline*, Schleiermacher advised that practical theology should involve a mix of "church interest and the scientific spirit."[47] He described a possible scientific foundation for practical theology, one on which his students—including Hagenbach, Schweizer, and Nitzsch—relied on in their own work.[48] Nitzsch made important contributions to practical theology by addressing links between practical and other branches of theology. In his three-volume *Praktische Theologie*, he (like Schleiermacher) described practical theology as the "crown of theological studies," while presenting it in a comprehensive and methodological manner.[49] When asserting that ecclesiastic science could be perfected by applying Christian theory, he emphasized his belief that all theology is practical, and that its main task is to serve the "Christian church and life."[50]

---

[42] Karl R. Hagenbach, *Encyklopädie und Methodologie der theologischen Wissenschaften*, 10th ed., ed. Emil Kautzsch (Leipzig: Hirzel, 1880), p. 284.
[43] Hagenbach, *Encyklopädie*, pp. 114, 118, 204, 312, 376.
[44] Hagenbach, *Encyklopädie*, p. 281.
[45] Hagenbach, *Encyklopädie*, pp. 316–317; Howard, *Protestant Theology*, p. 318.
[46] Hagenbach, *Encyklopädie*, p. 318.
[47] Friedrich Schleiermacher, *Kurze Darstellung des theologischen Studiums zum Behuf einleitender Vorlesungen* (Berlin: Reimer, 1830), p. 99.
[48] Dorner, *Geschichte*, pp. 882–883.
[49] Carl Immanuel Nitzsch, *Praktische Theologie*, 2nd ed., vol. 3 (Bonn: Adolph Marcus, 1868), p. v.
[50] Carl Immanuel Nitzsch, *Praktische Theologie*, 2nd ed., vol. 1 (Bonn: Adolph Marcus, 1859), pp. 1, 5, 31.

31.4 METHODOLOGY, RELIGION, AND CHRISTIANITY: SCHLEIERMACHER, CARL NITZSCH, AND CARL ULLMANN

Scholars have studied the ways that mediating theologians adopted and responded to Schleiermacher's method and ideas. Schleiermacher built a foundation for a new theological method that stood in opposition to Protestant scholastic and Enlightenment theologies. During the eighteenth century, dogmatic theology received less attention as historical-critical research methods emerged and expanded. Rational theology started with philosophical principles, but in contrast to both rationalist theologians and Immanuel Kant (1724–1804), and to a greater degree than any of his contemporaries, Schleiermacher emphasized faith and "Christian feeling" rather than standard proofs.[51] The reactions to Schleiermacher of mediating theologians and scholars in other fields were varied. For example, when responding to criticisms of Schleiermacher's *Glaubenslehre* and theological method, Nitzsch argued that Schleiermacher's method should not be perceived as a formal philosophy due to its religious knowledge and "the highest unity of [that] knowledge."[52]

Whereas Schleiermacher assigned objective knowledge to philosophy, some of his students who were influenced by Hegel felt a need to advance shared discussions of theology and philosophy. In an 1843 essay entitled "Vierzig Sätze" on theological academic freedom, Ullmann emphasized objective truth when commenting, "The marriage between faith and knowledge was formed in heaven."[53] He, like Schleiermacher, believed in establishing a strong connection between Christianity and science, but he also acknowledged the existing contrast between the church, which demanded "unity and authority," and science, which advocated "freedom, development, and autonomy."[54] But Ullmann did not believe that this should hinder either a positive outlook on faith and knowledge or a stronger presence in the church of science resulting from academic efforts. He was preoccupied with objectivity, and this resulted in a closer link between mediating theology and philosophy.[55] Nitzsch agreed, regarding philosophy as an opportunity for "religion as a moment of philosophical knowledge."[56]

Religious thematization in new philosophical and theological contexts emerged during the nineteenth century.[57] Mediating theologians built on Schleiermacher's emphasis on

---

[51] Carl Immanuel Nitzsch, "Delbrück über Schleiermachers christliche Glaubenslehre," *Theologische Studien und Kritiken* 1 (1828), pp. 655–656.

[52] Nitzsch, "Delbrück," p. 656.

[53] Carl Ullmann, "Vierzig Sätze, die theologische Lehrfreiheit innerhalb der evangelisch-protestantischen Kirche betreffend," *Theologische Studien und Kritiken* 16, no. 1 (1843), p. 9.

[54] Ullmann, "Vierzig Sätze," p. 8.

[55] Walther Hoffmann, "Vermittlungstheologie," in *Die Religion in Geschichte und Gegenwart. Handwörterbuch in gemeinverständlicher Darstellung*, vol. 5, ed. Hermann Gunkel, Otto Scheel, and Leopold Zscharnack (Tübingen: J. C. B. Mohr, 1913), p. 1644.

[56] Carl Immanuel Nitzsch, *System der christlichen Lehre*, 5th ed. (Bonn: Adolph Marcus, 1844); Wilhelm Dilthey, *Vom Aufgang des geschichtlichen Bewusstseins: Jugendaufsätze und Erinnerungen* (Göttingen: Vandenhoeck & Ruprecht, 1972), p. 54.

[57] Johannes Zachhuber, *Theology as Science in Nineteenth-Century Germany: From F. C. Baur to Ernst Troeltsch* (New York: Oxford University Press, 2013), p. 111.

psychological aspects of religion, including human self-awareness, when determining its core.[58] Nitzsch, one of the mediating school's more independent thinkers, believed that definitions of religion prior to Schleiermacher were incomplete, and he therefore welcomed the idea of religion being linked to human self-awareness and based on absolute dependence. He commended Schleiermacher, Jakob Friedrich Fries (1773–1843), and Friedrich Heinrich Jacobi (1743–1819) for their contributions to the idea of the "existence of religion" in human self-awareness, and for offering a more profound comparison to empiricism.[59] Nitzsch modified Schleiermacher's concept of religion (which emphasized absolute dependence) by describing it in objective terms that highlighted ethics.[60] While Schleiermacher believed that religious piety entailed neither knowledge nor action, and that the doctrine of faith could be disconnected from Christian ethics,[61] Nitzsch felt that Christian religion could not be separated from objective knowledge and moral action.[62] Nitzsch also commented on the close relationship between religious ideas and revelation, as well as the advancements he recognized in Schleiermacher's biblical theology.

Nitzsch engaged with Schleiermacher's concept of religion in his *System der christlichen Lehre* (1844). Addressing supporters of the speculative Hegelian school, he expressed disagreement with their intellectual definition of religious faith, and insisted that any religious archetype must have a real-life component.[63] He agreed with Schleiermacher that religious feeling includes a vital "religious-spirit life," but felt that Schleiermacher's view of such a feeling was limited, and believed instead that the "totality of the spirit-life ... [must include] reason and will."[64] Still, he did not reject Schleiermacher's use of religious feeling as a core starting point. In his *System of Christian Doctrine*, he offered a new understanding based on the premise that "the original feeling of religion is the unity of reason and conscience, and the living energy of the one function influences the vivacity of the other.... It is only within the confines of these movements that all the essential changes and perfections of religious life take place."[65]

Even though Nitzsch criticized Schleiermacher's view of religion for being too subjective in its emphasis on feelings and consciousness, he believed it had potential for moving toward a more objective position. Believing that Schleiermacher's "conscious dependence upon God" was incomplete,[66] he turned to Hegelian philosophy to argue that Schleiermacher's concept could be improved by accepting a position in which original divine feeling is objective and purified "upon the varying and blended life and perception."[67] He added that "the original God-feeling ... also has an original power to make itself objective."[68]

---

[58] Holte, *Vermittlungstheologie*, pp. 48, 69.
[59] Nitzsch, *System der christlichen Lehre*, p. 13.
[60] Nitzsch, *System der christlichen Lehre*, p. 3.
[61] CG^2, pp. 14, 146.
[62] Nitzsch, *System der christlichen Lehre*, p. 3.
[63] Nitzsch, *System der christlichen Lehre*, pp. 25–26.
[64] John P. Lacroix, "Carl Immanuel Nitzsch," *Methodist Review* 55 (1873), pp. 582–584.
[65] Carl Immanuel Nitzsch, *System of Christian Doctrine*, trans. Robert Montgomery (Edinburgh: T&T Clark, 1849), p. 25.
[66] Nitzsch, *System der christlichen Lehre*, pp. 6, 8.
[67] Nitzsch, *System der christlichen Lehre*, p. 24; Holte, *Vermittlungstheologie*, p. 64.
[68] Nitzsch, *System der christlichen Lehre*, p. 24; Nitzsch, *System of Christian Doctrine*, pp. 24–25.

Schleiermacher promoted the vital essence of Christianity by defining it as consciousness of redemption.[69] Mediating theologians took their cues from Schleiermacher when writing about the essence of Christianity. While some theologians explored Christianity in relation to other religions and in the contexts of historical and philosophical studies, a mythical form of Christology as expressed by David Friedrich Strauss (1808–1874) in his *Life of Jesus* (1835) fueled interest in discussing the essence of Christianity. Ullmann, a disciple of Schleiermacher who was arguably the best-known and most influential advocate of mediating theology, published *Das Wesen des Christenthums* (1845), a text that served as a mediating theology manifesto. He was one of many nineteenth-century theologians who became preoccupied with the topic of the essence of Christianity, and he engaged with historical and philosophical ideas in support of it. Whereas Johann Gottfried Herder (1744–1803) emphasized the "human character" of Christianity, Ullmann argued that Christianity emerged with a "new life" in association with its founder.[70] He characterized Christianity using Johannine terminology of a union between God and humanity rather than the Pauline terminology of redemption.[71]

Ullmann believed that the new epoch in theology required theologians to clarify the essence of Christianity because individuals in the past "lived in Christendom," but those in the present merely studied or reflected on it.[72] Accordingly, a better understanding of Christianity was required in order to correctly address its origination compared to other religious concepts and institutions. Like Schleiermacher, Ullmann wanted to show how Christianity differed from other religions in its status as a living and influential entity rather than simply a doctrine.[73] Ullmann believed that Schleiermacher's description of the essence of Christianity as a life-restoring power was an important advancement. Given his concern for mediation between orthodoxy and Enlightenment ideas, Ullmann was especially drawn to Schleiermacher's assertion that Christianity was not merely an appeal to doctrinal knowledge or moral law, but an extension "from the central point of feeling that penetrates the whole inner man."[74] Ullmann considered this a more complete and profound concept of religion, but felt that Schleiermacher did not go far enough in making sure that Christianity did not lapse into an Enlightenment religion dominated by subjectivity and reductionism.

31.5 THE DOGMATIC TASK: SCHLEIERMACHER AND ALEXANDER SCHWEIZER

One of Schleiermacher's most talented and faithful students was Alexander Schweizer (1808–1888), a native of Switzerland who served as Professor of Theology at the University

---

[69] Carl Ullmann, *Das Wesen des Christenthums: Mit Beziehung auf neuere Auffassungsweisen desselben von Freunden und Gegnern; Eine Erörterung auch für gebildete Nicht-Theologen*, 3rd ed. (Hamburg: Perthes, 1849), p. 44.
[70] Ullmann, *Das Wesen des Christenthums* (1849), pp. 5, 11.
[71] Ullmann, *Das Wesen des Christenthums* (1849), pp. 9, 18.
[72] Ullmann, *Das Wesen des Christenthums*, 4th ed. (1854), p. 4.
[73] Ullmann, *Das Wesen des Christenthums* (1854), pp. 6–7.
[74] Ullmann, *Das Wesen des Christenthums* (1849), p. 45.

of Zurich. In formulating independent ideas on mediation, Schweizer emphasized a strong connection between traditional theology and contemporary society, and believed that meditating theology could connect church beliefs with aspects of modernity. In terms of apologetics, he surpassed Schleiermacher in mediating between established Protestantism and progressive knowledge. Whereas Schleiermacher perceived mediation as an evolving act, Schweizer viewed it as an established condition.[75]

Schweizer wrote a pair of two-volume works that were clearly inspired by Schleiermacher's desire to bridge old and new theology. In the first, *Die Glaubenslehre der reformierten Kirche* (1844, 1847), Schweizer emphasized his former teacher's efforts to recast dogmatics according to Reformation traditions—that is, in accordance with a "Reformed consciousness."[76] Based on this dogmatic premise, Schweizer reaffirmed his teacher's position that piety should not be reduced to objective theological knowledge, but should rather be approached as a feeling conditioned by self-awareness.[77] Schweizer disagreed with his mediating theology peers who preferred greater objectivity. Like Schleiermacher, Schweizer was thorough in his treatment of absolute dependence, but unlike Schleiermacher he willingly addressed and, in some cases, agreed with ideas offered by certain Reformed authorities.[78] Schweizer further developed his theological views in the two-volume *Die christliche Glaubenslehre* (1863, 1872). In this work Schleiermacher's influence is evident, especially in terms of a concern for method. Schweizer created a theological system focused on Christian consciousness, in which he merged Schleiermacher's notion of absolute dependence with the doctrine of predestination. He relied on Schleiermacher's dogmatic work when applying "freedom in appropriating traditional dogmas"—an approach that acknowledged modern ideas.[79]

In *Die christliche Glaubenslehre*, mediation is clearly present in Schweizer's balancing of old theology in an initial historical phase and modern thought during a second phase.[80] He presented fully developed ideas from earlier dogmatic works when arguing that the feeling of absolute dependence is at the center of dogma. His definition of dogma, as the "science of church doctrine" belonging to the Protestant tradition, and as a symbol of historical theology, was similar to Schleiermacher's description.[81] Schweizer also used his *Glaubenslehre* to argue that the Bible's authority was not dependent on verbal inspiration, but on the historical situations of its authors.[82] As part of his response to traditional doctrines, Schweizer agreed with Richard Rothe (1799–1867) that it was no longer necessary to maintain biblical inspiration, the divinity of Christ, and the doctrine of satisfactory atonement.[83] In the last section of this text he gives a detailed description of Christianity as "the religion of redemption."[84]

---

[75] Barth, *Protestant Theology*, pp. 555, 557.

[76] Alexander Schweizer, *Die Glaubenslehre der evangelisch-reformierten Kirche, dargestellt und aus den Quellen belegt*, vol. 1 (Zurich: Orell, Füssli, 1844), pp. 91–92.

[77] Alexander Schweizer, *Die christliche Glaubenslehre nach protestantischen Grundsätzen*, vol. 1 (Leipzig: Hirzel, 1863), p. 145.

[78] Gerrish, *Tradition and the Modern World*, pp. 122–123.

[79] Otto Pfleiderer, *The Development of Theology in Germany since Kant*, trans. J. Frederick Smith (New York: Macmillan, 1890), p. 125.

[80] Barth, *Protestant Theology*, p. 556.

[81] Schweizer, *Die christliche Glaubenslehre nach protestantischen Grundsätzen*, vol. 1, p. 24.

[82] Schweizer, *Glaubenslehre*, vol. 1, pp. 160–161.

[83] Schweizer, *Glaubenslehre*, vol. 1, p. 111.

[84] Schweizer, *Glaubenslehre*, vol. 1, p. 384.

31.6 History of Dogma and Christology: August Neander and Carl Ullmann

German universities increasingly applied the new historical methods emerging in the 1820s to theology and other disciplines. Regarding the topic of historicism, Thomas Howard describes the change in emphasis from theology to history as a "paradigmatic event."[85] In *Brief Outline*, Schleiermacher explained his view of a scientific-academic theology focused on speculative and historical trends. The text underscores his status as a "mediator for historicism."[86] With historical characteristics playing a vital role, Schleiermacher insisted that the primary task of dogmatic scholarship was to present doctrinal developments in their historical contexts, with the added factor of "the inner life of the Christian principle."[87] Following his lead in emphasizing the organic nature of doctrine, Dorner, Neander, and Hagenbach wrote pioneering texts on historical theology and church history that clearly reflected Schleiermacher's concerns.

As Schleiermacher's student at the University of Halle, August Neander (1789–1850) learned about the organic metaphor and its scientific implications.[88] He would later use the organic concept in many of his manuscripts. In his multivolume *General History of the Christian Religion*, he described Christianity in terms of "continuing organic development" advancing through different stages.[89] He acknowledged that his own approach involved understanding church history not as a collection of external facts, "but as a development proceeding from within [that provided] an image of internal history."[90] In Neander's view, church history was best approached as an ongoing process of development emphasizing life over doctrine. His goal was to merge ideas from Schleiermacher and Romanticism—as well as from F. W. J. Schelling—when presenting church history in terms of organic development.

Schleiermacher's impact can be seen in the ways in which his fellow mediating theologians pursued a "development concept" for the history of dogma influenced by romanticism, idealism, and organic historicism—ideas linked with Herder and Hegel. Ullmann, for example, embraced the motif of progress when addressing topics such as the sixteenth-century Reformation, which he described as "essentially the principle of vital progress, of a continual purifying and perfecting alike of practice and of doctrine, of the Church and of science."[91] In *A History of Christian Doctrines*, Hagenbach insisted that the primary purpose of historical

---

[85] Howard, *Religion*, pp. 1–2, 6.

[86] Zachary Purvis, *Theology and the University in Nineteenth-Century Germany* (Oxford: Oxford University Press, 2016), p. 164.

[87] Schleiermacher, *Kurze Darstellung*, p. 41; *BO*, p. 42.

[88] Friedrich Schleiermacher, *Vorlesungen über die Kirchengeschichte*, KGA 2.6, ed. Simon Gerber (Berlin: de Gruyter, 2006); KGA 2.6, p. 9.

[89] August Neander, *Allgemeine Geschichte der christlichen Religion und Kirche*, vol. 5 (Hamburg: Perthes, 1845), p. 840.

[90] August Neander, *General History of the Christian Religion and Church: From the German of Dr. Augustus Neander*, vol. 1, trans. Joseph Torrey (Boston: Crocker & Brewster, 1851), p. v.

[91] Carl Ullmann, *Reformers before the Reformation: Principally in Germany and the Netherlands*, trans. Robert Menzies (Edinburgh: T&T Clark, 1855), p. xviii.

KGA 2.6, studies of doctrine was to understand the development of "particular doctrinal statements, opinions, and representations of the faith, in which the Church teaching of each period is unfolded."[92]

Whereas rationalist thinkers were uncomfortable with the idea of a sinless Jesus, mediating theologians were willing to discuss—and defend—the assertion. When Strauss rejected Jesus' sinlessness on the foundation of its a priori unfeasibility, they agreed with Schleiermacher in acknowledging the important implications of this idea—not only for Christology, but for the entire system of Christianity.[93] In his *Glaubenslehre*, Schleiermacher affirmed Jesus' sinlessness as part of a system of Christianity in which "redemption is achieved through his communication of his sinless perfection."[94] This belief is also evident in Ullmann's contention that the perfect nature of Jesus must be viewed in light of his perceptions of redemption and associated implications for humanity. According to Ullmann, the person of Jesus represented a new and complete ethical creation that served as the basis for a new creation for all humanity.[95] The apologetic model of Ullmann's work was used by several mediating theologians responding to Strauss' *Life of Jesus*[96]—for example Neander in a book entitled *Das Leben Jesu Christi* (1837) and Tholuck's *Die Glaubwürdigkeit der evangelischen Geschichte* (1837).

31.7 CONCLUSION

For theology, the nineteenth century was an important transition period focused on the concepts of progress and mediation. Faced with intellectual and scientific changes in academia, Protestant theologians turned to mediation in hope of establishing a middle ground between old and new theology, with a mediating approach considered helpful for addressing concerns involving post-Enlightenment ideas and modernity. However, any reading of nineteenth-century theology as a movement dominated by a single form of mediation is in danger of overlooking the mediating theology created by Schleiermacher and his students. With the help of Schleiermacher's principle, mediation was situated between various positions within Protestantism, as well as between religion and culture.[97]

Although Schleiermacher never intended to create a school that carried his name, there is truth in assertions made by Barth and others that all nineteenth-century efforts to link theology with science were influenced by Schleiermacher's mediating system. The mediating school originated with the 1827 publication of the journal *Theologische Studien und Kritiken*, one of several publications promoting a mediating agenda. Schleiermacher's version of mediation was modified by a select group of scholars who offered views balancing liberalism

---

[92] Karl R. Hagenbach, *A History of Christian Doctrines*, vol. 1 (Edinburgh: T&T Clark, 1880), p. 20.
[93] Carl Ullmann, *Die Sündlosigkeit Jesu: Eine apologetische Betrachtung*, 6th ed. (Hamburg: Perthes, 1853), pp. 24–25.
[94] *CG²*, p. 18.
[95] Ullmann, *Die Sündlosigkeit Jesu*, 7th ed. (1863), p. 10.
[96] Hirsch, *Geschichte*, vol. 5, p. 507.
[97] Christian Lülmann, *Schleiermacher, der Kirchenvater des 19. Jahrhunderts* (Tübingen: J. C. B. Mohr, 1907), p. 56.

with orthodoxy and philosophical theology with dogmatic traditionalism.[98] They expressed their interest in overcoming old theological arguments while defending Schleiermacher's scientific definition of theology, the importance of Christian consciousness, a discussion on the nature of religion, and an organic understanding of Christian doctrine.[99]

Important questions for future research include the broader intellectual roots of mediating theologians and their (dis)continuity with Schleiermacher's theology. Differences between Schleiermacher and his students are clear, especially those concerning his theory of religion. Whereas the agendas of many mediating theologians fit well with Schleiermacher's scientific outlook and method, they were subject to religious reassessments and to more objective theological development.[100] Though mediating theologians agreed with Schleiermacher's psychological foundation of religion, they also integrated a theoretical approach and directed at strengthening ties between theology and philosophy. Hagenbach was among encyclopedists pursuing a nuanced effort that resisted a disproportionately historicized analysis of theology, and Nitzsch offered a more complete and systematic discussion of the discipline of practical theology. More speculative mediating theologians also attempted to combine the ideas of Hegel and Schleiermacher. The mediating school arguably offered the richest form of Protestant theology during the first half of the nineteenth century, based on views that moved between opposing theological positions as well as between faith and modernity.[101]

Suggested Reading

Aubert, Annette G. *The German Roots of Nineteenth-Century American Theology* (New York: Oxford University Press, 2013).
Hagenbach, Karl R. *Ueber die sogenannte Vermittlungstheologie: Zur Abwehr und Verständigung* (Zurich: Meyer & Zeller, 1858).
Voigt, Friedemann. *Vermittlung im Streit: Das Konzept theologischer Vermittlung in den Zeitschriften der Schulen Schleiermachers und Hegels* (Tübingen: Mohr Siebeck, 2006).

Bibliography

Aubert, Annette G. *The German Roots of Nineteenth-Century American Theology* (New York: Oxford University Press, 2013).
Aubert, Annette G. "Protestantism." In *The Oxford Handbook of Nineteenth-Century Christian Thought*, ed. Joel D. S. Rasmussen, Judith Wolfe, and Johannes Zachhuber (Oxford: Oxford University Press, 2017), pp. 504–523.
Barth, Karl. *Protestant Theology in the Nineteenth Century*. Trans. by Brian Cozens and John Bowden (Grand Rapids: Eerdmans, 2002).

---

[98] Zachhuber, *Theology as Science*, p. 16.
[99] Nitzsch, *System of Christian Doctrine*, pp. 2, 15.
[100] Aubert, *German Roots*, p. 94.
[101] Friedemann Voigt, "Die Schleiermacher-Rezeption (1834–1889)," in *Schleiermacher Handbuch*, ed. Martin Ohst (Tübingen: Mohr Siebeck, 2017), p. 445.

Christophersen, Alf. *Friedrich Lücke (1791–1855)*, vol. 2: *Dokumente und Briefe*. Theologische Bibliothek Töpelmann 94.1 (Berlin: de Gruyter, 1999).

Clayton, John. "Theologie als Vermittlung—Das Beispiel Schleiermachers." In *Internationaler Schleiermacher-Kongreß Berlin 1984*, Teilband 2, ed. Kurt-Victor Selge (Berlin: de Grutyer, 1985), pp. 899–915.

Cross, George. *The Theology of Schleiermacher: A Condensed Presentation of His Chief Work, "The Christian Faith"* (Chicago: University of Chicago Press, 1911).

Dilthey, Wilhelm. *Vom Aufgang des geschichtlichen Bewusstseins: Jugendaufsätze und Erinnerungen* (Göttingen: Vandenhoeck & Ruprecht, 1972).

Dorner, Isaak A. *Geschichte der protestantischen Theologie besonders in Deutschland* (Munich: Cotta, 1867).

Dorner, Isaak A. *History of Protestant Theology*, vol. 2. Trans. George Robson and Sophia Taylor (Edinburgh: T&T Clark, 1871).

Dorner, Isaak A. *System der Christlichen Glaubenslehre*, vol. 1 (Berlin: Hertz, 1886).

Gerrish, Brian A. *Tradition and the Modern World: Reformed Theology in the Nineteenth Century* (Chicago: University of Chicago Press, 1978).

Hagenbach, Karl R. *A History of Christian Doctrines*, vol. 1 (Edinburgh: T&T Clark, 1880).

Hagenbach, Karl R. *History of the Church: In the Eighteenth and Nineteenth Centuries*, vol. 2. Trans. John F. Hurst (New York: Scribner, 1869).

Hagenbach, Karl R. *Encyklopädie und Methodologie der theologischen Wissenschaften*, 10th ed. Ed. Emil Kautzsch (Leipzig: Hirzel, 1880).

Heussi, Karl. *Kompendium der Kirchengeschichte* (Tübingen: J. C. B. Mohr, 1909).

Hirsch, Emanuel. *Geschichte der neueren evangelischen Theologie im Zusammenhang mit den allgemeinen Bewegungen des europäischen Denkens*, vol. 5 (Gütersloh: C. Bertelsmann, 1954).

Holte, Knut Ragnar. *Die Vermittlungstheologie: Ihre theologischen Grundbegriffe kritisch untersucht*. Trans. Björn Kommer (Uppsala: Almquist & Wiksells, 1965).

Hoffmann, Walther. "Vermittlungstheologie." In *Die Religion in Geschichte und Gegenwart. Handwörterbuch in gemeinverständlicher Darstellung*, vol. 5, ed. Hermann Gunkel, Otto Scheel, and Leopold Zscharnack (Tübingen: J. C. B. Mohr, 1913), pp. 1642–1646.

Howard, Thomas Albert. *Protestant Theology and the Making of the Modern German University* (Oxford: Oxford University Press, 2006).

Howard, Thomas Albert. *Religion and the Rise of Historicism: W. M. L. de Wette, Jacob Burckhardt, and the Theological Origins of Nineteenth-Century Historical Consciousness* (Cambridge: Cambridge University Press, 2000).

Lacroix, John P. "Carl Immanuel Nitzsch." *Methodist Review* 55 (1873), pp. 576–595.

Lange, Johann P. *Grundriss der theologischen Encyklopädie mit Einschluss der Methodologie* (Heidelberg: Carl Winter, 1877).

Lempp, Otto. "Schleiermachersche Schule." In *Die Religion in Geschichte und Gegenwart. Handwörterbuch in Gemeinverständlicher Darstellung*, vol. 5, ed. Hermann Gunkel, Otto Scheel, and Leopold Zscharnack (Tübingen: J. C. B. Mohr, 1913), pp. 313–316.

Lücke, Friedrich. "Erinnerungen an Dr. Friedrich Schleiermacher." *Theologische Studien und Kritiken* 7 (1834), pp. 745–813.

Lülmann, Christian. *Schleiermacher, der Kirchenvater des 19. Jahrhunderts* (Tübingen: J. C. B. Mohr, 1907).

Neander, August. *Allgemeine Geschichte der christlichen Religion und Kirche*, vol. 5 (Hamburg: Perthes, 1845).

Neander, August. *General History of the Christian Religion and Church: From the German of Dr. Augustus Neander*, vol. 1. Trans. Joseph Torrey (Boston: Crocker & Brewster, 1851).

Nitzsch, Carl Immanuel. "Delbrück über Schleiermachers christliche Glaubenslehre." *Theologische Studien und Kritiken* 1 (1828), pp. 640–668.

Nitzsch, Carl Immanuel. *Praktische Theologie*, 2nd ed., vol. 1 (Bonn: Adolph Marcus, 1859).

Nitzsch, Carl Immanuel. *Praktische Theologie*, 2nd ed., vol. 3 (Bonn: Adolph Marcus, 1868).

Nitzsch, Carl Immanuel. *System der christlichen Lehre*, 5th ed. (Bonn: Adolph Marcus, 1844).

Nitzsch, Carl Immanuel. *System of Christian Doctrine*. Trans. Robert Montgomery (Edinburgh: T&T Clark, 1849).

Pfleiderer, Otto. *The Development of Theology in Germany since Kant, and Its Progress in Great Britain since 1825*. Trans. J. Frederick Smith (New York: Macmillan, 1890).

Purvis, Zachary. *Theology and the University in Nineteenth-Century Germany* (Oxford: Oxford University Press, 2016).

Rothermundt, Jörg. *Personale Synthese: Isaak August Dorners dogmatische Methode* (Göttingen: Vandenhoeck & Ruprecht, 1968).

Schleiermacher, Friedrich. *Der christliche Glaube nach den Grundsätzen der evangelischen Kirche im Zusammenhange dargestellt*. Zweite Auflage (1830/1831). 7th ed. Ed. Martin Redeker (Berlin: de Gruyter, 1999).

Schleiermacher, Friedrich. *Kurze Darstellung des theologischen Studiums zum Behuf einleitender Vorlesungen* (Berlin: Reimer, 1830).

Schleiermacher, Friedrich. *Predigten, 1790–1808*, KGA 3.3, ed. Günter Meckenstock (Berlin: de Gruyter, 2013).

Schleiermacher, Friedrich. *Reden und Abhandlungen, der Königlichen Akademie der Wissenschaften vorgetragen von Friedrich Schleiermacher aus Schleiermachers handschriftlichem Nachlasse herausgegeben von Ludwig Jonas* (Berlin: Reimer, 1835).

Schleiermacher, Friedrich. *Theologische Enzyklopädie (1831/1832)*. Ed. Walter Sachs. Schleiermacher-Archiv 4 (Berlin: de Gruyter, 1987).

Schleiermacher, Friedrich. *Theologische-dogmatische Abhandlungen und Gelegenheitsschriften*. KGA 1.10, ed. Hans-Friedrich Traulsen, in collaboration with Martin Ohst (Berlin: de Gruyter, 1990).

Schleiermacher, Friedrich. *Vorlesungen über die Kirchengeschichte*. KGA 2.6, ed. Simon Gerber (Berlin: de Gruyter, 2006).

Schweizer, Alexander. *Die Glaubenslehre der evangelisch-reformierten Kirche, dargestellt und aus den Quellen belegt*, vol. 1 (Zurich: Orell, Füssli, 1844).

Schweizer, Alexander. *Die christliche Glaubenslehre nach protestantischen Grundsätzen*, vol. 1 (Leipzig: Hirzel, 1863).

Troeltsch, Ernst. "Protestantisches Christentum und Kirche in der Neuzeit." In *Die Kultur der Gegenwart: Ihre Entwicklung und Ziele*, ed. Paul Hinneberg (Berlin: Teubner, 1922), pp. 431–792.

Twesten, August. *Zur Erinnerung an Friedrich Daniel Ernst Schleiermacher: Vortrag gehalten in der Königlichen Friedrich-Wilhelms-Universität zu Berlin* (Berlin: Buchdruckerei der Königlichen Akademie der Wissenschaften, 1869).

Ullmann, Carl. "Ueber Partei und Schule, Gegensätze und deren Vermittlung." *Theologische Studien und Kritiken* 9, no. 1 (1836), pp. 5–61.

Ullmann, Carl. "Vierzig Sätze, die theologische Lehrfreiheit innerhalb der evangelisch-protestantischen Kirche betreffend." *Theologische Studien und Kritiken* 16, no. 1 (1843), pp. 7–35.

Ullmann, Carl. *Die Sündlosigkeit Jesu: Eine apologetische Betrachtung*, 6th & 7th eds. (Hamburg: Perthes, 1853, 1863).

Ullmann, Carl. *Das Wesen des Christenthums: Mit Beziehung auf neuere Auffassungsweisen desselben von Freunden und Gegnern; Eine Erörterung auch für gebildete Nicht-Theologen*, 3rd & 4th eds. (Hamburg: Perthes, 1849, 1854).

Ullmann, Carl. *Reformers before the Reformation: Principally in Germany and the Netherlands*. Trans. Robert Menzies (Edinburgh: T&T Clark, 1855).

Voigt, Friedemann. *Vermittlung im Streit: Das Konzept theologischer Vermittlung in den Zeitschriften der Schulen Schleiermachers und Hegels* (Tübingen: Mohr Siebeck, 2006).

Voigt, Friedemann. "Die Schleiermacher-Rezeption (1834–1889)." In *Schleiermacher Handbuch*, ed. Martin Ohst (Tübingen: Mohr Siebeck, 2017), pp. 442–455.

Weidner, Revere Franklin. *An Introduction to Dogmatic Theology: Based on Luthardt* (Rock Island: Augustana, 1888).

Welch, Claude. *Protestant Thought in the Nineteenth Century*, vol. 1: *1799–1870* (New Haven: Yale University Press, 1972).

Zachhuber, Johannes. *Theology as Science in Nineteenth-Century Germany: From F. C. Baur to Ernst Troeltsch* (New York: Oxford University Press, 2013).

CHAPTER 32

SCHLEIERMACHER AND PROTESTANT LIBERALISM

ARNULF VON SCHELIHA

32.1 Concept and Use

There is an opinion frequently held that Friedrich Schleiermacher is the father of Protestant liberalism. This opinion seems at first glance to be correct. On closer inspection, however, we have to bear in mind that Schleiermacher himself did not call his theology a "liberal theology," nor did the other Protestant theologians who, without being his academic disciples, followed Schleiermacher in his way of thinking.[1]

The first mention of the term "liberal theology" can already be found in the book by Johann Salomo Semler (1725–91), *Institutio ad doctrinam Christianam liberaliter discendam* (1774).[2] Here, Semler uses the term to refer to the strict historical interpretation of the New Testament without dogmatic obstacles with the aim of perfecting Christianity and strengthening private piety in contrast to official clergy guidelines.[3] In the nineteenth century, only Karl Gottlieb Bretschneider (1776–1848), a critic of Schleiermacher's, suggested using "liberalism" to denote his program of theological rationalism, and combined it with political liberalism.[4] This is similar to the suggestion made by the outsider David Friedrich Strauß (1808–1874), who in 1848 published a treatise, *Der politische und der theologische Liberalismus*, in which he affirmed a "pure humanism" that he called theological liberalism.[5] The term is used in the sense of church politics, for example, to characterize Daniel Schenkel (1813–1885) and the *Protestantenverein* that he co-founded in 1863. In the late

---

[1] See Hans-Joachim Birkner, "Liberale Theologie" (1974/1976), in Hans-Joachim Birkner, *Schleiermacher-Studien*, ed. Hermann Fischer (Berlin: Walter de Gruyter, 1996), pp. 51–62.

[2] See Johann Salomo Semler, *Institutio ad doctrinam Christianam liberaliter discendam, auditorum usui destinate* (Halle: Hemmerde, 1774).

[3] See Markus Iff, *Liberale Theologie in Jena. Ein Beitrag zur Theologie- und Wissenschaftsgeschichte des ausgehenden 19. Jahrhunderts* (Berlin: Walter de Gruyter, 2011), pp. 1–2.

[4] See Karl Gottlieb Bretschneider, "Die Ultra's und die Liberalen in der Theologie," in *Für Christenthum und Gottesgelahrtheit. Eine Oppositionsschrift*, vol. 3 (Jena, 1820), pp. 195–204.

[5] See David Friedrich Strauß, *Der politische und der theologische Liberalismus* (Halle: Kümmel, 1848).

nineteenth century, Alois Emanuel Biedermann (1819–1885), Richard Adalbert Lipsius (1830–1892), and Otto Pfleiderer (1839–1908) were often seen as belonging to "liberal theology."[6] Biedermann himself also used the term "free theology."[7] But these representatives of the so-called "free theology" were far removed from Schleiermacher's theological focus and interests. They are therefore not considered in this essay, despite their affiliation with Protestant liberalism.

The increasing tendency to use the term "Protestant liberalism" or "theological liberalism" only became visible in the twentieth century, when it was put into circulation and used in three dimensions. First, representatives of the so-called theology of crisis used it in a polemical way to distinguish themselves from the kind of theological thinking that had begun with Schleiermacher and ended with Adolf von Harnack (1851–1930) and Ernst Troeltsch (1865–1923), with the terms "liberal theology" and "cultural Protestantism" (*Kulturprotestantismus*) often being used synonymously in this context. The second dimension is the opposite assessment of the period from Schleiermacher to Troeltsch that has emerged since the 1970s. Backed by the so-called "Schleiermacher-Renaissance" that has been visible since the 1960s,[8] "Protestant liberalism" has since acquired an increasingly positive reputation.[9] Third, the Swiss scholar Ulrich Neuenschwander (1922–1977) drew the distinction between "old and new liberalism." On the one hand, he identified the period from Schleiermacher to Harnack as being in continuity with the "free theology" (to which he also saw himself as belonging), while on the other emphasizing the experiences of disharmony and crisis between humankind, the world and God, without thereby resorting to orthodox teaching or church creeds.[10]

The history of the concept of Protestant liberalism and the actual phenomenon do not coincide. In this chapter, the term is understood in an analytical way that makes it possible to name Schleiermacher's basic theological insights and to identify on this basis a main stream in the history of theology in the nineteenth century inspired by him. Doing so is to bear in mind that this kind of theology did not form a uniform movement, because later theologians diverged from Schleiermacher's unfolding of his basic insights responding to new intellectual and cultural challenges. That means as well that under repeatedly changed conditions, these essential features are still effective in the present and enjoy widespread recognition.

---

[6] Examples are given by Iff, *Liberale Theologie in Jena*, pp. 4–6.
[7] See Alois Emanuel Biedermann, *Die freie Theologie oder Christentum und Philosophie in Streit und Frieden* (Tübingen: Fuess, 1844).
[8] A leading venue for this new interest in Schleiermacher was the Göttingen Faculty of Theology and its prominent teachers such as Emanuel Hirsch, Wolfgang Trillhaas, Hans-Joachim Birkner, and Hans-Walter Schütte. Another important figure was Gerhard Ebeling, the last leader of the hermeneutic school who discovered Schleiermacher during these years. See Jana Huisgen, *Der christliche Glaube als reflektierte Erfahrung. Eine Studie zur Schleiermacherrezeption Gerhard Ebelings* (Berlin: Peter Lang, 2020).
[9] See Jörg Lauster, "Liberale Theologie. Eine Ermunterung," *NZSThR* 50 (2007), pp. 291–307.
[10] See Ulrich Neuenschwander, *Die neue liberale Theologie. Eine Standortbestimmung* (Bern: Stämpfli, 1953), pp. 1–3.

32.2 CONCEPT AND CONTENT

The first essential feature had already been established by Semler and was then continued by Schleiermacher: namely, the historical interpretation of the biblical tradition. Schleiermacher had held a chair in Dogmatics and the New Testament at Berlin University since 1809. Almost 50 percent of his theological lectures he gave were on the books of the New Testament, including on *The Life of Jesus*.

The systematic result of Schleiermacher's exegetical work forms the second essential feature that is visible in his major work, *The Christian Faith*.[11] As an object of historical interpretation, the Bible can no longer exercise formal authority with regard to doctrine. Thus, Schleiermacher replaced the doctrinal *De Sacra scriptura* as the fundamental article of the dogmatic prolegomena with the "distinctive nature"[12] of Christianity (*Wesen des Christentums*), which he construed by using a methodological mixture of historical and conceptual arguments.[13] Schleiermacher's famous formula is christologically founded and reads, "Christianity is a monotheistic mode of faith belonging to the teleological bent of religion. It is distinguished essentially from other such modes of faith in that within Christianity everything is referred to the redemption accomplished through Jesus of Nazareth."[14] This approach to doctrine through the "distinctive nature of Christianity" is the second feature of Protestant liberalism and of great significance to that which would come.

The third feature established by Schleiermacher and characteristic of Protestant liberalism is the founding of doctrine in a general concept of religion, combined with a theory of religious diversity. Schleiermacher contributed pioneering work to this field in the "Propositions Borrowed from the Philosophy of Religion" that he wrote in the introduction to his doctrine of faith (*Glaubenslehre*).[15] The feeling of absolute dependency is an essential element of human self-consciousness. It is the core and "selfsame nature of piety"[16] or religion, but is only present or realized in the historical variety of real religions. In this context, Schleiermacher suggests the formula that "Christianity is a monotheistic mode of faith belonging to the teleological bent of religion."[17] This formulation is embedded in a religious-historical comparison with other monotheistic modes of faith (Judaism, Islam), and with polytheistic and primitive modes of faith.[18] The consequence for dogmatic methods is that Christian doctrine has the status of expressing a specific religious experience founded by the redeemer Jesus Christ and communicated by the common spirit of Christianity.

---

[11] See *CF (2016)*.

[12] *CF (2016)* §11, p. 79.

[13] See Markus Schröder, *Die kritische Identität des neuzeitlichen Christentums. Schleiermachers Wesensbestimmung der christlichen Religion* (Tübingen: Mohr Siebeck, 1996).

[14] *CF (2016)* §11, p. 79.

[15] *CF (2016)* §§7–10.

[16] *CF (2016)* §4, p. 18.

[17] *CF (2016)* §11, p. 79.

[18] See Arnulf von Scheliha, "Schleiermacher als Denker von Pluralität," in *Reformation und Moderne. Pluralität–Subjektivität–Kritik. Akten des Internationalen Kongresses der Schleiermacher-Gesellschaft in Halle (Saale) März 2017*, ed. Jörg Dierken, Arnulf von Scheliha, and Sarah Schmidt (Berlin/Boston: De Gruyter, 2018), pp. 25–44.

The fourth feature introduced by Schleiermacher is the equality and the interdisciplinarity of all theological disciplines. In his theological encyclopedia *Brief Outline of the Study of Theology*, he designs in an elaborated way a differentiated ensemble of theological disciplines that cannot substitute or ignore one another. Each discipline is theological in a full sense, and it is only in collaboration that all disciplines can fulfil their specific function of preparing students for church government (*Kirchenleitung*), which, as a "positive science," is precisely the function of academic theology.[19] Furthermore each theological discipline is assigned to a respective academic discipline outside theology (for example history, philology, philosophy, psychology), with which it shares methods and themes. The academic status and interdisciplinarity of theological disciplines are for Schleiermacher and liberal Protestants the means to modernize theology, church, and society.

The fifth feature is Schleiermacher's attempt to raise the status of theological ethics and to furnish it with the same range as doctrine. Both, the Christian doctrine of faith and Christian ethics, "taken together, present the whole reality of Christian life."[20] The growing "ethical interest had to effect a divorce between the two disciplines."[21] His formula of the "distinctive nature of Christianity" as a "mode of faith belonging to the teleological bent of religion" requires unfolding the ethical dimension of Christian faith because the term "teleological" means "that the predominant relation to a moral task forms the fundamental typus of religious states of mind and heart."[22] For Schleiermacher, this typus "is most clearly marked in Christianity, less completely in Judaism."[23] Both Christian doctrine and ethics are embedded in Schleiermacher's theory of culture, which he called "philosophical ethics." This speculative and fundamental science provides the concept for empirical studies in human culture and for historical analysis. As theological disciplines, doctrine and ethics are linked to philosophical ethics by the concept of the Christian church that is founded in Schleiermacher's well-known "Propositions Borrowed from Ethics" at the beginning of his "Introduction" to his doctrine of faith.[24] Hence, ethics appears twice in Schleiermacher's system of sciences, which shows its great importance. Protestant liberalism in the nineteenth century followed Schleiermacher's lead and emphasized the significance of ethics for modern Christianity in strengthening the individual personality that realizes the Christian spirit in society by performing the tasks given by God in the domains of family, work, and state.

Related to this theological-ethical thought is the sixth feature, which is the religious assumption that human deeds inspired by Christianity and performed by Christians will improve the world and all societies that have contact with the Christian faith and ethics. It is this belief in the progress of history that characterizes Protestant liberalism and that allows it to overcome the pessimistic anthropology of old Protestantism. "The Augustinian explanation of origin and universality of sin was no longer credible."[25] Schleiermacher and his followers interpret the doctrine of sin anew, cultivating the opinion that Christianity as

---

[19] *BO* §1.
[20] *CF (2016)* §26.2, p. 164.
[21] *CF (2016)*, p. 165.
[22] *CF (2016)* §9.1, p. 63.
[23] *CF (2016)* §9.2, p. 67.
[24] *CF (2016)* §§3–6.
[25] Walter E. Wyman, Jr., "Rethinking the Christian Doctrine of Sin: Ernst Troeltsch and the German Protestant Liberal Tradition," *ZNThG/JHMTh* 1 (1994), p. 227.

a spiritual power can combat and reduce the individual and social influence of human sin.[26] The Christian history of salvation is being transformed into a history of development that is achieving real and visible results in human civilization. For Christians,

> something new enters into precisely this world with Christ's appearance, thus something that stands in contrast with the old situation. It follows that, for us, only that part of the world that is at one with the Christian Church then becomes the locus of what perfection has come into being thereby or of what is good, and, for us, with respect to latent self-consciousness, only that part has become the locus of blessedness.[27]

This optimism is a legacy of the theology and philosophy of the Enlightenment, but Schleiermacher and Protestant liberalism gave it a christological foundation in the redeemer, with the effect that the doctrine of eschatology became less important for faith and doctrine. The Kingdom of God (*Reich Gottes*) becomes the goal of history in general, taking hold of Christianity and eternity.

32.3 Main Representatives in the Nineteenth Century

The tradition established by Schleiermacher was taken up by Richard Rothe (1799–1867) and Albrecht Ritschl (1822–1889) in the mid-nineteenth century, with each focusing on the ethical side of Schleiermacher's thinking in a different way. But both also adopted and adapted ideas from other thinkers such as Georg Friedrich Wilhelm Hegel (1770–1831), Ferdinand Christian Baur (1792–1860) and the Tübingen School,[28] and Hermann Lotze (1817–1881).[29] Thus, the way that Rothe and Ritschl updated Schleiermacher's ideas also represented a new start, with Ritschl in particular seeing his theology as opposing not only the prevailing theologies of the second half of the century, but also parts of Schleiermacher's theology.[30]

32.3.1 Richard Rothe

Richard Rothe held a chair in the New Testament and dogmatics at Heidelberg University (1837–1849 and 1854–1867), interrupted by a period when he was professor of practical

---

[26] See Derek R. Nelson, "Schleiermacher and Ritschl on Individual and Social Sin," *JHMTh/ZNThG* 16 (2009), pp. 131–154.
[27] *CF (2016)* vol. 2, §113.3, pp. 753–754.
[28] See Johannes Zachhuber, *Theology as Science in Nineteenth-Century Germany: From F.C. Baur to Ernst Troeltsch* (Oxford: Oxford University Press, 2013).
[29] See Matthias Neugebauer, *Lotze und Ritschl. Reich–Gottes–Theologie zwischen nachidealistischer Philosophie und neuzeitlichem Positivismus* (Frankfurt Main: Lang, 2002).
[30] See Arnulf von Scheliha, "Albrecht Ritschls Deutung von Friedrich Schleiermachers Reden 'Über die Religion,'" in *200 Jahre "Reden über die Religion," Akten des 1. Internationalen Kongresses der Schleiermacher-Gesellschaft Halle 14.–17. März 1999*, ed. Ulrich Barth and Claus-Dieter Osthövener (Berlin/New York: De Gruyter, 2000), pp. 728–747.

theology in Bonn. The liberal atmosphere in the Grand duchy of Baden was a suitable context for Rothe's liberal way of thinking about theology, and for his ecclesiastical and political engagement.

In his major work, *Theological Ethics*, Rothe adopts Schleiermacher's ethical approach to the philosophy of culture and theory of Christianity,[31] and seeks to interpret the totality of reality meaningfully as leading to the Kingdom of God. This *magnum opus* represents more than a theory of culture or an ethic in a narrow sense. Rather, Rothe combines in a dynamic synthesis philosophical speculation on cosmology and the theory of subjectivity, dogmatic reflection, historical vision, and the formulation of ethical norms.

Rothe's view of human cultural history as salvation history aims at the eschatological goal of a perfect spiritual community between God and humanity. God, the absolute subject of authentic personhood, reveals to humanity the perfect *communio* of spiritual beings, which opens itself to God in free religious and ethical self-determination. The religious and moral processes run parallel to one another. The religious process is directed towards God, while moral acts shape the culture. The point of both is the proximate and in the end eschatologically complete realization of the Kingdom of God. Rothe conceives the Kingdom as a universal organism made up of Christian states, all of which have transcended national and ecclesiastical particularism.

One driving force behind Rothe's socio-eschatological utopia of the universal religious and ethical community of all humanity is his diagnosis of the growing social polarization and the crisis of traditional ecclesiastical Christianity.[32] Hence, he argues that the national state should be responsible for social welfare, moral education, and religious life on the basis of Christian values. The state institutions should be made open to civil participation. Political freedom and sovereignty of the people are fundamental norms of Rothe's political thinking. Prince and parliament should cooperate. Religious pluralism could be granted in modern society in a restricted sense. On the one hand, a special combination of theological and national-political liberalism becomes visible here. On the other, the moral competence that Rothe attributes to the state cannot be deemed classically liberal in the sense of advocating the functional separation of religion and state that is specific to the liberal program.

32.3.2 *Allgemeiner Deutscher Protestantenverein*

The *Allgemeiner Deutscher Protestantenverein*, founded in 1863, was the branch of Protestant liberalism in civil society and regional churches for roughly thirty years. Rothe was a co-founder of the association, other leading figures were Daniel Schenkel, its co-founder and vice president until 1874, the renowned Swiss scholar Johann Caspar Bluntschli (1808–1881), co-founder and president until 1874, and Adolf Sydow (1800–1882), who studied theology under Schleiermacher in Berlin and became a pastor in several higher positions. The aim of the *Protestantenverein* was to meet the challenges of modern culture and life, and its members were convinced that Protestant churches could only cope with modernization if

---

[31] See Richard Rothe, *Theologische Ethik*, 3 vols. (Wittenberg: Zimmermann, 1845–1848); 2nd ed., 5 vols. (Wittenberg: Zimmermann, 1867–1871); reprint, ed. Jürgen Albert (Waltrop: Spenner, 1991).

[32] See Arnulf von Scheliha, *Protestantische Ethik des Politischen* (Tübingen: Mohr Siebeck, 2013), pp. 132–144.

the "alliance of throne and altar" is dissolved, if churches organize their life separately from the state, open their doctrines and structures to laypeople, and also grant them the chance to participate and cooperate. This was a position that Schleiermacher had already taken.

After the foundation of the empire the *Protestantenverein* saw itself as part of the Protestant civil religion of the new state, which was to be integrated through a unified Protestant culture. Those who opposed that goal, especially the Catholics faithful to Rome, were seen as enemies of the empire, excluded from the cultural state. The association therefore supported the government in the *Kulturkampf* (1881–1887) between the Prussian state and the Roman Catholic Church. But, when Bismarck ended the *Kulturkampf*, the *Protestantenverein* reacted with disappointment and, like political liberalism, increasingly lost its influence. The *Protestantenverein* is a good example of the connection between Protestant liberalism and political liberalism. Its political allies were the liberal parties, with the *Protestantenverein* being connected to them both on a personal level and through a symbiosis of ideas regarding political and ecclesiastical reform.

32.3.3 Albrecht Ritschl

Unlike Rothe, Ritschl founded an influential academic school. His academic influence covers almost all theological disciplines. In 1852 he became Professor of New Testament and Early Church History in Bonn, and in 1864 he was appointed to a chair in dogmatics and ethics in Göttingen. The three volumes of Ritschl's main work, *The Christian Doctrine of Justification and Reconciliation*, represent these three steps.[33] The first volume reconstructs "the history of the doctrine"; the second, "the biblical matter of the doctrine"; the third, "the positive unfolding of the doctrine." As Zachhuber argues, Ritschl's "work on doctrine must be seen in its conjunction with his historical theology."[34] His theological work inspired two generations of theologians, which continued until about 1930. Like Schleiermacher Ritschl's work was inspiring because it combined and integrated different streams of thought. He was therefore able to discuss the problems of his time with great sophistication, and especially to respond to the challenges posed by the modern criticism of religion, the incipient de-Christianization of society, the increasing prevalence of materialistic or naturalistic ideologies (*Weltanschauungen*), the visible tension between the humanities and the flourishing natural sciences, and the effects that the modernization of society had on people's lives. Ritschl's project was to use late Idealist philosophy to provide an extensive theological apology of Christianity. In fact, he addressed his theology to Germany's educated middle class, whose most prominent feature was their historical consciousness.[35]

Like Schleiermacher, Ritschl founded his theology on a general theory of religion.[36] Although he always rejected the concept of a natural religion, he began from 1874 to work

---

[33] See Albrecht Ritschl, *Die christliche Lehre von der Rechtfertigung und Versöhnung*, 3 vols. (Bonn: Adolph Marcus, 1870–1874).

[34] Zachhuber, *Theology as Science*, p. 133.

[35] See Leiff Svensson, *A Theology for the Bildungsbürgertum: Albrecht Ritschl in Context* (Berlin/Boston: Walter de Gruyter, 2020).

[36] See the analytic reconstruction of Ritschl's theory of religion by Kevin W. Hector, *The Theological Project of Modernism: Faith and the Conditions of Mineness* (Oxford: Oxford University Press, 2015), pp. 179–211.

out a general or "formal, metaphysical" concept of religion.[37] The task of all religion is a "solution of the contradiction in which man finds himself, as both a part of the world of nature and a spiritual personality claiming to dominate nature."[38] All world religions deal with this gap between natural and spiritual life, and suggest different solutions. The Christian solution cannot be given from a standpoint beyond Christianity, and nor can it be proven philosophically; rather, it can only be explained from within the Christian perspective itself. This is the reason that Ritschl switched to a dogmatic perspective and presented the Christian solution of the general religious answer referring to the Kingdom of God.

Ritschl's concept of the Kingdom of God combines the different historical, theological, and philosophical elements of his thinking. He concedes that Schleiermacher had already combined the philosophical doctrine of ethical goods with the theological doctrine of the Kingdom of God,[39] but he noted that Schleiermacher's doctrinal unfolding of this approach lacked a "firm hand," which he saw himself as being responsible for providing. His interpretation of the Kingdom of God refers to the philosophical distinction of spirit and nature and integrates his historical contribution to New Testament research. Here, he focuses on Jesus' activity as well as the first generation of the church and brings out the central theological relevance of the New Testament. The most important religious themes of Jesus' activity are the propagation of the Kingdom of God and the forgiveness of sins, which becomes reality for those who accept it in the authority of Jesus. Like Schleiermacher, Ritschl affirms an effective interpretation of justification and reconciliation, and emphasizes the visibility of Christian ideas in human deeds. Again like Schleiermacher, Ritschl rejects in this context the premodern doctrine of sin. Instead he emphasizes the developmental and social dimension of sin, whose power can be stopped and reduced by the progressive advent of the Kingdom of God. This underlines Ritschl's liberal idea of Protestantism, with its immense range of application.

His understanding of the Kingdom of God aims for a complete coincidence of proclamation and practice. Thus, Jesus' proclamation of the Kingdom of God corresponds to his foundation of the church, while the disciples' acceptance of the forgiveness of sins correlates with their readiness to live a new life in the divine kingdom. The Kingdom of God is thus both religious *and* ethical; it is a divine gift *and* the product of human effort. This leads to his formula of the essence of Christianity:

> Christianity, then, is the monotheistic, completely spiritual, and ethical religion, which, based on the life of its Author as Redeemer and as Founder of the Kingdom of God, consists in the freedom of the children of God, involves the impulse to conduct from the motive of love, which aims at the moral organisation of mankind, and grounds blessedness on the relation of sonship to God, as well as on the Kingdom of God.[40]

---

[37] See Ruth Görnandt, *Die Metaphysikkritik Gerhard Ebelings und ihre Vorgeschichte* (Tübingen: Mohr Siebeck, 2016), pp. 16–61; and Svensson, *A Theology for the Bildungsbürgertum*, pp. 200–214.

[38] Albrecht Ritschl, *The Christian Doctrine of Justification and Reconciliation: The Positive Development of the Doctrine*, trans. A. B. Macaulay and H. R. Mackintosh (Edinburgh: T&T Clark, 1902), p. 199.

[39] Ritschl, *The Christian Doctrine of Justification and Reconciliation*, p. 199: "It remained for Schleiermacher first to employ the true conception of the teleological nature of the Kingdom of God to determine the idea of Christianity."

[40] Ritschl, *The Christian Doctrine of Justification and Reconciliation*, pp. 13–14.

This Kingdom of God is realized in history by the Christian community founded by Jesus, which always remains dependent on him. The aim of Christian faith is to constitute ethical individuals and to strengthen them in struggling against nature and nurturing culture and society. Ritschl understands faith as trust in God's forgiveness and in his providence.[41] This trust helps to overcome obstacles and contingencies, and Christians thereby "become free vis-à-vis the world."[42] The individual contribution to the Kingdom of God and the improvement of society are fulfilled through the commandment to love one's neighbor, which Ritschl interprets strictly in the perspective of the Protestant "ethics of vocation" (*Berufsethik*).[43]

The goal or telos of the Christian history of salvation as a whole is to approximate to history of the world. Christianity argues for the superiority of spirit over nature, and performs the task of all religions, which is to solve "the contradiction in which man finds himself, as both a part of the world of nature and a spiritual personality claiming to dominate nature."[44] The nucleus of this teleology is the doctrine of God. Here, Ritschl follows Schleiermacher's principle that God is only and purely love. God's will and love are the reason for creation and the aim of human history. The divine teleology aims for the moral organization of humanity in the Kingdom of God. While Rothe argues that the liberal and cultivated state could take over the role of the church, Ritschl insists that the church has its own role independent of the state. Ritschl differentiates between the religious, ethical and legal dimensions of the church, and emphasizes the invisible community of Christians, a community that works differently to an ethical or legal community.

32.3.4 Ritschl's Followers

Ritschl's followers added different aspects to the Protestant liberalism inspired by Schleiermacher.

Wilhelm Herrmann (1846–1922), Professor of Systematic Theology at the University of Marburg from 1879, combines Luther's theological insights with ideas from Kant's philosophical ethics and designs a program of theological ethics that considers modern life and the crisis of moral consciousness.

Herrmann follows Kant's critical philosophy and denies the possibility of reaching knowledge of God through metaphysics or pure reason.[45] Rather, divine revelation is the only mode of access to God. The theological task is to show the anthropological and moral plausibility of this experience, and not to prove that it has universal validity. Unlike Schleiermacher and Ritschl, who favored an harmonious agreement of all scientific disciplines, Herrmann saw metaphysics, science, and religion in a more or potentially antagonistic relationship.[46]

---

[41] See Arnulf von Scheliha, *Der Glaube an die göttliche Vorsehung. Eine religionssoziologische, geschichtsphilosophische und theologiegeschichtliche Untersuchung* (Stuttgart: W. Kohlhammer, 1999), pp. 214–274.

[42] See Hector, *The Theological Project of Modernism*, p. 210.

[43] On Ritschl's concept of ethics, see Helga Kuhlmann, *Die theologische Ethik Albrecht Ritschls* (Munich: Chr. Kaiser, 1992).

[44] Ritschl, *The Christian Doctrine of Justification and Reconciliation*, p. 199.

[45] See Mark D. Chapman, "'Theology within the Walls.' Wilhelm Herrmann's Religious Reality," *NZSThR* 34 (1992), pp. 69–84.

[46] See Görnandt, *Die Metaphysikkritik Gerhard Ebelings*, pp. 62–119.

For him, they represent separate spheres, and the danger for human and religious life is that the sciences in the form of scientific monism, or politics in the form of materialistic ideologies, try to occupy or replace the religious sphere or the higher life. In reaction to this, Herrmann develops a dualistic view of reality. Religion, and especially Christianity, is no longer seen as a function of theoretical understanding, but rather as a higher "reality of an individual experience" through "attending to inner perceptions."[47] This religious reality is opened by a direct personal impression of Jesus, which creates a life-history in the individual of being in steady communion with God. "Jesus himself becomes a real power to us when he reveals in his authority over us his inner life to us."[48] This experience evokes an unconditional trust in God, including a true knowledge of God as love and at one and the same time as love for one's neighbor. Thus, Herrmann understands faith in God as a special expression of ethical conviction. Religion is the power to do good.

The Christian faith is therefore the instrument to overcome the moral crisis of modern society and to strengthen individuals. Furthermore Herrmann does not refrain from making political suggestions to improve the social conditions of work and life. He was involved in the *Evangelisch-Sozialer Kongress* and in 1891 he gave a lecture at the second annual meeting that programmatically dealt with economic and religious matters. For Herrmann, the so-called "social question" is a political and a theological one, and he cautiously pleads for the church to forge links with the socialist movement.[49]

Julius Kaftan (1848–1926), who held chairs in Basel (from 1874) and Berlin (from 1883),[50] understands religion in a universal and general sense as a practical science of value in its relatedness to God as the highest good. Christian dogmatics is a science of Christian truth recognized in faith that is nurtured by Scripture and represents an autonomous sphere of the spiritual in contrast to theoretical sciences. In contrast to Schleiermacher and Ritschl, Kaftan emphasized the mystical element of faith. As a member of the high consistory of the Old Prussian Evangelical Church (1904–1925), he dealt with the new constitution of the church after the revolution and the separation of state and church. He rejected the "irreligious" republic of Weimar and appealed to people to resist it. Here, theological and political liberalism begin to separate.

32.4 Adolf Harnack and Ernst Troeltsch as Scholarly Politicians of a Liberal Hue

Adolf Harnack and Ernst Troeltsch are those representatives of Protestant liberalism in the long nineteenth century whose influence exceeded the borders of academic

---

[47] Wilhelm Herrmann, "Religion," in *Schriften zur Grundlegung der Theologie*, vol. 1, ed. Peter Fischer-Appelt (Munich: Chr. Kaiser, 1966) p. 289.
[48] Wilhelm Herrmann, *Der Verkehr des Christen mit Gott im Anschluss an Luther dargestellt*, 6th ed. (Stuttgart/Berlin: J.-G. Cottasche Buchhandlung Nachfolger, 1908), p. 59.
[49] See Wilhelm Herrmann, "Religion und Sozialdemokratie," *ZThK* 1 (1891), pp. 254–286.
[50] See Folkart Wittekind, *Geschichtliche Offenbarung und die Wahrheit des Glaubens. Der Zusammenhang von Offenbarungstheologie, Geschichtsphilosophie und Ethik bei Albrecht Ritschl, Julius Kaftan und Karl Barth* (Tübingen: Mohr Siebeck, 2000).

theology. They personified the type of scholarly politician in the fields of scientific organization (*Wissenschaftsorganisation*; Harnack), cultural policy (*Kulturpolitik*; Harnack and Troeltsch), parliament, and post-revolutionary state administration (Troeltsch).[51]

Harnack picked up and developed the historical feature of liberalism inspired by Schleiermacher. Alter professorships in Leipzig (1876), Giessen (1882), and Marburg (1996) he accepted an appointment to the university of the imperial capital Berlin in 1888. He became a member of the Prussian Academy of Sciences in 1890. From 1905 to 1921, Harnack was the General Director of the Royal (from 1918, Prussian State) Library in Berlin. In 1911, Harnack was one of the moving spirits behind the founding of the *Kaiser Wilhelm Gesellschaft* (today, the Max Planck Society), and became its first president.

In his major work, *Lehrbuch der Dogmengeschichte*,[52] Harnack reconstructs the rise of Christian dogma, which he understands as the doctrinal system of the church with a legal framework, and its development from the fourth century to the Protestant Reformation. His historiographic thesis is that Christian faith and Greek philosophy were from their earliest origins so closely intermingled that the resultant system included many beliefs and practices that were tied to the respective epoch. The significance of Protestantism is that it rejected the Greek understanding of dogma and reduced Christian thinking to essential and basic insights. The liberation of Christian thinking from Greek philosophy would set free the power of the Gospel in the present time.

In this historical perspective Harnack delivers his specific contribution to the debate on the distinctive nature of Christianity that Schleiermacher had launched in his famous "What Is Christianity?" lectures (*Das Wesen des Christentums*). This brief outline of the history of Christianity pursues the goal of "de-Hellenizing Christianity" and "distinguishing the wheat from the chaff" of Christianity. As a phenomenon, Christianity can only be analyzed by "a comprehensive induction that shall cover all the facts of its history."[53] But "the chief matter" is to focus on the founder of Christianity, the life and work of Jesus of Nazareth, and on classical epochs. It is a liberal concept because Harnack's historical reconstruction of Jesus' words and deeds offers three different but equal possibilities for conceiving the "Essence of Christianity": "the kingdom of God and its coming," "God the Father and the infinite value of the human soul," and "the higher righteousness and the commandment of love."[54] This inner plurality of the "kernel of Christianity" corresponds to a plurality of different interpretations of doctrines, and to the plurality of Christian denominations of his time. Harnack might be the first liberal theologian after Schleiermacher to acknowledge the plurality of denominations and to criticize all denominations (which exceeds Schleiermacher's approach). The history of Christian denominations is for Harnack a history of profit and loss that includes Protestantism. At the end of the series of lectures, Harnack defined the kernel of Christianity in the following terms: "the Gospel is the knowledge and recognition

---

[51] See Gangolf Hübinger, *Kulturprotestantismus und Politik. Zum Verhältnis von Liberalismus und Protestantismus im wilhelminischen Deutschland* (Tübingen: Mohr Siebeck, 1994).

[52] See Adolf von Harnack, *Lehrbuch der Dogmengeschichte*, 3 vols., 4th ed. (Tübingen: J.C.B. Mohr, 1909).

[53] Adolf von Harnack, *What Is Christianity? Lectures Delivered in the University of Berlin During the Winter-Term 1899–1900*, trans. Thomas Bailey Saunders, 2nd ed. (New York: G.P. Putnam's Sons, 1901), p. 12. Concerning the systematic concept behind Harnack's historical reconstruction see Claus-Dieter Osthövener, "Adolf von Harnack als Systematiker," *ZThK* 99 (2002), pp. 296–331.

[54] Harnack, *What Is Christianity?*, p. 55.

of God as the Father, the certainty of redemption, humility and joy in God, energy and brotherly love."[55] This formulation exemplifies the continuity with and the transformation of Schleiermacher's impulse.

It was Ernst Troeltsch who completed and extended the Protestant liberalism of the nineteenth century.[56] After a short appointment as a professor in Bonn (1892–1894), Troeltsch held a chair in systematic theology at the University of Heidelberg. He was appointed to a professorship in Berlin in 1915, where he lectured in the philosophical department as a philosopher for "the philosophy of religion, social sciences, and history, and for the history of the Christian religion." After the First World War, Troeltsch was elected member of the Prussian parliament for the liberal German Democratic Party (DDP) and worked as an (under)secretary of state in the Prussian ministry of science, art, and education (1919–1920).

Troeltsch took Schleiermacher's ideas and transformed them into a methodological concept.[57] *Firstly*, he designed a methodology by which he based dogmatics and ethics on a general concept of religion, which he did through his theory of the so-called *religious a priori*.[58] Religion is an essential and independent element in human consciousness, manifested in the historical religions as a coexistence of human and divine spirit. *Secondly*, unlike Ritschl, he states that

> Christianity is ... a theoretical abstraction. It presents no historical uniformity, but displays a different character in every age, and is, besides, split up into many different denominations, hence it can in no wise be represented as the finally attained unity and explanation of all that has gone before, such as religious speculation seeks.[59]

Troeltsch constructs a methodology by which he establishes the essence of Christianity in a critical debate with Harnack.[60] On the one hand, Troeltsch sees himself as a dogmatist of the so-called "history of religions" school, and underlines the significance of a historical criticism of Bible, tradition, and dogmatics.[61] "Once applied to the scientific study of the Bible and church history, the historical method acts as a leaven, transforming everything

---

[55] Harnack, *What Is Christianity?*, p. 320.

[56] See Mark D. Chapman, *Ernst Troeltsch and Liberal Theology: Religion and Cultural Synthesis in Wilhelmine Germany* (Oxford: Oxford University Press, 2001).

[57] See Hermann Fischer, "Systematische Theologie in liberaler Perspektive. Zu den Prinzipien der Dogmatik als Glaubenslehre," in *Liberale Theologie. Eine Ortsbestimmung*, ed. Friedrich Wilhelm Graf (Gütersloh: Gütersloher Verlagshaus, 1993), pp. 32–51.

[58] See Ulrich Barth, "Religionsphilosophisches und geschichtsmethodologisches Apriori," in *Gott als Projekt der Vernunft* (Tübingen: Mohr Siebeck, 2005), pp. 359–394.

[59] Ernst Troeltsch, "The Place of Christianity among World Religions," in *Christian Thought: Its History and Application*, ed. Baron F. von Hügel (London: University of London Press, 1923), p. 13; and Troeltsch, "Die Stellung des Christentums unter den Weltreligionen," in *Der Historismus und seine Überwindung. Fünf Vorträge*, ed. Baron Friedrich von Hügel (Berlin: Heise, 1924), pp. 62–83.

[60] See Ernst Troeltsch, "'Wesen des Christentums'?" (1903), in *Zur religiösen Lage, Religionsphilosophie und Ethik*, vol. 2, Gesammelte Schriften, 2nd ed. (Tübingen, J. C. B. Mohr (Paul Siebeck), 1922), pp. 386–451; and B. A. Gerrish, "Ernst Troeltsch and the Possibility of a Historical Theology," in *Ernst Troeltsch and the Future of Theology*, ed. John Powell Clayton (Cambridge: Cambridge University Press, 2009), pp. 100–135.

[61] See Ernst Troeltsch, "Die Dogmatik der 'religionsgeschichtlichen Schule," in *Zur religiösen Lage, Religionsphilosophie und Ethik*, vol. 2, Gesammelte Schriften, 2nd ed. (Tübingen, J.C.B. Mohr (Paul Siebeck), 1922), pp. 500–524.

and ultimately exploding the very form of earlier theological methods."[62] On the other, he argues as a philosopher of history that the essence of Christianity cannot be formulated in a perpetual sense, but only as a developing matter. Hence, it is necessary to combine nuanced historical insights with a philosophical approach, which Troeltsch does by using the philosophy of value. Thus, the essence is not to be identified with the origins of Christianity, but is instead a principle that develops in history and that reflects each moment in the present. "Determining essence is designing essence."[63] The *third* methodological step is the comparison of world religions. In this context, Troeltsch formulates his famous thesis that there is no absoluteness of Christianity, but only a relatively higher validity. It is only in Western civilizations that Christianity is seen as a "relative-absolute" point of climax in the history of religions, since it has unfolded the idea of personal redemption.[64] The Christian principle is the rebirth of humankind affected by divine revelation and developed in human history. The *fourth* step is developing dogmatic themes from a theory of religious experience.[65] Troeltsch implements this in his dogmatic "doctrine of faith" in a correlation of divine revelation and individual faith. Troeltsch's concept of revelation refers to the "effects of divine life." Thus, "the Bible, or rather the history witnessed by it, is the fundamental and central revelation; the historical tradition of the Church and the modern religious sentiment, the progressive revelation; and the present religious experience, the present revelation. Revelation therefore has its stages and is never finished."[66] The aspect of progressive revelation legitimizes the methodological subjectivism of the dogmatic perspective, which is perhaps the reason that Troeltsch limited the academic rank of this theological discipline and cut back the ecclesiastical relevance of his dogmatics.[67]

All representatives of German Protestant liberalism in the nineteenth century sought a modern theology that differed from the so-called positive theology of the conservative Lutherans and from neo-pietist theology (*Erweckungsbewegung*). Although inspired by Schleiermacher, they varied the essential features with the result that the inner spectrum of Protestant liberalism was very broad. So Protestant liberalism in the nineteenth century was less a uniform movement than the sum of numerous attempts to design a theology that was open to the scientific sphere and modern life in different ways. In doing so, those involved criticized and competed with one another.[68] This competition was the prerequisite

---

[62] Ernst Troeltsch, "On the Historical and Dogmatic Methods in Theology" (1898), in *Religion in History*, trans. James Luther Adams and Walter F. Bense (Edinburgh: T&T Clark, 1991), p. 12.

[63] Troeltsch, "'Wesen des Christentums'?," p. 451.

[64] See Ernst Troeltsch, "Die Absolutheit des Christentums und die Religionsgeschichte" (1902), in *Die Absolutheit des Christentums und die Religionsgeschichte (1902/1912)*, vol. 5, ed. Trutz Rendtorff (Berlin/New York: Walter de Gruyter, 1998).

[65] See Arnulf von Scheliha, "'Dogmatik, ihre Zeit in Gedanken gefaßt'? Die dogmatische Aufgabe zwischen historischer Kritik und christologischer Gegenwartsdeutung," in *Systematische Theologie heute. Zur Selbstverständigung einer Disziplin*, ed. Hermann Deuser and Dietrich Korsch (Gütersloh: Gütersloher Verlagshaus, 2004), pp. 60–84.

[66] Ernst Troeltsch, *Glaubenslehre, Nach Heidelberger Vorlesungen aus den Jahren 1911 und 1912* (Munich/Leipzig: Duncker and Humblot, 1925), p. 40.

[67] See Hans-Joachim Birkner, "Glaubenslehre und Modernitätserfahrung. Ernst Troeltsch als Dogmatiker," in *Schleiermacher-Studien*, ed. Hermann Fischer (Berlin: Walter de Gruyter, 1996), pp. 77–78.

[68] See, for example, Brent W. Sockness, *Against False Apologetics: Wilhelm Herrmann and Ernst Troeltsch in Conflict* (Tübingen: Mohr Siebeck, 1998); and Christophe Chalamet, "Ernst Troeltsch's

for allowing the new theological movement of dialectical theology, whose leaders initiated a new mode of theology while also remaining heirs to liberalism, to overcome Protestant liberalism after the First World War.

32.5 CURRENT PERSPECTIVES

After the Second World War, Protestant liberalism was increasingly reanimated, which can be seen in the fact that the work of both Friedrich Schleiermacher and Ernst Troeltsch are being published in a complete edition. Hermann Fischer has argued that the fundamental assumptions of liberal theology have found their way into Protestant theology today,[69] showing in detail how the essential insights of Troeltsch's program are realized in a modified form by Karl Barth (1886–1968), Paul Tillich (1886–1965), Emanuel Hirsch (1888–1972), Friedrich Gogarten (1887–1967), and Gerhard Ebeling (1912–2001).[70] Especially Paul Tillich's *Systematic Theology*, published 1951–1953, is often seen as being in line with the liberal approach.

Today, however, the profiles of theological schools are no longer as distinct as was the case at the beginning of the century. Protestant theologians of almost all hues increasingly accept the need to historicize biblical and ecclesiastical traditions, to embrace theological pluralism and a theory of religions, and to focus on freedom as the main issue of modern life. Thus, the essential features of Protestant liberalism have become part of many theological concepts on an academic level, with Protestant liberalism thereby gaining general acceptance—and in a way that is broader than Neuenschwander's "new liberalism." Markus Buntfuß sees these functions of Protestant liberalism as now being completely fulfilled.[71] But this assertion might be too optimistic. On the one hand, Protestant Evangelicalism and Pentecostalism have grown considerably in recent decades, seemingly at the proportional expense of those areas of Christianity that have been respective to liberalism. On the other hand, secularization combined with the social marginalization of religions is a new and strong opponent of the basic insights of Protestant liberalism in the present and future.

Protestant liberalism became an international phenomenon in the twentieth century, as the range of countries covered in the volume edited by Lauster, Schmiedel, and Schüz shows.[72] Shelli Poe shows that Schleiermacher's basic dogmatical insights and impulses dovetail to a remarkable extent methodically and content-wise with motives and topics of contemporary womanist, feminist, queer, ecological, and postcolonial theologians.[73]

Break from Ritschl and His School," *Journal for the History of Modern Theology / Zeitschrift für Neuere Theologiegeschichte* 19, no. 1 (2012), pp. 34–71.

[69] See Fischer, "Systematische Theologie in liberaler Perspektive," p. 40.
[70] See Fischer, "Systematische Theologie in liberaler Perspektive," pp. 40–51.
[71] See Markus Buntfuss, "Liberale Theologie. Eine Erinnerung und eine Ergänzung," in *Liberal Theology Today*, ed. Jörg Lauster, Ulrich Schmiedel, and Peter Schüz (Tübingen: Mohr Siebeck 2019), pp. 291–301.
[72] See Jörg Lauster, Ulrich Schmiedel, and Peter Schüz, eds., *Liberal Theology Today* (Tübingen: Mohr Siebeck, 2019), pp. 7–81.
[73] See Shelli Poe, *The Constructive Promise of Schleiermacher's Theology* (New York: Bloomsbury, 2021).

Another historical influence of Protestant liberalism can be seen in Roman Catholic theology,[74] and in Liberal or Progressive Judaism.[75] Whether Protestant liberalism could have effects on modern Islam and other religious communities in the modern world is an open question. As the period from Schleiermacher to Troeltsch already shows, however, the history of Protestant liberalism is the history of the transformation not only of religion, but also of itself.

Suggested Reading

Buntfuss, Markus. "Liberale Theologie. Eine Erinnerung und eine Ergänzung." In *Liberal Theology Today*, ed. Jörg Lauster, Ulrich Schmiedel, and Peter Schüz (Tübingen: Mohr Siebeck 2019), pp. 291–301.
Chapman, Mark D. *Ernst Troeltsch and Liberal Theology: Religion and Cultural Synthesis in Wilhelmine Germany* (Oxford: Oxford University Press, 2001).
Fischer, Hermann. "Systematische Theologie in liberaler Perspektive. Zu den Prinzipien der Dogmatik als Glaubenslehre." In *Liberale Theologie. Eine Ortsbestimmung*, ed. Friedrich Wilhelm Graf (Gütersloh: Gütersloher Verlagshaus, 1993), pp. 32–51.
Hector, Kevin W. *The Theological Project of Modernism: Faith and the Conditions of Mineness* (Oxford: Oxford University Press, 2015).
Scheliha, Arnulf von. "Schleiermacher als Denker von Pluralität." In *Reformation und Moderne. Pluralität–Subjektivität–Kritik. Akten des Internationalen Kongresses der Schleiermacher-Gesellschaft in Halle (Saale) März 2017*, ed. Jörg Dierken, Arnulf von Scheliha, and Sarah Schmidt (Berlin: Walter de Gruyter, 2018), pp. 25–44.
Zachhuber, Johannes. *Theology as Science in Nineteenth-Century Germany: From F. C. Baur to Ernst Troeltsch* (Oxford: Oxford University Press, 2013).

Bibliography

Barth, Ulrich. "Religionsphilosophisches und geschichtsmethodologisches Apriori." In *Gott als Projekt der Vernunft* (Tübingen: Mohr Siebeck, 2005), pp. 359–394.
Biedermann, Alois Emanuel. *Die freie Theologie oder Christentum und Philosophie in Streit und Frieden* (Tübingen: Fuess, 1844).
Birkner, Hans-Joachim. "Glaubenslehre und Modernitätserfahrung. Ernst Troeltsch als Dogmatiker." In *Schleiermacher-Studien*, ed. Hermann Fischer (Berlin: Walter de Gruyter, 1996), pp. 63–78.

---

[74] See Eilert Herms, "Schleiermacher's Encyclopedia, Philosophical Ethics, Anthropology, and Dogmatics in German Protestant Theology," in *Schleiermacher, the Study of Religion, and the Future of Theology. A Transatlantic Dialogue*, ed. Brent W. Sockness and Wilhelm Gräb (Berlin: Walter de Gruyter 2010), pp. 361–362.

[75] See Christian Wiese, *Wissenschaft des Judentums und Protestantische Theologie im wilhelminischen Deutschland. Ein Schrei ins Leere?* (Tübingen: Mohr Siebeck, 1999); and Imke Stallmann, *Abraham Geigers Wissenschaftsverständnis. Eine Studie zur jüdischen Rezeption von Friedrich Schleiermachers Theologiebegriff* (Frankfurt am Main: Peter Lang, 2013).

Birkner, Hans-Joachim. "Liberale Theologie" (1974/1976). In Hans-Joachim Birkner, *Schleiermacher-Studien*, ed. Hermann Fischer (Berlin: Walter de Gruyter, 1996), pp. 51–62.
Bretschneider, Karl Gottlieb. "Die Ultra's und die Liberalen in der Theologie." In *Für Christenthum und Gottesgelahrtheit. Eine Oppositionsschrift*, ed. Wilhelm Schröter und Friedrich August Klein vol. 3 (Jena, 1820), pp. 195–204.
Buntfuss, Markus. "Liberale Theologie. Eine Erinnerung und eine Ergänzung." In *Liberal Theology Today*, ed. Jörg Lauster, Ulrich Schmiedel, and Peter Schüz (Tübingen: Mohr Siebeck 2019), pp. 291–301.
Chalamet, Christophe. "Ernst Troeltsch's Break from Ritschl and His School." *Journal for the History of Modern Theology / Zeitschrift für Neuere Theologiegeschichte* 19, no. 1 (2012), pp. 34–71.
Chapman, Mark D. *Ernst Troeltsch and Liberal Theology: Religion and Cultural Synthesis in Wilhelmine Germany* (Oxford: Oxford University Press, 2001).
Chapman, Mark D. "'Theology within the Walls.' Wilhelm Herrmann's Religious Reality." *NZSThR* 34 (1992), pp. 69–84.
Fischer, Hermann. "Systematische Theologie in liberaler Perspektive. Zu den Prinzipien der Dogmatik als Glaubenslehre." In *Liberale Theologie. Eine Ortsbestimmung*, ed. Friedrich Wilhelm Graf (Gütersloh: Gütersloher Verlagshaus, 1993), pp. 32–51.
Gerrish, B. A. "Ernst Troeltsch and the Possibility of a Historical Theology." In *Ernst Troeltsch and the Future of Theology*, ed. John Powell Clayton (Cambridge: Cambridge University Press, 2009), pp. 100–135.
Görnandt, Ruth. *Die Metaphysikkritik Gerhard Ebelings und ihre Vorgeschichte* (Tübingen: Mohr Siebeck, 2016).
Harnack, Adolf von. *Lehrbuch der Dogmengeschichte*, 3 vols., 4th ed. (Tübingen: J.C.B. Mohr, 1909).
Harnack, Adolf von. *What Is Christianity? Lectures Delivered in the University of Berlin During the Winter-Term 1899-1900*. Trans. Thomas Bailey Saunders, 2nd ed. (New York: G.P. Putnam's Sons, 1901).
Hector, Kevin W. *The Theological Project of Modernism: Faith and the Conditions of Mineness* (Oxford: Oxford University Press, 2015).
Herrmann, Wilhelm. "Religion." In *Schriften zur Grundlegung der Theologie*, vol. 1, ed. Peter Fischer-Appelt (Munich: Chr. Kaiser, 1966), pp. 283–297.
Herrmann, Wilhelm. "Religion und Sozialdemokratie." *ZThK* 1 (1891), pp. 254–286.
Herrmann, Wilhelm. *Der Verkehr des Christen mit Gott im Anschluss an Luther dargestellt*, 6th ed. (Stuttgart/Berlin: J.-G. Cottasche Buchhandlung Nachfolger, 1908).
Herms, Eilert. "Schleiermacher's Encyclopedia, Philosophical Ethics, Anthropology, and Dogmatics in German Protestant Theology." In *Schleiermacher, the Study of Religion, and the Future of Theology. A Transatlantic Dialogue*, ed. Brent W. Sockness and Wilhelm Gräb (Berlin: Walter de Gruyter 2010), pp. 361–374.
Hübinger, Gangolf. *Kulturprotestantismus und Politik. Zum Verhältnis von Liberalismus und Protestantismus im wilhelminischen Deutschland* (Tübingen: Mohr Siebeck, 1994).
Huisgen, Jana. *Der christliche Glaube als reflektierte Erfahrung. Eine Studie zur Schleiermacherrezeption Gerhard Ebelings* (Berlin: Peter Lang, 2020).
Iff, Markus. *Liberale Theologie in Jena. Ein Beitrag zur Theologie- und Wissenschaftsgeschichte des ausgehenden 19. Jahrhunderts* (Berlin: Walter de Gruyter, 2011).
Kuhlmann, Helga. *Die theologische Ethik Albrecht Ritschls* (Munich: Chr. Kaiser, 1992).
Lauster, Jörg. "Liberale Theologie. Eine Ermunterung." *NZSThR* 50 (2007), pp. 291–307.

Lauster, Jörg, Ulrich Schmiedel, and Peter Schüz, eds. *Liberal Theology Today* (Tübingen: Mohr Siebeck, 2019).

Nelson, Derek R. "Schleiermacher and Ritschl on Individual and Social Sin." *JHMTh/ZNThG* 16 (2009), pp. 131–154.

Neuenschwander, Ulrich. *Die neue liberale Theologie. Eine Standortbestimmung* (Bern: Stämpfli, 1953).

Neugebauer, Matthias. *Lotze und Ritschl. Reich-Gottes-Theologie zwischen nachidealistischer Philosophie und neuzeitlichem Positivismus* (Frankfurt Main: Lang, 2002).

Nottmeier, Christian. *Adolf von Harnack und die deutsche Politik 1890–1930*, 2nd ed. (Tübingen: Mohr Siebeck, 2017).

Osthövener, Claus-Dieter. "Adolf von Harnack als Systematiker." *ZThK* 99 (2002), pp. 296–331.

Poe, Shelli. *The Constructive Promise of Schleiermacher's Theology* (New York: Bloomsbury, 2021).

Ritschl, Albrecht. *The Christian Doctrine of Justification and Reconciliation: The Positive Development of the Doctrine*. Trans. A. B. Macaulay and H. R. Mackintosh (Edinburgh: T&T Clark, 1902).

Ritschl, Albrehct. *Die christliche Lehre von der Rechtfertigung und Versöhnung*, 3 vols. (Bonn: Adolph Marcus, 1870–1874).

Rothe, Richard. *Theologische Ethik*, 3 vols. (Wittenberg: Zimmermann, 1845–1848). 2nd ed., 5 vols. (Wittenberg: Zimmermann, 1867–1871). Reprint, ed. Jürgen Albert (Waltrop: Spenner, 1991).

Scheliha, Arnulf von. "Albrecht Ritschls Deutung von Friedrich Schleiermachers Reden 'Über die Religion.'" In *200 Jahre "Reden über die Religion." Akten des 1. Internationalen Kongresses der Schleiermacher-Gesellschaft Halle 14.–17. März 1999*, ed. Ulrich Barth and Claus-Dieter Osthövener (Berlin/New York: De Gruyter, 2000), pp. 728–747.

Scheliha, Arnulf von. "'Dogmatik, ihre Zeit in Gedanken gefaßt'? Die dogmatische Aufgabe zwischen historischer Kritik und christologischer Gegenwartsdeutung." In *Systematische Theologie heute. Zur Selbstverständigung einer Disziplin*, ed. Hermann Deuser and Dietrich Korsch (Gütersloh: Gütersloher Verlagshaus, 2004), pp. 60–84.

Scheliha, Arnulf von. *Der Glaube an die göttliche Vorsehung. Eine religionssoziologische, geschichtsphilosophische und theologiegeschichtliche Untersuchung* (Stuttgart: W. Kohlhammer, 1999).

Scheliha, Arnulf von. *Protestantische Ethik des Politischen* (Tübingen: Mohr Siebeck, 2013).

Scheliha, Arnulf von. "Schleiermacher als Denker von Pluralität." In *Reformation und Moderne. Pluralität–Subjektivität–Kritik. Akten des Internationalen Kongresses der Schleiermacher-Gesellschaft in Halle (Saale) März 2017*, ed. Jörg Dierken, Arnulf von Scheliha, and Sarah Schmidt (Berlin/Boston: De Gruyter, 2018), pp. 25–44.

Schröder, Markus. *Die kritische Identität des neuzeitlichen Christentums. Schleiermachers Wesensbestimmung der christlichen Religion* (Tübingen: Mohr Siebeck, 1996).

Semler, Johann Salomo. *Institutio ad doctrinam Christianam liberaliter discendam, auditorum usui destinate* (Halle: Hemmerde, 1774).

Sockness, Brent W. *Against False Apologetics: Wilhelm Herrmann and Ernst Troeltsch in Conflict* (Tübingen: Mohr Siebeck, 1998).

Stallmann, Imke. *Abraham Geigers Wissenschaftsverständnis. Eine Studie zur jüdischen Rezeption von Friedrich Schleiermachers Theologiebegriff* (Frankfurt am Main: Peter Lang, 2013).

Strauß, David Friedrich. *Der politische und der theologische Liberalismus* (Halle: Kümmel, 1848).

Svensson, Leiff. *A Theology for the Bildungsbürgertum: Albrecht Ritschl in Context* (Berlin/Boston: Walter de Gruyter, 2020).

Troeltsch, Ernst. "Die Absolutheit des Christentums und die Religionsgeschichte" (1902). In *Die Absolutheit des Christentums und die Religionsgeschichte (1902/1912)*, vol. 5, ed. Trutz Rendtorff (Berlin/New York: Walter de Gruyter, 1998).

Troeltsch, Ernst. "Die Dogmatik der 'religionsgeschichtlichen Schule.'" In *Zur religiösen Lage, Religionsphilosophie und Ethik*, vol. 2, Gesammelte Schriften, 2nd ed. (Tübingen, J.C.B. Mohr (Paul Siebeck), 1922), pp. 500–524.

Troeltsch, Ernst. *Glaubenslehre, Nach Heidelberger Vorlesungen aus den Jahren 1911 und 1912* (Munich/Leipzig: Duncker and Humblot, 1925).

Troeltsch, Ernst. "On the Historical and Dogmatic Methods in Theology" (1898). In *Religion in History*. Trans. James Luther Adams and Walter F. Bense (Edinburgh: T&T Clark, 1991), pp. 11–32.

Troeltsch, Ernst. "The Place of Christianity among World Religions." In *Christian Thought: Its History and Application*, ed. Baron F. von Hügel (London: University of London Press, 1923), pp. 1–36.

Troeltsch, Ernst. "Die Stellung des Christentums unter den Weltreligionen." In *Der Historismus und seine Überwindung. Fünf Vorträge*, ed. Baron Friedrich von Hügel (Berlin: Heise, 1924), pp. 62–83.

Troeltsch, Ernst. "'Wesen des Christentums'?" (1903). In *Zur religiösen Lage, Religionsphilosophie und Ethik*, vol. 2, Gesammelte Schriften, 2nd ed. (Tübingen, J. C. B. Mohr (Paul Siebeck), 1922), pp. 386–451.

Wiese, Christian. *Wissenschaft des Judentums und Protestantische Theologie im wilhelminischen Deutschland. Ein Schrei ins Leere?* (Tübingen: Mohr Siebeck, 1999).

Wittekind, Folkart. *Geschichtliche Offenbarung und die Wahrheit des Glaubens. Der Zusammenhang von Offenbarungstheologie, Geschichtsphilosophie und Ethik bei Albrecht Ritschl, Julius Kaftan und Karl Barth* (Tübingen: Mohr Siebeck, 2000).

Wyman, Jr., Walter E. "Rethinking the Christian Doctrine of Sin: Ernst Troeltsch and the German Protestant Liberal Tradition." *ZNThG/JHMTh* 1 (1994), pp. 226–250.

Zachhuber, Johannes. *Theology as Science in Nineteenth-Century Germany: From F.C. Baur to Ernst Troeltsch* (Oxford: Oxford University Press, 2013).

CHAPTER 33

SCHLEIERMACHER, NEO-ORTHODOXY, AND DIALECTICAL THEOLOGY

PAUL DAFYDD JONES

At present, English-language scholarship on Schleiermacher stands at the intersection of two interpretative trajectories—one long-standing, lamentable, and in decline, the other relatively novel, laudable, and on the rise. On the one hand, there is the well-known fact that twentieth-century theologians often treated Schleiermacher harshly. It was Schleiermacher who encouraged theologians to submit to the protocols of the Enlightenment and German Romanticism; Schleiermacher who lost sight of Scripture; Schleiermacher who exchanged doctrine for a muddy appeal to experience, questioning Christ's divinity and rendering the Trinity an afterthought; Schleiermacher who disaffiliated systematics and ethics and collapsed Christianity into culture; Schleiermacher who endorsed habits of mind that culminated in the dead-end of liberal Protestantism. On the other hand, Schleiermacher is now being read with fresh, admiring, and rather more perceptive eyes. Yes, he was alert to the philosophical and cultural trends of his day, but he was never governed by them; Schleiermacher is better read as a thinker who transposed Reformed insights into a pietist key.[1] No, Schleiermacher did not sideline Scripture,[2] nor did an interest in experience lead him to slight Christ's divinity or dismiss the Trinity.[3] No, Schleiermacher was not

---

[1] See, for instance, B. A. Gerrish, *Tradition and the Modern World: Reformed Theology in the Nineteenth Century* (Chicago: University of Chicago Press, 1978), pp. 13–48, and *Continuing the Reformation: Essays on Modern Religious Thought* (Chicago: University of Chicago Press, 1993), pp. 145–216.

[2] See Paul T. Nimmo, "Schleiermacher on Scripture and the Work of Jesus Christ," *International Journal of Systematic Theology* 31 (2015), pp. 60–90.

[3] See Kevin W. Hector, "Actualism and Incarnation: The High Christology of Friedrich Schleiermacher," *International Journal of Systematic Theology* 8 (2006), pp. 307–322; Paul DeHart, "*Ter mundus accipit infinitum*: The Dogmatic Coordinates of Schleiermacher's Trinitarian Treatise," *Neue Zeitschrift für Systematische Theologie und Religionsphilosophie* 52 (2010), pp. 17–39; and Shelli M. Poe, *Essential Trinitarianism: Schleiermacher as Trinitarian Theologian* (London: T&T Clark, 2017).

uninterested in ethics; he had a vital grasp of Christian life in community and his thought allows for constructive conversation with diverse liberationist perspectives.[4]

Given this state of affairs, it is tempting to view the earlier interpretative trajectory—a calling card for scholars associated with "neo-orthodoxy" and "dialectical" theology—as a relic from the past. Why bother with outmoded critiques when, at long last, Schleiermacher is being treated fairly? Why bother, too, when those critiques are associated with a paradigm (neo-orthodoxy) that collapses under scrutiny and a term of art (dialectical) that is something of a moving target? I would offer two responses. First, the misreadings of Schleiermacher that dominated twentieth-century scholarship have proven hard to dispatch. They continue to shape ecclesial and academic discussion, largely because they are woven into the fabric of a "founding narrative of twentieth-century theology"—one that supposes that Karl Barth initiated a much-needed "revolt" against the liberalism of his teachers, whose errors can be tracked back to the "father of modern theology," and put Protestantism theology back on course.[5] So we are not yet in a position to rest on any interpretative laurels. Second, it is possible to convert interpretative missteps into interpretative gains. There is instructive mischief to be had: demonstrating that Schleiermacher's theology is often consonant with, and perhaps even supportive of, Christian theology in its neo-orthodox and dialectical modes.

This chapter proceeds straightforwardly. The first section sketches and rejects neo-orthodoxy as a paradigm for engaging twentieth-century theology, while granting that this term captures the mood of much mid-century Anglophone scholarship. It then shows that, if one *were* to take the paradigm of neo-orthodoxy seriously, Schleiermacher would best be read as an ally, not an opponent. The second section considers the more serviceable notion of dialectical theology. Focusing on early writings by Barth and Rudolf Bultmann, I show that Schleiermacher anticipates key dimensions of their programs, even as those programs put his thought under valuable pressure. Finally, I argue that scholarship ought to look beyond talk of neo-orthodoxy and dialectical theology and imagine a different framework for thinking about Schleiermacher and his successors.

33.1 Schleiermacher and Neo-Orthodoxy

In many surveys of twentieth-century theology, neo-orthodoxy is associated with a clutch of European theologians who rose to prominence in the 1920s: Karl Barth, Emil Brunner, Rudolf Bultmann, Friedrich Gogarten, and Paul Tillich. Its ranks later swelled to include Reinhold Niebuhr and H. Richard Niebuhr in the United States, and Donald Baille, John Baille, and T. F. Torrance in the United Kingdom. To be sure, scholars often acknowledge that this compound word has limitations. Beyond the fact that its principal referent is obscure—what "orthodoxy" is being renewed here?—there are obviously better

---

[4] See Paul Dafydd Jones, "Liberation Theology and 'Democratic Futures' (by way of Karl Barth and Friedrich Schleiermacher)," *Political Theology* 10 (2009), pp. 261–285, and Shelli M. Poe, *The Constructive Promise of Schleiermacher's Theology* (London: T&T Clark, 2021).

[5] Gary Dorrien, *The Barthian Revolt in Modern Theology: Theology without Weapons* (Louisville, KY: Westminster John Knox Press, 2000), p. 3. Schleiermacher as the "father of modern theology" is a common, if unhelpful, turn of phrase.

ways to describe these authors' preoccupations. In the 1920s and 1930s, one might refer to the "theology of the Word," "crisis theology," or "dialectical theology"; after World War II, one might follow Tillich and talk of "kerygmatic theology," or think in terms of Barthians, Brunnerians, Christian realists, and so on. Even so, neo-orthodoxy was an established part of the theological lexicon for many decades. Langdon Gilkey offered a bracing summary of this "movement" in the influential *Handbook of Christian Theology* (1958), lauding its capacity to tether historical awareness, acceptance of scientific inquiry, and social concerns with the basic insights of the Reformation.[6] David Tracy treated it as a "basic model" for theological inquiry in his influential *Blessed Rage for Order* (1975).[7] And, while acknowledging its "denigrative connotation," H. Martin Rumscheidt supplied a deft précis in the important *Encyclopedia of the Reformed Faith* (1992).[8] Although used less frequently in recent years, the term is still employed on occasion.[9]

What are neo-orthodoxy's distinguishing characteristics? Taking Gilkey, Tracy, and Rumscheidt as guides, one might identify four concerns. First, neo-orthodoxy sought to make theological exegesis—not historical-critical research—central to dogmatic work, while reasserting doctrines of the magisterial Reformation. Second, neo-orthodoxy critiqued the conventions of Protestant "liberalism." It challenged those who downplayed human sinfulness and, correspondingly, exposed the folly of endeavors to coordinate Christian faith with modern philosophical, ethical, and political norms. Third, there was a massive amplification of the place of revelation in theological work, this being a concept that emphasized the epistemological consequences of God's justification of sinners, against those who approached faith in terms of religious experience, morality, and/or historical consciousness. Fourth, there was an insistence that Christian theology should proceed on its own terms. It need not defer to auxiliary disciplines; it should comport itself in a forthright, unapologetic manner.

Now this quartet of characteristics immediately raises questions. Generally, none of the authors associated with this "movement" identified themselves as neo-orthodox, and each would resist the claim that his project was consistent with that of his colleagues, even granted certain points of convergence. (In September 1939, Barth sounded an almost wistful note: "as the sun went up . . . fellowships which had not really been fellowships at all were dissolved like the morning mist").[10] It seems apt, in fact, to view neo-orthodoxy as a label foisted on authors from the *outside*—a shorthand, designed to impose order on a cluster of German-language research programs and their Anglophone offshoots. But recognizing this fact does not render the shorthand serviceable; it only exposes it as a sloppy generalization. To claim that major nineteenth-century theologians were uninterested in the doctrinal heritage of

---

[6] Landon B. Gilkey, "Neo-Orthodoxy," in *A Handbook of Christian Theology: Definition Essays on Concepts and Movements of Thought in Contemporary Protestantism*, ed. Marvin Halversen and Arthur A. Cohen (Cleveland, OH: World Publishing Company, 1958), pp. 256–261.

[7] David Tracy, *Blessed Rage for Order: The New Pluralism in Theology* (Chicago: University of Chicago Press, 1996).

[8] H. Martin Rumscheidt, "Neo-Orthodoxy," in *Encyclopedia of the Reformed Faith*, ed. Donald McKim (Louisville, KY: Westminster/John Knox Press, 1992), p. 253.

[9] See, for instance, Chad Meister and J. B. Stump, *Christian Thought: A Historical Introduction* (London: Routledge, 2010), pp. 441–454.

[10] Karl Barth, "How My Mind Has Changed in This Decade (Part One)," *The Christian Century* 56, no. 37 (1939), p. 1098.

the Reformation, for instance, is patently false. Albrecht Ritschl, Wilhelm Herrmann, and, later, Adolf von Harnack never wanted to jettison the past; they sought only to make it intelligible in an altered political and philosophical context. Opposition to putatively "liberal" conventions, equally, does not really tell us much. Which creditable twentieth-century theologians do *not* worry about the relationship of historical-critical research to doctrine, caution against rosy estimates of "progress," or decry an uncritical embrace of "modern" norms? Finally, the unapologetic rhetoric of neo-orthodoxy did not, in and of itself, betoken an uncomplicated reassertion of sixteenth-century insights. Barth is a case in point: one cannot understand his thought without reference to various philosophical trajectories—neo-Kantianism, German Idealism, and dialogical personalism, in particular—or without noticing his reprisal of claims in the programs he inveighed against.[11]

So is talk of neo-orthodoxy useless? If approached as a category that summarily lumps together Barth, Brunner, the Niebuhrs, and putative allies, one must reply in the affirmative. It does not shed light; even the heat it emits is dubious. That this term became a fixture in scholarly discourse, however, does speak to the *mood* of much mid-twentieth-century Anglophone theology. Generally, it served as a statement of intent in a century roiled by conflict and change: building bridges with the sixteenth century, not developing the achievements of the nineteenth, was thought to be the best way forward. More particularly, it was an occasion to negotiate local pressures. In North America, it disclosed a concern to challenge the optimism of much nineteenth-century scholarship—exemplary targets being Albrecht Ritschl, Horace Bushnell, and their epigones—while heeding Walter Marshall Horton's impassioned call for a "realistic theology,"[12] set apart from the modernist programs of Shailer Mathews et al., on the one side, and the folly of fundamentalism, on the other.[13] In the United Kingdom, it pointed to a revival in the fortunes of the Reformed tradition, both within the Church of England and in nonconforming communities—something made evident by the fact that it was Scottish and Welsh theologians who championed Barth's thought (H. R. Mackintosh, the Baille brothers, John E. Daniel, T. F. Torrance, and Donald McKinnon being especially important).[14] Finally, neo-orthodoxy adverted to a desire, on both sides of the Atlantic, to challenge the growing distance between biblical studies and systematic theology. It had a function parallel to "biblical theology" in its heyday: it enabled those trained in the historical-critical method to challenge the naturalistic drift of biblical studies, and it

---

[11] See, for example, Bruce L. McCormack, *Orthodox and Modern: Studies in the Theology of Karl Barth* (Grand Rapids: Baker, 2008), pp. 21–41 and 63–88; Matthias Gockel, *Barth and Schleiermacher on the Doctrine of Election* (Oxford: Oxford University Press, 2006); and Christoph Chalamet, "Barth and Liberal Protestantism," in *The Oxford Handbook of Karl Barth*, ed. Paul Dafydd Jones and Paul T. Nimmo (Oxford: Oxford University Press, 2019), pp. 132–146.

[12] William Marshall Horton, *Realistic Theology* (New York: Harper & Brothers, 1934). I should add that Horton did not commend neo-orthodoxy in this book. He was wary of Barth, while sympathetic toward Brunner. My point is that neo-orthodoxy was one way to respond to Horton's call for "realistic" theology.

[13] A point made nicely by Charles Clayton Morrison in "The Liberalism of Neo-Orthodoxy," Parts 1–3, *The Christian Century* 67 (1950), pp. 697–699, 731–733, and 760–763. William Hordern thinks similarly; see Hordern, *The Case for a New Reformation Theology* (Philadelphia: The Westminster Press, 1959), pp. 11–30.

[14] For more detail, see D. Densil Morgan, *Barth Reception in Britain* (London: T&T Clark, 2010).

enabled those engaged in dogmatics to weave exegetical claims into the fabric of theological inquiry.[15]

Even if one treats neo-orthodoxy more as a mood than a movement, the opprobrium heaped on Schleiermacher remains noteworthy. He was tagged as the principal villain in the narrative of modern theology, the thesis against which twentieth-century scholars ought to position themselves as antitheses. Barth bears some responsibility for this. Although the *Church Dogmatics* offered nuanced criticism, earlier writings traded in sweeping judgments. The critique of religion as the "supreme competence of human possibility" in the second edition of *Romans*, for instance, presents Schleiermacher as a forerunner of *Kulturprotestantismus*, as do many essays in *The Word of God and Theology*: two texts widely read in German and quickly (if not entirely accurately) translated into English. Emil Brunner's *Die Mystik und das Wort*—a text that Barth referenced positively in his teaching, while worrying about in correspondence, then challenging in the pathbreaking journal *Zwischen den Zeiten*—also exerted a good deal of influence.[16] And the culminative impact of these critiques was considerable. J. Arundel Chapman's *Introduction to Schleiermacher* (1932), for instance, commits an entire chapter to *Die Mystik und das Wort* before offering a call to arms: "Theology needs to-day a fresh start which must be a return to the old start. We must start with God, with the revelation of God of the Bible, and supremely Jesus Christ."[17] While Hugh Ross Mackintosh's *Types of Modern Theology* (1937) is more measured, it adopts a similar line. On one side, we have an author who "put discovery in place of revelation" and set "religious consciousness in the place of the Word of God"; on the other, a thinker (Barth) whose works "are a treasure-house of . . . incorruptibly Christian convictions" with "incalculable import for the Church."[18]

At precisely this point, however, an irony comes into view. Notwithstanding the limits of neo-orthodoxy as an interpretative paradigm, a more careful reading of Schleiermacher—one that dispenses with the binary of antithesis/thesis, hero/villain—might have allowed those attracted to this paradigm to relate to him as an *ally*, not an enemy. Looking again at the four concerns noted above shows why.

Consider first the place of Scripture in theological inquiry. It is well known that the *Glaubenslehre* does not begin by foregrounding the principle of *sola scriptura*. It opens with a delicate analysis of the "feeling of absolute dependence" that Schleiermacher takes to be ingredient to self-consciousness, which segues into a clarification of the church, a comparative discussion of Abrahamic faiths, and a statement about Christianity's distinctiveness, before concluding with reflections on how best to articulate dogmatic claims—all facilitated by an annexation of insights from the (idiosyncratically construed) realms of ethics, philosophy

---

[15] See, for instance, G. Ernest Wright, "Neo-Orthodoxy and the Bible," *Journal of Bible and Religion* 14 (1946), pp. 87–93.

[16] Emil Brunner, *Die Mystik und das Wort* (Tübingen: J. C. B. Mohr, 1924). See also Karl Barth, *The Theology of Schleiermacher: Lectures at Göttingen, Winter Semester of 1923/4*, ed. Dietrich Ritschl, trans. Geoffrey W. Bromiley (Grand Rapids: Eerdmans, 1982); Bruce L. McCormack, *Karl Barth's Critically Realistic Dialectical Theology, 1909–1936* (Oxford: Clarendon, 1995), p. 397; and Karl Barth, "Brunners Schleiermacherbuch," in *Karl Barths Gesamtausgabe*, vol. 3, no. 19: *Vorträge und kleinere Arbeiten 1922–1925*, ed. Holger Finze (Zürich: TVZ, 1990), pp. 401–425.

[17] J. Arundel Chapman, *An Introduction to Schleiermacher* (London: The Epworth Press, 1932), p. 164.

[18] Hugh Ross Mackintosh, *Types of Modern Theology: Schleiermacher to Barth* (New York: Charles Scribner's Sons, 1937), pp. 100, 317, 318, and 319.

of religion, and apologetics. Schleiermacher opens his account thus for good reasons. In a fast-moving philosophical and ecclesial context, with the union of the Reformed and Lutheran churches and the launch of the University of Berlin in view, he thought it prudent to offer a gradual circumscription of the Protestant faith that he hoped to understand. He sought, that is, to describe the "lay of the land" before embarking on dogmatics proper. Does it follow that Schleiermacher was uninterested in or uncommitted to the scriptural witness? No. Later in the *Glaubenslehre*, Schleiermacher presents the Bible as a *conditio sine qua non* for piety. Christians would likely not have any consciousness of Jesus apart from the preaching of his earliest followers, and this preaching supplied the raw, authoritative material from which the New Testament was constructed. And even if one ought not to say that the redeeming work of Christ and Christ's Spirit *depends* on the biblical witness (that would make literacy and/or audition a precondition of faith, ignoring the fact that God evokes faith through diverse means), Scripture is the *typical* way that Christ, in the Spirit, presents himself to us as the living Lord. Alongside the sacraments and preaching, it is a principal instrument that God uses to stimulate, shape, and sustain piety, and it is a principal medium through which Christ's body relates to its head. But is not the deferral and brevity of Schleiermacher's bibliology a sign of Scripture's marginality? Again, no. Schleiermacher's bibliology is terse because Scripture is considered an uncontroversial means of divine instruction, foremost among the "essential and invariable features of the church."[19] Just as the Spirit indwells the church now, so the Spirit animated Christian communities after Christ's death and resurrection: she supported the writing of individual books, as well as their formation into a canon, and rendered that canon an "authentic" and "sufficient" instrument that "can lead us into all truth."[20] But—our neo-orthodox interlocutor will not quit!—isn't it *still* the case that Schleiermacher seems reluctant to integrate exegetical reflection and dogmatic inquiry, and doesn't that speak volumes? Once more, no. Although Schleiermacher's employment of biblical verses, books, and idioms doesn't resemble Calvin or Luther, that hardly makes his work *un*scriptural. *The Life of Jesus*, for instance, draws attention to the *Glaubenlehre*'s deep reliance on John's presentation of the incarnation as a gracious action that ramifies across history, with Christ being the one who "desired nothing else than [the] transformation of the world into the Kingdom of God" and who acted "to effect it" through "pure self-communication."[21] And Schleiermacher's doctrine of election might be read as an extended gloss on Eph. 1:5 ("he chose us in Christ before the beginning of the foundation of the world"): a challenge to the Reformed tradition's overdependence on Romans, as well as a nice reminder that the postulation of protological adoption needn't have eternal reprobation as its complement.

Consider, second, the charge that Schleiermacher initiates a movement of thought whose *terminus ad quem* is the "anthroposophical chaos" of *Kulturprotestantismus*: an endorsement of "modern" conventions that loses sight of a distinctively Christian account of God's ways and works.[22] The first item for the defense would be the *Speeches* of 1799: a text that uses the rhetoric of the Enlightenment and German Romanticism not to honor but to

---

[19] *CF* (1928), p. 586.
[20] *CF* (1928), p. 606.
[21] *LJ*, p. 126.
[22] Karl Barth, *Der Römerbrief*, 2nd. ed. of 1922 (Zürich: TVZ, 2005), p. xxi. All translations are my own.

parody those intellectual and artistic moments. Indeed, if the initial addresses aim to wean Berlin's intelligentsia from uncritical habits of mind, the final speech boldly—one might say, unapologetically—commends Christianity as a determinate, "positive" religion, centered in Christ's mediation of the finite and the infinite.[23] The second item for the defense would be the *Glaubenslehre*. Although Schleiermacher writes about "an eternal covenant" between faith and "independent scientific inquiry,"[24] his dogmatics is aptly read as a riposte to the inflated philosophical anthropologies that gained currency in the early decades of the nineteenth century. Rather than viewing human beings primarily in terms of the autonomous exercise of theoretical and practical reason—a Kantian claim, extravagantly developed by Fichte—Schleiermacher emphasizes our *receptivity* to God's prevenient operations. The famous description of piety as "the consciousness of being absolutely dependent, or, which is the same thing, of being in relation with God"[25] is a case in point. It does not center the human being; it serves as a prelude to the acclamation of divine primacy that dominates the later sections of the *Glaubenslehre*. Combine the items, and one might even argue that Schleiermacher challenged the secularizing philosophical culture of northern Europe. If material was "borrowed from elsewhere," it was always "twisted and turned" to support a decidedly Christian end:[26] an affirmation of divine primacy and the salvation wrought in Christ.

This brings me to revelation and the eschewal of apologetics, the third and fourth dimensions of neo-orthodoxy. I consider them in turn.

One cannot reasonably expect Schleiermacher to conceive revelation along the lines of Barth and his followers. That would require him to anticipate the terminology of German Idealism and the thought-world of neo-Kantianism; that would require that he foresee an account of revelation as an act of divine self-communication, the material content of which is God's triunity and the historical point of reference for which is Jesus' life, death, and resurrection. One can say, however, that the *Glaubenslehre* shares the neo-orthodox commitment to doing theology theocentrically, and that many of the impulses that underwrote Barth's account of revelation are present in the *Glaubenslehre*. Generally, there is a constant drive to foreground God's sovereignty. So, having considered creation and providence in light of God's all-encompassing "divine causality," Schleiermacher takes pains to emphasize that Christ does not arise from a nexus of conditions immanent to history, even as Christ's influence ramifies across history.[27] For those with eyes to see, he is the product of "a creative divine act" that results in a perfected God-consciousness—a God-consciousness coextensive with the "perfect indwelling of the Supreme Being as His peculiar being and His inmost self."[28] Likewise the church: a body that "springs from no other individual life than that of the Redeemer," having a "divine origin" and standing in contrastive relationship with the sinful world, "the unorganized mass to which it is opposed."[29] More particularly,

---

[23] *Speeches*[1], pp. 119–121.
[24] *OG*, p. 64.
[25] *CF (1928)*, p. 12.
[26] Kathryn Tanner, *Theories of Culture: A New Agenda for Theology* (Minneapolis: Fortress, 1997), p. 112.
[27] See *CF(1928)*, pp. 360, 365, and 367.
[28] *CF (1928)*, pp. 381 and 388.
[29] *CF (1928)*, pp. 525 and 528.

Schleiermacher shows more interest in Christians' knowledge of God than is sometimes thought. If the *Glaubenslehre* begins by identifying "feeling" as a dimension of human being that bespeaks our receptivity to God, Schleiermacher is quick to note that feeling cannot be cleanly disaggregated from "knowing" and "doing." And while the "feeling of absolute dependence" is so named because it is a consequence of the antecedent fact of divine causality (a consequence unavailable to knowing and doing: these dimensions of the person entail an active "passing-beyond-self"), the modification of feeling that is piety can and does "stimulate Knowing and Doing, and every moment in which piety has a predominant place will contain within itself one or both of these in germ."[30] Feeling, knowing, and doing coinhere; and the stimulation of feeling that is piety, the substance of which is the act of God in Christ and the Spirit, can and does issue in knowledge. Indeed, knowledge of God is *exactly* what comes into view when, at the end of the *Glaubenslehre*, Schleiermacher declares that "God is love," that "love and wisdom . . . can claim to be not mere attributes but also expressions of God," and that those incorporated into Christ's body "come to knowledge [*Erkenntnis*] of the divine love."[31] Although Schleiermacher does not draw attention to the point, then, the (literal!) bookends of his masterwork pay tribute to the opening of Calvin's *Institutes of the Christian Religion*. "Knowledge of self" is secured through an awareness of the divine "whence" that precedes us; "knowledge of God" is elaborated, slowly but surely, by attending to God's creative and redemptive action, the culmination of which is a frank statement about God's very being.

Finally, I would suggest that Schleiermacher be read as an unapologetic theologian *avant la lettre*, albeit of a curious kind.[32] As noted already, Schleiermacher does not allow standards external to faith to govern dogmatic reflection. The Introduction to the *Glaubenslehre* is clear on this point: while it borrows from auxiliary fields to circumscribe the scope and meaning of piety, borrowing does not determine the content of piety. One finds here an updated application of Augustine's account of the Israelites' plunder of the Egyptians as a warrant for Christians' annexation of philosophical insights, with a shift from "pagan" wisdom to the realm of *Geisteswissenschaft*.[33] At the same time, Schleiermacher uses the intellectual currents of his day for his own purposes. Consider again the "feeling of absolute dependence." If, say, a philosopher accepted that this feeling is indeed ingredient to self-consciousness and was sufficiently intrigued by Schleiermacher's elucidation of it to keep reading, they would soon discover that this feeling's "whence" cannot be understood without reference to a distinctively Christian account of God. They would then find the formal, pre-dogmatic beginning of the *Glaubenslehre* enveloped in a grand vision of divine sovereignty—one that begins with a statement about divine causality, then moves on to the incarnation and the church, and concludes with the claim that God is love. An unapologetic explication of piety, then, goes hand in hand with an expansion of thought, one that

---

[30] *CF (1928)*, pp. 8f.

[31] *CF (1928)*, pp. 730, 731–732, and 729. Although the Introduction to the *Glaubenslehre* employs the triplex of *Gefühl*, *Tun*, and *Wissen*, the reference to *Erkenntnis* (*CF (1928)*, p. 729) does not lack for cognitive import.

[32] I allude to William C. Placher, *Unapologetic Theology: A Christian Voice in a Pluralistic Conversation* (Louisville, KY: Westminster John Knox, 1989).

[33] Augustine of Hippo, *On Christian Teaching*, trans. R. P. H. Green (Oxford: Oxford University Press, 1997), p. 64.

shows a philosopher what faith makes intellectually (and affectively) available. But instead of this expansion of thought being turned against the philosopher, there is a transcending of the "limitations proper to the philosophical foundations," the condition of possibility for which is "a realistically conceived divine act": namely, God's presence in Christ and the church.[34] The result is an theology whose "unapologeticism" goes hand in hand with a high degree of "accessibility": a presentation of faith that begins on grounds comprehensible to nonbelievers and ends with a perspective that subsumes those same grounds, showing them to be a symptom of something much more basic—God's action to create and redeem the world in Christ, through the Spirit.

33.2 SCHLEIERMACHER AND DIALECTICAL THEOLOGY

Although "dialectical theology" stakes a stronger claim to interpretative utility than "neo-orthodoxy," its meaning is neither self-evident nor fixed. One might, for instance, use this phrase to encompass work undertaken by Barth, Brunner, Gogarten, and their allies in the 1920s, noting that these authors treated what was widely viewed as a "crisis of culture" as a byproduct of the more fundamental crisis of humanity before God.[35] One might also use it as an interpretative device to track Barth's thinking from the mid-1910s onwards, as neo-Kantian epistemological conventions are put in service of a distinctive brand of critical realism.[36] Or, to turn to Bultmann, one might use the phrase to describe a powerful fusion of doctrine, exegesis, and proclamation: a correction of liberal Protestantism, undertaken from within, that sets an interest in history and experience in a theocentric, existentialist, and missional frame.[37] Finally, one might treat dialectical theology not as a twentieth-century phenomenon but as a mode of discourse: a style of writing that prefers paradox, tensions, and contrasts to (seemingly) rationalistic doctrinal formulations, and that counts among its ranks authors as diverse as Melito of Sardis, Martin Luther, Søren Kierkegaard, and Simone Weil.

I will not attempt a definition of dialectical theology here. I want instead to build on the previous section by identifying three emphases in Barth's and Bultmann's writings in the 1920s. Doing so provides the leverage needed to engage the *Glaubenslehre*, and to substantiate

---

[34] McCormack, *Orthodox and Modern*, p. 15.

[35] See, for instance, Friedrich Gogarten, "Between the Times" and "The Crisis of Our Culture," in James M. Robinson, ed., *The Beginnings of Dialectical Theology*, vol. 1, trans. Keith R. Crim and Louis De Grazia (Richmond: John Knox, 1968), pp. 277–282 and 283–300.

[36] See McCormack, *Critically Realistic Dialectical Theology*, and more recently, D. Paul La Montagne, *Barth and Rationality: Critical Realism in Theology* (Eugene, OR: Cascade, 2012).

[37] See especially Rudolf Bultmann, "Liberal Theology and the Latest Theological Movement" and "The Significance of 'Dialectical Theology' for the Scientific Study of the New Testament," in Bultmann, *Faith and Understanding*, ed. Robert W. Funk, trans. Louis Pettibone Smith (Philadelphia: Fortress, 1987), pp. 28–52 and 145–164. See also David W. Congdon, *The Mission of Demythologizing: Rudolf Bultmann's Dialectical Theology* (Minneapolis: Fortress, 2015).

my suggestion that Schleiermacher's masterwork anticipates dialectical concerns, even as this same masterwork is put under critical pressure by later authors.

The first emphasis has to do with the objectivity and nonobjectifiability of God.[38] "Objectivity" refers to the vivid sense of divine reality that courses through Barth's and Bultmann's writings, manifest particularly in the tendency to describe the incarnation and the outpouring of the Spirit as disclosive of God as "wholly other," who "break[s] . . . in upon us 'perpendicularly from above.'"[39] "Nonobjectifiability" is a shorthand way to note that human beings cannot possess God's otherness. While God certainly uses creaturely media to reveal Godself, God is hidden in and distinct from those media. It is therefore impossible to comprehend God as such, and impossible to encounter God as an object that could be grasped or manipulated. (Bultmann puts it well: "God is not a given entity"; revelation is no "establishable, objective fact"; and even "justification by faith is not a demonstrable fact of existence").[40] Now, given all this, it stands to reason that dialectical theology contests the assumption that historical-critical examinations of the Bible could supply a definitive, operationalizable sense of Jesus' "personality" (a hallmark of liberal Protestantism) and expresses wariness toward systems of doctrine (a hallmark of Protestant scholasticism). Both risk domesticating God; both risk converting divine objectivity into a usable "thing." Barth will therefore tell Harnack that "we no longer know Christ according to the flesh" and will insist that the "firm connection and blood relationship" of theology and *Geisteswissenschaft* be severed, and Bultmann will declare that an "interest in the personality of Jesus" has no place in his work.[41] And Barth, having questioned the viability of religion, dogmatism, *and* dialecticism as pathways for thought, will insist that, because the "task of theology is the Word of God," it foretells the "certain *defeat of all* theology and *of every* theologian."[42] Only God can speak for Godself.

A second emphasis is the pairing of sin and grace. On one level, dialectical theology challenges those inclined to underrate the gravity and extent of sin. Sin must not be viewed as a "manageable" impediment to relationship with God. It is a radical distortion of human existence whose effects permeate every dimension of life—social, political, ecclesial, and theological. Accordingly, attempts to coordinate Christian faith with "modern" Western values must be resisted. The "civilized" world isn't a complement to God's sanctification of the individual; it must be approached, like everything else, in light of God's "total annulment of man."[43] On another level, this account of sin is juxtaposed with a compelling affirmation

---

[38] These terms are not my own. For the first, see George Hunsinger, *How to Read Karl Barth: The Shape of his Theology* (Oxford: Oxford University Press, 1991); for the second, see David W. Congdon, *Rudolf Bultmann: A Guide to His Theology* (Eugene, OR: Cascade, 2015), pp. 32–51.

[39] Karl Barth, *The Humanity of God*, trans. Thomas Wieser and John Newton Thomas (Richmond: John Knox, 1960), p. 42.

[40] Bultmann, "Liberal Theology," p. 45; "The Question of 'Dialectic' Theology: A Discussion with Erik Peterson," in Robinson, ed., *The Beginnings of Dialectical Theology*, pp. 257–274, at p. 266; and "The Problem of 'Natural Theology,'" in *Faith and Understanding*, pp. 313–331, at p. 329.

[41] The exchange of letters between Barth and Harnack in 1923 is reproduced in Robinson, ed., *The Beginnings of Dialectical Theology*, pp. 165–187; the quotation is from p. 170. See also Rudolf Bultmann, *Jesus and the Word*, trans. Louise Pettibone Smith and Erminie Huntress Lantero (New York: Charles Scribner's Sons, 1958), p. 8.

[42] Karl Barth, *The Word of God and Theology*, trans. Amy Marga (London: T&T Clark, 2011), p. 196.

[43] Bultmann, "Liberal Theology," p. 46. Emphases removed.

of the reality and efficacy of grace. While Bultmann tended to connect grace with the faith of the individual, Barth's interests were more ontological. He insisted that the "complementary dialectic" of God and world, which identifies these realities as unsublate-able contrasts, be paired with a "supplementary dialectic," wherein sin is consistently surpassed and overturned by God's gracious advance, the material content of which is Christ as the "new human."[44] Here is a striking passage from the famous second edition of *Romans*:

> Grace is the power of obedience. It is *the* theory, which as such is also practice; *the* taking, which is also being taken. It is *the* indicative, which has as its meaning the absoluteness of the categorical imperative. And it is *the* imperative, *the* call, *the* command, *the* advance that one cannot *not* obey, which has the power of an unambiguous conclusion.

At issue here is the most momentous "nevertheless" to sin imaginable, as our unflagging hostility toward God is overmastered by our enclosure in Christ's body, and the "now" of sin is outmatched by the eschatological reality of Christ's resurrection. It is for this reason that I am emboldened "to take up arms against the world of men and against the men of the world," even as "I myself, as subject, am made the subject of this very attack."[45]

A third emphasis, while continuous with the preceding, brings into view a further dimension of dialectical theology in the 1920s: a reimagining of Luther's *theologia crucis*, wherein "true theology and recognition of God" hinge on a willingness to encounter Christ crucified.[46] With this *theologia crucis*, Barth and Bultmann advanced perhaps the deepest challenge to liberal Protestantism, exchanging an acclamation of Christ's inauguration of the Kingdom for the claim that the abyssal event of the cross should serve as the point of departure for thought. Another passage from *Romans*:

> The faithfulness of God is Jesus' entering into and remaining in the deepest human ambiguity and darkness . . . He stands as a sinner among sinners. He stands entirely under the judgment under which the world stands. He stands in the place where God can only be present as a question. He takes the form of a slave. He goes to the cross, to death. At the height of his life, his purpose is negative. In no respect is he a genius, one who bears manifest or occult psychic powers; he is not a hero, leader, poet, or thinker. And precisely in this negation ("My God, my God, why have you forsaken me?"), precisely as an impossible *More*, as an imperceptible *sacrifice* of everything that is genius-like, heroic, aesthetic, philosophical—all human possibilities—he is the fulfilment of every elevated human possibility of progress, as the law and the prophets view it. *Precisely there* God exalts him, *precisely there* is he recognized as the Christ, whereby the light of the last things illuminates all humankind and all things. We see in him God's faithfulness actually in the depths of hell. The messiah is the end of humankind. Even here, God is faithful. The new day on which the righteousness of God breaks in is the day in which humankind is *remade*.[47]

---

[44] The "complementary" and "supplementary" types of dialectic are important for McCormack in *Critically Realistic Dialectical Theology*. See also Michale Beintker, *Die Dialektik in der "dialektischen Theologie" Karl Barths* (Munich: Chr. Kaiser Verlag, 1987).
[45] Barth, *Der Römerbrief*, p. 205.
[46] Martin Luther, "Heidelberg Disputation (1517)," in *Martin Luther's Basic Theological Writings*, ed. Timothy F. Lull (Minneapolis: Fortress Press, 1989), p. 44.
[47] Barth, *Der Römerbrief*, p. 78.

Christ, then, must *not* be viewed as the founder of an ethical kingdom (contra Ritschl), as a mediator who enables our relationship with the Father (contra Herrmann), or as the embodiment of the highest ethical and religious values (contra Harnack). Christ is the ultimate site of judgment, and his death exposes the hubris of humankind in general and liberal Protestantism in particular. At the same time—and note, in the quotation above, how Barth encloses the "no" of judgment in a space that begins and ends with God's gracious "yes"—it is in Christ that God's solidarity with and commitment to humankind is most evident. And, once again, for those who live into the cross, it is this solidarity and commitment that licenses critique, permitting theological reflection to serve as a distant echo of God's judgment by intensifying the "crisis of culture" to the point at which we are "distrustful right to our fingertips of everything which in any way is the work of man."[48]

What might Schleiermacher say in response? If he can be read as an unapologetic, neo-orthodox theologian before the fact, does he really anticipate the emphases of dialectical theology? The answer to the question is arguably more complex than with neo-orthodoxy, but valuably so: it becomes impossible to think in terms of an either/or here, and the possibility of a both-and begins to present itself as a pathway for thought.

Notice, first, that Schleiermacher shares the desire to balance an affirmation of God's objectivity with a sense of God's nonobjectifiability. Divine objectivity, to be sure, is not described with an eye to jolting the reader out of her immersion in the quotidian and driving her toward an encounter with divine transcendence. Nor is it elevated into a dogmatic theme, as in *Romans*. But, as noted already, the *Glaubenslehre*'s initial analysis of religious consciousness is quickly overwritten with an expansive account of God's ways and works. And by the text's end, it is pretty much impossible to view faith to a "state of consciousness," immanent to a patch of time and space.[49] Faith is a gracious *determination* of consciousness: a "local" receipt of the history-spanning impartation of redeeming grace, grounded in God's elective decree and grasped in Spirit-led fellowships that acclaim the "union of the Divine Essence with human nature in the Person of Christ."[50] Internal to faith, moreover, is the awareness that insight into the "whole" is always *partial*. So just as Schleiermacher's pre-dogmatic analysis of the feeling of absolute dependence includes the caveat that this feeling always occurs in combination with a determinate formation of self-consciousness, so Schleiermacher insists that a piety ordered to God's ways and works is always inflected by and tethered to the quotidian. Even as the *Glaubenslehre*'s philosophical apparatus can distract from this point, then, an affirmation of nonobjectifiability therefore lies close to hand: Schleiermacher insists that "consciousness of God" is always "combined with, and related to, the sensible self-consciousness ... carry[ing] with it such determinations as belong to the realm of the antithesis in which the sensible self-consciousness moves."[51] We do not know God as God knows Godself; our apprehension is always conditioned by finitude. Or, as Bultmann puts it, "If the proclamation of God's forgiving love is really valid for *me*, i.e., for me in my concrete life situation, then it is not at all understandable apart from that situation."[52] Granted, then, that Schleiermacher does not share Bultmann's historicism or

---

[48] Gogarten, "Between the Times," p. 281.
[49] Bultmann, "Liberal Theology," p. 50. Emphasis removed.
[50] *CF (1928)*, p. 724.
[51] *CF (1928)*, p. 25; cf. p. 47.
[52] Rudolf Bultmann, *Existence in Faith: Shorter Writings of Rudolf Bultmann*, trans. Schubert M. Ogden (Cleveland, OH: World Publishing Company, 1960), p. 56.

interest in Luther's *pro me*, are we not in the same neck of the dogmatic woods? Doesn't Schleiermacher, like Bultmann, pair an affirmation of God's all-encompassing activity with an awareness that we receive that activity *in media res*? Isn't there an analogous pairing of divine objectivity and nonobjectifiability?

Notice, second, the dialectic of sin and grace. On the one hand, there is clear continuity. Sin and grace comprise the poles of the "antithesis" that underpins the entirety of the second part of the *Glaubenslehre*: God's redemptive activity being juxtaposed with humanity's hostility, and our state of "God-forgetfulness" being overcome by the imputation of "God-consciousness." "God-forgetfulness," further, is neither akin to an individual losing track of time or blanking on a name, nor an event that pertains solely to the "affections" of a believing community. Schleiermacher is far more realistic. As an obstruction of the "spirit" by the "flesh," God-forgetfulness is a far-reaching, historical *fact*, discerned in faith: a "derangement of our nature"[53] that precedes our actions and incurs guilt. Grace, correspondingly, is an event of divine condescension. It cannot be produced or evoked by us; it is always grounded in God's initiative. And, again, it has concrete consequences. The Spirit ensures that Christ's "person-forming divine influence"[54] ramifies across time and space, drawing increasing numbers into Christ's body. So much so—and here we have Schleiermacher's application of the "supplementary dialectic," noted above—that the church will eventually subsume all creation, and Jesus will have fully "overcome the world" (John 16:33, KJV).

On the other hand, there are certainly discontinuities. One pertains to the different rhetorical strategies of the authors. In the *Glaubenslehre*, Schleiermacher favors a stately prose style, reminiscent of the Protestant scholastics who preceded him. Systolic expressions of a "poetic" sort and diastolic, "rhetorical" reactions are subsumed under a "descriptively didactic" mode of discourse, with dogmatic claims being the result of a "logically ordered reflection upon the immediate utterances of the religious self-consciousness."[55] Barth and Bultmann, by contrast, worry that "logically ordered reflection" risks a "religious" mindset that is liable to lose sight of God's nonobjectifiability. As such, their prose flits between dogmatic, poetic, and rhetorical registers of expression. Christian existence, as an uneasy simultaneity of sin and gracious justification, is rhetorically performed; the line separating the "scientific" and the dramatic, the intellectual and the existential, is consistently blurred. And this difference in rhetorical form adverts to a difference in dogmatic content. On one side, there is Schleiermacher's boundless confidence in the outworking of redemption, the endpoint of which is the world's envelopment by the church. And while this confidence does not permit one to assume that portion of the world is more-or-less redeemed, the affinity between Schleiermacher's sense of the enlarging sphere of the Spirit-led church and some nineteenth-century visions of progress is hard to deny. It becomes tempting, arguably, to imagine that God's action in the church might be complemented by God's stimulation of sociocultural norms, political programs, and philosophical advances in the wider world. On the other side, Barth and Bultmann make resistance to such a temptation an imperative, refusing to think of a straightforward application of God's redemptive work in history. Instead of pairing redemption and providence, they connect redemption with eschatology. And instead of redemption being construed as "spirit" overcoming worldly "flesh," it is

---

[53] *CF (1928)*, p. 275.
[54] *CF (1928)*, p. 427.
[55] *CF (1928)*, pp. 78 and 81.

frequently figured as God's *killing* the "old" and *raising* the "new" human—an event invisible to sight yet beheld, haltingly, in the context of a future-oriented faith.

With the third emphasis, Christ crucified, the differences become acute. That is probably already evident: Barth and Bultmann prefer to think in terms of dying and being made alive, given God's "faithfulness . . . in the depths of hell," while Schleiermacher discerns a movement from flesh to spirit; Barth and Bultmann tend to foreground justification, offering only sketchy remarks on sanctification, while Schleiermacher follows Calvin in treating sanctification before justification. Even so, difference does not necessarily mean disagreement. It raises, rather, the prospect of a striking synthesis: Schleiermacher's account of Christ's inauguration of the Kingdom, which spreads out across history, being paired with Barth's and Bultmann's account of the cross as the basis of judgment and redemption. And this dialectic of Kingdom and cross might be paired with another one, which moves between Schleiermacher's protological imagination and Barth and Brunner's eschatological focus. On this reckoning, the "undivided eternal divine decree"[56] that identifies Christ as the second Adam would be paired with the acclamation of the future that impinges on the present—the future of "Jesus Christ, the new human of the new world, who appears on the threshold of my existence, demanding entrance."[57] Granted that Barth eventually moves closer to Schleiermacher on election, then, it might be possible to read Barth's and Bultmann's work in the 1920s as a dialectical counterpoint to the *Glaubenslehre* and the *Church Dogmatics*—the result being a dizzying, stereoscopic view, with the lamb slain before the foundation of the world *also* being the one who is coming soon, the one whose futurity unmakes and remakes human life into what it is originally intended to be.

33.3 Conclusion

This comparison of Schleiermacher with his most renowned critics could certainly be extended. One might wish for the interpretative mischief I have sought to make with respect to neo-orthodoxy to turn serious, perhaps through a consideration of how Schleiermacher draws on Protestant confessions or through an analysis of how various paragraphs of the *Glaubenslehre* engage in quiet, respectful controversy with Protestant scholasticism. Or one might consider Schleiermacher's sermons and homilies, while reading dialectical theology in terms of the proclamation of the Word. Or one might ask, finally, if the charge that Schleiermacher sidelines the Hebrew Bible ought to be paired with a critique of dialectical thinkers. Are we not choosing between two bad options, both of which make evident the long-standing failure of Christian thinkers to think clearly about Israel: *either* a lightly theorized supersessionism, *or* a stark association of ancient Israel with sinful, rejected humankind?

I want to conclude, however, with two broader points. First, it seems fair to say that this essay remains beholden to a somewhat parochial vision of historical theology, since it lets doctrinal concerns—the doctrine of God, justification, analyses of Christ's person and work,

---

[56] *CF (1928)*, p. 389.
[57] Barth, *Der Römerbrief*, p. 230.

and so on—set the parameters for analysis. Now these concerns and parameters are not, in and of themselves, illegitimate. They arise organically from the texts; they are usefully brought back to bear on those texts. But the risk is that a doctrinal focus draws attention away from newer lines of inquiry, many of which have proven invaluable for understanding luminaries from the past. Why not consider Schleiermacher, Barth, Bultmann, et al. in terms of their treatments of (say) sexual difference, colonialization, race, class, and the transnational ideology of whiteness? Why not reckon with the fact that, while these axes of interpretation will home in on uneven, occasional, and disquieting parts of these authors' writing, those instances of unevenness, occasionalism, and disquiet can shed new and important light on the whole? Why not, to put it more generally, embed the hermeneutics of suspicion within the domain of historical theology, with an eye to gaining new angles of vision on the past?

Second, I think it fair to say that this treatment of what has sometimes been viewed as a "debate" between Schleiermacher, neo-orthodoxy, and dialectic theology—a debate that, by the end of the previous section, became a constructive conversation—suggests that established ways of engaging modern theology stand in need of revision. To be sure, what Gary Dorrien has called the "founding narrative of twentieth-century theology," wherein Barth launches a "revolt" against a liberal theological establishment, was not plucked out of thin air; it is a standard feature of many treatments of modern Christian thought. But it is not clear that this founding narrative is interpretatively helpful. On one level, the preceding analysis has shown that the dialectical "revolt" against figures like Ritschl, Herrmann, Harnack, and Ernst Troeltsch involved not a repudiation of Schleiermacher's insights but, ironically, a quiet *reassertion* of those insights, albeit with a shift in rhetoric. It is not simply that Schleiermacher is *not* a "liberal"; it is also the case that Schleiermacher anticipates the concerns of neo-orthodoxy and dialectical theology. On another level, and more broadly, it is worth asking if the dialectical endeavors of the 1920s foretold a still more consequential transformation of the theological imagination, initiated in the late 1960s and continuing in the present, wherein Christian thought is roused from its ecclesial captivity and freed up to reckon with a host of sociopolitical issues: white supremacism, patriarchal dominance, environmental exploitation, the cruelties of global capitalism, and, more recently, the resurgence of ethnonationalist ideologies. If that *is* the case, to draw now on a periodization popularized by Eric Hobsbawm, might it be that the long nineteenth century (1789–1914: from the French revolution to the beginning of the Great War) was *not* followed by a shorter twentieth century (1918–1991: the end of the World War I to the collapse of Soviet totalitarianism), and that we must understand that the project of twentieth-century theology is still unfolding? And what place should Schleiermacher be afforded? How does one think about an intruder from the past who, despite the scorn heaped toward him, remains a constant presence in the thoughts and writings of his descendants?

Suggested Reading

Barth, Karl. *Der Römerbrief*. 2nd ed. of 1922 (Zürich: TVZ, 2005).
Bultmann, Rudolf. *Faith and Understanding*. Ed. Robert W. Funk, trans. Louis Pettibone Smith (Philadelphia: Fortress, 1987).

McCormack, Bruce. *Orthodox and Modern: Studies in the Theology of Karl Barth* (Grand Rapids: Baker, 2008).
Morgan, D. Densil. *Barth Reception in Britain* (London: T&T Clark, 2010).

Bibliography

Augustine of Hippo. *On Christian Teaching*. Trans. R. P. H. Green (Oxford: Oxford University Press, 1997).
Barth, Karl. "Brunners Schleiermacherbuch." In *Karl Barths Gesamtausgabe*, vol. 3, no. 19: *Vorträge und kleinere Arbeiten 1922–1925*, ed. Holger Finze (Zürich: TVZ, 1990), pp. 401–425.
Barth, Karl. "How My Mind Has Changed in This Decade (Part One)." *The Christian Century* 56, no. 37 (1939), pp. 1097–1099.
Barth, Karl. *The Humanity of God*. Trans. Thomas Wieser and John Newton Thomas (Richmond: John Knox, 1960).
Barth, Karl. *Der Römerbrief*. 2nd. ed. of 1922 (Zürich: TVZ, 2005).
Barth, Karl. *The Theology of Schleiermacher: Lectures at Göttingen, Winter Semester of 1923/4*. Ed. Dietrich Ritschl, trans. Geoffrey W. Bromiley (Grand Rapids: Eerdmans, 1982).
Barth, Karl. *The Word of God and Theology*. Trans. Amy Marga (London: T&T Clark, 2011).
Beintker, Michale. *Die Dialektik in der "dialektischen Theologie" Karl Barths* (Munich: Chr. Kaiser Verlag, 1987).
Brunner, Emil. *Die Mystik und das Wort* (Tübingen: J. C. B. Mohr, 1924).
Bultmann, Rudolf. *Existence in Faith: Shorter Writings of Rudolf Bultmann*. Trans. Schubert M. Ogden (Cleveland, OH: World Publishing Company, 1960).
Bultmann, Rudolf. *Faith and Understanding*. Ed. Robert W. Funk, trans. Louis Pettibone Smith (Philadelphia: Fortress, 1987).
Bultmann, Rudolf. *Jesus and the Word*. Trans. Louise Pettibone Smith and Erminie Huntress Lantero (New York: Charles Scribner's Sons, 1958).
Chalamet, Christoph. "Barth and Liberal Protestantism." In *The Oxford Handbook of Karl Barth*, ed. Paul Dafydd Jones and Paul T. Nimmo (Oxford: Oxford University Press, 2019), pp. 132–146.
Chapman, J. Arundel. *An Introduction to Schleiermacher* (London: The Epworth Press, 1932).
Congdon, David W. *The Mission of Demythologizing: Rudolf Bultmann's Dialectical Theology* (Minneapolis: Fortress, 2015).
Congdon, David W. *Rudolf Bultmann: A Guide to His Theology* (Eugene, OR: Cascade, 2015).
DeHart, Paul. "*Ter mundus accipit infinitum*: The Dogmatic Coordinates of Schleiermacher's Trinitarian Treatise." *Neue Zeitschrift für Systematische Theologie und Religionsphilosophie* 52 (2010), pp. 17–39.
Dorrien, Gary. *The Barthian Revolt in Modern Theology: Theology without Weapons* (Louisville, KY: Westminster John Knox Press, 2000).
Gerrish, B. A. *Continuing the Reformation: Essays on Modern Religious Thought* (Chicago: University of Chicago Press, 1993).
Gerrish, B. A. *Tradition and the Modern World: Reformed Theology in the Nineteenth Century* (Chicago: University of Chicago Press, 1978).
Gilkey, Landon B. "Neo-Orthodoxy." In *A Handbook of Christian Theology: Definition Essays on Concepts and Movements of Thought in Contemporary Protestantism*, ed. Marvin Halversen and Arthur A. Cohen (Cleveland, OH: World Publishing Company, 1958), pp. 256–261.

Gockel, Matthias. *Barth and Schleiermacher on the Doctrine of Election* (Oxford: Oxford University Press, 2006).

Hector, Kevin W. "Actualism and Incarnation: The High Christology of Friedrich Schleiermacher." *International Journal of Systematic Theology* 8 (2006), pp. 307–322.

Hordern, William. *The Case for a New Reformation Theology* (Philadelphia: The Westminster Press, 1959).

Horton, William Marshall. *Realistic Theology* (New York: Harper & Brothers, 1934).

Hunsinger, George. *How to Read Karl Barth: The Shape of his Theology* (Oxford: Oxford University Press, 1991).

Jones, Paul Dafydd. "Liberation Theology and 'Democratic Futures' (by way of Karl Barth and Friedrich Schleiermacher)." *Political Theology* 10 (2009), pp. 261–285.

La Montagne, D. Paul. *Barth and Rationality: Critical Realism in Theology* (Eugene, OR: Cascade, 2012).

Luther, Martin. "Heidelberg Disputation (1517)." In *Martin Luther's Basic Theological Writings*, ed. Timothy F. Lull (Minneapolis: Fortress Press, 1989), pp. 30–49.

Mackintosh, Hugh Ross. *Types of Modern Theology: Schleiermacher to Barth* (New York: Charles Scribner's Sons, 1937).

McCormack, Bruce L. *Karl Barth's Critically Realistic Dialectical Theology, 1909–1936* (Oxford: Clarendon, 1995).

McCormack, Bruce L. *Orthodox and Modern: Studies in the Theology of Karl Barth* (Grand Rapids: Baker, 2008).

Meister, Chad, and J. B. Stump. *Christian Thought: A Historical Introduction* (London: Routledge, 2010).

Morgan, D. Densil. *Barth Reception in Britain* (London: T&T Clark, 2010).

Morrison, Charles Clayton. "The Liberalism of Neo-Orthodoxy." Parts 1–3. *The Christian Century* 67 (1950), pp. 697–699, 731–733, and 760–763.

Nimmo, Paul T. "Schleiermacher on Scripture and the Work of Jesus Christ." *International Journal of Systematic Theology* 31 (2015), pp. 60–90.

Placher, William C. *Unapologetic Theology: A Christian Voice in a Pluralistic Conversation* (Louisville, KY: Westminster John Knox, 1989).

Poe, Shelli M. *The Constructive Promise of Schleiermacher's Theology* (London: T&T Clark, 2021).

Poe, Shelli M. *Essential Trinitarianism: Schleiermacher as Trinitarian Theologian* (London: T&T Clark, 2017).

Robinson, James M., ed. *The Beginnings of Dialectical Theology*. Vol. 1. Trans. Keith R. Crim and Louis De Grazia (Richmond: John Knox, 1968).

Rumscheidt, H. Martin. "Neo-Orthodoxy." In *Encyclopedia of the Reformed Faith*, ed. Donald McKim (Louisville, KY: Westminster/John Knox Press, 1992), pp. 253–254.

Tanner, Kathryn. *Theories of Culture: A New Agenda for Theology* (Minneapolis: Fortress, 1997).

Tracy, David. *Blessed Rage for Order: The New Pluralism in Theology* (Chicago: University of Chicago Press, 1996).

Wright, G. Ernest. "Neo-Orthodoxy and the Bible." *Journal of Bible and Religion* 14 (1946), pp. 87–93.

CHAPTER 34

SCHLEIERMACHER'S INFLUENCE ON ROMAN CATHOLIC THEOLOGY

GRANT KAPLAN

34.1 INTRODUCTION

WHEN treating the topic of this chapter, the logical place not only to start, but to abide, is with his influence on the first generations of the Catholic theology faculty in Tübingen, sometimes known as the Catholic Tübingen School. Schleiermacher's influence on the Catholic Tübingen School constituted in many ways his most direct, resounding, and also the deepest, in the sense that this embedded influence was transmitted through its own century, and into the twentieth century, most directly via the *ressourcement* theology of the mid-twentieth century, and, more broadly, through post-Second Vatican Council theology. This chapter makes the case for Schleiermacher's influence on two of the most important members of the Catholic Tübingen School, Johann Sebastian Drey and his student and later colleague, Johann Adam Möhler, in dialogue with key contributors, positive and negative, to the discussion of influence. As a coda, it will then offer some reflections on how this influence has been refracted into more recent Catholic theology.

34.2 THE ANXIETY OF INFLUENCE

Hanging over this question of influence are the value judgments about the influencer. For some, Schleiermacher represents all that is wrong in modern theology; therefore, depending on their sympathies with a given Catholic figure, they either downplay or exaggerate Schleiermacher's hand in things. Other scholars seem desperate to find this influence in an effort to legitimate modern Catholic theology, which when left to its own devices was internally moribund. Therefore, anything good in it must have arrived via a confessional version of something like interlibrary loans. Neither agenda will be likely to produce a clear judgment or logic about influence. One finds this dilemma already articulated by Möhler. In his 1825 *Unity in the Church*, he only cites Schleiermacher one time, but in a noted passage he talks of "a great theologian of our time," and clearly intends Schleiermacher.[1] In a book review two years later, Möhler complains about this question, or accusation, of influence. Noting that such Catholics as Francis de Sales and François Fènelon had expressed ideas about an *intimus conscientia fundus*, which foretell Schleiermacher's foregrounding of God-consciousness, Möhler laments,

> It is thus only on account of the predictable ignorance on the part of Protestant authors of Catholic literature that causes them to claim . . . that Catholic ideas grew on Protestant soil. They never leave the Protestant terrain, and thus do not know what goes on elsewhere. Therefore, they speak of Catholic theologians *Schleiermacherizing*, when they should say instead that Schleiermacher *Catholicizes*.[2]

As we will see, this complaint does not go away.

While Catholicizing might be adulatory for some, it was pejorative for others, including the most important narrator of nineteenth-century theology: Karl Barth. Barth's Schleiermacher incarnated perfectly the deleterious spirit of "neo-Protestantism," which rejected the preferred theological form given by the Reformers. In a densely packed section in the *Church Dogmatics*, Barth called Möhler "the man who is rightly honoured as the father of modern German Catholicism."[3] Regarding the influence of Schleiermacher, Barth says that Möhler knew Schleiermacher's thought "particularly well," and adds that Möhler's achievement was done "with the help of Hegel and Schleiermacher." Barth concurred with Möhler's judgments about Schleiermacher: "It was really a waste of time for Protestant critics of Möhler's system to accuse him of 'Schleiermacherising' and to charge him with transmuting Catholic doctrine. . . . Möhler did represent Catholic doctrine and in doing so understood Schleiermacher at the deepest possible level . . . Do we not have to admit that he is right?"[4] Barth argues that Möhler recognized a kinship with Schleiermacher because the latter Catholicized. The boldness here is stunning, even for Barth: Schleiermacher, as reflexively Protestant as imaginable, could be written off as having a greater similarity to Catholicism—a denomination against which Schleiermacher held many of the predictable prejudices—than to his own Protestant tradition.

When someone of Barth's stature weighs in on this question, it has the capacity of altering the scholarly direction of the topic. More recent commentators have acknowledged the staying power of Barth's claims while also correcting them. John Thiel writes, "Indeed, the

---

[1] Johann Adam Möhler, *Unity in the Church or the Principle of Catholicism*, trans. Peter Erb (Washington, DC: Catholic University of America Press, 1995), §8; The full citation reads, "There is a beautiful thought of a great theologian of our time, who states that by the communication of the Holy Spirit through Christianity the creation of humanity was first perfected" (Erb, 98, n. f; slightly amended); Himes comments, "'great theologian' is, of course, Schleiermacher," in Michael Himes, "'A Great Theologian of Our Time': Möhler on Schleiermacher," *Heythrop Journal* 37 (1996), p. 25.

[2] Johann Adam Möhler, "Rezension von Adam Gengler, Über das Verhältnis der Theologie zur Philosophie," *Theologische Quartalschrift* 9 (1827), pp. 514–515; I was made aware of this passage by the reference to it in Himes, "'A Great Theologian of Our Time,'" p. 25.

[3] Karl Barth, *The Doctrine of the Word of God*, vol. I.2 of *Church Dogmatics*, trans. G. T. Thomson and Harold Knight, ed. G. W. Bromiley and T. F. Torrance (Edinburgh: T&T Clark, 1956), p. 561

[4] Barth, *The Doctrine of the Word of God: Church Dogmatics* I/2, p. 563.

well-known twentieth-century portrait of Schleiermacher as the embodiment of the spirit of modernity was largely the work of Brunner and Barth, and this portrait has influenced not only the history of Schleiermacher scholarship but also our notion of modern theology itself."[5] As Thiel shows, conflating Schleiermacher's theology to Catholic theology was not a one-off comment, but more of a running theme in Barth.[6] Yet Barth's reading was hobbled by an inadequate understanding of Catholic Tübingen in general and of Möhler in particular. More critical comments come from other scholars. Michael Himes, for one, questions how well Barth understood Möhler: "Barth seems unaware that the perspective of [*Unity in the Church*] and that of the later Möhler in *Symbolik* are very different," although Barth "quotes from the two books indiscriminately."[7] Max Seckler, meanwhile, takes umbrage at Barth's claim of Möhler (rather than his teacher Drey) being the father of modern German Catholicism. Barth's summary of Möhler reveals him to be "not yet at the level of the scholarship" published at the time when Barth made his claims.[8] Barth's influence, unfortunately, also led to confusion, for Barth, at least in this passage, described the influence in a way that was dismissive of both Schleiermacher and Catholic Tübingen. The challenge at hand, then, is to wade through these historiographic landmines and present Schleiermacher's impact as accurately as possible.

34.3 SCHLEIERMACHER'S INFLUENCE ON JOHANN SEBASTIAN DREY

The great task facing German Catholics was to construct a theology equipped to confront modern and Enlightenment critiques. No theologian did this more creatively and skillfully than Johann Sebastian Drey (1777–1853), contemporary of Schleiermacher, and perhaps the best example of Schleiermacher's influence on Catholic theology. Drey's role in the development of fundamental theology has been acknowledged in the *Dictionary of Fundamental Theology*, which states, "J.S. Drey's theological significance is evident from the fact that today, by consensus, he is accorded the role of 'founder' or 'father of modern fundamental theology.'"[9] This section focuses on four locations of Schleiermacher's influence: first, in a

---

[5] John Thiel, "Schleiermacher as 'Catholic': A Charge in the Rhetoric of Modern Theology," *Heythrop Journal* 37 (1996), p. 67.

[6] Thiel, "Schleiermacher as 'Catholic,'" pp. 70–72.

[7] Michael Himes, "Divinizing the Church: Strauss and Barth on Möhler's Ecclesiology," in *The Legacy of the Tübingen School*, ed. Donald Dietrich and Michael Himes (New York: Crossroad/Herder, 1997), p. 96.

[8] Max Seckler, "Einleitung," in Johann Sebastian Drey, *Nachgelassene Schriften. Vierter Band*, ed. Max Seckler (Tübingen: Francke Verlag, 2015), p. 423.

[9] Abraham Peter Kustermann, "Drey, Johann Sebastian von (1777–1853)," in *Dictionary of Fundamental Theology: English-Language Edition*, ed. René Latourelle (New York: Herder & Herder, 1994), p. 247. In his overview of early nineteenth-century apologetics, Avery Dulles calls Drey "The most outstanding German Catholic apologist of the period." See Dulles, *A History of Apologetics* (San Francisco: Ignatius Press, 1999), p. 238. Perhaps the greatest living scholar who works explicitly in the field of fundamental theology, Max Seckler, has devoted much of his retirement to preserving the legacy of Drey, another indication of Drey's status.

theological method that addressed the need for theology to think historically; second, and related to the first point, in a nascent theory of the development of doctrine; third, in a creative hermeneutical approach; fourth, in a theology of orthodoxy that would allow greater room for the preceding three points. In all of these, Drey's reimagining of these theological topoi leave a discernible Schleiermacherian trace.

34.3.1 Theological Architectonics

In the course of the eighteenth century, the explosion of knowledge demanded that faculty in universities develop courses that would allow students to get an overview of the field. The resulting textbooks were called "encyclopedia," and the genre of theological encyclopedia exploded during the century. Toward the end of the century, the Enlightenment model of knowing, which privileged rationality and superimposed mechanistic models onto different disciplines, gained prominence. Both these occurrences—the explosion of knowledge, and the demand for greater rationality—challenged theology to justify its existence in the university. Schleiermacher sought to address these challenges in his groundbreaking work of theological encyclopedia, *Brief Outline of the Study of Theology*, which appeared in 1811. Drey had been professor at a seminary in Ellwangen, but the faculty and its students were relocated, in 1817, to Tübingen and placed in the university alongside the renowned Protestant Faculty of Theology. In response, Drey published his *Brief Introduction to the Study of Theology*, which one commentator calls, "a fascinating Catholic analogue to Schleiermacher's *Kurze Darstellung*."[10] In the opening paragraphs of the "Foreword," Drey contrasts Schleiermacher's with Gottlieb Jakob Planck's approach to theological encyclopedia, and it is obvious that Drey prefers the former. Space constrains prevent any detailed, or even brief, comparison of many overlapping themes in the encyclopedia of Drey and Schleiermacher.[11]

Drey had studied the growing field, both Protestant and Catholic, of theological encyclopedia. These encyclopediae traditionally divided theology into four disciplines: exegesis, history, dogmatics, and practical theology.[12] Schleiermacher realigned this structure by keeping practical theology, adding philosophical theology, and folding exegesis, history, and dogmatics under historical theology.[13] Historical theology herewith becomes a master field, and Schleiermacher teases its exalted place in the "Introduction," when he writes, "Theology is a positive science."[14] Later, Schleiermacher describes historical theology as follows: "It is at once not only the foundation of practical theology but also the verification of philosophical

---

[10] Bradford E. Hinze, "Johann Sebastian Drey's Critique of Friedrich Schleiermacher's Theology," *Heythrop Journal* 37 (1996), p. 4.

[11] Two fine monographs in English do this. See Bradford E. Hinze, *Narrating History Developing Doctrine: Friedrich Schleiermacher and Johann Sebastian Drey* (Oxford: Oxford University Press, 1993), and John Thiel, *Imagination & Authority: Theological Authorship in the Modern Tradition* (Minneapolis: Fortress Press, 1991).

[12] For this point see Zachary Purvis, *Theology and the University in Nineteenth-Century Germany* (Oxford: Oxford University Press, 2016), p. 147.

[13] For this and what follows, see *BO*.

[14] *BO* §1, p. 1; his emphasis on the positivity of religion stretches all the way back to the "Fifth Speech" in *On Religion*.

theology"; "Historical theology is the actual corpus of theological study."[15] This move allowed theology to encounter its own positivity and to think about it with historical consciousness.

Drey also exchanges the fourfold structure for a threefold one, but replaces "philosophical theology" with "scientific theology," where he allocates not just polemics and apologetics, but also doctrinal theology. Drey bookends the scientific with the historical and the practical. Like Schleiermacher, Drey stresses the *positive* nature of Christianity, by which he means the historical: "This positive character of Christianity must not be overlooked or given cursory attention by anyone who intends to offer a fully accurate and authentic account of it." Later in the opening section he affirms this point: "Christianity is a particular positive religion."[16] For Drey (though perhaps less clearly for Schleiermacher), the positivity in Christianity is directly bound up with the historical nature of its reality.[17] Though God, the true object of theology, can be known through abstract, necessary truths of reason, the study of theology must take into account that God appeared in particular times and places, became incarnate in Jesus Christ, and the particular witness of God's ongoing presence can be chronicled through the history of religion and specifically of the Christian church.

Drey clearly borrowed Schleiermacher's threefold division of the field and accented, as did Schleiermacher, the centrality of historical study in the study of theology. Both Schleiermacher in Berlin and Drey in Tübingen felt external pressures to justify the place of theology in the university and to do so by writing a theological encyclopedia. Their works, the *Brief Outline* and the *Brief Introduction*, are considered landmarks in the field two hundred years later.

34.3.2 Development of Doctrine

The expanding field of history impacted the way these two titans organized the discipline of theology; it also changed the way theologians thought about the relationship between truth and time. For Drey, growing historical consciousness made the older and static scholastic framework untenable. In his flawed but still canonical account of doctrinal development, Owen Chadwick cites a famous passage from Jacques Bossuet, an archetypical post-Tridentine thinker: "The Church's doctrine is always the same ... The Gospel is never different from what it was before. Hence, if at any time someone says that the faith includes something which yesterday was not said to be of the faith, it is always heterodoxy, which is any doctrine different from orthodoxy."[18] The modern explosion of historical data and understanding cast doubt on Bossuet's truism, a doubt that posed grave problems for those

---

[15] *BO* §§27, 28, p. 13.

[16] Johann Sebastian Drey, *Brief Introduction to the Study of Theology*, trans. Michael J. Himes (New York: Crossroad, 1997), §§34, 48, pp. 14, 20.

[17] For a helpful comparison of positive religion in Schleiermacher and Drey, see Hinze, *Narrating History*, pp. 220–225.

[18] Owen Chadwick, *From Bossuet to Newman*, 2nd ed. (Cambridge: Cambridge University Press, 1987), p. 17. For Chadwick on Drey, and Schleiermacher's influence, see ibid., pp. 102–111. For a delightful counterweight to the often presumptively negative account of Catholic Tridentine theology, see Trent Pomplun, "Early Modern Catholic Theology (1500–1700)," in *The Oxford Handbook of Catholic Theology*, ed. Lewis Ayres and Medi Ann Volpe (Oxford: Oxford University Press, 2019), pp. 563–576.

wedded to a worldview in which the authority of churches rested on their having taught the same thing, in the same way, for the duration of their existence.[19] If "what the Church teaches" concerning marriage has changed, then current teaching is subject to change, and it would seem difficult to reconcile the mutability of church teaching with the divine authorship undergirding these teachings.

Both Schleiermacher and Drey understood the urgency of the situation and sought to address it not just by stepping into the dogmatic controversies of the day, but by highlighting methods and theories that would provide a theological grammar to articulate whether and how doctrine develops. By locating dogmatic theology within historical theology, Schleiermacher already tipped his hand about his concerns with an understanding of doctrine that purported to be timeless. Doctrines were the product of a historical process. John Thiel helpfully summarizes Schleiermacher's orientation:

> Historical theology, [Schleiermacher] judged, needed to embrace a more creative explanation of tradition, one that could serve as an alternative to the long-held notion of tradition as an unchanging deposit of faith contained in the letter of the scriptural text or the dogmatic formula...[20]

The task here, of course, is not to describe how Schleiermacher did this, but rather to show what debt Drey's theology of doctrinal development owed to the Berlin theologian.[21] The development of doctrine occupied Drey from the outset of his academic career, and before he encountered Schleiermacher.[22] As Thiel notes, Drey favored organic metaphors during this period.[23] This preference changed by the time of the *Brief Introduction*, and Schleiermacher's influence can be traced in two ways: first, in Drey's adoption of the language of *construction* and *reconstruction* to illuminate how the individual theologian takes an active role in the actual development of doctrine; second, through a dialectical model that accounts for the movement of doctrine from the variable to the fixed.

---

[19] For this shift, see Bernard Lonergan: "The Transition from a Classicist World-View to Historical-Mindedness," in *A Second Collection*, ed. William Ryan and Bernard Tyrrell (Toronto: University of Toronto Press, 1996), pp. 1–9.

[20] John Thiel, "Naming the Heterodox: Interconfessional Polemics as a Context for Drey's Theology," in *Revision der Theologie—Reform der Kirche*, ed. Abraham Peter Kustermann (Würzburg: Echter, 1994), p. 129; on the same page, see note 30 for bibliography regarding Schleiermacher's influence on Drey's understanding of doctrinal development.

[21] Drey's contribution to this question is not just acknowledged in scholarship on Drey, but also in larger studies on doctrinal development: see Jan Hendrik Walgrave, *Unfolding Revelation: The Nature of Doctrinal Development* (Philadelphia: Westminster, 1972), pp. 285ff.; Chadwick, *From Bossuet to Newman*, pp. 102–111; Grant Kaplan and Holly Taylor Coolman, "The Development of Doctrine," in *The Oxford Handbook of Catholic Theology*, ed. Lewis Ayers and Medi Ann Volpe (Oxford: Oxford University Press, 2015), pp. 612–629.

[22] See, for instance, the 1812 essay, Johann Sebastian Drey, "Revision des gegenwärtigen Zustandes der Theologie," in *Revision von Kirche und Theologie: Drei Aufsätze*, ed. Franz Schupp (Darmstadt: Wissenschaftliche Buchgesellschaft, 1984), pp. 1–24.

[23] Thiel, *Imagination & Authority*, p. 80.

34.3.3 Creative Hermeneutics

In the *Brief Introduction*, Drey describes the vocation and task of theology as "nothing less than the construction of religious faith through knowledge."[24] This construction can take on a historical shape: Christians in the first century believed "x," and by the fourth century believed "x + y" about the nature of Jesus. It can also take on a "scientific shape," and Drey insists on the necessity of the latter. He writes, "We regard a rigorously scientific construction of theology as a necessity, given the spirit of our age and the current stage not only of theology but of Christianity itself."[25] An example of scientific construction would be the division of theology presented in the *Brief Outline*. The history of theology does not divide itself; it is done through the creative act. Drey gives a longer explanation of this task in his section on hermeneutics (§§152–161), which echoes Schleiermacher's famous divinatory hermeneutic: "The interpreter must put himself completely in the author's position, must transform himself into the author, so to speak, and then construct anew what the author created originally; this is called reconstruction [*Nachconstruieren*]."[26] This act is creative, not mechanical or rote. For this reason, the vocation for theology requires more than ordinary piety: "The unequivocal vocation for theology consists in . . . what by analogy could be called religious genius."[27] The concern with genius strongly marked Romanticism, and by extension Schleiermacher, with its emphasis on individual creativity.[28] Thiel relays Drey's evident reliance on Schleiermacher's hermeneutics: "Anyone familiar with Schleiermacher's writings cannot help but be struck by the similarities between Drey's account of the interpretive act and Schleiermacher's," right down to the language of *Nachconstruieren*.[29]

34.3.4 Dialectics of Orthodoxy

Both Drey and Schleiermacher had an understanding of history and of historical consciousness too advanced to accept a static view of Christianity. In this view, being orthodox in the here and now means adherence to whatever period in Christian history, or formulation, or text is deemed essentially Christian. Yet if one imagined Christianity as a living tradition, as Drey did, then Christianity was not always the same thing at every time. In order for Christianity to be meaningful, however, it cannot be in a constant state of flux. The task then, was to identify what was mobile and what was fixed in Christianity. To do so, both

---

[24] Drey, *Brief Introduction*, §45, p. 19.
[25] Drey, *Brief Introduction*, §46, p. 23.
[26] Drey, *Brief Introduction*, §161, p. 75.
[27] Drey, *Brief Introduction*, §102, p. 47.
[28] For the theme of genius in Romanticism, see Darrin McMahon, *Divine Fury: A History of Genius* (New York: Basic Books, 2013), pp. 113–149.
[29] John Thiel, "The Universal and the Particular," in *The Legacy of the Tübingen School*, ed. Donald Dietrich and Michael Himes (New York: Crossroad/Herder, 1997), p. 61. For a comparison between Drey's divinatory hermeneutic and Schleiermacher's psychological interpretation, see Thiel, *Imagination & Authority*, pp. 85–90; Hinze takes particular issue with Gadamer's now canonical assessment of Schleiermacher's hermeneutics (Hinze, *Narrating History, Developing Doctrine*, pp. 141–143).

theologians had to swim against the current, and in Drey's case an extremely strong current, to sway readers toward a wider notion of doctrinal acceptability.[30]

Famously, in the *Brief Outline*, Schleiermacher liberates the term "heterodox" from its normally pejorative connotation. He associates orthodoxy with a fixed (*festhalten*) state and mobility (*beweglich*) with what is heterodox.[31] He goes on to note the characteristics of both false orthodoxy and false heterodoxy. Schleiermacher's new and improved orthodoxy, as he intended it for the Protestant Church of his day, will possess a "mobility [*Beweglichkeit*] of the letter," in spite of which it will "still be able to be orthodox in all the major points of doctrine."[32] The validity of a given doctrine depends on its capacity to navigate a state of oscillation "above and between its orthodox and heterodox poles," the fixed and the mobile.[33] To understand what Schleiermacher might have in mind, take a term like "consubstantiation." It presents a problem because, for the modern sensibility, substance means matter, whereas for a medieval Aristotelean, an "immaterial substance" would not present a contradiction. The fixed might be some understanding of how Christ could be present, but it would be a mistake to insist on a formula, like "consubstantiation," that does not carry the same weight in a post-Aristotelean worldview. The task of the theologian is to sift the fixed from the mobile, to preserve the essence of Christianity in each new historical setting.

Drey treats this problem in the subheading "System of Christian Doctrine" under the branch of "Scientific Theology." In the attempt to give scientific coherence to Christian teaching, the theologian must take into account the nature of what is taught. For Drey, it is not a "dead tradition [*todte Ueberlieferung*]" but a living one, and thus its teaching develops, and "has two elements: a fixed and a mobile [*ein fixes und ein bewegliches*]."[34] While borrowing the framework of fixed and mobile,[35] Drey does not go as far as Schleiermacher in associating the mobile with the heterodox. Instead he prefers to associate what is fixed with dogma, and the mobile with opinion (§258). Unlike Schleiermacher, Drey still prefers orthodoxy to heterodoxy, for orthodoxy regards what is fixed as fixed, and what is mobile as mobile, while heterodoxy wants what is fixed to be mobile. Drey balances this judgment by describing an equally problematic position, *hyperorthodoxy*: "Whoever denies the mutability of doctrine either because he rejects the idea altogether or elevates opinion into dogma is called *hyperorthodox*."[36] Despite their purported zeal for truth, the hyperorthodox fall short because they do not grasp the basic reality that Christianity is a living tradition, and its body of teachings are necessarily *in via*.

---

[30] For a reliable account of Drey's theology of orthodoxy, see the section "Fixed and Moving Elements: Orthodoxy, Heterodoxy, and Hyperorthodoxy," in Hinze, *Narrating History*, pp. 114–130.

[31] BO, §203.

[32] BO, §207.

[33] For this point, see Thiel, *Imagination & Authority*, p. 50.

[34] Drey, *Brief Introduction*, §256, p. 116.

[35] Thiel calls Schleiermacher's influence on Drey regarding this point "unmistakable" (Thiel, "Naming the Heterodox," p. 131). Hinze calls Drey "clearly mindful of and influenced by the distinctions Schleiermacher makes" (Hinze, *Narrating History*, p. 115). Both also note how Drey borrows from but also distinguishes Schleiermacher's position.

[36] Drey, *Brief Introduction*, §260, p. 118.

34.4 Reviewing the Historiography

Having analyzed key points of overlap between Drey's *Brief Introduction* and Schleiermacher's *Brief Outline*, the question of influence can be taken up again more critically.[37] Drey admitted almost two decades later, in his *Apologetik*, that he was swayed in his *Brief Introduction* by Schleiermacher's idea of apologetics.[38] Yet was Drey covering his tracks, even while admitting influence, in order to stay in the good graces of Catholic authorities? Here it bears noting that, beginning in the 1830s, many leading authorities regarded German Catholic theology as a hotbed of error, stemming from easily contracted infections caught from German philosophy. Things only worsened during the Catholic Modernist crisis, which peaked in the early 1900s, but remained in the air until the eve of the Second Vatican Council. In this environment, many authorities regarded the "nouvelle théologie" of de Lubac, Congar, and others as a return to Modernism. And when these *ressourcement* theologians claimed lineage to Tübingen, they were informed that the Catholic Tübingen School was simply a precursor to Modernism.[39] After Catholic Anti-Modernism fell from its privileged perch, it became safer to trace this influence positively. In the post-Second Vatican Council era, when Tübingen's historically attentive and non-scholastic method no longer instigated accusations of Modernism, scholars turned anew to this question and answered it affirmatively.[40]

This consensus received a shake-up in 2007 when Max Seckler reissued the *Kurze Einleitung* in the third volume of Drey's *Nachgelassene Schriften*. Seckler challenged much of the status quo in the section of his introduction titled, "The Problem of Drey's Schleiermacher-Connection."[41] Seckler begins by surveying reviews of Drey's *Brief Introduction*, ranging from 1820 to 1822. Only one reviewer draws any connection to Schleiermacher, and the connection is not highlighted.[42] He also notes that the confluence between the two can be explained, at different points, by the mutual influence of Schelling and Jacobi.[43] Seckler rightly complains about vague suggestions that do not properly

---

[37] For an earlier attempt, see Nico Scheurs, "Johann Sebastian Drey und Friedrich Schleiermacher: Ein Forschungsbericht," in *Revision der Theologie—Reform der Kirche: Die Bedeutung des Tübinger Theologen Johann Sebastian Drey (1777–1853) in Geschichte und Gegenwart*, ed. Abraham Peter Kustermann (Würzburg: Echter, 1994), pp. 140–149.

[38] Johann Sebastian Drey, *Philosophie der Offenbarung*, vol. 1 of *Die Apologetik als wissenschaftliche Nachweisung der Göttlichkeit des Christentums in seiner Erscheinung* (Mainz: Kupferberg, 1838), at p. iv: "I myself for a time found acceptable the account of apologetics given by Schleiermacher, which is reflected in the section on apologetics in my *Brief Introduction* (§§230ff), and also in the in the lectures [on apologetics] where it had initially served as a foundation [for my approach]."

[39] For a retracing of these steps, see Grant Kaplan, "Retrieval and Renewal: Chenu, the Tübingen School, and the Renewal of Theological Method in *Optatam Totius*," *Theological Studies* 77, no. 3 (September 2016), pp. 567–592.

[40] Much of this literature appears in the bibliography and in the essay by Scheurs, "Johann Sebastian Drey."

[41] Max Seckler, "Das Problem der Schleiermacher-Connection Dreys," in Seckler, "Bandeinleitung," in Johann Sebastian Drey, *Nachgelassene Schriften. Dritter Band*, ed. Max Seckler (Tübingen: Francke Verlag, 2007), pp. 70–106.

[42] Seckler, "Bandeinleitung," pp. 70–73.

[43] Seckler, "Bandeinleitung," p. 55, n28; p. 75, n7.

demonstrate influence, but instead assume it and thus avoid any burden of demonstration. Seckler then echoes a historiographic tendency already highlighted by Möhler, "to derive the best elements of recent Catholic theology from Protestant sources," which eventually led to an unintended *mésalliance* between Protestant historians of theology and neo-scholastics, both of whom had a vested interest (with quite different ultimate goals) of linking the Tübingen School to Schleiermacher.[44] Only in the 1840s did Protestant theologians begin to make the connections between Drey and Schleiermacher more direct. Seckler then argues that the claim that the *Brief Introduction* was merely a Catholic echo of the *Brief Outline*, was part of larger battle to discredit Catholic Tübingen by showing its debt to (or perhaps infection from) Schleiermacher's neo-Protestant theology.

Despite Seckler's efforts, the argument fails to convince, largely because Seckler attributes too much weight to influence. He rightly insists on Drey's originality and notes the many ways that Drey's encyclopedia departs from Schleiermacher's. Such claims do not undermine or even moderate claims of influence. Hume woke Kant from his dogmatic slumber, and that point stands no matter the difference between Humean skepticism and Kant's transcendental Idealism. Seckler is right, however, to push back against claims that Drey simply borrowed from Schleiermacher, as though he did not forge his own path.[45] Both Seckler and Leonhard Hell point us back to the point Möhler made already in 1827, that the tendency, especially in Protestant historiography, to downplay Drey's originality reveals a habit of regarding developments in Catholic theology as derivative of the Protestant spirit.[46]

34.5 Schleiermacher's Influence on Johann Adam Möhler

Schleiermacher's influence on Möhler compares to that on Drey, but Möhler's pronounced and public turn from Schleiermacher complicates the assessment. His earlier work, *Unity in the Church* (1825), bears a clear stamp of Schleiermacher. Despite his subsequent hesitation about the youthful enthusiasm on display in *Unity in the Church*, it remains a landmark in modern ecclesiology, representing perhaps the greatest post-Tridentine attempt to rethink the church in a way that did not identify it with the hierarchy.[47] Möhler's retrieval

---

[44] Seckler, "Bandeinleitung," p. 77. Seckler laments that this tendency took on a political dimension in the *Kulturkampf* and lasted into the anti-Modernism episode.

[45] See his concluding remarks in Seckler, "Bandeinleitung," pp. 101–106. Here we can mention the work of Leonhard Hell, which Seckler praises exceedingly, to highlight the originality of Drey's encyclopedic project. Hell concludes that, whatever similarity, there is a greater dissimilarity between Drey and Schleiermacher. See Leonhard Hell, "Der Beitrag Johann Sebastian Drey zur Architektur der Theologie," in *Theologie als Instanz der Moderne*, ed. Michael Kessler and Ottmar Fuchs (Bern: Francke Verlag, 2005), p. 50.

[46] Hell ends a recent essay on this topic by lamenting examples of Protestant theology that suffered from a failure to think and read outside of Protestant contours. See Leonhard Hell, "Dogmatische Theologie als Wissenschaft: Johann Sebastian Drey im Gespräch mit Friedrich Schleiermacher," *Trierer Theologische Zeitschrift* 126, no. 2 (2017), pp. 135–149.

[47] For this element of his ecclesiology, as well as his influence on Congar, see Thomas F. O'Meara, "Beyond 'Hierarchology': Johann Adam Möhler and Yves Congar," in *The Legacy of the Tübingen*

of pre-scholastic sources also served as a methodological model for twentieth-century *ressourcement*. His direct influence on these figures has already been demonstrated;[48] suffice to say, Möhler has cast a significant theological shadow, and the case for Schleiermacher's influence on *him* makes a de facto case for Schleiermacher's indirect influence on the two centuries of Catholic theology since *Unity in the Church*.

As a student of Drey, it is no surprise that Möhler would have had some esteem for Schleiermacher, whom the letters from Möhler's 1823 visit to the Protestant faculty in Berlin mention. Möhler identified himself as a church historian, and saved most of his praise of the Berlin faculty for his counterpart there, August Neander, although he names Schleiermacher, along with Marheineke, as its leading lights.[49] Möhler saw in Neander a model for a church historian, but when he published *Unity in the Church* three years later, little doubt remained about the influence of Schleiermacher. Michael Himes summarizes this point: "Möhler's contemporaries, both Catholic and Protestant, accepted it as an established fact that the Catholic theologian had been heavily influenced by the Berlin theologian. Where those early readers of *Einheit* saw Schleiermacher's influence most clearly was not in any particular treatment of doctrine so much as in the foundation of Möhler's whole view of Christianity."[50] This judgment is confirmed in the memorial reflection by Möhler's former student, Joseph Martin Mack: "For Möhler . . . the writings of and encounter with [Schleiermacher] in the winter of 1822/23 were all the same not without influence as Möhler began to write his first book, *Unity in the Church*, although it was an influence that admittedly provoked opposition."[51] Himself a Catholic hardliner who lost his job over his protest against mixed-marriage policy in Wurttemberg, Mack's remarks about influence, even if geared toward narrating Möhler's break from Schleiermacher, serve perhaps as the strongest external evidence for Schleiermacher's influence on Möhler.

According to Himes, §31 of *Unity* offers perhaps the best example of Schleiermacher's unacknowledged influence. Möhler writes,

> The human being is set in a great whole to act and to view himself as a member in it. . . . This is what the schools call oneness with the universe, the harmony of individual and universal life. This oneness with the universal whole is at the same time true being in God, the condition of true knowledge of God, of the creator of the universe, for the universe as such is grounded in God and is his total revelation.[52]

The only reference in this section is to an obscure theologian, Franz Joseph Seber, not to Schleiermacher. Yet the passage echoes Schleiermacher's panentheistic vision, most famously presented in "Second Speech" in *On Religion*. Möhler's *Unity* claims to exposit patristic theology—the full title adds, "Presented in the Spirit of the Church Fathers of the First Three Centuries"—and it is striking that this section omits patristic references and takes up

---

School: *The Relevance of Nineteenth-Century Theology for the Twenty-First Century*, ed. Donald Dietrich and Michael Himes (New York: Crossroad/Herder, 1997), pp. 173–191.

[48] See Kaplan, "Retrieval and Renewal," pp. 567–592.
[49] See Johann Adam Möhler, *Gesammelte Aktenstücke und Briefe. Band I*, ed. Stephan Lösch (Munich: Verlag Josef Kösel & Friedrich Pustet, 1928), pp. 83, 89.
[50] Himes, "'A Great Theologian of Our Time,'" p. 25.
[51] Mack, "Zum Gedächtnis an Möhler," in *Gesammelte Aktenstücke und Briefe*, p. 539.
[52] Möhler, *Unity in the Church*, §31 (Erb, 153 with emendations).

a Romantic idiom. In the same paragraph, Möhler talks about *Gottesbewusstsein*, a term popularized by Schleiermacher (for prominent usage, see *Glaubenslehre*, §§32–34.) Möhler's appropriation of Schleiermacher in §31 demonstrates not just one instance of borrowing, but how Schleiermacher's theology helped form Möhler's rethinking of the church from the ground up.[53]

Besides adopting Romanticism's organic monism over atomistic individualism, Möhler also transformed ecclesiology by accenting the role of the Holy Spirit in creating Christian unity. Möhler's church begins at Pentecost, not the Last Supper, for it was here the Holy Spirit descended on those gathered, and "the same divine Spirit would never again leave believers, would never come again but would continually be present. Because the Spirit fills her, the Church, the totality of believers that the Spirit forms, is the unconquerable treasure of the new life principle, ever renewing and rejuvenating herself."[54] The Spirit abides, connecting the church of the present day with the church gathered in Jerusalem. The Spirit is the animating principle that makes the community a living reality. Geiselmann writes, "On this point Möhler is without a doubt inspired by Schleiermacher, for whom the Christian common spirit forms itself to the one and always the same life principle of the totality of believers."[55]

Through this pneumatocentric orientation, Möhler was able to reimagine the church and to push back against post-Tridentine Catholicism's overwhelming influence on visibility.[56] In an oft-cited book review of 1823, Möhler had complained about an author, Theodor Katerkamp, who explained the church solely through the divine institution of the hierarchy, as though that alone would account for the reality of the church.[57] In Schleiermacher, Möhler found a model (certainly not the only model, as he would complain in his 1827 review) for imagining the church as beginning with an internal reality that would express itself externally. This approach flew in the face of the default position of Catholic ecclesiology after the Reformation, with its insistence of externality of profession and magisterial office.

By moving toward a pneumatocentric approach, Möhler was applying Drey's notion of living tradition to ecclesiology. Despite disavowing the Tridentine ecclesiological approach oriented toward an anti-Protestant apologetic, Möhler had his own apologetic interests in play. His approach problematized the principle of *sola scriptura*, a point that Möhler would make throughout his career. In an earlier draft of *Unity*, Möhler remarks, "We say [against the Reformers] that without the Spirit of Christianity they never would have found what they found [in Scripture]."[58] This Spirit animates believers, both individually and collectively, and Catholics are as wide of the mark as Protestants when they replace this Spirit with magisterial

---

[53] Möhler indicates the centrality of §31 in the opening sentence. Himes highlights this point ("'A Great Theologian of Our Time,'" p. 25).

[54] Möhler, *Unity in the Church*, §2 (Erb, 84).

[55] Josef Rupert Geiselmann, "Johann Adam Möhler und die Entwicklung seines Kirchenbegriffs," *Theologische Quartalschrift* 112 (1931), p. 47. See *CF (1928)* §140.

[56] For this point see Michael Himes, *Ongoing Incarnation: Johann Adam Möhler and the Beginnings of Modern Ecclesiology* (New York: Crossroad, 1997), pp. 50–59.

[57] Johann Adam Möhler, "Rezension von Theodor Katerkamp, Des ersten Zeitalters der Kirchengeschichte erste Abteilung: Die Zeit der Berfolgngen," *Theologische Quartalschrift* 5 (1823), pp. 484–532, at p. 497. For a translation of the passage in question, see Himes, *Ongoing Incarnation*, p. 66.

[58] Johann Adam Möhler, *Die Einheit in der Kirche oder das Prinzip des Katholizismus*, ed. Josef Rupert Geiselmann (Cologne: Jakob Hegner, 1957), pp. 385–386.

authority that must be subsequent to it. In the passage just cited, Möhler mentions three contemporary Protestants, including Schleiermacher, who see the need for some kind of theology of tradition.[59] Schleiermacher, as Möhler rightly saw, *Catholicized* in certain ways that made his influence on the Tübingen faculty more understandable, if less original. Möhler read Schleiermacher, and the central ecclesiological themes in *Unity in the Church* arose from Möhler's encounter with him. Himes's assessment is worth repeating: "While the number of direct citations may be few, Schleiermacher's presence is pervasive. Möhler's contemporaries, both Catholic and Protestant, recognized that presence and accepted as an established fact that he had been heavily influenced by the Berlin theologian."[60]

Möhler was a theologian in a hurry, and by 1828 he had written a massive study of Athanasius, two long articles on Anselm, and a defense of celibacy. The latter two have been translated and printed as books in English.[61] At the end of the "Third Book" of his study of Athanasius, Möhler took issue with Schleiermacher's preference for Sabellius' trinitarian theology over that of Athanasius. This disagreement, seemingly quite removed from the pressing issues in *Unity*, led Möhler to rethink elements of his ecclesiology. Even here though, Möhler maintained his reverence for Schleiermacher, calling him "one of the most brilliant Protestant theologians."[62] Möhler would rethink key aspects of his theology, and by the time he published *Symbolik* in 1832, his ecclesiological focus accented christological elements. Although these changes were matters of emphasis, it is fair to say that Möhler had distanced himself from Schleiermacher. Still, Schleiermacher's thought continued to hold sway.

34.6 Conclusion: Charting Schleiermacher's Subsequent Influence

When it became acceptable for the Catholic theologians to engage Protestant authors as part of the new, ecumenical orientation called for by the Second Vatican Council, Catholics took up the works of Tillich, Barth, Bultmann, and Schleiermacher, among other Protestant authors, to say nothing of Orthodox thinkers like Alexander Schmemann. This newly sanctioned encounter with non-Catholic sources extended into theological curricula, when the aforementioned authors, as well as leading non-Catholic exegetes, found their way onto

---

[59] Möhler, *Einheit in der Kirche*, p. 386. This omission from the printed version is part of the evidence that leads Geiselmann to conclude, "The name 'Schleiermacher' appears with much greater frequency than in the published text. The influence of Schleiermacher on Möhler's *Unity* was immediately noted by the more attuned contemporaries" (Josef Rupert Geiselmann, "Sachlicher Kommentar," in Johann Adam Möhler, *Die Einheit in der Kirche oder das Prinzip des Katholizismus*, ed. Geiselmann (Cologne: Jakob Hegner, 1957), p. 586).

[60] Himes, *Ongoing Incarnation*, p. 88.

[61] For an account of Möhler's development in this period, see Grant Kaplan, "Between Rome and Tübingen: Rethinking Johann Adam Möhler's Political Theology," *Journal of Church and State* 58, no. 2 (Spring 2016), pp. 234–260.

[62] Johann Adam Möhler, *Athanasius der Grosse und die Kirche seiner Zeit, besonders im Kampfemit dem Arianismus* (Mainz: Floriam Kupferberg, 1827), I, p. 305.

reading lists and syllabi. In short, borrowing from non-Catholic sources no longer seemed eccentric or questionable, even though the longer Catholic tradition lent countless examples from early Christianity (Plato, Philo), medieval Catholicism (Aristotle, Avicenna), and even the supposedly insular modern Catholicism, which borrowed more from figures like Christian Wolff and Isaac Newton than they sometimes let on.

Schleiermacher's appeal to religious experience has certainly found resonance among Catholic theologians seeking to expand theological *loci* beyond Scripture and tradition, narrowly understood. A theological project like Karl Rahner's, although materially less indebted to Schleiermacher than to Kant or Heidegger, still bears a kind of formal similarity to Schleiermacher. Here we can recollect an article by Francis Fiorenza on the subject.[63] Although not focused on tracing influence, Fiorenza notes the parallels between certain projects in modern Catholic fundamental theology and the work of Schleiermacher. By eschewing the neo-scholastic paradigm, the discipline of fundamental theology itself ended up working in the grooves already laid by Schleiermacher: Fiorenza admits that his own work took shape in conscious dialogue with Schleiermacher and his critics, admitting, "I was attempting to reformulate a Roman Catholic fundamental theology in relation to Schleiermacher's work."[64] His article is not just confessional about his motives, but also locates themes found in Schleiermacher and already mentioned above, including the idea of the Holy Spirit animating the communal life of believers: "Others, such as Karl Rahner and Joseph Ratzinger have argued that the presence of the Sprit in the ongoing life of the church determines what is normative."[65] The influence on Rahner stands out for Fiorenza: "Rahner's fundamental theology is a radical transformation with elements of the tradition version. . . . [I]t approximates Schleiermacher's *Glaubenslehre* by explicating the whole range of Christian doctrine in relation to human subjectivity."[66] Fiorenza believes that Rahner worked in a Schleiermacherian key: "If one compares Schleiermacher's *Glaubenslehre* with Rahner's *Foundations of Christian Faith*, then it is not simply the introduction or even the introductory sections of dogmatic method, but the whole *Glaubenslehre* that correlates with Roman Catholic foundational theology."[67]

This chapter began with Catholic appeals to Schleiermacher's greatness. As long as Catholics continue to read Schleiermacher, we can expect more of the same: exaltation, curiosity, aversion, and even repulsion. He is an enduring figure, a giant in the history of Western religious thought. Each generation will come to grips with Schleiermacher and make their judgments about his merits. In turn, each era will be judged by what they make of this prince of the church.

---

[63] Francis Schüssler Fiorenza, "Schleiermacher and the Construction of a Contemporary Roman Catholic Foundational Theology," *Harvard Theological Review* 89, no. 2 (1996), p. 176.

[64] Fiorenza, "Schleiermacher and the Construction," p. 190; he refers to Fiorenza, *Foundational Theology: Jesus and the Church* (New York: Crossroad, 1984).

[65] Fiorenza, "Schleiermacher and the Construction," p. 193.

[66] Fiorenza, "Schleiermacher and the Construction," p. 181; for a more recent comparison of Rahner and Schleiermacher, see Allen G. Jorgenson, *The Appeal to Experience in the Christologies of Friedrich Schleiermacher and Karl Rahner* (New York: Peter Lang, 2007).

[67] Fiorenza, "Schleiermacher and the Construction," p. 194.

Suggested Reading

Drey, Johann Sebastian. *Brief Introduction to the Study of Theology*. Trans. Michael J. Himes (New York: Crossroad, 1997).
Möhler, Johann Adam. *Unity in the Church or the Principle of Catholicism*. Trans. Peter Erb (Washington, DC: Catholic University of America Press, 1995).
Thiel, John. *Imagination & Authority: Theological Authorship in the Modern Tradition* (Minneapolis: Fortress Press, 1991).

Bibliography

Barth, Karl. *The Doctrine of the Word of God*. Vol. I.2 of *Church Dogmatics*. Trans. G. T. Thomson and Harold Knight. Ed. G. W. Bromiley and T. F. Torrance (Edinburgh: T&T Clark, 1956).
Chadwick, Owen. *From Bossuet to Newman*. 2nd ed. (Cambridge: Cambridge University Press, 1987).
Drey, Johann Sebastian. *Philosophie der Offenbarung*. Vol. 1 of *Die Apologetik als wissenschaftliche Nachweisung der Göttlichkeit des Christentums in seiner Erscheinung* (Mainz: Kupferberg, 1838).
Drey, Johann Sebastian. "Revision des gegenwärtigen Zustandes der Theologie." In *Revision von Kirche und Theologie: Drei Aufsätze*, ed. Franz Schupp (Darmstadt: Wissenschaftliche Buchgesellschaft, 1984), pp. 1–24.
Dulles, Avery. *A History of Apologetics* (San Francisco: Ignatius Press, 1999).
Fiorenza, Francis Schüssler. "Schleiermacher and the Construction of a Contemporary Roman Catholic Foundational Theology." *Harvard Theological Review* 89, no. 2 (1996), pp. 1175–1194.
Geiselmann, Josef Rupert. "Johann Adam Möhler und die Entwicklung seines Kirchenbegriffs." *Theologische Quartalschrift* 112 (1931), pp. 1–91.
Geiselmann, Josef Rupert. "Sachlicher Kommentar." In Johann Adam Möhler, *Die Einheit in der Kirche oder das Prinzip des Katholizismus*, ed. Geiselmann (Cologne: Jakob Hegner 1957), pp. 585–628.
Hell, Leonhard. "Der Beitrag Johann Sebastian Drey zur Architektur der Theologie." In *Theologie als Instanz der Moderne*, ed. Michael Kessler and Ottmar Fuchs (Bern: Francke Verlag, 2005), pp. 41–52.
Hell, Leonhard. "Dogmatische Theologie als Wissenschaft: Johann Sebastian Drey im Gespräch mit Friedrich Schleiermacher." *Trierer Theologische Zeitschrift* 126, no. 2 (2017), pp. 135–149.
Himes, Michael. "Divinizing the Church: Strauss and Barth on Möhler's Ecclesiology." In *The Legacy of the Tübingen School*, ed. Donald Dietrich and Michael Himes (New York: Crossroad/Herder, 1997), pp. 95–110.
Himes, Michael. "'A Great Theologian of Our Time': Möhler on Schleiermacher." *Heythrop Journal* 37 (1996), pp. 24–46.
Himes, Michael. *Ongoing Incarnation: Johann Adam Möhler and the Beginnings of Modern Ecclesiology* (New York: Crossroad, 1997).
Hinze, Bradford E. "Johann Sebastian Drey's Critique of Friedrich Schleiermacher's Theology." *Heythrop Journal* 37 (1996), pp. 1–23.

Hinze, Bradford E. *Narrating History Developing Doctrine: Friedrich Schleiermacher and Johann Sebastian Drey* (Oxford: Oxford University Press, 1993).

Jorgenson, Allen G. *The Appeal to Experience in the Christologies of Friedrich Schleiermacher and Karl Rahner* (New York: Peter Lang, 2007).

Kaplan, Grant. "Between Rome and Tübingen: Rethinking Johann Adam Möhler's Political Theology." *Journal of Church and State* 58, no. 2 (Spring 2016), pp. 234–260.

Kaplan, Grant. "Retrieval and Renewal: Chenu, the Tübingen School, and the Renewal of Theological Method in *Optatam Totius*." *Theological Studies* 77, no. 3 (September 2016), pp. 567–592.

Kaplan, Grant, and Holly Taylor Coolman. "The Development of Doctrine." In *The Oxford Handbook of Catholic Theology*, ed. Lewis Ayers and Medi Ann Volpe (Oxford: Oxford University Press, 2015), pp. 612–629.

Kustermann, Abraham Peter. "Drey, Johann Sebastian von (1777–1853)." In *Dictionary of Fundamental Theology: English-Language Edition*, ed. René Latourelle (New York: Herder & Herder, 1994), pp. 247–251.

Lonergan, Bernard. "The Transition from a Classicist World-View to Historical-Mindedness." In *A Second Collection*, ed. William Ryan and Bernard Tyrrell (Toronto: University of Toronto Press, 1996), pp. 1–9.

McMahon, Darrin. *Divine Fury: A History of Genius* (New York: Basic Books, 2013).

Möhler, Johann Adam. *Athanasius der Grosse und die Kirche seiner Zeit, besonders im Kampfemit dem Arianismus* (Mainz: Floriam Kupferberg, 1827).

Möhler, Johann Adam. *Die Einheit in der Kirche oder das Prinzip des Katholizismus*. Ed. Josef Rupert Geiselmann (Cologne: Jakob Hegner, 1957).

Möhler, Johann Adam. *Gesammelte Aktenstücke und Briefe. Band I*. Ed. Stephan Lösch (Munich: Verlag Josef Kösel & Friedrich Pustet, 1928).

Möhler, Johann Adam. "Rezension von Adam Gengler, Über das Verhältnis der Theologie zur Philosophie." *Theologische Quartalschrift* 9 (1827), pp. 498–522.

Möhler, Johann Adam. "Rezension von Theodor Katerkamp, Des ersten Zeitalters der Kirchengeschichte erste Abteilung: Die Zeit der Berfolgngen." *Theologische Quartalschrift* 5 (1823), pp. 484–532.

O'Meara, Thomas F. "Beyond 'Hierarchology': Johann Adam Möhler and Yves Congar." In *The Legacy of the Tübingen School: The Relevance of Nineteenth-Century Theology for the Twenty-First Century*, ed. Donald Dietrich and Michael Himes (New York: Crossroad/Herder, 1997), pp. 173–191.

Pomplun, Trent. "Early Modern Catholic Theology (1500–1700)." In *The Oxford Handbook of Catholic Theology*, ed. Lewis Ayres and Medi Ann Volpe (Oxford: Oxford University Press, 2019), pp. 563–576.

Purvis, Zachary. *Theology and the University in Nineteenth-Century Germany* (Oxford: Oxford University Press, 2016).

Scheurs, Nico. "Johann Sebastian Drey und Friedrich Schleiermacher: Ein Forschungsbericht." In *Revision der Theologie—Reform der Kirche: Die Bedeutung des Tübinger Theologen Johann Sebastian Drey (1777–1853) in Geschichte und Gegenwart*, ed. Abraham Peter Kustermann (Würzburg: Echter, 1994), pp. 140–149.

Schleiermacher, Friedrich. *Brief Outline of Theology as a Field of Study*. 3rd ed. Trans. Terrence N. Tice (Louisville, KY: Westminster John Knox, 2011).

Seckler, Max. "Bandeinleitung." In Johann Sebastian Drey, *Nachgelassene Schriften. Dritter Band*, ed. Max Seckler (Tübingen: Francke Verlag, 2007), pp. 70–106.

Seckler, Max. "Einleitung." In Johann Sebastian Drey, *Nachgelassene Schriften. Vierter Band*, ed. Max Seckler (Tübingen: Francke Verlag, 2015). pp. 396–452.

Thiel, John. "Naming the Heterodox: Interconfessional Polemics as a Context for Drey's Theology." In *Revision der Theologie—Reform der Kirche*, ed. Abraham Peter Kustermann (Würzburg: Echter, 1994), pp. 114–139.

Thiel, John. "Schleiermacher as 'Catholic': A Charge in the Rhetoric of Modern Theology." *Heythrop Journal* 37 (1996), pp. 61–82.

Thiel, John. "The Universal and the Particular." In *The Legacy of the Tübingen School*, ed. Donald Dietrich and Michael Himes (New York: Crossroad/Herder, 1997), pp. 56–74.

Walgrave, Jan Hendrik. *Unfolding Revelation: The Nature of Doctrinal Development* (Philadelphia: Westminster, 1972).

B
CONSTRUCTIVE USES

CHAPTER 35

CONSTRUCTIVE THEOLOGY

SHELLI M. POE

BECAUSE of persistent and widespread critiques of Friedrich Schleiermacher's theology in the twentieth century, many contemporary theologians do not herald his work as influential for their own. That makes it difficult to trace Schleiermacher's influence on constructive forms of theology. His influence has indeed been felt, but as Linn Tonstad puts it in reference to her own work, that influence is often "subterranean."[1] In this chapter, I will argue that significant aspects of Schleiermacher's theology have been carried on and developed in many constructive theologies, even when his name is not mentioned.

The chapter begins by offering a brief overview of constructive theology, attending to its basic features as outlined in the publications of the Workgroup on Constructive Theology. It argues that constructive theologians are formed by two streams of thought: modern liberal theology and liberation theology. Constructive theologians early in the Workgroup's history drew on the inheritance of modern theology left to them by Schleiermacher, and they are forthright in their acknowledgement of his influence. Within a decade of the Workgroup's founding, prominent liberation theologians and scholars substantially influenced by liberation theology began to identify as constructive theologians and/or join the Workgroup.[2] Wittingly or unwittingly, they offer doctrinal approaches and content that were prefigured in Schleiermacher's theology. Taking these two streams of thought together, we can see the significant influence of Schleiermacher's work within constructive theology in the twentieth and twenty-first centuries.

35.1 CONSTRUCTIVE THEOLOGY

The Workgroup on Constructive Theology was founded at Vanderbilt Divinity School in 1975 as a place for theologians who were interested in teaching theology in ways relevant to the present moment to gather cross-institutionally. As Jason A. Wyman documents its

---

[1] Linn Marie Tonstad, *God and Difference: The Trinity, Sexuality, and the Transformation of Finitude* (New York: Routledge, 2016), p. 287.

[2] I am using the term "liberation theology" widely to include not only Latin American perspectives but a variety of theologies that foreground a concern for social justice in particular contexts.

history,[3] the Workgroup began with about fifteen members, and its numbers increased to twenty-seven by 1994, fifty by 2005, and seventy by 2016.[4] The original Vanderbilt members included Sallie McFague, Peter Hodgson, Edward Farley, and others.[5] Gordon Kaufman and David Tracy were instrumental for the formation of the group.[6] Most participants were North American, although Dorothee Soelle was involved early on.[7] Over the years, others emerged as its leaders, including Sharon Welch, Catherine Keller,[8] and Kathryn Tanner. By 2005, the Workgroup's demographics became more diverse than in its beginning because its leadership sought out "a mix of races, ethnicities, and genders, and a mix between Protestants and Catholics."[9]

The Workgroup's first textbook and companion reader sought to show how the Christian tradition "has been challenged and transformed under the pressures of modern thought."[10] In this effort, each chapter of *Christian Theology: An Introduction to Its Traditions and Tasks* (1982) includes the Enlightenment as a watershed moment that requires new ways of doing theology.[11] The Workgroup then published *Reconstructing Christian Theology* (1994), which took up liberation theology as a second watershed moment.[12] The Workgroup has published one volume approximately every ten years since its founding, and each one remains in touch with these two watershed moments. The editors of the third volume, *Constructive Theology: A Contemporary Approach to Classical Themes* (2005), write that the Workgroup "continues to be inspired by the liberal theological agenda expressed in the first set of volumes, and we share the political and social concerns of the second volume as well, but we find ourselves living in different times and speaking to a very different generation of students."[13] This generation included students who were relatively unfamiliar with Christian Scripture and theology, and were not engaged in religious communities or political organizations, on the whole.[14] Though the volume aims at this particular audience, engagement with both liberal theology and liberation theology can be seen in the structure of its chapters, each of which treats classical doctrines and their history, including inevitable references to the Enlightenment and its aftermath, followed by contemporary perspectives that include reference to social and political issues at hand. Contributing authors to the fourth volume, *Awake to the Moment* (2016), continue to express a commitment to both Christianity after the Enlightenment and also contemporary issues. "Christian theologians today embody

---

[3] See Jason A. Wyman Jr., *Constructing Constructive Theology: An Introductory Sketch* (Minneapolis: Fortress Press, 2017).

[4] Ibid., pp. 54, 61, 66, 71.

[5] Wyman relies on Gary Dorrien's account of these names in Wyman, *Constructing Constructive Theology*, p. 35.

[6] Ibid., pp. 51, 58.

[7] Ibid., p. 36.

[8] Ibid., p. 60.

[9] This is a quotation from Paul Lakeland, in Wyman, *Constructing Constructive Theology*, p. 66.

[10] Peter C. Hodgson and Robert H. King, "Preface," in Hodgson and King, eds., *Christian Theology: An Introduction to Its Traditions and Tasks* (Minneapolis: Fortress, 1994), p. ix.

[11] Ibid., p. xi.

[12] Rebecca S. Chopp and Mark Lewis Taylor, eds., *Reconstructing Christian Theology* (Minneapolis: Fortress Press, 1994).

[13] Serene Jones and Paul F. Lakeland, *Constructive Theology: A Contemporary Approach to Classical Themes* (Minneapolis: Fortress, 2005), p. 4.

[14] Ibid.

the heritage both of Enlightenment reasoning *and* of Christian storytelling," they write.[15] Tapping into the liberation strand of constructive theology, the editors also claim that there is no point to theology "if it does not enter fully into all of what it means to be alive and present in these days of change, wonder, and challenge."[16] The structure and content of the fourth volume bring constructive theology's liberation emphasis heavily to the forefront.

Wyman argues that constructive theology is a form of theology that (a) highlights the fact that its claims are created by human beings in conversation with tradition and other human beings in particular contexts, (b) uses an interdisciplinary approach, and (c) aims at social justice.[17] Based on his analysis, "most, but not all, liberation theologies today are forms of Constructive theology, while all Constructive theology holds in sight liberationist aspirations, yet has not always succeeded in fully incorporating liberation theologies."[18] As an emerging discipline, then, both a survey of the publications of the Workgroup and Wyman's analysis show that constructive theology is closely related to liberal theology and liberation theology, attending to the challenges brought to the fore by modernity in the eighteenth and nineteenth centuries and movements for social justice in the twentieth and twenty-first centuries.[19]

35.2 Schleiermacher and Constructive Theology

Schleiermacher's relationship to constructive theology's first watershed moment is well known, as he is widely considered the progenitor of modern theology. Schleiermacher was one of the first Christian theologians to critically engage with the insights and questions of modernity in such a way as to contribute both to the history of modern thought and to a transformation of Christian theology in the modern period. Robert King, co-editor of *Christian Theology*, picks him out as of particular importance: "if any individual can be said to have set theology on a new course in response to the challenges of the modern age, it was Schleiermacher."[20] King's assessment of Schleiermacher's role in the history of Christian doctrine is worth duplicating at length. He highlights Schleiermacher's transformation of the Christian theological tradition while standing within it:

---

[15] Laurel C. Schneider and Stephen G. Ray Jr., eds., *Awake to the Moment: An Introduction to Theology* (Louisville: Westminster John Knox, 2016), p. 94.

[16] Ibid., p. 5.

[17] Wyman, *Constructing Constructive Theology*, p. xxx.

[18] Wyman, "Constructive Theology," p. 5. "A partial list of some of the most influential Black theologians who have been a part of the Workgroup or call themselves 'constructive' theologians include: James Cone, . . . Victor Anderson, Dwight Hopkins, Stephen Ray, . . . M. Shawn Copeland, . . . James H. Evans Jr, Sheila Briggs, Andrea C. White, . . . Anthony Pinn and many others who could be included" (p. 11).

[19] There are, of course, theologians who are not part of the Workgroup but identify their work as "constructive" and define the field differently. It is an emerging field, and this chapter does not attempt to treat the subject in a comprehensive manner.

[20] Robert H. King, "Introduction: The Task of Theology," in *Christian Theology: An Introduction to Its Traditions and Tasks*, ed. Peter C. Hodgson and Robert H. King (Minneapolis: Fortress, 1994), p. 12.

> If one considers the primacy given to self-consciousness as the foundation of [Schleiermacher's] system or to consciousness of redemption as its chief organizing principle, then clearly there has been a break with tradition. No longer can it be assumed that salvation history provides the objective ground for systematic theology. Nor must it be supposed that every doctrine previously included in the compendium of theology will necessarily find a place within a contemporary formulation of faith. In fact, even those that are included may be expected to take on new meaning in view of the radically different perspective taken toward them. In retrospect, what we seem to have here is the beginning of a new theological paradigm by one who stands within the tradition of Augustine and the Reformation, but who realizes that the tradition must be transformed if it is to be responsive to the challenges of the modern age.[21]

In line with King's recognition of the significance of Schleiermacher's role in constructing modern theology, ten of thirteen chapters in the Workgroup's first volume refer to Schleiermacher's work as of signal importance for the transformation of the doctrine on which they focus. In four of these chapters, Schleiermacher's approach, doctrinal content, and/or later streams of thought indebted to him are explicitly endorsed.[22] Furthermore, all but four chapters in *Christian Theology* list Schleiermacher's work in its suggestions for further reading.[23]

In the rest of this chapter, I turn to Schleiermacher's relation to liberation theology. Schleiermacher lived and worked on a different continent, in a different political situation, in another language and culture, and approximately a century-and-a-half before liberation theology and the Workgroup were founded. I do not intend to argue, therefore, that Schleiermacher should be considered a proto-liberationist. His work is centuries (to name only one metric) away from theological reflection done from the perspective of the oppressed, marginalized, and excluded. Although Schleiermacher does not seem to have been particularly racist, sexist, or colonialist, some of his work did in fact contribute to just those ideologies, and aspects of his theology would need alteration in order to be adopted by constructive theologians.[24] Furthermore, it would be difficult to trace a direct genetic relation between his theology and the foundational work of prominent liberation theologians. His theology does not feature as an important resource, for example, in Gustavo Gutierrez's *A Theology of Liberation*, Mary Daly's *Beyond God the Father*, Delores S. Williams' *Sisters in the Wilderness*, or Ada María Isasi-Díaz's *Mujerista Theology*. When Schleiermacher is mentioned in James H. Cone's *A Black Theology of Liberation*, criticism is not far behind.

Nevertheless, Schleiermacher's work is remarkably resonant with the doctrinal approaches and content offered in many prominent liberation theologies. Whether liberation theologians recognize Schleiermacher as one of their theological forerunners, he offered a number of transformations in theological method and doctrine that are being taken up by liberation theologians within and apart from the Workgroup on Constructive Theology. The rest of this chapter treats four themes, showing significant ways in which

---

[21] Ibid., p. 14.
[22] Hodgson and King, *Christian Theology*, chapters 2, 4, 7, 10.
[23] See Chapter 32 in this volume, "Schleiermacher and Protestant Liberalism."
[24] See Theodore Vial, *Modern Religion, Modern Race* (New York: Oxford, 2016); Joerg Rieger, *Christ and Empire: From Paul to Postcolonial Times* (Minneapolis: Fortress Press, 2007); Iain G. Nichol, ed., *Schleiermacher and Feminism: Sources, Evaluations, and Responses*, Schleiermacher Studies and Translations 12 (Lewiston, NY: Edwin Mellen Press, 1992).

Schleiermacher's proposals prefigure trends in liberation theology. The first two themes are methodological, while the last two are doctrinal.

35.2.1 Theology as a Historical Discipline

In his *Summa Theologiae*, Thomas Aquinas wrote that "sacred doctrine" is knowledge of "certain truths which exceed human reason" that are made known to humanity by divine revelation.[25] Theology thus consists in an explication of the facts of divine revelation, and is of the utmost importance, since humanity's salvation "depends upon the knowledge of this truth."[26] Departing from this view, Schleiermacher reconceived of theology as a historical discipline.[27] Rather than viewing theology as an elucidation of divinely revealed and otherwise inaccessible truths, he understood theology as a description of historical Christian piety. As he wrote in the *Brief Outline*, "Historical theology... forms the proper body of theological study; and is connected with science, strictly so called, by means of philosophical, and with the active Christian life by means of practical theology."[28] All three branches of theology are intertwined with one another, but historical theology—which includes knowledge of the early church, of the history of Christianity, and of contemporary Christianity[29]—offers a view of the whole enterprise that is required for guidance of the church.[30] Theology is, therefore, second-order descriptive and regulative reflection on already-existing Christian piety.[31] As Schleiermacher described it in *Christian Faith* (or *Glaubenslehre*), "Dogmatic theology is the science concerned with the interconnection of whatever doctrine has currency in a given social organization called a Christian church at a given time."[32] Thus, although it has been "seldom expressly acknowledged,"[33] Schleiermacher maintained that theologies are temporally limited. It is clear, he wrote, "that today doctrinal treatises from the seventeenth century can no longer serve the same purpose as they did then but that much that was purveyed by them belongs now only to a presentation of the history of doctrine, and that only dogmatic presentations different from them can possess the same ecclesial value today that they had then."[34] For Schleiermacher, theology needs continual revision as it takes account of current church doctrines and contexts.[35]

Theology is therefore not simply descriptive and interpretive, for Schleiermacher, but is also critical and regulative. Although the dogmatic theologian is constrained to give an account of doctrines that are confessed in public, it is nonetheless the case that the theologian can have "a distinctly singular influence on the form of a presentation and on one's

---

[25] Thomas Aquinas, *The Summa Theologiae of Saint Thomas Aquinas*, Latin–English ed., vol. 1 (Scotts Valley, CA: NovAntiqua, 2008), q.1, a.1, p. 2.
[26] Ibid., p. 3.
[27] BO §69, p. 120. Historical theology is "part of the science of modern history."
[28] Ibid., §28, p. 102.
[29] Ibid., §85, p. 125.
[30] Ibid., §26, pp. 101–102.
[31] Ibid., §11, p. 95.
[32] *CF (2016)*, §16, p. 119.
[33] Ibid., §19.2, p. 134.
[34] Ibid., §19.2, p. 135.
[35] See Chapter 16, "Brief Outline."

mode of handling it," or even step "forward in particular matters by way of deliberately correcting customary statements. Thus, already on this account, our definition in no way excludes improvements and new developments in Christian doctrine."[36] The purpose of improving and developing Christian doctrine is to "be able rightly and appropriately to work upon what is healthy and upon what is morbid, as well as to help forward any members of the organization that have remained behind; and also to employ what is applicable, out of other departments, in connexion with our own."[37]

Schleiermacher also maintained the notion of an "eternal covenant between the living Christian faith and completely free, independent scientific inquiry."[38] This covenant stipulates that "faith does not hinder science and science does not exclude faith."[39] Schleiermacher held that the basis for this covenant had been established in the Reformation, and that it was of the utmost significance for his own day. If an approach does not honor this eternal covenant, for Schleiermacher, it "fails to meet adequately the needs of our time and we need another one."[40] Schleiermacher was writing his dogmatic theology in the context of advances in natural sciences and historical criticism. He sought to create a theology that would not run afoul of the knowledge of the world developed by natural sciences. He therefore questions and reconceives the traditional notions of creation and miracles. In addition, Schleiermacher was concerned about the "traditional views of the messianic prophecies" and revelation, which he thought historical criticism would not bear out.[41] As such, his *Glaubenslehre* provides a view of revelation in Christ that relies, instead, on "trust in the inner power of Christianity."[42]

Though the issues that were at the forefront of Schleiermacher's day might be different than those confronting contemporary constructive theologians, both parties maintain that theology has a constructive task. As Schleiermacher wrote, theology

> should not be constructed as though its chief task were to receive and hand on in a continuous tradition as much of the previous material as possible. Instead, in times such as these our primary concern should be to take into account what appears to me to be the inevitable and immediate future. To be sure, we ought not to sacrifice or even obscure anything essential to evangelical [Protestant] Christianity. But we must in good time rid ourselves of everything that is obviously only secondary and based on presuppositions that are no longer valid, so that we might avoid becoming ensnared in useless controversies that might lead many easily to give up hope of ever grasping what is essential.[43]

As this passage shows, Schleiermacher's conception of theology is quite resonant with that of constructive theologians in the twentieth and twenty-first centuries. Not only do they conceive of theology along these same lines, but they have also explicitly referred to Schleiermacher in doing so. For example, Rebecca Chopp and Mark Lewis Taylor write that "Christian theology is a historical discipline, as Friedrich Schleiermacher argued, because it

---

[36] *CF (2016)*, §19.3, pp. 135–136.
[37] *BO*, §81, p. 124.
[38] *OG*, p. 64.
[39] Ibid.
[40] Ibid.
[41] Ibid., p. 65.
[42] Ibid., p. 66.
[43] Ibid., p. 67.

has to do with ongoing reflection on the historically dynamic life of Christians."[44] Liberation theologians have focused particularly on the importance of recent history and the contemporary life of the church, in and with its context. They recognize that theology is written out of and for particular times and places, and that it must be continually reconsidered and revised. As Stephen Ray and Laurel Schneider state, "theologians undertake the challenge of interpreting Christian ideas as best they can for their own age and the specific challenges that face that age, without losing the wisdom and revelatory messages embedded in the long histories and traditions of Christians who have sought to be faithful in the past."[45] Furthermore, they maintain that constructive theologians "apply a critical lens to the many ways that Christian ideas participate in making the world, both for good and for bad."[46]

35.2.2 Theology's Subject Matter as the Church's Reception of Redemption

Schleiermacher organized the material in *Christian Faith* (1830/1831) in terms of the Christian's religious self-consciousness (*unseres frommen Selbstbewußtseins*). This phrase refers to the Christian's awareness of the universe's absolute dependence upon God. In the first part of the *Glaubenslehre*, Schleiermacher discussed the development of the religious self-consciousness, as it is always already presupposed by and contained in every religious affection (*Gemütserregung*). He did so in three sections, each of which refers to the religious self-consciousness insofar as it expresses the relation between the world and God: a description of our religious self-consciousness; a description of the divine attributes, which refers to the religious self-consciousness; and a description of the constitution of the world, which is indicated in the religious self-consciousness. After detailing the development of the Christian religious self-consciousness, Schleiermacher turned to the facts of the religious self-consciousness as they are determined through the contrast between sin and grace. Within this second part of the *Glaubenslehre*, there are also three sections treated within each side of the contrast. In the development of the consciousness of sin, the first section treats sin as the condition of humanity; the second treats the composition of the world in relation to sin; and the third treats the divine attributes that are related to the consciousness of sin. In the development of the consciousness of grace, the first section discusses the state of the Christian insofar as they are conscious of divine grace; the second discusses the condition of the world in relation to redemption; the third discusses the divine attributes insofar as they are related to redemption.[47]

By organizing the material this way, Schleiermacher is spinning a theological web using two stabilizing lines: the Christian's awareness of the world's absolute dependence upon God, and the Christian's awareness of a contrast between sin and grace. In other words, Schleiermacher organized the material in terms of the Christian's understanding of creation

---

[44] Rebecca S. Chopp and Mark Lewis Taylor, "Introduction: Crisis, Hope, and Contemporary Theology," in *Reconstructing Christian Theology*, p. 13.

[45] Stephen G. Ray Jr. and Laurel Schneider, "Introduction," in *Awake to the Moment*, ed. Laurel C. Schneider and Stephen G. Ray Jr. (Louisville: Westminster John Knox, 2016), p. 3.

[46] Ibid., p. 12.

[47] See Chapter 18, "*The Christian Faith* as Liberal Theology."

and redemption. Between these stabilizing lines, he worked round and round, discussing the state of humanity and the Christian, the composition and condition of the world, and divine attributes. Moreover, the second part of the *Glaubenslehre* fills in distinctly Christian content that is not yet introduced in the first part. As such, Schleiermacher organized Christian doctrines "relative to the experience of redemption."[48] While experience is of signal importance for Schleiermacher's understanding of the theological task, he did not appeal to generic human experience in the *Glaubenslehre* proper. Rather, the relevant experience is the Christian's reception of redemption, situated within particular histories and contexts. Schleiermacher therefore prefers the term "dogmatic theology" to "systematic theology," since the latter conceals, "to the detriment of the subject, not only the historical character of the discipline before us, but also its relation to Church-Guidance as constituting its purpose and aim."[49]

For Schleiermacher, biblical texts and early church documents are part of historical theology insofar as they are used to gain knowledge of early Christianity.[50] The theologian must also know about "the history of the system of doctrine and the history of the Christian community."[51] Schleiermacher wrote that "all propositions that claim a locus within a body of Evangelical [Protestant] doctrine must gain warranty, in part, by appeal to Evangelical confessional documents and, where these are found wanting, to Scriptures of the New Testament."[52] The appeal to Scripture comes second here only because a direct appeal to Scripture would demonstrate that a doctrine is Christian, whereas Schleiermacher is interested in demonstrating the distinctively Protestant character of the doctrines he presents. In his dogmatic theology, then, Schleiermacher organizes the material in relation to a reception of redemption, and he appeals to Scripture and tradition throughout.

This means that a simple reading of the principle of *sola scriptura* is not adequate to Christian reality, in Schleiermacher's view. As Edward Farley and Peter Hodgson argue with reference to Schleiermacher's work,

> A community whose actual social duration is based on testimony to the gospel, the experience of salvation mediated by the presence of the risen Christ, and the inauguration of God's promised eschatological rule cannot have a literature construed as an atomistic collection of authoritative texts containing a deposit of revelation confined to a special time in the past.... The question of scripture and tradition is therefore closely intertwined with that of ecclesiology.[53]

One way to explain the intimate connection between Scripture, tradition, and ecclesiology in Schleiermacher's thought is to point to his understanding of divine revelation. For him, "the concept 'revelation' designates the originative character of the fact that underlies a given religious community, insofar as this fact, viewed as conditioning those contents of an individual nature regarding the religious stirrings that are coming forth within that community,

---

[48] King, "Introduction," p. 13.

[49] *BO*, §97, p. 130. Wyman also points out the aversion to "systematic" theology that some constructive theologians demonstrate. See Wyman, *Constructing Constructive Theology*, pp. xviii–xxvi.

[50] *BO*, §88, p. 127.

[51] Ibid., §90, p. 128.

[52] *CF (2016)*, §27, p. 166.

[53] Edward Farley and Peter C. Hodgson, "Scripture and Tradition," in Hodgson and King, *Christian Theology*, p. 75.

is not itself to be understood, in turn, simply based on the earlier interconnected historical context referred to just above."[54] Christianity's revelatory basis is the fact of the existence of Jesus of Nazareth, insofar as the Christian community is originated and conditioned by him.[55] As such, for Schleiermacher, "revelation" does not refer to propositional content, but to a person and his activity. In *Christian Theology*, George Stroup reflects on Schleiermacher's view of revelation, saying that "what is revealed is not so much truths about God as the reality of redemption, which in turn becomes the basis for indirect discourse about God. For Schleiermacher, God cannot be known directly. Redemption, however, does provide a legitimate basis for language and knowledge about God. What is known as a consequence of redemption is that God's nature is love."[56] Because Schleiermacher takes the church's experience of redemption as the object of theology, his theological method tethers Christian claims about God to the Christian community's reception of redemption by God in and through Jesus of Nazareth and his Spirit in the church. While critics influenced by Karl Barth may suggest that Schleiermacher's theological method decenters the true object of theology (i.e. God as revealed in Scripture) and centers the human subject, his theological method actually places the living Christ at the very center of not only his theology but also his theological epistemology.

Constructive theologians address the notion of God revealed in Scripture in various ways. Elisabeth Schüssler Fiorenza, for instance, argues that much of modern biblical scholarship assumes that it is possible for biblical scholars to step outside of their own interests and contexts in order to study the text objectively. She notes that supposedly "disinterested and dispassionate scholarship"[57] only "denies its particular perspective and rhetorical aims."[58] Even further, Schüssler Fiorenza suggests that this academic posture legitimates injustice and oppression. She offers, instead, a "critical process of feminist biblical interpretation for liberation."[59] Another approach is taken by the writers of *Awake to the Moment*, who discuss the revelation of God within Scripture by pointing to a Bible study group in Dallas that includes Walmart workers and construction workers. They note that "in these situations, it is rare that the Bible is read in search of absolute truth claims, for personal self-gratification, or for the sake of learning some interesting facts about the past. Rather, the Bible is read in search for answers in everyday struggles, which are the struggles of the community."[60] These authors' theories regarding divine revelation in Scripture reflect their conviction that God is revealed in the thick of real-life experience and conversation with the biblical text.

Liberation theologians are also well known for attending to the redemptive experiences of Christian communities. Delores Williams, in her landmark book *Sisters in the Wilderness*, begins "constructing theology from the point of view of black women's experience" by starting "with the black community (composed of females and males) and its understanding

---

[54] *CF (2016)*, postscript to §10, pp. 75–76.

[55] See *CF (2016)*, §13, p. 93.

[56] George Stroup, "Revelation," in Hodgson and King, *Christian Theology*, p. 128.

[57] Elisabeth Schüssler Fiorenza, "The Bible, the Global Context, and the Discipleship of Equals," in Chopp and Taylor, *Reconstructing Christian Theology*, p. 82.

[58] Ibid., p. 82.

[59] Ibid., pp. 90–91.

[60] Shannon Craigo-Snell, Joerg Rieger, Cynthia L. Rigby, and Kathleen Sands, "What Do We Know and How? Context and Questions," in Schneider and Ray Jr., *Awake to the Moment*, pp. 59–60.

of God's historic relation to black female life."⁶¹ Drawing on the anthropological work of Lawrence Levine, she argues that "black people used the Bible to put primary emphasis upon God's response to the community's situations of pain and bondage."⁶² Williams focuses particularly on Black women in the church, and uses Hagar's story as "the community's analogue for African-American women's historic experience."⁶³ She argues that God responds to Black women in situations of oppression by giving them resources to survive and is involved in developing a quality of life "appropriate to their situation and their heritage."⁶⁴ Drawing on and critiquing earlier Black liberation theologians' work, Williams argues that God is not primarily a God of liberation, but participates in promoting the survival and quality of life of oppressed people. She therefore places the religious self-consciousness of Black American women at the forefront of her theology, exploring the history of Black women's oppression in the Americas and its biblical analogue in the Hagar story, and surveying relevant Christian history, including Black liberation theology, feminist theology, and Black churches. Throughout, Williams highlights what we might call the Living God, a God who is present with Black women as they struggle for survival and quality of life.

While Williams' book does not reiterate the language or structure of Schleiermacher's *Glaubenslehre*, the theological methodologies at work in both are strikingly similar. Schleiermacher's theological method also intertwines religious self-consciousness with claims about God such that the two cannot be separated without losing significant meaning. For both Schleiermacher and Williams, revelation does not simply refer to propositional content, but to a this-worldly process of redemption and a living relationship with the divine, in which the particularity of the present moment is of the utmost importance.

35.2.3 Expanding Trinitarian Discourse

Moving now to the doctrinal overlap between Schleiermacher's theology and trends in liberation theology, we begin with Schleiermacher's call for a renewal of trinitarian doctrine. A full consideration of Schleiermacher's treatment of the doctrine of the Trinity is presented elsewhere.⁶⁵ Here, suffice it to say that Schleiermacher was not satisfied with the traditional presentation of the doctrine and called for a renewed Protestant treatment of it. Particularly concerning for Schleiermacher was the fact that the technical formulations involved in trinitarian thought are so far removed from the experience of redemption that "our faith in Christ and our living communion with him would be the same even if we had no knowledge of this transcendent fact [i.e., of the eternal divine being in itself] or if this fact were different."⁶⁶ In Schleiermacher's wake, theologians of the twentieth century have taken great pains to show how the doctrine of the Trinity is connected to Christian life.

---

⁶¹ Delores S. Williams, *Sisters in the Wilderness: The Challenge of Womanist God-Talk* (Maryknoll, NY: Orbis, 1993), p. 3.
⁶² Ibid., p. 4.
⁶³ Ibid.
⁶⁴ Ibid., p. 5.
⁶⁵ See Shelli M. Poe, *Essential Trinitarianism: Schleiermacher as Trinitarian Theologian* (New York: Bloomsbury, 2017). See also Chapter 21 of the present volume, "Trinitarian Thought."
⁶⁶ *CF (2016)*, §170.3, p. 1023.

Social trinitarians are foremost among them. Jürgen Moltmann, for instance, recounts that "from the time of Melanchthon, and particularly since Schleiermacher and the moral theology of the nineteenth century, the doctrine of the Trinity seems to have been regarded in Protestantism as no more than a theological speculation with no relevance for life, a kind of higher theological mystery for initiates."[67] Moltmann refers to Schleiermacher's call for a Protestant reformulation of the doctrine of the Trinity:

> Schleiermacher was open to a complete reshaping of the doctrine of the Trinity. "We have the less reason to regard this doctrine as finally settled since it did not receive any fresh treatment when the Evangelical (Protestant) Church was set up; and so there must still be in store for it a transformation which will go back to its very beginnings." Precisely this must be attempted today.[68]

Following Schleiermacher, Moltmann holds that the doctrine of the Trinity does not "belong in the 'consideration of the divine majesty,' quite separately from the revelation of God through Christ for us, in our history and our flesh."[69] In fact, he claims that "once this distinction is made, it is correct to turn from the doctrine of the Trinity as pure speculation and apply ourselves to the history of law, sin and grace with which we are concerned. But such a distinction is itself fundamentally false."[70] He therefore does not hold out a doctrine of the Trinity that attempts to make affirmations about God as God is in Godself: "we can only say who he is for us in the history of Christ which reaches us in our history."[71] Although Moltmann follows Schleiermacher in calling for a reformulation of trinitarian doctrine that emphasizes the importance of the doctrine of the Trinity for Christian lives, his own proposal would run afoul of Schleiermacher's doctrine of God not least because of Schleiermacher's commitment to divine impassibility and strong apprehensions about undue anthropomorphism. In addition, Schleiermacher's theology steers clear of the kind of hierarchy and subordination that remains in Moltmann's trinitarian theology despite his attempts to overcome it, and Schleiermacher does not give the cross pride of place in his theology.

As such, Schleiermacher's legacy with regard to the doctrine of the Trinity is more in line with what we find in some feminist, womanist, and queer forms of liberation theology. Linn Tonstad's work is a prime example. In *God and Difference*, she argues that "grounding sexual difference in the trinity [by gendering the God–world relation] does not rescue sexual difference from hierarchical inequality; it can just as easily demonstrate the inequality of Father and Son."[72] Such inequality is one reason Schleiermacher rejected the doctrine of the immanent Trinity. Tonstad therefore refers to Schleiermacher's argument that the equality stipulated by the doctrine of the immanent Trinity is undermined by the way in which the persons of the Trinity are distinguished, namely, by relations of origin.[73] She writes,

---

[67] Jürgen Moltmann, *The Crucified God: The Cross of Christ as the Foundation and Criticism of Christian Theology* (Minneapolis: Fortress, 1993), p. 237. See also Moltmann, *The Trinity and the Kingdom: The Doctrine of God* (Minneapolis: Fortress, 1993).
[68] Moltmann, *The Crucified God*, p. 238.
[69] Ibid., p. 237.
[70] Ibid.
[71] Ibid., p. 238.
[72] Tonstad, *God and Difference*, p. 4.
[73] Ibid., p. 10.

the development Schleiermacher describes may be a central trinitarian problem. Immanent divine paternity and filiation first developed to counter categorical subordinationism. Now that such subordinationism has been vanquished in theory, paternity and filiation may advance subordination rather than counter it, or so I have argued. This is one of the many sites where trinitarian theologians need to be schooled by radical feminist, womanist, and queer thinkers.[74]

At a more basic level, we can also see Schleiermacher's thought at work in Tonstad's work where she argues that the doctrine of the Trinity should not be used as a standard to determine "the boundaries of communities of discourse."[75] She points out that this happens in theological debates whenever theologians insist that particular trinitarian doctrinal formulations distinguish "believers from idolaters or theologians worth engaging from those who may safely be ignored."[76] Her book is therefore "a critique of how getting the trinity right (e.g., speaking and praying Father rightly) becomes a pious cudgel protecting the wielder from seriously engaging the questions and concerns raised by those relegated to the pile of tares [see Matthew 13] left to rot outside the church door."[77] While Tonstad is clearly indebted to feminist and queer theologies and is focused here on the debate in ecclesial circles surrounding the inclusion or exclusion of LGBTQ + individuals in Christian communities, Schleiermacher, too, was of the opinion that more diversity is needed in trinitarian thought. As a sequel to the trinitarian conclusion of his *Glaubenslehre*, he attended to Sabellius' position in his 1822 essay "On the Discrepancy." After offering a nonstandard interpretation of Sabellianism, he argues that Sabellius' position was too hastily dispensed with.[78] Schleiermacher's own reinterpretation of Sabellianism and the trinitarian thought he presents in his *Glaubenslehre* are attempts to expand the boundaries of legitimate trinitarian discourse. His legacy in this regard can be found in contemporary attempts at rethinking trinitarian doctrine.

35.2.4 Collective Understanding of Sin and Grace

Liberation theologians are well known for their attention to and analyses of structural sin and evil. Rather than thinking of sin as a problem primarily to be dealt with by and within individuals, liberation thinkers have pointed out how sinful structures perpetuate racism, sexism, ableism, colonialism, classism, and so on. For example, Emilie Townes identifies structural evil with the cultural production of evil.[79] She draws on H. Richard Niebuhr's work to "make sense of structural evil by categorizing and looking for the pattern and meaning of

---

[74] Ibid., p. 288.
[75] Ibid., p. 4.
[76] Ibid., p. 5.
[77] Ibid.
[78] Schleiermacher's view of boundary-making in Christian theology can be found in *Christian Faith*, paragraphs 20–22. It should be noted that instead of creating a list of propositions that all Christians must assent to, and instead of relying on prior historical ecclesial declarations, Schleiermacher identifies just four positions that seem to contradict the distinctive nature of Christianity. See *CF [2016]*, §22.2, pp. 145–146.
[79] Emilie M. Townes, *Womanist Ethics and the Cultural Production of Evil* (New York: Palgrave Macmillan, 2006), p. 7.

life as we have currently constructed it."⁸⁰ She looks particularly at the stereotyping of Black femaleness in order to understand the way "a society can produce misery and suffering in relentlessly systematic and sublimely structural ways."⁸¹ Townes calls for a dismantling of "the fantastic hegemonic imagination," a phrase she coined by blending Michel Foucault's use of "fantasy" and "imagination" with Antonio Gramsci's understanding of "hegemony."⁸² Such dismantling can occur by "holding on to justice and peace as relevant, vital, necessary, and indispensable values that we can craft into faithful action in our scholarship, in the lives of those in our religious communities, and in the worlds we live in."⁸³ This is, for Townes, a "group project"⁸⁴ that happens in daily life.⁸⁵ Townes works out in detail how evil is collectively produced, collectively embodied and enacted, and susceptible to collective dismantling. In this regard, her work can be seen as a development of Schleiermacher's own understanding of sin and evil as collective. In *Reconstructing Christian Theology*, Chopp and Taylor identify Schleiermacher's corporate understanding of sin and grace as of particular importance for constructive theologians today. They write, "perhaps we are called as theologians to point toward emancipatory praxis as what Schleiermacher in another context referred to as the 'corporate grace' that is necessary to address today's all-pervasive 'corporate evil.'"⁸⁶

Schleiermacher understood both sin and grace in collective terms. That is not to say that he disregarded the individual when discussing these topics. He clearly stated that "we are then able to trace the way in which God-consciousness takes shape in and with stirred self-consciousness only to the deed of an individual."⁸⁷ In this paragraph, he defines sin as turning away from God, and grace as the dependence of any communion with God upon a communication from the redeemer. Nonetheless, when Schleiermacher detailed sin further, he noted that "we are conscious of sin, in part, as grounded in ourselves [*in uns selbst gegründet*], and, in part, as having its ground somewhere beyond our own individual existence [*teils als ihren Grund jenseits unseres eignen Daseins haben*]."⁸⁸ Sin is partially grounded in the ways that human beings are raised and socialized, with later generations learning from earlier ones.⁸⁹ Schleiermacher reconceived of "original sin" based on this insight. He then noted that "if, on the one hand, the susceptibility to sin that precedes every deed is effected in each individual by the sin and susceptibility of the sin of others, but if, at the same time, it is also both propagated in others and secured in them by each individual through one's own free actions, then sinfulness is of a thoroughly collective nature."⁹⁰ Schleiermacher is offering here a Christian perspective on sin that broadens its focus to include the whole of humanity.

Schleiermacher carried this collective understanding of sin through to its resolution in a collective understanding of gracious redemption. For him, Christ is the completion of

---

⁸⁰ Ibid., p. 6.
⁸¹ Ibid., p. 12.
⁸² Ibid., p. 18.
⁸³ Ibid., p. 161.
⁸⁴ Ibid., p. 160.
⁸⁵ Ibid., p. 164.
⁸⁶ Chopp and Taylor, "Introduction," p. 22.
⁸⁷ *CF (2016)*, §63, p. 385.
⁸⁸ Ibid., §69, p. 413.
⁸⁹ Ibid., §69.1, p. 414.
⁹⁰ Ibid., §71.2, p. 428.

the creation of humanity. In Christ, "an absolutely strong God-consciousness is originally given, and if he enters within the continuing historical interconnectedness of human nature as such a person by virtue of a creative divine causality, then, according to the law governing this historical interconnectedness of human nature, his higher perfection must work in a stimulating and communicating way upon this same human nature."[91] In this passage, Schleiermacher is outlining how he thinks Christ's person is redemptive: "he, as well as his entire efficacious action, stands under the law of historical development, and that development is completed through its gradual spread outward from the point of his appearance over the whole of humanity."[92] In short, Schleiermacher held that Christ's person and work infuse into humanity a newly strong and consistent awareness of humanity's absolute dependence upon God, and this awareness is transmitted historically in such a way that the consciousness of sin decreases and consciousness of grace increases. The result is a new collective life. In paragraph 112, he describes it this way: "once we allow ourselves to be taken up into community with Christ, we are deeply stirred, with him, by the union of what is divine with the human nature in Christ's person, and our consent to this situation becomes a steadfast, active will to hold firm to this union and to spread its impact further."[93]

Although Townes and Schleiermacher are, of course, operating in different contexts, the way in which they both understand sin and grace to be collective and culturally promulgated is striking. Both Townes and Schleiermacher conceive of sin as intergenerational and collective, and these notions can contribute to contemporary efforts at dismantling structures of sin and evil at least insofar as they draw attention to the ways in which sinfulness resides not only in individuals but also in all manner of sociocultural activities.

35.3 CONCLUSION

This chapter has argued that those engaging in constructive forms of theology are knowingly or unknowingly carrying on and developing Schleiermacher's legacy, in two related directions—engaging modern challenges and engaging social justice. To demonstrate how contemporary liberation theologies echo portions of Schleiermacher's approach and doctrinal proposals, I have surveyed Schleiermacher's understanding of theology as a historical discipline, his focus on the church's reception of redemption as theology's proper subject matter, his call for a renewal of trinitarian doctrine, and his collective understanding of sin and grace, and I have correlated these with trends in liberation theology. Though the space of this chapter has not allowed an investigation of Schleiermacher's Christology, atonement theory, and his understanding of the noncompetitive relationship between God and the world, these are further fruitful areas of research for those who wish to draw on Schleiermacher's theology constructively.[94]

[91] Ibid., §89.2, p. 555.
[92] Ibid., §89.2, p. 555.
[93] Ibid., §112.1, p. 742. See Chapter 19 in the present volume, "Sin and Redemption."
[94] For a more fully developed argument, see Shelli M. Poe, *The Constructive Promise of Schleiermacher's Theology*, T&T Clark Rethinking Theologies Series (New York: Bloomsbury, 2021), and Poe, ed., *Schleiermacher and Sustainability: A Theology for Ecological Living* (Louisville: Westminster John Knox Press, 2018).

Suggested Reading

Poe, Shelli M. *The Constructive Promise of Schleiermacher's Theology* (New York: Bloomsbury, 2021).
Poe, Shelli M., ed. *Schleiermacher and Sustainability: A Theology for Ecological Living* (Louisville: Westminster John Knox, 2018).
Soskice, Janet Martin. "Being and Love: Schleiermacher, Aquinas and Augustine." *Modern Theology* 34, no. 3 (2018), pp. 480–491.
Streufert, Mary J. "Reclaiming Schleiermacher for Twenty-first Century Atonement Theory: The Human and the Divine in Feminist Christology." *Feminist Theology* 15, no. 1 (2006), pp. 98–120.

Bibliography

Aquinas, Thomas. *The* Summa Theologiae *of Saint Thomas Aquinas*. Latin–English ed., vol. 1 (Scotts Valley, CA: NovAntiqua, 2008).
Chopp, Rebecca S., and Mark Lewis Taylor. "Introduction: Crisis, Hope, and Contemporary Theology." In *Reconstructing Christian Theology*, ed. Rebecca S. Chopp and Mark Lewis Taylor (Minneapolis: Fortress, 1994), pp. 1–24.
Chopp, Rebecca S., and Mark Lewis Taylor, eds. *Reconstructing Christian Theology* (Minneapolis: Fortress Press, 1994).
Craigo-Snell, Shannon, Joerg Rieger, Cynthia L. Rigby, and Kathleen Sands. "What Do We Know and How? Context and Questions." In *Awake to the Moment: An Introduction to Theology*, ed. Laurel C. Schneider and Stephen G. Ray Jr. (Louisville, KY: Westminster John Knox, 2016), pp. 19–67.
Farley, Edward, and Peter C. Hodgson. "Scripture and Tradition." In *Christian Theology: An Introduction to Its Traditions and Tasks*, ed. Peter C. Hodgson and Robert H. King (Minneapolis: Fortress, 1994), pp. 61–87.
Hodgson, Peter C., and Robert H. King, eds. *Christian Theology: An Introduction to Its Traditions and Tasks* (Minneapolis: Fortress, 1994).
Jones, Serene, and Paul F. Lakeland. *Constructive Theology: A Contemporary Approach to Classical Themes* (Minneapolis: Fortress, 2005).
King, Robert H. "Introduction: The Task of Theology." In *Christian Theology: An Introduction to Its Traditions and Tasks*, ed. Peter C. Hodgson and Robert H. King (Minneapolis: Fortress, 1994), pp. 1–27.
Moltmann, Jürgen. *The Crucified God: The Cross of Christ as the Foundation and Criticism of Christian Theology* (Minneapolis: Fortress, 1993).
Moltmann, Jürgen. *The Trinity and the Kingdom: The Doctrine of God* (Minneapolis: Fortress, 1993).
Nichol, Iain G., ed. *Schleiermacher and Feminism: Sources, Evaluations, and Responses*. Schleiermacher Studies and Translations 12 (Lewiston, NY: Edwin Mellen Press, 1992).
Poe, Shelli M. *The Constructive Promise of Schleiermacher's Theology*. T&T Clark Rethinking Theologies Series (New York: Bloomsbury, 2021).
Poe, Shelli M. *Essential Trinitarianism: Schleiermacher as Trinitarian Theologian* (New York: Bloomsbury, 2017).
Poe, Shelli M., ed. *Schleiermacher and Sustainability: A Theology for Ecological Living* (Louisville: Westminster John Knox Press, 2018).

Ray, Stephen G., Jr., and Laurel Schneider. "Introduction." In *Awake to the Moment*, ed. Laurel C. Schneider and Stephen G. Ray Jr. (Louisville: Westminster John Knox, 2016), pp. 1–18.

Rieger, Joerg. *Christ and Empire: From Paul to Postcolonial Times* (Minneapolis: Fortress Press, 2007).

Schneider, Laurel C., and Stephen G. Ray Jr., eds. *Awake to the Moment: An Introduction to Theology* (Louisville: Westminster John Knox, 2016).

Schüssler Fiorenza, Elisabeth. "The Bible, the Global Context, and the Discipleship of Equals." In *Reconstructing Christian Theology*, ed. Rebecca S. Chopp and Mark Lewis Taylor (Minneapolis: Fortress, 1994), pp. 79–98.

Stroup, George. "Revelation." In *Christian Theology: An Introduction to Its Traditions and Tasks*, ed. Peter C. Hodgson and Robert H. King (Minneapolis: Fortress Press, 1994), pp. 114–140.

Tonstad, Linn Marie. *God and Difference: The Trinity, Sexuality, and the Transformation of Finitude* (New York: Routledge, 2016).

Townes, Emilie M. *Womanist Ethics and the Cultural Production of Evil* (New York: Palgrave Macmillan, 2006).

Vial, Theodore. *Modern Religion, Modern Race* (New York: Oxford, 2016).

Williams, Delores S. *Sisters in the Wilderness: The Challenge of Womanist God-Talk* (Maryknoll, NY: Orbis, 1993).

Wyman, Jason A., Jr. *Constructing Constructive Theology: An Introductory Sketch* (Minneapolis: Fortress Press, 2017).

Wyman, Jason A., Jr. "Constructive Theology, Black Liberation Theology, and Black Constructive Theology: A History of Irony and Resonance." *Black Theology* 16, no. 1 (2018), pp. 4–12.

Wyman, Jason A., Jr. *What Is Constructive Theology? Histories, Methodologies, and Perspectives* (New York: Bloomsbury, 2020).

CHAPTER 36

THINKING ABOUT RACE

THEODORE VIAL

36.1 INTRODUCTION

I once heard Dwight Moody Smith give a lecture entitled, "Is the Gospel of John Anti-Semitic?" The first sentence of the talk was, "Yes, of course." And then he went on to talk about something more interesting. It would be hard to find a nineteenth-century European intellectual whose writings on race did not fall outside the range of attitudes towards race that we find acceptable today. This is true of Schleiermacher, too, though in complicated ways. It would be easy to pick out some quotes of his and answer the question, "Is Schleiermacher racist?" with "Yes, of course." But we would lose a lot by answering too quickly. For one thing, the category of race as we use it today did not exist in Schleiermacher's day, but it was in the process of being formed. And another thing—if bumper stickers existed during his lifetime, the bumper sticker on the back of Schleiermacher's carriage in Berlin would say, "Celebrate diversity!" He played an important role in theorizing what it means to be human in such a way that diversity is a strength. So there is much that is appealing to us in Schleiermacher, and he raises the question for us of whether there are problematic aspects to what we normally think of as progressive or justice-oriented framing of race and racism in our own time. When we are thinking about race and Schleiermacher, we are thinking about ourselves.

This chapter unfolds in four sections (and a couple of subsections). In the first I argue that, while race often seems to be a biological category (it is, in part, the grouping of people based on heritable physical characteristics), there is another important aspect to what race means in the modern West. Race is not just a grouping; it is also a set of assumptions about what those groupings mean. It is the attribution, sometimes conscious, often simply assumed, that the groups we have created share certain characteristics that I will call "cultural" in this chapter—beliefs, tendencies to behave in certain ways, differing dialects, cuisines, patterns of behavior, and patterns of thought. To understand the construction of the category of race fully and to analyze how it functions in societies today we must attend to the cultural side of the concept of race as much as the biological side. In the second section I turn to the development of the idea of culture, and Schleiermacher's role in constructing that idea. In particular, I spend some time on his theory of sociability. Johann Gottfried Herder, a rough contemporary of Schleiermacher's, also plays a role here. In the third section I analyze parts of an unpublished manuscript of Schleiermacher's on the British settlement of Australia. I am making an assumption here about my readers, that most will have approved of what Schleiermacher had to say about culture, and so will be surprised (and likely experience other emotions) by how he describes Australians. This is one place where Schleiermacher challenges us to think about ourselves. There has been very little scholarship on the topic of Schleiermacher and race. In the fourth section I raise several topics related to race that are important for us today and propose some ways in which further work on Schleiermacher could help us in our own thinking about race.

36.2 BACKGROUND

36.2.1 What Did Race Mean in Germany in the Eighteenth and Nineteenth Centuries?

Race is a social construct, as everyone now says. But the history of its construction is complex. When and why was it constructed? Is it an appropriate category to apply to the ancient or medieval worlds? J. Kameron Carter locates the origins of race in the supersessionist theology of second-century Gnostics.[1] Willie James Jennings locates it in the bodies of European explorers and conquerors in the fifteenth and sixteenth centuries, whose sense of self was dislocated from (European) native landscapes.[2] Thandeka locates the origins of race in seventeenth-century Virginia laws that created the categories of "white" and "black" in order to divide and weaken the economic servant class in their struggles against the wealthy planter class.[3] I argue that post-Kantian philosophers (this includes Schleiermacher) add a very important stratum to these genealogies of the development of race.

As with all genealogies, the result of doing the difficult close work is not to fix a concept in some essentialist way, but to show how semantic layers shift and accrete. The word "race" enters English in the late sixteenth century, and German in the late seventeenth. I argue that in the early nineteenth century two important layers are added to the concept of race and combined in a way not seen before: a biological and a cultural layer.[4] We can see this combination in the famous 1897 address of W. E. B. Du Bois to the American Negro Academy: Du Bois stated that race is "a vast family of human beings, generally of common blood and language, always of common history, traditions and impulses, who are both voluntarily and involuntarily striving together for the accomplishment of certain more or less vividly conceived ideals of life."[5] Du Bois' definition combines biological and cultural categories.

---

[1] J. Kameron Carter, *Race: A Theological Account* (New York: Oxford University Press, 2008).
[2] Willie James Jennings, *The Christian Imagination: Theology and the Origins of Race* (New Haven: Yale University Press, 2010).
[3] Thandeka, *Learning to Be White: Money, Race, and God in America* (New York: Continuum, 1999).
[4] For a fuller discussion, see Theodore M. Vial Jr., *Modern Religion, Modern Race* (New York: Oxford University Press, 2016), especially chapter 5: "Herder and Schleiermacher as Unfamiliar Sources of Racism."
[5] W. E. B. Du Bois, "The Conservation of Races," in *W. E. B. Du Bois Speaks: Speeches and Addresses, 1890–1919*, ed. Philip S. Foner (New York: Pathfinder, 1970), pp. 73–85.

Blood is a biological category. But traditions, impulses, and striving for ideals are cultural. Both are central to Du Bois' definition of race.

To think of race biologically—as a group of genetically heritable characteristics—requires a theory of heritable characteristics like Gregor Mendel's (1822–1884) genes, and to think of humans as a species shaped by genetically heritable characteristics requires an idea of species changing over time like Charles Darwin's (1809–1882) theory of evolution. As we will see, to think of race as predictive of certain behavioral characteristics or traditions and impulses requires that we assume that groups of people can be defined by a common culture. The common usage of race in the modern Western world is in alignment with Du Bois' definition: race is a combination of biology and culture. Kwame Anthony Appiah has shown how this idea of race, and Du Bois' specifically, is incoherent.[6] And yet this combination of biology and culture is how race gets used in our world, incoherence notwithstanding.

Biologists now tell us that race is not a salient category. The genetic variation within a group typically identified as a race is as great as the genetic variation between members of that group and other races. And yet, as my use of the word "race" in the previous sentence shows, we still know what race is and it still operates in our world to distinguish groups of people. It is the second aspect of race, the cultural, that has such a grip on our minds. Schleiermacher plays a significant role in inventing the idea of culture, and so in thinking about race with Schleiermacher we are learning about the tenacious presence of thinking in terms of culture in our own thinking and behaviors that we take for granted.

36.2.2 Biology

Mendel had not yet planted his peas (1856–1863) when Schleiermacher died (1834), and Darwin was still traveling on *The Beagle* (1831–1836). But Immanuel Kant (1724–1804) had proposed a theory of race that, though it likely sounds preposterous to most people today, functionally fulfills many of the same theoretical needs of Mendel's and Darwin's theories on the biological side of our idea of race.

Kant entered the heated debate about whether human difference could be understood as the result of separate creations (in which case different races constitute different species) with an adamant "no." Agreeing with Georges-Louis Leclerc, Compte de Buffon, Kant argued that species were defined by the ability of individual members of the species to mate (roughly how most of us would define it today). Humans are one species. How then to account for the great diversity of physical appearances among humans? Kant argued, as many have, that one important factor in human differentiation is environment: some human body types are well adapted to hot climates, some to cold, some to dry, and some to moist. But Kant accurately observed that fair-skinned humans transplanted to hot climates, or dark-skinned humans transplanted to cold, do not change colors, nor do their offspring. There is something within humans that makes physical adaptations to climate relatively permanent. In Darwin's theory this relative permanence is the result of fitness selection that takes many generations. In Kant's theory, which predates the idea of human evolution, he posited four "germs" (*Keime*)

---

[6] Kwame Anthony Appiah, *In My Father's House: Africa in the Philosophy of Culture* (Oxford: Oxford University Press, 1992), chapter 2.

with which nature endowed the original humans, each one activated by different climates as humans migrated to different geographical areas. These germs caused the adaptive physical characteristics. Once activated, they were permanent. The germs take the theoretical place of Mendel's genes, and the fact that they are activated but then permanent takes the place of Darwin's theory of species that change to adapt to their environment, but over vast stretches of time. There are, Kant argues, four races (he calls them variations, reserving the word race for the one human race): white, negro, hunnish, and hinduish. Human populations whose physical appearances fall somewhere between the characteristics of these groups (and Kant acknowledged that the empirical range of human appearances is more analogue than digital) are either the result of sexual mixing, or incomplete development of a type.

Though Kant's mechanisms seem odd to us, he essentially codifies the biological aspect of modern concepts of race (Du Bois' "blood"). Kant also attributes different impulses and ideals to different races, characteristics that I am calling cultural—some kinds of people are more intelligent, some lazy, some passionate—in ways typical of how eighteenth-century Europeans viewed people not like them. But Kant has no theory to account for these cultural differences in the way his theory can account for physical differences. The theory of adaptation to climate accounts for physical differences, but what about different values, habits, work ethics, moral tendencies, and so on? It is the attributing of these cultural characteristics based on physical characteristics that makes race racism. This detour into Kant has been necessary to highlight the extent to which race, as a modern construction, relies on culture as a category. But where does the idea of culture enter?

36.3 SCHLEIERMACHER AND CULTURE

We use culture in roughly two senses, which may seem unconnected but, as we will see, are not: We use "culture" in the sense of "high culture" (opera, the MoMA) and in the sense of shared worldview ("Culture . . . denotes an historically transmitted pattern of meanings embodied in symbols, a system of inherited conceptions expressed in symbolic forms by means of which men communicate, perpetuate, and develop their knowledge about and attitudes towards life").[7] "Culture" in this second sense is largely a creation of eighteenth- and nineteenth-century Germans. Johann Gottfried Herder (1773–1803) is a key figure, as are the participants in the loose group of people often referred to as the "early German Romantics." Schleiermacher was greatly formed by this group as a young man in Berlin, and made significant contributions to this influential movement.

Schleiermacher's legacy on race is more complicated than Kant's in many ways. It is not a word he uses often. Jörg Rieger characterizes him as follows: "Schleiermacher is not free from racist influences," but "he does not resonate with the stronger forms of racism of his day."[8] Schleiermacher was a pluralist who tended to celebrate diversity rather than rank it hierarchically. In *On Religion: Speeches to Its Cultured Despisers* (1799) he argued, at least as far

---

[7] Clifford Geertz, "Religion as a Cultural System," in Geertz, *The Interpretation of Cultures* (New York: Basic Books, 1973), p. 89.

[8] Jörg Rieger, *Christ and Empire: From Paul to Postcolonial Times* (Philadelphia: Fortress Press, 2007), p. 225.

as religion is concerned, that the more religions the better—the more different ways people have of sharing their experiences of the infinite, the richer sense all of us have of the infinite.[9] As far as nations and national cultures are concerned, Schleiermacher was again an enthusiastic pluralist. One of the reasons he opposed Napoleon's invasion of Prussia so strongly is that the world was better off with both a robust French and a robust Prussian people, but they belonged on different sides of the Rhein. When France occupied Prussia diversity was in danger of being reduced. The debate in Schleiermacher's day that we would most likely hear as a debate about race was over the civic status of Jews. Schleiermacher was one of the few, and first, public intellectuals to argue that membership in a religious group was distinct from national citizenship—he saw no reason why Jews could not be full Prussian citizens.[10]

Schleiermacher's views on religions, nations, and Jewish equality are some of the factors that led into my statement above that Schleiermacher is appealing to us. He strikes us as a progressive, as one of the early champions of values of equality we hold dear. Schleiermacher's principle for discerning meaningful groupings of humans among the larger human race was not biological but linguistic. Like Herder, Schleiermacher believed that the most salient human groups were nations (*Völker*). (Note that a "nation" in this context is a culturally coherent group of people, not necessarily a state. For example, Schleiermacher believed that there was a German nation with a common language and history, but the German state did not exist until 1871. Schleiermacher lived in Prussia, a kingdom that was part of the Holy Roman Empire until that political entity was dissolved by Napoleon.) Schleiermacher noted something with which most of us are familiar: people who hang out together a lot begin to adopt each other's speech and mannerisms. In his *Lectures on the State* Schleiermacher gave the hypothetical case of a group of strangers thrown together on a desert island after a shipwreck. Over time, they begin to speak and gesture in ever more similar ways.[11] Schleiermacher observed that people's internal states often are expressed externally in speech and gesture, and further that humans have a tendency towards "lively imitation."[12] While Schleiermacher did not often use the word "culture" (*Kultur*), he clearly had such a concept in mind when he wrote of his hypothetical shipwreck survivors: "[T]here must the people live together, and finally get along; have a language and also conduct a common way of living."[13]

For Schleiermacher, culture or nationality is more than a layer of icing on the cake of human nature. Like eggs, they are a constituent part of what makes each of us what we are—they are central to our identity. Though Schleiermacher was deeply influenced by Kant's epistemology, agreeing that we do not have direct access to objects in the world but that our

---

[9] While Schleiermacher holds that it is better for each *Volk* or culture to have the religion appropriate for it, and is against proselytizing, it is also the case, in his later *The Christian Faith*, that the core intuition of Christianity places it at a higher level of development than other religions. He expects, over the course of human history, for all peoples to gravitate slowly towards Christianity.

[10] Schleiermacher, "Letters on the Occasion of the Political-Theological Task and the Open Letter of Jewish Householders," in David Friedländer, Friedrich Schleiermacher, and Wilhelm Abraham Teller, *A Debate on Jewish Emancipation and Christian Theology in Old Berlin*, ed. and trans. Richard Crouter and Julie Klassen (Indianapolis: Hackett Publishing Company, 2004), pp. 80–112, esp. p. 100.

[11] *LvS*, p. 515.

[12] *CG (Redeker)* §6.2, pp. 42–43.

[13] *LvS*, p. 515.

perceptions are shaped for us by the categories of our minds,[14] he disagreed with Kant that these categories are universal across humanity. They are, Schleiermacher argued, linguistic. We think in language. The categories our minds use to create how we experience the world are linguistic. Language is not the glove put on the hand of thought, in Isaiah Berlin's apt phrase (referring to Herder). Rather, "thought clings to language" (Herder's apt phrase).[15] Schleiermacher writes, "we must admit that the difference in thinking that takes place in all is that which is laid down by language."[16] If one thinks about the generally acknowledged impossibility of "perfect" translations, one will see evidence to support this view. It is not as though what we think preexists the language with which we express it. Were that the case, it would be easier to express precisely the same thoughts in different languages, like saving a Word file as a PDF.

Herder and Schleiermacher are the good guys of the early nineteenth century, from today's progressive perspective. They are the celebrators of difference, the anti-Eurocentric/ethnocentric philosophers. Herder argues that the criteria by which each culture makes judgments are themselves part of that culture. There is no Archimedean point outside of language and culture. Of course ancient Greeks think they are superior to ancient Egyptians—they are using Greek values to make the judgment. The Egyptians use their own values, and find themselves superior to Greeks.[17] Herder thinks it is absurd for nineteenth-century Europeans to place themselves at the top of a racial/cultural hierarchy. If we value the utilitarianism of early industrialization, then Europeans (especially the English) look pretty good. By other values, Europeans are sorely lacking and could learn much from other peoples.

36.3.1 Sociability: A Double-edged Sword

I want to return to Schleiermacher's thought experiment about a shipwreck in his argument about how peoples (*Völker*, cultural/linguistic groupings) form. Schleiermacher argued that humans are fundamentally expressive and fundamentally mimetic beings. We naturally make our internal states external in sound and gesture, and we naturally imitate the sounds and gestures of those around us. Sounds and gestures of others shape our internal states. This is why, over time, the shipwrecked passengers, thrown together in close proximity to each other and needing to survive, begin to develop a common language. Because we think and experience in categories of language, this also leads to the passengers developing a common set of values—a culture. Schleiermacher performed this thought experiment because he argues that something like this is the origin of all human peoples—but the origins of most of these groupings are beyond the reach of historical science.

This is not a "just-so story" for Schleiermacher. It goes to the core of his theories about what humans essentially are, and what religion essentially is. In 1799, the same year that his *On Religion* was published, Schleiermacher published an essay entitled, "Toward a Theory

---

[14] Peter Grove, *Deutungen des Subjekts: Schleiermacher's Philosophie der Religion* (Berlin: Walter de Gruyter, 2004), p. 32.
[15] Isaiah Berlin, *The Roots of Romanticism* (Princeton: Princeton University Press, 2001), p. 44.
[16] *Dial.* 2, p. 159.
[17] Johann Gottfried Herder, "Abhandlung über den Ursprung der Sprache," in *Werke*, vol. 1, *Frühe Schriften, 1764–1772*, ed. Ulrich Gaier (Frankfurt: Deutscher Klassiker Verlag, 1985), p. 28.

of Sociable Conduct" ("Versuch einer Theorie des geselligen Betragens"). "Geselligkeit" can be translated into English as both "sociability" and "conviviality." As we will see, sociability is not merely a pleasant social grace. Schleiermacher, a great taxonomist, places sociability in its own category alongside other fundamental human activities such as politics, science, and religion. What distinguishes the activity of "free sociability" is that it "is neither tied to nor determined by any external purpose." No matter how interesting and important one's profession may be, no matter how rewarding one's domestic life may be, both these arenas of human activity have purposes or ends that rein in the activity of the mind. "The highest and most complex of professions, therefore, like the simplest and lowest, produce one-sidedness and limitation. Domestic life places us in contact with only a few individuals and always with the same ones."[18]

A non-constrictive space is necessary both for full personal development and for criticizing and changing unjust social norms and structures. A free-flowing exchange of feelings and ideas allows one to imagine and know different ways of being and to "unsettle [] familiar categories formed by one's professional or domestic obligations."[19] For this activity to succeed, it must be reciprocal (a *Wechselwirkung*). One must listen as well as talk. One must express oneself freely, but not so idiosyncratically that one is inaccessible to those with whom one is socializing.[20] If one conceives of this activity as a means to an end outside of the activity itself (e.g., it builds good citizens or creates the glue that holds society together), then the society will not really be free.

> It can, therefore, be conceived as nothing other than the free play of thoughts and feelings whereby all members mutually stimulate and enliven each other. The reciprocal action accordingly is self-constrained and complete. The form as well as the purpose of sociable activity is contained in the concept of reciprocal action and this action constitutes the entire essence of society.[21]

Schleiermacher did not work out this theory of sociability in an ivory-tower vacuum. He was an active participant in the emerging "salon" society in Berlin in the late eighteenth century. Jürgen Habermas points to these salons as one of the spaces in the emerging political and social imaginary where the "public sphere," so important to democratic systems of government, was created.[22] One of the regular gatherings Schleiermacher frequented was hosted by Henriette Herz, a young Jewish woman married to Markus Herz, a prominent Berlin physician. Markus, seventeen years her elder, had already been hosting scientific and

---

[18] Friedrich Schleiermacher, "Versuch einer Theorie des geselligen Betragens," in *Studien, Materialen, Register*, ed. K. Feilchenfeldt et al. (Munich: Matthes & Steitz, 1983). Cited in Ulrike Wagner, "Schleiermacher's Geselligkeit, Henriette Herz, and the 'Convivial Turn,'" in *Conviviality at the Crossroads*, ed. Oscar Hemer et al. (Palgrave Macmillan, 2020; Open Access, Cham. https://doi.org/10.1007/978-3-030-28979-9_4), pp. 65–87.
[19] Wagner, "Schleiermacher's Geselligkeit," p. 71.
[20] Andrew Dole, *Schleiermacher on Religion and the Natural Order* (New York: Oxford University Press, 2010), p. 107.
[21] Wagner, "Schleiermacher's Geselligkeit," p. 72; citing Schleiermacher's "Versuch einer Theorie."
[22] "It was the world of the men of letters but also that of the salons in which 'mixed companies' engaged in critical discussions; here, in the bourgeois homes, the public sphere was established." Jürgen Habermas, *The Structural Transformation of the Public Sphere: An Inquiry into a Category of Bourgeois Society*, trans. Thomas Burger (Cambridge: The MIT Press, 1991), p. 106. Italics in original.

philosophical demonstrations and lectures (he had been one of Kant's favorite students) in his home before his marriage to Henriette. There was at that time no university in Berlin, and Herz's lectures were one of the venues where scientists and scholars gathered to learn the latest advances in various fields. Henriette, fluent in five languages as well as knowledgeable about physics, began hosting discussions of literature and music at the same time in a separate room in their home, and over time more and more of Berlin's intelligentsia began shifting from Markus's lectures to Henriette's discussions.

Schleiermacher and Henriette Herz became close friends, meeting daily to walk and talk, in addition to the weekly gatherings she hosted. They undertook a translation together.[23] The friendship of a young married Jewish woman and a young unmarried Reformed minister caused some gossip and scandal, though both Schleiermacher and Herz insisted throughout their lives that the relationship was Platonic. It was one of the reasons the church hierarchy in Berlin decided to move Schleiermacher to a parish in a remote village (there were also passages in *On Religion* that pushed the boundaries of what was then theologically acceptable to say in public).

The creative arts were much valued in these gatherings, and many participants published novels and poems or were musicians. Schleiermacher tried fiction (*The Christmas Eve Dialogues*), but while these dialogues are theologically interesting, it is clear that fiction is not his gift. What the participants in these gatherings did consider to be his gift was his conversational abilities. Friedrich Schlegel wrote that "what Goethe is to poetry, and Fichte is to philosophy, Schleiermacher is to humanity."[24] In a letter Henriette Herz wrote, "Schleiermacher is a rare appearance to me . . . so much understanding, so much knowledge, so full of love and yet so tender, so totally a beautiful nature. If ever something be made of me, so it will happen through him, who takes so much trouble to make something of me."[25]

Why all this fuss about parlor conversation, and what does it have to do with race? For Schleiermacher, sociability is the key to the full development of a person's individuality, and as we have seen (remember the shipwreck), it is the key to the converging values, language, and gestures that constitute the culture of a people, that makes them what they are. It is hard to disagree with the value Schleiermacher places on the free and respectful exchange of ideas. And yet there are downsides to this view. First, although Schleiermacher is a pluralist, for cultures to develop fully they must offer opportunities for sociability. Societies that cannot do this for any reason end up being ranked as less developed, or as lower, for Schleiermacher. Second, it is sociability that allows for the development of culture ("a common way of living," "the entire essence of society"); and culture turns out to be the way that we attribute "common history, traditions and impulses" to groups of people we have identified (based on appearance) as distinct. Kant's theory of race can account for physical differences between groups of people, much the same way genetics and natural selection can. That is the "blood" half of Du Bois' definition. But Kant goes on to make assumptions about groups' nonphysical characteristics (habits, mores, work

---

[23] Isaac Weld Jr., *Travels thought the States of North America, and the Provinces of Upper and Lower Canada, during the Years 1795, 1796, and 1797* (London: Printed for John Stockdale, 1799).

[24] Cited in James M. Brandt, *All Things New: Reform of Church and Society in Schleiermacher's Christian Ethics* (Louisville: Westminster John Knox Press, 2001), p. 3.

[25] Cited in Kurt Nowak, *Schleiermacher: Leben, Werk und Wirkung* (Göttingen: Vandenhoeck & Ruprecht, 2001), p. 81.

ethic, intelligence, etc.) that he really has no way to account for theoretically. These are characteristics that we would categorize as "culture," a category that was only beginning to be created in Kant's day. This is the "traditions, impulses, and ideals" part of Du Bois' definition. While Schleiermacher and Herder did not themselves use the category of race much, they do play a significant role in the creation of "culture" in the second sense listed above, the sense in which Geertz means "culture." In other words, even though Schleiermacher did not use "race" as a category of human difference the way Kant does, or we do, Schleiermacher provided the theoretical justification for attributing nonphysical characteristics to groups of people. In "race," we differentiate human groups based on appearance, but the assumptions about behavior, values, attitudes, and so on we make stem from the cultures we attribute to these groups.

I will turn now to the descriptions Schleiermacher gives of a particular people, or *Volk*, the indigenous inhabitants of Australia. But before I do that, I want to raise a question, to which I will return after my discussion of Schleiermacher and Australians. I have offered two definitions of culture: "high" culture of socially valued art and music, and the commonalities of assumptions and knowledge that joins a group of people. Are these two unrelated uses of the same word, or are they linked in some way?

36.3.2 Schleiermacher and Australians

I have argued that our category of race depends on both a biological factor (we group people by a select set of physical characteristics) and a cultural factor (conceptions expressed in symbolic form shared and passed down among a group of people). In other words, we tend to expect people who look a certain way to act or be a certain way (and this, sometimes, despite our best efforts not to expect this). Further, Schleiermacher argues that sociability—the free and mutual expression of thoughts and feelings as an end in itself, not a means to some other end—is necessary for the full development of individuality and the healthy development of the culture of a people. I turn now to a book Schleiermacher prepared, but never published, at the same time that he was writing his *Speeches*. This book allows us to see some of the ways Schleiermacher's theories about culture and sociability play out when used to analyze a non-European group of people.

One of the phenomena that feeds into the development of modernity in the West is the growth of a certain kind of market. Social orders undergo significant shifts in the eighteenth and nineteenth centuries, with a growing middle class asserting power and a desire for recognition that really had no place in the traditional three estates of Europe. It is often noted that print material plays a significant role in these economic and social shifts. There is an analogy to the sudden development of internet commerce with which we are familiar. A growing and reading middle class created a market for the mass publication of newspapers, journals, and books. We can see a great deal of anxiety at the time about what kind of reading material might have beneficial, edifying, social effects, or whether some reading created a dumbing down of popular culture. One of the genres of mass publication that fed this growing demand of middle-class readers was travel literature. In the late eighteenth and early nineteenth centuries Europe experienced a kind of craze for reports of travelers to places far from the European continent (I mentioned above the travel narrative of which Schleiermacher and Herz undertook a translation).

In 1799, Schleiermacher was approached by a publisher who had a series intended to supply books to meet the demand of travel literature. The publisher proposed that Schleiermacher translate David Collins's *An Account of the English Colony in New South Wales* from English into German.[26] Schleiermacher proposed, instead, that he write a complete history of English settlement in Australia, and he asked the publisher to send him more materials on the subject. Schleiermacher delivered a manuscript of about 135 pages to the publisher in the summer of 1800, but the publisher apparently decided to suspend the series for which Schleiermacher's book was intended. On May 30, 1802, Schleiermacher, having not heard from the publisher for a while, returned the materials on Australia, offering to take up the project again if the publisher were interested.[27]

What remains of the manuscript is mostly about the voyages of discovery and attempts at colonization by Europeans, and the flora and fauna they found in Australia. There are three brief passages in which Schleiermacher reports on the indigenous inhabitants of Australia. I translate them (clumsily, but literally) in full here.

The first passage describes the impressions of Dutch explorers arriving on the west coast of Australia:

> The inhabitants, the most miserable kind of human who can only be compared to the Tierra del Fuegans, [are] completely without clothes, and what is more [without] shelter, worse off in that regard than the ants, whose domiciles, never so big seen, filled the plain; without the first beginnings of field or garden technology, indeed without tools, it appeared, to catch the fish that nature had so richly assigned to them, and so pitifully tortured from flying pests that they barely wanted to open their eyes.[28]

The second passage reports on European impressions of native Australians on the southeast coast of Australia:

> First, the inhabitants were everywhere on the whole the same kind [*Geschlecht*] as those seen by Dampier on the northwest coast and by Tasman in van Diemens Land [the people described in the first passage], with few and insignificant differences; a people [*Volk*] spread very thinly over the land—never were even 50 seen together at one time—without any trace of laws or civil constitution, of religion or superstition or agriculture or arts, in every regard on the lowest step of human development [*Bildung*]; black in color and on narrower examination also woolly from hair, but without the characteristic adverse facial features of the negroes, medium size neither fleshy nor strong in bone structure; going around completely naked, at least as far as the necessities of comfort or modesty are under discussion; for from makeup were they nowhere bare, their skin was in part painted red or white, in part decorated with sublime work of artistic stripes [scars or calluses]. Some also wore bones in their earlobes or in the septum of their noses, and near the Endeavor River [they wore] necklaces of pieces of mussel and armbands of human hair. And these few decorations served them better than their

---

[26] David Collins, *An Account of the English Colony in New South Wales: With Remarks on the Dispositions, Manners, etc. of the Native Inhabitants of that Country. To Which Are Added, Some Particulars of New Zealand; Compiled, by Permission, from the MSS. Of Lieutenant-Governor King* (London: Printed for T. Cadell Jun. and W. Davies, in the Strand, 1798).

[27] Günter Meckenstock, "Einleitung des Bandherausgebers," in *KGA* 1.3, p. xcii. In "Zur Siedlungsgeschichte Neuhollands (Australiens)," *Schriften aus der Berliner Zeit 1800–1802, KGA* 1.3, pp. 269–270.

[28] "Zur Siedlungsgeschichte Neuhollands (Australiens)," *KGA* 1.3, pp. 269–270.

southern brothers, [with their] more lively eyes, whiter teeth, a softer voice and great agility in using their organs to imitate the tones of the foreigners—these were observable physical advantages. If in this the western New Hollanders were found without domicile or any house structure or tools; here in the east . . .[29]

The third passage describes the attempt to found a satellite colony on the Island of Norfolk, led by Philipp Gidley King. Schleiermacher reports that King decided to proceed in a friendly manner, using weapons only for self-defense, and to trying to encourage free trade (*Verkehr*) and mutual trust:

> [This way of proceeding] did not require a feeling of original equality to recommend to the new Hollanders a more peaceful procedure that would prohibit treating the undeveloped [*ungebildeten*] son of the opposing earth-side as a contemptuous being with no rights; nor [did this way of proceeding require] a higher feeling of honor which is a better marker of the morals than earlier races [in other words, an appeal to the higher nature of the Europeans]; nor an unassuming upright and paternal frame of mind, by which Arthur Philipp always distinguished himself. Rather it was merely the highly natural calculation led to by the composition of these people and the particular situation of the colony that would have been produced in any guard of the same of commonest intelligence. There was nothing to be won from the old inhabitants by the new, whatever type of struggle and whatever the outcome of the same one might presuppose. Their possessions were as miserable as the first discoverers had found; they led in every aspect a wretched life, and had added to this the smallest possible and simplest institutions, and had expended only so much of the human capacity for invention, out of which the progressive development of humans developed that kept the original spark of existence from going out, without actually being able to see any development or progress. With their simple standing still on the lowest level of enjoyment and activity it was probable that they would never pose a hindrance to the taking possession of the treasures of the land, were they yet to be discovered, an event that was not very likely. Just as little could they [themselves] be a desirable possession. Even when the colony needed more helping hands (of which, surely, the greatest part of the colony included), of what use could one make of these people? Those who from real need (because the climate and the pests demanded to be sure a better shelter) had not yet been compelled to devise better more comfortable dwellings as their huts and caves which didn't even protect them from moisture and not infrequently . . .[30]

There are clearly passages here that raise alarm bells for our current racial sensitivities. Like Kant, Schleiermacher has no doubts about the Australians as conspecies with Europeans. They had "the original spark of [human] existence," and were inventive enough to keep it from being extinguished. But Schleiermacher's summary of the conditions of the Australians' lives smacks of the discredited language of "the primitive." They are "wretched." They had no technology or agriculture or tools with which to fish. Their ability to provide themselves shelter did not even reach the technological level of ants. Schleiermacher does call the body modifications of the people on the southeast coast "sublime art," but it is not the kind of cultural expression that allows him to see any kind of civic organization or religious meaning. He does not see civil institutions or religion.[31]

---

[29] Ibid., p. 271. The passage breaks off here.
[30] Ibid., pp. 278–279. The passage breaks off here.
[31] See David Chidester, *Savage Systems: Colonialism and Comparative Religion in Southern Africa* (Charlottesville: University of Virginia Press, 1996).

Schleiermacher does not attribute what he takes to be the Australians' place on the lowest level of development or progress to any innate characteristic like Kant's germs. Their characteristics as a people is not based on biology. This is an important reminder to us that we need to move our contemporary discussions about race beyond biology to understand race's effects in our world. Rather, Schleiermacher points to sociability as a factor explaining the state of Australian culture, a culture that leaves them "the most miserable kind of human." Never did they gather in a group of even 50 people. The conditions for sociability do not exist among the indigenous Australians. In contrast to his shipwreck thought experiment, Australians do not gather at the critical mass at which their expression of their internal states in speech and gesture and their lively imitation of each other enables the personal and communal process of development. There is not a sufficient free-flowing exchange of feelings and ideas that would allow them to imagine and know different ways of being and to "unsettle familiar categories formed by one's professional or domestic obligations."[32] They are *ungebildet*, "undeveloped." Recall Henriette Herz's comment that "If ever something be made of me, so it will happen through him [Schleiermacher]." The unconstrained exchange of sociability is precisely what allows individuals to develop (*bilden*) into their true and full selves. For the Australians there is no possibility of personal development, and thus no possibility of social development of this people (*Volk*).

How are we to judge this? One possibility is to place Schleiermacher on the balance arm of our racial values and weigh him as too problematic to use (I have students and colleagues who react negatively to the presence of people like Schleiermacher on a syllabus) or with a kind of "handle with care" warning ("Schleiermacher is not free from racist influences, but he does not resonate with the stronger forms of racism of his day"; Rieger). We could stop with labeling John an anti-Semite and move on to another Gospel. But that would close off an important conversation partner, not just in the sense of a trade-off—Schleiermacher is problematic on race but that may be outweighed by his Christology or his pluralism—but a partner who can teach us something important about race. Once we have judged we can continue to think: we would not use language like Schleiermacher's. But he poses to us the question: If we value sociability, if we agree that the free exchange of ideas is worth promoting, does it lead us too to ranking people (*Völker*) as more and less developed, as more and less deserving of respect? In the final section of this chapter I will raise this question again in terms of assemblages, and the way our values get taken up and shaped by global systems of power and economy.

A more nuanced reckoning would include the following: it would be difficult to hold Schleiermacher responsible for his judgments about the complexity of Australian society, given his sources. We might wish that he had assumed complexity, and therefore been more skeptical of his sources. I'll return to this issue below. It is disappointing that Schleiermacher does not see the rich cultural expressions that are present in his sources. He notes the body modifications and decorations of the Australians, but in the same passage cannot see that they have any art or religion. Despite being one of the main people to teach us that each culture has its own values, and so there is no real angle from which one culture can judge another, he fails to see the possibilities of Australian culture. The two definitions of the word "culture" seem to be collapsing into one another. Schleiermacher's location in the "high"

---

[32] Wagner, "Schleiermacher's Geselligkeit," p. 71.

culture of the Berlin salons, where literature and music and politics were discussed and the goal was simply to draw one another out, to express oneself and to help others in their self-expression, is so far removed from the culture of the Australians in the Geertzian sense that Schleiermacher has trouble seeing it as a culture at all.

We might think that Schleiermacher was guilty of a failure of the imagination, or that his values were admirable, but he was unable to live up to them. But I think something deeper and more important is going on. I want to conclude with some preliminary reflections on three topics that we need to work through ourselves, and that we can take up in conversation with what we have learned about Schleiermacher.

36.4 Thinking with Schleiermacher

The scholarship on Schleiermacher and race is scanty. Leora Batnitzky makes insightful use of Schleiermacher as constructor of the category of religion, a category not well suited to many forms of Judaism (which is also an ethnicity and a nationality, among other things).[33] Steven Jungkeit offers a fascinating analysis of the reconfiguration of space in Schleiermacher's theology. For Jungkeit, Schleiermacher offers resources for disrupting an imperial imaginary. While not explicitly about race, the connection of imperialism and racism makes this book quite relevant.[34] Jörg Rieger situates Schleiermacher's theory of religion as part of the rise of a specific phase of bourgeois capitalism—again, adjacent to but important for the discussion of race.[35] The two scholars perhaps most influential in arguing that race is a product of Christian theological histories and mistakes, Willie James Jennings and J. Kameron Carter, do not take up Schleiermacher as part of this theological genealogy (Carter discusses him in the context of hermeneutics).

36.4.1 Pluralism

In his carefully worked out epistemology, Schleiermacher accepts Kant's theory that we do not have direct access to things as they are, but only to how they appear to us. He argues, with Herder, that the categories of our minds that shape our experience are not universal, as Kant had argued, but linguistic. This entails that one's mother tongue shapes, at the deepest levels, the way one experiences the world, the way one thinks, and the possibilities available for what kind of individual self one can be. Because a people (*Volk*) shares a common language, each people has a culture that is made up of what and how they experience and think. Living at a time in the wake of the Enlightenment, when many Europeans believed that they had achieved a level of rationality and science that set them at a more advanced level than the rest of the world, Schleiermacher argued that the shared cultural values of a

---

[33] Leora Batnitzky, *How Judaism Became a Religion: An Introduction to Modern Jewish Thought* (Princeton: Princeton University Press, 2011).

[34] Steven R. Jungkeit, *Spaces of Modern Theology: Geography and Power in Schleiermacher's World* (New York: Palgrave Macmillan, 2012).

[35] Rieger, *Christ and Empire*, p. 197.

people contain within them the criteria by which they make all their judgments. The inflated sense of worth of Europeans corresponded to what they held to be important. But each culture had its own values, its own judgments. Schleiermacher is one of the first to argue against Euro- and ethno-centrism.

Although an ordained Reformed minister in the age of imperialism, Schleiermacher argued against colonialism, and against proselytizing and converting others. Because religion is a sense of the infinite, "[e]ach person must be conscious that his religion is only a part of the whole," and "there are [other] views just as pious." Other religions offer the chance to experience a "sense for which he may be completely lacking."[36]

And yet Schleiermacher is not a complete relativist. Each culture is valuable, but every culture requires certain conditions in order to flourish and reach its full expression. Underpinning the whole philosophy of pluralism is a commitment to the values of free expression, non-coercion, sociability. These are values that I also hold. And yet they lead me, and us, to some vexing contradictions. There are cultures that have much more sharply defined and policed gender roles than mine, for example. It is hard not to judge this as an abridgment of freedoms, of the full humanity of women and sexual minorities and men trapped in narrow models of masculinity. It seems to be a coercive or artificial restraint on sociability and personal development. To be a consistent anti-ethnocentrist or pluralist, however, would block any place from which to make these judgments. This is not necessarily an insolvable conundrum. But it is an unavoidable conundrum if we begin, as many of us do, with Schleiermacher's philosophy of culture and cultural diversity.[37] Perhaps, in Schleiermacher's day, it would be plausible to argue that the British ought to stay in Britain and leave the Australians to themselves. In our ever-increasingly globalized world, staying in Britain would not erase the cultural contact and economic impacts of different peoples upon each other. What is our responsibility here? Rather than simply judging Australians to be "wretched" from a European perspective, one could enter into dialogue with foreign cultures. And if they themselves purport to be wretched? What forms of "development," of "foreign aid," do we owe to others? What do they owe to us? Are there indigenous values that would make Westerners healthier, our relationships more humane, our relationship to the environment more sustainable? Where is the line of cultural appropriation that we ought not cross? How can material assistance avoid cultural "contamination"? Some of Schleiermacher's answers to these questions trouble us. Here it is more fruitful to continue on beyond criticizing Schleiermacher's judgments and ask ourselves about our own judgments or abnegation of judgment.

36.4.2 Intersectionality

Schleiermacher and Herder are often accused of promoting a dangerous kind of cultural homogeneity. If the human tendency to express and mimic forms a people over time, there

---

[36] *Speeches¹*, p. 27.

[37] For a brilliant analysis of the way Western liberal and feminist values block us from seeing different kinds of agency, particularly in the women's mosque movement in Egypt, see Saba Mahmood, *The Politics of Piety: The Islamic Revival and the Feminist Subject* (Princeton: Princeton University Press, 2011).

is a danger that particularities of groups within the larger group could be erased. This is precisely the issue at stake in the debate about whether there is a place for a Jewish subculture in Prussia. This is a real danger of the cultural diversity stance taken by Herder and Schleiermacher. Let a thousand flowers bloom, but each flower ought to be pure, not mixed. While Herder and Schleiermacher do not fall into this trap, some of their followers do, with disastrous consequences for Germany. It does not take long for the cultural and linguistic bases of peoplehood to become a blood basis—Germany for the Germans. Ernst Moritz Arndt and Friedrich Ludwig Jahn (the founders of the gymnastics movement), for example, were liberal compatriots of Schleiermacher's in fighting against French occupation. In both, nationalism soon became German ethnocentrism and antisemitism. Schleiermacher, in contrast, argued that Germany was a cultural/linguistic *Volk*, not defined by blood. He has a sense of what today we call intersectionality. Identity is not singular. One can be Prussian and Jewish. This set of issues is not just historical: in the contemporary United States there are life and death struggles over who belongs, what defines an "American"—is it a certain kind of ethnicity, or religious background, or cultural heritage? Must everyone speak English? What history should we teach in public schools? Do we emphasize "e pluribus unum" or "In God we trust"?

Schleiermacher offers excellent resources here—he does not fall into the trap some accuse him of laying. He is profoundly aware that some classes of people in Prussia have less opportunity for sociability and self-development than others. There is an intersectionality of national identity, gender, and labor. In some forms of labor humans become a mechanism, which is for him dehumanizing.[38] He argues for the unification of German states into a larger cultural and political entity that would include Catholic and Protestant regions. One can be German and Catholic, or German and Protestant. One can be a hyphenated German (Bavarian-German, Prussian-German, Jewish-German) and truly be both. Being a woman in Prussia is not the same as being a man, but both are truly Prussian.

Schleiermacher's thinking on these issues is always penetrating and instructive, even when we end up disagreeing. There is a robust debate among scholars about the extent to which Schleiermacher is or is not a helpful resource for feminists. Though he advocates Jewish citizenship, he recommends "improvements" to Judaism that strike us as inappropriate (though they did not strike his Jewish friends as inappropriate—a reminder to us to be as aware as possible of our own perspectives).

But there is something in the logic of intersectionality, the idea that people have more than one identity and that their multiple identities intersect, that is limiting at the same time that it is liberating. And both the limiting and the liberating aspects stem from the ideas of culture and cultural diversity we inherit from Schleiermacher. Kimberlé Crenshaw's legal arguments in *DeGraffenReid v General Motors* (1976) that General Motor's seniority-based system of layoffs, while not discriminating against women or against Black people, did unjustly discriminate against Black women, showed the critical need for intersectional analysis.[39] Intersectionality provided a powerful tool for diversity, especially in the academy in the 1980s and 1990s as universities sought to strengthen their academic work by increasing the experiences and perspectives present on their faculties and student bodies.

---

[38] Brandt, *All Things New*, p. 123.

[39] Kimberlé W. Crenshaw, "Race, Gender, and Sexual Harassment," *Southern California Law Review* 65 (1992), pp. 1467-1476. Available at https://scholarship.law.columbia.edu/faculty_scholarship/2867.

But there seems to be a limit to what intersectionality can accomplish. My own institution has done a very good job of diversifying its faculty across metrics of race, gender, and queerness. We have achieved a high level of what a former faculty colleague and diversity officer referred to as "zoological diversity." We have checked many boxes. But intersectionality works differently in different environments. It is an excellent tool in the legal environment to work towards equity in hiring, promotion, and compensation. It gives a finer grain of analysis to root out bias. This is as true in academia as it is at General Motors. But, Schleiermacher teaches us, the fact of difference is not enough. We also need reciprocal and non-coercive interaction. Schleiermacher asks us to consider what social and material conditions are necessary for genuinely sociable interactions between very different people.

36.4.3 Assemblage

While intersectionality has taught us to see and act on very important factors, the limits of intersectionality as the sole basis for thinking about our identities, racial and otherwise, are beginning to emerge. One limit of intersectionality I point to above: the fact of a more nuanced way of thinking about identity can lead to more boxes to be checked, without the hard work of creating systems and cultures that allow these identities to interact and flourish. Aisha Beliso De-Jesús argues that "[u]nlike the radical social movements that have served strategic purposes in disrupting Western regimes of knowledge and Euro-centrism by creating openings in university institutions since the 1980s, academic identity-thinking sequesters identity-based subjects into ghettoized enclaves of representation, and has become a neutralizing system used to manage difference."[40]

Beliso De-Jesús draws on the work of Jasbir Puar and others, who in turn draw on the work of Giles Delueze and Pierre-Félix Guattari on assemblages. We have been thinking about racial identity in terms of the culture of a group, and in terms of the individual identities of members of various groups. Assemblage asks us to analyze larger systems and dynamics in which groups and individuals are swept up. Puar argues, in *Terrorist Assemblages*, that the identities of homosexuals in the US is not simply a matter of the intersection of nationality and sexual orientation. These identities are caught up in and formed in part by global movements of economics, foreign relations, and military interventions. A tolerance of (certain kinds of) homosexual identity in the US reinscribes "stagings of U.S. nationalism via a practice of sexual othering, one that exceptionalizes the identities of U.S. homosexualities vis-à-vis Orientalist constructions of 'Muslim sexuality.'"[41] One of the justifications for military intervention around the world is concern for the way "they treat their women and gays." Back home, as Janet Jakobsen argues, one is free to be gay if (following *Obergefell v Hodges*, 2015) one commits to a long-term monogamous relationship modeled on traditional heterosexual marriage, and one is free since 2011 to join the military and protect US interests abroad. "[T]he movement for 'gay liberation,' initially understood by many as freeing gays

---

[40] Aisha Beliso-De Jesús, "Confounded Identities: A Meditation on Race, Feminism, and Religious Studies in Times of White Supremacy," *Journal of the American Academy of Religion* 86 (2018), pp. 325–326.

[41] Jasbir Puar, *Terrorist Assemblages: Homonationalism in Queer Times* (Durham: Duke University Press, 2017), p. 4.

and lesbians from the oppression of the family and pushing back against the regulatory state, has led so inexorably toward both gay marriage and service in the military."[42]

In contrast to pluralism and intersectionality, there is less explicit wrestling in Schleiermacher with anything like assemblages. And yet Schleiermacher is still a good person to think with here. The secondary literature on Schleiermacher and race, Schleiermacher and nationalism, Schleiermacher and gender, could be greatly enhanced by sustained attention to the global dynamics in which he was caught up. The salons in which he formulated his ideas were in part created by rapid changes in an early stage of capitalism that produced a powerful middle class outside of the traditional estates system, a group of highly educated socially engaged Jewish women from economically powerful families, and a need for new structures of sociability in which new national and religious identities can be worked out. While Schleiermacher was against colonialism, he worked out his ideas of culture (and race) in the context of a mass market for travel literature and the imperial drive for non-European resources and markets. Careful analysis of how these factors play into Schleiermacher's thoughts on human nature, race, gender, nationalism, and so on would be an important resource for drawing our attention to the assemblages with which our own thoughts and feelings about race are entangled.

SUGGESTED READING

Grove, Peter. *Deutungen des Subjekts. Schleiermachers Philosophie der Religion* (Berlin: Walter de Gruyter, 2004).

Jennings, Willie James. *The Christian Imagination: Theology and the Origins of Race* (New Haven: Yale University Press, 2010). See especially chapter 3, "Colenso's Heart."

Jungkeit, Steven R. *Spaces of Modern Theology: Geography and Power in Schleiermacher's World* (New York: Palgrave Macmillan, 2012).

Vial, Theodore. *Modern Religion, Modern Race* (New York: Oxford University Press, 2016).

Voegelin, Eric. *The History of the Race Idea: From Ray to Carus. The Collected Works of Eric Voegelin*, vol. 3. Trans. Ruth Hein (Baton Rouge: Louisiana State University Press, 1998).

BIBLIOGRAPHY

Appiah, Kwame Anthony. *In My Father's House: Africa in the Philosophy of Culture* (Oxford: Oxford University Press, 1992).

Batnitzky, Leora. *How Judaism Became a Religion: An Introduction to Modern Jewish Thought* (Princeton: Princeton University Press, 2011).

Beliso-De Jesús, Aisha. "Confounded Identities: A Meditation on Race, Feminism, and Religious Studies in Times of White Supremacy." *Journal of the American Academy of Religion* 86 (2018), pp. 307–340.

Brandt, James M. *All Things New: Reform of Church and Society in Schleiermacher's* Christian Ethics (Louisville: Westminster John Knox Press, 2001).

---

[42] Janet Jakobsen, *The Sex Obsession: Perversity and Possibility in American Politics* (New York: New York University Press, 2020), p. 50.

Carter, J. Kameron. *Race: A Theological Account* (New York: Oxford University Press, 2008).

Chidester, David. *Savage Systems: Colonialism and Comparative Religion in Southern Africa* (Charlottesville: University of Virginia Press, 1996).

Collins, David. *An Account of the English Colony in New South Wales: With Remarks on the Dispositions, Manners, etc. of the Native Inhabitants of that Country. To Which Are Added, Some Particulars of New Zealand; Compiled, by Permission, from the MSS. Of Lieutenant-Governor King* (London: Printed for T. Cadell Jun. and W. Davies, in the Strand, 1798).

Crenshaw, Kimberlé W. "Race, Gender, and Sexual Harassment." *Southern California Law Review* 65 (1992), pp. 1467-1476. Available at: https://scholarship.law.columbia.edu/faculty_scholarship/2867.

Dole, Andrew. *Schleiermacher on Religion and the Natural Order* (New York: Oxford University Press, 2010).

Du Bois, W. E. B. "The Conservation of Races." In *W. E. B. Du Bois Speaks: Speeches and Addresses, 1890–1919*. Ed. Philip S. Foner (New York: Pathfinder, 1970), pp. 73–85.

Friedländer, David, Friedrich Schleiermacher, and Wilhelm Abraham Teller. *A Debate on Jewish Emancipation and Christian Theology in Old Berlin*. Ed. and trans. Richard Crouter and Julie Klassen (Indianapolis: Hackett Publishing Company, 2004).

Geertz, Clifford. "Religion as a Cultural System." In Geertz, *The Interpretation of Cultures* (New York: Basic Books, 1973), pp. 87–125.

Habermas, Jürgen. *The Structural Transformation of the Public Sphere: An Inquiry into a Category of Bourgeois Society*. Trans. Thomas Burger (Cambridge: The MIT Press, 1991).

Herder, Johann Gottfried. "Abhandlung über den Ursprung der Sprache." In *Werke*, vol. 1, *Frühe Schriften, 1764–1772*, ed. Ulrich Gaier (Frankfurt: Deutscher Klassiker Verlag, 1985), pp. 695–810.

Jakobsen, Janet. *The Sex Obsession: Perversity and Possibility in American Politics* (New York: New York University Press, 2020).

Jennings, Willie James. *The Christian Imagination: Theology and the Origins of Race* (New Haven: Yale University Press, 2010).

Jungkeit, Steven R. *Spaces of Modern Theology: Geography and Power in Schleiermacher's World* (New York: Palgrave Macmillan, 2012).

Mahmood, Saba. *The Politics of Piety: The Islamic Revival and the Feminist Subject* (Princeton: Princeton University Press, 2011).

Puar, Jasbir. *Terrorist Assemblages: Homonationalism in Queer Times* (Durham: Duke University Press, 2017).

Rieger, Jörg. *Christ and Empire: From Paul to Postcolonial Times* (Philadelphia: Fortress Press, 2007).

Thandeka. *Learning to Be White: Money, Race, and God in America* (New York: Continuum, 1999).

Wagner, Ulrike. "Schleiermacher's Geselligkeit, Henriette Herz, and the 'Convivial Turn.'" In *Conviviality at the Crossroads*, ed. Oscar Hemer et al. (Palgrave Macmillan, 2020; Open Access, Cham. https://doi.org/10.1007/978-3-030-28979-9_4), pp. 65–87.

Weld, Isaac Jr. *Travels thought the States of North America, and the Provinces of Upper and Lower Canada, during the Years 1795, 1796, and 1797* (London: Printed for John Stockdale, 1799).

CHAPTER 37

GENDER

RUTH JACKSON RAVENSCROFT

37.1 INTRODUCTION

THIS chapter has two parts. In the first, I offer a survey of the understanding of gender that Schleiermacher develops in his ethical writings. I highlight what I perceive to be the profound limitations of his account, including the sexist and heterosexist assumptions underpinning his dimorphic approach to gender. I also, however, begin to open up a critical conversation with Schleiermacher's work, drawing on his wider ethical thought to suggest some resources internal to his corpus for challenging these assumptions.

In the second part of the chapter, having established that there is room to challenge Schleiermacher's views "from within" his own body of work, I will focus on two important facets of his theology: his expression of divine transcendence (i.e. God is beyond all differences of sex and gender) and his understanding of the God-world relationship—a relationship underpinned by divine transcendence. In contrast to the narrow perspectives on gender we find in Schleiermacher's ethics, I suggest that his theological account of the God-world relationship facilitates a more open conception of human relationality and difference, where multiplicity and the cultivation of individuality is integral to his account of what it means to be human. As Schleiermacher writes in his 1799 *Speeches on Religion* for example, "just as nothing is more irreligious than to demand uniformity in humanity generally, so nothing is more unchristian than to seek uniformity [*Einförmigkeit*] in religion."[1] It will also become clear in what follows that Schleiermacher's understanding of the divine does not contain either the root of, or a reflection of, the view he articulates elsewhere that masculinity can be aligned with a tendency toward activity and rationality, and femininity with a tendency toward passivity and feeling. Nor does the way that Schleiermacher codes gender expression within human society, according to two fixed poles of masculinity and femininity, find its root in his understanding of God.

Nowhere in this essay will I seek to use Schleiermacher's work to provide the basis of a constructive theology of gender. The nineteenth-century terminology and frameworks that Schleiermacher employs for thinking about sex and gender are of course significantly

---

[1] *Speeches*[1], p. 123; *Reden*[1], p. 325.

distinct from the developing discourse in the twenty-first century.[2] And it is also the case that his own use of words is what Patricia Guenther-Gleason calls "slippery," in the sense that "it is not always possible to know with certainty the manner in which his concepts of 'femininity' and 'masculinity' relate to biological referents."[3]

In terms of the assumptions and ethical stance on gender that I myself bring to this study, it is worth explaining at the outset that I understand gender to be a historical category or designation, and that I take gender identities and roles not to be fixed or rigid or essential, but to entail a dynamism, even a kind of volatility. Gender roles and identities are established through time, generated by complex patterns of human language and behavior, by bodies acting and being acted upon within particular contexts. To use a formula from Judith Butler's early work, gender occurs in repeated and sustained action. Unlike biological sex, which is a category more narrowly used to refer to anatomical distinctions between human beings, gender is a *doing*, Butler writes—it refers to the "cultural meaning and form that [a] body acquires, the variable modes of [a] body's acculturation."[4] Indeed, as Denise Riley has argued (her own thinking indebted to Sojourner Truth's refrain "Ain't I a woman?," which underscored the complex, interlocking series of identities that constitutes "womanhood"), there are differing temporalities of "women," and "the effects of lived gender are sometimes unpredictable and fleeting."[5] Writing schematically, Riley notes that as a category, "women" for example is "historically, discursively constructed, and always relatively to other categories which they themselves change... 'women' is both synchronically and diachronically erratic as a collectivity, while for the individual, 'being a woman' is also inconstant, and can't provide an ontological foundation."[6]

It is with the above assumptions in mind that I find the attitudes to sex and gender that Schleiermacher articulates in his ethics to be damagingly narrow. And in the approach I take in the following, I also remain mindful of Rosi Braidotti's assertion that built into feminist practice is the task of resisting any negative or disparaging implications that are associated with the notion of difference, and relations of difference.[7] For Braidotti, "the subject of feminism is not Woman as the complementary and specular *other* of Man, but rather a complex and multilayered embodied subject that has taken her distance both from the institutions of femininity and masculinity, unhinging them both."[8] It is in relation to these claims that my critical focus in this chapter does not remain simply negative, in terms of outlining the limitations of Schleiermacher's account, but becomes constructive in its claim that Schleiermacher's narrow ethical views on gender are not integral to the structure of his thought, but can be resisted and destabilized by other principles at play in his work.

---

[2] The editors of the English translation of the *Brouillon* note that Schleiermacher would understand "gender," "sex," and "sexual" as "virtual synonyms." See *NOE*, p. 79, n84.

[3] Patricia E. Guenther-Gleason, *On Schleiermacher and Gender Politics* (Harrisburg, PA: Trinity Press International, 1997), pp. 36–37.

[4] Judith Butler, "Sex and Gender in Simone de Beauvoir's *Second Sex*," *Yale French Studies* 72 (1986), p. 35.

[5] Denise Riley, *"Am I That Name?"* (Hampshire: Macmillan Press, 1988), p. 6.

[6] Riley, *"Am I That Name?"*, pp. 1–2.

[7] Rosi Braidotti, "*Allegro, ma non troppo*: On Feminist Becomings," in *Intermedialities: Philosophy, Arts, Politics*, ed. Henk Oosterling and Ewa Plonowska Ziarek (Plymouth: Lexington Books, 2011), p. 99. Emphasis my own.

[8] Braidotti, "*Allegro, ma non troppo*: On Feminist Becomings," pp. 99–100.

I propose that the framework Schleiermacher offers us for thinking about human relations of difference, and how these relations of difference are sustained by a loving God, serves both to undermine the limitations of his own perspective, and is also one of the most valuable aspects of the rich philosophical and theological legacy that he has left us. (And in rooting my own observations in Schleiermacher's theology, I do also note the discrepancy between my position and Braidotti's Deleuzean framework, as well as her resistance to transcendence and teleology, even if I share and support the lines of analysis and critique I have quoted above.)

By proceeding in this way, I also admit to being uninterested in exploring the question "Is Schleiermacher a feminist?"—a query engaged with in a cluster of essays during the 1990s,[9] but in my view a dead end for thinking constructively *after* Schleiermacher. This is especially so given the difficulty of honoring each new wave of feminist insight and activism that will break anew onto the reception history of his work. Moreover, just as it is beyond the scope of this essay to profile Schleiermacher's contemporaries, the great women whose hospitality and friendship Schleiermacher enjoyed in Berlin close to 1800, including Henriette Herz, Caroline Schelling, and Dorothea Veit,[10] I have not committed to exploring Schleiermacher's admission in his early 30s that he tended to "attach himself more closely to women than to men."[11] While undoubtedly of historical and biographical interest, this tendency has less to contribute on a constructive level in the present discussion.

37.2 THE PROBLEM WITH GENDER IN SCHLEIERMACHER'S ETHICS

Across Schleiermacher's writings in ethics, politics, and philosophy, as well as in his pastoral theology and sermons, his characterization of human experience reveals a dimorphic conception of sex and gender—a polarization of humanity into masculine and feminine subjects. This theorization of gender is pervasive in his work. It patterns his appreciation of how societies function, how institutions are formed, and how humans on the individual level think, act, communicate, and form relationships with one another.

In some of his early lectures on ethics, for example, Schleiermacher is interested in describing "the science of history"—of "intelligence as manifestation."[12] He explores how humans act in the world as rational "organs," bringing institutions into being, establishing social order and ways of living together in community. And here, both in his *Brouillon zur Ethik* of 1805/1806, and his philosophical ethics of 1812/1813 and 1816/1817, Schleiermacher explains that gender differences "permeate all organic systems" and belongs to the bodies

---

[9] See for example the essays in Iain G. Nichol, ed., *Schleiermacher and Feminism: Sources Evaluations, and Responses* (Lewiston/Queenston/Lampeter: The Edwin Mellen Press, 1992).

[10] For a study of these remarkable women see Barbara Becker-Cantarino, *Schriftstellerinnen der Romantik: Epoche-Werke-Wirkung* (Munich: Beck, 2000).

[11] See his letter to his sister Charlotte in 1799, in Frederica Rowan, ed., *The Life of Friedrich Schleiermacher as Unfolded in His Autobiography and Letters*, 2 vols. (London: Smith, Elder, 1860), pp. 197–199.

[12] *NOE*, p. 34.

and souls of all human beings. Even the way that reason itself is individuated in the lives of discrete persons is "split" (*zerspalten*), Schleiermacher states, according to "gender characteristics" (*Geschlechtscharaktere*).[13] It is worth noting that Schleiermacher's distinctive take on ethics leads him to argue that the appropriate "form" the discipline should take is one of simple description and illumination of the laws and principles governing human action in the world. In his lectures he does not, in other words, seek to undertake a normative account of what *should* or *ought* to be the case.[14] Nevertheless, as part of this attempt at "narrating" the laws of human action in history,[15] Schleiermacher mirrors assumptions about gender roles and norms that became pervasive in the Prussian nineteenth century, including the notion of a "feminine soul," higher and nobler than the "masculine soul" in regard to religion and the spiritual. He ascribes attributes primarily associated with receptivity to femininity, and attributes primarily associated with spontaneity to masculinity.[16] These distinctions of gender follow sexual function, he states, so that in female cognition we find a facility for feeling (*Gefühl*) and appropriation, whereas in male cognition we find a greater facility for fantasy (*Fantasie*) and invention.[17]

What Thandeka has called Schleiermacher's "constricted cultural imagination" thus contributes to his presumption that gender is universally polarized or dyadic in character, and likewise to the heterosexist and heteronormative assumptions governing his conception of how communities are formed and ordered.[18] For the theologian or philosopher tasked with engaging constructively with Schleiermacher on the theme of gender, as I am in this chapter, we thus far seem to be without resources: his conceptions of sex and gender are unequivocally unsuitable for importing directly into our contemporary conversations. Indeed, since the 1980s and 1990s, feminist Schleiermacher scholars have drawn attention to his complicity in the contemporary understanding that it was the male who would take his place at the head of a household, would represent his family as a whole in matters civic and political, and could expect his wife and daughters to be subordinate to him.[19] Dawn DeVries has referred readers to Schleiermacher's 1818 sermon on marriage to this end, where he reflects on the domestic order described in Ephesians 5. In this context, DeVries explains, Schleiermacher teaches that "a woman's public influence is, and should be, limited to what she can accomplish through her influence over her husband in private."[20]

The proposal that Schleiermacher can offer a distinctive and valuable contribution to the philosophy of gender, however, has nevertheless had a number of advocates, DeVries included. Ruth Drucilla Richardson, the author of a major study in the 1990s concerning

---

[13] *BzE*, p. 54; *NOE*, p. 79.

[14] *NOE*, pp. 34–35.

[15] *NOE*, p. 34.

[16] For a historical study of the emergence of this notion of a feminine soul see Marilyn Chapin Massey, *Feminine Soul: The Fate of an Ideal* (Boston: Beacon Press, 1985).

[17] *Ethik (Birkner)*, pp. 81–83; *PE*, pp. 61–62.

[18] "Schleiermacher, Feminism, and Liberation Theologies: A Key," in *The Cambridge Companion to Friedrich Schleiermacher*, ed. Jacqueline Mariña (Cambridge: Cambridge University Press, 2005), p. 301.

[19] See for example *CE (Brandt)*, p. 111. For commentary, see the essays by Sheila Briggs and Katherine M. Faull in Nichol, *Schleiermacher and Feminism*.

[20] Dawn deVries, "Schleiermacher's 'Christmas Eve Dialogue': Bourgeois Ideology or Feminist Theology?," *The Journal of Religion* 69, no. 2 (Apr., 1989), p. 171. For the sermon in question see *Serm. (DeVries)*, pp. 181–195.

the role of women in Schleiermacher's thought, argues that a series of Schleiermacher's early ethical writings, including his review of Friedrich Schlegel's controversial novel *Lucinde*, his Christmas Eve dialogue, and his *Brouillon zur Ethik*, evidence his acute awareness of the *limitations* of gendered existence—its partial nature.[21] In her evaluation of Schleiermacher's early writings, Richardson establishes that he understands the "extinction" of characteristics of sex and gender to be the objective of human life and ethical society. And the way that this extinction is achieved, she explains—the way such a partial existence can be overcome—is via the institution of marriage, a relationship of love providing the opportunity for reciprocal engagement, and for sexual union understood as an "absolute fusion of consciousness" (*eine absolute Verschmelzung des Bewußtseins*).[22] Richardson writes,

> To become full human beings, each sex needs to acquire the *Geschlechtscharaktere* of the other. This occurs in a mature love relationship in which the sensual and the spiritual are united. As Schleiermacher explains: "in love's highest moments the exchange of consciousness, the entire transposition into the other, is the highest and most necessary" (KGA 1.3, p. 201).[23]

With the above point in view, Thandeka pithily describes the implications of Schleiermacher's perspective thus: "autonomous gender experiences are impossible in Schleiermacher's practical scheme of things . . . Man cannot be complete alone; woman cannot be complete alone. Each requires the other for completeness."[24] Yet here, rather than deliver Schleiermacher as a fruitful dialogue partner for philosophies of gender, we do of course run in to further problems. For in light of the long reception of Luce Irigaray's philosophy of sexual difference, and given a series of scholarly engagements with the concepts of femininity and the Eternal Feminine in the final decades of the twentieth century, feminist critiques of the feminine other as a tool and construal of patriarchy are now long established.[25] Following such critiques, Thandeka establishes a major issue with Richardson's work on Schleiermacher: both Schleiermacher's view that dimorphic gender perspectives can be gainfully overcome in a loving marriage, and Richardson's endorsement of that view, risk rendering the feminine principle here simply as that which is "other" to the male; a salve and a supplicant able to complete and assuage masculine incompleteness and limitation.[26]

---

[21] See Ruth Drucilla Richardson, *The Role of Women in the Life and Thought of the Early Schleiermacher 1768–1806* (Lewiston/Lampeter/Queenston: The Edwin Mellen Press, 1990).

[22] *BzE*, p. 57; *NOE*, p. 82.

[23] Ruth Drucilla Richardson, "Schleiermacher's 'Vertraute Brief': A Momentary Aberration or a Genuine Schleiermacherian Ethical Treatise," in *Schleiermacher und die Wissenschaftliche Kultur des Christentums*, ed. Günter Meckenstock (Berlin/Boston: De Gruyter, 1991), p. 462.

[24] Thandeka, "Schleiermacher, Feminism, and Liberation Theologies: A Key," in Mariña, *The Cambridge Companion to Friedrich Schleiermacher*, p. 300.

[25] See Luce Irigaray, *Speculum of the Other Woman*, trans. Gillian C. Gill (Ithaca, NY: Cornell University Press, 1985). For theological analysis see e.g. Elizabeth Johnson, *She Who Is: The Mystery of God in Feminist Theological Discourse* (New York: Crossroad, 1992), p. 49: "Is it not the case that the very concept of the 'feminine' is a patriarchal invention, an ideal projected onto women by men and vigorously defended because it functions so well to keep men in positions of power and women in positions of service to them?"

[26] For a developed discussion of these concerns regarding Schleiermacher's perception of femininity, see Julie K Ellison, *Delicate Subjects: Romanticism, Gender, and the Ethics of Understanding* (New York: Cornell University Press, 1990), and Guenther-Gleason, *On Schleiermacher and Gender Politics*.

Furthermore however, and just as significantly and insidiously for the present analysis, it is also clear that Richardson's approving analysis of Schleiermacher ensures that a heterosexist ideal is instantiated as a cultural norm that governs human flourishing. Richardson asserts that love is at the heart of human existence—"the primary goal" of life. "It is through love," she explains, that in Schleiermacher's view "one is enabled to move beyond partial womanhood or manhood to become a complete human being or *Mensch*."[27] Marriage between man and woman here thus becomes the idealized and total state of union for all individuals—the exclusive means to achieving fulfilment. Complementarity is similarly enshrined as the basis for harmony in that marriage, and the biological family established as the smallest unit of religious and political life.

37.3 Unfastening Schleiermacher's Assumptions

If Richardson's reading serves only to deepen the disquieting assumptions concerning differences of sex and gender in Schleiermacher's account, then for her part, Thandeka has pointed out a different way in which he could be said to move past the perception of an absolute masculine/feminine binary in his thought, while avoiding the notion that feminine flourishing is subordinate or even instrumental to masculine fulfilment. This way forward concerns Schleiermacher's conception of the subject in his *Affektenlehre*—his exploration of how music can be used to stir the affections.[28] She explains that in his work on aesthetics, he points to a protogender of humanity, which represents the primal "artistic" state of the psyche *before* it is split into masculine and feminine genders. This "original" gender, which Schleiermacher refers to as the "artist," writes Thandeka, "is neither male nor female nor androgynous (since the use of these gender dimorphic terms represents the split self and thus cannot be used to define the self before it is split)."[29] In sharp contrast to Richardson's analysis, then, Thandeka's attention to Schleiermacher's notion of an artistic protogender does not render human wholeness as an exclusive achievement of the institution of marriage, and thus does not necessarily enshrine a heterosexist (and in practice also sexist) principle at the heart of Schleiermacher's vision of human flourishing.

Although Thandeka does not make the link herself, this notion of a protogender is resonant, I think, with the allusive imagery of "infinite humanity" that Schleiermacher includes in a piece he wrote in 1798 for the journal *Athenaeum*, which was edited by the Schlegel brothers. This fragment, entitled "Idea for a Reasonable Catechism for Noble Women" (*Idee zu einem Katechismus der Vernunft für edle Frauen*), raises the issue of women's emancipation in an ironical manner. We can reasonably suppose that in this piece, Schleiermacher is drawing on his knowledge of the frustrations facing his female contemporaries in the literary salons of Berlin—some of them noble (*edle*) and all of them educated women, a number of

---

[27] Richardson, "Schleiermacher's 'Vertraute Brief,'" p. 462.
[28] See Friedrich Schleiermacher, *Ästhetik (1832/33); Über den Begriff der Kunst (1831–33)*, ed. Holden Kelm (Hamburg: Felix Meiner Verlag, 2018).
[29] Thandeka, "Schleiermacher, Feminism, and Liberation Theologies: A Key," pp. 292–293.

them part of the upper echelons of Berlin's Jewish community too—whose creativity and aesthetic ambition he knew to be stultified by gendered norms and institutional practices. Rather than tackle the issue of women's civil liberties directly, what Schleiermacher achieves in this text is to poke and prod away at existing expectations regarding women and their roles and duties in life *indirectly*, by employing a distinctive literary form: a parody of a traditional Protestant teaching document, alongside a creed and a set of ten commandments for educated Prussian women of polite society.

These commandments that Schleiermacher offers in the text constitute a series of ironical recommendations, driving at the shortcomings of contemporary expectations about the behavior and role of women. "Thou shalt long for what men have in education, art, wisdom and honor," we read. "Thou shalt not enter into a marriage, if it is inevitable that it will be broken."[30] But toward the end of the fragment, Schleiermacher uses the imagery I am specifically interested in for the purposes of this discussion—he invites his audience to "believe in the infinite humanity [*unendliche Menschheit*], which was there, before it adopted [*annahm*] the garments [*die Hülle*] of masculinity and femininity."[31] In doing so, he uses imagery that suggests the temporary and even flimsy nature of gender roles, as well as the societal structures that generate expectations and practices around sex and gender. They are merely a "wrapping" or a "cover" (*Hülle*) to be put on. The "infinite humanity" Schleiermacher alludes to in this text is thus once again not posited as the outcome of a male-female sexual union within the context of marriage, but styled instead as the original status of humanity as a whole.

Schleiermacher's *Affektenlehre* and his catechism are not the only points in his corpus to offer a possible opening for critical dialogue on his views concerning relationality, difference, and the structuring role that gender has in the composition of human societies. Regarding Schleiermacher's philosophy of friendship for example, Graham Ward and Matthew Robinson have both demonstrated the deep regard he had for relationships outside of the marriage context—relationships not limited to those between a male-female dyad, or bound to perceptions of feminine passivity and masculine activity—in terms of their ability to develop the *Bildung* of individuals.[32] Indeed, Schleiermacher carves out a distinctive conception of "free sociality" (*freie Geselligkeit*) in his ethical and political writings, which, in a way much influenced by his time frequenting the salons of Berlin at the turn of the century, refers to a realm of society outside of the institutions of the academy, the family, the church, and the state. In Schleiermacher's view, such a "free" social domain enabled interaction between individuals without reference to the "limitations of [their] domestic and *bürgerliche* relationships."[33] And the reciprocity engendered in this sphere of life was, in his view, crucial to the task of individual cultivation and fulfilment.

---

[30] Schleiermacher, "Idee zu einem Katechismus der Vernunft für edle Frauen", in *KGA* 1.2, ed. Günter Meckenstock (Berlin: De Gruyter, 1984), p. 153.

[31] Schleiermacher, "Idee zu einem Katechismus", p. 154.

[32] See e.g. Graham Ward, "Schleiermacher and the Theology of Friendship," in *Beyond Tolerance: Schleiermacher on Friendship, Sociability and Lived Religion*, ed. Kevin Vander Schel and Matthew Ryan Robinson (Berlin: De Gruyter, 2019), pp. 11–23, and Matthew Ryan Robinson, *Redeeming Relationship, Relationships That Redeem: Free Sociability and the Completion of Humanity in the Thought of Friedrich Schleiermacher* (Tübingen: Mohr Siebeck, 2018).

[33] *TSC*, p. 21.

A further opening for critical conversation on these themes can be found in his novella about Christmas Eve. Published in 1806, in this text Schleiermacher stages a dialogue between multiple individuals.[34] We meet a cast of eight adults and a little child, Sofie, who between them tell stories and play music (the women of the party) and make speeches and invite debate (the men of the party)—each person making their own particular contribution to a reflection on the significance of Christmas. On a surface level, as his critics have noted, the dialogue seems to offer Schleiermacher another opportunity to uncritically align religious femininity with domesticity and passivity, while uniting masculinity with rational and dialectical activity.[35] Yet significantly, the narrative also features a series of ironical comments about the behaviors and expectations attached to masculinity and femininity (Sofie turns her nose up at sewing, the men are made to look genuinely absurd in their speechmaking), which arguably serve to expose traditional norms, opening them to discussion and critique.[36]

The above samples from Schleiermacher's corpus offer evidence to indicate that the narrow attitudes to sex and gender we find articulated in his ethics are not integral to the structure of his thought but can be challenged and undermined by other principles at play in his work. And in the second part of this chapter, I will now seek to test this idea further by focusing in on his religious and theological writings. Here, I argue, we find the basis for a much more open approach to human difference and relationality—an approach according to which, Schleiermacher declares, the symbol of "infinite and living nature is multiplicity and individuality."[37]

37.4 A God beyond Finite Difference

Enshrined across Schleiermacher's theological writings is the teaching that God is radically transcendent—a God who cannot be placed under those limits belonging only to finite life in the created sphere, including differences of sex and gender.[38] And in his two-volume dogmatics project *Christian Faith* (first edition 1821–1822, second edition 1830–1831), Schleiermacher introduces a methodological approach and an attitude to theological language that ensures this teaching on transcendence can be upheld, and that anthropomorphizing patterns of imagination with regard to the divine can be avoided.[39] In her 2015 book *God and Difference*—a critical appraisal of classical and contemporary approaches to the doctrine of the Trinity—Linn Marie Tonstad explains why these aspects

---

[34] See *CEC*.

[35] See e.g. Karl Barth's reading of the dialogue in *Die Theologie Schleiermachers 1923/4*, ed. Dietrich Ritschl (Zurich: Theologischer Verlag, 1978).

[36] I discuss this further in Ruth Jackson Ravenscroft, *The Veiled God: Friedrich Schleiermacher's Theology of Finitude* (Leiden: Brill, 2019), chs. 7–9.

[37] *Speeches¹*, p. 24.

[38] *CG²*, §40, pp. 230–231; *CF (2016)*, §40, p. 217.

[39] Shelli M. Poe has also argued that Schleiermacher's transcendental reasoning about redemption by God in Christ enables feminist theologians to develop a fruitful model of envisaging divine personhood. See "Schleiermacher's Transcendental Reasoning: Toward a Feminist Affirmation of Divine Personhood," *Feminist Theology* 24, no. 2 (2016), pp. 139–155.

of Schleiermacher's work provide a framework able to sustain ways of thinking fruitfully about gender in a theological mode, and for tackling questions about God and difference. Tonstad writes, "Instead of reading elements of finitude and sin into the divine nature, Schleiermacher emphasizes the transformation of finitude wrought by a God beyond contrast and comparison with the world, yet to whom the human being is always intrinsically related."[40]

The significance of Tonstad's point lies firstly in the principle that, given his commitment to a transcendent God beyond all finite difference, Schleiermacher's understanding of the divine when properly understood cannot contain either the root of, or a reflection of, his view that finite masculinity is aligned with a tendency toward activity and rationality, and finite femininity with a tendency toward passivity and feeling. Nor does Schleiermacher root in his conception of God the narrow way that he codes gender expression within human society according to two poles of masculinity and femininity. In Schleiermacher's appeal to transcendence then, we thus find another opening for working to destabilize the sexist and heterosexist assumptions current in his work—for maintaining, that is, that they are not a necessary element in his theological system.

Secondly however, what Tonstad also indicates helpfully here is that since Schleiermacher's God transcends all worldly boundaries and qualifications, this transcendence enables the agency of God in the world such that it does not clash with, resist, or oppose different forms of human difference and relationality. To invoke a felicitous a turn of phrase used by Thomas Aquinas—in Schleiermacher's view, "grace does not destroy nature, but perfects it."[41] It is here, I submit, that we find the real fruits of the theological framework for thinking about human difference-in-relation that Schleiermacher has bequeathed to us. And it is here that we also see how Schleiermacher's theological thinking can chime with the feminist cause of attending positively to difference, which I outlined above in relation to Braidotti's philosophical stance.

The theological logic of a divine grace that perfects worldly relationships rather than destroys them matches a companion point that Schleiermacher establishes in *Christian Faith*, namely that affirming absolute divine otherness does not mean evacuating the world of divine "presence." To suppose such a divine withdrawal to be symptomatic of transcendence is to misconstrue the divine nature: it is to speak of God in spatialized terms, as if God partakes in the limits of embodied creaturely existence, where to be in one place means one cannot be elsewhere.[42] Instead, Schleiermacher explains that in human existence, recognizing oneself to be absolutely dependent upon God as the transcendent source of all finite becoming, and "being conscious of oneself as in relation with God," amount to exactly the same thing.[43] Just as creation and divinity cannot be placed on the same scale of being and reality, there is also no ontological opposition or friction between creatures and God. And it is this quality of the God-world relationship that enables God in God's transcendence

---

[40] Linn Marie Tonstad, *God and Difference: The Trinity, Sexuality, and the Transformation of Finitude* (New York: Routledge, 2015), p. 19.

[41] *ST* I, q. 1, a. 8, ad. 2.

[42] For an archetypal statement of the relation between divine transcendence and divine immanence, that they are not "mutually exclusive," see Kathryn Tanner, *God and Creation in Christian Theology: Tyranny or Empowerment?* (Minneapolis: Fortress Press 2005).

[43] CG^2, §4, p. 40; $CF(2016)$, §4.4, p. 26.

to eternally sustain and love all of creation in its continued becoming. The work of God, at once radically transcendent and radically immanent to creation, is thus also in a position to overcome creaturely suffering and hurt—instances of where sin has inflicted those differences-in-relation, rendering them sore, prejudicial, and oppressive—by redeeming humanity from within and without.[44] And this work of healing and redemption is of course, for Schleiermacher, achieved in the Incarnation, toward which the whole of creation is ordered.[45]

It is worth taking a little space here to establish Schleiermacher's strategy for upholding divine transcendence, and how this helps him develop a framework for describing the God-world relationship where God is established as the steadfast creator, sustainer, and lover of the world. Crucially, doing so will allow me to establish the theological groundwork according to which Schleiermacher understands difference and multiplicity to be integral to what it means to be human. It will also underscore the consistency with which Schleiermacher resolutely avoids anthropomorphizing language to appeal to the work and nature of God in his *Glaubenslehre*—abandoning what he refers to as "poetic" and "rhetorical" language, for the "presentational-didactic" language he understands is pivotal for the precise scientific task of dogmatics.[46] The result is that at no point in Schleiermacher's theological scheme can we detect any sort of "blueprint" in the divine life for how we are to express and negotiate differences of sex and gender within human society.

Schleiermacher's strategy for upholding transcendence is inaugurated in the very introduction to his *Glaubenslehre*, which includes his discussion of how the relationship central to religion, between the Infinite and the finite, is one humans recognize via the sphere of feeling (*Gefühl*) and intuition (*Anschauung*). (God is not, for Schleiermacher, to be reduced to the outcome of human speculation—simply a concept or object to be rationally deduced, or worse constructed, by the knowing mind).[47] It is in this introduction that Schleiermacher famously establishes that it is in the "feeling of absolute dependence" (*das schlechthinnige Abhängigkeitsgefühl*) that Christians recognize themselves as the creaturely recipients of their existence, unable to provide the stimulus and continuing grounds for own their lives, agency, and flourishing in the world. Schleiermacher's appeal to the word *Gefühl* does not signal an understanding of religion as reducible to an activity or projection of the human psyche.[48] Instead, the "feeling" of absolute dependence is a recognition of the transcendent: it is a response to God, who in faith Christians know as *Der Woher*—the eternal *Whence* of their receptive and active existence. This *Whence* in Schleiermacher's telling is not the world "in the sense of the totality of finite being," and nor is God any aspect of that totality. Rather, Schleiermacher recognizes God as the absolutely *un*conditioned source of everything conditioned, creaturely, and created.[49]

Schleiermacher also uses this vocabulary of absolute dependence to frame the first doctrinal proposition in his *Glaubenslehre*: his doctrine of creation. When we combine the

---

[44] Tonstad, *God and Difference*, p. 17.
[45] See Schleiermacher's exegesis of Col. 1:16 in CG^2, §164.3, p. 496; *CF (2016)*, §164, p. 999.
[46] See *CF (2016)*, §17, p. 127.
[47] See *Speeches*[1], p. 24.
[48] See for example Julia A Lamm, "The Early Philosophical Roots of Schleiermacher's Notion of *Gefühl*, 1788–1794," *Harvard Theological Review* 87, no. 1 (1994), pp. 67–105.
[49] CG^2, §4, p. 39; *CF (2016)*, §4, p. 24.

teaching that God creates out of nothing with the doctrine that God *preserves* the world in its becoming, Schleiermacher explains, then this is simply an alternative way of saying that the *totality* of finite being is absolutely dependent upon God for its existence not just now or then, but at every moment without qualification.[50] The significance of this way of reflecting on the God-world relationship is that it enables Schleiermacher to think in a distinctive way about the proper "object" of the divine creation and preservation. Indeed, as Brian Gerrish has put it, for Schleiermacher it is more apt to say that the "the unit of divine care" is creation as a *whole*, rather than creation's particulars, individuals, objects, and creatures.[51]

Let us consider what Schleiermacher's emphasis on the *whole* of creation as the object of the divine will means for his conception of how divine agency relates to the particularities of human history. Essentially, it means that Schleiermacher's understanding of divine action is modulated by his attention to the interconnectedness of finite reality—his recognition that everything finite has the conditions for its occurrence in the full scope of what has come before it in that same finite reality. The result is that in Schleiermacher's view, everything that happens in the created sphere falls under what one might describe as a mediated (*mittelbare*) exercise of divine omnipotence.[52] This does not mean that in Schleiermacher's view, God wills some things absolutely and others only in a conditional sense, dependent on certain finite conditions pulling one direction or the other. Instead, Schleiermacher proposes a way of perceiving divine action whereby "one and the same divine will encompasses the entire mutually conditioning domain of finite being."[53] The world as willed by God in its totality constitutes an ever-expanding and intimately interrelated nexus of finite causality.

It is in this formulation, where God wills creation as a whole (and not the various parts of creation in abstraction from each other), that we also see the facility of Schleiermacher's scheme to conceptualize human freedom, human creativity, and human individuality as qualities and activities that are enabled in the world *within* the creative act of God, who orders all things as an interconnected nexus of activity and change. Katherine Sonderegger has suggested that Schleiermacher would have esteemed the modern notion of the ecosystem, which "offers a picture of interconnection, each species dependent on the next for its life."[54] The human in this scenario cannot experience themselves or "their world" in abstraction, writes Sonderegger; "they take up the world, 'the other,' into themselves, recognising it and themselves in this act of experience."[55] And so in Schleiermacher's portrayal of the world's dynamic ecology, held in its constant becoming by God, we thus have a foundation for a theological understanding of difference, relationality, and particularity as aspects to the human condition that do not lie in tension or opposition to the divine purpose for Schleiermacher, but are enabled and inherent in the totality of finite creation through the very conditions supplied by divine governance.

---

[50] *CF (2016)*, §36, p. 205.

[51] Brian Gerrish, *Tradition and the Modern World: Reformed Theology in the Nineteenth Century* (Chicago: University of Chicago Press, 1978), pp. 108–109.

[52] CG^2, §54.4, pp. 329–330; *CF (2016)*, §54.4, p. 310.

[53] CG^2, §54.4, p. 331; *CF (2016)*, §54.4, pp. 311–312.

[54] Katherine Sonderegger, "The Doctrine of Creation and the Task of Theology," *The Harvard Theological Review* 84, no. 2 (1991), p. 193.

[55] Sonderegger, "The Doctrine of Creation and the Task of Theology," p. 194.

If Schleiermacher's doctrines of creation and preservation help him to establish a coherent framework for speaking about God's involvement with the world, then in the second part of his *Glaubenslehre* this framework is renewed and completed with his doctrine of redemption. The full teleological context Schleiermacher sets up for his doctrine of redemption is his witness to the biblical axiom that God is Love (1 John 4:16). God, says Schleiermacher, is known in faith to be absolutely omnipotent, eternal, and omniscient. Honoring the teachings bound up with these "general" divine attributes is what helps us to avoid using anthropomorphic imagery to speak of the divine nature. And yet, Schleiermacher stresses, it is the divine attribute of Love alone that Christians should understand to be identical with the essence of the divine nature.[56] It is by love and in love and through love that God makes Godself known to creation.[57] For God has only one purpose in willing the world into being: to unite human nature with the divine. This is a purpose inaugurated in the Incarnation and ongoing in human history, while in Christ through the Spirit the reign of God is extended and developed in the life of the church (§164.2). In Schleiermacher's theology, nature never proceeds in isolation from grace; there is no splintering in the divine will between that which is divined absolutely, before all time, and that which takes place amid the particular circumstances of human history.[58] Divine responsibility for the whole human race seen from the perspective of eternity, he writes, and the specific set of circumstances governing the time when Christ would come, "are *one* undivided revelation of divine omnipotence."[59] And since this is Schleiermacher's interpretation of Galatians 4:4—the notion that Christ was born "in the fulness of time"—I am not surprised to read that Julia Lamm has seen connections between the theological logic of Schleiermacher's scheme and that of the English mystic Julian of Norwich, for whom in the Love of God "all shall be well."[60]

In stark contrast to Julian's theology however, we do not find in Schleiermacher's *Glaubenslehre* a litany of kinship metaphors—mother, father, spouse, brother—such as Julian uses in her *Revelations* to describe how the work of God in and through Christ is known and felt by human beings.[61] Indeed, Schleiermacher's emphasis on divine transcendence stimulates in his method a turn to apophatic restraint: a painstaking avoidance of any terminology that would introduce the conditions and limits of finite nature and finite relationality into language used of God. It is I think reasonable to say that in Julian's writings, the cataphatic and apophatic work in dialectical tension. Any danger we might be in of idolatrous practice—of assuming motherhood in God in a way that takes its cue from a creaturely model or referent—is quelled by the rolling excess of a multiplicity of metaphors. To use the words of Catherine Keller on the topic, who invokes the pattern of Pseudo-Dionysius the Areopagite, "Negative theology is that self-conscious strategy of unnaming that accompanies, from Denys on, the exuberant multiplication of names. . . . The doxological

---

[56] CG^2, §127.

[57] CG^2, §166.

[58] CG^2, §164.3, p. 496; *CF (2016)*, §164.3, p. 1001.

[59] CG^2, §118.1, pp. 250–251; *CF (2016)*, §118.1, pp. 772–773.

[60] See Julia A. Lamm, "Casting Out Fear: The Logic of 'God is Love' in Julian of Norwich and Friedrich Schleiermacher," in *Saving Fear in Christian Spirituality*, ed. Ann Astell (Notre Dame, IN: Notre Dame Press, 2020), pp. 231–257.

[61] Julian of Norwich, *Revelations of Divine Love*, ed. Barry Windeatt (Oxford: Oxford University Press 2016). For theological engagement with Julian's theological language see Janet Soskice, *The Kindness of God* (Oxford: Oxford University Press, 2007).

dimension of the mysticism of unnaming pervades its discourse, its fertility of names, from the start."[62]

But if what we find in Schleiermacher is the restraint of unnaming without the corresponding plenitude of metaphorical language used of the divine, does this mean Schleiermacher's God, who is absolutely beyond all finite difference, is also rendered a mystery beyond mystery for human beings?—a God utterly opaque and enigmatic to the rational creatures who seek God in worship? I do not think this is the case. In the following passage, which I provide as a sample of Schleiermacher's way of communicating the radical transcendence of God beyond any worldly characterization or designation, we see his capacity for combining the sense that the divine confounds all human attempts at description or conception, with a direct account, nevertheless, of how God is intimately involved in human history. Here, Schleiermacher is describing how when applied to God the terms freedom and necessity will always sit in unresolved dialectical tension with one another. The divine causality, he argues, must be described in ways that do not repeat, untroubled, a set of specifically human presuppositions regarding what it means to be "free" in one's actions. He writes,

> We must not think anything to be necessary in God without, at the same time, positing it as free, and we must not think anything to be free in God in such a way that it is not, at same time, necessary. . . . Just as little can we also think God's willing of Godself and God's willing of the world to be separated from each other. This is so, for if God wills Godself, God also wills Godself to be creator and preserver, with the result that God's willing of the world is already included in God's-willing-of-Godself.[63]

Schleiermacher's denial here that any human conception of freedom or necessity can be suitably applied to the divine nature does seem to rest in the non-resolution of the terminology—God is *both* free and determined, even as these terms cancel each other out in the human intellect in apophatic aporia. And yet at the crux of this passage is also a resolute statement about the intimacy between God and creation. "For if God wills Godself," writes Schleiermacher, then "God also wills Godself to be creator and preserver." Creation of the world is included in God's very desire to be God.

Refraining from rooting relations of gender and finite difference in the Godhead thus does not for Schleiermacher suffocate the ability to speak concretely about the work of God in creation. Instead, it is the work of recognizing and upholding the transcendent nature of the divine, beyond all finite difference, that facilitates Schleiermacher's theology of love.

37.5 Human Difference and Relationality: A Way Forward

In the reading of Schleiermacher's *Glaubenslehre* I offered in the previous section, I explored how his conception of the God-world relationship is governed by a conception of divine

---

[62] Catherine Keller, "The Apophasis of Gender: A Fourfold Unsaying of Feminist Theology," *Journal of the American Academy of Religion* 76, no. 4, (2008), p. 913.

[63] *CG²*, §54.4, pp. 332–333; *CF (2016)*, §54.4, pp. 313–314.

transcendence. Schleiermacher understands creation as a *whole* to be the object of divine causality and divine love. The framework he sets up thus sustains the idea that human freedom and individuality—the development of human persons in time—is enabled in the world *within* the creative act of God. And at the same time, Schleiermacher's strategy for upholding transcendence means that in his theological scheme we find no necessary root or reflection of the views he offers in his ethics concerning gendered difference in creation. Appealing to the God who is beyond all finite difference can provide us with a way of undermining the narrowly heterosexist and sexist assumptions about human reciprocity and flourishing that we saw earlier in Schleiermacher's ethics, then, while also opening up a channel for finding in Schleiermacher a much more fruitful and open conception of human difference and relationality. I will now bring the discussion in this chapter to a close by drawing further attention to the promise in Schleiermacher's theology for offering a positive account of human relations of difference, including those differences belonging to the categories of sex and gender. This promise is rooted in Schleiermacher's understanding of human beings as creatures-in-relation.

Indeed, in Schleiermacher's view, human beings are creatures who are not only always already in relation to God (upon whom they are absolutely dependent), but also inherently embedded in a sphere of continual reciprocal activity and passivity with other creatures. The created world is a nexus of pulsating life for Schleiermacher, within which humans fluctuate between relative dependence (or receptivity) and relative freedom (or activity) in constant relation to other creatures.[64] To parse this apprehension of finite relationality in the language of Schleiermacher's dogmatics, we could say that to live in acknowledgement of the "immediate self-consciousness of absolute dependence" on God does not entail eschewing an involvement in the world, or its trappings and relationships.[65] Rather, Schleiermacher understood religious feeling to "accompany every human deed as a holy music,"[66] and stressed that "the efficacious action of God-consciousness within us is given only in a process of interconnectedness with our physical and bodily organism."[67] In other words, Schleiermacher stresses in his *Glaubenslehre* that although absolute dependence upon God is a relation established underneath all human reflection, action, and speech, and cannot be reduced to any of these activities, it is nevertheless a relation linked up with bodies, places, and the to-and-fro of human communication for its full articulation and constitution. God is known by human individuals *with* the world, and *within* the context of the whole spectrum of their worldly relationships. Schleiermacher understands human difference and individuality to be firmly a part of how we know and love God.

We see these principles at work in Schleiermacher's conviction that piety is inherently intersubjective, and that religion is always communal—central motifs in his 1799 *Speeches*. Here, as part of challenging the assumptions of the "cultured despisers" of religion he addresses in the text, Schleiermacher explains that it is impossible for religion to be private (confined to an individual's own self-expression in the world), general (without root in shared faith and practices), or pure (lived in abstraction from the events of history, and the shaping influence of human language). To be religious is inevitably to belong to the

---

[64] CG^2, §4–5, CF (2016), §4–5.
[65] CG^2, §4.4, p. 40; CF (2016), §4.4, p. 24.
[66] *Reden*[1], p. 219; *Speeches*[1], p. 30.
[67] CG^2, §61; CF (2016), §61, p. 372.

"determinate shape" of a religious community.[68] And it is only by dwelling within a historical religious tradition—what he calls the "positive" religions—that Schleiermacher thinks a person can "attain their individuality."[69] This exploration of the nature of religion and individual commitment to the religious life gives Schleiermacher the context for writing the line I quoted at the outset of this chapter, that "just as nothing is more irreligious than to demand uniformity in humanity generally, so nothing is more unchristian than to seek uniformity [*Einförmigkeit*] in religion."[70] To put it another way, Schleiermacher's theological scheme rejects a vision of human fulfilment that requires a person to be conformed to a single universal standard, whether that standard be a masculine ideal, or a particular level of rationality, culture, or learning.

Indeed, Schleiermacher's stress on the shared and socially structured life of religion tells us something about the negotiation of human identities in the material world of time and place. My self-understanding as a social and political agent comes from my knowledge of myself as a particular life that emerges as part of a greater whole. My fluctuation in finite existence is between receptivity and activity; between what others make of me, and what I make of myself. "We always find ourselves to exist only in coexistence with some other," Schleiermacher writes in the opening sections of *Christian Faith*.[71] And later on in the same section, he also contends that individual freedom only truly occurs through the process of time, where a person's development is defined by "being composited on the part of some 'other' in the process."[72] As development happens in relation for Schleiermacher, personal identities in his view will thus always be inflected and affected by the norms, codes, and habits of a particular societal context. But they are not controlled and regulated entirely by these norms and codes—instead, the dynamic fluctuation of freedom and dependence in the finite sphere ensures that in my individuality, I am continually expanding, deepening, and challenging what it means to be a member of the numerous groups, institutions, or communities of which I am part. I am not defined absolutely from without, and so likewise there cannot by any one ideal or homogenous experience of being a woman (for example), and no one identical way of being a spouse or a sibling or a friend.

It is in Schleiermacher's attention to the reciprocal dynamic between finite self and other, and his grasp of how this dynamic constitutes the process of personal identity formation, that we have, I contend, another resource in his thought for undermining and challenging the fixed, dyadic view of gender that we find articulated in his ethics. Indeed, according to the logic of Schleiermacher's theological thought, differences between human beings should not be understood as static or rigidly delineated, just as they are not to be denied, disparaged, or ironed out. Difference is instead integral to the expression of the fulness and vibrancy of creation. At this juncture, I would like to return to a point that I raised at the outset of the chapter, and to ask, Does Schleiermacher's scheme have the means to support something akin to Braidotti's notion of the feminist subject—a "complex and multilayered embodied subject, that has taken her distance both from the institutions of femininity and masculinity, unhinging them both"?[73]

[68] *Reden¹*, p. 308; *Speeches¹*, p. 108.
[69] *Reden¹*, pp. 305–309; *Speeches¹* pp. 106–109.
[70] *Speeches¹*, p. 123; *Reden¹*, p. 325.
[71] CG^2, §4.1; *CF (2016)*, §4.1, p. 20.
[72] CG^2, §4.2; *CF (2016)*, §4.2, p. 21.
[73] Braidotti, "*Allegro, ma non troppo*: On Feminist Becomings," pp. 99–100.

One of the moments where we see a possible opportunity for this kind of "unhinging" or distancing in Schleiermacher's thought, however slight, is a passage from his *Soliloquies*—a short text he published in 1800. In this book, at the age of 32, Schleiermacher reveals his "highest intuition" (*Anschauung*) as the following—that "each human being [*Mensch*] should represent humanity in his own way, combining its elements uniquely, so that humanity may reveal itself in every mode, and all that can issue from its womb [*Schooße*] be made actual in the fullness of unending space and time [*in der Fülle der Unendlichkeit*]."[74] I draw attention to this passage both for Schleiermacher's spotlight on the uniqueness of each human person, and for his stress that individual uniqueness, borne out of their development in a particular time, place, and set of interpersonal relationships, can redefine and develop the meaning of the whole to which that individual belongs—even when that whole is as vast as humanity itself. If we carry this insight over into the question of gender, we have a platform in Schleiermacher's work for suggesting, with Denise Riley, that labels like "woman" or "man" will always be inadequate and provisional, and that "it is neither possible nor desirable to live solidly inside" any sexed or gendered designation.[75] And furthermore, in Schleiermacher's understanding of the world as constantly developing, fluxing, and expanding within the love of God, we can also see how Schleiermacher's theological scheme might embrace and support the notion that our categories concerning gender might too be ever-expanding, and ever-redefined.

***

My aim in this chapter has been to offer a critical response to the understanding of gender Schleiermacher articulates in his ethics. In service of this aim, I have explored two important features of Schleiermacher's theological thinking: his expression of divine transcendence (i.e. God is beyond all differences of sex and gender) and his understanding of the God-world relationship underpinned by divine transcendence. At the close of the chapter, my proposal remains that the theological framework Schleiermacher offers us for thinking about human relations of difference, and how these relations of difference are sustained by a loving God, not only serves to undermine the limitations of his own narrow articulation of gender roles in his ethics, but is also one of the most fruitful dimensions of the rich philosophical and theological legacy that he has left us.

Suggested Reading

Ellison, Julie K. *Delicate Subjects: Romanticism, Gender, and the Ethics of Understanding* (New York: Cornell University Press, 1990).

Guenther-Gleason, Patricia E. *On Schleiermacher and Gender Politics* (Harrisburg, PA: Trinity Press International, 1997).

Poe, Shelli M. *The Constructive Promise of Schleiermacher's Theology* (London: T&T Clark, 2021).

Schleiermacher, Friedrich. *Christmas Eve Celebration: A Dialogue*, ed. and trans. Terrence Tice (Eugene, OR: Cascade, 2010).

---

[74] *Monologen¹*, p. 18; *Solil.*, p. 31.
[75] Riley, *"Am I That Name?"*, p. 112.

Schleiermacher, Friedrich. "Idee zu einem Katechismus der Vernunft für edle Frauen." In *KGA* 1.2, ed. Günter Meckenstock (Berlin: De Gruyter, 1984), pp. 153–154.

Tonstad, Linn Marie. *God and Difference: The Trinity, Sexuality, and the Transformation of Finitude* (New York: Routledge, 2015).

Bibliography

Barth, Karl. *Die Theologie Schleiermachers 1923/4*. Ed. Dietrich Ritschl (Zurich: Theologischer Verlag, 1978).

Becker-Cantarino, Barbara. *Schriftstellerinnen der Romantik: Epoche–Werke–Wirkung* (Munich: Beck, 2000).

Braidotti, Rosi. "*Allegro, ma non troppo*: On Feminist Becomings." In *Intermedialities: Philosophy, Arts, Politics*, ed. Henk Oosterling and Ewa Plonowska Ziarek (Plymouth: Lexington Books, 2011), pp. 99–111.

Butler, Judith. "Sex and Gender in Simone de Beauvoir's *Second Sex*." *Yale French Studies* 72 (1986), pp. 35–49.

DeVries, Dawn. "Schleiermacher's 'Christmas Eve Dialogue': Bourgeois Ideology or Feminist Theology?" *The Journal of Religion* 69, no. 2 (1989), pp. 169–183.

Ellison, Julie K. *Delicate Subjects: Romanticism, Gender, and the Ethics of Understanding* (New York: Cornell University Press, 1990).

Gerrish, Brian. *Tradition and the Modern World: Reformed Theology in the Nineteenth Century* (Chicago: University of Chicago Press, 1978).

Guenther-Gleason, Patricia E. *On Schleiermacher and Gender Politics* (Harrisburg, PA: Trinity Press International, 1997).

Irigaray, Luce. *Speculum of the Other Woman*. Trans. Gillian C. Gill (Ithaca, NY: Cornell University Press, 1985).

Johnson, Elizabeth. *She Who Is: The Mystery of God in Feminist Theological Discourse* (New York: Crossroad, 1992).

Julian of Norwich. *Revelations of Divine Love*. Ed. Barry Windeatt (Oxford: Oxford University Press 2016).

Keller, Catherine. "The Apophasis of Gender: A Fourfold Unsaying of Feminist Theology." *Journal of the American Academy of Religion* 76, no. 4 (2008), pp. 905–933.

Lamm, Julia. "Casting Out Fear: The Logic of 'God is Love' in Julian of Norwich and Friedrich Schleiermacher." In *Saving Fear in Christian Spirituality*, ed. Ann Astell (Notre Dame, IN: Notre Dame Press, 2020), pp. 231–257.

Lamm, Julia A. "The Early Philosophical Roots of Schleiermacher's Notion of Gefühl, 1788–1794)." *Harvard Theological Review* 87, no. 1 (1994), pp. 67–105.

Massey, Marilyn Chapin. *Feminine Soul: The Fate of an Ideal* (Boston: Beacon Press, 1985).

Nichol, Iain G. ed. *Schleiermacher and Feminism, Sources Evaluations, and Responses* (Lewiston/Queenston/Lampeter: The Edwin Mellen Press, 1992).

Poe, Shelli M. "Schleiermacher's Transcendental Reasoning: Toward a Feminist Affirmation of Divine Personhood." *Feminist Theology* 24, no. 2 (2016), pp. 139–155.

Ravenscroft, Ruth Jackson. *The Veiled God: Friedrich Schleiermacher's Theology of Finitude* (Leiden: Brill, 2019).

Richardson, Ruth Drucilla. *The Role of Women in the Life and Thought of the Early Schleiermacher 1768–1806* (Lewiston/Lampeter/Queenston: The Edwin Mellen Press, 1990).

Richardson, Ruth Drucilla. "Schleiermacher's 'Vertraute Brief': A Momentary Aberration or a Genuine Schleiermacherian Ethical Treatise?" In *Schleiermacher und die Wissenschaftliche Kultur des Christentums*, ed. Günter Meckenstock (Berlin: De Gruyter, 1991), pp. 455–462.

Rieger, Joerg. "Power and Empire in the Study of Nineteenth-Century Theology: The Case of Schleiermacher." *Journal for the History of Modern Theology / Zeitschrift for Neuere Theologiegeschichte* 20, no. 1 (2013), pp. 44–60.

Riley, Denise. *"Am I That Name?"* (Hampshire: Macmillan Press, 1988).

Robinson, Matthew Ryan. *Redeeming Relationship, Relationships That Redeem: Free Sociability and the Completion of Humanity in the Thought of Friedrich Schleiermacher* (Tübingen: Mohr Siebeck, 2018).

Rowan, Frederica, ed. *The Life of Friedrich Schleiermacher as Unfolded in His Autobiography and Letters*. 2 vols. (London: Smith, Elder, 1860).

Schleiermacher, Friedrich. *Ästhetik (1832/33); Über den Begriff der Kunst (1831–33)*. Ed. Holden Kelm (Hamburg: Felix Meiner Verlag, 2018).

Schleiermacher, Friedrich. "Idee zu einem Katechismus der Vernunft für edle Frauen." In *KGA* 1.2, ed. Günter Meckenstock (Berlin: De Gruyter, 1984), pp. 153–154.

Sonderegger, Katherine. "The Doctrine of Creation and the Task of Theology." *Harvard Theological Review* 84, no. 2 (1991), pp. 185–203.

Soskice, Janet. *The Kindness of God* (Oxford: Oxford University Press, 2007).

Tanner, Kathryn. *God and Creation in Christian Theology: Tyranny or Empowerment?* (Minneapolis: Fortress Press 2005).

Thandeka. "Schleiermacher, Feminism, and Liberation Theologies: A Key." In *The Cambridge Companion to Friedrich Schleiermacher*, ed. Jacqueline Mariña (Cambridge: Cambridge University Press, 2005), pp. 287–306.

Tonstad, Linn Marie. *God and Difference: The Trinity, Sexuality, and the Transformation of Finitude* (New York: Routledge, 2015).

Ward, Graham. "Schleiermacher and the Theology of Friendship." In *Beyond Tolerance: Schleiermacher on Friendship, Sociability and Lived Religion*, ed. Kevin Vander Schel and Matthew Ryan Robinson (Berlin: De Gruyter, 2019), pp. 11–23.

CHAPTER 38

SCHLEIERMACHER AND THE POLITICS OF ANGLOPHONE RELIGIOUS STUDIES

ANDREW C. DOLE

38.1 INTRODUCTION

Schleiermacher's writings were addressed in many cases to the controversies of his time in both church and academy. And his contributions were not infrequently understood quite differently by those on different sides of those controversies. The passing of time and the fading of the energies of particular disputes have the effect of making the distorting effects of partisan commitments more visible; but truncated and cartoonish portrayals of Schleiermacher are not yet relics of the distant past. In this chapter I want to trace the fortunes of one such portrayal that circulated for several decades within Anglophone scholarship (and may still be in circulation, if only weakly) and identify the conditions that seem to have given it purchase within the literature. I will also advance claims about specific ways in which this portrayal gets Schleiermacher wrong, though my work in this area will of necessity be brief.

Here I am interested in ways Schleiermacher appears in literature that is distant from his writings—the way he is understood at second or third hand, on the basis of the authority of interpretive authorities or traditions. So in this chapter I will not be concerned with Schleiermacher specialists, but with those whose area of expertise is the study of religion in broad compass. And I am concerned with English scholarship here largely because two of its characteristics seem to me to be crucial for understanding the possibility of the portrayal of Schleiermacher I will explore below. First, for monolingual scholars working during the period in which this portrayal emerged, the language barrier forced a dependence on a small selection of dated translations and secondary works animated by their own concerns. And second, professional anxieties localized within the North American academy generated a context in which a caricatured Schleiermacher was polemically useful.

The history I will survey here begins in the late twentieth century. I will need to assume as background a history through which the Anglophone literature inherited the notion that

Schleiermacher's conception of religion was a strictly individual affair—that Schleiermacher had nothing to say about religion as a social phenomenon.[1] This notion is in place by the early twentieth century, and its arrival in English coincides with Rudolf Otto's appropriation of the legacy of Schleiermacher for his own purposes. Given additional space, I would set the stage more thoroughly by discussing secondary literature on Schleiermacher that was in circulation during this period, because much of it took place under the shadow of Karl Barth and some of it was animated by a concern to appease neo-orthodox sensibilities. But for now that work remains undone.

38.2 RELIGIOUS EXPERIENCE

Wayne Proudfoot's *Religious Experience*, published in 1985, was a major event in the reception of Schleiermacher's work for Anglophone scholars of religion. The work positioned Schleiermacher as an early proponent—in fact the principal architect—of a program dedicated to the "protection" of religion from critical scrutiny from "external" perspectives.

The general project of *Religious Experience* is to present a set of recent advances in understanding, including post-positivistic philosophy and attribution theory, as correctives to claims about "religious experience" that had figured prominently within religious studies. Schleiermacher appears primarily in the early stages of the work as the progenitor of the discourse of religious experience, one whose positions (and agenda) have had a formative influence on that discourse. I will focus on three of Proudfoot's main claims. The first is that for Schleiermacher, religious experience is independent of concepts and beliefs. The second is that Schleiermacher understood religious language to be directly expressive of religious experience, unconditioned by knowledge or cultural values. And the third is that Schleiermacher's aim in maintaining these positions was to ensure that religion would only ever be analyzed "from within."

(1) According to Proudfoot, Schleiermacher took the "core" of religion—religious experience—to be "prior to concepts and beliefs." The principal textual evidence Proudfoot cited for this claim is from the *Speeches* in the English edition available at the time (John Oman's translation of the fourth edition), the second speech in particular. According to Proudfoot Schleiermacher's position was an attempt to surmount Kantian skepticism of religious ideas: "Religion is a sense, a taste, a matter of feeling and intuition. Consequently, it remains unscathed by Kant's contention that our experience is structured by the categories and thoughts we bring to it and thus that we produce rather than reproduce the world we think we know." Maintaining the independence of religious experience from concepts and beliefs was an antireductionist strategy: "For Schleiermacher and the tradition that derived from him, descriptive accuracy is to be obtained and reductionism is to be avoided by insisting on the immediacy of religious experience, and on its radical independence from beliefs and practices. It is a moment in human experience which remains unstructured by, though it is expressed in, thoughts and actions."[2]

---

[1] See Andrew Dole, "'The Case of the Disappearing Discourse': Schleiermacher's Fourth Speech and the Field of Religious Studies," *The Journal of Religion* 88 (2008), pp. 1–28.

[2] Wayne Proudfoot, *Religious Experience* (Berkeley: University of California Press, 1985), pp. 2, 3.

While most of the texts Proudfoot cited are drawn from the *Speeches*, other representatives of the "tradition," such as William James and Rudolf Otto, were also recruited to assist in his reconstruction of Schleiermacher's position. I have space here only for the briefest of comments on the adequacy of Proudfoot's textual case. Schleiermacher did not use the vocabulary of concepts and beliefs—nor, for that matter, the vocabulary of religious experience—so Proudfoot's case turns on the translation of Schleiermacher's terminology into his own. There are passages that work well for Proudfoot's purposes; perhaps the best is Schleiermacher's claim that the religious consciousness "has not yet passed through the stage of the idea, but has grown up purely in feeling."[3] But there are also problems, the main one being that Proudfoot treated claims in the text about different things—intuition, feeling, religious consciousness, the "first mysterious moment," and piety—as all generically about "religious experience," such that what Schleiermacher said about any one of these can be extended to the others.

Before moving on I want to note that Proudfoot saw a tension within Schleiermacher's position. He accused Schleiermacher of incoherence because piety "requires reference to God, to all, or the universe," and "piety cannot be independent of concepts and beliefs and at the same time an intentional state that can only be specified by reference to objects of thought and explanatory claims."[4] I regard this observation as instructive, since it calls attention to claims by Schleiermacher that do not square with the position that Proudfoot ascribed to him. A similarly instructive moment occurs in Proudfoot's examination of the *Glaubenslehre*, which he regarded as more sophisticated than the *Speeches*, but still committed to the position that "piety is independent of thought and practice."[5] Proudfoot noted that there are two ways of reading Schleiermacher's claims about the feeling of absolute dependence. Reading Schleiermacher in one way, "many have criticized Schleiermacher for equating religious experience with a subjective feeling that has no cognitive content and may be an artifact of personal or cultural factors" (no names are mentioned). In contrast to this position Proudfoot cited Robert Williams, who had recently (in *Schleiermacher the Theologian*) argued that the feeling of absolute dependence is "a direct, prereflective apprehension of reality."[6] Proudfoot did not resolve this interpretive dilemma, but it is fairly clear that it is Williams' reading that coheres with Proudfoot's own; the alternative, which allows "religious experience" to be conditioned by historical factors, does not return after this first mention.

(2) Proudfoot ascribed to Schleiermacher the "doctrine" that "religious language is determined by the religious affections and not by antecedent thought."[7] The central thesis of this doctrine, for Proudfoot, is that "more reflective figurative expressions gain their authority from the fact that they are extensions of natural expressions." This is because, according to Proudfoot, "to characterize [an] expression as natural is to deny that it is governed by convention, and thus to assert that the connection between the religious consciousness and linguistic expression is independent of cultural influences and constructive thought."[8] Even after a survey of Schleiermacher's discussion in the *Glaubenslehre* of the way

---

[3] Proudfoot, *Religious Experience*, p. 10, citing *Speeches*², p. 54.
[4] Proudfoot, *Religious Experience*, p. 15.
[5] Proudfoot, *Religious Experience*, p. 17.
[6] Proudfoot, *Religious Experience*, p. 22.
[7] Proudfoot, *Religious Experience*, p. 24.
[8] Proudfoot, *Religious Experience*, pp. 24, 32.

religious doctrine develops within religious communities through reflection over the course of time, Proudfoot concluded that "Schleiermacher has here offered a theory of religion in which religious language and practice are derived from religious experience conceived as feeling, and not the other way around."[9]

From this textual basis Proudfoot advanced claims about how, according to Schleiermacher, religion is properly to be studied. On his account, for Schleiermacher the primary goal of the study of religion should be the identification of religious experience in its most original form. Because the causal relationship between religious experience and religious language runs in only one direction ("religious language is to be explained by reference to the religious affections, and not vice-versa") religious discourse offers a window on religious experience without offering any explanatory purchase over it; "Schleiermacher is convinced that piety is an original and underived moment of consciousness, and that the study of religion and of religious thought ought to be approached as the attempt to describe that experience through an examination of its expressions."[10]

(3) Proudfoot connected Schleiermacher's position on the "autonomy" of religion to the project of protecting religion from critical examination. On this point the relationship between Schleiermacher and the tradition that follows from him is not perfectly clear. Some of Proudfoot's passages stop short of ascribing to Schleiermacher himself a desire to protect religion: "Schleiermacher was the earliest and most systematic proponent of the autonomy of religious experience and of religious judgments and doctrines," which claim of autonomy "has become the chief strategy for protecting religious beliefs and practices from the possibility of conflict with the conclusions of science or with the assumptions that inform our perceptual and moral experience."[11] But in other places this motivation is immediately connected to Schleiermacher's position: "As a sense that precedes and is independent of all thought . . . religion can never come into conflict with the findings of modern science or with the advance of knowledge in any realm. It is an autonomous moment in human experience and is, in principle, invulnerable to rational and moral criticism."[12] And elsewhere Schleiermacher is just included in the category of "protectivists":

> others have followed Schleiermacher in viewing religious language as expressive and consequently not subject to the critical questions and requests for justification which are appropriately applied to language that is employed to make assertions.
> . . . from our perspective, Barth, Schleiermacher, and [D.Z.] Phillips employ similar strategies to limit all inquiry and reflection on Christian faith, or religious experience and belief, to internal elucidation and analysis.[13]

In the next section I will describe the influence *Religious Experience* seems to have had on the interpretation of Schleiermacher in the Anglophone literature; and in the final section I will offer some criticisms. I am certainly not the first to see shortcomings in Proudfoot's early portrayal of Schleiermacher. Ted Vial, for instance, has devoted an essay to an assessment of the adequacy of Proudfoot's claims (and also those of George Lindbeck); and

---

[9] Proudfoot, *Religious Experience*, p. 26.
[10] Proudfoot, *Religious Experience*, pp. 23, 13.
[11] Proudfoot, *Religious Experience*, p. 6.
[12] Proudfoot, *Religious Experience*, p. 2.
[13] Proudfoot, *Religious Experience*, pp. 26, 236.

below I will mention developments in Proudfoot's own understanding of Schleiermacher since 1985, as well as work on both sides of the issue by Terry Godlove.[14]

38.3 AFTER PROUDFOOT

Proudfoot's main purpose in *Religious Experience* was not to reconstruct Schleiermacher's position on the academic study of religion. Rather, Schleiermacher figured in the book as one member of a set of scholars who collectively serve as a foil for his own position on religious experience. The book enjoyed considerable influence within religious studies over the next several decades, and one consequence of its influence is that a recognizably Proudfootian Schleiermacher entered the literature of Anglophone religious studies.

It is at this point that academic politics enters my narrative. *Religious Experience* was published during a time that saw the rise of a sharply polarized view of the academic study of religion in North America—an episode I am inclined to label a "theology panic." For those who subscribe to this view, on one side stand scholars who want to study religion "objectively" or "critically"; on the other stand scholars—in particular theologians or phenomenological "crypto-theologians"—who want to protect religion from such study. Ivan Strenski's essay of 1987, "Our Very Own 'Contras,'" describes an academic "revolution" whose aim, "the emergence of a discipline of 'religious studies' as distinct from theology," was (prematurely) declared accomplished by Claude Welch in 1971, now threatened by "counter-revolutionary forces" entrenched within the American Academy of Religion. These "contras," however, did not openly advertise themselves as theologians: "without lapsing into a discredited positivism," Strenski advised, "we in religious studies must resist its re-theologizing—even if these days the new theology speaks often in the seductive pseudo-universal language of continental Hermeneutics, the archaic religion of Eliade, or the post-critical faith of Ricoeur."[15]

Criticism of Rudolf Otto and Mircea Eliade as "antireductionists" and defenders of the "autonomy" of religion was well established before 1985. So, for example, an influential essay from 1972 by Hans Penner and Edward Yonan, "Is a Science of Religion Possible?," attributed to Otto and Eliade the position that religion is unique, irreducible, and *sui generis*, and presents this position as an obstacle to attempts to explain religion.[16] In 1973 Strenski had published a lengthy essay on Eliade, arguing that he "makes religion independent of culture and its study independent of cultural and historical disciplines"; Eliade postulates "a heavenly world of rationally unassailable archetypes" primarily as a strategy for deflecting

---

[14] Ted Vial, "Anschauung and Intuition, Again (or, 'We Remain Bound to the Earth')," in *Schleiermacher, the Study of Religion, and the Future of Theology: A Translatlantic Dialogue*, ed. Brent Sockness and Wilhelm Gräb (Berlin: De Gruyter, 2010), pp. 39–50. George Lindbeck's *The Nature of Doctrine*, which describes Schleiermacher as an "experiential-expressivist," was published in 1984, and while it deserves consideration alongside *Religious Experience*, its influence outside theological circles has been minimal.

[15] Ivan Strenski, "Our Very Own 'Contras': A Response to the 'St. Louis Project,'" *Journal of the American Academy of Religion* 54 (1986), pp. 331f.

[16] Hans Penner and Edward Yonan, "Is a Science of Religion Possible?" *Journal of Religion* 52 (1972), p. 130.

criticisms of religion from logical positivism.[17] And Donald Wiebe's important 1984 AAR paper, "The Failure of Nerve in the Academic Study of Religion," pointedly asked "who or what it is that ought to set the agenda for, and hence control," the academic study of religion—"the scholar-scientist or the scholar-devotee, the church or the academy, the procedures of science or the (supposed) transcendent subject-matter of that science," identifying Otto and Eliade as members of the opposition.[18]

The year 1985 saw this polarization institutionalized with the founding of the North American Association for the Study of Religion (NAASR), for which Wiebe's essay came to be something of a manifesto. In 2005, two of that organization's founders, Wiebe and Luther Martin, wrote retrospectively that the motivation for its formation was the perception that the American Academy of Religion had failed to live up to its scholarly mission:

> As [Claude] Welch had feared . . . the Academy fell back into the arms of religiously oriented interests where it has largely remained to this day. There were some in the AAR who by this time had become frustrated with the Academy's inability to transform itself into an institution that was able to encourage the development of a genuine scientific/scholarly approach to the study of religion, free from religious influence. The original membership of NAASR, consequently, sought to establish an alternative venue in which to work toward the establishment of a sound, academic study of religion, not in opposition to the AAR but complementary to it.[19]

On this account, then, NAASR was founded to be the institutional embodiment of the position that "religious interests" are naturally antithetical to the "sound, academic" study of religion.[20]

Thus the idea that theologians, practically by definition, are dedicated to the program of sheltering religion from objective scrutiny, and so are the natural enemies of the academic study of religion, predates Proudfoot's work on Schleiermacher. Schleiermacher makes no appearance in any of the works I have mentioned in this section, which were almost exclusively conversant with twentieth-century literature. *Religious Experience* appears to have been instrumental in extending the historical reach of the portrayal of theologians as "protectivists" further back than Otto, and thus for facilitating the construction of longer historical narratives to justify the program of purging the academy of theological influences.

J. S. Preus' *Explaining Religion: Criticism and Theory from Bodin to Freud*, published in 1987, was one of the first books to draw on Proudfoot's portrayal of Schleiermacher. The project of the book was to offer a deep history of the development of a naturalistic-explanatory approach to the study of religion. The framework for this project was the struggle for

---

[17] Ivan Strenski, "Mircea Eliade: Some Theoretical Problems," in Strenski, *Religion in Relation: Method, Application and Moral Location* (Columbia: University of South Carolina Press, 1993), pp. 23, 40.

[18] Donald Wiebe, "The Failure of Nerve in the Academic Study of Religion," in *Failure and Nerve in the Academic Study of Religion*, ed. William Arnal et al. (New York: Routledge, 2012), pp. 6f.

[19] https://naasrreligion.files.wordpress.com/2014/01/establishingabeachhead.pdf (accessed June 9, 2020).

[20] In 2013, at a moment of high tension regarding the program and identity of NAASR, Wiebe offered a set of reflections on its history and prospects, paying particular attention to its relationship to (and influence on) the AAR. See Donald Wiebe, "Change the Name! On the Importance of Reclaiming NAASR's Original Objectives for the Twenty-First Century," *Method & Theory in the Study of Religion* 25 (2013), pp. 350–361.

control within the academic study of religion, and early on Preus made a point of noting his agreement with the position of Strenski's "Our Very Own 'Contras.'"[21] The naturalistic-explanatory approach, as described by Preus, represents an "alternative tradition" to a "purely descriptive" approach that "stems historically from nineteenth-century apologetic theology, exemplified by Schleiermacher's effort to describe the contents of the religious self-consciousness to its 'cultured despisers.'"[22] Preus' narrative begins in the eighteenth century, with Jean Bodin, Herbert of Cherbury, Bernard Fontenelle, and Giambattista Vico, and with David Hume representing the first clear emergence of the naturalist paradigm. After Hume, however, the next figure to appear is August Comte; while theologians contribute to the naturalistic paradigm early on, by the nineteenth century, theology is generally positioned as operating in the "apologetic" mode and is not part of Preus' narrative. His primary reference to Schleiermacher late in the book is simply an adjunct to a claim about Otto: "Schleiermacher and Otto fixed a theological notion of 'the sacred' that has been very durable and popular until now: essential religion (which strongly implies authentic religion), rooted in an apprehension of 'the holy', is utterly prior to either conceptual or moral formulation and elaboration."[23] No works by Schleiermacher appear in Preus' bibliography; *Religious Experience* does.

A recognizably Proudfootian Schleiermacher begins to appear with some regularity after 1985 in the context of discussions about the difference between "naturalistic," "scientific," or "reductionistic" approaches to religion and their alternatives. So, for example, Terry Godlove leaned on Proudfoot in his contribution to the 1990 essay collection *Religion and Reductionism*. According to Godlove Schleiermacher is the originator of "apologetic eliminativism," defending the claim that the essence of religion "is a mode of immediate awareness, having no conceptual, propositional, dogmatic or doctrinal components."[24] Godlove also echoed Proudfoot's claim that Schleiermacher's position is obviously incoherent: "Schleiermacher either never saw or, as part of a wider apologetic strategy, deliberately obscured the fact that his descriptions of the state of 'immediacy' show it to be shot through with beliefs and concepts."[25]

Some moments of this history are interesting. In a 1977 book review Robert Segal praised scholars who "confront directly and honestly the challenge posed by science and analytic philosophy," who engage in critical reflection not "to justify casting aside science and scientific language as the standards of objectivity and cognitive meaningfulness but on the contrary to enable religion and religious language to meet those standards. In their attempt to reconcile religion with science and, broadly secular culture they continue a tradition which goes back to Schleiermacher and even to Philo."[26] But in 1991 Segal criticized scholars who offer "religious" rather than "naturalistic" accounts of religion, stating flatly that

---

[21] J. Samuel Preus, *Explaining Religion: Criticism and Theory from Bodin to Freud* (New Haven: Yale University Press, 1987), p. xix n36.

[22] Preus, *Explaining Religion*, p. xx.

[23] Preus, *Explaining Religion*, p. 200. At this point in the text Preus mentions Schleiermacher, but cites only texts by Otto and Eliade.

[24] Terry Godlove Jr., "The Instability of Religious Belief: Some Reductionistic and Eliminative Pressures," in *Religion and Reductionism: Essays on Eliade, Segal, and the Challenge of the Social Sciences for the Study of Religion*, ed. Thomas Idinopolous and Edward Yonan (Leiden: Brill, 1994), pp. 51, 49.

[25] Godlove, "The Instability of Religious Belief," pp. 49f.

[26] Robert A. Segal, *Metaphor and Myth in Science and Religion*, by Earl MacCormac (review), *Journal of Religion* 57 (1977), p. 423.

a naturalistic account, however inadequate, is more adequate than a religious one, which amounts to the litany that religion originates as a response to the transcendent. Feuerbach, Freud, and Durkheim provide a host of processes and entities like projection, wish fulfillment, complexes, collective representations, and symbols to account for how and why religion originates and functions. Friedrich Schleiermacher, Rudolf Otto, and Mircea Eliade, their religious counterparts, provide nothing.[27]

When David Ray Griffin pointed out that Schleiermacher had in fact offered explanations of how the feeling of absolute dependence arises, Segal retrenched—"But what needs to be explained is the step *from* the feeling to religion"—which sentence seems to assume that Schleiermacher said nothing on this subject.[28]

The scholar who has made the most consistent use of this view of Schleiermacher has been Russell McCutcheon, whose graduate studies with Wiebe were subsequent to the publication of *Religious Experience* and the formation of NAASR. Schleiermacher appears in 1997 as one of the progenitors of the "discourse of *sui generis* religion," which McCutcheon described as the "regnant discourse" of the field of religious studies. In Louis Jordan's statement that "in every man, Religion in its essence is one and the same thing," McCutcheon espied an "aspect of the discourse on sui generis religion apparent at least as early as Schleiermacher: religion constitutes a private, interiorized dimension of experience that, although manifested outwardly in varying forms, is shared across all religions regardless of their historical differences."[29] In 1999: "Schleiermacher firmly placed religion within the interior, private, and personal realm of experience, emotion, and feeling"; "the implication for the insider/outsider problem is that religious feelings are preeminently a matter for the insider . . . the outsider, the one who emphasizes the role to be played by rationality, simply misses the point if they think that one can study religion objectively from afar."[30] In 2001: "Schleiermacher defended religion against its so-called cultured despisers by re-conceiving of it as a nonquantifiable individual experience, a deep feeling, or an immediate consciousness," an understanding that "takes what is all too public and social and tries to secure and protect it within the private and inscrutable realm of subjectivity and pure consciousness"; for the "'private affair' tradition" pioneered by Schleiermacher (proximately represented by Martin Marty), "religion, or the sacred, is itself somehow pure, internal, intentional, creative, socially autonomous, and efficacious and therefore can be studied only though its various secondary, symbolic manifestations. In a word, religious feelings can be considered to be a cause, but never simply an effect."[31]

The preface to *Religious Experience: A Reader* (2008), which McCutcheon edited with Craig Martin, begins with the claim that Schleiermacher "argued as far back as 1799 that the core of religion is an awe-inspiring *experience* of God"; where Kant had placed God beyond

---

[27] Robert A. Segal, "Religion as Interpreted Rather than Explained", *Soundings: An Interdisciplinary Journal* 74 (1991), pp. 282-283.

[28] Robert A. Segal, "Response: In Defense of Social Scientific Naturalism: A Response to David Ray Griffin," *Journal of the American Academy of Religion* 68 (2000), p. 140.

[29] Russell McCutcheon, *Manufacturing Religion: The Discourse on Sui Generis Religion and the Politics of Nostalgia* (Oxford: Oxford University Press, 1997), p. 60.

[30] Russell McCutcheon, ed., *The Insider/Outsider Problem in the Study of Religion: A Reader* (London: Cassell, 1999), p. 68.

[31] Russell McCutcheon, *Critics Not Caretakers: Redescribing the Public Study of Religion* (Albany: SUNY Press, 2001), pp. 4f.

human knowing, "Schleiermacher would bring his god back in by saying that we have *direct experiences* of this god."³² The same year McCutcheon claimed that a set of strategies that are "among the more successful, and thus persuasive and pervasive, techniques employed within social formations for reproducing dominant forms of organization" can be traced back to Schleiermacher, who "effectively protected—and thereby, some would say, simultaneously marginalized—those dimensions of social life then labeled as 'religion' from what he saw as the cynical, prying eyes of Enlightenment rationality, by claiming that religion was essentially a personalistic, affective experience."³³ For Schleiermacher, "religious experiences are exclusively the causes of other things; they cannot be explained as merely the effects of other ordinary human behaviors. Such experience is understood as irreducible, primary, and utterly unique (i.e. sui generis)." Schleiermacher's tradition contrasts with one dedicated to "studying the causes, functions, and consequences of human behavior and organization," a program now represented in the academy by NAASR.³⁴ And in 2015, Schleiermacher appears as the originator of the position expressed most prominently by Otto, that "religious institutions are simply a secondary site where a prior, pristine, and personal experience is expressed publicly." Schleiermacher's position, like Otto's, was motivated by a desire to shield religion from criticism: for Schleiermacher "religion was first and foremost about 'feeling' and as such, was neither a rational nor an irrational element of the human .... [F]eelings are non-rational, personal, and thus not prone to logical critique."³⁵

Two features of these uses of Schleiermacher I have surveyed here are worth noting. First, these references to Schleiermacher are not substantive. Unlike Proudfoot, Preus, Segal, and McCutcheon do not engage in the exegesis of Schleiermacher's texts; rather, they advance claims about Schleiermacher that, if they are supported at all, are supported by secondary literature. And second, these scholars' purposes in citing Schleiermacher are purely positional, part of boundary-fixing exercises where "critical" or "scientific" approaches to the study of religion fall on one side, and "theological" approaches fall on the other.

Having described the appearance and persistence of a "Proudfootian Schleiermacher" in the literature after 1985, I want to note that its significance appears to be fairly limited. A "protectivist" Schleiermacher appeared prominently in NAASR-adjacent polemics around the turn of the twentieth century, and it is impossible to know the extent to this portrayal's influence outside the sphere of scholarly publications—so for example within the academic classroom. But within the literature this figure seems largely to have enjoyed at best a brief moment in the sun. While in recent years the occasional glimpse can be found in NAASR's house journal, I have not found references to a recognizably Proudfootian Schleiermacher in works by Donald Wiebe, Luther Martin, or younger scholars such as Craig Martin.³⁶ Also, Proudfoot's own understanding has developed; in recently published essays he has voiced doubts about the soundness of his earlier views, and has stated flatly

---

³² Craig Martin and Russell McCutcheon, eds., *Religious Experience: A Reader* (Taylor & Francis Group, 2014), p. vii.

³³ Russell McCutcheon, "Critical Trends in the Study of Religion in the United States," in *New Approaches to the Study of Religion*, vol. 1, ed. Peter Antes et al. (Berlin: De Gruyter, 2008), p. 325.

³⁴ McCutcheon, "Critical Trends", p. 325.

³⁵ Russell McCutcheon, *A Modest Proposal on Method: Essaying the Study of Religion* (Leiden: Brill, 2015), pp. 171–173.

³⁶ See, for example, Lieve Orye, "'It's about Us': Religious Studies as a Human Science," *Method & Theory in the Study of Religion* 13 (2001), p. 356. I should note that while Proudfoot's Schleiermacher

that "Schleiermacher does not say that religious intuitions are prelinguistic and therefore untouched by grammatical rules and connections."[37] The same is true of Terry Godlove, who has recently reexamined Proudfoot's (and his own) earlier views at length.[38] It is possible that at present McCutcheon is the sole remaining subscriber to the "protectivist" rendering of Schleiermacher.

Before I offer my own response to the (early) Proudfootian portrayal of Schleiermacher, consider a few brief mentions of his work written in English that have a significantly different flavor. In a 2003 publication, Jeppe Sind Jensen remarked that "I consider religion to have been relegated from the transcendent and otherworldly by—preeminently—Kant, Schleiermacher, and Feuerbach. The 'locus' of religion was removed from gods to humans." In 2014 he remarked, "although more critical of Enlightenment ideas than of religion and the established churches, the Romanticist emphasis on religiosity, experience and emotion inadvertently turned religion into a very human affair. This, in fact, helped pave the way for ever more naturalistic explanations of the nature and origin of religion."[39] And Arie Molendijk has stated that "Schleiermacher's account of religion established a revaluation of the historical character of religion and of its positivity. Such views were of great importance to the rise of the scientific study of religion, because they awakened the awareness that religions are to be studied in their own right and not as instances of either superstition or natural (rational) religion."[40]

Jensen and Molendijk have much in common with the "mentioners" of Schleiermacher I have surveyed above. They are not Schleiermacher specialists; they are participants in the Anglophone study of religion (i.e. they read English sources and write in English); and they position a development away from theology as a necessary step for the emergence of the academic study of religion. I am inclined to say that what accounts for the very different character of their sense of what Schleiermacher was about is simply that they are located in Europe rather than in North America—a location that places them closer to German

---

does not appear in the broader NAASR literature, neither generally does a more adequately understood Schleiermacher.

[37] Wayne Proudfoot, "Intuition and Fantasy in 'On Religion,'" in *Interpreting Religion: The Significance of Friedrich Schleiermacher's Reden über die Religion for Religious Studies and Theology*, ed. Dietrich Korsch and Amber L. Griffioen (Tübingen: Mohr Siebeck, 2011), p. 92. In this essay Proudfoot refines his criticism of Schleiermacher's position in the *Speeches*, focusing now on his claim that religious intuitions are independent of each other, a position Proudfoot regards as difficult to sustain in relation to Schleiermacher's attention to "the development of linguistic skills and the cultivation of social practices that assume grammatical and conceptual connections with other beliefs and practices" (p. 98). See also Wayne Proudfoot, "Immediacy and Intentionality in the Feeling of Absolute Dependence," in *Schleiermacher, the Study of Religion, and the Future of Theology: A Translatlantic Dialogue*, ed. Brent Sockness and Wilhelm Gräb (Berlin: De Gruyter, 2010), p. 28: "I continue to think that Schleiermacher regarded the distinctive moment in piety as one that is unstructured by the Kantian forms and categories, but I am now unsure whether or not he regarded it as independent of concepts."

[38] Terry Godlove Jr., "Nonconceptualism and Religious Experience: Kant, Schleiermacher, Proudfoot," in *Pragmatism and Naturalism: Scientific and Social Inquiry*, ed. Matthew Bagger (New York: Columbia University Press, 2018), pp. 252–276.

[39] Jeppe Sind Jensen, *The Study of Religion in a New Key* (Arhus: Arhus University Press, 2003), p. 43 n31.; Jensen, *What Is Religion?* (New York: Routledge, 2014), pp. 17f.

[40] Arie Molendijk, "Introduction," in *Religion in the Making: The Emergence of the Sciences of Religion*, ed. Arie Molendijk and Peter Pels (Leiden: Brill, 1998), p. 4.

literature on Schleiermacher and the history of academic theology, and farther away from North American anxieties about who "controls" the study of religion.

38.4 SCHLEIERMACHER AND THE STUDY OF RELIGION

In response to the claims about Schleiermacher that are downstream of *Religious Experience* I will address three broad issues. The first of these concerns how Schleiermacher's positions on religion and "religious experience" should be understood; the second, the place of an "academic study of religion" in his corpus; and third, the question of whether and how his claims about religion were motivated by a desire to protect it from critical examination.

38.4.1 Religion and "Religious Experience"

The claim that for Schleiermacher religion *just is* a feeling, or a type of feeling, cannot withstand the examination of more than a few decontextualized passages from his writings.[41] Feeling does occupy a privileged position within religion as Schleiermacher understood it; but religion itself extends beyond feeling, both within the minds of persons and into interpersonal relations—into ideas, claims, social practices, artifacts, and institutions. Feeling (intuition, immediate self-consciousness) defines religion not by being coextensive with it but by being essential to it—not by being the entirety of the phenomenon but by being its core.

Schleiermacher did not make prominent use of the idea of "religious experience," but neither is it absent from his thinking. The young Schleiermacher did position a distinct kind of experience—a moment of contact between person and universe—as a source of religious intuitions and feelings. But it is important to note that the essence of a religion is not some such experience, but the intuition (or, later, feeling) that results when this is "grasped, apprehended, and conceived according to one's own nature" and which becomes the common possession of groups of persons when shared through discourse and other forms of expression.[42] The later *Glaubenslehre*'s feeling of absolute dependence is not a "religious experience" because it is not an experience, but rather a component or aspect of some (or possibly all) experience that can be identified by abstraction from experience. There is one religious experience that figures importantly in Schleiermacher's mature thinking: it is the "experience of redemption." But I do not think that early-Proudfootian criticisms can be mounted against this Schleiermacher on this point. The experience of redemption is not a pan-religious phenomenon, but is distinctive to the Christian tradition; it cannot plausibly be claimed to be prior to concepts and beliefs (and Schleiermacher nowhere claims that it

---

[41] See, in particular, chapter 2 of Andrew Dole, *Schleiermacher on Religion and the Natural Order* (Oxford: Oxford University Press, 2010), "Religion in Outline."

[42] *Speeches¹*, pp. 24f. This passage was absent from *Religious Experience*, but Proudfoot's 2011 essay, "Intuition and Fantasy," devotes a good deal of attention to it.

is); and Schleiermacher takes great pains to point out that this experience results not from some direct and unmediated action of a supernatural agent but rather from participation in Christian community (which we might now redescribe as engagement in Christian social practices).[43]

38.4.2 The Study of Religion

In *Religious Experience* Proudfoot's claims about Schleiermacher's position on the study of religion bypass (for the most part) what Schleiermacher wrote about the relationship between religion and the sciences.[44] In his wider corpus Schleiermacher positioned theology as the recipient of information about religion (and about human beings generally) developed within history, psychology, ethics, and other academic disciplines. The text where this is set out most explicitly is the *Brief Outline*; readers of the *Glaubenslehre* also know that in the second edition Schleiermacher labeled the main components of his understanding of religion, and Christianity, as "propositions borrowed from" these sciences. Schleiermacher also gave a novel meaning to the term "philosophy of religion," defining it as a discipline that studies the different forms that religious communities assume "and how what is distinctive in the various faith-based associations that have arisen in history relates to these differences," in the *Glaubenslehre* borrowing from this field a schematism of the different forms and developmental stages of religion in general.[45] And famously (as well as controversially), he distinguished between two standpoints from which Christianity could be examined. The extra-theological sciences generally, and also those parts of theology that are dedicated to the identification of the essence of the Christian religious tradition, view it "from above," that is, as an instance of "the general concept of a religious community or a community of faith"; in the *Glaubenslehre* it was only after the methodological introduction, in the "first part of the system of doctrine," that Schleiermacher wrote "we are definitely not moving outside of the domain of Christian piety any longer."[46] In other words, a view of Christianity "from above" is internal to theology up to the point where it moves into the specific mode of dogmatics.

Perhaps the greatest failing of the portrayal of Schleiermacher's place in the academic study of religion that one finds in, for example, McCutcheon is that it erases from the historical record Schleiermacher's insistence on—and his role in establishing—the idea that religion is a rightful object of investigation, "from above" *rather than "from within"*, by the full range of the *Wissenschaften*.

---

[43] Andrew Dole, "What Is 'Religious Experience' in Schleiermacher's Dogmatics, and Why Does It Matter?," *Journal of Analytic Theology* 4 (2016), pp. 44–65.

[44] In *Religious Experience* Proudfoot did mention Schleiermacher's understanding of philosophy of religion (p. 17), but entirely without comment.

[45] *BO*, p. 11; *CF (2016)*, pp. 45–79.

[46] *BO*, p. 15; compare §6 in *CG1*, p. 20; *CF (2016)*, p. 190.

38.4.3 "Protectivism"

I think it best to address the "protectivism" charge by way of a lengthy analogy. Imagine that in some city there is an old, complex, and much-beloved building—call it "the Hall"—that a community considers its collective possession. Suppose that some areas of the Hall are in poor repair, such that some parties are worried about the possibility of structural failures. Now imagine that a person within this community proposes a program of renovation. The Hall is to be assessed with an eye for issues of structural integrity; repairs are to be made where this is possible, and this might result in more than cosmetic changes. Parts of the building that are found to be irreparable are to be demolished. And imagine that this program contains specific recommendations—this part is to be modified like so, this part is basically fine, this part is beyond saving.

There is certainly a sense in which our would-be renovator would be acting "protectively": she is motivated by a concern for the well-being of the Hall, and wants to forestall possible events that would impinge upon this. But I do not think it could be said that what such a person is trying to "protect" the Hall from is critical examination. This is because critical examination is an essential part of her own program. The renovator believes that an *absence* of critical examination will do the Hall no favors, for time will have its way with the structure regardless.

Now imagine that there are parties who will object to making any significant changes to the Hall. Imagine our renovator deploying the following argument:

> The Hall has a long history, and has looked very different at different times. And yet it has been the Hall through all of these changes. So what makes the Hall the Hall, really? I think what makes the Hall the Hall is that it reflects its architect's desire to be a spacious and gracious gathering-place for our community, and a repository for our historical records and artifacts. The sad fact is that in its current condition, the Hall cannot effectively serve those purposes. My proposed renovations will make the Hall more truly what it was always meant to be, even if it differs in significant ways from its current form.

This modification basically makes our renovator an essentialist about the Hall, and this modification gives the charge of "protectivism" more purchase. For consider the criticism that the Hall is an embarrassment in virtue of its dilapidated condition. Our renovator might respond, "well, dilapidation is an embarrassment, certainly. But the Hall's dilapidated condition is accidental rather than essential: the Hall is more than its sagging floors or its crumbling facade. However embarrassing its current state, the Hall *in itself* is not an embarrassment." This rhetoric does have the effect of deflecting criticism, in a way, by grounding the identity of "the Hall" in something that could not, in fact, be the object of the criticism in question.

Schleiermacher deployed his essentialism for purposes analogous to those of our imagined renovator. He used his claims about essences as criteria for discriminating between "healthy" and "diseased" conditions in religion, and for recommending alterations aimed at making it possible for religion to do what, on his account, it was properly meant to do. There are senses in which he was a "protectivist" about religion: his strategy in the *Speeches*, for example, was to argue that those features of religion that motivated the negative evaluations of its "despisers" were accidental rather than essential, such that their criticism missed the thing itself. But I do not think that either the claim that his intention was to protect religion from critical examination or that his understanding of religion accomplishes this can be defended. As with our imagined renovator, the critical examination of religion is internal to his program of reform.

In fact I cannot imagine any charge of protectivism against Schleiermacher that would not also apply to a very different kind of figure. Consider the one who argues that unsavory features of the academic study of religion are products of failures to conform to its proper (perhaps "scientific") program, and that properly understood, much of what passes for the study of religion is really something else (perhaps "theology") in disguise. To argue in this way would be to protect the study of religion against criticism to the same extent that Schleiermacher, properly understood, so protects religion.

38.5 CONCLUSION

Aside from whatever can be said about Schleiermacher himself, there is no denying that some elements of his positions were attractive to, and appropriated by, later thinkers with projects different from his. And in fact there is a more interesting history to be related in this area, one about the historical fortunes of the view that Schleiermacher was far too anthropological a thinker to be "safe" for Christian theology. I suspect that the tendency to oversimplify the past in self-serving ways is a natural temptation for those with an impulse to draw sharp boundaries between sound and unsound in the present. It may be that the rendering of Schleiermacher I have surveyed here is nearing the end of its run in our literature. But given Schleiermacher's dedication to "mediating" between positions that others, then and now, have seen as irreconcilable, it is likely that caricatures of his position will continue to appear wherever programs of constructing unbridgeable polarities, whether within the church or the academy, would be inconvenienced by his actual positions.

SUGGESTED READING

Byrne, Peter. *Natural Religion and the Nature of Religion* (London: Routledge, 1989).
Strenski, Ivan. "On 'Religion' and Its Despisers." In *What Is Religion? Origins, Definitions, and Explanations*, ed. Thomas Idinopolous and Brian Wilson (Leiden: Brill, 1998), pp. 113–132.
Tilley, Terrence W. "Review: Polemics and Politics in Explaining Religion." *The Journal of Religion* 71 (1991), pp. 242–254.
Wiebe, Donald. *The Politics of Religious Studies: The Continuing Conflict with Theology in the Academy* (New York: St. Martin's, 1999).

BIBLIOGRAPHY

Dole, Andrew. "'The Case of the Disappearing Discourse': Schleiermacher's Fourth Speech and the Field of Religious Studies." *Journal of Religion* 88 (2008), pp. 1–28.
Dole, Andrew. *Schleiermacher on Religion and the Natural Order* (Oxford: Oxford University Press, 2010).

Dole, Andrew. "What Is 'Religious Experience' in Schleiermacher's Dogmatics, and Why Does It Matter?" *Journal of Analytic Theology* 4 (2016), pp. 44–65.

Godlove, Terry Jr. "The Instability of Religious Belief: Some Reductionistic and Eliminative Pressures." In *Religion and Reductionism: Essays on Eliade, Segal, and the Challenge of the Social Sciences for the Study of Religion*, ed. Thomas Idinopolous and Edward Yonan (Leiden: Brill, 1994), pp. 49–64.

Godlove, Terry Jr. "Nonconceptualism and Religious Experience: Kant, Schleiermacher, Proudfoot." In *Pragmatism and Naturalism: Scientific and Social Inquiry*, ed. Matthew Bagger (New York: Columbia University Press, 2018), pp. 252–276.

Jensen, Jeppe Sind. *The Study of Religion in a New Key* (Arhus: Arhus University Press, 2003).

Jensen, Jeppe Sind. *What Is Religion?* (New York: Routledge, 2014).

Martin, Craig, and Russell McCutcheon, eds. *Religious Experience: A Reader* (Taylor & Francis Group, 2014).

McCutcheon, Russell. "Critical Trends in the Study of Religion in the United States." In *New Approaches to the Study of Religion*, vol. 1, ed. Peter Antes et al. (Berlin: De Gruyter, 2008), pp. 317–343.

McCutcheon, Russell. *Critics Not Caretakers: Redescribing the Public Study of Religion* (Albany: SUNY Press, 2001).

McCutcheon, Russell. *Manufacturing Religion: The Discourse on Sui Generis Religion and the Politics of Nostalgia* (Oxford: Oxford University Press, 1997).

McCutcheon, Russell. *A Modest Proposal on Method: Essaying the Study of Religion* (Leiden: Brill, 2015).

McCutcheon, Russell, ed. *The Insider/Outsider Problem in the Study of Religion: A Reader* (London: Cassell, 1999).

Molendijk, Arie. "Introduction." In *Religion in the Making: The Emergence of the Sciences of Religion*, ed. Arie Molendijk and Peter Pels (Leiden: Brill, 1998), pp. 1–27.

Orye, Lieve. "'It's about Us': Religious Studies as a Human Science." *Method & Theory in the Study of Religion* 13 (2001), pp. 355–373.

Penner, Hans, and Edward Yonan. "Is a Science of Religion Possible?" *Journal of Religion* 52 (1972), pp. 107–133.

Preus, J. Samuel. *Explaining Religion: Criticism and Theory from Bodin to Freud* (New Haven: Yale University Press, 1987).

Proudfoot, Wayne. "Immediacy and Intentionality in the Feeling of Absolute Dependence." In *Schleiermacher, the Study of Religion, and the Future of Theology: A Translatlantic Dialogue*, ed. Brent Sockness and Wilhelm Gräb (Berlin: De Gruyter, 2010), pp. 27–37.

Proudfoot, Wayne. "Intuition and Fantasy in 'On Religion.'" In *Interpreting Religion: The Significance of Friedrich Schleiermacher's Reden über die Religion for Religious Studies and Theology*, ed. Dietrich Korsch and Amber L. Griffioen (Tübingen: Mohr Siebeck, 2011), pp. 87–98.

Proudfoot, Wayne. *Religious Experience* (Berkeley: University of California Press, 1985).

Segal, Robert A. *Metaphor and Myth in Science and Religion*, by Earl MacCormac (review). *Journal of Religion* 57 (1977), p. 423.

Segal, Robert A. "Religion as Interpreted Rather than Explained." *Soundings: An Interdisciplinary Journal* 74 (1991), pp. 275–288.

Segal, Robert A. "Response: In Defense of Social Scientific Naturalism: A Response to David Ray Griffin." *Journal of the American Academy of Religion* 68 (2000), pp. 133–141.

Strenski, Ivan. "Mircea Eliade: Some Theoretical Problems." In Strenski, *Religion in Relation: Method, Application and Moral Location* (Columbia: University of South Carolina Press, 1993), pp. 15–41.

Strenski, Ivan. "Our Very Own 'Contras': A Response to the 'St. Louis Project.'" *Journal of the American Academy of Religion* 54/2 (1986), pp. 323–335.

Vial, Ted. "Anschauung and Intuition, Again (or, 'We Remain Bound to the Earth')." In *Schleiermacher, the Study of Religion, and the Future of Theology: A Translatlantic Dialogue*, ed. Brent Sockness and Wilhelm Gräb (Berlin: De Gruyter, 2010), pp. 39–50.

Wiebe, Donald. "Change the Name! On the Importance of Reclaiming NAASR's Original Objectives for the Twenty-First Century." *Method & Theory in the Study of Religion* 25 (2013), pp. 350–361.

Wiebe, Donald. "The Failure of Nerve in the Academic Study of Religion." In *Failure and Nerve in the Academic Study of Religion*, ed. William Arnal et al. (New York: Routledge, 2012), pp. 6–33.

CHAPTER 39

FRIEDRICH SCHLEIERMACHER AND THE POSTSECULAR

"Pacemaker for the Consciousness of a Postsecular Society"?

MATTHEW RYAN ROBINSON

Schleiermacher is the pacemaker for the consciousness of a postsecular society that accepts the continued existence of religion in an environment that is becoming progressively more secular.

—Jürgen Habermas, "The Boundary between Faith and Knowledge"[1]

39.1 INTRODUCTION

THE "postsecular" first becomes a topic of social-critical discourse in the 1960s—one hundred thirty years after Schleiermacher's death. Yet Jürgen Habermas, one of the thinkers most famously associated with postsecular theory, called Schleiermacher "the pacemaker for the consciousness of a postsecular society."[2] That Schleiermacher might have been a prototypical postsecular thinker is suggested already by the title of his most famous work, *On Religion: Speeches to Its Cultured Despisers*.[3] Was Schleiermacher not addressing an audience of enlightened deists quite similar to the audience of secularization theorists addressed

---

[1] Jürgen Habermas, "The Boundary between Faith and Knowledge," in Jürgen Habermas, *Between Naturalism and Religion: Philosophical Essays*, trans. Ciarin Cronin (Malden: Polity Press, 2008 [2005]), pp. 209–247, here p. 242.

[2] Habermas, "The Boundary between Faith and Knowledge," p. 242. Concerning to what extent Habermas is unique with this assessment, see note 37 below.

[3] Cf. Gunter Scholz, "Religion und Säkularisierung bei Schleiermacher und Steffens," in *System und Subversion. Friedrich Schleiermacher und Henrik Steffens*, ed. Sarah Schmidt and Leon Miodonski (Berlin and Boston: De Gruyter, 2018), pp. 233–252.

by postsecular thinkers? Also like many of the latter, he was arguing for the non-reducible, unique vitality of religion. Yet, as a reading of Schleiermacher, categorizing him as a prototypical theorist of the postsecular would be too thin and associative. Reading Schleiermacher in relation to the postsecular requires constructing a conceptual linkage between core concerns of discourses on the postsecular and those of Schleiermacher's time and context.

Such a constructive reading of Schleiermacher in relation to the postsecular might involve two tasks. The first task would be to reconstruct empirical and practical engagements of Schleiermacher's thought with issues categorized under the contemporary term "postsecular." Only then, second, should attempts be made at extrapolating points of relevance for the contemporary moment from his work. The present chapter is devoted to only the first of these two tasks.

39.2 The (Post)Secular: Religion, Values, and Social Solidarity

The title of sociologist Peter Berger's 1999 edited volume *The Desecularization of the World* implies some kind of fading away of secularity. In his introduction, however, Berger observes that "the world today ... is as furiously religious as it ever was."[4] The discourses making use of the terminology of the "postsecular" are many and varied[5]—enough so that many have questioned the concept's internal coherence or usefulness.[6] Broadly speaking, "secularity" refers, on the one hand, to the legal transfer of duties and properties from religious to nonreligious purview and, on the other hand, to the emergence of nonbelief in modernity as a serious option for individuals and even whole societies. Against this background, the postsecular refers not to a break or a rupture with secularization processes and secular worldviews, but, quite the opposite, to the ongoing working-out, over the course of at least two centuries, of normative requirements for organizing social spaces and institutions populated by multiple, competing religious worldviews while remaining social spaces and institutions that do not themselves espouse any particular religious worldview. As such the terminology of the secular and the postsecular refer to a complex set of interrelations of ideas, values, and their (de)institutionalization unfolding over time as well as to the analytic and practical challenges these interrelations have produced. Secularity presupposes postsecularity, while postsecularity relies on secularity.[7]

---

[4] Peter Berger, "The Desecularization of the World: A Global Overview," in *The Desecularization of the World: Resurgent Religion and World Politics*, ed. Peter Berger (Grand Rapids: William B. Eerdmans, 1999), pp. 1–18, here p. 2.

[5] For reviews of literature on the postsecular, see James A. Beckford, "SSSR Presidential Address: Public Religions and the Postsecular: Critical Reflections," *Journal for the Scientific Study of Religion* 51, no. 1 (2012), pp. 1–19; Alex Cistelecan, "The Theological Turn of Contemporary Critical Theory," *Telos* 167 (2014), pp. 8–26; Gregor McLennan "Towards a Postsecular Sociology?," *Sociology* 41, no. 5 (2007), pp. 857–870; McLennan, "The Postsecular Turn," *Theory, Culture & Society* 27, no. 4 (2010), pp. 3–20.

[6] See Umut Parmaksiz, "Making Sense of the Postsecular," *European Journal of Social Theory* 21, no. 1 (2018), pp. 98–116, esp. p. 99.

[7] Cf. Klaus Eder in "Europäische Säkularisierung—Ein Sonderweg in die postsäkulare Gesellschaft? Eine theoretische Anmerkung," *Berliner Jahrbuch der Soziologie* 3 (2002), pp. 331–343.

Amid the existentialist anomie and social-scientific positivism of the post-World War II period, Catholic sociologist Andrew Greeley predicted in a 1966 article, "After Secularity," that the Christian church would be needed for offering "Gemeinschaft"-oriented social forms (meaning, personal forms of "community") in a world increasingly structured as "Gesellschaften" (by which he meant the more impersonal "society").[8] The argument of the article works on the basis of the givenness of secularity, not its disappearance. In this way, Greeley's analysis bears similarity to that of theologian Harvey Cox in his 1965 book *The Secular City*, which sought to diagnose the future of religion *in*, not *after*, the presence of the secular.[9] Eugene Borowitz's 1970 "The Postsecular Situation of Jewish Theology" outlined the ways secular forms of modernity failed Jewish people throughout the West. Here, too, Borowitz did not call into question the emergence of a secular option, nor did he predict its disappearance; rather, he observed that the offer of a secular emancipation had been rejected by Jewish people throughout the West because of a secular society's inability to produce and sustain values: "The root difficulty is that there is little or nothing in the secular approach to things today which is productive and empowering of human value."[10] So there is a concern evident in early discourses on postsecularity to preserve social values and the ability to cultivate ultimate meaning, and this is, interestingly, not rooted in the expectation that religion is disappearing, but also not in the expectation that the secular will either. How is this to be understood? A similar struggle is evident in the efforts of some postmodern theologians in the 1990s, from John Milbank[11] to Graham Ward.[12] Milbank, Catherine Pickstock, and Ward opened their introduction to the much-discussed project of Radical Orthodoxy by announcing that "the logic of secularism is imploding ... It proclaims ... its own lack of values and lack of meaning."[13] But here, too, as Milbank himself writes in his preface to the 2006 second edition of his 1990 *Theology and Social Theory*, the concern for values after the secular leads to a "new recognition of a need for a universal discourse if we are to sustain any political hope."[14]

Jürgen Habermas[15] has turned to religion more often in his work since the beginning of the new millennium because religions present "cultural sources that nurture citizens' solidarity"[16] and produce "mentalities that [the liberal state] cannot produce from its own resources."[17] This is similar to the postsecular concern already evident

---

[8] Andrew M. Greely, "After Secularity: The Neo-Gemeinschaft Society: A Post-Christian Postscript*," *Sociological Analysis* 27, no. 3 (1966), pp. 119–127.

[9] Harvey Cox, *The Secular City: Secularization and Urbanization in Theological Perspective* (Princeton: Princeton University Press, 2013 [1965]).

[10] Eugene Borowitz, "The Postsecular Situation of Jewish Theology," *Theological Studies* 31, no. 3 (1970), pp. 460–475, here p. 470.

[11] John Milbank, *Theology and Social Theory: Beyond Secular Reason* (Oxford: Blackwell Publishing, 2006 [1990]).

[12] Graham Ward, *The Postmodern God* (Oxford: Blackwell Publishers, 1997).

[13] John Milbank, Catherine Pickstock, and Graham Ward, eds., *Radical Orthodoxy: A New Theology* (London and New York: Routledge, 1999), p. 1.

[14] Milbank, *Theology and Social Theory*, p. xxii.

[15] Cf. Habermas' most famous articulation of the postsecular in Jürgen Habermas, "Notes on a Post-Secular Society," *New Perspectives Quarterly* 25, no. 4 (Fall 2007), pp. 17–29.

[16] Jürgen Habermas, "Prepolitical Foundations of the Constitutional State?," in Habermas, *Between Naturalism and Religion*, pp. 101–113, here p. 111.

[17] Jürgen Habermas, "Introduction," in Habermas, *Between Naturalism and Religion*, p. 3.

in Cox and Greeley, except that it represents the perspective of a secular citizenry rather than religious concerns about the place of religion in society. But in Habermas' work, in fact, these at first seemingly opposite perspectives and sets of concerns are revealed to be inseparable. At the core of Habermas' turn to religion as an important phenomenal field for sociological and political-theoretical analysis lie both sides of the paradox that "the ideologically neutral exercise of secular governmental authority" and "different communities of belief" need one another, indeed, that they are necessary for guaranteeing and nurturing one another's well-being.[18] The framing within which this "post-metaphysical" position develops is that postsecularity—the ongoing presence of religious worldviews in public—relies on the maintenance of secular norms to guarantee "equal rights and mutual tolerance."[19] At the same time, the principles of secular governance themselves presuppose postsecularity in that the normative contents of the ideal of a secular society demand forms of publicness that do not privilege *any* claim "to structure a form of life in its entirety"[20]—including secularist claims of that nature—that are, instead, accessible to all, and that guarantee space for both religious and nonreligious worldviews. The postsecular remains secular, while the secular itself—as a set of norms with attending institutions serving to manage a pluralism of competing, comprehensive claims to life—was always already "postsecular."

The postsecular can, in summary, be understood as the set of civic and political challenges entailed in managing religious pluralism addressed to modern societies, namely, challenges concerning: the plurality of competing confessions in one society, the sociopolitical management thereof, structural transformations of society, and, finally, the formation of social values. These are questions of politics and law, on the one hand, and of religious communication, on the other hand. If this is correct, then the specific language of the "postsecular" should not be understood as referring to an "age" in the more recent history of modern societies that follows a "secular" one, but rather as referring to the recent development of discourses, particularly academic discourses, concerning religion seeking to analyze the simultaneity of religious pluralism and secular state apparatuses. In other words, the postsecular refers to a problem, not a period, and that problem is much older than the term itself. Having recognized this structure of the challenges of the postsecular, it becomes possible to inquire after Schleiermacher's own characterization of the problem and proposed approaches to addressing it.

---

[18] Habermas, "Introduction," p. 3.
[19] Habermas, "Introduction," p. 3.
[20] Jürgen Habermas, "Religious Tolerance as Pacemaker for Cultural Rights," in Habermas, *Between Naturalism and Religion*, pp. 251–270, here p. 261.

39.3 Schleiermacher's Description of His "Postsecular" Context: Illustrated through His Sociology of "Church Geography and Statistics"

Schleiermacher came of age in a period of revolutions driven in part by universalistic social ideals—the American (1776–1778) across the Atlantic and the French (1789) west of the Rhein—each under banners of the equality and the attending right to self-determination of all persons.[21] Later as an adult, Schleiermacher experienced firsthand the violence and terror of war, as Napoleon drove through Prussia, overwhelming first the city of Halle in 1806, where Schleiermacher was a professor at the time. In the wake of his march through Europe, Napoleon secularized countless churches, monasteries, and convents, making literal secularization a most concrete experience in Schleiermacher's day. The turmoil of incessant wars and shifting borders was at least temporarily put to rest by the Congress of Vienna after the defeat of Napoleon, which from 1815 joined the German states into the German Confederation. These events, then, might be said to form Schleiermacher's "postsecular" situation. Note that it was in the immediate aftermath of these events that in 1817 Schleiermacher held his first lectures on politics and a theory of the state at the university in Berlin.

So Schleiermacher himself had significant personal experience with the issues just mentioned and wrote about them in his capacities both as a scholar and as a churchman. One thinks additionally of his response to the question of Jewish conversion to Christianity, emancipation, and then citizenship;[22] or of his role in negotiating forms of union for the Lutheran and Reformed confessions in Prussia;[23] or again of his lecture courses in Berlin on the state as well as on church history and sociology of the church.[24] And that is to say nothing of the theories of religions he outlines in the fifth speech in *On Religion*[25] and in §§7–10 of *The Christian Faith*.[26] However, a more textured interpretation of Schleiermacher's thinking in relation to the central issues at stake in discussions of the postsecular is possible by looking at his empirical research on Christian confessions in relation to the state in his day as well as at his theory of the state and the place of religion in it. An analysis of

---

[21] See Andreas Arndt, *Reformation der Revolution. Friedrich Schleiermacher in seiner Zeit* (Berlin: Mathes & Seitz, 2020). See also: Miriam Rose, *Schleiermachers Staatslehre* (Tübingen: Mohr Siebeck, 2011), p. 221; Matthias Wolfes, *Öffentlichkeit und Bürgergesellschaft. Friedrich Schleiermachers politische Wirksamkeit*, 2 vols. (Berlin and New York: De Gruyter, 2004).

[22] Friedrich Schleiermacher, *Briefe bei Gelegenheit der politisch-theologischen Aufgabe und des Sendschreibens jüdischer Hausväter* (1799), in *KGA* 1.2, pp. 327–361.

[23] Friedrich Schleiermacher, *Zwei unvorgreifliche Gutachten in Sachen des Protestantischen Kirchenwesens, zunächst in Beziehung auf den Preußischen Staat* (1804), in *KGA* 1.4, pp. 359–408.

[24] Friedrich Schleiermacher, *Vorlesungen über die kirchliche Geographie und Statistik*, in *KGA* 2.16; Friedrich Schleiermacher, *Vorlesungen über die Kirchengeschichte*, in *KGA* 2.6; Friedrich Schleiermacher, *Vorlesungen über die Lehre vom Staat*, in *KGA* 2.8.

[25] *Reden¹*, pp. 293–326. English translation: *Speeches¹*, pp. 95–124.

[26] *CG²* and *CF (2016)*, §§7–10, pp. 60–93.

Schleiermacher's thought in relation to the postsecular may be approached in consulting these texts and by distinguishing between Schleiermacher's characterization of political and legal questions related to religious pluralism and, in the following section, his practical theory of religion in society.

The multiplicity of Christian confessions as well as the intense conflicts among them were as familiar to Schleiermacher as interreligious conflicts are to readers in the twenty-first century. The Thirty Years War and the Peace of Westphalia (1648), with its reaffirmation of the Peace of Augsburg's *cuius regio, eius religio* doctrine (1555), lay 150 years in the past already in Schleiermacher's day. However, events in Schleiermacher's own lifetime provided recent reconfirmations of the necessity of such principles—as well as of the complexity involved in implementing them. That complexity in particular is evident in Schleiermacher's lectures on "Church Geography and Statistics" (held in 1826/1827 and 1833/1834)—an attempt at what might be called a sociology of the Christian churches in which Schleiermacher described the current situation of Christian churches throughout the world (from Asia to Africa to the Americas), though especially in Europe, documenting even numbers of bishoprics, parishes, and clergy, as well as the extent of diocesan territories, and the various churches' legal relations to secular authorities. These lectures provide many examples of the complexity and difficulty Schleiermacher perceived in sorting out church–state relations in his context, but two can suffice for present purposes: the legal implementation of religious tolerance and the outworking of the Congress of Vienna.

In several places Schleiermacher refers to the *Toleranzedikte* of Emperor Joseph II (1781, 1782, 1785), to that of Louis XVI in France (1788) granting legal tolerance to Protestants, and to the laws issued by Maximillian IV in Bavaria between 1801 and 1803 secularizing monasteries and also extending legal tolerance to Protestants.[27] These declarations increased the religious freedoms of Protestants throughout vast sections of western Europe, in France, in the free state of Bavaria, and in the Holy Roman Empire, including what is today Austria and northern Italy to the south and east of Schleiermacher and the present-day Netherlands on the northwestern side. At the same time, as Schleiermacher points out, this often worked better in theory than in practice: The fact that cities like Prague or Vienna were home to important universities and the seat of important bishoprics, and that in Vienna the bishop was also rector of the university, meant that certain challenges remained unresolved. Schleiermacher perceived a certain resistance on the part of Roman Catholic authorities to permit their clerics to pursue advanced university studies, while on the Protestant side, prohibitions against Protestant clergy in Bohemia (present-day Czech Republic) and Austria studying for church ministry outside of their own territory, in combination with the severely limited number of Protestant educational institutions, made preparation for church leadership difficult to say the least.[28]

In other places, Schleiermacher summarizes the effects of the Congress of Vienna, both on Roman Catholic bishoprics and on Protestant churches within the territories of the new German Federation (*Bund*).[29] He notes that with the loss of their status as imperial states or estates (*Reichsstände*) through a process known as mediatization, several important bishoprics now lost their legal right to appeal directly to the emperor. That status had allowed

---

[27] KGA 2.16, pp. 293–301, 438, 449.
[28] KGA 2.16, pp. 438–439.
[29] KGA 2.16, pp. 289–293.

them, for example, to maintain dioceses that extended across the borders of more than one territory and also to maneuver in non-church matters on a more equal footing with electors and princes in the Empire. After the Congress of Vienna, however, they became subject in temporal matters to their German state, and the princes unsurprisingly were decidedly opposed to a bishop from another state ruling a diocese that extended into their own state. Among Protestants a new legal question arose after Vienna concerning the reorganization of the legal status of churches in the event that a prince converted from one confession to another. Until Vienna, but since Augsburg (*cuius regio, eius religio*), the churches' contacts with the government were organized by the confession of the prince, such that, for example, a Protestant upper consistory might answer ultimately to a Roman Catholic minister of the interior in a Roman Catholic state. How would this be handled after Vienna, when with the conversion of a prince the whole state no longer was also administratively converted?[30]

Answers to this question could carry significant consequences for legal issues such as state recognition of church examinations and ordination to churchly offices as well as for the collection of church taxes. Moreover, solutions could vary so much from state to state and from period to period that, as Schleiermacher observes, it might seem quite impossible to identify real principles for the development of a programmatic approach to church–state relations that would be valid at all times and everywhere. The structural relationships (*Verhältnisse* is the word he uses throughout) were too complicated. In index of the situation he observed around him, Schleiermacher says that "the contested question: in which relationship the church stands to the state" is, as a question of political theory, a task that is important "only to the theorists," and "those who stand in the middle of things [i.e., clergy, politicians and so on] don't even bother with it."[31] Principles concerning the relationship of church and state that proceed from agreement upon starting presuppositions will not be found; instead, as Schleiermacher observes, "the founding of principles proceeds from where the power is."[32]

Nevertheless, two principles might be distilled from Schleiermacher's characterization of the complications just summarized: First, Schleiermacher's frame of analysis in this text is not to look at a religion *én bloc*, but to look at geographically, politically, and to some extent culturally demarcated units. In describing the religious landscape of his day, he did not see *a* Lutheran church, but many churches—for example Bavarian, Saxonian, Württenburgian, Bohemian, Swiss, Dutch, Danish, and Swedish—who shared a Lutheran confession to some extent, but who alongside one another exhibited an "infinite diversity" and whose forms of mutual recognition (e.g., of one another's ordained ministers or for admission to communion) developed in politically ad hoc ways and according to circumstance.[33] Second, the religious diversity of Schleiermacher's day and the re-formation of the political landscape meant that "the religious relationships [to the state] now had to reform themselves."[34] Throughout the lectures on a sociology of the Christian churches, Schleiermacher is sorting through the effects of the differentiation of the societal sphere of the state from that of church and the solutions proposed in result—a process through which, as Gunter Scholz describes, "religion

---

[30] KGA 2.16, p. 387.
[31] KGA 2.16, pp. 387–388.
[32] KGA 2.16, p. 389.
[33] KGA 2.16, pp. 388–389.
[34] KGA 2.16, p. 289.

and church [were] losing their social power and were being demarcated as a societal subsystem."[35] So, beyond secularization as a procedural, legal act, we might say that secularization in Schleiermacher's world, on a theoretical level, refers to the social transformations that were taking place in the relationships of church and governance to one another leading to "the reduction of the religious sphere to one sub-area of society," alongside politics, science, and economy.[36] Schleiermacher's version of the question of the "postsecular," then, might be understood as a question concerning how "to think through the ways in which religion and secular culture might be compatible."[37]

39.4 Schleiermacher's Proposals for His "Postsecular" Context: Illustrated through His Lectures on the State

One place Schleiermacher addresses this question is in his lectures on a theory of the state. As in his philosophical ethics (being Schleiermacher's theory of society), so too in his lectures on a theory of the state Schleiermacher presents a minimalistic conception of the state as the organization of the particular property (*Eigentum*) of a particular group in its (at least seemingly) irreducible uniqueness (its *Eigentümlichkeit*) and in the group's striving toward the realization of its full potential for rational action in harmony with nature, or what he calls the *Naturbildungsprozess*.

The state does not *fundamentally* serve the purpose of maintaining a monopoly on violence (whether in policing within or defending from without), nor of safeguarding the equality and rights of individuals, although both of these constitute necessary tasks in what *is* fundamental, namely, the *Naturbildungsprozess*. Also for this same reason, as Andreas Arndt notes, for Schleiermacher "it is not law that constitutes the state, but rather *Eigentum*."[38] Schleiermacher states this perspective rather directly when he says in the 1805/1806 lectures on ethics, "If one is involved in the formation of *Eigentum*, one is also engaged in the founding of a state."[39] *Eigentum* and *Eigentümlichkeit* refer to the irreducible uniqueness—what is *eigen*, or proper to oneself—of a particular group and its expressions

---

[35] Scholz, "Religion und Säkularisierung," p. 233. See also Gunter Scholtz, *Ethik und Hermeneutik. Schleiermachers Grundlegung der Geisteswissenschaften* (Frankfurt am Main: Suhrkamp, 1995), pp. 35–64. A key move that made this insight possible for Schleiermacher was his perception of the need to extend the concept of the "individual" to groups, organizations, and institutions for analysis of contemporary societies. Cf. Rudolf Stichweh, "The History and Systematics of Functional Differentiation in Sociology," in *Bringing Sociology to International Relations: World Politics as Differentiation Theory*, ed. Mathias Albert, Barry Buzan, and Michael Zürn (Cambridge: Cambridge University Press, 2013), pp. 50–70.

[36] Scholz, "Religion und Säkularisierung," p. 239.

[37] Scholz, "Religion und Säkularisierung," p. 241.

[38] Andreas Arndt, "Der Begriff des Rechts in Schleiermachers Ethik-Vorlesungen," in *Wissenschaft, Kirche, Staat und Politik. Schleiermacher im Preussischen Reformprozess*, ed. Andreas Arndt, Simon Gerber, and Sarah Schmidt (Berlin and Boston: De Gruyter, 2019), p. 221.

[39] Friedrich Schleiermacher, "Brouillon zur Ethik (1805/06)," in Schleiermacher, *Entwürfe zu einem System der Sittenlehre*, ed. Otto Braun, vol. 2 of *Werke. Auswahl in vier Bänden* (Leipzig: Felix Meiner, 1913), pp. 75–239, here p. 143.

of itself.⁴⁰ For the state to be inseparable from the *Eigentümlichkeit* of particular groups, as Schleiermacher suggests, means a state is tied to the historical experience and cultural ethos of a particular people and place, not based on a constitution. As Schleiermacher remarks, "The development of the state is its present condition; and this is the constitution, actually; usually, however, when one thinks of a constitution, one thinks of a piece of paper (on which I place hardly any value at all)."⁴¹ This means, as Miriam Rose summarizes, that law is actually cultural sanctioned custom,⁴² and the legitimacy of the state consists in its representation of the *Gesinnung* of the *Gemeinschaft*, that is, of its constituent communities' "unique spirit" (*eigenthümlicher Geist*),⁴³ their specific sense of themselves. Note that this is not to equivocate between the state and a particular group; Schleiermacher, in fact, seems to think that the need for and function of a state is to provide structures for managing interactions of groups that differ from one another. He refers in the 1817 lectures, for example, to practical challenges like interrelating different languages or incorporating settled and nomadic peoples into one state, and marks confrontation (in war) and-or conjunction (via peaceful joining) of distinct groups, along with a hierarchization of ruler and subject, as the moments of state formation.⁴⁴

The state has an interest in religious communities, according to Schleiermacher, because of their particular ability to provide a "unifying principle" for "peoples of the most diverse heritage,"⁴⁵ specifically by cultivating a common spirit (*Gemeingeist*) of a people—and of subordinating foreign difference to domestic custom.⁴⁶ As something that preexists the state's existence and always exceeds the state's functional-bureaucratic role,⁴⁷ the cultivation of a people's sense of itself is not ultimately within the control of the state, in Schleiermacher's view. So the state has a serious interest in religion for the role the latter plays in cultivating the *Gemeingeist* and thereby shaping "public life" (*öffentliches Leben*). "Religion," says

---

⁴⁰ The word *eigen* and related compound words in German cover a large semantic range. Roughly speaking, *eigen* and related words indicate the idea of "that which is specific to." Hence, they can be used possessively in referring to *property*, but more basic to such referents is a reflexive referent to a subject's *properties*, that which is specific to a personality or "one's own" ideas, intentions, freedom, and so on. Thus, when Schleiermacher writes of that which is in some way *eigen*—whether *Eigentum* or *Eigentümlichkeit* or even of *das Eigene*—he might be speaking specifically about property, for example, but he is always also referring more fundamentally to the individual subject (whether person, group, or other) to whose total profile the *eigene* thing or quality contributes. Thus, the *Eigentum* of a state consists not only in its commerce but also its culture, not only in its lands, but also its laws or even its loves.

⁴¹ *KGA* 2.8, pp. 855, 191; quoted in Arndt, "Der Begriff des Rechts in Schleiermachers Ethik-Vorlesungen," p. 220.

⁴² Rose, *Schleiermachers Staatslehre*, p. 221.

⁴³ From an anonymous student transcript of Schleiermacher's 1805/1806 lectures on philosophical ethics, the *Brouillon zur Ethik*, Evangelisch-reformierte Gemeinde Lübeck, Bibliothek KIII 26, p. 305.

⁴⁴ *KGA* 2.8, pp. 384–385.

⁴⁵ *KGA* 2.8, pp. 214–215, 266 (1817 student transcript of Varnhagen).

⁴⁶ *KGA* 2.8, p. 72 (Schleiermacher's manuscript); *KGA* 2.8, p. 912 (student transcript of Waitz). Cf. Rose, *Schleiermachers Staatslehre*, pp. 190–201. Note that with this language, Schleiermacher is engaging a much larger set of discourses in his day, including Johann Gottfried Herder's *Volksseele*, Montesquieu's *esprit général*, Hegel's understanding of *Volksgeist*, and Friedrich Heinrich Jacobi's *Gemeingeist*. See: Andreas Grossmann, "Volksgeist; Volksseele," in *Historisches Wörterbuch der Philosophie*, ed. Joachim Ritter, Karlfried Gründer, and Gottfried Gabriel (Basel: Schwabe AG, 1971–2007).

⁴⁷ *KGA* 2.8, p. 323 (1817 student transcript of Varnhagen).

Schleiermacher, is one of "the two basic elements of the formation of a people."[48] The other, he says, is formal or technical schooling. Both begin within the private sphere of the family, but, unlike schooling, religion carries within it a potential with fundamental significance for public life, namely, the ability to produce "a new common principle of life" for a state, in the production of which religious activity takes a leading role until such time as this principle has become a common holding. The state can then "connect to everything that is intellectual in it for the people and separate it from religion"[49]—for example in the form of schooling and knowledge production.

For Schleiermacher, the common spirit (*Gemeingeist*) of a people by turns contributes to the political sensibility (*Gesinnung*) in a state and becomes the law of the land, punchily summarized in the refrain "what is custom becomes law" (*was Sitte ist, Gesetz wird*).[50] But it is rooted in soil, family, and the language and ways of life (the practices or *Gebräuche* that form the basis of technical training and formal schooling) that are characteristic of the particular peoples inhabiting that soil. Law, we might say, is rooted in claims to cultural dominance. It is, thus, sadly not surprising that Schleiermacher's assessment of people whose religion and ways of life did not fit with those of his leading Protestant Prussian culture is pockmarked by troubling cracks between principle and practice—especially as regards Jews and nonreligious persons (though it is also difficult to read his characterization of the Roman Catholic Church as very approbatory).

Schleiermacher does explicitly speak in opposition to theocracy and even to a Christian government, he regularly insisted on a clear separation of church and state (and had since his youth), and he professed strong support for the freedom of religion, such that the state not direct the affairs of religious communities.[51] These convictions are consistent, on the one hand, with his opposition to requiring to Jews to convert to Christianity in order to receive political emancipation.[52] One reason for his position is that the state "can have no influence on the religion of the individual."[53] He maintains, further, that it is obvious that non-Christian persons can make important contributions to the good of the state: "No one will say it would be advantageous to have significant and, moreover, educated groups of people

---

[48] KGA 2.8, p. 321 (1817 student transcript of Varnhagen).

[49] KGA 2.8, p. 323 (1817 student transcript of Varnhagen).

[50] Among numerous occurrences, with slight variations, see KGA 2.8, pp. 513, 629 (1829 student manuscript of Hess and Willich).

[51] See KGA 2.8, pp. 104–107 (1829–1833 Schleiermacher's manuscript). One thinks also of Schleiermacher's declaration in his 1799 *On Religion*: "Away, therefore with every such union of church and state!" Friedrich Schleiermacher, *On Religion: Speeches to Its Cultured Despisers*, ed. and trans. by Richard Crouter (Cambridge: Cambridge University Press, 1996), p. 90.

[52] See also Schleiermacher's 1799 *Briefe bei Gelegenheit der politisch-theologischen Aufgabe und des Sendschreibens jüdischer Hausväter* (1799), in KGA 1.2. English translation: David Friedländer, Friedrich Schleiermacher, and Wilhelm Abraham Teller, *A Debate on Jewish Emancipation and Christian Theology in Old Berlin*, ed. and trans. Richard Crouter and Julie Klassen (Indianapolis: Hackett Publishing Company, 2004). Among scholarly receptions of this work, see: Richard Crouter, "Friedrich Schleiermacher's *Letters on the Occasion* and the Crisis of Berlin Jewry," in Crouter, *Friedrich Schleiermacher: Between Enlightenment and Romanticism* (Cambridge: Cambridge University Press, 2005), pp. 123–139; and Gunter Scholtz, "Friedrich Schleiermacher über das Sendschreiben jüdischer Hausväter," in *Judentum im Zeitalter der Aufklärung*, ed. Vorstand der Lessing-Akademie (Wolfenbüttel: Jacobi Verlag, 1977), pp. 297–351.

[53] KGA 2.8, p. 444 (1817/1818 student manuscript of Goetsch).

in a state who are however excluded from legal participation in that state."⁵⁴ And yet, on the other hand, he also wants to distinguish in other places between what is legal and what is prudent. Although a state cannot legally discriminate on the basis of religion, when it comes to important business of the state requiring trustworthiness, "this must and should be the case. A government will lose much when it makes as members people who have no claim to a religion."⁵⁵

As is already well known,⁵⁶ Schleiermacher's logic with regard to Jews is especially alarming. The positions Schleiermacher reaches stem from and reinscribe both problematic characterizations of Jewish religion and the exclusivist nature of his political environment. In the 1833 lectures on the state, Schleiermacher concludes that Jews hold fundamentally and unchangeably to a theocratic political orientation, and that (here quoting at length) "only through a complete change can it cease to be so. If now the question should be raised, how they are to be treated, since they hold to an obstructive kind of political principle, then it is not in this situation the case that they can participate in the state equally with other residents."⁵⁷ As Rose summarizes, Schleiermacher holds the view that "in order for the state to be able to maintain the distinction it itself draws between church and state, for the benefit of religious freedom, religious communities must also themselves maintain this distinction. Those religious communities that cannot, those that, as a religion, strive for state power, . . . are excluded from the right to freedom of religion."⁵⁸

Schleiermacher's pseudonymously written *Letters on the Occasion of the Political Theological Task* and the *Sendschreiben of Jewish Heads of Households* have been read by some interpreters as presenting a more liberal political position: He underscores the importance of the separation of church and state, opposes making conversion to Christianity a criterion of citizenship, and supports emancipation, writing that "reason demands all should be citizens, but does not at all require that all should be Christians, and there must be a variety of ways to be a citizen and a non-Christian."⁵⁹ He says he is "completely serious" about the possibility of Jews becoming citizens.

His liberal attitude and seriousness about Jewish citizenship are, however, deeply questionable. He only wishes not to require Jewish conversion to Christianity because the converted Jews would bring their religious "sensibilities" (*Gesinnungen*) with them and "that would be a serious sickness against which we should inoculate ourselves!"⁶⁰ As for a concrete proposal for Jewish citizenship, he stipulates two criteria that the state must insist

---

[54] KGA 2.8, p. 107 (1829–1833 Schleiermacher's manuscript).
[55] KGA 2.8, pp. 444–445 (1817/1818 student manuscript of Goetsch).
[56] Much has been written on Schleiermacher's anti-Judaism. See, among other works: Matthias Blum, *"Ich wäre ein Judenfeind?" Zum Antijudaismus in Friedrich Schleiermachers Theologie und Pädagogik* (Köln, Weimar, and Wien: Böhlau, 2010); Gorazd Andrejč, "Schleiermacher and Tillich on Judaism: A Structural Comparison," in *Returning to Tillich: Theology and Legacy in Transition*, ed. Russel Re Manning and Samuel Shearn (Berlin and Boston: De Gruyter, 2018), pp. 152–157; Wolfes, *Öffentlichkeit und Bürgergesellschaft*, vol. 2, pp. 326–390; Roderick Barth, Ulrich Barth, and Claus-Dieter Osthövner, eds., *Christentum und Judentum. Akten des internationalen Kongresses der Schleiermacher Gesellschaft in Halle* (Berlin and Boston: De Gruyter, 2012).
[57] KGA 2.8, p. 916 (1833 student manuscript of Waitz).
[58] Rose, *Schleiermachers Staatslehre*, p. 198; cf. p. 180.
[59] KGA 1.2, p. 335. First Letter.
[60] KGA 1.2, p. 347. Third Letter.

upon: that they subordinate Jewish ceremonial law to the law of the state and that they publicly denounce their hope for the messiah. The reason given is the same one Schleiermacher would give thirty years later: Such commitments bespeak citizenship to a different country and a compromised and untrustworthy loyalty to the Prussian state. So it is difficult to see in what meaningful sense Schleiermacher felt the "variety of ways to be a citizen and a non-Christian" were possible for Jews. The fact that these letters were published pseudonymously, that there is a significant element of satire to them, that they are sarcastic and derisive in their tone throughout toward the state and in places also toward Christians—all of this does little to make their message and its communication to Schleiermacher's reading public less poisonous.

39.5 Conclusion

It is important for any assessment of Schleiermacher in relation to the postsecular to approach the topic via areas of his work exhibiting more historical-empirical and practical interests rather than primarily, let alone solely, via his more theoretical works. An exclusive focus on the latter risks enabling readers to overlook the details of how he worked out his theories in practice, or failed to do so; including the former challenges readers, instead, to address those practical details directly and ask whether they might even be intrinsic to the theory. This chapter has made such an approach by focusing on Schleiermacher's sociological presentation of the relations of states and churches in his lectures on church geography and statistics and his practical understanding of the relationship of the state to religious communities in his lectures on the state.

Schleiermacher's sociological lectures on the situation of the Christian churches show how complicated the political organization of churches was in Schleiermacher's day, both in their relationships to one another and in their relationships to the state. It is one thing to advocate for the separation of church and state as a matter of principle, but a more complicated thing to sort out in practice what states and churches need from one another in terms of mutual recognition and how this is to be handled in swiftly evolving legal-political contexts like that of Europe after the Congress of Vienna. The complexity of church–state relations reveals on a structural level that a differentiation of social spheres was quickly unfolding in Schleiermacher's day. Schleiermacher attempts a political-theoretical analysis of this differentiation of the state from religion in his lectures on the state. The lectures reveal the importance of the concepts of *Eigentum* and *Gemeingeist* and of the role of religion in cultivating the *Gemeingeist* that is necessary for the formation of a new political *Lebensprinzip* or *Gesinnung* in Schleiermacher's political theory. Specifically, these concepts help him to make sense of the way constitutions crystallize custom (à la "was Sitte ist, Gesetz wird").

Note how similar this sounds, in a way, to Habermas' reasons for looking to religion in the context of the postsecular, namely as a source for the cultivation of values that produce social solidarity—values the state cannot *de jure* prescribe but on which it depends. However, Schleiermacher's identification of the significance of religion in relation to the *Gemeingeist* of a people is not what Habermas wishes to highlight when he describes Schleiermacher as the "pacemaker for the consciousness of a postsecular society": Habermas interprets Schleiermacher as trying to place religion *within* while remaining differentiated *from* the state, rooted not in society but in a transcendental *a priori* of its own. Schleiermacher's own position, however, continues to give priority in religious matters to what he imagines as societies' core cultures. This point would need to be squarely addressed in an evaluation of the helpfulness of Schleiermacher's thinking for negotiating contemporary complexities of religious pluralism in civic and political settings.

Suggested Reading

Friedländer, David, Friedrich Schleiermacher, and Wilhelm Abraham Teller. *A Debate on Jewish Emancipation and Christian Theology in Old Berlin*. Ed. and trans. Richard Crouter and Julie Klassen (Indianapolis: Hackett Publishing Company, 2004).
Habermas, Jürgen. *Between Naturalism and Religion: Philosophical Essays*. Trans. Ciarin Cronin (Malden: Polity Press, 2008 [2005]).
Rose, Miriam. *Schleiermachers Staatslehre* (Tübingen: Mohr Siebeck, 2011).
Scholtz, Gunter. "Religion und Säkularisierung bei Schleiermacher und Steffens." In *System und Subversion. Friedrich Schleiermacher und Henrik Steffens*, ed. Sarah Schmidt and Leon Miodonski (Berlin and Boston: De Gruyter, 2018), pp. 233–252.

Bibliography

Andrejč, Gorazd. "Schleiermacher and Tillich on Judaism: A Structural Comparison." In *Returning to Tillich: Theology and Legacy in Transition*, ed. Russel Re Manning and Samuel Shearn (Berlin and Boston: De Gruyter, 2018), pp. 152–157.
Arndt, Andreas. "Der Begriff des Rechts in Schleiermachers Ethik-Vorlesungen." In *Wissenschaft, Kirche, Staat und Politik. Schleiermacher im Preussischen Reformprozess*, ed. Andreas Arndt, Simon Gerber, and Sarah Schmidt (Berlin and Boston: De Gruyter, 2019), pp. 219-232.
Arndt, Andreas. *Reformation der Revolution. Friedrich Schleiermacher in seiner Zeit* (Berlin: Mathes & Seitz, 2020).
Barth, Roderick, Ulrich Barth, and Claus-Dieter Osthövner, eds. *Christentum und Judentum. Akten des internationalen Kongresses der Schleiermacher Gesellschaft in Halle* (Berlin and Boston: De Gruyter, 2012).
Beckford, James A. "SSSR Presidential Address: Public Religions and the Postsecular: Critical Reflections." *Journal for the Scientific Study of Religion* 51, no. 1 (2012), pp. 1–19.
Berger, Peter. "The Desecularization of the World: A Global Overview." In *The Desecularization of the World: Resurgent Religion and World Politics*, ed. Peter Berger (Grand Rapids: William B. Eerdmans, 1999), pp. 1–18.
Blum, Matthias. "Ich wäre ein Judenfeind?" *Zum Antijudaismus in Friedrich Schleiermachers Theologie und Pädagogik* (Köln, Weimar, and Wien: Böhlau, 2010).
Borowitz, Eugene. "The Postsecular Situation of Jewish Theology." *Theological Studies* 31, no. 3 (1970), pp. 460–475.
Cistelecan, Alex. "The Theological Turn of Contemporary Critical Theory." *Telos* 167 (2014), pp. 8–26.
Cox, Harvey. *The Secular City: Secularization and Urbanization in Theological Perspective* (Princeton: Princeton University Press, 2013 [1965]).

Crouter, Richard *Friedrich Schleiermacher: Between Enlightenment and Romanticism* (Cambridge: Cambridge University Press, 2005).

Eder, Klaus. "Europäische Säkularisierung—Ein Sonderweg in die postsäkulare Gesellschaft? Eine theoretische Anmerkung." *Berliner Jahrbuch der Soziologie* 3 (2002), pp. 331–343.

Friedländer, David, Friedrich Schleiermacher, and Wilhelm Abraham Teller. *A Debate on Jewish Emancipation and Christian Theology in Old Berlin*. Ed. and trans. Richard Crouter and Julie Klassen (Indianapolis: Hackett Publishing Company, 2004).

Greely, Andrew M. "After Secularity: The Neo-Gemeinschaft Society: A Post-Christian Postscript*." *Sociological Analysis* 27, no. 3 (1966), pp. 119–127.

Grossmann, Andreas. "Volksgeist; Volksseele." In *Historisches Wörterbuch der Philosophie*, ed. Joachim Ritter, Karlfried Gründer, and Gottfried Gabriel (Basel: Schwabe AG, 1971–2007), pp. 1102-1107.

Habermas, Jürgen. *Between Naturalism and Religion: Philosophical Essays*. Trans. Ciarin Cronin (Malden: Polity Press, 2008 [2005]).

Habermas, Jürgen. "Notes on a Post-Secular Society." *New Perspectives Quarterly* 25, no. 4 (Fall 2007), pp. 17–29.

McLennan, Gregor. "The Postsecular Turn." *Theory, Culture & Society* 27, no. 4 (2010), pp. 3–20.

McLennan, Gregor. "Towards a Postsecular Sociology?" *Sociology* 41, no. 5 (2007), pp. 857–870.

Milbank, John. *Theology and Social Theory: Beyond Secular Reason* (Oxford: Blackwell Publishing, 2006 [1990]).

Milbank, John, Catherine Pickstock, and Graham Ward, eds. *Radical Orthodoxy: A New Theology* (London and New York: Routledge, 1999).

Parmaksız, Umut. "Making Sense of the Postsecular." *European Journal of Social Theory* 21, no. 1 (2018), pp. 98–116.

Rose, Miriam. *Schleiermachers Staatslehre* (Tübingen: Mohr Siebeck, 2011).

Schleiermacher, Friedrich. *Briefe bei Gelegenheit der politisch-theologischen Aufgabe und des Sendschreibens jüdischer Hausväter* (1799). In *KGA* 1.2, pp. 327–361.

Schleiermacher, Friedrich. [anonymous student transcript] *Brouillon zur Ethik* (Evangelisch-reformierte Gemeinde Lübeck, Bibliothek KIII).

Schleiermacher, Friedrich. "Brouillon zur Ethik (1805/06)." In Schleiermacher, *Entwürfe zu einem System der Sittenlehre*, ed. Otto Braun, vol. 2 of *Werke. Auswahl in vier Bänden* (Leipzig: Felix Meiner, 1913), pp. 75–239.

Schleiermacher, Friedrich. *Vorlesungen über die Lehre vom Staat*, KGA 2.8, ed. Walter Jaeschke (Berlin: De Gruyter, 1998).

Schleiermacher, Friedrich. *Vorlesungen über die kirchliche Geographie und Statistik*, KGA 2.16, ed. Simon Gerber (Berlin: De Gruyter, 2005).

Schleiermacher, Friedrich. *Zwei unvorgreifliche Gutachten in Sachen des Protestantischen Kirchenwesens, zunächst in Beziehung auf den Preußischen Staat* (1804). In *KGA* 1.4, pp. 359–408.

Scholtz, Gunter. *Ethik und Hermeneutik. Schleiermachers Grundlegung der Geisteswissenschaften* (Frankfurt am Main: Suhrkamp, 1995).

Scholtz, Gunter. "Friedrich Schleiermacher über das Sendschreiben jüdischer Hausväter." In *Judentum im Zeitalter der Aufklärung*, ed. Vorstand der Lessing-Akademie (Wolfenbüttel: Jacobi Verlag, 1977), pp. 297–351.

Scholtz, Gunter. "Religion und Säkularisierung bei Schleiermacher und Steffens." In *System und Subversion. Friedrich Schleiermacher und Henrik Steffens*, ed. Sarah Schmidt and Leon Miodonski (Berlin and Boston: De Gruyter, 2018), pp. 233–252.

Stichweh, Rudolf. "The History and Systematics of Functional Differentiation in Sociology." In *Bringing Sociology to International Relations: World Politics as Differentiation Theory*, ed. Mathias Albert, Barry Buzan, and Michael Zürn (Cambridge: Cambridge University Press, 2013), pp. 50–70.

Ward, Graham. *The Postmodern God* (Oxford: Blackwell Publishers, 1997).

Wolfes, Matthias. *Öffentlichkeit und Bürgergesellschaft. Friedrich Schleiermachers politische Wirksamkeit*, 2 vols. (Berlin and New York: De Gruyter, 2004).

CHAPTER 40

SCHLEIERMACHER AND THE PHILOSOPHY OF CULTURE

WILHELM GRÄB

40.1 THE PROGRAM OF A PHILOSOPHY OF CULTURE, WITH REFERENCE TO SCHLEIERMACHER

IN the first decades of the twentieth century, philosophy attempted to describe its task anew under the rubric of a "philosophy of culture," in order to distinguish it from the sciences. This was the context in which Schleiermacher was first regarded as a cultural philosopher, and his philosophical ethics in particular was interpreted as a cultural-philosophical blueprint. The significance Schleiermacher's philosophy of culture has had until today can best be understood with regard to this context. I will therefore explain his approach in that historical context first. Then I will show what justifies the view that Schleiermacher's philosophical ethics in particular is an interesting and still sustainable cultural-philosophical draft. I will also attend to the profiling of Schleiermacher's philosophy of culture in the context of his time in comparison with Rousseau, Kant, Herder, and Hegel. Next I will point out that Schleiermacher's cultural philosophy is complemented by a cultural theology that presents the practice of a good life, supported by the Christian spirit, within modern culture. Finally, I will highlight the impulses Schleiermacher still gives to both a critical diagnosis and a practical treatment of the crisis of modern culture.

Georg Simmel and Ernst Cassirer are the two most important representatives of the cultural-philosophical renewal of philosophy in the first half of the twentieth century. In the winter semester of 1906/1907 Simmel gave a lecture on "Philosophie der Kultur."[1] Three years later, largely initiated by Simmel, the interdisciplinary journal *Logos*, with the subtitle *Internationale Zeitschrift für Philosophie der Kultur*, was founded. Ernst Troeltsch was appointed chair of the philosophy of culture department at the University of Berlin, and Paul Tillich received an honorary professorship in the philosophy of religion and culture at the University of Leipzig in 1927. In a way already marking the end of this philosophical

---

[1] Georg Simmel, "*Philosophie der Kultur* (1906/07)," in *Kolleghefte und Mitschriften*, ed. Angela Rammstedt and Cécile Rol, Gesamtausgabe Bd. 21 (Berlin: Suhrkamp, 2012), pp. 57–571.

direction, in 1944 Cassirer, who had returned from exile in America, published a complete overview of the question of a philosophy of culture: *An Essay on Man: An Introduction to a Philosophy of Human Culture*.[2] In this book, he also offered a summary of his own cultural-philosophical life's work, which culminated in the *Philosophie der symbolischen Formen*.[3]

The philosophy of culture, which appeared programmatically in the first half of the twentieth century, aimed primarily at cultural criticism. Taking up the impulses of Neo-Kantianism as well as of a philosophy of life, the criticism was directed at a modern society that no longer seemed able to combine the tremendous progress in science and technology with an understanding of their meaning and purposes. The impression was reinforced that the dynamic developments in science and technology, as well as the forms of production of the capitalist economy pervading all areas of life, increasingly obeyed their own internal dynamics, while discourse about their value and significance for human life was largely absent. Literature and theater, film and art were becoming autonomously operating cultural systems. They too were obeying the laws of the development of their own aesthetic forms more than they reflected the basic interests of people interpreting their life experiences.

This perception of a crisis of culture marked the emergence of a philosophy of culture at the beginning of the twentieth century. Georg Simmel even spoke of the "Tragödie der Kultur"[4] that grew out of a disintegration of material and symbolic culture and an increasing distance between the factual developments in the fields of aesthetic-symbolic culture and the culture of people's ways of life. The "philosophy of culture" aimed to counteract this. In order to do so, it mobilized a concept of culture that was based on holding together or reuniting material and symbolic culture—so the formation of things and the formation of communication about their meaning, purpose, and significance.

Nevertheless, Cassirer published his philosophy of culture under the title "Philosophie der symbolischen Formen."[5] What was still striking about its conception was that material culture, and thus the organization of elementary living conditions, hardly played a role in it. The reason for this was that at a time when people were fascinated by the progress in science and technology and economics, Cassirer was interested in bringing to light the cultural significance of symbolic communication in myths, literature, religion, and arts, and thus in developing a critical understanding of the meaning and purpose of scientific-technical and economic "progress." Likewise, Simmel also made certain developments of modern society—a society in which material culture and intellectual culture, the culture of things and the culture of critical understanding about their meaning and purpose for human life, were at risk of falling apart—a subject of criticism.[6]

---

[2] Ernst Cassirer, *An Essay on Man: An Introduction to a Philosophy of Human Culture* (New Haven: Yale University Press, 1944).

[3] Ernst Cassirer, *Philosophie der symbolischen Formen*, Part 1: *Die Sprache* (1923) (Darmstadt: Wissenschaftliche Buchgesellschaft, 1994); Part 2: *Das mythische Denken* (1925) (Darmstadt: Wissenschaftliche Buchgesellschaft, 1994); Part 3: *Phänomenologie der Erkenntnis* (1929) (Darmstadt: Wissenschaftliche Buchgesellschaft, 1994).

[4] Georg Simmel, "Der Begriff und die Tragödie der Kultur (1911)," in *Aufsätze und Abhandlungen 1909-1918*, ed. Rüdiger Kramme and Angela Rammstedt, GA 12 (Frankfurt am Main: Suhrkamp, 2001), pp. 194-223.

[5] Cassirer, *Philosophie der symbolischen Formen*.

[6] Georg Simmel, "Persönliche und sachliche Kultur," in Ders. *Aufsätze und Abhandlungen. 1894 bis 1900*, ed. Heinz-Jürgen Dahme and David P. Frisby, GA 5 (Frankfurt am Main: Suhrkamp, 1992), pp. 560-584.

In their search for ways to counter the crisis of modern culture, the protagonists of the new philosophy of culture at the beginning of the twentieth century looked back to its beginnings in the spirit of the Enlightenment. Kant, Herder, and also Schleiermacher became important points of reference for them.

The first studies on "Schleiermacher's Philosophy of Culture" emerged in the historical context of a search for a concept of culture that was as comprehensive as it was integral. One such study was *Schleiermachers Kulturphilosophie*, a book by Albert Reble published in 1935. The book was in fact his doctoral dissertation, which had been supervised by Theodor Litt at the University of Leipzig.[7] Litt (1880–1962), himself a student of Wilhelm Dilthey (1833–1911), was one of the most important representatives of the new philosophy of culture, alongside Simmel and Cassirer. As Litt wrote in his "preface" to Albert Reble's book, the dissertation was intended to show that Schleiermacher had presented a philosophy of culture that remained still viable. Dilthey had previously defended the same claim. Now, Litt argued, it was important to incorporate Schleiermacher's fruitful deliberations into the contemporary debates about a new philosophy of culture.[8]

Reble did not seek to present a detailed historical-philological study as much as he sought to subject Schleiermacher's philosophical-theological work as a whole to a cultural-philosophical reading. He noted that Schleiermacher had not spoken directly of a "philosophy of culture," even in his drafts for the lecture on philosophical ethics. Reble also did not ignore the fact that Schleiermacher made only sparse use of the term "culture." Nevertheless, he made every effort to show that Schleiermacher's entire philosophical-theological work deserved rigorous cultural-philosophical attention. He showed that already in the "Reden über die Religion"[9] and in the "Monologen"[10] Schleiermacher had drawn religion and morality into a culturally integrative theory of the connectedness of life ("Theorie des Lebenszusammenhanges").[11] Accordingly, he interpreted Schleiermacher's Philosophical Ethics as a "System der Kulturphilosophie" by means of which he developed a theory of the connectedness of sense ("Theorie des Sinnzusammenhanges")[12] of the history of humankind.

Reble wanted to show that in Schleiermacher's "philosophy of culture" the modern world, despite its differentiation into various cultural dimensions, forms a "context of meaning" and a "context of life." In Schleiermacher, he found an interesting appropriation and development of the Enlightenment view that there is a normative and ultimate purpose to human history, which every human being as well as all major social institutions assist in realizing. Inspired by Reble, other scholars discovered in the first decades of the twentieth century that not only Kant and Herder but also Schleiermacher had formulated important cultural-philosophical principles, and thus that a cultural-theoretical reading of Schleiermacher's philosophical ethics was both viable and important.[13]

---

[7] Albert Reble, *Schleiermachers Kulturphilosophie. Eine entwicklungsgeschichtlich-systematische Würdigung*, Sonderschriften der Akademie gemeinnütziger Wissenschaften zu Erfurt, Heft 7 (Erfurt: Stenger, 1935).
[8] Reble, *Schleiermachers Kulturphilosophie*, p. v.
[9] *Speeches²*.
[10] *Monologen¹*.
[11] Reble, *Schleiermachers Kulturphilosophie*, pp. 24–72.
[12] Reble, *Schleiermachers Kulturphilosophie*, pp. 73–244.
[13] Cf. Hermann Mulert, *Schleiermacher-Studien I. Schleiermachers geschichtsphilosophische Ansichten in ihrer Bedeutung für seine Theologie*, Studien zur Geschichte des neueren Protestantismus

40.2 SCHLEIERMACHER'S PHILOSOPHICAL ETHICS AS PHILOSOPHY OF HISTORY AND PHILOSOPHY OF CULTURE

Schleiermacher's philosophical ethics not only represents Schleiermacher's most important philosophical achievement: it also documents an original draft in the history of ethics. It grew out of Schleiermacher's examination of Kant's and Fichte's ethics. Schleiermacher criticized these two authors for having envisaged human life from a one-sided legal perspective and then making formal moral demands without taking into account the historical reality of moral life.

In the "Grundlinien einer Kritik der bisherigen Sittenlehre" (1803)[14] Schleiermacher subjected the history of philosophical ethics to criticism even from its ancient beginnings. The critical question he asked about the ethical reflections of Plato and Aristotle aimed at determining the relationship between moral standards and lived morality. Ethics must not stop at merely establishing the standards or principles of moral action. If ethics understands practical reason as an aspect of human nature, then ethics must also take into account the historical effectiveness of practical reason. It is not enough to draw up a catalogue of duties and virtues. It is necessary to describe the human action that has led and leads to the construction of culture in the history of humankind. The achievements of culture are manifested in cultural goods. Only an ethics that is not restricted to the norms and principles of moral actions, but also goes on to describe the cultural goods these actions produce in the course of history, will do justice to its claim to grasp moral action in all its dimensions. An ethics of goods that complements the ethics of duties and virtues can represent the whole field of human moral action. These were, in short, the guiding principles of an ethics developed in the "Grundlinien einer Kritik der bisherigen Sittenlehre" (1803), which, as Schleiermacher later said in his Halle lectures on philosophical ethics (1805/1806),[15] should be able to appear as the "Wissenschaft der Geschichte."[16]

For Schleiermacher's own conceptualization of ethics, a starting point that we would today call an anthropological one was decisive. He worked on the assumption that with the specific constitution of human nature, moral and practical reason were also effective historically as creative powers. This accounts for the constructive character of Schleiermacher's philosophical ethics. It does not claim to depict the empirical reality of the historical world of human beings; rather, it is concerned with developing the categories whereby it is possible to judge which human actions contribute to the ethical process of the historical realization of cultural goods, and with discerning their moral value. As an ethical process, history emerges from

---

3 (Berlin: Töpelmann, 1907); Hans Lorenz Stoltenberg, "Friedrich Schleiermacher als Soziologe," *Zeitschrift für die gesamte Staatswissenschaft* 88 (1930), pp. 77–113; Gerda von Bredow, *Wertanalysen zu Schleiermachers Güterethik* (Phil Diss., Berlin, 1941).

[14] GKS.

[15] Friedrich Schleiermacher, *Brouillon zur Ethik 1805/1806*, in *Entwürfe zu einem System der Sittenlehre*, ed. Otto Braun, Newprint of 2. Edition Leipzig 1927 (Aalen: Scientia-Verlag, 1967), pp. 75–240 (hereafter PhE (1805/1806)).

[16] PhE (1805/1806), p. 80.

rational, human engagement with nonhuman nature that has not yet been "rationalized"—that is, rationally examined, analyzed, and acted upon or responded to communicatively; in Schleiermacher's words, the ethical process starts with "the human nature already united with reason and inspired by it."[17] Such engagement aims at the realization of the highest good by means of a progressive mastery of nature by human beings endowed with reason.

Conceived of as an ethics of goods, Schleiermacher's philosophical ethics links three traditional ideas that have influenced the modern understanding of history and culture: (1) the biblically-theologically founded topos of the *dominium terrae*, humanity's dominion over the earth (Genesis 1:28); (2) the Aristotelian doctrine of the highest good, in which all goods resulting from ethical actions come together; and (3) the teleological understanding of history and culture that prevailed in the Enlightenment, according to which humankind progressively subjects nature to its ends and makes nature the means of realizing human freedom.

However, in contrast to other approaches of his time, Schleiermacher's philosophical ethics does not develop a theory of stages and steps outlining the development of history culminating in the present. Nor does it address the empirical diversity of cultures and their respective historical development. As Schleiermacher understood it, a speculative ethics operating at the level of conceptual construction is not able to describe or narrate historical facts, events, and courses. He described the relationship between the speculative concept of his ethics and the empirical facts of history in the following way: "For each other, history is the picture book of ethics and ethics the formula book of history."[18] It is therefore correct to say that Schleiermacher's philosophical ethics provides "the categories that make the understanding of history possible in the first place,"[19] or that it forms a "structural theory of history."[20] It is not the gradual progress in the realization of the "highest good" that he addresses, but rather the fundamental forms of human action that underlie the construction of human culture through and in human history.

Schleiermacher follows a dialectical, conceptual procedure adopted by Plato. He forms conceptual pairs of opposites, which he then relates to each other again crosswise. One basic distinction is between organizing action and symbolizing action. Organizing action leads to the domination and cultural formation of nature by reason. In symbolizing action, on the other hand, reason manifests itself as the force that transforms nature into culture. Reason also makes nature the object of its knowledge. Thus, reason becomes its own symbol in which it recognizes itself as an effective, culture-forming force. The other basic distinction Schleiermacher makes is between identical actions and individual actions. Identical action is action that connects people with each other and in which they participate together. It presupposes a like-minded community and at the same time creates that community. Individual action, in contrast, is an action that is determined by the individuality of those who act and express it.

---

[17] Cf. PhE (1805/1806), p. 85.

[18] Friedrich Schleiermacher, *Ethik 1816*, in *Entwürfe zu einem System der Sittenlehre*, pp. 513–626 (p. 549).

[19] Hans-Joachim Birkner, *Schleiermachers Christliche Sittenlehre im Zusammenhang seines philosophisch-theologischen Systems* (Berlin: Töpelmann, 1964), p. 38.

[20] Cf. Wilhelm Gräb, *Humanität und Christentumsgeschichte. Eine Untersuchung zum Geschichtsbegriff im Spätwerk Schleiermachers* (Göttingen: Vandenhoek und Ruprecht, 1980).

Table 40.1 Schleiermacher's Ethic of Goods

	Organizing	Symbolizing
Identical	State, law, economy	Language, science
Individual	Free sociability	Religion, church, arts

These two pairs of opposites are not to be understood as mutually exclusive. Schleiermacher rather works with the idea of an oscillation of opposites, which means that the organizing always participates in the symbolizing action, and the identical in the individual action, and vice versa. By crossing the two pairs of opposites, Schleiermacher creates a fourfold structure of cultural action. This structure enables him to categorize corresponding cultural goods or cultural spheres within the fourfold structured action of human reason.

Action that is predominantly identical and organizing in nature forms the cultural spheres of state and economy, transport and law. Action that is predominantly individual and organizing in nature enables the private sphere, the sphere of personal property and the social interaction of people participating in it. Action that is predominantly identical and symbolic in nature is the prerequisite for people to be able to communicate linguistically; identical symbolization has also produced its own cultural sphere in science and its institutions. Finally, action that is predominantly individual and symbolic in nature brings religious feeling to symbolic expression. It finds its institutional form in the church and the forms of its representation in the wider fields of the arts.

The four-part scheme into which Schleiermacher has rendered the cultural-philosophical program of his ethics of goods can thus be represented diagrammatically (Table 40.1).

40.3 SCHLEIERMACHER'S CONCEPT OF CULTURE

In Schleiermacher's first lecture on philosophical ethics as the ethics of goods, which he gave in Halle in the winter semester of 1805/1806, he identified his point about the highest good as the goal of history with the "idea of a perfect culture that has come back in recent times."[21] Two transcripts of this lecture that have now become available show that behind Schleiermacher's inclusion of the concept of culture lies a critical examination of Jean Jacques Rousseau's (1712–1778) negative view of culture, followed by a rigorous attempt to give the concept of culture an ethically normative meaning.[22]

Schleiermacher was able to assimilate the whole of what ethics is into to the concept of culture: "The result of all that has been said so far about the formation of the faculties of reason

---

[21] PhE (1805/1806), p. 92.
[22] Andreas Arndt kindly made available to me these two transcripts, which are not yet published but are intended for the critical edition of Schleiermacher's lectures on philosophical ethics, one by Fr. C. Köpke, the other by August Böckh. They are titled as follows: "Friedrich Daniel Ernst Schleiermacher. Ethikvorlesung (Halle 1805/1806) Collegienheft der Ethik ausgearbeitet von August Böckh". The manuscripts of the transcripts are in the possession of the archives of Berlin-Brandenburgischen Akademie der Wissenschaften (BBAW): "Nachlaß Schleiermacher 585/1 © der Transkription Klaus

we call culture."[23] Culture is the whole process of "forming and shaping the world under the pressure of ideas,"[24] everything that "belongs to the realization of the highest good."[25]

By being able to speak of the "idea of a perfect culture" instead of the "highest good," Schleiermacher indicates the comprehensive meaning he wanted to give to the concept of culture. In the transcripts of the lecture of 1805/1806 Schleiermacher explicitly distances himself from an understanding of culture according to which it is the privileged domain of those who have intellectual access to education, science, and art. The fundamental achievements of the management of material life, craftsmanship, and technology should also be regarded as cultural phenomena. The fact that the notion of culture is not so strongly used in Schleiermacher's later ethics lectures is probably due to the fact that this narrow understanding of culture, which he opposed in the early lecture, continued to dominate the common usage of the term. But even in the absence of the term, the conception of culture developed in the lecture of 1805/1806 shaped Schleiermacher's mature philosophical ethics as well.

"Without clothing, dwelling etc. there will be not a higher culture. So do not separate, but leave the whole as a whole: the whole is, after all, culture."[26] Everything that is produced by the action of human reason on nature—all transformations of nature for the purposes of sustaining and improving human life, everything that is touched by human hands in order to invest it with meaning or to shape it for the purpose of preserving and developing the human species—becomes culture.

Through organizing action, the production of material and social goods, the state and the economy, free association, sociability and domestic property form material culture. Symbolic and spiritual goods, science and the academy, religion and the church form symbolic culture. Organizing and symbolizing actions refer to each other dialectically. Neither exists without the other—there is no mastery of nature without knowledge and cognition, nor without religion and art. By including the concept of culture in the program of his philosophical ethics, Schleiermacher gives "culture" a meaning that is so comprehensive that it integrates the material and symbolic dimensions of society and the whole history of humanity.

At the same time, Schleiermacher introduces an ethical-normative dimension into the concept of culture.[27] This becomes evident from a remark directed against Rousseau and his contempt for culture. As the transcripts of the lecture show,[28] Rousseau's critique of culture

---

Grotsch 1989–1994" (hereafter Transcript Böckh); "Ethik. Nach dem Vortrage des Herrn Professor Schleiermacher. Michaelis 1805–Ostern 1806. Fr. C. Köpke" (hereafter Transcript Köpke).

[23] Transcript Köpke, p. 19.
[24] Transcript Köpke, p. 19.
[25] Transcript Köpke, p. 19.
[26] Transcript Böckh, p. 31.
[27] Brent Sockness, in particular, has recently pointed out that Schleiermacher's ethics in its cultural-philosophical orientation nevertheless wants to be understood as ethics. Cf. Brent Sockness, "Cultural Theory as Ethics," in *Christentum–Staat–Kultur. Akten des Kongresses der Internationalen Schleiermacher-Gesellschaft in Berlin März 2006*, ed. Andreas Arndt, Ulrich Barth, and Wilhelm Gräb (Berlin/New York: De Gruyter, 2008), pp. 517–526.
[28] Transcript Köpke, p. 20; Transcript Böckh, p. 31.

is the target when Schleiermacher says that "culture" is to be despised "only if reason is abandoned and everything is meant to serve the personality; otherwise, however, it is equal to the highest, comprehending everything moral in itself."[29]

In this way, Schleiermacher makes it clear that since not all persons participate equally in advancing culture and civilization, humans' dominion over nature leads to the domination of some people over other people. This was the reason for the negative view of culture held by Rousseau, who recognized the possession of property—which he understood as implied in the concept of culture—as having particularly dangerous potential. In contrast, Schleiermacher explicitly articulated his positive understanding of culture (as the shaping of nature by human reason interested in moral goods) in terms of ethically normative claims that reasonable human beings place on themselves.[30] Through the ethical structure around which he constructed his understanding of culture, Schleiermacher distanced himself from the negative consequences that Rousseau saw associated with the process of civilization.

Schleiermacher also drew attention to the value of the historical particularity and plurality of cultures. Individual and identical actions characterize the construction of culture as much as organizing and symbolizing actions do. These differences do not justify cultural differences in value. Cultures develop differently, but they all have their origin and their center of strength in the one faculty of reason that is present in the same way within all people.

It is therefore also questionable whether the specific teleological disposition of Schleiermacher's philosophy of history and culture operates on the ultimately colonial, imperialist, and racist logic of the superiority of European culture.[31] Such an interpretation is only plausible if one overlooks the kind of ethical foundation on which Schleiermacher builds his concept of culture. In his criticism of Schleiermacher (and of Herder), Ted Vial overlooks the fact that the ethical categories for understanding human culture give every culture a reason to appreciate culture wherever and however it develops. Schleiermacher was of course of the opinion that not all cultures are equally advanced on the way to the realization of the highest good. However, the differences are due to geographical and climatic conditions for which human beings cannot be held responsible. In any case, no one is entitled to look down on other cultures or even to want to rule over others because of a supposed cultural superiority. For all cultures presuppose rational human nature and have the same goal of promoting the common good.

---

[29] PhE (1805/1806), p. 92.

[30] "The newer idea of the establishment of a general culture, as soon as it is calculated not on personality but on reason, is also the realization of the highest good, namely on the part of forming and shaping the world under the form of ideas" (Transcript Böckh, p. 17).

[31] Cf. Theodore Vial, *Modern Religion, Modern Race* (New York: Oxford University Press, 2016).

40.4 SCHLEIERMACHER'S CONCEPT OF CULTURE IN THE CONTEXT OF THE CULTURAL PHILOSOPHY OF THE ENLIGHTENMENT

Schleiermacher made no claim to originality with his concept of culture. He took up the concept of culture because it seemed to him to be suitable for clarifying the equally normative and far-reaching claim of his ethics of goods. He deliberately appropriated two assumptions from the cultural philosophy of his time. Firstly, the substantive use of "culture," as opposed to "cultivation" as an ennobling activity, had already been introduced into philosophy during the Enlightenment. In Kant and Herder "culture" describes that which specifically distinguishes humans from other living beings and enables them to create a world designed to meet their purposes. Schleiermacher was able to connect this account of culture with his ethics of goods. And secondly, the Enlightenment defined the concept of culture normatively and understood it as a teleological determination of human action. The idea that the history of humankind is a history of cultural development oriented toward the idea of attaining the highest good requires people who adopt this orientation for themselves and base their actions on it.

In order to make it clear how Schleiermacher nevertheless contributed in an independent way to contemporary debates on the concept of culture, I will briefly present the historical context of the discussion.

Emanuel Hirsch (1888–1972) has pointed out that the broad and integrative concept of culture that Schleiermacher favored was first mentioned in the work of Samuel Pufendorf (1632–1694), a teacher of natural law and early forerunner of the Enlightenment.[32] Almost 100 years later Johann Gottfried Herder (1744–1803), in his "Ideen zur Philosophie der Geschichte der Menschheit,"[33] took up the broad and socio-anthropologically fundamental understanding of culture that Pufendorf had posited. For Herder, human beings are inherently cultural beings. Even in their original state, they are conceivable only as socially acting beings, always communicating and cooperating with others, and dependent on their upbringing and education in their development.

For Herder, culture is the form that human beings give to nature in order to make it serve their purposes. Culture is therefore anything but a luxury. Culture is that which makes human beings viable in the first place and enables them to survive in the succession of generations. Culture takes the place of instinct, which is what controls the behavior of animals. Human beings must compensate for their lack of instincts by inventing tools that enable them to control nature and put it at the service of their life interests. Human beings "had . . . to come into the world weak to learn reason."[34]

Herder's concept of culture is based on his anthropology. Because humans have language, they also have history and traditions: "So it is from language that reason and culture begin."[35]

---

[32] Emanuel Hirsch, "Der Kulturbegriff. Eine Lesefrucht," *Deutsche Vierteljahresschrift für Literaturwissenschaft und Geistesgeschichte* 3 (1925), p. 298.

[33] Johann Gottfried Herder, *Ideen zur Philosophie der Geschichte der Menschheit* (1784–91), ed. Martin Bollacher, Werke Bd. 6 (Frankfurt am Main: Suhrkamp, 1989) (hereafter FHA 6).

[34] Herder, FHA 6, p. 143

[35] Herder, FHA 6, p. 141.

Every new generation grows into their culture through teaching and learning, through the development of abilities and skills, through the adoption of customs and traditions. Each generation must develop what it receives from the previous one, but must do so by its own use of reason.

Each individual culture—which for Herder always represents the culture of a people characterized by its distinctive language, traditions, and customs—has its own history and goes through certain stages of development. Since all individual cultures and all stages of their developments contribute in their own way to progress in the realization of human possibilities, cultures cannot to be judged by a superior (extra-cultural or beyond-cultural) standard, for such a position does not exist.

The teleological view of history also does not lead Herder to posit differences in rank between cultures. Every culture, no matter what stage of development it may have reached, contributes to the ultimate purpose of human history by bringing to light the wealth of possibilities that humanity can realize. Herder certainly did not want to make his own culture the yardstick for evaluating other cultures. He also distanced himself from a division of humanity into races in a way that Kant and Hegel did not.[36]

Schleiermacher did not mention Herder by name in his ethics lectures. However, it is quite clear from his comments on the "view" that has "come back in recent times," namely, that a final perspective on the meaning of history carries the "idea of a perfect culture"[37] within itself, that this view refers to suggestions he received from Herder. Just how intensively Schleiermacher engaged with Herder's "Ideen" is shown in his text "Über den Wert des Lebens" (1792/1793),[38] written only one year after Herder's publication of the "Ideen." In this text, as in "Über die Freiheit" (written between 1790 and 1792),[39] Schleiermacher writes, as Herder did, of "education and culture" as that which "should be possible in all states and among all peoples."[40]

Like Herder, Schleiermacher gave positive recognition to the individuality, and thus also to the pluralism, of cultures. Individuality and generality are mutually dependent. Every individual culture enriches the cultural advancement of humanity in general. Schleiermacher therefore criticizes those among his Enlightenment contemporaries who represent an elitist understanding of their own culture and evaluate other cultures in terms of their own:

> It is shallow one-sidedness, childish pride, when we are only willing to find a culture of spirit where our own form of culture is dominant: Worse than the Greeks, for whom everything non-Greek was barbarian, for us everything is uncultured that does not have our style of paint and finish...[41]

Schleiermacher could not imagine a humanity that had not already entered the state of culture and thus the rational and purposeful treatment of nature. Whoever doubted this, the

---

[36] Cf. Anne Löchte, *Johann Gottfried Herder. Kulturtheorie und Humanitätsidee der Ideen, Humanitätsbriefe und Adrastea* (Würzburg: Königshausen & Neumann, 2005); Karin Priester, *Rassismus—Eine Sozialgeschichte* (Leipzig: Reclam, 2003).
[37] PhE (1805/1806), p. 92.
[38] *UWL*.
[39] *UF*.
[40] *UWL*, p. 449.
[41] *UWL*, p. 456.

young Schleiermacher scolded, "Scatter a little of the mist before your eyes and you will find among all nations rich and charitable traces of humanity."[42]

Despite a great deal of factual agreement with Herder, Schleiermacher used the term "culture" in a much more circumscribed way. This is probably in response to the negative connotations that Rousseau had introduced into the concept of culture. Schleiermacher critically addressed Rousseau's contempt for culture in the two transcripts of his lecture on the ethics of goods (1805/1806) (which have not yet been critically edited).[43]

As already noted, Rousseau claims that the cultural and civilizing progress that the Enlightenment recognized above all in the arts and sciences and in social manners has had negative societal consequences. Those who gain access to cultural education, science, and the arts because of their social position, he claims, gain an advantage in power and influence over others. This leads to an inequality between people, which is most evident in the acquisition of property and the claim to personal possessions.

Rousseau did not want to go "back to nature"—an attitude that has often been attributed to him incorrectly. Like Herder later on, he saw people as completely dependent on the formation of culture or civilization. However, for Rousseau, one of the shortcomings of human nature was precisely this selfish striving for personal advantage. He recognized the danger that cultural and civilizational progress would primarily benefit the ruling classes in society. Instead of trusting in cultural and civilizing progress alone, Rousseau demanded better education and better politics. Education, laws, and a reasonable religion must create the conditions for people who are living together in a state to have equal access to the goods produced by society. With his theory of the social contract and a civil religion committed to common values, Rousseau therefore also became the philosophical precursor for the proponents of the French Revolution (1789).[44]

Schleiermacher's objection to Rousseau's negative view of culture must not be understood as a plea for a naïve optimism about progress that denies the associated social problems. Schleiermacher countered Rousseau's negative view of humans as antisocial beings primarily focused on their individual advantage with a more positive image of humanity. According to Schleiermacher, humans have always striven for social cooperation because of their inherent faculty of reason. Their individuality does not contradict their sociality. Individuality and sociality are mutually dependent on each other in human action that is oriented toward the highest good. Then a positive view of culture is possible, Schleiermacher argues against Rousseau, if we consider practical reason as the force determining human action.

Here it becomes clear once again why Schleiermacher has cast his cultural philosophy in the form of a speculative ethics. This formulates the conditions that must be fulfilled if history is to be seen as continuously making progress in the realization of the general and individual good. Schleiermacher did not give his ethics of goods an imperative form, however;

---

[42] *UWL*, p. 457.

[43] Cf. Transcript Böckh, pp. 31f.: "If one, like Rousseau, considers culture to be destructive, this is because one considers individual parts of it and not the whole, or that one considers it only from the point of view of the psychic and not the physical"; as well as Transcript Köpke, pp. 19f.: "It is very well known that there is a hostile view of the same [of culture] which Rousseau in particular represented and tried to defend with all his distinctive eloquence."

[44] Cf. Wolfgang Kersting, *Jean-Jacques Rousseaus "Gesellschaftsvertrag"* (Darmstadt: GRIN Verlag, 2002).

rather, he articulated it in the form of a descriptive ethics. Instead of the ethical imperative, Schleiermacher relies on reason as an effective force in human action.

Furthermore, in place of the moral imperative, Schleiermacher relied on the power of lived religion to motivate and enable moral action. Religion, more precisely the church, which Schleiermacher understood to be the institutional form of every religion, is only one of the four cultural spheres, alongside the state, science, and free sociability. Yet, like the other cultural spheres, religion has a constitutive function for the whole of culture. "Each [of these spheres] in a certain sense also has all the others in itself; the state, in how far they [these spheres] have an external existence, the church, in how far they rest on attitude [*Gesinnung*], science, in how far they must have an identical medium, and free sociability as a general binding agent."[45]

Religion, with its function of individual symbolization, plays a constitutive role in being human. Its significance for the construction of culture lies in the fact that it provides the mindset on which all cultural work rests. One could also say that lived religion makes the claim that practical reason places on human beings generally understandable on the individual level.

40.5 Schleiermacher's Philosophy of Culture and Christianity

Schleiermacher rejected the "natural religion" of the Enlightenment. Where religion is lived, it is always positive, historical religion. Religion exists in the diversity of historical religions. Schleiermacher welcomed this diversity; for example, in contrast to Hegel's philosophy of history, from the point of view of his philosophical theory of religion (which differs from the standpoint of the Christian faith) he did not accept a construction of the history of religion that would culminate in Christianity as the ultimate religion.[46]

Nevertheless, Schleiermacher's philosophy of culture must also be seen in close connection with his conception of Christianity and its importance in world history. He was of the opinion that, from the point of view of the Christian faith, Christianity is regarded as superior to other religions. In a theological perspective, based on the Christian certainty of faith, Christianity is not only one religion among many. Schleiermacher saw in Christianity "the actual completion of religious consciousness"[47] and thus the completion of the ethos that the building of culture demands.

Within the framework of his theology, which reflects the self-understanding of the Christian faith, Schleiermacher supplemented the formal-structural philosophy of history and culture of his philosophical ethics with a conception of Christianity as an authentic

---

[45] Friedrich Schleiermacher, *Ethik 1812/13*, in *Entwürfe zu einem System der Sittenlehre*, pp. 241–372 (pp. 273f.).

[46] Cf. Wilhelm Gräb, "Religion 'ist nicht anders möglich als in einer unendlichen Menge verschiedener Formen.' Schleiermacher und die Vielfalt der Formen des Religiösen," in *Religion und Religionen im Deutschen Idealismus. Schleiermacher–Hegel–Schelling*, ed. Friedrich Hermanni, Burkhard Nonnenmacher, and Friederike Schick (Tübingen: Mohr Siebeck, 2015), pp. 65–84.

[47] *Sitte*.

historical agent of the cultural process of human history.[48] The appearance of Christ and the Christian movement emanating from him, which is not restricted to the institutionalized church but embraces the Christian world, leads to the realization of the Kingdom of God and thus, in religious terminology, to the completion of the highest good. Christ, he says, is "the creation of human nature which is only now complete,"[49] and is thus the condition for the completion of humanity.

Schleiermacher placed the Christian ethics next to the philosophical ethics. The Christian ethics reflects the Christian faith, showing how, through the Christian Church, it becomes a culture-forming force by permeating the entire cultural process with the Christian spirit. Other perspectives from different cultural spheres would also be possible. Religion does not stand for the whole of culture. Nor is it presented in the philosophical ethics as the foundation or even the substance of culture at all. Nevertheless, Schleiermacher demonstrates in his Christian ethics that he believes the Christian religion to be a force that transforms culture in all its dimensions. Therefore, in Christian ethics he states that the cultural sphere of religion has a morally oriented impact on other cultural spheres, such as the state, the economy, or science.

This Christian view on culture remains positional and particular. Schleiermacher assumes that those who belong to the Christian church and live the Christian faith take up this view. As long as they live the Christian faith in the spirit of Jesus, they do so in the vastness of a culture of humanity whose orientation Schleiermacher unfolds in his philosophy of culture.

Nevertheless, one has to admit critically that Schleiermacher's conception of Christianity also has religious-imperial traits. Christianity is after all intended to unite all humankind in itself and help to realize the "idea of a perfect culture."[50] Today we can no longer understand this claim to the cultural superiority of the Christian religion in this way, and we will certainly not want to defend it.

40.6 Schleiermacher's Philosophy of Culture and Modern Society

Schleiermacher presented his philosophy of culture independently of its Christian interpretation. Regarded in the context of contemporary history, his particular achievement can be recognized in the fact that he drew attention to the functional differentiation of cultural spheres. This has now become a structural characteristic of our understanding of modern culture in particular.

On the one hand, Schleiermacher distinguished between cultural spheres and institutions (economy/state; free sociability/privateness; sciences/academy; religion/church) whose function for society as a whole was to ensure the material and social maintenance of life in the succession of generations. This function is fulfilled by organizing action. On the other hand, there are cultural spheres whose function for the whole of society lies in enabling

---

[48] Cf. Gräb, *Humanität und Christentumsgeschichte*.
[49] CG², §89, pp. 27f.
[50] PhE (1805/1806), p. 92.

social communication and morally responsible interaction. This function is fulfilled through symbolizing action. Each of the cultural spheres stands for functional areas that perform a service for the whole of society. However, each of the functional spheres also contains all the others in itself, contributing in a specific way to the achievement of the common good.

Gunter Scholz pointed out that Schleiermacher had thus succeeded in presenting a theory of the functional differentiation of modern society, an idea developed later by Talcott Parsons (1902–1979) and Niklas Luhmann (1927–1998).[51] In contrast to Hegel, according to Scholz, Schleiermacher's notion of cultural development does not lead to the moral-cultural state finally gaining sole power of control by orienting the economy and law, science, religion, and art toward its own purposes.[52] Instead, Schleiermacher had indicated that the various functional areas of modern society have (relative) autonomy. In this way, he had already taken into account the dynamics of modern society and developed a constructive approach toward understanding the process of functional differentiation between social organizations.[53]

However, Scholz also pointed out that Schleiermacher attributed the differentiated social functional areas to the actions of reasonable people who were aware of their moral responsibility.[54] This integration of the differentiated cultural world stems from Schleiermacher's principled presuppositions concerning the unity of reason among human beings and the moral obligations that follow from this. If one acknowledges the ethical imperative, then one can indeed say that Schleiermacher's philosophy of culture not only already offers a theory of functionally differentiated modern culture, but can also be regarded as "an orienting guideline for practice in this culture."[55]

The philosophy of culture, which flourished in the first half of the twentieth century, diagnosed a deep crisis in modern culture. For Simmel and Cassirer, this crisis consisted in particular in the fact that the enormous progress in science, technology, and economic productivity was countered by a decline in social communication about how to deal with this progress in a responsible manner. In the search for ways to overcome the crisis of modern culture, Schleiermacher as a cultural philosopher also came into view. His cultural-philosophical concept is in fact still interesting today—on the one hand because of his early insight into the functional differentiation of modern culture, and on the other hand because he insisted that this modern culture only serves the common good if the functionally differentiated areas are not left to their own inherent functional logics. What remains important is that people, both as individuals and as a society, are aware that the unity of their rationality gives them the opportunity and the ability to work for a world that promotes the well-being of all.

---

[51] Cf. Gunter Scholz, *Ethik als Theorie der modernen Kultur. Mit vergleichendem Blick auf Hegel*, in: Gunter Scholz, *Ethik und Hermeneutik. Schleiermachers Grundlegung der Geisteswissenschaften* (Frankfurt am Main: Suhrkamp, 1995), pp. 35–64.

[52] Scholz, *Ethik als Theorie der modernen Kultur*, pp. 36f.

[53] Scholz, *Ethik als Theorie der modernen Kultur*, pp. 36f.

[54] Scholz, *Ethik als Theorie der modernen Kultur*, p. 37.

[55] Scholz, *Ethik als Theorie der modernen Kultur*, p. 39.

Suggested Reading

Birkner, Hans-Joachim. *Schleiermachers Christliche Sittenlehre im Zusammenhang seines philosophisch-theologischen Systems* (Berlin: Töpelmann, 1964).
Scholz, Gunter. "Ethik als Theorie der modernen Kultur. Mit vergleichendem Blick auf Hegel." In Gunter Scholz, *Ethik und Hermeneutik. Schleiermachers Grundlegung der Geisteswissenschaften* (Frankfurt am Main: Suhrkamp, 1995), pp. 35–64.
Vial, Theodore. *Modern Religion, Modern Race* (New York: Oxford University Press, 2016).

Bibliography

Birkner, Hans-Joachim. *Schleiermachers Christliche Sittenlehre im Zusammenhang seines philosophisch-theologischen Systems* (Berlin: Töpelmann, 1964).
Bredow, Gerda von. *Wertanalysen zu Schleiermachers Güterethik* (Phil Diss. Berlin, 1941).
Cassirer, Ernst. *An Essay on Man: An Introduction to a Philosophy of Human Culture* (New Haven: Yale University Press, 1944).
Cassirer, Ernst. *Philosophie der symbolischen Formen*, Part 1: *Die Sprache* (1923) (Darmstadt: Wissenschaftliche Buchgesellschaft, 1994); Part 2: *Das mythische Denken* (1925) (Darmstadt: Wissenschaftliche Buchgesellschaft, 1994); Part 3: *Phänomenologie der Erkenntnis* (1929) (Darmstadt: Wissenschaftliche Buchgesellschaft, 1994).
Gräb, Wilhelm. *Humanität und Christentumsgeschichte. Eine Untersuchung zum Geschichtsbegriff im Spätwerk Schleiermachers* (Göttingen: Vandenhoeck und Ruprecht, 1980).
Gräb, Wilhelm. "Religion 'ist nicht anders möglich als in einer unendlichen Menge verschiedener Formen.' Schleiermacher und die Vielfalt der Formen des Religiösen." In *Religion und Religionen im Deutschen Idealismus. Schleiermacher–Hegel–Schelling*, ed. Friedrich Hermanni, Burkhard Nonnenmacher, and Friederike Schick (Tübingen: Mohr Siebeck, 2015), pp. 65–84.
Herder, Johann Gottfried. *Ideen zur Philosophie der Geschichte der Menschheit* (1784–91). Ed. Martin Bollacher. Werke Bd. 6 (Frankfurt am Main: Suhrkamp, 1989).
Hirsch, Emanuel. "Der Kulturbegriff. Eine Lesefrucht." *Deutsche Vierteljahresschrift für Literaturwissenschaft und Geistesgeschichte* 3 (1925), pp. 398-400.
Kersting, Wolfgang. *Jean-Jacques Rousseaus "Gesellschaftsvertrag"* (Darmstadt: GRIN Verlag, 2002).
Löchte, Anne. *Johann Gottfried Herder. Kulturtheorie und Humanitätsidee der Ideen, Humanitätsbriefe und Adrastea* (Würzburg: Königshausen & Neumann, 2005).
Mulert, Hermann. *Schleiermacher-Studien I. Schleiermachers geschichtsphilosophische Ansichten in ihrer Bedeutung für seine Theologie*. Studien zur Geschichte des neueren Protestantismus 3 (Berlin: Töpelmann, 1907).
Priester, Karin. *Rassismus—Eine Sozialgeschichte* (Leipzig: Reclam, 2003).
Reble, Albert. *Schleiermachers Kulturphilosophie. Eine entwicklungsgeschichtlich-systematische Würdigung*. Sonderschriften der Akademie gemeinnütziger Wissenschaften zu Erfurt, Heft 7 (Erfurt: Stenger, 1935).
Schleiermacher, Friedrich. *Brouillon zur Ethik 1805/1806*. In *Entwürfe zu einem System der Sittenlehre*. Ed. Otto Braun, Newprint of 2. Edition Leipzig 1927 (Aalen: Scientia-Verlag, 1967), pp. 75–240.

Schleiermacher, Friedrich. *Ethik 1812/13*. In *Entwürfe zu einem System der Sittenlehre*. Ed. Otto Braun. Newprint of 2. Edition Leipzig 1927 (Aalen: Scientia-Verlag, 1967), pp. 241–372.

Schleiermacher, Friedrich. *Ethik 1816*. In *Entwürfe zu einem System der Sittenlehre*. Ed. Otto Braun. Newprint of 2. Edition Leipzig 1927 (Aalen: Scientia-Verlag, 1967), pp. 513–626.

Scholz, Gunter. "Ethik als Theorie der modernen Kultur. Mit vergleichendem Blick auf Hegel." In Scholz, *Ethik und Hermeneutik. Schleiermachers Grundlegung der Geisteswissenschaften* (Frankfurt am Main: Suhrkamp, 1995), pp. 35–64.

Simmel, Georg. *Der Begriff und die Tragödie der Kultur* (1911). In *Aufsätze und Abhandlungen 1909–1918*, ed. Rüdiger Kramme and Angela Rammstedt. GA 12 (Frankfurt am Main: Suhrkamp, 2001), pp. 194–223.

Simmel, Georg. *Persönliche und sachliche Kultur*. In Ders. *Aufsätze und Abhandlungen. 1894 bis 1900*, ed. Heinz-Jürgen Dahme and David P. Frisby. GA 5 (Frankfurt am Main: Suhrkamp, 1992), pp. 560–584.

Simmel, Georg, *Philosophie der Kultur* (1906/07). In *Kolleghefte und Mitschriften*, ed. Angela Rammstedt and Cécile Rol. Gesamtausgabe Bd. 21 (Berlin: Suhrkamp, 2012), pp. 57–571.

Sockness, Brent. "Cultural Theory as Ethics." In *Christentum–Staat–Kultur. Akten des Kongresses der Internationalen Schleiermacher-Gesellschaft in Berlin März 2006*, ed. Andreas Arndt, Ulrich Barth, and Wilhelm Gräb (Berlin/New York: De Gruyter, 2008), pp. 517–526.

Stoltenberg, Hans Lorenz. "Friedrich Schleiermacher als Soziologe." *Zeitschrift für die gesamte Staatswissenschaft* 88 (1930), pp. 77–113.

Vial, Theodore. *Modern Religion, Modern Race* (New York: Oxford University Press, 2016).

Index

For the benefit of digital users, indexed terms that span two pages (e.g., 52–53) may, on occasion, appear on only one of those pages.

Tables are indicated by *t* following the page number

A

absolute, concept of 42, 71–72, 205–6, 215–16
absolute dependence, feeling of 64–65, 86–87, 273–74, 276, 292, 331–32, 515, 545–47, 620, 631, 639–40
action/activity 158–59, 160–64
  as broadening/propagative 307–8, 357–58, 359–60
  as efficacious 358, 405
  as purifying 95, 307–8, 357
  as re/presentational 95, 357–58, 360–61, 405
  of reason, organizing 96–97, 161–62, 162*t*, 228, 230–31, 664–65, 665*t*
  of reason, symbolizing 96–97, 161, 162, 162*t*, 205–6, 228, 230–31, 354–55, 665*t*, 667, 672–73
aesthetics xxvii–xxviii, 200–1, 437–38
  and mood xxvii–xxviii, 86–87, 114, 151–52, 175–76, 207, 209–12
Agendenstreit, the (agenda controversy) 330
Ammon, Christof Friedrich von 59–60
anthropology 32, 177, 221–23, 297, 320–21, 668–69
antitheses 49–50, 70–71, 88, 91–92, 96–97, 664–65
Aristotle 6, 9–10, 106, 127, 155, 158, 163, 167–68, 174–76, 177, 214, 220, 238–39, 246, 425–26, 487–88, 494, 500, 569–70, 663
Arminianism 56–57
art 9–10, 15–16, 17–18, 97–98, 121–22, 127, 139, 150, 194, 205–7, 209–10, 228, 265–66, 354–55, 399–400, 404–5, 406, 418–19, 425–26, 427, 603, 604–5, 666
  as religion (*Kunstreligion*) 97–98, 121–22, 204
Athenaeum (journal) 72, 73, 204, 221

B

Barth, Karl xxiv–xxv, 53, 265–66, 289, 311, 323–24, 346–47, 461, 473–74, 475–76, 505–6, 535, 548–54, 558–59
Baur, Ferdinand Christian 323–25, 331–32, 336–37, 460, 526
beatific vision 278, 281–82
beauty/the beautiful 119, 209, 214, 227
Bekker, Immanuel 500
Berlin, University of xxiii–xxiv, 85–86, 101–2, 109–11, 114–15, 204–5, 368–69, 400–1, 660–61
  faculty of theology 109–11, 114–15, 126–27
biblical scholarship 192–93, 199–200, 326, 367, 372–73, 394, 524, 543–45
Bildung (formation/enculturation) 14, 46–41, 180, 183–85, 410, 440–41, 444–45, 604–5, 617
Birkner, Hans-Joachim 263, 264, 266–67, 268, 289–90, 331–32, 354
Blackwell, Albert 17
blessedness 277–78, 312, 357–58, 479, 526, 529
Boeckh, August 6, 488, 500–1
Bossuet, Jacques 561–62
Braidotti, Rosi 612–13, 625
Bretschneider, Karl Gottlieb 64, 522–23
Brief Outline of Theology as a Field of Study 74, 101, 109–10, 112, 351, 397–98, 402–3, 404–5, 511, 525, 560, 563, 581, 640
Brunner, Emil xxiv–xxv, 304, 541–42, 543–44, 548, 553
Bultmann, Rudolf 289n.14, 548–53
Butler, Judith 612

C

Calvin, Jean 62, 64, 546–47
Carlsbad Decrees 79–80
Cassirer, Ernst 660–61
causality, absolute/divine 64–65, 292–93, 300, 310, 340–41, 343–44, 546–48
Christian Faith, see *Glaubenslehre*
Christmas Eve Dialogue 16, 204, 466, 600, 614–15, 618
Christology 63–64, 294, 297–98, 346–47, 452, 474–75, 509
    person of Christ 63–64, 294, 319, 338–39, 359, 509, 551–52
    work of Christ 312–14, 319, 357, 460, 544–45
church
    as institution 60–62, 260–61, 265–66, 398–400, 402–4, 650 *DialektikDialektik*
    Lutheran 53–65, 309, 544–45, 651–52
    Reformed 53–65, 309, 544–45, 651–52
    Roman Catholic 54–55, 57–58, 62, 119, 267, 408, 536, 557, 650–51
    Trinity (*Dreifaltigkeitskirche*) 54, 78, 237, 258–59, 450–51, 460–61, 489–90
    unification of, *see* unification, of Lutheran and Reformed churches
    see also community, religious
colonialism/colonization 316, 360, 363–64, 602–3, 667
communication 95, 96–97, 190–92, 195, 210, 250, 403, 435, 438–40, 443, 672–73
community, religious 80, 159–60, 327–28, 363, 378, 403–4, 440–41, 478–79, 624–25
confessions, creedal 54, 56–58, 110, 293–94, 313, 459, 553, 570, 649–51
Congress of Vienna 79–80, 179, 650–51
creation, of world 129, 168, 284–85, 291–95, 300–1, 306, 312–13, 315, 327, 329–30, 332–33, 338–39, 517, 530, 583–84, 619–22
culture 106–7, 151, 162–64, 166–67, 174–75, 188, 200–1, 227, 237, 363–64, 429, 525, 527, 596–98, 600–1, 660

D

decree, divine 56–57, 64, 301, 327, 329, 331, 332–33, 340–41, 551–52, 553
determinism 39, 293, 623
De Vries, Dawn 451, 452–53, 454–55, 461–62, 477, 614–15

Dialektik 15–16, 49–50, 77, 114, 137, 196–97, 206–7, 229–31, 352–54, 423n.31–24, 499–500
dialectical theology 261–62, 267–68, 289–90, 304, 435, 534–35, 541, 548–53, 554
dialogue 6, 7–8, 128–29, 139–41, 147–48, 149, 150, 156, 190–92, 196–97, 353, 466–67, 472–74, 477, 489–91, 492, 498, 614–15, 618
Dilthey, Wilhelm 49, 69, 70, 171–72, 190–91, 198–99, 201, 224, 430–31, 662
divination (hermeneutical) 179–80, 197–98
doctrine 54–56, 107, 264–65, 298, 455–56, 524, 562, 631–32
    see also dogmatic propositions
dogmatic propositions 295–96, 552–53
dogmatics 112–13, 264, 273, 274–75, 356
Dorner, Isaak A. 336–37, 509–10
Dorrien, Gary 290–91, 554
Drey, Johann Sebastian 267, 369, 559–66
Du Bois, W. E. B. 594–95
Durkheim, Émile 181, 182–83, 636

E

Ebeling, Gerhard 326, 329–30
Eberhard, Johann August 22, 23–24, 75, 203–4, 418, 487
education 171, 238
    see also *Bildung* (formation)
election, *see* predestination
Eliade, Mircea 633–43
encyclopedia, theological 112, 113, 258–59, 267–68, 270, 510–11, 560–61
Enlightenment, European 57, 183, 188–89, 257–58, 668, 670
epistemology 137, 188–89, 190–91, 201, 605–6
eschatology 294–95
essence
    of Christianity 299, 320–21, 398–99
    of religion, *see* absolute dependence, feeling of; intuition, of the universe
ethics
    Christian 112, 206, 307, 316, 351, 525, 527, 672
    philosophical 14–15, 104, 106–7, 114, 149–50, 155, 200–1, 205–7, 208–9, 220–21, 230–31, 237, 663–66, 672
Eucharist 62–63
Eusebius, of Caesarea 389–90
evil 183–84, 309–11, 427, 588–89
exegesis 263

F

family 163–64, 178–79, 184–85, 241, 309, 359, 360, 420, 422–23, 467, 469, 525, 616, 617–18
feeling 88, 92–93, 143, 207, 209, 225–27, 273–74, 275–80, 325, 352, 438–40, 442–43, 513, 613–14, 620
  religious 181, 205–6, 225, 227, 639
  see also absolute dependence, feeling of
feminism 476–77, 613
Feuerbach, Ludwig 325, 636, 638
Fichte, Johann Gottlieb 70, 71–72, 74, 87–88, 104–6, 123–24, 125–26, 127, 137, 139–40, 188, 211–12, 215, 427, 436, 437–38
Fiorenza, Elisabeth Schüssler 585
Fiorenza, Francis Schüssler 342, 570
formation, see *Bildung*
Frank, Manfred 198–99
freedom 71–72, 156, 181–82, 183–85, 276, 277–78, 623
French Revolution/occupation xxiii–xxiv, 71, 74, 103, 121–22, 129–30, 467–68, 596–97, 670
Friedrich Wilhelm III, King of Prussia 58–59, 78, 102
Friedrich Wilhelm IV, King of Prussia 80–82
friendship 617

G

Gadamer, Hans-Georg 194, 198–99
Gaß, Joachim Wilhelm 369
gender 228, 469–70, 476–77, 611
Gerrish, Brian A. 53, 289
Geiselmann, Josef Rupert 568
Glaubenslehre (*Christian Faith*) 113, 208–9, 211–12, 272, 288, 306–7, 435, 544–47
gnosticism 324–25, 594
God
  doctrine of 88–90, 94, 142–43
  knowledge of 220–21, 225, 277–80, 437, 441, 546–47
  and world 50–51, 92–94, 220–21, 275–76, 284–85, 291–92, 332–33, 343–28, 362–63, 456, 515, 550, 583–84, 618–23

G

God-consciousness 63–64, 227, 275–83, 294, 297–98, 312–13, 322–23, 329, 373–74, 376, 452–53, 456, 458, 546–47, 567–68, 589–90, 624

God-forgetfulness 297–90, 306, 552
Godlove, Terry 635, 637–38
Goethe, J.W. 71, 73, 103, 182, 213
Gogarten, Friedrich 535, 541–42, 548
good, highest 183–85, 230–31, 354–55, 665–66, 671–72
grace 299, 306–7, 312–15, 549–50, 589–90, 619
Graf, Friedrich Wilhelm 289–90
Grünow, Eleanore 76, 422–23, 467
Günthenke, Constanze 9

H

Habermas, Jürgen 191–92, 445–46, 599–600, 645, 647–48, 656–57
Hagenbach, Karl 267, 510–11, 516–17, 518
Halle, University at xxiii, 13, 75–77, 102–3, 112, 203–4, 382–83, 418, 460–61, 467, 487, 500–1, 665
Harms, Claus 59–60, 292
Harnack, Adolf von 290, 336–37, 531–33, 549, 551
Hase, Karl von 366
Hegel, George Wilhelm Friedrich 37–38, 70, 85, 111, 114, 124–25, 159, 188, 207–8, 211–12, 215–16, 248, 323–24, 430–31, 437, 506, 513, 526, 558, 671
Heraclitus 40, 493–98
Herder, Johann Gottfried 8–9, 37–38, 147–48, 190, 191–92, 514, 597–98, 606–7, 668–70
heresey/heresies 129, 262, 320–21
hermeneutics 13–14, 114, 118, 126–27, 147–49, 188, 263, 319–20, 386, 387, 493–94, 498, 563, 633
  general and special 14, 188–93, 386
  grammatical and technical 195–98
Herrmann, Wilhelm 336–37, 530–31, 551, 554
Herz, Henriette 7, 119–20, 123, 436, 599–600, 601, 604, 613
Herz, Markus 599–600
Heß, Johann Jakob 369
Himes, Michael 558–59, 567
Hirsch, Emanuel 86–87, 535, 668
historical consciousness 13, 268, 298, 352, 364, 367–68, 398, 531, 561–62
history
  of art 214–16
  of church 13, 57, 112, 263, 264, 506, 516, 533–34, 649–50
  study of 107, 163–65, 324–25, 326–27, 354, 367–68, 525–26, 663–65
Hölderlin, Friedrich 71

Holy Spirit 37, 167, 189, 293, 306, 338–42, 346–47, 358, 373–74, 376–77, 386, 451, 557–58, 568
Humboldt, Wilhelm von 46–47, 85–86, 108, 147–48, 172–73, 191–92, 400–1

I
idealism 27–28, 33, 43, 125–26, 220
immortality, see soul, immortality of
imperialism 667, 672
individuality 40, 41–42, 45–48, 93–94, 142, 156–57, 162t, 180–82, 183–85, 195–97, 225–27, 228, 237, 354–55, 383, 420, 426, 441, 623–25, 669
inspiration, biblical 189, 386, 515
interpretation 6–7, 14, 188–201
  see also hermeneutics
intuition xxvi–xxvii, 17, 43–44, 72–73, 197, 204, 276–80, 438–40, 442–43, 620, 630–31, 639–40
  highest 156, 420, 626
  of the universe 40, 41–42, 45, 73, 204, 438–39, 442–43, 478
Islam 274, 283

J
Jackson Ravenscroft, Ruth 475–76
Jacobi, Friedrich Heinrich 37–42, 90–91, 120–21, 437, 512–13
Jena, University of 71, 105, 366, 489
Jena circle 72–73
Jensen, Jeppe 638–39
Jesus of Nazareth
  as historical figure 327–28, 367–68, 371–72, 392–94, 470–71
  as ideal figure 328, 371–72
  as Redeemer 262, 299, 312–13, 322–23, 362–63, 517, 546–47
  see also Christology
Jonas, Ludwig 139, 356–57
Judaism 263, 274, 283, 320, 378, 394, 446–47, 525, 606–7
Julian of Norwich 622–23

K
Kant, Immanuel 21, 42–44, 70, 87–88, 104–5, 123–24, 156–57, 164, 180, 190–91, 208, 211–12, 214, 221, 276–77, 296, 362, 418–19, 423, 425, 436–37, 441, 530–31, 595–96, 662, 668
Kierkegaard, Søren 311, 430–31, 548

kingdom of God 261, 300, 377, 526, 527, 529–30, 671–72
knowledge/knowing 14–16, 92–93, 126, 141–46, 190–92, 194, 196–97, 353, 546–47
Krämer, Hans Joachim 12–13

L
Lamm, Julia 293, 304–5, 313, 472–73, 477, 622
language 147–49, 189–97, 198–99, 212–13, 442–43
Leibniz, Gottfried Wilhelm 24, 40, 103, 121, 156, 214, 418
Lessing, Gotthold Ephraim 37–38, 103, 203, 361, 367–68, 387–88, 437
liberalism 289–91, 301–2, 517–18, 522, 544–46, 550
Life of Jesus (lectures) 111, 112–13, 326, 366, 388, 391–94, 524, 544–45
love 64, 123–24, 277–78, 332, 343–45, 360–61, 422–23, 470, 546–47, 584–85, 614–15, 622
Lücke, Friedrich 54, 270, 272, 290–91, 293, 306, 390, 508, 510
Luhmann, Niklas 182–83, 445–46, 673
Luther, Martin 54–56, 62, 359, 392, 469, 530, 550

M
Mack, Joseph Martin 567
Marheineke, Philipp 110, 336–37, 510, 567
Mariña, Jacqueline 322
McCutcheon, Russell 636–38, 640
McGrath, Alister 323–24, 325–26
mediation 145–46, 314–15, 322, 507–9, 514–15, 517–18
Mendelssohn, Moses 37–38, 203–4
metaphysics 27, 29–31, 33–34, 441–42
miracles 284, 290–91, 292–93, 329, 375, 376–77, 393–94
modernity 98–99, 166, 319, 331, 441–42, 517, 579–80, 646
Möhler, Johann Adam xxx–xxxi, 557–59, 566–69
Molendijk, Arie 638–39
Monologen, see *Soliloquies*
monotheism 274, 282–83
Moravians 58–59
music 210–11, 444–45, 469, 475

N

Napoleon 77–78, 79–80, 102, 467–68, 649
nationalism 360, 606–7
nationality 597–98, 606–7
natural religion, *see* religion, natural
naturalism 288–89, 290–91, 634–37, 638
Neander, August 110, 516, 517, 567
neo-orthodoxy 304, 541–48
Niebuhr, H. Richard 363, 541–42
Niebuhr, Reinhold 311, 541–42
Nietzsche, Friedrich 188–89
Nitzsch, Karl Immanuel 508, 511, 512–13, 518
Novalis (Friedrich von Hardenberg) 71, 72, 73, 124, 239

O

objectivity 438–40, 512, 515, 549, 551–52
Occasional Thoughts on the University in the German Sense 74, 78, 106–9, 113–14, 172–73
oppositions, *see* antitheses
orthodoxy 53, 63–64, 65, 564
Otto, Rudolf 633–35, 637

P

pantheism 50–37, 87–88, 93–94, 164
pastoral care 407–9
Patsch, Hermann 126–27, 474–129
Paulus, Heinrich Gottlob 366, 369, 393–94
Peace of Tilsit (1807) 77–78, 102
pedagogy 114, 171, 204–5, 238, 258
  lectures on 173–74, 176–77
philosophical writings
  (Schleiermacher's) 106–7, 113–14, 137–41, 155–57, 172–76, 188–93, 205–7, 352–54
philosophy
  of art 205–7, 208–9
  classical German 93–94, 130, 204–5, 207, 216
  of culture 174–75, 188, 199, 211–12, 425, 527, 606, 660
  of life 224
  of nature 14–15, 71–72, 76–77, 129, 130, 215
  speculative 129, 513
physics 11–12, 17–18, 45–46, 150, 157–58, 160–61, 221, 230–31, 353–54, 429, 499–500
pietism 56–57
piety, *see* self-consciousness, pious

Plato 5, 76, 121, 128–29, 139–41, 155–56, 175–76, 177, 214, 220, 278–79, 425–26, 440–41, 472–73, 477, 488–92, 497–98, 664
Platonic dialogues
  authenticity of 10–11
  ordering of 11–12, 12*t*, 13
pluralism, religious 59–60, 301, 398–99, 527, 596–97, 606, 657
pneumatology 95, 346–47
poetry 205–6, 212–13, 389, 600
practice, religious 398–99, 401, 404–9, 631–32
preaching 237, 273, 406–7, 450–53, 456–60, 544–45
predestination 56–57, 64–65
Preus, J. Samuel 634–35
progress 315–16, 443–44, 510–11, 516–17, 525–26, 542–43, 670–71, 673
Proudfoot, Wayne 280, 281–82, 630–33, 637–38
providence 300–1, 621
Prussia xxiii–xxiv, 54, 59–62, 78–76, 102–3
Prussian Union (1817) 58–60, 80, 175–76, 649–50
Prussian Academy of Sciences 205, 211, 237, 489–90, 532
pseudonymity (in Scripture) 385, 386, 391, 392
psychology 114, 147, 166–67, 180, 184–85, 207, 208–9, 219, 496–97, 525, 640
Puar, Jasbir 608–9

R

race 593, 669
racism 667
Rahner, Karl 570
rationalism 39, 351, 361–62, 479
Rauschenbusch, Walter 311
Reble, Albert 174–75, 662
redemption 93–94, 266, 279, 297, 306–7, 312–15, 320–21, 357–58, 362–63, 471, 622
Reformation, Protestant 359
Reformed tradition 53, 543–44
regeneration 313, 360
Reimarus, Hermann Samuel 361, 367
religion
  academic study of 14, 89–90, 93–94, 261–62, 434–35, 632, 633–39

Religion (cont.)
  concept of 70, 71, 205–6, 282, 283, 436–37, 438–40, 441–43, 524, 633–39, 649–50, 653–55, 665t
  and morality 29, 95, 436–37, 662
  natural 446, 671
religious experience 304, 533–34, 570, 630–33, 636–37, 639–40
revelation 43–44, 324–25, 331–33, 533–34, 544, 546–47, 584–85
  see also inspiration, biblical
Richardson, Ruth Drucilla 476, 614–16
Ricoeur, Paul 190–91, 633
Rieger, Joerg 316, 363–64
Riley, Denise 612, 626
Ritschl, Albrecht 289–90, 308, 336–37, 363, 528–30, 542–44, 551
Romanticism 70–73, 82, 130, 203–4, 213, 220, 436, 444–45
Rothe, Richard 166, 509–10, 515, 526–27, 530
Rousseau, Jean-Jacques 163, 665, 666–67, 670
Rütenik, Karl August 369–70

S
Sack, August Friedrich Wilhelm 59–60
Sack, Friedrich Samuel Gottfried 54, 59–60
salvation see redemption
sanctification 313, 360, 553
Schelling, Friedrich Wilhelm Joseph 69, 103, 105–6, 107–8, 208, 210, 211–12, 220, 428–29, 437, 473–74
Schiller, Friedrich 74, 208, 211–12, 213, 221
Schlegel, August Wilhelm 71–72, 73, 118, 221, 616–17
Schlegel, Caroline 73, 123
Schlegel, Friedrich 7–8, 12, 71, 73, 118, 204, 383, 422, 436, 467, 474–75, 488–90, 616–17
Schleusner, Johann Friedrich 384–85
Schmid, Johann Wilhelm 366
Scholz, Gunter 651–52, 673
Schweitzer, Albert 112–13, 366, 371, 378
Schweizer, Alexander 53, 514–15
Science [Wissenschaft] 106–9, 115, 230–31, 283–84, 353, 436–37, 582
Seckler, Max 558–59, 565–66
Segal, Robert 635–36
self-consciousness 27–28, 31, 93–94, 143, 211–12, 223–27, 231, 328–29

immediate 143, 211–12, 216, 227, 275–76, 283–84, 324, 353, 639
pious 220–21, 273–75, 282, 297, 305, 306, 325, 328–29, 352, 356, 357, 377, 437–38, 583–84, 631
sensible 275–76, 297, 328–20, 551–52 Speeches (On Religion)
Semler, Johann Salomo 367–68, 522–23
Shorey, Paul 13
Simmel, Georg 660–62
sin 297–98, 299, 306–11, 360, 549–50, 588–89
  actual 296–97, 308–9
  original 293–94, 308–9, 589
  as social 304–5, 308–9
slavery 249, 360, 426
sociality/sociability 180–82, 206, 226, 227, 228, 354–55, 439, 445–46, 598–601, 604, 617
  free 354–55
society 163–64, 174–76, 182–84, 600–1, 617, 645–46, 661, 670, 672–73
sociology 95, 182–83, 649–52
Soliloquies 156–57, 181–82, 417–21
Sonderegger, Katherine 621
soul
  doctrine of 111, 147, 219–21, 225–29, 232–33, 497
  immortality of 29–30, 362, 441, 444
  operations of 225–27
Speeches (On Religion) xxiv–xxv, 17–18, 45, 89–91, 109, 123–24, 164, 351, 434, 507, 545–46, 611, 630–31
Spinoza, Baruch 14, 37, 70, 71–72, 89–90, 277–78, 279–80, 426, 437–38
Staatslehre 114, 236, 597, 652–56
Stapfer, Johann Friedrich 64–65, 171, 203, 220, 384–85
state 71–72, 79–80, 96, 109–10, 114, 183–85, 227, 233, 236, 445–46, 652–53
  relationship to church 79–80, 237, 239–40, 653–55
Steffens, Henrik 69–82, 103, 137–38, 210
Stein, Heinrich Friedrich Karl vom und zum 60–61, 102–3, 108
Strauss, David Friedrich 111, 112–13, 366, 370, 371, 392–93, 473–74, 517
Strenski, Ivan 633–35
subjectivity 71–72, 180, 182, 198–99, 208, 304, 315, 319–20, 325–26, 328–29, 420, 438–40

supernaturalism 288–89, 290–91, 292–93, 325, 351, 361–63

T
Tennemann, Wilhelm Gottlieb 8–10, 490–91
Thandeka 594, 614, 615, 616–17
theology
    constructive 577–83
    historical 112, 260, 263–65, 355–56, 399–400, 581–82, 584
    philosophical 112, 260, 261–63, 297, 355–56, 399–401
    as a positive science 74, 105–7, 260–61
    practical 112, 206, 260, 265–66, 355–56, 397
    study of 112–13
    see also *Brief Outline of Theology as a Field of Study*
Thiel, John 558, 562–64
Tice, Terrence N. xxxii, 257–58, 295–96, 337, 452
Tillich, Paul 42–43, 290, 535, 541–42, 569–70, 660–61
Tonstad, Linn Marie 347–48, 577, 587, 588, 618–19
Trinity, doctrine of 63–64, 322, 335, 540–41, 586–88
Troeltsch, Ernst 166, 302, 505, 533–34, 554, 660–61
Tübingen, University of xxiv, 366

Twesten, August Detlev Christian 127, 139, 267, 508–10

U
Ullmann, Carl 507, 512, 514, 516–17
understanding 147–52, 155–57, 188–200
unification, of Lutheran and Reformed churches xxiii, 58–60, 288–89, 467–68
university, idea of 74, 102–8, 410

V
Vial, Ted 276–77, 279, 316, 632–33, 667

W
Wars of Liberation 79
Weil, Simone 548
Wiebe, Donald 633–34
Williams, Delores 585–86
Williams, Robert 341–42, 631
Wolf, Friedrich August 75, 383, 487, 491–92, 500
Wolff, Christian 22, 26, 219–20
world, idea of 45, 92–94, 142–43, 225–26, 328–29, 353–54, 441–44, 496
worship 59–61, 206, 264, 358, 404–6, 451, 457–636

Z
Zwingli, Huldrych 55–56, 62, 64